THE OXFORD HANDBOOK OF

MODERN CHINESE LITERATURES

This volume's cover features an image of avant-garde Taiwanese author Hsia Yü's 夏宇 2007 poetry collection *Pink Noise* (粉紅色噪音). The latter is a self-published volume printed in pink and black text on a set of transparent polyurethane pages, producing a palimpsestic effect whereby the reader sees multiple layers of text overlaid onto one another. The volume's poetry consists of a set of English and French text Hsia Yü has culled from the Internet and then fed multiple times through an Apple translation and search software called Sherlock, yielding extremely idiosyncratic Chinese equivalents. The resulting multilingual, boundary-crossing text nicely captures some of the taxonomical concerns that animate this Oxford Handbook. In particular, we approach modern Chinese literature as a fundamentally heterogeneous category that is not necessarily limited to texts composed in Chinese or originating from China, nor to ones that are "literary" in the traditional sense of the word. Finally, although we focus on the modern period, broadly defined, we are nevertheless attentive to the ways in which all texts function as palimpsests, inflected with virtual traces of the various literary and textual traditions that precede them.

We are grateful to Hsia Yü for giving us permission to use this photograph of the cover of *Pink Noise* as the cover image for our own volume.

THE OXFORD HANDBOOK OF

MODERN

CHINESE

LITERATURES

Edited by

CARLOS ROJAS

and

ANDREA BACHNER

OXFORD

UNIVERSITY PRESS

OXFORD
UNIVERSITY PRESS

Oxford University Press is a department of the University of Oxford. It furthers
the University's objective of excellence in research, scholarship, and education
by publishing worldwide. Oxford is a registered trade mark of Oxford University
Press in the UK and certain other countries.

Published in the United States of America by Oxford University Press
198 Madison Avenue, New York, NY 10016, United States of America.

CIP data is on file at the Library of Congress
ISBN 978-0-19-938331-3

1 3 5 7 9 8 6 4 2
Printed by Sheridan Books, Inc., United States of America

Contents

PART I STRUCTURE

PART II TAXONOMY

PART III METHODOLOGY

Descriptive Table of Contents

PART I STRUCTURE

PART II TAXONOMY

PART III METHODOLOGY

ACKNOWLEDGMENTS

THE editors would like to acknowledge the support of the CCK Foundation Inter-University Center for Sinology, the Shewo Memorial Fund, and Duke's Asia/Pacific Studies Institute, Department of Asian and Middle Eastern Studies, Franklin Humanities Institute, Critical Asian Humanities program, and the Program in Literature for funding a workshop in Spring 2014, at which earlier versions of many of the papers in this volume were presented.

About the Contributors

Nick **Admussen** is Assistant Professor of Chinese Literature and Culture at Cornell University. He is a poet and translator of poetry, and his first scholarly book, *Recite and Refuse: Contemporary Chinese Prose Poetry*, is forthcoming from the University of Hawai'i Press.

Andrea **Bachner** is Associate Professor of Comparative Literature at Cornell University. Her research explores comparative intersections between Sinophone, Latin American, and European cultural productions in dialogue with theories of interculturality, sexuality, and mediality. She is the author of *Beyond Sinology: Chinese Writing and the Scripts of Cultures* (Columbia University Press).

Mark **Bender** is Professor of Chinese Literature and Folklore at The Ohio State University. He is the author of *Plum and Bamboo* (Illinois), the co-editor of *The Columbia Anthology of Chinese Folk and Popular Literature* (Columbia), and translator of *Butterfly Mother* (Hackett).

Brian **Bernards** is Assistant Professor of East Asian Languages and Cultures at the University of Southern California. He is the author of *Writing the South Seas: Imagining the Nanyang in Chinese and Southeast Asian Postcolonial Literature* (University of Washington Press) and co-editor (with Shu-mei Shih and Chien-hsin Tsai) of *Sinophone Studies: A Critical Reader* (Columbia University Press).

Kwok Kou Leonard **Chan** is Chair Professor of Chinese Literature at the Hong Kong Institute of Education. He is the author of the Chinese-language volumes *On Lyrical China* (Hong Kong), *How Did Literature Become Knowledge? Literary Criticism, Literary Studies, and Literary Education* (Beijing), and *Structuring Chinese Literary Tradition* (Wuhan); he is also the chief editor of the twelve-volume *Compendium of Hong Kong Literature 1919–1949* (Hong Kong).

Shelby Kar-yan **Chan** is Associate Professor of Translation at Hang Seng Management College. She is author of *Identity and Theatre Translation in Hong Kong* (Springer), and is the co-editor of *Islands or Continents*, *Words and the World*, and *The Other Voice* (all published by the Chinese University Press).

CHANG Cheng is a journalist in Taiwan and is one of the founding editors of the multilingual newspaper *Sifang Bao* (*Four-Way Voice*). In 2015, he established an event called "Bringing Back Books That You Cannot Read," to encourage people to bring back books for migrants. He also established a Southeast Asia–themed bookstore in Taiwan called Brilliant Time.

Sung-sheng Yvonne Chang is Professor of Asian Studies at the University of Texas, Austin. She is the author of *Modernism and the Nativist Resistance: Contemporary Chinese Fiction from Taiwan* (Duke University Press) and *Literary Culture in Taiwan: Martial Law to Market Law* (Columbia University Press), and co-editor (with Michelle Yeh and Ming-ju Fan) of *The Columbia Sourcebook of Literary Taiwan* (Columbia University Press).

CHEN Pingyuan is Professor of Chinese Literature at Peking University. His books in Chinese include *The Transformation of Narrative Models in Chinese Fiction; The Literati's Chivalric Dreams: Narrative Models of Chinese Knight-Errant Literature; Establishing Modern Chinese Scholarship; Touches of History: An Entry into "May Fourth" China; Pictures on the Left, History on the Right: A Study of Late Qing Picture Magazines*; and *History of Literature as an Academic Discipline*.

Xiaomei Chen is Professor of Chinese and Comparative Literature at the University of California at Davis. She is the author of *Occidentalism: A Theory of Counter-discourse in Post-Mao China* (Oxford University Press; Rowman and Littlefield), *Acting the "Right" Part: Political Theater and Popular Drama in Contemporary China* (University of Hawai'i Press) and the editor of the *Columbia Anthology of Modern Chinese Drama* (Columbia University Press) and *Reading the Right Text: An Anthology of Contemporary Chinese Drama with a Critical Introduction (*University of Hawai'i Press).

Rey Chow is Anne Firor Scott Professor of Literature at Duke University. Her publications in the past decade include *The Age of the World Target* (Duke University Press, 2006), *Sentimental Fabulations, Contemporary Chinese Films* (Columbia University Press, 2007), *Entanglements, or Transmedial Thinking about Capture* (Duke University Press, 2012), and *Not Like a Native Speaker: On Languaging as a Postcolonial Experience* (Columbia University Press, 2014).

John A. Crespi is Luce Associate Professor of Chinese at Colgate University. He is the author of *Voices in Revolution: Poetry and the Auditory Imagination in Modern China* (University of Hawai'i Press).

Kirk A. Denton is Professor of East Asian Languages and Literatures at The Ohio State University. He is author of *The Problematic of Self in Modern Chinese Literature: Hu Feng and Lu Ling* (Stanford University Press) and *Exhibiting the Past: Historical Memory and the Politics of Museums in Postsocialist China* (University of Hawai'i Press). His edited books include *Modern Chinese Literary Thought: Writings on Literature, 1893–1945* (Stanford University Press), (with Michel Hockx), *Literary Societies in Republican China* (Lexington), and the *Columbia Companion to Modern Chinese Literature* (Columbia University Press). He is also editor of the journal *Modern Chinese Literature and Culture*.

Gilbert C. F. Fong is Professor of Translation at Hang Seng Management College. He has translated many plays by Gao Xingjian into English, which were published in *The Other Shore, Snow in August, Cold Literature: Selected Works by Gao Xingjian* (with Mabel Lee), *Escape and The Man Who Questions Death*, and *Of Mountains and Seas*. He is also co-editor of *Islands or Continents* and *Words and the World: An Anthology of Poetry Translation* (both published by University of Hong Kong Press), among other volumes.

Matthew Fraleigh is Associate Professor of East Asian Literature and Culture at Brandeis University. His research concerns the literature of early modern and modern Japan, especially *kanshibun* (Sinitic poetry and prose). He is the author of *Plucking Chrysanthemums: Narushima Ryūhoku and Sinitic Literary Traditions in Modern Japan* (Harvard University Asia Center) and has published annotated translations of some of Ryūhoku's best-known works, including *New Chronicles of Yanagibashi and Diary of a Journey to the West: Narushima Ryūhoku Reports From Home and Abroad* (Cornell East Asia Series).

Junning Fu is a doctoral candidate in Comparative Literature at Cornell University.

GE Zhaoguang is Professor of History at Fudan University. His Chinese-language publications include *Chan Religion and Chinese Culture, Daoist Religion and Chinese Culture, Intellectual History of Chan Buddhism*, and *History of Chinese Thought*.

Jonathan Christopher Hamm is Associate Professor of Asian Languages and Literatures at the University of Washington. He is the author of *Paper Swordsmen: Jin Yong and the Modern Chinese Martial Arts Novel* (University of Hawai'i Press) and *Book, Sword, and Nation: Jin Yong and the Modern Chinese Martial Arts Novel* (University of Hawai'i Press).

Michael Gibbs Hill is Associate Professor of Chinese and Comparative Literature, University of South Carolina. He is the author of *Lin Shu, Inc.: Translation and the Making of Modern Chinese Culture* (Oxford University Press) and the translator of Wang Hui's *China from Empire to Nation-State* (Harvard University Press).

Nathaniel Isaacson is Assistant Professor of Modern Chinese Literature at North Carolina State University. He is currently completing a book on colonial modernities and Chinese science fiction.

JI Jin is Professor of Chinese Literature at Suzhou University, and is the author, in Chinese, of *Qian Zhongshu and Modern Western Thought, The Sage in Fortress Besieged, Dialogues between Ji Jin and Leo Ou-Fan Lee, Chen Quan: A Borrowed Mirror from a Foreign Land, Another Kind of Voice: Interviews with Foreign Sinologists*, and *Reciprocal Perspectives*. He is the editor of the Chinese-language volume *Letters Between C.T. Hsia and T.A. Hsia*, and editor-in-chief of the series "Collection of Canonical Works by Modern Western Critics" and "Collection of Overseas Chinese Literary Studies."

Belinda Kong is Associate Professor of Asian Studies and English at Bowdoin College. She is the author of *Tiananmen Fictions Outside the Square: The Chinese Literary Diaspora and the Politics of Global Culture* (Temple University Press).

Jie Li is Assistant Professor of East Asian Languages and Civilizations at Harvard University. She is the author of *Shanghai Homes: Palimpsests of Private Life* (Columbia University Press) and co-editor of *Red Legacies: Cultural Afterlives of the Communist Revolution* (Harvard Asia Center).

LIAO Chaoyang is Professor of Foreign Languages at the National Taiwan University. He has been consistently interested in the intersection between Western theory and Asian traditions, and has published numerous articles in academic journals.

Ping-hui Liao is Professor of Literary and Critical Studies and Chuan Lyu Endowed Chair in Taiwan Studies at the University of California, San Diego. He is the author of *Keywords 200 in Literary and Critical Studies* (in Chinese) (Ryefield), and co-editor (with David Wang) of *Taiwan under Japanese Colonial Rule* (Columbia University Press) and (with Ackbar Abbas) of *Internationalizing Cultural Studies* (Blackwell).

LIAO Yun-chang is a journalist in Taiwan and previously served as acting deputy editor-in-chief of the Taiwan newspaper *Lihpao Daily*. She is dedicated to the promotion of multicultural reading, and currently works at *CommonWealth Magazine* Education Foundation as director of research and development.

Jianmei Liu is Associate Professor of Chinese Literature at the Hong Kong University of Science and Technology. She is the author of *Zhuangzi and Modern Chinese Literature* (Oxford University Press) and *Revolution Plus Love: Literary History, Women's Bodies, and Thematic Repetition in Twentieth-Century Chinese Fiction* (University of Hawai'i Press).

MEI Chia-ling is Professor of Chinese Literature at National Taiwan University. Her Chinese-language publications include *New Criticism on the Literature of the Six Dynasties: Pastiche, Narrator as the Author's Mouthpiece and Interchange Poetry, Language and Narrative in a New Account of Tales of the World, Gender or Nation? Criticism on Taiwan Fiction of the 50's and the 80's–90's*, and *From China's Youth to Taiwan's Youth*.

Viren Murthy is Assistant Professor of Transnational Asian History at the University of Madison-Wisconsin. He is the author of *The Philosophy of Zhang Taiyan: The Resistance of Consciousness* (Brill) and co-editor (with Axel Schneider) of *The Challenge of Linear Time: Nationhood and the Politics of History in East Asia* (Brill) and (with Prasenjit Duara and Andrew Sartori) of *A Companion to Global Historical Thought* (Blackwell).

Laikwan Pang is Professor of Cultural Studies in the Department of Cultural and Religious Studies at the Chinese University of Hong Kong. She is the author of *Building a New China in Cinema: The Chinese Left-wing Cinema Movement, 1932–37* (Rowman and Littlefield), *Cultural Control and Globalization in Asia: Copyright, Piracy, and*

Cinema (Routledge), *The Distorting Mirror: Visual Modernity in China* (University of Hawai'i Press), and *Creativity and Its Discontents: China's Creative Industries and Intellectual Property Right Offenses* (Duke University Press).

David Porter is Professor of English and Comparative Literature at the University of Michigan. He is the author of *The Chinese Taste in Eighteenth-Century England* (Cambridge University Press) and *Ideographia: The Chinese Cipher in Early Modern Europe* (Stanford University Press), and the editor of *Comparative Early Modernities* (Palgrave), *Internet Culture* (Routledge), and *Between Men and Feminism* (Routledge).

Carlos Rojas is Professor of Chinese Cultural Studies, Women's Studies, and Arts of the Moving Image at Duke University. He is the author of *Homesickness: Culture, Contagion, and National Transformation* (Harvard University Press), *The Great Wall: A Cultural History* (Harvard University Press), and *The Naked Gaze: Reflections on Chinese Modernity* (Harvard University Asia Center). He is also the co-editor (with Eileen Cheng-yin Chow) of *The Oxford Handbook of Chinese Cinemas* (Oxford University Press), among other volumes, and has translated book-length literary fiction by Yu Hua, Yan Lianke, and Ng Kim Chew.

Tze-lan Deborah Sang is Professor of Chinese Literature and Media Studies at Michigan State University. She is the author of *The Emerging Lesbian: Female Same-Sex Desire in Modern China* (Chicago University Press) and co-editor (with Sylvia Li-chun Lin) of *Documenting Taiwan on Film: Issues and Methods in New Documentaries* (Routledge).

Shuang Shen is Associate Professor of Comparative Literature and Chinese at the Pennsylvania State University. She is the author of *Cosmopolitan Publics: Anglophone Print Culture in Semi-Colonial Shanghai* (Rutgers University Press).

Haun Saussy is University Professor and Professor of Comparative Literature at the University of Chicago. He is the author of *The Problem of a Chinese Aesthetic* (Stanford University Press) and *Great Walls of Discourse and Other Adventures in Cultural China* (Harvard University Asia Center) and co-editor (with Kang-I Sun Chang) of *Chinese Women Poets, An Anthology of Poetry and Criticism from Ancient Times to 1911* (Stanford University Press), (with Eric Hayot and Steven Yao) of *Sinographies: Writing China* (University of Minnesota Press), and (with Roger des Forges, Chiao-mei Liu, and Gao Minglu) of *Chinese Walls in Time and Space* (Cornell Asia Center), among other volumes.

Mingwei Song is Associate Professor of Chinese Literature at Wellesley College. He is the author of *Young China: National Rejuvenation and the Bildungsroman, 1900-1959* (Harvard University Asia Center) and, in Chinese, of *Criticism and Imagination* (Shanghai) and *The Sorrows of a Floating World: A Biography of Eileen Chang* (Taipei). He is the guest editor of *Renditions 77/78*, a special issue that features Chinese science fiction.

E. K. Tan is Associate Professor of Comparative Literature and Cultural Studies in the Department of Cultural Analysis and Theory at the State University of New York, Stony Brook. He is the author of *Rethinking Chineseness: Translational Sinophone Identities in the Nanyang Literary World* (Cambria).

Karen Thornber is Professor of Comparative Literature and of East Asian Languages and Civilizations at Harvard University. She is the author of *Empire of Texts in Motion: Chinese, Korean, and Taiwanese Transculturations of Japanese Literature* (Harvard University Asia Center) and *Ecoambiguity: Environmental Crises and East Asian Literatures* (University of Michigan Press). She is also the editor of *World Literature and Health* (Literature and Medicine, Johns Hopkins University) and the translator of *Tōge Sankichi and Poems of the Atomic Bomb* (Center for East Asian Studies, University of Chicago).

Xiaofei Tian is Professor of Chinese Literature at Harvard University. She is the author of *Tao Yuanming and Manuscript Culture: The Record of a Dusty Table* (University of Washington Press), *Beacon Fire and Shooting Star: The Literary Culture of the Liang (502–557)* (Harvard University Asia Center), and *Visionary Journeys: Travel Writings from Early Medieval and Nineteenth-century China* (Harvard University Asia Center), as well as several volumes in Chinese. She is also co-editor of the *Oxford Handbook of Classical Chinese Literature (1000 BCE–900 CE)* and the translator of a late-nineteenth-century memoir, *The World of a Tiny Insect: A Memoir of the Taiping Rebellion and Its Aftermath* (University of Washington Press).

Chien-Hsin Tsai is Associate Professor of Asian Studies at the University of Texas, Austin. He is co-editor (with Shu-mei Shih and Brian Bernards) of *Sinophone Studies: A Critical Reader* (Columbia University Press).

Ban Wang is William Haas Professor in Chinese Studies at Stanford University. He is the author of *The Sublime Figure of History* (Stanford University Press) and *Illuminations from the Past* (Stanford, 2004), editor of *Words and Their Stories* (Brill), and co-editor of *Trauma and Cinema* (University of Hong Kong Press), *China and New Left Visions* (Lexington, 2012), and *Debating the Socialist Legacy and Capitalist Globalization* (Palgrave Macmillan, 2014).

David Der-wei Wang is Edward C. Henderson Professor of Chinese Literature at Harvard University. He is the author of *The Lyrical in Epic Time: Modern Chinese Intellectuals and Artists Through the 1949 Crisis* (Columbia), *The Monster that is History: History, Violence, and Fictional Writing in Twentieth-Century China* (University of California Press), *Fin-de-Siècle Splendor: Repressed Modernities in Late Qing Fiction, 1849–1911* (Stanford University Press), and *Fictional Realism in 20th-Century China* (Columbia University Press), and the editor of *Harvard New Literary History of Modern China* (Harvard University Press).

WANG Hui Professor in the Department of Chinese Language and Literature at Tsinghua University, Beijing. His English-language publications include *The End of*

Revolution: China and the Limits of Modernity (Verso), *China's New Order: Society, Politics, and Economy in Transition* (Harvard University Press), *The Politics of Imagining Asia* (Harvard University Press), and *The Rise of Modern Chinese Thought* (Harvard University Press).

Xiaojue Wang is Associate Professor of Modern Chinese Literature and Culture at Rutgers University. She is the author of *Modernity with a Cold War Face: Reimagining the Nation in Chinese Literature across the 1949 Divide* (Harvard University Asia Center).

XIA Xiaohong is Professor of Chinese Literature at Peking University. Her books in Chinese include *Late Qing baihua Vernacular Literature and Enlightenment Readings, Liang Qichao: Between Politics and Scholarship, Enlightenment and Inheritance: Liang Qichao's Literary Routes, Late Qing Literati's Ideas on Women, Late Qing Women and Modern China, Reading Liang Qichao,* and *Fragmented Records from Late Qing Shanghai.*

YAN Lianke is an author and professor at Renmin University in Beijing. English translations of his novels include *Serve the People!, Dream of Ding Village, Lenin's Kisses,* and *The Four Books* (all published by Grove Atlantic).

Yingjin Zhang is Distinguished Professor of Modern Chinese Literature at the University of California, San Diego. He is the author of *Cinema, Space, and Polylocality in a Globalizing China* (University of Hawai'i Press), *Chinese National Cinema* (Routledge), *Screening China: Critical Interventions, Cinematic Reconfigurations, and the Transnational Imaginary in Contemporary Chinese Cinema* (Center for Chinese Studies, University of Michigan), and *The City in Modern Chinese Literature and Film: Configurations of Space, Time, and Gender* (Stanford University Press), and co-author (with Kuei-fen Chiu) of *New Chinese-Language Documentaries: Ethics, Subject and Place* (Routledge). His edited books include *A Companion to Chinese Cinema* (Wiley-Blackwell) and *A Companion to Modern Chinese Literature* (Wiley-Blackwell).

THE OXFORD HANDBOOK OF

MODERN
CHINESE
LITERATURES

INTRODUCTION

The Limits of Wen (文)

CARLOS ROJAS

> He named his creation *corporeal writing* (*wenshen* 文身), but remarked
> that to call these *wen* 紋 [meaning "marks"] would have been an anach-
> ronistic mistake.
>
> (Ng Kim Chew, "Inscribed Backs")

THE Malaysian Chinese author Ng Kim Chew's 2001 short story "Inscribed Backs"
opens with a description of a set of mysterious marks tattooed on the back of a Chinese
coolie, including one fragment that appears to read "Ah, South Seas, you are my mother's homeland" (325–326). The source and meaning of these tattoos is a mystery that
drives Ng's narrative as a whole, and I propose that we may similarly use this figure of
the nearly illegible tattoos to reexamine our understanding of the category of modern
Chinese literature.

At one level, these markings are arguably modern, Chinese, and literary, though
each of these designations underdetermines the complexity of the text in question.
For instance, although the tattoos were clearly written during the coolie's lifetime, and
hence during the modern period, the story nevertheless suggests that they take their
inspiration from sources as ancient as Shang dynasty oracle bone inscriptions from
the second millennium BCE. Similarly, although the tattoos are technically written in
Chinese script, the characters are nevertheless so badly mangled as to be virtually illegible. Finally, although the form of the tattoos resembles that of literary text, their location on the back of an anonymous coolie positions them as almost the precise antithesis
of orthodox literature. I propose, accordingly, that we may view these tattoos as a peculiar form of modern Chinese literature, and furthermore that we may use these fictional
texts to help reassesses what precisely makes a text modern, Chinese, and even literary
in the first place. By considering a fictional text seemingly positioned at the outer margins of conventional understandings of the category of modern Chinese literature, in

other words, it is possible to reassess the structural conditions and the taxonomic logic of the category itself.

In Ng's story, the tattoos are first glimpsed by a Chinese scholar surnamed Yu, who is a history professor from Malaysia specializing in the migration patterns of Chinese coolies in Southeast Asia.[1] Fascinated by these mysterious markings, Mr. Yu becomes determined to track down their origins, but for many years he has difficulty obtaining funding for the investigation. Indeed, it is not until decades later, after Mr. Yu has retired from his position at the university, that he is finally able to assemble a research team and travel to regions throughout the former Straits Settlements to track down leads on the source of the tattoos. At one point Mr. Yu and his team see an elderly coolie whose back is inscribed with "many, many characters, including countless 每, 母, 水, 毋, and 海, suggesting that all of the other characters were derived from this final one"—referring to the character 海, which is pronounced *hai* in Mandarin and means "sea" (334).

Not long afterwards, Mr. Yu is badly injured in a car accident, but while he is lying in a coma in the hospital one of his assistants (who is also the story's narrator) runs across the man with variants of 海 tattooed on his back, and follows him home. It turns out that the man lives with an elderly Chinese lady, who offers to tell the narrator the story of her life over a series of leisurely afternoon teas. The old lady recounts how, when she was eighteen years old, she met an Englishman named Mr. Fu.[2] They became romantically involved and proceeded to open a high-end brothel in Singapore, which attracted a variety of elite clients. One of their customers was a Chinese man who was using ancient oracle bone inscription techniques to compose what he described as "a modern-day *Dream of the Red Chamber*" on the backs of ten thousand turtle shells. Mr. Fu was inspired by this venture to embark on a similarly quixotic project of his own—but in place of tortoise shells he instead decided to inscribe his masterpiece on the backs of thousands of Chinese coolies, by which he hoped to write "a novel as great as *Ulysses*" (354).

The lady notes at one point that Mr. Fu called his text "tattoos," or literally "corporeal writing." In her remark, the lady uses the term *wenshen* (文身) in Chinese, but immediately adds that it would have been an anachronistic mistake to refer to these tattoos as *wen* (紋), or "markings" (353). To help appreciate the distinction being drawn here between the homophonous and nearly synonymous characters 文 and 紋, we may turn to one of China's earliest dictionaries, Xu Shen's *Shuowen jiezi* (說文解字 [Explanation of simple and compound graphs], circa 100 CE), which contains a postface that recounts how the legendary figure Cang Jie allegedly invented Chinese writing from animal and bird tracks and the "patterns on the plumage of birds and the pelts of animals" (鳥獸之文). In this description of how the semantically meaningful patterns that form the basis of the Chinese writing system are derived from the nonlinguistic patterns found in nature, the same 文 character is used to refer to both sets of patterns. Although it is now conventional to use the homophonous variant *wen* (紋) to refer to the former (nonlinguistic patterns), this graphic distinction is in fact merely a retrospective attribution, and originally the same character, 文, was used to refer to both writing and nontextual markings, as well as to the process of differentiating between the two.

We find a similar set of issues in the entry for *wen* in the *Shuowen jiezi* itself. The *Shuowen* does not offer the sorts of definitions that we find in modern dictionaries; instead it illustrates the meaning of the character under consideration by gesturing toward the character's putative etymology, its visual form, and the ways in which it may be used. The entry for 文 begins by noting that the character is literally the product of a chiasmus of intersecting lines, then specifies what the character looks like and how the corresponding graph may be used within other characters:

> [The character] *wen* is a set of intersecting lines, and it resembles a crisscross pattern (*wen*). All characters relating to "writing/markings" (*wen*) are derived from this 文 graph.
>
> 文錯畫也,象交文, 凡文之屬皆从文 。

While at first glance this definition might appear to be rather tautological ("*wen* ... resembles *wen*, and all *wen* are derived from *wen*"), in practice it offers several distinct yet overlapping ways of understanding the character. Rather than attempting to specify precisely what the character means, the *Shuowen* entry instead describes the character's form, appearance, and use.

Like the *Shuowen jiezi* definition of *wen*, our objective in this volume is not to offer a definition of modern Chinese literature, nor is it to provide a comprehensive survey of all that the category might entail; instead we propose to use a series of strategic interventions to illustrate the structural conditions out of which modern Chinese literature has emerged, how it is viewed, and how it may be interpreted. Our goal, in other words, is to showcase a set of methodologies that may be used to approach modern Chinese literature, while in the process offering different ways of reassessing what modern Chinese literature is in the first place. We contend that modern Chinese literature is not a static category but rather a dynamic entity whose significance and limits are continually being reshaped through the process of interpretation itself. Similarly, modern Chinese literature is not a singular, unitary category, but rather a plurality of overlapping categories—of modern Chinese literatures.

PART I: STRUCTURE

The first clause of the *Shuowen jiezi* definition of *wen* specifies that the graph consists of a pair of intersecting lines—which may be read as a reference either to how the graph itself is written or to the patchwork of intersecting marks out of which legend holds that Chinese writing originally emerged. This initial portion of the *wen* entry, in other words, specifies the structural conditions on which both the written character *wen* and the entire Chinese writing system (also known as *wen*) are grounded. In Part I of this volume, we similarly consider some of the structural conditions from which modern Chinese literatures have been produced, circulated, and consumed, and specifically how these conditions may inform our understanding of individual texts as well as of the sociocultural environment within which they are positioned.

To begin with, writers inevitably write about what they know, even as they tend to be drawn inexorably to the unknown. Kirk Denton and Ping-hui Liao examine this dialectics of familiarity and unfamiliarity by considering some of the ways in which a thematics of home and travel have informed the writings of authors such as Lu Xun, Eileen Chang, and Wu Zhuoliu. Denton and Liao consider not only the ways in which these works deploy a thematics of home and travel, but also how the relationship between the space of the home and a process of travel provides some of the enabling conditions for literary production itself. First, Denton notes that beneath the familiar narrative of the May Fourth period as a liberatory movement from one's rural hometown to the metropolis, there was in fact a complicated set of attachments to the space of the hometown, and Denton offers a detailed analysis of several of Lu Xun's works to show how the ambivalent space of the hometown continued to maintain a complicated hold on the author's May Fourth imagination. Liao, meanwhile, considers Lu Xun and an array of other authors, and argues that for many of them the act of traveling away from home was marked by "a profound sense of psycho-social deprivation, reluctance, and loss, rather than empowerment or recreational escape." Liao concludes by considering diasporic figures like Ha Jin and Gao Xingjian, who use their position as migrant authors as a starting point from which to explore issues of identity and emancipation.

It is not only people who travel; so do knowledge and the epistemological paradigms within which it is embedded, and in their chapters XIA Xiaohong, Nathaniel Isaacson, and CHEN Pingyuan consider how the circulation of knowledge in the early modern period helped shape the conditions under which literature was produced and consumed. First, Xia offers a detailed genealogical account of the modern Chinese concept of *xiju*, or "drama." She notes that although historically Chinese had a variety of terms that partially overlapped with our contemporary concept of drama, a concept corresponding more precisely to Western "drama" did not begin to emerge until early-nineteenth-century Western missionaries such as Robert Morrison and Joseph Edkins, together with late-nineteenth and early-twentieth-century Chinese scholars' exposure to new drama movements in Japan. Next, Isaacson offers a close analysis of Xu Nianci's 1904 science-fiction story "New Tales of Mr. Braggadocio" to examine the conflicted relationship between modern scientific epistemological paradigms and more traditional Confucian and Daoist ones, together with a complementary set of tensions between capitalism and modernization. Finally, Chen Pingyuan considers the emergence in China of the genre of literary historiography and its implications for how we approach and interpret literature itself. Noting that traditional China did not have literary histories as we understand them today, Chen argues that the practice of writing literary histories began to proliferate in the early twentieth century as a result of curricular demands placed on scholars teaching literature at the university. This process has continued in the contemporary era, with an explosion of literary histories by China-based scholars. Chen considers the ramifications of this reliance on literary histories, and asks what might result if China were to move away from its current reliance on literary histories. He is asking, in other words, how literary histories provide the conceptual grounds on which our understanding of literature itself is predicated.

Literature is often assumed to be defined by its reliance on language, and the chapters by Andrea Bachner and Michael Hill examine issues of language and translation, while those by MEI Chia-ling and by Shelby Kar-yan Chan and Gilbert C. F. Fong consider related concerns with voice and dialect. Xiaomei Chen and John Crespi, finally, turn their attention to the status of partially nonlinguistic elements within textual works. First, Bachner considers the work of contemporary Taiwanese poet Chen Li, whose poems often revolve around a strategic fragmentation of Chinese characters themselves. Bachner discusses Chen's claim that his poetry is effectively untranslatable, and puts his work into dialogue with similar experiments using Western alphabetic languages. In these and other instances, she concludes, language is not merely a communicative medium, but rather an integral part of the message itself. Hill, meanwhile, approaches a related set of questions of untranslatability through the prism of the translational practices pioneered by Lin Shu, the prolific turn-of-the-century translator who didn't know any foreign languages and instead had to rely on intermediaries to provide preliminary oral translations of the works in question. Hill uses these early-twentieth-century Chinese translational practices to reassess some of the assumptions implicit in views on translation that are currently dominant within the North American academy.

Mei Chia-ling brings the metaphor of voice—as popularized by Lu Xun in his famous early-twentieth-century critique of China as "voiceless"—to bear on the 1930s "recited poetry" movement, focusing on how this emphasis on oral recitation helped dramatize dialect differences latent within the written text. Shelby Chan and Gilbert Fong, meanwhile, approach issues of dialect from a different perspective in their discussion of the contemporary Hong Kong drama translator Rupert Chan, who is the first translator to rely exclusively on Cantonese (or what he calls "Hongkong-speak") in his drama translations for stage performance. Chan and Fong argue that Rupert Chan's work offers a revealing glimpse into the complicated language and dialect politics that characterize contemporary Hong Kong.

Xiaomei Chen and John Crespi, on the other hand, consider the obverse of this focus on language, by examining the status of nonlinguistic elements embedded in literary texts. Chen, for instance, takes as her starting point several iconic invocations of "The Internationale" in Chinese literary, dramatic, and cinematic works, and notes that although the song has a linguistic component, its primary significance in these works lies in its purely (nonlinguistic) *sonic* status. On a similar note, John Crespi takes Zhang Guangyu's midcentury work *Journey to the West in Cartoons* as a starting point for reflecting on the status of illustrated cartoons as a literary genre in its own right. With cartoons, the semantic valence of the textual captions is complemented by the nontextual status of the illustrations themselves.

Needless to say, a key element within the system of literary production involves the mechanisms that permit literature to be published in the first place, and as Laikwan Pang, YAN Lianke, Jie Li, and Junning Fu illustrate, these mechanisms frequently reflect the complex intersection of state, market, and technological factors, which may restrict the availability of some types of works while actively promoting others. Looking at the Mao and post-Mao eras, respectively, Laikwan Pang and Yan Lianke consider the imbricated relationship between state power and literary production in modern China. First, Laikwan Pang looks at the work of Tian Han, one of modern China's most influential dramatists. While Tian Han established his reputation in the Republican period in the 1930s and 1940s, Pang turns here to three historical dramas Tian wrote during the Great Leap Forward in the late 1950s, emphasizing the ways in which the allegorical qualities of these works are closely intertwined with contemporary state doctrine. Pang emphasizes not only the ways in which Tian used historical dramas to comment allegorically on the present, but also how this sort of allegorical logic opens up these texts to a wide range of possible interpretations. Yan Lianke, meanwhile, is a prize-winning contemporary author whose works have often been either censored, self-censored, recalled, or deliberately sidelined, and in his chapter he argues that China is currently undergoing an important shift from what he calls a "hard" censorship regime to a "soft" one. In contrast to a hard censorship regime in which the state plays an aggressive role in restricting the publication of works deemed problematic, under a soft censorship regime the onus of exercising this oversight is instead shifted to publishers and the authors themselves. Yan argues, moreover, that the effects of this soft censorship regime are even more pernicious than those of a hard censorship regime, in that they encourage authors and publishers to internalize repressive state ideologies.

One result of these shifting modalities of state control is the production of literary works that cannot be published at all (or at least not until much later). In her chapter, Jie Li considers a category that she, following Chinese literature scholar Chen Sihe, calls "invisible writing" or "drawer literature"—which is to say texts that cannot be officially published at the time they are written, and instead must be kept hidden in private drawers or circulated privately only among a small group of acquaintances. Conversely, the explosive growth of the Internet in China over the past couple of decades has had a transformative influence on authors' ability to distribute literary works outside of the state-authorized publication system. Junning Fu, meanwhile, considers the status of contemporary Internet literature through the lens of a novel, *Dream of Returning to 1997*, that comments metatextually on the structural conditions of its own creation. In particular, the novel describes a protagonist who jumps back in time from 2004 to 1997 and proceeds to establish a vast media empire by rewriting from memory popular Internet novels that he had read in the "future," and even creates the dominant Internet platform on which many of those novels would be distributed. The explosive growth of the Internet in China over the past couple of decades has had far-reaching implications for the production, circulation, and consumption of literary works, and Fu's chapter examines some of these ramifications with respect to shifting dialectics of elite and popular literature.

These sorts of structural considerations are not located strictly outside the text but rather may be seen as a direct extension of it—positioned as an array of paratextual concerns that simultaneously provide the enabling conditions on which literary production is itself necessarily predicated. Through an analysis of these various structural conditions, accordingly, it is possible to gain a more nuanced understanding not only of the resulting literary texts themselves but also of what it means to interpret a text in the first place.

PART II: TAXONOMY

The second portion of the *Shuowen jiezi* definition discussed above closely resembles the first, in that they both point to the graph's chiasmatic status as a product of intersecting lines. The primary difference is that while the definition's first clause emphasizes the graph's compositional structure, the second underscores instead its visual appearance. In particular, the latter clause draws on an approach that the dictionary calls *xiangxing* (象形), literally "giving an image of the shape," which operates on the assumption that the appearance of a character reflects its meaning. This approach reflects the common belief that form carries meaning and significance, and in Part II of this volume we similarly adopt what could be described as a *xiangxing* approach to literary taxonomy. In particular, some of the most influential taxonomical categories are ones grounded on surface resemblances, and here we consider a set of historical, ethno-regional, and formal factors on which a corresponding array of taxonomic categories are grounded. In so doing, it is not our intention to privilege any set of taxonomies over others but rather to illustrate different ways in which one may think about taxonomies and their logics in the first place, and our ultimate objective is to explore some of the assumptions behind the category of modern Chinese literature itself.

First, David Porter, Xiaojue Wang, and Xiaofei Tian each offer a novel perspective on a seemingly familiar historical period. For Porter, the period is the "early modern," by which he means not the late imperial era that Chinese literature scholarship usually refers to as *jindai* (literally "near modern"), but rather an earlier period that might parallel the European early modern era from the early sixteenth century to the late eighteenth century. Noting that in both China and Europe this period was characterized by increasing commercial prosperity, imperial expansion, and a burgeoning of fiction writing, Porter proposes that we might use the European notion of *early modern* to reassess a contemporary body of literary production from China, while at the same time reflecting on what this sort of comparative methodology might entail. Next, Xiaojue Wang observes that literary production from the mid-twentieth century is often grouped into categories based on its political affiliations (including nationalist, Communist, and anti-Communist literature), but proposes that it might be useful to consider these works within the larger historical category of the Cold War, by looking comparatively at works of different ideological backgrounds. Finally, Xiaofei Tian uses the fiction of Hao Ran to offer an alternative perspective on what Tian calls the Cultural Revolution period—by which she means not only the 1966–1976 Cultural Revolution proper but also earlier periods that were similarly characterized by an emphasis on cultural-political transformation. In particular, she identifies the early twentieth century's New Culture movement, the events surrounding Mao's 1942 Yan'an Forum talks, and the first year of the Great Leap Forward (1958), which is also the year Hao Ran published the story "The New Bride," which Tian examines. Tian argues that the socialist content of Hao Ran's work is often at odds with the literary, and frequently erotic, language he uses, and that part of the interest of his works lies in the resulting dialectics of subversion and sublimation.

The next cluster of chapters consider literary taxonomies informed by regional or ethnonational characteristics, which attempt to reexamine the naturalized category of "Chinese" literature by considering alternative configurations of regional and ethnonational characteristics. In particular, Matthew Fraleigh, Kwok Kou Leonard Chan, and Sung-sheng Yvonne Chang consider bodies of literary production that challenge, in different ways, conventional assumptions about what constitutes a national literature. First, Fraleigh looks at a body of poetry written in what he calls Literary Sinitic—which is to say, poetry written in Chinese by non-Chinese authors who typically did not speak Chinese. These poems follow Chinese-language conventions (including rhyme-schemes based on the Chinese pronunciations of the characters), but were designed to be read aloud in other languages. Fraleigh argues that this body of literature, together with the compositional and reading practices that accompanied it, complicates our assumptions about the taxonomic limits of "Chinese literature." Leonard Chan and Yvonne Chang look at literary production from the geopolitical border regions of Hong Kong and Taiwan. Opening with a poem by former Hong Kong governor Cecil Clementi, for instance, Leonard Chan examines the ways in which the colony is portrayed in poetry from the 1920s and 1930s, focusing specifically on how poets may "construct an identity for themselves and their place by finding expression for their urban experience." Chang, in turn, uses a case study centered around the diaries of Lü Heruo to consider the literary scene of the final years of colonial Taiwan, and to think more broadly about the structural conditions that may help shape the literary field. In particular, she considers the ways in which the literary scene in the final years of colonial Taiwan was shaped by some distinctive local features that operated at variance with more general literary and cultural phenomena from that period.

The following three chapters extend a similar set of concerns to bodies of literary production defined not so much by geographic place, but more importantly by patterns of migration. First, Taiwan-based journalists CHANG Cheng and LIAO Yun-chang consider writings by Southeast Asian migrant workers and marriage migrants living in Taiwan. Although these texts are mostly composed by nonprofessional authors who are neither from Taiwan nor writing in Chinese, Chang and Liao nevertheless argue that these texts should be considered part of the broader category of Taiwan literature on the grounds that the writers live in Taiwan and their works offer an important perspective on contemporary Taiwan society and culture. Next, Shuang Shen turns to the same Cold War period that Xiaojue Wang considers in her chapter, though Shen focuses more explicitly on a set of transregional considerations, including trans-Pacific migration and a phenomenon that Shen, following the critic Djelal Kadir, describes as the "worlding" of Chinese literature in a trans-Pacific context. Shen then concludes with a comparative analysis of two trans-Pacific works: the U.S.-based author C. Y. Lee's Anglophone novel *Lover's Point* and Malaysian Chinese author Jin Zhimang's Chinese-language novel *Hunger*. Finally, Belinda Kong looks at a similar migrational pattern in her discussion of Xiaolu Guo, a young author who was born in a fishing village in Zhejiang province but who relocated to London in 2002. Trained as a film director, Guo has also written several novels in both Chinese and English, and here Kong considers two of Guo's English-language novels, using them not only to help rethink the limits of the category of Anglophone literature, but also to reflect on the institutional and geopolitical dimensions of English in a global context.

Finally, Mark Bender's and JI Jin's chapters return us to Mainland China, though each approaches the category of Chinese literature from a rather unconventional perspective. Bender focuses on works by the ethnically Yi poet Aku Wuwu, who writes in both Mandarin Chinese and the Nuosu dialect of Yi, examining how Aku presents different identities through his work as he draws on an eclectic archive of cultural allusions ranging from Yi mythology to Native American culture. Ji Jin considers the status of Western literature in Chinese translation in Mainland China during the post-Mao period. Under Deng Xiaoping's Reform and Opening Up campaign that began in 1978, there was a surge of Chinese translations of Western literary works, which had a transformative impact on a new generation of Chinese authors interested in exploring modes of literary expression. Ji Jin notes that in many instances the influence of these translated works within the contemporary literary field was comparable to, or even greater than, that of corresponding works originally written in Chinese, and therefore argues that they should be regarded as an integral part of contemporary Chinese literature.

The last four chapters in this section consider categories of literary production based on two different understandings of the concept of genre. First, Chris Hamm and Mingwei Song consider two popular genres defined by their thematic focus. Hamm uses Xiang Kairan's midcentury martial arts novel *Righteous Heroes of Modern Times* to reflect on some of the narrative, thematic, and rhetorical conventions of the Chinese martial arts genre, suggesting that the work's treatment of martial arts traditions—which are defined by a process of inheritance and transformation—offers a suggestive metaphor for the cultural logic of genre itself. Mingwei Song looks at the contemporary resurgence of science fiction in Mainland China, arguing that the dialectics of visibility and invisibility developed in many of these works may be viewed as a commentary on the status of contemporary science fiction itself, insofar as it is a popular genre positioned at the margins of the literary establishment.

In addition to genres defined primarily by their thematic focus, there are also ones defined by their mode of writing, such as prose, poetry, and drama. In their chapters, Rey Chow and Nick Admussen examine some issues relating to the genres of poetry and prose poetry, respectively. First, Chow offers a detailed analysis of some poems by the prolific Hong Kong author Leung Ping-kwan, who published not only poetry but also essays, short stories, novels, and criticism, focusing in particular on Leung's use of *shuqing*, or lyricism, to develop "an inward turning vision in which the self as such becomes objectified—or thing-ified—through a controlled act of composition and, in that process, merged with the external world." Admussen, meanwhile, turns to the hybrid genre of prose poetry, and argues that whereas contemporary Chinese prose poetry has a strong generic identity, this was less true during the Republican period. Admussen looks specifically at Bing Xin's early-twentieth-century translations of poems by Rabindranath Tagore (many of which Tagore originally composed in Bengali and then translated into English, which Bing Xin in turn retranslated into Chinese)— arguing that the resulting translations provided an influential model for later Chinese prose poetry, despite the fact that the "prose poetry" dimension of Bing Xin's texts emerged primarily in the process of translation itself.

Each of the taxonomic categories discussed above is seemingly grounded on a set of formal resemblances, though in each case these surface similarities occlude a more complex and contradictory underlying structural logic. It is, however, precisely by starting with these formal resemblances that it then becomes possible to critically reexamine their corresponding structural logics, and in the process to consider a variety of alternative taxonomical categories.

PART III: METHODOLOGY

While the first two portions of the definition of *wen* in the *Shuowen jiezi* focus on the graph's structure and its appearance, the third turns to the graph's meaning, and specifically the ways it may be used as a component within other Chinese characters with a similar semantic valence. This final clause points to an exercise in interpretation, wherein the meaning of a constituent portion of a character contributes to the meaning of the character itself. In Part III of this volume, we similarly showcase a number of different methodological approaches to interpreting a literary work, including not only approaches associated with modern literary theory, but also ones grounded in traditional Chinese poetics.

One set of interpretative approaches focuses on issues of history and historiography, and in the first four chapters of Part III, David Der-wei Wang, Jianmei Liu, Haun Saussy and GE Zhaoguang, and Yingjin Zhang take historical considerations as a starting point for their analyses. First, David Wang challenges the common equation of literary theory with paradigms originating from the West, and examines how three analytical concepts rooted in traditional Chinese literary thought have been deployed by twentieth-century authors and scholars. Wang's argument is not that these autochthonous literary concepts, and their attendant theoretical paradigms, should supplant the corresponding body of "Western" concepts and theories, but rather that the two may be productively put in dialogue with one another. Jianmei Liu then pursues a similar approach in examining how contemporary expatriate author Gao Xingjian invokes and engages with the classic Taoist text the *Zhuangzi*, pointing in particular to the resonances between Gao Xingjian's focus on issues of exile and Zhuangzi's concept of absolute spiritual freedom. In their essay, Haun Saussy and Ge Zhaoguang consider the early-twentieth-century trend in "new historical studies." This historiographic turn helped transform not only contemporary perspectives of Chinese history but also understandings of the historiographic process, revealing the fictional dimensions of many earlier writings as well as the persistent discursive dimension of even contemporary historiography. Finally, looking more specifically at issues of *literary* historiography, Yingjin Zhang notes that while there has been a veritable explosion of literary histories written by scholars in China, North America–based scholars appear to have little interest in writing these sorts of studies. From this, Zhang proceeds to reflect more broadly on literary historiography as an interpretive methodology in its own right, and particularly its role in helping negotiate between competing interpretive tendencies to emphasize a dialectics of "structure and rupture" while approaching a seemingly coherent body of literary or cultural production.

In the modern period, two dominant modes of literary analysis emphasize political and psychological considerations, respectively, and Viren Murthy, WANG Hui, Chaoyang Liao, and Ban Wang deploy methodologies partially inspired by one or both of these approaches. First, Viren Murthy considers two of the essays Lu Xun wrote in 1908 while still in Japan, and argues that in these early works—both of which antedate Lu Xun's explicit engagement with Marxism by several years—we find an exploration of a set of methodological considerations that are in fact at the heart of Marxist analysis, and specifically his pursuit of what Wang Hui calls a "depoliticized politics." In the following chapter, Wang Hui himself turns to the novella *The True Story of Ah Q*, which Lu Xun wrote about twenty years after his Japan essays, and asks how we might reconcile the protagonist's status as an archetypal figure of self-defeatism with his eventual attempt to join the revolution. In particular, Wang Hui takes as his starting point the narrator's remark, in the novella's preface, that "as though my thoughts were possessed by a ghost, I always return to the idea of writing the story of Ah Q," from which Wang offers a reading of the work that examines a series of "ghostly" moments where the narrative folds back upon itself. Chaoyang Liao continues this interest in ghosts in proposing a Lacanian reading of the short story collection *Seeing Ghosts* by contemporary Taiwan author Li Ang. In particular, Liao notes that psychoanalysis is a rather peculiar methodology, insofar as its pursuit of "truth" is merely tactical, and once the knowledge produced by this method has served its purpose, it may be set aside. Finally, Ban Wang takes Ding Ling's 1930s fiction to examine a process he calls "positive sublimation"—which is to say the translation of libidinal energy into political passion. Wang argues that this notion of positive sublimation offers a way of releasing psychoanalysis from a narrow focus on individual sexual desire in order to examine a set of broader sociopolitical considerations.

Another set of approaches takes as their starting point a cluster of social and communal concerns, and in their chapters Tze-lan Deborah Sang, E. K. Tan, and Karen Thornber focus on gender, sexuality, and environmental issues, respectively. Sang opens her chapter with a discussion of a young Eileen Chang's account of her frustrations with being unable to live up to her mother's (gendered) expectations, and then takes this reflection on the "trauma of normative femininity" as a starting point for a critical rethinking of the feminist implications of Chang's work as a whole. In the following chapter, E. K. Tan turns to the novel *A Wife's Diary* by contemporary Taiwanese lesbian author Chen Xue, looking at the work's treatment of a thematics of what he calls "queer homecoming," which takes as its goal a generative rethinking of kinship relations in modern society. In particular, Tan draws on recent work on "queer phenomenology" by Sara Ahmed and others, and focuses on the novel's treatment of furniture, arguing that furniture represents the sorts of objects in space that we necessarily rely on to orient ourselves, even as the possibility of literally rearranging one's furniture represents the possibility of challenging and restructuring traditional kinship assumptions and family affinities. Finally, Karen Thornber opens her chapter with another homoerotically themed novel, Chu T'ien-wen's *Notes of a Desolate Man*, though Thornber's primary interest here is not with sexuality, but rather with a broader set of ecological considerations. Following an introductory discussion of the treatment, in *Notes of a Desolate Man*, of life and death in the shadow of the HIV/AIDS pandemic, Thornber turns to a more detailed analysis of the relationship between human and ecological crises in Yan Lianke's *Dream of Ding Village*.

The final cluster of essays focuses on issues of temporality and ethnopolitical identity. First, Brian Bernards considers a body of literary production that emerges out of a similar tension between competing claims of national and ethnic identity. Bernards looks at what is known as Mahua literature—which is to say, Chinese literature from Malaysia. Bernards does not merely make this body of Mahua literature his object of analysis; he proposes that it offers *a mode* of analysis—what he calls "Malaysia as method"—with broader implications for how we understand the relationship between regional and ethnonational attributes. Next, Chien-hsin Tsai uses a notion of "post-loyalism" to analyze Singaporean author Chia Joo Ming's novella *Ambon Vacation*. Building on David Der-wei Wang's recent discussion of (post-)loyalism—in which Wang brings the Chinese term for loyalist (*yimin*) into dialogue with two other homophonous terms meaning "migrant" and "savage," respectively, to argue that post-loyalism combines a sense of loyalty to the former homeland, a desire to set down roots in a new one, and a residual quality of outsideness or alienation—Tsai illustrates how "Ambon Vacation" interweaves themes of loyalism, migration, and localism to reassess the very notions of heritage and identity that the concept of loyalism would seem to invoke in the first place. Finally, in the last chapter I consider some recent works by Hong Kong author Dung Kai-Cheung, focusing specifically on the ways that they deploy a simultaneously anticipatory and belated sense of temporality. Drawing on Freudian notions of the fetish and of deferred action, wherein the present is viewed through the prism of either an anticipated future loss or through a belated reassessment of a past event, I consider the ways in which Dung weaves together issues of sexuality, textuality, and Hong Kong identity.

The interpretive methodologies we showcase here are necessarily finite, and there are countless other hermeneutic strategies that we could have chosen instead. In the end, however, our intention is not to privilege any specific set of methodologies, but rather to encourage a critical reexamination of the assumptions implicit in existing methodologies. We are inviting, in other words, a meta-methodology, which simultaneously examines both the literary phenomena under consideration and the interpretive paradigms used to help make sense of them.

CODA

Ng Kim Chew's "Inscribed Backs" concludes with two unexpected revelations. First, the female narrator learns that the tattoos on the back of Ah Hai—the former coolie who led her back to his home—are actually not the handiwork of the Englishman known as Mr. Fu, but rather of a Peranakan Chinese man whose ancestors had migrated from China to Southeast Asia centuries earlier. The latter had to have seen some of Mr. Fu's "creations" and been deeply impressed, though he knew only one Chinese character— the character 海. For reasons that are left unspecified in the story, Ah Hai offers his back as a writing tablet, on which the other man proceeds to inscribe countless miswritten variants of the character in question. Second, shortly after learning about the source of Ah Hai's tattoos, the narrator returns to Mr. Yu's hospital room and finds he has just died. He is lying naked on the bed, and the narrator is shocked and bewildered to discover that his back, too, is covered in Chinese characters:

> Some of the characters were as large as a fist, others were as tiny as the tip of a needle, and they were all written in irregular strokes of different thicknesses. They were, however, all the same character: 海. They were all written in a very infantile style, as though from a practice book kept by a child who was just learning how to write.

It is revealed, in other words, that Mr. Yu's back was inscribed with the very text he had spent the final decades of his life trying to track down. The story concludes shortly after this revelation, without specifying how or why Mr. Yu's back came to be marked in this way, but one intriguing possibility is that he had been tattooed without knowing it, and that his fascination with the coolie's tattoos was in fact an unwitting manifestation of an attempt to make sense of his own identity.

As the narrator is still attempting to assimilate this discovery of Mr. Yu's tattoos, an object resembling a human vertebra suddenly rolls out of a box that she had just been given, and she notices that the bone is covered with undecipherable Chinese characters. She speculates that "perhaps these were symbols that antedated the Chinese written language, like the traces left by birds and animals which, legend holds, provided the inspiration for the earliest Chinese characters," alluding to the legend of Cang Jie's invention of the Chinese writing system, discussed above. Like the tattoos on Mr. Yu's back, the significance and origin of the illegible markings on the vertebra-like bone are never explained in the story, though the work's allusion to the Cang Jie legend suggests that they represent the historical origins of the Chinese writing system as well as the array of nonlinguistic markings against which it is structurally opposed.

In this respect, the bone markings capture a crucial tension at the heart of Ng's story, insofar as the narrative's various sets of tattoos are presented as being nearly illegible for two different sets of reasons. On one hand, the tattoos appear to be inspired by Shang dynasty oracle bone inscriptions (in that Mr. Fu originally took inspiration from the man trying to compose a modern-day *Dream of the Red Chamber* written entirely in oracle bone script), which is a very early version of the Chinese language that is virtually unintelligible to modern readers without specialized training. On the other hand, the tattoos appear to be written by individuals (ranging from the expatriate Mr. Fu to the unnamed Peranakan Chinese) positioned at the outer margins of the Chinese geocultural sphere, each of whom is obsessed with a Chinese script that they themselves barely understand. These mutually opposed sets of connotations, in turn, underscore the way in which the tattoos signify both identity and alienation. They mark both a set of aspirational identities and inverse processes of subjugation and reification. They represent the possibility that individuals may create new identities for themselves, but also the ways in which these same individuals frequently remain defined by social categories of which they themselves may not be fully aware.

Ensconced between these two mutually opposed limit points of an ancient script from China's historical heartland and a very contemporary script from China's outer margins, we find an eclectic body of textual production that may be variously viewed as "modern," "Chinese," and "literary." It is this hybrid and plural category of modern Chinese literatures that is our focus here, and we are specifically interested in the ways in which these texts, like Ng's tattoos, invite and simultaneously resist a process of analysis and interpretation.

At a more practical level, in the following chapters we provide Chinese characters for all proper names and titles, and for select technical terms, but not for place names or fictional characters (unless required by the context of the discussion). We do the same for titles and terms from other languages, including Japanese, Vietnamese, and the Nusuo dialect of Yi. We provide both the original text and an English translation of all quoted poetry, but for prose block quotes we provide only the English translation. In the interest of readability, and also in recognition of the eclectic origins of many of the texts under discussion, we have tried to keep the use of pinyin to a minimum—offering Chinese characters for those readers who read Chinese and English translations for those who do not. Similarly, we have tried, wherever possible, to use the accepted transliterations of authors' names rather than the default pinyin romanizations. So, for instance, the author of "My Dream of Being a Genius" is always referred to as Eileen Chang, and not Zhang Ailing.

NOTES

Epigraph taken from Ng Kim Chew 黃錦樹, "Kebei" 刻背 [Inscribed backs] in *Youdao zhidao* 由島至島 [From island to island] (Taipei: Rye Field Publishing Company, 2001), 325–359. See "Inscribed Backs," in Ng Kim Chew, *Slow Boat to China and other Stories by Ng Kim Chew*, ed. and trans. Carlos Rojas (New York: Columbia University Press, 2016). Subsequent quotes from this story will be referenced parenthetically in the main text, with page numbers corresponding to the 2001 Chinese edition of the work.

1. In my translation of this story, the protagonist's surname is transliterated as "Yur," to differentiate it from another character in the story with a precisely homophonous surname.
2. Ng Kim Chew has indicated that "Fu," here, is short for "Faulkner."

WORKS CITED

Ng Kim Chew 黃錦樹. "Kebei" 刻背 [Inscribed Backs]. In *Youdao zhidao* 由島至島 [From island to island]. Taipei: Maitian, 2001. 325–359. English translation available in Ng Kim Chew, *Slow Boat to China and Other Stories by Ng Kim Chew*. Ed. and trans. Carlos Rojas. New York: Columbia University Press, 2016.

PART I

STRUCTURE

CHAPTER 1.1

....

LU XUN, RETURNING HOME, AND MAY FOURTH MODERNITY

....

KIRK A. DENTON

A new emotion gradually possessed Juehui. He didn't know whether it was joy or sorrow, but one thing was clear—he was leaving his family. Before him was an endless stretch of water sweeping steadily forward, bearing him to an unfamiliar city. There, all that was new was developing—new activities, new people, new friends. . . . For the last time, he looked back. "Goodbye," Juehui said softly. He turned to watch the on-rushing river, the green water that never for an instant halted its rapidly advancing flow.

(Ba Jin, *Family*)

When I was a kid, I used to think that bees and flies were absurd and pathetic. I'd watch the way they'd light someplace, get spooked by something, and then fly away. After making a small circle, they'd always come back again and land just exactly where they had been before. Who could have imagined that someday, having made my own small circle, I would fly back too? And who would ever have expected that you would do the same thing? Couldn't you have managed to fly a little farther away?

(Lu Xun, "Upstairs in a Wineshop")

THE two epigraphs above express a sense of the deeply ambiguous relationship May Fourth writers and intellectuals had with their homes and hometowns. On one hand, there is the exultant and regretless departure from home expressed at the end of Ba Jin's 巴金 *Family* (家; 1933), when Gao Juehui, its protagonist, decides to escape from his oppressively traditional family and make his way to the freedom the modern metropolis seems to offer. On the other hand, the two characters in Lu Xun's 魯迅 story "Upstairs in a Wineshop" (在酒樓上; 1924) have abandoned the path taken by Juehui and returned home, if only temporarily. This is a return filled with regret and disappointment, but also tinged with nostalgia and an element of sincere attachment to the past and tradition.

Juehui's heroic renunciation of family and tradition and his triumphant departure from home are the quintessential gestures of May Fourth literary modernity.[1] By *modernity*, I mean the values that were seen to stand in opposition to a moribund tradition: individualism, science, rule of law, a teleological view of historical progress, democracy, nationalism, revolution, enlightenment, and so forth, as well as the physical spaces, technology, and commercial culture of the modern metropolis. But as the quotation from Lu Xun's "Upstairs in the Wineshop" suggests, this gesture of leaving home and embracing the metropolis is not the whole picture: even as they left home, modern intellectuals like Lu Xun returned to it again and again in literary texts.

When we look closely at these two sides of the literary representations of home, the conventional view that May Fourth intellectuals boldly renounced their pasts and embraced modernity with an unwavering spirit of optimism—in the prototypical manner of Juehui—begins to unravel. Stories such as "Upstairs in a Wineshop" thus problematize May Fourth pretensions to a radical rupture with the past. We find instead a much more complex and nuanced picture. Loaded as it is with so many emotionally charged layers of meaning, home offers a useful lens through which to explore this complex experience of modernity. In this chapter, I look at the trope of home in May Fourth literature, with a focus on Lu Xun, not simply as a foil to modernity, but as a site for an ideological, cultural, political, and psychic struggle.

Much attention has been paid of late in the scholarship on modern Chinese literature to debunking this discourse of modernity and questioning the hubris of its values of enlightenment, revolution, and nationalism.[2] We should add to this list of values "iconoclasm." In this chapter, I hope to question May Fourth claims about its own radical rupture from the past and its parallel optimism about Western modernity. In reading literary works in ways that do not seek to gloss over or smooth out paradox and ambiguity, I hope to present a May Fourth that is far more problematic than its own polemical discourses allow us to see. Literary texts can reveal that Chinese intellectuals' experience with modernity was complex and manifold, difficult and uneasy. Modernity was, then, not simply the intellectual project of nation building, progress, revolution, and iconoclasm; it was a psychic and emotional experience that was disturbing and traumatic. Of course, in addition to questioning the metanarratives of modernity, I also want to broaden what we mean by "tradition" when we talk about "Chinese tradition" in the context of the May Fourth. These metanarratives of modernity were largely constructed in opposition to a reified and simplified tradition; dismantling them means looking at tradition with fresh eyes.[3]

My focus is a body of fictional works that depict intellectuals returning from the metropolis to their rural homes.[4] Let me say, before going into my argument and analysis, that by "home" I mean a cluster of ideas associated with *jia* (家, "home" or "family"), *jiating* (家庭, "family"), and *guxiang* (故鄉, "hometown"), which include a range of sometimes conflicting values linked with tradition, nation, selfhood, and gender.

There is in Chinese no all-encompassing term such as the English word *home* or the German *Heim*. Yet the word *jia* is as culturally potent as *home* or *Heim* in their respective cultural contexts. *Jia* in modern Chinese is generally translated as "family," but the word can also refer to the physical place where the family resides—the family home—and clearly evokes the broader emotional and cultural resonances associated with this space. *Jiating*, meanwhile, is the set of relations that constitute the family, and *guxiang* is the hometown, the village of one's ancestry, especially of the patriarchal lineage, and the realm of ancestral spirits. *Guxiang* is in this sense an extension of *jia* and *jiating*. Like all objects of representation, home in modern China is unstable and contested, a site for the investment of a variety of meanings: personal nostalgia, local identity, nationhood, tradition, patriarchy, and so forth.

Perhaps more than any other fictional genre, stories about returning home show us that the move away from tradition and the embrace of Western values and discourses were not in any way emotionally or psychologically easy or even satisfying for the iconoclasts and Westernizers we associate with the May Fourth movement. Western scholarship has tended to ignore or dismiss modern Chinese ties to tradition as forms of emotional self-deception, rationalizations in response to the Western impact[5]—perhaps because denying the place of tradition confirms the essential rightness of Western social and political values. I am not suggesting that these "return-home" stories undermine at the emotional level what these intellectuals believed at the rational or intellectual levels; rather, I argue that they embody the very difficult and problematic experience that Chinese intellectuals had with modernity in the early twentieth century. Tradition emerges in these stories not as something to fall back on in the face of modernity, but as a kind of return of the repressed and the source of psychic struggle. As Xiaobing Tang has put it in his analysis of Lu Xun's story "Hometown" (故鄉, 1921) and his "native-land" (*xiangtu* 鄉土) fiction more generally, "As a literary form that explores the incidental and remembered fragments of experience, native-land literature compels as well as accomplishes an inquiry into the realm of the unconscious. In engaging in the discourse of alterity, nostalgic writings antithetically outline large and external forces that drive memories and desires inward and into the unconscious."[6] The return-home story forefronts this encounter with the repressed as a psychic conflict and tends to lack the easy nostalgia of "imagined" homelands that can be found in other native-land texts (such as some stories by Shen Congwen 沈從文).[7]

Though I focus here on Lu Xun, the trope of returning home is prevalent in the works of a broad range of writers of the 1920s and beyond. Far from being a marginal theme in modern Chinese literature, returns home are central to it. If leaving home was the quintessential gesture of modernity, returning to it reveals the flipside of that modernity. It is during moments of returning home, coming face to face with the repressed other of tradition, that the psychic/cultural/historical crisis of modernity appears most visibly and most painfully. Stories in this mode are often, though by no means always, in the form of a first-person reminiscence by a modern intellectual of a return to his rural hometown from the modern metropolis, usually Shanghai or Beijing. During the return, memories of the narrator's past flood into his or her mind; these stories embody a complex web of remembering, and the home and the hometown become the spatial projection of those memories. As Gaston Bachelard and others argue, space contains compressed time, and time can only be established through spatial imagery.[8] These stories' representation of space, and the movement of characters through space, may reflect a "memory crisis" at the heart of modernity, when a society moves into a period in which established forms of social identification are collapsing.[9] Dislocating from the metropolis to the hometown provokes memories, memories that are a product of the present as much as they are a reflection of the past.

Returning home necessarily entails a return to the past and tradition. Beneath modernity's metanarrative of iconoclasm lie deep ties to a tradition that May Fourth intellectuals sought to repress; to return home is to confront the repressed, thus giving rise to a web of psychic/cultural/historical conflicts. Freud's essay "The Uncanny" can help frame this complex relationship with home. In the essay, Freud discusses the interrelationship between the German terms unheimlich (uncanny, or literally "unhome-like") and heimlich ("canny," or more literally, "home-like" or "familiar"). *What is known and familiar is associated with the home, but for Freud, as Samuel Weber puts it, "heimlich and unheimlich are not simply opposites, . . . heimlich itself is the repository of ambivalent meanings, signifying on one hand, the familiar and domestic, on the other and simultaneously the concealed and the hidden."*[10] Freud defines *unheimlich* as "something familiar and old-established that has been estranged only by the process of repression";[11] it is "that class of the terrifying which leads back to something long known to us, once very familiar."[12] The paradoxical relationship of May Fourth writers to their homes is similar: home is at once a place that is familiar and a place of terrifying estrangement.

Just as there is no tradition without modernity, there is no home without the metropolis. Leaving home is thus intertwined with the desire to return. But there is no real home to return to, and modern Chinese intellectuals found themselves in a state of "homelessness," where the sense of rootedness to place and of the shared community of the likeminded gives way to feelings of alienation and exile, perhaps a universal condition of modernity.[13] The split from home that modernity entailed provoked in modern Chinese intellectuals a tremendous amount of anxiety, because after breaking with home and family and associating them with a pernicious tradition, home could then not be sought out as a space of comfort from the onslaught of modernity. At the same time that the "hearth" is associated with a narrow and parochial tradition, the city emerges as the new "cosmos," to borrow Yifu Tuan's term, the site of a universal modernity. But there is no longer any happy medium between the two places—they have become almost antagonistic, even as the one cannot exist without the other.

HOME IN PREMODERN CHINA

Although it seemed to offer for some literati a comforting embrace from the onslaught of the universal culture of empire, bureaucracy, and obligatory political loyalism/

activism, home was also the site for the propagation of the Confucian values that constituted, at least in late imperial times, official state ideology.[14] The home was where
young boys read and memorized the canonical Confucian texts and where family
members practiced rituals that, as Patricia Ebrey notes, "legitimated the social and
political structure, making social distinctions part of what is taken to be the nature
of things."[15] In the ancestral hall, the physical and symbolic center of elite homes,
family members carried out rituals that expressed their respect to their forebears
and their obligation to carry on the ancestral line. Not only was the home the place
where Confucian values were learned, the house itself and the "complex structuring
of domestic space . . . embodied in microcosm the hierarchies of gender, generation
and rank inherent in the Chinese social order, tying all its occupants into the mac-
rocosm of the polity," as Francesca Bray puts it.[16] In premodern Chinese society, the
home was never a space for purely familial or private concerns; it was already at least
partly co-opted by the Confucian state and Confucian-inspired social values.

The topos of home occupied a prominent place in traditional Chinese literature, and
it is important, in trying to sort out the modern in literary modernity, to see modern
representations of home in terms of this tradition, both to mark differences that might
help us clarify that modernity and to problematize that modernity by drawing attention
to similarities. Yi-fu Tuan, a geographer who has written extensively on spatiality in
China, sees a split between what he calls "cosmos" and "hearth."[17] Cosmos is the universalist world of the scholar-bureaucrat; hearth, the particularist world of home and
local identity. The values of the cosmos were strongest among the literati and those of
hearth most pronounced among the uneducated classes, but all classes had affinities
to both. There was by no means an absolute split between the two worlds; as we have
seen, the "hearth" was precisely the site for the propagation of the values associated
with a universalizing Confucian "cosmos." The anthropologist Charles Stafford argues
that "separation and reunion"—manifested not only in leaving and returning home, but
in everyday social encounters and etiquette, rituals of kinship, ancestor worship, and
political discourse—are central to Chinese culture, and one can never be understood
without the other.[18]

Given the practices of posting officials to regions far from their natal homes and
of exiling political subversives to far-flung regions of the empire, the desire to return
home was a common theme in premodern literature. Home in these representations
is often equated with family, community, a sense of belonging, and stable cultural
values. It signifies an ideal that is at once personal and public: both the particularity
of the family and one's local culture and the universalist values of the Confucian tradition. Longing to return home is a sentiment expressed in much Chinese poetry: in
the Book of Odes (詩經), especially those poems written in a woman's voice; in
"Encountering Sorrow" (離騷), a third-century BCE narrative poem by Qu Yuan
屈原, who in exile laments his lord's lack of appreciation of his talent; and in the
poems of Tao Yuanming 陶淵明, to name but a few examples. In exile poetry, the
representation of home is more fraught, with the poet caught between perfect personal ideals and an imperfect homeland. So even in imperial times the relation to

home for the Chinese intellectual could be rife with tensions. In the modern period, as I argue below, it becomes deeply problematic.

HOME AS TRADITION: LEAVING HOME AND MODERNITY

With the national crisis engendered by Western imperialism and the weakening of the Chinese state through the late Qing period and early Republic, May Fourth intellectuals launched an all-out assault on the Chinese tradition, in particular Confucianism and its promotion of familial and social hierarchies. May Fourth polemical discourse sometimes makes an absolute equivalence between home and tradition. Home was for the iconoclasts a symbolic space through which they could both construct and then tear down tradition, a discursive starting point from which they sought to forge a Chinese modernity. A typical example is Wu Yu's 吳虞 essay "Theory of the Family System as the Basis of Totalitarianism" (家族制度為專制主義之根據論; 1917).[19] Wu argues that filial piety is the foundation of the totalitarian state and that the traditional family system inevitably reproduced the "right kind of people" to support that state. The moral code governing ruler and subject and father and son had a mutually reinforcing, complementary relationship, writes Wu. The family system was an instrument of authoritarian control, and the servile morality it nurtured in the population was the factor most responsible for two thousand years of acquiescence under despotic rule. Filiality was the establishment's ideology for producing a people submissive toward authority; the family system was nothing more than the means of production (and reproduction) of such a people.[20] Chen Duxiu 陳獨秀, Gao Yihan 高一涵, and other iconoclasts associated with the journal *New Youth* (新青年) wrote similar polemical essays denouncing Confucianism and the "ethics of *li*" (*lijiao* 禮教), as well as the family system that put them into practice. To put it into Lu Xun's rhetoric, the home (here, meaning family, hometown, and tradition) was an "iron house" (鐵屋) in which people live slumbering lives without self-consciousness and with no great desire to leave it or destroy it.[21] Viewed through these polemical texts, modernity in China can be seen as a process of constructing a certain idea of the home for the purposes of nation building and modernization. The various tribal ties that characterize home—family, clan, local filiations—sometimes get lost in this larger discourse of nation as the only true *Gemeinschaft*.

Leaving this patriarchal and traditional home has conventionally been the defining topos of Chinese literary modernity. The paradigmatic statement of this escape from home was expressed for May Fourth intellectuals in a Western literary text—Henrik Ibsen's play *A Doll's House*, which was translated into Chinese by Hu Shi 胡適 and Luo Jialun 羅家倫 and published in a special 1918 issue of *New Youth*. Stuck in a stifling relationship with an overbearing husband, Nora willfully leaves home at the end of the play to start, we presume, her own life without the encumbrances of family obligations. Nora's leaving home was a model of a liberating escape from tradition for Chinese writers and readers, most of whom were male. Leaving home was the paradigmatic act of modernity that marked a rejection of tradition, convention, and oppression. Many intellectuals made this modern gesture in their real lives, leaving their rural home-towns for study in the coastal metropoles or abroad.[22] We also see this played out in literary texts that self-consciously imitated Nora's escape. A year after his translation was published, Hu Shi wrote his own version of the Nora story, *Greatest Event in Life* (終身大事; 1919), a short play that ends with the female protagonist leaving her parents' home to pursue true love. Ouyang Yuqian's 歐陽予倩 *The Shrew* (破婦; 1922) follows the Nora story even more closely: it concerns a woman who makes the radical decision to take her baby and leave her husband after he abandons their youthful ideals and gives in to tradition. In Ba Jin's *Family*, cited in the first epigraph of this chapter, Gao Juehui leaves his home and multigenerational family in the interior province of Sichuan and makes his way to the modern metropolis.

For May Fourth writers, leaving home was a necessary step in forging a modern identity through which to break from the past, an exhilarating liberation from an oppressive and deadening tradition and its hierarchical ethics. Leaving home was the spatial equivalent of enlightenment, forging a subject position outside the dark and stifling confines of the family. Like their counterparts in the West, modern Chinese writers were in a sense homeless, physically and spiritually deracinated from their natal homes. Like Joyce and his recreation of Dublin from the distance of Paris, Chinese writers wrote their homes from the modern metropoles.

Lu Xun and Returning Home in May Fourth Literature

Lu Xun was rather more pessimistic than many of his contemporaries about the pos-sibility of leaving or breaking free of the "iron house" of tradition. His "madman" in "Diary of a Madman" (狂人日記; 1918) seems to represent this possibility: he sees through the façade of Confucian ethics, finding home and family to be the source of social violence and cannibalism. On the other hand, the madman himself may have unwittingly consumed human flesh and, as we learn in the story's classical-language preface, he has subsequently been cured, is awaiting assignment to a position in the state bureaucracy, and has himself given the diary its name, thus accepting society's labeling him mad. The madman cannot escape the claustrophobic confines of the fam-ily home. In his celebrated essay "What Happens after Nora Leaves?" (娜拉走後怎樣; 1924), Lu Xun questions the value of empty proposals for women leaving home when society has remained largely unchanged and unreceptive to change. For Lu Xun, one is always, in a sense, destined to return home, to return to the iron house from which one came.

Lu Xun's returning-home stories reinforce this notion that subject positions outside the iron house are impossible. At the same time, the characters who return home in these stories are not the same as they were before they left, and the home to which they return appears not to be the same as when they lived there. It is this state of limbo between the city and home, modernity and tradition, *heimlich* and *unheimlich* that is explored in Lu Xun's returning home stories.

Lu Xun wrote three stories centered on the return home of a first-person narrator: "Hometown" (1921), "Upstairs in a Wineshop" (1924), and "New Year's Sacrifice" (祝福; 1924). In each of these works, the narrator encounters in his hometown something uncanny, something that is at once familiar and strangely unknown. Although less obviously a returning-home story—it takes place entirely in the metropolis of Beijing—I also discuss "Regret for the Past" (傷逝; 1925) in terms of its first-person narrator's return to a "native-place hostel" (會館), a kind of substitute hometown. Finally, I look briefly at how in his autobiography—*Dawn Blossoms Plucked at Dusk* (朝花夕拾)—Lu Xun structures his own life around leaving and, finally, returning home. All of these stories juxtapose their narrators' present and past selves and highlight their psychic dilemmas or crises.

The paradigmatic story in this returning home vein is "Hometown." Its first-person narrator recounts his return home after twenty years of absence and his encounter with a childhood friend, Runtu. Xiaobing Tang rightly recognizes the complex relationship the narrator has with his hometown. Though deeply alienated from the world, the narrator finds upon his return that "the native land necessarily participates in the formation of the narrator's selfhood or subjectivity. An absent presence, the native land has become the other that is always within the narrating subject and in terms of which he needs to tell his story and narrate his origins. It thus stakes a permanent claim on his existence and self-consciousness. No matter how far he may drift away from this landscape, he cannot escape, just as he is not equipped to step outside his own body."[23] Home and the past cannot be squeezed out of one's subjectivity no matter how much one might try to do so.

The narrator is drawn to his hometown with a nostalgic anticipation that is quickly deflated by the dark and lifeless reality he finds upon arrival:

> It was in the depth of winter and as I drew closer to the place where I'd grown up, the sky clouded over and a cold wind whistled into the cabin of my boat. Through a crack in the canopy, I peered out into the distance. Scattered across the distant horizon, towns and villages came into view under the vast and graying sky: they were drab, desolate, devoid of any semblance of life. I was assailed by a depression against which I was utterly powerless.[24]

The narrator experiences a disturbing disjunction between the reality before his eyes and his memories of the place, memories that were "far more lovely." He recognizes that it may not be the place that has changed, but he himself.

The narrator tell us that his "sole purpose in coming back this time was to bid my home an everlasting farewell" (1: 476; 89), and we learn that he plans to sell the family home and move his mother and nephew to his new home in the north. But this bold gesture of bidding an "everlasting farewell" is undermined at the psychic level. The central plot of the story is the narrator's meeting with Runtu. Before the meeting, the narrator recalls fondly the fantastic outdoor world to which Runtu had introduced him—a seaside world of jade-colored watermelons, fierce badgers, various species of birds, and all manner of colorful seashells—when they were children:

> Wow! Runtu's mind was an inexhaustible treasure-house of exotic things, things my everyday friends knew nothing about, for while Runtu was out there by the sea, they—like me—had nothing to look out on but the square patch of sky that was visible above the high walls of a family courtyard. . . . Now, when my mother said that Runtu might drop by, memories of my boyhood suddenly came alive again as though illumined by a brilliant flash of lightning. For a fraction of a second, I even seemed to recapture that beautiful homeland I thought I had lost. (1: 479; 93–94)

But when he finally meets the now middle-aged Runtu, the narrator sees a tall man whose "round and ruddy face of yesteryear had already turned pale and grey, and it was etched with deep wrinkles. . . . He was wearing a battered old felt hat, and his cotton clothes were so thin that he was shivering" (1: 481–482; 96). After a long, awkward silence, Runtu finally addresses the narrator as "Master," thus establishing a hierarchical relationship between them that does not mesh with the narrator's memories of their unfettered friendship.

What marks the story off from some other native-place literature is its explicit critique of the nostalgic impulse that enshrouds home in a happy, idyllic aura.[25] Lu Xun wants the reader to see that the narrator has repressed the dark side of the past in favor of carefree memories, memories that are as much a reflection of his own present disenchantment with the modern metropolis as they are an authentic account of the past. Runtu, this poor peasant man, stands at once as a counter to the nostalgic impulse of the alienated narrator and as an emblem of the way the past insistently inserts itself into and continues to shape the psyche of the modern intellectual. The narrator in "Hometown" is content with neither the present nor the past. He is tied to the past through memories that are an integral part of his psychic makeup, and those memories are at the same time shaped by present feelings of discontent and despair. It is the subaltern—Runtu, the poor peasant—who is the center of this memory crisis for the narrator, suggesting that happy images of home are intertwined with a hierarchical social structure that places peasants on the bottom and intellectuals on the top, with some positioned as masters and others as slaves. The narrator's confrontation with the past in the figure of Runtu is an encounter with an unjust social system, to be sure, but a social system that also offers space for a magical union through play between two boys of different social classes.

Like "Hometown," "New Year's Sacrifice" is about an encounter between a first-person intellectual narrator and a subaltern. The first-person narrator returns during a New Year's holiday to Lu Town, a place he "still calls home, though his immediate family no longer lives there" (2: 5; 219). While there, he learns the history of Xianglin Sao, a poor peasant woman who, after her first husband died, escaped her in-laws to work as a servant in the house of the narrator's uncle. When her mother-in-law found her, Xianglin Sao was taken back to their mountain village and sold, against her will, to another man to be his wife. Her second husband also died and a wolf devoured her son from that marriage. Xianglin Sao ends up working once again at the uncle's home, though she is by this time a shadow of her former vigorous self. Eventually, she is relieved of her duties, becomes a beggar, and dies of poverty.

Before the reader knows any of this, however, the narrator describes a disturbing encounter he has with Xianglin Sao, now a beggar. The encounter is centered on a series of questions Xianglin Sao asks of the narrator, who in her eyes is educated and should therefore have ready answers: Is there a soul after death? Does hell exist? And do family members meet in hell? Unsure of why she is asking these questions and wary of giving her information that might distress her, the narrator equivocates, offering vague answers or avoiding the issue altogether with the safe phrase "can't say for sure" (說不清). The encounter makes the narrator extremely "uneasy" (不安): "Even after a good night's sleep I couldn't get her out of my mind. It was as though I had a premonition of disaster. The wearisome atmosphere of my uncle's study melded with the gloom of the snow-filled skies to intensify my anxieties" (2: 8; 224).

Like Runtu, Xianglin Sao is a figure of the uncanny, the repressed. She represents something that is to the modern intellectual narrator at once other and familiar. For the narrator, dealing with Xianglin Sao's disturbing questions means confronting his own complicity in her oppression, something he is apparently reluctant to do.[26] At the end of the story, having narrated the sordid and tragic tale of Xianglin Sao's life and death, the narrator feels refreshed and able to enjoy the snowy New Year's night "conscious of nothing except that the various gods of heaven and earth were enjoying the ritual offerings and all the incense that burned in their honor" (2: 21; 241). He is immersed in the very superstitions that have isolated Xianglin Sao from the community and led to her death. For the narrator, returning home means facing his own ties to an unjust social system that is founded on superstitions and makes no room for human warmth and sympathy. That same system offers intellectuals a privileged social position, but one whose ideals the narrator fails to live up to.

The narrator may be alienated from his hometown, but Xianglin Sao is truly homeless. The community of Lu Town has excluded her because she has been tainted by her marriages (in a society that favored chastity and loyalty) and the deaths of her two husbands. In a sense, Lu Xun may be suggesting that the narrator's existential wandering between the city and the rural home pales in comparison to a woman who truly has no home.

"In the Wineshop" may be the most complex of these return-home stories, because it involves returns home by two different narrators. Lin Yu-sheng argues that the story problematizes Lu Xun's iconoclasm. Following Zhou Zuoren 周作人, Lin equates Lu Xun with the character Lü Weifu, who serves throughout much of the story as a narrator, and says that Lü Weifu's filial acts reveal Lu Xun's attitude of "cherishing old ties" (念舊).[27] Lin seems to want to make Lu Xun into a traditionalist, or at least to deconstruct his modern iconoclasm. I would rather see this story as emblematic of a crisis of modernity—a crisis embodied in the parallel themes of leaving and returning home.

The story is about an unnamed first-person narrator returning to his hometown after years of absence. Bored and listless, he goes to an old drinking haunt where he meets by chance his old friend, Lü Weifu, who to the narrator looks tired and aging. They order food and wine, and Weifu slowly perks up and begins to tell stories of how he came to return home. At one point he utters the words cited in the second epigraph above about how bees and flies "always come back again and land just exactly where they had been before" (2: 27; 246).

Modernity for the May Fourth intellectual is ultimately a state of homelessness, a state captured in the image of the flies and bees that leave and return in an endless cycle. Although the two modern intellectuals in this story are often considered opposite characters—with Weifu fallen from his modern ideals and the first-person narrator steadfastly, at least in his own mind, holding on to those ideals—they have much in common: both are drawn inexorably back to their hometowns, where they feel estranged, and neither feels at home in the modern metropolis. Lu Xun captures this sense of homelessness with images of north and south. The north in the story represents the narrator's present and the metropolis of Beijing where he now lives. The south is his hometown, the past, tradition. The north has a dry powdery snow, whereas the snow in the south is moist and clinging. The narrator is alienated from both places: "It occurred to me that while it was true that the north wasn't my home, the south wasn't my home either anymore, for I was treated as a mere guest here too. No matter how the dry snow of the north scattered in the wind, no matter how the moist snow of the south clung to things—none of that had anything to do with me" (2: 25; 244). The modern intellectual is a homeless wanderer caught between north and south, metropolis and hometown, present and past, modernity and tradition. He is at once attracted to and repelled by both.

For the first-person narrator, home is bleak, colored only with the "pallor of a leaden sky" (2: 24; 242). Next to the tavern lies an abandoned garden that would seem to parallel the bleak landscape he finds throughout the town. But though it is late winter and the garden has been untended, winter plum and camellia blossoms brighten the lifeless atmosphere of the garden. As Theodore Huters has suggested, these flowers represent the inflated self-image of the first-person narrator as he seeks to distance himself from the degradation of Weifu, who is now teaching the Confucian classics to young children in the provincial city of Taiyuan.[28] The winter plum blossoming in the snow is a common symbol, often found in premodern works of art and poetry, of the moral fortitude of the literatus. As such, the winter plum in this abandoned garden can also stand for the lingering value of the past in a dark and dreary world. As the narrator puts it, these flowers are "well worth marveling at." Lu Xun's relationship with the past was a complex and dynamic one that, as Eileen Cheng observes, "challenged reductive uses of the categories 'traditional' and 'modern' by exposing the ways in which the two are mutually imbricated."[29] The flowers in the abandoned garden can represent at once the narrator's modern subjectivity *and* his ties to the past; they highlight the mutually intertwined relation of modernity and tradition. One might even see the flowers as representing Weifu's sincere attachment to the past through the filial acts he recounts to the narrator.

The narrator's encounter with Lü Weifu is centered on the latter's narration of two stories, which are offered as explanation for why he had come to return home. The first-person narrator's return home thus involves listening to the narration of Lü Weifu's own return home. Like Xianglin Sao's story, both of Weifu's stories are centered on death. First, he recounts his attempt, requested by his anxious mother, to rebuild the grave of his younger brother, who had died as a child many years earlier. At the anxious moment when he pulls back the fragments of the original coffin, he finds no trace of the corpse, which had probably been washed away by the rising waters of the adjacent river. Still, out of filial duty to his mother, he gathers some dirt from the spot where the corpse had been and scatters it in a newly bought coffin that he has placed next to his father's grave. This act, which he says was done merely to please his mother, implicitly links Weifu to his father, home, and the ancestral village.

Lü Weifu's second story tells of a more pleasant task—presenting red velvet flowers to Ah Shun, daughter of a boatman in the town. Again, Weifu's mother, who recalled that Ah Shun had desperately wanted some velvet flowers when she was a girl, instigates the task, asking Weifu to buy the flowers in the city before he sets out on his trip home. But this task, though undertaken happily by Weifu, also ends in failure and deception. When he learns that the girl had died—she fell sick after a relative, angry that Ah Shun refused to lend him money, lied to her that her betrothed was a despicable person—he can only give the flowers to a neighbor to pass on to Ah Shun's younger sister. To his mother, he says simply that the younger sister was delighted with the flowers.

Although he may have abandoned the ideals of youth and ended up teaching the Confucian classics to young children, Lü Weifu confronts his past with a courage and vigor that the first-person narrator cannot muster. He carries out his two missions with extreme care and depth of feeling and embodies in his actions a form of filial piety that is sincere and authentic. In this sense, Weifu represents the best of the Confucian tradition: compassion for others and sincere filial devotion, not empty rituals in the name of authority and social hierarchy. The first-person narrator sits largely silent as Weifu narrates the stories of the two acts of filial piety. In this sense, his return home involves an encounter with a tradition that disturbs his modern subject position and his sense of his own distance from tradition. That Weifu is a modern intellectual who behaves in traditional ways blurs the clear lines the narrator seems to draw between the present and the past, modernity and tradition, the metropolis and home.

"Regret for the Past" is, in my reading, a kind of play on the return-home genre. As we have seen, the norm in this genre is for the first-person narrator to have left the metropolis, return to his hometown, and then make his way back to the city. "Regret" reverses this movement. Written after the death of his former lover, Zijun, the "notes" that constitute the story first recount the narrator's life in the native-place hostel, where Zijun would later come to visit him. After an awkward declaration of love, the two decide to move to a new home and live together. For a while, they are happy, but their relationship deteriorates rapidly as the narrator comes to see Zijun as having abandoned her former ideals and become a parochial housewife, preoccupied with the daily routine of cleaning, shopping, and eating. Juansheng, the narrator, increasingly avoids home, escaping to a library where he fantasizes about his future:

> In the library, I often saw a brilliant flash illuminating a new road that lay stretched out before me. I imagined Zijun bravely coming to her senses as she resolutely strode forth and left our icy home. And on her face one could not see the slightest trace of rancor or resentment. At such times I felt light and free as a drifting cloud. Above me would appear a blue sky; below, deep mountains and vast oceans. I would see towering skyscrapers; battlefields; motorcars; the stock exchange; bright sunny streets bustling with people; and deep black nights. I had a genuine premonition that this new life of mine was not far off. (2: 124; 356)

One day, Juansheng abruptly tells Zijun that he no longer loves her, a declaration that is greeted by stony silence. Not long after, Zijun's father comes to take her back home, and we learn that she dies, though we are not told how.

In returning home, Zijun seems to fulfill Lu Xun's observation, in "What Happens After Nora Leaves," that the only options open to modern women in China are to return home or become a prostitute. But what interests me is that Juansheng also returns "home." He goes back to the native-place hostel in which he formerly lived, a decision that is starkly at odds with his repeated remarks about the "many new roads" open to him. Like women, men in China are destined to return home. In Juansheng's case, returning home entails a repression of the memory of his relationship with Zijun. Near the end of the story, he says: "I must take the first step and make my way silently down that new road, hiding the truth within my heart's deepest wound and taking falsehood and forgetfulness as my guides" (用遺忘和說謊做我的前導). In light of the fact that Lu Xun's reviled "national character" (國民性), as depicted in "The True Story of Ah Q" (阿Q正傳; 1921) and other texts, is rooted in forgetfulness and not facing reality, Juansheng's "new road" suggests, ironically, a road right back home—to the past and to a patriarchal system that gives men options not offered to women. The story reveals the modern home—where a man and a woman can share a love relationship based on equality and mutual respect—to be a sham, built on a false sense of male entitlement and female oppression.

In Lu Xun's fiction, home—leaving it and returning to it—is a central trope. Leaving home seems to allow for the birth of a modern subject, but that subject is forever tethered to the past and destined to return home. "New roads" that lead away from home have a way of ending back where they started, like the flies and bees that "land exactly where they had been before." The narrators in "Hometown," "New Year's Sacrifice," and "Upstairs in a Wineshop" encounter something uncomfortable in their returns home, and each somehow fails to fully recognize or tries to deny their ties to tradition. Lu Xun questions the modern pose of the intellectual disentangled from the past and other fantasies of heroic modernity.

The trope of home—being home, leaving it, and returning to it—also structures Lu Xun's autobiography, *Dawn Blossoms Plucked at Dusk*. The volume narrates episodes from Lu Xun's childhood in his hometown of Shaoxing, his studies in Nanjing and then Japan, and finally his return to Shaoxing. In the preface, Lu Xun explicitly draws attention to home and memories of it, suggesting that it is key to an understanding of the volume as a whole:

> "At one point, I frequently recalled the fruits and vegetables I ate as a child in my native home. . . . These were all extremely beautiful and savory memories, all of which ensnared me in thoughts of home (都曾是使我思乡的蛊惑). Afterwards, only long after I had departed, I found that it was little more than this: only in memory did these past sentiments exist. Perhaps they will delude me for a lifetime, inducing me to look back at them now and then."[30]

Delusive as these memories might be, they exert a powerful influence on the narrating self.

The final text in the collection (excluding the long "postface") is "Fan Ainong" (範愛農), a recollection of a complex friendship Lu Xun had with the enigmatic titular character, also a native of Shaoxing. They first met when the two were students in Japan. Lu Xun found Fan reprehensible for opposing the sending of a telegram to protest the Qing execution of the revolutionary Xu Xilin 徐錫麟, who had been Fan's teacher. Lu Xun quotes Fan as saying: "Those killed have been killed, those dead have died—what's the use of sending a stinking telegram?" Several years later, first in Hangzhou and then in Shaoxing, where Lu Xun takes up a teaching position, the two become close. But Fan is something of an eccentric who drinks too much, is socially awkward, and has descended into poverty. In the end, he drowns, his corpse found "upright in a creek" among the water chestnuts. Like the deaths in the stories discussed above, Fan's death—it could be suicide or simply an accident while trying to urinate off the edge of a boat in a state of inebriation—contributes to the enigma and to the pull that this character has on Lu Xun.

As Eileen Cheng discusses, the figure of Fan Ainong in Lu Xun's rendering recalls various images of outspoken and unconventional poets from the premodern past: Qu Yuan, who drowned himself in protest against a corrupt political world that failed to appreciate his talents and criticisms, and Ruan Ji 阮籍, who like Fan was an eccentric nonconformist who liked to drink and who would angrily regard the uncouth with "more white than black in his eyes."[31] As Cheng concludes, Fan becomes "readable in historical terms, as one who belongs to a long lineage of talented nonconformists unappreciated in their times."[32] One could add to this lineage the poet Li Bai 李白, who legend has it drowned in a drunken state while trying to embrace the reflection of the moon.

Lu Xun's return home and re-encounter with Fan Ainong parallel the return home of the narrator in "Upstairs in the Wineshop" and *his* encounter with Lü Weifu. In *Dawn Blossoms Plucked at Dusk*, Lu Xun narrates his own life as both a return home and a re-encounter with a fellow native. The return entails yet another death, yet another uncanny element from the past. The pull of Fan on Lu Xun's mind suggests the attraction that the best of the past had to offer the present: a person who is unconventional, forthright, sincere, and incorruptible. Like Weifu, Fan Ainong is an enigmatic character who defies neat categories of "traditional" or "modern." Just as Weifu is an ironic counter to the narrator's own delusions of modernity, Fan represents a questioning of youthful radicalism and, as Eileen Cheng puts it, narratives of "self-consoling gestures or . . . heroic self-fashioning."[33] That Lu Xun narrates his own life as such a return home suggests how central it was to his self-understanding and to his creative motivations as a writer.

CONCLUSION

The various returns home and encounters with the past discussed above reveal the problematic nature of Lu Xun's radical iconoclasm and Nietzscheanism, forged in his late Qing texts and developed in some of his May Fourth writings. Nietzsche, it will be recalled, rejected home as one of the "pitiable comforts" used by the common man to avoid confronting reality. For Zarathustra, Nietzsche's superman, solitude becomes a new home: "O solitude! O my *home*, solitude! Too long have I lived wildly in wild strange places not to return home to you in tears. Now you may threaten me with your finger, as mothers threaten; now you may smile at me, as mothers smile."[34] As William Connolly writes:

> He [Nietzsche] defines ineliminable sources of the urge to find a home, but sometimes he also seems to look to a world where the urge itself disappears; he attends to the struggle within the self to overcome belief that the world is designed to become a home, and sometimes he acts as though those who do not or cannot conquer it should be subordinated to those who do; he exposes what happens when moderns try to master the world, but many of his formulations then seem to call upon a 'overman' to master it more completely.[35]

But Connolly also finds a "shadow of longing" in Nietzsche's rejection of home and homesickness. Is there a similar "shadow" hovering over Lu Xun's narrators and their returns homes? Like Nietzsche, Lu Xun questions such nostalgic longings as ultimately a memory construct that alienates us from the real, but home is not just something one can willfully reject with an easy iconoclastic gesture. As the spatial embodiment of one's past and one's memories, home is an integral part of the personal psyche and the collective cultural consciousness. One leaves it because it can be oppressive, but is drawn back to it because, ultimately, it will not be completely repressed.

As Huters describes him, Lu Xun is far from typical of May Fourth writers in terms of the complexity of his moral vision and the depth of his introspection.[36] From this perspective, Lu Xun's literary returns home might be seen to reflect a unique sensitivity to the inseparability of tradition and modernity. But the pervasiveness of returns home in May Fourth literature suggests, to the contrary, that the psychic and cultural tensions embodied in the stories analyzed here were shared by a wide range of writers. Though I have focused here on Lu Xun, I want to underline that returning home is central to Chinese literary modernity and that this centrality complicates the binary of tradition and modernity that has often shaped our understanding of modern Chinese literature.

NOTES

Epigraphs taken from Ba Jin, *Family*, Sidney Shapiro, trans. (Beijing: Foreign Languages Press, 1978); and Lu Xun, "Upstairs in the Wineshop," in *Diary of a Madman and Other Stories*, William A. Lyell, trans. (Honolulu: University of Hawaii Press). Here, and throughout this chapter, romanizations have been modified to conform to the pinyin transcription system.

1. Here I am using the term *May Fourth literature* in a broad sense: the "new literature" that emerged from the May Fourth movement.

2. Some have, for example, looked beneath the May Fourth feminist rhetoric and found deep ties to traditional patriarchy in the way May Fourth writers used images of women and women's bodies for the nationalist agenda. See, for example, Dai Jinhua 戴錦華 and Meng Yue 孟悦, *Fuchu lishi dibiao* 浮出歷史地表 [Emerging from the horizon of history] (Kaifeng: Henan renmin chubanshe, 1989). Prasenjit Duara has questioned two central categories of May Fourth modernity—the Nation and a Hegelian conception of a teleological History—and proposed a "bifurcated" history that looks at once at the Nation and what it represses. See *Rescuing History from the Nation: Questioning Narratives of Modern China* (Chicago: University of Chicago Press, 1995). Others, such as David Wang, argue that the hegemonic discourse of May Fourth nationalism repressed incipient modernities that existed already in the late Qing period. Instead, he proposes a radical rereading of late Qing texts as examples of what Chinese modernity could have been but for the hegemonic May Fourth modern subject. See *Fin-de-siècle Splendor: Repressed Modernities of Late Qing Fiction, 1848–1911* (Stanford: Stanford University Press, 1997). In her *Zhou Zuoren and an Alternative Chinese Response to Modernity* (Cambridge: Harvard University Asia Center, 2000), Susan Daruvala sees Zhou Zuoren as representing an "alternative" literary response to modernity, one that rejected nationalism and iconoclasm. In my own work on modern Chinese literary criticism, I have scrutinized the iconoclastic stance of May Fourth intellectuals and tried to lay bare some of their deep ties to tradition, in particular how traditional epistemological orientations shaped their reception of Western literary modes such as realism, romanticism, and aestheticism. See Kirk A. Denton, "Introduction," in *Modern Chinese Literary Thought: Writings on Literature, 1893–1945* (Stanford: Stanford University Press, 1996), 1–60.

3. Eric Hobsbawn and Terence Ranger, among others, have shown us that the very concept of "tradition" is a modern invention, which reflects a modern anxiety about changing relations with the past. See *The Invention of Tradition* (Cambridge: Cambridge University Press, 1983).

4. A similar scholarly endeavor has been undertaken by Stephen Dodd in the context of modern Japanese literature. See *Writing Home: Representations of the Native Place in Modern Japanese Literature* (Cambridge: Harvard University Asia Center, 2004). For discussions in modern Chinese literature of "home" and the "returning" theme, see Zhao Yuan 趙園, "*Huigui yu piaopo: Guanyu Zhongguo xiandangdai zuojia de xiangtu*

yishi" 回歸於漂潑關於中國現當代作家的鄉土意識 [Returning and wandering: on modern and contemporary Chinese writers nativist consciousness]. *Wenyi yanjiu* 文藝研究 [Literary research] 4 (1989): 56–65; and Bai Peilan 白佩蘭. "Weiji zhong de jiating: 1920–1940 nian Zhongguo zhishifenzi lun jiating" 危機中的家庭: 1920–1940 年中國知識分子論家庭 [The home in crisis: Chinese intellectuals on the home from 1920 to 1940] Trans. Zheng Lulin 鄭魯琳, in *Xingbie yu Zhongguo* 性別與中國 [Gender and China], ed. Li Xiaojiang (Beijing: Sanlian, 1994), 38–62.

5. See, for example, Joseph R. Levenson, *Confucian China and Its Modern Fate: A Trilogy* (Berkeley: University of California Press, 1968).

6. Xiaobing Tang, "Beyond Homesickness: An Intimate Reading of Lu Xun's 'My Native Land,'" in *Chinese Modernism: The Heroic and the Quotidian* (Durham: Duke University Press, 2000), 86.

7. On the concept of "imaginary homelands," see David Der-wei Wang, *Fictional Realism in Twentieth-Century China: Mao Dun, Lao She, Shen Congwen* (New York: Columbia University Press, 1992). For more on "native place" literature, see Rosemary Haddon, "Chinese Nativist Literature of the 1920s: The Sojourner-Narrator." *Modern Chinese Literature* 8.1–2 (Spring/Fall 1994): 97–126; and Tao Tao Liu, "Local Identity in Modern Chinese Fiction and Fiction of the Native Soil (Xiangtu Wenxue)," in *Unity and Diversity: Local Cultures and Identities in China*, ed. Liu and David Faure (Hong Kong: Hong Kong University Press, 1996), 139–160. For a historical study of the role of "native place" in modern China, see Bryana Goodman, *Native Place, City and Nation: Regional Networks and Identities in Shanghai, 1853–1937* (Berkeley: University of California Press, 1996).

8. Bachelard writes: "Memories are motionless, and the more securely they are fixed in space, the sounder they are." See *The Poetics of Space* (New York: The Orion Press, 1994), 9.

9. On the modern memory crisis, see Richard Terdiman, *Present Past: Modernity and the Memory Crisis* (Ithaca: Cornell University Press, 1993) and Pierre Nora, "Between Memory and History," *Representations* 26 (Spring 1989): 7–25.

10. Samuel Weber, "The Sideshow, or: Remarks on a Canny Moment," *Modern Language Notes* 88.6 (1973): 1105.

11. Sigmund Freud, "The Uncanny," in *Freud on Creativity and the Unconscious* (New York: Harper and Row, 1968): 148.

12. Freud, "The Uncanny," 123–124.

13. On homelessness as a condition of modernity, see Rosemary Marangoly George, *The Politics of Home: Postcolonial Relocations and Twentieth Century Fiction* (Cambridge: Cambridge University Press, 1996); Edward Relph, *Place and Placelessness* (London: Pion, 1976); Peter Berger, Brigitte Berger, and Hansfried Kellner, *The Homeless Mind: Modernization and Consciousness* (New York: Vintage, 1974); and Andrew Gurr, *Writers in Exile: The Identity of Home in Modern Literature* (Atlantic Highlands, N.J.: Humanities Press, 1981).

14. Patricia Buckley Ebrey, *Confucianism and Family Rituals in Imperial China: A Social History of Writing about Rites* (Princeton: Princeton University Press, 1991).

15. Ebrey, *Confucianism*, 4.

16. Francesca Bray, *Technology and Gender: Fabrics of Power in Late Imperial China* (Berkeley: University of California Press, 1997), 4.

17. Yi-fu Tuan, *Cosmos and Hearth: A Cosmopolite's Viewpoint* (Minneapolis: University of Minnesota Press, 1996).

18. Charles Stafford, *Separation and Reunion in Modern China* (Cambridge: Cambridge University Press, 2000).

19. Wu Yu 吳虞, "Jiazu zhidu wei zhuanzhi zhuyi zhi genju lun" 家族制度為專制主義之根據論 [Theory of the family system as the basis of totalitarianism], *Xin qingnian* 新青年 [New youth] 2.6 (February 1917): 10–13.

20. For a discussion of this text, see Ono Kazuko, *Chinese Women in a Century of Revolution* (Stanford: Stanford University Press, 1989), 96. Interestingly, Wu Yu quotes Montesquieu on Chinese filial piety as an obstacle to democracy, reflecting a general tendency in the May Fourth to draw on the authority of Western intellectuals for their own attacks on tradition.

21. See *"Nahan zixu"* 吶喊自序 [Preface to *Call to Arms*], in *Lu Xun quanji* 魯迅全集 [Complete works of Lu Xun], 16 vols. (Beijing: Renmin wenxue, 1981), vol. 1: 415–421.

22. Leaving home was a much less radical act for Chinese male intellectuals than it is made out to be in literary representations, because it could be done under the old guise of going off to take the civil service exam or assuming some official post somewhere away from home, a common phenomenon for the literati class in premodern times. Leaving home for women, such as Qiu Jin's 秋瑾 decision to leave her husband and family to study in Japan, was a far more difficult and wrenching experience.

23. Tang, "Beyond Homesickness," 78.

24. *Lu Xun quanji*, vol. 1: 476; and Lu Xun, *Diary of a Madman and Other Stories*, trans. William A. Lyell (Honolulu: University of Hawai'i Press, 1990), 89. Subsequent references to Lu Xun's stories will give page numbers parenthetically, with the *Lu Xun quanji* reference first (including volume number and page number separated by a colon), followed by the page number from the William Lyell translation.

25. See Tang, "Beyond Homesickness."

26. See, for example, Theodore Huters, "Blossoms in the Snow: Lu Xun and the Dilemma of Modern Chinese Literature," *Modern China* 10.1 (1984): 49–77.

27. Yu-sheng Lin, *The Crisis of Chinese Consciousness: Radical Anti-traditionalism in the May Fourth Era* (Madison: University of Wisconsin Press, 1979), 142–151.

28. Huters, "Blossoms."

29. Eileen J. Cheng, *Literary Remains: Death, Trauma, and Lu Xun's Refusal to Mourn* (Honolulu: University of Hawai'i Press, 2013), 8.

30. *Lu Xun quanji*, vol. 2: 229–230. This is a modified translation from *Dawn Blossoms Plucked at Dusk*, trans. Yang Hsien-yi and Gladys Yang (Beijing: Foreign Languages Press, 1976), 2.

31. Cheng, *Literary Remains*, 65–68.

32. Cheng, *Literary Remains*, 83.

33. Cheng, *Literary Remains*, 66.

34. Friedrich Nietzsche, *The Portable Nietzsche*, ed. and trans. Walter Kaufman (New York: Penguin, 1976), 295.

35. William Connolly, "Nietzsche: Politics and Homesickness," in *Political Theory and Modernity* (Oxford: Oxford University Press, 1988), 140–141.

36. Huters, "Blossoms."

WORKS CITED

Bachelard, Gaston. *The Poetics of Space*. New York: Orion Press, 1994.

Bai Peilan 白佩蘭. "Weiji zhong de jiating: 1920–1940 nian Zhongguo zhishifenzi lun jiat-ing" 危機中的家庭：1920–1940 年中國知識分子論家庭 [The home in crisis: Chinese intellectuals on the home from 1920 to 1940] Trans. Zheng Lulin 郑鲁琳. In *Xingbie yu Zhongguo* 性別與中國 [Gender and China]. Ed. Li Xiaojiang. Beijing: Sanlian, 1994. 38–62.

Berger, Peter, Brigitte Berger, and Hansfried Kellner. *The Homeless Mind: Modernization and Consciousness*. New York: Vintage, 1974.

Bray, Francesca. *Technology and Gender: Fabrics of Power in Late Imperial China*. Berkeley: University of California Press, 1997.

Cheng, Eileen J. *Literary Remains: Death, Trauma, and Lu Xun's Refusal to Mourn*. Honolulu: University of Hawai'i Press, 2013.

Connolly, William. "Nietzsche: Politics and Homesickness." In Connolly, *Political Theory and Modernity*. Oxford: Oxford University Press, 1988. 137–174.

Daruvala, Susan. *Zhou Zuoren and an Alternative Chinese Response to Modernity*. Cambridge: Harvard University Asia Center, 2000.

Denton, Kirk A. "Introduction." In *Modern Chinese Literary Thought: Writings on Literature, 1893–1945*. Ed. Kirk Denton. Stanford: Stanford University Press, 1996. 1–61.

Dodd, Stephen. *Writing Home: Representations of the Native Place in Modern Japanese Literature*. Cambridge: Harvard University Asia Center, 2004.

Duara, Prasenjit. *Rescuing History from the Nation: Questioning Narratives of Modern China*. Chicago: University of Chicago Press, 1995.

Ebrey, Patricia Buckley. *Confucianism and Family Rituals in Imperial China: A Social History of Writing about Rites*. Princeton: Princeton University Press, 1991.

Freud, Sigmund. "The Uncanny (1919)." In *Freud on Creativity and the Unconscious*. New York: Harper and Row, 1968. 122–160.

George, Rosemary Marangoly. *The Politics of Home: Postcolonial Relocations and Twentieth Century Fiction*. Cambridge: Cambridge University Press, 1996.

Goodman, Byrna. *Native Place, City and Nation: Regional Networks and Identities in Shanghai, 1853–1937*. Berkeley: University of California Press, 1996.

Gurr, Andrew. *Writers in Exile: The Identity of Home in Modern Literature*. Atlantic Highlands, N.J.: Humanities Press, 1981.

Haddon, Rosemary. "Chinese Nativist Literature of the 1920s: The Sojourner-Narrator." *Modern Chinese Literature* 8.1–2 (Spring/Fall 1994): 97–126.

Hobsbawm, Eric, and Terence Ranger, eds. *The Invention of Tradition*. Cambridge: Cambridge University Press, 1983.

Huters, Theodore. "Blossoms in the Snow: Lu Xun and the Dilemma of Modern Chinese Literature." *Modern China* 10.1 (1984): 49–77.

Kazuko, Ono. *Chinese Women in a Century of Revolution*. Stanford: Stanford University Press, 1989.

Levenson, Joseph. *Confucian China and Its Modern Fate: A Trilogy*. Berkeley: University of California Press, 1968.

Lin, Yu-sheng. *The Crisis of Chinese Consciousness: Radical Anti-traditionalism in the May Fourth Era*. Madison: University of Wisconsin Press, 1979.

Liu, Tao Tao. "Local Identity in Modern Chinese Fiction and Fiction of the Native Soil (Xiangtu Wenxue)." In *Unity and Diversity: Local Cultures and Identities in China*. Ed. Liu and David Faure. Hong Kong: Hong Kong University Press, 1996. 139–160.

Lu Xun 鲁迅. *Dawn Blossoms Plucked at Dusk*. Trans. Yang Hsien-yi and Gladys Yang. Beijing: Foreign Languages Press, 1976.

Lu Xun 魯迅. *Lu Xun quanji* 魯迅全集 [Complete works of Lu Xun], 16 vols. Beijing: Renmin wenxue, 1981.

Lu Xun 魯迅. *Diary of a Madman and Other Stories*. Trans. William A. Lyell. Honolulu: University of Hawai'i Press, 1990.

Nietzsche, Friedrich. *The Portable Nietzsche*. Ed. and trans. Walter Kaufman. New York: Penguin, 1976.

Nora, Pierre. "Between Memory and History." *Representations* 26 (Spring 1989): 7–25.

Relph, Edward. *Place and Placelessness*. London: Pion, 1976.

Stafford, Charles. *Separation and Reunion in Modern China*. Cambridge: Cambridge University Press, 2000.

Tang, Xiaobing. "Beyond Homesickness: An Intimate Reading of Lu Xun's 'My Native Land.'" In *Chinese Modernism: The Heroic and the Quotidian*. Durham: Duke University Press, 2000. 49–96.

Terdiman, Richard. *Present Past: Modernity and the Memory Crisis*. Ithaca: Cornell University Press, 1993.

Tuan, Yi-fu. *Cosmos and Hearth: A Cosmopolite's Viewpoint*. Minneapolis: University of Minnesota Press, 1996.

Wang, David Der-wei. *Fictional Realism in Twentieth-Century China: Mao Dun, Lao She, Shen Congwen*. New York: Columbia University Press, 1992.

Wang, David Der-wei. *Fin-de-siècle Splendor: Repressed Modernities of Late Qing Fiction, 1848–1911*. Stanford: Stanford University Press, 1997.

Weber, Samuel. "The Sideshow, or: Remarks on a Canny Moment." *Modern Language Notes* 88.6 (1973): 1102–1120.

Wu Yu 吳虞. "Jiazu zhidu wei zhuanzhi zhuyi zhi genju lun" 家族制度為專制主義之根據論 [Theory of the family system as the basis of totalitarianism]. *Xin qingnian* 新青年 [New youth] 2.6 (February 1917): 10–13.

Zhao Yuan 趙園. "Huigui yu piaopo: Guanyu Zhongguo xiandangdai zuojia de xiangtu yishi" 回歸於漂泊關於中國現當代作家的鄉土意識 [Returning and wandering: On modern and contemporary Chinese writers nativist consciousness]. *Wenyi yanjiu* 文藝研究 [Literary research] 4 (1989): 56–65.

CHAPTER 1.2

....

TRAVELS IN MODERN CHINA

From Zhang Taiyan to Gao Xingjian

....

PING-HUI LIAO

WHY do people travel? Sigmund Freud thinks that it has to do with our "early wishes" to escape "the family and especially the father"—or, as Paul Fussell puts it, to steer away from "the boss" and work.[1] Anthropologists such as Mary Helms and Claude Lévi-Strauss suggest that travelers move not only across space and time but also in the social hierarchy, to "overcome distance" and thereby to obtain moral as well as epistemological authority.[2] For Mary Pratt, however, journeying to a foreign land often involves a colonial "planetary consciousness" to dominate and conquer the primitive others and to catalogue new flora or fauna.[3] With regard to the interrelationship between travel and "long-distance nationalism," Benedict Anderson mentions quite a few factors that contribute to modern exoduses, including kidnapping, slavery, international trade, tourism, political asylum, war, famine, job opportunities, religious freedom, study abroad, and so forth.[4]

I argue that when modern Chinese intellectuals and writers travel, they are often shaped by a profound sense of psychosocial deprivation, reluctance, and loss rather than empowerment or recreational escape. In contrast to what Freud proposes, Chinese people are obliged to show filial piety and to stay near their parents. Confucius famously warns, "So long as one's parents are alive, one should never travel far."[5] Modern Chinese artists and writers have often viewed journeys away from the fatherland as particularly painful and humiliating, because their departures have often been propelled by foreign invasion, colonial discrimination, national division, land pollution, reeducation of the elite, and so forth. Travels in modern China are not only about displacement and exile, but in many ways are informed by a sense of inadequacy and betrayal, with the desire to stay close (or return) to the fatherland constantly being frustrated and negated.

Zhang Taiyan 章太炎 (1868–1936) fled to Taiwan after the failure of the Wuxu Reform and realized that his Confucian utopian vision of a new Qing state was on the verge of collapse. Later, when Zhang returned to China in 1903 from Japan, he was incarcerated for three years because of his attempts to subvert the empire. Zhang is hardly alone.

Liu Na'ou 劉吶鷗, Jiang Wenye 江文也, Wu Zhuoliu 吳濁流, Yang Jizeng 楊基振, Zhong Lihe 鍾理和, and many other intellectuals from Taiwan were spied on, tortured, imprisoned, and even murdered after returning to the fatherland. On the mainland, hundreds of thousands migrated due to the Sino-Japanese war in the late 1930s and again, on a more massive scale, during the clashes between the Nationalist and Communist regimes. Xiao Hong 蕭紅, Eileen Chang 張愛玲, Nieh Hualing 聶華苓, Pai Hsien-yung 白先勇, Ya Xian 瘂弦, Ang Lee 李安, and Hou Hsiao-hsien 侯孝賢, to name a few, are among the artists who write or produce works around such diasporic experiences, works that feature haunting, traumatic images of their home, country, and world order vanishing or destroyed.

In Wu Wenguang's 吳文光 2014 documentary film *Investigating My Father* (調查父親), for instance, the memory of the father is overshadowed by differential, conflicting accounts—official and unofficial, archival and anecdotal, familial and communal—of a nation divided, of untold (or underrepresented) stories about the Great Famine, the Cultural Revolution, June Fourth, and other large and small tragedies. The father's passage through time and place is riddled with gaps, intrigues, and secrets, to the point that "when Father returns from travel, he appears to be a different person, a stranger." Even those who now return to China from abroad, the so-called *haigui* (海歸; the term means "returned from overseas," but it also puns on the homophonous word for "sea tortoise," 海龜), are regarded suspiciously, as if they were double agents—working for the CIA or for the Cyber Units of the Liberation Army, or simply coming back to grab huge grants and bigger portions of pension and benefits. Evidently, travels in modern China prove to be more truncated, complicated, and convoluted than many theorists have imagined.

Before we examine such truncated routes of travel in modern China, perhaps we should raise the question of the ways in which travel affects a nation or, more specifically, Chinese people's lives. Here, we also have a plethora of possibly revealing situations. Gilles Deleuze, for instance, draws on the story of Achilles overtaking the tortoise (a sea tortoise?) to observe that any inner or outer vital motion inevitably involves change and "relates the objects of a closed system to open duration."[6] James Clifford suggests that travel goes hand in hand with translation and brings about a sense of "discrepant cosmopolitanism" in the form of cultural critique on top of unsettling the psychosocial structure of identification in partial response to the political economy of movement.[7] Edward W. Said credits those who travel or steer away from home with more innovative capacities and utopian impulses to bring about reform and social change, in contrast to those "potentates" who stay behind and cling onto the status quo. But Said also highlights the pain and "terminal loss" one has to endure while in exile.[8] In relation to modern China, Anderson's perspective resonates perhaps more strongly with Said's here in claiming that national fathers tend to be travelers who rearticulate cultural identity and introduce an "inverted" telescopic vision by reinventing the tradition, coming up with imaginative ways in which they can bring home what they might have at first deemed "foreign." In blending the alien with the local, these national fathers hope to strengthen the national spirit. This is most apparent in modern China, a nation that was struggling to redefine itself against the backdrop of the Opium War and the long shadow it cast.

Travel literature has, of course, a long tradition in Chinese literature, though often in the form of human geography, mountain and river mapping, literati's retreats or inner exile experiences, dream adventures, pilgrimages, and border crossings in time of war. These motifs persist in modern Chinese literature, but travel writings in the twentieth-century Chinese and Sinophone communities tend to be constituted by a desire to be on an equal footing with and even to overtake the West, to such an extent that the journeys are often perpetuated by themes of cultural translation, colonial encounter, diasporic mediation, modernity and identity, frontier consciousness, and cosmopolitanism.

Modern writers from Liang Qichao 梁啟超 to Ma Jian 馬健 deploy tropes of travel—including travel to Taiwan, Japan, Britain, the United States, and New Zealand, as well as within China—to construct new imaginaries and alternate paths in cognitive mapping. Zhang Taiyan, for instance, began to thematize issues of travel after undergoing a dramatic transformation when, from September 1898 to May 1899, he made a short visit to Taiwan, then a Japanese colony, to take up a post at the *Taiwan Daily News* (台灣日日新報; *Taiwan Nichinichi Shinpo*) as a columnist and editor. Before fleeing to Taiwan to escape persecution by Empress Dowager Cixi 慈禧 on account of the Wuxu Reform that Zhang had initiated with his teacher Kang Youwei 康有為, Zhang established himself as a neo-Confucian with little idea of how a modern nation-state functioned in terms of governance and political economy. It was in Taiwan that Zhang experienced firsthand Japanese colonial modernity and as a result revised his utopian visions of popular sovereignty and national spirit. In a number of newspaper articles, he considered ways in which Chinese philosophical tradition might be illuminated by individualistic thought and Western logic. He decided to move to Japan in May 1899 to meet with many radical intellectuals of the time. There, he began to formulate the notion of a new republic, which he later on introduced (with a profound influence on Dr. Sun Yat-sen 孫中山) under the name *zhonghua minguo* (中華民國), which would bring the five ethnic groups together in a democratic and harmonious manner.

On December 16, 1898, Zhang published a short but emotional commentary in the *Taiwan Daily News* in response to a Japanese friend's thoughtful reflections on leaving the small colony to return home, hailing the friend's poem as a melancholic master-piece reminiscent of the famous lyrics by such Tang poets as Wang Wei 王維 and Li Shangyin 李商隱, with its imagery of the "enormous, deep space of clouds and waters" that evokes lingering sensations of pain and loss.[9] Like his Japanese friend, Zhang found Taiwan to be a tiny, misty island "with sea gulls filling the sky," a place in the "barbaric south" providing only "temporary" shelter. However, drifting lonely souls on such a marginal island quickly acquaint themselves with colleagues in similar diasporic predicaments: "They eagerly shake hands but soon sail on to a distant metropolis to fulfill their ambitions."[10] This is not the only commentary Zhang made on friends going back home for more important posts. On December 24, 1898, for instance, Zhang wrote that "lyrics on lives in Taiwan actually are about the poet's otherworldly enterprise."

His commentaries show vibrant resonances with those Japanese colonial officers who were returning to contribute to their home country. Apparently, even as Zhang traveled in Taiwan, his loyalty remained with the Qing emperor and his ailing dynasty; he envisioned and was tormented by a homologous analogy and even uncanny parallel between Japan and Qing China.

In a long poem dated December 27, 1898, Zhang also compared his displacement and diasporic experience to that of Liu Bei 劉備, the founder of Shu who had attempted to revive the Han dynasty when the nation collapsed and split into three kingdoms. Zhang spent time reading documents of the colonial government, so as to expand his horizons. In a newspaper article published on December 18, 1898, Zhang admitted that the colonial government's educational, land, and market reforms, together with the constitution of the local literati society as a public space, enabled Taiwan to become more advanced than the mainland. He provided eyewitness accounts of how Chinese and Western civilizations were successfully reproduced in Taiwan, placing the island ahead of China itself. He presented details concerning the land survey, public schools, sales tax, and salons that were set up across the island, indicating that Taiwan might well serve as a model for the Chinese government back home in the mainland. He was very impressed that Taiwanese intellectuals could get together to recite poems, discuss public concerns, and disseminate scientific or professional knowledge throughout the island. Because of such exposure to colonial modernity, Zhang felt very much drawn to Western learning and democracy, and remarked that "different kinds of people would come to the salon, to express themselves and to be enlightened by others, were all abiding by general rules to behave properly and to aim to be better persons."[11] Meantime, Zhang was also entertained by the Japanese (and, to him, probably more subtle) ways of retelling traditional Chinese supernatural tales, finding a story about a Taiwanese fruit (the column essay dated December 18, 1898) to be revealingly succinct (*miao* 妙) and marvelous (*shen* 神) in narrative structure.

In many ways, Zhang's travel away from his home country is significant for our understanding of modern Chinese cultural history. First, Zhang was a strong believer in modernizing the ailing Qing dynasty and enabling it to compete with the West. That is why he played an active role in the Wuxu Reform, eager to transform Kang Youwei's Confucian vision of the "Great Harmony" into a political reality. But as the Reform was blocked by Empress Dowager Cixi, Zhang recognized that travel to Taiwan would entail a separation not only from the Qing Empress Dowager but also from the Qing dynasty and its political order, leaving him no hope of returning to the fatherland in the immediate future. For him, traveling to Taiwan must have meant coming to terms with the abrupt end of his philosophical and political aspirations, but it also meant a journey to a new world and new system of colonial governance. In realizing this, he actually moved closer to the radical position represented by Liang Qichao instead of that upheld by his old master and mentor Kang Youwei, more along the line of appropriating Meiji and Western ideas than reinventing traditional notions of patriarchy and statehood. Second, he was fascinated by what he saw in Taiwan and decided to move to Japan in May 1899, so that he might acquire new learning and become a student of global modernity. He coined the phrase *Zhonghua minguo* (Chinese Republic), which was later introduced by Sun Yat-sen as the official name of the Republic of China.

Third, as a result of his travel to Japan, Zhang developed the concept of *guoxue* (national learning) to boost the national spirit, advocating more fruitful ways to blend scientific and philological approaches to Chinese classics. He came up with a new phonetic system for the Chinese language, which ironically was carried over to Taiwan and many parts of the world while not available in China, his fatherland. Fourth, Zhang taught from 1902 to 1903 at a Japanese prep school, the Kobun Gakuin (Hongwen Institute), and had several distinguished students there who planned on pursuing advanced study in Japan, including Lu Xun 魯迅 (1881–1936) and Qian Xuantong 錢玄同. Because of his writings and teaching in Japan, Zhang made friends with Japanese scholars and was seen as a leading Chinese intellectual of the time. However, in *Travels in China*, Akutagawa Ryunosuke (1892–1927) portrayed Zhang as a boring and superficial figure when they met in Shanghai in 1921, using Zhang as a relatively well-known and hence symbolic character to represent China as regressive and cumbersome. In critical response to such derogatory comments and negative portraits, writers such as Wu Zhuoliu tried to offer more sympathetic accounts when they traveled back to China. Fifth, Zhang helped construct a new China while in Japan, but soon after his return he was horrified by the Nationalist Party's corruption and found himself once again a stranger in his home country. Finally, and perhaps most importantly, Zhang's exile in Taiwan and later on in Japan can be seen as an important case of Sinophone rearticulation, as an alternative mode of writing back to China from abroad. He even suggested in an article that in terms of temporality, Taiwan was very much ahead of China.

Significantly, Zhang's eight-month sojourn in Taiwan transformed his mindset and prepared him for a journey to Japan in 1902 to learn more about Meiji reforms and to befriend liberals as well as revolutionaries such as Liang Qichao, Huang Kan 黄侃, and members of the China United Society (同盟會), including Sun Yat-sen. Dr. Sun himself is another traveler, who discovered his identity while in Honolulu and eventually went on to become the founding father of the Republic of China. Leaving China in 1894, Sun had gone to Hawai'i, where he founded the China Revival Society (興中會). He moved the organization's headquarters to Hong Kong early in 1895. After several failed uprisings, he was forced to leave for Europe and became internationally famous when Qing agents attempted to kidnap him in London. Europe soon became too dangerous, so Sun traveled to Japan, where he met Zhang Taiyan while propagandizing among the large community of Chinese students, political exiles, and businessmen. Both Sun and Zhang testify to the complex situations in which their travel accounts gain meaning, as they are very much informed by foreign travelogues on China while their experiences abroad helped constitute their political visions. Sun draws on the lessons of American democracy to formulate his "three principles," while Zhang revises his Confucian notion of national unity and ethnic harmony after acquiring materials in Japanese on related topics.

Among Zhang's students at Kobun Gakuin between 1902 and 1903 was Lu Xun, who had gone to Japan with the hope of becoming a physician. Lu Xun attended Sendai

Medical Academy and was soon attracted to the professional manners and meticulous attention to detail of his teacher Fujino Genkuro. This was Lu Xun's first exposure to Japanese modernity in everyday practice. However, it was a slide about the decapitation of a Chinese spy in the classroom that shocked him to the core as it showcased his home country's backwardness. Lu Xun changed his path after the traumatic scene, advocating that the Chinese mind rather than the body had to be transformed and rescued: modern literature, not medicine, would function as a spiritual antidote (a pharmakon). Thus, Lu Xun launched his literary career in Sendai, Japan, and went on to view Confucianism as backward and even cannibalistic. But it was Yu Dafu 郁達夫 who mourned his country's inferior status and painfully meditated over the fate of China, drawing on the sinking feeling of a depressed male protagonist who studied in Japan. Yu Dafu was only reiterating what numerous Japanese writers of the time said about China, such as accounts by Akutagawa Ryunosuke and Yosano Akiko (1878–1942) of their travels to China and Manchuria, where they saw only poverty and corruption. Yu's short story "(沈淪)" ends with this lament: "O China, my China, you are the cause of my death! . . . I wish you could become rich and strong soon! . . . Many, many of your children are still suffering."[12]

In *Travels in China*, Akutagawa criticizes Zhang Taiyan when he meets the supposedly most respectable Chinese intellectual of the era, who actually tried to offer him a warm welcome. In 1921, Akutagawa spent four months in China. He got sick the day after arriving, and was touched when he woke up at the hospital to see bouquets lined up at his bedside. He suddenly realized that he "had quite a few friends" in Shanghai, but that didn't prevent him from dismissing the modern Chinese intellectual world as "barren and wasted," and lacking any literary talents who could rival the acclaimed Tang-Song poets or Ming-Qing fiction writers.[13] Akutagawa seemed to have treated his conversation with Zhang Taiyan as the explanations of a tour guide rather than viewing it as an insightful intellectual dialogue. Akutagawa admired ancient China and would frequently contrast the old and the new. However, he seemed to have felt that if there was anything good about contemporary China it was necessarily derivative and at best only reminiscent of something much better in his home country.

For instance, he observes at one point that when he saw a "sea of blue young barley" through the window of the East Asia Common Culture Academy, he fancied himself back home: "I felt as though I was in Japan. . . . But when I approached the window, I saw Chinese farmers working in the barley field before my eyes. I felt angered as though they weren't supposed to be there. Coming all this way to see a Japanese carp streamer in the Shanghai sky gave me a bit of joy."[14] Thus, Akutagawa both saw and failed to see Chinese farmers working in the barley field, because he shifted his attention to an imaginary center and envisioned something that resided elsewhere and was out of place in the present.

Like Akutagawa, Yosano Akiko traveled in 1928 across Manchuria, but she went even further, to Mongolia. Akutagawa was traveling under the aegis of the Osaka News news agency, while Akiko and her husband were supported by the South Manchurian Railway Company. The mission of these famous writers was to familiarize Japanese readers with what was going on in China, and it is understandable that they would often underscore exotic elements in order to highlight Japan's status as a forerunner in modern ways of life and as a colonial power suggesting notions of efficiency and civility for its backward or corrupt Asian brothers. Joshua Fogel has noted that Yosano "had to fashion a travel narrative that reflected both her pressing creative needs and her distinctive responses to the fascinating but often tense worlds in which she traveled."[15] According to Fogel, Yosano "met with few Chinese and with not a single Chinese writer or poet. There were Japanese-speaking Chinese guides at several places and a prolonged, lovely meeting with the wives of two Chinese warlords. Otherwise her encounters in Manchuria were exclusively with other Japanese—innkeepers, businessmen and their wives, and especially the many employees of the South Manchurian Railway Company and their wives."[16] As a result, "China, Manchuria, Mongolia—in the form of their mountains, their temples and shrines, their natural beauty, their cities and thoroughfares—are there to be seen, but only rarely interacted with."[17]

Yosano is particularly celebrated for her contributions to Japan's early feminist thought. She was an "outspoken proponent of women's education and suffrage, and in 1921 she became dean and professor at Bunka Gakuin, a free coeducational school, which she founded together with her husband and others" (3). In spite of her liberal and feminist stance, Akiko decided to remain silent about the pain and suffering she witnessed in China, especially with regard to the native women and subalterns in Manchuria. As Fogel comments, "Yosano Akiko never once mentions that all the extraordinary courtesies she and her husband received during their weeks in Manchuria and Mongolia might in any way influence what she was writing about Japanese activities there."[18] Apparently, she was not only complacent but also complicit with the Japanese empire as a prestigious member of the colonizing power, writing only for a Japanese readership.

A number of Sinophone writers have reacted strongly to the negative images of China recorded by these Japanese travel writers, in order to help foster a sense of self-esteem and identity. Consequently, Chinese travel literature has taken on many different forms and ideologies, ranging from anticolonialism to double consciousness and self-assertion. In *Mixed Feelings about Nanjing* (南京雜感), for instance, Wu Zhuoliu quotes a Tang poem, "Perching by the Maple Bridge at Night" (夜泊楓橋), to criticize Japanese derogatory accounts that portrayed China as full of misery and corruption in the 1920s and 1930s.[19] He suggests a dual perspective—to move close while maintaining an imaginative distance—in order to be more appreciative and to develop local knowledge. Another example is Xiao Hong, who highlights her travel routes with deep roots in Manchuria.

In contrast to Yosano, Xiao Hong (1911–1942) writes about life in Northeastern China and Manchuria. Xiao Hong herself was forced to travel and migrate from Harbin to Beijing to Chongqing to Macao and Hong Kong. Lu Xun helped her publish her first major novel in Shanghai by supplying a foreword discussing women suffering from the changing fate of life and death. Xiao Hong went on to complete her masterpiece on her hometown of Harbin while residing in Hong Kong.

In many ways, Zhong Lihe's accounts of travel across Manchuria and China complement the stories by Xiao Hong. A Hakka writer who couldn't get approval from his
parents for his marriage, Zhong decided to move with his fiancée to Manchuria in
1940, advertised by the Japanese colonizers as a "brave new world" and a "land of equal
opportunity." After a year, Zhong became disenchanted with the colonial regime and
racial discrimination there, so he moved to Beijing, where he stayed for six years (1941–
1946). There he witnessed all sorts of political corruption and the incompetence of the
government. One diary entry, dated October 13, 1945, compares contemporary corruption to disgusting scenes from a classical novel that discloses the "true insolent faces of
the offices," and suggests they are even uglier: "No way will such horrendous, obscene
Chinese stories end." And in another bitter entry, he indicated that the Chinese officials
on both sides of the civil war were totally indifferent to people's suffering: "KMT and
Communist forces fought on near Chongqing, accompanied by the civilians' helpless
cries and painful screams; they would temporarily hold their fire, so as to stuff more
foreign bills into their pockets."[20] Even the Koreans were confused as to whether they
should celebrate China's new future under the Republican government, because they
couldn't tell the KMT from the Communists, as the tables had been turned several
times and neither seemed to do any better.

Zhong Lihe returned to Taiwan in March 1946, but was hospitalized in January 1947
for tuberculosis. While in National Taiwan University Hospital, he was able to observe
and offer firsthand accounts regarding the uprising as well as the February 28 Incident.
As he had no paper at his disposal, he recorded his concerns and confusions on the
margins and backs of prescription notes. He was shocked by the bloody violence and
chaos, and suddenly found his homeland to be a very strange place, torn apart by sheer
brutality and madness.

Given the wars and hardships that have plagued modern China, it is small wonder that countless Chinese moved to other parts of the world: Hong Kong, Malaysia,
Indonesia, Australia, New Zealand, Canada, California, and so forth. The poems,
letters, and graphics inscribed on the walls of the immigration detention center on
Angel Island, off the coast of San Francisco, are especially insightful, as they reveal
the Chinese immigrants' hopes and fears as they anxiously waited for weeks and even
years at the doorstep to their dreamland—America (the "Beautiful Country"). These
Angel Island poems were originally written by immigrants from China detained in the
Immigration Station just outside of San Francisco during the period 1910–1940, when
the majority of 175,000 immigrants used this site as their port of entry into the United
States. First written down and then carved on the wooden walls by immigrants on
their way to the United States, these poems were almost lost when the immigration station was destroyed in a fire in 1940. In 1970, park ranger Alexander Weiss accidentally
discovered the archives, but it was not until 1976, through the concerted effort of the
Asian American community, that the building was reconstructed and preserved as a
living monument to the history of the Asian American immigrants. "As a result, these
poems have become the textual evidence of one of the saddest chapters in the history
of American immigration" (Shan 385).

The poems, 135 in number, are mostly written in the style of regulated verse, with more than half (73) in seven-character quatrains. The writers are not famous poets, but they make revealing allusions to classical Chinese narratives of hostages or captives who later become heroes (such as King Wen of the Zhou and Su Wu of the Han dynasty) as well as to modern Western political figures like Napoleon Bonaparte, whose name in Chinese transliteration suggests "breaking the island" or "conquering the hill"—a reference to the Gold Mountain (San Francisco, and by implication, California and the entire United States). These immigrants desired to build new careers in the United States and to seek recognition or even revenge, so as to surprise or to surpass their American hosts. While a number of them committed suicide, the majority managed to get admitted to the United States. According to the Angel Island website that was put up later, these Chinese immigrants and their descendants have done well. Shan Te-hsing 單德興 and the poetry anthology editors highlight gloomy scenes of frustration and despair, but on the website there are interviews and memoirs that show brighter sides of the detainees' diasporic experience on Angel Island. One detainee, for example, said that he found the almonds on the island to be the juiciest and that he made good friends there, even learning a lot of things American from the guards. But overall, these Angel Island poems lament the weakness of China as a political entity while expressing confidence and even pride in being Chinese as distinct from the Western "barbarians" whose history is short and culture is shallow.[21]

In fact, this sort of double rhetoric—of seeking shelter in America while retaining a Chinese cultural identity—is also evident in a work like Pai Hsien-yung's "Winter Night" (冬夜; 1970), in which a University of California history professor confesses to a dual and ambivalent role of being a "plain deserter." To those who stayed to educate Chinese people, "how could I have mustered enough self-respect to stand up and speak for the May Fourth Movement?" he asks. "That's why, too, in all my expatriate days, I've never talked about the history of the Republican period," he continues, "That time at the University of California I saw how excited the students were in the middle of their movement, so I mentioned May Fourth only to humor them—it was merely a joke." But Professor Wu is still proud of being Chinese, especially in relation to ancient China: "The glories of the past are easy to talk about. I don't feel ashamed when I tell my students, 'The Tang dynasty created what must have been the most powerful, and culturally the most brilliant, empire in the world at that period in history.'"[22]

Like Pai, Eileen Chang came to California from Hong Kong in 1955 on a visit arranged by the US Information Service Agency, so that she could write about the corruption in Communist China in order to endorse America's interventions across the Pacific. But Eileen Chang's English novels were not well received in America. Many scholars have tried to explain Chang's years in the United States in terms of American Orientalism or her self-translation project. Eileen Chang's English-language ethnographic articulation of Chinese peasant consciousness, *Rice-Sprout Song* (1955), for example, is not only suggestive of a new global order established by the US defeat of prior colonial powers, but is also reminiscent of colonial cartography and Orientalist desires. As David Der-wei Wang points out, Eileen Chang wrote three novels in English: *Rice-Sprout Song* and

Naked Earth (1957) were written during Chang's sojourn in Hong Kong from 1952 to 1955, as "part of an anti-Communist literary campaign sponsored by the United States Information Service," while *The Rouge of the North* (1967) was a result of Chang's long period of work toward launching her career as a writer of English fiction after coming to the United States in 1955.[23] For Wang, the two supposedly "anti-Communist" novels by Eileen Chang "flaunt politics in ways Chang would not have chosen," and even Chang's last novel in English, *The Rouge of the North*, is "a novel not of national politics but about politics as a daily practice of life," not only probing the reactionary meaning of "Chinese obsessiveness" but "a last imaginary refuge after [Chang] had taken political asylum in the US," in a new country where Chang found that "fictional experience had infiltrated lived experience, and that she herself might finally have become the embittered woman."[24] Wang considers Chang's English fiction as part of her translation (and transgression) project, so that the novelist can reinvent early stories and characters, renegotiate the "fates of Chinese women," and rethink the significance of remembrance and repetition.[25] "Shifting back and forth on linguistic, cultural, gender, and temporal territories," he suggests, Chang is able to find that "between memory and reality an awkward disharmony frequently arises."[26]

In fact, during her stay in the United States, Eileen Chang was attracted to her new environment, especially Hollywood's screwball comedy. She wrote about all kinds of foods she had enjoyed, including not only homemade food back in Shanghai but also international and ethnic cuisines ranging from Spanish tapas to Japanese sushi, Italian pizza, and American steak. In California, she gradually discovered the difference between Chinese and Chinese American restaurants. She documented her travel experiences and her change to a more receptive perspective. In other words, she developed a "late style" to start her diasporic project to reconnect with Hong Kong and Shanghai by rewriting or retranslating some of her early novels. How do we come to terms with all these conflicting interpretations, particularly now as more and more posthumous material by Chang is coming to light that is calling for renewed critical inquiries regarding her late years in the United States? The correspondence exchanged between Chang and Song Qi 宋淇, William Tay's 鄭樹森 memoirs, and Chen Zishan's 陳子善 commentaries, together with Yingjin Zhang's illuminating discussion of Chang's use of Hollywood screwball comedies, not to mention some of Chang's late novels and journals, all help shed a different light on Chang's Cold War days in the United States. In this regard, Chang's late work is not just about "reminiscence" or about Shanghai and even China, as David Wang and Leo Ou-fan Lee noted. Rather, her multilingual and polyphonic project aims at piecing together the fragments of her life in a new home. It is a Sinophone writer's attempt to reach out to the Anglophone world in spite of a profound sense of being deserted and estranged: what matters are her discoveries, her travels across time and space. Chang tried her hand at new genres and media, at writing film scripts, at appropriating Hollywood comedies and musicals, and readjusted her textual strategies in response to the demands of the film industry. To paraphrase Theodor Adorno (speaking of Beethoven), we may say that Chang's late works are processes in which extremes and catastrophes are forced together, to produce moments of friction and dissonance.[27]

Along these lines, the works of expatriate authors such as Ha Jin 哈金 and Gao Xingjian 高行健 may be read not primarily as accounts of trauma and memory, or simply reminiscences of China, since both authors actually write about their travels in China and beyond. Ha Jin (who takes the first character in his penname from his favorite city, the multilingual Harbin) relocated to the United States and decided to write in English in a gesture of self-exile and self-emancipation. In his work, the Sinophone meets the Anglophone, whereas in Gao's work the Sinophone is brought into contact with the Francophone. Evoking literary giants such as Joseph Brodsky, Vladimir Nabokov, and Joseph Conrad, Ha Jin indicates that his choice of English as a medium differs from that of Lin Yutang 林語堂, who "served as a 'cultural ambassador' and who spoke to the West about China and to the Chinese about the West."[28] Rather than depending on China for his literary existence, Ha Jin instead opts for a model set by Conrad and Nabokov, "who didn't represent their native countries and instead found their places in English." As a migrant and a writer, Ha Jin thus employs English as a mode of communication and of expression to "speak truth to power."[29] In the same way, Gao Xingjian turns to French writers like Marguerite Duras for inspiration. He experiments with different genders and pronouns to narrate real and imaginative accounts of travels in China during the Cultural Revolution, appropriating the stories of Moses, Jonah, and many others to give voice to migrant subjects and accidental travelers. It seems that we are now at a crossroads in which travels in China often lead us to other parts of the world. Indeed the diverse travel routes and diasporic experiences of Eileen Chang, Gao Xingjian, and Ha Jin, following in the footsteps of Zhang Taiyan in many ways, indicate that these modern and contemporary Chinese writers are not only traveling to other places, but settling down, however uncomfortably, elsewhere and into another language/world.

NOTES

1. Sigmund Freud, quoted in Paul Fussell, ed., *Norton Book of Travel* (New York: Norton, 1987), 13.
2. See Mary Helms, *Ulysses' Sail: An Ethnographic Odyssey of Power, Knowledge, and Geographic Distance* (Princeton: Princeton University Press, 2014), and Claude Lévi-Strauss, *Tristes Tropiques* (Paris: Plon, 1955).
3. See Mary Louise Pratt, *Imperial Eyes: Travel Writing and Transculturation*, 2nd ed. (New York: Routledge, 2007).
4. See Benedict Anderson, *Spectre of Comparisons: Nationalism, Southeast Asia, and the World* (London: Verso, 1998).
5. Analects: Liren 19 (論語•里仁).
6. Gilles Deleuze, *Cinema 1: The Movement-Image* (Minneapolis: University of Minnesota Press, 1986), 11.

7. See James Clifford, *Routes: Travel and Translation in the Late Twentieth Century* (Cambridge: Harvard University Press, 1997).

8. See Edward W. Said, *Reflections on Exile and Other Essays* (Cambridge: Harvard University Press, 2002).

9. Zhang, 12-16-1898 column commentary, *Nichinichi Shinpo*, Chinese Section, 1.

10. Zhang, 12-16-1898 column essay.

11. Zhang, 12-18-1898 column essay.

12. Yu Dafu, "Sinking," trans. Joseph S. M. Lau and C. T. Hsia, in *The Columbia Anthology of Modern Chinese Literature*, ed. Joseph S. M. Lau and Howard Goldblatt, 2nd ed. (New York: Columbia University Press, 2007), 69.

13. Ryonosuke Akutagawa, *Travels in China*, trans. Joshua Fogel, *Chinese Studies in History* 30.4 (1997): 24–25.

14. Akutagawa, *Travels in China*, 37.

15. Akiko Yosano, *Travels in Manchuria and Mongolia*, trans. Joshua Fogel (New York: Columbia University Press, 2001), 5.

16. Yosano, *Travels in Manchuria and Mongolia*, 6–7.

17. Yosano, *Travels in Manchuria and Mongolia*, 7.

18. Yosano, *Travels in Manchuria and Mongolia*, 4.

19. Wu Zhuoliu 吳濁流, *Nanjing zhagan* 南京雜感 [Mixed feelings about Nanjing] (Taipei: Yuanxin, 1977).

20. Zhong Lihe 鍾理和, *Riji shujian* 日記書簡 [Diaries and letters] (Tainan: Taiwan Literature Center, 2009), entry dated October 13, 1945.

21. Shan Te-hsing, "At the Threshold of the Gold Mountain: Reading Angel Island Poetry," in *Sinophone Studies: A Critical Reader*, ed. Shu-mei Shih, Chien-hsin Tsai, and Brian Bernards (New York: Columbia University Press, 2013), 385.

22. Bai Xianyong [Pai Hsien-yung], "Winter Nights," in *The Columbia Anthology of Modern Chinese Literature*, ed. Joseph S. M. Lau and Howard Goldblatt (New York: Columbia University Press, 2007), 217.

23. David Der-wei Wang, "Foreword," in Eileen Chang, *The Rouge of the North* (Berkeley: University of California Press, 1998), vii.

24. Wang, "Foreword," vii, vii, xxviii, and xxix respectively.

25. See Wang, "Foreword," xxvii–xxviii.

26. Wang, "Foreword," xxix.

27. See Theodor Adorno, "Beethoven's Late Style," in *Night Music: Essays on Music, 1920–1962,* ed. Rolf Tiedemann (New York: Seagull, 2009), 18.

28. Ha Jin, "Exiled to English," *New York Times*, May 30, 2009, retrieved February 2, 2015, from http://www.nytimes.com/2009/05/31/opinion/31hajin.html?_r=0.

29. Ha Jin, "Exiled to English."

WORKS CITED

Adorno, Theodor W. "Beethoven's Late Style." In *Night Music: Essays on Music, 1920–1962.* Ed. Rolf Tiedemann. New York: Seagull, 2009.

Akutagawa, Ryonosuke. *Travels in China.* Trans. Joshua Fogel. *Chinese Studies in History* 30.4 (1997).

Anderson, Benedict. *Spectre of Comparisons: Nationalism, Southeast Asia, and the World.* London: Verso, 1998.

Bai, Xianyong [Pai Hsien-yung]. "Winter Nights." In *Columbia Anthology of Modern Chinese Literature.* Ed. Joseph S. M. Lau and Howard Goldblatt. New York: Columbia University Press, 2007. 210–223.

Clifford, James. *Routes: Travel and Translation in the Late Twentieth Century.* Cambridge: Harvard University Press, 1997.

Deleuze, Gilles. *Cinema 1: The Movement-Image.* Minneapolis: University of Minnesota Press, 1986.

Fussell, Paul, ed. *Norton Book of Travel.* New York: Norton, 1987.

Helms, Mary W. *Ulysses' Sail: An Ethnographic Odyssey of Power, Knowledge, and Geographic Distance.* Princeton: Princeton University Press, 2014.

Ha Jin. "Exiled to English." *The New York Times,* May 30, 2009. Retrieved February 2, 2015, from http://www.nytimes.com/2009/05/31/opinion/31hajin.html?_r=0.

Levi-Strauss, Claude. *Tristes Tropiques.* Paris: Plon, 1955.

Pratt, Mary Louise. *Imperial Eyes: Travel Writing and Transculturation.* 2nd ed. New York: Routledge, 2007.

Said, Edward W. *Reflections on Exile and Other Essays.* Cambridge: Harvard University Press, 2002.

Shan Te-hsing, "At the Threshold of the Gold Mountain: Reading Angel Island Poetry." In *Sinophone Studies: A Critical Reader.* Ed. Shu-mei Shih, Chien-hsin Tsai, and Brian Bernards. New York: Columbia University Press, 2013. 385–396.

Wang, David Der-wei. "Foreword." In Eileen Chang, *The Rouge of the North.* Berkeley: University of California Press, 1998. vii–xxx.

Wu Zhuoliu 吳濁流. *Nanjing zhagan* 南京雜感 [Mixed feelings about Nanjing]. Taipei: Yuanxin, 1977.

Yosano, Akiko. *Travels in Manchuria and Mongolia.* Trans. Joshua Fogel. New York: Columbia University Press, 2001.

Yu Dafu. "Sinking." Trans. Joseph S. M. Lau and C. T. Hsia. In *The Columbia Anthology of Modern Chinese Literature.* Ed. Joseph S. M. Lau and Howard Goldblatt, 2nd ed. New York: Columbia University Press, 2007. 44–69.

Zhong Lihe 鍾理和. *Riji shujian* 日記書簡 [Diaries and letters]. Tainan: Taiwan Literature Center, 2009.

CHAPTER 1.3

....

THE CONSTRUCTION OF THE MODERN CHINESE CONCEPT OF *XIJU* ("DRAMA")

....

XIA XIAOHONG

LIKE many academic concepts, the contemporary Chinese notion of *xiju* (戲劇; "drama") is effectively a modern invention. There have been numerous studies examining the relationship between *xiju* and *xiqu* (戲曲; "opera"), but the vast majority focus on premodern sources, while the ones that do turn to the early modern period generally consider only the work of Wang Guowei 王國維. The lacunae in this body of research are obvious, and in this chapter I will examine the notion of *xiju* with respect to the introduction of Western concepts of drama and performance conventions into China, focusing on terms such as *xi* (戲), *ju* (劇), and *qu* (曲), together with more recent binomes such as *xiju* (戲劇) and *xiqu* (戲曲). I will consider how these terms intersected with the Western concept of drama in the early modern period, thereby creating a new epistemological category with uniquely modern implications.

By *early modern* (近代), I am referring to the century-long period from around 1820 to around 1920, which is to say from the late Qing to the May Fourth period. I am primarily interested in tracing the acceptance of Chinese notions of *xiqu* by Western observers such as the British missionary Robert Morrison (1782–1834), who discussed Chinese *xiqu* in an entry in a 1822 Chinese-English dictionary. Beginning in June of 1926, the "drama" section of the *Morning Post Supplement* (晨報副刊) published a thoughtful discussion of the National Theater Movement, which offers a convenient endpoint for our examination. I will draw on materials from a fairly broad historical period in order to demonstrate an underlying set of causal relations, and will use analyses of newspapers and journal articles, literary taxonomies, dictionary and encyclopedia entries, literary histories, and major literary debates on the grounds that these sorts of texts played a fundamental role in shaping early modern discourse, and are therefore much more useful in revealing historical patterns than are studies by contemporary scholars.

WESTERN WRITINGS ON DRAMA
FROM THE LATE QING

There is no doubt that the early modern Chinese concept of *xiju* is a product of the eastward spread of Western culture, and more specifically of a process of Sinification of the Western concept of *drama*. This process followed two basic trajectories, one of which is oriented outward and the other inward. During the late Qing, many Chinese scholars traveled abroad, watched dramas, and recorded their impressions. However, these sorts of reflections and critiques derived mostly from a Chinese discursive environment, and therefore were molded to fit that perspective. Although Chinese travelers found these Western works innovative and were impressed by the Western use of stage sets and the status of actors, the resulting travelogues by Chinese ambassadors, merchants, and scholars did not play a very significant role in helping introduce Western notions of drama into China. We should, therefore, focus instead on contributions by Western missionaries.

Needless to say, an analysis of the missionaries' introduction of the concept of drama into China is necessarily grounded in a consideration of the discursive environment in the West. As contemporary models of experience, Western concepts of literary form have already been deeply internalized into Chinese attitudes, but by using these sorts of "tinted glasses" to examine Chinese theater, or comparing a Western notion of drama with Chinese correlates, we may develop a new perspective on translation as mediated by processes of cultural dissemination. To this end, the English missionaries Robert Morrison and Joseph Edkins (1823–1905) deserve particular attention.

In the early nineteenth century, Robert Morrison composed and edited a six-volume *Dictionary of the Chinese Language* that was enormously influential within Western Sinology. In 1822, Part 3 was published in Macao, and unlike Parts 1 and 2, which focused on defining Chinese characters in English, Part 3 used English combined with some Chinese to explain a number of Chinese terms. These detailed explanations went far beyond what one would expect from a conventional dictionary, and instead were more like encyclopedia entries. The entry *drama*, for instance, opens with a capsule history of Chinese theater and proceeds to cite an array of Chinese and Western sources, including *One Hundred Yuan Dramas* (元人百種曲), the nine standard character types in Chinese theater, and the twelve standard theatrical narrative structures. The entry notes that the Song dynasty used the term *xiqu* (戲曲) to refer to drama, and unlike what the Tang dynasty called *chuanqi* (傳奇) and what the Jin dynasty called *yuanben zaju* (院本雜劇), Song *xiqu* managed to escape the limits of historical periodization and came to assume the same significance as what Morrison characterizes as "the drama [that] began to prevail in the time of the [Sui]"—which is to say, the word developed from a technical term into a widely used one.[1] Meanwhile, Chinese *xiqu* was able to find an appropriate position in Western literary taxonomies.

However, Edkins, who was very interested in introducing Western classical learning into China, began discussing ancient Greek notions of drama in 1857 in the Shanghai journal *Shanghae Serial* (六合叢談). Most of these famous tragedies and comedies were classified under the Chinese category of *chuanqi*,[2] but when Edkins examined the origins of ancient Roman drama in another article titled "A Brief Discussion of Roman Poets" (羅馬詩人略說), he characterized the latter works as "Roman plays based on the scripts of Greek plays (*xiju*)."[3] Not only was it convenient to use the Chinese term *chuanqi* (which at the time was usually used to refer to *kunqu* opera) to refer to the ancient Greek plays, this usage also had the advantage of being readily intelligible to Chinese readers. At the same time, however, this practice could also confuse Chinese readers who had never before encountered Greek drama, thereby leaving them with a completely erroneous understanding of what was being discussed. Accordingly, one should focus on the works' underlying form, and not merely the term used to refer to them.

Edkins's most important study was his *Brief Description of Western Learning* (西學略述; 1885), portions of which were subsequently reprinted in countless other works. In volume four, on "literature," there are three sections on drama from Spain, France, England, Germany, and ancient Greece, and all three of these sections use the term *ciqu* (詞曲) to refer to these Western plays[4]—a usage that is obviously borrowed from the seventeenth-century author Li Yu's 李漁 *Reflections at Leisure Hours* (閑情偶寄), in which Li Yu distinguishes between *ciqu* and *yanxi* (演習). In particular, Edkins, in his discussion of German theater, groups both poetry and drama under the heading of "German poetics" (德國詩學), which is equivalent to what we now call "poetics" (詩學). These three sections were subsequently all grouped under the category of "literature" (文學類) in the 1897 volume *A Comprehensive Summary of Current Affairs by Category and for All Nations* (萬國分類時務大成). Of these, the sections "*Ciqu*" (詞曲) and "Investigation on Recent *Ciqu*" (近世詞曲考) were reprinted in the *Compilation of Western Politics* (西政通典) portion of the *Three Compilations of Western Learning* (西學三通).[5]

Although the preceding overview is obviously not exhaustive, it should suffice to demonstrate the wide dissemination of the concept of *ciqu* during this late-nineteenth-century period. After China was defeated by Japan in 1895 in the first Sino-Japanese War, Chinese enthusiasm for saving the nation reached a climax, and a strong demand for these sorts of Western texts developed, which would permit reformers "to satisfy urgent contemporary demands by selecting publications from many different Western nations."[6] After multiple reprints of Edkins's *Brief Description of Western Learning*, the Western drama structure that Edkins outlined based on Greek tragedies and comedies gradually came to be known and accepted by many late Qing intellectuals. At the same time, the existence of a variety of different terms for the Western concept of drama in Chinese discourse at the time demonstrates that a definitive translational correlate had not yet emerged.

THE INTERRELATIONSHIP BETWEEN DRAMA, FICTION, AND POETRY

Although it may be difficult to differentiate drama from fiction and poetry based solely on their textual form, it is actually not hard to appreciate their intertwined nature, given that drama and fiction share an emphasis on narrative, while drama and poetry share an emphasis on rhythm and rhyme. Prior to the late Qing, however, this kind of intermixing was virtually impossible. Apart from poetry's status as an elite genre and drama's status as a popular one, the fact that the former is written in rhyme while the latter is written in prose effectively prevented fiction from merging with drama. But with the introduction into China of Western ideas of literature, new questions of literary taxonomy began to emerge. In the process of reformulating the literary categories of poetry, prose, fiction, and drama, previous hierarchical distinctions were relaxed or destroyed, and it was only then that a peculiar intermixing of literary categories began to emerge, with *xiqu* being one of the most obvious examples.

We should note that although the term *xiqu* had been in use since the Song-Yuan transition, it typically referred to a type of musical performance, and it was not until the beginning of the twentieth century that it began to be used as a broad literary category. Prior to that, the words used in place of *xiqu* included the single-character terms *xi, ju,* and *qu* and the binomes *ciqu, quben,* and *chuanqi.* Of these, *ciqu* and *quben* referred specifically to written texts, while the other terms referred to a type of performance as well as a type of text.

As early modern scholars were reexamining China and reconstructing literary taxonomies based on their comparison of Chinese and Western traditions, the boundaries between these different categories should in theory have become more distinct, though in practice they ended up becoming more blurred than ever. The reason for this is that as types of literary production that had previously been positioned on the margins began to move toward the center, it became necessary to recruit more resources to study these literary considerations—and clearly an effective strategy involves expanding the reach of existing taxonomical categories.

A key catalyst in this late Qing intermixing of drama and poetry was the essay "A Record of Observing Drama" (觀戲記) published in 1902 in the San Francisco newspaper *Mon Hing Po* (文興報) by Kang Youwei's 康有為 student, Ou Jujia 歐榘甲. The following year, another of Kang Youwei's students, Liang Qichao 梁啟超, reprinted this essay in his newspaper *Qingyi Paper, Complete Edition* (清議報全編), as well as in the revolutionary text *Spirit of the Yellow Emperor* (黃帝魂), thereby enabling the essay to circulate widely.[7] Ou Jujia's essay traced a narrative tradition linking *xiqu* back to the *Book of Odes* (詩經), arguing that "*banben* [班本; "drama scripts"] derived from ancient *yuefu* [樂府; "music bureau poetry"], while *yuefu* in turn derived from ancient poetry."[8] The implication was that theater and poetry shared a common origin.

Late Qing commentators adopted this same perspective, in accordance with their practical enlightenment needs and their desire to help promote the category of theater (*xiqu*). Theater came to be viewed as a key weapon in helping enlighten lower-class society: "Conquering hundreds of thousands of performances! Conquering hundreds of thousands of articles!"[9] Or, to put it more directly, they argued that *xiqu* "is capable of moving all of society. Even if you are deaf you can still see it, and even if you are blind you can still hear it. There is no better means of improving society."[10] In order to improve the lowly status of *chuanqi* and *quben* in Chinese culture, the easiest way was to borrow from the prestige of poetic prose. The fondness of late Qing scholars of *xiqu* for tracing its origins can be explained by this same motivation.

In January of 1904, as Liang Qichao was writing his "Colloquy on Fiction" (小說叢話), he challenged the long-standing distinction between "poetry" (*shi* 詩) and "drama" (*qu* 曲), and instead grouped plays (*xiqu* 戲曲) under a broader category of "poetry" (*shi*):

> As for Westerners and their different forms of poetry, we translated them all with the single word *shi* (詩). For instance, our traditional Chinese categories of *sao* [騷; "lament"], *yuefu*, *ci*, and *qu*, can all be regarded as kinds of poetry. I think that if we adopt the narrowest understanding of the concept, then it would only include the "three hundred odes" [in the classic *Book of Odes*], but if we adopt the broadest understanding, then all lyrical categories (詞曲之類) could be called poetry.[11]

By adopting this new standard whereby plays (*quben*) fall under the "broadest understanding" of poetry, theatrical works by figures such as the dramatists Tang Xianzu 湯顯祖 and Kong Shangren 孔尚任 could naturally be called "ten-thousand word poems." Liang Qichao, accordingly, is able to praise these works as being "in no way inferior, in either their imagination or their power, to the works of Byron or Milton." Furthermore, Liang argued that what he called "drama poetry" (曲本之詩) had the advantage of being superior to other poetic forms, to the point that it would eventually be raised to the pinnacle of the poetry world: "We don't know how Chinese rhythmic prose will develop in the future, but if we look back at the developmental path it has taken to reach this point, we must consider *quben* as the heavyweight." This highest form of poetry—namely, theatrical literature (戲曲文學)—was regarded as one of the most powerful and effective enlightenment tools, and therefore the status of theater was immediately elevated.

An even greater intermixing of literary categories can be found in the introduction of theater into the category of fiction. Although vernacular fiction and theater had previously been tightly intertwined, they were nevertheless called by different names. Late Qing scholars' inclusion of theater under the category of fiction could be traced back to the popularization of Qing dynasty *tanci* (彈詞), whereupon *tanci* gradually became a kind of reading genre that was, as Xia Cengyou 夏曾佑 observed, "removed from the field of singing and performance. . . . As musical scripts have become like this, they become more and more like fiction, and the only thing distinguishing one from the other is that one is rhymed and the other isn't."[12] This assessment is not incorrect, though from the perspective of the specific conditions of the late Qing, more important factors included the development of enlightenment consciousness, and particularly the introduction of Western concepts of fiction.

The essay "How our Press Started Publishing Literary Supplements" (本館附印說部緣起), which was serialized in the Tianjin journal *Guowen Daily* (國聞報) in 1897, announced that "when Europe, America, and Japan initially began to develop, it was always with the help of fiction." The essay, furthermore, grouped dramatic works such as *Romance of the Western Chamber* (西廂記), *Peony Pavilion* (牡丹亭), and *The Palace of Eternal Youth* (長生殿) together with fictional works such as *Romance of the Three Kingdoms* (三國演義) and *The Water Margin* (水滸傳)—and called them all "narratives" (說部) or "novels" (小說).[13] In this way, drama joined ranks with fiction with respect to its contribution to the project of "enlightening the masses," to the point of even being folded into the category of fiction. Even in later years, Liang Qichao, who described himself as a mad lover of fiction, never forgot this ambitious claim, and continued calling for a revolution by fiction.

In his 1902 essay "On the Relationship between Fiction and Government of the People" (論小說與群治之關係), which has often been described as a manifesto for fictional revolution, Liang Qichao appealed to the new perspective that "when Westerners discuss literature, they prioritize fiction," and granted fiction the highest praise. He argued that fiction has assets associated with both the "idealist school" and the "realist school," which permit it to take readers to a different setting and help them enjoy a different perspective. Liang praised fiction's powers of enveloping, immersion, stimulation, and lifting, and also celebrated fiction's ability to surpass other forms of literature. However, he emphasized that fiction, having been elevated to such an exalted level, also bore a heavy responsibility, and concluded: "If one wishes to improve the government of the people, one must begin by revolutionizing the literary world; and if one wants to establish a new people, it is necessary to first have a new literature." Liang also argued that a "literary revolution" was the catalyst and the heart of the late Qing literary reform movement, and it was therefore natural that theater would become connected to fiction. Then, as in the 1897 discussion that appeared in *Guowen Daily*, Liang cited an array of different examples, intermixing fictional texts like *Dream of the Red Chamber* (紅樓夢) and *The Water Margin* with dramatic works like *Romance of the Western Chamber* and *Peach Blossom Fan* (桃花扇).[14] The journal *New Fiction* (新小說), of which Liang Qichao was the editor, even had a column for "*chuanqi*-style fiction" (傳奇體小說), to provide a space wherein "revolutionary soldiers for China's theater world" could be cultivated.

It was on the model of *New Fiction*, which published its inaugural issue in November of 1902, that the journals *Illustrated Fiction* (繡像小說), *The Fiction Monthly* (月月小說), and *Fiction Forest* (小說林) were established. In these four journals—which are known collectively as the "four fiction journals of the Late Qing"—*chuanqi* and other drama forms made frequent appearances, and this editorial approach continued until the early Republican period. Even as late as 1921, the year before Shen Yanbing 沈雁冰 (a.k.a., Mao Dun 茅盾) and others designated *Fiction Monthly* (小說月報) as the official journal of the Literature Study Society, dramatic fiction had not yet fully disappeared from the pages of this "fiction" journal—though by that point the column titles had already been changed from "new theater" (新劇) and *chuanqi* to *quben* and finally to *juben*. From this, we can see how strong and persistent the late Qing subsumption of theater under the category of fiction had been.

The highest poetic form included in Liang Qichao's literary taxonomy—*quben* (曲本)—was still considered a type of "fiction" (小說).[15] Similarly emerging from a desire to elevate the status of fiction, Liang Qichao's friend Di Baoxian 狄葆賢 attempted to trace the origins of "fiction." Di Baoxian nevertheless followed a different approach from that of Ou Jiaju, in that Di used music to trace a genealogy stretching from the *Book of Odes* to "Han dynasty songs, Tang dynasty *yuefu*, Song lyric poetry (*ci*), Yuan drama (*qu*), and Ming dynasty *kunqu*." He also proposed the curious theory that "the *Book of Odes* may be viewed as the ancestor of fiction, and Confucius may be viewed as the antecedent of the novelist." Regardless of whether or not this sort of genealogy seems credible today, it was only by playing up to the *Book of Odes*, which Confucian scholars regarded as a classic, that drama was finally able to gain respect. But this perspective was clearly not possible until after the literary category of "fiction" had already been established.[16] Furthermore, from this we can see that poetry provided a crucial basis on which fiction and drama were elevated, and it remained positioned above them.

On the surface, to absorb drama into either poetry or fiction might appear to diminish its independence as a literary genre. However, if one observes more carefully, drama's very transmutability could accord it greater capital as a literary resource, while also being emblematic of the shifting understanding of literature in the early modern period.

The Relationship between *Xiqu* and *Xiju*

If we trace the origins of *xiju*, it turns out that the term's use actually antedates that of *xiqu*. From the classic dictionary *Ciyuan* (辭源) we learn that the Tang dynasty poet Du Mu 杜牧 refers to *xiju* in his poem "Reminiscing the Past while at Xijiang" (西江懷古),[17] while the *History of the Early Tang* (舊唐書) also contains a cluster of references to *xiju*, though in these two texts *xiju* is used primarily to refer to a form of entertainment. However, scholars agree that by the mid-Tang, *xiju* was used to refer to theatrical works, and furthermore was in much wider circulation than *xiqu* (which does not appear at all in any of the twenty-six dynastic histories).[18] It was not until the late Qing that this finally began to change.

Contemporary scholarship generally traces the term *xiqu* back to the work of Wang Guowei. For instance, the Shanghai Theater Academy professor Ye Changhai 葉長海

argues, "During the Yuan, Ming, and Qing, the term *xiqu* generally referred to theatrical scripts (*quben* 曲本) or texts (*benzi* 本子). It should be noted, however, that
scholars in antiquity very rarely used the word *xiqu*, and it was not until Wang Guowei
that the term began to enter wider circulation."[19] In this respect, the significance and
influence of Wang's *Study of Xiqu from the Song and the Yuan* (宋元戲曲考) cannot
be overstated. However, if we return to the discursive environment of the late Qing, it
turns out that Wang Guowei's use of the term is actually in response to contemporary
realities. Periodicals and newspapers, such as *Alarm Bell Daily* (警鐘日報), played an
important role in this process.

On April 22, 1904, an announcement titled "A Plan for Improving Theater"
(改良戲劇之計畫) appeared in the "Annals" (紀事) section of *Alarm Bell Daily*, officially ushering in the early modern discourse on "theater reform." The announcement
stated that in Chaozhou, a Mr. Fang "went to the provincial government and asked
to meet with all of the local officials, and requested that *chao* drama (潮戲) be either
reformed or prohibited." It adds that "this request was granted and was about to be
implemented."[20] This announcement attracted the attention of an author writing under
the penname Jian He 健鶴, who proceeded to publish an essay with the same title,
which was serialized in the same newspaper over a three-day period beginning on May
30.[21] Jian He's project was divided into five components, of which the portions relating
to theatrical companies, scripts, and performance all took Japan as their model. In fact,
on the second day of serialization, the title of the article switched from the term *xiju* to
yanju (Japanese *engeki* 演劇), which was popular in Meiji Japan.

On August 7 and 8 of that year, *Alarm Bell Daily* published two articles titled "General
Regulations for Committees on Theater Reform" (戲劇改良會開辦簡章) and "General
Regulations for the Committees on the Reform of Shaoxing Theater" (紹興戲曲改良
會簡章).[22] The establishment of these committees can be seen as evidence that they
were taking up Jian He's suggestion that a central drama bureau should be established
in Shanghai, with branch bureaus in the province under its purview. The purpose of the
reform movement was to enlighten the lower classes.[23] On August 21, Chen Qubing's
陳去病 essay "Discussing the Uses of Theater" (論戲劇之有益) was published. This
essay continued Jian He's earlier call for a "new theater" to support the call for a "surge
in nationalism,"[24] while also demanding that theater "expand its nationalism" so that
it might contribute to the anti-Qing revolution.[25] When this essay was reprinted in the
new *Great Stage of the Twentieth Century* (二十世紀大舞台), Chen proudly described
how it had already been posted in *Alarm Bell Daily*, where it had been "very effective."[26]
The effect to which he was referring must have included the essay "Discussing Theater"
(論戲曲) that Chen Duxiu 陳獨秀 published in the September issue of the *Anhui
Vernacular Newspaper* (安徽俗話報). Chen Duxiu's advocacy of theater reform took
as its starting point the principle that "theater is the school of the masses, and actors
are the instructors." He therefore hoped that there would be more new dramas that
indirectly addressed contemporary events and introduced new ideas in order to move
the masses, and "transform them into red-blooded and knowledgeable citizens."[27] After
the essay was translated into classical Chinese, it was published in *New Fiction*, where it

had an even greater impact. This essay's repeated references to *xiqu*, however, marked a departure from Chen Qubing's use of *xiju* in his earlier essay.

From its initial conception in *Alarm Bell Daily*, the journal *Great Stage of the Twentieth Century* was launched in October of 1904, making it China's first journal devoted specifically to theater. Liu Yazi's 柳亞子 opening preface and the journal's public announcement both referred to the goal of Theater Reform, and invited "comrades from China and overseas ... to submit poems, new scripts, songs, and so forth."[28] In this way, Theater Reform was able to claim a space of its own. In December, *Alarm Bell Daily* published Liu Shipei's 劉師培 "The Origins of Theater" (原戲). The article repeatedly used the term *xiqu* but never mentioned *xiju*.[29] At the time, Liu Shipei was the newspaper's editor and Chen Qubing was a contributor, and therefore the article may well have been one that was left over from *Great Stage of the Twentieth Century* after it ceased publication.

Thanks to the efforts of *Alarm Bell Daily*, and particularly Chen Qubing's full-throated advocacy, the idea of theater reform spread widely and received considerable attention. Its responses included an essay by Wang Zhongqi 王鍾麒 titled "On the Relationship between Theater Reform and Government of the People" (論戲曲改良與群治之關係), which was published in 1906 in the newspaper *Shun Pao* (申報).[30] The essay not only attracted attention by troping on the title of Liang Qichao's famous 1902 essay on fiction, it also capitalized on the broad circulation of *Shun Pao* to spread its message of theater reform.

With this promotion of theater reform, the term *xiqu* became increasingly widespread, and from the different uses of the term in Liang Qichao's "Colloquy on Fiction," which was serialized in *New Fiction*, we can find some clues as to its significance. Liang Qichao used *quben* (曲本) and Di Baoxian used *gequ* (歌曲), while Xu Dingyi 許定一 used *xiqu* (戲曲) when he wrote, "If you want to reform theater (*xiqu*), you must first reform fiction."[31] A comprehensive search of the archive of all the articles published in *Shun Pao* reveals that between 1872 and 1904, the word *xiqu* appeared in twenty-two articles, while in the seven years from 1905 through the end of 1911 the corresponding number of articles increased to forty-six. In contrast, the word *xiju* appeared in 270 *Shun Pao* articles prior to 1905, while between 1905 and 1911 it appeared in fifty-nine—meaning that after 1905 *xiju* appeared at virtually the same rate as *xiqu*.

Although the words *xiqu* and *xiju* can both be found in ancient texts, the modern popularization of *xiqu* was largely a result of its use in Japan, unlike the contemporary reappropriation of *xiju*. In Meiji-era Japan, theatrical works from both China and the West were all called *xiqu*. This can be seen, for instance, in an article published in 1883 in the newspaper *Nihon Rikken Seitō Shinbuns* (日本立憲政黨新聞), which cites Shakespeare's works as a model for contemporary theatrical reform.[32] In Sasakawa Rinpu's 笹川臨風 discussion of literature from the Jin, Yuan, Ming, and Qing dynasties in his 1898 volume *A Chinese Literary History* (支那文學史), there are subsections devoted to "the development of fiction and drama (*xiqu*)," "fiction and drama (*xiqu*)," and "critique of fiction and drama (*xiqu*)."[33] These studies, and particularly Meiji-era works on Chinese literature, must have impressed Chinese students and others living in Japan, as a result of which the term *xiqu*, which had previously been quite rare in Chinese, quickly became as common as the parallel term *xiju*.

Initially, *xiqu* and *xiju* were used in somewhat different ways. Jian He and Chen Qubing emphasize *xiju* because Japan's new theater had left a deep impression on them when they were studying in Japan, and, as Jian He puts it,

> At the time, I watched Japanese theatrical performances, where modern theater is quite different from classical theater. In the past, the theater would be divided into singing and performance, interspersed with narrative explanation. In general, this could be perceived as the sister of Chinese theater. In modern Japan, however, all of these theaters are performing modern drama, which uses wild dialogue (which is to say narration with a humorous quality) and mimicry.[34]

This is obviously quite different from a traditional understanding of the status of the character *qu* in the term *xiqu*. Accordingly, *xiju* became the preferred term, while the use of *xiqu* in "General Regulations for the Conference on the Reform of Shaoxing Theater" and in Chen Duxiu's works continued to follow the term's original meaning (which is due in part to the influence of Chen's study in Japan). As mentioned in the "General Regulations," the "existing dramas" that some wanted to reform in order to "create a new type of *xiqu*" encompassed many regional forms, including all sorts of local ditties, songs, and *xiqu*—all of which featured a combination of performance and singing.[35] Chen Duxiu, meanwhile, defined *xiqu* as a form of "contemporary music" from the preceding two centuries, divided into the operatic forms of *bangzi* (幫子), *erhuang* (二黃), and *xipi* (西皮), by which he was clearly referring to Shaanxi opera and Peking opera, which at the time were the two major new forms of regional theater.[36]

However, there isn't a very significant difference in a contemporary Chinese context between the growing popularity of *xiqu* resulting from its status in Japan, on one hand, and the continued prominence of *xiju* resulting from its traditional importance in China, on the other. It was common to see the terms being used interchangeably. However, for most people who still preferred *xiqu*, the boundary between the two terms was relatively clear in that—in the context of Chinese history—many scholars followed Liu Shipei's assertion that "*xiqu* originates from classical musical dance performances."[37] Moreover, Wang Guowei, in his 1908 essay "An Investigation of the Origins of *Xiqu*" (戲曲考原), published in *Journal of National Essence* (國粹學報), took this a step further and proposed that "*xiqu* refers to a musical dance performance that tells a story."[38] This definition subsequently came to be widely accepted, and Xie Wuliang 謝無量 adopted it in his 1918 volume *A Comprehensive Literary History of China* (中國大文學史).[39] Singing was therefore still a necessary element of *xiqu*. In Huang Renbian's 黃人編 1911 volume *A Popular Encyclopedic Dictionary* (普通百科新大辭典), the entry for *chuanqi* specifies that "*chuanqi* scripts are now classified as literature, while their performances are classified as *xiqu*."[40] In discussions of Western theater, meanwhile, the term *xiqu* is always closely related to a singing performance. For instance, in Sun Yuxiu's 孫毓修 "An Essay on European and American Fiction" (歐美小說叢談), which was serialized in *Fiction Monthly* in 1913, each section includes a discussion of *xiqu*. This is particularly true of the section on "The Origins of English *Xiqu*" (英國戲曲之發源), which states that "English *xiqu* [drama] originated around 1100 CE." The essay argues that the term originated in liturgical performances, and specifically Roman performances of Biblical scenes.[41] The attention to the use of singing in these sorts of *xiqu* suggests that *xiju* had a broader meaning than *xiqu*.

XIJU EMBRACES THE TREND FOUND IN *XIQU*

Perhaps even more interesting than the growing popularity of the word *xiqu* in the late Qing as a result of its prominence in Japan is the contemporary reinvention of the older term *xiju*. Apart from the late Qing's borrowing from Japan and its imitation of Europe's and American's new drama, which helped drive an alliance between musical *xiqu* and old-style theater, two significant early Republican discussions of literary history—namely, the critique of old-style theater in the journal *New Youth* (新青年) and the "national theater movement" that appeared in the pages of the *Morning Post Supplement*—played a decisive role in shaping the eventual meaning of *xiju*.

In October of 1918, *New Youth*, which had already established a reputation for promoting "literary revolution," published a special issue on "Theater (*xiju*) Reform." The special issue included Hu Shi's 胡適 "The Concept of Literary Evolution and Theater Reform" (文學進化觀念與戲劇改良), Fu Sinian's 傅斯年 "Differing Perspectives on Theater Reform" (戲劇改良各面觀) and "Another Consideration of Theater Reform" (再論戲劇改良), and Song Chunfang's 宋春舫 "A Hundred Perspectives on Contemporary Drama" (近世名戲百種目). The special issue also included Ouyang Yuqian's 歐陽予倩 "Perspectives on Theater Reform" (戲劇改良各面觀) and Zhang Houzai's 張厚載 "My Views on Old-Style Chinese Theater" (我的中國舊戲觀). However, although this special issue was certainly not lacking in constructive perspectives on "reform," what was perhaps more striking was its critique of old-style Chinese theater. This was really fomented earlier, in March of that year, with a letter submitted by Zhang Houzai, titled "New Literature and Old-Style Chinese Theater" (新文學及中國舊戲). This letter immediately elicited responses in *New Youth* from Hu Shi, Chen Duxiu, Qian Xuantong 錢玄同, and Liu Bannong 劉半農.[42] In the Letters to the Editor section of the August issue of the journal, Liu Bannong and Qian Xuantong debated this question,[43] and the controversy continued with Zhou Zuoren's 周作人 letter "On the Rise and Fall of Old-Style Chinese Theater" (論中國舊戲之應廢) together with Qian Xuantong's response.

Ever since Liang Qichao advocated a revolution in fiction, the category of "fiction" (*xiaoshuo*), which included *xiqu*, had been criticized for being "the root of the corruption of China's government of the masses."[44] But if one compares these various critiques, the New Culture critique advanced in the pages of *New Youth* was the strongest. Furthermore, Liang Qichao's critique was primarily directed at the level of literary works' *content*, while the formal structure of *xiqu* continued to be widely respected. The New Culture critique of old-style theater, by contrast, offered a comprehensive negation of the works' ideas as well as their artistic status—a critique of traditional Chinese *xiqu* that was not expected by the participants of the earlier discussions of "theater reform" and "new theater."

The *New Youth* attack on old-style theater focused on its allegedly barbaric character. This was actually based on a Western standard of civilization, wherein theater, in the form of spoken drama, functions as an affirmation of civilization. Therefore, from the very beginning Chen Duxiu had stated, "The reason why Europeans value theater is because it represents the fruit of literature, art, and science." But Chen claimed that "Chinese theater"—whether viewed from a literary, artistic, or scientific perspective— lacks "even a single iota of value."[45] Hu Shi and Fu Sinian, in their respective essays, repeatedly appealed to "pure *xiju*," which clearly referred to a spoken drama tradition beginning with Ibsen. As Fu Sinian put it, "the elements that make up pure theater necessarily include movement and language, with movement referring to ordinary human movement and language referring to ordinary human language." Following this trajectory, and using realistic theater as a standard, Fu Sinian asserted that old-style Chinese theater was fundamentally backward:

> Over the seven or eight centuries from the Song dynasty up to the present day, the pathetic Chinese theatrical world has yet to produce true theater. It even treated acrobatics and variety shows as a theatrical standard! ... Acrobatic and variety performances all have an athletic and playful dimension, which entails a set of movements and language that are far removed from ordinary human movement and language—[Old-style Chinese theater] is incapable of depicting actual human emotion.

This work was based on the premise that "if the belief in old-style theater is not destroyed, new theater will not be possible."[46] In contrast to Fu Sinian's energetic advocacy of "new theater," Zhou Zuoren offered similar praise of "European-style new theater," which he argued was the only possible constructive option for undertaking theater reform.[47]

Viewed from the perspective of European spoken theater, the singing, makeup, and fighting associated with traditional Chinese *xiqu* all came under suspicion, as old-style Chinese theater was critiqued for being "a synthesis of all sorts of different kinds of variety performances." It was therefore deemed necessary to wait "until these sorts of elements are completely eliminated, and only then would it be possible for pure theater to emerge."[48] Regardless of how Zhang Houzai may have tried to promote the aesthetic qualities of old-style theater, accordingly, the *New Youth* writers still took the position that it lacked "even a single iota of value," and "they had nothing more to say about it."[49]

Given that *New Youth* was the primary forum where this debate was played out, it was a very one-sided contest. Apart from Zhang Houzai, virtually all of the other contributors were basically in agreement. From the titles of their essays, we can discern the key point of the debate, in that those by Hu Shi, Fu Sinian, and Ouyang Yuqian all feature the phrase *theater reform*. This, along with Zhou Zuoren and Qian Xuantong's energetic exchange on "Discussing the Rise and Fall of Old-Style Chinese Theater" and Chen Duxiu and Liu Bannong's agreement—but notably contrasted with Zhang Houzai's two essays adopting an opposing perspective—offered a stark contrast between theater reform and old-style Chinese theater. One should also note that virtually all of these reform-minded writers held positions at Peking University, while Zhang Houzai was a former Peking University student who had been dismissed before graduation. It was therefore hardly a fair competition, and as a result the term *xiju* (戲劇; "theater") came to achieve wide currency, in contrast to *jiuxi* (舊劇; "old-style theater").

Although the 1918 *New Youth* critiques of old-style Chinese theater could not convert a devoted fan of traditional theater like Zhang Houzai, this had changed by the time the theater section of the *Morning Post Supplement* was published on June 17, 1926. This brought together a group of scholars including Yu Shangyuan 余上沅, Zhao Taimou 趙太侔, Wen Yiduo 聞一多, Xiong Foxi 熊佛西, and Zhang Jiazhu 張嘉鑄, who all came together to discuss the question of "national theater." With this, the famous earlier debate about theater reform finally received a new hearing.

Yu Shangyuan, Zhao Taimou, Wen Yiduo, and Zhang Jiazhu had all gone to the United States to study either theater or fine arts, and before returning to China they wrote and performed the English-language play *Yang Guifei* (楊貴妃). Excited by the success of the performance, they gathered in Yu Shangyuan's kitchen and came up with the slogan National Theater Movement.[50] By *national theater* (*guoju* 國劇), they were referring neither to old-style theater (*jiuju* 舊劇) nor to new theater (*xinju* 新劇), but rather to the practice of "having Chinese people use Chinese materials to perform Chinese dramas for Chinese audiences."[51] This position, combined with the fact that each of these scholars had been influenced by Western symbolist art, left them dissatisfied with the realist drama of Ibsen that had been embraced by the New Culture movement. They felt that the issue-driven plays promoted and admired by the *New Youth* contributors would lead drama down the wrong path, wherein "the causal relationship between art and life would be inverted." "Thought," they argued, "would thereby become the soul of drama," and forgotten would be the fact that drama "also has a more pure . . . artistic value."[52]

In the view of Yu Shangyuan and his colleagues, drama should not pursue realism as its highest objective, given that "the movement and language that are performed on stage are already not the kind of movement and language that one encounters in daily life." Accordingly, "expressionism" (*xieyi* 寫意)—which is viewed as the opposite of "realism" (*xieshi* 寫實) and which "approaches the status of pure art"—came to be revered. This conflict between Western-originated realist art and nonrealist or expressionist art became magnified and put into the context of a difference between East and West:

> In broader terms, Western art values realism and the direct depiction of life, and
> as a result it easily adapts to shifting times, though it is difficult for it to maintain

a transcendent style. Its biggest weakness is that it emphasizes only reality, and not art. Eastern art, on the other hand, emphasizes form and meaning, and is quite rigid in terms of its mode of expression and therefore has a tendency to stick to prior models and become an unchanging imitation. On the upside, its aesthetic content is more expansive. However, by mimicking [reality] for a long time, it can depart from life entirely, leaving behind only a dead shell of art.[53]

This recognition of a combination of the West's newest modernism with traditional Chinese art is certainly forward-looking.

It is precisely by beginning from a question of aesthetic value that Chinese old-style theater was regarded as "containing a relatively pure artistic dimension," and furthermore it became an important source of "national theater."[54] While the *New Youth* contributors denounced old-style theater's makeup, stage props, craftsmanship, and so forth, Yu Shangyuan and Zhao Taimou nevertheless found old-style theater to be full of aesthetic significance. This is particularly true of its highly stylized nature, for which these commentators offered their highest praise: "The stylization of Chinese old-style theater is art itself. It is not merely stylization, but rather it could be called symbolization." This old-style theater "surpasses not only daily life, but even nature itself."[55] Although these commentators also had some critiques of this old-style theater, because the National Theater Movement supporters viewed "movement" as theater's core element, old-style theater still received special attention on account of its craftsmanship and its visual appeal. This, meanwhile, was a key premise of Yu Shangyuan's argument that "to create a National Theater, one cannot but draw on old-style theater."[56]

Around the time of the "Theater Supplement" discussion of the National Theater Movement, Yu Shangyuan wrote an essay in English titled "Drama," the latter half of which was translated into Chinese and published under the title "National Theater" (國劇). Although the general content of the essay had already appeared in Yu's "Preface to 'The National Theater Movement'" (「國劇運動」序) and "Critique of Old-Style Theater" (舊戲評價), the structure and clarity of the English-language essay helped Yu present his National Theater ideal in a more complete fashion. Its objective was for "the National Theater we are in the process of establishing to be a new theater located between the two extremes of 'expressionism' and 'realism.'"[57] It is precisely in National Theater, located at the interstices of Chinese old-style theater's expressionism and European theater's realism, that we find what Yu Shangyuang and his colleagues described as "the perfect theater of which we all dreamed, from antiquity to the present."[58]

Although the attitudes of *New Youth* and *Morning Post Supplement* might appear to be diametrically opposed in other respects, both publications nevertheless frequently published essays with the word *xiju* in the title. For instance, there was Wen Yiduo's "At the Crossroads of *Xiju*" (戲劇的歧途), Deng Yizhe's 鄧以蟄 "The Evolution of *Xiju* and Morality" (戲劇與道德的進化) and "*Xiju* and Sculpture" (戲劇與雕刻), Yang Zhensheng's 楊振聲 "Chinese Language and Chinese *Xiju*" (中國語言與中國戲劇), Liang Shiqiu's 梁實秋 "The Differentiation of *Xiju* Art" (戲劇藝術辨正), Yang Shengchu's

楊聲初 "Shanghai *Xiju*" (上海的戲劇), Yu Shangyuan's "On *Xiju* Critique" (論戲劇批評) and "A List of Works on *Xiju*" (戲劇參考書目), Xiong Foxi's "Beijing *Xiju* from Ninety Years Ago" (九十年前的北京戲劇) and "A Summary of the Transformations that *Xiju* has Undergone since the Ming-Qing Period" (明清以來戲劇的變遷說略). From this, one can see that the term *xiju* was indeed far more versatile than *xiqu*.

The sorts of discussions cited above were ultimately aggregated in various new dictionaries. For instance, the *Encyclopedic New Dictionary* (百科新辭典) that Hao Xianghui 郝祥輝 edited in 1921 differentiates between *wenxue* (文學; which the entry translates as "literature") and *wenyi* (文藝; which the entry translates as "literature and art") as follows:

> *Wenxue* (*Literature*): *Wenxue* refers to an art form that is expressed through written language, which is to say fiction, drama (*xiju*), and poetry.
> *Wenyi* (*Literature and Art*): *Wenyi* refers to aesthetic objects that display an ideological dimension—which is to say, it is a generic term for poetry, drama (*xiju*), fiction, painting, sculpture, and so forth.[59]

In this definition, *xiju*—and not *xiqu*—is considered a literary or literary/artistic category alongside fiction, poetry, painting, and so forth.

In *Dictionary of Literature and Art* (文藝辭典), which Sun Lianggong 孫俍工 compiled in 1927 in Tokyo, all of the entries are related to foreign terms. The volume includes an entry for *xiju*, for which it also provides the English term *Drama*:

> *Xiju* (*Drama*)
> Synonymous with *xiqu*.
> Usually used to refer to works in a poetic or prose format that are performed on a stage. In more general terms, however, it is a composite art form that brings together many other art forms, including poetry, music, painting, architecture, and so forth.[60]

Although this text states that *xiju* and *xiqu* are synonyms, the fact that it takes as its main entry not *xiqu* (which was the more common term in Japan at the time) but rather *xiju*, points to the difference in perspective between the editor and contemporary society.

The *Chinese Encyclopedic Dictionary* (中華百科辭典), which it took the lead editor Shu Xincheng 舒新城 ten years to complete, includes lengthy entries for both *xiqu* and *xiju*, which it defines as follows:

> *Xiqu*: An art form that uses song and dance to perform a story.
> *Xiju*: An art form that uses movement to perform stories on stage, and which attracts the audience's sympathy. This is the most complex art form, in that it brings together construction, sculpture, painting, dance, and music.[61]

This definition of *xiqu* is largely drawn from Wang Guowei's "An Investigation of the Origins of *Xiqu*," while the definition of *xiju* not only includes that of *xiqu* but also includes a section on Western theater. Even spoken drama and its manifestation in China, known as "new drama" (*xinju*), can be included.

Dictionary of Literature and Art and *Chinese Encyclopedic Dictionary* were both later supplemented and reprinted, and went on to have a wide impact. They obviously played a key role in contributing to the subsequent differentiation between the terms *xiqu* and *xiju*.

From the consolidation of the term *xiju* beginning in the late Qing, we can see that the Sinification of the Western concept of drama was a very complicated process that involved the introduction of Western knowledge, the reconstruction of aesthetic categories, theater reform, the development of new theater, the critique of old-style theater, and so forth. Moreover, this process opened up a new form of Chinese theater, while breaking through the longstanding formal constraints found in the West. Though taking Western theater as our starting point, we still need to return to the efforts to establish a Chinese subjectivity. Over a century-long period, the development of views on, and the implementation of, early modern theater offers a rich source of insight and inspiration.

(translated by Carlos Rojas)

Notes

1. Robert Morrison, *A Dictionary of the Chinese Language*, Part III (Macao: East India Company Press, 1822), 129–130.
2. Joseph Edkins 艾約瑟, "Luoma shiren lüeshuo" 羅馬詩人略說 [A brief discussion of Roman poets], *Liuhe congtan* 六合叢談 [Shanghae serial] 3, March 26, 1857.
3. Edkins, "A Brief Discussion of Roman Poets."
4. Edkins, "Ciqu" 詞曲 [Ciqu], "Jinshi ciqu kao" 近世詞曲考 [Investigation on recent *ciqu*] and "Deguo shixue" 德國詩學 [German poetics], in *Xixue lüeshuo* 西學略述 [Brief description of Western learning], vol. 4. Part of Edkins, trans., *Xixue qimeng shiliuzhong* 西學啟蒙十六種 [Sixteen forms of Western enlightenment] (Shanghai: Zhuyitang shuju, 1896).
5. *Geguo wenzi* 各國文字 [Writings from various nations], in Qian Feng 錢豐, ed. *Wanguo fenlei shiwu dacheng* 萬國分類時務大成 [A comprehensive summary of current affairs by category and for all nations], vol. 20 (Shanghai: Xiuhai shanfang, 1897). See also "Ciqu yuepu" 詞曲樂譜 [*Ciqu* scores] and "Taixi ciqu" 泰西詞曲 [Western *ciqu*], in Yuan Zonglian 袁宗濂 and Yan Zhiqing 晏志清, eds. *Xizheng tongdian* 西政通典 [Compilation of Western politics], vol. 16 (Shanghai: Cuixin shuguan, 1902).
6. Qian Feng 錢豐, *Fan lie* 凡例 [Book guide], *A Comprehensive Summary of Current Affairs by Category and for all Nations*, vol. 1.
7. Huangdi zisun zhi yige ren 黃帝子孫之一個人 (penname of Huang Zao 黃藻), ed. *Huangdi hun* 黃帝魂 [Spirit of the Yellow Emperor], printed in December 1903, published in January 1904.
8. Wu Yasheng 無涯生 (Ou Jujia 歐榘甲), "Guanxi ji" 觀戲記 [A record of observing drama], originally published in *Wenxing bao* 文興報 [*Mon Hing Po*], reprinted in *Qingyibao quanbian* 清議報全編 [Qingyi paper, complete edition], vol. 25, appendix 1.

9. Wu Yasheng, "A Record of Observing Drama."

10. San Ai 三愛 (Chen Duxiu 陳獨秀), "Lun xiqu" 論戲曲 [Discussing *xiqu*], *Xin xiaoshuo* 新小說 [New literature] 14 (March 1905).

11. Yinbing 飲冰 (Liang Qichao 梁啟超) et al., *Xiaoshuo conghua* 小說叢話 [Colloquy on fiction], *Xin xiaoshuo* 新小說 [New literature], no. 7. This is listed as having been published in September 1903, but in actuality it was not published until after January 1904.

12. Bieshi 別士 (Xia Cengyou 夏曾佑), "Xiaoshuo yuanli" 小說原理 [The principles of fiction], *Xiuxiang xiaoshuo* 繡像小說 [Illustrated fiction] 3 (June 1903).

13. "Benguan fuyin shuobu yuanqi" 本館附印說部緣起 [How our press started publishing literary supplements], *Guowen bao* 國聞報 [Guowen daily], December 11, 1897.

14. Liang Qichao, "Lun xiaoshuo yu qunzhi zhi guanxi" 論小說與群治之關係 [On the relationship between fiction and government of the people], *Xin xiaoshuo* 新小說 [New literature] 1 (November 1902).

15. See Xia Xiaohong 夏曉虹, "Liang Qichao de wenlei gainian bianxi" 梁啟超的文類概念辨析 [An analysis of Liang Qichao's concept of literary taxonomy], in *Guoxue yanjiu* 國學研究 [Guoxue studies], vol. 15 (Beijing: Peking University Press, 2005).

16. Ping Zi 平子 (Di Baoxian), "Colloquy on Literature," *New Literature* 9 (dated August 1904, but the actual publication was delayed).

17. Entry "*Xiju*" 戲劇 [Drama], in *Ciyuan* 辭源 [Ciyuan], rev. ed., vol. 2 (Beijing: Shangwu yinshuguan, 1980), 1195.

18. See Wang Tingxin 王廷信, "'Ershiliu shi' zhong de 'xiju' gainian lüekao" "二十六史"中的"戲劇"概念略考 [An examination of the concept of *xiju* in the twenty-six dynastic histories], *Zhonghua xiqu* 中華戲曲 [Chinese drama] 1 (2003).

19. Ye Changhai 葉長海, "*Xiqu kao*" 戲曲考 [An investigation of *xiqu*], *Xiju yishu* 戲劇藝術 [Theatrical arts] 4 (1991).

20. "Gailiang xiju zhi jihua" 改良戲劇之計畫 [A plan for improving theater], *Jingzhong ribao* 警鐘日報 [Alarm bell daily], April 22, 1904.

21. Jian He 健鶴, "Gailiang xiju zhi jihua" 改良戲劇之計畫 [A plan for improving theatrical performance] (the title was later changed to "Yanju gailiang zhi jihua" 演劇改良之計畫 [A plan for improving theatrical performance]), *Alarm Bell Daily*, May 30–June 1, 1904.

22. Jian He, "A Plan for Improving Theatrical Performance."

23. "Xiju gailianghui kaiban jianzhang" 戲劇改良會開辦簡章 [General regulations for committees on theater reform] and "Shaoxing xiqu gailianghui kaiban jianzhang" 紹興戲曲改良會簡章 [General regulations for the committees on the reform of Shaoxing theater], *Alarm Bell Daily*, August 7–8, 1904.

24. Jian He, "A Plan for Improving Theatrical Performance."

25. "Lun xiju zhi youyi" 論戲劇之有益 [Discussing the uses of theater], *Chenzhong bao* 晨鐘報 [Morning bell daily], August 21, 24, 26, 1904. The passage quoted here was published on August 21.

26. Pei Ren 佩忍 (Chen Qubing 陳去病), "Lun xiju zhi youyi" 論戲劇之有益 [Discussing the uses of theater], *Ershi shiji dawutai* 二十世紀大舞台 [Great stage of the twentieth century] 1 (October 1904).

27. San Ai (Chen Duxiu), "Discussing *Xiqu*."

28. Ya Lu 亞盧 (Liu Yazi 柳亞子), "'Ershi shiji dawutai' fakan ci" 〈二十世紀大舞台〉發刊詞 [Opening preface to *Great Stage of the Twentieth Century*], in *Great Stage of the*

Twentieth Century 1 (October 1904), "'Ershi shiji dawutai congbao' zhaoguqi bing jian-zhang" 〈二十世紀大舞台叢報〉招股啟並簡章 [Great stage of the twentieth century journal announcement and regulations] 2 (November 1904).

29. "Yuanxi" 原戲 [The origins of theater], *Morning Bell Daily*, December 24–25, 1904. This essay was initially published anonymously, but was subsequently published under Liu Shipei's name in *Guocui xuebao* 國粹學報 [Journal of national essence], no. 34, 1907.

30. Lu Sou (Wang Zhongqi 王鍾麒), "Lun xiqu gailiang yu qunzhi zhi guanxi" 論戲曲改良與群治之關係 [On the Relationship between Theater Reform and Government of the People], *Shun Pao* 申報, September 22, 1906.

31. Yinbing (Liang Qichao), Ping Zi (Di Baoxian), Ding Yiyu 定一語, *New Literature*, no. 7, 9, 13 (September 1903, August 1904, and February 1905).

32. Originally published in *Nihon Rikken Seitō Shinbuns* (日本立憲政黨新聞) on June 9, 29, 1883; reprinted in Yoshida Seiichi 吉田精一 and Asai Kiyoshi 淺井清, eds., *Jindai wenxue pinglun daxi* 近代文學評論大系 [Collection of early modern literary criticism], vol. 1 (Tokyo: Kadokawa Shoten, 1971), 15–19.

33. Sasakawa Rinpu, 笹川臨風, *A Chinese Literary History* 支那文學史 (Tokyo: Hakubunkan, 1898).

34. Jian He, "A Plan for Improving Theatrical Performance."

35. "General Regulations for the Committees on the Reform of Shaoxing Theater."

36. San Ai (Chen Duxiu), "Discussing *Xiqu*."

37. "Yuanxi" 原戲 [The origins of drama], *Alarm Bell Daily*, December 12, 1904.

38. Wang Guowei 王國維, "Xiqu kaoyuan" 戲曲考原 [An investigation of the origins of *xiqu*], *Guocui xuebao* 國粹學報 [Journal of national essence] 48 (December 1908).

39. Xie Wuliang 謝無量, *Zhongguo da wenxueshi* 中國大文學史 [A comprehensive literary history of China], 4th ed. (Shanghai: Zhonghua shuju, 1918), 79.

40. Huang Renbian 黃人編, *Putong baike xin dacidian* 普通百科新大辭典 [A popular ency-clopedic dictionary] (Shanghai: Guoxue fulunshe, 1911), 61.

41. Sun Yuxiu 孫毓修, *Oumei xiaoshuo congtan: Yingguo xiqu zhi fayuan* 歐美小說叢談: 英國戲曲之發源 [An essay on European and American fiction: The origins of English *xiqu*], *Fiction Monthly* 4.7 (November 1913).

42. Zhang Houzai 張厚載 et al., "Xinwenxue ji Zhongguo jiuxi" 新文學及中國舊戲 [New literature and old-style Chinese theater], *New Youth* 4.6 (June 1918).

43. Liu Bannong 劉半農 and Qian Xuantong 錢玄同, "Jin zhi suowei 'Pingjujia'" 今之所謂評劇家 [Contemporary so-called "theater critics"], *New Youth* 5.2 (August 1918).

44. Liang Qichao, "On the Relationship Between Fiction and the Government of the People."

45. Chen Duxiu, letter in response to Zhang Houzai's "New Literature and Old-style Chinese Theater," *New Youth* 4.6 (June 1918).

46. Fu Sinian 傅斯年, "*Xiju gailiang gemianguan*" 戲劇改良各面觀 [Various perspectives on theater reform] and "Zailun xiju gailiang" 再論戲劇改良 [Another discussion on theater reform], and see also Hu Shi 胡適, "Wenxue jinhua guannian yu xiju gailiang" 文學進化觀念與戲劇改良 [Literary evolution and theater reform], in *New Youth* 5.4 (October 1918).

47. Zhou Zuoren 周作人, "Lun Zhongguo jiuxi zhi yingfei" 論中國舊戲之應廢 [On the rise and fall of old-style Chinese theater], *New Youth* 5.5 (November 1918).

48. Fu Sinian, "Various Perspectives on Theater Reform" and Hu Shi, "Literary Evolution and Theater Reform."

49. Fu Sinian, "Another Discussion on Theater Reform," and Qian Xuantong's letter in response to Zhang Houzai's "'Lianpu'—'da bazi'" 臉譜—打把子 ['Masks'—'Acrobatics'], *New Youth* 5.4 (October 1918).

50. Yu Shangyuan 余上沅, "Yu Shangyuan zhi Zhang Jiaju shu" 余上沅致張嘉鑄書 [Letter from Yu Shangyuan to Zhang Jiazhu], *Guoju yundong* 國劇運動 [National theater movement] (Shanghai: Xinyue shudian, 1927), 274.

51. Yu Shangyuan, "Xu" 序 [Preface], *National Theater Movement*, 1.

52. Yu Shangyuan, "Preface," and Wen Yiduo 聞一多, "Xiju de qitu" 戲劇的歧途 [At the crossroads of theater], *National Theater Movement*, 3 and 55–56.

53. Zhao Taimou 趙太侔 "Guoju" 國劇 [National theater] and Yu Shangyuan, "Jiuxi pingjia" 舊戲評價 [Evaluation of old-style theater], in *National Theater Movement*, 11, 196, 193, and 10 respectively.

54. Yu Shangyuan, "Preface," 6.

55. Zhao Taimou, "National Theater" and Yu Shangyuan, "Evaluation of Old-style Theater," in *National Theater Movement*, 16 and 197.

56. Yu Shangyuan, "Evaluation of Old-style Theater," 197; and "Zhongguo xiju de tujing" 中國戲劇的途徑 [The trajectory of Chinese theater], in *Xiju yu wenyi* 戲劇與文藝 [Theater and the Arts] 1.1 (May 1929). Yu Shangyuan writes, "Although the theatrical elements of these works are so weak, the reason old-style theater has managed to endure for so long lies in the fact that it emphasizes action rather than script, and watching rather than listening." See his "Evaluation of Old-Style Theater," 201.

57. Yu Shangyuan, "Guoju" 國劇 [National theater]; Chinese translation published in *Morning Post* (晨報) (April 17, 1935). Cited from Zhang Yu 張余, ed. *Yu Shangyuan yanjiu zhuanji* 余上沅研究專集 [Collected studies on Yu Shangyuan] (Shanghai: Shanghai Jiaotong University Press, 1992), 77.

58. Yu Shangyuan, "The Trajectory of Chinese Theater."

59. Hao Xianghui 郝祥輝, ed., *Baike xin cidian* 百科新辭典 [Encyclopedic new dictionary] (section on literary arts) (Shanghai: Shijie shuju, 1922), 25 and 26.

60. Sun Lianggong 孫俍工, ed., *Wenyi cidian* 文藝辭典 [Dictionary of literature and art] (Shanghai: Minzhi shuju, 1928), 2 and 915.

61. Shu Xincheng 舒新城, ed., *Zhonghua baike cidian* 中華百科辭典 [Chinese encyclopedic dictionary] (Shanghai: Zhonghua shuju, 1930), 7 and 1098.

Works Cited

Bieshi 別士 (Xia Cengyou 夏曾佑). "Xiaoshuo yuanli" 小說原理 [The principles of fiction], *Xiuxiang xiaoshuo* 繡像小說 [Illustrated fiction] 3 (June 1903).

"Benguan fuyin shuobu yuanqi" 本館附印說部緣起 [How our press started publishing literary supplements]. *Guowen bao* 國聞報 [Guowen daily], December 11, 1897.

Ciyuan 辭源 [Ciyuan], rev. ed., vol. 2. Beijing: Shangwu yinshuguan, 1980.

Edkins, Joseph 艾約瑟. "Luoma shiren lüeshuo" 羅馬詩人略說 [A brief discussion of Roman poets]. *Liuhe congtan* 六合叢談 [Shanghae serial] 3, March 26, 1857.

Edkins, Joseph, trans. *Xixue qimeng shiliuzhong* 西學啟蒙十六種 [Sixteen forms of Western enlightenment]. Shanghai: Zhuyitang shuju, 1896.

Fu Sinian 傅斯年. "Xiju gailiang gemianguan" 戲劇改良各面觀 [Various perspectives on theater reform]. *Xin qingnian* 新青年 [New youth] 5.4 (October 1918).

Fu Sinian 傅斯年. "Zailun xiju gailiang" 再論戲劇改良 [Another discussion on theater reform]. *Xin qingnian* 新青年 [New youth] 5.4 (October 1918).

"Gailiang xiju zhi jihua" 改良戲劇之計畫 [A plan for improving theater], *Jingzhong ribao* 警鐘日報 [Alarm bell daily], April 22, 1904.

Hao Xianghui 郝祥輝, ed. *Baike xin cidian* 百科新辭典 [Encyclopedic new dictionary] (section on literary arts). Shanghai: Shijie shuju, 1922.

Hu Shi 胡適. "Wenxue jinhua guannian yu xiju gailiang" 文學進化觀念與戲劇改良 [Literary evolution and theater reform]. *Xin qingnian* 新青年 [New youth] 5. 4 (October 1918).

Huangdi zisun zhi yige ren 黃帝子孫之一個人 (penname of Huang Zao 黃藻), ed. *Huangdi hun* 黃帝魂 [Spirit of the Yellow Emperor], 1904.

Huang Renbian 黃人編. *Putong baike xin dacidian* 普通百科新大辭典 [A popular encyclopedic dictionary]. Shanghai: Guoxue fulunshe, 1911.

Jian He 健鶴, "Gailiang xiju zhi jihua 改良戲劇之計畫 [A plan for improving theater] (the title was later changed to "Yanju gailiang zhi jihua" 演劇改良之計畫 [A plan for improving theatrical performance]). *Jingzhong ribao* 警鐘日報 [Alarm bell daily], May 30–June 1, 1904.

Liang Qichao 梁啟超. "Lun xiaoshuo yu qunzhi zhi guanxi" 論小說與群治之關係 [On the relationship between fiction and government of the people]. *Xin xiaoshuo* 新小說 [New literature] 1 (November 1902).

Liu Bannong 劉半農 and Qian Xuantong 錢玄同. "Jin zhi suowei 'Pingjujia'" 今之所謂評劇家 [Contemporary so-called 'theater critics']. *Xin qingnian* 新青年 [New youth] 5.2 (August 1918).

[Liu Shipei 劉師培]. "Yuanxi" 原戲 [The origins of theater]. *Chenzhong bao* 晨鐘報 [Morning bell daily], December 24–25, 1904.

Lu 僇 (Wang Zhongqi 王鍾麒). "Lun xiqu gailiang yu qunzhi zhi guanxi" 論戲曲改良與群治之關係 [On the relationship between theater reform and government of the people]. *Shun Pao* 申報, September 22, 1906.

"Lun xiju zhi youyi" 論戲劇之有益 [Discussing the uses of theater]. *Chenzhong bao* 晨鐘報 [Morning bell daily], August 21, 24, 26, 1904.

Morrison, Robert. *A Dictionary of the Chinese Language.* Part III. Macao: East India Company Press, 1822.

Pei Ren 佩忍 (Chen Qubing 陳去病). "Lun xiju zhi youyi" 論戲劇之有益 [Discussing the uses of theater]. *Ershi shiji dawutai* 二十世紀大舞台 [Great stage of the twentieth century] 1 (October 1904).

Qian Feng 錢豐, ed. *Wanguo fenlei shiwu dacheng* 萬國分類時務大成 [A comprehensive summary of current affairs by category and for all nations], vol. 20. Shanghai: Xiuhai shanfang, 1897.

San Ai 三愛 (Chen Duxiu 陳獨秀). "Lun xiqu" 論戲曲 (Discussing *xiqu*). *Xin xiaoshuo* 新小說 [New literature] 14 (March 1905).

Sasakawa Rinpu, 笹川臨風. *A Chinese Literary History* 支那文學史. Tokyo: Hakubunkan, 1898.

Shu Xincheng 舒新城, ed. *Zhonghua baike cidian* 中華百科辭典 [Chinese encyclopedic dictionary]. Shanghai: Zhonghua shuju, 1930.

Sun Lianggong 孫俍工, ed. *Wenyi cidian* 文藝辭典 [Dictionary of literature and art]. Shanghai: Minzhi shuju, 1928.

Sun Yuxiu 孫毓修. *Oumei xiaoshuo congtan: Yingguo xiqu zhi fayuan* 歐美小說叢談: 英國戲曲之發源 [An essay on European and American fiction: The origins of English *xiqu*]. *Fiction Monthly*. 4.7 (November 1913).

Wang Guowei 王國維. "Xiqu kaoyuan" 戲曲考原 [An investigation of the origins of *xiqu*]. *Guocui xuebao* 國粹學報 [Journal of national essence] 48 (December 1908).

Wang Tingxin 王廷信. "'Ershiliu shi' zhong de 'xiju' gainian lüekao" "二十六史"中的 "戲劇"概念略考 [An examination of the concept of *xiju* in the twenty-six dynastic histories]. *Zhonghua xiqu* 中華戲曲 [Chinese drama] 1 (2003).

Wu Yasheng 無涯生 (Ou Jujia 歐榘甲). "Guanxi ji" 觀戲記 [A record of observing drama], originally published in *Wenxing bao* 文興報 [*Mon Hing Po*], reprinted in *Qingyibao quanbian* 清議報全編 [Qingyi paper, complete edition], vol. 25 (1902), appendix 1.

"Xiju gailianghui kaiban jianzhang" 戲劇改良會開辦簡章 [General regulations for committees on theater reform] and "Shaoxing xiqu gailianghui kaiban jianzhang" 紹興戲曲改良會簡章 [General regulations for the committees on the reform of Shaoxing theater]. *Jingzhong ribao* 警鐘日報 [Alarm bell daily], August 7–8, 1904.

Xia Xiaohong 夏曉虹. "Liang Qichao de wenlei gainian bianxi" 梁啟超的文類概念辨析 [An analysis of Liang Qichao's concept of literary taxonomy]. *Guoxue yanjiu* 國學研究 [Guoxue studies], vol. 15. Beijing: Peking University Press, 2005.

Xie Wuliang 謝無量. *Zhongguo da wenxueshi* 中國大文學史 [A comprehensive literary history of China], 4th ed. Shanghai: Zhonghua shuju, 1918.

Ya Lu 亞盧 (Liu Yazi 柳亞子). "'Ershi shiji dawutai' fakan ci" 〈二十世紀大舞台〉發刊詞 [Opening preface to *Great Stage of the Twentieth Century*]. *Great Stage of the Twentieth Century* 1 (October 1904).

Ya Lu 亞盧 (Liu Yazi 柳亞子). "'Ershi shiji dawutai congbao' zhaoguqi bing jianzhang" 〈二十世紀大舞台叢報〉招股啟並簡章 [Great stage of the twentieth century journal announcement and regulations] 2 (November 1904).

Ye Changhai 葉長海. "Xiqu kao" 戲曲考 [An investigation of *xiqu*]. *Xiju yishu* 戲劇藝術 [Theatrical arts] 4 (1991).

Yinbing 飲冰 (Liang Qichao 梁啟超) et al. "Xiaoshuo conghua" 小說叢話 [Colloquy on fiction]. *Xin xiaoshuo* 新小說 [New literature] 7 [1903].

Yinbing (Liang Qichao), Ping Zi 平子 (Di Baoxian 狄葆賢), and Ding Yiyu 定一語. *New Literature*, no. 7, 9, 13 (September 1903, August 1904, February 1905).

Yu Shangyuan 余上沅. "Yu Shangyuan zhi Zhang Jiaju shu" 余上沅致張嘉鑄書 [Letter from Yu Shangyuan to Zhang Jiazhu]. In *Guoju yundong* 國劇運動 [National theater movement]. Shanghai: Xinyue shudian, 1927.

Yuan Zonglian 袁宗濂 and Yan Zhiqing 晏志清, ed. *Xizheng tongdian* 西政通典 [Compilation of Western politics], vol. 16. Shanghai: Cuixin shuguan, 1902.

Zhang Houzai 張厚載 et al. "Xinwenxue ji Zhongguo jiuxi" 新文學及中國舊戲 [New literature and old-style Chinese theater]. *Xin qingnian* 新青年 [New youth] 4.6 (June 1918).

Zhou Zuoren 周作人. "Lun Zhongguo jiuxi zhi yingfei" 論中國舊戲之應廢 [On the rise and fall of old-style Chinese theater]. *Xin qingnian* 新青年 [New youth] 5.5 (November 1918).

CHAPTER 1.4

··

ORIENTALISM, SCIENTIFIC PRACTICE, AND POPULAR CULTURE IN LATE QING CHINA

··

NATHANIEL ISAACSON

Xu Nianci's 許念慈 (1875–1908) "New Tales of Mr. Braggadocio" (新法螺先生譚; 1904) features two moments of Fanonian double consciousness in its opening pages.[1] A preface in the voice of the author's pseudonym, *Juewo* 覺我 ("The Awakened One"), refers to the work as "gossip heard through the bean trellis" and a "ludicrous attempt at imitation."[2] This pseudonymous disavowal opens the text up to at least two modes of reading: as a work of art that is mere entertainment, or as a work of art that contains a serious message. This instance of narratological distancing is immediately followed by a series of moments of doubled consciousness in the plot itself. The narrator, Mr. Braggadocio, becomes distraught upon realizing that all worldly phenomena can be described in terms of scientific law, and proceeds to flee his home and ascend Mt. Everest. The 360,000-foot-high summit is so lofty that the gravitational field of earth is compromised by neighboring planets and stars, causing his corporeal body and his soul to become separated. Upon regaining his composure, he undertakes a series of experiments on these two bodies. Shaoling Ma notes that "what is more fantastical than his out-of-body *and* out-of-spirit experience is the first-person narration that is simultaneously a third-person reference to his 'selves,' an 'I' as a third-person to himself."[3] Mr. Braggadocio is a figure literally torn between fields of knowledge, the narrator of a whimsical romp about the solar system with a message of national salvation.

Xu Nianci's sequel to Iwaya Sazanami's 岩谷小波 (1870–1933) "Tales of Mr. Braggadocio" (Japanese "*Hora Sensei*" 法螺先生), published by Forest of Fiction (小說林) press, straddles a number of intellectual realms: Chinese folk beliefs, Christian theology, *wenyan* (文言) fiction, Meiji-era *shōsetsu* (小說), the emergence of children's fiction as a literary category in Japan, Liang Qichao's "new literature" (新小說), Social

Darwinism, Zhuangzian irrationalism, and scientific rationalism, to name but a few. As a sequel to a loose translation of a Meiji-era Japanese short story by Iwaya Sazanami, which Takeda Masaya 武田雅哉 identifies as a loose translation of the stories of Baron von Münchhausen,[4] the story and its translated prequels bear many of the thematic and historical hallmarks of colonial modernity—globally circulated Baudrillardian homages to translations of translations long divorced from any originary "master text." Though his didactic purpose and desire to write in a vernacular style were in concert with other writers of the *genbun-itchi* (言文一致; "unification of spoken and written language") movement, Sazanami is recognized as the first author of modern Japanese children's literature (initially through translation), placing him at the margins of canonical literature as a writer of adventure hoping to appeal to a juvenile audience.[5] "Mr. Braggadocio" bridges the gap between serious literature and entertainment, in dialogue with the anxiety engendered by the universality of scientific knowledge.[6] While the story's scientific "discoveries" may stand out as either disproven or pure fabrication to a contemporary lay reader, many of the scientific elements of Xu Nianci's story represent developments contemporary to the author.

In this chapter, I examine a set of interrelated issues. First, drawing on Lydia Liu's *Translingual Practice*, I examine how "New Tales of Mr. Braggadocio" reflects processes of cultural exchange that imbricated science and associated terms into the vocabulary of colonial modernity. In this context, science and scientific institutions were translated into late Qing fiction and culture as tools of social transformation. These translations drew upon the vocabulary of neo-Confucian positivism, but Daoist language and concepts were also used in attempts to describe, refute, or enculturate Western science. Through popular media, late Qing intellectuals pondered if Daoism or Confucianism could serve as epistemic frame for science or whether the reverse was true—could science be contextualized and explained by indigenous modes of thought, or was science the ultimate field of knowledge? Second, the short story also reflects on the relationship between capitalism and modernization, suggesting that while there were potential avenues for resistance to or reframing of the philosophical rubric of science, there were no such alternatives to the sociopolitical logic of global capital. Finally, I contend that this fictional failure to resist incorporation into the global economy is symptomatic of a deep-seated anxiety about the emancipatory potential of a genre closely associated with the colonial effort. Late Qing authors were ambivalent about the question of whether Orientalism could be turned against itself in any of its incarnations.[7] Science, science fiction, and engagement with global capital were seen as necessary components of modernization, but regarded with suspicion for their complicity in the colonial project.

SCIENCE AND EMPIRE

Kexue (科學; "science") is a key term that helped constitute the lexicon of late Qing colonial modernity.[8] Originally meaning simply "knowledge," in the late Qing it came to be linked to the European Enlightenment's scientific method and a corresponding field of knowledge production. Science was first understood through the vocabulary and philosophical orientation of the Neo-Confucian interpretation of the "Greater Learning" (大學), and was designated by phrases such as "investigation-extension" (*gezhi* 格致), "investigation of things" (*gewu* 格物), "the study of probing thoroughly the principle" (窮理之學), and "investigating things so as to extend knowledge" (格物致知). *Gezhi*, in particular, refers to an internal process of individual cultivation and cognition that leads to the subjective apprehension of knowledge and results in a capacity to achieve universal order. During the late Qing, however, conceptualizations of science began to shift toward a sense of objective understanding of the material world.

Not originally a Chinese term, *kexue* was a Japanese import, a product of Japan's Meiji restoration and another example of translingual practice. It was during this period that the term *kexue*, and its associations with categorizing knowledge, began to come into widespread usage. *Kexue*, though more closely associated with notions of observation and factual experiment, continued to be associated with positivism and an overarching cosmic order. Thinkers like Yan Fu 嚴復 (1854–1921) saw in science, and especially in sociology, the "science of sciences," and the ability to unveil the inherent interrelation between natural and social order.[9] Wang Hui explains that *kexue* and *gezhi* were two key terms that fell into the nebula of terms associated with the West. Terms like *kexue*, *wenming* (文明; "civilization"), *keji* (科技; "technology"), *minzhu* (民主; "democracy"), and *xixue* (西學; "Western learning") as well as notions of civic and political involvement, evolution, and Social Darwinism—all of which were firmly rooted in a Weberian/Marxist model that privileges the development of European institutions and economic systems as a teleological historical standard—were often viewed as foreign imports and perceived in a nebulous cluster of overlapping associations, conflating a number of modern calques with the more long-standing traditions from which they had been repurposed. Likewise, the term *wenming* was transplanted from a Japanese term pronounced *bunmei*, which was closely grounded on notions of modernity and Westernization.[10] Like the hegemonic narrative of Said's "universalizing historicism," civilization was also a concept associated with the imagination of a single historical trajectory and a universal valuation of cultural worth. Science and civilization were not merely discourses deployed to justify the expansion of empire, they effectively served as Empire's swords. Modern science was inextricably intertwined with the growth of European and Japanese empires, the expansion of global capital, and the "three masses" of modernity: mass production, mass consumption, and mass destruction.[11]

Turn-of-the-century Chinese intellectuals saw social Darwinism as a political reality. These same figures were also aware of the complicity of scientific institutions and science fiction in the production of Orientalist discourse and the colonial project. Decades before Edward Said's influential critique of Orientalism, late Qing intellectuals were already cognizant of the fact that the natural and social sciences were often deployed in the service of the imperial effort, and that the uneven relationship between the West and the rest was not merely discursive but instead was a material reality reinforced by a number of institutional formations. To paraphrase Said, they recognized that "Orientalism [*was*]—and [did] not simply represent—a considerable dimension of modern political-intellectual culture."[12]

Theodore Huters and Marston Anderson have delineated the ways in which permutations of modernism and realism were closely associated with one another from the late Qing into the May Fourth era.[13] As a close cousin of realism, modernism entailed the adoption of realistic narrative writing practices. Material modernization and the adoption of realistic narrative modes to promote modernization were understood as the most viable alternative to a failing imperial system, and were paradoxically associated with Westernization at the same time as repurposed terminologies kept them moored to neo-Confucian positivism. Late Qing intellectuals understood the popularization of science to be an engine of modernization. The urgency of translation and promotion of science for the sake of national salvation was tempered by deep-seated anxieties about the relationship between science and empire. This cultural double bind produced a schizophrenic discourse of modernity visible in the popular media of the era. In the context of a theoretical understanding of science fiction as a product of Orientalism expressing the conscious and unconscious desires of the colonial imagination,[14] Chinese science fiction was the product of two converging intellectual trends of turn-of-the-twentieth-century China: the imperialist imagination of global exchanges and conquest that led to the emergence of the genre in the West and its translation into Chinese via Japan, and the crisis of epistemological consciousness spurred on by China's semi-colonial subjugation to European powers.

"New Tales of Mr. Braggadocio" also makes a number of gestures to more practical elements of the colonial effort, including the race to discover and map uncharted territories on the surface of the earth; it extended this fantasy into outer space, reflecting the fantasy of colonial accumulation engendered by the era of European empire that was so common to Victorian science fiction—what Giovanni Arrighi and Prasenjit Duara refer to as the logics of accumulation and territoriality, reflecting the rising tide of global capitalism.[15] Late Qing popular culture featured a number of fictional and real attempts to create museums, exhibition halls, libraries, and other apparatuses of cultural modernization. This focus on exploration, collection, and dissemination of knowledge reflects an evolving vision of Western science whose focus shifted from material technology to institutions of colonial modernity—what Andrew Jones and Alan Rauch theorize as the "knowledge industry."[16] The reconfiguration of private collections into institutional symbols of empire and the colonial accumulation that accompanied these aims were also understood to be a key component of scientific modernity. The protagonist's success in producing a pseudoscientific discovery that obviates the material trappings of industrial technology results in a paradoxical defeat, suggesting that while modern science may potentially be resisted, the cycles of production, accumulation, and destruction at the heart of capitalism cannot.

Lu Xun heralded the translation of science fiction, arguing in the preface to his translation of Jules Verne's *De la terre a la lune* (From the earth to the moon; 1903) that Chinese science fiction, while "as rare as unicorn horns," possessed the potential to educate the public in the otherwise tedious subject of science, and he encouraged concerted efforts in the translation of science fiction.[17] In the same year, in his preface to *Iron World* (鐵世界), the translation of Jules Verne's *Les cinq cents millions de la Bégum* (The Begum's Fortune), Bao Tianxiao 包天笑 (1876–1973), a colleague of Xu Nianci at *Forest of Fiction*,[18] wrote, "science fiction is the vanguard of the civilized world," adding that "there are those in the world who don't like to study, but there are none who don't appreciate science fiction, thus it is an adroit mechanism of importing civilized thought, and its seeds quickly bear fruit."[19] Haitian Duxiaozi 海天獨孝子 wrote in a similar vein that "in our country today, the tide of imported Western knowledge, and books volume upon volume would make the ox carrying them break a sweat or fill a library to the rafters. To get twice the result with half the effort, what might we choose to make popular throughout the land? I implore you to begin with science fiction."[20] Xu Nianci's original work followed soon after.

FICTIVE ARCHAISM

Linguistically, Xu Nianci's story combines vernacular and literary Chinese, translating scientific concepts using a preexisting philosophical vocabulary common to the world of late Qing letters.[21] "New Tales of Mr. Braggadocio" is written in the style of the Daoist classic, the *Zhuangzi*, which we can date to around the third century BCE. On a number of occasions, Mr. Braggadocio uses direct quotations from the *Zhuangzi*. The story's appearance in the popular press and ostensibly frivolous subject matter stand in stark contrast to the deliberate archaism of the text and the philosophical tone that it invokes. In his analysis of the creolized religious practice of French spiritualism and mesmerism, John Monroe argues that a newly emerging (often scientific) "vocabulary" of practices, doctrines, and institutional formations is grafted onto a relatively stable "grammar" of deep religious structures.[22] The thematic content of "Mr. Braggadocio" enacts a similar creolization, taking Daoist metaphysics as an ontological "grammar" for understanding the universe, the rhetorical style of *Zhuangzi* as a textual model, and the vocabulary of modern science as the vocabulary of evolutionary history and scientific discovery. Mr. Braggadocio describes two attempts at overturning colonial modernity: by "making room" for the totalizing force of scientific taxonomy within the realm of Daoist thought, and by seizing the reins of global capital. The narrative most successfully overturns the realities of colonial modernity in linguistic, rather than narrational, terms.

Istvan Csicsery-Ronay, riffing on Darko Suvin's concept of the *novum*, has argued that the literary texture of science fiction produces a chronoclastic effect, "embody[ing] cultural collisions between the usage of words familiar in the present (a neologism's 'prehistory') and the imaginary, altered linguistic future asserted by the neology."[23] Xu Nianci takes a different (albeit familiar) tack, opting to present science through the rhetorial structure of a pre-Han model. This form of linguistic invention puts the reader in the position of an imagined past rather than an imagined future history.

In the language of the *Zhuangzi*, we see the modern world as Zhuangzi would have seen it. What are the implications of Xu Nianci's deployment of philosophical Daoism as the language of his own fictive neology? What is indicated when science fiction is written in precisely the opposite linguistic register—fictive archaism, rather than fictive neology? Where Jia Baoyu, in *New Story of the Stone* (新石頭記; 1904), attempts to counter the colonial threat by resuscitating Confucian tradition and embalming the unknowable universe of Daoist myth and the unpredictable wilds beyond China's borders of the *Classic of Mountains and Seas* (山海經), Mr. Braggadocio revives Daoist language. This narrative and thematic repurposing of the *Zhuangzi* attempts to place science within the context of Daoist hermeneutics and to assert the precedence of an unknowable universe over the clockwork predictability of scientific ontology.

This language attempts to establish the authority of a very specific form of literary Chinese as the most suitable language for writing about and comprehending the universe and Western science. Like Lu Xun, who lamented that his translation of Verne's *De la terre a la lune* could not achieve sufficient sophistication without recourse to literary Chinese, Xu Nianci suggests that the best way to speak of the present is to rescucitate the language of a bygone era. The *Zhuangzi* is a text (or accumulation of texts) that denies the capacity of human reason to understand the true nature of the Dao/universe. To this extent, we could read Mr. Braggadocio as antiscientific, or at least as antimodern and against language reform.

The story's use of Zhuangzian diction and syntax, and the occasional direct quotation, are contrasted with a catalogue of modern translated terms, many of which are rendered in transliteration only. When the narrator visits the surface of Venus, for instance, the text offers an extended treatise on an alternate theory of evolution, peppered with biological terms like *coelenterates* (腔腸動物), *echinoderms* (棘皮動物), and *molluscs* (軟體動物).[24] Along with an ability to name and categorize the world using contemporary scientific terms, the author also demonstrates a keen attention to time and the measurement of it, regularly observing the duration and speed of events in the story. In these aspects, the language of the story distances itself from its philosophical model text.

Some of the most important vocabulary in the text, however, can be traced neither to the language of Chinese philosophical antiquity nor to that of translated scientific modernity. In particular, Xu Nianci uses the term *linghun* (靈魂) to mean "soul," stating, "I have no word for it, but it would be referred to in the common language of religion as the 'soul.'"[25] This calls to mind popular Chinese beliefs in a *hun* (魂) and *po* (魄) soul. Chinese folk belief disagrees on how many *hun* and *po* souls one has, what their relationship is to the living body, where they go after death, and whether they live on forever after the death of the body.[26] While the usage of "my soul-body" (*yu linghun zhi shen* 余靈魂之身) to refer to his 'soul' and "my corporeal-body" (*yu quqiao zhi shen* 余軀殼之身) to refer to his body is unique to this text, the story seems to confirm that they conform roughly to associations in the classic *Book of Rites* (禮記) of the *hun* with vital energy and the ascent to heaven and the *po* with the physical body and a descent into the earth.[27] Neither of these terms corresponds very well at all to the vocabularies of either Christian theology or Chinese thanatology. In short, even in a "pure Chinese" context, it is very unclear just what a *linghun* is.

It is equally possible, however, that in spite of his idiosyncratic vocabulary, Xu Nianci is also appealing to a Judeo-Christian theological understanding of body and soul. Late-nineteenth-century journals like *Chinese Serial* (遐邇貫珍) and *Shanghae Serial* (六合叢談) were among the wide range of missionary publications that offered readers Christian theological discussions of the body-soul duality alongside scientific tracts on subjects like human anatomy, articles on mesmerism, and news pieces about the completion of a trans-Atlantic telegraph cable.[28] Emerging scientific knowledge about the human body was presented alongside theological arguments about the immortal soul, further muddying the dividing line between science and religion or metaphysics. Xu Nianci blurs the distinction between Chinese and Christian spirituality and science by placing the figure of the *linghun* within the context of empiricism and scientific knowledge. The *linghun* in the text is indeed a *shen*, or a body endowed with a physical presence that the narrator is able to weigh and quantify. The text's borrowing from Daoist philosophy and Han thanatology sets it apart from other late Qing intellectuals, who framed science in terms of Neo-Confucianism (*lixue* 理學), but it shares the tendency to understand science in the context of established ontological categories that implicate science in a broader moral and metaphysical universe. Thus, "New Tales of Mr. Braggadocio" attempts to vitiate science's claims to universal knowledge by subsuming it under the rubric of Daoist cosmology. Under the Daoist rubric of an ineffable universe, the text also subverts Christianity's claims to theological preeminence by blurring the lines between Christian and Chinese folk religious practice. In other words, the *Zhuangzi* is positioned as both a potential conduit for and a counter to Western science.

TIME, SPACE, CAPITAL

Mr. Braggadocio's fictional discovery of conditions on Venus that contradict Darwinian theories of evolution, and his mission to uncover evidence subverting science's claims to universality, are also borne out thematically in the text. On a corporeal journey to what he first believes to be a facsimile of China at the center of the earth, Mr. Braggadocio encounters an elderly man named Huang Zhongzu (黃種族, lit. "Yellow Race"), the benevolent overseer of a precise simulacrum of Mr. Braggadocio's national homeland. Underground, time is refracted: one second equals 216,000 above-ground seconds, allowing Mr. Braggadocio and Huang Zhongzu to see the progress of Darwinian deep time. He calculates:

> reckoning by Huang Zhongzu's clock, one second took two and a half days, and one minute was equal to one hundred and fifty days. One hour was equivalent to twenty-five of our years, and twenty-four hours equaled six hundred of our years. And thus the oldest people among them live for only four hours. 'The morning

mushroom knows nothing of twilight and dawn, the summer cicada knows nothing of spring and autumn.' In apprehension of the universe, so vast the gulf 'twixt thee and I![29]

This passage juxtaposes the rational segmentation of time based on the European horological system and the sublime nature of geologic time, with the Daoist notion of time as fundamentally ineffable that is implicit in Zhuangzi's parable of the morning mushroom and the cicada.[30] Another iteration of Mr. Braggadocio's double consciousness is thus temporal double consciousness; a fastidious attention to the measurement of rational, industrial time is juxtaposed with the language of Daoism as a hermeneutic tool for explicating the mysteries of deep time.

Beneath the earth, time is slowed down, allowing Mr. Braggadocio and Huang Zhongzu to perceive generations of social transformation occurring before their very eyes. For China, the clockwork machinery of time ticks inexorably forward, but at a different pace. Coevality is expressed as a geological metaphor—deep beneath the planet's surface, where geologists unearth the past, Mr. Braggadocio discovers the "truth" of China's decay. Social decline is sited underground—the place of both the past and of an undeveloped, troglodyte society, paralleling the inhabitants of the island of Le'erlaifu 勒而來複 in Huangjiang Diaosou's 黃江釣叟 *Tales of the Moon Colony* (月球殖民地小說; 1904–1905) and the Morlocks in H. G. Wells's *The Time Machine* (1885).[31] Despite the fact that time is slowed down in this underground facsimile of China, the future still looms on the horizon as an inevitable catastrophe. This episode, as well as an earlier failed attempt to awaken his own countrymen "from their muddled dreams, wipe the sleep from their eyes, push them to catch up and create a new civilization," leads him to remark that he would like to cause a holocaust in East Asia, "leaving a new uncharted territory to a future Columbus."[32] Rhetorically, the text insists upon the explanatory power of Daoism while the plot details discoveries that subvert certain details of Darwinian evolution. These inversions are undermined by intruding visions of a society that is indeed devolving, causing the narrator to imagine himself as the harbinger of a Social-Darwinian catharsis. This moment of double consciousness parallels similar passages in Huangjiang Diaosou's *Tales of the Moon Colony* and Wu Jianren's *New Story of the Stone*, where China's benighted populace is either left to die or falls victim to a mercy killing, and prefigures Lu Xun's iconic iron house metaphor. The perceived logic of social Darwinism is presented as one facet of Western science that cannot be overcome.

Benjamin Schwarz has noted that in translating Thomas Huxley's work on Social Darwinism, Yan Fu misapprehended the text's critical stance, and—perhaps not surprisingly, given China's semicolonial plight—transformed a critique of social Darwinism into a system of moral and social valuation.[33] The perception that the law of survival of the fittest applied to societies and nations hung over late Qing intellectual life like the Sword of Damocles. However exaggerated the actual threat of national extinction, the effects of this anxiety were quite profound. Whatever they might be, intellectual and practical justifications for the adoption of things foreign had to be formulated.

Social-Darwinian racial evolution becomes a visible and actively influential process as Huang Zhongzu employs a collection of elixirs to alter the behavior of the denizens of underground China. Huang at first appears to be a contemporary, "scientific" iteration of *Mencius's* proponent of neutral human nature, Gaozi, informing Mr. Braggadocio that the human capacity for good and evil is innate, and can be changed based upon the environmental conditions one is raised in. As Huang explains how he manipulates human behavior in his laboratory, the vision of human nature takes on a Xunzian turn, suggesting that the Warring States philosopher's opinion that "man's nature is evil," was correct.[34] The substances associated with good moral qualities are nearly all used up, while those associated with sloth, avarice, and self-interest are still in ample supply and are more efficacious. Showing Mr. Braggadocio a jar filled with morphine, Huang Zhongzu informs him,

"This one also brightens and purifies society through the understanding of principles and eschewing hypocrisy. It is a solid, and all of it is contained in this bottle, of which only five ten-thousandths remain." He pointed to a large bottle, saying "This bottle contains a liquid, of which sixty-five percent remains. It is called *morphine*, the most poisonous of substances. If one is poisoned by it he'll lose all ambition and his flesh will waste away, cutting short his lease on life. I'd hate to be poisoned by it, but many have already come to such an end. This substance is the desire for money, and this is superstitious faith in spirits. And this gas is unbridled arrogance, while this one is benighted ignorance. This liquid is aimless wandering, and over here we have indecision. This yellow solid is the cause of encephalitis and pneumonia, and this violet colored liquid is desire for fame. All in all, the roots of human good are being eaten away and only eight or nine ten-thousandths remain. What hope do I have?"[35]

The lab filled with various substances for the manipulation of human behavior calls into question both Mencius's and Xunzi's visions of human nature perfected through education and moral cultivation, replacing human agency with chemical reactions.

When Mr. Braggadocio realizes that he himself is one of Huang Zhongzu's doomed progeny, and that he is seeing China itself rather than a subterranean facsimile, his epiphany leads to a narrative rupture that leaves behind Mr. Braggadocio's corporeal body and the intractable decay of life on earth that he has discovered, switching to the journey of his soul-body through space. He witnesses a group of Mercurian doctors replacing an old man's cerebral tissue in order to restore his youth. Mr. Braggadocio remarks,

My Lords! I am quite certain that this is their method of making people. The human faculties of life, motion and cognition are all accumulated in the brain. Now, if we were to take out the old and replace it with new cerebral matter, lost teeth would grow anew, hunched backs would straighten, and greying pates return to lustrous black. Aged men awaiting the tolling bells could be reborn as vibrant youth. Alas, I was not able to learn the method of this art. Had I been able to, upon my return home I would have amassed the necessary capital to open a brain-matter renewal company in Shanghai, and the makers of Mr. Ailuo's Brain Tonic would have had to close their doors at once. All of those outdated, polluted and contemptible customs of this country would be completely washed clean.[36]

The competition between an ineffable universe and the taxonomized universe of the knowledge industry is thereby juxtaposed with a concern with the accumulation of capital. Mr. Braggadocio's revealing remark at the end of the passage—that he would "wash clean" the intractable customs of his countrymen—is one of the moments where his own double consciousness is revealed. Remarks like these foreground that there is much more at stake than money, and that revitalizing China is more than a matter of displacing the hegemony of scientific knowledge.

   The temptations of capital continue to assert themselves as Mr. Braggadocio traverses the solar system. In outer space, Mr. Braggadocio demonstrates that, as Viren Murthy has observed in his analysis of Tan Sitong 譚嗣同 and Zhang Taiyan's own attempt to address the disparities between Confucian and evolutionary models of time, "equality, abstract time, and evolution are intimately associated with the logic of global capitalism."[37] When he discovers a trove of precious gems on the surface of Venus, he says,

> my heart raced as I began to plan how I would gather them up and steal away to Earth. When compared to so-called wealthy men, their jaws would drop as they conceded the superior vastness of my riches. Unfortunately, I stood there empty-handed, unable to devise a method to do so.[38]

He discovers that the gems are a form of living mineral, which become superheated if they are shattered, and begins a series of experiments into their nature. His exploration of the gems leads him to a series of further discoveries, contradicting a number of theories of the evolution of life on earth and throughout the universe. First, he surmises that heat was inherent in matter at the creation of the universe, and that younger planets and earlier stages of matter contain more potential energy than older ones. Second, he discovers that extinct and present-day species are able to coexist, disproving theories of evolution through distinct stages that asserted that some species could no longer exist. Finally, he infers that elements are brought together as a result of the planet's revolutionary motion. All of these discoveries fulfill the fantasy that inspired his original flight to the top of Mt. Everest desiring to find knowledge beyond the ken of Western science. While Mr. Braggadocio does make inroads in wresting the knowledge industry from its European "owners," he is less successful in overturning another aspect of colonial modernity: the imperatives of global capitalism.

Brain Electricity

After his body and soul are reunited, shortly after his arrival in Shanghai, Mr. Braggadocio attends a conference on mesmerism (催眠術), where he invents the technique of producing and transmitting "brain electricity" (腦電). Mesmerism, animal magnetism, and other "spiritual sciences" had been more or less disproven in Europe and the United States by this time,[39] but remained relatively popular in Japan and continued to gain a foothold in China after Xu Nianci's story was published. Luan Weiping has suggested that sources of inspiration for Xu Nianci included Tan Sitong's syncretic concept *yitai* (以太; "ether") in his *Exposition of Benevolence* (仁學; 1899) and John Fryer's translation of Henry Wood's (1834–1909) *A Method of Avoiding Illness by Controlling the Mind* (治心免病法; 1896).[40] The year Xu Nianci's story was printed, the *China Press* (大陸報) featured a report on a Shanghai conference on mesmerism hosted by a Mr. Tao (likely Tao Chengzhang).[41] In the decades following the publication of "Mr. Braggadocio," a number of texts on mesmerism made their way into China via translation from Japanese.[42] These texts were produced by a wide range of institutional apparatuses dedicated to mesmerism that sprang up during the second decade of the twentieth century. Many of these societies started in Japan and were soon transplanted to mainland China. These institutions buttressed their teaching efforts with a number of publications on the subject; in total, more than eleven publishing companies produced over forty texts on mesmerism, mentalism, and spiritism between 1916 and 1935.[43] These texts focused on mesmerism as a rationalized set of bodily practices, giving ordered, detailed instructions for both the hypnotist and his subject. While many aspects of mesmerism have been discredited, the core practice of hypnotism and hypnotic suggestion continues to be an important aspect of some approaches to contemporary psychotherapeutic practice.

As a matter of personal discipline, Mr. Braggadocio's perfection of the techniques of "brain electricity," and his intense focus on measurements of distance, time, and even numbers, depict science as part of the category Marcel Mauss refers to as "techniques of the body"[44]—ritualized and patterned behaviors that the scientist deploys to gain control of his own body and to understand and effect change in the world. Mr. Braggadocio opens a school in Shanghai, and soon demand for his six-day training program is so great that he has to open a series of schools across China and eventually throughout the globe. These techniques also resemble a Fordist-Taylorist mode of scientific management of the individual and social body. Brain electricity is neither the product of an idiosyncratic genius, nor is it the product of a unique cultural tradition. Instead, mastery of brain electricity derives from rationalized labor broken down into a series of prescribed, specialized, and repetitive tasks overseen by the narrator. Mr. Braggadocio's schools follow a similar model, churning out graduates with the measurable efficiency of an assembly line as soon as unnecessary distractions have been eliminated.

"Brain electricity" allows the practitioner to produce light and heat and to send and receive messages, eliminating the need for lightbulbs, telephone and telegraph, heating devices, and even the newly invented wireless. A global economic crisis ensues; trains, ships, telecommunications, lightbulbs, and the mining and forestry industries are all rendered redundant by brain electricity, and they collapse. One-third of the world's population is left unemployed, and Mr. Braggadocio is forced to go into hiding after an enormous angry mob gathers and threatens his safety. This episode again allegorizes science as a practice of institutional discipline and a socioeconomic endeavor.

Shaoling Ma, examining the narrative in terms of the relationship between modern subjectivity and the Marxist conception of social labor, has argued that the story moves from an allegory of primitive accumulation to one that "foresees the future postindustrial or information society in which the technological knowledge of brain electricity creates surpluses in both capital and labor."[45] While China's full incorporation into the system of global capital did not happen until eighty-five years later, "New Tales of Mr. Braggadocio" boldly predicts the inevitability of this eventuality. Nearly dismantling international networks of capital, Mr. Braggadocio discovers he is part of a system whose destruction would spell his own demise.

CONCLUSION

Mr. Braggadocio's adventuresome whimsy masks a serious meditation on global knowledge and capital. Careening through space in one body and falling to the center of the earth in another, he is dual consciousness personified. Mr. Braggadocio's soul is a projection of the fantasy of scientific and colonial exploration taken to its logical conclusion. Meanwhile, miles beneath the surface of the earth his corporeal body turns its gaze back on himself and his nation, engaged in an act of self-discovery through which he becomes aware of the severity of China's national plight. Again, the text features the figure of the man of knowledge viewing China's social crisis from afar as its people near their impending doom, this time in the form of the old man whom Mr. Braggadocio meets beneath the Earth. The old man has the power to intervene, but it is clear that his efforts are destined to fail. Mr. Braggadocio's world is yet another uninhabitable narrative space.

The narrative style of the work suggests that the attainment of utopia and true understanding of the universe is a matter of returning to a state of Daoist inaction, but the narrator's actions are anything but an embodiment of quiescence. The temporal perspective that is evoked through this language subverts the notion of linear-chronological progress, while the narrator lays claim to the observation of phenomena outside the realm of known scientific laws of planetary and animal evolution. As much as the story does suggest a successful dethroning of Western science and the ability to make new discoveries that overturn previous theories, colonial capital insists on the primacy of a new world order and its inescapable logic, Mr. Braggadocio's real motivation proves to be personal profit rather than national renewal. Many of his failures are characterized as an inability to capitalize on what he sees and learns. While what he sees on Venus and Mercury and his invention of "brain-electricity" fictionally overturn theories of evolution and biology contemporary to the text. Mr. Braggadocio nevertheless attempts to have them work within the logic of global capitalism. His eventual unsettling of the planet's economic system suggests that such an act would be a form of suicide, in that he is already so deeply imbricated in the global economy that a disruption of the system constitutes an inevitable threat to his own well-being.

NOTES

1. Xu Nianci was born in Changshu, Jiangsu, and also published under the pennames Juewo 覺我 and Donghai Juewo 東海覺我. He mastered Japanese at a young age, and excelled in mathematics and writing. Around 1898, he became involved in the "new studies" movement (新學潮流) and went to work for the China Education Society (中國教育會). He was an active translator and writer, known for mastery of a number of different literary styles. He has also been recognized for his interest in modernism, realism, and Hegelian aesthetics, having published a number of works on the subject, including "My Outlook on Fiction." See Sun Wenguang, ed., *Zhongguo jin dai wen xue da ci dian 1840–1919* 中國近代文學大辞典, 1840–1919 [Dictionary of modern Chinese literature, 1840–1919] (Hefei: Huangshan shu she, 1995), 383; Li Shengping et al., *Zhongguo jin xian dai ren ming da ci dian* 中國近現代人名大辭典 [Dictionary of modern Chinese biography] (Beijing: Zhongguo guoji guangbo chubanshe, 1989), 572.

2. Xu Nianci, "Xin Faluo xiansheng tan" 新法螺先生譚 [New tales of Mr. Bragadoccio] (Shanghai: Xiaoshuo lin, 1905), 1.

3. Shaoling Ma, "'A Tale of New Mr. Bragadoccio': Narrative Subjectivity and Brain Electricity in Late Qing Science Fiction," *Science Fiction Studies* 40. 1 (March 2013): 59.

4. Takeda Masaya 武田雅哉, *Tobe! Daishin tekoku: Kindai chūgoku no gensō kagaku* 飛べ～！大清帝国:近代中国の幻想科学 [Fly! The Qing empire: Modern China's fantastic science] (Tokyo: Riburopōto, 1988), 78–80. Takeda notes that Xu Nianci also published translations of work by Jules Verne. See also Shaoling Ma, "'A Tale of New Mr. Bragadoccio,'" 55.

5. For more on Japanese children's literature, see Judy Wakabayashi, "Foreign Bones, Japanese Flesh: Translations and the Emergence of Modern Children's Literature in Japan," *Japanese Language and Literature* 42.1 (April 2008): 227–255.

6. Xu Nianci appears to have been inspired by both Iwaya Sazanami and Inoue Tsutomu (the Japanese translator of Verne's *From the Earth to the Moon*), who were in turn inspired by Johann Wolfgang von Goethe's vision of "a fuller integration of poetic and scientific sensibilities that would provide a way of experiencing nature both symbolically and scientifically, simultaneously." See Miller, "Introduction" to Goethe, *The Metamorphosis of Plants* (Cambridge: MIT Press, 2009), xi. See also Xu Nianci, "Yu zhi xiaoshuo guan" 余之小說觀 [My outlook on fiction], *Xiaoshuo lin* 小說林 [Forest of fiction] (January 1908): 1–8; (March 1908): 19–15 [page numbering is continuous; individual articles in each issue have their own numbering].

7. For more on the relationship between early Chinese science fiction and Orientalism, see Isaacson, "Science Fiction for the Nation: *Tales of the Moon Colony* and the Birth of Modern Chinese Fiction," *Science Fiction Studies* 40.1 (March 2013): 33–54.

8. See Lydia Liu, *Translingual Practice: Literature, National Culture and Translated Modernity China 1900–1937* (Stanford: Stanford University Press, 1995), 1–42.

9. Benjamin Elman, *From Philosophy to Philology: Intellectual and Social Aspects of Change in Late Imperial China* (Cambridge: Harvard University Press, 1984). See also Wang Hui, "The Fate of Mr. Science: The Concept of Science and Its Application in Modern Chinese Thought," *positions: east asia cultures critique* 3.1 (Spring 1995): 2–28.

10. Although precise dating of the first usage of the term *kexue* (科學) is clouded by Kang Youwei's penchant for forging memorials, it is clear that the use of this term as a translation for "science" did not emerge until the early twentieth century, most likely in the year

1911, with the fall of the Qing Dynasty. Wang Hui, "The Fate of Mr. Science in China," 27–28. See also Liu, *Translingual Practice*, 265–378.

11. While Rieder does not use this particular phrasing, I have borrowed this concept from his analysis of the material conditions that led to the emergence of science fiction in Europe in *Colonialism and the Emergence of Science Fiction* (Wesleyan, CT: Wesleyan University Press, 2008), 28.

12. Edward Said, *Orientalism* (New York: Vintage Books, 1979), 12. On "universalizing historicism," see Said, "Orientalism Reconsidered," *Cultural Critique* 1 (Autumn 1985): 89–107.

13. Marston Anderson, *The Limits of Realism: Chinese Fiction in the Revolutionary Period* (Berkeley: University of California Press, 1990), 24–37. Ted Huters, "Ideologies of Realism in Modern China," in *Politics, Ideology, and Literary Discourse in Modern China: Theoretical Interventions and Cultural Critique,* ed. Liu Kang and Tang Xiaobing, (Durham: Duke University Press, 1993), 147–172.

14. See Istvan Csicsery-Ronay, "Science Fiction and Empire," *Science Fiction Studies* 30.2 (July 2003): 231–245; Patricia Kerslake, *Science Fiction and Empire* (Liverpool: Liverpool University Press, 2007); and Rieder, *Colonialism and the Emergence of Science Fiction.*

15. Giovanni Arrighi, *The Long Twentieth Century: Money, Powern and the Origins of Our Times* (London and New York: Verso Press, 1994); Prasenjit Duara, *Sovereignty and Authenticity; Manchukuo and the East Asian Modern* (Lanham, MD: Rowman & Littlefield Publishers, 2003)

16. See Andrew Jones, *Developmental Fairy Tales: Evolutionary Thinking and Modern Chinese Culture* (Cambridge: Harvard University Press, 2011), 42–43. Jones's analysis of "knowledge texts" in the context of the late Qing is based on Alan Rauch's *Useful Knowledge: the Victorians, Morality and the March of Intellect* (Durham: Duke University Press, 2001). See also Qin Shao, "Exhibiting the Modern: The Creation of the First Chinese Museum, 1905–1930," *The China Quarterly* 179 (September 2004): 684–702.

17. Lu Xun, *Lu Xun quanji* 魯迅全集 [Complete works of Lu Xun], vol. 10 (Beijing: Renmin wenxue chubanshe, 2005), 163–167.

18. Bao Tianxiao was born Qing Zhu 清柱, in Jiangsu province; he also wrote under the names Gongyi 公毅, Xiao 笑, Tianxiao 天笑, Weimiao 微妙, Kaye 迦葉, and others. He attained the degree of *xiucai* at nineteen. He worked as an editor and writer for more than ten journals. In 1906, he went to work for the *Shanghai Times* 上海時報 as the editor of the supplement *Yuxing* 餘興. In 1931, he became editor of *Xiaoshuo huabao* 小說畫報 at Wenming shuju, editor of *Xingqi* 星期 for Dadong shuju, and editor of *Nü xuesheng* 女學生 at Wenhua yinshua gongsi (Li Shengping, et al., *Dictionary of Modern Chinese Bibliography*, 111; Wei Shaochang et al., eds., *Zhongguo jindai wenxue cidian* [Dictionary of modern Chinese literature], Zhengzhou, Henan jiaoyu chubanshe, 1993, 113.

19. Quoted in Takeda, "Cong Donghai juewo Xu Nianci de 'Xin Faluo xiansheng tan' shuo qi" [Beginning with Donghai Juewo Xu Nianci's "New Tales of Mr. Braggadocio"], trans. Qian Wei 錢瑋, *Ming Qing xiaoshuo yanjiu* 明清小說研究 [Ming and Qing fiction research] 2.13 (1986): 46. For more on Xu Nianci and the purpose of science fiction, see Shaoling Ma, "Narrative Subjectivity," 56.

20. Quoted in Wang Shanping 王姍萍, "Xixue dongjian yu wanqing kexue xiaoshuoqianlun" 西學東漸與晚清科學小說淺論 [A preliminary discussion of the "Eastward Advance of Western Knowledge" and late Qing science fiction], "Baoding shifan zhuanke xuexiao xuebao" 保定師範專科學校學報 [Baoding college journal] 19.1 (Jan. 2006): 54; see also Chen Pingyuan and Xia Xiaohong, "Tuxiang wanqing: Dianshizhai huabao" 圖像晚

清："點石齋畫報 [Picturing the late Qing: Dianshizhai huabao] (Tianjin: Baihua wenyi chubanshe), vol. 1, 58–63. For more on the history of translations of science fiction from Japanese to Chinese, see Takeda Masaya and Hayashi Hisayuki 林久之, *Chūgoku kagaku gensō bungakukan* 中国科学幻想文学館 [Compendium of Chinese scientific fantasy literature], vol. 1 (Tokyo: Taishūkan Shoten, 2001), 45–72.

21. Shaoling Ma, "Narrative Subjectivity," 55.

22. John Warner Monroe, *Laboratories of Faith: Mesmerism, Spiritism and Occultism in Modern France* (Ithaca: Cornell University Press, 2008), 7–8.

23. Csicsery-Ronay contends that the language of science fiction is one of futurism and invention, deploying neology to place the reader in an imagined future. Science fiction texts engage in a form of world-building whose language often invokes a sense of a historical trajectory that made such language possible. Fictive neology names imagined technologies and social conditions, but also hints at the social and material conditions that led to their emergence. Csiscery-Ronay, "Science fiction and Empire," 13–46.

24. For a more comprehensive list of terms, see Takeda, "Beginning with Donghai Juewo," 445, and Luan Weiping 欒偉平, "Jindai kexue xiaoshuo yu linghun: You 'Xin Faluo xiansheng tan' shuo kaiqu" 近代科學小說與靈魂: 由'新法螺先生譚'說開去 [Modern science fiction and the soul: Starting with "New Tales of Mr. Braggadocio"], *Zhongguo jindai wenxue yanjiu congkan* 中國現代文學研究叢刊 [Modern Chinese literature studies] 3 (2006): 47.

25. Xu Nianci, "New Tales of Mr. Braggadocio," 3

26. Stevan Harrell, "The Concept of Soul in Chinese Folk Religion," *Journal of Asian Studies* 38.3 (May 1979): 519–528.

27. K. E. Brashier, "Han Thanatology and the Division of Souls," *Early China* 21 (1996): 125–158.

28. See for example, a discussion of whether the brain is equivalent to the soul in an explication of the brain's function in the human body appearing in *Xia'er guan zhen* 遐邇貫珍 [Chinese serial] 6.23 (1855). Discourses on the soul and Christian salvation were featured regularly in *Jiaohui congbao* 教會叢報 [The church news]—after 1875 the journal appeared under the name *Wanguo gong bao* 萬國公報 [The globe magazine]—alongside translations of passages from the Bible, but scientific treatises well outnumbered Christian content in the journal.

29. Xu Nianci, "New Tales of Mr. Braggadocio," 14–15. Translation modified.

30. See *Zhuangzi jinzhujinyi* 莊子今注今譯 [The *Zhuangzi* with contemporary exegesis and translation], ed. Chen Guying 陳鼓應, vol. 1 (Beijing: Zhonghua shuju, 2001), 1–18; Burton Watson, *The Complete Works of Chuang Tzu* (New York: Columbia University Press, 1968), 30.

31. Nathaniel Isaacson, "Science Fiction for the Nation: *Tales of the Moon Colony* and the Birth of Modern Chinese Fiction," *Science Fiction Studies* 40.1 (March 2013): 45; Paul Alkon, "Cannibalism in Science Fiction," in *Food of the Gods: Eating and the Eaten in Fantasy and Science Fiction*, ed. Gary Westfahl, George Edgar Slusser, and Eric S. Rabkin (Athens: Georgia University Press, 1996), 145–147.

32. Xu Nianci, "New Tales of Mr. Braggadocio," 9.

33. Benjamin Schwarz, *In Search of Wealth and Power* (Cambridge, MA: Belknap Press, 1964), 45–48.

34. This famous debate in Confucian philosophy centers on the question of whether human nature is inherently good or evil. In *Mencius*, Gaozi argues against his mentor that human nature is neutral. See *Mengzi zhengyi* 孟子正義 [Correct meanings of the *Mencius*], ed.

Jiao Xun 焦循, vol. 2 (Beijing: Zhonghua Shuju, 1987), 731–733; Bloom, *Mencius* (New York: Columbia University Press, 2009), 121–124. Xunzi, on the other hand, argues that man's nature is "evil" (*e* 惡). See *Xunzi jijie* 荀子集解 [Collected commentaries to the Xunzi], ed., Liang Yunhua 梁運華, vol. 2 (Beijing: Zhonghua shuju, 1988), 434–448; Eric L. Hutton, *Xunzi: The Complete Text* (Princeton, NJ: Princeton University Press, 2014), 248–257.

35. Xu Nianci "New Tales of Mr. Braggadocio," 19.
36. Xu Nianci "New Tales of Mr. Braggadocio," 22.
37. Murthy, "Ontological Optimism, Cosmological Confusion, and Unstable Evolution: Tan Sitong's *Renxue* and Zhang Taiyan's Response," in *The Challenge of Linear Time: Nationhood and the Politics of History in East Asia*, Leiden Series in Comparative Historiography 7 (Boston: Brill, 2014), 50.
38. Xu Nianci, "New Tales of Mr. Braggadocio," 24.
39. For more on the relationship between mesmerism, the Catholic Church, and scientific practice in France in the eighteenth and nineteenth centuries, see Monroe, *Laboratories of Faith.*
40. Luan, "Modern Science Fiction," 52.
41. Luan, "Modern Science Fiction," 49.
42. Tao Chengzhang 陶成章 published his translation on mesmerism in collaboration with Cai Yuanpei, *Cuimianshu jiangyi* 催眠術講義 [Explanation of mesmerism], at roughly the same time. See Takeda, *Feixiang ba!*, 87.
43. Li Xin 李欣, "Zhongguo lingxue huodong zhong de cuimianshu" 中國零學活動中的催眠術 [Mesmerism in the Chinese psychics movement], *Ziran kexue yanjiu* 自然科學研究 [Studies in the history of natural science] 28.1 (2009): 12–23.
44. Marcel Mauss, *Techniques, Technology and Civilization* (New York: Durkheim Press, 2006 [1968]).
45. Shaoling Ma, "Narrative Subjectivity," 67.

Works Cited

Alkon, Paul. "Cannibalism in Science Fiction." In *Food of the Gods: Eating and the Eaten in Fantasy and Science Fiction.* Ed. Gary Westfahl, George Edgar Slusser, and Eric S. Rabkin. Athens: Georgia University Press, 1996. 142–159.

Anderson, Marston. *The Limits of Realism: Chinese Fiction in the Revolutionary Period.* Berkeley: University of California Press, 1990.

Brashier, K. E. "Han Thanatology and the Division of Souls." *Early China* 21 (1996): 125–158.

Chen Pingyuan 陳平原 and Xia Xiaohong 夏曉虹. *Tuxiang wanqing*: Dianshizhai huabao 圖像晚清: "點石齋畫報" [Picturing the late Qing: Dianshizhai huabao]. Tianjin: Baihua wenyi chubanshe, 2006.

Csicsery-Ronay, Istvan, Jr. "Science Fiction and Empire." *Science Fiction Studies* 30.2 (July 2003): 231–245.

Davis, Wade. *Into the Silence: The Great War, Mallory, and the Conquest of Everest.* New York: Alfred A. Knopf, 2012.

Elman, Benjamin. *From Philosophy to Philology: Intellectual and Social Aspects of Change in Late Imperial China.* Cambridge: Harvard University Press, 1984.

Goethe, Johann Wolfgang von. *The Metamorphosis of Plants.* Cambridge: MIT Press, 2009.

Harrell, Stevan. "The Concept of Soul in Chinese Folk Religion." *Journal of Asian Studies* 38.3 (May 1979): 519–528.

Huters, Theodore. "Ideologies of Realism in Modern China: The Hard Imperatives of Imported Theory." In *Politics, Ideology, and Literary Discourse in Modern China: Theorectical Interventions and Cultural Critique*. Ed. Liu Kang and Tang Xiaobing. Durham: Duke University Press, 1993. 147–172.

Isaacson, Nathaniel. "Science Fiction for the Nation: *Tales of the Moon Colony* and the Birth of Modern Chinese Fiction." *Science Fiction Studies* 40.1 (March 2013): 33–54.

Jones, Andrew. *Developmental Fairy Tales: Evolutionary Thinking and Modern Chinese Culture*. Cambridge: Harvard University Press, 2011.

Li Xin 李欣. "Zhongguo lingxue huodong zhong de cuimianshu" 中國零學活動中的催眠術 [Mesmerism in the Chinese Psychics Movement]. *Ziran kexue yanjiu* 自然科學史研究 [Studies in the history of natural sciences], 28.1 (2009): 12–23.

Lu Xun 魯迅. *Lu Xun quanji* 魯迅全集 [Complete works of Lu Xun], vol. 10. Beijing: Renmin Wenxue Chubanshe, 2005.

Kerslake, Patricia. *Science Fiction and Empire*. Liverpool: Liverpool University Press, 2007.

Krakauer, John, *Into Thin Air: A Personal Account of the Mount Everest Disaster*. New York: Villard Books, 1997.

Landes, David S. *Revolution in Time: Clocks and the Making of the Modern World*. Cambridge, MA: Belknap Press, 1983.

Li Shengping, et. al. *Zhongguo jin xian dai ren ming da ci dian* 中國近現代人名大辭典 [Dictionary of modern Chinese biography]. Beijing: Zhongguo guoji guangbo chubanshe, 1989.

Liu, Lydia. *Translingual Practice: Literature, National Culture, and Translated Modernity—China, 1900–1937*. Stanford: Stanford University Press, 1995.

Luan Weiping 欒偉平. "Jindai kexue xiaoshuo yu linghun: You 'Xin Faluo xiansheng tan' shuo kaiqu" "近代科學小說與靈魂: 由'新法螺先生譚'說開去" [Modern science fiction and the soul: Starting with "New Tales of Mr. Braggadocio"]. *Zhongguo jindai wenxue yanjiu congkan* 中國現代文學研究叢刊 [Modern Chinese literature studies] 3 (2006): 46–60.

Ma, Shaoling. "'A Tale of New Mr. Braggadocio': Narrative Subjectivity and Brain Electricity in Late Qing Science Fiction." *Science Fiction Studies* 40.1 (March 2013): 55–72.

Mauss, Marcel. *Techniques, Technology and Civilization*. Ed. Nathan Schlanger. New York: Durkheim Press, 2006.

Mencius [Mengzi]. *Mencius*. Trans. Irene Bloom. Columbia University Press, 2009.

Mengzi 孟子. *Mengzi Zhengyi* 孟子正義 [Correct meanings of the *Mencius*]. Ed. Jiao Xun 焦循, 2 vols. Beijing: Zhonghua Shuju, 1987.

Monroe, John Warner. *Laboratories of Faith: Mesmerism, Spiritism and Occultism in Modern France*. Ithaca: Cornell University Press, 2008.

Murthy, Viren. "Ontological Optimism, Cosmological Confusion, and Unstable Evolution: Tan Sitong's *Renxue* and Zhang Taiyan's Response." In *The Challenge of Linear Time: Nationhood and the Politics of History in East Asia*. Leiden Series in Comparative Historiography 7. Boston: Brill, 2014. 49–82.

Qin Shao. "Exhibiting the Modern: The Creation of the First Chinese Museum, 1905–1930." *The China Quarterly* 179 (September 2004): 684–702.

Rauch, Alan. *Useful Knowledge: The Victorians, Morality and the March of Intellect*. Durham: Duke University Press, 2001.

Rieder, John. *Colonialism and the Emergence of Science Fiction.* Middletown, CT: Wesleyan University Press, 2008.

Schwarz, Benjamin. *In Search of Wealth and Power.* Cambridge, MA: Belknap Press, 1964.

Song Puzhang et al., eds. *Xia'er guanzhen fujie ti, suoyin* 遐邇貫珍附解題,索引 [Chinese serial with explanations and index]. Shanghai: Shanghai cishu chubanshe, 2005.

Sun Wenguang, ed. *Zhongguo jin dai wen xue da ci dian*1840–1919 中國近代文學大辭典, 1840–1919 [Dictionary of modern Chinese literature, 1840–1919]. Hefei: Huangshan shu she, 1995.

Takeda Masaya 武田雅哉. *Tobe! Daishin tekoku: Kindai chūgoku no gensō kagaku* 飛べ〜! 大清帝国:近代中国の幻想科学 [Fly! The Qing empire: Modern China's fantastic science]. Tokyo: Riburopōto, 1988. Translated as Takeda Masaya, *Feixiang ba! Daqing diguo: Jindai zhongguo de huanxiang kexue* 飛翔吧! 大清帝國: 近代中國的幻想科學, trans. Ren Junhua 任鈞華, Taibei: Yuanliu chubanshe, 2008.

Takeda Masaya. "Cong Donghai juewo Xu Nianci de 'Xin Faluo xiansheng tan' shuo qi" [Beginning with Donghai juewo, Xu Nianci's "New Tales of Mr. Braggadocio"]. Trans. Qian Wei 錢瑋. *Ming Qing xiaoshuo yanjiu* 明清小說研究 [Ming and Qing fiction research] 2.13 (1986): 440–450.

Takeda Masaya and Hayashi Hisayuki 林久之. *Chūgoku kagaku gensō bungakukan* 中国科学幻想文学館 [Compendium of Chinese scientific fantasy literature], 2 vols. Tokyo: Taishūkan Shoten, 2001.

Wang Hui. "The Fate of 'Mr. Science' in China: The Concept of Science and Its Application in Modern Chinese Thought." *positions: east asia cultures critique* (Spring 1995) 3.1: 1–68.

Wakabayashi, Judy. "Foreign Bones, Japanese Flesh: Translations and the Emergence of Modern Children's Literature in Japan." *Japanese Language and Literature* 42.1 (April 2008): 227–255.

Wang Shanping 王姍萍. "Xixue dongjian yu wanqing kexue xiaoshuoqianlun" 西學東漸與晚清科學小說淺論 [A preliminary discussion of the "Eastward Advance of Western Knowledge" and late Qing science fiction]. *Baoding shifan zhuanke xuexiao xuebao* 保定師範專科學校學報 [Baoding college journal] 19.1 (January 2006): 53–56.

Wilkinson, Alec. *The Ice Balloon: S. A. Andrée and the Heroic Age of Arctic Exploration.* New York: Alfred A. Knopf, 2011.

Wright, David. "John Fryer and the Shanghai Polytechnic: Making Space for Science in Nineteenth-Century China." *The British Journal for the History of Science* 29.1 (March 1996): 1–16.

Xu Nianci 徐念慈. *Xin faluo xiansheng tan* 新法螺先生譚 [New Tales of Mr. Braggadocio]. Shanghai: Xiaoshuo lin, 1905.

Xu Nianci. "Yu zhi xiaoshuo guan" 余之小說觀 [My outlook on fiction]. *Xiaoshuo lin* 小說林 (January 1908): 1–8; (March 1908): 19–15.

Xu Nianci. *Xin faluo xiansheng tan.* In *Zhongguo jindai wenxue daxi* 1840–1929: *xiaoshuo ji* 中國近代文學大系 1840–1919: 小說集 [A treasury of modern Chinese literature 1840–1929: fiction collection], ed. Wu Zuxiang 吳組緗 et al., vol. 6. Shanghai: Shanghai shudian, 1991. 323–343.

Xu Nianci. "New Tales of Mr. Braggadocio." Trans. Nathaniel Isaacson. *Renditions* 75 (Autumn 2011): 15–38.

Xunzi. *Xunzi jijie* 荀子集解 [Collected commentaries to the Xunzi]. Liang Yunhua梁運華, ed. 2 vols. Beijing: Zhonghua shuju, 1988.

Xunzi. *Xunzi: The Complete Text.* Trans. Eric. L. Hutton. Princeton: Princeton University Press, 2014.

Zhuangzi 莊子. *Zhuangzi jinzhu jinyi* 莊子今注今譯 [The *Zhuangzi* with contemporary exegesis and translation]. Ed. Chen Guying 陳鼓應, 3 vols. Beijing: Zhonghua Shuju, 2001.

Zhuangzi. *The Complete Works of Chuang Tzu.* Trans. Burton Watson. New York: Columbia University Press, 1968.

CHAPTER 1.5

THE STORY OF LITERARY HISTORY

CHEN PINGYUAN

APART from being a famous writer and thinker, Lu Xun 魯迅 was also an eminent scholar of literary history. His *A Brief History of the Chinese Novel* (中國小說史略) and *A Concise Outline of Chinese Literary History* (漢文學史綱要), as well as his preface to the second volume, on narrative, of the *Compendium of New Chinese Literature* (中國新文學大系：小說二集序), are still regarded by the Chinese academic world as standard works. But why was Lu Xun ultimately unable to complete the *History of Chinese Literature* (中國文學史) that he had planned to write, despite his repeated emphasis, in his later years, on his desire to do so?

In letters to Li Xiaofeng 李小峰, Cao Qinghua 曹靖華, Cao Juren 曹聚仁, Zeng Tianshe 增田涉, and others in the 1930s, Lu Xun repeatedly addressed the question of why it was impossible to write a literary history. He cited lack of time, the inaccessibility of the necessary research material, and the enormous scope of the project, as well his own "dearth of ideas."[1] The first three reasons refer to exterior circumstances, but the fourth merits a different treatment, since it is connected to Lu Xun's evaluation of scholarly work. In this chapter, I will first focus on why Lu Xun was unable to write a literary history, and then turn to the reason he did not write it.

The writing of literary history is an academic endeavor that has emerged as a cultural necessity in conjunction with the rise of Western-style learning, and which was promoted by the new educational system. If there had not been academic teaching, or if teaching institutions had not taught literary history as a subject, Lu Xun and other scholars would probably not have engaged in writing literary histories. Lu Xun notes that in antiquity there were works that "examined the origin of literary genres and evaluated their craft" (such as the *Literary Mind and the Carving of Dragons* [文心雕龍]), as well as others that "established chronologies of writers and traced influences" (such as the *Grades of Poetry* [詩品]). Until the modern era, however, there had not been any "research that covered the complete history of Chinese literature." Zheng Zhenduo 鄭振鐸 claimed that until the modern era literary history "had not really become the subject of research,"[2] and while Zheng's assertion may not be completely accurate, it is nevertheless clear that research on literary history was a product of early modern China's process of Westernization. Even today, most literary histories of China are still written because of educational needs.

Lu Xun wrote *A Brief History of the Chinese Novel* because he needed lecture notes for his courses at Peking University, and he observed that "I wrote *A Brief History of the Chinese Novel* because I had to make a living by teaching."[3] Similarly, he completed *A Concise Outline of Chinese Literary History* as required course content when he was teaching at Xiamen University. During his ten-year stay in Shanghai, however, when he did not plan to return to teaching, what need was there for him to persist in writing a literary history? To write a literary history was an integral part of the teaching duties of a university professor, but one could not make a living from the publication of teaching materials alone. A freelance writer like Lu Xun must have calculated the investment-profit ratio of doing research on literary history—this being without a doubt a long-term project without quick profit from royalties. Since Lu Xun had neither the time nor the money, this was the kind of project he really should not have chosen. When he was teaching at Xiamen University, Lu Xun taught six hours of classes and was able to dedicate the remainder of his time to reading and research, so writing 4,000–5,000 characters of lecture notes a day on literary history was not a problem.[4] But he did not have the same kind of leisure while in Shanghai; political and economic pressures did not allow him to dedicate himself to research, and furthermore he was faced with a lack of research materials. Therefore, in spite of his long-standing desire to write a literary history, Lu Xun should have realized that it was not really possible to do academic research in those circumstances.[5]

This is not to say that writing literary history was only possible within an academic system, and in fact there were quite a few literary histories written by editors of publishing houses or freelance writers, but Lu Xun was unable to stomach the kind of large-scale compilational method they used.[6] He felt that "the method of the Confucian intellectuals of the Qing" was unacceptable; instead, one had to "begin by writing at length oneself," and yet "writing a long piece was quite difficult," especially the writing of literary history in which "one writer had to account for the changes from the past to the present."[7]

Under similar economic conditions, others were able to write the literary histories that Lu Xun was unable to complete. Because his standards were too high, the time and energy that he needed to dedicate to this endeavor far exceeded what others required. Lu Xun was definitely able "to write a reasonably good literary history" and "to point out some things that others had not seen," but the problem was that this would have required him to sacrifice his other work.[8] Therefore, we have to ask if writing a literary history such as he had wanted to do for a long time was really that important to Lu Xun. Even though he already had several years of university teaching experience, Lu Xun remained positioned at the margins of academia. He supported the student movement, encouraged "the path to do good," and subverted the power of the existing system. If we add to this his scathing critique of "famous scholars" who occupied a central position,

Lu Xun was quite unlikely to collaborate with the academic mainstream. He had no regrets about this, and instead pursued a path of resistance to the mainstream.

In his essay "On the Power of Mara Poetry" (摩羅詩力說), Lu Xun celebrated "those . . . who were committed to resistance, whose purpose was action but who were little loved by their age," and this pursuit of being a "warrior of the spirit" pervaded Lu Xun's whole life.[9] His scholarship was no exception, as Lu Xun lauded heterodoxy and occupied a heterodox position himself. Heterodoxy, in contrast to orthodoxy, has its value as well as its limitations. The writing of "random thoughts" (zawen 雜文) can encourage extremism, caustic critique, and strategic controversy, while academic research needs to strive for equanimity, general communicability, and evenhandedness. These are not merely different projects, but also involve different styles and ways of thinking. In his early years, when he dedicated himself to scholarship, Lu Xun was very selective about his zawen production, but in his later years, when he delighted in writing combative essays, it was difficult for him to engage in academic research with tranquility. Lu Xun's rebellious stance determined his position in a line of writers and intellectuals through the ages. Clearly, his way of thinking inclined him toward the writing of zawen and distanced him from formal scholarship. This state of mind was not productive for the writing of literary history.

To write zawen requires passion and emotional involvement, whereas to do research requires calm and balance. Therefore, at the end of 1926 Lu Xun hesitated, feeling that "to write literature one needs passion, to teach one needs equanimity," to engage in both means putting the two at odds with one another. "To teach," here, encompasses the writing of literary history. Lu Xun, equally good at writing and research, decided in the end that "it might be better to write some useful essays and to leave research for when there is time left."[10]

Over the following decade, Lu Xun wrote many "useful essays" on the nation and its people, but his attempt to write literary history in his spare time inevitably fell behind— not only since Lu Xun had no way of committing a large amount of time and energy to it, but more so because the way of thinking he adopted for his essays was not suitable for more formal academic research. Under irreconcilable circumstances, Lu Xun chose to continue writing zawen, yet he felt uneasy about abandoning his goal of writing literary history. It is difficult to imagine Lu Xun, as a successful writer of zawen, with the necessary calm to sift through heaps of old books. Whether people who pursue a lofty goal finally reach it or not is not for those who live after them to decide, but the absence of what would have been an interesting Literary History of China is regrettable.

THE INSTITUTION OF LITERARY HISTORY

Ancient China had no literary history, since this was a new phenomenon that gradually took shape along with the rise of modern schools. The goal of setting up schools according to Western models in the late Qing, for the transmission of Western learning and culture, was originally meant to foster useful talent for the successful administration of the country and the ensuring of national security. From the perspective of the late Qing, Western culture was limited to the sciences and applied sciences, and Western learning did not include literature and the arts.[11] Even though Chinese technology, institutions, and education were deemed deficient, it was still impossible to believe that even what was viewed as the best "system of morality and literature" in the world would also turn out to be embarrassing. It now seems almost inconceivable that people at the time even needed to import the notion of literature. And yet, with the help of reforms of university regulations, the importance of literary education was gradually recognized. In addition, the way in which literature was taught in the modern, Western-style schools began to distance itself from the study of rhetoric of traditional schools. Even though there was then no way to establish the subject of "Western literature," even the subject of "Chinese literature" and its research methods were radically new for Chinese scholars.

When the 1902 "Regulations for the Imperial University of Peking" (京師大學堂章程) mentioned the curriculum of the art of poetry and prose, it only described it as "different types of Chinese poetry and prose." In the 1903 "University Regulations" (大學堂章程), by contrast, the same topic was discussed at great length. In addition to covering general methodology in the section "Short Explanation of Research Methods on Chinese Literature," each course came with detailed information. In the "University Regulations," the most important courses on Chinese literature in the field of literary studies included "Methods of Literary Research" (文學研究法), "A Study of the *Shuowen*" (《說文》學), "Study of Rhyme and Prosody" (音韻學), "Examples of Prose Writing from Different Dynasties" (歷代文章流別), "Overview of the Writings of Antiquity" (古人論文要言), "Famous Prose Writers from the Zhou and Qin to Today" (周秦至今文章名家), "Overview of the Complete Library in Four Sections (*Siku*)" (四庫集部提要), "History of Western Literature" (西國文學史), and sixteen others. What is most remarkable is that the teachers of "History of Western Literature" and "Examples of Prose Writing from Different Dynasties" were advised to use a Japanese *History of Chinese Literature* (中國文學史) as their model. Those who had taught "the art of poetry and prose" in the past paid attention to the cultivation of literary skills, and consequently recitation, appreciation, emulation, and composition were at the center; in contrast, the new discipline of literary history was mainly a transmission of knowledge, not accompanied by the study of writing. To discard literary writing meant to bring such disciplines as "Examples of Prose Writing" or "Literary History" as defined in the world of literary education closer to the methodology of Japanese and Western Sinology.

Once the literary education in new-style schools stopped relying on traditional collections such as *A Collection of Tang Poetry* (唐詩別裁集) or *A Compilation of Classical Prose* (古文辭類纂), how were the students to acquire the necessary knowledge in an ocean of books? After all, one could no longer require them to search through the *Siku* (四庫) or the *Qilüe* (七略) bibliographies on their own. At the time, people compared Chinese and Western education and were very appreciative of the teaching materials of foreign schools that advocated a method of "a gradual deepening of knowledge and of a systematic approach," and thought that they could spare students the work of trying to orient themselves in the dark.[12] And yet there were still many obstacles to putting this into practice—especially with regard to the compilation of teaching material for the humanities.

In 1902, when Zhang Baixi 張百熙 was in charge of university teaching, he addressed teaching materials as a central issue. According to Zhang, translation was of the utmost importance for the teaching of Western politics and Western culture, and one had only to erase "those parts that were not compatible with the Chinese spirit or were too immersed in religion." However, no adequate teaching material could be found for teaching the "study of Chinese culture." Therefore, Zhang was keen on promoting the writing of "survey-style manuals and the establishing of chronologies for the 'books of a hundred writers,' " as well as of "survey lecture notes according to the course schedule for the students' instruction." The aim was "to give support to teachers and provide guidance for students," which made it "necessary to follow a sequential order leading to a gradual deepening of knowledge. Therefore, the writing of teaching material was one of the most important tasks of institutions of higher learning."[13] According to this train of thought, the Imperial University of Peking not only used teaching material in translation but also urged each discipline to produce its own course materials. Not much of those teaching materials has survived, however, and in fact we only have Zhang Heling's 張鶴齡 "Lectures on Ethics" (倫理學講義), Wang Zhouyao's 王舟瑤 "Lectures on the Study of the Classics" (經學科講義) and "Lectures on Chinese History" (中國通史講義), Du Qi's 屠寄 "Lectures on the Study of History" (史學科講義), Zou Daijun's 鄒代鈞 "Lectures on Chinese Geography" (中國地理講義), Chen Fuchen's 陳黻宸 "Lectures on Chinese History" (中國史講義), and a few others. Only fragments of Chen's "Lectures on Chinese History" survive, since the rest were destroyed on the grounds that they "promoted democracy."[14]

The teaching materials developed for the Imperial University of Peking were not only used at this particular institution, they were also disseminated throughout the country. For instance, the original 1904 edition of *A History of Chinese Literature* (中國文學史) by Chinese literature scholar Lin Chuanjia 林傳甲 was difficult to obtain, but a 1910 reprint became quite popular. Lin's work is an invaluable example that helps us understand the production of teaching materials at the Imperial University of Peking and the conditions for the teaching of literature under the new educational system.

As the first example of a history of Chinese literature that drew on and used a Western understanding of literary history, Lin's *A History of Chinese Literature* has received a great deal of attention.[15] Given its status as a pathbreaking work, shortcomings and flaws were difficult to avoid, and therefore critics treat this work leniently, even making an effort to excuse its lack of a novel structure or original design. The admonition of the "University Regulations" and Lin's own explanation make scholars focus on the relationship of this work with the Chinese translation of Sasakawa Taneo's 笹川種郎 *Dynastic History of Chinese Literature* (歷朝文學史). This is of course correct, and yet Lin's emulation of Sasakawa's literary history, and his reworking of it into "a history of classical Chinese prose," was definitely not a result of a sudden inspiration, but rather had its roots in a broader context.[16]

If we compare Lin's *History of Chinese Literature* and the mandates of the "University Regulations," we find that the sixteen chapters in Lin's table of contents and the first sixteen clauses of the regulations on "research and the substance of literature" correspond perfectly. Lin had initially planned to follow them closely and to implement all forty-one clauses, but for the sake of structural clarity he eventually dispensed with the final twenty-five clauses. The beginning of Lin's *History of Chinese Literature* explains his writing strategy quite clearly.[17] In fact, among the known lectures from the Imperial University of Peking, Lin's was exemplary for following the model of the "Regulations." The structure and organization of the lectures by Wang Zhouyao, Du Qi, Chen Fuchen, Zou Daijun, and others generally differed quite significantly from the "University Regulations." Perhaps this can be explained by the uneasy, still undetermined position of research on literary history at the time. It did not have the self-defined, independent standard of "study of the classics," nor did it resemble a discipline such as geography, with its basic copying of foreign texts, and therefore it had to mechanically follow the ready-made model of the university regulations.

As a university lecture, Lin's literary history was necessarily dependent on university regulations. Those who followed Lin did not lack in erudition and daring, and their writing was far more brilliant than Lin's. More importantly, the strife between different factions in academia directly influenced the literary tendencies of the era, and it had clear connections to the emergence of the May Fourth New Literature Movement. I am referring to how Lin Shu 林紓 and Yao Yongpu 姚永樸, as representatives of the Tongcheng school, were replaced by Liu Shipei 劉師培 and Huang Kan 黃侃 of the Xuanxue school. If we compare Lin Shu's *Research on Classical Prose from Chunjuezhai* (春覺齋論文) and Yao Yongpu's *A Method for Literary Research* (文學研究法) with Liu Shipei's *A Chinese Literary History of the Middle Ages* (中國中古文學史) and Huang Kan's *Notes on the Literary Mind and the Carving of Dragons* (文心雕龍札記), we can see that the first two focused on literature of the Tang and Song dynasties, while the latter favored literature from the Six Dynasties period. Each of these four works is excellent, so why did the latter two triumph while the former two suffered a devastating defeat?

Apart from historical changes and personal vicissitudes, two factors merit attention. First, the feel of Six Dynasties prose was relatively easy to bring together with the newly imported Western contexts. Second, the way of thinking and university teaching of the Xuanxue School, as well as the form of literary history they produced, were relatively easy to accept in this context. Therefore, the study of Chinese literary history over the following decades would follow Liu and Huang rather than Lin and Yao.

In the early years of the Republic, the Tongcheng and Xuanxue schools were at war with each other at Peking University; the outcome of this battle was the victory of the Xuanxue school and its attention to Six Dynasties prose. But the rapidly emerging New Culture wiped out the strife of the literary schools left over from the Qing dynasty and engaged in new topics of intellectual warfare. The school of Liu and Huang that had just achieved victory now became the target of attack of the proponents of the New Culture Movement. There is no clearer evidence for this than the slogan "the scoundrels of the Tongcheng, the evildoers of the Xuanxue."[18]

The Tongcheng school withdrew from the stage of history, whereas the Xuanxue school underwent changes but remained active after the proponents of the New Culture Movement gained the upper hand at Peking University after 1917. According to Peking University's regulations, each official course had to provide students with course materials, even if they were merely cursory. Instructors had the double duty of writing lectures and of teaching classes. After editing, these lecture notes would be officially published and would often become important works in academic history. For instance Zhou Zuoren's 周作人 "History of European Literature" (歐洲文學史), Lu Xun's *A Brief History of the Chinese Novel*, Wu Mei's 吳梅 "Lectures on Drama" (詞餘講義, later renamed "An Overview of Theater Study" [曲學通論]), were all cutting-edge works whose contribution cannot be overlooked. Hu Shi's 胡適 *Chinese Literature of the Past Fifty Years* (五十年來中國之文學) fundamentally changed people's tendency to worship the past and made contemporary literature worthy of study and consideration. This slim book, published in 1922, was not really based on lecture notes but was nevertheless closely related to Hu Shi's work at Peking University, and therefore helps us understand that the teaching and research of literary history, unlike the traditional practice of literary criticism, constitutes a type of organization of knowledge in need of the support of a new scholarly system as well as the unceasing effort of generations of scholars.

Rearranging the National Heritage and Literary Studies

New approaches to teaching old and new literature, both Chinese and foreign, constituted an important context for the production of knowledge. This involved radical paradigm shifts and was determined by educational aims and the support of literary traditions, as well as the regulations of education, economic concerns, teachers' salaries, and other pragmatic constraints. But if literary studies supported "literary history," "literary theory," "literary criticism," and other related disciplines, why did literary history finally gain the upper hand?

A look at the 1917 "Curriculum" for Chinese literature at Peking University and the 1918 "Overview of the Humanities at Peking University" (北京大學文科一覽) reveals the four major changes achieved at Peking University by the New Culture Movement: "Literary History" became a key course in the department of Chinese literature; students of the department of Chinese literature could not avoid "European Literature"; "Literature of the Modern World" was increasingly taken seriously; and genres such as drama and narrative, which had not been previously viewed as serious literature, became compulsory subjects for university students.[19] Even though the atmosphere at Peking University underwent a profound change, when faced with a choice between the "avant-garde" and the "national past," the majority of teachers and students of Chinese culture chose the latter. Only with the changes of time and based on the accounts of Fu Sinian 傅斯年, Yang Zhensheng 楊振聲, and Yu Pingbo 俞平伯 did the impression emerge that the former was victorious.

Even though the strife between classical and vernacular Chinese in Peking University's Chinese Literature Department gradually subsided in the 1920s, the history of foreign literatures was not approved of, and courses in new literature were slow in developing. What held these back was the attitude of teachers and students toward literary study. Later historians speak of the New Culture Movement at Peking University's Chinese Literature Department either by critiquing the "superficiality of their learning" or lamenting "literature's loss of language."[20] Even though both have their justification, these views are not devoid of prejudice. Together they underline the impasse of the Chinese Literature Department—was what was needed in the end literary studies or an appreciation of literary art? All this involved the profound rift between Literary Revolution and the movement of "Rearranging the National Heritage." Even as the latter gained a depth of research, its interest went contrary to the current of the times.

When the Literary Revolution began to subside in 1919, Hu Shi wrote "The Importance of New Thought" (新思潮的意義), "On National Learning—in Response to Mao Zishui" (論國故學——答毛子水), "The Politics of Qing Scholars" (清代學者的治學方法), and other essays expressing a fascination with history, and raised the banner of "Rearranging the National Heritage." The fact that Hu Shi, who had originally been known for "important modern academic principles," turned to "Rearranging the National Heritage" baffled the young scholars who had just been awakened and rushed away from the heaps of old books. From the perspective of Hu Shi's own scholarship, the transition from A Short History of Chinese Philosophy (中國哲學史大綱) to A Study of The Water Margin (水滸傳考証) did not seem such a radical turn. And yet, from the perspective of cultural thought, the shift from New Youth (新青年) to National Studies Monthly (國學季刊) was quite radical. Even though there were many controversies over this within society at large, the academic world simply continued in its accustomed direction. But the problem is that the research of literature is not the same as the scrutiny of the classics and of history, and textual criticism can by no means solve all problems. Hu Shi succeeded in elevating research on narrative "to the same level as traditional studies of the classics and of history," but the excessive belief in science that made evidentiary methods the golden rule of academic research necessarily repressed the "interest in literariness."

That same year, Fu Sinian, a student of Peking University's Chinese Literature Department, took up Hu Shi's direction and declared categorically: "research on national culture is an academic issue, not a literary issue."[21] But doesn't literary research also count as knowledge? In other words, how can one discuss the Book of Odes (詩經), The Songs of the South (楚辭), and The Dream of the Red Chamber (紅樓夢) without any thought of their literariness? No one would explicitly say so, but the standard of criticism underwent profound changes. At first glance, the importance of "textual criticism" overrode both "argumentation" and the study of the "art of poetry and prose" in academia. Consequently, in the teaching of philosophy and literature, dating, editions, and plot became all-important, but this rarely involved reflections on conceptual thought or aesthetic judgment. People sometimes resisted this tendency, but their voices were too weak and were easily smothered. Even in the early 1940s, Shen Congwen's 沈從文 "The Re-establishment of the Literary" (文運的重建) and Cheng Qianfan's 程千帆 "On the Problems of Teaching in Today's Chinese Literature Departments" (論今日大學中文系教學之蔽) did not have much of an impact. Shen critiqued Peking University, where the May Fourth Literary Revolution originated, noting that "after 1927 we were forced to dispense with Peking University's progressive spirit, and instead direct the energy of teachers and students toward philology, critical interpretation, and textual criticism," and adding that "of course its result occupied a place in scholarship—the place of a 'museum piece.'"[22] Other scholars paid Shen's critique little heed, dismissing it as the mere ramblings of a novelist. Cheng's critique of "the use of the method of textual criticism to eliminate the teaching of the aesthetics of verse and prose," pointing out that what Chinese literature departments taught "were only authors' life stories, the truth or falsity of literary works, the tradition of words and phrases, and important information about context," was completely justified, but the writer's attitude was too lenient. What he wanted to argue was that "textual criticism was not only not harmful to the enjoyment of literature, but in fact was necessary for it. And yet, its use has its limits. We cannot eternally tarry in the process of textual criticism."[23] Moreover, Cheng Qianfan favored classical verse rather than new literature, and this was where he parted ways with Shen Congwen.

Of course we cannot blame Hu Shi for this development, but such a shift could only occur once "Rearranging the National Heritage" had become a general trend. To borrow from Hu Shi, the Literary Revolution needed "daring hypotheses," but once the movement of "Rearranging the National Heritage" had started to develop, this had to be changed into "careful investigation." The former underscores "talent," whereas the latter insists on "skills." By promoting the scientific method of evidentiary criticism, even though it was only Hu Shi's personal formulation, Chinese academia of the 1920s elevated the worship of textual criticism into a blind belief, which directly led to a profound change in the forms of knowledge, namely the decline of the study of literature and literariness and the rise of the study of history. Without a doubt, any kind of scholarship needs "profound imagination," and the intellectual current linked to "Rearranging the National Heritage" became an important turning point for the emergence of new studies of history, but this had a negative impact on literary studies as they were going through major changes.

When the Literary Revolution was in decline and after the current of "Rearranging the National Heritage" had rapidly gained prominence, Peking University's Chinese Literature Department, which had clearly profited from its association with the New Culture Movement, gradually implemented changes in literary studies by regulating curricula, selecting teachers, promoting the lecture format, reforming schools, and so forth, but key among these was the continual increase of the territory of literary history.[24] In the following decades, literary history as a self-evident system of knowledge became the most important required course in Chinese literature departments in universities across China.

THE MYTH OF LITERARY HISTORY

The transition from poetry and prose critique and biographies of scholars to the writing and teaching of literary history was an intentional choice of Chinese scholars from the late Qing onward. The importance of literary history in Chinese academia in the twentieth century was mostly due to the introduction of what was characterized as a scientific and progressive perspective and a more "systemic" approach, but its advantages and disadvantages have not yet been thoroughly analyzed. Zhang Taiyan 章太炎 argued that the new-style education was too focused on the speed of learning by using classroom teaching as its main method, which made students "focus on aural learning and discard visual learning," so that no profit could come of it "beyond the lecture."[25] Likewise, Liu Yongji 劉永濟 complained that "today's learning imitates the West; literature has become a science, and becomes established as history," and that so-called literary history was nothing but a compilation of scattered knowledge, indiscriminately copying from foreign countries and borrowing the dross of the ancients.[26] Even though Zhang and Liu "vented their discontent" in strong terms, they had no way of shaking the foundations of the monumental structure of literary history that had already become the standard. Those who teach at universities in China today, especially those who teach literature, cannot avoid writing and lecturing on literary history.

Only in the past few decades, following the publication of several works discussing a century's worth of writing of literary history in China from the vantage point of intellectual history or the archeology of knowledge, has a more profound reflection on the advantages and disadvantages, and the merits and demerits, of literary history as a science, as a system of knowledge, and as a form of writing begun to emerge. Unfortunately, this kind of reflection still stagnates at the level of abstract reflection, and has not yet influenced the reality of university classrooms today.

The core of literary studies has been transformed from the training of skills in "literary style and composition" to the accumulation of knowledge of literary history. It is not based on individual writers' or scholars' sense of aesthetics, but has become an integral part of the process of modernization of China as a whole. Literary history has become a system of knowledge, of great use and importance for expressing national sentiment, for uniting the national spirit, for absorbing foreign cultures and for entering "world literature."

I do not wish to discuss why the writing of literary history has succumbed to this monumental narrative over the past century, nor do I want to excavate the discursive supremacy that secretly underpins this discourse of unification. Even less do I want to doubt history's veracity or the value of the existence of literature. As a university teacher, I just want to ask a few basic questions. What is the aim of training students in a Chinese literature department? How can we evaluate the suitability of literary studies? Over the past century, the Chinese have made literary history (or rather, the general history of literature) the core discipline of Chinese literature departments at the university level, but is this choice in need of being reevaluated?

Of course I am not denying the value of literary history; what I want is to question literary history's blind faith in the present, and to affirm the need to question literary studies in modern China, to see if we really want to make literary history the core of our curriculum. For some scholars, to write a literary history for the university classroom is certainly a good way of gaining fame and fortune.[27] But I don't trust this to be the pinnacle of scholarship. I suspect that this inclination within Chinese academia (and the publishing world) toward writing all kinds of literary histories is motivated by economic considerations, and perhaps even a kind of vanity, rather than constituting an intellectual scholarly pursuit. The "systemic writing of teaching material" of the past has turned into an autocracy of thought and established a monopoly of knowledge. Today's monumental national literary histories, in turn, take a different path, in that in addition to constituting an unnecessary waste, they also risk poisoning the academic atmosphere.

One cannot approach the myth of literary history from the perspective of either national pride or postmodern theories; instead, one must do so through a careful attention to educational and intellectual history. In 1918, Peking University stipulated that "as part of the humanities, the field of Chinese literary studies has two disciplines, literary history and literature, and since their aim is completely different, their teaching methods must also differ." The aim of the former is "to endow students with a knowledge of the changes and different movements in the literature of each epoch"; in contrast, the objective of the latter is "to endow students with a sense of literary beauty, to appreciate the writers' dedication and indirectly enhance their own literary art."[28] A year and a half later, the Assembly of Professors of Chinese Literary Studies—consisting of fifteen professors, including Qian Xuantong 錢玄同, Liu Bannong 劉半農, Ma Youyu 馬幼漁, Shen Jianshi 沈兼士, Zhu Xizu 朱希祖, and Wu Mei—once again debated the reform of teaching material and methods. In order to facilitate exchange and consultation, the assembly decided to divide participants into five categories: teachers of literary history, teachers of literature, teachers of Chinese philology, teachers of calligraphy, and teachers of preparatory national culture.[29] In the early years of Peking University's literary studies, the study of the historical changes of literature and the analysis of literature each had its own place. To stress literature and literary history equally is a good idea. Unfortunately, after the 1950s and following the rise of the curriculum of literary history—which became ever more pronounced as it accrued more importance and produced increasingly prominent professors—the superficiality of teaching and the cursory character of lecturing did great harm to literary study.

We have just started to understand Hu Shi's intellectual trajectory—Hu Shi called his own scrutiny of narrative a perspective that was "entirely that of literary history, but not one of literary research."[30] On the basis of such a direction of reading, he even defied world opinion by questioning the value of *The Dream of the Red Chamber* and finding it "conceptually" less interesting than *The Scholars* (儒林外史) and "artistically" less sophisticated than *The Sing-song Girls of Shanghai* (海上花列傳) and *The Travels of Lao Can* (老殘遊記).[31] One can certainly critique Hu Shi's aesthetic taste, but one must still admire his courage and independence of opinion. It required considerable courage for Hu Shi to express these unorthodox opinions while knowing full well that all Chinese revere *The Dream of the Red Chamber*.

Qian Zhongshu 錢鍾書 was even more decisive: apart from writing the Tang and Song part of the *History of Chinese Literature* (中國文學史) commissioned by the Chinese Academy of Social Sciences and Humanities in the early 1960s, he never published any work of a general historical nature. To choose an attitude of independent reading and writing was due to his insight that his own study of literary history, far from being of universal influence and applicability, was a hermetically closed theoretical edifice that would eventually collapse. He therefore preferred to turn his attention to the "fragments of civilization," and read from them the mysteries and meanings of the universe. Of course "what remains of a whole theoretical system and has value are only a couple of ideas," and what reason is there to "heed only lengthy discourses and writings" and to "dismiss single words or phrases"?[32] There is no general history that is not based on grand systems, and it is an author's conscious choice to emphasize theory and neglect practice.

This represents the attitude and strategy of academics, but what about students? From the students' perspective, literary history is not necessarily the best reading material. In fact, the courses and writings on literary history are merely a crutch by way of which we conduct literary studies, in order to lead students gradually into the palace of literature. But we are still in a situation in which teaching materials pose as scholarship, and even though the serving maid has become a lady, she is still in attendance.

If Literary History Did Not Exist . . .

From another perspective, though, if there were no literary history, how would we think, teach, and write? From my perspective, the most direct results would be the following:

(1) Devoid of a systemic form, knowledge would fragment. This would be the case not only for university teachers and students, but for society's structure of knowledge in general. It is common knowledge that Tang *shi* poetry was followed by Song *ci* lyric poetry, that Li Bai's 李白 and Du Fu's 杜甫 genius had a lasting impact, and that *The Plum in the Golden Vase* (金瓶梅) influenced *The Dream of the Red Chamber*; everybody understands the different styles of thought and writing of the Zhou brothers (Lu Xun and Zhou Zuoren) and the

aesthetic characteristics of ancient style and regulated verse. The difference is that the people of an era can pay attention to the style of an author or to a literary form, but they are not familiar with, nor can they be aware of, the so-called "style of an era"—for instance the totality of characteristics of Ming literature or all the facets of the literary scene of the 1930s. What is taught in Chinese literature classrooms today as "common knowledge of literary history" (even though it does not include foreign literature) is probably more complete than that of the erudite traditional scholar. And yet, one cannot avoid asking if we can really have "the whole history at our command," to talk with knowledge about the past and the present, from Qu Yuan 屈原 to Lu Xun. We should remind ourselves of Chen Yinke's 陳寅恪 caveat in "A Report on Feng Youlan's Examination of the First Volume of *History of Chinese Philosophy*" (馮友蘭中國哲學史上冊審查報告): "The more his words follow a systemic method, the further he strays from the truth of the knowledge of the ancients."[33]

(2) Giving priority to reading would elevate the canon to an all-important position. From the *Four Books* and *Five Classics* (四書五經), to the *Records of the Historian* (史記), the *Selection of Refined Literature* (文選), the *Three Hundred Tang Poems* (唐詩三百首), and the *Compilation of Classical Prose*, a canonical approach to literary studies privileges anthologies. This is by no means democratic, since it constitutes a history of winners with no place for the losers, and consequently many writers and works have been lost, and the complexity and multifaceted nature of literature remains muted. And this does not take into account the potentially enormous influence that considerations of profit or prejudice have on the determination of what constitutes the canon and on the selections made by editors. To orient one's reading by way of the canon might lead to a partial eclipse for posterity, even to an ignorance of the totality of historical progress. To "teach" anew or to "read closely" anew leads to the emergence of different structures of knowledge. Because of publication profits and changes in scholarly fashion, what today's scholars say or write is above their actual level of erudition; in the past the exact opposite was true. The past focused on reading, understanding, learning, and transmitting knowledge, whereas today we focus on writing, making pronouncements, and creating.

(3) Without literary history we might risk focusing on one point while ignoring the larger picture. Without the framework of literary history, it would be difficult to construct the big picture, to trace the evolution of what cannot be known or might not be worth understanding, or to pay attention to epistemic breaks. On the other hand, one would gain an extreme freedom with regard to reading. One might choose not to read Han *fu* but still enjoy Yuan drama, just as one might not understand *Romance of the Western Chamber* (西廂記) but still appreciate The *Peony Pavilion* (牡丹亭). Nonprofessional readers could thus choose to follow their interests and read at will. For professional researchers, however, some loss would inevitably ensue, since everybody "would be a master only in their special field." But from the perspective of the reading of literature and of literary

study, individualism and eclecticism would probably become more viable. To focus too much on systematicity will necessarily lead to a false understanding of what one doesn't understand, and threatens to produce merely an overview instead of true research.

(4) By not following conventions, one would risk entering a "false path." This does not imply criticizing individual interest, but rather freeing oneself from old conventions and predetermined directions of development. In that way, what would have meaning and what not would depend solely on individual interest, and would allow from time to time "an operation of transgressing conventions." But this is not a bad thing. The most established field of literary research is that on *The Dream of the Red Chamber*, but in the past Hu Shi ridiculed university president Cai Yuanpei 蔡元培 as a representative of a method of searching for hidden meaning, of "guessing obscure riddles." Nevertheless, Cai persisted in his research, and his work has been influential. Even within the confines of a specialty, there are many instances of doing one thing while pretending to do something else. Enjoining somebody to comply with literary history will yield good results, avoid waste, and prevent students from being led astray. But this approach also lacks imagination, and will lead to very few pleasant surprises.

(5) This would allow one to stick to one's opinion and disregard the consensus. In the form of teaching material, literary history subordinates individual taste to the collective will. What I call "collective will" includes the common knowledge of the academic world, the audience's needs, as well as economic profit. An overly individual formulation can only be limited to specific academic contexts, and is unlikely to be widely accepted. If one hopes for the endorsement of the Ministry of Education and the recognition of academic colleagues, one has to compromise. This is the case even for quite successful works, such as *Thirty Years of Modern Chinese History* (中國現代文學三十年) by Qian Liqun 錢理群 and others, or Hong Zicheng's 洪子誠 *A History of Contemporary Chinese Literature* (中國當代文學史). Upon comparison, their literary histories and the individual works of each author differ quite radically. When Chen Xiying 陳西瀅 claimed that the English were not really cultured but merely posed as culture lovers, nobody dared say publicly that they liked Shakespeare.[34] Likewise, when writing literary history for the purpose of teaching, one does not have the right to an independent opinion. Would one dare to say that *The Dream of the Red Chamber* is not particularly great, or that Hu Shi is much greater than Lu Xun? In contrast, while not writing material for the purpose of teaching, one can stick to one's own opinion and write "peculiar" individual works or even ones that "are full of prejudice"—as long as one can justify them to oneself, that is enough.

Of course, this is all merely speculation. China's academic world cannot return to the era of "notes on classical poetry," "comments on *ci*," or "reflections on *wen*." Literary history became an academic discipline and a systematic discourse from 1903 onward, and it still maintains a leading position now, even though its aura has begun to fade and its function has started to change, as scholars are increasingly redirecting their attention and grow in experience and training, subtlety, and reflection.

The writing of literary history certainly has its high and low points, being excellent at times and mediocre at others, but of course no ideal literary history exists anywhere in the world. And thus scholars of every era dedicate themselves to rewriting literary history—this is indeed a common strategy of literary revolution or reform, since it has close connections to the implementation of new ideologies and the emergence of readers of a new era. Therefore, it is probably more fitting to speak of "reinventing literary history" rather than "rewriting literary history," since this process involves not only the literary evaluation of writers or scholarly thought and academic positions but also reading and training, academic disciplines and writing, scholarly research and ideology, educational institutions, and the market, among other factors. To consider, contest, and restructure the image of literary history with which we are familiar aims at calling forth the deep layers that lie submerged under scholarship, such as affect, poetic feeling, imagination, and critical spirit.

(translated by Andrea Bachner)

NOTES

1. See Lu Xun 魯迅, *Lu Xun quanji* 魯迅全集 [The complete works of Lu Xun] (Beijing: Renmin wenxue chubanshe, 1981), vol. 12, 44, 130, and 184, and vol. 13, 582.

2. Zheng Zhenduo 鄭振鐸, "Yanjiu Zhongguo wenxue de xin tujing" 研究中國文學的新途徑 [A new path for the research of Chinese literature], in *Zhongguo wenxue yanjiu* 中國文學研究 [Research on Chinese literature] (Beijing: Zuojia chubanshe, 1957), 4.

3. Lu Xun, "Liu Wuji lai xin an yu" 柳無忌來信按語 [Answer to Liu Wuji's letter], in *Lu Xun quanji* 魯迅全集 [The complete works of Lu Xun], vol. 8, 299.

4. See Lu Xun, *Lu Xun quanji* 魯迅全集 [The complete works of Lu Xun], vol. 11, 117, 123, and 136.

5. See Lu Xun, "Zhi Li Xiaofeng" 致李小峰 [Letter to Li Xiaofeng] and "Zhi Hu Jinxu" 致胡今虛 [Letter to Hu Jinxu], in *Lu Xun quanji* 魯迅全集 [The complete works of Lu Xun], vol. 44, 207.

6. For instance, in the preface to his *Zhongguo wenxue jinhua shi* 中國文學進化史 [A history of the progress of Chinese literature] (Shanghai: Guangming shuju, 1929) Tan Zhengbi 譚正璧 writes: "What counts as writing may also mean to use good available material."

7. Lu Xun, "Zhi Cao Juren" 致曹聚仁 [Letter to Cao Juren], in *Lu Xun quanji* 魯迅全集 [The complete works of Lu Xun], vol. 12, 184.

8. See Lu Xun, "Liang di shu" 兩地書 [Letters between two places], in *Lu Xun quanji* 魯迅全集 [The complete works of Lu Xun], vol. 11, 117 and 184.

9. Lu Xun, "Moluo shi li shuo" 摩羅詩力說 [On the power of Mara poetry], in *Lu Xun quanji* 魯迅全集 [The complete works of Lu Xun], vol. 1, 66 and 100; trans. Shu-ying Tsau and Donald Holoch as "On the Power of Mara Poetry," in *Modern Chinese Literary Thought:*

Writings on Literature 1893–1945, ed. Kirk A. Denton (Stanford: Stanford University Press, 1996), 96–109, quotation at 99 and 108. Translation revised.

10. See Lu Xun, "Letters between Two Places," 184.

11. Zhang Zhidong 張之洞 writes: "schools, geography, finance, taxation, war preparation, law, public works, commerce are part of Western governance; mathematics, painting, mining, medicine, sound technology, light, chemistry, electricity are part of the Western arts": *Quan xue bian: She xue* 勸學篇 • 設學 [Encouraging learning: Organization of education] (Shanghai: Shanghai Shudian, 2002), 41.

12. "Zongli Yamen zoupi Jingshi Daxuetang zhangcheng" 總理衙門奏擬京師大學堂章程 [Regulations for the Imperial University of Peking by the Zongli Yamen], chap. 1, "Zong gang" 總綱 [Overview], in *Beijing daxue shi liao* 北京大學史料 [Material on the history of Peking University], ed. Beijing Daxue jiaoshi yanjiu shi (Beijing: Beijing daxue chubanshe, 1993), vol. 1, 81.

13. Zhang Baixi 張百熙, "Zou chouban Jingshi Daxuetang qingxing shu" 奏籌辦京師大學堂情形疏 [Memorandum of the state of the Imperial University of Peking], in *Beijing Daxue shi liao* 北京大學史料 [Material on the history of Peking University], ed. Beijing daxue jiaoshi yanjiu shi (Beijing: Beijing daxue chubanshe, 1993), vol. 1, 54.

14. See Chen Fuchen's 1904 entry citing Li Shizhen's 李士楨 "Lament" (挽詩), in Chen Fuchen 陳黻宸, "Chen Fuchen nianpu" 陳黻宸年譜 [Chronicle of Chen Fuchen], in *Chen Fuchen ji* 陳黻宸集 [Works by Chen Fuchen] (Beijing: Zhonghua Shuju, 1995), 1192.

15. For instance, Zheng Zhenduo's 鄭振鐸 *Illustrated History of Chinese Literature* 插圖本中國文學史, Rong Zhaozu's 容肇祖 *An Outline of Chinese Literary History* (中國文學史大綱), and others all mention this as the first history of Chinese literature written by a Chinese; see Xia Xiaohong 夏曉虹, "Zuowei jiaokeshu de wenxueshi: Du Lin Chuanjia *Zhongguo wenxueshi*" 作為教科書的文學史——讀林傳甲〈中國文學史〉 [Literary history as teaching material: Lin Chuanjia's *A History of Chinese Literature*], in *Wenxue shi* 文學史 [Literary history], 2nd ed. (Beijing: Beijing Daxue Chubanshe, October 1996), 329–333; and Dai Yan 戴燕, "Wenxue, wenxue shi, Zhongguo wenxue shi: Lun ben shiji chu 'Zhongguo wenxue shi' xue de faren" 文學 • 文學史 • 中國文學史——論本世紀初 "中國文學史" 學的發軔 [Literature, literary history, Chinese literary history: On the undertaking of the study of "Chinese literary history" at the beginning of the century], *Wenxue yichan* 文學遺產 [Literary legacy] 6 (1996): 4–15 for a more detailed analysis of Lin's work.

16. See Huang Lin 黃霖, *Jindai wenxue piping shi* 近代文學批評史 [A history of early modern literary criticism] (Shanghai: Shanghai guji chubanshe, 1993), 783–785.

17. Lin Chuanjia 林傳甲, *Zhongguo wenxue shi* 中國文學史 [A history of Chinese literature] (Wulin mouxinshi, 1910), 1.

18. Qian Xuantong 錢玄同 himself was quite satisfied with this "invention" and mentioned it repeatedly in letters to Chen Duxiu 陳獨秀 and Hu Shi; see the correspondence section of *New Youth* (新青年), 2.6, 3.5, and 3.6 (1917).

19. See Chen Pingyuan 陳平原, "Xin jiaoyu yu xin wenxue—cong Jingshi Daxuetang dao Beijing Daxue" 新教育與新文學——從京師大學堂到北京大學 [New education and New Literature: From the Imperial University of Peking to Peking University], *Xueren* 學人 [The scholar], 14th ed. (Nanjing: Jiangsu wenyi chubanshe, 1998); a different version of this essay was published as chap. 1 of *Zuowei xueke de wenxueshi* 作為學科的文學史 [Literary history as academic discipline] (Beijing: Beijing daxue chubanshe, 2011).

20. See Sang Bing 桑兵, "Jindai Zhongguo xueshu de diyuan yu liupai" 近代中國學術的地緣與流派 [The locations and schools of early modern Chinese academia], in *Wanqing minguo de Guoxue yanjiu* 晚清民國的國學研究 [Research on national learning in the late Qing and Republican period] (Shanghai: Shanghai guji chubanshe, 2001), 28–64, and Luo Zhitian 羅志田, "Wenxue de shiyu: Zhengli Guogu yu wenxue yanjiu de kaojuhua" 文學的失語：整理國故與文學研究的考據化 [How literature lost its language: Rearranging the National Heritage and literary research in the era of textual criticism], in *Liebian zhong de chuancheng: Ershi shiji qianqi de Zhongguo wenhua yu xueshu* 裂變中的傳承——20世紀前期的中國文化與學術 [Legacy amidst rupture: Chinese culture and academia in the early twentieth century] (Beijing: Zhonghua shuju, 2003), 255–321.

21. Fu Sinian 傅斯年, "Mao Zishui 'Guogu he kexue de jingshen' fuzhi" 毛子水〈國故和科學的精神〉附識 [On Mao Zishui's *The Spirit of the National Past and Science*], *Xinchao* 新潮 [Avant-garde] 1.5 (May 1919).

22. Shen Congwen 沈從文, "Wenyun de chongjian" 文運的重建 [The reestablishment of the literary], in *Shen Congwen quanji* 沈從文全集 [The complete works of Shen Congwen] (Taiyuan: Beiyue Wenyi Chubanshe, 2002), vol. 12, 81–82, first published in *Zhongyang ribao* 中央日報 [Zhongyang daily], May 4, 1940.

23. See Cheng Huichang 程會昌 (Qianfan 千帆), "Lun jinri daxue Zhongwenxi jiaoxue zhi bi" 論今日大學中文系教學之蔽 [On the problems of teaching in today's Chinese literature departments], *Siwen* 斯文 [Refined] 3.3 (February 1943), and "Guanyu 'Lun jinri daxue Zhongwenxi jiaoxue zhi bi'" 關於〈論今日大學中文系教學之蔽〉[On "On the Problems of Teaching in Today's Chinese Literature Departments"], *Guowen yuekan* 國文月刊 [National culture monthly] 68 (June 1948).

24. See Chen Pingyuan, "Zhishi, jineng yu qinghuai: Xin wenhua yundong shiqi Beida Guowenxi de wenxue jiaoyu" 知識、技能與情懷——新文化運動時期北大國文系的文學教育 [Knowledge, skills, and feelings: Literary education at Peking University's National Literature Department during the New Culture Movement], *Beijing daxue xuebao* 北京大學學報 [Academic journal of Peking University] (2009 and 2010): 97–118 and 133–157

25. See Zhang Taiyan 章太炎, "Qiu xue bi lun" 救學弊論 [On the disadvantages of promoting learning], in *Zhang Taiyan quanji* 章太炎全集 [The complete works of Zhang Taiyan] (Shanghai: Shanghai renmin chubanshe, 1985), vol. 5, 98.

26. See Liu Yongji 劉永濟, *Shisi chao wenxue yaolüe* 十四朝文學要略 [An outline of the literature of fourteen dynasties] (Harbin: Heilongjiang renmin chubanshe, 1984).

27. Influential literary histories, such as Liu Dajie's 劉大杰 *A History of the Development of Chinese Literature* (中國文學發展史) and *A History of Chinese Literature* (中國文學史), edited by You Guo'en 游國恩, as well as commercially successful literary histories such as *A History of Chinese Literature* (中國文學史) edited by Yuan Xingpei 袁行霈, *A History of Chinese Literature* (中國文學史) by Zhang Peiheng 章培恆 et al., and *Thirty Years of Modern Chinese Literature* (中國現代文學三十年) by Qian Liqun 錢理群 et al. underline the appeal of literary history.

28. "Wenke Guowen xuemen wenxue jiaoshou an" 文科國文學門文學教授案 [A record for professors of literary studies in the national humanities], *Beijing Daxue rikan* 北京大學日刊 [Periodical of Peking University], May 2, 1918.

29. "Guowen jiaoshouhui kaihui jishi" 國文教授會開會紀事 [Notes on the assembly of university professors of national learning], *Beijing daxue rikan* 北京大學日刊 [Periodical of Peking University], October 17, 1919.

30. Hu Shi 胡適, "Shenme shi 'guoyu de wenxue', 'wenxue de guoyu'?" 什麼是國語的文學, 文學的國語? [What is "national-language literature" and "a national literary language"?], in *Hu Shi zuopin ji* 胡適作品集 [Writings by Hu Shi] (Taipei: Yuanliu Chuban, 1986), vol. 24, 240.

31. Hu Shi 胡適, "Da Su Xuelin shu" 答蘇雪林書 [Response to Su Xuelin's letter] and "Yu Gao Yang shu" 與高陽書 [Letter to Gao Yang], in *Hu Shi Hongloumeng yanjiu lunshu quanbian* 胡適紅樓夢研究論述全編 [A complete edition of Hu Shi's research on *The Dream of the Red Chamber*] (Shanghai: Shanghai Guji Chubanshe, 1988), 279–280 and 290.

32. Qian Zhongshu 錢鍾書, "Du Laaokong" 讀拉奧孔 [Reading Laokoon], in *Qi zhui ji* 七綴集 [Seven pieces patched together], 2nd rev. ed. (Shanghai: Shanghai guji chubanshe, 1994), 34.

33. Chen Yinke 陳寅恪, "Feng Youlan *Zhongguo zhexueshi* shang ce shencha baogao" 馮友蘭中國哲學史上冊審查報告 [A Report on Feng Youlan's examination of the first volume of the *History of Chinese Philosophy*] in *Jinminghuan conggao erbian* 金明館叢稿二編 [Writings of Jinmingguan], vol. 2 (Shanghai: Shanghai Guji Chubanshe, 1980), 274.

34. See Chen Xiying 陳西瀅, "Ting qin" 聽琴 [Listening to the *qin*], in *Ling Shuhua, Chen Xiying sanwen* 凌叔華、陳西瀅散文 [Essays by Ling Shuhua and Chen Xiying], ed. Liu Hong 柳紅 and Xia Xiaofei 夏曉非 (Beijing: Zhongguo Guangbo Dianshi Chubanshe, 1992), 257.

WORKS CITED

Chen Fuchen 陳黻宸. "Chen Fuchen nianpu" 陳黻宸年譜 [Chronicle of Chen Fuchen]. In *Chen Fuchen ji* 陳黻宸集 [Works by Chen Fuchen]. Beijing: Zhonghua Shuju, 1995.

Chen Pingyuan 陳平原. "Xin jiaoyu yu xin wenxue—cong Jingshi Daxuetang dao Beijing Daxue" 新教育與新文學——從京師大學堂到北京大學 [New education and New Literature: From the Imperial University of Peking to Peking University]. In *Xueren* 學人 [The scholar], 14th ed. Nanjing: Jiangsu wenyi chubanshe, December 1998.

Chen Pingyuan 陳平原. "Zhishi, jineng yu qinghuai: Xin wenhua yundong shiqi Beida Guowenxi de wenxue jiaoyu 知識、技能與情懷——新文化運動時期北大國文系的文學教育 [Knowledge, skills, and feelings: Literary education at Peking University's National Literature Department during the New Culture Movement]. *Beijing Daxue xuebao* 北京大學學報 [Academic journal of Peking University] (2009 and 2010): 97–118 and 133–157.

Chen Xiying 陳西瀅. "Ting qin" 聽琴 [Listening to the qin]. In *Ling Shuhua, Chen Xiying sanwen* 凌叔華、陳西瀅散文 [Essays by Ling Shuhua and Chen Xiying]. Ed. Liu Hong 柳紅 and Xia Xiaofei 夏曉非. Beijing: Zhongguo guangbo dianshi chubanshe, 1992.

Chen Yinke 陳寅恪. "Feng Youlan *Zhongguo zhexueshi* shang ce shencha baogao" 馮友蘭中國哲學史上冊審查報告 [A report on Feng Youlan's examination of the first volume of the *History of Chinese Philosophy*]. In *Jinmingghuan conggao erbian* 金明館叢稿二編 [Writings of Jinmingguan], vol. 2. Shanghai: Shanghai guji chubanshe, 1980.

Cheng Huichang 程會昌 (Qianfan 千帆). "Guanyu 'Lun jinri daxue Zhongwenxi jiaoxue zhi bi'" 關於〈論今日大學中文系教學之蔽〉 [On "On the problems of teaching in today's

Chinese literature departments"]. *Guowen yuekan* 國文月刊 [National culture monthly] 68 (June 1948).

Cheng Huichang 程會昌 (Qianfan 千帆). "Lun jinri daxue Zhongwenxi jiaoxue zhi bi" 論今日大學中文系教學之蔽 [On the problems of teaching in today's Chinese literature departments]. *Siwen* 斯文 [Refined] 3.3 (February 1943).

Dai Yan 戴燕. "Wenxue, wenxue shi, Zhongguo wenxue shi: lun ben shiji chu 'Zhongguo wenxue shi' xue de faren" 文學・文學史・中國文學史——論本世紀初 "中國文學史" 學的發軔 [Literature, literary history, Chinese literary history: On the undertaking of the study of "Chinese literary history" at the beginning of the century]. *Wenxue yichan* 文學遺產 [Literary legacy] 6 (1996): 4–15.

Fu Sinian 傅斯年. "Mao Zishui 'Guogu he kexue de jingshen' fuzhi" 毛子水〈國故和科學的精神〉附識 [On Mao Zishui's *The Spirit of the National Past and Science*]. *Xinchao* 新潮 [Avantgarde] 1.5 (May 1919).

"Guowen jiaoshouhui kaihui jishi" 國文教授會開會紀事 [Notes on the assembly of university professors of national learning]. *Beijing Daxue rikan* 北京大學日刊 [Periodical of Peking University], October 17, 1919.

Hu Shi 胡適. "Da Su Xuelin shu" 答蘇雪林書 [Response to Su Xuelin's letter]. *Hu Shi Hongloumeng yanjiu lunshu quanbian* 胡適紅樓夢研究論述全編 [A complete edition of Hu Shi's research on *The Dream of the Red Chamber*]. Shanghai: Shanghai guji chubanshe, 1988. 279–280.

Hu Shi 胡適. "Shenme shi 'Guoyu de wenxue', 'wenxue de Guoyu'?" 什麼是國語的文學, 文學的國語? [What is "national-language literature" and "a national literary language"?]. In *Hu Shi zuopin ji* 胡適作品集 [Writings by Hu Shi], vol. 24. Taipei: Yuanliu chuban, 1986.

Hu Shi 胡適. "Yu Gao Yang shu" 與高陽書 [Letter to Gao Yang]. In *Hu Shi Hongloumeng yanjiu lunshu quanbian* 胡適紅樓夢研究論述全編 [A complete edition of Hu Shi's research on *The Dream of the Red Chamber*]. Shanghai: Shanghai guji chubanshe, 1988. 290.

Huang Lin 黃霖. *Jindai wenxue piping shi* 近代文學批評史 [A history of early modern literary criticism]. Shanghai: Shanghai guji chubanshe, 1993.

Lin Chuanjia 林傳甲. *Zhongguo wenxue shi* 中國文學史 [A history of Chinese literature]. Wulin mouxinshi, 1910.

Liu Yongji 劉永濟. *Shisi chao wenxue yaolüe* 十四朝文學要略 [An outline of the literature of fourteen dynasties]. Harbin: Heilongjiang renmin chubanshe, 1984.

Lu Xun 魯迅. *Lu Xun quanji* 魯迅全集 [The complete works of Lu Xun]. Beijing: Renmin wenxue chubanshe, 1981.

Lu Xun 魯迅. "On the Power of Mara Poetry." Trans. Shu-ying Tsau and Donald Holoch. In *Modern Chinese Literary Thought: Writings on Literature 1893–1945*. Ed. Kirk A. Denton. Stanford: Stanford University Press, 1996. 96–109.

Luo Zhitian 羅志田. "Wenxue de shiyu: Zhengli Guogu yu wenxue yanjiu de kaojuhua" 文學的失語：整理國故與文學研究的考據化 [How literature lost its language: Rearranging the National Heritage and literary research in the era of textual criticism]. In *Liebian zhong de chuancheng: Ershi shiji qianqi de Zhongguo wenhua yu xueshu* 裂變中的傳承——20世紀前期的中國文化與學術 [Legacy amidst rupture: Chinese culture and academia in early twentieth century]. Beijing: Zhonghua shuju, 2003. 255–321.

Qian Zhongshu 錢鍾書. "Du Laaokong" 讀拉奧孔 [Reading Laokoon]. In *Qi zhui ji* 七綴集 [Seven pieces patched together], 2nd rev. ed., Shanghai: Shanghai guji chubanshe, 1994.

Sang Bing 桑兵. "Jindai Zhongguo xueshu de diyuan yu liupai" 近代中國學術的地緣與流派 [The locations and schools of early modern Chinese academia]. In *Wanqing minguo de*

Guoxue yanjiu 晚清民國的國學研究 [Research on national learning in the late Qing and Republican period]. Shanghai: Shanghai guji chubanshe, 2001. 28–64.

Shen Congwen 沈從文. "Wenyun de chongjian" 文運的重建 [The reestablishment of the literary]. In *Shen Congwen quanji* 沈從文全集 [The complete works of Shen Congwen], vol. 12. Taiyuan: Beiyue wenyi chubanshe, 2002; first published in *Zhongyang ribao* 中央日報 [Zhongyang daily], May 4, 1940.

Tan Zhengbi 譚正璧. *Zhongguo wenxue jinhua shi* 中國文學進化史 [A history of the progress of Chinese literature]. Shanghai: Guangming shuju, 1929.

"Wenke guowen xuemen wenxue jiaoshou an" 文科國文學門文學教授案 [A record for professors of literary studies in the national humanities]. *Beijing Daxue rikan* 北京大學日刊 [Periodical of Peking University], May 2, 1918.

Xia Xiaohong 夏曉虹. "Zuowei jiaokeshu de wenxueshi: Du Lin Chuanjia *Zhongguo wenxueshi*" 作為教科書的文學史——讀林傳甲〈中國文學史〉 [Literary history as teaching material: Lin Chuanjia's *A History of Chinese Literature*]. In *Wenxue shi* 文學史 [Literary history], 2nd ed. Beijing: Beijing daxue chubanshe, 1996. 329–333.

Zhang Baixi 張百熙. "Zou chouban Jingshi Daxuetang qingxing shu" 奏籌辦京師大學堂情形疏 [Memorandum of the state of the Imperial University of Peking]. In *Beijing Daxue shi liao* 北京大學史料 [Material on the history of Peking University]. Ed. Beijing Daxue jiaoshi yanjiu shi, vol. 1. Beijing: Beijing daxue chubanshe, 1993.

Zhang Taiyan 章太炎. "Qiu xue bi lun" 救學弊論 [On the disadvantages of promoting learning]. In *Zhang Taiyan quanji* 章太炎全集 [The complete works of Zhang Taiyan], vol. 5. Shanghai: Shanghai renmin chubanshe, 1985.

Zhang Zhidong 張之洞. *Quan xue bian: She xue* 勸學篇·設學 [Encouraging learning: Organization of education]. Shanghai: Shanghai shudian, 2002.

Zheng Zhenduo 鄭振鐸. "Yanjiu Zhongguo wenxue de xin tujing" 研究中國文學的新途徑 [A new path for the research of Chinese literature]. In *Zhongguo wenxue yanjiu* 中國文學研究 [Research on Chinese literature]. Beijing: Zuojia chubanshe, 1957.

"Zongli Yamen zoupi Jingshi Daxuetang zhangcheng" 總理衙門奏擬京師大學堂章程 [Regulations for the Imperial University of Peking by the Zongli Yamen]. *Beijing Daxue shi liao* 北京大學史料 [Material on the history of Peking University]. Ed. Beijing Daxue jiaoshi yanjiu shi, vol. 1. Beijing: Beijing daxue chubanshe, 1993.

THE SECRETS OF LANGUAGE

Chen Li's Sinographic Anagrams

ANDREA BACHNER

IN one of his poems from the 2009 collection *Light/Slow* (輕 / 慢), Taiwanese poet Chen Li 陳黎 formulates a critical genealogy of nationalism on the basis of a "found object," the Chinese character for "country" (國):

國

國破衰亡簡史：
國,或,戈,弋
匕, 乚, 、,¹

Country

abbreviated history of a country's decline:
country, or, spear, arrow
dagger, hook, dot,

In this poem, Chen Li stages the "abbreviated history of a country's decline" as an exercise in graphic form. The Chinese character for country, 國, is stripped of its power, one element, one stroke at a time, until nothing is left but a single dot without any conventional semantic meaning. That the elements of the Chinese character for country refer to weapons—spear (戈), arrow (弋), and dagger (匕)—transforms the second line and the beginning of the third line into an appositional phrase, rather than a mere series in which 國 loses more and more of its elements. The dot, the last remnant of the character 國, together with the commas that separate the different stages of decay, invokes an image of blood drops. This felicitous formal structure leads to the execution of the word *country* and, by extension, of the idea of nationhood, as if the graphic elements of this Chinese character determined its semantic meaning. The implication is that the idea of *country*—and perhaps, more specifically, the Chinese nationalism invoked by the character's use of the terms 國家 for "nation" and 中國 for "China"—is bound to lead to violence and to self-destruction.

Chen Li's "Country," with its graphically executed critique of violence and nationalism, is reminiscent of one of the poet's best-known concrete experiments, his "War Symphony" (戰爭交響曲) of 1995.[2] In "War Symphony," Chen Li used only four characters—兵 ("soldier"), 丘 ("tomb"), and the onomatopoetic compound 乒乓 ("ping pang")—to criticize the injury and death that are inevitable outcomes of war. As the ranks of soldiers (rows of the character 兵) are wounded and killed in combat—the onomatopoetic compound 乒乓 symbolizes both the sound of guns and, via a fake graphic reading, the soldiers' (兵) loss of limbs—they give way to rows of tombs (丘). Although formal experimentation is a constant poetic force in Chen Li's work, *Light/ Slow* returns to graphic experiments with a vengeance. Many of its poems toy with the graphic force of Chinese characters, from poems reminiscent of "War Symphony" that abandon Chinese syntax to invest in the visual force of Chinese characters, to experiments that harken back to traditional Chinese genres in their play with the material and graphic characteristics of the Chinese script.[3] Two distinct poetic genres drive Chen Li's attention to a Chinese poetic tradition: poems constructed with Chinese characters from famous Tang poems, and poems such as "Country" in the tradition of the hidden-character poem (*yinzi shi* 隱字詩), a kind of poetic riddle based on anagrammatic principles. Both types of poems work with a reselection and recombination of elements, either on the basis of existing poems or, in the case of the hidden-character poems, on the basis of the graphic components of Chinese characters. Whereas Chen Li's twist on Tang poetry exploits a highly canonical Chinese form—with the original poems visible on the page, though printed in a slightly faded font so as to highlight Chen Li's recycled creations—the hidden-character poems hail from a more marginal Chinese tradition.

Although hidden-character poems are mentioned in Liu Xie's 劉勰 literary treatise *The Literary Mind and the Carving of Dragon* (文心雕龍), Liu Xie grants them only conditional entrance among canonical literary genres under the heading "Humor and Enigma" (諧隱 [讔]), as a poetic form that may serve an expressive or moral purpose but is also prone to be used for frivolity and ribaldry.[4] Indeed, even as poetry in Chinese became increasingly invested in the poetic and graphic possibilities of the Chinese script under the influence of Western modernism, for instance in the context of modernist experiments in Taiwan of the 1950s and 1960s, Chinese forms of graphic play received short shrift. While poets and critics drew heavily on Western models such as Ezra Pound, Guillaume Apollinaire, or E. E. Cummings, or even earlier forms such as George Herbert's pattern poetry, by contrast Chinese pattern poetry, such as *huiwen* (回文 or 廻紋), or riddle poems, were dismissed as mere linguistic games, if they were mentioned at all.[5] Chen Li's use of the hidden-character poem in *Light/Slow*—they constitute one of three parts of the collection, which has more than seventy short poems in total—reactivates a marginalized genre.[6] It claims literary nimbleness for this genre of riddle poetry in which the character or characters to be guessed are given in the text of the riddle in disaggregated form.[7]

Unlike most riddles, hidden-character poems contain clues that are not merely related to content but, reminiscent of a rebus, concern the very linguistic materiality of the term or character that is the solution to the riddle.[8] Most of Chen Li's riddle poems contain a threefold strategy for helping the reader to guess the correct answer: (1) the poem hints at the semantic content of the hidden character; (2) the poem includes a description of the shape of the character or its components; (3) the poem contains characters that are visually reminiscent of the hidden character. Usually, the title of each poem, when it is not the target character itself, features an element of the target character (for instance 口 for 品, 木 for 柳, or 氏 for 氐). To solve the riddle, a reader needs to think of the Chinese characters concerned in concretely visual terms, reading for graphic elements and not only for semantic meaning. The poetic text often highlights such a graphic reading that requires a reader to put a character's elements back together. For instance, the description "比晶還要精" ("even purer than 晶 [also 'clear']") allows a reader to guess that the character in question is 品 ("product" or "commodity"), which resembles 晶 but, lacking the middle strokes, looks more transparent.[9] To point a reader to the character 目, related to vision and eyesight, another poem describes it as "日復一日的凝視" ("a gaze that adds a 日 [also 'day' or 'sun'] to a 日"), literally a doubling of the character 日 dependent on a gaze or fixed stare that results in a partial superimposition of both elements.[10] Whereas this example works by combining two characters, others—such as the play on 晶 and 品—work by subtraction. 目 is not only the partial doubling of 日, but also, as Chen Li's poem puts it, an instance of "斷肢的耳" ("a 耳 [also: 'ear'] that has had its extremities cut off").[11] In this way, Chen Li's hidden-character poems invite a reader's appreciation of the graphic conceits at the heart of each poem, as well as the combinatorial creativity of Chinese characters themselves. Not only does Chen Li's title for the section, "Hidden-Character Poems," point directly to the genre of riddle and invite the reader to engage in (controlled) guesswork, the poet's comments after each poem or group of poems contain the solution to the riddles, or the titles directly reveal the target character. The aim of the poems is not to leave the reader puzzled, but rather to allow a reader to reconstruct the ingenious crafting of language in each poem and to celebrate the combinatorial creativity of the Chinese language and its components.

That Chen Li's Sinographic riddles depend on their linguistic material, namely the concrete form and components of the Chinese script, becomes clear in my attempts at translation, which are more description and commentary than translation proper and cannot do without the presence of at least some of the Chinese original, such as the Chinese characters that are most essential to Chen Li's graphic puns. In his postface, Chen Li effectively points to the profound untranslatability of the graphically invested poems in *Light/Slow*. As poetic experiments that highlight their graphic material, they are limited to a linguistically and culturally specific medium, the Chinese script:

這本詩集裏的詩其實很多是無法翻譯的 (譬如輯二裏那些詩),部份因為從詩集《苦惱與自由的平均律》 以來,我嘗試在詩中挖掘中文字特性或中文性 (Chineseness) 所致。[12]

> Many of the poems in this collection are actually untranslatable (for instance the poems in the second part). In part this is because, from my collection *Worries and Freedom Well-Tempered* onward, I have been trying to unearth the specificity of Chinese writing or of *Chineseness* in my poems.

The poems Chen Li refers to here rely on their linguistic medium, the Chinese language, even more specifically than does poetry in general. To attempt a translation of poems in general presents the challenge of expressing content in another language and replicating some of the poetic features of the original, such as rhyme, rhythm, or assonance. Since the graphic shape of a poem or part of a poem, of a Chinese character or part of a Chinese character, is exploited for poetic effect in Chen Li's poems, however, translation hinges not only upon a difference in language, but also upon a difference in writing system. Once the graphic qualities of a text become meaningful via the distribution and form of textual elements, rather than forming arbitrary textual contingencies, translation exposes the problems of transcription: not as a supposedly transparent, smooth transition between different scripts, but as the challenge of carrying across meaning (understood as signification and aesthetic impact) between different textual media.

And yet, Chen Li phrases the cultural specificity, and hence untranslatability, of his work in and through translation: the decisive factor of this type of poetic experiment, its "Chineseness," is expressed in Chen Li's text both in Chinese, as *zhongwenxing* (中文性), and (parenthetically) in English as "Chineseness"—a bilingual maneuver that my English translation of Chen Li's "Chinese" original cannot adequately communicate. Whereas the English noun *Chineseness*, built on the basis of the adjective "Chinese," remains open to different semantic values of "Chinese"—as an ethnic, cultural, national, or linguistic descriptor—the Chinese term, based on *zhongwen* (中文), functions as a linguistic category, one that highlights the Chinese written language (*zhongwen*) rather than speech, and thus repeats the even more specific phrase *zhongwenzi texing* (中文字特性; the specificity of Chinese writing or Chinese written characters) that precedes it. The juxtaposition of three similar terms in two languages seems to raise a fundamental question. How are we to read Chen Li's insistence on Chineseness as the basis for untranslatable poetic material, indeed as a marker of untranslatability?

Chen Li's assertion might strike readers as an essentialist highlighting of the putative uniqueness of the Chinese language, thereby resonating with the notion of Chinese writing as the other script par excellence, alterity given concrete medial form—only now as a celebration of Chinese uniqueness from within a Sinophone tradition. And yet, as a poet from Taiwan, Chen Li has repeatedly underlined the hybridity of Taiwanese culture, in which the "Chinese" element is, at best, a placeholder for one strain of cultural influence among others.[13] Indeed, Chen Li's design on the Chinese script often counters any nationalist instrumentalization of the Chinese writing system.

His use of the Chinese script, such as the graphic "execution" of the idea of nationalism in his poem "Country," carefully dissociates the creativity of the Chinese character
and Chinese nationalism. Even as the poem activates the Sinographic mystique of the
character 國—suggesting a connection between meaning and written sign beyond an
arbitrary and conventional link—it sacrifices the Sinograph to execute 國. However,
this "sacrifice" works only by invoking the mimetic force often attributed to Chinese
characters by observers both within and outside the Chinese cultural sphere—namely,
that characters in the form of pictographs or ideographs forge a nonarbitrary link
between the written sign and its signified. But a strategic exploitation of ideographic
appeal allows Chen Li to question essentialist notions of culture and language even
more radically. In "Country," Chen Li finds in the Chinese written signifiers the basis
for undermining the idea of nation. In order to do so, he parasitically uses the aura of
the Chinese script, only to de-sign it by parsing the elements down to its basic strokes,
no longer imbued with meaning and thus no longer part of an ideographic reading that
derives signification from a mere combination of equally meaningful parts. Even as the
unique graphic creativity of written Chinese is highlighted in Chen Li's poetic experiments that celebrate the materiality of the Chinese script, an analytical thrust can reach
the extreme of pulverizing the Sinographic material, as in "Country."[14] What can Chen
Li's poetic riddles tell us about the status of the Chinese script, about translation, and
about poetic language in general?

Poetic Transmediation

One famous reflection on the graphic specificity of the Chinese script, Ernest Fenollosa's
essay "The Chinese Written Character as a Medium for Poetry," edited and published
by Ezra Pound in 1919, also raises the question of writing's graphic materiality and
translation. Fenollosa's essay contrasts English and Chinese as poetic media, credit-
ing Chinese characters with special expressive power, one that highlights movement
rather than stasis and concretion rather than abstraction. As the model for a poetic
language closer to nature, understood as an infinite dynamic network of phenomena
in action, Chinese stands in stark contrast to English as well as pointing the way to
recuperating English as a powerful poetic language. For Fenollosa, under the Latinate
straitjacket that constricts English, a different, more poetic English tries to fight free,
one that could potentially function like Chinese.

In spite of many comparative examples in Fenollosa's essay that show the dormant
power of English, one of the most important traits that make Chinese a good medium
for poetry is conspicuously absent from Fenollosa's discussion of the English language: its graphic component. Unlike other linguistic characteristics of English that
resemble Chinese according to Fenollosa, its alphabetic letters cannot compare to the
graphic, indeed ideographic, potential of Chinese characters. What fascinated Fenollosa
about Chinese poetry was its graphic creativity, the fact that the complexity of Chinese

characters allowed a vaster playing field for the poetic manipulation of language. If the formalist critic Roman Jakobson in his essay "Linguistics and Poetics" defined the poetic function of language as the application of paradigmatic criteria on a syntagmatic level, as an added constraint of similarity and contrast that determined (consciously or unconsciously) the selection of contiguous words, Fenollosa's examples show an interest in a similar understanding of linguistic poeticity with regard to graphic elements.[15] The following example concludes Fenollosa's essay (in Pound's edition):

> The overtones vibrate against the eye. The wealth of composition in characters makes possible a choice of words in which a single dominant overtone colors every plane of meaning. That is perhaps the most conspicuous quality of Chinese poetry. Let us examine our line.

日	昇	東
Sun	Rises (in the)	East

> The sun, the shining, on one side, on the other the sign of the east, which is the sun entangled in the branches of a tree. And in the middle sign, the verb "rise," we have further homology; the sun is above the horizon, but beyond that the single upright line is like the growing trunk-line of the tree sign. This is but a beginning, but it points a way to the method, and to the method of intelligent reading.[16]

What Fenollosa describes in the synesthetic metaphor of visually vibrating overtones in this passage is, to put it more prosaically, the fact of the repetition of one graphic element in the three contiguous characters of a poetic line: 日 or *sun*. Of course, somebody who does not read Chinese cannot spontaneously "parse" Chinese characters on the basis of its components (as Ezra Pound would have it on the basis of Fenollosa's theory). Nor would a native reader of Chinese necessarily consciously reflect on each graphic element, as opposed to taking in a character as a gestaltic whole. Irrespective of the etymological (or etymographic) valence of Fenollosa's reading, the poetic repetition of one graphic element in this example poses a distinct challenge for translation.[17] Can this poetic phenomenon work with other linguistic and graphic material, such as the alphabetic script of English?

The synesthesia in Fenollosa's discussion of visual "overtones" in his Chinese example seems to indicate one possible translational direction, from graphic form to sound. If Chinese poetry resonates visually, maybe the overtones and poetic echoes in other languages can be rendered by way of sonic resonances rather than graphic similarity. This is an approach that the Brazilian concrete poet Haroldo de Campos espouses in his essay on Fenollosa, "Ideogram, Anagram, Diagram: A Reading of Fenollosa" ("Ideograma, anagrama, diagrama: Uma leitura de Fenollosa"), the introductory piece to the 1977 edited volume *Ideogram: Logic, Poetry, Language* (*Ideograma: Lógica, poesia, linguagem*), which contains a translation of Fenollosa's essay and other works relevant to an ideographic interest in the Chinese script. De Campos asks about the possibility of putting into action a poetic practice of resonances like the one Fenollosa describes as the ideographic method for "a phonetic language, written with alphabetic digits, noniconic in itself."[18] Influenced by Roman Jakobson's definition of the poetic function and Ferdinand de Saussure's work on anagrams, de Campos proposes a "structural translation" that would allow an apparent disregard for semantic content in order to "take hold of the semiotic process of 'saturation' of 'visible and active' *intracode*."[19] To illustrate this kind of translation, de Campos reiterates Fenollosa's example and juxtaposes it with a line from the long poem *The Wandering Guesa* (*O Guesa errante*), written between 1858 and 1888 by the Brazilian poet Joaquim de Sousândrade. Fenollosa's example appears with two types of "translations," even before the appearance of the poetic line by Sousândrade that de Campos offers as the "result" of a structural translation. In addition to the translation of the three Chinese characters into English and Portuguese, de Campos also provides a schematic transcription of the characters in which 日 is replaced by the circular form of the sun while the other character elements are transformed into stick figures. This graphic translation—the schematization of 日—highlights the resonances with Sousândrade's line:

> The sun at sundown (sad askunce!)
> The SUN at SUNdown (sad aSkUNce!)
>
> O sol ao pôr-do-sol (triste soslaio!).
> O SOL ao pôr-do-SOL (triste SOsLaio!)[20]

As in the example of "日昇東, " the word *sol*, made visible by de Campos's highlighting in big letters, appears three times in one line, from its appearance as stand-alone word to its combination (*pôr-do-sol*) to its latent presence in the word *soslaio*. For de Campos, the transformation of *sol* reproduces the repetition of 日 in the Chinese example: "In the syntagmatic sequence of the verse, the intermittent incidence of the 'sonic figure' SOL seems to reproduce, directly or in transformed shape, the same play of 'harmonies' that Fenollosa caught on the graphematic level of Chinese characters."[21] In other words, since de Campos's emphasis is on the way the elements of a poetic text are interrelated, since they create internal echoes—they form, in de Campos's words, a "relational intracode"—it does not matter if such a resonance happens on the level of sound or graphic elements.[22]

But there is one fundamental problem in this equation. For Fenollosa, the beauty of the ideographic method did not simply reside in the added aesthetic emphasis achieved by the repetition of elements, but rather in an added layer of meaning. In other words, the point of repeating 日 in Fenollosa's example lies in the way this illustrates the image of the rising sun. One condition needs to be in place for this poetic gamble to work: the repeated element needs to have semantic value (that its semantic value is motivated, i.e. that the relation between "日" and the meaning "sun" is wrought iconically, is an added bonus, of course). In other words, graphic repetition as envisioned by Fenollosa and de Campos has to be graphemic; it cannot simply reduplicate random graphic elements, but only those that are suggestive of a meaning. This is why de Campos highlights the word *SOL* as an element of his graphic rendition of Sousândrade's poetic line, instead of going for the (lower-hanging) graphic fruit of underlining the letter *o*, such as:

O sOl aO pÔr-dO-sOl (triste sOslaiO!)

This alternative emphasis also highlights one of the underlying problems of de Campos's "structural translation." Rather than conceiving of letters and Chinese characters as signs with graphic and phonic components, de Campos seems unable to think beyond phonemes or graphemes, which is to say elements that carry semantic meaning. De Campos's translation sets out on a quest for similarity with the aim of finding a method in alphabetic writing that would match the creativity of the graphic method that Fenollosa had seen in evidence in the Chinese script in general, and in its poetic uses in particular. However, by underlining the semantic-phonetic unit *sol* rather than graphic and phonic units such as the *o*, de Campos disavows the multiplicity of poetic resonances that are possible in Chinese and in Portuguese: graphic, semantic, and phonic. De Campos's "translation" of Fenollosa's Chinese example into Brazilian Portuguese ends up cementing the difference between the two languages and the two scripts at work. Since de Campos limits the scope of translation to elements with conventionalized meaning—the character and radical 日 and the word *sol*—even in translation Chinese and Portuguese remain inevitably at odds, one confined to its graphic facet, the other enshrined in its phonetic straitjacket. In other words, even in a tradition that seeks in the Chinese script a new source for poetic and graphic inspiration, Chinese is Chinese and English is English (or Portuguese is Portuguese). And this difference finds its basis in erecting the difference between the graphic and the phonetic into a symbolic absolute, rather than dwelling on the components shared by all languages and their scripts.

In spite of Fenollosa's and de Campos's interest in the poetic potential of the Chinese script in order to push their own languages beyond their comfort zones, their reflections still naturalize the fundamental difference between Chinese (equated with its graphic form) and English or Portuguese (as spoken languages). In spite of their fascination with graphic form, they end up echoing Ferdinand de Saussure's phonetic bias in his *Course in General Linguistics* (*Cours de linguistique générale*).[23] Before working on what would become one of the most influential reflections on language of the twentieth century, one that continues to define the way in which we think about language in the context of literary and cultural studies, Saussure was deeply interested in anagrammatic phenomena. Much of his research, unpublished during his lifetime and made partly available as late as 1971 by Jean Starobinski in *Words upon Words* (*Les mots sous les mots*), was dedicated to the hypothesis that much of Indo-European poetry (Saussure's examples were drawn mostly from Latin, Ancient Greek, and Vedic) functioned in anagrammatic ways—where strict rules of phonetic repetition regulated poetry and, if such phonetic repetitions were traced and parsed, a secret text would start to appear. Poetry, in other words, was hiding key words, often proper names, under its surface meaning.

These "hypograms" or "paragrams"—Saussure never quite settled on one term—were not pure anagrams in which all the letters or components have to be rearranged to form new meaning, but a distribution or scattering of fragments of a key term or proper name over (and under) several lines or verses. In spite of the fact that the poetic material under scrutiny came to Saussure in written form—Starobinski underlines the importance of the critic's eye and ear for a successful anagrammatic reading—Saussure insists on the phonetic nature of this process, making phonemes the units of the anagrammatic process of permutation.[24] Saussure's phonetic turn (not only in linguistics as such, but also in relation to the anagram) swerves away from the conventional graphic dimension of the anagram with its focus on letters as graphic, rather than phonetic units. As Starobinski emphasizes, this *research will have only a link of distant analogy with the traditional anagram, which functions only through graphic signs. Reading, in this instance, applies to deciphering combinations of phonemes not of letters.*[25] Even though Saussure abandoned his anagrammatic work, probably because he started to distrust his findings as he begun to see the same structures everywhere, almost as a kind of combinatorial paranoia, the implications of unearthing words under words would haunt Western theoretical approaches for several decades—as in the work of Julia Kristeva, Jean Riffaterre, or Haroldo de Campos.[26]

What is striking in Saussure's work on anagrams for my purpose here is not the problem of the pervasive appearance of his hypograms, nor necessarily the related question of whether these phenomena were intentional poetic creations, unconscious artifacts of poetic processes, or a product of a reader's combinatorial fixation, but rather what appears to be a phonetic bias that underpins his reflections on the basic building blocks of language. For Saussure, the language that lies beneath language is necessarily the same as the language under which it hides: phonetic and not graphic, speech and not writing, double entendre, not double vision. In spite of the uncanny strangeness of anagrammatic processes, their linguistic alterity is relative as long as surface text and hidden text are thought of as confined to the same (type of) language and as functioning according to the same understanding of language. Privileging the combination of phonetic units, rather than graphic ones, downplays the multiplicity of linguistic expression in favor of sound. Saussure's definition of the hypogram as phonetic rather than graphic introduces a division in the realm of language (and different languages), one that pits scripts against speech and language against language.

BEYOND (AND BELOW) THE SINOGRAPHIC

Do Chen Li's hidden character poems, with their reference to a Chinese poetic tradition, similarly cement a vision of absolute linguistic difference, albeit from within a Chinese scriptworld rather than fueled by a Western desire for alterity? Even though Chen Li's insistence on the untranslatability and the putative Chineseness of his experiments might suggest as much, his poetic practice opens up a wider, more complex perspective on work with the Chinese script and thus on linguistic difference in general. Chen Li invokes Chineseness to point to the material and medial specificity of his poetic experiments. At the same time, his poems effectively open up the category of Chineseness to include its margins.

As Chen Li embraces the marginal genre of the poetic riddle, he not only dignifies this genre as high literature, but at times engages intentionally in an irreverent, even ribald tone. He thus reforges the negative connection of riddle poems and uncouth humor that Liu Xie had critiqued in *The Literary Mind and the Carving of Dragons* and gives it a positive, affirmative twist. For instance, Chen Li presents one subgroup of hidden-character poems that toys with Chinese characters for sexual organs or human excrement and turns abjection into carnivalesque pleasure as one of the examples of the genre par excellence. The five poems that graphically explicate the characters 屄 ("vagina"), 屌 ("penis"), 屁 ("fart"), 屎 ("shit"), and 尿 ("urine") are, as Chen Li explains in his commentary, *yinsi shi* (隱私詩, "poems about private, or hidden, parts"), but furthermore, as such, by way of near homophony, they point to the genre of *yinzi shi* (隱字詩, "hidden-character poems"). Not only are these poems doubly "hidden"—both share the character *yin* (隱, "hidden"). As the commentary explains, they also point to another underlying riddle. The key characters of the five poems all share the same radical, 尸, which is the simplified form of the character 屍 (*shi*), meaning "corpse." Not only do these poems conceal characters (隱字, *yinzi*) or private parts (隱私, *yinsi*), they also conceal (the Chinese characters for dead) bodies (隱屍, *yinshi*).[27]

In contrast to such examples of tongue-in-cheek humor that gives poetic form to taboo topics, some of Chen Li's hidden-character poems, such as "Country," take up much more serious issues, such as the reinvestment of the margins of Chinese culture and a critique of sinocentrism. In such instances, the specifically sinographic technique of the hidden-character poem is often employed by Chen Li to problematize the idea of cultural and national essence, for instance in a group of five poems that thematize and contest Chinese visions of the cultural other, the non-Chinese: "Five Savages" (五胡). These five poems, written from the perspective of the "savage" produced through the culturally biased lens of sinocentrism, also debunk the concept of the "savage" as a discursive production. The genre of the hidden-character poem with its sophisticated play with and comprehension of the Chinese written character becomes the perfect instrument for a critique of Chinese ethnocentrism. "Five Savages" uses sinographically oriented poetic strategies to criticize the Han-centrism of Chinese culture. The first poem, "勹," provides a particularly striking etymography of cultural bias:

勹

你開口咬定我是
凶惡之徒

勹 ——

不, 我不凶

勹

You assert loudly that I am
a ferocious guy [凶惡, or 兇惡]

勹 ——

No, I am not ferocious (凶)

我是割下肉
祖匈與你們交心的
平常人[28]

I am—flesh (肉) cut off,
my breast [匈＝胸] on your breast, baring my heart—
just a man

As in so many of Chen Li's hidden-character poems, the title of the work refers to a kind of reading, rather than to the poem's content. The key lies in one of the components of the word that the text describes: 匈 (pronounced "xiong") as in 匈奴 *Xiongnu*, the name of a nomadic non-Han ethnicity in the northwest, which a Chinese Central Plains tradition had always treated as barbaric. The poem proceeds through a (pseudo-)analytical series, not only presenting the character in question in its component parts, but also alluding to the character itself as a truncated and biased form: 匈 is composed of the elements 勹 and 凶, where the latter (better known in its alternative form 兇) signifies "ferocious." As a counter to the ethnocentric equation of the Other with savagery and the scripting of ethnic difference as ethic turpitude, Chen Li reminds his readers that 匈 is, after all, an alternative, "mutilated" version of 胸, meaning "breast" but also "person": when you cut off one of its parts, its humanity— the radical for flesh, 肉—you reduce 匈 to the inhuman notion of the ferocious savage, 凶 or 兇. Here, racial profiling is likened to a process of castration, where the "human" part of the other is denied while also offering a clever pun in the poem's rebus-like logic. In the end, the other (匈) reveals himself or herself to have been human all along: as Chen Li explains in a footnote, the character 匈, pronounced "qun," means "people" in the language of this ethnic group. Through the graphic logic of this poem, notions of cultural and ethnic centrality are revealed as only a matter of perspective, and thus ethnocentrism should be given up for a wider, more inclusive definition of humanity.

Chen Li's sinographic work in this poem stands out for its (pseudo-)etymographic wit that dissects a character into its parts, as well as drawing on alternative character versions. The seemingly superfluous component 勹 is filled with meaning through a different process: its graphic resemblance to ㄅ—which is one of the signs in Taiwan's Zhuyin phonetic transcription system and is pronounced "b"—allows the character 匈 to be read as meaning not only "human" but also "not evil" (勹 or rather 勹 +凶), since 勹 = ㄅ = b = bu = 不 (meaning "not").[29] The poetic conflation of 勹 and ㄅ is purely graphically motivated, yet it only becomes meaningful after a process of voicing.[30] This example illustrates that Chen Li's script poetics are not invested in a nostalgic return to a recovered graphic purity of the sinograph. The poet does not provide an etymography so much as trace a critical genealogy. Rather than exhuming the true meaning of Chinese characters by moving closer to their origin, the poet activates the possibility of the sinograph to point beyond its own scriptural and cultural tradition, while at the same time revealing its ethnocentric bias. It is in this sense that "a tiny Chinese character is often a miniature of the cosmos or its parts," as the poet asserts in his postface[31]—as material for poetic experimentation, not because of any mimetic claim inherent in the writing system as such.

As is customary in the tradition of Chinese riddle verse, Chen Li's anagrammatic experiments work with graphic, rather than phonetic, material. Its basic units are strokes, radicals, and characters, rather than phonemes or syllables. And yet, the graphic pun with 冖 and 勹 also pushes the unity of Chen Li's Chinese elements to the extreme: 冖 is not a character in its own right, but only a radical with a vaguely semantic charge; 勹, derived from 冖, is a sign in the character-derived Zhuyin phonetic script, and as such is stripped of any semantic value and reduced to a purely phonetic value. A similar process is at work in Chen Li's "Country," where the radical ㄴ and the stroke 丶 become invested with new semantic meaning, as are the commas that punctuate the series of Chinese characters, thus signaling that they form part of a syntactic construction, as well as constituting (pseudo-)iconic elements—with the dot 丶 and the commas reminiscent of drops of blood. These elements—at once integral parts of and foreign intruders to the script in which they appear—accrue meaning only by way of their juxtaposition and contextualization, only because they require a reader to activate different facets and strategies of reading.

In Chen Li's poetic experiments, the language beneath language, then, does not simply constitute a superficial mirror and equivalent of its surface language. Rather, it produces meaning, not only through different combinations, but mainly because its building blocks are mutable and flexible: not merely graphemes or phonemes, but bits of language that can function in more than one way and that can be broken down into more than one type of unit. It is here that the language beneath language does not stabilize or naturalize its surface language, but rather opens up and contests conventional notions of what constitutes a specific language (such as Chinese), and, by analogy, of what constitutes or counts as language as such.

UNTRANSLATABILITY REVISITED

From the vantage point of his poetic practice, Chen Li's insistence on the untranslatability of his graphic poetry needs rephrasing. Instead of simply reiterating the age-old cliché of the untranslatability of poetry or entrenching Chinese in a position of linguistic incommensurability, Chen Li's riddle poems enact an alternative way of conceiving of linguistic difference. This difference—hence Chen Li's emphasis on the materiality of the Chinese script—is not only a question of meaning, of semantic non-coincidence, but also of the graphic and phonic materiality of a language, a question of sound as well as script. However, in order to circumvent the danger of solidifying barriers around languages and essentializing different languages and scripts, the radicalization of linguistic difference has to be accompanied by a complementary gesture of relativization: the difference between languages is not one of essences, of *phone* versus *graphe*, and thus a difference that is still peddled as the mainstay of the complete alterity of the Chinese script. Rather, languages are different because they mix the facets at play in all linguistic communication in unique ways. The very fact that spells the radical untranslatability of linguistic expression, its unique phonic and graphic shape, also makes linguistic difference relative, a question of similar components in different selections and combinations rather than an essential divide.

One of the poems in *Light/Slow*, "A Difficult Poem that Is Easy to Read" (一首容易讀的難詩), addresses the question of translation directly by rephrasing it as an oscillation between untranslatability and commensurability. This poem contains four lines of cryptic characters, pseudographs that look like Chinese characters because they follow the graphic and combinatorial conventions of sinographs though without forming part of the Chinese lexicon. The pseudographs of "A Difficult Poem" are quoted from one of Chen Li's earlier poems, "A Love Poem" (情詩), a poem entirely crafted from cryptic characters.[32] The last lines of "A Love Poem" are quoted in "A Difficult Poem," which is imagined as an opaque Chinese poem cherished by Pindar, the famously difficult ancient Greek poet:

他喜歡讀一首叫「情詩」的中文詩
因為這詩, 據說
翻不翻成希臘文都一樣難懂[33]

He liked to read a Chinese poem called "Love Poem"
because this poem, so they say,
was equally difficult to read irrespective of if it was translated into Greek or not

At first glance, Chen Li's strange characters seem to embody the very idea of untranslatability: how can something that is unreadable in a given language be translated? At a second glance, even as Chen Li's pseudographic creations push untranslatability to an extreme, they circumvent translation altogether. Since these signs are "fake," they are not in need of translation; they are as cryptic to native readers of Chinese as to somebody who reads and writes in ancient Greek, such as Pindar.[34] But even as these lookalike characters do not need translation, they are untranslatable, since how would one translate, or, indeed, transgraph pseudo-Chinese into pseudo-Greek?

But instead of merely celebrating the opacity of pseudographic text that would transcend the limits of specific languages in its universal unreadability, Chen Li's translational practice goes a step further. A group of his hidden-character poems actually gloss the supposedly unreadable characters from "A Love Poem" and "A Difficult Poem," using them as the key terms of poetic riddles. On one hand, this makes the character at the center of each riddle verse doubly cryptic, the core of an unsolvable riddle, since it calls on a reader to identify an unknown character, one that did not exist prior to the poet's creation. On the other hand, via the author's comment at the end of the group of poems, these Chinese characters are imbued with semantic and phonetic value: each of the cryptic characters is granted a pronunciation and signification.[35] What had seemed unintelligible is now given meaning and context; what had seemed outside the bounds of language proper is now intelligible as one of its integral parts. Once we as readers have taken in Chen Li's character glosses, his inventions have become part of our

Chinese lexicon. Irrespective of the doubtful facticity of these glosses, Chen Li thus underlines the virtual limitation as well as openness of any linguistic system: linguistic strangeness does not lurk outside of the limits of our own language; rather, the linguistic unknown is a constant in our process of learning and reactivating what we perceive as our own language.[36]

At the same time, to push the boundaries of one's language and explore beyond its symbolic limits might be a conduit to linguistic enrichment and creativity. One of these lines of inquiry leads away from a consideration of language as a symbolic, ideological structure to a scrutiny of language as linguistic material for selection and combination. Anagrammatic experiments and reflections such as Ferdinand de Saussure's work on a phonetically understood anagrammar of Indo-European poetry, the reflections on poetic resonances in logographic and alphabetic scripts by Brazilian concrete poet Haroldo de Campos, or Chen Li's poetic revitalization of the genre of the hidden-character poem embark upon this route. Where not tempered by preconceived notions of total linguistic difference (between sound and script), interest in words under words, in the components of (and below) language that constitute language as a concrete practice, potentially conceives of language as duplicitous and multilayered. As Jacques Derrida reminds us in *Shibboleth: For Paul Celan* (*Schibboleth: Pour Paul Celan*), only a text that consists of multiple languages is truly untranslatable, since not only the linguistic specificity of one language, but the specific differences between the languages in play, will be lost in translation.[37] But viewing language through an anagrammatic lens means not only potentially discovering another meaning below the linguistic surface, but also engaging in linguistic movement below and beyond our conventional relation to language as a medium of communication invested in expressing meaning without much detour. Anagrammatic work points to language not as a transparent medium of communication, but rather as a protean material reservoir that depends on the flexibility and malleability of its elements. If language is duplicitous—not other to itself, but other to our linguistic routines and expectations—then difference lies at the very heart of language and questions the possibility of linguistic ownership. While this pragmatically exacerbates the problem of translation, it also precludes discourses of untranslatability from erecting symbolic walls of incommensurability between languages: linguistic expression is already multiply in translation, even before another language comes into play.

Anagrammatic practices have a particular relationship to language. They highlight in miniature how language works. With their emphasis on the basic building blocks of language they can cement linguistic othering by discovering that what lies beneath language simply replicates our preconceived notion of (our own or another's) language, such as in Saussure's insistence on the phonetic nature of anagrams in Indo-European poetry or de Campos's strategic blindness (at least in his essay on Fenollosa) to the graphic force of the alphabetic script. And yet, since these practices push the possibilities of linguistic creation to their limits and open up a dimension of language below language, they can also render a language other to itself by putting into play the basic units of language and its basic rules of combination. For instance, many of Chen Li's hidden-character poems, while hinging upon graphic combinations, also probe phonic elements or those that lie at the margins of linguistic significance, such as single strokes and dots or punctuation marks.[38] The untranslatability of Chen Li's sinographic anagrams—both as pragmatic extreme and in their symbolic relativity—resonates with Emily Apter's celebration of untranslatability as a "linguistic form of creative failure," albeit with a much stronger emphasis on creativity than on failure.[39] It also teaches us as readers that we have to pay attention to linguistic specificity even as, or whenever, we want to think of language or translation in general. Being alert to specific textual turns, even down to the placement of a dot or a comma, will allow us to think about language without downplaying internal differences potentially disruptive to theoretical coherence, but without erecting linguistic difference into a fetish of incommensurability either.

NOTES

I would like to express my profound gratitude to Chen Li 陳黎 for permission to reprint and translate the poems analyzed in this chapter.

1. Chen Li, *Qing/man* 輕／慢 [Light/slow] (Taipei: Erya wenhua, 2009), 82. Unless indicated otherwise, all translations are my own.
2. See Chen Li, *Daoyu bianyuan* 島嶼邊緣 [The edge of the island] (Taipei: Jiuge, 2003), 102–104.
3. For a discussion of the ideographic fascination of the Concrete Poetry movement, especially the Brazilian Noigandres group, see Andrea Bachner, *Beyond Sinology: Chinese Writing and the Scripts of Culture* (New York: Columbia University Press, 2014), 74–82.
4. See Liu Xie 劉勰, *Wenxin diaolong yizhi* 文心雕龍譯旨 [The literary mind and the carving of dragons, annotated], ed. Jiang Shuge 姜書閣 (Jinan: Zhailu shushe, 1984), 51–54; trans. Vincent Yu-chung Shih as *The Literary Mind and the Carving of Dragons* (New York: Columbia University Press, 1959), 78–83.
5. See, for instance, the unequal discussion of European and Chinese pattern poetry in Yu Guangzhong 余光中, "Gudongdian yu weituoxing zhijian" 古董店與委託行之間 [Between antique store and pawn shop], in *Lin Hengtai yanjiu ziliao huibian* 林亨泰研究資料彙編 [Materials for the study of Lin Hengtai], vol. 1, ed. Lü Xingchang 呂興昌 (Zhanghua: Zhangxian Wenhua, 1994), 32–37; Luo Qing 羅青, *Cong Xu Zhimo dao Yu Guangzhong* 從徐志摩到余光中 [From Xu Zhimo to Yu Guangzhong] (Taipei: Erya, 1978), 54ff.; and Wen Renping 溫任平, "Zhongguozi de shiyi zuoyong yu zhongguo shi" 中國字的示意作用與中國詩 [The use of Chinese characters as allusions in Chinese poetry"], *Chuangshiji* 創世紀 [The epoch poetry quarterly] 37 (November 1974): 29–37.
6. Even though the whole second section of *Light/Slow* bears the title "Hidden-Character Poems," this section also includes other examples of visual poetry as well as Chen Li's poetic recycling of Tang poems.
7. For a thorough discussion of riddle poems and other anagrammatic structures in Chinese literature and their terminological vicissitudes, such as *xi zi* (析字, "analyzing characters")

or *li he* (離合, "dividing and joining"), see John Marney, *Chinese Anagrams and Anagram Verse* ([Taipei]: Chinese Materials Center Publication, 1993).

8. In *The Interpretation of Dreams*, as well as other writings, Sigmund Freud likened the work of the unconscious in dreams both to the visual and textual riddle of the rebus and to non-Western scripts, such as hieroglyphs or Chinese characters. For a discussion of the graphic facets of Freud's dream work, see Jean-François Lyotard, *Discours, figure*, 2nd ed. (Paris: Klincksieck, 2002), 238–270; trans. Antony Hudek and Mary Lydon as *Discourse, Figure* (Minneapolis: University of Minnesota Press, 2011), 233–267.

9. Chen Li, *Light/Slow*, 55.

10. Chen Li, *Light/Slow*, 56.

11. Chen Li, *Light/Slow*, 56. In this case, 目 is only part of the solution, as a component of the character 具.

12. Chen Li, "Houji: Pianmian zhi ci" 後記：片面之詞 [Postface: Biased words], *Light/Slow*, 169–175, quotation at 174.

13. For instance, in Chen Li's epilogue to the collection *Daoyu bianyuan* 島嶼邊緣 [The edge of the island], he dwells on the special energy of Taiwan due to a history of transculturation and hybridity; see "Zai daoyu bianyuan (Ba)" 在島嶼邊緣(跋) [At the edge of the island (Epilogue)], in *Daoyu bianyuan*, 189–193.

14. Another poem in *Light/Slow* also toys with a dissection of the idea of nationhood. The poem "Nation" (國家) plays with the second part of this two-character word, "家," whose root meaning is related to the ideas of family and home. When you take away the character's roof element, what remains? A series of hogs (豕) under the cover of the nation. The signification of "nation" thus produced communicates deep sarcasm, not only vis-à-vis the idea of nation but also in relation to the ideographic myth attached to Chinese writing. See *Light/Slow*, 101.

15. See Roman Jakobson, "Linguistics and Poetics," in *Style in Language*, ed. Thomas Sebeok (Cambridge: MIT Press, 1960), 350–377.

16. Ernest Fenollosa and Ezra Pound, *The Chinese Written Character as a Medium for Poetry*, ed. Haun Saussy, Jonathan Stalling, and Lucas Klein (New York: Fordham University Press, 2008), 60.

17. Jan Assman coins the term *etymography* as a graphic pendant to etymology; see "Etymographie: Zeichen im Jenseits der Sprache," in *Hieroglyphen: Altägyptische Ursprünge abendländischer Grammatologie*, ed. Aleida Assmann and Jan Assmann (Munich: Fink, 2003), 37–63.

18. Haroldo de Campos, "Ideograma, anagrama, diagrama: Uma leitura de Fenollosa," in *Ideograma: Lógica, poesia, linguagem*, ed. Haroldo de Campos (São Paulo: Editora Cultrix, 1977), 9–113, quotation at 61.

19. de Campos, "Ideograma, anagrama, diagram," 62.

20. I am bending orthographic rules here in order to express the combinatorial force of the line in my English translation.

21. de Campos, "Ideograma, anagrama, diagrama," 62.

22. de Campos, "Ideograma, anagrama, diagrama," 60.

23. Saussure treats writing in general only to distinguish its interference from what he sees as the true linguistic object, spoken language. Even then, with the exception of some remarks on nonphonetic scripts, his focus is on phonetic writing systems. See Ferdinand de Saussure, *Cours de linguistique générale*, ed. Tullio de Mauro (Paris: Payot, 1982), 40–54,

trans. Roy Harris as *Course in General Linguistics* (Peru, IL: Open Court, 2006), 21–31. For a critique of Saussure's phonocentrism, see Jacques Derrida, *De la grammatologie* (Paris: Minuit, 1967), trans. Gayatri Chakravorty Spivak as *Of Grammatology* (Baltimore and London: The Johns Hopkins University Press, 1976).

24. Luzia Braun and Klaus Ruch foreground Saussure's analysis as an engagement with written text; see "Das Würfeln mit den Wörtern: Geschichte und Bedeutung des Anagramms," *Merkur* 42.4 (1988): 225–236, quotation at 228.

25. Jean Starobinski. *Les mots sous les mots: Les anagrammes de Ferdinand de Saussure* (Paris: Gallimard, 1971), 27–28, trans. Livia Emmet as *Words upon Words: The Anagrams of Ferdinand de Saussure* (New Haven: Yale University Press, 1979), 15.

26. For a discussion of the importance of Saussure's work on anagrams for theoretical reflection, especially in the work of Michael Riffaterre, see Paul de Man, "Hypogram and Inscription," *Diacritics* 11.4 (Winter 1981): 17–35.

27. See Chen Li, *Light/Slow*, 78.

28. Chen Li, *Light/Slow*, 57.

29. Chen Li's procedure here is reminiscent of some of the strategies used in Chinese Internet language, the so-called Martian Script (火星文).

30. Even though Chen Li's poetic practice highlights the graphic creativity of Chinese characters, sound asserts its importance constantly, for example in the glosses of rare or invented characters that indicate their voicing, or in the form of homophonic play, for instance in a group of hidden-character poems whose key characters share a common pronunciation; see *Light/Slow*, 90–92.

31. Chen Li, "Postface," 172.

32. Chen Li, *Kunao yu ziyou de pingjunlü* 苦惱與自由的平均律 [Worries and freedom well-tempered] (Taipei: Jiuge, 2005), 125–126.

33. Chen Li, *Light/Slow*, 9.

34. A similar play with untranslatability is at work in Xu Bing's 徐冰 installation "A Book from the Sky" (天書) with its massive display of made-up Chinese characters. For a discussion of Xu Bing's politics of translation, see Stanley Abe K., "No Question, No Answers: China and A Book from the Sky," *boundary 2* 25.3 (Fall 1998): 169–192.

35. Some of these signs are imagined and defined by Chen Li as characters of regions or ethnicities at the margins of Chinese culture. Only very few of them lend themselves to being parsed ideographically.

36. This assertion of the alterity of all language resonates with Jacques Derrida's dictum "I have only one language, it is not mine" (*Je n'ai qu'une langue, ce n'est pas la mienne*), through which Derrida describes the politically fraught tension between language use and identity politics in order to theorize about the structural dispossession or alterity of and in language. See Jacques Derrida, *Le monolinguisme de l'autre, ou la prothèse d'origine* (Paris: Galilée, 1996), 13, trans. Patrick Mensah as *Monolingualism of the Other; or, The Prosthesis of Origin* (Stanford: Stanford University Press, 1998), 1, translation slightly altered.

37. See Jacques Derrida, *Schibboleth: Pour Paul Celan* (Paris: Galilée, 1986), 54–55, trans. Joshua Wilner as "Shibboleth: For Paul Celan," in Jacques Derrida, *Sovereignties in Question: The Poetics of Paul Celan*, ed. Thomas Dutoit and Outi Pasanen (New York: Fordham University Press, 2005), 1–64, quotation at 29.

38. This is a radical understanding of anagrammatic processes, one that makes the anagram a meeting place of different sign systems and implies that the elements of an anagram can go beyond (or rather, fail to measure up to) conventional units required for

signification. In the context of a discussion of Jean Ricardou's literary practice, Lynn Higgins points out that "words are but one of many possible signifying systems upon which anagrams can operate"; see "Literature 'à la lettre': Ricardou and the Poetics of Anagram," *Romanic Review* 73.4 (1982): 473–488, quotation at 473. For a discussion of the importance of anagrammatic tropes in psychoanalysis, see Andrea Bachner, "Anagrams in Psychoanalysis: Retroping Concepts by Sigmund Freud, Jacques Lacan, and Jean-François Lyotard," *Comparative Literature Studies* 40.1 (2003): 1–25.

39. Emily Apter, *Against World Literature: On the Politics of Untranslatability* (London and New York: Verso, 2013), 20.

WORKS CITED

Abe, Stanley K. "No Question, No Answers: China and A Book from the Sky." *boundary 2* 25.3 (Fall 1998): 169–192.

Apter, Emily. *Against World Literature: On the Politics of Untranslatability*. London and New York: Verso, 2013.

Assman, Jan. "Etymographie: Zeichen im Jenseits der Sprache." *Hieroglyphen: Altägyptische Ursprünge abendländischer Grammatologie*. Ed. Aleida Assmann and Jan Assmann. Munich: Fink, 2003. 37–63.

Bachner, Andrea. "Anagrams in Psychoanalysis: Retroping Concepts by Sigmund Freud, Jacques Lacan, and Jean-François Lyotard." *Comparative Literature Studies* 40.1 (2003): 1–25.

Bachner, Andrea. *Beyond Sinology: Chinese Writing and the Scripts of Culture*. New York: Columbia University Press, 2014.

Braun, Luzia, and Klaus Ruch. "Das Würfeln mit den Wörtern: Geschichte und Bedeutung des Anagramms." *Merkur* 42.4 (1988): 225–236.

Chen Li 陳黎. *Daoyu bianyuan* 島嶼邊緣 [The edge of the island]. Taipei: Jiuge, 2003.

Chen Li 陳黎. *Kunao yu ziyou de pingjunlü* 苦惱與自由的平均律 [Worries and freedom well-tempered]. Taipei: Jiuge, 2005.

Chen Li 陳黎. *Qing/man* 輕 / 慢 [Light/slow]. Taipei: Erya Wenhua, 2009.

de Campos, Haroldo. "Ideograma, anagrama, diagrama: Uma leitura de Fenollosa." In *Ideograma: Lógica, poesia, linguagem*. Ed. Haroldo de Campos. São Paulo: Editora Cultrix, 1977. 9–113; partial trans. Kevin Mundy and Marc Benson as "Poetic Function and Ideogram/ The Sinological Argument" in Haroldo de Campos, *Novas: Selected Writings*, ed. Antonio Sergio Bessa and Odile Cisneros (Evanston: Northwestern University Press, 2007), 287–311.

Derrida, Jacques. *De la grammatologie*. Paris: Minuit, 1967; trans. Gayatri Chakravorty Spivak as *Of Grammatology*. Baltimore and London: The Johns Hopkins University Press, 1976.

Derrida, Jacques. *Le monolinguisme de l'autre, ou la prothèse d'origine*. Paris: Galilée, 1996; trans. Patrick Mensah as *Monolingualism of the Other; or, The Prosthesis of Origin*. Stanford: Stanford University Press, 1998.

Derrida, Jacques. *Schibboleth: Pour Paul Celan*. Paris: Galilée, 1986; trans. Joshua Wilner as "Shibboleth: For Paul Celan" in Jacques Derrida, *Sovereignties in Question: The Poetics of Paul Celan*, ed. Thomas Dutoit and Outi Pasanen. New York: Fordham University Press, 2005, 1–64.

Fenollosa, Ernest, and Ezra Pound. *The Chinese Written Character as a Medium for Poetry*. Ed. Haun Saussy, Jonathan Stalling, and Lucas Klein. New York: Fordham University Press, 2008.

Higgins, Lynn. "Literature 'à la lettre': Ricardou and the Poetics of Anagram." *Romanic Review* 73.4 (1982): 473–488.

Jakobson, Roman. "Linguistics and Poetics." *Style in Language*. Ed. Thomas Sebeok. Cambridge: MIT Press, 1960. 350–377.

Liu Xie 劉勰. *Wenxin diaolong yizhi* 文心雕龍譯旨 [The literary mind and the carving of dragons, annotated]. Ed. Jiang Shuge 姜書閣. Jinan: Zhailu shushe, 1984. 51–54; trans. Vincent Yu-chung Shih as *The Literary Mind and the Carving of Dragons*. New York: Columbia University Press, 1959.

Luo Qing 羅青. *Cong Xu Zhimo dao Yu Guangzhong* 從徐志摩到余光中 [From Xu Zhimo to Yu Guangzhong]. Taipei: Erya, 1978.

Lyotard, Jean-François. *Discours, figure*. 2nd ed. Paris: Klincksieck, 2002; trans. Antony Hudek and Mary Lydon as *Discourse, Figure*. Minneapolis: University of Minnesota Press, 2011.

de Man, Paul. "Hypogram and Inscription." *Diacritics* 11.4 (Winter 1981): 17–35.

Marney, John. *Chinese Anagrams and Anagram Verse*. [Taipei]: Chinese Materials Center Publication, 1993.

de Saussure, Ferdinand. *Cours de linguistique générale*. Ed. Tullio de Mauro. Paris: Payot, 1982; trans. Roy Harris as *Course in General Linguistics*. Peru, IL: Open Court, 2006.

Starobinski, Jean. *Les mots sous les mots: Les anagrammes de Ferdinand de Saussure*. Paris: Gallimard, 1971; trans. Livia Emmet as *Words upon Words: The Anagrams of Ferdinand de Saussure*. New Haven: Yale University Press, 1979.

Wen Renping 溫任平. "Zhongguozi de shiyi zuoyong yu zhongguo shi" 中國字的示意作用與中國詩 ["The use of Chinese characters as allusions in Chinese poetry"]. *Chuangshiji* 創世紀 [The epoch poetry quarterly] 37 (November 1974): 29–37.

Yu Guangzhong 余光中. "Gudongdian yu weituoxing zhijian" 古董店與委託行之間 [Between antique store and pawn shop]. *Lin Hengtai yanjiu ziliao huibian* 林亨泰研究資料彙編 [Materials for the study of Lin Hengtai], vol. 1. Ed. Lü Xingchang 呂興昌. Zhanghua: Zhangxian Wenhua, 1994. 32–37.

CHAPTER 1.7

....

ON NOT KNOWING

Translation, Knowledge Work, and Modern Literature

....

MICHAEL GIBBS HILL

IN a wry, provocative essay, "Thou Dost Not, and Shalt Not Speak My Language" (*Lan tatakellama lughatī*), the Moroccan critic 'Abd al-Fattāḥ Kīlīṭū (Abdelfattah Kilito) freely admits that he does not like to hear foreigners speak Arabic. Upon meeting an American woman who spoke flawless Moroccan Arabic, he confesses: "I was surprised, and for the first time I felt that my language was slipping from me. Fortunately, I did not speak to her in standard Arabic, for if she spoke that too, what would have been left for me?"[1] This desire for a space of ownership, which persists despite all efforts to embrace foreignness, otherness, or, to use another term of late capitalism, "diversity," speaks to an uneasiness about the way language comes to reflect larger power relations: the American woman's fluent Arabic echoes the long history of the alliance between Orientalism and colonial incursions in North Africa and the Middle East.

This relationship between power and possession of knowledge has long been the focus of literary and cultural critique, whether in discussions of Orientalism or more recent attempts to think beyond area studies. But what of the other side of the coin: what happens when one does not know the language of another person, yet hopes ardently to communicate, appreciate, and understand? As with the uncanny Arabic skills of the American woman, the *unavailability* of a foreign language also carries historical meanings and burdens. So, too, do the routes taken to move around the lack of access to foreign languages. It might be useful, then, to stick with Kīlīṭū a bit longer, and compare his words on the American woman to his discussion in a different essay of Muṣṭafā Luṭfī al-Manfalūṭī (1876–1924), a famous Egyptian translator who, unimpeded by his lack of a knowledge of French, relied on a number of collaborators to rewrite well-known works of French literature, such as *La Dame aux camélias* by Alexandre Dumas, fils and Jacques-Henri Bernardin de Saint-Pierre's *Paul et Virginie,* into literary Arabic.[2] Although Kīlīṭū seems sympathetic to al-Manfalūṭī, he is ultimately repelled by the sentimental traditionalism that suffused al-Manfalūṭī's writings, and chides him for hiding the "unspeakable secret" of his desire to be European, as al-Manfalūṭī's ignorance of French and adherence to traditionalist literary Arabic serves as a sign of his distance from the contemporary cosmopolitan intellectual.[3]

In an odd coincidence of world literature, al-Manfalūṭī died in the same year as Lin Shu 林紓 (1852–1924), the wildly prolific "translator" who also knew no foreign languages and, like al-Manfalūṭī, relied on friends, acquaintances, and rarely idle "assistants" to render English- and French-language fiction and drama—including *La Dame aux camélias* and *Paul et Virginie*—into literary Chinese. He, too, was disavowed by subsequent generations of intellectuals and literary writers.[4] At this point I admit that I lack the training and knowledge needed to offer a comparison of the writings of al-Manfalūṭī and Lin Shu as literary texts. Nonetheless, I believe the convergence of their stories points to a significant historical question of the relationship between translation as *techne* and the position of translation in debates about world literature. Drawing from my own knowledge of the archives of modern China and leaving behind, for now, Lin Shu's Egyptian counterpart, I will also discuss how the problem of the lack of access to foreign languages bears on twentieth-century Chinese history.

Emily Apter's book *Against World Literature* argues that scholarly discussions of world literature, especially as they relate to methods for understanding the global circulation of literary texts, "rely on a translatability assumption" that serves to suppress or exclude "the Untranslatable" and underwrites "tendencies . . . toward reflexive endorsement of cultural equivalence and substitutability, or toward the celebration of nationally and ethnically branded 'differences' that have been niche-marketed as commercialized 'identities.'"[5] By pointing to many significant cases of untranslatability, Apter offers new insight into the conditions of the circulation of literature, art, and film in the contemporary world. Taking Apter's cue—and perhaps arguing, in the spirit of mistranslation, in geographical and historical directions that are unanticipated by her work—this essay explores a different set of "translatability assumptions" in China from the late nineteenth century through the middle of the twentieth.

These translatability assumptions addressed the problem of how to translate a text from a source language when the translator does not know that language. Faced with this problem, two methods emerged in modern China. The first was "tandem translation" (*duiyi* 對譯), which involved two or more persons working together to translate a text, usually in a configuration where one person who knew the language of the source text offered a rough verbal translation while the other person (who usually did not know the foreign language) transcribed the text into written Chinese. The second was "retranslation" or "relay translation" (*chongyi* 重譯 or *zhuanyi* 轉譯), which involved retranslating a text that had already been translated—for example, Mao Dun's 茅盾 translations of Russian novels that were published in the 1950s were all translated from English versions of these novels, and many other Russian works were translated through German.[6] These ostensibly irregular practices of translation were extremely common in China in the roughly seven decades from the 1880s through the 1950s. Their commonness—and their ability to be taken by important critics, writers, and readers as full-fledged translation—suggests that these practices offer an opportunity to think through not only some of the fundamental questions of translation in modern world literature but also to reconsider the practice of comparative literature in the academy today.

Most scholars who have studied the history of translation in China in the early twentieth century (myself included) have tended to see the extensive use of relay translation or retranslation in terms of the divide between prominent late-Qing intellectuals and major figures of the New Culture and May Fourth movements, as well as their successors in the late 1920s and through the 1930s.[7] Within this framework—inherited directly from the "May Fourth paradigm," which asserted the virtually absolute novelty of the political and cultural positions taken by a small number of intellectuals in Beijing in the late 1910s—one important question emerges: to what extent did the means that May Fourth intellectuals used to produce translations *really* demonstrate their differences from the practices of the late Qing, especially those personified by Lin Shu? If we phrase the question this way, the answer is: not very much. In previous work, I've taken a sociological perspective on this issue, arguing that the persistence of these irregular practices of translation should reduce in our eyes the extreme differences that were often assumed to exist between older-style scholars such as Lin Shu and his later rivals, including Zheng Zhenduo 鄭振鐸 (1898–1958), Mao Dun (1896–1981), and Lu Xun 魯迅 (1881–1936).[8]

But this conclusion is partial at best, and, for me, unsatisfying. When we move beyond judgments about the accuracy of assertions made by the "new camp" and the various "old camps" in the 1910s and 1920s and focus instead on the common threads in their arguments, we see how some of the broader trends in modern Chinese literature might relate to problems of comparative literature and world literature. Examining "untranslatability"—which these writers and critics faced regularly in their work—does not necessarily lead us away from the easy simplifications of niche-marketed cultural identities (and all of the connections to a neoliberal economic order) that Apter finds in contemporary discussions of world literature. The tendencies within the practice of "world literature" in China between 1870 and 1950 suggest that many of the same strategies were present. The persistence of identity marketing and targeted modes of representing difference in Chinese literature might also point to larger trends in global culture that are beyond language and literature itself.

Rather than focus on the commonplace assumption that the translator should know the foreign language from which he or she translates, I want to turn instead to assumptions that are embedded in the practice of literary criticism in North America and elsewhere. Erich Auerbach, a founding figure in the field of comparative literature, saw the limitations of world literature as one and the same as the limits of the individual scholar, who faces a vast, multilingual archive that is "virtually impossible" for an individual to master.[9] Nonetheless, Auerbach believed that the most important understandings of world literature must come from the individual: "The historical synthesis of which I am speaking, although it has significance only when it is based on a scholarly penetration of the material, is a product of personal intuition and hence can only be expected from an individual."[10] Auerbach stuck to this principle, pointing to the limitations of his own vision in his magisterial study *Mimesis*: "We must, unfortunately, forego discussing the rise of modern Russian realism . . . even in the most general way; for our purpose, this is impossible when one cannot read the works in their original language."[11]

Scholars of literature usually heed Auerbach's advice. Few reliable statements about a literary work can be made, it seems, without direct reference to "the original." But in this offhand comment, we might ask, what is *our purpose*? And what are the cases in which the purpose at hand makes reading in translation, and *translating in translation*, justifiable on an aesthetic and ethical level? To answer these questions, we must look through and beyond the modern "regime of translation" described by Naoki Sakai, in which "translation *articulates* languages so that we may postulate the two unities of the translating and translated languages as if they were autonomous and closed entities through *a certain representation of translation*."[12] This representation of translation shapes our commonsense assumption that translators must know the language of the source text intimately in order to do justice to the source text, the author, and readers of the translated text. (Auerbach, too, argues that critics need the same level of knowledge even to interpret a text.) Broadly speaking, all of the examples I discuss below test this regime of translation and seek to find ways either through or around it. They also show how translation—however defined—always undermines the propositions that lie behind it: translation constantly happens where it supposedly cannot or should not. In these moments of improbable or ostensibly impossible translation, we find useful insights into the history of modern Chinese literature and culture.

The first of these insights concerns the institutional history of translation and the end of the Qing dynasty. The particular circumstances of language education in the final years of the Qing state—a state that was by no means monolingual, and whose languages, such as classical Chinese, Manchu, Mongolian, and Tibetan, spanned a vast territory—always loomed over discussions of translation and, more broadly, the standards by which to train and judge educated professionals. Indeed, if we apply Sakai's notion of the modern regime of translation to the particular history of the Qing state, we see that the regime of translation must deny the Qing any status as a modern state. As Wang Hui has pointed out, the multipolar, multilingual "universal empire" did not perform the linkage between a single national language and the unitary, sovereign power of the modern nation-state as it was defined in Western Europe and elsewhere in the nineteenth century.[13] The ability to translate from one national language into another, then, was bound up with the larger problems of China's status as a modern state and culture. Although ample attention has been devoted to the problem of the national language and its role in translation, this essay looks for how ideas about sources and source languages connect to the construction of modern Chinese literature and the languages in which it is written.

Second, we also see the translators' ideas about what was transmitted through these irregular translations. Although translation is often seen as a secondary or derivative activity, these arguments about what comes across in translation are nonetheless arguments about the essential functions of literature and literary writing. In particular, they show connections to the history of language reform. Of course, it would be a commonsense observation to say that ideas about translation are closely linked to more general problems of language and representation, but in the early decades of the twentieth century, debates over the future of the written Chinese language itself were particularly prominent, so elucidating these connections between translation and language reform is of particular value for tracing the role of translation in the formation of self-consciously or avowedly modern literature in China.

FOOTSTEPS FROM AFAR: LIN SHU AND TANDEM TRANSLATION

Of all the late Qing translators, Lin Shu was the most famous and prolific practitioner of tandem translation. Although Lin occasionally expressed reservations about his ignorance of a foreign language, he believed that he could nonetheless perceive the most important traits of the works he translated with his collaborators. His preface to *The Biography of Nell, a Filial Girl* (孝女耐兒傳), a translation of Dickens's *The Old Curiosity Shop*, which he prepared with his collaborator Wei Yi 魏易, reveals much about his understanding of the process and his beliefs in his own ability as critic and interpreter:

> I do not understand Western languages. When I venture to work in the area of translation, I depend on two or three gentlemen who convey the meaning of a text to me orally. My ears hear it, and my hand keeps pace. When they fall silent and my hand stops, [we find that] after working for four hours, we have translated 6,000 words. Flaws and mistakes are to be found throughout, yet I am fortunate that famous men of learning in our country accepted them in spite of their crudeness; this is my great fortune. Once, I tried sitting silently in a room; after a month, I could easily tell the footsteps of my family from those of people outside, even though I had not laid eyes on them once. Nowadays a few gentlemen who share my goals occasionally show me the writings of Western scholars. Although I do not understand Western languages, as I hear them translate aloud to me each day, I can also distinguish their different schools of writing—like telling apart footsteps of people in my family. They can be lofty, clear and modest, graceful and calm, imposing and strong, grieved and distressed, or lascivious and rude; the most important aspects all lie in their rightness of sentiment and rectitude in judging good and evil. These are universal principles (*gongli* 公理) for all times; nothing Chinese or foreign can exceed it.[14]

This rich description, which we might see as more of a semifictional account of Lin's work as a translator, echoes "The Xiangji Studio" (項脊軒志), an essay by the Ming dynasty writer Gui Youguang 歸有光 (1506–1571), and places Lin Shu and his collaborators in an idealized scene where men of letters (*wenren* 文人) work in a leisurely, disinterested fashion quite different from the quick pace at which Lin produced his translations.[15]

Lin's preface also makes two important arguments about the work of translation. The first concerns what the work of translation can bring across languages: despite the language barrier, when great literary works meet sensitive readers, they activate within these readers a sense of the "universal principles" (*gongli*) of literary writing and the shared moral and ethical values behind them. These "universal principles" of literature—a phrase rich with resonances that relate to the translation of law and the social sciences in late Qing China—make, in this case, English literature and Chinese literature comparable with one another.[16]

Beyond this, Lin Shu also makes an argument about the translator, suggesting that when the right measures are put into practice by the gentlemen he works with, the "rightness" and "rectitude" of a literary work that is expressed in a foreign language remain translatable even to those who do not have access to that language. Because translation is tied metaphorically to the sensory experience of listening to what one cannot see, the hermeneutic of apprehending these principles lies, like the universal principles themselves, on another level beyond reading the words on the page. This double abstraction places the translator in the position of the ideal reader who is able to guide the reading of others in their encounter with the foreign text. By displacing the value of the technical knowledge of a foreign language, Lin Shu asserts a modified and narrowed version of what Joseph Levenson called the "amateur ideal," which revered "the educated gentleman, prepared for the world of affairs and his place in the governing class by a course of humane letters, with nothing crudely purposive about it."[17] Unlike the amateur ideal described by Levenson, however, Lin Shu does not reject technical learning but retains a certain authority over such learning that is, ultimately, aesthetic and moral. (In the case of a reformist writer like Dickens, in whose work Lin Shu so clearly heard the footsteps of universal principle, the translator gains the authority to make literature that intervenes in politics.) Such authority does not seem limited to Lin Shu himself: there is no reason that one of his collaborators who knows the foreign language would be incapable of discerning footsteps in the same way, as long as they exercised the same aesthetic and moral judgment wielded by Lin Shu. In this case, then, perceptive readers with the ability to discern these universal principles become arbiters of their true meaning, giving the translator (or the person whose work passes for translation) an unusually large voice in debates about literature in both the foreign language and the host language.

BEYOND THE "PITIFUL HORIZON": MAY FOURTH WRITERS AND RELAY TRANSLATION

As in many other areas of intellectual activity, the intellectuals associated with the New Culture and May Fourth movements of the 1910s and 1920s drew sharp lines to distinguish their translations from the works of their predecessors. Lin Shu and Yan Fu 嚴復 (1854–1921) in particular served as targets of their attacks, whether, as in Lin's case, for their ignorance of foreign languages or, as in Yan Fu's case, for their use of classical Chinese as the primary language of their translations. Lin Shu was also singled out for his prolific publishing record as a leading author for the Commercial Press (Shangwu Yinshuguan 商務印書館) in Shanghai.[18] Nonetheless, the intellectuals who decried the commercialism and traditionalism of Lin Shu's cultural enterprise found themselves stuck on one point: even as they championed the literatures of oppressed peoples around the globe, they also relied uncomfortably on intermediaries to produce translations. Rather than huddle with their linguistic informants in the same room, however, they usually relied on translations produced in English or Japanese to make a new Chinese translation.

In light of earlier practices, this particular use of intermediary languages changed and, perhaps, raised the stakes of translation. The use of English, Japanese, and German to access literary works that were not written in those languages functioned as a creative mode of resistance against these high-prestige languages, all of which served as markers of a cosmopolitan education and, particularly for English, a sign of a bourgeois family background. In his study on Russian literature in China, Mark Gamsa has noted that many important figures from the May Fourth period avoided English-language literature because of its association with Lin Shu and commercialized entertainment literature. In particular, he argues that Lu Xun's "refusal to deal with English and American literature was complete" and opted instead to "put his German and Japanese mainly in the service of translating the works of Russian authors."[19] Stepping outside the frame of translation studies, we might also see that this practice is implicitly linked to the deep enthusiasm for interlanguages like Esperanto among New Culture and May Fourth intellectuals.[20] The dream of communicating through and making art with a neutral interlanguage that would not be subject to the political or historical tensions between states and nations was destined to be overwhelmed by precisely the power dynamics between languages that Esperanto sought to escape. Relay translation, then, offered another, quietly audacious solution: using a language *not* to study the literature of that language but to *go around* the cultures and power relations it represents.

The widespread use of relay translation, which overlapped with disavowals of the previous generation's ways of translating, required a conceptual justification—or a theory of literature and translation—to support its continued development. Beyond the usual acknowledgments that relay translation was not an "ideal" method, key figures in the production of modern Chinese literature regularly appealed to an essence that was beyond language—a combination of human experience and the "essence" of a people (*minzu* 民族) that, like the "rightness" and "rectitude" that Lin Shu found in the best works he translated, would not be lost in translation.

As Mao Dun took over the editorship of *Short Story Monthly* (小説月報) in 1921, the translations in the magazine, like the short stories it published, took a decidedly different direction, disavowing so-called Mandarin Ducks and Butterfly fiction in favor of works that adhered to the standards of literature set forth by May Fourth intellectuals.[21] During this transition, the young critic Zheng Zhenduo worked to establish new standards for translation in the magazine and, by dint of the magazine's status in the publishing world, for the whole literary field. His long essay "Three Problems in the Translation of Literature" (譯文學書的三個問題) addresses translation as practice and the institutional issues related to relay translation.[22] Faced with the task of finding new models for literary writing, Zheng complained about the lack of resources at hand:

> At the present time, when literary tastes are so weak and when the voices of people on the literary scene are so quiet, how can we find people with the skills to translate directly from original languages? If we wait for them to appear before we take up translating, then we must ask: "How long must a man live until he sees the Yellow River run clear?" In these times, if we do not want to sever relations with the literature of the entire world, then we can only say that "a little comfort is better than nothing" and use this incomplete and dangerous means to translate.[23]

At stake for Zheng is the chance to have access to the literature of *the whole world*; the price of admission, however, is to take all of the chances that come along with indirect translations. The only other option is endless isolation and belatedness. Zheng's version of a universal value for literature stands in clear contrast to Lin Shu's: unlike Lin Shu, who believed he heard the echoes of "universal principles" rooted in ethics and aesthetics, Zheng asserts a universal value in terms of space and geography. To some extent, Zheng's argument exposes the limitations to Lin Shu's own ideas of the "universal," which were rooted in the "Western Learning" (*xixue* 西學) of the late Qing; for Lin, the possibility of a literary work conforming to "universal principles" is almost always circumscribed by its origin either in China or the metropolitan West.

Beyond this question of the techniques and practices needed to engage with "the literature of the whole world," Zheng's essay also offers a theory of what is essential in a work of literature. As he composed "Three Problems in the Translation of Literature," Zheng leaned heavily on *Elements of Style: An Introduction to Literary Criticism* (1915), a book by the now-forgotten American scholar David Watson Rannie. Many of the formulations in Zheng's essay come directly from Rannie or appear with only minor changes.[24] Throughout the book, Rannie asserted that literary expression is *not* bound by language—ideas or "thought" always lie behind it and are most important. Following this argument closely in his essay, Zheng almost completely sets aside the question of formal expression: it is "thought" that holds paramount importance, especially in translation. Zheng uses the following passage to great effect. In my translation below, the first sentence from Zheng's essay quotes directly from Rannie, while the second, underlined sentence is Zheng's addition to the argument:

> Style is only another word for *expression*, and that expression in literature means *the translation of thought into language*. . . . Thought is shared among humans, and can be transferred from one type of written language into another.[25]

For Rannie, however, the status of "thought" and meaning are far more important than what transmits them. Rannie argued that it was possible to "waive consideration of the ultimate problem of thought and expression, and assume (what is at all events practically certain) that a great deal of expression is optional and therefore separable from meaning."[26] This assumption, in turn, would license translation, because, according to this line of thought, "There is no reason why meaning should not be expressed in more languages than one."[27]

Rannie's argument about the separability of meaning and expression proved to be very important for Zheng's own assessment of the possibility of how literature is transmitted. Departing from straight translation (or cribbing) from Rannie, Zheng makes the following leap in his argument:

> In *Elements of Style*, Rannie shows that "a great deal of *expression* is optional and therefore separable from thought." For example, then, if thought is like water, then "expression" is a means for carrying that water. Regardless of how the form or shape of the vehicle might change, the fundamental characteristics and quantity of the water will never be reduced.[28]

The theory Zheng developed through Rannie can at least console his colleagues and his readers about the lack of adequately trained translators: if thought/*sixiang* (思想) is separable from the text and capable of being used in "multiple expressions," or if thought/*sixiang* is like water that can be transferred through multiple vessels, then relay translation can in fact deliver the badly desired access to the most important aspects of literatures that are not written in the languages most commonly studied by elite Chinese intellectuals and professionals, that is, English, German, or Japanese. In other words, it is only by the *reduction* of literary writing to an instrument for carrying knowledge that it becomes possible for translation to serve as a tool for reforming literature and pursuing social change.

The "whole world" that Zheng beckons toward is not bound to the languages of the world but to the techniques that make them transferrable or fungible. The literature of the world can only be accessed by a faith that the relay language is neutral enough to transfer ideas and expression without fundamentally altering them. This theory sidesteps the modern regime of translation described by Sakai by appealing to a higher category—thought—that exists on a plane that is beyond the regulation of national character or national essence that otherwise takes place in a single language. If thought is separable from language and linguistic expression, then the performance of the work of translation no longer requires a translator who knows the foreign language of the source text. Zheng's translatability assumption also displays far greater certainty than Lin Shu's method: whereas Lin Shu admits to making many errors in his work and stresses the indirect ways in which he senses the "rightness of sentiment" and "rectitude of judgment" found in the works he translated, Zheng suggests that the repeated transfer of thought through language is possible without serious alterations.

Mao Dun's role in debates around translation is of particular importance, not only for his initial contributions as an editor and translator but also for his work to form the canon of modern Chinese literature and culture when he served as the first Minister of Culture for the People's Republic of China from 1949 to 1965. In the editor's introduction to the 1921 special issue of *Short Story Monthly* that focused on oppressed peoples

(被損害民族)—a group that included the peoples of Poland, Ireland, the African diaspora, and Zionist Jews in Palestine—Mao Dun argued that the value of literary works by these writers lay in the way they carried a certain kind of historical experience:[29]

> The cries of oppressed peoples for justice and fairness are indeed truly just and fair. The humanity (*renxing* 人性) that is left over when it has been drawn through the wringer is a truly precious humanity, a humanity that bears no resemblance to the oppressor. . . . We are even more certain that flecks of gold can be found in the sand of humanity; even more certain that light shines behind the darkness in the road ahead.[30]

The far-flung origins of these works and the particular language skills of their translators—who included Zhou Zuoren 周作人, who read Japanese and English, and Mao Dun himself, who read English—made it clear that the stories featured here had to be the products of retranslation. Mao Dun's outlook on translation and the role and of language provided a straightforward justification to this practice: "Language and writing are mere tools; the essence of a nation's literature is not in fact found here" (語言文字不過是一種工具而已, 民族的文學之特質, 實不在此).[31]

As with Zheng Zhenduo, the instrumentalization of language serves as an overriding justification for retranslation: it is not the language of literary writing that matters, for that is a mere tool, but the inner expression and essence (*tezhi* 特質) that resides elsewhere, outside or beyond language. By pushing away completely from philological knowledge, Mao Dun's theory of translation estranges itself both from the philological tradition that had persisted into the late Qing and beyond and from the kind of attention to language and close reading mentioned earlier in the work of Mao Dun's contemporary, Eric Auerbach.[32] (Indeed, the argument that language is nothing but a tool would be used by later language reformers who believed that the Chinese script could be abolished altogether in favor of another tool.[33]) By refusing to acknowledge significant differences between works of literature written in different languages and engaging in none of the usual handwringing about what is lost in translation—a gesture that even Zheng Zhenduo felt he had to make—Mao Dun also attributes extraordinary power to translations and their readers. Mao Dun argues that, like panning for gold, readers surely will encounter *in any text* those words, images, and pieces of narrative that mean little to them; only when those pieces of the "essence" of a writer or the people he or she represents come into focus will the audience see the value of a translated literary work.

CONCLUSION

Lu Xun had himself practiced retranslation in his very first collection of translations he produced with his brother, Zhou Zuoren, and later by translating Russian fiction and theoretical writings through Japanese, including works by authors such as Alexander

Fadeyev (1901–1956) and Anatoly Lunacharsky (1897–1933). In his recent study of Lu Xun's technique of "hard translation" (*ying yi* 硬譯), a technique of translating from Japanese that closely followed the syntax and (where possible) the vocabulary of the Japanese original, Wang Pu has argued that the "dense and clumsy sentences, present everywhere in Lu Xun's texts of 'hard translation,'" confronted both reader and translator with instances of defamiliarization that open a space for the translator's agency and leave traces of the translator's agency in the translated text.[34] Speaking more broadly of the possibilities for translation in the 1930s, Lu Xun vigorously defended the practice of retranslation:

> The foreign languages most widely known by Chinese people are probably English, and then Japanese. Without retranslation then we would only see a lot of literature from England, America, and Japan. Not only would we miss [Henrik] Ibsen and [Vicente Blasco] Ibáñez, we would also have no way to read even very well-known works such as [Hans Christian] Anderson's tales or Cervantes's *Don Quixote*. What sort of pitiful horizon is this? Naturally, China does not necessarily have people fluent in Danish, Norwegian, or Spanish, and no one up until now has translated from those languages—they are all from English. Even Soviet works are largely retranslated from English and French.[35]

Lu Xun's short catalog of world literary works from Spanish, Norwegian, and Swedish shows the senselessness of *not* engaging in relay translation at this moment in history. Of course, there is always the possibility that institutional supports will develop for directly working with these languages; in evoking this possibility, however, he did so (as almost always) with a dose of healthy skepticism. In this sense, Lu Xun endorsed a practice of making works of literature that anticipated or beckoned to other practices that would bring about its own disappearance. The best example of this mode of writing can be found in works on language reform such as "The Vernacular is the Root of Reform" (論白話為維新之本) by Qiu Tingliang 裘廷梁 or "Some Modest Proposals for the Reform of Literature" (文學改良芻議) by Hu Shi 胡適, both of which used literary Chinese or *wenyan* (文言) to call for the demise of literary Chinese and the social structures that had grown up around it.[36] For Lu Xun, as well as Zheng Zhenduo and Mao Dun, the use of English or Japanese as an intermediary by which to understand Russian literature and the works of weak and wounded peoples—seen as redemptive, exemplary, even revolutionary—follows a similar process of anticipating its own disappearance.

To return to the question of translation, I see productive difficulties in reconciling the translation practices of this long line of Chinese translators with the ethics that have come to be so important in North American scholarship on translation. Walter Benjamin's "The Translator's Task," one of the most widely cited works in Anglophone scholarship on translation, appears on the surface to argue against virtually every stated justification for tandem translation or relay translation described above. The interest in oppressed peoples—and the search for the "essence" of peoples that (according to

Mao Dun) lie in a literary work—runs directly counter to Benjamin's approach to the problem of "content" in literary translation. Benjamin argued:

> What does a poetic work 'say,' then? Very little, to a person who understands it. Neither message nor information is essential to it. However, a translation that aims to transmit something can transmit nothing other than a message—that is something inessential. And this is also the hallmark of bad translations.[37]

Benjamin also argued later in the essay that "one can extract from a translation as much communicable content as one wishes, and this much can be translated; but the element toward which the genuine translator's efforts are directed remains out of reach."[38] When we contrast Benjamin's comments with the agenda put forward by Lin Shu, Zheng Zhenduo, and Mao Dun, it seems that all three might fall into Benjamin's category of misguided translators, because all three were interested in "extracting . . . communicable content" that related to the specific texts they translated. Likewise, Benjamin's insistence on the minimal importance of whether a work of literature "will find, among the totality of its readers, an adequate translator" radically downplays the importance of how institutions of literature operate:[39] in particular, how literature circulates and how "an adequate translator" might acquire knowledge of the language of the original in the first place.

Rather than pronounce these views on translation to be irreconcilable or incommensurable, however, we might try using these practices of translation from this particular period in Chinese history to read "The Translator's Task" against itself. We can do this by turning to the most famous concept in the essay, "pure language" (*die reine Sprache*), and Benjamin's suggestion that some of the most important work of both translators and their translations is to "express the most intimate relationships among languages."[40] What if that "most intimate relationship" can only be found in languages' separation from one another? To use Lu Xun's examples, if we consider Norwegian and Chinese, the number of speakers who could operate between those languages in the 1930s (or perhaps even now?) was close to zero. Although "The Translator's Task" questions the work of those who are interested in moving mere "content" between French and German (the languages in which Benjamin was working when he wrote the essay), we have to ask what other options were available to Mao Dun and Zheng Zhenduo, other than to focus on the "communicable content" that can be transmitted by the "tool" of language. Returning to the arguments of Lin Shu and Mao Dun, it appears that "universal principles" (for Lin) or "essence" (for Mao Dun) serves as a supplement to "pure language," one that acknowledges far more explicitly than Benjamin's essay the historicity of literary texts, their translators, and the process of translation. Large-scale translation projects that are undertaken by people who are aware that the knowledge that Benjamin calls "essential" (that which is "neither message nor information") *will never be available on those terms* might be seen as a utopian attempt to overcome the historical divides between languages that are reinforced by a strict insistence that only a knowledge of the source language will enable a person to understand a literary work.

The "translatability assumptions" of both Lin Shu and Mao Dun also go beyond the model of extraction and informational communication in important ways. Lin Shu listens for footsteps beyond his door; Zheng Zhenduo ladles water; and Mao Dun insists that the "essence of a people's literature" is not found in language, but elsewhere. The "universal principles" that Lin Shu heard in those footsteps, or the "essence" that Mao Dun found in the literatures of oppressed peoples, were projections made by the translators themselves; those projections offered a way to glimpse beyond what Sakai calls the modern regime of translation. As Sakai notes, "The particular representation of translation in which translation is understood to be communication between two particular languages is, no doubt, a historical construct."[41] So, too, is the representation of the position of the translator as a person who must be able to negotiate one kind of difference in a text—the difference between languages—in order to be able to make other aspects of the text (e.g., its ideas, descriptions, etc.) comprehensible to the reader. The extent to which Lin Shu and Mao Dun acknowledged that notions like "universal principle" or "essence" were projections is less important than how these projections gave these thinkers a path around the modern regime of translation. In all cases, whether in Lin Shu's assertion of universal principle, in Zheng Zhenduo's arguments about the effortless transmissibility of meaning, or in Mao Dun's delinking of language and essence, we see these translators resist a key aspect of the modern regime of translation described by Sakai: that is, each translator denies that knowledge of the foreign language in question (and the literary works made in that language) carries an ineluctable relation to a single nation, people, or culture. This move authorizes the translator's own projection of new meaning onto the works and opens the translated works themselves to embracing and containing new meaning beyond accuracy or fidelity to the original.

It is here, however, that the two generations of translators part ways. Although Lin Shu often lamented the situation of Chinese letters and learning, he would never find it as weak as Zheng Zhenduo, who thought the entire literary scene was "nothing but a few bald peaks and high cliffs, with twisted pines dotting the barren landscape."[42] Indeed, Lin saw certain translated works, such as the writings of Washington Irving, as material to build new supports for his own literary traditionalism. Indeed, through his praise of Irving, Lin argued that traditionalist literary style—including the use of classical Chinese prose—was not only compatible with modern literature but fundamental to such a literary outlook.[43] For both Zheng Zhenduo and Mao Dun, this technique is a way of filling what they believed was a very real void in the literature of China and to engage with "the whole world." The disavowal of the importance of language makes it possible for these translators to present "the world" to readers. If, as David Damrosch argues, "world literature" is primarily a mode of reading, then this particular disavowal of the importance of the specificities of language makes it possible for these translators to present "the world" to readers and to forge their own new practice of world literature. In particular, Mao Dun's lack of anxiety over not knowing the foreign languages from which he translated relied on a sense of the neutrality of the interlingual transaction that makes the "essence" of another literature that much more visible.

The varying responses to the problem of access—of knowing and not-knowing—offered by Lin Shu, Zheng Zhenduo, Mao Dun, and Lu Xun all lead me to suggest that we have in this period a practice of understanding "world literature" that remains unaccounted for in the history of world literature itself. As I suggested at the beginning of this essay, the correspondences between Lin Shu and Luṭfī al-Manfalūṭī, two widely influential men of letters who never met, knew nothing of the other's language, and who cannot be connected through the usual epistemological frameworks of "contact" and "translation" that are so important in contemporary practices of comparative literature, might also provide us with another way of drawing modern Chinese literature together with other histories of literature and culture in the nineteenth and twentieth centuries. For now, my attempt to set them beside one another is my own act of scholarly "retranslation"—a gesture beyond the horizon of our accepted ways of understanding literature.

NOTES

1. Abdelfattah Kilito, *Thou Shalt Not Speak My Language*, trans. Waïl S. Hassan (Syracuse: Syracuse University Press, 2008), 91–92.
2. See Paul Starkey, "Muṣṭafā Luṭfī al-Manfalūṭī," in *Essays in Arabic Literary Biography, 1850–1950*, ed. Roger Allen (Wiesbaden: Harrasowitz, 2010), 200–207.
3. Kilito, *Thou Shalt Not Speak My Language*, 4–5. See also Shaden Tageldin, *Disarming Words: Empire and the Seductions of Translation in Egypt* (Berkeley: University of California Press, 2011), 1–2.
4. For treatments of Lin Shu's career, see my *Lin Shu, Inc.: Translation and the Making of Modern Chinese Culture* (New York: Oxford University Press, 2013), and Hu Ying, "The Translator Transfigured: Lin Shu and the Cultural Logic of the Late Qing," *positions: east asia cultures critique* 3.1 (Spring 1995): 69–96.
5. Emily Apter, *Against World Literature: On the Politics of Untranslatability* (London: Verso, 2013), 2–3.
6. See Nicolai Volland, "Translating the Socialist State: Cultural Exchange, National Identity, and the Socialist World in the Early PRC," *Twentieth Century China* 33.2 (April 2008): 51–72.
7. See, for example, Wang Yougui 王有貴, "Zhongguo fanyi chuantong: Cong zhuanyi dao cong yuanwen fanyi (1949–1999)" 中國翻譯傳統研究: 從轉譯到從原文譯 (1949–1999) [China's tradition of translation: From retranslation to translation from source texts, 1949–1999], *Zhongguo fanyi* 中國翻譯 [Translation in China] 1 (2008): 27–32.
8. See my brief discussion in *Lin Shu, Inc.*, 233–235. For similar observations on Zhou Zuoren, see Michel Hockx, *Questions of Style: Literary Societies and Literary Journals in Modern China, 1911–1937* (Leiden: Brill, 2003), 181–183.
9. Erich Auerbach, "Philology and *Weltliteratur*," trans. M. and E. W. Said, in *The Princeton Sourcebook on Comparative Literature*, ed. David Damrosch et al. (Princeton: Princeton University Press, 2009), 125–138.
10. Erich Auerbach, "Philology and *Weltliteratur*," 133.
11. Erich Auerbach, *Mimesis: The Representation of Reality in Western Literature*, trans. Willard R. Trask (Princeton: Princeton University Press, 1953), 492. For this quotation

and discussions of the archive of literary history, I am indebted to Jonathan Zwicker, *Practices of the Sentimental Imagination: Melodrama, the Novel, and the Social Imaginary in Nineteenth-Century Japan* (Cambridge: Harvard University Asia Center, 2006), 1–12.

12. Naoki Sakai, *Translation and Subjectivity: On "Japan" and Cultural Nationalism* (Minneapolis: University of Minnesota Press, 1997), 2.

13. See Wang Hui, *China from Empire to Nation-State*, trans. Michael Gibbs Hill (Cambridge: Harvard University Press, 2014), 38–53.

14. Lin Shu 林紓, "Xu" [序], in Lin Shu, trans. *Xiaonü Nai'er zhuan* 孝女耐兒傳 [The biography of Nell, a filial girl] (Shanghai: Shangwu yinshuguan, 1908), 1.

15. See Hill, *Lin Shu, Inc.*, 95–96.

16. Hill, *Lin Shu, Inc.*, 68–72.

17. Joseph Levenson, *Confucian China and Its Modern Fate: A Trilogy* (Berkeley: University of California Press, 1968), 16–19.

18. See Hill, *Lin Shu, Inc.*, 203–217.

19. Mark Gamsa, *The Reading of Russian Literature in China: A Moral Example and Manual of Practice* (New York: Palgrave Macmillan, 2010), 14–15.

20. For one illuminating discussion of this phenomenon, see Gregor Benton, *Chinese Migrants and Internationalism: Forgotten Histories, 1917–1945* (London: Routledge, 2007), 92–114.

21. For a discussion of this larger dynamic in Commercial Press journals, which included *The Eastern Miscellany* (東方雜誌), see Theodore Huters, "Culture, Capital, and the Temptations of the Imagined Market: The Case of the Commercial Press," in *Beyond the May Fourth Paradigm: In Search of Chinese Modernity*, ed. Kai-wing Chow et al. (Lanham, MD: Lexington Books, 2008), 27–50.

22. Uganda Sze-pui Kwan argues that Zheng's essay was the first systematic discussion of translation in the Republican period. See Kwan, "Xiandaixing yu jiyi—Wusi dui Lin Shu wenxue fanyi de zhuiyi yu yiwang" 現代性與記憶——五四對林紓文學翻譯的追憶與遺忘 [Modernity and memory—how May Fourth writers remembered and forgot Lin Shu's literary translation], *Xiandai Zhongguo* 現代中國 [Modern China] 11 (September 2008): 103–106.

23. Zheng Zhenduo, "Yi wenxue shude sange wenti" 譯文學書的三個問題 [Three problems in literary translation] *Xiaoshuo yuebao* 小說月報 [Short story monthly] 12.3 (March 1921): 24.

24. Here it should be noted that, as with several other works of criticism from this period in his career, Zheng translated directly from other critics' work; although he does acknowledge these sources, he does not tell the reader that he is borrowing extensively from these critics and presenting their words as his own. Jing Tsu has shown how Zheng borrowed heavily from early twentieth-century critics such as Richard Green Moulton and John Drinkwater; much of the information in Zheng's *Outline of Literature* (文學大綱) was cribbed from a book by Drinkwater of the same title. See Tsu, "Getting Ideas About World Literature in China," *Comparative Literature Studies* 47.3 (2010): 305–314.

25. Zheng Zhenduo, "Three Problems of Translation," 2. See also David Watson Rannie, *The Elements of Style: An Introduction to Literary Criticism* (London and Toronto: J. M. Dent, 1915), 2.

26. Rannie, *The Elements of Style*, 31.

27. Rannie, *The Elements of Style*, 31.

28. Zheng Zhenduo, "Three Problems of Translation," 5.

29. For a thorough background discussion of these translations, see Irene Eber, *Voices from Afar: Modern Chinese Writers on Oppressed Peoples and their Literature* (Ann Arbor: University of Michigan Center for Chinese Studies, 1980), 1–62.

30. Mao Dun 茅盾, "Yinyan" 引言 [Introduction], *Xiaoshuo yuebao* 12.10 (October 1921): 2–3.

31. Mao Dun, "Introduction," 7.

32. Meng Yue argues, for example, that *bianyi* (編譯; "translation and compilation") practiced in Shanghai in the late Qing drew heavily from the philological practices of Jiangnan elites. See *Shanghai and the Edges of Empires* (Minneapolis: University of Minnesota Press, 2006), 33–42.

33. One reformer argued: "Writing is a kind of tool. If the tool is not suited to the times, then it is completely acceptable to set it aside and create a new one. Hanzi [漢字; Chinese characters] were shown long ago to be old pieces of trash completely unsuited [to the times], and we should get rid of them and make them into a thing of the past." See Michael Gibbs Hill, "New Script and a New 'Madman's Diary'," *Modern Chinese Literature and Culture* 27.1 (Spring 2015): 83–84.

34. Pu Wang. "The Promethean Translator and Cannibalistic Pains: Lu Xun's 'Hard Translation' as a Political Allegory," *Translation Studies* 6.3 (2013): 328–329.

35. Lu Xun 魯迅, "Lun chongyi" 論重譯, in *Lu Xun quanji* 魯迅全集 [Complete works of Lu Xun] (Beijing: Renmin wenxue chubanshe, 1995), 5: 505.

36. Qiu Tingliang 裘廷梁, "Lun baihua wei weixin zhi ben" 論白話為維新之本 [Vernacular writing is the root of reform], in *Jindai wenlun xuan* 近代文論選 [Selected essays from the early modern period], ed. Shu Wu 舒蕪 et al. (Beijing: Renmin wenxue chubanshe, 1999), 176–180. For a discussion of this anticipatory rhetoric, see Hill, "New Script," 77–81.

37. Walter Benjamin, "The Translator's Task," trans. Steven Rendall, in *The Translation Studies Reader*, ed. Lawrence Venuti, 3rd ed. (New York: Routledge, 2012), 75.

38. Benjamin, "The Translator's Task," 79.

39. Benjamin, "The Translator's Task," 76.

40. Benjamin, "The Translator's Task," 77.

41. Sakai, *Translation and Subjectivity*, 15.

42. Zheng Zhenduo, "Three Problems of Translation," 22.

43. For a discussion of Lin Shu and Washington Irving, see Hill, *Lin Shu, Inc.*, 126–155.

WORKS CITED

Apter, Emily. *Against World Literature: On the Politics of Untranslatability*. London: Verso, 2013.

Auerbach, Erich. *Mimesis: The Representation of Reality in Western Literature*. Trans. Willard R. Trask. Princeton: Princeton University Press, 1953.

Auerbach, Erich. "Philology and Weltliteratur." Trans. M. and E. W. Said. In *The Princeton Sourcebook on Comparative Literature*. Ed. David Damrosch et al. Princeton: Princeton University Press, 2009. 125–138.

Benjamin, Walter. "The Translator's Task." Trans. Steven Rendall. In *The Translation Studies Reader*. Ed. Lawrence Venuti. 3rd. ed. New York: Routledge, 2012. 75–83.

Benton, Gregor. *Chinese Migrants and Internationalism: Forgotten Histories, 1917–1945*. London: Routledge, 2007.

Eber, Irene. *Voices from Afar: Modern Chinese Writers on Oppressed Peoples and their Literature*. Ann Arbor: University of Michigan Center for Chinese Studies, 1980.

Gamsa, Mark. *The Reading of Russian Literature in China: A Moral Example and Manual of Practice*. New York: Palgrave Macmillan, 2010.

Hill, Michael Gibbs. *Lin Shu, Inc.: Translation and the Making of Modern Chinese Culture*. New York: Oxford University Press, 2013.

Hill, Michael Gibbs. "New Script and a New 'Madman's Diary.'" *Modern Chinese Literature and Culture* 27.1 (Spring 2015): 75–104.

Hockx, Michel. *Questions of Style: Literary Societies and Literary Journals in Modern China, 1911–1937*. Leiden: Brill, 2003.

Hu Ying. "The Translator Transfigured: Lin Shu and the Cultural Logic of the Late Qing." *positions: east asia cultures critique* 3.1 (Spring 1995): 69–96.

Huters, Theodore. "Culture, Capital, and the Temptations of the Imagined Market: The Case of the Commercial Press." In *Beyond the May Fourth Paradigm: In Search of Chinese Modernity*. Ed. Kai-wing Chow et al. Lanham, MD: Lexington Books, 2008. 27–50.

Kilito, Abdelfattah. *Thou Shalt Not Speak My Language*. Trans. Waïl S. Hassan. Syracuse: Syracuse University Press, 2008.

Kwan, Uganda Sze-pui 關詩珮. "Xiandaixing yu jiyi—Wusi dui Lin Shu wenxue fanyi de zhuiyi yu yiwang" 現代性與記憶——五四對林紓文學翻譯的追憶與遺忘 [Modernity and memory—how May Fourth writers remembered and forgot Lin Shu's literary translation]. *Xiandai Zhongguo* 現代中國 [Modern China] 11 (September 2008): 91–119.

Levenson, Joseph. *Confucian China and Its Modern Fate: A Trilogy*. Berkeley: University of California Press, 1968.

Lin Shu 林紓, trans. *Xiaonü Nai'er zhuan* [The biography of Nell, a filial girl]. Shanghai: Shangwu yinshuguan, 1908.

Lu Xun 魯迅. "Lun chongyi" 論重譯 [On relay translation] (1934). In *Lu Xun quanji* 魯迅全集 [Complete works of Lu Xun]. Beijing: Renmin wenxue chubanshe, 1995. 504–506.

Mao Dun 茅盾. "Yinyan" 引言 [Introduction]. *Xiaoshuo yuebao* 小說月報 [Short story monthly] 12.10 (October 1921): 1–7.

Meng, Yue. *Shanghai and the Edges of Empires*. Minneapolis: University Minnesota Press, 2006.

Qiu Tingliang 裘廷梁. "Lun baihua wei weixin zhi ben" 論白話為維新之本 [Vernacular writing is the root of reform]. In Shu Wu 舒蕪 et al., eds., *Jindai wenlun xuan* 近代文論選 [Selected essays from the early modern period]. Beijing: Renmin wenxue chubanshe, 1999. 176–180.

Rannie, David Watson. *The Elements of Style: An Introduction to Literary Criticism*. London and Toronto: J. M. Dent, 1915.

Sakai, Naoki. *Translation and Subjectivity: On "Japan" and Cultural Nationalism*. Minneapolis: University of Minnesota Press, 1997.

Starkey, Paul. "Muṣṭafā Luṭfī al-Manfalūṭī." *Essays in Arabic Literary Biography, 1850–1950*. Ed. Roger Allen. Wiesbaden: Harrasowitz, 2010. 200–207.

Tageldin, Shaden. *Disarming Words: Empire and the Seductions of Translation in Egypt*. Berkeley: University of California Press, 2011.

Tsu, Jing. "Getting Ideas About World Literature in China." *Comparative Literature Studies* 47.3 (2010): 305–314.

Volland, Nicolai. "Translating the Socialist State: Cultural Exchange, National Identity, and the Socialist World in the Early PRC." *Twentieth Century China* 33.2 (April 2008): 51–72.

Wang, Pu. "The Promethean Translator and Cannibalistic Pains: Lu Xun's 'Hard Translation' as a Political Allegory." *Translation Studies* 6.3 (2013): 324–338.

Wang Hui. *China from Empire to Nation-State*. Trans. Michael Gibbs Hill. Cambridge: Harvard University Press, 2014.

Wang Yougui 王有貴. "Zhongguo fanyi chuantong: Cong zhuanyi dao cong yuanwen fanyi (1949–1999) 中國翻譯傳統研究：從轉譯到從原文譯 (1949–1999) [China's tradition of translation: From retranslation to translation from source texts, 1949–1999]. *Zhongguo fanyi* 中國翻譯 [Translation in China] 1 (2008): 27–32.

Zheng Zhenduo. "Yi wenxue shude sange wenti" 譯文學書的三個問題 [Three problems in literary translation]." *Xiaoshuo yuebao* 小說月報 [Short story monthly] 12.3 (March 1921): 1–25.

Zwicker, Jonathan. *Practices of the Sentimental Imagination: Melodrama, the Novel, and the Social Imaginary in Nineteenth-Century Japan*. Cambridge: Harvard University Asia Center, 2006.

CHAPTER 1.8

....

VOICE AND THE QUEST FOR MODERNITY IN CHINESE LITERATURE

....

MEI CHIA-LING

In February of 1927, Lu Xun 魯迅 gave a talk at the Hong Kong Youth Association with the title "Voiceless China" (無聲的中國). Why and in what sense could China be described as "voiceless"? According to Lu Xun, the classical Chinese used in the past had become completely irrelevant in the present, and furthermore "it expressed anti-quated thoughts, and therefore its voice belonged entirely to the past and amounted to nothing." Instead, Lu Xun urged the nation's youth "to transform China into a nation with a voice, to speak with daring and to advance boldly," and "to speak with a modern voice, a voice of their own, and use a living speech to freely voice their own thoughts and feelings." For Lu Xun, there were only two possible roads after this: "to hold on to classical Chinese and die, or to do away with classical Chinese and live."[1]

The main objective of Lu Xun's talk was to emphasize processes of literary renewal, which is to say, "the abolition of classical Chinese and adoption of a modern Chinese vernacular." Upon further reflection, however, this assertion appears quite problematic. To begin with, the concepts of *voice* and *voicelessness* are being used figuratively here, to designate language's ability (or inability) to adequately express feelings and convey meaning. And yet, should we understand literary renewal as being only the renewal of *wen* (文), which is to say, of the written language? Whereas literary history usually views China's literary revolution as a transition from classical to modern vernacular Chinese, by focusing on a notion of "China *with* a voice" we may ask the following questions: Is the concept of voice, especially in the context of language, also in need of modernization? What kind of voice counts as modern? Has the question of voice really entered into the project of literary renewal, and if so, how? Given that Hong Kong's primary language at that time was Cantonese and Lu Xun was from Shaoxing, in which variant of Chinese did Lu Xun give voice to his thoughts when he spoke of China's voice during his speech in Hong Kong? Was he speaking in Cantonese, in his own Shaoxing dialect, or in the national language (*guoyu* 國語) promoted by the Nationalist government? What kind of dialogue did the movement for literary renewal and this national language policy maintain?

In the context of Chinese literature's pursuit of modernity, this issue of voice also invites us to reconsider several widely accepted beliefs, such as:

(1)   The myth of the opposition of classical Chinese and modern vernacular Chinese: Are classical Chinese and the modern vernacular really completely opposed to one another? How exactly does the modern vernacular define itself vis-à-vis traditional literary Chinese?

(2)   The myth of the competition between the national language and regional languages: Does a modern literature necessarily have to be written in the national language? Can regional languages also be used to write literature?

(3)   The myth of the unity of speech and writing: Can spoken language and written language really ever become one? Does the modern written vernacular really coincide with spoken language?

In what follows, I will take poetic discourses from the 1930s and the resulting problems of aesthetics and politics as my entry point into a consideration of the issues outlined above, and then will use the development of "New Poetry's new poetry," namely the development of the movement of "recited poetry" (朗誦詩), to analyze the agonic and dialectical relationship between voice and writing. Finally, by focusing on the notion of language education achieved by Zhu Ziqing 朱自清 and others, I will analyze their theories of voicing and their focus on recitation, and how these shaped the modern voice in the literary history of China by way of their forceful promotion in the context of national-language education.

Aesthetics and Politics in the Poetic Discourse of the 1930s: The Poetry Reading Society, the China Poetry Society, and the Poetry Recitation Movement

A key objective of the May Fourth New Culture Movement involved the replacement of traditional literary Chinese with a modern vernacular, though different genres developed in an uneven fashion. Many critics have pointed out that literary renewal was particularly fraught for the development of new poetry during the literary revolution. Zhu Guangqian 朱光潛, for instance, observed that although "old forms had been destroyed, new forms had yet to be established," while Zhu Ziqing specified that "a modern Chinese poetic tradition was still too impoverished, whereas the tradition of old poetry was too persistent; therefore, poetic language often followed old patterns and showed few innovations."[2] This caused New Poetry to stagnate from the very beginning of its development.[3] Consequently, a key issue for the development of the modern Chinese poetry movement involved using poetry recitation to help search for new forms and establish a new critical discourse.

However, even as writers and critics from a variety of different backgrounds emphasized recitation in order to help the fledgling New Poetry movement advance, they nevertheless differed with respect to their advocacy of methods of practicing poetry and the concepts for its study. Among these, the Poetry Reading Society established by Zhu Guangqian, Zhu Ziqing, and others, as well as the China Poetry Society that was later run by writers from the Creation Society and the Sun Society, represent two different directions. In particular, the Poetry Reading Society's recitation experiment was extremely important for the aesthetic pursuit of New Poetry; in contrast, the emphasis on the masses favored by the China Poetry Society can be seen as the harbinger of the poetry recitation movement's emphasis on politics and education.

Between 1932 and 1933, Zhu Ziqing and Zhu Guangqian returned from Europe to China and proceeded to recruit like-minded intellectuals to establish the Poetry Reading Society, which met regularly in Zhu Guangqian's house in Beijing to recite poetry. One of the society's most important members, Shen Congwen 沈從文, described its activities in his essay "On Reciting Poetry" (談朗誦詩):

> The Northern *Poetry Journal* (詩刊) had been closed for over ten years. ... But in Beiping a new group of poets and aficionados established another society for reading poetry. This group met at Zhu Guangqian's home in Beiping's Houmen district, and its participants included Liang Zongdai 梁宗岱, Feng Zhi 馮至, Sun Dayu 孫大雨, Luo Niansheng 羅念生, Zhou Zuoren 周作人, Ye Gongchao 葉公超, Fei Ming 廢名, Bian Zhilin 卞之琳, He Qifang 何其芳, Xu Fang 徐芳 from Beijing University, Zhu Ziqing, Yu Pingbo 俞平伯, Wang Liaoyi 王了一, Li Jianwu 李健吾, Lin Geng 林庚, Cao Baohua 曹葆華 from Qinghua University, as well as Miss Lin Huiyin 林徽因, Mister Zhou Xuliang 周煦良, among others. They participated in poetic discussions and recited, read, discussed, and hummed old poetry, New Poetry, as well as foreign poetry. Everybody excitedly discussed the following questions: What was the potential for the success of the recital of New Poetry? How much progress had been made in the recitation of New Poetry? Could New Poetry be recited? To have almost everybody who practiced or cared about New Poetry in the North united in one place in this society was no small accomplishment. ...
>
> Those in attendance who took turns reciting poetry included Yu Pingbo, who was good at singing *Tianci*; Zhu Ziqing, who was one of the foremost practitioners of modern Chinese; Liang Zongdai and Li Jianwu, who had extensive knowledge of French poetry; Feng Zhi, who was very familiar with German poetry; and Ye Gongchao, Sun Dayu, Luo Niansheng, Zhou Xuliang, Zhu Guangqian, and Lin Huiyin, who had all studied poetry in English, as well as Miss Xu Fang, who

confidently recited poetry with her loud, resonant voice. Zhu and Zhou recited new and old poetry in their Anhui accent, Yu in his Zhejiang accent, and Miss Lin Huiyin read some poems with a Fujian accent.[4]

The members of the Poetry Reading Society are often called *Jingpai*, meaning "Beijing school," and critics have primarily focused on the scholarly status of its members and the aesthetic standards and creative practices of their lyricism, as well as their publishing activities (such as the *Da Gong Bao* or *General Newspaper* [大公報] and the *Journal for Literature* [文學雜誌]). In contrast, the Poetry Reading Society has not received much attention, even though it was regarded as one of the most distinguished scholarly associations of the 1920s and 1930s. However, Shen Congwen's description shows that the link between refining New Poetry and recitation was in fact the foremost interest of its members. This group of literati, most of whom were from an academic background, came together to discuss the recitation of poetry, and they devoted their efforts to using vocal practices in order to help promote the modernization of New Poetry.

This focus was a reflection of the academic background of its leaders Zhu Guangqian, Zhu Ziqing, and others, and particularly their experience of participating in the Poetry Reading Society in London. In the 1930s, British poet Harold Monro organized a poetry recitation circle, and every Thursday afternoon he would invite local poets to his Poetry Bookstore to recite their own work or that of earlier poets. The influence of these gatherings on the Chinese scholars in London was profound, and they would frequently mention this experience in their writings.[5] The members of the Poetry Reading Society similarly experimented with the voice of modern poetry and applied themselves to the honing of prosody and rhythm. For instance, Zhu Guangqian writes:

> Poetry and music alike are born from rhythm. Rhythm is the phenomenon of the alteration between rising and falling tones, light and strong stresses. . . . The harmonious changes of tones and the differences of light and strong, long and short, the rules of putting a stress here but not there are by no means arbitrary; rhythm in language is this pattern of strong and light stresses, of long and short syllables. . . .
>
> Western and Chinese poetry have both arrived at an era in which the words themselves seek out music, but there is a huge difference between them that is particularly worthy of our attention: this being the art of recitation. Since poetry can no longer be sung, the art of poetry recitation emerged in the West, but in China little emphasis has been placed on recitation. But where there is no art of recitation, the word remains mute. Only where there exists the art of recitation can poetry become living language.[6]

At the same time, the China Poetry Society and its members similarly stressed the practice of reciting poetry, though their philosophy was completely different from the elitism and the pursuit of pure poetry of the members of the Poetry Reading Society. The China Poetry Society aimed at creating poetry for the masses by way of the physical performance of reciting poetry: on one hand it was intended to carry New Poetry to the masses, but on the other it proposed to adopt the language of the masses in order to re-energize poetry, which had been stagnating. This group was established in 1932 in Shanghai by Yang Sao 楊騷, Mu Mutian 穆木天, Ren Jun 任鈞, and Pu Feng 蒲風, among others, and with the journal *New Poetry* (新詩歌) as their official organ they became very influential, with sections in Guangzhou, Beiping, Qingdao, and Ximen. The group inherited its ideology and style from the revolutionary perspective and the realism of the Creation Society and the Sun Society, and emphasized that "poetry is a reflection of society's reality, as well as the engine for the progress of society, and should thus be able to transmit the sense of a time." The group attacked the Crescent Moon and Modernist groups for their flight from and whitewashing of reality, which they believed "needed to be corrected and eradicated." At the same time, the group used the slogan "conversion of New Poetry into folk ballads" to promote the integration of popular language and slang into poetry as its final goal in order to "bring the New Poetry movement to its completion." Mu Mutian wrote a poem on the occasion of launching the first issue of the society's journal, *New Poetry*, using a poetic form to proclaim the journal's aim:

我們要捉住現實，
歌唱新世紀的意識；
工人農人是越法地受剝削，
但是他們反帝熱情也越法高漲。
我們要歌唱這種矛盾和他的意義，
從這種矛盾中去創造偉大的世紀；
我們要用俗言俚語，
把這種矛盾寫成民謠小調鼓詞兒歌，
我們要使我們的詩歌成為大眾歌調，
我們自己也成為大眾的一個。 [7]

We want to seize reality,
Sing the meaning of a new era;
Workers and peasants are ever more oppressed,
But their spirit of resistance surges Ever more strongly.
We want to sing this contradiction and its meaning,
And from this contradiction create a mighty era;
We want to use popular language and slang
To transform this contradiction into ballads, ditties, drum songs, and nursery rhymes,
We want our poems to become the tunes of the masses,
We want to become part of the masses ourselves.

The recitation of poetry advocated by Mu Mutian had to leave the scholar's study and face the masses. As Ren Jun observes: "On one hand, this entailed bringing one's work directly to the masses so as to achieve its intended result. On the other hand, it meant gradually returning poetry to an oral and aural art, after the new poetry of that time had already more or less become a visual art."[8]

The China Poetry Society's emphasis on turning over poetry to the masses by transforming a visual art into an oral and aural art originated from a concern with social reality, and resulted in poetry's becoming a mouthpiece for the working and peasant classes. This differed clearly from the elitism and aesthetic concerns of the members of the Poetry Reading Society. However, after the War of Resistance erupted in China, the attention paid to the masses not only found its justification in spreading propaganda and educating the masses, it also incited a wave of recited poetry and related discussions, and even encouraged intellectuals like Zhu Ziqing to begin addressing the problem of recited poetry from the perspective of propaganda and education. When we ponder the transition from the recitation of poetry to recited poetry, however, the problematic role of the concept of voice in modern literature becomes even more evident.

The Literature of War and the Voice of Politics: The Tension between the Recitation of Poetry and Recited Poetry during the War of Resistance

On July 7, 1937, the eruption of gunfire at Marco Polo Bridge marked the beginning of the war between China and Japan. It was a time of crisis during which China's very survival was at stake, and a crucial time for the mobilization of the whole nation. In contrast to previous wars, this conflict involved the entire nation and not only led to chaos, destruction, and death, but also witnessed the emergence of a variety of new literary genres under the aegis of a spirit of enlightenment and democracy.[9] These new literary forms aimed at uniting the nation and strengthening its determination to resist the enemy. From these circumstances emerged such phenomena as the recitation of poetry directed at the masses, as well as the genre of recited poetry and the movement for the recitation of New Poetry.

The emergence of recited poetry as a new poetic genre for the masses helped transform poetry recitation from an individual performance into a mass movement. The concept of poetry of the China Poetry Society was consonant with this objective. As Ren Jun explained in his essay "A Brief Discussion of the Duties of Poetry Workers" (略論詩歌工作者當前的工作和任務):

> Why should we take up and advance the practice and work of reciting poetry? Of course there are two main reasons for this. First, from the perspective of the nature of poetry: poetry is by no means composed for the eyes, but rather for the ears. As the British poet Bottomley observes, "Only poetry that is recited and heard is real poetry." But what about our New Poetry? There is no way around it: most of it has become a kind of "visual art," a "mute art," and has lost the essence of poetry. Therefore, we want to promote the recitation of poetry in order to return poetry to its status of "oral and

aural art." Second, from the perspective of the use of poetry, we want to transform poetry again into an "oral and aural art," or at least into an art that does not only appeal to the eyes. Only when it appears before the masses can poetry be disseminated more widely and more effectively develop its role as a weapon in the service of the War of Resistance. Therefore, to initiate and advance the work of reciting poetry in the history of China's New Poetry movement really marks the significance of our epoch.[10]

The China Poetry Society's concept of recitation was evidently different from that of the Poetry Reading Society. However, given the need to stimulate national sentiment and appeal to the populace in order to resist the Japanese, and given that everybody was affected by the war, the cultural elite of the salons as well as teachers and students left their studies to join the masses and participate in propaganda and education work. Consequently, members of the Poetry Reading Society who had initially gathered to appreciate poetry's beauty also began to attend to its real-world significance, and even established links with the poetic theories developed by the China Poetry Society. For instance, Zhu Ziqing's essay "On Recited Poetry" (論朗誦詩) points out that the pressing realities of the War of Resistance had created the need for recited poetry as an activity to become a collective movement ("we must do propaganda, we must educate the masses"), while also explaining that the creation of poetry had to become collective instead of individual in order to bring forth an independent genre of recited poetry:

> In the past, New Poetry still had one thing in common with traditional poetry, which is that its main starting point was the individual. Consequently, it could only be enjoyed in solitude, and could not please the crowd; it could only appeal to oneself or one's friends, but not to the masses. I think this is why the poetry recitation movement was unable to unfold before the war. But with the War of Resistance came a turning point where the recitation movement not only developed widely, it also generated the independent genre of recited poetry.
>   Recited poetry is poetry of the masses, which is to say collective poetry. Even though the writers are individuals, their starting point is the masses, they are only the mouthpieces of the masses. Their works have to be read in front of the masses and to grow in the intense atmosphere of the collective.[11]

During the war, the recited poetry and the poetry recitation movements developed together, and soon poets started to write recited poetry to boost morale and keep up the spirit of resistance. Without a doubt, the injunction to create poetry for the masses was a central aim. For instance, Gao Lan 高蘭, one of the poets who put great effort into composing recited poetry, dedicated his poem "Developing Our Recited Poetry" (展開我們的朗誦詩歌) to the form of recited poetry and called upon other poets to promote its composition. His use of language and poetic form resonates with Ren Jun or Zhu Ziqing's ideals:

新時代點起了新的烽火，
這烽火照耀著祖國的山河！
來吧! 詩人們!

展開咱們朗誦的詩歌,
全民的抗戰裡有你也有我。
惟有朗誦的詩歌,
才是我們的詩歌,
惟有朗誦的詩歌,
它才不再僅是嘆息花飛和葉落,
惟有朗誦的詩歌,
它才能不再是剖白自我的吟哦,
它是
奴隸們怒吼的喉舌,
它是
爭取民族解放,
抗戰的隊伍中,
文化的鐵甲列車![12]

A new era has lighted a new beacon
A beacon that shines on our country's mountains and rivers!
Come, poets!
Let's develop our recited poetry,
Both you and I have joined the whole nation's War of Resistance.
Only recited poetry
Is truly our poetry,
Recited poetry
No longer bemoans drifting petals and falling leaves,
Recited poetry
No longer fixates on the self,
It is
The howling mouthpiece of the slave,
It is
Culture's tank
In the army of the War of Resistance
That fights for the nation's freedom!

The conviction that "recited poetry is the poetry of the masses, it is collective poetry" foregrounded the collective *we* as the enunciating subject of recited poetry, in a solemn vow of allegiance to the collective spirit and feeling in the face of the masses.

In the process of the modernization of New Poetry, the voice emerged as one of the most important factors. Recited poetry was composed for recitation in front of the masses, and the characteristics and uses of this newly emerging poetic genre were markedly different from those of earlier periods. This is why critics called it "New Poetry's new poetry."[13] From a different perspective, however, the development of this poetic form responded to the nation's war needs, and its strong political nature cannot be overlooked. But how did this political and educational dimension enter into dialogue with poetry's aesthetic qualities? And what was the interaction between voice and writing?

Recited poetry was an important part of war literature as well as a demonstration of the politics of voice. It emerged during wartime and, transmitted orally, was endowed with a propagandist and educational duty. Thus, from the outset recited poetry appeared in the guise of a struggle; consequently even in its written form it continually foregrounded the importance of voice, even as it implied an antagonism between the reciting voice and the written poem, which leads us to the following questions: does voice control writing, or does writing control voice? And how did recited poetry perform its political mission of resistance and national rescue in the interaction of writing and voice?

Without a doubt, the emphasis of poetic theory during the war years was on how to develop principles of composition suited to the recitation of poetry and the needs of aurality. Zhu Ziqing, Xi Jin 錫金, Li Guangtian 李廣田, Xu Chi 徐遲, Lin Geng, and others all weighed in on this issue. For instance, Li Guangtian's essay "Poetry and Recited Poetry" (詩與朗誦詩) illustrates the limitations imposed by written content on voicing through a comparison of three poems: Dai Wangshu's 戴望舒 "Autumn Dream" (秋天的夢), Zang Kejia's 臧克家 "Old Horse" (老馬), and He Qifang's "I Sing for the Young" (我為少男少女們歌唱). Li points out that the tone of "Autumn Dream" is cold and gloomy, "causing dejection," and it "simply cannot be read aloud." "Old Horse" expresses a general ideal of humanism, and reading it yields better results than "Autumn Dream," though it is not suited for recitation either. Li observes that He Qifang's poem, meanwhile, sings of the morning, of hope, of the future in a "joyous and excited key," adding that, "of course, this kind of poem lent itself to being read, even with a loud voice." Li nevertheless doubted whether He Qifang's poem was suited to being recited in front of the masses, given that the poet only purports to sing for "the young," without embracing a more momentous tone or aspiring to a wider audience. Finally, Li offers a poem by an unknown fourteen-year-old girl, "They Accuse Me" (他們在控訴我), as an ideal example of recited poetry because, he contends, it is not directed to only a small group of people, but rather addresses workers, peasants, and the masses, and also because "it does not sing of the future or of happiness, but of the blood-soaked reality and of action without fear of death."[14]

Of course, according to Li Guangtian, the content and the written words of a poem determine the form and vocal expression of recited poetry. On one hand, a poetic composition can only be recited if it has certain political and collective characteristics, and its most important aim is to achieve a political effect by way of the voice. On the other hand, by focusing on poetic register and linguistic form Zhu Ziqing emphasized the interaction of written word and voice:

The audience of recited poetry neither has patience nor education; it aims to immerse itself in happiness and desires force—images are of course good, but they should be dynamic, such as "grenades" and "fuses." Static images such as "axis," "fortress," and "ropes" are simply not powerful enough.

Dialogue should be simple; sentences should be short and somewhat standard. If they are too uneven they become prose, if they are too neat they no longer sound

natural. Language has to be carefully selected, like the dialogue in a play. . . . Just
as a drama script is not complete until it has been performed, recited poetry is not
complete until it has been recited. This kind of verse often feels long when one reads
it, but does not seem long at all when it is being recited. This is because reading is a
spatial operation, whereas listening is a temporal one.[15]

Zhu's reflections underscore the dialectical relationship between voice and writing, in
that the temporality of speech trumps the spatiality of written composition. A poem can
only be completed through being recited, and yet the fact that Zhu favors words such
as *grenades* and *fuses* over *axis, fortress,* and *ropes* alerts us to the fact that the imagery
or meaning of the written word controls the performative outcome of the voice. At the
beginning of the War of Resistance, for instance, Gao Lan's "It's Time, My Comrades"
(是時候了,我的同胞), which called the whole nation to resist the Japanese, is filled
with forceful imagery and short phrases:

> 是時候了, 我的同胞!
> 敵人的飛機大炮,
> 又大舉屠殺我們來了!
> 我們早已是炸裂的火藥,
> 還禁得住這樣的燃燒?
> 爆炸!
> 爆炸!
> 爆炸了吧!
> 一切不願做亡國奴的人喲!
> 假如你還不曾把恥辱忘掉,
> 假如你還不再想作苟且偷生的膿包,
> 是時候了, 我的同胞![16]

> It's time, my comrades!
> The enemy with war planes and bombs,
> Has come again in force to slaughter us!
> We are already dynamite at the point of ignition,
> So how will we bear this burning?
> Explode!
> Explode!
> Let's explode!
> O all who do not want to be the slaves of a fallen nation!
> If you have not yet wiped out the shame,
> If you no longer want to live ignobly,
> Then it's time, my comrades!

Recited verse from this period either called upon the whole nation to take up the
fight and to put all effort into the War of Resistance, or evoked the homeland with nostalgia and mourned family and friends who had become victims of the war; it either
glorified the heroism of the fighters and praised the wisdom of the leaders, or it called
on the enemy soldiers to return home in the name of humanity and shared human

sentiment. In addition, it typically featured the following characteristics: (1) relying heavily on a collective *we* as enunciating subject; (2) using affect to appeal to a spirit of resistance; (3) using dialogue as well as theatrical and performative components.

Xi Jin, Gao Lan, Tian Jian 田間, Ai Qing 艾青, and Ke Zhongping 柯仲平 were prominent writers of recited poetry during the War of Resistance. Among these, Ke Zhongping and Gao Lan were the most representative creators of recited poetry at the homefront and in Yan'an, respectively. Gao Lan was from the Northeast and experienced the extreme hardships of being a refugee in the aftermath of the Mukden Incident of September 18, 1931. His poem "My Home is at the Heilong River" (我的家在黑龍江) from that year was recited over the radio and moved the hearts of millions. It unites many of the strategies of recited verse and can be regarded as a classic of the genre:

> 你的家呢, 老鄉?
> 在吉林?
> 在瀋陽?
> 在萬泉河邊?
> …
> 我的家呀!
> 我的家在興安嶺之陽,
> 在黑龍江的岸上;
> 江北是那遼濶而自由的西伯利亞,
> 江南便是我生長的家鄉。
> 天哪! 九一八!
> 九一八!
> 日本帝國主義的大炮, 刀槍,
> 擊碎了這老實的夢想,
> 搗毀了多少年的希望!
> 這個日子永生也不能忘;
> …
> 從此!
> 完了!
> 完了!
> 我的兄弟爹娘,
> 我生長的家鄉,
> 雖然
> 依舊是冰天雪地,
> 依舊是山高水長,
> 可是,
> 三千萬人民成了牛馬一樣,
> 雪原成了地獄, 再沒有天堂!
> 被奸淫!
> 被擄搶!
> 被屠殺!
> 被滅亡!
> 然而, 荒莽的人,

有著荒莽的力量,
那力量因了熬煎,
因了苦難,
更為加速度的成長!¹⁷

Where is your home, my friend?
In Jilin?
In Shenyang?
By the Wanquan River?
By the Yalu River?
. . .
My home?
My home is in the lee of Kinghan Range,
On the banks of the Heilong River;
North of the river is the vast, free Siberia,
South of the river is the home where I grew up.
Alas! September 18!
September 18!
The canons and bayonets of Japanese imperialism
Smashed this dear dream,
Destroyed the hopes of so many years!
We must never forget that day;
. . .
Since then!
All has been lost!
All lost!
My brothers and parents,
The home where I grew up,
Even though
It is still a place of cold skies and snowy ground,
Of high mountains and big rivers,
But,
Thirty million citizens became beasts of burden,
The snowy plain has become a hell, no longer a heaven!
It was raped!
Plundered!
Slaughtered!
Annihilated!
And yet, a desperate people
Also has a desperate kind of strength,
Because of suffering
Because of hardship that strength
Will grow ever faster!

This poem is several hundred verses long, and the two sections quoted above appear at the beginning of the poem. Using a question and answer about home and family, the poem stirs up longing and nostalgia for one's own home. "At Jilin?/At Shenyang?/ By the Wanquan River?/By the Yalu River?" constitute rhyming parallel structures; the detailed descriptions of the homeland's scenery and characteristics and the multiple elaborations of human feeling and natural features so as to evoke abundance, beauty, peace, and happiness that follow are reminiscent of Han dynasty *fu* poetry. The line "Alas! September 18!" constitutes a crucial turning point for the whole poem, using an apostrophe to emphasize the sorrow and anger at the enemy soldiers' cruel abuse of the homeland, and to emphasize that the people will persevere as a whole and continue to fight fervently, even in the face of death.

This kind of strategy emphasizes affect and uses the cadence of the voice during recitation to create a strong emotional effect, which helped make Gao Lan's recited poetry so popular and widely broadcast during the war. The recited poetry that was composed in Yan'an, such as Ke Zhongping's verses, came even closer to the earlier practices of the China Poetry Society, using colloquial and popular language and adopting forms close to popular songs and ballads to establish links with people and places. Ke Zhongping's famous poem "United Defense Army of the Border Region" (邊區自衛軍), which Mao Zedong 毛澤東 praised, is a long epic-style poem that narrates how Han Wa of the United Defense Army of the border region fought against the Japanese with courage and cunning. The poem begins as follows:

> 左邊一條山，
> 右邊一條山，
> 一條川在兩條山間轉;
> 川水喊著要到黃河去,
> 這裡碰壁轉一轉,
> 那裡碰壁彎一彎;
> 它的方向永不改,
> 不到黃河心不甘。[18]

> A mountain on the left,
> A mountain on the right,
> A winding river in between;
> The river's water shouts that it wants to reach the Yellow River,
> But hits an obstacle here and turns and turns,
> Hits an obstacle there and churns and churns;
> And yet its direction will never change,
> Until it reaches the Yellow River it won't be content.

The poem is suited for recitation precisely because it is reminiscent of folk ballads and folk songs. In other words, it is no longer purely in the realm of language meant for recitation, but rather comes close to being chanted as a song.[19]

In reality, such a hybrid of recitation and song had already made its appearance when Guang Weiran 光未然 composed the "Yellow River Cantata" (黃河大合唱). When Zhu Ziqing talked about the poetry recitation movement during the war, he pointed out that

> even though the recitation movement takes poetry as its main focus, it is by no means limited to poetry. . . . If the recitation movement before the war constituted a kind of aesthetic education, during the war it constituted a political education.

The audience for political education, it goes without saying, is much larger than that for aesthetic education, and so the educational material has to follow suit; even the recitation societies of that time sometimes brought songs for recitation.[20]

Furthermore, since recited poetry depended on the performance of recitation, it also developed many similarities with theatrical performance. In January 1938, Yan'an organized a huge poetry recital that proved quite unsuccessful. Participants were of the opinion that one of the reasons for its failure was an "excessive emphasis on movement and posture during recitation."[21] What this phenomenon suggests is that, even as poetry recitation and recited poetry pursued similar political aims, their inner tensions had not yet been resolved. This prompts us to consider whether the recited poetry movement should be considered recitation or poetry, and whether it emphasizes the voice of the original written verse or the resulting theatrical performance.

After the War of Resistance, Ke Zhongping wrote the poem "Workers Will Ensure the Construction of an Industrialized Nation—Congratulations on Behalf of the Workers on the Occasion of the 28th Anniversary of the Chinese Communist Party" (創造工業國工人敢保險--為中國工人慶祝中國共產黨二十八周歲作), which foregrounds these questions even more clearly. The poem begins by glorifying the Chinese Communist Party and its role in changing the fates of workers and peasants, then turns to industrial development, and concludes with a strong acclamation of Chairman Mao and the Chinese Communist Party. The poem's vocabulary is accessible, its syntax smooth, and it is easy to pronounce, but what is particularly noteworthy are Ke's remarks at the end:

> This poem can be recited in a free allegro pace, even accompanied by drumming or the sounds of the two-stringed fiddle. It might be even more suitable to sing it to any tune popular among the workers. Whatever proves unsuitable can be changed. This poem is meant as a small token and gift for my comrade workers.[22]

In order to dedicate it to his comrade workers, the poet's creation can be sung "to any tune popular among the workers," and "whatever proves unsuitable can be changed." This is no longer the transformation of poetry for the masses, but rather the almost complete erasure of the written words of poetry.

NATIONAL-LANGUAGE LITERATURE, NATIONAL LITERARY LANGUAGE, AND MODERN CHINA'S NATIONAL-LANGUAGE EDUCATION

Throughout literary history, the dialectical development of speech (voice) and language (writing) has been quite precarious. When we focus on recitation, we see that the Qing dynasty Tongcheng School's notions of "using voice to seek the spirit" (因聲求氣) and its pursuit of "harmony of content and sound" (神氣音節) also emphasized recitation as a medium for literary learning. Zhu Ziqing and Lu Zhiwei 陸志韋 both addressed the role of voice for literature and education, with Zhu observing that

> since May Fourth, people have been fond of using the saying of "nodding one's head and wagging one's tail" (搖頭擺尾) to describe those infatuated with the old literature. To nod one's head and wag one's tail indicates the shameful posture while reciting literature, even though one does not need to nod one's head or wag one's tail while reciting.[23]

Lu Zhiwei elaborated:

> I was born in Nanlu Village in Zhejiang's Wuxing County. The language of my hometown was only used and understood within several square kilometers. . . . For thirty years I was not aware of what dialect I was speaking, and it wasn't until very recently that I started to study the national language with much effort, though my level is still far from qualifying me to write poetry in the modern vernacular. But I studied continuously and tried over and again. . . . Initially, I used a kind of mongrel official language to write poetry in the vernacular. . . . I should have realized much earlier that I had to study the national language first.
>
> From 1901 until 1912 or 1913, I experimented with rhythm for the first time, resulting in the pieces collected in *Crossing the River* (渡河集). The effort of that time was utterly wasted. Zhu Peixian 朱佩弦 said that it was still too early for me to produce mature works, but I blame my dialect.[24]

Zhu Ziqing observed that there was a difference between an emphasis on voicing during recitation for traditional and modern literature, while Lu Zhiwei claimed that a standard national language was a necessary condition for the creation of poetry in the modern vernacular. By focusing on different issues, they foregrounded at least two ways in which modern literature and classical literature differ: the first concerns a choice of language, namely the need to use the national language for literature (in contrast to local languages and dialects); the second concerns cadence and linguistic rhythm and is thus a question of genre, namely that the voicing of literature (in the modern vernacular national language) and traditional classical literature were quite different. These two factors played an important role in the national language movement and literary revolution from the beginning of the Republican period onward.

The national language movement originated in the late Qing and gained momentum in the Republican period, yet each period had a different focus. During the early period, the emphasis was on using transliteration systems and character simplification, and promoting the use of a modern vernacular. The difficulty of traditional literary Chinese proved an obstacle for reading, literacy, and the acquisition of new knowledge, and therefore one of the movement's key aims became the "unity of speech and writing" (言文一致). As the concept of a democratic nation gained ideological importance in China and in the context of Japan's Meiji Restoration, however, the inspiration and impact of the national language movement and its aspiration to nurture the people's patriotism by way of the unification of language came to surpass even that of the "unity of speech and writing." During this late Qing period, however, the language reform movement was not promoted by the government or any official organ, and the question of whether or not to improve the literary language was never raised.[25]

The most important differences between the national literature movement of the late Qing and the Republican period were that linguistic unity was endorsed by the government and began to converge with literary revolution. Once national language (as speech) was opposed to national culture (as written language), these two perspectives became dialectically united. In 1913, as part of the Republic's new government plan, the government convoked a Conference on the Unification of Reading and Sound, to establish a framework for a common national language, during which the unification of the zhuyin romanization system and the standard pronunciation of Chinese characters were decided. In 1920 the Ministry for Education mandated that every school change the curriculum of first- and second-year students from National Culture (*guowen* 國文) to National Language (*guoyu* 國語). In this way, linguistic unity and general education became parallel government strategies.[26]

Literary revolution was mainly promoted by journals such as *New Youth* (新青年) and *Avantgarde* (新潮), both of which were based at Peking University. Chen Duxiu 陳獨秀, Qian Xuantong 錢玄同, Liu Bannong 劉半農, Hu Shi 胡適, Fu Sinian 傅斯年, and others debated how to improve literature. They originally focused on writing rather than speech, and therefore what they initially called *national language* in fact referred to writing in the vernacular (as opposed to classical Chinese or *wenyan*) rather than to standard Mandarin (as opposed to local dialects). Among these early reformers, Qian Xuantong took the lead in advocating the use of a written language suitable for being a national language (以國語為之). In fact, he elevated the earlier notion of literature in the modern vernacular to the status of the formal written language among intellectuals. The main focus of Hu Shi's essay "Toward a Constructive Theory of Literary Revolution" (建設的文學革命論) was also for literature in the modern vernacular to be considered literature in the national language, and thus to elevate the position of the modern vernacular. Literary reform required the establishment of a Chinese national-language literature, since "only with a national-language literature can there be a literary national language." Hu Shi's emphasis was clearly on writing rather than on speech.

After Hu Shi and others joined the Association for the Study of the National Language and the Society for the Implementation of National Language Unity, Fu Sinian proposed the two paths of spoken language and a Europeanized national language as ways of enriching the literature in the modern vernacular.[27] It is here that the national language movement and the literary revolution converged, as the language spoken around Beijing became the basis for the standard language (spoken vernacular) as well as the main language used by the new literature from May Fourth onward.[28] Even so, at the beginning of the development of new literature, writing in local languages or dialects was not rejected outright, as evidenced by Shen Congwen's reference, in his essay "On

Reciting Poetry," to Yu Pingbo and Lin Huiyin, who used their Zhejiang and Fujian dialects to read poetry.

This brings us back to Lu Zhiwei. Lu was dissatisfied with his early writings, and blamed his dialect. According to him, the most important reason for his lack of success was the differences in the rhythm of the national language and regional dialects. Since the language was not the same, sound and tone, cadence, and rhythm were transformed during recitation, and this also influenced the writing process. As the national language became the official language of the nation, accordingly, the national-language literature came to supersede literature written in other regional languages and dialects, and modern vernacular literature was only able to flourish when it became part of the national educational system.

However, can classical Chinese and the modern vernacular really be rigorously differentiated, and does literature in the modern vernacular really completely coincide with the spoken vernacular? Even though Hu Shi, Chen Duxiu, and others vigorously opposed traditional literary Chinese at the beginning of the new literature movement, seeing it as the complete opposite of literature in the modern vernacular, scholars who have researched national-language education realized fairly early that the modern spoken vernacular and the so-called modern literary vernacular Chinese were actually not the same at all, given that modern literary Chinese contained no small amount of traditional literary Chinese. As Wei Jiangong 魏建功, chairperson of the Committee for the Implementation of the National Language, observed,

> Literature in the modern vernacular became an important slogan at one moment in literary history; but the works under this label were not yet truly [national] language literature. When we read many new literary works, poetry, narrative, or drama, most of these are merely new stuff that seems neither written in Chinese nor to use the Chinese language.[29]

Zhu Ziqing elaborated, "Everyday speech and writing cannot become one," given that "the written modern vernacular is not the same as the language we speak, and the modern literary vernacular is even less like what we speak. Writing and speaking are two fundamentally different things."[30] He explained that

> early poetry in the modern vernacular was unable to avoid the influence of traditional literary Chinese and added in some European influences, but spoken Chinese was only a very small part of it. Afterward, spoken Chinese gradually eliminated traditional literary Chinese while continuing to develop a European flavor, and only in recent years [in the '30s and '40s] has there been more use of purely spoken Chinese—which is to say the national language, the language spoken around Beijing.[31]

In short, "the Europeanized components and the literary Chinese components of modern literary Chinese seemed unavoidable."[32] But it was also in the context of such a linguistic reality that voicing and reading accrued their special signification, namely to fuse traditional literary Chinese and Europeanized language with the vernacular and establish a new linguistic status quo through sustained training in reading. Zhu Ziqing cites New Poetry as an example here:

> The language of New Poetry is not the language of the people, but rather a Europeanized or modernized language. Therefore, when one reads it aloud, it doesn't appear smooth to the tongue and the ear. Of course, other literature written in the modern vernacular suffers the same problem, but literature other than poetry tends to be longer, so awkward passages can be easily concealed. In contrast, because of poetry's brevity, a harmonious reading is more difficult. . . . Our New Poetry proceeds toward a new nature by means of old ways . . . the focused training of reading aloud can shorten the process somewhat, but by how much depends on our effort.[33]

What merits attention here is that many of the important members of the Poetry Reading Society later participated in the elaboration of educational material for all school levels as well as in the practice of modern reading, since they believed that a modern national literary language could be achieved by means of national-language education.

Toward the end of 1946, a group of scholars interested in language education convened at Peking University at the invitation of Wei Jiangong to hold a conference on "Methods for Reading Chinese." Many former members of the Poetry Reading Society, such as Zhu Ziqjing, Zhu Guangqian, Shen Congwen, and Feng Zhi, participated and shared their personal experiences, stressing the importance of reading for language education. For instance, Zhu Ziqing emphasized the importance of a national literary language to explain the relationship between the modern written vernacular and the spoken national language:

> If we focus on recitation in the modern vernacular from elementary school onward, even Europeanized syntax can gradually become amenable to voicing. Thus, we can achieve a "national literary language" if the content of our future national language becomes richer day by day.[34]

Consequently, the meaning of voice for modern Chinese literature was not merely an index of literary accomplishment nor simply a means of rousing the emotions of the masses. Rather, in the form of the language that readers of the new generation studied, it became an important road to literary creation. It not only played a role in the development of New Poetry and recited poetry, it also became a key element in the shaping of a national-language literature as well as a national literary language. The unity of speech and writing promoted by the new literature movement was directed toward a convergence of speech and writing, as well as the elevation of the literariness of the modern vernacular. Reading out loud was regarded as one of the best means of training.

CONCLUSION

I will conclude by returning once again to Lu Xun's dictum that China needs a modern voice—a voice of its own. This "voice" is not a mere metaphor, but rather a biological and material phenomenon. It is the standard that intellectuals and writers use to perfect themselves, and has managed, by means of national educational politics and academic curricula, to put down roots in the present and develop toward the future. In literature's pursuit of modernization, there is not only writing but also the voice, and because of this voice, the literary landscape was transformed, leading China from the past to the present, from being a voiceless nation to a nation with a voice.

(translated by Andrea Bachner)

NOTES

1. Lu Xun 魯迅, "Wusheng de Zhongguo" 無聲的中國 [Voiceless China], in *Lu Xun quanji* 魯迅全集 [The complete works of Lu Xun], vol. 4 (Beijing: Renmin wenxue chubanshe, 2005), 12 and 15.

2. Zhu Guangqian 朱光潛, "Xiandai Zhongguo wenxue" 現代中國文學 [Modern Chinese literature], in *Zhu Guangqian quanji* 朱光潛全集 [The complete works of Zhu Guangqian], vol. 9 (Hefei: Anhui Jiaoyu Chubanshe, 1993), 328. Zhu Ziqing 朱自清, "Xin shi de jinbu" 新詩的進步 [The progress of New Poetry], in *Zhu Ziqing quanji* 朱自清全集 [The complete works of Zhu Ziqing], vol. 2 (Jiangsu: Jiangsu jiaoyu chubanshe, 1988), 319.

3. Hu Shi's 胡適 first volume of New Poetry was called *Experiments* (嘗試集). One of its poems, "Butterfly" (蝴蝶), composed in 1916 and arguably the earliest poem of the collection, espouses the form of five-character verse throughout, thus clearly showing the influence of the formal constraints of traditional poetry. See *Hu Shi zuopinji 27: Changshi ji* 胡適作品集27：嘗試集 [The collected works of Hu Shi, vol. 27: Experiments] (Taibei: Yuanliu Chubanshe, 1986), 58.

4. Shen Congwen 沈從文, "Tan langsong shi" 談朗誦詩 [On reciting poetry], in *Shen Congwen quanji* 沈從文全集 [The complete works of Shen Congwen], vol. 17 (Shanxi: Beiyue wenyi chubanshe, 2002), 247–248.

5. For instance, Wu Mi 吳宓 records in his diary how he went to Monro's bookstore, T. S. Eliot's introduction card in hand, and listened with effort to Monro's recitation of William Blake's poems. Zhu Ziqing writes of Monro's Poetry Bookshop in his *London Travels: Three Bookstores*. In his diary during his travels in England (1931–1932), he frequently mentions that he bought books there, listened to poetry recitations, or meditated on the problem of the comparison of Chinese and Western poetry. In "The Special Role of Literature in the Language-Based Arts" (文學作為語言藝術的特殊地位), "A Plea for Poetic Rhythm" (替詩的音律辯護), and other essays, Zhu Guangqian often uses the example of London's "Poetry Society" to make his points.

6. Zhu Guangqian, "Ti shi de yinlü bianhu" 替詩的音律辯護 [A plea for poetic rhythm], originally published in *Dongfang Zazhi* 東方雜誌 [Asia journal] 30.1, then republished

under the title "Zhongguo shi heyi zoushang lü de lu" 中國詩何以走上律的路 [How Chinese poetry discovered rhythm] as chapter 12 of *Shi lun* 詩論 [A discussion of poetry] in *Zhu Guangqian quanji* 朱光潛全集 [The complete works of Zhu Guangqian], vol. 3, 237 and 245.

7. See Ren Jun 任鈞, "Guanyu Zhongguo Shige Hui" 關於中國詩歌會 [On the China Poetry Society], in *Xin shi hua: liangjian wenyi* 新詩話：兩間文藝 [New Poetry: Between two arts] (Shanghai: Xin Zhongguo Chubanshe, 1946).

8. Ren Jun, "On the China Poetry Society."

9. These new literary genres comprised reportage literature (報告文學), "living newspaper" skits (活報劇), street performance (街頭劇), street poetry (街頭詩), and recited poetry, among others. See Lan Hai 藍海, *Zhongguo kangzhan wenyi shi* 中國抗戰文藝史 [A history of Chinese literature during the war of resistance] (Jinan: Shandong wenyi, 1984), 73–166.

10. See Ren Jun, *New Poetry: Between Two Arts*, 101–102.

11. Zhu Ziqing, "Lun langsong shi" 論朗誦詩 [On recited poetry], in *Zhu Ziqing quanji* 朱自清全集 [The complete works of Zhu Ziqing], vol. 3, 253–262.

12. Gao Lan 高蘭, *Gao Lan langsong shi* 高蘭朗誦詩 [Gao Lan's recited poems], new ed. (Zhongqing: Jianzhong Shuju, 1942), 36–41. The whole poem comprises nine stanzas. The verses cited here comprise the first stanza, which is repeated at the end of the poem.

13. See Zhu Ziqing, "On Recited Poetry"; and Li Guangtian 李廣田, "Shi yu langsong shi" 詩與朗誦詩 [Poetry and recited poetry], in Jian Tierao 簡鐵浩 ed., *Langsong yanjiu lun-wen ji* 朗誦研究論文集 [Research on recitation] (Hong Kong: Songhua Chuban Gongsi, 1978), 281–292.

14. Li Guangtian, "Poetry and Recited Poetry."

15. Zhu Ziqing, "On Recited Poetry."

16. Gao Lan, *Recited Poetry by Gao Lan*.

17. Gao Lan. "Wo de jia zai Heilong jiang" 我的家在黑龍江 [My home is at the Heilong River], *Dagong bao* 大公報, January 17, 1939.

18. Ke Zhongping 柯仲平, *Ke Zhongping wenji: Shige juan* 柯仲平文集・詩歌卷 [The collected works of Ke Zhongping: Poetry] (Kunming: Yunnan renmin chubanshe, 2002), 304.

19. This is foregrounded by Ke Zhongping himself; see *The Collected Works of Ke Zhongping: Poetry*, 135.

20. Zhu Ziqing, "On Recited Poetry."

21. See Ke Zhongping 柯仲平, "Ziwo pipan (genju zhan ge shehuiyi jilu)" 自我批判 (根據戰歌社會議記錄) [Self-criticism (According to the records of the conference of the War Poetry Society)], in *Shi de langsong yu langsong de shi* 詩的朗誦與朗誦的詩 [Reciting poetry and poetry in recitation], ed. Gao Lan 高蘭 (Shandong: Shandong daxue chubanshe, 1987), 66–67.

22. *The Collected Works of Ke Zhongping: Poetry*, 135.

23. Zhu Ziqing, "Lun langdu" 論朗讀 [On reading], in *Zhu Ziqing quanji* 朱自清全集 [The complete works of Zhu Ziqing], vol. 2, 56.

24. Lu Zhiwei 陸志韋, "Lun jiezou" 論節奏 [On rhythm]. *Wenxue zazhi* 文學雜誌 [Journal of literature] 1.3 (July 1937): 14–15 and 18.

25. In 1902, Wu Rulun 吳汝綸, who was then superintendent of pedagogy at the Imperial University of Peking (which later became Peking University), went to Japan to investigate school governance. In a conversation with Wu, the famous Japanese educator Isawa Shūji 伊澤修二 emphasized: "The best way . . . of educating the patriotism of the people is lin-guistic unification." He even suggested that Chinese institutions of higher learning "should

eliminate other subjects and add the subject of national language instead." Wu was profoundly impacted by this experience. When he returned to China, he submitted a statement to the minister of education Zhang Baixi 張百熙 in favor of linguistic unity. Soon afterward, students of the Imperial University of Peking, such as Wang Fenghua 王鳳華 and others also submitted a statement to Yuan Shikai, then Minister of Beiyang, "asking for the implementation of an alphabet for the official language and for the establishing of the subject of the common national language, so as to lead the people to wisdom and to save the nation." Even though it was not put into practice then, the concept of a national language had taken shape. See Wang Ermin 王爾敏, "Zhongguo jindai zhishi pujihua zhi zijue ji Guoyu yundong" 中國近代知識普及化之自覺及國語運動 [The consciousness of the spread of knowledge and the national language movement in China's early modern period]. *Jindaishi yanjiu jikan* 近代史研究集刊 [Journal of research on early modern China] 11 (July 1982): 13–45, and Wang Feng 王風, "Wanqing pinyinhua yu baihuawen cuifa de Guoyu sichao" 晚清拼音化與白話文催發的國語思潮 [Phonetization in the late Qing and the implementation of the modern Chinese vernacular in the context of the trend toward a national language], in Xia Xiaohong 夏曉虹, Wang Feng, et al. *Wenxue yuyan yu wenzhang tishi* 文學語言與文章體式 [The language of literature and the form of writing] (Hefei: Anhui jiaoyu chubanshe, 2006), 20–45.

26. For an account of the development of the national language movement, see Li Jinxi 黎錦熙, *Guoyu yundong shigang* 國語運動史綱 [An outline of the national language movement] (Shanghai: Shangwu yinshuguan, 1935), and Ni Haishu 倪海曙, *Zhongguo pinyin wenzi yundong shi jianbian* 中國拼音文字運動史簡編 [A short history of China's phonetization movement] (Shanghai: Shidai chubanshe, 1950).

27. See Fu Sinian 傅斯年, "Zeyang zuo baihuawen" 怎樣做白話文 [How to write literature in the modern vernacular], *Xinchao* 新潮 [Avantgarde] 1.2 (February 1919): 171–184.

28. See Wang Feng 王風, "Wenxue geming yu Guoyu yundong zhi guanxi" 文學革命與國語運動之關係 [The relation between literary reform and the national language movement], in Xia Xiaohong, Wang Feng, et al. *The Language of Literature*, 46–70.

29. Wei Jiangong 魏建功, "Zhongguo chun wenxue de xingtai yu Zhongguo yuyan wenxue" 中國純文學的形態與中國語言文學 [The condition of pure literature in China and literature in Chinese], originally published in *Wenxue* 文學 [Literature] 2.6 (1934), included in *Wei Jiangong wenji* 魏建功文集 [The collected works of Wei Jiangong], vol. 5 (Jiangsu: Jiangsu jiaoyu chubanshe, 2001), 299.

30. Zhu Ziqing, "Lun songdu" 論誦讀 [On reciting], in *The Complete Works of Zhu Ziqing*, vol. 3, 189.

31. Zhu Ziqing, "On Reading," 59–60.

32. See Zhu Ziqing's talk in "Zhongguo yuwen songdu fangfa zuotanhui jilu" 中國語文誦讀方法座談會記錄 [Records of the conference on methods of recitation in Chinese], recorded by Chen Shilin 陳士林 and Zhou Dingyi 周定一, *Guowen yuekan* 國文月刊 [Chinese language monthly] 53 (March 1947): 5.

33. Zhu Ziqing, "Recitation and Poetry," *The Complete Works of Zhu Ziqing*, vol. 2, 392.

34. Zhu Ziqing, "Records of the Conference on Methods of Recitation in Chinese," 5.

Works Cited

Chen Shilin 陳士林 and Zhou Dingyi 周定一, eds. "Zhongguo yuwen songdu fangfa zuotanhui jilu" 中國語文誦讀方法座談會記錄 [Records of the conference on methods of recitation in Chinese]. *Guowen yuekan* 國文月刊 [Chinese language monthly] 53 (March 1947): 5.

Fu Sinian 傅斯年. "Zeyang zuo baihuawen" 怎樣做白話文 [How to write literature in the modern vernacular]. *Xinchao* 新潮 [Avantgarde] 1.2 (February 1919): 171–184.

Gao Lan 高蘭. *Gao Lan langsong shi* 高蘭朗誦詩 [Gao Lan's recited poems], new ed. Zhongqing: Jianzhong Shuju, 1942.

Gao Lan 高蘭. "Wo de jia zai Heilong jiang" 我的家在黑龍江 [My home is at the Heilong River]. *Da Gong Bao* 大公報. January 17, 1939.

Hu Shi 胡適. *Hu Shi zuopinji 27: Changshi ji* 胡適作品集 27：嘗試集 [The collected works of Hu Shi, vol. 27: Experiments]. Taibei: Yuanliu Chubanshe, 1986.

Ke Zhongping 柯仲平. *Ke Zhongping wenji: Shige juan* 柯仲平文集. 詩歌卷 [The collected works of Ke Zhongping: Poetry]. Kunming: Yunnan renmin chubanshe, 2002.

Ke Zhongping 柯仲平. "Ziwo pipan (genju zhan ge she huiyi jilu)" 自我批判(根據戰歌社會議記錄) [Self-criticism (According to the records of the conference of the War Poetry Society)]. In *Shi de langsong yu langsong de shi* 詩的朗誦與朗誦的詩 [Reciting poetry and poetry in recitation]. Ed. Gao Lan 高蘭. Shandong: Shandong daxue chubanshe, 1987. 66–67.

Lan Hai 藍海. *Zhongguo kangzhan wenyi shi* 中國抗戰文藝史 [A history of Chinese literature during the War of Resistance]. Jinan: Shandong Wenyi, 1984.

Li Guangtian 李廣田. "Shi yu langsong shi" 詩與朗誦詩 [Poetry and recited poetry]. In *Langsong yanjiu lunwen ji* 朗誦研究論文集 [Research on recitation]. Ed. Jian Tierao 簡鐵浩. Hong Kong: Songhua chuban gongsi, 1978. 281–292.

Li Jinxi 黎錦熙. *Guoyu yundong shigang* 國語運動史綱 [An outline of the national language movement]. Shanghai: Shangwu yinshuguan, 1935.

Lu Xun 魯迅. "Wusheng de Zhongguo" 無聲的中國 [Voiceless China]. In *Lu Xun quanji* 魯迅全集 [The complete works of Lu Xun], vol. 4. Beijing: Renmin wenxue chubanshe, 2005. 12–15.

Lu Zhiwei 陸志韋. "Lun jiezou" 論節奏 [On rhythm]. *Wenxue zazhi* 文學雜誌 [*Journal of literature*] 1.3 (July 1937): 14–15.

Ni Haishu 倪海曙. *Zhongguo pinyin wenzi yundong shi jianbian* 中國拼音文字運動史簡編 [A short history of China's phonetization movement]. Shanghai: Shidai chubanshe, 1950.

Ren Jun 任鈞. "Guanyu Zhongguo Shige Hui" 關於中國詩歌會 [On the China Poetry Society]. In *Xin shi hua: Liangjian wenyi* 新詩話：兩間文藝 [New Poetry: Between two arts] (Shanghai: Xin Zhongguo chubanshe, 1946). 101–102.

Shen Congwen 沈從文. "Tan langsong shi" 談朗誦詩 [On reciting poetry]. In *Shen Congwen quanji* 沈從文全集 [The complete works of Shen Congwen], vol. 17. Shanxi: Beiyue Wenyi Chubanshe, 2002. 247–248.

Wang Ermin 王爾敏. "Zhongguo jindai zhishi pujihua zhi zijue ji Guoyu yundong" 中國近代知識普及化之自覺及國語運動 [The consciousness of the spread of knowledge and the national language movement in China's early modern period]. *Jindaishi yanjiu jikan* 近代史研究集刊 [Journal of research on early modern China] 11 (July 1982): 13–45.

Wang Feng 王風. "Wanqing pinyinhua yu baihuawen cuifa de Guoyu sichao" 晚清拼音化與白話文催發的國語思潮 [Phonetization in the late Qing and the implementation of the modern Chinese vernacular in the context of the trend toward a national language]. In *Wenxue yuyan yu wenzhang tishi* 文學語言與文章體式 [The language of literature and the form of writing]. Ed. Xia Xiaohong 夏曉虹, Wang Feng, et al. Hefei: Anhui jiaoyu chubanshe, 2006. 20–45.

Wang Feng 王風. "Wenxue geming yu Guoyu yundong zhi guanxi" 文學革命與國語運動之關係 [The relation between literary reform and the national language movement]. In *Wenxue yuyan yu wenzhang tishi* 文學語言與文章體式 [The language of literature and the form of writing]. Ed. Xia Xiaohong 夏曉虹, Wang Feng, et al. Hefei: Anhui jiaoyu chubanshe, 2006. 46–70.

Wei Jiangong 魏建功. "Zhongguo chun wenxue de xingtai yu Zhongguo yuyan wenxue" 中國純文學的形態與中國語言文學 [The condition of pure literature in China and literature in Chinese]. In *Wei Jiangong wenji* 魏建功文集 [The collected works of Wei Jiangong], vol. 5. Jiangsu: Jiangsu jiaoyu chubanshe, 2001. 299.

Zhu Guangqian 朱光潛. "Ti shi de yinlü bianhu" 替詩的音律辯護 [A plea for poetic rhythm], *Dongfang zazhi* 東方雜誌 [Asia journal] 30.1; republished as "Zhongguo shi heyi zoushang lü de lu" 中國詩何以走上律的路 [How Chinese poetry discovered rhythm] (chapter 12 of *Shi lun* 詩論 [A discussion of poetry]) in *Zhu Guangqian quanji* 朱光潛全集 [The complete works of Zhu Guangqian], vol. 3 (Hefei: Anhui jiaoyu chubanshe, 1993), 237 and 245.

Zhu Guangqian 朱光潛. "Xiandai Zhongguo wenxue" 現代中國文學 [Modern Chinese literature]. In *Zhu Guangqian quanji* 朱光潛全集 [The complete works of Zhu Guangqian], vol. 9. Hefei: Anhui jiaoyu chubanshe, 1993. 328.

Zhu Ziqing 朱自清. "Lun langdu" 論朗讀 [On reading]. In *Zhu Ziqing quanji* 朱自清全集 [The complete works of Zhu Ziqing], vol. 2. Jiangsu: Jiangsu jiaoyu chubanshe, 1988. 53–62.

Zhu Ziqing 朱自清. "Lun langsong shi" 論朗誦詩 [On recited poetry]. In *Zhu Ziqing quanji* 朱自清全集 [The complete works of Zhu Ziqing], vol. 3. Jiangsu: Jiangsu jiaoyu chubanshe, 1988. 253–262.

Zhu Ziqing 朱自清. "Lun songdu" 論誦讀 [On reciting]. In *Zhu Ziqing quanji* 朱自清全集 [The complete works of Zhu Ziqing], vol. 3. Jiangsu: Jiangsu jiaoyu chubanshe, 1988. 53–62.

Zhu Ziqing 朱自清. "Songdu jiaoxue yu 'wenxue de guoyu'" 誦讀教學與文學的國語 [The study of reading and the "national literary language"]. In *Zhu Ziqing quanji* 朱自清全集 [The complete works of Zhu Ziqing], vol 3. Jiangsu: Jiangsu jiaoyu chubanshe, 1988. 181, 182, and 184.

Zhu Ziqing 朱自清. "Xin shi de jinbu" 新詩的進步 [The progress of New Poetry]. In *Zhu Ziqing quanji* 朱自清全集 [The complete works of Zhu Ziqing], vol. 2. Jiangsu: Jiangsu jiaoyu chubanshe, 1988. 319.

CHAPTER 1.9

HONGKONG-SPEAK

Cantonese and Rupert Chan's Translated Theater

SHELBY KAR-YAN CHAN AND GILBERT C. F. FONG

RUPERT Chan 陳鈞潤, the famous Hong Kong drama translator, once lamented that two particular lines had been omitted from the performance script of his Cantonese adaptation of Alan Ayckbourn's *A Small Family Business*. In Act 1, Hoh Bitdaat, a private detective from Shenzhen, arrives to confront the Hong Kong businessman Mak Chaiga with the fact that he has caught Mak's daughter Mak Maanha shoplifting in a supermarket.

> MAK CHAIGA.   *(to Mak Maanha)* 人地有你嘅菲林! [They've caught you on film!]
> HOH BITDAAT.   *(corrects Mak Chaiga)* 唔係膠卷, 係錄像。 [It's not film; it's video.]

Hongkongers usually refer to photographic film as *feilam* (菲林), which is a loose Cantonese transliteration of the word *film*, while Mainland Chinese refer to film as *jiaojuan* (膠卷). The former preserves the original sound and thus the foreignness of the term, while the latter is a semantic translation that insists on sinicization. To Rupert Chan, the dialogue illustrates not just the difference in terminology between Cantonese and Mandarin, but also a discrepancy—rooted in the differences in values, culture, and lifestyle—between Hong Kong and Mainland China. This is precisely the reason why Chan insists on translating foreign plays into Hong Kong–styled Cantonese and rendering them as colloquial as possible.

Cantonese has been used in "spoken drama" performances since its inception in the 1910s, but in script writing and translations, standard Chinese had always been employed for its prestige. Rupert Chan was among the first to translate Western plays into colloquial Cantonese, and as this became a trend, it started to play an important role in the legitimization of Cantonese as a written language. After the 1997 Handover, Cantonese has been promoted by some as a symbol of resistance against Mainland

Chinese hegemony in linguistic and political terms. Through a study of Rupert Chan's use of Hong Kong Cantonese in his drama translations, this chapter illustrates the burgeoning of the awareness of Hong Kong identity in the 1980s and 1990s.

It has been argued that Hong Kong, with its lack of authentic historic roots, defines itself through two negativities: it is neither Chinese nor British, therefore it is.[1] This was the feeling in the 1980s and early 1990s, immediately preceding the Handover, during which Hongkongers found themselves in a state of not belonging to any nation, as they were only colonial subjects. Then came the Handover, and under Chinese rule ever since that transition, Hongkongers have been "learning to belong to a nation."[2] However, the negativity lingers on, and feelings of antipathy are targeted at the new sovereign, the Chinese government, and all that is associated with it. With the Umbrella Movement in 2014, the city has entered a period of "trying *not* to belong to a nation." Having been alienated by the heavy-handed tactics of the Beijing government and the government of the Special Administrative Region (SAR), it struggled for more political independence in the form of a free general election of the Chief Executive. Recently, a heightened rhetoric of Hong Kong nationalism has emerged as a new discursive force, but it remains unclear what constitutes Hong Kong nationhood. It seems that the idea of Hongkongness is based once again on negativity, predicated on differences (we are not Chinese) and the rejection of cultural or ethnic fraternity.

The 1997 Handover, according to Rey Chow, might appear to represent the end of colonialism, but in fact it merely resulted in a transfer from one colonialism to another:

> My point is, of course, not a defense of British colonialism, but rather that we need to dispel as well the myth of a Chinese nationalism masquerading as savior and possessor of a community that has, in fact, very little in common with the People's Republic at this point. And this, I think, is the most unique feature of Hong Kong's postcoloniality: the end of British colonialism will be followed by a new colonialism, that of its "motherland."[3]

The predicament of this consecutive colonialism has created a situation of "homelessness at home" in Hong Kong.[4] This feeling is aggravated by the increasing dominance of Mandarin and the potential disappearance of Cantonese. Since the sense of being at home is closely linked to the linguistic safe zone of the mother tongue, the threat to Cantonese also involves the culture and the way of life and thinking it embodies. The Cantonese movement, in this sense, represents an attempt to restore a "feeling at home" by way of linguistic practice.

In a world in which constructions of individual identity tend to be based on "natural facts," grounded in bodily configuration, the fact of where one and one's parents were born, or the mother tongue one speaks (properties that associate one's origin with a place of origin—which is to say, one's home—and a group identity as a denominator that links up these natural facts), the identity of Hong Kong people becomes fuzzy and ambiguous. According to Said, nationalism may be reduced to the sense of belonging: "an assertion of *belonging in and to* a place, a people, a heritage," which also "affirms the home created by a community of language, culture, and customs."[5] The problem for Hong Kong is, as Mathews, Ma, and Lui argue, precisely how to learn to belong to the Chinese nation, and this has many manifestations.[6] First, the Mainland Chinese membership hits a raw nerve for Hongkongers because it is imposed upon Hong Kong and wills itself to be incommensurate with other expressions of identity. The Beijing government has been increasing its intensity in imposing a monolithic PRC identity and its concomitant systems and values throughout the entire country, and especially on the outlying "prodigal son," Hong Kong. This is met with resistance on the part of Hongkongers. Second, as Rey Chow notes, Hong Kong and China have very little in common, especially in terms of political systems, social values, and cultural habits. Third, these differences are mainly driven by the distance between Mandarin and Cantonese, which has been compared to that between English and Swedish.[7] Cantonese becomes one of the important sites where Hong Kong people deal with external influences and build up their own culture, with good results. Cantonese has been viewed as a highly visible symbol that makes Hong Kong special and distinguishable from the mainland.

SUSPENSION OF IDENTITIES

For Hong Kong, the idea of the territory as home can no longer be conceived as reflecting a coherent and distinct identity; instead, as Nikos Papastergiadis has observed, identity becomes "spread across considerable distances and redefined through exchange across multiple geopolitical and cultural borders."[8] There is a need to "reterritorialize"[9]—to establish affiliations, to fill the gaps that result from the decoupling of physical location and cultural identity, and to reimagine the possibilities of establishing a larger, stronger home. Deterritorialization and reterritorialization are conjoined, with the latter occurring immediately after the former. Through various means of reaching out—such as emigration, studying abroad, overseas business connections, or simply developing a passion for things foreign—one is able to acquire more affiliations, downplaying the importance of filiations. As a result, the notion of home is situated in multiple locations, and images of home become ambivalent. There is more than one home, and each home takes on more or less importance at different times. With multiple homes come multiple identities. The concept of identity, for Hongkongers, is less a pure and unitary entity than a variegated network.

One may recall Stuart Hall's description of cultural identity as a hybrid, the result of a process of social transformation, where ideas, worldviews, and other forces interact.[10] Dissatisfied with the notion of a single unitary identity, Hall also elucidates the identity politics of a postmodern subject who contains and assumes different identities at different times, giving rise to a state of constant flux.[11] In fact, Hongkongers, given their unique history and multiple loyalties, wear many masks, but a mask connotes concealment and has a false ring to it, and with the suspension of identities, the identity being deployed, which is to say that which is not being suspended, actually belongs to and forms part of the self.[12] A temporary stabilization of subject positions can come about only when a certain constituent identity discourse rises to prominence and thus leaves others in a state of dormancy. This strategy celebrates self-determination, enabling one to freely select and put on as many identities as one wishes depending on the circumstances.

The concept of suspension of identities is particularly useful in understanding the relationship between Hong Kong and the PRC. With their particular ethnic, regional, linguistic, and cultural links, Hongkongers have been able to find various occasions to confirm, express, and sometimes even forge their own brand of Chineseness. David Faure describes this Chineseness as an "ideology and religion" comparable to "what Christendom was to the West."[13] Although Faure is referring to the pre-1997 situation, this description remains apt even after the Handover. Faure distinguishes between a cultural and a political China—one may be culturally Chinese without necessarily embracing the Chinese regime on the mainland:

> Like most people in most places, Hong Kong people wanted to be left alone to get on with their lives. Unlike most people in most places, they were faced with the certainty of a sharp break in their political culture. . . . However, from 1 July 1997 when sovereignty returns to China, Hong Kong people will be not only Chinese by culture by also by nationality. They will find a government that has every right to claim not only the right to rule but the right to demand and debate in the name of Chinese culture and identity. Integrating Hong Kong into China has required the Hong Kong Chinese people to come to the realization that politics does matter. It does matter because in the context of nationalism, the central element in political culture is not respect for tradition but patriotism.[14]

For the people of Hong Kong, the estrangement from mainland China may enable what Mikhail Bakhtin calls an "exotopy," a vision from the "outside" that overcomes the limitations of a point of view situated "inside" a particular locale or culture:

> In order to understand, it is immensely important for the person who understands to be *located outside* the object of his or her creative understanding—in time, in space, in culture. . . . In the realm of culture, outsideness is a most powerful factor in understanding. It is only in the eyes of *another* culture that foreign culture reveals itself fully and profoundly (but not maximally fully, because there will be cultures that see and understand even more).[15]

More than half a century has passed since Bahktin made these observations, and exotopy may no longer have the same significance. Culturally speaking, it is harder today to delineate where "in" and "out" are located: in a world of interdependencies or within the intertexts of cultural imaginaries, can there ever really be an outside? Timothy Weiss suggests it might be more accurate to translate the term *exotopy* as "to the side" rather than as "outside," arguing that this retranslation may explain better the situation of Hong Kong, which consistently positions itself *to the side* of the dominant Chinese culture and of world culture as a whole.[16] First, while its ethnic, linguistic, and geopolitical link with China cannot be denied, Hong Kong does not consider itself as an insider per se, but as an entity that stands at one remove. Second, the territory relies heavily on a broad cultural imagination that cuts across and includes transcultural elements. It mixes things Eastern and Western, but not without a certain skepticism and pragmatism; it often transforms imported elements and adapts them to the local situation. In the context of a suspension of identities, the Chinese identity is to be taken up and fitted in with a network of other identities when it is profitable to do so, often economically or politically, sometimes socially or culturally. In other words, Hong Kong identity can be compartmentalized. Locating Hong Kong's own identity within the Chinese "motherland" might be an easy choice for ethnic, economic, and political reasons, yet this is not actually happening. What Hongkongers aspire to is a democratic future that allows them the status of subjects, rather than remaining confined in the colonial past and the pan-colonial present in which they are mere objects.

Most discourses on Hong Kong identity describe it as modern, Western-influenced, materialist, and predominantly urban. Due to the fact that Hong Kong's development has been produced despite a lack of access to political power and an erosion of tradition following its isolation from China, Hong Kong identity is often considered a rejection from and of traditional Chinese culture.[17] While this is generally true, we should also note Hong Kong's selective attachment to any culture or identity discourse. Hong Kong identity thrives on change and a constant repudiation of unitary identity discourses. As mercurial and opportunistic as any city-dwellers, Hongkongers tend to enthusiastically welcome foreign elements (which may include English, Japanese, Korean, or Southeast Asian), but ultimately retain only those that fit their local needs. Once adopted, these elements are subject to revision and replacement when circumstances change. In other words, the development of a Hong Kong identity can be described as a cycle of suspension, sedimentation, and substitution. In the hodgepodge of identity discourses, there remain some "stubborn chunks," which refuse to be rejected, displaced, or dispelled— one of which is Chinese culture. The debates that focus on the negative correlation between Hong Kong and Chinese sociocultures are probably and justifiably fueled by Beijing's increasingly visible and heavy-handed tactics to impose a state-oriented monolithic national identity on Hong Kong, which sets out to eclipse Hong Kong's local identity. The result is a survival strategy that combines diversified exposure and discriminating attachment to and adoption of diverse cultural discourses.

LANGUAGE

Benedict Anderson famously describes the nation as an "imagined political community," the growth of which is mainly "horizontal," as every citizen is, in a sense, an equal member. Everyone searches for "a new way of linking fraternity, power and time meaningfully together." The new self-conceptions found a ready-made template from which to work: the national languages that, Anderson believes, began to emerge in the sixteenth century "as a gradual, unselfconscious, pragmatic, not to say haphazard development.[18] Michael Billig develops Anderson's position further, arguing that the term *imagined community* suggests that the nation "depend[s] upon continual acts of imagination for its existence."[19] The original "imagining" is reproduced sometimes by using national symbols purposefully, but often through daily routines of which we may not be conscious.[20] An identity may be found in the "embodied habits of social life,"[21] including language, which enables groups of people to become an "interpretive community" by managing or manipulating not only what their possessors project, but also how such projections are received and interpreted. What is thereby created is not only a nation but an entire history, based on particular interpretations of recorded events. This constitutes what Billig terms "banal nationalism," which refers to the "endemic condition" under which the concept of the nation is indicated or flagged in the daily lives of its citizenry.[22] The use of the local language in everyday life serves as a "forgotten reminder" whose significance is forgotten by the observer yet remembered in the depths of one's mind.[23]

CANTONESE

Prior to 1997, Hong Kong's two official languages were English and Chinese, which were often used in a complementary fashion, and this has remained largely unchanged after the Handover.[24] English has long enjoyed a prestigious status as the working language for the formal institutions of government, law, education, and international commerce, but is perceived less as an alien property of British colonial legacy than as a useful, neutral, international language. For the people of Hong Kong, Chinese has always been problematic, as reflected in the government's wording of its 1974 ruling on official languages that ambiguously identifies "Chinese" as the co-official language. The ambiguity usefully allows for the interpretation of "Chinese" as referring to Cantonese in its spoken form and to Mandarin in its written form. After 1997, the bilingual setting has been transformed into a trilingual one, where Mandarin was formally introduced into the sociolinguistic scene of Hong Kong through the policy of "Biliteracy and Trilingualism," which refers to the consistent use of standard English and Chinese as official written languages and English, Cantonese, and Mandarin as the spoken varieties.[25] This tripartite system is becoming clearer and more entrenched—English serving as the de facto lingua franca, Mandarin becoming increasingly important due to the political and economic prowess of China, and Cantonese retaining a strong but marginal presence. The paradox is that Cantonese is simultaneously situated at the center of everyday life but on the periphery of the official realm.

It has been argued that Cantonese has been on the scene in certain high-domain functions since the 1980s.[26] Nevertheless, Cantonese has never been promoted or extensively adopted as a regular official language. Thanks to the fairly widespread bilingual proficiency of the local people and their willingness to accommodate themselves to different linguistic situations (which is to say, they are willing to speak the language of their interlocutors whenever possible, and do not insist on speaking Cantonese all the time), one can live and get around Hong Kong without knowing Cantonese at all. All public announcements are made in English, Mandarin, and Cantonese, and most television programs are bilingually dubbed and/or subtitled. It is reported that more and more local schools are using Mandarin instead of Cantonese as the medium of instruction in Chinese lessons.

Rupert Chan and Staging Hongkongness

Rupert Chan is the first translator to use Cantonese exclusively and directly to translate plays for stage performance. He is also the linchpin of the school of localization and colloquialization in Hong Kong theater. His work illustrates that Cantonese is considered a distinct, vibrant, and creative language that is close to the heart and everyday life of Hongkongers as an emblem of their independent identity. Chan's strategy of translation affirms the importance of the local, and more importantly it shows how various cultures are compartmentalized and consolidated to buttress a Hong Kong identity, debunking the myth of purity, heritage, and opposition in the case of identity construction.

In 1991, Rupert Chan wrote a book titled *Hongkongers Speak* (港人自講) in which he discusses various aspects of the Cantonese spoken in Hong Kong, for which he coins the term *Hongkong-speak* (香港話), as opposed to the Cantonese (廣府話) that originated and is spoken in Guangzhou, China. The book's title provides an insight into the cultural identity of people in the territory. As a witty pun it can be translated as either "Hongkongers speak *to* themselves" or "Hongkongers speak *for* themselves." The title also suggests a shared membership based on the language spoken in the territory. In other words, Hongkong-speak is the language with which Hongkongers communicate among themselves, as much as it is the language they use to express themselves to the rest of the world. Second, in Cantonese the phrase 港人自講 is a homophone of 港人治港 (literally, "Hongkongers govern Hong Kong"), which was the basis of the HKSAR's Basic Law imposed by Beijing.[27] Through this title Chan attempts to relate the autonomy of Hongkong-speak to the autonomy of the territory, although his writing involves much tongue-in-cheek banter, intending to achieve rhetorical rather than political effect. Chan believes that Hongkong-speak is characteristic of the common mentality of the Hong Kong people. He describes Hongkong-speak as "the hodgepodge mixing the East, the West, the South, the North and the Middle (as in the game of mah-jongg), which is the richest of the richest and the trickiest of the trickiest."[28] Thanks to their power of amalgamation and conversion, foreign or Chinese words will become uniquely "Hong Kong" when they fall into the hands of Hongkongers.[29] He compares Hongkong-speak to Hong Kong–style fusion-cuisine quails marinated in soy sauce (豉油乳鴿).[30] Cantonese transliterations from English become commonly used phrases, and after citing numerous examples he concludes that Hongkong-speak is an important linguistic construction. Even mistranslations and mispronunciations of foreign terms, either conscious or unintended ones, reflect to a large extent the values and lifestyle of contemporary Hong Kong. For Chan, purity is an anomaly in the case of Hongkong-speak, since multilingualism and multiculturalism, as reflected in the language, are necessary conditions in the territory.[31] Written in 1991, the book also hints at Chan's nostalgia for old language use, the folk art performances of Canton, and the cultural diversity chiefly brought about by the outgoing British colonization.

The book *Hongkongers Speak* not only reflects Chan's take on the local language and identity, but also sheds light on his translations for the theater. As stated in the title of one of his more famous articles, Chan has been "Translating Drama for the Hong Kong Audience" (為香港觀眾翻譯戲劇; 1992). He dismisses scholarly translations and embraces a localized approach, in which the aim is to enhance audience identification with the story and to ensure the actors' accurate delivery of theatrical discourse.[32] He asserts that Hongkongers speak a unique and beautiful language, and posits that

> no matter whether it is translated or original drama, as long as it is produced for the Hong Kong audience, it should adopt the local language [Hongkong-speak] in order to highlight its local flavor. Personally, I adore the liveliness of Hongkong-speak, which is in a process of continuous evolution and innovation. Now that our local language has dominated the advertising field, how can the theater choose languages other than Hongkong-speak?[33]

Chan's insistence on using Hongkong-speak to translate drama reveals his strong affiliation with the local language that is shared between the translator, the actors, and the audience, allowing identification with other members of the local community. At the same time, the use of Hongkong-speak is representative of the difference between Hong Kong and Mainland China. It is symbolic of the pride and sense of belonging to the local community. This is akin to R. J. Watts's notion of an ideology of dialect, which he uses to refer to

> any set of beliefs about language in which, in a scenario in which a standardized written language coexists with a number of non-standard oral dialect varieties, the symbolic value of the dialects in the majority of linguistic marketplaces in which they are in competition with the standard is not only believed to be much higher than that of the standard but is also deliberately promoted as having a higher value.[34]

The way Chan values and promotes Hongkong-speak over the standard written form of the Chinese language is, perhaps unwittingly, linked to the desire to value and promote a sense of Hong Kong identity. For the Cantonese-speaking Hongkongers, the dialect functions, in other words, as a badge of Hongkongness, an emblem of belonging to Hong Kong.

LOCAL COLOR

For Chan, the primary goals of using the local tongue are to facilitate on-the-spot comprehension by the local audience and to manifest and accentuate the region's "local color" (本土特色). His famous puns, quips, double entendres, riddles, and ditties all have to be delivered in Hongkong-speak to fully develop their efficacy and pungency. Sometimes his translation is a hybrid of various languages and cultures (other than Chinese and English), which precisely reflects the flexibility of Hongkong-speak. In *Fooling Around with Heaven and the Emperor* (胡天胡帝; 1990), a translation of Alfred Jarry's *Ubu Roi*, Chan renders the French word *merde* ("shit") as 卡拉疴茄 (*ka¹-la¹ oh¹-ke¹*)—using a near homophone of the Japanese word *karaoke*, which was all the rage in Hong Kong in the 1990s, but with two characters, 疴茄, that in Hongkong-speak mean "to take a dump."

While the Hongkong-speak Chan uses in his theater translations signifies a sense of belonging and allegiance to the territory and its people, the strong Hong Kong identity evinced by this language also represents an attachment to the lifestyle in Hong Kong. The complicated nature of Hongkong-speak, as discussed in Chan's own book, is evidence of the prevalence of things foreign in the daily life of Hongkongers, such as Hollywood films, Japanese television drama, and Indian security guards. He also frequently inserts references to popular culture. For instance, in his adaptation of Alan Ayckbourn's *A Small Family Business*, he often uses popular and newly coined phrases like "final answer" (最後答案) and "past the safety line" (過咗保險綫) from the Hong Kong version of *Who Wants to Be a Millionaire*.

Chan's domestication agenda is somewhat self-contradictory, however. On one hand, he aims to be as "true" to the original Western plays as possible. Almost all the scenes, actions, and dialogues are retained. On the other hand, he also wants to eradicate all traces of "Westernness." The story's settings are relocated to China or Hong Kong, and the title of the play and the names of the events, places, and characters are thoroughly sinified. He renders the dialogue in a distinctly Hong Kong Cantonese style, and by way of the substitution of cultural markers and the frequent use of slang and sexual innuendo, adroitly maneuvers his translations close to a model familiar to Cantonese-speaking audiences.

DOMESTICATED SETTING

Chan's espousal of Hongkong-speak has determined his predilection for transplanting the settings of foreign plays to locations and contexts familiar to the local audience. Of his forty theater translations from 1983 to 2007, eleven have their backgrounds relocated to Hong Kong and six to China; Chan calls the former works of *localization* and the latter works of *sinification*.[35] One feature of his relocations is that the new setting is rarely modern-day Hong Kong, but rather usually either prewar Hong Kong (which is to say the 1920s–1940s) or Guangdong province at the turn of the twentieth century. Such a preference for prewar Hong Kong and old Guangdong, according to Chan, stems primarily from his nostalgia for his grandmother's language and the Hong Kong dialect, which, especially in the Japanese occupation era, was a fusion of archaic and vernacular Cantonese, with an occasional sprinkling of broken English.

Another recurring setting for Chan's translations is Tang-dynasty Guangdong, as seen, for instance, in his translation of Shakespeare's *Twelfth Night* (元宵). On many occasions, Chan expresses his fondness for Tang poetry—for its musicality, its narrative capacity, and its ability to retain the formal beauty of Shakespearean prose. He also finds the Tang poetic form, when delivered in Cantonese on stage, to be a viable substitute for archaic Western poems and ballads. For example, in the concluding scene (Act V) of his translation of *Cyrano de Bergerac* (1990), he uses three *lüshi* (律詩, "regulated poems") and one *jueshi* (絕詩, "quatrain poem") to replace the three ballads and one refrain spoken by Cyrano in the English version (see Table 1). Chan's translated poems cannot be said to be full translations; they are doggerel containing semantic items roughly similar to the originals. According to Chan, *xinshi* (新詩, "new poetry," written in free verse) sounds closer to the English version, yet he insists on adopting the classical poetic form. Diligent efforts are made to reproduce the original sound pattern by following the line length and tonality of the English ballads. The lengths of the source and of the translated poems are similar: the number of lines in each stanza is a multiple of four. The first three translated poems have eight lines, with the final syllables of the first, second, fourth, sixth, and eighth lines rhyming with the ~*ung* sound in Cantonese, while the refrain repeats the same rhyme in its second and fourth lines. All the English poems end with the same line, as do the Chinese poems.

Linguistic concerns, however, are only half the picture; other factors affecting the choice of setting include performability and plausibility. The new setting should justify the actions and mannerisms of the characters in the foreign plays. In *Cyrano de Bergerac*, for instance, the protagonist is a duelist, poet, and musician in seventeenth-century France. The plot involves many scenes where he combats various foes while composing ballads. It would appear strange for Chinese actors to duel and recite verses simultaneously in modern attire, but not when they are in period costume. In the Tang dynasty, swordplay and poetry were both popular pursuits among men of letters; it is thus a sensible substitute for the time setting.

At first sight, Chan's relocation of settings might not appear to be a strategy designed to maximize intimacy with the audience, though in practice the temporal distance produced by the period setting may actually help to facilitate reception on the part of the audience by affording them a sense of their heritage and of a multiplicity of selfhood. More generally, Chan's setting relocations, his use of Tang poetry, and his adoption of a performance style inspired by Cantonese opera evince an obvious link with the cultural heritage of classical China, or what Tu Wei-ming terms "cultural China." At the same time, there is a synchronic alignment with modern-day Hong Kong. The translated dialogues are in vernacular Hong Kong Cantonese. Chan believes his theater translations principally serve the local audience, and he feels obliged to cater to them.[36] He regards Hong Kong Cantonese as the most expressive communicative medium in Hong Kong, so he declines to translate into modern standard Chinese.

Despite the strong linguistic connection with present-day Hong Kong, Chan appears to shy away from contemporary sociopolitical issues, content to be a firm believer in the idea that theater is art and entertainment.[37] Even when producers want political comments, Chan tones them down. He states that his priority is not "using the past to allude to the present" (借古喻今) or "using the West to allude to the East" (借西喻東).[38] However, his translations and adaptations do not run short of indirect and subtle allegory. For instance, with his translation of Alan Ayckbourn's *A Small Family Business* for the Hong Kong Repertory Theatre in 2004, the director Fredric Mao initially requested that he set the story in modern-day Hong Kong, but Chan later decided to switch it to Shenzhen, China, on the rationale that with a Shenzhen setting, "a sense of distance could be maintained while certain bizarre aspects pointing to the situation in Hong Kong could be subtly reflected."[39] He emphasizes that the story is "universal" and the audience members should "withdraw themselves from the story's specific context while watching the play."[40] In the story, a security guard bribes and blackmails the protagonist's family and triggers the downfall of the family and its business. Chan thinks that the existence of the Independent Commission Against Corruption means that an act of such flagrant corruption could not possibly happen in Hong Kong.[41] This can be perceived as a rejection of political China, where corruption and bribery are rife and commonplace, and an indirect hint of the preference for a cultural China as symbolized by his adaptation of Shakespeare's *Twelfth Night*, the story background of which is set in the *Lantern Festival*'s Tang-dynasty China and old Hong Kong, rather than the present-day Communist regime.

NEOCULTURATION

Theater translation is a process and a product of transculturation. It is instructive to draw on the Cuban ethnologist Fernando Ortiz's differentiation between the interrelated notions of *transculturation* and *neoculturation*:

> I am of the opinion that the word *transculturation* better expresses the different phases of the process of transition from one culture to another because this does not consist merely in acquiring another culture, which is what the English word *acculturation* really implies, but the process also necessarily involves the loss or uprooting of a previous culture, which could be defined as a deculturation. In addition it carries the idea of the consequent creation of new cultural phenomena, which could be called neoculturation. In the end, as the school of Malinowski's followers maintains, the result of every union of cultures is similar to that of the reproductive process between individuals: the offspring always has something of both parents but is always different from each of them.[42]

Rupert Chan's affirmation of Hong Kong's local identity through translations into Cantonese is not achieved through replacing or subverting the hierarchy of the official language, nor is the local identity highlighted at the expense of a broader national (or ethnic) identity. The concept of China appeared to him to be compartmentalized, and from its different compartments he takes what is suitable for his adaptation, his audience's taste and hermeneutic competence, and his conception of the relationship between the Hong Kong identity and Mainland China. The result is a kind of quasi-allegiance to China, and the product—both his translation and the local identity represented therein—is a hyphenation as much as a hybrid.

Chan's approach could thus be described as partial and functional, with an aim to create something new and beneficial for the growth of the language and culture of Hong Kong: "Through domesticated adaptations, I connect the stems and leaves of foreign species into the trunks of local trees, enabling a kind of 'transplant' chemical action, so that a new hybridized species will come into being."[43] His localized theater translations can be considered processes of neoculturation, as they go beyond the syncretic model of an uneasy fusion between two cultures and languages. They simultaneously note the coexistence of Western and Eastern elements and highlight the loss that occurs in each of these systems when a third system is created. Chan replaces the cultural markers in the source text and gives prominence to the local language and culture. By juxtaposing two cultural origins, he underlines the historic specificity and artistic originality of the neocultural product. Without concealing the fact that his works are adaptations of foreign drama, he artfully reveals the cultural divide and convinces the audience that it is indeed surmountable. While one may say that the two cultures merge with one another, it may be more precise to say that they assimilate, substitute, and alter each other to (re)produce a third, hybridized cultural form. The process involves both loss and gain, although neither is absolute—the loss is partial and the gain creates a new cultural product. Chan's Hongkong-speak is a schizophrenic contextual combination of vernacular Cantonese, other Chinese dialects, different forms of written Chinese (drawn from sources ranging from Cantonese opera to Tang poetry), and cheeky transliterations of English. This hybrid language might be viewed as a legacy of the colonial past, a linguistic predicament, or a sign of linguistic incompetence, but it is also an opportunity to create a critical discourse against the purist Chinese nationalistic tradition and to problematize the conventional binary opposition of East and West.[44]

HONGKONG-SPEAK AND IDENTITY

Rupert Chan's domesticated translations blazed a trail in the history of theater in Hong Kong, not only because he started the trend of using local dialect to translate foreign plays for the stage, but also because in doing so he highlighted the role of Cantonese in the development of Hong Kong identity. That the use of Cantonese was popularized and its status elevated from the 1980s through the 1990s was opportune, especially as the

promotion of a fully national and socialist culture in Hong Kong by the Chinese government from the 1980s onwards threatened the survival of the former's Cantonese culture
rooted in regionalism. At the same time, the success and buoyancy of popular music,
films, and television shows in Hong Kong boosted local confidence in the superiority of
Hong Kong's own culture and facilitated the assimilation of speakers of other varieties
of Cantonese in the territory and across the border into Hongkong-speak. There used
to be a variety of Cantonese accents heard in the territory before the 1990s, but it has
since diminished and bred a kind of linguistic discrimination. Even if one is able to
speak Cantonese, if it is not the particular Hong Kong variety with its unique accent,
syntax, and vocabulary, one is almost immediately identified as a non-Hongkonger.[45]

The self-value evinced by Cantonese in Hong Kong points to a "horizontal" growth
of communal identity, in the Andersonian sense of the word. The dominance of
Cantonese, despite its subjugated status with regard to English and Mandarin, offers its
speakers "a new way of linking fraternity, power and time meaningfully together," making it possible for Hongkongers "to think about themselves, and to relate themselves
to others, in profoundly new ways."[46] The buoyancy of Hong Kong popular culture
fostered a sense of pride and solidarity among Hong Kong people during the 1980s
and 1990s. After the new millennium, the local entertainment industry lost most of
its lustre and vitality, and it is being increasingly outshone by its Taiwanese, Japanese,
and Korean counterparts, to which many investors and audiences have shifted their
attention and loyalty. With dwindling earning power and audience base overseas, the
popular culture in Hong Kong has started to turn inwards, focusing on the local market and developing a new and even quirkier brand of Cantonese. The clear division
of roles and functions between Cantonese (mainly oral or informal) and English and
written Chinese (mainly written or formal) brings about the almost automatic assignment of casual, light-hearted, and flippant utterances to Cantonese. The tone of such
tongue-in-cheek utterances is mostly irreverent, sometimes purposefully sarcastic and
even subversive. At the same time, the informal settings in which Cantonese is used
allow the speakers to blend in a few foreign-language phrases and invent new slang and
idioms, giving off a cosmopolitan and somewhat nonchalant flavor. The malleability of
Cantonese makes its discourses current and highly responsive. Therefore, Cantonese
has become the designated medium in creative culture and performance for the local
residents. In this way, Hong Kong Cantonese, the Cantonese-based popular culture,
and the everyday life of Hong Kong enjoy a dynamic symbiotic relationship. Their
interactions are invariably rapid, straightforward, and unpredictable.

This brings us to another characteristic of Hong Kong Cantonese, which is its relative exclusivity to the local Cantonese-speakers. The coinage of new Cantonese idioms
has always been popular, and in recent years this trend has been further accelerated by
the prevalence among the younger generation of online forums and chat rooms (the
best-known one being the Hong Kong Golden Forum [香港高登討論區]). *Chiuyu*
潮語 (which refers to vogue words, not the Teochew dialect)[47] is the term Hong Kong
speakers use to refer to their own brand of Cantonese, and they have produced numerous websites, publications, and even flash cards that collate and explain the meaning of
newly coined words and phrases.[48] This phenomenon gives rise to an intricate web of

intertextuality in Cantonese popular culture. One must be familiar with the language, the current topics and affairs, and the popular culture of the territory before being able to enjoy and participate in the conversation. Non-Cantonese speakers and those who are not familiar with the local popular culture, even the most competent students and scholars of Chinese language and literature, might be bewildered at the quirky and intractable syntax of the kind of Cantonese used on the local popular culture scene. Gone is the inferiority of Cantonese-based writings vis-à-vis those written in standard Chinese, as the former is often considered crude, vulgar, and not worth reading; on the contrary, there are more and more signs pointing to the fact that Hong Kong people have developed a sense of pride and ownership vis-à-vis their own language. There are more and more Cantonese novels that are able to find favor with audiences and are studied by university scholars. The exclusive use of Cantonese in the Umbrella Movement is another example of Hong Kong people's ownership of the dialect and solidarity among its speakers. The Chinese title of the movement—*Zedaa wandung* (遮打運動)—and the attendant slogans use a wide array of puns, jokes, curses, and other wordplay in Cantonese to emphasize the distinct identity that they see as under threat from the mainland.[49]

In his 1997 adaptation of George Bernard Shaw's *Pygmalion* (窈窕淑女), Chan offers two endings, in one of which the Hong Kong flower girl parts with the Oxford professor. Chan explains why she is determined to leave:

> You taught me English manners, so that I am transformed into a high-class lady. For that I owe you my gratitude. Yet at the end of the day I am still a Hongkonger. From now on I want to choose my own way.[50]

Chan thinks that this line to a certain extent reflects Hongkongers' sentiment regarding the 1997 Handover. While his compatriots in Mainland China were enthusiastically celebrating the Handover as a patriotic triumph, an act to "redress a hundred years of national shame" (洗雪百年國恥), Chan believes that Hongkongers instead viewed it as an opportunity to go their own way, to be distinct from both Britain and China. The quote is representative of the sentiment of the Hongkongers in the 1980s and 1990s; perhaps alternatively it was an expression of the frustration and helplessness prevalent in the community and a harbinger of the more belligerent regionalism in Hong Kong, such as the Umbrella Movement which made news around the world in 2014.

Translated theater, as an act of translation, is a site of contestation and construction. As an interstice, it is an apt analogy and embodiment of the encounter between cultures and languages. In the case of Hong Kong, this manifests itself as the meeting of the foreign with a more or less indigenous Chineseness. In the 1980s and 1990s, there was neither overt rejection nor repulsion of the authority of the ruling sovereign. Such an attitude remains unchanged in present-day Hong Kong, except that the demands of the Self have become more vocal and visible.

Rupert Chan went to Queen's College for high school and the University of Hong Kong for college, both of which are bastions of colonial education. He is an expert in Western opera (he regularly hosts a program on opera on Radio Hong Kong). On the

Table 1 Poems at the end of Act V, *Cyrano de Bergerac*

Source text	Translation [Literal translation]
Lightly I toss my hat away,	春意闌珊酒意濃 (*nung*^{4}) [Spring fades yet drinking mood grows stronger]
Languidly over my arm let fall	美人如玉劍如虹 (*hung*^{4}) [A beauty is like jade, and a sword is like a rainbow.]
The cloak that covers my bright array—	輕舒猿臂懲鷹犬 [Gently stretch the ape-like arm to punish the hawkish dog.]
Then out swords, and to work withal!	小試牛刀弄狗熊 (*hung*^{4}) [Try my bull knife to tease the hound-like bear.]
A Launcelot, in his Lady's hall . . .	項伯項莊空舞劍 [Xiang Bo and Xiang Zhuang brandished their swords to no avail.]
A Spartacus, at the Hippodrome! . . .	鍾紳鍾縉枉爭鋒 (*fung*^{1}) [Zhong Shen and Zhong Jun competed with each other in vain.]
I dally awhile with you, dear jackal,	龍泉飛舞龍吟和 [Dragon fountain dances and dragons sing in chorus.]
Then, as I end the refrain, thrust home!	亂既終時爾亦終 (*jung*^{1}) [When the chaos ends, so will you.]
Where shall I skewer my peacock? . . . Nay,	紫電青霜映白虹 (*hung*^{4}) [Purple lightning and blue frost shone against the white rainbow.]
Better for you to have shunned this brawl!—	莫邪干將化游龍 (*lung*^{4}) [Mo Xie and Gan Jiang became dragons.]
Here, in the heart, thro' your ribbons gay?	解牛焉用庖丁技 [To carve a cow, you do not need Pao Ding's technique.]
—In the belly, under your silken shawl?	屠狗何需朱玄功 (*gung*^{1}) [To slaughter a dog, you do not need the kung-fu of Zhu Xuan.]
Hark, how the steel rings musical!	錯捋虎鬚應有悔 [You should regret for tugging at tiger whiskers wrongly.]
Mark how my point floats, light as the foam,	敢撩龍性實難容 (*yung*^{4}) [You should not be tolerated for teasing dragons.]
Ready to drive you back to the wall,	君誠有幸朝聞道 [One is fortunate to hear Dao in the morning.]
Then, as I end the refrain, thrust home!	亂既終時爾亦終 (*jung*^{1}) [When the chaos ends, so will you.]

Source text	Translation [Literal translation]
Ho, for a rime! . . . You are white as <u>whey</u>—	詩興爭如酒興濃 (*nung⁴*) [The mood for poetry is as strong as the mood for wine.]
You break, you cower, you cringe, you . . . <u>crawl</u>	葡萄先染錦袍<u>紅</u> (*hung⁴*) [The grapes dye the robe red.]
Tac!—and I parry your last essay:	左支、右絀、連連退 [Charge in the left, withdraw in the right; you retreat again and again.]
So may the turn of a hand fore<u>stall</u>	直砍、橫揮、步步攻 (*gung¹*) [Slash vertically, gash horizontally; you attack step by step.]
Life with its honey, death with its <u>gall</u>;	架隔遮攔攔不住 [Partitions cannot block the assaults.]
So may the turn of my fancy <u>roam</u>	驚惶惱恨恨無窮 (*kung⁴*) [What a shame that fear and remorse see no ends.]
Free, for a time, till the rimes <u>recall</u>,	荊軻悔未師勾踐 [Jing Ke regretted not learning from Gou Jian.]
Then, as I end the refrain, thrust <u>home</u>!	亂既終時爾亦終 (*jung¹*) [When the chaos ends, so will you.]
Refrain:	亂曰： [Refrain:]
Prince! Pray God, that is Lord of <u>all</u>,	最是倉皇辭廟日 [It will be most hasty and sad on the day you depart the temple.]
Pardon your soul, for your time has come!	酬詩送爾入溟濛 (*mung⁴*) [The odes will accompany you into oblivion.]
Best—pass—fling you aslant, <u>asprawl</u>—	去冠、撒劍、朝天……跌 [Toss your crown, hurl your sword, towards the sky . . . and you fall down.]
Then, as I end the refrain . . .	亂既終時—— [When the chaos ends,]
—Thrust home! (Act V; Hooker 1950)	——爾亦終 (*jung¹*) [so will you.] (Rupert Chan 1990)

other hand, as seen in his translations, he also has a fondness for classical Chinese culture and literature. As such, not untypical for a Hongkonger, his is an interstitial identity. Unlike Chung King Fai 鍾景輝, who strove to preserve the distinctive "sauce and flavor" of Western theater, or the xenophilia of the Seals Theatre, Chan refuses to accept a literal translation of the source texts.[51] Nor is he willing to succumb to the might of

Chineseness as defined by the PRC, which is increasingly tainted with chauvinism. However, his brand of negativity, as is typical of Hong Kong culture, is not absolute. Like any translator, he takes raw materials from the foreign (in his case Western, especially British, drama), and renders them (using the Cantonese dialect) into something suited to the local context. The resulting products are different from their source texts but familiar to Hongkongers in form and language, their tone purposefully charged with the irreverence and irrelevance of many local movies. Yet as something new and unique to Hong Kong, they maintain an open-minded attitude vis-à-vis other cultural expressions and absorb, appropriate, and transform them, which is characteristic of the writing of Hong Kong identity.

NOTES

1. Gilbert C. F. Fong 方梓勳, "Jia zai Xianggang: Xianggang huaju de bentu xingxiang" 家在香港：香港話劇的本土形象 [Home in Hong Kong: The local image of Hong Kong drama], in *Xianggang huaju lunwenji* 香港話劇論文集 [Collection of essays on Hong Kong drama], ed. Gilbert C. F. Fong and Hardy Tsoi 蔡錫昌 (Hong Kong: Chung Tin Productions Ltd., 1992), 99–118.
2. See Gordon Mathews, Eric Kit-wai Ma, and Tai-lok Lui, *Hong Kong, China: Learning to Belong to a Nation* (London : Routledge, 2008).
3. Rey Chow, "Between Colonizers: Hong Kong's Postcolonial Self-Writing in the 1990s," in *Ethics after Idealism: Theory, Culture, Ethnicity, Reading* (Bloomington: Indiana University Press, 1998), 174.
4. See Shelby Kar-yan Chan, *Identity and Theatre Translation in Hong Kong* (Berlin: Springer, 2015), chap. 1.
5. Edward Said, "Reflections on Exile," in *Reflections on Exile: and Other Literary and Cultural Essays* (London: Granta, 2001), 176.
6. Mathews, Ma, and Lui, *Hong Kong, China*.
7. John E. Joseph, "Case Study 1: The New Quasi-Nation of Hong Kong," in *Language and Identity: National, Ethnic, Religious* (London: Palgrave Macmillan, 2004), 133.
8. Nikos Papastergiadis, "The Limits of Cultural Translation," in *The Turbulence of Migration: Globalization, Deterritorialization and Hybridity* (Cambridge: Polity Press, 2000), 116.
9. Papastergiadis, "The Limits of Cultural Translation," 115.
10. Stuart Hall, *The Hard Road to Renewal: Thatcherism and the Crisis of the Left* (London and New York: Verso, 1988), 5.
11. Stuart Hall, "The Question of Cultural Identity," in *Modernity and Its Futures*, ed. Stuart Hall, David Held, and Tony McGrew (Cambridge: Polity Press, 1992), 277; and Chris Barker, "Issues of Subjectivity and Identity," in *Cultural Studies: Theory and Practice* (London: SAGE, 2005), 224.
12. Gilbert C. F. Fong 方梓勳, "Xuanzhi de ziwo rentong: Xianggang xiju fanyi de beihou" 懸置的自我認同：香港戲劇翻譯的背後 [Suspension of identities: Behind drama translation in Hong Kong], *Hong Kong Drama Review* 5 (2007): 3.
13. David Faure, "Reflections on Being Chinese in Hong Kong," in *Hong Kong's Transitions, 1842–1997*, ed. Judith M. Brown and Rosemary Foot (London: Macmillan Press, 1997), 105.
14. Faure, "Reflections on Being Chinese in Hong Kong," 117.

15. Mikhail Bakhtin, "Response to a Question from the *Novy Mir* Editorial Staff," in *Speech Genres and Other Late Essays*, trans. Vern W. McGee, ed. Caryl Emerson and Michael Holquist (Austin: University of Texas Press, 1986), 7.

16. Timothy Weiss, "The Living Labyrinth: Hong Kong and David TK Wong's *Hong Kong Stories*," in *Translating Orients: Between Ideology and Utopia* (Toronto: University of Toronto Press, 2004), 83.

17. See, for example, Khun Eng Kuah and Wong Siu-lun, "Dialect and Territorial-Based Associations: Cultural and Identity Brokers in Hong Kong," in *Hong Kong Reintegrating with China: Political, Cultural and Social Dimensions*, ed. Lee Pui-tak (Hong Kong: Hong Kong University Press, 2001); and Andrew Simpson, "Hong Kong," in *Language and National Identity in Asia*, ed. Andrew Simpson (Oxford: Oxford University Press, 2007), 173.

18. Benedict Anderson, *Imagined Communities: Reflections on the Origin and Spread of Nationalism*, 2nd ed. (London and New York: Verso, 1991), 6, 36, 42.

19. Michael Billig, *Banal Nationalism* (London: Sage, 1995), 70.

20. Billig, *Banal Nationalism*, 75.

21. Billig, *Banal Nationalism*, 8.

22. Billig, *Banal Nationalism*, 6.

23. Billig, *Banal Nationalism*, 8.

24. See Martha Pennington, "Perspectives on Language in Hong Kong at Century's End," in *Language in Hong Kong at Century's End*, ed. Martha Pennington (Hong Kong: Hong Kong University Press, 1998).

25. Mee Ling Lai, "Cultural Identity and Language Attitudes—Into the Second Decade of Postcolonial Hong Kong," *Journal of Multilingual and Multicultural Development* 32.3 (2011): 250.

26. See, for example, Don Snow, *Cantonese as Written Language: The Growth of a Written Chinese Vernacular* (Hong Kong: Hong Kong University Press, 2004); and Simpson, "Hong Kong," 178–182.

27. In Cantonese, both phrases are pronounced *gong²-yan⁴ ji⁶ gong²*.

28. Rupert Chan 陳鈞潤, *Gangren zi jiang* 港人自講 [Hongkongers-speak] (Hong Kong: Breakthrough, 1991), 155.

29. Chan, *Hongkongers Speak*, 142.

30. Rupert Chan 陳鈞潤, "Zhizuzhe, bin yi le" 知足者，頻譯樂 [Happy is he who frequently translates], in *Wenxue zuopin de fanyi guocheng: Lilun yu shijian* 文學作品的翻譯過程：理論與實踐 [The translating process of literary works: Theory and practice], ed. Nga-lai Cheng 鄭雅麗 (Hong Kong: School of Chinese, The University of Hong Kong, 2000), 109.

31. Chan, "Happy Is He Who Frequently Translates," 98–99, 117–119, 147–149.

32. Rupert Chan, in an interview by Shelby Kar-yan Chan, December 12, 2009, Hong Kong.

33. Rupert Chan, *Hongkongers Speak*, 216.

34. R. J. Watts, "The Ideology of Dialect in Switzerland," in *Language Ideological Debates*, ed. J. Blommaert (Berlin and New York: Mouton de Gruyter, 1999), 69.

35. See Chan, *Identity and Theatre Translation*, chap. 6.

36. Rupert Chan, "Rupert Chan 陳鈞潤" (interview by Sze-wai Shing 盛思維; Hong Kong, August 1997), in *Xianggang huaju fangtanlu* 香港話劇訪談錄 [Collection of interviews with theatre practitioners in Hong Kong], ed. Gilbert C. F. Fong (Hong Kong: Hong Kong Theatre Works, The Chinese University of Hong Kong, 1997), 147.

37. Chan, Interview by Shelby Kar-yan Chan.

38. Chan, Interview by Shelby Kar-yan Chan.

39. Chan, Interview by Shelby Kar-yan Chan.

40. Rupert Chan, "Cong Yingguo yizhi dao Dai Zhonghua de *Jiating zuonie*" 從英國移植到大中華的《家庭作孽》 [*A Small Family's Business* transplanted from Britain to Greater China], presented at "Tashan zhi shi" xiju yantao hui 「他山之石」戲劇研討會 ["Rock on another mountain" drama conference] (The Chinese University of Hong Kong, Hong Kong, August 16–18, 2006), 3.

41. Chan, "*A Small Family's Business* Transplanted," 3.

42. Fernando Ortiz, *Cuban Counterpoint: Tobacco and Sugar* (Durham: Duke University Press, 1995), 102–103.

43. Chan, "*A Small Family's Business* Transplanted," 4.

44. David C. S. Li, *Issues in Bilingualism and Biculturalism: A Hong Kong Case Study* (New York: Peter Lang, 1996), 11–23.

45. For example, in her sensationally titled paper "'I Am Not Qualified to Be a Honkongese Because of My Accented Cantonese': Mainland Chinese Immigrant Students in Hong Kong" (2011), Mingyue Gu demonstrates that mainland Chinese immigrant students are aware of the social distinctions brought about by the different language ideologies between Hong Kong Cantonese and other Chinese dialects, and they tend to include the sub-cultures of different places in Mainland China in a single cultural "package" while seeing Hong Kong culture as existing independently. Mingyue (Michelle) Gu, "'I Am Not Qualified to be a Honkongese Because of My Accented Cantonese': Mainland Chinese Immigrant Students in Hong Kong," *Journal of Multilingual and Multicultural Development* 32.6 (2011): 515-529.

46. Anderson, *Imagined Community*, 36.

47. For the definition, characteristics, and development of *Chaoyu* and its use in writing, see Lau (2009: 1–53). Tak-him Lau, "The Use of Hong Kong Vogue Words in Writing and the Development of Language Education in Hong Kong" (MA thesis, University of Hong Kong, 2009), accessed January 31, 2015 at http://hdl.handle.net/10722/56696.

48. Most advertisements, comic books, and leisure and entertainment magazines and some popular paperbacks are written in Cantonese. In mass circulation Chinese papers, such as *Apple Daily, Oriental Daily, ST Headline*, and *Metro*, Cantonese plays a significant role. Even more serious political and cultural newspapers (e.g., *Ming Pao Daily, Hong Kong Economic Times, Hong Kong Economic Journal*) and journals (e.g., *Ming Pao Monthly, City Magazine*) contain some feature articles written partially or completely in Cantonese. For a detailed investigation on Cantonese publications in Hong Kong, please refer to Don Snow's *Cantonese as Written Language*. For the use of Cantonese in advertisement and public announcement and the relationship with the Hong Kong identity, see Shelby Kar-yan Chan, "*Vive la differance*! Gangshi Yueyu guanggao yu shenfen rentong" 港式粵語廣告與身份認同 [Vive la differance! Hongkong-styled Cantonese advertisements and cultural identity], in *Shangdao yu rendao: Hengguan renyu* 商道與人道：恒管人語 [Words of HSMC on business and the humanities], ed. Hang Seng Management College (Hong Kong: Chung Hwa Books, 2013), 149–151.

49. Gywnn Guilford, "Here's Why the Name of Hong Kong's 'Umbrella Movement' is So Subversive," *Quartz*, October 23, 2014, accessed February 1, 2015 at http://qz.com/283395/how-hong-kongs-umbrella-movement-protesters-are-using-their-native-language-to-push-back-against-beijing/.

50. Chan, "Happy Is He Who Translates," 108.

51. For an analysis of the translated theater of Chung King-fai and The Seals Theatre, see Chan, *Identity and Theatre Translation*, chap. 3.

WORKS CITED

Anderson, Benedict. *Imagined Communities: Reflections on the Origin and Spread of Nationalism.* 2nd ed. London and New York: Verso, 1991.

Bakhtin, Mikhail. "Response to a Question from the *Novy Mir* Editorial Staff." In *Speech Genres and Other Late Essays*. Trans. Vern W. McGee. Ed. Caryl Emerson and Michael Holquist. Austin: University of Texas Press, 1986. 1–9.

Billig, Michael. *Banal Nationalism.* London: Sage, 1995.

Barker, Chris. "Issues of Subjectivity and Identity." In *Cultural Studies: Theory and Practice.* London: SAGE, 2005. 215–247.

Chan, Rupert 陳鈞潤. *Gangren zi jiang* 港人自講 [Hongkongers speak]. Hong Kong: Breakthrough, 1991.

Chan, Rupert 陳鈞潤. "Rupert Chan 陳鈞潤" Interview by Sze-wai Shing 盛思維. Hong Kong, August 1997. In *Xianggang huaju fangtanlu* 香港話劇訪談錄 [Collection of interviews with theater practitioners in Hong Kong]. Ed. Gilbert C. F. Fong. Hong Kong: Hong Kong Theatre Works, The Chinese University of Hong Kong, 1997. 145–153.

Chan, Rupert 陳鈞潤. "*Zhizu zhe, bin yi le*" 知足者,頻譯樂 [Happy is he who frequently translates]. In *Wenxue zuopin de fanyi guocheng: Lilun yu shijian* 文學作品的翻譯過程：理論與實踐 [The translating process of literary works: Theory and practice]. Ed. Nga-lai Cheng 鄭雅麗. Hong Kong: School of Chinese, The University of Hong Kong, 2000. 103–139.

Chan, Rupert 陳鈞潤. "*Cong Yingguo yizhi dao Dai Zhonghua de Jiating zuonie*" 從英國移植到大中華的《家庭作孽》 [*A Small Family's Business* transplanted from Britain to Greater China]. Paper presented at "Tashan zhi shi" xiju yantao hui 「他山之石」戲劇研討會 ["Rock on another mountain" drama conference]. The Chinese University of Hong Kong, Hong Kong, August 16–18, 2006.

Chan, Rupert 陳鈞潤. Interview by Shelby Kar-yan Chan. Hong Kong, December 12, 2009.

Chan, Shelby Kar-yan 陳嘉恩. "Vive la différence! Gangshi Yueyu guanggao yu shenfen rentong" 港式粵語廣告與身份認同 [Vive la différence! Hongkong-styled Cantonese advertisements and cultural identity]. In *Shangdao yu rendao: Hengguan renyu* 商道與人道：恒管人語 [Words of HSMC on business and the humanities]. Ed. Hang Seng Management College. Hong Kong: Chung Hwa Books, 2013. 149–151.

Chan, Shelby Kar-yan. *Identity and Theatre Translation in Hong Kong.* Berlin: Springer, 2015.

Chow, Rey. "Between Colonizers: Hong Kong's Postcolonial Self-Writing in the 1990s." In *Ethics after Idealism: Theory, Culture, Ethnicity, Reading.* Bloomington: Indiana University Press, 1998. 149–188.

Faure, David. "Reflections on Being Chinese in Hong Kong." In *Hong Kong's Transitions, 1842–1997.* Ed. Judith M. Brown and Rosemary Foot. London: Macmillan Press, 1997. 103–120.

Fong, Gilbert C. F. 方梓勳. "Jia zai Xianggang: Xianggang huaju de bentu xingxiang" 家在香港：香港話劇的本土形象 [Home in Hong Kong: The local image of Hong Kong drama]. In *Xianggang huaju lunwenji* 香港話劇論文集 [Collection of essays on Hong Kong drama]. Ed. Gilbert C. F. Fong and Hardy Tsoi 蔡錫昌. Hong Kong: Chung Tin Productions, 1992. 99–118.

Fong, Gilbert C. F. 方梓勳. "Xuanzhi de ziwo rentong: Xianggang xiju fanyi de beihou" 懸置的自我認同：香港戲劇翻譯的背後 [Suspension of identities: Behind drama translation in Hong Kong]. *Hong Kong Drama Review* 5 (2007): 1–14.

Gu, Mingyue (Michelle). "'I Am Not Qualified to Be a Honkongese Because of My Accented Cantonese': Mainland Chinese Immigrant Students in Hong Kong." *Journal of Multilingual and Multicultural Development* 32.6 (2011): 515–529.

Guilford, Gywnn. "Here's Why the Name of Hong Kong's 'Umbrella Movement' is so Subversive." *Quartz* October 23, 2014. Accessed February 1, 2015 at http://qz.com/283395/how-hong-kongs-umbrella-movement-protesters-are-using-their-native-language-to-push-back-against-beijing/.

Hall, Stuart. *The Hard Road to Renewal: Thatcherism and the Crisis of the Left.* London and New York: Verso, 1988.

Hall, Stuart. "The Question of Cultural Identity." *Modernity and Its Futures.* Ed. Stuart Hall, David Held, and Tony McGrew. Cambridge: Polity Press, 1992. 274–316.

Joseph, John E. "Case Study 1: The New Quasi-Nation of Hong Kong." *Language and Identity: National, Ethnic, Religious.* London: Palgrave Macmillan, 2004. 132–161.

Kuah, Khun Eng, and Wong Siu-lun. "Dialect and Territorial-Based Associations: Cultural and Identity Brokers in Hong Kong." In *Hong Kong Reintegrating with China: Political, Cultural and Social Dimensions.* Ed. Lee Pui-tak. Hong Kong: Hong Kong University Press, 2001. 203–218.

Lai, Mee Ling. "Cultural Identity and Language Attitudes—Into the Second Decade of Postcolonial Hong Kong." *Journal of Multilingual and Multicultural Development* 32.3 (2011): 249–264.

Lau, Tak-him. "The Use of Hong Kong Vogue Words in Writing and the Development of Language Education in Hong Kong." MA thesis. University of Hong Kong, 2009. Accessed January 31, 2015 at http://hdl.handle.net/10722/56696.

Li, David C. S. *Issues in Bilingualism and Biculturalism: A Hong Kong Case Study.* New York: Peter Lang, 1996.

McKay, Sandra L., and Sau-ling C. Wong, eds. *New Immigrants in the United States: Readings for Second Language Educators.* Cambridge and New York: Cambridge University Press, 2000.

Mathews, Gordon, Eric Kit-wai Ma, and Tai-lok Lui. *Hong Kong, China: Learning to Belong to a Nation.* Oxon: Routledge, 2008.

Papastergiadis, Nikos. "The Limits of Cultural Translation." In *The Turbulence of Migration: Globalization, Deterritorialization and Hybridity.* Cambridge: Polity Press, 2000.

Pennington, Martha. "Perspectives on Language in Hong Kong at Century's End." In *Language in Hong Kong at Century's End.* Ed. Martha Pennington. Hong Kong: Hong Kong University Press, 1998. 3–40.

Said, Edward. *The World, the Text and the Critic.* Cambridge: Harvard University Press, 1983.

Said, Edward. "Reflections on Exile." In *Reflections on Exile and Other Literary and Cultural Essays.* London: Granta, 2001. 173–186.

Simpson, Andrew. "Hong Kong." In *Language and National Identity in Asia.* Ed. Andrew Simpson. Oxford: Oxford University Press, 2007. 173–180.

Snow, Don. *Cantonese as Written Language: The Growth of a Written Chinese Vernacular.* Hong Kong: Hong Kong University Press, 2004.

Watts, R. J. "The Ideology of Dialect in Switzerland". In *Language Ideological Debates.* Ed. J. Blommaert. Berlin and New York: Mouton de Gruyter, 1999. 67–104.

Weiss, Timothy. "The Living Labyrinth: Hong Kong and David TK Wong's *Hong Kong Stories*." In *Translating Orients: Between Ideology and Utopia.* Toronto: University of Toronto Press, 2004. 79–108.

....

SINGING
"THE INTERNATIONALE"

From the "Red Silk Road" to the Red Classics

....

XIAOMEI CHEN

IN a successful attempt to combine the theatrical conventions of modern spoken drama with Peking opera, the 2006 operatic drama *Qu Qiubai* (瞿秋白) illustrates the power of sound, which, in the words of Jacques Attali, "reflects the manufacture of society" and "prompts us to decipher a sound form of knowledge."[1] Centered on the emotional power of Qu's "Superfluous Words" (多餘的話), written in a Nationalist Party (KMT) prison in 1935, the opera probed his "traitorous" thoughts against Chinese communist history, which had resulted in a mass criticism against Qu before and during the Cultural Revolution in the 1960s. In the 1980s, Qu was gradually restored to his original status as an important early leader of the CCP and his "Superfluous Words" has been celebrated as an insightful treatment of the international socialist movements, which had questioned the problematic nature of their early leadership. It is therefore no wonder that thirty years later, this opera focuses on the last days before Qu's death, when he puts down his mask as a former Chinese Communist Party (CCP) leader and uses paragraphs from his "Superfluous Words" in speaking to his mother, two wives, and his potential lover Ding Ling 丁玲 about his private feelings.

Qu regretted having led an "actor's" career in the political theater of the CCP power struggle, when he was entrusted with presiding over the CCP's politburo at a time of crisis in 1927, after the KMT had openly turned against the party. In this process of criticizing the CCP while denying his role as a true believer, however, the sonic background of "The Internationale" throughout the performance underscores the fact that Qu *did* die heroically—while singing "The Internationale," as numerous communist martyrs did before their executions. To borrow from Jonathan Sterne's discussion of sound studies, we see in this instance how sonic practice "*redescrib[es]* what sound does in the human world, and what humans do in the sonic world": Qu should be reinscribed by his communist culture as a heroic leader because, in the final analysis, his sonic expression overpowered his "confessional" words, and his action spoke louder than his writing.[2]

By the same token, the 2010 film *Seal of Love* (秋之白華)[3] also explores a sonic imagination to reflect on Qu's creative and critical capacities as a writer, translator, and literary critic, especially in the context of his friendship with Lu Xun 魯迅 and his leadership of the leftist literary movement in the 1930s. With the motif of "The Internationale" periodically emerging at critical moments, the film highlights Qu's quiet despair when he was captured and imprisoned by the KMT after having been "abandoned" by the Red Army troops upon their retreat from Jiangxi to embark on the Long March. Both the opera and the film restored Qu to his identity as a passionate lover, a literary giant, and a committed socialist, even though he had questioned the very fundamentals of the communist ideology and the exhausting internal strife within the CCP central leadership, which had persecuted him time and again as a "leftist opportunist" and a "rightist opportunist" at different moments of crisis in early CCP history. Most significantly, both the opera and the film dramatize his execution, at which he courageously sang "The Internationale" in Russian and in Chinese on his way to the execution ground, touching many onlookers with his unflinching faith. This Chinese story expands the critical landscape of some Western scholars' work on North America and Europe, where, as Sterne observes, "in most times and places, sonic culture is characterized by the tensions held within its configuration of difference and sameness."[4] In this Chinese context, "The Internationale" harmonized Qu's opposing desires; his questioning of his own experience as a communist leader did not contradict his faith expressed in "The Internationale," which strove for the happiness of all suffering people.

In theatrical representations of Qu's life journey, "The Internationale" enabled him to express his multiple voices and multifaceted selves as a modern intellectual in search of a utopian state for the oppressed and the poor and a May Fourth literary scholar "toiling to free himself from the dilemma of *isms*."[5] Whereas the emotional power of his "Superfluous Words" expressed his putatively traitorous critique of communist doctrine, for example, the sonic power of his singing "The Internationale" paradoxically confirmed his identity as an international socialist, whose commitment to the liberation of "all the slaves of the world"—a key phrase in "The Internationale"—ultimately protected his reputation against future attacks as a "traitor."[6] Both in reallife and in artistic representations, Qu's singing of "The Internationale" transcended rigid ideological boundaries and permitted intellectuals to underscore their own humanity and dignity, while also praising the revolutionary masses as masters of their own fate. In Qu's case, singing "The Internationale" expressed his complex life, which was deeply affected by his early Soviet experience of listening to the mass singing of the song, his later life when he taught it to others, as well as his feelings of having no regret in his life upon execution. The song also "expanded" the legacy of Qu, and the paradoxical stories centering on his close relationship to it.

Taking these two performances as my point of departure, in this chapter I examine the preoccupation of Chinese intellectuals, translators, writers, and performers with the power of voice and sound. I explore soundscape as an interdisciplinary approach that links visual, sonic/aural, musical, and performative texts as a site of cultural memory and construction of knowledge, power, and historical narratives. In particular, this chapter focuses on a number of critical issues related to the prominent role of "The Internationale." For instance, how did "The Internationale" evolve from its French and Soviet roots into a Chinese nationalist song of promise, change, and progress? How did it become a rally song to mobilize the Chinese masses and convert people to the CCP cause? Why did it preserve its popularity in a way that other red classic songs did not in the zigzagging historical transitions from the high Maoist period to the heyday of the Cultural Revolution, the early Reform Era, and finally postsocialist disillusionment? I argue that despite the song's historical involvement in the construction of revolutionary discourse, such as CCP leaders' tales, war stories, socialist constructions, and postsocialist deconstructions of party history, "The Internationale" has retained its function as a song of memory and of counterculture for manipulating the very revolutionary beliefs it had helped promote in the first place. Most importantly, as a site of sonic construction of knowledge and power, "The Internationale" embodies and manifests complex and paradoxical impulses, which can at once legitimize and challenge the status quo and its authoritarian system. In the changing landscape of modern and contemporary Chinese cultural performance, "The Internationale" has captured immense emotional power, promoting a nation's political alignment with the communist movement before and after the founding of the PRC in the Maoist socialist culture; it has also expressed a Maoist nostalgia in the postsocialist period, and by remapping mediascapes and soundscapes has at once intensified and harmonized the contradictions inherent in a present in which socialist and capitalist values interact with each other in producing a unique culture that does not fit the usual binary claims of either camp.

SONIC "ORIGINS," LEADERS' POWER, AND THEIR SONG STORIES

I begin with a sonic reading of a few stories of "beginnings" with regard to the glorious life stories of the CCP founding fathers. I argue that sonic imagination has occupied a central position in their own autobiographical writings as well as in biographies and Party histories authored by others. In Qu Qiubai's own words, it was the power of "The Internationale" that first formed his socialist identity, before he had read books written by Marx, Engels, and Lenin. The profound impact of sonic power lured him into the pursuit of socialist theories and, to a large extent, changed his life trajectory from a major literary figure to the national leader of an emerging political party.

In November 1920, during his fifty-day stay in Harbin on his way to visit the Soviet Union as a newspaper reporter dispatched by *Morning News* (晨報) in Beijing and *New Current Affairs* (時事新報) in Shanghai, Qu heard "The Internationale" for the first time, sung passionately by a large crowd in Russian at the Harbin Labor Party's celebration of the third anniversary of the founding of the Soviet Union. He was deeply affected by its solemn melody.[7] "It was the first time I heard 'The Internationale,' and since then, I have enjoyed hearing it numerous times again in the Soviet Union everywhere and all the time," Qu observed, adding "It was indeed the Soviet anthem."[8] During his sojourn in the Soviet Union, "The Internationale" touched him again and again on his subsequent visits to workers' gatherings and socialist and communist congresses.

As occurred with many of Qu's contemporaries, a sonic imagination of "The Internationale" constructed a world citizen in a global socialist movement, binding an intellectual in search for "truth" to the cause of liberating the world's proletariat. It was amid the roaring singing of "The Internationale," for example, that Qu attended the First Congress of the Far East Communist and Revolutionary Parties in St. Petersburg in February 2, 1922, where "the laboring people of Petrograd" and their comrades from faraway countries shouted "long live the Soviets" to deafening applause in the magnificent imperial palace of the former regime, "shaking the great wall of an ancient kingdom with a history of four thousand years."[9] Similarly, on June 22, 1921, Qu was impressed by the music of "The Internationale" that spontaneously arose upon the declaration of the opening of the Third Congress of the Comintern in Moscow.[10] Even though after the ceremony he succumbed to tuberculosis, which he had contracted when he was sixteen or seventeen,[11] Qu wrote his *Spiritual Journey to the Red Capital* (赤都心史)—a classic piece of "red reportage" and the first of its kind in Chinese literary history—and left behind a lasting image of Lenin speaking to the audience on July 6, 1921, his silhouette reflected on the wall against red banners.[12] Qu reported to Chinese readers this exhilarating scene of Lenin speaking to the proletariat in fluent German, with the earnest and dramatic air of a "true" proletariat leader. Together with his description of the audial power of "The Internationale," Qu preserved in his writing a quintessential symbol of Russia's October Revolution, which was later captured in countless paintings, films, and performances and has influenced many generations of Chinese audiences.

Based largely on Qu's own words, biographers and party historians have credited him as the first Chinese journalist to report on the October Revolution.[13] They describe him as one of the earliest and most spirited "red ambassadors," who first travelled on the "red silk road" through Manchuria and Siberia between mid-October 1920, when he left Beijing, to January 25, 1921, when he arrived in Moscow.[14] When Chen Duxiu 陳獨秀 and Li Dazhao 李大釗 cofounded the CCP in 1921, as the result of having studied the Soviet revolution from translated writings and imported ideas from the Soviet agents sent to China by the Comintern, Qu had already witnessed the Soviet revolutionary life firsthand, and published on the postrevolutionary society with its promises and problems. Having reported these events before or around the time of the founding of the CCP, Qu became not only a pioneer in introducing Leninism to the Chinese people, but also the first teacher to instruct the first group of Chinese students dispatched by the CCP to study in the Soviet Union, and his students included many future leaders and writers in the CCP, such as Liu Shaoqi 劉少奇, Ren Bishi 任弼時, Luo Yinong 羅亦農, Jiang Guangci 蔣光慈, and Peng Shuzhi 彭術之.[15]

Interestingly, the stories of Qu being one of the CCP's "founding fathers" have often returned to his sonic experience. Although details varied, party historians and early participants who witnessed revolutionary history highlighted Qu's role in revising the Chinese translation of the lyrics of "The Internationale." Liu Jingren 劉靜仁, for example, noted how, in November 1921, Chen Duxiu, Qu Qiubai, and Liu himself witnessed the tremendous applause Lenin received when he appeared at the Fourth Congress of the Comintern, with the spontaneous singing of "The Internationale" in numerous foreign languages and accents. Chen and Qu regretted that they could not join the singing in Chinese for lack of a quality translation, which in turn prompted Qu to translate the lyrics upon his return to China.

Other memoirs describe Qu translating the lyrics from the original French in front of an organ in his cousin's residence in Beijing during 1923, testing each word against the beat of the music. As the newly appointed editor-in-chief of the journal *New Youth* (新青年), Qu published his lyrics in his journal in June 15, 1923, which popularized the Chinese version.[16] A contemporary television drama series captures this historic moment: Part 15 of *The Sun Rises from the East* (日出東方), premiered in 2001 as part of the celebration of the eightieth anniversary of the founding of the CCP, staged a scene in which Qu visited Mao Zedong's residence in Guangzhou where Qu tells Mao about his plan to publish his new translation of "The Internationale." With Cai Hesen 蔡和森, Qu recites his newly rendered lyrics with poetic zest:

> Arise, slaves, arise!
> Do not say that we have nothing,
> We shall be the masters of the world!
>
> This is the final struggle,
> Unite together towards tomorrow,
> The Internationale
> Shall certainly be realized.[17]

> 奴隸們起來, 起來!
> 不要說我們一無所有,
> 我們要做天下的主人!
>
> 這是最後的斗爭,
> 團結起來到明天,
> 英特納雄耐爾
> 就一定要實現!

In response to Cai's question, Qu explains that he did not translate the word *Internationale* into Chinese but instead rendered it as *yingtenaixiongnaier* (英特納雄耐爾) because this worked best with the beat of the music and could be understood and shared with people speaking different languages. Qu emphasized a linkage of sounds to what Sterne calls one's "cultural moments and the crises and the problems of their time"[18] and also, I would add, to the cross-cultural transformative affects of sonic power. Upon hearing that Qu had first heard the song in a worker's gathering in Manchuria for a celebration of the founding of the Soviet Union, Mao suggested in the television drama *The Sun Rises from the East* that the song be taught to "our workers, peasants and all the revolutionaries." While Qu is teaching Mao and Cai to sing the song, a montage appears with scenes from *Lenin in October* (列寧在十月), when Russian workers stormed the Winter Palace in 1917 amidst the roaring music of "The Internationale," familiar images to many Chinese audiences who had lived through the Maoist period, when the movie was very popular. Qu's teaching scene repeated itself in a subsequent episode that shows him leading Mao Zedong, Zhou Enlai 周恩來, Zhang Guotao 張國燾, and others in singing "The Internationale" during the Third Congress of the CCP, with more than thirty representatives singing the song in chorus. The continuous appeal of "The Internationale" found its expression eighty years later in 2007 in Guangzhou, which declared itself the city where the founders of the CCP first sang "The Internationale" in Chinese.

Whereas the singing of "The Internationale" became an integral part of the story of the founding of the PRC, the tales of martyrs also evoked the song as a defining moment of their lives in order to justify socialist idealism. Party histories as well as personal memoirs presented Li Dazhao as having played a key role in spreading the lyrics of "The Internationale." Li Xinghua 李星華, Li Dazhao's daughter, recalled how the first song her father taught his children was "The Internationale," and how he explained key lines such as "Do not say that we have nothing/We shall be the masters of the world" and "Who is the creator of the world?/Only us, hard working labors and farmers."[19] The sonic power of "The Internationale" appealed to Li because it best expressed his earlier ideals; in an essay written on July 23, 1920, he had explained this idea of the masses, not their "masters," having created the world. Other memoirs recorded that in January 1923, Li Dazhao and Qu Qiubai attended a gathering to commemorate the fourth anniversary of the death of German socialist leader Karl Liebknecht, where Qu sang "The Internationale" and Li delivered a speech. Li heard "The Internationale" everywhere during his July 1924 visit to Moscow, and he led his students and colleagues to sing it in training sessions for socialist activists from 1925 to 1926. Upon Li's execution by a Northern warlord in 1927, 700 mourners attended his funeral in Beijing, and once again sang "The Internationale." In countless twenty-first-century dramas, films, and television representations of Li's life and the early history of the CCP, Li is always shown singing "The Internationale" before his execution.

A 2005 spoken drama, *Searching for Li Dazhao* (尋找李大釗), however, expressed a post-socialist disillusionment with communist utopia through a clever "play-within-a-play," with the framed play depicting Li's life story and the framing play showing how a director rehearses the framed play with his cast. Employing a Brechtian alienation effect, the unfolding of the framed play is often interrupted by the director, who criticizes her cast members for lacking a basic understanding of revolutionary history. For instance, in a scene dramatizing the first meeting of the CCP in 1921, all thirteen founding members passionately sing "The Internationale," the de facto Party song at the time. The director finds that her cast can only sing contemporary Chinese pop songs, and therefore she has to teach them how to sing "The Internationale." A Brechtian interruption punctuating the loss of communist appeal ninety years after the founding of the PRC prompts the audience to reflect on the failure of the Party's mission and the senseless loss of people's lives.

The sonic effects of "The Internationale" have once again played multiple roles: it can support a "main-melody play" (主旋律戲劇) in which a selfless and noble Li helps promote the CCP campaign to battle corruption and power abuse, while at the same time revealing its very irrelevance to contemporary society, in which the CCP leadership's victory in the revolutionary war before 1949 can no longer validate its legitimacy in holding on to political power in the twenty-first century. The director's frustration in producing a revolutionary drama in a nonrevolutionary time reveals the artists' exhaustion in pursuing an aesthetic form of realist drama.

The artists' fatigue on stage echoes the ruling party's concerns with its lingering and problematic legacy in postsocialist China, as seen in recent internet coverage of the history of "The Internationale" by the CCP website cps.people.com.cn. A post titled "How Did Mao Zedong and Deng Xiaoping Teach 'The Internationale'?" (毛澤東鄧小平怎樣親自教唱國際歌?) repeats the familiar stories about the song, including Qu Qiubai's translation, Mao's teaching of it to the Red Army soldiers in Jinggangshan in 1927, his ending a poem with it to celebrate the victory of a key battle,[20] his leading a collective singing during a New Year celebration in Yan'an in 1938, and his discussing its educational role during a speech at the Seventh Party Congress in Yan'an in 1945. This online essay likewise lists Zhu De 朱德, Liu Shaoqi, Zhou Enlai, and Deng Xiaoping's invocations of the song at different historical moments, with intriguing detail that reveals a clever use of the song by one state leader to counter the mainstream ideology in the early 1960s. Chen Yun 陳雲, for example, quoted the line "we can only rely on our own efforts" to justify his approval of a controversial policy known as "allocating land to individual peasants" in order to raise agricultural production during the economic crisis after the failure of the Great Leap Forward. In the realm of aesthetic pursuits, moreover, the essay argues that the beginning lyrics in the national anthem, such as "Arise, those unwilling to be slaves" (起來, 不願做奴隸的人們) were inspired by the first line of "The Internationale": "Arise, slaves, arise!" (起來, 飢寒交迫的奴隸).[21] The frequent and even contradictory uses of "The Internationale" support Sterne's description of sonic phenomena and their interpretation as "a product of changes in thought,"[22] but most importantly, the song's rich history and never-ending transformations in contemporary China highlight the historical conditions unique to the Chinese revolutionary experience and its characteristic differences from other nations, formerly socialist or otherwise.

"FOREIGN" SONG, CHINESE "RED CLASSICS," AND THEIR SOUNDSCAPE

While the founding fathers' stories intersect with "The Internationale," the dawning years of the PRC culture industry have likewise been linked to preserving and developing the sonic power of this rally song. In this section, I consider a few examples of "red classic" performances in the early years of the PRC, bearing in mind a few critical questions. How did this foreign song become popularized as a virtual CCP "Party song"? What was the appeal of Maoist discourse as a tool in producing devoted citizens and a shared mission that crossed international boundaries and historical periods? How was "The Internationale" used in PRC performance art in the form of a theme song, a piece of background music, a stage line, or visual representations of the Paris Commune and Eugène Pottier (author of the song's lyrics) in propaganda posters? I argue that key lyrics of "The Internationale," such as "Arise, ye oppressed people all over the world!"; "Do not say that we have nothing,/We shall be the masters of the world!" and "This is the final struggle,/Unite together towards tomorrow" best explained to the Chinese people some of the central concepts of the Maoist discourse of equality of class, gender, and race, as well as its global vision of emancipating all mankind after the Chinese people's own emancipation.

"The Internationale" certainly helped construct the collective identities of Chinese socialists in the early period of Chinese revolution, the Maoist period, and especially during the Cultural Revolution. In addition, "The Internationale" redefined the Chinese revolution as "a continuous revolution" to lead Third-World countries in their struggle against Western imperialism and Soviet revisionism in the Cold War era. Throughout the decades following the collapse of the Berlin Wall and the disintegration of both the former Soviet Union and the Eastern European socialist bloc, "The Internationale" has maintained its sonic power in advocating a new brand of "socialist China" in the reform era, transforming China into a capitalist economy with "socialist characteristics." This can be seen in the song's permanent positioning as a concluding piece in three revolutionary music and dance epics from 1964 (*The East is Red*; 東方紅), 1984 (*The Song of the Chinese Revolution*; 中國革命之歌), and 2009 (*The Road to Prosperity*; 復興之路).[23] In all three epics, "The Internationale" speaks to the Maoist socialist blueprint in liberating the oppressed slaves, the Dengist march toward modernization and prosperity as "the final struggle," and the post-Deng leaders' pursuit of the "Chinese dream" so that the Chinese people will truly become "the masters of the world!"

I start with the importance of several Soviet films and their role in popularizing "The Internationale" in the beginning years of the PRC. At least three films on Lenin—each featuring "The Internationale" at key moments—were translated and released in China between 1950 and 1952. The construction of the Maoist discourse in early PRC films, therefore, partially drew its inspiration from Soviet cinema, which was ingeniously combined with the May Fourth new music and leftist mass composition, benefiting from what Andrew F. Jones calls "the hierarchized 'music historical field' of the Republican period."[24] It was not until the mid-1950s that "The Internationale" began to appear in execution scenes of CCP martyrs in domestic films, and it reached its peak appearance in 1960s film, in the background music of model theater, and in sessions of mass singing of revolutionary songs.

Produced in 1936 by the Moscow Film Studio and dubbed in Chinese in 1950 by China's Northeast Film Studio, *Lenin in October* dramatized Lenin's secret arrival in St. Petersburg following his 1917 winter exile in Finland, his convincing coleaders to stage a military uprising to seize political power against the argument for delaying such action made by Trotsky, his sleeping on the floor of his bodyguard's apartment the night before the onset of the October Revolution, and its final victory. The movie features "The Internationale" twice: in a "martyr scene" when a driver kills a policeman who is on the way to capture Lenin, and in a "celebration scene" when Lenin declares the eventual realization of the long-cherished dream of a "mass revolution" in the victory rally at the conclusion of the movie.[25]

Lenin in 1918 (列寧在一九一八), produced by Moscow Film Studio in 1939 and released to Chinese audiences in 1951, depicts the dramatic events in the year after the October Revolution and Lenin's determination to defend the first socialist state against imperialist forces and the "White army."[26] "The Internationale" emerged at the electrifying moment upon Lenin's entering a factory to mobilize the cheering crowd against the reactionaries' rebellion; the sound track of "The Internationale" stops after Lenin is shot by a woman assassin, signifying a painful and dramatic moment in the course of the Bolshevik revolution.

Together with the audio and visual effect of "The Internationale," Lenin's statement to the workers during his speech that "preserving a political regime is more difficult than winning it" became a well-known slogan in the 1960s to justify Mao's call to "never forget class struggle," especially during the Cultural Revolution, as films on Lenin became even more popular at a time when most domestic and foreign films were banned. The music of "The Internationale" in *Lenin in 1918* around the assassination scene now took on a new significance, suggesting that the hidden agents of the bourgeoisie were the most dangerous enemies of the people. That is why, in the subsequent scene, Lenin convinced Gorky never to show mercy for the class enemies: "We were too soft in the past; the bullets of the intellectuals are still lodged in my body," a warning which justified persecutions of the "bourgeois intellectuals" before and during the Cultural Revolution.

Less popular than the two preceding films, *The Unforgettable 1919* (難忘的一九一九), produced in 1952 and dubbed by the China Northeast Film Studio in 1952, dramatized the Soviet Red Army's 1919 defeat of the White Army at the battle to defend Petrograd against British, American, and French forces, with the dominant presence of Stalin as a key leader, a manifestation of the cult of Stalin in the 1930s.[27] Despite its departure from its precursors, *The Unforgettable 1919* similarly concludes with the rising music of "The Internationale" at a mass rally, together with the crowd cheering "Long live Stalin!"

The prominence of "The Internationale" in these Soviet films, however, did not transplant itself immediately into the making of a new cinema in the beginning years of the PRC. Among the Chinese films released in 1950, at least three martyr movies could have used "The Internationale" for their execution scenes, but they resorted instead to the popular music of the Republican period and Western musical instruments. *Zhao Yiman* (趙一曼), for instance, depicts the heroic story of the title heroine, a CCP woman commander in the Northeastern Allied Force against the Japanese invaders, and her eventual capture and torture in the enemy's prison. Before her execution, Zhao calmly puts on her best attire, combs her hair, encourages her cellmates to carry out their unfinished tasks, and bravely shouts, "Long live the Chinese Communist Party" on her way to the execution ground. This execution scene closely resembles the familiar act of Jiang Jie in the well-known 1965 film *Living Forever in Burning Flames* (烈火中永生).[28] While Zhao was accompanied by the music of the film's theme song, characterized by mixed tones of leftist and popular music before 1949, Jiang Jie instead marched to the execution ground with the rising music of "The Internationale," arm-in-arm with her comrade, while shouting "Long live the Chinese Communist Party" and "Long live Chairman Mao" before the enemy's gunshots. In this latter film, an obvious Mao cult in the 1960s resulted in the slogan switch from pledging loyalty to the party to the supreme leader himself—as seen in Jiang Jie's bravery before execution. A parallel switch from pre-1949 leftist popular music to "The Internationale" likewise intensified the symbols and performative style of 1960s cinema, which connected a new Maoist nation with global socialist and communist movements through a vibrant visual and audial tradition of the red classics. Thanks to the more radical policies in the 1960s, the exploration of the "new music" of the May Fourth period and of the Chinese folkloric tradition present in the early 1950s film receded into history and was replaced by the more "purely" communist song of "The Internationale."

Zhao Yiman was not alone in drawing from cultural and artistic traditions of the Republican period. In *Shangrao Prison* (上饒集中營), also released in 1950, the multiple execution scenes do not include "The Internationale" but use the choral singing popularized in Yan'an and elsewhere during the war, featuring leftist musical tunes pioneered by Nie Er 聶耳 and Xian Xinghai 冼星海, accompanied by piano, violin, cello, and other Western symphonic instruments for dramatic, tragic, and heroic affect. *Steel-Made Soldiers* (鋼鐵戰士), released in 1950, shares many features with *Shangrao Prison*; its lengthy story line in a prison setting with repeated torture and execution scenes did not call for any use of "The Internationale," despite its popularity in the political life of the Chinese people during the same period.

Although the films released in 1950 did not feature "The Internationale," one work did feature a key line from the lyrics, as seen in the film's title: *Unite Together Toward Tomorrow* (團結起來到明天). Starring Bai Yang 白楊 dressed in a textile worker's uniform as a representative of the oppressed proletariat, the film dramatizes workers' strikes against the KMT government in 1948 in an effort to protect their factory on the eve of Shanghai's liberation. The movie concludes with a victory rally featuring a theme song expressing the workers' will: "Unite together toward tomorrow/ our glorious struggle, brave and firm/not afraid of countless difficulties/only the CCP can bring us the glory of victory" (團結起來到明天/我們光榮鬥爭勇敢堅強/千難萬苦不怕阻擋/有了共產黨才有勝利的榮光). Both the visual power of the movie stars of the Republican era and the popular songs of the early 1950s—such as "The Bright Sky in the Liberated Areas" (解放區的天是晴朗的天) and the PLA march song, "Our Troops March Toward the Sun" (我們的隊伍向太陽)—seemed sufficient in highlighting the mood and spirit of the film without having to resort to the actual music of "The Internationale," whose key phrase in the film's title already featured a new Chinese nationalism "toward tomorrow."

One of the earliest uses of the "The Internationale" may be found in the 1956 film *Mother* (母親), which dramatized the story of a migrant worker who moves from a poverty-stricken rural area to Shanghai, only to lose her husband to the foreigners' cruel exploitation of steel workers; she devotes the rest of her life to the CCP underground work under dangerous conditions while raising three children to become dedicated communists. At the low ebb of the revolution, Mother witnesses the brutal arrest of Lao Deng, the underground leader of the workers' movement, but Lao Deng refuses to betray his comrades and—after repeated torture—he fearlessly walks out of his prison cell, singing "The Internationale" on the police truck and all the way to the execution ground.

This direct use of "The Internationale," however, did not preclude the movie from also incorporating popular songs of the Republican period, as seen in variations of the theme song "How Can I Not Miss Her" (叫我如何不想她), originally written by Zhao Yuanren 趙元任, and played as background music throughout different moments in the movie. According to Andrew Jones, Zhao belonged to "the luminaries of May 4th era literature and culture," who were also "active in promoting new music" and shared the mission of "the nation-building enterprise."[29] In addition, Zhao's song accompanied the love scene between the mother's oldest son and her future daughter-in-law, both underground CCP members, who discuss their secret work while rowing a boat on the lake at Beihai Park in Beijing. Using "How Can I Not Miss Her" was both historically accurate, because of its popularity in Beijing at the time of the film's setting, and thematically appropriate for a budding romantic love. The star power of the Republican period, as seen in the captivating performances by Zhang Ruifang 張瑞芳 and Jin Yan 金焰 in *Mother*, also provided the movie with a transnational, transhistorical, and perhaps even transideological appeal.

Following a similar story line of a courageous mother, the 1960 film *A Revolutionary Family* (革命家庭) portrays Zhou Lian, an illiterate woman in an arranged marriage, who finds in her husband a loving man and a patient teacher who teaches her how to read and write as well as "the revolutionary truth." A local CCP leader working tirelessly in organizing peasant and workers' movements in 1927, her husband dies of fatigue and illness, but the mother takes over his underground work while raising their three children. In a moving scene, she enjoys listening to her oldest son's story of having witnessed "a brand new life" in the Soviet Union, where workers no longer suffer from oppression and exploitation. Shortly thereafter, on his way to the Jiangxi Red Army area, he is captured, tortured by the KMT, and heroically embraces his death, singing "The Internationale" as he walks out of his prison cell, soon joined by a chorus of all the prisoners, and witnessed by his mother in a nearby cell. Heartbroken by her son's death, yet proud of his loyalty to the party, the mother becomes even more determined to fight for the common cause of all the proletariat, which now includes avenging her own son.

In *A Revolutionary Family*, the singing of "The Internationale" unites two generations of revolutionaries, as the mother and son's farewell ritualizes sacrifice and redefines the family connection as secondary to the class relationship. A new revolutionary family also accidentally "confirms" the value of an arranged marriage of the traditional culture, which happened to provide the mother with a loving husband who appreciated her for who she was. This sort of possible "patriarchal" reading, however, could be countered by the real life story of Yu Lan 于藍, who played the role of Zhou Lian. In the 1930s, at age seventeen, Yu had walked for fifty days to reach Yan'an, where she trained at the Lu Xun Art Academy and debuted in her protagonist role of another revolutionary mother in the 1951 film *Red Flag over Green Hill* (翠崗紅旗). Her spectacular performance of Zhou Lian won her the best actress award in the second Moscow International Film Festival. In contrast to her dramatic character Zhou, whose marriage was arranged according to the mandate of the traditional ethics, Yu Lan's falling in love with Tian Fang 田方 in Yan'an, their shared limelight in pioneering a new cinema in the early years of the PRC, and happy marriage testified to the enduring "truth" of "The Internationale"; as its second stanza proclaimed:

> There has never been any savior of the world,
> Nor deities, nor emperors on which to depend.
> To create Mankind's happiness
> We must entirely depend on ourselves!
>
> 從來就沒有什麼救世主,
> 也不靠神仙皇帝。
> 要創造人類的幸福,
> 全靠我們自己!

"The Internationale" became increasingly prominent in mid-1960s cinema, particularly in "red classics" such as *The Red Detachment of Women* (紅色娘子軍) and *Living Forever in Burning Flames*. As Barbara Mittler observes, during the Cultural Revolution "The Internationale" appeared in most of the model works at their execution scenes, such as *The Red Detachment of Women*, in which Hong Changqing is burned to death by rich landlords, and *On the Dock* (海港), when "The Internationale" became "an important leitmotif" to highlight the spirit of internationalism in support of the oppressed peoples of the world.[30] In the most radical claim by the official media during the Cultural Revolution, "The Internationale" was even cited as the only revolutionary song since the birth of the Paris Commune of 1871; according to this claim, all the works produced in the 100 years from "The Internationale" to the model theater were nothing but expressions of feudalist, capitalist, and revisionist arts and should therefore be eliminated.[31] "The Internationale" was therefore explored in the sweeping ideological campaign against literary and artistic achievements of the May Fourth period and the first seventeen years after the founding of the PRC in order to carry out "the Great Proletarian Cultural Revolution." If Roderick MacFarquhar was correct in concluding that perhaps part of Mao's motive to initiate the Cultural Revolution was to "galvanize the country" after "routine replace[d] voluntarism" and "responsibility clog[ged] idealism,"[32] "The Internationale" apparently rallied the masses toward achieving that rebirth of a Chinese revolution. Ironically, right after September 13, 1971, when Lin Biao—Mao's chosen successor—was believed to have escaped to the Soviet Union and the entire country was under a secret military alert, the Central Radio Station was told to repeatedly broadcast "The Internationale" and "Three Main Rules of Discipline and the Eight Points for Attention" (三大紀律八項注意)[33] in an attempt to maintain order and stability after this shocking event. In early post-Mao China, however, when new plays, operas, and films criticized the Gang of Four and their drastic policy of litera-ture and art, "The Internationale" once again gained popularity in shows about CCP leaders who had been persecuted during the Cultural Revolution. Several performance pieces on Zhou Enlai dramatized his waning days before his death, when he sang "The Internationale" with his wife to express his revolutionary resolve despite being indicted as a "contemporary Confucius" by the members of the Gang of Four. Numerous theater works and films also staged early historic events such as the Nanchang Uprising and Autumn Peasant uprisings of 1927, with their frequent use of "The Internationale."

Lesser-known events, such as the Guangzhou Uprising, were also staged in early post-Mao China, as seen in a spoken drama titled *Guangzhou Thunder* (廣州驚雷). Unlike the troops in the Nanchang Uprising, who quickly retreated from the city to pre-serve its forces, the participants in the drama occupy key spots in Guangzhou, such as the telegraph station, the police department, the train station, the electricity plant, and the central bank, just as (the fictional) Lenin had advocated in *Lenin in October*. They defend their posts against the gunshots of the imperialist forces of America, Britain, Japan, and France after three days of fierce combat in the city, in the spirit of the Paris Commune of 1871. In one dramatic scene, Zhou Wenyong, a leader of the uprising, declared to his ex-lover that contrary to her obsession with bourgeois Western music, such as Beethoven's Symphony No. 5 with its "Fate" motif, it was "The Internationale," the "militant song of the starving slaves, which would be heard all over the world to inspire the proletariat to achieve victory in the realization of communism."[34] In real history, upon the defeat of the Guangzhou Uprising, Zhou was imprisoned, and he had only one request before his execution: to have a picture taken with Chen Tiejun, who had pretended to be his wife as a cover for their underground activities. They had fallen in love, but were too busy for romance. On the execution ground, however, they finally declare their love, sing the "Internationale," and perform their own wedding in front of their enemies. A 1980 film titled *A Wedding at the Execution Ground* (刑場上的婚禮), which accurately presents this real-life story, has been adapted into a "Guangdong opera" (粵劇), a "dance drama" (舞劇), a "Peking opera" (京劇), and other theatrical pieces, all featuring the leitmotif of "The Internationale."

Early tales of love and revolution in the last two decades eulogized Deng Xiaoping as an even more supreme leader than Mao—according to the popular saying, "Mao brought us liberation, but Deng brought us happiness" (毛主席為我們得解放, 鄧小平為我們謀幸福). Ironically, in the new era, when prosperity justified a res-toration to capitalism, which ran against the communist spirit expressed in "The Internationale," the song still occupied a central position in deifying Deng Xiaoping in numerous performances, which Mao would have called "revisionist poisonous weeds" engineered by agents of the "number-one capitalist roader," as Mao had called Deng in 1976. The award-winning 2004 film *My Years in France* (我的法蘭西歲月),

for instance, depicts a young Deng, unemployed and too poor to enroll in a school in France, between 1920 and 1925. He befriends Zhou Enlai, Zhao Shiyan 趙世炎, Li Fuchun 李富春, Cai Chang 蔡暢, Nie Rongzhen 聶榮臻, and other future leaders of the CCP, and throws himself enthusiastically into the Bolshevik cause. Focusing on Deng's adolescent life, the film demonstrates the energy, passion, and utopian appeal of the socialist movement in the 1920s that turned a group of foreign students into determined communists.

While portraying Deng's experience growing up in France, the film explores a rarely represented event in the history of the founding of the European branch of the Young Chinese Communist Party.[35] With youthful energy and a romantic spirit, the charismatic and handsome Zhou Enlai, together with his young friends such as Zhao Shiyan, Zhang Shenfu 張申府, and Liu Qingyang 劉清揚, climbs to the top of Notre Dame to enjoy the enchanting bird's-eye view of Paris while celebrating their having finally found in each other "true comrades-in-arms and true isms." Proud of their zealous endeavors to establish the Paris communist group in "the heart of European culture and politics" for the sake of promoting a Chinese communist movement, they recall Marx and Engels's lonely efforts to rely on each other in developing the theories of communism. The five are now confident that in a few years' time the "fire of the Chinese communist movement will spread to every corner of the Chinese soil, and to wherever Chinese sons and daughters live."[36] They decide to educate overseas Chinese students and laborers about a Marxist approach to a Chinese revolution, and to establish contact with the French Communist Party and the Soviet Union. Accompanied by the captivating tolling of Emmanuel, the great bell of the cathedral, the young founding fathers sing "The Internationale" to their heart's content, which Xiao San, a young communist enthusiast and a romantic poet, vows to translate into Chinese so that the proletariat back home can enjoy a song of its own.[37] A cinematic view of a romantic, exotic Paris points to the irony of a youthful group from a backward China who became the vanguard of a proletariat movement of which they had little knowledge but to which they nevertheless devoted their lives. The power of "The Internationale" and its translation into another language once again defined a critical moment in the founding history of the CCP and, most significantly, in a new era which evoked communist idealism and its symbolic songs to validate the legitimacy of a one-party system in postsocialist China.

EMOTIONAL POWER, MOBILIZATION, POLITICIZATION, AND COUNTERCULTURAL RALLY

As demonstrated above, performances of "The Internationale"—both in everyday life and in theatrical representations—became expressions of the communist movement against KMT rule before 1949 as well as a rally song in the socialist experience that would define CCP rule. Such wide and complex implications of "The Internationale" have also become integral parts of contemporary theater history. "The Internationale" has been featured prominently in the writing of the official history of the early revolutionary military base areas in Jiangxi Province and in Yan'an, and in particular in the context of the "red theater movement." As recorded in his *Red Star Over China*, Edgar Snow was impressed by the Red Army amateur performances of drama skits and a harvest dance for the local peasants, with leaders such as Mao Zedong, Lin Biao 林彪, Liu Bocheng 劉伯承, and their wives sitting among the cadets, workers, clerks, and villagers on the ground in the open fields in 1936 Bao'an. At the end of a three-hour-long variety show, a children's chorus concluded the evening by singing "The Internationale," while the young women dancers stood erect with their "fists upraised as the song ended."[38]

Snow was told that red theater drama troupes had begun in Ruijin, Jiangxi, in 1931, where the Gorky School recruited and trained approximately sixty theater troupes; as a result, every army unit had its own performance group. Snow observes that "even though it was 'propaganda in art' carried to the ultimate degree," the red theater was able to meet "a genuine social need" for the local peasant starving for any cultural event, as it "calmed the fears of the people, gave them rudimentary ideas of the Red program, and dispensed great quantities of revolutionary thoughts, to win the people's confidence."[39] Snow effectively pinpointed the close connection between propaganda art and the victory of the communist revolution, stating, "One could think of the whole history of the Communist movement in China as a grand propaganda tour, and the defense, not so much of the absolute rightness of certain ideas, perhaps, as of their right to exist."[40] This practice of singing "The Internationale" as part of CCP propaganda would become more fully developed over the following decades, and furthermore would become popular in local social events, public education, and war mobilizations, as well as oral and performance culture.

This powerful sonic culture was developed further with the institutional practice of providing a Red Army unit with a performance team, which became an essential part of the process of politicization of CCP soldiers from the 1930s to contemporary times. A remainder of this practice persists in the twenty-first century, when a professional army theater troupe staged the spoken drama *Music from Heaven* (天籟). The play depicts a Red Army performance team, which carries a gramophone through numerous and fierce battles during the Long March. In a central scene of the play, a young soldier loses her life protecting the instrument that was a gift from the Soviet Red Army, and had been treasured as one of the most precious "weapons" in fulfilling their mission in political mobilization for the army units on the war front. In another scene, a woman team leader plays "The Internationale" from a record she had brought back from the Soviet Union in an attempt to educate her coleader on the mission of their performing team, which was deemed as important as any fighting unit engaged in actual combat. At the end of the scene, fellow performers join her in singing "The Internationale" while a revolving stage displays them in a group sculpture, with each of them performing their skits while mobilizing fighters on the battlefield. According to the reviews, *Music*

From Heaven was successfully premiered in 2007 by Comrade Theater attached to the political department of the Guangzhou Military Region, and this "autobiographical" play dramatized the history of this particular army theater: it was first organized as a propaganda team of the Fourth Red Army in Jinggangshan in 1928, when high-ranking commanders such as Nie Rongzhen, Luo Ronghuan 羅榮桓, and Luo Ruiqing 羅瑞卿 occasionally served as directors, scriptwriters, or actors.[41] It was later renamed Soldier's Theater and accompanied the Red Army troops through all key battles during the Long March, as portrayed in *Music from Heaven*. The celebration of "The Internationale" in the play as a unifying song, therefore, dramatized its circulation through a record from the Soviet Union to the Chinese war fronts in order to emphasize the equally important function of "a cultural army" (文化大軍) and its talented creation of "a red culture" (紅色文藝) since the 1930s. The play created a theatrical monument that eulogized the contributions and sacrifices of the army performers in the revolutionary past and a unique theater tradition during the war period.

In the twenty-first century, joining an army performance troupe has remained a dream job for many aspiring artists, even though each group of performers is required to perform at least 100 shows for grass-roots army units, some stationed in extremely remote areas under very difficult circumstances.[42] While singing "The Internationale" and other red songs defines the troupes' repertoire, an army stage provides a golden opportunity for budding stardom and an entry path into the commercial circle of movie and television dramas. Those faithful in following their seemingly less rewarding careers in the army might on occasion eventually find stardom on a greater stage, such as the actress Peng Liyuan 彭麗媛. Peng tested into an army troupe at age fifteen, and went on to become one of the best singers in contemporary China. One Internet article celebrated Peng's thirty-two years of performing "classic red songs" (精品紅歌), which includes "The Song of the Heroes" (英雄贊歌), the theme song of a 1964 popular film entitled *Heroic Sons and Daughters* (英雄兒女) about the Korean war. In this film, the protagonist Wang Fang, an army performer, succeeds in her painful assignment of scripting and singing about the heroic death of Wang Cheng, her stepbrother, who had thrown himself into South Korean troops with his last explosive device in an effort to defend his post as the last surviving soldier on the battlefield. Peng Liyuan's performance of Wang Fang's famous song in praise of the selfless soldiers of the Chinese volunteer army in support of North Korea in the war against the US imperialists and the South Korean capitalist regime fulfilled multiple tasks. It celebrated the revolutionary traditions of fearless soldiers as well as the talented performers who had encouraged them at the front and spread their deeds to the entire army, the nation, and the world. Singing a revolutionary song during not-so-revolutionary times also validates the ruling party's right to power since, as the article proclaimed, Peng expressed the "positive energies of the CCP's founding principle of serving the public and ruling for the people's interests in her coming out into the world to sing the red songs."[43] Not surprisingly, Peng appeared at the 2014 Spring Festival Eve Gala, which opened with the singing of "The Internationale."

Despite the seminal role of "The Internationale" in maintaining the hegemony of the dominant CCP ideology, its symbolic and emotional power could also rally a countercultural movement to challenge the official culture. The story of the song, therefore, would not be complete without mentioning its countercultural and subversive role in the 1989 Tiananmen student demonstration by way of example. The Cui Jian 崔健 phenomenon is a case in point. During the early years of the reform era, Cui's rock-and-roll song "I Have Nothing" (*yiwu suoyou* 一 無所有) captured a generation of the Chinese people who shared his feeling of possessing nothing in a society rapidly moving away from its socialist past. Having grown up in the Maoist period with an inspiring message such as "don't say that we have nothing/we will become the masters of the world" from the "The Internationale," many from Cui's generation felt profoundly disillusioned by communist idealism after the end of the Cultural Revolution, because they owned nothing with which to compete in a world intent on the pursuit for material wealth. Originally written as a love song for his girlfriend, Cui's confessional song simultaneously expressed a deep sense of loss, and has thus been interpreted as a political allusion and a protest against the status quo. Cui's electrifying performance of the song in Tiananmen Square became a central event in the 1989 student demonstration against the government's corruption and refusal for political reform. Ironically, "The Internationale" has retained an equally powerful appeal; when the occasion arose, it blended perfectly with "I Have Nothing" as timely expressions of a rebellious generation. As Yang Fan recalled, "The Internationale" reminded him and his fellow students of their responsibilities and inspired them to "stand up to the highest authority in China"; "I was ready to die for the great cause"—when the song "superseded all sound on the square," he "grew up and became a man."[44]

In one of the most memorable moments during the government crackdown of the demonstrations on June Fourth, 1989, the last group of students reluctantly retreated from Tiananmen Square at gunpoint while singing "The Internationale." Liu Xiaobo 劉曉波 recalled how the students' command headquarter repeatedly broadcast the oath "Heads may be chopped off, blood may flow, but democratic liberty may not be lost": "The sad strains of the official song of the Chinese Communist Party, the 'Internationale'; the heavy atmosphere of martyrdom; and the spirit of sacrifice blended together perfectly."[45] From a slightly different perspective, Andrew Jones also pointed out the political use of rock music in student demonstration "as a means for affective empowerment, cultural critique, *and* as a conduit for explicitly political protest."[46]

Despite Cui's denial that his lyrics concerned the Chinese people's lack of freedom and democracy, his "I Have Nothing" was understood by some listeners as "an ironic response to the Chinese lyrics of the 'Internationale,'" which proclaimed "Slaves rise up, rise up!/We cannot say that we have nothing [*yiwu suoyou*]/We will be masters of all under heaven."[47] The previously oppressed slaves in the pre-1949 "old society," who had supposedly become "masters of a new socialist China" in the Maoist discourse, were paradoxically transformed into images of rebellious slaves against the Dengist regime in their persistent search for individualism, freedom, and democracy, the original blueprints of the May Fourth movement of 1919. The history of singing "The Internationale" now has completed a full and vicious cycle: when the students retreated from Tiananmen Square and their tragedy gradually disappeared from the national consciousness, did their cherished dreams also perish in history? Did their aspiration of becoming the master of their own destiny deconstruct the very logic of the Chinese communist revolution from the inside out, and dramatize the futility of such revolution?

Much has happened in the twenty-five years since the government repression of the student demonstrations in 1989. China's emergence as the second economic power in the world still called for the collective singing of "The Internationale," as seen in the commercial success of the Beijing concert "Shocking" (震撼) featuring Liu Han 劉歡, Liao Changyong 廖昌永, and Mo Hualun 莫華倫, three talented and acclaimed singers in contemporary China. In spite of their brilliant singing of classic songs from the Chinese and foreign repertoires, they did not truly stir the emotions of the audience until they sang "The Internationale" at their second curtain call, when the audience finally joined their solemn singing in a contemporary theater community, in which one song connected all.

I hope this chapter has demonstrated the complex intersection between the emergence of a political song, the reiterating of its importance, and its related performances as being rich cultural and everyday practices, which reveal contradictions, inconsistencies, and deconstructive clues to question conventional wisdom. Propaganda performance, as partly created through a century-long history of singing "The Internationale," has not always been forced upon writers, actors, and artists through strict censorship and political suppression. This chapter cautions against the conventional wisdom that socialist China suppressed artists and their creative energies, as seen in their unproductive years during the Maoist period. On the contrary, I argue that Chinese intellectuals and performance artists at times also took it upon themselves to visualize and perform a socialist blueprint and actively participate in the formation of modern and contemporary canons, with performance pieces on revolutionary history. Without their pioneering achievements, we would not have the long history of performing "The Internationale," with its complexities, multiple voices, and diverse traditions.

Notes

1. Jacques Attali, "Noise: The Political Economy of Music," in *The Sound Studies Reader*, ed. Jonathan Sterne (New York: Routledge, 2012), 30.
2. Jonathan Sterne, "Sonic Imaginations," in *The Sound Studies Reader*, 2.
3. The film's Chinese title *Qiu zhi bai hua* was inspired by a seal Qu carved for his wife Yang Zhihua. *Bai* is from Qu's surname Qiubai and *hua* is from Yang's given name Zhihua. *Qiu zhi* means "that which belongs to Qiubai," indicating their desire to be together forever.
4. Sterne, "Sonic Imaginations," 1.
5. Xinmin Liu, *Signposts of Self-Realization* (Leiden: Brill, 2014), 122.
6. I use quotation marks here to indicate that Qu was indeed charged as a traitor before and during the Cultural Revolution. Even then, his singing of "The Internationale" at the execution ground helped soften his image as a traitor.
7. Qu Qiubai, "Xin Eguo youji" 新俄國遊記 [A travel report from the new Russia], in Qu Qiubai, *Duoyu ren xinshi* 多餘人新史 [A new history of a Superfluous man], ed., Qiu

Sang 丘桑 (Beijing: Dongfang chubanshe, 1998), 69–149, 117; cited in Wang Tiexian 王鐵仙 and Liu Fuqin 劉福勤, eds., *Qu Qiubai Zhuan* 瞿秋白傳 [A biography of Qu Qiubai] (Beijing: Renmin wenxue chubanshe, 2011), 66.

8. Qu Qiubai, "Xin Eguo youji," 117.

9. Wang Guanquan 王觀泉. *Yige ren he yige shidai* 一 個人和一個時代 [A man and his era] (Tianjin: Tianjin renmin chubanshe, 1989), 244.

10. Qu Qiubai, *Chidu xin shi* 赤都心史 [Spiritual journey to the red capital], in Qu Qiubai, *Duoyu ren xinshi* 多餘人新史 [A new history of a superfluous man], ed. Qiu Sang 丘桑, 153–266, 191; Comintern refers to the Communist International (共產國際, 1919–1943).

11. Wang, *A Man and His Era*, 188.

12. Qu Qiubai, *Spiritual Journey to the Red Capital*, 194, cited in Wang, *A Man and His Era*, 162.

13. Wang, *A Man and His Era*, 206, 207–208.

14. Wang, *A Man and His Era*, 170; Zhou Yongxiang 周永祥, *Qu Qiubai nianpu* 瞿秋白年譜 [A chronology of Qu Qiubai] (Guangzhou: Guangdong renmin chubanshe, 1983), 15–16, 19.

15. Wang and Liu, *A Biography of Qu Qiubai*, 94.

16. Jin Dianqiang 金點強 "Zhongwen 'Guoji ge' xiugai hao ji bian" [中文《國際歌》修改好幾遍] [Several revisions of the Chinese version of "The Internationale"], http:/big5.cri.cn/gate/big5/gb.cri.cn/12764/2007/08/15/2865@1719269_1.htm (last accessed, 11/20/2008).

17. Here is a case of a typical media misrepresentation of the history of translating "The Internationale": the translation used in this television drama series, as well as in other films and dramas, was not penned by Qu Qiubai; it was revised by other writers and finalized after 1949 as the "official" version. Zheng Zhenduo 鄭振鐸 and Xiao San 蕭三 were cited as translators of "The Internationale," among others. See note 37 for more information.

18. Sterne, "Sonic Imaginations," 3.

19. Li Xinghua 李星華, "Huiyi wo de fuqin Li Dazhao" 回憶我的父親李大釗 [Remembering my father Li Dazhao], http://blog.sina.com.cn/s/blog_636ea8510100lsxr.html (last accessed, 4/29/2013).

20. Mao Zedong 毛澤東,"Dielianhua: Cong Dingzhou xiang Changsha" 蝶戀花·從汀州向長沙 [March from Tingzhou to Changsha—to the tune of Dielianhua]. The poem ends with these two lines: "To the Internationale's stirring strains/A wild whirlwind swoops from the sky" (國際悲歌歌一曲,狂飆為我從天落). English translation quoted from "March from Tingchow to Changsha," in *Mao Zedong Poems* (Open Source Socialist Publishing, 2008), (https://socialistpublishing.files.wordpress.com/2010/05/maopoems-newsetting.pdf (last accessed, 4/24/2015).

21. Wang Cui 王翠, "Mao Zedong Deng Xiaoping zenyang qinzi jiaochang 'Guoji ge'?" 毛澤東鄧小平怎樣親自教唱國際歌? ["How did Mao Zedong and Deng Xiaoping teach 'The Internationale'?"], http://dangshi.people.com.cn/GB/18060862.html (last accessed, 4/10/15).

22. Sterne, "Sonic Imaginations," 2–3.

23. For more information and analysis of these three epics, see chap. 3 of Xiaomei Chen, *Performing Chinese Revolution: Founding Fathers, Red Classics and Revisionist Histories* (New York: Columbia University Press, forthcoming).

24. Andrew F. Jones, *Yellow Music* (Durham: Duke University Press, 2001), 16.

25. According to Patricia Wilson, in 1939, Zhou Enlai brought back to Yan'an from the Soviet Union a film projector and some Soviet films such as *Lenin in October* and *Lenin in 1918*; he taught others how to operate the projector. See her "The Founding of the Northeast Studio," in *Chinese Film: The State of the Art in the People's Republic,* ed. George Stephen Semsel (New York: Praeger, 1987), 15–33.

26. *Lenin in 1918* was directed by Mikhail Romm with Boris Shchukin playing the role of Vladimir Lenin, produced in 1939, and translated by the Shanghai Film Studio attached to the Central Film Bureau.

27. Starring Mikheil Gelovani as Joseph Stalin and Pavel Molchanov as Vladimir Lenin, and directed by Mikheil Chiaureli, *The Unforgettable 1919* was produced by Mosfilm Studio in 1952; it was much less popular in China than the other two films on Lenin.

28. *Living Forever in Burning Flames* was produced by the Beijing Film Studio in 1965 and directed by Shui Hua 水華, with Xia Yan 夏衍, Luo Guangbin 羅廣斌, and Yang Yiyan 楊益言 as coscriptwriters, starring Zhao Dan 趙丹, Yu Lan 于藍 and Zhang Ping 張平.

29. Jones, *Yellow Music*, 35.

30. Barbara Mittler, *A Continuous Revolution* (Cambridge: Harvard University Asian Center, 2012), 112–113.

31. Chen Baichen 陳白塵 and Dong Jian 董健. *Zhonguo xiandai xiju shigao* 中國現代戲劇史稿 [A draft history of modern Chinese drama] (Beijing: Zhongguo xiju chubanshe, 1989), 3.

32. Roderick MacFarquhar, *The Origins of the Cultural Revolution*, Vol. 3: *The Coming of the Cataclysm* 1961–1966 (New York: Columbia University Press, 1997), 469.

33. As Barbara Mittler noted, this "Red Army Song" was "based on disciplinary points made by Mao in 1928" in order to remind "the army to help and support the people and never abuse their power when stationed in a village." It was also one of the four most popular songs promoted during the Cultural Revolution, together with "The East is Red," "The Internationale," and "Sailing the Seas Depends on the Helmsman" (大海航行靠舵手); they were remembered as "sounds of the Cultural Revolution." See Mittler, *A Continuous Revolution*, 69, 112.

34. Tan Yiyuan 潭儀元 and Xu Hongsheng 許宏盛, *Guangzhou jinglei* 廣州驚雷 [Thunder in Guangzhou], in *Guangdong huaju xuan* 廣東話劇選 [Selected plays from Guangdong], ed., Zhongguo Xijujia Xiehui Guangzhou Fenhui 中國戲劇家協會廣州分會 [Guangzhou branch of Chinese Dramatist Association] (Guangzhou: Guangdong renmin chubanshe, 1981), 279–370, 326. The play was premiered by Guangdong Theater (廣東話劇團) in 1977.

35. Zhao Baohua 趙葆華, *Wode Falaixi suiyue* 我的法蘭西歲月 [My years in France], in *Deng Xiaoping juben xuan* 鄧小平電影劇本選 [Selected film scripts on Deng Xiaoping], ed. Li Mengxue 李夢學 (Beijing: Zhongguo dianying chubanshe, 2004), 27.

36. Zhao, *My Years in France*, 29.

37. For more information about Xiao San being one of the translators of "The Internationale" and other possible translators in addition to Qu Qiubai, see "*Guoji Ge* jiqi zhongwen yizhe" 《國際歌》及其中文譯者 ["The Internationale" and its Chinese translators], http://news.xinhuanet.com/ziliao/2007-11/15/content_7078808_3.htm (last accessed, 4/29/2013).

38. Edgar Snow, *Red Star over China* (London: Left Book Club, Victor Gollancz, 1937), cited in *Radical Street Performance: An International Anthology*, ed. Jan Cohen-Cruz

(London: Routledge, 1998), 26–30, 29. Cohen-Cruz was "astonished that actors were so integrated into the major events of the times" and noted Snow's depiction of the "vitality of these theatre contingents in the 1930s and 1940s," 26.

39. Snow, *The Red Star over China*, cited in Cohen-Cruz, ed. *Radical Street Performance*, 29–30.

40. Snow, *The Red Star over China*, cited in Cohen-Cruz, ed. *Radical Street Performance*, 30.

41. http://baike.baidu.com/view/2259284.htm (last accessed, 4/7/2015).

42. "Jielu budui wengong tuan shengcui zhuangkuang" 揭露部隊文工團生存狀況 [Revealing the existing conditions of performance troupes in the People's Liberation Army], http://ent.qq.com/original/guiquan/g105.html (last accessed, 4/7/2015).

43. http://club.china.com/data/thread/12171906/2768/18/20/1_1.html (last accessed, 4/7/2015).

44. Joanna T. Pecore, Ken Schweitzer, and Yang Fan, "Telling the Story with Music: The Internationale at Tiananmen Square," http://www.asian-studies.org/EAA/EAA-Archives/4/1/229.pdf (last accessed, 3/19/2015).

45. Liu Xiaobo, "That Holy Word, Revolution," in *Popular Protest and Political Culture in Modern China*, ed. Jeffrey N. Wasserstrom and Elizabeth J. Perry, 2nd ed. (Boulder, CO: Westview Press, 1992), 316.

46. Andrew F. Jones, "The Politics of Popular Music," in *Popular Protest and Political Culture in Modern China*, ed. Wasserstrom and Perry, 155.

47. Jones, "The Politics of Popular Music," 157.

Works Cited

Attali, Jacques. "Noise: The Political Economy of Music." In *The Sound Studies Reader*. Ed. Jonathan Sterne. New York: Routledge, 2012. 29–39.

Chen Baichen 陳白塵 and Dong Jian 董健. *Zhonguo xiandai xiju shigao* 中國現代戲劇史稿 [A draft history of modern Chinese drama]. Beijing: Zhongguo xiju chubanshe, 1989.

Cohen-Cruz, Jan, ed. *Radical Street Performance: An International Anthology*. London: Routledge, 1998.

Jones, Andrew F. "The Politics of Popular Music." In *Popular Protest and Political Culture in Modern China*. Ed. Jeffrey N. Wasserstrom and Elizabeth J. Perry. Boulder, CO: Westview Press, 1992. 2nd ed. 148–165.

Jones, Andrew F. *Yellow Music*. Durham: Duke University Press, 2001.

"Jielu budui wengong tuan shengcui zhuangkuang" 揭露部队文工团生存状况 [Revealing the existing conditions of performance troupes in the People's Liberation Army], http://ent.qq.com/original/guiquan/g105.html (last accessed, 4/7/2015).

Jin Dianqiang 金點強. "Zhongwen 'Guoji ge' xiugai hao ji bian" [中文《國際歌》修改好幾遍] [Several revisions of the Chinese version of "The Internationale"], http://big5.cri.cn/gate/big5/gb.cri.cn/12764/2007/08/15/2865@1719269_1.htm (last accessed, 11/20/2008).

Li Xinghua 李星華. "Huiyi wo de fuqin Li Dazhao" 回憶我的父親李大釗 [Remembering my father Li Dazhao], http://blog.sina.com.cn/s/blog_636ea85101000lsxr.html (last accessed, 4/29/2013).

Liu Xiaobo. "That Holy Word, Revolution." In *Popular Protest and Political Culture in Modern China*. Ed. Jeffrey N. Wasserstrom and Elizabeth J. Perry. 2nd ed. Boulder, CO: Westview Press, 1992. 309–324.

Liu, Xinmin. *Signposts of Self-Realization*. Leiden: Brill, 2014.

Mao Zedong 毛澤東. "Dielianhua: Cong Dingzhou xiang Changsha" 蝶戀花·從汀州向長沙 [March from Tingzhou to Changsha—to the tune of Tieh Lien Hua—July 1930]. In *Mao Zedong Poems*. Open Source Socialist Publishing, 2008. (https://socialistpublishing.files.wordpress.com/2010/05/maopoems-newsetting.pdf (last accessed, 4/24/2015).

Mittler, Barbara. *A Continuous Revolution*. Cambridge: Harvard University Asian Center, 2012.

Qu Qiubai 瞿秋白. *Chidu xin shi* 赤都心史 [Spiritual journey to the red capital]. In Qu Qiubai, *Duoyu ren xinshi* 多餘人新史 [A new history of a superfluous man]. Ed. Qiu Sang 丘桑. Beijing: Dongfang chubanshe, 1998. 153–266.

Qu Qiubai 瞿秋白. "Xin Eguo youji" 新俄國遊記 [A travel report from the new Russia]. In Qu Qiubai, *Duoyu ren xinshi* 多餘人新史 [A new history of a superfluous man]. Ed. Qiu Sang 丘桑. Beijing: Dongfang chubanshe, 1998. 69–149.

Qu Qiubai 瞿秋白. *Qu Qiubai*. Beijing: Zhongguo shehui kexue chubanshe, 2003.

Qu Qiubai 瞿秋白. *Qu Qiubai you ji: E xiang ji cheng; Chi du xin shi* 瞿秋白遊記: 餓鄉紀程, 赤都心史 [Qu Qiubai's travel reports: Journey to the starving land; Journey of heart to the red capital). Beijing: Dongfang chubanshe, 2007.

"*Guoji Ge* jiqi zhongwen yizhe" 《國際歌》及其中文譯者 ["The Internationale" and its Chinese translators], http://news.xinhuanet.com/ziliao/2007-11/15/content_7078808_3.htm (last accessed, 4/29/2013).

Semsel, George Stephen. ed., *Chinese Film: The State of the Art in the People's Republic*. New York: Praeger, 1987.

Snow, Edgar. "China" [excerpt from *Red Star over China*]. In *Radical Street Performance: An International Anthology*. Ed. Jan Cohen-Cruz. London: Routledge, 1998. 26–30.

Sterne, Jonathan. "Sonic Imaginations." In *The Sound Studies Reader*. Ed. Jonathan Sterne. New York: Routledge, 2012. 1–18.

Tan Yiyuan 潭儀元 and Xu Hongsheng 許宏盛. *Guangzhou jinglei* 廣州驚雷 [Thunder in Guangzhou]. In *Guangdong huaju xuan* 廣東話劇選 [Selected plays from Guangdong], ed., Zhongguo Xijujia Xiehui Guangzhou Fenhui 中國戲劇家協會廣州分會 [Guangzhou branch of Chinese Dramatist Association]. Guangzhou: Guangdong renmin chubanshe, 1981.

Wang Cui 王翠,"Mao Zedong Deng Xiaoping zenyang qinzi jiaochang 'Guoji ge?" 毛澤東鄧小平怎樣親自教唱國際歌? ["How Did Mao Zedong and Deng Xiaoping Teach 'The Internationale'"], http://dangshi.people.com.cn/GB/18060862.html (last accessed 4/10/15).

Wang Guanquan 王觀泉. *Yige ren he yige shidai* 一個人和一個時代 [A man and his era]. Tianjin: Tianjin renmin chubanshe, 1989.

Wang Tiexian 王鐵仙 and Liu Fuqin 劉福勤, eds. *Qu Qiubai Zhuan* 瞿秋白傳 [A biography of Qu Qiubai]. Beijing: Renmin wenxue chubanshe, 2011.

Wilson, Patricia. "The Founding of the Northeast Studio." In *Chinese Film: The State of the Art in the People's Republic*. Ed. George Stephen Semsel. New York: Praeger, 1987.

Zhao Baohua 趙葆華. *Wode Falaixi suiyue* 我的法蘭西歲月 [My years in France]. In *Deng Xiaoping juben xuan* 鄧小平電影劇本選 [Selected film scripts on Deng Xiaoping]. Ed. Li Mengxue 李夢學. Beijing: Zhongguo dianying chubanshe, 2004. 3–90.

Zhou Yongxiang 周永祥. *Qu Qiubai nianpu* 瞿秋白年譜 [A chronology of Qu Qiubai]. Guangzhou: Guangdong renmin chubanshe, 1983.

CHAPTER 1.11

BEYOND SATIRE

The Pictorial Imagination of Zhang Guangyu's 1945 Journey to the West in Cartoons

JOHN A. CRESPI

WHEN in November 1945 Chongqing newspapers announced Zhang Guangyu's 張光宇 (1900–1965) exhibition *Journey to the West in Cartoons* (西遊漫記), those in the know had a good idea what to expect. Everyone, from peasant to professor, was of course familiar with the classic novel *Journey to the West* (西遊記), which was written in the Ming dynasty and has permeated the folk religion and popular culture of China ever since. But now that famous title was interrupted by another word: *man* (漫). This variation introduced a separate history, a much shorter one, measured in decades, not centuries, and sent an unmistakable message: that Zhang would present not a straight retelling of the classic story, but a fractured fairy tale cast in a particular genre—that of the modern image-text of *manhua* (漫畫) or "cartoon."

Existing studies describe *Journey to the West in Cartoons* as a colorful, whimsical, but also trenchant lampoon of politics and society, what Edward Gunn has called a representation of "Nationalist China in a state of complete moral and social bankruptcy."[1] *Journey* is indeed a masterful example of Republican-era political satire, but it is also a remarkable work of *manhua*, a genre of verbal-visual art that flourished in China's cosmopolitan treaty ports during the first several decades of the twentieth century. In this chapter, I propose that when viewed in conversation with the history of Chinese *manhua, Journey to the West in Cartoons* comes into renewed focus at a level beyond satire. It is, I argue, also an allegorical look back at the relationship of *manhua* with the popular print genre of the pictorial magazine, the medium in which *manhua* thrived during the interwar years.

I construct this alternative reading of *Journey* through several mutually supportive angles. First, after describing the creation and exhibition of *Journey*, I review the career of Zhang Guangyu as a Republican-era artist-entrepreneur who actively developed the relationship between *manhua*, which he pioneered, and pictorial magazines, which he prolifically founded and edited. Examining Zhang's early work in publishing and *man-hua* up to 1945 suggests two things. First, his creative identity and professional network grew out of pictorial magazines; and second, Zhang's bringing of *manhua* into popular pictorials redefined the meaning of *manhua* by linking this visual genre to the print genre of the pictorial magazine. I then turn to *Journey to the West in Cartoons* itself, reading it not for its satirical messages, which are already well understood, but for how Zhang in the opening chapter frames *Journey* as a metacommentary on the pictorial press, and in particular the *manhua* pictorial to which he had devoted much of his career. I conclude with some thoughts on the place of pictorial magazines in the modern Chinese literary canon.

Journey to the West in Cartoons as Political Satire

Zhang Guangyu created *Journey to the West in Cartoons* over a period of about four months during the second half of 1945. At the time, he was settled temporarily with his wife and four children, aged seven to eighteen, in Beiwenquan, a quiet mountain village on the outskirts of Chongqing, China's wartime provisional capital. Writing in 1946, Zhang remarks that the idea of illustrating and adapting the Ming dynasty novel *Journey to the West* came to him fortuitously. Having exhausted his stock of bedtime stories, he purchased a copy of the original *Journey* in the nearby town of Beibei, a local cultural center and the wartime site of Fudan University. He would read one chapter of the novel during the day, and then retell it to his children in the evening. This ritual revealed, as he puts it, a level of meaning in the legendary tale he had never noticed before: that of anti-bureaucratic satire. Specifically, Zhang notes that the Jade Emperor's ruse of granting the Monkey King Sun Wukong the bogus title of Superintendent of Stables

> means that the Jade Emperor's Heavenly Palace was riddled with bribery and corruption ... such that Sun Wukong's raising havoc in heaven was a deed of heroic proportions. Likewise, the novel hints at how all the demons and monsters that Tripitaka encounters are, without exception, either relatives of the Jade Emperor or sons-in-law of the Dragon King, sent down to earth as punishment for misdeeds in Heaven.[2]

Zhang's reinterpretation of *Journey to the West* as satire resonated with a broad trend in the arts and literature of the Nationalist-controlled regions during the later war years, what has been called "a loosely coordinated shift from resistance literature back to social criticism."[3] In other words, after several years of wartime alignment with the state's goal of national defense, creators of fiction, drama, poetry, and visual art went back to an independent, critical stance directed against the misrule of the state authorities, in this case the regime of Chiang Kai-shek. The return to critique was not lost among cartoonists, who had specialized in political satire from the 1920s through the 1930s. For veteran cartoonists, like Ding Cong 丁聰, Ye Qianyu 葉淺予, Liao Bingxiong 廖冰兄, Huang Yao 黃堯, and of course Zhang Guangyu, it was a time of exhibitions, both joint and individual, staged in cities like Chongqing, Chengdu, Guiyang, and Kunming. Exhibiting their work, rather than publishing in magazines or books, was driven by circumstance. With severe materials shortages, lack of printing facilities, and strict censorship by the Nationalist authorities making publication in print next to impossible, cartoon artists of the time turned to public exhibition as the most effective way to reach their audiences.[4]

The adaptation of traditional materials in Zhang's *Journey* was not unique either. The early years of the War of Resistance had seen extensive experimentation with popular forms, or "putting new wine in old bottles," as a way to spread wartime propaganda among the general populace.[5] Although this trend declined in the Nationalist-controlled areas later in the war as the intended audiences for literature and art moved away from the illiterate or semiliterate and back toward the educated population, *manhua* artists did not discard traditional forms and techniques, but employed them in ways that enhanced and refined their own distinct styles. For instance, Ding Cong combined social caricature with the scroll-painting format, complete with colophons, to create his eight-foot-long *Images of Today* (現象圖), exhibited in 1944, while Liao Bingxiong's *Spring and Autumn in the Cat Kingdom* (貓國春秋) was influenced by Chinese folk art.[6] Huang Yao, meanwhile, adapted the traditional "ink and wash" (水墨) technique on rice paper to create the sixty-four panels of his gently tinted but satirically sharp *Contradiction Collection* (矛盾集).[7]

As originally exhibited, Zhang's *Journey* comprised sixty panels, with color illustrations mounted above the accompanying narrative text, which was handwritten by Zhang Guangyu's younger brother Zhang Zhengyu 張正宇 in decorative *li* (隸) style calligraphy (Fig. 1). The first exhibition of *Journey* took place from November 22 to mid-December 1945 in Chongqing's Sino-Soviet Cultural Center, with another showing in Chengdu two months later. Exhibitions planned for Shanghai and Nanjing in 1946 were banned by the authorities, but the series was successfully displayed once more in Hong Kong in June 1947.[8]

The poster Zhang designed for the exhibition labels the work a "color, long-form mythical *manhua*" (長篇神話彩色漫畫).[9] In the press, however, *Journey* was in at least one instance advertised under a slightly different name, as a "color, long-form mythical picture-story" (長篇神話彩色連環畫).[10] The term *picture-story* (*lianhuanhua* 連環畫) refers to a popular genre of illustrated storybooks that by the 1930s was being used to present everything from traditional moral tales to martial arts movies.[11] *Journey*'s structural affinity to the picture-story genre distinguishes it from the exhibited work of Ding, Ye, Liao, and Huang, which did not depend on extended narrative format. At the same time, the story's ten sections or *hui* 回, each six panels long, are linked quite loosely, similar to the episodic structure of *Journey to the West* the novel.[12] Adding further to the open-endedness of Zhang's narrative is that the ten *hui* comprise the

FIGURE 1 Zhang Zhengyu (left) and Zhang Guangyu preparing for the 1945 Chongqing exhibition of *Journey to the West in Cartoons*. (Courtesy of Huang Dagang and Tang Wei.)

first part of what he originally intended to be a multipart work, so the story itself ends inconclusively.[13] Further resonances with the Ming novel are the introductory couplets introducing each *hui*, as well as the overall linguistic style, which emulates the idiom of a traditional vernacular novel.

As in the original novel, the various subplots in the 1945 *Journey* come together around a quest: Sun Wukong (Monkey), Zhu Bajie (Pig), Sha Heshang (Monk Sha), and Tripitaka (Tang Xuanzang) are traveling in search of the *Book of Heaven* (天書), a boon whose precise meaning and value is left to the reader's imagination. The four pilgrims move through five locales, with characters and events in each place alluding to issues of corruption and misrule in wartime and postwar society. Moolaland (紙幣國), for instance, is the Orientalist confection of a country where paper money grows on government-owned trees and Pig, who spits up gold ingots on request, is wined and dined by caricatured versions of then-Minister of Finance H. H. Kung 孔祥熙, his wife Song Ailing 宋愛玲, and her brother, the high-ranking politician T. V. Soong 宋子文. In the Kingdom of Ancient Aegysine (埃秦古國), vicious humanoid crows—most in Egyptian garb, but one drawn in Disneyesque style as a cigar-smoking hooligan—represent minions of the Nationalist police state who delight in arresting and enslaving the populace. The city of Dream Hedonia ("夢得快樂"城), meanwhile, is a futuristic, aerial pleasure zone of beauty salons, funhouse mirrors, and dance halls restricted to the rich and politically connected—a dig at the exclusive and Americanized lifestyles of Chongqing's refugee elite. From Hedonia the travelers ride steel-clad zeppelins over the "Qin Puppet" Demon Empire ("偽秦" 妖國), a reference to the Japanese-occupied regions of wartime China. There Monkey uses his supernatural powers to bomb the Demon Empire into submission, but then must flee, along with his three comrades, because the Hedonian leaders determine the quartet to be "dangerous elements" who oppose continued collaboration with the defeated enemy, a policy that the Mayor of Hedonia announces at a grand but politically bogus surrender ceremony. After a narrow escape, the travelers' shadows are suddenly sucked into a miasmic cloud, symbolizing the black market. Inside the cloud they discover "jackpot" carp in a fetid, muddy pool, and are ingested by a gigantic skeleton, whose capacious stomach is filled with money and contraband. The pilgrims break free from the skeleton, return to their bodies, and continue their quest. In the final chapter, Monkey impetuously smashes an "evil egg" (孽蛋), thus releasing a clutch of serpents. The last of the sixty panels depicts a giant Napoleon emerging from a great gust of wind to upbraid Monkey for setting loose the dragonets of fascism, which the Jade Emperor had assigned Napoleon to guard.

Journey's elaborate burlesque of wartime figures and events places it squarely in the genre of political satire. Yet the work as a whole, with its lavish visual impact and absurdist storyline, has always pointed to something more. Commentators have, for instance, singled out the strong, even distracting, design elements of Zhang's imagery, noting how his "exploration into the comparatively systematic language of decorative forms" overshadows his satirical attacks on reality.[14] Others emphasize how *Journey* unrelentingly reflects "social reality" "*despite* the surface trappings of a seemingly rather preposterous mythical story" (italics added), or how Zhang's extensive and bizarre formal experimentation in some cases "falls short in terms of imaginative expression."[15] This kind of ambiguous viewing experience was described as early as 1947 by the modernist writer and erstwhile colleague of Zhang, Ye Lingfeng 葉靈鳳. In a review of the Hong Kong exhibition, Ye posits two kinds of spectators:

> One kind will feel that it is quite good indeed, a feast for the mind and the eye, rather like looking at a beautiful woman. Another kind of viewer, beyond finding it attractive and interesting, will get a strange sensation of déjà vu from everything pictured. . . . He will feel that much of what appears in the illustrations he has either experienced himself, or at the very least has heard others talking about. Some are events of the past, others the burning issues of the day.[16]

In part, Ye's comments reflect what he, as a Shanghai cultural sophisticate, perceived as the cultural ignorance of the Hong Kong audience. At the same time, he evokes the visual pleasure of viewing *Journey*, how the sheer surface entertainment elicited by its colorful, at times even sexually arousing, imagery tends to obscure more serious underlying messages. This doubled viewing experience intimates a level of allegory in Zhang's *Journey* that shifts attention away from political satire and toward the aesthetics of the popular, crowd-pleasing, pictorial-based genre of *manhua*.

Zhang Guangyu and the Making
of *Manhua*

To understand why *Journey* asks to be read beyond satire, it helps to trace Zhang's career over the three decades preceding 1945. Growing interest in Zhang Guangyu over the past decade or so has shown him to be a treaty-port Renaissance man in the field of commercial art: a designer of advertisements, cigarette cards, and calendar posters for companies likes Nanyang Tobacco and British-American Tobacco, a pioneer in modern Chinese furniture design, a costume designer for early film, an innovator in modernizing Chinese-language typography, author of China's first comprehensive book on international commercial design, and, of course, an accomplished cartoonist and caricaturist.[17] But if we seek the center of gravity of Zhang's creative identity among all these activities, we find it in his work with pictorial magazines. In fact, the nexus between *manhua* and pictorials was largely engineered by Zhang, as we can see in a review of his active role in Shanghai's pictorial press.

Turning first to Zhang's early career, we discover how he used the medium of the pictorial to construct his public identity as an artist. That process began in 1918 and 1919, during his apprenticeship at the arts and variety magazine *World Pictorial* (世界畫報), a publication of the Shanghai Shengsheng Fine Arts Company.[18] The pages of *World Pictorial* include a variety of illustrations signed by Zhang as well as sketches explicitly depicting him as an artist. In one sketch, for instance, Zhang is shown painting *en plein air*, brush in hand and palette balanced on his forearm (Fig. 2). It was also at *World Pictorial* that he invented the pen name Guangyu that he used for the rest of his artistic career. His signature, which he included on his illustrations in the magazine from cover pictures to advertisements to fashion and current event sketches, has particular prominence. In one case Zhang even hides his English-language initials, K. Y., in the corner of a painting drawn in the background of a cover illustration, thus adding a curious depth to his image of creative ownership. The signatures also draw attention to themselves for their experimental flourishes, inspired by the elaborate signatures of the American illustrators, like Harrison Fisher and Charles Dana Gibson, whom Zhang and his colleagues emulated (Fig. 3).

After establishing his professional presence on the pages of *World Pictorial*, Zhang soon struck out on his own in the rough-and-tumble world of Shanghai's pictorial press. In 1921, he cofounded China's first film magazine, *The Motion Picture Review* (影戲雜誌). Between 1925 and 1927, while working his day job at Nanyang Tobacco, he worked very briefly at *Pictorial Shanghai* (上海畫報) before founding and editing *China Camera News* (三日畫報), an arts and society tabloid featuring photography and cartoons that ran for 169 issues.[19] Beyond helping establish a professional artistic persona, and of course generating income, making and marketing pictorials attracted a network of like-minded associates. Zhang, for instance, came to know an important future coeditor, Ye Qianyu, after Ye was hired as an assistant in the

FIGURE 2 A sketch of the young Zhang Guangyu. *World Pictorial*, November 1918, no. 4.

production of *China Camera News*.[20] Not long afterward, in 1927, Zhang organized his circle of acquaintances—photographers, illustrators, and commercial artists—around a company called China Fine Art Printing and Publishing to launch *Shanghai Sketch* (上海漫畫) (1928–1930).[21] Acting as general manager and chief editor for *Shanghai Sketch*, Zhang oversaw this large-format, color weekly's publication from April 1928 to June 1930. Under his leadership, *Shanghai Sketch* also functioned as a networking node for the recently founded Shanghai Sketch Association, a loose confederation originally comprising eleven young, mostly amateur, commercial artists, for whom Zhang and another veteran commercial artist, Ding Song 丁悚, acted informally as mentors.[22]

Shanghai Sketch has for several reasons been foregrounded as a key moment in the consolidation of the genre of Chinese *manhua*.[23] First, as mentioned above, the magazine was directly linked to the Shanghai Sketch Association, comprised mostly of cartoonists; second, *Shanghai Sketch* stood out among peer publications because it committed a relatively large amount of its content to cartoons, both single-panel and series, including Ye Qianyu's celebrated and long-running comic *Mr. Wang* (王先生). In terms of professional affiliations and content, *Shanghai Sketch* did indeed lay a foundation for the "golden age" of *manhua* of the mid-1930s. Not to be overlooked, however, is that the histories singling out *Shanghai Sketch* as a step forward in the formation of *manhua* as a free-standing genre are all written in hindsight; that is, during or after the

FIGURE 3 An early signature by Zhang Guangyu, emulating the style of American illustrators. *World Pictorial*, August 1918, no. 1.

consolidation of *manhua* during its peak of popularity from 1934 to 1937. The eventual success of *manhua* art prompted its advocates to write histories of the genre, and those historical surveys tend to place the magazine within a teleology of generic development. Obviously, such histories were not a part of the discourse of *manhua* in the late 1920s, during the two-year run of *Shanghai Sketch* when, in China, the genre was young and its future unclear. A wide-angle look at *Shanghai Sketch* in fact challenges the notion that the meaning of *manhua* can even be delimited to what we think of as "cartoons."

While *Shanghai Sketch* was not the first Chinese magazine to include *manhua* in its content, it was the first to use the word *manhua* in its name. In that specific context— the title of a pictorial variety magazine—the word *manhua* does not directly refer to the cartoons in their own right. Rather, it is a lexeme derived interculturally, from the global semantic framework of early-twentieth-century pictorials. In China, as well as various metropolitan centers throughout Asia, the names for such magazines, and illustrated satire magazines in particular, were typically transliterations or transformations of Euro-American satire magazines like *Puck* or *Punch*.[24] Indeed, China's first periodical fully dedicated to illustrated satire had the bilingual English and Chinese

FIGURE 4 Cover of *Shanghai Sketch*, April 13, 1929.

name *Shanghai Puck* 上海潑克 (1918–1919), making it "an integral part of global trends and circulations of satirical journalism."[25] Such was also the case for *Shanghai Sketch*, where the word *sketch* in the Chinese magazine's English title was likely borrowed from a British weekly called *The Sketch: A Journal of Art and Actuality* (1893–1959), which circulated among Shanghailanders and other English-speaking members of China's treaty-port communities (Figs. 4, 5). Like *Shanghai Sketch*, *The Sketch* was a profusely illustrated arts and society magazine, thick with advertisements, that aimed to keep its readers up to date with the latest in fashion, celebrity lifestyle, entertainment, and current events. Caricature and illustration were featured in both, as were short written pieces including fiction, travel notes, portraits of socialites, film reviews, foreign or domestic oddities, and light humor. In fact the similarities between the two magazines

FIGURE 5 Cover of *The Sketch*, October 12, 1921.

strongly suggest that the word "sketch" in both titles refers not exclusively to the humorous or satirical drawings they contained, which in the case of *Shanghai Sketch* amounted to less than half the layout, but rather to the full range of visual *and* verbal infotainment found therein, from fashion and current events to celebrity lifestyles, art, literature, all manner of literary or semiliterary vignettes, and, of course, humorous and satirical illustration.

One can argue, then, that as a linguistically split term, *manhua*/sketch points not simply to the genre of the cartoon per se, but also to a "visual emporium of cosmopolitanism" to be found in Republican-era Shanghai pictorials.[26] According to this view, popular pictorials, and most prominently the long-running *Young Companion* (良友畫報; 1926–1945), represent a "kaleidoscopic" treaty-port print phenomenon that is "trans-locally networked, hybrid, heterogeneous, future-oriented, and unabashedly flaunting conceptual and visual curiosities and novelties."[27] *Shanghai Sketch* was, of course, not the first pictorial magazine produced in China; but as figures 6 and 7 illustrate, it very much lived up to the adjective "kaleidoscopic," and did so by aggressively blending the art of caricature and cartoon illustration with the kind of textual and photographic content that otherwise dominated the pages of pictorial magazines.

Zhang continued contributing to and editing pictorial magazines through the early 1930s. In late 1929, along with Ye Qianyu and Ye Lingfeng, he founded and edited what was to become, behind *The Young Companion*, the second largest pictorial in Shanghai, *Modern Miscellany* (時代畫報; 1929–1937), into which *Shanghai Sketch* along with much of its *manhua* content was soon merged.[28] Several years later, in 1933, Zhang partnered in the founding of the illustrated variety magazine *Decameron* (十日談). After quitting his full-time design work with British-American Tobacco in 1934, his career in pictorials accelerated. During the next three years, before the war with Japan broke out in mid-1937, he worked as chief editor for *Van Jan* (萬象; 1934) and *Thrice-monthly Magazine* (十日雜誌; 1935–1936), edited two *manhua* monthlies, *Oriental Puck* (獨立漫畫; 1935–1936) and *Shanghai Puck* (上海漫畫; 1936–1937), and coedited with Ye Qianyu the short-lived *manhua* magazine *Puck* (潑克; 1937). Zhang also contributed extensively to the leading *manhua* publications of the time. For the most famous and influential of these, *Modern Sketch* (時代漫畫; 1934–1937), he designed the cover of the inaugural issue (Fig. 8), a bricolage horseman assembled from the tools of the cartoonist's and magazine editor's trades, which became the informal emblem of the Chinese cartoon during the 1930s.

When artists and writers turned to creating wartime propaganda full-time following the outbreak of hostilities with Japan in July 1937, Zhang remained in Shanghai until the city was invaded in November, editing magazines such as *New Life Pictorial* (新生畫報) and *Resist Japan Pictorial* (抗日畫報) and serving on the editorial board of *Resistance Cartoons* (救亡漫畫). Zhang then fled to Hong Kong to work as arts director for the *Sing Tao Daily* (星島日報) and editor for the *Sing Tao Pictorial* (星島畫報). Following a brief sojourn in Chongqing in 1940–1941, he returned to Hong Kong to continue work for *Sing Tao Daily*, but with the fall of the British colony to the Japanese he moved to Guangzhou, and then to Guilin. When the latter city was taken over by the Japanese during the 1944 Ichigo Offensive, Zhang and his family made the difficult trek through Liuzhou and Guiyang to Chongqing, where he created *Journey to the West in Cartoons*.[29]

FIGURE 6 Cartoon-style illustration dominated the four color pages of *Shanghai Sketch*. Zhang Guangyu's contribution is the vision of "Future Shanghai" on the left, above the advertisement for the fabric company Tarantulle. *Shanghai Sketch*, January 4, 1930, no. 89.

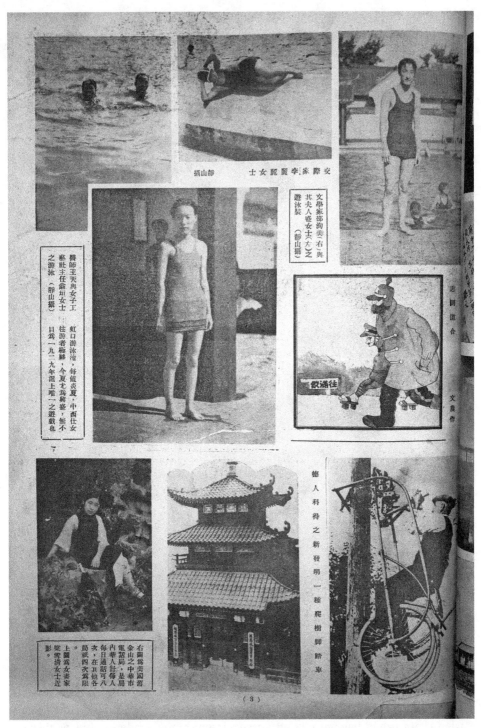

FIGURE 7 The monochrome pages of *Shanghai Sketch* were mostly devoted to photographs, including celebrity lifestyles and international "news of the weird," such as the German tree-climbing bicycle shown bottom right. But this portion of the magazine also incorporated current events cartoons, as seen in the right-center panel. *Shanghai Sketch*, August 10, 1930, no. 68.

FIGURE 8 Zhang Guangyu's cover design for the inaugural issue of *Modern Sketch*, January 1934.
Courtesy of Special Collections and University Archives, Colgate University Libraries.

Journey to the West in Cartoons: Beyond Satire

On its own, Zhang Guangyu's decades-long commitment to founding and editing pictorial magazines, and *manhua* pictorials in particular, does not of course prove that he created *Journey to the West in Cartoons* as an allegory of the pictorial genre. Such a claim would have to rely on purely circumstantial evidence. But neither can *Journey to the West in Cartoons* be understood as simply a piece of political satire. This is because the strictly satirical interpretation leaves out Chapter One, an episode of crucial importance in that it functions as a narrative frame for all the ensuing chapters. This frame is, in fact, double. At the level of diegetic function, it stages the main narrative by presenting a story within a story, a strategy that conveniently allows Zhang to launch his tale in progress, without lengthy buildup. But, as a work of *manhua, Journey* is a predominantly visual text, and it is at the level of illustration that the first chapter of *Journey* generates *another* frame, a conceptual one born of transcultural encounter and defined by a certain practice of reading. This double framing acts as the governing structure of Zhang's *Journey*. Its prominence alerts us to view the main narrative not just as political satire, but as a retrospection upon the kaleidoscopic imagination of pictorial magazines, and in particular *manhua* pictorials.

Turning first to the written narrative of Chapter One, we find a fairy tale of sorts. A wise king of antiquity dreams of a visit from the Elder of History (歷史老人), who carries a crystal orb in one hand and holds the *Book of Heaven* under his arm. Giving the orb to the king, the Elder announces: "The world is vast and filled with wonders. Your puny kingdom, what does it amount to? I bestow upon you this orb. Look carefully within, and behold the myriad changes!" The rather greedy king demands to have the *Book* as well, but is rebuffed by the Elder, who promptly "disappears without a trace." The narration to the second panel describes the king awakening to find the orb is in fact real. It rests in his hands, smooth and featureless on its surface but aglow with shifting patterns in its depths. The third panel's narration, just one sentence long, tells of the king seeing within the orb a *shanhai yuditu* (山海輿地圖), or *mappa mundi*, in which he spots his own country. At first delighted by observing his lands in living detail, even down to the doings of his own court and officials, the king is suddenly perturbed by the implications of a device that can, beyond his power, represent the inner workings of his state. Just as he is about to smash the orb, the Elder of History "bursts from a corner of the room in a flash of auspicious light." In the narration to the next panel, the Elder tells the king to stay his hand, explaining that the *Book of Heaven* is inside the orb. In the sixth and final panel of Chapter One, the king asks how he is to read the *Book* if it is inside the orb. At this the Elder, with a laugh, points into the orb and tells the king that Monkey and his three colleagues are even now on their way to obtain the *Book* for him from *Sukhāvatī* (極樂世界), the Buddhist "Land of Bliss" or "Western Paradise."

Where the written portion of Chapter One gets the main narrative up and running by identifying the main characters' quest for the *Book of Heaven*, the accompanying visual narrative does two things. On one hand, it tells the story of a transcultural encounter, expressed in the transfer of the orb from the Elder to the king. At the same time, the illustrations in Chapter One introduce a mode of reading. That mode, constructed as a visual relation between the king and the orb, duplicates the visual relation between reader and pictorial magazine. Most critically, in the sixth and last panel of the first chapter Zhang manipulates point of view in a way that frames the subsequent, satirical chapters as if occurring *within* the allegorical space of an imaginary *manhua* pictorial writ large.

The most striking feature of the first panel is Zhang's caricature of both the king and the Elder of History. The former is clad in the orientalized garb of the First Qin

FIGURE 9 *Journey to the West in Cartoons,* Chapter 1, panel 1.

Emperor, while the latter wears a cartoonishly Westernized Biblical robe and sports a golden halo, long beard, and white angel wings (Fig. 9). The two figures appear in a dream balloon, with the king shown as a supplicant, arms outstretched to eagerly receive the orb, upon which his eyes are fixed intently. The Elder, meanwhile, holds the orb high as he rather condescendingly urges the ruler of this "puny kingdom" to view the world of "wonders" and "myriad changes." Panel two, which might be described in cinematic language as a medium shot, repeats the trope of the gaze by showing the king sitting in bed, his eyes still fixed on the orb, which compositionally dominates the center of the panel by emitting beams of golden light that radiate out to fill the panel's background (Fig. 10). Also in this panel the king is shown holding the globe before his eyes, very much in the position of a reader—in this case, a reader of leisure reclining in bed.

The third panel reiterates the posture of reading by providing a frontal close-up of the king, only his eyes, ears, and fingers visible around the edges of the orb, which fills the frame to reveal the oceans and continents of the *mappa mundi* (Fig. 11). The king, in other words, is shown viewing the orb precisely as one would view a book or magazine. The orb as shown is not "reading" matter, strictly speaking, but a picture, and more specifically a "world-picture" of sorts that includes China, as implied by the Sinicized image of the king. Panel four shows the king, still sitting in bed, raising the orb over his head in order to smash it. The Elder, meanwhile, is drawn rushing out of the upper

FIGURE 10 Chapter 1, panel 2.

FIGURE 11 Chapter 1, panel 3.

left corner of the panel, gesturing urgently at the king (Fig. 12). Panel five then shifts to a close-up of the Elder's hand, framed by blue lightning bolts, pointing into the orb, where the *Book of Heaven* floats among white clouds (Fig. 13). As for the king, he is again depicted in the posture of reading, with only his face and elongated fingers visible in the panel's bottom right corner as he holds up the orb and looks intently within it at the *Book*. In the sixth and final panel of Chapter One, the point of view shifts to that of the king, so that we, like him, gaze into the orb as if inches from its surface (Fig. 14). We see what the king sees: Monkey, Tripitaka, Monk Sha, and Pig depicted in profile, moving through clouds and mountains on their quest to retrieve the *Book* from the Western Paradise.

As the summary above already suggests, several features of Chapter One invite us to read it as an allegory of the introduction of pictorial magazines, and specifically the *manhua* pictorial, to China. The first of these features is, of course, the exchange of the orb from the Western Elder to the Sinicized king. Zhang Guangyu and other *manhua* artists of the 1930s regarded their art as a Western import whose popularization and elaboration depended heavily on the medium of the pictorial magazine, which was also considered a Western cultural import.[30] In his 1935 article "The Development of Chinese *Manhua*," cartoonist Huang Shiying 黃士英 unequivocally refers to Chinese *manhua* as "a product of western culture" that originated from the publication of China's first illustrated supplement, *Dianshizhai Pictorial* (點石齋畫報), founded in 1884 by the British businessman Ernest Major (Fig. 15). Huang's historical narrative of the genre over the ensuing five decades finds the high points of *manhua*'s development coinciding with the publication of pictorial magazines dedicated to this visual form, from Shen Bochen's 沈伯塵 (1889–1920) *Shanghai Puck* to *World Pictorial*, through *Shanghai Sketch*, and then on to the mid-1930s boom in *manhua* pictorials.[31] In a companion piece to Huang's history, another cartoonist, Wang Zimei 汪子美, deemphasizes the nineteenth-century pictorial roots of *manhua*, stressing instead how in the early 1930s the consolidation of *manhua* as an independent visual art form depended "parasitically" upon the magazine market. According to Wang, *manhua* survived the termination of *Shanghai Sketch* in 1930 because of a rise in demand for "fresh" content from popular magazines, most notably China's leading pictorials *The Young Companion* and *Modern Miscellany*. Chinese *manhua*, Wang continues, advanced from "bud to splendid blossom, even magnificence" with the appearance of the *manhua* pictorial *Modern Sketch* in 1934, the publication that led the way for a raft of related magazines in which new and veteran cartoonists developed their art.[32] Read against Huang's and Wang's histories, panel one of *Journey* opens the way toward interpreting the orb as much more than a diegetic prop for the main, satirical narrative.

Further reinforcing the parallel between the orb and the pictorial magazine is the sensationalist and global nature of the orb's visual scope. When Huang Shiying referred to *Dianshizhai Pictorial* as the starting point of China's *manhua*, he was pointing to a new form of popular illustration designed to excite and inform a popular audience. *Dianshizhai* succeeded because of its emphasis on the "new" and "sensational," much of it comprising fanciful depictions of the "west."[33] That sensational, visual, kaleidoscopic style defined the pictorial magazine as a mass-market commodity in China's

FIGURE 12 Chapter 1, panel 4.

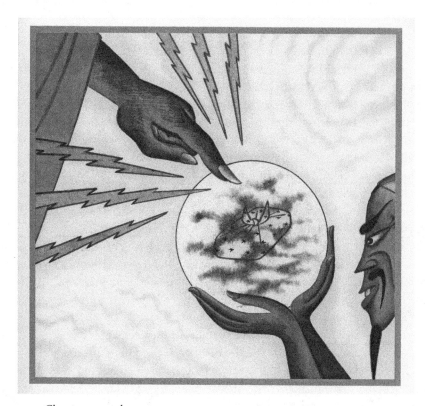

FIGURE 13 Chapter 1, panel 5.

FIGURE 14 Chapter 1, panel 6.

treaty ports. Like the Elder's orb, it allowed its readers to "behold the myriad changes" in a world "vast and filled with wonders."

Panel three, a frontal close-up of the king peering closely at the *mappa mundi*, gives visual emphasis to precisely the "worldview" offered by this kind of pictorial infotainment. In fact, five of the six panels in Chapter One show the king looking directly at the orb, and in four of those Zhang draws him reading a book or magazine in the posture of a consumer of light, leisure-time reading—precisely the market niche of pictorial magazines. Following through on this pattern of visual positioning, the sixth and final panel of Chapter One, which aligns the spectator's point of view with that of the king, invites us to "read" the remainder of *Journey* as if it were a pictorial magazine.

Another element of Zhang's allegorical layering is the *Book of Heaven*. What precisely is it? The conventional explanation, first broached by Zhang's cartoonist colleague Liao Bingxiong upon the first exhibition of *Journey* in Chongqing, proposes that the book Monkey and company seek is actually the "Sutra of Democracy" (民主真經).[34] From that perspective, *Journey to the West in Cartoons* represents the strictly political quest of delivering a just and democratic regime to the oppressed people of China. The other approach, of course, is to understand the *Book of Heaven*, the prize so strongly desired by the king in Chapter One, as the *manhua* pictorial writ large. And indeed, the ensuing nine chapters of Zhang's *Journey* revisit the cosmopolitan, kaleidoscopic "visual emporium" of an entire print genre.

中國漫畫發展史

黃士英

導言

本論

漫畫，一西洋文化的產物，流傳於中國的歷史比其他姊妹藝術皆遲，流傳於中國的浮世畫比較晚，雖然也包含着濃刻意味，與漫畫的性質相似，然而不能發揮而適應於大衆的需要，纔經過了艱苦的歷程，到近代便漸漸成熟起來了。

漫畫在人類社會的活動裏面發掘資料的題材，而抓住一個時代的社會興趣與含意的描寫，表現着時間上存有常的歷史背景。他所發表的漫畫，就合在有常時的社會情形與社會狀態，若具過去的漫畫加以檢討治的、流水帳的記錄。一本社會進化史之或一本政的途中，在時代的過程裏，在文化的領域內透達永久不滅的光芒。

近代漫畫界的活躍，漫畫發展的路線之廣泛性，已深得廣大讀者的同情，漫畫在急切的進步的光芒。

中國漫畫第一步開步走的時候，首推清光緒十三年出版的點石齋畫報了，點石齋畫報為中國畫報的始祖，主編人吳友如，錢病鶴，為以繪畫代醫照相的時代，內容取圖文對照方法，一面文字線路迷寫的不是狗單痴出版之小說，新聞，一面加揷繪畫，那時繪畫還沒有獨立成為漫畫的價值，可是揷用繪畫的力量來表現文字的不足為彌漫的揷圖，定期刋物的揷石齋畫報却是繪畫與實際社會生活的起點，亦可說是中國漫畫界的胚胎時代，諸如水滸，紅樓夢，三國誌一類小說的揷圖，用線條鐵刻工正，楷圖細密，十足表現君主封建時代士大夫階級控制下之人民生活。

漫畫史的發展的歷程可以時代區分為四個階段。

第一階段：──繪畫時代之辛亥革命階段。──平民元

第二階段：──文化革命開始的五四運動時期。──民十

第三階段：──五冊慘案革命文學時代──民八

第四階段：──九一八後變的民族復興時期──民

昔

維新運動以前及辛亥革命以後

D.木板手工印刷時代
C.石印時代
B.銅鋅板鎬印刷時代
A.橡皮板印刷時代

漫畫與印刷的進步又把着連帶作用，我們可以在印刷的範圍內把漫畫的進展劃為四個時代。

在辛亥革命以前的點石齋畫報出版之前，還有未成名的畫報是用小板手工印刷的。取材與繪畫巧妙與點石齋畫報大同小異，不過這以後有正式發行，用以備點整壁等用，古典型技巧較精美，體點石齋之後於光緒二十三年便有求新，印刷頗見精美，求新報臨用圖文與圖之照之外，更用繪畫介紹西洋的科學【圖】二技巧雖仍是中國古典型而取用繪畫，亦是這一個時期的漫畫別名之日木板手工印刷時代，

走上了實際生活的道途。
自從新聞紙日報林立，光緒十九年的新聞日報，民元年的大共和日報亞洲日報等出現，漫畫亦垂登上了報紙的地位，辛亥革命之潮澎湃全國，人民受了新思潮的刺激漫畫力於維新運動，西洋新文化源源流入，新興藝術便容易發見內智識界所接受，漫畫亦就在這維新運動之中挺起幼小的苗芽來。

那時漫畫界人才萃出了，新興畫家沈泊塵丁悚陳抱一張聿光江小鶼等都是活躍於當時日報的漫刺畫的中心人物。

大共和日報──沈泊塵丁悚
神州日報──張聿光沈泊塵丁悚
民立報──錢野鶂
新申報──丁悚沈泊塵
亞洲日報──江小鶼
新聞報──島星驄

FIGURE 15 The first page of Huang Shiying's 1935 history of Chinese *manhua*. *Dianshizhai Pictorial* is shown center right. The two images below it are from *World Pictorial*, where Zhang Guangyu apprenticed in 1918–1919.

When read against, or alongside, the political satire of the remaining fifty panels, the visual narrative of *Journey* very much reproduces the mélange of transcultural, cosmopolitan imagery that defined the golden age of the *manhua* pictorial. Moolaland is a critique of the Nationalist regime's inflationary economic policy, but it is also a showcase for political caricature, exotic locales, and lavish celebrity lifestyles. The Kingdom of Ancient Aegysine is an exposé of the secret police, but one whose multifarious visual style—quoting Disney, Pharaonic Egyptian art, and traditional Chinese motifs—celebrates the global eclecticism of *manhua* at its peak in the 1930s. And true, Dream Hedonia does unmask the decadent, pleasure-seeking society of Chongqing's wartime elite. But the imagery of this fanciful city, from space-age floating pleasure palaces to modernist beauty salons and an extravagant masquerade ball, revisits the visual emporium of the pictorials Zhang had spent his career editing and designing. As for the "False Qin" Demon Empire, here Zhang confounds the photojournalistic imagery of grand state ceremony often seen in pictorials by portraying the surrender of the Demon Empire in exaggerated, even grotesque, *manhua* style.

These many parallels between the visual field of *Journey to the West in Cartoons* and the kaleidoscopic content and format of *manhua* pictorials are, I suggest, quite deliberate. Shanghai pictorials of the 1920s and 1930s were, as Richard Vinograd asserts, "layered mediascapes" guided by an "esthetics of unpredictability," "fragmented and delirious virtual spaces" akin to dreamworlds, or to Foucauldian heterotopias that represent, contest, and invert.[35] As perhaps *the* chief architect of this pictorial aesthetic, Zhang Guangyu constructed *Journey* as a tour de force retrospection upon an entire unruly genre of popular-political discourse.

CONCLUSION

Shortly after the four pilgrims arrive in Hedonia, the Mayor orders his Secretariat to produce for them a travel guide to the city (Fig. 16). The second panel of the fifth chapter shows Pig reading this guide, which Zhang has drawn as a large-format magazine (indeed, larger than Pig himself) whose cartoonish cover features a high-kicking showgirl, a hula dancer, fireworks, and several Hedonian dirigibles. The grinning, drooling, thoroughly delighted Pig announces to Tripitaka, "Master, the *Book of Heaven* has been right here all along!"[36]

We might dismiss Pig's response to the guide as no more than a gag; he is, after all, a figure of legendary lust and impetuousness. But why not take Pig at his word? Perhaps Zhang is telling us, through Pig, that, yes, the oversized, *manhua*-festooned, infotainment pictorial truly *is* the *Book of Heaven*, and that the crowd-pleasing, colorful genre of the pictorial should indeed be considered a Sutra of Democracy. If so, Zhang would not be the first to take that position. His friend and colleague in the pictorial business, Shao Xunmei 邵洵美 (1906–1968), had said much the same in late 1934, not long after he had begun collaborating with Zhang to launch a flotilla of high-profile

FIGURE 16 Pig reads the travel guide to Hedonia.

pictorials under Shao's new company, Modern Publications Ltd.[37] In an article published in *Modern Miscellany*, Shao relates his response to someone who asks why he was committing his energies to pictorial magazines rather than "serious publications devoted purely to literature and art." Current literary magazines, Shao observes, are aimed at such a tiny, highly educated segment of the population that "it barely makes a difference if they exist or not."[38] Moreover, he adds, in contrast to avant-garde literary journals, with circulations from 1,000 to at most 10,000, pictorials like *Modern Miscellany* and *The Young Companion* enjoy print runs reaching 60,000 to 70,000. Shao goes on to express a particular disdain for the democratic pretensions held by proponents of "mass language" (大眾語言) literature, which he describes as a "plaything of a leisured class" that not only fails to understand literature but treats the masses like "apes they can forcibly train."[39] Pictorials, however, use images to attract people to letters, making reading a pleasure rather than a chore. As Shao puts it, "Only after using pictures to satisfy their eyes and humor to relax their nerves can you irrigate their souls with ideas."[40] Shao Xunmei, as a publisher, and Zhang Guangyu, as an artist-entrepreneur, both invite us to take another look at the print genre of pictorials as an intellectually influential and politically significant element of the culture of reading in Republican-era China. For all their mass appeal, or perhaps because of it, pictorials were intellectually sidelined by the more "serious" pursuit of engaged literature. Today, too, pictorial magazines fall between cracks in the academic division of labor because "they do not belong to the disciplines of history, literature, or visual arts proper."[41] As for *manhua*, Zhang's visually evocative, profoundly heterogeneous, and fundamentally self-reflexive cartoon journey prompts us to examine more closely those hybrid verbal-visual forms that confound traditional generic boundaries.

NOTES

I would like to thank Karl Jackson and Samantha Lee for their hard work in producing an English translation of *Journey to the West in Cartoons*, the Colgate University Research Council for providing a Major Grant to help me track down information in Shanghai and Beijing, and Huang Dagang and Tang Wei in Beijing for their generous assistance in my hunt for materials on Zhang Guangyu's life and work.

1. Bi Keguan 畢克官 and Huang Yuanlin 黃遠林, *Zhongguo manhua shi* 中國漫畫史 [A history of Chinese cartoons] (Beijing: Wenhua yishu chubanshe, 2006), 190–191; Edward M. Gunn, "Literature and Art of the War Period," in *China's Bitter Victory: The War with Japan, 1937–1945*, ed. James C. Hsiung and Steven I. Levine (Armonk: M. E. Sharpe, 1993), 249; Chang-tai Hung, *War and Popular Culture*, 126–127; Shen Xueli 申雪莉, "Zhang Guangyu lianhuanhua *Xiyou manji* yinyushi fengge tanxi" 張光宇連環漫畫"西遊漫記"隱喻式風格探析 [An examination of the metaphorical style in Zhang Guangyu's series-*manhua Journey to the West in Cartoons*], *Meishu daguan* 美術大觀 [Art panorama] 3 (August 2013); Michael Sullivan, *Art and Artists of Twentieth-Century China* (Berkeley: University of California Press. 1996), 120–121.

2. Zhang Guangyu 張光宇, "Zixu *Xiyou Manji*" 自序"西遊漫記" [Author's preface to *Journey to the West in Cartoons*], *Qingming* 清明 3 (July 16, 1946).

3. Gunn, "Literature and Art of the War Period," 247.

4. Cartoons were exhibited frequently during the first several years of the war, but primarily as a government-supported arm of the anti-Japanese propaganda movement directed at the illiterate or semiliterate population outside major cities. The exhibitions of the mid-1940s, by contrast, were aimed more toward the kind of middlebrow audience that had been fans of political satire in *manhua* through the prewar years. Examples include Ding Cong's participation in the Modern Art Exhibition alongside Paris-trained painters like Pang Xunqin 龐薰琹 (1906–1985), as well as his showing of the satirical scroll *Images of Today* (現象圖), also in Chengdu, during the winter of 1944 (see Sullivan, *Art and Artists of Twentieth-Century China*, 15); Huang Yao held two cartoon exhibitions in Kunming in 1944, one benefiting a middle school and another featuring lighthearted sketches of people and places in the city of Kunming itself (see "Zheng": Liangcheng 鄭良誠, "*Niubizi Huazhan* kan hou" "牛鼻子畫展"看後 [*Upon viewing the Niubizi Exhibition*]. *Zhengyibao* 正義報, September 17, 1944: 4; Zhengyibao 正義報, "*Weilao Rongjun Zhan* shiri qi juxing" 慰勞榮軍展十日起舉行 [Veterans' Benefit Exhibition to open on the 10th], Zhengyibao 正義報, September 8, 1944: 3; and Zhengyibao, "*Niubizi Huazhan* wei Wuhua Zhongxue mujuan." 牛鼻子畫展為 五華中學募捐 [*Niubizi Exhibition* donates to Wu Hua Middle School], Zhengyibao 正義報, September 30, 1944: 3). Zhang Guangyu contributed to the eight-artist Joint Cartoon Exhibition (漫畫聯展) which opened on March 15, 1945 at Chongqing's Sino-Soviet Culture Center and later toured surrounding schools, factories, and suburbs before moving on to Chengdu in early 1946 (see Bi and Huang, *Zhongguo manhua*

shi, 190). Liao Bingxiong's satirical *Spring and Autumn in the Cat Kingdom* debuted in the spring of 1946 in Chongqing, followed by a tour of Chengdu and Kunming (see Bi and Huang, *Zhongguo manhua shi,* 194–200). The most important prewar *manhua* exhibition was the First National Cartoon Exhibition (第一屆全國漫畫展覽會) held in Shanghai in November 1936, with subsequent shows in Nanjing, Hangzhou, and Suzhou. The opening in Shanghai is described in *Manhuajie* 漫畫界 [Modern Puck] 7 (November 5, 1936).

5. Chang-tai Hung, *War and Popular Culture: Resistance in Modern China, 1937–1945* (Berkeley: University of California Press, 1994), 187–220.

6. See Chang-tai Hung, "The Fuming Image: Cartoons and Public Opinion in Late Republican China, 1945 to 1949," *Comparative Studies in Society and History* 36.1 (January 1994).

7. *Images of Today* can be viewed on the website of the Spencer Museum of Art at http://collection.spencerart.ku.edu/eMuseumPlus. *Contradiction Collection* is posted in its entirety on the Huang Yao Foundation website, http://huangyao.org/866.html.

8. Nan Huang 南黃, "Zhang Guangyu Zhengyu kunzhong—manhua jiezuo *Xiyou manji* jiang zai Hu zhanlan" 張光宇正宇昆仲一漫畫傑作"西遊漫記"將在滬展覽 [Cartoon masterpiece *Journey to the West in Cartoons* by brothers Zhang Guangyu and Zhengyu to be exhibited in Shanghai], *Wanhuatong* 萬花筒 [Kaleidoscope] 11 (1946); Tang Wei 唐薇, "Nianbiao" 年表 [Chronology], in *Zhang Guangyu wenji* 張光宇文集 [Selected writings of Zhang Guangyu], ed. Tang Wei 唐薇 (Jinan: Shandong meishu chubanshe, 2011), 228; Zhang Guangyu 張光宇, *Xiyou manji* 西遊漫記 [Journey to the west in cartoons], ed. Tang Wei 唐薇 and Huang Dagang 黃大剛 (Beijing: Renmin meishu chubanshe, 2012), 129. *Journey to the West in Cartoons* was also displayed for a week in Beijing's Chinese Artists Association Exhibition Hall in April 1957, as reported in *Manhua* 漫畫 [Cartoon], "*Xiyou manji* zai Beijing zhanchu" "西遊漫記"在北京展出 [*Journey to the West in Cartoons* shown in Beijing] 88 (May 8, 1957), 6. The original work is still extant, held by Zhang Guangyu's eldest son, Zhang Dayu, in his home in Beijing (Huang Dagang and Tang Wei, personal communication, June 8, 2014).

9. Zhang Guangyu, *Xiyou manji,* 137.

10. Nan Huang, "Zhang Guangyu Zhengyu kunzhong—manhua jiezuo *Xiyou manji* jiang zai Hu zhanlan." As noted above, Zhang in the 1945 exhibition poster used the term *manhua.* This choice indicates his preference for the word *manhua,* whose generic range is much broader than that of *lianhuanhua.* Zhang retains this usage in the "Author's Preface" to the 1958 publication of *Journey,* calling *Journey* a *lianxu manhua* (連續漫畫), that is, a "continuous" or "series" *manhua.*" See Zhang Guangyu, *Zhang Guangyu wenji,* 1.

11. See Kuiyi Shen, "*Lianhuanhua* and *Manhua*: Picture Books and Comics in Old Shanghai."

12. Zhang writes that the loose episodic structure was a deliberate choice on his part meant to emulate the original novel's open-ended "sausage-link" organization according to which "if you cut off a length, or add a length, it's still a string of sausages." See Zhang Guangyu, "Zixu *Xiyou Manji.*"

13. Zhang Guangyu, *Zhang Guangyu wenji,* 2.

14. Zou Jianlin 鄒建林, "Minguo wenyi zhong de 'gaixie jingdian' xianxiang: Cong Liao Bingxiong *Maoguo Chunqiu* tan qi" 民國文藝中的"改寫經典"現象: 從廖冰兄"貓國春秋"談起 [The phenomenon of "rewriting the classics" in Nationalist-era literature and art: The case of Liao Bingxiong's *Spring and Autumn in the Cat Kingdom*], *Wenyi yanjiu* 文藝研究 [Literature and art studies] 6 (2011): 126.

15. Gan Xianfeng 甘險峰, *Zhongguo manhua shi* 中國漫畫史 [A history of Chinese cartooning] (Jinan: Shandong huabao chubanshe, 2008), 163; Ma Ke 馬克, "Meiyou shiqu guangcai de huaduo: Lüetan manhua *Xiyou manji* 沒有失去光彩的花朵：略談"西遊漫記" [A blossom that has not lost its splendor: A brief discussion of *Journey to the West in Cartoons*], in *Xiyou manji* 西游漫記 [Journey to the west in cartoons], ed. Tang Wei 唐薇 and Huang Dagang 黃大剛 (Beijing: Renmin meishu chubanshe, 2012), 136.

16. Ye Lingfeng 葉靈鳳, "Jieshao Guangyu de *Xiyou Manji*" 介紹光宇的 "西遊漫記" [Introducing Guangyu's *Journey to the West in Cartoons*], in *Xiyou manji* 西遊漫記 [Journey to the west in cartoons], ed. Tang Wei 唐薇 and Huang Dagang 黃大剛 (Beijing: Renmin meishu chubanshe, 2012), 133.

17. See Tang Wei, "Nianbiao," 219–226. For further discussion of Zhang's career in design, see Ellen Johnston Laing, *Selling Happiness: Calendar Posters and Visual Culture in Early Twentieth-Century Shanghai* (Honolulu: University of Hawai'i Press, 2004), 196–197; Lynn Pan, *Shanghai Style: Art and Design Between the Wars* (San Francisco: Long River Press, 2008), 245–247; Ye Qianyu 葉淺予, *Ye Qianyu zizhuan: Xi jiangxu cangsang ji liunian* 葉淺予自傳：細講敘滄桑記流年 [Autobiography of Ye Qianyu: A detailed account of vicissitudes through fleeting years] (Beijing: Zhongguo shehui kexue chubanshe, 2006), 62–63; and Mao Zhiming ed., *Shanghai manhua* (passim). Zhang's book on commercial design, *Modern Commercial Arts* (近代工藝美術) was published in 1932 by the Fine Arts Publishing Company (中國美術刊行社).

18. Where possible I have used the original English titles of the periodicals mentioned here and below. Where English titles cannot be located or do not exist, I have translated directly from the Chinese.

19. See Julia F. Andrews, "*Pictorial Shanghai* (*Shanghai Huabao*, 1925–1933) and Creation of Shanghai's Modern Visual Culture," *Yishuxue yanjiu* 藝術學研究 (Journal of art studies) 12 (September 2013): 9, 17; Zhang Guangyu, *Zhang Guangyu wenji*, 220.

20. Ye Qianyu, *Ye Qianyu zizhuan*: 58–59; Huang Shiying 黃士英, "Zhongguo manhua fazhan shi" 中國漫畫發展史 [The development of the cartoon in China], *Manhua shenghuo* 漫畫生活 [Cartoon life] 13 (September 20, 1935).

21. See Ye Qianyu, *Ye Qianyu zizhuan*, 63; Ye Feng 葉風, "Zhongguo manhua de zaoqi zhen-gui wenxian: *Shanghai manhua*" 中國漫畫的早期珍貴文獻：上海漫畫, in Mao Zhiming ed., *Shanghai Sketch*, vol. 1, 1–2.

22. Bi Keguan and Huang Yuanlin date the founding of the Association to Autumn 1927 (see Bi and Huang, *Zhongguo manhua shi*, 96). Based on an announcement in Shanghai's *Shun Pao* (申報), Gan Xianfeng places the founding of the Association in December 1926 (see Gan Xianfeng, *Zhongguo manhua shi*, 109).

23. See Bi Keguan and Huang Yonglin, *Zhongguo manhua shi*, 99–102; Gan Xianfeng, *Zhongguo manhua shi*, 111; Huang Shiying, "Zhongguo manhua fazhan shi"; and Wang Zimei 汪子美, "Zhongguo manhua zhi yanjin ji zhanwang" 中國漫畫之演進及展望 [China's *manhua*: Evolution and future prospects], *Manhua shenghuo* 漫畫生活 [Cartoon life] 13 (September 20, 1935).

24. See Hans Harder, "Prologue: Late Nineteenth and Twentieth Century Asian *Punch* Versions and Related Satirical Journals," in *Asian Punches: A Transcultural Affair*, ed. Barbara Mittler and Hans Harder (Heidelberg: Springer, 2013); John A. Lent, "Introduction," in *Illustrating Asia: Comics, Humor Magazines, and Picture Books*, ed. John A. Lent (Honolulu: University of Hawaii Press, 2001), 4; and Barbara Mittler, "Epilogue: Ten Thousand *Pucks* and *Punches*: Satirical Themes and Variations Seen

Transculturally," in *Asian Punches: A Transcultural Affair*, ed. Barbara Mittler and Hans Harder (Heidelberg: Springer, 2013).

25. Yi-wei Wu, "Participating in Global Affairs: The Chinese Cartoon Monthly *Shanghai Puck*," in *Asian Punches: A Transcultural Affair*, ed. Barbara Mittler and Hans Harder (Heidelberg: Springer, 2013), 372.

26. Paul G. Pickowicz, Kuiyi Shen, and Yingjin Zhang, "Introduction: *Liangyou*, Popular Print Media, and Visual Culture in Republican Shanghai," in *Liangyou: Kaleidoscopic Modernity and the Shanghai Global Metropolis, 1926–1945*, ed. Pickowicz, Shen, and Zhang (Leiden and Boston: Brill, 2013), 3.

27. Paul G. Pickowicz, Kuiyi Shen, and Yingjin Zhang, "Introduction: *Liangyou*, Popular Print Media, and Visual Culture in Republican Shanghai," 3.

28. Shen Xueli, "Zhang Guangyu lianhuanhua *Xiyou manji* yinyushi fengge tanxi," 135, 141.

29. Tang Wei, "Nianbiao," 225–226.

30. In the words of Richard Vinograd, these *manhua* artists were experiencing "a kind of historical amnesia" about the uniqueness of the pictorial. Vinograd lists a number of "print-and-image" publications that are formally similar to pictorial magazines, with some dating back to the late Ming period. See Vinograd, "Multi-Medium, Site, and Dream-World: Aspects of Shanghai Pictorials of the 1920s and 1930s," *Yishuxue yanjiu* 藝術學研究 [Journal of art studies] 12 (September 2013): 175–178.

31. Huang Shiying, "Zhongguo manhua fazhan shi."

32. Wang Zimei, "Zhongguo manhua zhi yanjin ji zhanwang."

33. Xiaoqing Ye, *The* Dianshizhai *Pictorial: Shanghai Urban Life, 1884–1898* (Ann Arbor: Center for Chinese Studies, The University of Michigan, 2003).

34. See Zhang Guangyu, "Zixu *Xiyou Manji*." Following Liao's interpretation are Gan Xianfeng, *Zhongguo manhua shi*, 164; Shen Xueli, "Zhang Guangyu lianhuanhua *Xiyou manji* yinyushi fengge tanxi," 52; and Michael Sullivan, *Art and Artists of Twentieth-Century China*, 121.

35. Richard Vinograd, "Multi-Medium, Site, and Dream-World: Aspects of Shanghai Pictorials of the 1920s and 1930s," 193–198.

36. Zhang Guangyu, *Xiyou manji*, 58.

37. John A. Crespi, "China's *Modern Sketch*-1: The Golden Era of Cartoon Art, 1934–1937," MIT Visualizing Cultures [online database] (Cambridge: MIT, 2011).

38. Shao Xunmei 邵洵美, "Huabao zai wenhuajie de diwei" 畫報在文化界的地位 [The place of pictorials in the culture world], in *Yige ren de tanhua* 一個人的談話 [Conversations alone] (Shanghai: Shanghai shudian chubanshe, 2012), 74.

39. Shao Xunmei, "Huabao zai wenhuajie de diwei," 75.

40. Shao Xunmei, "Huabao zai wenhuajie de diwei," 76.

41. Pickowicz, Shen, and Zhang, "Introduction: *Liangyou*, Popular Print Media, and Visual Culture in Republican Shanghai," 2.

Works Cited

Andrews, Julia F. "*Pictorial Shanghai (Shanghai Huabao*, 1925–1933) and Creation of Shanghai's Modern Visual Culture." *Yishuxue yanjiu* 藝術學研究 (Journal of art studies) 12 (September 2013): 43–128. Retrieved January 11, 2015 from http://art.ncu.edu.tw/journal/words/%E7%AC%AC12%E6%9C%9F02-Julia%20F%20Andrews.pdf.

Bi Keguan 畢克官 and Huang Yuanlin 黃遠林. *Zhongguo manhua shi* 中國漫畫史 [A history of Chinese cartoons]. Beijing: Wenhua yishu chubanshe, 2006.

Crespi, John A. "China's *Modern Sketch*-1: The Golden Era of Cartoon Art, 1934–1937." MIT Visualizing Cultures [database online]. Cambridge, MA, 2011. Retrieved August 20, 2014, from http://ocw.mit.edu/ans7870/21f/21f.027/modern_sketch/ms_essay01.html.

Ding Cong 丁聰. *Xianxiang tu* 現象圖 (Images of today). Spencer Museum of Art, "Collections" [database online]. Kansas City, 2013. Retrieved July 25, 2014 from http://collection.spencerart.ku.edu/eMuseumPlus.

Gan Xianfeng 甘險峰. *Zhongguo manhua shi* 中國漫畫史 [A history of Chinese cartooning]. Jinan: Shandong huabao chubanshe, 2008.

Gunn, Edward M. "Literature and Art of the War Period." In *China's Bitter Victory: The War with Japan, 1937–1945*. Ed. James C. Hsiung and Steven I. Levine. Armonk: M. E. Sharpe, 1993. 235–274.

Harder, Hans. "Prologue: Late Nineteenth and Twentieth Century Asian *Punch* Versions and Related Satirical Journals." In *Asian Punches: A Transcultural Affair*. Ed. Barbara Mittler and Hans Harder. Heidelberg: Springer, 2013. 1–11.

Huang Shiying 黃士英. "Zhongguo manhua fazhan shi" 中國漫畫發展史 [The development of the cartoon in China]. *Manhua shenghuo* 漫畫生活 [Cartoon life] 13 (September 20, 1935).

Huang Yao 黃堯. *Maodun ji* 矛盾集 [Contradiction collection]. Huang Yao Foundation, "Resource Center" [database online]. Retrieved July 25, 2014 from http://huangyao.org/866.html.

Hung, Chang-tai. "The Fuming Image: Cartoons and Public Opinion in Late Republican China, 1945 to 1949." *Comparative Studies in Society and History* 36.1 (January 1994): 122–145.

Hung, Chang-tai. *War and Popular Culture: Resistance in Modern China, 1937–1945*. Berkeley: University of California Press, 1994.

Laing, Ellen Johnston. *Selling Happiness: Calendar Posters and Visual Culture in Early Twentieth-Century Shanghai*. Honolulu: University of Hawai'i Press, 2004.

Lent, John A. "Introduction." In *Illustrating Asia: Comics, Humor Magazines, and Picture Books*. Ed. John A. Lent. Honolulu: University of Hawai'i Press, 2001. 1–10.

Ma Ke 馬克. "Meiyou shiqu guangcai de huaduo: Lüetan manhua *Xiyou manji*" 沒有失去光彩的花朵：略談 "西遊漫記" [A blossom that has not lost its splendor: A brief discussion of *Journey to the West in Cartoons*]. In *Xiyou manji* 西游漫記 [Journey to the west in cartoons]. Ed. Tang Wei 唐薇 and Huang Dagang 黃大剛. Beijing: Renmin meishu chubanshe, 2012. 135–136. Originally published in *Meishu* 美術 [Fine arts], June 1957.

Manhua 漫畫 [Cartoon]. "*Xiyou manji* zai Beijing zhanchu" "西遊漫記"在北京展出 [Journey to the West in Cartoons shown in Beijing] 88 (May 8, 1957): 6.

Manhuajie 漫畫界 [Modern Puck] 7 (November 5, 1936).

Mao Zhiming 毛志明, ed. *Shanghai manhua* 上海漫畫 [Shanghai sketch]. 1928–1930. Shanghai: Shanghai shudian chubanshe, 1996 [reprint].

Mittler, Barbara. "Epilogue: Ten Thousand *Pucks* and *Punches*: Satirical Themes and Variations Seen Transculturally." In *Asian Punches: A Transcultural Affair*. Ed. Barbara Mittler and Hans Harder. Heidelberg: Springer, 2013. 423–444.

Nan Huang 南黃. "Zhang Guangyu Zhengyu kunzhong—manhua jiezuo *Xiyou manji* jiang zai Hu zhanlan" 張光宇正宇昆仲一漫畫傑作"西遊漫記"將在滬展覽 [Cartoon masterpiece *Journey to the West in Cartoons* by brothers Zhang Guangyu and Zhengyu to be exhibited in Shanghai]. *Wanhuatong* 萬花筒 [Kaleidoscope] 11 (1946).

Pan, Lynn. *Shanghai Style: Art and Design Between the Wars*. San Francisco: Long River Press, 2008.

Pickowicz, Paul G., Kuiyi Shen, and Yingjin Zhang, eds. "Introduction: *Liangyou*, Popular Print Media, and Visual Culture in Republican Shanghai." In *Liangyou: Kaleidoscopic Modernity and the Shanghai Global Metropolis, 1926–1945*. Leiden and Boston: Brill, 2013. 1–13.

Shao Xunmei 邵洵美. "Huabao zai wenhuajie de diwei" 畫報在文化界的地位 [The place of pictorials in the culture world]. In *Yige ren de tanhua* 一個人的談話 [Conversations alone], Shanghai: Shanghai shudian chubanshe, 2012. 73–77.

Shen, Kuiyi. "*Lianhuanhua* and *Manhua*: Picture Books and Comics in Old Shanghai." In *Illustrating Asia: Comics, Humor Magazines, and Picture Books*. Ed. John A. Lent. Honolulu: University of Hawaii Press, 2001. 101–120.

Shen Xueli 申雪莉. "Zhang Guangyu lianhuanhua *Xiyou manji* yinyushi fengge tanxi" 張光宇連環漫畫"西遊漫記"隱喻式風格探析 [An examination of the metaphorical style in Zhang Guangyu's series *manhua Journey to the West in Cartoons*]. *Meishu daguan* 美術大觀 [Art panorama] 3 (August 2013): 52–53. Retrieved August 16, 2014 from Cnki.net.

The Sketch: A Journal of Art and Actuality. London: Ingram Brothers [etc.]. Hathi Trust Digital Library [database online]. Retrieved July 10, 2014 from http://hdl.handle.net/2027/mdp.39 015085551375?urlappend=%3Bseq=71.

Sullivan, Michael. *Art and Artists of Twentieth-Century China*. Berkeley: University of California Press, 1996.

Tang Wei 唐薇. "Nianbiao" 年表 (Chronology). In *Zhang Guangyu wenji* 張光宇文集 [Selected writings of Zhang Guangyu]. Ed. Tang Wei 唐薇. Jinan: Shandong meishu chubanshe, 2011. 219–235.

Vinograd, Richard. "Multi-Medium, Site, and Dream-World: Aspects of Shanghai Pictorials of the 1920s and 1930s." *Yishuxue yanjiu* 藝術學研究 Journal of art studies 12 (September 2013): 171–214. Retrieved January 11, 2015 from http://art.ncu.edu.tw/journal/words/%E7%AC%AC12%E6%9C%9F04-RichardVinograd.pdf.

Wang Zimei 汪子美. "Zhongguo manhua zhi yanjin ji zhanwang" 中國漫畫之演進及展望 [China's *manhua*: Evolution and future prospects] *Manhua shenghuo* 漫畫生活 [Cartoon life] 13 (September 20, 1935).

Wu, I-Wei. "Participating in Global Affairs: The Chinese Cartoon Monthly *Shanghai Puck*." In *Asian Punches: A Transcultural Affair*. Ed. Barbara Mittler and Hans Harder. Heidelberg: Springer, 2013. 365–387.

Ye Feng 葉風. "Zhongguo manhua de zaoqi zhengui wenxian: *Shanghai manhua*" 中國漫畫的早期珍貴文獻: 上海 漫畫 [A precious document of early Chinese cartooning: *Shanghai Sketch*]. In *Shanghai manhua* 上海漫畫 [Shanghai sketch]. 1928–1930. Ed. Mao Zhiming. Vol. 1. Shanghai: Shanghai shudian chubanshe, 1996 [reprint]. 1–3.

Ye Lingfeng 葉靈鳳. "Jieshao Guangyu de *Xiyou Manji*" 介紹光宇的 "西遊漫記" [Introducing Guangyu's *Journey to the West in Cartoons*]. In *Xiyou manji* 西遊漫記 [Journey to the west in cartoons]. Ed. Tang Wei 唐薇 and Huang Dagang 黃大剛. Beijing: Renmin meishu chubanshe. 2012. Originally published in *Xinsheng wanbao* 新生晚報 [New life evening news] (Hong Kong), June 13, 1947.

Ye Qianyu 葉淺予. *Ye Qianyu zizhuan: Xi jiangxu cangsang ji liunian* 葉淺予自傳：細講敘滄桑記流年 [Autobiography of Ye Qianyu: A detailed account of vicissitudes through fleeting years]. Beijing: Zhongguo shehui kexue chubanshe, 2006.

Ye, Xiaoqing. *The Dianshizhai Pictorial: Shanghai Urban Life, 1884–1898*. Ann Arbor: Center for Chinese Studies, University of Michigan, 2003.

Zhang Guangyu 張光宇. "Zixu *Xiyou Manji*" 自序"西遊漫記" [Author's preface to *Journey to the West in Cartoons*]. *Qingming* 清明 3 (July 16, 1946).

Zhang Guangyu 張光宇. *Xiyou manji* 西遊漫記 [Journey to the west in cartoons]. Ed. Tang Wei 唐薇 and Huang Dagang 黃大剛. Beijing: Renmin meishu chubanshe, 2012.

Zheng Liangcheng 鄭良誠. "*Niubizi Huazhan* kan hou" "牛鼻子畫展"看後 [Upon viewing the *Niubizi Exhibition*]. *Zhengyibao* 正義報, September 17, 1944: 4.

Zhengyibao 正義報. "*Weilao Rongjun Zhan* shiri qi juxing" 慰勞榮軍展十日起舉行 [Veterans' Benefit Exhibition to open on the 10th]. *Zhengyibao* 正義報, September 8, 1944: 3.

Zhengyibao 正義報. "*Niubizi Huazhan* wei Wuhua Zhongxue mujuan" 牛鼻子畫展為五華中學募捐 [*Niubizi Exhibition* donates to Wu Hua Middle School]. *Zhengyibao* 正義報, September 30, 1944: 3

Zou Jianlin 鄒建林. "Minguo wenyi zhong de 'gaixie jingdian' xianxiang: Cong Liao Bingxiong *Maoguo Chunqiu* tan qi" 民國文藝中的"改寫經典"現象: 從廖冰兄"貓國春秋"談起 [The phenomenon of "rewriting the classics" in Nationalist-era literature and art: The case of Liao Bingxiong's *Spring and Autumn in the Cat Kingdom*]. *Wenyi yanjiu* 文藝研究 (Literature and art studies) 6 (2011): 125–133.

THE ALLEGORY OF TIME AND SPACE

Tian Han's Historical Dramas in the Great Leap Forward Period

LAIKWAN PANG

FOUR months before the publication of the "May 16 Notification" that officially announced the advent of the Cultural Revolution, we already find in a drama journal a long article criticizing Tian Han 田漢.[1] The author argues that historical dramas like Tian Han's *Xie yaohuan* (謝瑤環)

> appear to disgrace the Emperor, humiliate the powerful, and celebrate those officials who spoke for the people. But in reality what they really applaud is the rightists, with the aim of waging a war against the party and against socialism. They wear the coat of "praising the left" and "returning to the ancient," but in essence they are "anti-party," "anti-socialism," and "anti-people" big poisonous weeds.[2]

Such a radical, tendentious interpretation, which would soon overwhelm the entire cultural world of China, is obviously based on the logic of allegory—the most basic understanding of allegory is precisely "speaking otherwise than one seems to speak."[3] Although allegory is itself a Western concept, there are comparable notions of *bi* 比 (metaphor) and *xing* 興 (affective evocation) in the Chinese context. These literary methods can be traced all the way back to the *Book of Odes* (詩經), the first collection of poems in Chinese history, and they refer to a figurative use of language, to a use of words that point to some other meaning beyond the apparent one.[4] The Maoist critic in 1966 undoubtedly believed that Tian Han and other allegedly reactionary writers wrote in such a manner, and that, consequently, their works put up a deceptive façade, appearing to express something while actually saying something else.

This kind of criticism is now generally criticized as overpoliticized and skewed, and allegory is seen as something forced by the critic onto the writer's work. In other words, such a reading depends on a violent appropriation of writing by reading. But the whole-sale condemnation of the critic could also be naive. In highly politicized Maoist China, writing and reading, the writer and the critic, could not be easily dichotomized, as both practices and agents were caught in the same ideological environment. The notion of "allegory" (*yuyan* 寓言) can help us explore authorship and, by extension, the meaning of writing, at a time when censorship and self-censorship were rampant and nothing could be taken at face value. Allegory is a site where writing and reading meet, where the authorial and the ideological are contested and confused.

To explore the politics of allegorical writing in Maoist China, in this chapter I focus on a highly political form of writing in a most turbulent period by an extremely ide-alistic writer: Tian Han's historical dramas during the Great Leap Forward period. Of all cultural forms, drama (both spoken drama and regional operas), probably more than cinema, was the single most politically effective and heavily utilized means of propaganda in modern and contemporary China until the television age. There was a long history preceding 1949 in which the theatrical stage overlapped with the political stage: while common folk, literate or not, loved traditional operas, intellectuals in the late Qing and early Republican period began to experiment with theater in order to express themselves, on one hand, and to enlighten the people, on the other.[5] The strong political orientation of spoken drama shaped the central concerns of modern Chinese drama in its formative age,[6] and the dramatic form would be heavily utilized again for agitation purposes during both the Sino-Japanese war and the civil war periods.[7]

Entering the so-called seventeen-year period (1949 to 1966), different kinds of drama and regional opera were seamlessly incorporated into the state ideological apparatus. What distinguishes this period from the following Cultural Revolution period was an acknowledgment of individual authorship, even if this had to be endorsed by the state through the author's voluntary submission to it. The seventeen-year period was a time when famous writers and dramatists, such as Tian Han, were still respected as pub-lic intellectuals. Their works embodied both the state and themselves as artists, and were mediated by state-sponsored professional associations, such as the Association of Dramatists, and by professional journals, such as *Drama News* (戲劇報) and *Scripts* (劇本), in the area of theatrical arts. This congenial condition did not last long, and the condemnation of two theatrical pieces, *Li Huiniang* (李慧娘) and *Hairui Dismissed from Office* (海瑞罷官), initiated the Cultural Revolution.[8] On the other hand, the *yangbanxi* (樣板戲; model performance pieces) project also sanctifies the dramatic form to infiltrate revolutionary ideology.[9] The notion of "authorship" would be entirely suppressed during the Cultural Revolution.[10]

Tian Han was a highly respected playwright in Maoist China, but the authorship marked in the works he produced, particularly in the late 1950s and early 1960s, can-not be taken for granted as being entirely his own. This was a time when artists' cre-ative autonomy had to be heavily sutured into the will of the state, but it was also the time when Tian Han's fame peaked, so he had to speak for both the state apparatus and himself. In the following I analyze the ways these works embody the struggle between authorship and state power by analyzing their allegorical portrayals of the "past" and the "outside." At the time, history was no longer meaningful in its own right, but had to be repeatedly written and interpreted to justify the socialist present and to be projected into the communist future. Tian Han's theatrical works also bring into focus socialist China's difficult projects of national unification, on one hand, and internationalism, on the other. The following discussion of the ways in which "other times" and "other people" were depicted and imagined in Tian Han's works provides a new understanding of the naiveté and struggles of critical intellectuals in the age of Maoism.

THE DRAMA OFFSTAGE

Tian Han is recognized as one of twentieth-century China's most idealistic and romantic writers. Among his left-wing intellectual peers in the 1920s and 1930s, Tian Han was also one of the most prolific, and the genres he handled ranged widely from spoken dramas to film scripts, poems to novellas, and lyrics to critical essays. Starting in 1949, however, his hitherto abundant creative energy seemed subtly curbed, and he became buried by the many official duties to which he was assigned. From 1949 to 1966, Tian Han served as Head of the Xiqu Reform Unit in the Ministry of Culture, Head of the Bureau of Art Affairs, and Inaugural Headmaster of the Institution of Chinese Xiqu, as well as Chair of the Association of Dramatists. Like most other upper-level bureaucrats, Tian Han had little time to focus on his literary career. But at the beginning of 1958, Mao passionately summoned the Chinese people to engage in production, the more the better. Not only were factories and communes committed to impossible missions, but cultural units and individual cultural workers also strove to become part of the Great Leap Forward. Disgraced by the low number of works he had produced since 1949, Tian Han vowed to write ten new theatrical scripts immediately. He was not able to meet his goal, but 1958 to 1959 was another peak of production for him, during which he wrote three spoken dramas—*Guan Hanqing* (關漢卿) (1958), *Shisanling Reservoir Fantasia* (十三陵水庫暢想曲) (1958), and *Princess Wencheng* (文成公主) (1959), as well as the Peking Opera *Story of the Western Chamber* (西廂記) (1959).

This period of creative rejuvenation should be contextualized within the wider political turbulences in which Tian Han was caught. Under the "Hundred Flowers" slogan, from 1956 to 1957 artists and authors had been encouraged to voice their own opinions and produce new works, and a pluralistic atmosphere had emerged after the allegedly successful completion of the PRC's First Five-Year plan.[11] In 1957 Tian Han was given the task of encouraging his fellow writers in the Association of Dramatists to voice opinions that might diverge from official discourse. He also wrote a few articles himself, such as "We Need to Attend to Artists and Improve Their Livelihood" (必須切實關心並改善藝人的生活), and "Pleading on Behalf of Performers' Youth"

(為演員的青春請命), to remind the state politely how it could improve its cultural governance.[12]

But creative workers and critics were quickly silenced, and many were punished, when the Anti-Rightist campaign was launched in 1957, and it was "decided" that 70 percent of the editorial staff of *Drama News*, the official publication of the Dramatists' Association, were rightists.[13] It is generally understood that the two movements were connected causally, that Mao was outraged by the large amount of criticism directed at various levels of the government during the Hundred Flowers campaign, and that he launched the Anti-Rightist campaign to halt a development that some believed was leading to a state crisis.[14] We can say that 1957 was a trying year for many Chinese intellectuals, when they were given the most honorable political duties only to be shoved aside immediately. There was a strong sense of having been betrayed by the state, and many began to realize that the regime was not the same one they had identified with.

During this period of confusion and disenchantment, intellectuals were hit with two other important and disorienting national events. First, the demand for the "Great Leap Forward" arrived in literary and artistic circles, and all cultural workers once again were plunged into a festive mode of cultural production. Meanwhile, many parts of China began to suffer the calamity of the great famine, which very soon would affect the entire country.[15] The political intention behind the works Tian Han produced during this period of intense personal and social unrest remains an enigma for Tian Han scholars.[16] As Chair of the Association of Dramatists, Tian Han not only witnessed but also was deeply entrenched in the political drama. He had believed in the congeniality promoted by the Hundred Flowers campaign, and encouraged many of his fellow dramaturges and writers to assert themselves before the state, for which they ended up being severely punished. Between July 1957 and March 1958, nearly one hundred theater workers were criticized in the seventeen issues of *Drama News* published in this period.[17] Tian Han was one of them, but after his confession he escaped the rightist label under which many of his colleagues in the Association of Dramatists, such as Wu Zuguang 吳祖光, had to suffer for the rest of their lives.[18] We do not know the extent to which Tian Han victimized his colleagues to safeguard himself, but allegations were not lacking.[19] Unable to wash his hands of the Anti-Rightist purgation, how could Tian Han then happily plunge into the Great Leap Forward gala?

Tian Han recounted that the overall atmosphere of the Great Leap Forward brought back his dearest wartime memory, when theatrical production served the very narrow political function of agitation for national defense. He was excited by this overall spirit of collectivity and youthfulness, and he felt that he was able to regain the creative energy he had lost in the 1950s.[20] In other words, Tian Han was highly aware that these Great Leap Forward pieces were political through and through, and he allowed one type of politics that he could handle and with which he could identify to displace another type with which he was not able to come to terms.[21] In 1958, Tian Han finally seemed to be able to resolve his dual identities as a party leader and as an independent writer by embracing the spirit of the Great Leap Forward, and he was able to find meaning in art after serving as a state bureaucrat for a decade. But can innocence be so easily conjured up and made to return? Escaping the political fad that was taking place in the real world, Tian Han fully exposed himself to the politics he created on stage.

THE ONSTAGE DRAMA: TEMPORAL SIGNIFICANCE

Let us now look more closely at the political dimensions of two of his works, *Guan Hanqing* and *Princess Wencheng*. *Guan Hanqing* is a metadrama that depicts the production and reception of a popular Yuan opera, *The Enmity of Doue* (竇娥冤), which was written by Guan Hanqing, one of the most famous opera writers in Chinese history. The story begins with Guan's courtesan, Zhu Lianxiu, outraged upon learning of an unjust homicide charge against Doue, a poor widow. Abused since childhood, Doue led a miserable but respectable life that came to an abrupt end after she was accused of killing a rascal so that the real murderer, the rascal's son, could get away scot-free. Guan Hanqing decides to write an opera to expose the crime and to criticize the corruption of the Yuan court. Tian Han created different versions of the ending, and the most popular one is tragic: both Guan and Zhu are captured and exiled to different places. This spoken drama was widely performed and acclaimed, and it was quickly adopted into different regional operas and staged all over China. It was also translated into English, Japanese, and Russian, and was performed in different countries.

Tian Han decided to write about Guan Hanqing because Guan was designated a World Cultural Celebrity in 1958 by the World Peace Council.[22] Tian Han was elated, and shared in the national pride of his fellow Chinese and particularly the Chinese dramatists. As his secretary Li Zhiyan 黎之彥 wrote:

> January 20, 1958. Tonight, with gusty winds from the west, Comrade Tian Han wore a long navy-blue leather gown, crouching at his desk and concentrating on writing. Shortly before midnight, he said to me: "The World Peace Council decided to crown Guan Hanqing as a World Cultural Celebrity, and the ceremony will be held in June this year, to celebrate the seventh centennial of this great dramatist's birth. Both China and the world will commemorate him. This is the glory of the Chinese race, and it is also the pride of our theater. I will prepare a speech to be delivered at the conference, starting tomorrow. We should take this opportunity to read more books, and to conduct a systematic study of Guan Hanqing and his writings." Mr. Tian added: "We have plenty of books here, and we should be able to find some related to the Yuan dynasty."[23]

Tian Han wrote not only a speech but also a full-length dramatic script about Guan Hanqing. We do not know much about Guan Hanqing, who lived in the thirteenth century. Although it is clear that he was already a famous and active dramaturge in his lifetime, there is no historical evidence to indicate that he was a dissident under

Mongol rule.[24] But Tian Han decided to portray Guan as a hero of the Chinese people, and he particularly emphasized the class and race struggles in the Yuan dynasty. Tian Han added the "universal" values of independent sovereignty and class equality to this historical story, so that Guan could become a universal hero transcending culture and history, corresponding to his newly confirmed "World Cultural Celebrity" status.

But the use of historical figures and historical stories was not a singular exercise unique to the writing of *Guan Hanqing*. All the works Tian Han created during the Great Leap Forward period are historical: both *Guan Hanqing* and *Story of the Western Chamber* take place during the Yuan dynasty, *Princess Wencheng* is a Tang story, while *Shisanling Reservoir Fantasia* combines historical and contemporary figures into a fantasia. In fact, many of the official duties Tian Han assumed since 1949 concerned the reform of *xiqu* (regional opera), and he had been very concerned about the revival of historical dramas and operas in new China. Sadly, a major indictment against him during the Cultural Revolution was precisely that he wrote historical dramas at a time when he was supposed to be producing stories celebrating contemporary socialist governance.

The question of allegory inevitably arises here: are these historical dramas simply literary reconstructions of historical events, or do they contain allegorical messages critical of current politics? Rudolf Wagner interprets *Guan Hanqing* in the latter way: "The relationship between the Han Chinese and the Yuan rulers resonates with that between the 'masses' and the Party [in contemporary China]. The Party is a self-perpetuating minority which rules over the former."[25] This straightforward reading is not unconvincing, based on the political conditions of the time and the long-standing tradition in Chinese literature and drama of using the past to criticize the present. In fact, when commenting on *The Enmity of Doue*, Tian Han asserted: "Obviously, in terms of both its intention and its method, Guan Hanqing used the past as an allegory (*yi gu yu jin* 以古喻今). He stood by the victimized woman as well as the ordinary people, and he vehemently cursed the rulers. That is why Guan Hanqing titled this piece Doue's 'enmity.'"[26] Although Doue was a contemporary of Guan Hanqing, Tian Han still used the notion of *yi gu yu jin* to describe Guan's writing, probably because he wanted to connect this piece to the venerable tradition of this literary practice in China, so that we can read Doue's story as one that symbolizes the deeper and universal moral significance of the people rising up against despotism.

But it is also problematic to assume that Tian Han simply adopted Guan Hanqing's literary technique and political intention of using the past to criticize the present political regime, because Tian Han himself was a part of this regime. Although Tian Han differed from his friend Guo Moruo 郭沫若, who held key government offices, he was clearly the party's spokesperson in the cultural world. Wagner emphatically states that Tian Han consciously utilized a variety of sophisticated and time-honored forms for airing his grievances against a regime of which he was critical.[27] But such a dichotomized model fails to account for the collaborative relationship between intellectuals and the government in 1950s China. *Guan Hanqing* was created after Mao's call for the Great Leap Forward, and Tian Han found an artistic rebirth for himself within this collectivist ideology. Wagner's allegorical reading does not account for Tian Han's own faithfulness and subjective identification with the regime.

Also, we must recognize that Tian Han himself was highly critical of the overpoliticization of history and literature that was the norm in his days, and he could not have been unaware of the problems of *yi gu yu jin*. Throughout the 1950s, Tian Han repeatedly emphasized the importance of accurate and thorough historical research for the writing of historical stories. Li Zhiyan recounts Tian Han's commitment to reading about Yuan history as background research for *Guan Hanqing*. Tian Han consulted major historical texts like *The History of Yuan* (元史), *A New History of Yuan* (新元史), and Marco Polo's travelogue to learn about contemporary life, and he deliberately added related details to his script, making sure the fictive and the historical blended together well.[28] Tian Han emphasized history not only to make the story believable, but also as a corrective to the contemporary tendency of focusing only on the heroic present and brushing the past aside. He repeatedly asserted that although scriptwriters were responsible for demonstrating the spirit of modern China and for praising the struggles of contemporary people, they must not ignore historical subjects and blur the line between contemporary topics and historical materials. He disliked the common practice among contemporary writers of freely appropriating history, and believed that contemporary political concerns should not be allowed to mask what actually had happened in the past.[29] However, and no matter how much he denied it, during the Cultural Revolution Tian Han would be charged with using his cultural works to criticize the Party allegorically, and this allegation would cost him his life.[30] In the end, the author's intentions do not matter, since the fates of the artwork and the artist are sealed by the political interpretations forced on them. Tian Han's tragic end reminds us not to take the concept of political allegory for granted as our prime hermeneutic framework.

We can say that Tian Han was caught in the dilemma of appropriating history on one hand and respecting it on the other, and was unable to use history to locate his authorial self clearly. A similar set of ambiguities emerges in the work of another famous intellectual, Wu Han 吳晗, who wrote the historical drama *Hairui Dismissed from Office* in 1959. The piece would be spotlighted several years later and criticized as an anti-Party allegory, and its purgation would mark the beginning of the Cultural Revolution. As one of the most famous historians of the time, Wu Han wrote a series of articles in 1959 criticizing the way history was sidelined by contemporary politics. He did not challenge the fundamental principle of contemporary historiography, concurring with the new intellectual view of the present as more worthy of study than the past. But he argued that the relative importance of the present should not be overemphasized, since understanding the present requires serious historical study.[31] He did not advocate history-writing for the sake of it, but argued that the two notions, "using the past for the present" (古為今用) and "privileging the present over the past" (厚今薄古), should be understood as two sides of the same coin, and that history should be read in terms of its value for present use. Interestingly, instead of reinforcing the importance of his profession by writing history, Wu Han ventured to write his first dramatic script, *Hairui*

Dismissed from Office. He presented this piece as an example of how the past can be used responsibly for approaching the present.

According to some stagnant versions of Marxist historicism prevalent at the time, history matters little because the past could only be regressive and depraved. Although Tian Han emphasized accurate historical details in his plays while Wu Han chose to present his historical research in a drama, they both stressed the importance of history in this age of ahistoricity, and they devoted themselves to fighting the intellectual crime of marginalizing history. But to be loyal to the kind of Marxism that prevailed then, they also asserted that history is meaningful only because it can help explain the present. This constructivist understanding of history allows history to be presented in ways that communicate effectively, so that it can be rendered dramatically with a coherent structure, romantic language, and heroic characters. History is both politicized and aestheticized at the same time, and the expertise of the creative writer and that of the historian become merged. For Wu Han, history must be heard, and he chose to demonstrate this by rendering it into a drama. For Tian Han, drama is always a powerful political tool, but he chose history to "package" drama during that unmanageable period so that he could submerge himself in a "purer" reality than the current murky one he did not know how to deal with. In both cases, a simple adoption of political allegory as a hermeneutic framework for reading the work misses the much more contrived struggle of the author. We should also recognize that these works embody not only the political struggles of the author but also, to a certain extent, those of the contemporary intellectual culture.

If critics of the Cultural Revolution and their contemporary counterparts slid back into the tendency against which Tian Han and Wu Han fought halfheartedly, the task for us is to engage with the framework of allegory even more vigorously in order to understand how Maoist intellectuals handled the contrived relations between arts and politics. Allegory operates not only along temporal differences but also spatial differences, and it was in this age of internationalism that the Chinese tradition of allegory found new manifestations. The historical dramas Tian Han produced during the Great Leap Forward period were clearly political, but the author did not direct the political message to the present regime; instead, the general feeling of unease was displaced outside the confines of China.

THE ONSTAGE DRAMA: SPATIAL SIGNIFICANCE

In a confession he wrote during the Cultural Revolution, Tian Han defended *Guan Hanqing* as a story that took place in the Yuan dynasty, a setting that had no resemblance at all to the contemporary PRC.[32] This assertion is clearly a defense against the charge of allegorical communication in his piece. What I find interesting is his further plea that if the story is to be read allegorically, it should be interpreted in terms of contemporary events in Japan, where the Japanese people were living under American occupation. Although he denied the accusation that *Guan Hanqing* was an allegory about the PRC state, he endorsed the allegorical reading of it as a criticism of American imperialism in Japan. This is what made the piece decidedly socialist and modern. In fact, Tian Han claimed that he did not plant this allegory in the piece; instead, he learned about it from his audience. It was letters from Japanese theatergoers that informed Tian Han of the extent to which these "foreigners" identified with his drama.

What Tian Han wrote about this in 1968 is confirmed by Chinese official reports published a decade earlier, which described the *Guan Hanqing* tour in Japan in this way:

> The piece was performed not only in Osaka, but also Kobe, Kyoto, Wakayama, Nagoya, Shizuoka, and Tokyo. The geographical reach and the length of the tour are almost unprecedented. Counting only the three months from early January to early April, more than ten million people attended the show in the theater or by listening to the live radio broadcast or the television broadcast. *Guan Hanqing* is so popular in Japan because Japanese viewers find in it echoes of their own tragic situation, and they see the unfortunate fate of the characters as reflecting their own. Otherwise the performance in Japan would not be so well received, and would not manifest such profound realist significance.[33]

Although the hyperbolic tone, which was common in news reportage at the time, cannot be trusted at face value, we can assume that the alleged popularity of *Guan Hanqing* in Japan was particularly meaningful to Tian Han, who had studied in Japan and was indebted to the education he received there. He was particularly influenced by the Japanese literary critic Kuriyagawa Hakuson 廚川白村 (1880–1923), whose promotion of Western literature as well as the value of art and love in society would influence Tian Han for the rest of his life. With his wide-ranging interests in Japanese and Western cultures, Tian Han was never a narrow-minded nationalist, and internationalism was dear to his heart. Between the historical story and the contemporary reception of *Guan Hanqing*, the Han resistance to Mongolian rule in the thirteenth century echoed the contemporary struggles of the Japanese against the Americans. It was probably art and love that made this transcultural and transhistorical leap possible.

Han–minority relations are featured not only in *Guan Hanqing* but also in *Princess Wencheng*, which stages the historical story of a famous Tang princess being married to a Tibetan king. Tian Han recounts how *Princess Wencheng* was created after the 1959 Tibetan riot. He attended an exhibition featuring Tibetan serfdom and was furious about the suffering incurred by the Tibetan people. He therefore decided to write a story to condemn such feudalistic practices. But instead of writing a contemporary story, he again returned to the Tang dynasty to explore the early life of Princess Wencheng. The princess was married by the Tang court to Songtsan Gampo, the king of the Yarlung dynasty of Tibet, to foster peace, and as the legend goes, she brought Buddhism and much of the Tang civilization to Tibet. Embodying kindness and culture, Princess

Wencheng has been revered in Tibet as the personification of the bodhisattva of mercy and compassion.

As with *Guan Hanqing*, Tian Han emphasized the importance of historical research in writing *Princess Wencheng*, and he consulted many historical documents to find out how people led their lives at the time.[34] But Tian Han did admit that this piece was written with a clear contemporary political message, which was the condemnation of Tibetan serfdom, a sentiment shared by many Chinese under the PRC propaganda. After the first version was produced, however, Tian Han was advised not to emphasize Tibetan class struggle, since that might create negative feelings among the Chinese audience about Tibet. Reluctantly, Tian Han had to forfeit a very important figure in the original version: the Tibetan girl Nima. Nima is a serf who runs away from her master and is rescued by another Tang princess also married to the Tibetan court, Princess Jincheng. Sympathetic to Nima, Wencheng decides to bring her back to her homeland and reunite her with her lover, but before she can do so Nima's master abducts her. When Wencheng finally saves Nima, the poor girl's eyes have been gouged out, and Wencheng is so upset that she vows to devote her life to protecting the poor in Tibet. This important part of the drama had to be edited out, because Tian Han was told that it would give a bad impression to the Chinese people about Tibet, at a time when the friendship of the two peoples was deemed to be of the utmost political importance.[35] Unlike with *Guan Hanqing*, which Tian Han composed almost in one breath, Tian Han wrote and rewrote the entire second part of *Princess Wencheng*, and was never happy with it.[36]

As indicated by his account of the writing process, Tian Han struggled to align himself with the state apparatus. Both the Tibetan serfdom exhibition he attended and the political pressure of promoting amity between the two peoples, although contradictory, were official political messages to which Tian Han submitted himself. His difficult process of rewriting indicates that he identified more with the former than the latter, and he stood by Nima, the disenfranchised serf. In fact, in *Guan Hanqing* there is a figure with similar symbolic significance, Sai Lianxiu, the disciple of Zhu Lianxiu. Outraged by her master's imprisonment, Sai sings: "When will the heaven open its eyes, and peel off the skin of the ruthless official?" The price Sai pays for singing this song is also her eyes, which are gouged out by the official she disparages. Although Guan Hanqing and Zhu Lianxiu are the protagonists of the drama, Sai is the true embodiment of courage and victimhood, as is Nima in *Princess Wencheng*. Tian Han's anger toward the Tibetan landlord was as ferocious toward the Mongolian oppressor, and he associated himself with both Sai Lianxiu and Nima. The association of blindness and justice is clear, and we can therefore understand why Tian Han was so reluctant to accede to the demand of the ideological apparatus to cut out the part of Nima.

Guan Hanqing and *Princess Wencheng* demonstrate not only the ways in which authorship was heavily negotiated, but also the conflicts between the ideologies of internationalism and of national unification. As mentioned above, Tian Han was not a narrow-minded patriot but rather valued international, intercultural, and interracial alliance. He could easily identify with the Japanese and the Tibetan people based on class affiliation, and the displacement of culture by class as one's major point of collective identification is also the principle of socialism. But when this principle risks national interests, he was told that the latter must come first.

During the Great Famine, when central leaders like Mao Zedong and Zhou Enlai gave up meat to express solidarity with the people, the PRC did not stop its financial support of Third World brother nations. It still provided 60,000 tons and 160,000 tons of grain to Albania and East Germany, respectively, while so many Chinese people died of hunger.[37] It was a time when the exportation of revolution was equivalent to the granting of material support, and only through "continual revolution" could the revolution in China be sustainable. As the Cultural Revolution *yangbanxi On the Dock* (海港) demonstrates, internationalism was a core part of Maoism, whose domestic and international powers reinforced each other.[38] However, when this ideal of internationalism based on universal class struggle meets national politics, the interest of the latter prevails, so that the list of PRC's friends changes constantly, and the national integrity of China is always more important than class struggles internationally.

Written right after the Tibetan Revolution, the original *Princess Wencheng* does not suggest much reflection on the part of Tian Han on the PRC's minority policy, even though he identified people's struggles in terms of class struggle, however much that identification was mediated by the PRC ideological apparatus. But even this hackneyed portrayal of the backwardness of the minority culture could not be allowed, since it might fan Han chauvinism and further drive Tibet's separatism. Tian Han's noble intention of promoting class amity between the Tibetan and the Han Chinese was aborted, largely because the regime recognized that such depiction would convey racial discrimination instead of class solidarity. At this point, the logic of national unification presided over that of universal class struggle, fundamentally challenging the basic principles of internationalism.

AUTHORSHIP IN MAOIST CHINA

The authorship embodied in *Guan Hanqing* and *Princess Wencheng* is a besieged one. On one hand, Tian Han did not forfeit his own name and autonomy, and he still believed in writing as a form of self-expression, paid for at a heavy price during the Cultural Revolution. But in reality it was increasingly difficult for any writer or artist to be autonomous, as long as that autonomy could only be granted through the endorsement of the state. In the case of Tian Han, his stagnant literary and political career in 1957 was salvaged by the Great Leap Forward, in which the faithful yet confused intellectual finally found a way to reunite with the state apparatus. The naive celebration of national construction as depicted in *Shisanling Reservoir Fantasia* and the condemnation of Tibetan serfdom in *Princess Wencheng* are clear evidence of this. But he would quickly become disillusioned all over again, with the state's interests continually surprising and overwhelming his own, so that the reunion he sought was never possible. By focusing on troubles outside the Han proper, Tian Han tried to escape his own intellectual duty of being critical of contemporary events in China, including the disaster created by the Anti-Rightist campaign, in which he participated. But as shown in the writing and rewriting of *Princess Wencheng*, this escape was of no avail. Tian Han seemed to be stuck in his struggle between being loyal to the party's demands and being loyal to his own aesthetic and moral impulses, which were also naive in their own ways.

In this context it is helpful to recall a controversial essay written by Fredric Jameson almost thirty years ago, which discusses precisely the importance of national allegory in modern Chinese literature.[39] While his argument that Third-World literatures are necessarily allegorical has already been discredited by many scholars, we can still explore how allegory might function for Chinese writers during such traumatized periods as the Great Leap Forward. Jameson demonstrates that the separation of the public and the private, and of the individual and society, are taken for granted in the West. This assumption directly impacts our reading of literature, dichotomized into the criticism of the world, on one hand, and an investigation of the self, on the other. For Jameson, this method of reading is culturally specific, and may not be reflected by other national literatures. I agree with Jameson that most Chinese writers and readers do not dichotomize society and individual in the same way, and indeed the relations involved are always convoluted. As I have argued above, China has a millennium-long literary practice of using history as an allegory of the present, and both writers and readers are trained to write and read accordingly, to such an extent that allegorical writing and reading can exceed authorial intention to become a collective unconsciousness. Modern socialist ideology further complicates this allegorical practice by introducing internationalism to the Chinese people, so that not only do the past and the present relate to each other politically, but things taking place inside and outside China can also be structurally connected.

What is most inspiring about Jameson's article is not what it has to say about the allegorical nature of Chinese literature, but rather its emphasis on the ways self and society can intersect and overlap, in contrast to most Western literatures, in which the exploration of the self and that of society are separated. But what Jameson has yet to probe is the connection between allegorical writings in China and those in the West. Clearly, allegory is not absent in contemporary Western literature. In fact, allegory has been practiced and discussed in a variety of contexts, from the hermeneutic tradition of theological studies to the heavy use of symbols and mythologies in romanticism, culminating in today's poststructuralist discourse in which no meaning can be taken for granted. In this literary and critical history, we find an increasing association of allegory with the internalization of language: the distance between the original word and the associated interpretations suggested in allegory only testifies to the system of language as a flow of empty signifiers that constantly defers meaning. This linguistic approach to allegory is elaborately discussed in Paul de Man's and Walter Benjamin's criticisms, in which the allegorical discourse is always displacing and disorienting, and therefore is always negative in itself.[40] As de Man puts it, "Whereas the symbol postulates the possibility of an identity or identification, allegory designates primarily a distance in relation to its own origin, and renouncing the nostalgia and the desire to coincide, it establishes its language in the void of this temporary difference."[41]

Juxtaposing the postcolonial and the poststructuralist discourses of allegory, we could interpret Jameson's celebration of allegorical writing in Third-World literatures as corrective to a deconstructive approach, so that allegory is no longer only meaningful to the challenge of the foundation of metaphysics but can become politically productive and socially engaging again. Jameson proposes that "Third-world texts, even those which are seemingly private and invested with a properly libidinal dynamic— necessarily project a political dimension in the form of national allegory: *the story of the private individual destiny is always an allegory of the embattled situation of the public third-world culture and society*."[42] Thus, allegory does not point back to oneself or the insecurity of the linguistic universe, it asks how the individual person is related to the collective, and vice versa. Examined from the opposite direction, the poststructuralist understanding of allegory also holds back Jameson's optimism of the allegorical power of third-world novels, as the allegorical message can never be securely grasped. It is laden with diverse meanings and yet wishes to be known, but any interpretations remains incomplete and unsettled, as the original text is always in danger of being radically rewritten beyond any control. As de Man reminds us, there is an implicit link between allegory and irony, as both are conscious in demonstrating the impossibility of presenting facts and our being in general.[43]

As demonstrated above, Tian Han's Great Leap Forward works were caught in the complicated cobweb of writings and interpretations, and they can be understood according to both ideas of allegory: they demonstrate the postcolonial connection between self and society as well as poststructuralism's perpetual sliding of meaning. From his formative years on, Tian Han himself always believed that his dramas were political, in the sense that there are always clear political messages to be told and to be received.[44] But this naivety could no longer be sustained in such a schizophrenic era, ridden with political idealism and despotic authoritarianism. Political writing in a hyperpolitical environment easily becomes excessively allegorical, cocooned within self-protective and self-expressive layers. This kind of writing is inevitably perilous and uncontrollable, as any meaning remains unstable and prone to being further appropriated. It is the negotiations and conflicts between society and individual, between meanings and *différance*, embodied in these dramas that make them so rich as allegorical texts. Although we will never know what exactly was in Tian Han's mind when he was writing these texts, we are sure that the texts are not transparent, and this opacity is the site where the author and the readers or critics invest their political messages, ethical struggles, and negotiated imaginations. Instead of struggling with the true "meanings" of Tian Han's texts, we might instead value the dense historicity of these texts, which is never settled and yet is always making connections.

NOTES

1. The full name of the notification is "Chinese Communist Party Central Committee Notification," which was issued on May 16, 1966.

2. Yun Song 雲松, "Tian Han de *Xie Yaohuan* shi yike daducao" 田漢的〈謝瑤環〉是一顆大毒草 [Tian Han's *Xie Yaohuan* is a big poisonous weed], *Juben* 劇本 [Script] (January 1966).

3. Erika Langmuir, *Allegory* (London: National Gallery; distributed by Yale University Press, 2010), 7.

4. For an interesting study of the use of metaphors in early Chinese poetry in terms of Chinese cosmology, see Martin Svensson Ekstroem, "Illusion, Lie, and Metaphor: The Paradox of Divergence in Early Chinese Poetics," *Poetics Today* 23.2 (Summer 2002): 251–289.

5. See Rebecca Karl, *Staging the World: Chinese Nationalism at the Turn of the Twentieth Century* (Durham: Duke University Press, 2002), 27–49; Hsiao-ti Li, "Making a Name and a Culture for the Masses in Modern China," *positions: east asia cultures critique* 9.1 (Spring 2001): 29–68.

6. Xiaomei Chen, "Introduction," in *Columbia Anthology of Modern Chinese Drama*, ed. Xiaomei Chen (New York: Columbia University Press, 2010), 3–4.

7. See Chang-tai Hung, *War and Popular Culture: Resistance in Modern China, 1937–1945* (Berkeley: University of California Press, 1994).

8. For a recent and thorough study of the politicization of the operatic arts during the seventeen-year period, see Zhang Lianhong 張煉紅, *Lilian jinghun: Xin Zhongguo xiqu gaizao kaolun* 歷練精魂：新中國戲曲改造考論 [Becoming spirits: A study of the xiqu reform in new China] (Shanghai: Shanghai renmin chubanshe, 2013).

9. On the model dramas of the Cultural Revolution, see Xiaomei Chen, *Acting the Right Part: Political Theatre and Popular Drama in Contemporary China* (Honolulu: University of Hawai'i Press, 2002), 17–158.

10. See Laikwan Pang, "Authorship versus Ownership: The Case of Socialist China," in *Media Authorship*, ed. Cynthia Chris and David A. Gerstner (New York: Routledge, 2012), 72–86.

11. While the "Hundred Flowers" slogan had been mentioned from time to time by Mao and other CCP leaders since the 1930s, the most important document promulgating this policy is the speech "Guanyu zhengque chuli renmin neibu maodun" 關於正確處理人民內部矛盾的問題 [On the correct handling of contradictions among the people], given by Mao in February 1957.

12. Tian Han, "Bixu qieshi guanxin gaishan yiren de shenghuo" 必須切實關心并改善藝人的生活 [We need to attend to artists and improve their livelihood], *Xijubao* 戲劇報 [Drama news] 7 (1956): 6–8; Tian Han, "Wei yanyuan de qingchun qingming" 為演員的青春請命 [Pleading on behalf of performers' youth], *Xijubao* 戲劇報 [Drama news] 11 (1956): 7.

13. Zhang Ying, an editor of *Drama News*, provides a comprehensive account of the unfolding of the Anti-Rightist Campaign within the Association of Dramatists. See Zhang Ying 張穎, *Wentan fengyun qinliji* 文壇風雲親歷記 [My personal experiences in turbulent literary circles] (Beijing: Sanlian, 2012), 107–113.

14. See Roderick MacFarquhar, Timothy Cheek, and Eugene Wu, ed., *The Secret Speeches of Chairman Mao, from the Hundred Flowers to the Great Leap Forward* (Cambridge: Harvard University Asia Center, 1989).

15. See Kimberley Ens Manning and Felix Wemheuer, ed., *Eating Bitterness: New Perspectives on China's Great Leap Forward and Famine* (Vancouver: University of British Columbia Press, 2011).

16. Li Hui 李輝, *Tian Han: Kuangbiao zhong luoye fanfei* 田漢：狂飆中落葉翻飛 [Tian Han: Falling leaves in the wild wind] (Zhengzhou: Daxiang chubanshe, 2002), 54.

17. Ge Yihong 葛一虹, *Zhongguo huaju tongshi* 中國話劇通史 [A general history of Chinese spoken dramas] (Beijing: Wenhua yishu chubanshe, 1990), 389.

18. Dong Jian 董健, *Tian Han zhuan* 田漢傳 [A biography of Tian Han] (Beijing: Shiyue wenyi chubanshe, 1996), 788–789.

19. Chen Mingyuan disagrees with Dong Jian and believes that Tian Han never betrayed Wu Zuguang, as most have assumed. Zhang Ying also asserts that Tian Han was by then already sidelined and had no authority for deciding who was a rightist. See Chen Mingyuan 陳明遠, *Wang nian jiao: Wo yu Guo Moruo, Tian Han de jiaowang* 忘年交：我與郭沫若、田漢的交往 [Friendships between generations: My contact with Guo Moruo and Tian Han] (Shanghai: Xuelin chubanshe, 1999), 234–237; Zhang Ying, *Wentan fengyun qinliji*, 110–113.

20. Tian Han, *Tian Han quanji* 田漢全集 [Complete works of Tian Han], vol. 16, (Shijiazhuang: Huashan wenyi chubanshe, 2000), 414–415.

21. Pledging complete loyalty to the regime, Tian Han finished *Guan Hanqing* in one month, and he wrote *Shisanling Reservoir Fantasia* in ten days.

22. For more about this World Peace Council and the background of *Guan Hanqing*, see Rudolf G. Wagner, *The Contemporary Chinese Historical Drama: Four Studies* (Berkeley: University of California Press, 1990), 8–13.

23. Li Zhiyan 黎之彥, *Tian Han chuangzuo zeji* 田漢創作側記 [A side-look at Tian Han's creative process] (Chengdu: Sichuan wenyi chubanshe, 1994), 70.

24. See Chinese Culture Research Institute, *Guan Hanqing yu Yuan zaju*, retrieved June 18, 2014, from http://hk.chiculture.net/0414/html/0414b11/0414b11.html.

25. Wagner, *The Contemporary Chinese Historical Drama*, 44–45.

26. Li Zhiyan, *Tian Han chuangzuo zeji*, 74.

27. Wagner, *The Contemporary Chinese Historical Drama*, 29–71.

28. Li Zhiyan, *Tian Han chuangzuo zeji*, 77.

29. Tian Han, "Ticai de chuli" 題材的處理 [Handling different subject matters], in Tian Han, *Tian Han lun chuangzuo* 田漢論創作 [Tian Han on creative writing] (Shanghai: Shanghai wenyi chubanshe, 1983), 503–507; originally published in *Wenyi bao* 文藝報 [News of literature and arts] 7 (1961).

30. During the Cultural Revolution, Tian Han was mostly criticized for the 1961 script *Xie Yaohuan*, which was considered a historical allegory condemning the Anti-Rightist campaign. He died in prison in 1968.

31. Wu Han, "Hou gu bo jin he gu wei jin yong" 厚古薄今和古為今用 [Privileging the present over the past and using the past for the present], in *Wu Han Shixue lunzhu xuanji* 吳晗史學選集 [Wu Han's collected historical studies], vol. 3 (Beijing: Beijing Renmin chubanshe, 1988), 44–49; originally published in *Wenshi jiaoxue* 文史教學 [Teaching literature and history] 1 (1959).

32. Tian Han, *Tian Han Zishu* 田漢自述 [Tian Han's autobiography] (Zhengzhou: Daxiang chubanshe, 2002), 206–207. See also *Tian Han quanji*, vol. 16, 415.

33. Li 黎, "Tian Han tongzhi de huaju *Guan Hanqing* zai Riben de wutai" 田漢同志的話劇《關漢卿》在日本的舞臺 [Comrade Tian Han's drama *Guan Hanqing* on the Japanese stage], *Juben* 劇本 [Script] 7 (1959): 102.

34. Tian Han, "Zhi Chen Mingyuan de yifeng xin" 致陳明遠的一封信 [A letter to Chen Mingyuan], in Chen Mingyuan, *Wang nian jiao*, 13.
35. Tian Han, *Tian Han zishu*, 202.
36. Lu Wei 陸煒, "Tian Han de Wencheng gongzhu yu lishi ticai kaijue wenti" 田漢的文成公主與歷史題材開掘問題 [Tian Han's *Princess Wencheng* and questions related to the exploration of historical subjects], in Chen Baichen 陳白塵 et al., ed., *Zhongguo huaju yanjiu* 中國話劇研究 [Research of Chinese spoken dramas], no. 6 (Beijing: Wenhua yishu chubanshe, 1993), 107–120.
37. Barbara Barnouin and Yu Changgen, *Zhou Enlai: A Political Life* (Hong Kong: Chinese University Press, 2006), 186–187. The exact death toll caused by the event remained controversial.
38. See Ban Wang, "Third World Internationalism and Chinese Cinema in the Chinese Cultural Revolution," in *Listening to China's Cultural Revolution: Translations between Music and Politics*, ed. Paul Clark, Laikwan Pang, and Tsan-huang Tsai (New York: Palgrave MacMillan, forthcoming).
39. Fredric Jameson, "Third-World Literature in the Era of Multinational Capitalism," *Social Text* 15 (Autumn 1986): 65–88.
40. See, for example, Walter Benjamin, *The Origin of German Tragic Drama*, trans. John Osborne (London: Verso, 1998); Paul de Man, "The Rhetoric of Temporality," in *Blindness and Insight: Essays in the Rhetoric of Contemporary Criticism* (Minneapolis: University of Minnesota Press, 1983), 187–228. For a comparison between the two theorists in their understandings of allegory, see Andrea Mirabile, "Allegory, Pathos, and Irony: The Resistance to Benjamin in Paul de Man," *German Studies Review* 25.2 (May 2012): 319–333.
41. De Man, *Blindness and Insight*, 206.
42. Jameson, "Third-World Literature in the Era of Multinational Capitalism," 69.
43. De Man, *Blindness and Insight*, 208–211. This understanding of allegory as opposed to a direct resemblance between the word, the object, and the idea is not only a Western concept, but the component of illusion is also always important in traditional Chinese poetic. See Ekstroem, "Illusion, Lie, and Metaphor."
44. Tian Han, *Tian Han zishu*, 176.

WORKS CITED

Barnouin, Barbara, and Yu Changgen. *Zhou Enlai: A Political Life*. Hong Kong: Chinese University Press, 2006.

Benjamin, Walter. *The Origin of German Tragic Drama*. Trans. John Osborne. London: Verso, 1998.

Chen Mingyuan 陳明遠. *Wang nian jiao: Wo yu Guo Moruo, Tian Han de jiaowang* 忘年交：我與郭沫若、田漢的交往 [Friendships between generations: My contact with Guo Moruo and Tian Han]. Shanghai: Xuelin chubanshe, 1999.

Chen, Xiaomei. *Acting the Right Part: Political Theatre and Popular Drama in Contemporary China*. Honolulu: University of Hawai'i Press, 2002.

Chen, Xiaomei. "Introduction." *Columbia Anthology of Modern Chinese Drama*. Ed. Xiaomei Chen. New York: Columbia University Press, 2010. 1–56.

Chinese Culture Research Institute. "Guan Hanqing yu Yuan zaju" 關漢卿與元雜劇 [Guan Hanqing and the zaju in the Yuan dynasty]. Retrieved June 18, 2014, from http://hk.chiculture.net/0414/html/0414b11/0414b11.html.

De Man, Paul. "The Rhetoric of Temporality." In *Blindness and Insight: Essays in the Rhetoric of Contemporary Criticism*. Minneapolis: University of Minnesota Press, 1983. 187–228.

Dong Jian 董健. *Tian Han zhuan* 田漢傳 [Biography of Tian Han]. Beijing: Shiyue wenyi chubanshe, 1996.

Ekstroem, Martin Svensson. "Illusion, Lie, and Metaphor: The Paradox of Divergence in Early Chinese Poetics." *Poetics Today* 23.2 (Summer 2002): 251–289.

Ge Yihong 葛一虹. *Zhongguo huaju tongshi* 中國話劇通史 [A general history of Chinese spoken drama]. Beijing: Wenhua yishu chubanshe, 1990.

Hung, Chang-tai. *War and Popular Culture: Resistance in Modern China, 1937–1945*. Berkeley: University of California Press, 1994.

Jameson, Fredric. "Third-World Literature in the Era of Multinational Capitalism." *Social Text* 15 (Autumn 1986): 65–88.

Karl, Rebecca. *Staging the World: Chinese Nationalism at the Turn of the Twentieth Century*. Durham: Duke University Press, 2002.

Langmuir, Erika. *Allegory*. London: National Gallery; distributed by Yale University Press, 2010.

Li 黎. "Tian Han tongzhi de huaju *Guan Hanqing* zai Riben de wutai" 田漢同志的話劇《關漢卿》在日本的舞臺 [Comrade Tian Han's spoken drama *Guan Hanqing* on the Japanese stage]. *Juben* 劇本 [Script] 7 (1959): 102.

Li, Hsiao-ti. "Making a Name and a Culture for the Masses in Modern China." *positions: east asia cultures critique* 9.1 (Spring 2001): 29–68.

Li Hui 李輝. *Tian Han: Kuangbiao zhong luoye fanfei* 田漢：狂飆中落葉翻飛 [Tian Han: Falling leaves in the wild wind]. Zhengzhou: Daxiang chubanshe, 2002.

Li Zhiyan 黎之彥. *Tian Han chuangzuo zeji* 田漢創作側記 [A side-look at Tian Han's creative process]. Chengdu: Sichuan wenyi chubanshe, 1994.

Lu Wei 陸煒. "Tian Han de Wencheng gongzhu yu lishi ticai kaijue wenti" 田漢的文成公主與歷史題材開掘問題 [Tian Han's *Princess Wencheng* and questions related to the exploration of historical subjects]. In *Zhongguo huaju yanjiu* 中國活劇研究 [Research of Chinese spoken dramas], vol. 6. Ed. Chen Baichen 陳白塵 et al. Beijing: Wenhua yishu chubanshe, 1993. 107–120.

MacFarquhar, Roderick, Timothy Cheek, and Eugene Wu, ed. *The Secret Speeches of Chairman Mao, from the Hundred Flowers to the Great Leap Forward*. Cambridge: Harvard University Asia Center, 1989.

Manning, Kimberley Ens, and Felix Wemheuer, ed. *Eating Bitterness: New Perspectives on China's Great Leap Forward and Famine*. Vancouver: University of British Columbia Press, 2011.

Mirabile, Andrea. "Allegory, Pathos, and Irony: The Resistance to Benjamin in Paul de Man." *German Studies Review* 25.2 (May 2012): 319–333.

Pang, Laikwan. "Authorship versus Ownership: The Case of Socialist China." In *Media Authorship*. Ed. Cynthia Chris and David A. Gerstner. New York: Routledge, 2012. 72–86.

Tian Han 田漢. "Bixu qieshi guanxin gaishan yiren de shenghuo" 必須切實關心并改善藝人的生活 [We need to attend to artists and improve their livelihood]. *Xijubao* 戲劇報 [Drama news] 7 (1956): 6–8.

Tian Han 田漢. *Tian Han quanji* 田漢全集 [Complete works of Tian Han]. Shijiazhuang: Huashan wenyi chubanshe, 2000.

Tian Han 田漢. *Tian Han zishu* 田漢自述 [Tian Han's autobiography]. Zhengzhou: Daxiang chubanshe, 2002.

Tian Han 田漢. "Ticai de chuli" 題材的處理 [Handling different subject matter]. In *Tian Han lun chuangzuo* 田漢論創作 [Tian Han on creative writing] (Shanghai: Shanghai wenyi chubanshe, 1983), 503–507; originally published in *Wenyi bao* 文藝報 [News of literature and arts] 7 (1961).

Tian Han 田漢. "Wei yanyuan de qingchun qingming" 為演員的青春請命 [Pleading on behalf of performers' youth]. *Xijubao* 戲劇報 [Drama news] 11 (1956): 7.

Tian Han 田漢. "Zhi Chen Mingyuan de yifeng xin" 致陳明遠的一封信 [A letter to Chen Mingyuan]. Chen Mingyuan, *Wang nian jiao*. 13.

Wagner, Rudolf G. *The Contemporary Chinese Historical Drama: Four Studies*. Berkeley: University of California Press, 1990.

Wang, Ban. "Third World Internationalism and Chinese Cinema in the Chinese Cultural Revolution." In *Listening to China's Cultural Revolution: Translations between Music and Politics*. Ed. Paul Clark, Laikwan Pang, and Tsan-huang Tsai. New York: Palgrave MacMillan, forthcoming.

Wu Han 吳晗. "Hou gu bo jin he gu wei jin yong," 厚古薄今和古為今用 [Privileging the present over the past and using the past for the present]. In *Wu Han shixue lunzhu xuanji* 吳晗史學選集 [Wu Han's collected historical studies] vol. 3. Beijing: Beijing Renmin chubanshe, 1988, 44–49; originally published in *Wenshi jiaoxue* 文史教學 [Teaching literature and history] 1 (1959).

Yun Song 雲松. "Tian Han de *Xie Yaohuan* shi yike daducao" 田漢的〈謝瑤環〉是一顆大毒草 [Tian Han's *Xie Yaohuan* is a big poisonous weed]. *Juben* 劇本 [Script] (January 1966).

Zhang Lianhong 張煉紅. *Lilian jinghun: Xin Zhongguo xiqu gaizao kaolun* 歷練精魂：新中國戲曲改造考論 [Becoming spirits: A study of xiqu reform in new China]. Shanghai: Shanghai renmin chubanshe, 2013.

Zhang Ying 張穎. *Wentan fengyun qinliji* 文壇風雲親歷記 [My personal experiences in turbulent literary circles]. Beijing: Sanlian, 2012.

CHAPTER 1.13

AN EXAMINATION OF CHINA'S CENSORSHIP SYSTEM

YAN LIANKE

IN a remarkable occurrence that up to this point has generally remained overlooked, in each of the four years from 2009 to 2013 a Chinese novel that had previously been banned was suddenly reprinted. In chronological order based on their date of original publication, these works included Jia Pingwa's 賈平凹 *Ruined City* (廢都; banned 1993, reprinted 2009), Mo Yan's 莫言 *Big Breasts and Wide Hips* (豐乳肥臀; banned 1997, reprinted 2012), the Henan author Li Peifu's 李佩甫 *The Gate for Sheep* (羊的門; banned 1998, reprinted 2012), and the Hunan author Wang Yaowen's 王耀文 *Chinese Painting* (國畫; banned 2000, reprinted 2010). The publication of these previously banned books should have attracted considerable attention, but instead it went virtually unnoticed. Why is this? In part, it is because the Chinese authorities do not want to bring undue attention to this practice of "unbanning," and in part it is because this phenomenon was presented as being more an issue of trust between authors and their publishers, as opposed to representing a major shift in literary and cultural policy. In fact, however, China's earlier hard censorship regime is being gradually transformed into one grounded on what may be called soft censorship.

The transition from hard censorship to soft censorship is the most significant and distinctive change in contemporary China's censorship regime, and while hard censorship uses a direct and forceful approach to control speech, publication, and other forms of artistic production, soft censorship instead relies on more tolerant methods. With respect to literature, the shift from hard censorship to soft censorship can produce a feeling of finally being released into the light after having long been buried in darkness.

Soft Censorship within a Regime
of Hard Censorship

Hard censorship is a means by which the state exerts control over literary production, and the procedure's ideological underpinnings are unrelated to the legal system. Although the legal system may have clear provisions for freedom of speech and freedom of the press, these are often mere fictions for public consumption. Under an authoritarian regime, all ideology operates in the service of the regime, as the invisible hand of power. Ideology operates above the law, but nevertheless remains subordinate to a dictatorial or autocratic power; it speaks for authority while defying the legal process. In the face of ideology, the law is nothing more than an overcoat that may be worn when it is needed and removed when it is not. Ideology is not held accountable to the law; it bows only to power. In order for power to achieve its goal of reforming history and reality, ideology must subject the press, the publishing industry, and various kinds of artistic production to a strict censorship policy, and consequently its efforts end up being directed toward the distortion of history and the suppression of reality—which is the ultimate objective of virtually all authoritarian systems.

Literature and art occupy a crucial position in this censorship process. Given that the press and public speech have a clear and direct relationship with social reality, it is easier for hard censorship to achieve its objectives. When art enters the domain of history and memory, however, it comes to have a more allusive and murky significance. Art uses stories, characters, symbols, allegories, allusions, and associations to create memory, and therefore is not nearly as direct as press coverage. After this sort of indirect and indeterminate memory enters people's consciousness, its effect can be far deeper and more powerful than that created by nonfictional works. For example, the treatment of the White Terror during the Russian Revolution in Boris Pasternak's *Doctor Zhivago*, of the Prague Spring in Milan Kundera's *The Unbearable Lightness of Being*, and of authoritarianism in George Orwell's *Animal Farm* and *1984* all helped strengthen the memory of events that autocratic power had attempted to cast into oblivion.

Art's greatness lies in part in its ability to facilitate the power of memory, and therefore many authoritarian regimes have been particularly strict in implementing a system of hard censorship. For instance, when an article is subjected to a spurious reading, its author could end up being executed (as was the case with Wang Shiwei 王實味, the author of "Wild Lilies" [野百合花]), and when a novel is found to have a bourgeois plot line, its author could be sentenced to exile and labor reform (as was the case with Wang Meng 王蒙, the author of *A Young Newcomer in the Organization Department* [組織部來了個年輕人]). This level of terror reveals the darkness at the heart of the autocratic regime.

In contemporary China, however, literary censorship is not nearly as rigid as press censorship, where all content that is perceived as potentially harmful is strictly prohibited. While these rules are clear as applied to the press, in the domain of literature the regime has instead followed a process of "reform and opening up" whereby it has begun to permit the publication of some works that are at best neutral with respect to power, the nation, and the ruling party. Because ideology wants to show the world its tolerant and enlightened approach and demonstrate the liberated and advanced attitudes of its ruling party, it has taken the opportunity to relieve the condition of oppression and darkness into which the censorship apparatus had previously brought writers and intellectuals. As a result, in contemporary China the state's censorship of literary production has been gradually transformed from an approach grounded in violence to one focusing on intent and sentiment.

Soft censorship is deliberately flexible and vague, in contrast to the sort of approach that was deployed in China during the Cultural Revolution and in the former Soviet Union, not to mention the violent approach found in contemporary North Korea. State institutions such as the Central Propaganda Department and the General Administration of Press and Publication set the parameters for the ideologically driven model of web censorship with which we are now familiar. The regime only issues directives and produces documents as general guidelines, and in addition to specifying which historical incidents may be discussed (such as the Cultural Revolution) and which may not (such as June Fourth), it also issues directives and regulations focusing on intent and sentiment. For instance, while it may have been possible to publish a certain type of anti-corruption novel, if you tried to write about Party officials you would encounter more regulations and restrictions. The highest cadres you could mention in these sorts of works are ones at the subprovincial level, and ideally the critique should be of a deputy governor rather than a deputy party secretary; furthermore, the work should emphasize that justice necessarily prevails. In any event, authors are not currently permitted to publish any anti-corruption novels at all, because even if they emphasize that justice inevitably prevails, these novels nevertheless give readers the impression that there exists widespread political corruption.

There are also "major melody" and "positivity" regulations, both of which operate at the level of intent and sentiment; these may also be seen as the product of a form of soft censorship relying on flexibility and ambiguity. After three decades of Reform and Opening Up, the Chinese state has managed to develop a set of more effective censorship methods that have far-reaching effects on its citizens, readers, and authors.

THE CONTRADICTIONS AND PARADOXES INVOLVED IN IMPLEMENTING A SOFT CENSORSHIP REGIME

Contemporary censorship practices are implemented through a set of top-down processes; they constitute an extension of an earlier system of hard censorship while also marking the beginning of a contemporary soft censorship approach. High-level departments closely tied to the ideological regime, such as central publication offices and propaganda departments, are the agents charged with establishing cultural policies. No matter how good or bad these policies might be, they all require these sorts of agents in order to be implemented—just as laws rely on the courts. These agents function as literature's judiciary and legal system, but with the difference that although China's legal system may be flexible, its legal code is quite strictly enforced—and if you want to use legal means to address a certain crime, you can generally find a way to do so. With respect to literary censorship, however, in the end it is not a question of matching a crime with a specific law, and there are no defense counsels to defend the accused or procuratorates to oversee the courts. Instead, the system proceeds based on individual agents' understanding of the relevant regulations.

These literary and cultural policies specifically prohibit the direct mention of certain post-1949 incidents such as the Anti-Rightist Movement, the Great Leap Forward, the Steel-Smelting Campaign, the Great Famine, and the Cultural Revolution—each of which brought China and its people tremendous hardship in the name of revolution. Because of a sense of artistic necessity and a sense of collective conscience, many authors have discussed and reimagined these events—but since their works are regarded as fictional artistic creations, many of them have succeeded in getting published. Examples include Li Rui's 李銳 *Trees Without Wind* (無風之樹), Wang Anyi's 王安憶 *Age of Enlightenment* (啟蒙時代), Jia Pingwa's *Ancient Furnace* (古爐), Yu Hua's 余華 *Brothers* (兄弟), Mo Yan's *Life and Death are Wearing Me Out* (生死疲勞), and my own novel *Hard Like Water* (堅硬如水)—all of which would have been unthinkable under a system of hard censorship but have nevertheless managed to get published under the current system, and furthermore have been widely praised. This is what we mean by the "softness" of the current censorship system. At the same time, there have also been many other works that were subsequently banned following publication, such as Zhang Yihe's 章詒和 *The Past is not like Smoke* (往事并不如烟), Chun Tao's 春 桃 *Chinese Peasant Investigation Report* (中國農民調查報告), Yang Jisheng's 楊繼繩 *Tombstone* (墓碑), as well as my own *Dream of Ding Village* (丁庄夢) and *The Four Books* (四書). This is what we mean by the "hardness" of the censorship system.

The ultimate standard for implementing a censorship regime is, of course, a set of policies specifying what may and may not be written. In practice, however, the censors are often permitted a considerable degree of flexibility in their implementation of these policies—whether in order to retain their official hat or their loyalty to the Party, or because they succumb to their emotions and their thirst for power. The flexible censorship system will invariably become more extensive and stricter—taking the expansiveness of Chinese-style social movements and revolutions, and applying them to a censorship system that becomes increasingly strict and exhaustive. For instance, the primary reason why novels like Wei Hui's 衛慧 *Shanghai Baby* (上海寶貝) and Mian Mian's 棉棉 *Candy* (糖) were banned was actually not on account of their content or their unorthodox style, but rather because of the censors' power and emotions. In particular, it is said that in writing these novels, these two authors got into a dispute over whether they had written about each other's experiences, and in the process they somehow managed to anger some censorship officials, who proceeded to ban the novels and halt the printing process. The publishers and editors, meanwhile, all kept their silence.

In implementing a set of censorship regulations, there is always the possibility of an abuse of power—which makes publishers cautious and encourages them to expand their own inspections. Abuse of power and expanded self-inspection are two key characteristics of the contemporary censorship regime. The former can be found throughout contemporary China, including presses and publishing houses. Previously, presses and publishing houses were some of the most active agents in the publishing industry, but due to abuses of power and stringent censorship requirements, many issues ranging from concerns with content to the use of specific words and phrases have increasingly come under the purview of the censors, and consequently many press directors and editors have been interrogated, suspended, or dismissed as a result of what they published. The agents charged with implementing censorship practices often single out a few authors in order to set an example for others, and as a result the entire industry has been transformed into one in which everyone is watching over everyone else. When a manuscript arrives, the first thing the press considers is not the work's literary value or its marketability, but rather whether or not it is politically sensitive. If the work's author has already attracted the attention of the authorities, the work will be judged more strictly. As a result, editors must serve not only as arbiters of a work's artistry and marketability, they must also serve as the first line of censors. As for works that are deemed to be particularly meritorious on artistic grounds but are perceived as carrying a certain degree of political risk, they are submitted to an even higher office to determine whether or not they are publishable. In this way, a work's slow journey through the censorship apparatus begins. Given the inherent ambiguity and indeterminacy of a work's artistic value and political sensitivity, the objective of the process is either to eliminate potential risk or to prevent it from developing further. The result is a pyramidal structure, with the censors at the center and the editors at the top.

It is not merely authors who are requesting greater freedom and looser oversight; there are also some conscientious publishers who feel the same way. This is especially true of those who must play the role of censors while also working on behalf of the press. These editors struggle with competing demands, and although they may have no choice but to apply this hard censorship policy in order to avoid creating even bigger problems for themselves, they nevertheless thirst for a more flexible and open policy that would permit them to seek out publishing possibilities in order to stimulate the publishing market while reassuring intellectuals that they can express themselves freely. In this way, they hope to promote a softening of the censorship apparatus, together with the possibility of freedom of the press and freedom of speech.

THE MEANS AND METHODS OF A SOFT CENSORSHIP APPARATUS

As China develops, it will inevitably continue to shift from a hard censorship system to a softer one, and while the ultimate objectives of these two approaches may be similar in that they both use concealment and deception to encourage amnesia and the creation of false memories, a soft system nevertheless employs more flexible methods that are more easily accepted. Precisely because the latter methods are more easily accepted, however, they are also more concealed, and may include tactics such as theoretical inducements, incentives, amnesty, education, self-censorship, and silence.

For instance, the nation's propaganda, cultural, and publishing departments continually use conferences and political directives to request that the press and cultural production organs follow the "main melody" and "positivity" directives. By bringing together large numbers of theorists to assess the significance of these directives for the future development of China and the Chinese people, the regime grants "main melody" and "positivity" an almost divine significance that is located at a moral pinnacle and at the heart of a seemingly infallible cultural and literary apparatus. These theorists seek to convince the nation that these sorts of works are the only ones that may be considered truly great, and that authors who write these sorts of works will serve as the backbone of the nation. From this, a new literary standard emerges, which in turn helps cultivate a new aesthetic sensibility. In this way, the regime is able to convince readers, authors, and theorists that if literature departs from this new standard, it will not be considered great; and even if it is not necessarily considered a bad work, it will still be quickly forgotten.

When literary works are classified based on whether they have positive or negative energy, this in turn provides a strict standard for assessing a work's worth. By conforming to this standard, a work may be recognized for its aesthetic value and receive a variety of literary prizes and public praise. For instance, there is the Five-One Project Prize, promoted by some propaganda departments, which recognizes novels, films, television programs, documentaries, and dramas that are not only "great, big, and high" but also "orthodox, red, and bright." Meanwhile, the most prestigious literary prizes awarded by the Chinese Writers' Association—namely, the Mao Dun Literary Prize and the Lu Xun Literary Prize—primarily recognize works whose aesthetic value is easily visible but which are also "positive" in their thought and content. Whenever one of these literary prizes is proposed, it must first be submitted to the propaganda office so that its standards for selection and evaluation may be reviewed and approved. As a result, these prizes are effectively stripped of their populist potential and are left only with their ideological significance with respect to the Party, the government, and a notion of "positive energy."

Apart from their role in promoting a process of assessment and censorship, these literary prizes may also include a large monetary award. For instance, the Mao Dun

Literary Prize awards the winner fifty thousand RMB and the Five-One Project Prize offers a hundred thousand. Afterwards, the winner may be invited to meet with a political leader and receive a commendation, and the local government may then reward him or her with free housing and job promotions (the army once had a policy whereby all army authors and artists who won this sort of major prize would automatically receive a promotion). Such prizes are therefore very appealing, but in order to win, an author must write works that accord with the government's ideological demands. Naturally, this has the effect of taking the objectives of the earlier hard censorship regime and reimplementing them using a new set of softer approaches.

One hallmark of a civilized, advanced, and modern society is its love and respect for its independent-minded authors. Any such nation must treasure its most creative authors and artists, but in China this sort of treatment becomes a means of domestication. For instance, most of the country's most prominent authors and artists currently serve as the directors or deputy directors of their writers' association or literary federation, and many of them also serve as representatives to the National People's Congress and the People's Political Consultative Conference. This is an extremely bizarre phenomenon whereby many authors, after they become famous by virtue of their writing, go on to become officials in writers' associations and literary federations that are nominally popular organizations but in practice function as arms of the state. After assuming this sort of official position, authors come to enjoy even greater recognition, prestige, and power, but their writings must accord with the Party's expectations, and as a result their independence will necessarily be curtailed. Meanwhile, the censorship regime—as it shifts its emphasis from formal support to a strategy of tacit domestication—achieves its objective of shifting the literary direction of these authors, and even if they do not write the sorts of so-called positive main melody works the regime desires, at the very least they won't write so-called negative works focusing on people's misfortune and the dark side of the country's history.

Of course, what an author writes is ultimately dependent on his or her personal interests, but in today's economy-driven society the market and readers play an increasingly important role. Every work must have a readership, just as every readership must have its own corresponding authors and literary works. In this way, readers may also come to function as a work's indirect censors, which in turn becomes one of the most effective methods of contemporary China's soft censorship system.

Most contemporary Chinese readers came of age after 1949, and consequently have a deep-rooted affection for socialist realism. Textbooks, newspapers, and literary works all function as forms of praise and eulogy, and when people are exposed to this sort of unitary doctrinal reading practice throughout their life, as readers they are likely to become hegemonic censors. Meanwhile, readers who grew up during the Reform Era in the 1980s and 1990s were exposed to a much wider range of imported reading material, though this reading material still had to go through the Chinese press and the censorship system. As a result, these new readers do not have the same revolutionary spirit as their elders, but neither do they have a truly critical attitude. Therefore, their sense of materialism has come to replace queries and goals. They have been educated by books, but have also been indirectly educated by ideology. More specifically, they have been educated by a process of reading and observation that is itself subject to censorship and control. The authors whom they idolize (including new-era authors such as Guo Jingming 郭敬明 and Zhang Jiajia 張佳家) all have a petit bourgeois quality. These readers are also contemporary China's most subjective readers, and by achieving control over them, the system thereby completes the process of acceptance and rejection that these subjective readers play with respect to some authors' writings. In an important respect, this helps realize an indirect but far-reaching objective of the soft censorship system—which is that when authors write for the sake of a group of readers, they ultimately come to accept the values held by those same readers. For instance, given that many contemporary readers are fond of hyper-nationalistic films, television programs, and novels, authors—if they wish to accommodate these interests in their writings—must necessarily accept the soft censorship role played by the readers.

A hard censorship system initially relies on legal regulations for its implementation, but over time it cultivates a system of self-censorship by fostering an environment of anxiety and terror. To the extent that an external censorship system is grounded on power and repression, an author's practice of self-censorship is driven by intuition, ignorance, and instinct. Self-censorship is in no way less destructive than the prohibitions implemented under hard censorship—because, like an unborn fetus under the One-Child Policy, a self-censored work effectively disappears from the world before it has even emerged.

Under a hard censorship regime, self-censorship arises out of an environment of terror, anxiety, and fear, and while it is predicated on unwillingness and resistance, it eventually generates a kind of intuitive response. Because it develops in reaction to outside pressure, it may eventually generate a sense of awakening or enlightenment following a change in the external conditions, thereby permitting writing to return to its original conditions. However, under a system of soft censorship, this sort of self-monitoring develops in response to the seduction of power, fame, and influence rather than being a product of fear and desperation. Its reflexive character, accordingly, is formed in response not only to the censorship system that has been in place for the past several decades, but more importantly to the author's own self-denigrating character. The self-censorship that develops under a regime of hard censorship has a fundamentally oppressive character, but as China's censorship system has begun to transition in recent years from a hard approach to a soft one, the practice of self-censorship has gradually become more voluntary and intuitive. In contrast to the self-monitoring that develops under a regime of hard censorship, the current system is no longer a product of a habitual process of self-observation, but rather is a result of the authors' own slave-like mentality. For the censors and the censorship system, the ultimate goal is for authors to voluntarily censor themselves, while for the authors and their works, this sort of voluntary self-censorship has a fundamentally hypocritical and self-deluded quality.

A good example of this sort of self-censorship is when Chinese authors write works that deliberately toe the line (these are known as "line ball" works, like a ping-pong ball that hits the line but is still considered in play). The greater artistic tragedy, however, lies in how this sort of self-censorship generates a new shared aesthetic that affects everyone—from authors to readers, and from government officials to censors—namely, that a harmless line ball work is the highest state of art. Actually, this kind of aesthetic understanding exemplifies a process of literary enslavement and degeneration that is driven by politics and ideology.

The silencing of public opinion means that works overlooked by the censorship process remain shrouded in silence. This is the most effective method of the contemporary censorship system. Previously, the policies implemented by the hard censorship regime were ones wherein the author was presumed to take responsibility for his or her own works, and therefore many Chinese writers and intellectuals were monitored, exiled, and even executed on account of their speech and writings. But in the Reform Era, policies emphasizing self-responsibility inaugurated a shift toward emphasizing a "freedom to write but restrictions on publication." When the current censorship system notices the appearance of inappropriate works, it will generally punish the publishing house, but not the author. My novel *Serve the People!* (為人民服務) is a good example of this, in that I myself was not subjected to any significant punitive measures after the novel was published in the Guangzhou literary journal *Huacheng* (花城), though the responsible parties at the press and the journal were subsequently fined, dismissed, and punished.

When publishers are held responsible for censoring the works they publish, the publishing industry becomes a massive filtration system. However, society is still developing, and given the size of the publishing industry there will inevitably be a large group of conscientious publishers who will see to it that most unjustly banned works eventually see the light of day. Moreover, under the contemporary censorship system, the authorities typically would not order that a book be banned or employees be dismissed, but instead would use secret talks, announcement prohibitions, and other indirect methods to ensure that the influence and sales of those inappropriate works are kept as low as possible.

My recent novel *The Explosion Chronicles* (炸裂志) encountered precisely this response. After a group of editors worked diligently to get it published, the censors deemed it inappropriate. The novel was not immediately banned as it would have been in the past, however, and instead it was reevaluated internally and subjected to a series of "gentle warnings," while publishers, journals, magazines, and awards agencies were forbidden from evaluating or even announcing it. Newspapers, television, web portals, and other government-controlled media were also uniformly silent about the novel, and were not permitted to make any announcements or promotions mentioning it. The result was that even though the work was in fact published, its influence and sales were nevertheless kept artificially low, and it quickly disappeared from view. Of course, a good work of literature does not necessarily require public acclamation, but for many authors this process of encouraging public opinion to maintain a collective silence can have the effect of suppressing a work without technically banning it. The use of silence to complete a process of prohibition is therefore truly one of the most effective methods of which a system of soft censorship may avail itself.

In contrast to the primitive methods used by a hard censorship regime, soft censorship is nominally enlightened and open, though certainly neither progressive nor free. China's current embrace of soft censorship does not mean that it has completely abandoned hard censorship, however, and in fact the former may be seen as an extension of the latter. If authors and intellectuals view this soft censorship regime as a sign of society's development and a product of an expanded freedom of speech and of the press, this will inevitably herald a new prison house of language and a return of a hard censorship system. It is important that one recognize that no matter how "soft" a regime might appear, in the end it is not fundamentally different from a hard censorship regime's attempts to erase memories and create false ones. Moreover, precisely because a soft censorship regime relies on hypocrisy and deceit, it is more effective in encouraging writers to adopt an attitude of compromise and only write for fame, fortune, or power. Consequently, while soft censorship might appear to mark an improvement on hard censorship, from the standpoint of the literary establishment and of the authors themselves it actually constitutes a greater threat.

An Examination of Censorship Is Actually a Deeper Study of Literature Itself

Although the best literary analysis is arguably a close reading, a work's significance is also shaped by the author's society and era, together with his or her frame of mind while the work was being composed. This is especially true of contemporary Chinese literature, wherein no work can ever escape the effects of the censorship system, and therefore a consideration of the censorship system can help yield a richer and more valuable understanding of the work itself.

First, a study of the censorship system requires an examination of the entire historical era in which the literary work was produced. Here, we find a people who have endured the darkness of a long revolution, including events like the anti-rightist cleansing, the so-called "three years of natural disaster," together with the decade-long Cultural Revolution, the effects of which persist up to the present day. However, China, a nation with a great literary tradition and civilization that can be traced back several millennia, conspicuously lacks extraordinary literary works like Boris Pasternak's *Doctor Zhivago*, George Orwell's *1984*, Alexandr Solzhenitsyn's *The Gulag Archipelago*, and Orhan Pamuk's *Snow*. In fact, contemporary China hasn't even produced a great satirical work like Orwell's *Animal Farm*. Wherein lies the reason for this enormous gap in modern China's literary tradition? Through a study of the censorship system, we can obtain a convincing answer.

Second, there are hardly any outstanding authors in China who have not at some point either been banned or become the subject of controversy. Accordingly, through a study of hard and soft censorship regimes, it is possible to obtain a deeper and fuller understanding of these authors, as well as of the trajectory and transformation of the broader cohort of authors to which they belong. Whether it is a question of artistic transformation itself or an adjustment at the level of the author's thought and the contents of his or her works, no authors have left more tracks or waves than those who have walked through the streams of censorship.

Returning to the four banned and republished novels mentioned at the beginning of this chapter, we can ask the following questions:

(1) Why were these specific authors first banned and then permitted to have their works republished?

(2) What types of works did these authors write before and after they were banned? After *Ruined City* was banned, for instance, Jia Pingwa wrote *Earth Gate* (土門), *White Night* (白夜), *Nostalgia for the Wolf* (懷念狼), *Gao laozhuang* (高老庄), and *Illness and Morbidity Report* (病相報告). However, none of these works can hold a candle to either *Ruined City* or some of his more recent works, such as *Ancient Furnace* or *The Lantern Bearer* (帶燈). Why did Jia Pingwa take such a long detour and why, after finally coming to his senses, was he then able to write works with even greater literary merit? Similarly, before *Big Breasts and Wide Hips* was banned, Mo Yan had written several novels dealing with contemporary China, including *Garlic Ballads* (天堂蒜臼之歌) and *Republic of Wine* (酒國), but after *Big Breasts* he produced a series of works like *Sandalwood Death* (檀香刑) and *Life and Death are Wearing me Out*, which had a greater historical significance but were nevertheless more distanced from contemporary concerns. The more interesting question, however, is why was Mo Yan so much more creative and inspired when working with historical subject matter, as opposed to when he was writing about more contemporary concerns? As for Li Peifu and Wang Yaowen, why did the banning of their works effectively mark the end of their careers as authors?

(3) To return to the literary text itself, if we select a banned work that nevertheless has considerable artistic value, we can derive even more insight from a close examination of the work itself. For instance, we may consider the banning of *Abandoned Capital* in conjunction with its artistic significance, or the process by which *Big Breasts and Wide Hips* was banned, unbanned, and then singled out by the Nobel Prize committee when it awarded Mo Yan the Nobel Prize for Literature. In both cases, an examination of China's censorship regime concerns

not merely the censorship regime itself, but more importantly offers important insight into the works and the authors themselves.

To put this another way, the study of China's censorship system permits a deeper understanding of contemporary Chinese literature that has to be created under the shadow of this censorship regime. This, in turn, permits us to undertake a deeper examination of the process of literary production itself.

(translated by Carlos Rojas)

CHAPTER 1.14

"ARE OUR DRAWERS EMPTY?"

Nie Gannu's Dossier Literature

JIE LI

"ARE our drawers empty?" In 1999, the modern Chinese literature scholar Chen Sihe 陳思和 asked this provocative question about literary production in Mainland China from 1949 to 1976. By *drawer literature* (抽屜文學) or "invisible writing" (潛在寫作), Chen refers to literary works that could not be published in their time and were instead kept in the drawer or circulated in small groups. Such invisible writing in a "deaf-mute era," he maintained, was also an "organic component of the spiritual life of that historical period." This critical intervention to examine subterranean, marginal, and nonofficial writings may help resurrect the literature of the Maoist era from easy dismissals of poverty and propaganda and help us see "the variety and richness of its zeitgeist."[1]

How are we to write the literary history of a time when reading and writing were subject to surveillance? Did waves of political movements "kill off" literature as personal expression, turning all art into propaganda and criticism into censorship? Or could literature still "survive" in the form of invisible writing, defined by subjective consciousness, artistic quality, and critical spirit? If, as Chen Sihe suggests, only the latter is worthy of the name *literature*, what are we to do with the enormous legacy of graphomania from this period that was not resistant against, but rather complicit with, state power? After all, even a writer of Shen Congwen's 沈從文 stature composed "mediocre poems of praise and celebration," and almost all intellectuals had to write confessions and denunciations addressed to the authorities and filed away in their dossiers.[2]

In an era when, to borrow a famous 1935 slogan often applied to intellectual life under tyranny, "for all its vastness China can no longer accommodate a quiet desk," a drawer to store away nonconforming thoughts was a risky luxury.[3] Since raids on homes were common during the Cultural Revolution, any "invisible writing" could turn into criminal evidence against its author, subject to confiscation and scrutiny as part of his or her dossier. Under the duress of existential threats or seduced by utopian ideologies, the dossiers of many writers and intellectuals contained not only testaments of courage and autonomous thinking, but also documents of unconditional surrender to the totalitarian regime. While agreeing with Chen Sihe's attempt to excavate great literary works from the rubble of the Mao era, I hesitate to exclude more ambivalent, even retrospectively shameful writings by intellectuals under communism—confessions and denunciations produced not *against* but *for* power—works that are difficult to reclaim in terms of "resistance" or "the sacred fire of literature."[4] Such a redemptive agenda might leave us with an overly romantic view of muffled dissident voices beneath a strident official culture.

Rather than looking only into "drawers"—the nooks and crannies of freedom overlooked by state power—this chapter proposes the category of *dossier literature*, which mines official archives as a museum of arrested thought.[5] I use this term to refer to the enormous body of writings collected in individual dossiers, including "invisible writing" confiscated from the writer as well as informer reports, interrogation notes, and confessions. A single dossier can have multiple authors and readers who may or may not be aware of one another's existence, some seeking out state power and others hiding unsuccessfully from it. Dossier literature is thus defined not by form, genre, or literary merit, but rather by its brush with state power, whose representatives are the only ones with a complete overview of a file's heterogeneous contents.

But are the contents of a dossier actually "literature"? Do they belong in the realm of literary studies, or should we sort its contents according to their historical or literary value? Chen Sihe excludes confessions produced by writers for authorities from his category of *invisible writing*, but beyond applying time-honored intellectual and aesthetic criteria to the task of literary canonization, the inextricable entanglement of aesthetics and politics demands critical examination of the very definition of literature.[6] Shifting the focus from resistance to complicity, the category of *dossier literature* calls attention to the ways the totalitarian state subjugated the practices of writing and reading to the policing and revolutionizing of hearts and minds. Put differently, dossier literature was literary insofar as literary composition and criticism were not just hindered by power, but were sometimes *in the service of* power. As I will show with the writer Nie Gannu's 聶紺弩 (1903–1986) dossier from the 1950s to the 1970s, a poetic circle could turn into an informer circle, literary interpretation could turn into criminal investigation, the author could become his own censor, while the censor could become his muse or the *zhiyin* (知音) reader who "knows the tone." A careful analysis of dossier literature undoes the dichotomy between "good literature" and "bad politics" to paint an ambivalent picture of intellectual survival under dictatorship.

NIE GANNU'S DOSSIER

The first item of any Chinese dossier is often basic personal data, taking the form of a list or a brief (auto-)biographical sketch. Nie Gannu's curriculum vitae includes his studies at the Huangpu Military Academy and Moscow Sun Yat-sen University as well as his working experience as a journalist and KMT official in the 1920s. After the Manchurian Incident in 1931, he moved to Shanghai and joined the League of Leftwing Writers in 1932 and the Communist Party in 1934. Working as an editor and writing many *zawen* (雜文, "miscellaneous essays"), he was a close friend to Lu Xun 魯迅 (1881–1936) and Hu Feng 胡風 (1902–1985). After the establishment of the People's Republic, Nie served as the vice editor-in-chief of the People's Literature Press. In 1955, he was implicated in the Anti–Hu Feng campaign, and in 1957 he was labeled a rightist along with his wife Zhou Ying 周穎 and sent to a farm in Northeast China to undergo "thought reform through labor" until 1962. In 1967, he would be arrested and imprisoned as a "counterrevolutionary," not to be released until 1976. After publishing several collections of classical-style verse in his old age, Nie Gannu died in 1986.[7]

Every line of this brief biography unravels into dozens, even hundreds of pages in Nie's dossier. Everyone in the People's Republic ever affiliated with a state institution—school, factory, or prison—has had a "dossier" (檔案) inaccessible to him or herself but which has held great sway over his or her past, present, and future. Personal files in China existed as early as the Eastern Zhou (770–221 BC) to ensure the genealogical appropriateness of court officials, while a system of criminal records, accompanied by surveillance and reprieves, already began in the Han (206 BC–220 AD). Under the communists, a personnel dossier system was instituted for party members in Yan'an in the early 1940s and was extended by the 1950s to other walks of life to include workers and students; they were consulted for promotions, welfare allocation, and selection of targets in political campaigns.[8]

Most worker and student dossiers were quite simple, containing no more than basic biographical data, family background, academic transcripts, organizational affiliations, and records of rewards and punishments.[9] By contrast, the dossiers of cadres, party members, and individuals considered politically suspect also contained extensive autobiographies, self-criticisms, leader evaluations, and informer reports on their political attitudes, lifestyle ethics, and day-to-day behavior. If an individual was placed under police surveillance or arrest, as in the case of Nie Gannu, his dossier would also be transferred to the Public Security Bureau. Given that Nie was a writer, his dossier included his publications plus whatever unpublished writings the authorities laid hands on, such as letters and diaries confiscated from his home. Interrogation notes, confessions and "thought summaries," further investigations into his history and social network, court verdicts, and warden reports all thickened his dossier, such that Nie quipped that it "knows more about me than I do about myself."[10]

Accumulated this way, the dossier of an intellectual such as Nie Gannu came to consist of a number of literary genres—old-style poems and their exegesis, dramatic dialogues (interrogation transcripts), interior monologues (confessions), and narrative prose (informer reports)—composed by a number of authors, including Nie himself, the authorities, and the informers. Its intended readership, however, was limited to the policing and judicial personnel, who might arrest, interrogate, try, and sentence individuals on the basis of "evidence" they attained in the files through a hermeneutics of suspicion.

What is extraordinary about Nie's dossier is that it has been "discovered" by a former member of the judicial authority who gave it a second reading through a hermeneutics of faith—not to establish facts or crimes but to affirm the spirit of a poet. This former member of the police decided to read Nie's file with literary appreciation and, in 2009, published extensive excerpts from it after careful selection, editing, annotation, and commentary. This heteroglossic text, titled *Nie Gannu's Case File* (聶紺弩刑事檔案), opens with a preface under the name Yu Zhen (寓真, literally "lodging the truth"), a pseudonym of the retired judge Li Yuzhen 李玉榛. His longstanding perusal of legal cases rendered him both nimble and numb, so that even though he had leafed through Nie Gannu's dossier "for several years," it was only after his retirement that he reread it with a different frame of mind:

> In the past the dossier appeared to be nothing more than a dense pile of words, but now, in the spring sunshine, a vivacious figure emerged from the pages. It was as if Mr. Nie Gannu were sitting across from me. I could listen to the Master's eloquent speech, his laughter or outrage; I could sense his penetrating gaze and animated gestures.
>
> Some years ago I had read Nie Gannu's poetry and the reminiscences and commentaries of his friends, so it seemed as if I had learned quite a bit about him, but such an understanding was general. It was not until I had tossed and turned in his case files for years and listened to his frank, earnest, incisive words that I felt that I really came to know the man, his poetry, and what makes him extraordinary.[11]

Yu Zhen acknowledges his own split identity, first as a judicial authority who saw only prosaic legal cases and later as a poetry lover whose discerning ear made him the poet's true *zhiyin*. Whereas published works by and on Nie Gannu are "without flesh and bones, without character," his police file tells us the more profound truth about the man.[12] The dossier's omniscience is largely due to the extensive reports of his conversations with friends as well as copies of his poetry submitted by informers with their annotations. Spoken or written, these words could not have survived the Cultural Revolution outside of the dossier, and since Nie himself was unaware of his friends' breach of trust, the dossier's omniscience even went beyond the poet's self-knowledge. Unlike the classical Chinese tragedy of the loyal minister who could not find a ruler who *knows* or *listens to* him, modern Chinese intellectuals suffered from persecution because they *were* listened *in on* and spied on, often by their best friends. If the police could become one's *zhiyin*, one's *zhiyin* could become the police. To give an example, one informer report, dated September 12, 1962, begins as follows:

> Yesterday I went to see Nie and had a "long, free chat." . . . Evening, we arrived at Xiyuan restaurant and sat outdoors following Nie's wishes. By 8 PM we ordered some food: baked wheat cakes, fried shrimp, pork liver, egg rolls, and tofu to go with some wine. I did not actively prompt him. After half a bottle of wine, Nie got a bit drunk and started a reactionary conversation . . . After ordering two more cold appetizers, Nie said he wanted some hot dishes, so we ordered some. We talked until

midnight snacks went on the market. / After midnight snacks, we walked over to the zoo. Nie called a rickshaw that took us to his house, where we talked some more. / After one evening I got quite a bit of information and spent quite some money, adding up to over 20 *yuan*. / Let me now write down his words as truthfully as I can remember them. [13]

With astute economic calculations, the informer was able to procure his report only through substantial investment—20 *yuan* was about an average cadre's weekly salary. When the inebriated man tossed words into the air, the sober man caught them, first in his mind and then on paper, complete with "stage directions" of hand gestures, tone, emphasis, and emotions. For instance, according to the report, Nie spoke thus of the persecution of intellectuals in the Anti-Rightist Campaign and of the ensuing catastrophe of the Great Leap Forward:

If you want to kill, then kill, but then what? Zhang Bojun 章伯鈞 told me from the start: "If it's good for the country and for the big picture, if you want to borrow my head I am also willing." Me too, if they want to borrow my (pointing to his own) head, I'm willing too, but I'm still going to talk. (With emphasis, in a tone of outrage) What have they done now? They have to be responsible. The whole nation has to be responsible. Only we are not responsible (knocking his fingers against the table).[14]

Without this friend-informer as a coauthor of his dossier, Nie Gannu might never have uttered such words, not to mention having such spontaneous verbal outbursts transmitted to posterity. Similarly, many poems Nie had written for or shared with his friends also found their way into his dossier even when he himself burned the poems, so that the police files contain the earliest extant copies of Nie's poems written between 1959 and 1966. Yu Zhen speaks of the fortuitous preservation of Nie's poetry, yet their very existence also bears obscene testimony to the underhanded internecine strife among intellectuals. After reading *Nie Gannu's Case File* in 2009, Zhang Yihe 章詒和, daughter of China's "No. 1 Rightist" Zhang Bojun, stirred up heated public discussion over informers with a passionate essay entitled "Who Sent Nie Gannu to Jail?":

I know most people mentioned in the text—some even very well, but Nie's file made their faces hazy and blurry, even strange. . . . Nie Gannu was not sent to jail by Red Guards or through the mischief of rebel factions. It was his friends who had "written" him into jail a stroke at a time.[15]

Once a victim and perpetrator of the pen's violence herself, Zhang Yihe recognizes that writing is power. In her 2004 bestselling memoir *The Past is Not Like Smoke* (往事並不如煙), Zhang reveals that, while in prison during the Cultural Revolution, she was given temporary reprieve from the excruciating physical labor of tea picking to follow a mentally ill fellow prisoner with a pen and notebook, writing down every word she uttered. The transcript became evidence for the prisoner's counterrevolutionary crime, and Zhang claims she only realized her own complicity when she heard the gunshot of execution.[16] Such instrumentalization of the written word provides the crudest illustration of Jacques Derrida's observation that "all clergies, exercising political power or not, were constituted at the same time as writing and by the disposition of graphic power."[17] Such "graphic power" accumulates in the archive, a kind of mnemotechnological invention that, as Michel Foucault points out, brings "everyday life into discourse" and deposits "the denunciation, the indictment, the inquiry, the report, the use of informers, the interrogation" in an "enormous documentary mass" in which they "build up through time as the endlessly growing memory of all the wrongs of the world."[18]

As a surveillance tool, the dossier's very production may be full of deceptions and betrayals, yet it may be the most transparent and faithful representation of an individual and his social network in the Mao era. The dossier presents an exceedingly intimate portrait of its subject through multiple perspectives and a variety of genres that blend into a strangely hybrid magnum opus. In treating the dossier as *literature*, I share the New Historicist approach of discovering the "unanticipated aesthetic dimension in objects without pretensions to the aesthetic."[19] This does not mean to endorse the violence of the dossier system, but rather to use literary interpretative strategies to probe the ideas and power relations, the fantasies and anxieties of an era through the vast textual archive it has bequeathed. Moreover, as I will elaborate in the following sections, literary composition, interpretation, and community could serve as both treacherous tools of and treasurable sanctuaries from totalitarian power.

THE CENSOR AS MUSE

We usually think of political tyranny as the nemesis of literary expression and production, but censorship has a much more complex impact on literary form, genre, and practice than simply banning, burning, or bowdlerizing books. Nie Gannu's own literary career presents an intriguing case in point. As a May Fourth intellectual, Nie had "promoted vernacular and opposed classical Chinese."[20] Instead of poetry, he was known for his *zawen*, the miscellaneous essay genre Lu Xun had forged into a biting weapon of social and political criticism. In the 1955 Anti–Hu Feng Campaign, however, Nie had to join the mass graphomania of "thought summaries" and confessions detailing past and present political views and associations. An old friend of the campaign's main target, he was compelled to write detailed reports about their interactions, recapitulating their conversations, ruminating over casual remarks, and psychoanalyzing every joke.[21] While Nie perfunctorily denounced Hu Feng, he also stood by his friend by denouncing himself as well, opening a confession with the line: "I am more of a Hu Feng element than any other Hu Feng element."[22] Condemned as a rightist in 1957, Nie was exiled to Manchuria to undergo "thought reform through labor."

As Xiaofei Tian mentions in her chapter for this volume, during the Great Leap Forward to accelerate the nation's industrial and agricultural production in 1958, Mao also called for a Great Leap Forward in cultural production, whereby everyone was called upon to write poetry. Nie's "intuitive response was to write classical verse," as he recalled later:

> Perhaps because the more removed I was from the literary scene, the more I felt as if only old poetry was poetry, with tradition, habit, national form, new wine in old bottles, and the like. I was already close to sixty, yet the scene of physical labor was new to me, and I was eager to write this down. . . . That night, I wrote about labor for the first time, a heptasyllabic "ancient-style" long verse.[23]

The following day, the cadre ordered Nie to write another thirty-two poems, and thus began the corpus of what he calls "literature produced by following commands" (遵命文學). Such a humorous label may also describe the broader literary landscape of the Maoist era. With the party as "muse," authors must write propaganda as well as confessions and denunciations with every political movement. In ways reminiscent of Christianity, the Party had consistently demanded from its members and followers praises of its glory or confessions of their innermost thoughts, or to "give one's heart to the Party" (向黨交心). Indeed, as the Romanian writer Stelian Tănase points out, "censorship does not limit itself to interdicting, to cutting some passages, etc. It asks for the creation of myths, themes, etc., which it projects (like a film on a screen) onto reality."[24]

Hence Nie began writing poetry in 1958 at the Party's call, with the intention to "eulogize labor" (歌頌勞動) and to show his thought reform, yet the authorities would later see even such eulogistic poetry as "venting" (發洩) his discontent with his exile.[25] To take as an example the poem "Weeding" (鋤草):

培苗每恨草偏長，
鋤草時將苗並傷。
六月百花初嫵媚，
漫天小咬太猖狂。
為人自比東方朔，
與雁偕征北大荒。
昨夜深寒地全白，
不知是月是春霜 。[26]

When cultivating seedlings one resents the growing weed
When hoeing the weed one often hurts the seedlings
In June hundreds of flowers just began to bloom
Covering the skies, a myriad midges bite with ferocity

I compare myself to the witty courtier Dongfang Shuo
Together with the wild geese I travel to Manchuria
Last night was bitter cold, the earth was all white
I do not know if it was the moon or the spring frost.

The poem found its way into Nie's dossier via a friend-informer, who also provided an interpretation of its "subversive" meaning: the poet longs for home on a snowy night, thus the allusion to Li Bai's 李白 "Night Thoughts" (夜思). He was banished because the "midges" of the Anti-Rightist Movement began attacking in June 1957, when the Hundred Flowers Movement had just gotten underway. The poet compares himself to the Han dynasty courtier Dongfang Shuo known for his satirical witticisms, now exiled to the Great Northern Wilderness with the wild geese.

If the Party was a muse in the positive sense of ordering people to write, it was also a muse in the negative sense of provoking "lyrical fury." As first formulated by Sima Qian 司馬遷, "one takes to writing to express one's anger" (發憤著書), or as Ouyang Xiu 歐陽修 (1007–1072) later put it, "great literature is the result of great suffering" (窮而後工). [27] In an interrogation in 1972, Nie admitted: "In the past I did not know how to write poetry. Bad mood made me learn, and when I felt my freedom restricted, I expressed my frustration through poetry." [28]

From the celebration of labor to the expression of personal grievances, Nie's exile to the Great Northern Wilderness during the Great Leap Forward gave rise to a new form of poetry. Connoisseurs like Shi Zecun 施蟄存 have praised Nie's old-style poems for their humorous curiosity (諧趣), often accompanied by a gloomy and reflective pathos (沈鬱) and hence to be distinguished from the banter (戲謔) of doggerel (打油詩).[29] Wang Xijian 王希堅 links the humor in Nie's poetry to his earlier miscellaneous essays, since both incorporate classical and modern, vernacular and elite language, and the humor derives in part from their incongruous juxtaposition.[30] As Xiaofei Tian puts it, "the poet deftly negotiates between the discourse of a traditional cultural elite and life in the 'brave new world' of socialism."[31] One frequent strategy is to relate his literal circumstances to classical literary tropes. For instance the poem "Gleaning with Zuguang, No. 1" (拾穗同祖光之一) contains the couplet:

一丘田有幾遺穗
五合米需千折腰

How many ears of grain are left over in a rice paddy?
To gather five *he* of rice, one must bow a thousand times.

Whereas Tao Yuanming 陶淵明 famously refused to "bow like a servant in return for five bushels of grain," the salary of a low-ranking official, Nie Gannu's modification suggests that, first, every grain of rice comes from hard toil; second, a real farmer may not be able to afford the proud posturing of an elite; and third, and most importantly, one could bow a thousand times without losing one's dignity. Certainly, premodern poets like Tao Yuanming, Wang Wei 王維, and Bai Juyi 白居易 also wrote "farmstead poetry" (田園詩) that dealt with the rustic world of agrarian labor.[32] Yet unlike the work of traditional literati who either chose a rustic life as reclusion or came to observe the farmers as local officials, Nie Gannu's poems from the Great Northern Wilderness focus on many minute and tedious details known only to an intellectual condemned to engage in agricultural toil. In this sense, his poetry also departs from the panoramic sceneries of collective labor that became a major trope of Mao's "revolutionary realism and revolutionary romanticism." While "writing to follow commands," what Nie Gannu wrote was far from formulaic propaganda, and even long after the end of the poetry-writing movement he continued to write classical-style poetry, even though his muse was no longer his intended reader.

Whereas "thought reform through labor" helped Nie Gannu develop a new poetic style, the political suppression of intellectuals also gave rise to a new kind of literary community. Ironically, one Maoist mass movement after another inspired Nie and fellow former May Fourth leftists to seek refuge in Chinese cultural traditions they had once considered decadent and feudal. After returning from the Great Northern Wilderness in 1962, Nie Gannu continued to write classical-style poetry until his 1967 arrest, mostly as gifts for his friends on various occasions.[33] As Xiaofei Tian points out, classical verse not only was "a way of dealing with and making sense of the radical changes China was undergoing," but also lent itself to "everyday social occasions" from festivals and birthdays to partings and funerals and thus enabled "active participation in a socio-literary community."[34] In China of the 1960s, such a literary community came to adopt some characteristics associated with a progressive public sphere.

Many of Nie Gannu's friends, once May Fourth leftists, were labeled rightists in 1957 and condemned for their speech crimes. Although publicly silenced, their marginality and irrelevance ironically allowed them to speak more frankly among themselves. As Nie saw it: "Those holding high offices suffer much more than we do as targets of proletarian dictatorship, because they have things to say but dare not. They have to act against their will for fear of losing their position."[35] By contrast, rightists had little to lose and could create discursive spaces apart from what Svetlana Boym calls, in the Soviet context, the "sphere of public authority." Whereas Soviet intellectuals from the 1960s and 1980s "challenged the official bureaucratic and political discourse" through "half words, jokes, and doublespeak," Nie and his rightist friends forged their alternative community around classical poetry with its rich and obscure allusions, as well as around calligraphy and painting whose appreciation required leisurely cultivation.[36]

This alternative public sphere, however, was neither explicitly dissident nor was it protected from the authorities, who frequently recruited informers from their midst in order to record subversive speech and writing for the dossiers. Thus, by the early 1960s the authorities who "eavesdropped" on their conversations were, in a sense, covert members of this public sphere. Writing of literature and the Stasi (East German secret police), Stephen Brockmann argues that many intellectuals joined the Stasi because it functioned as a "medium of communication" in "a society which increasingly has no language to deal with a considerable part of its own reality. . . . If newspapers like the Communist Party organ *Neues Deutschland* presented an unrelentingly optimistic picture of new production records and economic strengths, the Stasi concerned itself with failures and problems." The Stasi was a kind of "social unconscious," or even a "secret public sphere" where honest dialogue and debate took place in the form of spying and interrogations.[37] In a similar vein, since the platform for free speech shrank from newspapers and Party meetings to living rooms and restaurant gatherings between three or four friends, intellectuals entered into a strange, unidirectional dialogue with the authorities via the mediation of the informers.

LITERARY INQUISITION

Besides the secret police in the Soviet Union and Eastern Europe, another reference point for reading the dossiers of Nie Gannu and other Chinese intellectuals is that of the "literary inquisition" (文字獄) in premodern China, where poetic interpretation—or literary criticism—played an especially important role in the arrest and incarceration of writers. The most famous case of a Chinese literary inquisition was the 1079 Crow Terrace Poetry Trial (烏台詩案), when the prominent poet and literati-official Su Shi 蘇軾 (1037–1101), also known as Su Dongpo 蘇東坡, was charged with treason on account of his poetry. The resulting dossier contains the original indictments, copies of his allegedly slanderous writings, and depositions where the poet explicates the meanings of his poems. There is, as Charles Hartman points out, an "obvious affinity of the deposition to traditional Chinese commentary," as both identify allusions and quotations as well as relate these references to contemporary political events.[38]

In Nie Gannu's case, it was his friend-informers who provided the authorities with both his poems and the poetic interpretations that incriminated him. For instance, Dai Hao 戴浩, a fellow rightist and frequent beneficiary of Nie's hospitality, surrendered a poem Nie wrote for him and accused Nie of "borrowing my circumstances to vent his own indignant reactionary feelings."[39] Similarly, Nie's friend Xiang Sigeng 向思賡 reproduced Nie's poems on *The Dream of the Red Chamber* (紅樓夢) for the police and explicated their obscure personal meanings:

> Take the poem about Qingwen, the line "ripping off the red bodice" refers to [Nie's] expulsion from the party. "Mending the peacock-feathered cape" refers to his many contributions to the party. It would be unfair to call such poetry "reactionary." Still, ordinary people cannot see the problem with them, but we are his old friends and understand the references.[40]

Xiang was only able to understand Nie's poetry because he shared Nie's plight as an early member of the Communist Party later purged from its ranks. Brought before the authorities, however, such empathetic knowledge served to frame his friend as an "enemy of the people." Xiang died in 1994, shortly after receiving a copy of Nie's complete poems, which led Yu Zhen to speculate whether he had been "struck by a pang of contrition that killed him."[41] Dai Hao's and Xiang Sigeng's hermeneutics of Nie Gannu's poetry show that the *context* of interpretation matters more than its *content*. Before Nie's arrest, discerning the "hidden transcript" of discontent was a demonstration of compassion, but when facing the police, the same interpretation turned into betrayal, and appreciation turned into denunciation.

In the Chinese hermeneutic tradition, there has long been a tension between unraveling a poem's endless meanings and seeking out the author's original intention, between Dong Zhongshu's 董仲舒 (176–104 BC) dictum that "[*The Book of*] *Odes* has no direct interpretation" and Mencius's 孟子 (372–289 BC) belief that a poem's meaning is governed by the poet's intention and recoverable by a good reader who "knows the tone."[42] The censor, however, at once relentlessly pursues and utterly disrespects authorial intention in order to project onto the author the censor's own paranoia. Like premodern literary inquisitions, the Maoist censor engages in allegorical reading by politicizing the aesthetic, by detecting parallels between the past and the present, or by "supplying a definite signified for every poetic image."[43] Take for example the poem "Lulu Form, No. 2" (轆轤體之二) and its interpretation from Nie's dossier:

> 疏林映日复栖霞，
> 紫伞红旗十万家。
> 一夜云雷屯此地，
> 满城风雨涤新华。
> 居人旧有离人泪，
> 疏林映日復棲霞，
> 紫傘紅旗十萬家。
> 一夜雲雷屯此地，
> 滿城風雨滌新華。
> 居人舊有離人淚，
> 九月今開二月花。
> 不見白衣無酒暖，
> 山根掃葉且烹茶。

> Through sparse woods, the sun shines on Mount Qixia
> Purple canopy, red flags, a hundred thousand homes
> One night, cloud and thunder garrisoned here
> The city's wind and rain washed out a new China
> Former inhabitants left behind their tears
> In September bloom February flowers
> Nowhere in sight is the man dressed in white to warm the wine
> Sweeping leaves in the vale, let me cook some tea

For the unnamed interpreter in Nie's dossier, *thunder* and *rain* are code words for the impact of high politics on ordinary people, whereas "February flowers in September" is interpreted as referring to a state of time being out of joint, and therefore a veiled critique of socialism. Yu Zhen calls this reading a "farfetched distortion" and instead finds the line a vivid description of autumn foliage that innocently alludes to Du Mu's 杜牧 classical line "The frosted leaves are redder than February flowers" (霜葉紅于二月花). To render the poem politically benign in order to acquit Nie Gannu of his "counterrevolutionary" crimes, however, seems to confirm the legitimacy of the accusations. If Nie meant to be subversive, a more innocuous reading would seem to diminish the poem's value as political criticism. Yet to retrospectively celebrate the author as a heroic dissident would ignore the complexities of historical and personal contingencies.

Not only did the police and their informers read with a hermeneutics of suspicion. The authors themselves learned to read their own writings like their censors, so that authorial intention was always in dialogue with the authorities. When a friend asked him not to destroy "harmless" poems about *The Dream of the Red Chamber* and *The Water Margin* (水滸傳) in February of 1965, Nie replied: "What if they ask you to interpret the line: 'The hero's face singed with the convict's golden tattoo; smiling, he lightly enters the White Tiger Hall' (英雄臉刻黃金印，一笑身輕白虎堂)? If they look for a problem they would find it."[44] Knowing that the author has little authority over the interpretation of his own writing, Nie Gannu decided to burn all his poems on New Year's Eve of 1965, on which occasion he also wrote a poem:

自著奇書自始皇
乾坤袖手視詩亡
詩亡人豈春秋作
身賤吟須釜甑妨
自嚼吾心成嚼蠟
盡焚年草當焚香
鬥牛光焰知何似
但賞深宵爝火光

Writing wondrous books just for oneself, a practice dating back to the First Emperor[45]
Heaven and earth watch on indifferently as poetry perishes
After poetry perishes, would one really write the *Spring and Autumn Annals*?[46]
A man as lowly as I—must chanting poetry be thwarted by daily cooking[47]
Chewing my heart until it is like chewing wax
Burning the year's manuscripts as incense
The light going into the *Dou* and *Niu* stars, do you know what it is like?
Never mind, let me appreciate the torchlight deep into the night.[48]

In this poem, Nie plays the double role of the author and the censor, the tyrannical first emperor who burned books and buried scholars alive. Now that poetry has perished, there is no need to write history, for the author's own existence is precarious. On this New Year's Eve, burning his manuscripts becomes a devotional act like burning incense, whereas his mind's ruminations are as bland as wax. The light of the *douniu* stars suggests a defiant spirit, however ephemeral.[49] The final line references Zhuangzi's 莊子 "Free and Easy Wandering" (逍遙遊): "If, when the sun and moon are shining, you persist in lighting a torch, is not that a misapplication of fire?" While the blinding sun of Mao Zedong Thought eclipsed whatever illumination his own poetic torch might offer, the poet could still appreciate its light deep into the night. The recurring image of the fire stands at first for the censoring conflagration and then for the poems' fighting spirit. Thus a catastrophe turns into an aesthetic and philosophical experience, while destruction and loss give way to self-preservation and hope. A poem borne out of the burning of poetry, it speaks of literature's precarious condition under political tyranny, the conditions and (im)possibilities of its production and transmission. When it was no longer safe for an author to publish or even to keep manuscripts of his works in the drawer, the dossier ironically became the last haven for the preservation of literature.

IMPRISONED WRITING

Nie Gannu was arrested on January 25, 1967, shortly after the passage of a new "public security law" that considered a counterrevolutionary act any "attack or slander of the Great Leader Chairman Mao and his Dearest Comrade-in-Arms Lin Biao." His verdict, issued on May 8, 1974, sentenced him to lifelong imprisonment for

> stubbornly insisting on a reactionary and hostile stance toward the Party and Socialism. He often met with other "Rightist" elements to disseminate reactionary speech and vicious slander against the proletariat headquarters. Attacking the Party's various policies and the socialist system, they attempted in vain to topple the proletariat dictatorship and to restore capitalism. He also wrote voluminous amounts of counterrevolutionary poetry that cry out on behalf of the counterrevolutionary element Hu Feng, the Rightist element Ding Ling and others.[50]

Arresting the author for his thought crimes, the authorities confiscated all the writing Nie Gannu did not manage to destroy, but they did not immediately decipher all his poetry despite calling in Nie's friends to tease out their subversive intent. It was only several decades later that Yu Zhen discovered some poems Nie had scripted in cursive script between the lines of Mao Zedong's poems on what appeared to be calligraphic practice. Among them was a poem entitled "Tearing Up Some Poetry Drafts" (全撕某詩稿), which commemorates Nie's destruction of his poetic correspondence with Hu Feng between 1965 and 1967.[51] Another poem Yu Zhen discovered among Nie's "calligraphy" describes a target of persecution during the Cultural Revolution:

慈親獄母死還埋，
家譜續修萬死該。
三載退休都寫稿，
百篇歌頌爲貪財。
此真右派枉摘帽，
重扣高冠令掃街。
久在人文出版社，
蒼髯老賊張廣才。

Your dear mother-in-law died—how dare you bury her!
Continuing to compile the family genealogy—you ought to die ten thousand times!
Retired for three years and you kept writing
hundreds of odes to the Party—how greedy you are [for royalties]!
They should never have taken away your Rightist cap
Put on a dunce cap on him again and sweep the streets!
You've been around for some time at the People's Literature Press
Old scoundrel with a white beard like Zhang Guangcai [52]

By rendering the strident language of big-character posters into classical verse, the poem produces absurdist humor. One could also read empathy and self-mockery in its theatrical accusatory tone toward its subject, who is after all a rightist like Nie himself. Thus the poem is not only visually scripted between the lines of Mao's poetry, but also derives its meaning from the gaps in the pastiche of Maoist jargon.

During his decade-long incarceration, Nie Gannu's "literary" production consisted primarily of confessions. In her study of Stalinist and Romanian secret police files, Cristina Vatulescu points out that victims "were not just written about or, as in Kafka's *Penal Colony*, written on; rather they become the authors of their own files." This required victims to "internalize the ideology of the secret police" and produce "ventriloquized confessions."[53] Full of self-denouncing clichés, Nie Gannu's confessions certainly show such ventriloquism at work. Yet one might still discover hilarious subversion and ironic critiques of his interrogators in such sentences as: "I recognized that I am a non-power-holding capitalist-road-taking power-holder. All my views are wrong and reactionary, and I must really reform myself."[54]

Beyond confessions, Nie continued to compose and remember old-styled poetry surreptitiously in prison. He also taught his younger cellmate Li Shiqiang 李世強 to read and compose poetry starting in 1970. In the winter of 1972, Nie gave Li a few pieces of paper filled with tiny characters: "I am old and do not know if I will ever leave prison," Nie said. "These are some past and recent poems—I wrote down here everything I could memorize with the hope that my friends beyond these walls could read them some day. Why don't you read them first?"[55] Deeply moved, Li Shiqiang came up with three strategies to take the poems with him should he ever be released: to hide them in his cotton jacket, to memorize them, and to copy them into Mao's *Collected Works* with a hard pencil and then erasing the words afterwards, such that the pencil marks would stay but would not be easily detectable.[56] These methods succeeded, and Nie's poems managed to "escape" prison with Li Shiqiang's release in 1975.[57] A year later, with the end of the Cultural Revolution, Nie regained his freedom at the age of seventy-three and devoted the remaining decade of his life to the writing, recollection, and publication of poetry.[58]

Toward a Critical Reading
of Dossier Literature

In the cataclysmic decade of the Cultural Revolution, the dossier became the ultimate depository of literary works that could neither circulate in the public sphere nor be kept safe in private hands. The destruction of literature and incarceration of writers gave rise to a crisis of cultural memory as well as creative ways of transmission, especially the cases of poems literally and figuratively hidden between the lines of officially sanctioned texts. Such "writing between the lines" poignantly illustrates intellectual survival in the cracks of "proletariat dictatorship."

How was intellectual life possible under Communist dictatorship? Romanian writer Andrei Pleşu lists "resignation, sublimation of dissatisfactions, conjunctural cunning, melancholy, and humor" as "the props of our survival," which would not have been possible "if the Communist world had been a world of consistent evil."[59] In a similar vein, Nie Gannu opens his 1980 essay "Prison Nostalgia" (懷監獄) with the line: "Amidst its inhumanity the prison has some things that are humane, even very humane." He goes on to elaborate on the benefits of prison life, distributed between the three sites of his incarceration: Shanxi's Jishan prison was a Mecca for learning, since only inmates—regardless of their educational background—had the patience to read Marx's *Capital*; Linfen prison had the best health care, since imprisoned doctors continued their practice in jail and gave generous sick leaves; finally, Beijing prison's food was "not so bad"—once Nie even overheard a teenage inmate, addressing the warden as "uncle," asking him to please toast a steamed bun for her.[60] Nie might identify with the Romanian writer Nicolae Steinhardt, whose prison diaries were titled "Diary of Happiness": "Naturally the happiness possible in prison is different from pastoral happiness, but it is still a species of happiness, simultaneous and, at times, consubstantial with the tragedy of circumstances."[61] Moreover, recounting the brilliant analytical and rhetorical skills demonstrated by many prisoners during study sessions of Mao works, Nie might also agree with Pleşu that " 'The Captive Mind'—to recall Czesław Miłosz's formula from 1952—is still a mind and not necessarily a stupid one."[62]

To speak of happiness and intellectual life in prison, however, is not to trivialize the importance of freedom and the inhumanity of dictatorship. Rather, prison life seemed tolerable only in a broader context of material and spiritual deprivations. Some inmates saved up their meager prison income of two *yuan* a month to support their families, showing just how poor some parts of China were.[63] As for the loss of freedom, it was not as if high officials or ordinary people could speak their minds, so "prison nostalgia" ironically suggests the extent to which all of China had become a prison. Responding to criticisms of his essay for making prison life sound too good, Nie wrote:

> As if I should make prison sound scarier. . . . I know that there are very scary prisons where many people were tortured or murdered, but I had not gone to such a prison. . . . "Life is no life; death is no death / Hills are not hills; rivers not rivers." These are two lines from Wu Meicun's 吳梅村 gift of poetry to his friend to be exiled to Manchuria. Meicun had never been to Manchuria . . . but I had been there. Even if you cannot call it a paradise on earth, it also did not warrant Meicun's description.

As Nie recalled, he and hundreds of fellow rightists in the Great Northern Wilderness worked hard, ate well, and did not bemoan their fate. He self-deprecatingly calls his own optimism his "Ah Q Spirit," or sense of spiritual victory.[64] By contrast, literati such as the Ming loyalist Wu Meicun (1609–1671), who never suffered exile or incarceration, were so frightened by their own pathos-filled imagination of such places that they lost their backbones.[65] Sentimental hyperboles of suffering hardly serve to cultivate one's principles, but rather reinforce the Manichean dichotomy that an intellectual in the face of tyranny must always choose between being a courtier or a martyr, between death and disgrace. Turning punishments into opportunities to learn about new worlds, Nie also found a more supple dignity in prison and exile.

Still, Nie emphasizes that the so-called Ah Q spirit is a mutation of slavishness and a sign of adaptation to the conditions of dictatorship. After all, a major survival mechanism for intellectuals during the Maoist era was collaboration with the authorities, sometimes at the expense of family and friendship. Denouncing a friend under political pressure to demonstrate one's loyalty to the Party was all too common, but how should one come to terms with such "betrayal" after it resulted in decades of exile or imprisonment, or even death or suicide? Nie commented on such moral dilemmas in his correspondences with his friend Shu Wu 舒蕪 (1922–2009), notoriously known as a "traitorous disciple" of Hu Feng's who submitted to the authorities private correspondences that constituted the basis for the 1955 anti–Hu Feng campaign. Nie Gannu had remained friends with both Hu Feng and Shu Wu from the 1950s to the 1980s, and on Shu Wu's sixtieth birthday in 1982, Nie wrote a poem for him as a gift:

> 媚骨生成豈我儕，
> 與時無忤有何哉？
> 錯從耶弟方猶大，
> 何不紂廷咒惡來？
> 驢背尋驢尋到死，
> 夢中說夢說成灰。
> 世人難與談今古，
> 跳入黃河濯酒杯。

> There are those born sycophants—can they be our fellows?
> One cannot go against the times—what is to be done?
> Wrongly labeled a disciple of Jesus, you are compared to Judas
> Why did they not curse Elai at the court of the tyrant Zhou?[66]
> Looking for a donkey on a donkey's back until death
> Speaking of a dream in a dream until it turns into ashes
> With worldly people it is hard to speak of the present and past
> Can one leap into the muddy Yellow River to wash one's wine cup?

Nie took the fifth and sixth lines from an earlier poem he wrote for Hu Feng in 1966.[67] Bestowing the same words again on Shu Wu indicates the shared tragic destiny of Chinese intellectuals that might transcend personal scores. Nie further clarified his stance in a letter to Shu Wu:

> I have seen some compare you to Judas and got quite angry: Why is Shu Wu Judas? . . . Hu Feng *was* crucified, but then thousands and hundreds of thousands were crucified in all kinds of ways. Did you anticipate this? I certainly didn't, even after decades as a CCP member. I would never have dreamed of the ten years of catastrophe. Yet how strange that people hate Judas but not Pilate who sent him to the cross! I feel that the Judas story was invented so that people could change their target.[68]

For Nie Gannu, bickering over personal betrayals after the collective persecution of a whole generation of intellectuals only diverts guilt from an oppressive system that extorted denunciations and instigated internecine conflicts. Having passed away in 1986, Nie Gannu probably could not have anticipated the publication of his dossier twenty-some years later or the public uproar over his friend-informers, but his comments on Shu Wu's "betrayal" do give us a sense of how *he* would have liked posterity to read his dossier. Instead of retrying individuals as either innocent or guilty in a retrospective moral court, rereading the dossier could help us understand intellectual complicities—not so much their actual guilt but rather their entangled implications in the larger project of the communist revolution, their hopes, disillusionment, and choices made without the benefit of hindsight. Only in this way would we be able to discern the fluctuating relationship between the individual voice and the revolutionary chorus.

To propose the category of *dossier literature*, then, is not only to suggest the discovery of literary pearls from the Mao-era dossiers of writers, even though these files may hold the only extant copies of some great writing. Rather, it also suggests to what extent literature, literary criticism, and literati communities were implicated in the politics of this time, so much so that we must rethink time-honored literary definitions and criteria. Instead of a free and leisurely spiritual pursuit, literary creation and interpretation could be a matter of life and death in a time when the written word had the power to deceive, to imprison, and to kill. As propaganda, literature could inspire utopian illusions and conceal harsh realities. As confession or denunciation, poetry and its hermeneutics could incarcerate the poet for his thought crimes. As the dossier enfolded authors with censors, friends with informers, a looming hermeneutics of suspicion changed how readers read and how writers wrote, sometimes giving rise to new literary tropes and subtleties that reside between the lines. Reading dossier literature means attending not only to *what* is in the files—such as Nie's lost poetry and informer reports on his subversive speech—but also *how* the texts were created in the first place, how they got inside the dossier, as well as the impact of these texts on their authors. It also means being keenly conscious of the scholar's complicit alliances with the disciplinary powers that produced the files. Above all, dossier literature helps us recognize the banality of evil as well as the limits of virtue, the permeability of totalitarian power as well as how, in its imperfection, hope, humor, friendship, and great literature could still find a place.

NOTES

1. Chen Sihe 陳思和, "Women de chouti: Shi lun dangdai wenxue shi (1949–1976) de 'qian-zai xiezuo'" 我們的抽屜：試論當代文學史 (1949–1976) 的潛在寫作 [Our drawer: On invisible writing in contemporary literary history (1949–1976)], in *Zhongguo dangdai wenxue guanjianci shijiang* 中國當代文學關鍵詞十講 [Contemporary Chinese literature in ten keywords] (Shanghai: Fudan daxue, 2002), 65–92.
2. Chen Sihe's phrase; see "Our Drawer," 74. For examples of Shen Congwen's eulogistic poetry from the Cultural Revolution, see *Shen Congwen quanji* 沈從文全集 [Complete works of Shen Congwen] (Taiyuan: Beiyue wenyi, 2002), vol. 15.

3. I borrow the phrase from Jiang Nanxiang 蔣南翔 (1913–1988), a communist activist from Tsinghua University who famously proclaimed in 1935 that "for all of its vastness, North China can no longer accommodate a quiet desk" (華北之大,竟容不下一張安靜的書桌). See Ma Si 馬嘶, "Zheju 'mingyan' banquan guishui" 這句 "名言" 版權歸誰, *Zhonghua dushubao* 中華讀書報, Aug 8, 2001, http://www.gmw.cn/01ds/2001-08/08/01-A7E88FC845B3493E48256AA2000546E5.htm.

4. Chen Sihe, "Women de chouti," 75.

5. I borrow this phrase from an actual museum in Romania, the former site of Sighet prison, which incarcerated political prisoners under communism. See http://romaniatourism.com/sighetu-marmatiei.html.

6. Chen Sihe, "Women de chouti," 68–69.

7. For a concise overview of Nie's biography and oeuvre in English, see Xiaofei Tian, "Muffled Dialect Spoken by Green Fruit: An Alternative History of Modern Chinese Poetry," *Modern Chinese Literature and Culture* 21.1 (Spring 2009), 1–45.

8. Victor Shaw, *Social Control in China: A Study of Chinese Work Units* (Westport, CT: Greenwood Publishing Group, 1996), 72–83.

9. Zhengyuan Fu, *Autocratic Tradition and Chinese Politics* (Cambridge: Cambridge University Press, 1993), 225.

10. Yu Zhen 寓真, *Nie Gannu xingshi dang'an* 聶紺弩刑事檔案 [Nie Gannu's case files], *Zhongguo Zuojia* 中國作家 [Chinese writers] 4 (2009): 56.

11. Yu Zhen, *Nie Gannu xingshi dang'an*, 5.

12. Yu Zhen, *Nie Gannu xingshi dang'an*, 15.

13. Yu Zhen, *Nie Gannu xingshi dang'an*, 15.

14. Yu Zhen, *Nie Gannu xingshi dang'an*, 16.

15. Zhang Yihe 章詒和, "Shui ba Nie Gannu song jin le jianyu?" 誰把聶紺弩送進了監獄? [Who sent Nie Gannu to jail?], *Nanfang zhoumou* 南方週末 [Southern weekend], March 18, 2009.

16. Zhang Yihe, *Wangshi bingbu ruyan* 往事并不如烟 [The past is not like smoke] (Beijing: Renmin wenxue chubanshe, 2004), 245.

17. Jacques Derrida, *Of Grammatology* (Baltimore: Johns Hopkins University Press, 1976), 92.

18. Michel Foucault, "Life of Infamous Men," in *Michel Foucault: Power, Truth, Strategy*, ed. Meagham Morris and Paul Patton (Sydney: Feral Publications, 1979), 84.

19. Catherine Gallagher and Stephen Greenblatt, *Practicing New Historicism* (Chicago: University of Chicago Press, 2000), 10.

20. Nie Gannu, "Houji" 後記 [Afterword], in *Nie Gannu shi quanbian* 聶紺弩诗全编 [The complete poems of Nie Gannu] (Shanghai: Xuelin chubanshe, 1992), 163.

21. Nie Gannu, *Nie Gannu quanji* 聶紺弩全集 [The complete works of Nie Gannu], Vol. 10: *Yundong dang'an* 運動檔案 [Campaign files] (Wuhan: Wuhan chubanshe, 2004), 39.

22. Nie Gannu, *Yundong dang'an*, 43.

23. *Nie Gannu shi quanbian*, 8.

24. Quoted in Cristina Vatulescu, *Police Aesthetics: Literature, Film, and the Secret Police Archives in Eastern Europe* (Stanford: Stanford University Press, 2010), 65.

25. *Nie Gannu shi quanbian*, 430.

26. Yu Zhen, *Nie Gannu xingshi dang'an*, 18.

27. Martin Huang, *Literati and Self-Re/presentation: Autobiographical Sensibility in the Eighteenth-Century Chinese Novel* (Stanford: Stanford University Press, 1995), 17–18. See also commentaries for *The Complete Poems of Nie Gannu*, 489.

28. Yu Zhen, *Nie Gannu xingshi dang'an*, 12.

29. Shi Zecun's commentary in *Nie Gannu shi quanbian*, 446–449.

30. Wang Xijian's commentary in *Nie Gannu shi quanbian*, 487–489.

31. Tian, "Muffled Dialect Spoken by Green Fruit," 32.

32. Charles Kwong, "The Rural World of Chinese 'Farmstead Poetry' (*Tianyuan Shi*): How Far Is It Pastoral?" *Chinese Literature: Essays, Articles, Reviews (CLEAR)* 15 (December 1993): 57–84.

33. In 1978, Nie (re)collected these poems into a mimeographed book entitled *Zenda cao* 贈答草 [Gift poems].

34. Tian, "Muffled Dialect Spoken by Green Fruit," 20.

35. Yu Zhen, *Nie Gannu xingshi dang'an*, 39.

36. Svetlana Boym, *The Future of Nostalgia* (New York: Basic Books, 2001), 61–62.

37. Stephen Brockmann, *Literature and German Reunification* (Cambridge: Cambridge University Press, 1999), 86–88.

38. Charles Hartman, "Poetry and Politics in 1079: The Crow Terrace Poetry Case of Su Shih," *Chinese Literature: Essays, Articles, Reviews* (1990): 35.

39. Yu Zhen, *Nie Gannu xingshi dang'an*, 77.

40. Yu Zhen, *Nie Gannu xingshi dang'an*, 77.

41. Yu Zhen, *Nie Gannu xingshi dang'an*, 78.

42. Ming Dong Gu, "Literary Openness: A Bridge Across the Divide Between Chinese and Western Literary Thought," *Comparative Literature* 55.2 (Spring 2003): 126.

43. Longxi Zhang, *Allegoresis: Reading Canonical Literature East and West* (Ithaca: Cornell University Press, 2005), 61.

44. Yu Zhen, 13. The golden tattoo is the mark of the convict, but it is also what the heroes bear on their faces in *The Water Margin*, one of Mao Zedong's favorite classical novels. It was considered a glorification of rebellion/revolution except during the Cultural Revolution, when it was criticized for its ending, where all rebels submit to "pacification" (招安). Nie's poem may be read as counterrevolutionary because the power that brands the hero's face can be interpreted as the CCP. "White Tiger Hall" is where the enemies of hero Lin Chong set the trap for him, and the line could mean that Lin Chong/Nie Gannu comes to the trap unaware of the consequences, or alternatively it could mean that he actually knows the dire consequences but is willing to brave them.

45. Here Nie Gannu refers to those who have written books only for themselves with little expectation of being understood since the days of the First Emperor, who was famous for burning books and burying Confucian scholars.

46. The first three lines allude to *Mencius*, Book IV, Part B: "When all trace of the sage emperors had vanished, the *Songs* were no longer gathered from the people. After they stopped gathering the *Songs*, the *Spring and Autumn* was written" (王者之跡息而詩亡, 詩亡而後春秋作). Translation from David Hinton, *Mencius* (Washington, DC: Counterpoint, 1998), 147.

47. The two characters 釜甑 (*fuzeng*) mean "iron cauldron and earthenware pot," which are ancient cooking implements.

48. *Dou* and *niu* are names of asterisms. The poem can be found in Yu Zhen, 24.

49. The remainder of the line echoes Su Shi's famous poem "Brooding on Former Experiences at Mianchi" 和子由澠池懷舊, which opens with the line: "Do you know what it's like?—human life everywhere?" (人生到處知何似). This is followed by the metaphor of the traces left in the snow by a wild goose and the image of erased writing and lost poetry: "The old monk has died; a new pagoda is made; On his cell's fallen walls we've

no way to see poems written there long ago" (老僧已死成新塔/壞壁無由見舊題). See Stephen Owen, *Traditional Chinese Poetry and Poetics: Omen of the World* (Madison, University of Wisconsin Press, 1985), 131.

50. Yu Zhen, *Nie Gannu xingshi dang'an*, 11.
51. Yu Zhen, "Nie Gannu de liangye qiyi shigao" 聶紺弩的兩頁奇異詩稿 [Two extraordinary poetic manuscripts of Nie Gannu], *Zhonghua dushu bao* 中華讀書報, May 16, 2007.
52. Zhang Guangcai is a character from the Ming play *Pipa ji* 琵琶記 [Lute], an old neighbor who helps the female protagonist Zhao Wuniang to go look for her husband in the capital. Their dialogue before her departure is a famous episode in Peking opera.
53. Cristina Vatulescu, "Arresting Biographies: The Secret Police File in the Soviet Union and Romania," *Comparative Literature* 56.3 (Summer 2004): 250.
54. Yu Zhen, *Nie Gannu xingshi dang'an*, 13.
55. Li Shiqiang 李世强, "Jiadai shigao chuyu" 夾帶詩稿出獄 [Smuggling poetry drafts out of prison], in *Nie Gannu shi quanbian*, 597–599.
56. Li, "Jiadai shigao chuyu," 597–599.
57. Yu Zhen, *Nie Gannu xingshi dang'an*, 11.
58. In those years he also wrote many memorial poems and elegies for friends who had passed away or who were broken in spirit. An elegiac poem, a text of remembrance, often requires biographical context for proper decoding, so that the poem serves as a cue for memories by acquaintances as well as strangers, thus joining personal and public memory.
59. Andrei Pleşu, "Intellectual Life Under Dictatorship," *Representations* 49 (Winter 1995): 63.
60. Nie Gannu. "Jianyu yu wenren de Gutou," 6; and Nie Gannu, "Huai jianyu" 懷監獄 [Prison nostalgia] in *Nie Gannu zixu* 聶紺弩自序 [Autobiographical accounts by Nie Gannu] (Beijing: Tuanjie chubanshe, 1998), 490–499.
61. Pleşu, "Intellectual Life Under Dictatorship," 63–64.
62. Pleşu, "Intellectual Life Under Dictatorship," 63.
63. Nie, "Huai jianyu," 499.
64. *Nie Gannu shi quanbian*, 164–165.
65. Nie, "Letter to Shu Wu," August 15, 1984, in *Nie Gannu shi quanji*, 422–423. The criticism refers to the fact that Wu Weiye, instead of remaining a Ming loyalist, took office for almost two years under the Qing.
66. Elai was an evil minister at the court of the tyrant Zhou in the Shang dynasty.
67. See *Nie Gannu shi quanji*, 219. The original poem written for Hu Feng in 1966 can be found on 267. Nie also repeated the same line for himself in a poem titled "Zichao" 自嘲 [Self-mockery], 194.
68. *Nie Gannu shi quanbian*, 418–419.

Works Cited

Boym, Svetlana. *The Future of Nostalgia*. New York: Basic Books, 2001.

Brockmann, Stephen. *Literature and German Reunification*. Cambridge: Cambridge University Press, 1999.

Chen Sihe 陳思和. "Women de chouti: Shi lun dangdai wenxue shi (1949–1976) de 'qianzai xiezuo'" 我們的抽屜：試論當代文學史 (1949–1976) 的潛在寫作 [Our drawer: On invisible writing in contemporary literary history (1949–1976)]. In *Zhongguo dangdai wenxue guanjianci shijiang* 中國當代文學關鍵詞十講 [Contemporary Chinese literature in ten keywords]. Shanghai: Fudan daxue, 2002. 65–92.

Derrida, Jacques. *Of Grammatology*. Baltimore: Johns Hopkins University Press, 1976.

Foucault, Michel. "Life of Infamous Men." *Michel Foucault: Power, Truth, Strategy*. Ed. Meagham Morris and Paul Patton. Sydney: Feral Publications, 1979.

Fu, Zhengyuan. *Autocratic Tradition and Chinese Politics*. Cambridge: Cambridge University Press, 1993.

Gallagher, Catherine, and Stephen Greenblatt. *Practicing New Historicism*. Chicago: University of Chicago Press, 2000.

Gu, Ming Dong. "Literary Openness: A Bridge Across the Divide Between Chinese and Western Literary Thought." *Comparative Literature* 55.2 (Spring 2003): 112–129.

Hartman, Charles. "Poetry and Politics in 1079: The Crow Terrace Poetry Case of Su Shih." *Chinese Literature: Essays, Articles, Reviews (CLEAR)* 12 (December 1990): 15–44.

Huang, Martin. *Literati and Self-Re/presentation: Autobiographical Sensibility in the Eighteenth-Century Chinese Novel*. Stanford: Stanford University Press, 1995.

Kwong, Charles. "The Rural World of Chinese 'Farmstead Poetry' (*Tianyuan Shi*): How Far Is It Pastoral?" *Chinese Literature: Essays, Articles, Reviews (CLEAR)* 15 (December 1993): 57–84.

Nie Gannu. *Nie Gannu Shi Quanbian* 聶紺弩詩全編 [The complete poems of Nie Gannu]. Shanghai: Xuelin chubanshe, 1992.

Nie Gannu. *Nie Gannu quanji* 聶紺弩全集 [The complete works of Nie Gannu], Vol. 10: *Yundong dang'an* 運動檔案 [Campaign files]. Wuhan: Wuhan chubanshe, 2004.

Nie Gannu. *Nie Gannu zixu* 聶紺弩自序 [Autobiographical accounts by Nie Gannu]. Beijing: Tuanjie chubanshe, 1998.

Nie Gannu 聶紺弩. "Jianyu yu wenren de gutou: Nie Gannu zhi Shuwu de xin." 監獄與文人的骨頭：聶紺弩致舒蕪的信 [The prison and our bone: A letter from Nie Gannu to Shuwu], *Zawen xuankan* 雜文選刊 [Selections of miscellaneous essays] 6 (2010): 61.

Owen, Stephen. *Traditional Chinese Poetry and Poetics: Omen of the World*. Madison: University of Wisconsin Press, 1985.

Pleşu, Andrei. "Intellectual Life Under Dictatorship." *Representations* 49 (Winter 1995): 61–71.

Shaw, Victor. *Social Control in China: A Study of Chinese Work Units*. Westport, CT: Greenwood Publishing Group, 1996.

Tian, Xiaofei. "Muffled Dialect Spoken by Green Fruit: An Alternative History of Modern Chinese Poetry." *Modern Chinese Literature and Culture* 21.1 (Spring 2009): 1–45.

Vatulescu, Cristina. "Arresting Biographies: The Secret Police File in the Soviet Union and Romania." *Comparative Literature* 56.3 (Summer 2004): 243–261.

Vatulescu, Cristina. *Police Aesthetics: Literature, Film, and the Secret Police Archives in Eastern Europe*. Stanford: Stanford University Press, 2010.

Yu Zhen 寓真. *Nie Gannu xingshi dang'an* 聶紺弩刑事檔案 [Nie Gannu's case files], *Zhongguo Zuojia* 中國作家 [Chinese writers] 4 (2009): 4–81.

Yu Zhen 寓真. "Nie Gannu de liangye qiyi shigao" 聶紺弩的兩頁奇異詩稿 [Two extraordinary poetic manuscripts of Nie Gannu]. *Zhonghua dushu bao* 中華讀書報, May 16, 2007.

Zhang, Longxi. *Allegoresis: Reading Canonical Literature East and West*. Ithaca: Cornell University Press, 2005.

Zhang Yihe 章詒和. "Shui ba Nie Gannu song jin le jianyu?" 誰把聶紺弩送進了監獄? [Who sent Nie Gannu to jail?]. *Nanfang Zhoumou* 南方週末 [Southern weekend], March 18, 2009.

Zhang Yihe 章詒和. *Wangshi bingbu ruyan* 往事并不如烟 [The past is not like smoke]. Beijing: Renmin wenxue, 2004.

A DREAM OF RETURNING TO 1997

The Phenomenology of Chinese Web Fantasy Literature

JUNNING FU

THE Chinese web fantasy novel *A Dream of Returning to 1997* (夢回九七; hereafter *Dream*) was created and serialized between 2004 and 2005 by an author writing under the pseudonym Tonglingzhe 通靈者 on the web fantasy literature platform Qidian (起點).[1] It tells how the protagonist Yang Fan, an underdog figure, travels back in time from 2004 to 1997 and succeeds in founding a company named Qidian that specializes in serializing and publishing fantasy literature online. Through a series of fruitful business operations, Qidian becomes a gigantic entertainment empire, and toward the end of the novel readers are told that "in 2025 the Qidian Group dominated, on a global scale, publishing, cinema and most of the entertainment and culture industries."[2] In fact, by 2026 the Qidian Group had become the second-largest economic entity in the world, second only to China itself.

What's the reason for Qidian's marvelous success? Apart from the fascinating cultural commodities Qidian offers, it is the increase of consumers' investment in the entertainment industry (which further reflects the increase of global GDP and the improvement of people's livelihood), which contributed to Qidian's exponential expansion. However, as the narrator reminds us, it is important to notice that the development of this corporation, especially its exponential increase around 2019–2020, had a great deal to do with the poverty alleviation program it had launched in China years earlier, as a result of which the entire nation became rich and spent more and more time and money on the culture industry. Around this period, piracy—supposedly a predicament for the healthy development of creative industries—was eradicated. With Qidian's pioneering role in economic development, China's GDP had already surpassed that of the United States in 2018, and had since then enjoyed the status of the world's largest economic entity. Moreover, starting from 2025, Qidian's poverty alleviation pro-gram also extended to regions beyond China.

Dream belongs to the genre of what I call "Chinese web fantasy literature" (CWFL). This genre emerged in the late 1990s with certain online platforms as its primary medium of dissemination, and Qidian has been a leading figure in this industry, having spear-headed the successful commercialization of CWFL in 2003.[3] Moreover, such literature always contains a fantasy or imaginary narrative that accommodates readers' desire for self-fulfillment. For instance, most narratives feature a young protagonist who ascends to a godlike position. In the case of *Dream*, the protagonist Yang Fan transforms himself from an underdog figure to one of the most successful writers and businessmen in the world.

Dream offers a self-referential commentary on the genre itself. Not only was the novel serialized on the web fantasy literature platform Qidian, it also comments on a fictionalized version of the platform itself. Moreover, apart from fictionalizing the his-tory of this genre and the company that runs its major platform, the novel also projects an imaginary figure of the genre and the company into the future—speculating on how CWFL as a commercial institution might ultimately subsume other sectors of the cul-tural industry, and how the cultural industry might reconstitute itself as the condition of possibility of the economic realm itself, thus becoming a self-generating and auto-poietic figure as well. In other words, the novel is characterized by at least two levels of self-referentiality. On one hand, there is a referential relationship between the fictional work and the historical reality within which it is embedded. On the other hand, the two protagonists (Yang Fan and the company he launches) reconstitute themselves as self-referential figures that are both the origin and the end of history.

This chapter will read *Dream* through this twofold self-referentiality. It will trace the process of self-generation toward the absolute while reflecting on the gap between the fictional and the historical, and will argue that not only does *Dream* imagine a totalizing and absolute image of CWFL and its agent Qidian, in real life Qidian has also been pursuing its own version of commercial totalization. Both the novel and real life feature an elision of apparent binary oppositions between original and copy and between high literature and popular culture. I will argue that both in fiction and in reality CWFL and its commercial agent exhibit a reified history of capitalist modernity. To start my inquiry, let me begin with the question: why time travel? Why is time travel indispensable in a journey toward the absolute? What kind of constitutive relation does time-travel hold with regard to history? And why is the novel structured as a dream of traveling back in time, rather than forward?

RESTARTING A JOURNEY TOWARD THE "ABSOLUTE"

Dream opens with an episode in which a mediocre college graduate called Yang Fan travels back in time from 2004 to 1997. He retains his original memories, however, so that there is a seven-year gap between his rejuvenated body and his more experienced mind. It therefore occurs to Yang Fan that he might be able to find a way of capitalizing on his knowledge of the future in order to make a profit in the past to which he has now returned. The problem, however, is that he discovers he did not acquire much specialized knowledge on which he would be able to profit, and furthermore what knowledge he does have (for instance, of the outcomes of major sporting events, on which he could place bets) is not completely reliable, since it turns out that the events do not unfold precisely the same way as they did the first time around. He therefore feels that he has gained little advantage from having returned from the future, and begins to regret having wasted so much time reading web fantasy novels instead of studying. It then occurs to him, however, that he could use his interest in web fantasy fiction to his advantage by rewriting from memory novels that he had previously read in the "future," and serializing them for profit.

Moreover, Yang Fan proceeds to lay the foundation for China's web fantasy literature industry by creating the online platform Qidian before its original founders have a chance to do so. This platform and its parent company later play a key role in driving the commodification of web fantasy literature, and eventually Yang's business comes to include online gaming, publishing, cinema, and general entertainment, as Qidian becomes the most successful corporation in the world.

This brief summary illustrates the ambiguous and complicated status of Chinese web fantasy literature in the narrative. On one hand, Chinese web fantasy literature is presented as not only an object but also a cause of desire that shapes Yang Fan and other readers into desiring subjects. On the other hand, it is also retrospectively constituted as an abject figure that should have been expelled, since it had negatively affected Yang's movement up the social ladder in his previous life.[4] This contradiction—which is not an uncommon one for consumers who indulge in their beloved mass culture at the expense of their social success—is ultimately resolved by Yang's venture into the web fantasy literature industry.

Furthermore, if we reflect upon the fact that *Dream* is itself a web fantasy novel, the secret of Chinese web fantasy literature and the specificity of the aforementioned contradiction are revealed: what Chinese web fantasy literature fans such as Yang Fan consume is a vicarious enjoyment of social upward mobility, and ironically their habits of consumption can actually jeopardize their upward mobility in the social real.[5] As a metanarrative reflecting on Chinese web fantasy literature itself, *Dream* offers a symbolic solution to this apparent contradiction by imaginatively equating the practices of consumption with those of self-valorization.

At first glance, this sort of time-travel narrative exhibits a compensation effect: people arrive at a certain historical point, but when they look back, the mistakes they may have made or the historical trauma they may have encountered have not yet been successfully internalized, so that there is no possible reconciliation with the past. A fantasy novel with an underdog-like protagonist, traveling back in time and rearticulating his or her desire from an omniscient perspective, fulfills their fantasy of successfully coming to terms with this past. In this regard, a Chinese web fantasy novel such as *Dream* offers and promises an imaginary world of potential fullness and omnipotence in the future by returning to and recommencing from the past. On the other hand, by highlighting and capitalizing on the temporal difference between the future (from which the protagonist travels back) and the past (to which he returns), this time-travel genre, instead of just compensating for a historical loss, at the same time produces this same loss and makes it palpable. The awareness of loss, in other words, may be contemporaneous with the satisfaction that a compensational narrative offers.

What is effectively foreclosed in this process is history itself—which is to say, history as a process of heterogeneous becoming and as a traumatic encounter with the real.[6] An imaginary narrative of fullness and absoluteness like *Dream* embeds within itself a linear temporality of teleological progress and wish-fulfillment. Moreover, the relation between the "future" and the "past" is one of surplus value production that flattens history and reifies a process of historical becoming: It reduces singularity—difference-in-itself—into a difference between two value systems, and by capitalizing on this flattened difference a time traveler can produce surplus value.

How about the Qidian company in reality? Does it also attain a godlike and absolute status? While the pseudonymous author of *Dream*, Tonglingzhe, was imagining the Qidian group as an entertainment empire, Qidian itself had already been purchased by a Chinese online gaming company called SNDA (盛大) in October 2004, two months before the serialization of *Dream* began.[7] This does not undercut Tonglingzhe's fantasy, but rather reinforces his vision of the integration of web fantasy literature and other forms of entertainment: instead of being a single isolated culture form, CWFL is interwoven with other popular culture commodities, and together they form a capital machine that produces universal exchange value. In fact, several aspects of Tonglingzhe's vision came to pass within a decade of the completion of his novel. The company itself describes how "a complete commercial chain is formed through a cooperation between China's online gaming companies, film and television companies, and publishing houses: numerous excellent works on qidian.com have been successfully adapted into online games, films, TV series and dramas, and published offline."[8] In other words, commoditized and institutionalized CWFL plays an increasingly important role in producing narratives that may be reinvested into other cultural forms.

As a result, although the Qidian group in reality has not attained global business hegemony, its general trajectory mirrors that which is featured in the fictional plot of *Dream*, in that it reflects a tendency toward self-expansion and self-generation culminating in an absolute ideal. Such a totalizing gesture inevitably entails a tendency to unify binary dichotomies. In the next section, I will consider the binaries of original and copy and of high literature and popular culture as they are reflected in the story, and will argue that, despite its impulse to unify and totalize these binaries, *Dream* as a narrative totality consists of a number of gaps that can never be successfully reconciled within the narrative itself. I will also examine how Qidian and its parent company SNDA wrestle with these binaries institutionally and commercially.

UNITY OF OPPOSITES

One novel that Yang Fan writes after having returned to the past is inspired by a Japanese novel and manga titled *Full Metal Panic!* (フルメタル・パニック!), which he had read in the "future." Though taking inspiration from the original Japanese work, Yang reinvents the narrative in an anti-Japanese nationalist tone. In particular, while in the original work a Chinese character served as the embodiment of ultimate evil, in his recreation Yang Fan assigns this role to a Japanese figure. A Japanese pop culture company is uncannily charmed by his version of the story and offers to purchase the rights for a Japanese edition. The Japanese (re)adaptation, however, would obviously need to modify Yang's anti-Japanese nationalist narrative.

As Yang is engaged in these negotiations, his girlfriend Cao Linfang is diagnosed with an illness involving her hematopoietic stem cells and needs a bone marrow transplant to survive. Yang proceeds to mobilize his social and financial resources to assist her, but finds that he still faces a significant financial shortfall. The Japanese company's timely offer would solve his financial predicament and enable him to save Cao's life, and he therefore accepts—but only on the condition that no modification be made to his narrative. Unable to accept this condition, the Japanese company raises its bid several times, but ultimately fails to persuade Yang to change his mind. Yang offers an allegory to explain his reasoning, suggesting that if his mother and wife both were to fall into the sea and he were only able to save one of them, he would choose to rescue his mother and sink to death together with his wife.

This thematization of Cao's autoimmune disease brings together issues of literary originality, monetary exchange, national politics, corporeal illness, and romantic love, and specifically underscores the novel's negotiation of originality and derivation. A hematopoietic stem cell is not only capable of self-renewal but also may produce many different kinds of cells, and Yang Fan may be compared to such a cell insofar as he is transplanted back in time to reproduce himself while also generating a new global cultural industry. Actually, Yang has been "plagiarizing" other texts since his jump back in time, but the ethnonational politics implicit in this particular case of cultural borrowing (from the Japanese text) underscores particularly clearly the derivative nature of his literary practice.

Ultimately, it is Yang who is found to have a problem with his figurative bone marrow (lack of literary originality) that cannot be easily solved by a figurative hematopoietic stem cell transplantation (copying and depending on external originals), since this would further highlight his inability to create. In the narrative, Yang's and Cao's predicament is resolved with the assistance of Yang's friends and readers, who help with fundraising, publicity, and the search for a suitable donor. From that point on, Yang starts to write creatively on his own using refined literary techniques, and consequently can no longer be categorized as merely a popular author. It is at this point that the narrative contradiction between the original and the copy is partially displaced onto the confrontation between popular culture and high literature.

Yang's enterprise of plagiaristic literary production not only emblematizes the aporia of the original and copy but also underscores the fact that *Dream* offers a metacommentary on the production of surplus value and the accumulation of capital. Yang travels back in time and turns himself into an entrepreneur by utilizing his knowledge of the CWFL enterprise in the "future." When Yang Fan returns to 1997, he reproduces a body of web fantasy literature that enables him to accumulate his first reserve of capital. Moreover, this production of surplus value conditioned by the disequilibrium between two worlds bridged by time travel often generates considerable pleasure for its readers. In other words, this production of surplus value coincides with the generation of surplus pleasure, and by means of such a narrative schema a novel like *Dream* is able to attract readers and sustain itself economically.

At least two levels of capital accumulation are foregrounded here: on the level of content, the protagonist's time travel capitalizes on "future" literature and creates a self-sustaining cultural empire, while on the level of the work itself, the supplementary fantasy force of time travel has been internalized to sustain the work economically and to extract surplus value. As a result, instead of using time travel to explore alternate historical trajectories, the novel instead uses time travel to generate surplus value.

In reality, web fantasy literature has always been haunted by a different version of the problem of the original and the copy, namely the commercial conflict between the original and pirated copies. In general, readers of web fantasy fiction can only access a finite number of chapters of a novel for free, and must then pay in order to continue reading. Usually web fantasy literature writers update their work on a daily basis, since their income largely depends on the number of words they produce and the number of readers who purchase. In Qidian, registered users can purchase at a rate of 0.02 to 0.03 RMB per thousand words. In addition to direct consumption, web writers can obtain extra income by participating in various competitions organized by Qidian. Those competitions are generally judged on the basis of fan support, and writers have to negotiate with and mobilize their readers to vote. For instance, there is a monthly popularity contest among web fantasy novels, and winners benefit from the commercial and advertising visibility their novels acquire from being listed on the front page.

All these venues of income are menaced by the threat of piracy, so it is no wonder that at the end of *Dream* the possibility of a piracy-free world is celebrated. There are currently numerous piracy websites reproducing novels from commercialized platforms such as Qidian, Zhongheng, and Chuangshi.[9] Readers who are not willing to pay to read are able to access their beloved novels through those piracy websites, though they are subjected to popups and other advertisements. Those piracy websites are always in danger of being closed down, but they can never be completely eradicated. One special case is that of Baidu Tieba, a fan-based bbs founded by the giant search engine company Baidu. Readers can create a *tieba* for a specific theme, such as a popular idol, a novel, a philosopher, or an online game. People with similar interests will gather at a particular *tieba* to post, share, discuss online literature, and thereby form fan communities. As one of the most popular piracy websites for CWFL, Baidu Tieba affords free and easy access to basically all the popular web fantasy novels. One of the most popular web fantasy novels, *Zhetian* (遮天), has gathered more than two million registered fans at its *tieba*.[10] It seems that there is less an antagonism than a symbiosis between those CWFL platforms and Baidu Tieba, since the latter reciprocally contributes to the former's evolving fan culture.

Eventually, Yang Fan's refined style and use of literary motifs make it impossible to pigeonhole him as merely a writer of web fantasy literature. It is at this moment that the textual dialectics of the original and copy are displaced onto a confrontation between popular culture and high literature. In fact, the antagonism between CWFL and the literary establishment plays a major role in *Dream*'s narrative. People who support high literature in the story make several attempts to suppress the rise of CWFL as a culture form and Qidian as a commercial platform, while Yang Fan often stands up to defend the latter.

When Yang Fan's new work can no longer be categorized as mere fantasy literature, he becomes increasingly influential in literary circles while maintaining a low profile in real life, to the point that many people view him as a normal college student with an interest in fantasy literature. Manipulating this image of our protagonist, the novel introduces an interesting episode where Yang encounters a man called Wang Hai who prefers high literature to fantasy literature. Unaware of Yang's concealed identity, Wang belittles fantasy literature and Yang Fan himself, whom he views as a fan of this inferior cultural form. This struggle is mediated through the gaze of both parties' friends, many of whom are aware of Yang Fan's status as an important writer with a refined literary style. After being informed of Yang's other identity, Wang is deeply embarrassed.

From this episode we can abstract what I consider as another major generic feature of CWFL, which is that the protagonist or hero in a Chinese web fantasy novel is constantly dragged into existential struggles with a villain figure who underestimates the power of the former. These struggles are often mediated through the gaze of a third party and invariably conclude with the victory of the protagonist, who finally reveals his true identity or actualizes his hidden power. For instance, Yang Fan's identity before his temporal dislocation is that of merely a fan of web fantasy literature, but this subaltern identity functions as a return of the repressed—the reemergence of a repressed identity whose desire is always rejected. Consequently, while a Chinese web fantasy novel always caters to the fantasy of individual triumph (or the desire to be god, to be being-in-itself-for-itself, as Jean Paul Sartre might put it), at the same time it often produces a protagonist who appears to be free of desire or whose desire is foreclosed by maintaining a subaltern image. In fact, it is by constantly producing this subaltern or inferior image (the image the protagonist performs and the image his rivals misrecognize) that this desire of becoming god will be able to reproduce and reassert itself.

Later, when Yang Fan is humiliated by his antagonist, the persistence of this subaltern image signals that it is not only his desire that is foreclosed; actually, he himself desires external renunciation, which is essentially a desire for symbolic death. However, after the reversal during which Yang Fan undergoes a symbolic resuscitation by disclosing his other identity, we are invited to understand that the maintenance of a subaltern or inferior image serves as a seductive trap: the momentary identification with this image is only intended to induce an attack against which one is justified in reaffirming one's own superior identity (against that subaltern image, but also against the villain). Moreover, the spectating third party, in Yang Fan's case, serves two purposes. On one hand, some of the spectators are aware of Yang's other identity and are able to inform Wang Hai, thereby exempting Yang Fan from any need to announce himself. On the other hand, those spectators, especially those who are initially not aware of Yang's other identity, succeed in suturing the whole symbolic order by affirming that Yang's other identity is really desirable.

Suffice it to say that the ethical code implicated in a Chinese web fantasy novel is fundamentally ambiguous. The modest protagonist who maintains a harmless and even subaltern image appears to be an embodiment of good, while the aggressive and pretentious opponent appears to be an embodiment of evil; and yet, due to the fact that the provocative act initiated by a villain figure justifies the protagonist's ensuing act of disclosure of his much more respected identity, we may argue that this bullying villain is at the same time a helper or donor (to use the codes developed by Vladimir Propp in his study of folklore) who creates opportunities for our protagonist's self-staging.[11] Or we could even argue that the villain who never gives up on his desire is the embodiment of good, while the calculating protagonist who somehow sets up a delicate trap is an embodiment of evil.

Moreover, if we consider what is profaned during the encounter between the two figures, it is none other than the subaltern image with which the protagonist temporarily identifies. The protagonist's projective identification with this image is proven to be a strategic seduction during which the surplus value of this image is exploited. As a result, the passionate affinity manifested in this act of identification ironically turns out to be a betrayal. In the example considered above, it is CWFL itself that has been exploited, as it undergoes an uncanny transformation from an object cause of desire to an abject figure. However, the repetition of this plot throughout the story also reveals the untenability of the protagonist's new and hegemonic symbolic position or identity. More specifically, the repetitive (re)articulation of this hegemonic identity against a subaltern image or inferior figure not only reveals the contingency and fragility of this symbolic order itself, it also constantly revives or revitalizes this inferior figure as a haunting specter that one can never do away with. In other words, the mutually constitutive relationship between popular culture and high literature renders it impossible for one to exist without the other.

At one point, Yang Fan is called upon to mediate the strife between fantasy literature and the literary establishment, wherein it appears that CWFL still has a sense of inferiority with respect to the literary establishment. Ironically, it is only by distancing himself from CWFL that Yang Fan is able to acquire the legitimacy and cultural capital with which he might publically defend CWFL. However, at the end of *Dream* this antagonism is superseded, and while some readers might lament the fact that Yang Fan has not won the Nobel Prize for Literature, by this point the global status of the Nobel Prize for Literature has already been supplanted by the Qidian Fantasy Literature Award, which Yang proceeds to win three times.

Here we find a reunion between Yang Fan and CWFL, and this identity is predicated upon the fact that the power relation between the literary establishment (represented by the Nobel Prize) and popular culture (represented by CWFL) is reversed: while the Nobel Prize represents high literariness, literariness is no longer the benchmark against which a literary work is measured. What, then, is the new benchmark? The final paragraph of *Dream* provides an intriguing answer in its suggestion that "many people think it is precisely because Yang has not won the Nobel Literature Prize that we can claim him as successful. He does not aim at great literariness. He rejects inscrutable language or profound lessons. He is always oriented toward entertainment and manages to make everyone happy. This is the Way (Dao 道) of Qidian's success."[12]

In its commercial operation in the real world, Qidian attempted to resolve this antagonism by creating a subsite called Qidian Literature (起點文學) in November 2010, to feature more "realistic" and less "fantastic" works that are presented as being of greater literary quality.[13] This gesture of absorbing the literary establishment into itself uncannily rehearses what is imagined in *Dream*, wherein a gap is introduced between CWFL and Qidian that enables the latter to mediate between the literary establishment and CWFL. On the other hand, this gesture of commercial and categorical expansion simultaneously redefines and complicates our understanding of what CWFL is.

In addition to its ambiguous attitude toward piracy/plagiarism and high culture, *Dream* embodies an anxiety with regard to gender and sexual difference. For example, *Dream* apparently assumes its primary readership will be heterosexual men, and features narratives that they will tend to favor. For instance, a key plotline involves a love triangle between Yang Fan and two young women, which may be regarded as a common male fantasy. The seemingly narrow way in which the novel imagines its presumptive readership, however, might appear to be at odds with the narrative's own focus on the possibility of creating an all-encompassing entertainment empire.

In fact, the narrative of *Dream* appears to recognize the work's androcentrism, and how this might push away certain readers, particularly women. For example, after exposing his identity as a popular writer to his friend Zhao Fengping, Yang Fan warns Zhao that he should never tell anyone Yang's hidden identity. Yang is particularly concerned with the fact that his friend Chen Qianqian (who, together with Cao Linfang, will become Yang's life partner as the story unfolds) once expressed her disgust with his novel (without knowing he was actually the author). Similarly, when Yang's Chinese literature professor Miss Liu reads Yang's novel online (without knowing Yang is the author), she too initially finds it repulsive. But the novel's appeal quickly wins her over, and it turns out that she has always aspired to be a writer but was stymied by a lack of imagination. Another episode concerns how one of Yang Fan's female friends responds to his novel (again without knowing it is actually his), in that she cannot accept how the novel demeans female characters, but if she manages to overlook this aspect she finds that the work's description of a protagonist ascending to a godlike position is actually quite appealing. As a result, by folding back upon itself, *Dream* complicates the apparent androcentric tendencies of the narrative and the genre as a whole and imagines an inclusive reading community.

This narrative strategy of complicating gender binaries emblematizes the novel's broader attempts to construct a totalizing image of CWFL. In reality, novels such as *Dream* are confronted with competing narratives with regard to the imagination of gender and sexual difference. There is a flourishing culture industry featuring the production of online romantic stories—typically either a heterosexual romance featuring a female protagonist or a homoerotic narrative featuring two men. It is important to note, though, that many of those narrative features of CWFL, such as a young protagonist who ascends to a godlike position, are not incompatible with other novels belonging to the romantic genre. With regard to this emerging industry and presumably a large female readership, not only did Qidian create a new "Girls' Channel," its parent company SNDA also pursued a business acquisition to incorporate these profitable web literature sectors. In other words, while *Dream* attempts to accommodate and wrestle with incommensurable gender and sexual difference within the narrative, the Qidian company sets out to achieve a similar task by internalizing other genres—targeting and thus gendering a specific group of readers—into itself.

Coda

Though I read *Dream* as a commentary on the production of surplus value, it is undeniable that *Dream* also embeds within itself a utopian impulse, as its ending illustrates. Throughout the novel, the enterprise Qidian undergoes a process of becoming universal, such that it not only becomes a hegemonic cultural industry and global business empire but also radically alters the global economic condition at the end. According to the story, the Qidian Group helps to alleviate poverty and boost economic development. As a result, more and more people are capable of consuming web fantasy literature, which further leads to the exponential expansion of the Qidian group. Qidian thus becomes the origin of its own future prosperity and destiny. It is a story of capital accumulation as much as a utopian imagination of global well-being.

However, this utopian tale is very questionable. By narrating its maneuver to become its own condition of possibility, *Dream* offers a story of how Chinese web fantasy literature bootstraps itself by positing its presuppositions. Pierre Dardot and Christian Laval, in their book on Marx, describe the logic of capital as that of systematic constraint and turnover. More specifically, capitalism works by positing its own presuppositions, by claiming, for example, that what conditions and enables capitalism is logically always already the product of capitalism.[14] This immanent and autopoietic logic presents capitalism as a circular, enclosed, and self-generating myth. *Dream*'s imagination of a future utopia (is it a form of communism?), instead of being a result of political struggle or emerging from an alternative historical trajectory, reenacts capitalism's logic of positing its own presuppositions.

Having imagined the eradication of web fantasy literature piracy, Yang comes up with the idea that once society improves its economic well-being, all readers will be able to purchase all the literature they desire. At the end of the novel, Yang successfully fulfills this vision, though the question he forgets to ask is whether global readers who enjoy an affluent life will still be able to invest their libidinal energies into a fantasy narrative featuring the story of a young protagonist ascending to a godlike position. Will not the new social and economic conditions shut down the possibility of such a narrative and open a new spectrum of narrative possibilities? This indicates that, while fantasizing about the bright future of web fantasy literature and the arrival of social utopia in and beyond China, *Dream* simultaneously announces the death of the emerging genre to which it belongs.

Notes

I thank Carlos Rojas and Andrea Bachner for their encouragement, patience, and constructive criticism.

1. The novel can be found at http://free.qidian.com/Free/ShowBook.aspx?bookid=21036.
2. Tonglingzhe 通靈者. *Menghui jiu qi* 夢回九七 [A dream of returning to 1997], chap. 143, available at http://free.qidian.com/Free/ReadChapter.aspx?bookid=21036&chapte rid=660328.
3. By commercialization I refer to a sustainable commercial institution through which authors and platforms benefit economically from readers' online purchase and consumption of novels. See Qidian's "About Us," available at http://www.qidian.com/aboutus/aboutus.aspx.
4. Moreover, the fetishistic feature of CWFL is further highlighted by the fact that while after time travel, historical events no longer unfold the same way as before, the fate of CWFL (its popularity and so forth) is not subject to historical contingency. It sustains itself as a reliable source of capitalization despite the uncertainties introduced by time travel.
5. This can be understood as a version of what Lauren Berlant calls "cruel optimism," by which she means the irony of finding that something one desires constitutes an obstacle to one's own flourishing. See Lauren Berlant, *Cruel Optimism* (Durham: Duke University Press, 2011).
6. For history as a traumatic encounter with the real, see Fredric Jameson's "Imaginary and Symbolic in Lacan," in *The Ideologies of Theory* (New York: Verso, 2008), 77–124.
7. www.sdo.com.
8. http://www.qidian.com/aboutus/aboutus.aspx, my translation.
9. Zhongheng.com is a rising CWFL platform founded by an online gaming company in 2008, and Chuangshi.com is a CWFL platform newly created in May 2013, affiliated with Tencent, the biggest instant-message company in China. Ouyang Youquan, in his article on web literature "Review of Hot Issues in Web Literature" (2013), observed that in 2012 there were more than five hundred thousand piracy sites. Available at http://www.frguo.com/Info.aspx?ModelId=1&Id=5578.
10. "Zhetian ba" 遮天吧. Available at http://tieba.baidu.com/f?ie=utf-8&kw= %E9%81%AE% E5%A4%A9.
11. See Vladimir Propp, *Morphology of the Folktale* (Austin: University of Texas Press, 1968), 25–65.

12. Chap. 143, available at http://free.qidian.com/Free/ReadChapter.aspx?bookid=21036&chapterid=660328.
13. See Qidian's "About Us," available at http://www.qidian.com/aboutus/aboutus.aspx.
14. Pierre Dardot and Christian Laval, *Marx, Prénom Karl* (Paris: Gallimard, 2012).

WORKS CITED

"About Us." Qidian.com. Web. May 31, 2015. http://wwwploy.qidian.com/aboutus/aboutus.aspx.

Berlant, Lauren, *Cruel Optimism*. Durham: Duke University Press, 2011.

Dardot, Pierre, and Leval, Christian. *Marx, Prénom Karl*. Paris: Gallimard, 2012.

Jameson, Fredric. *The Ideologies of Theory*. New York: Verso, 2008.

Ouyang, Youquan. "Review of Hot Issues in Web Literature." March 2013 Web. May 31, 2015. http://www.frguo.com/Info.aspx?ModelId=1&Id=5578.

Propp, Vladimir. *Morphology of the Folktale*. Austin: University of Texas Press, 1968.

Tonglingzhe 通靈者. *Menghui jiu qi* 夢回九七 [A dream of returning to 1997]. Qidian.com. 2004–2005. Web. May 31, 2015 http://free.qidian.com/Free/ShowBook.aspx?bookid=21036.

"Zhetian ba" 遮天吧. Baidu.com. Web. May 31, 2015. http://tieba.baidu.com/f?ie=utf-8&kw=%E9%81%AE%E5%A4%A9.

PART II

TAXONOMY

EARLY MODERN COMPARATIVE APPROACHES TO LITERARY EARLY MODERNITY

DAVID PORTER

EARLY on in his pathbreaking novel *The Family* (家; 1931), two of Ba Jin's 巴金 young protagonists evoke, in a brief exchange, a familiar dichotomy that continues to shape our conceptions of Chinese literary history:

> "Our Chinese literature teacher is going to be the man who wrote that article, 'Cannibal Confucian Morality' in the *New Youth* magazine! Isn't that wonderful?"
>
> "You're really lucky," cried Qin, her face flushing with admiration. "We always get old-fashioned scholars for our 'lit' teachers, the kind whose favorite texts are books like *Selected Ancient Chinese Essays*."[1]

The contrast between the modernity of a popular reformist periodical and the obsolescence of a musty anthology of scholarly screeds is taken as being so obvious here as to be hardly worthy of note. And indeed, the idea of the "modern," like every periodizing rubric, derives much of its meaning from its perceived relation to the period it is taken to follow. Depending on one's disciplinary affinities and the breadth of one's historical view, one might quite plausibly define various features of the modern in a British context, for example, in contrast to the genteel artificiality of Victorian poetry, the animal-powered locomotion of the pre-steam era, the divine right of kings prior to the Glorious Revolution, or the experience of human subjectivity prior to Hamlet's oft-vaunted inauguration of modern self-consciousness. In the Chinese context, the modern is generally understood, as in the above example, to mark a considerably more decisive rupture from the past, and a transition spanning not centuries but only the two tumultuous decades encompassing the Boxer Uprising (1899–1901), the fall of the Qing (1911), and the New Culture Movement (1915–1921). In literature in particular, the early twentieth century was dominated by voices seeking to prescribe a course for literary modernity premised on a self-conscious rejection of the dominant conventions of the past with respect to language, style, and subject matter.

As in the British case, however, the precise connotations of this modernity depend on the delineation of the past to which it is opposed. In the most familiar account, inherited directly from the revolutionary rhetoric of May Fourth intellectuals, the past that literary modernity promises to transcend is that of an often undifferentiated Confucian tradition—leaden, stale, and soul-destroying in its rigid adherence to classical diction and feudal convention. The opposition between new- and old-style literary education that Ba Jin sketches in his dialogue is absolute, and one can only hope that the youthful Qin might eventually have replaced *old-fashioned, Confucian,* or *premodern* in her schema with the somewhat more nuanced designations *Qing, Ming-Qing,* or *late imperial,* in order to restore some degree of variegation to her vision of the past and to render the rupture of modernity a more contingent response to a more specific historical situation. And yet even a revised conception of the modern that emerges solely through a contrast with the final century of the Qing remains limited by the same structural dualism that shapes Qin's paradigm of old vs. new. That is to say, even this more nuanced periodization is premised on an assumption, grounded in revolutionary historiography, of thoroughgoing repudiation of the past and an a priori embrace of historical alterity as the fundamental principle underpinning any valid interpretation of China's twentieth-century experience.[2]

A considerable body of scholarship in recent decades has experimented with a still rather unorthodox period designation that, by dislocating this familiar presumption of historical alterity, may offer a fresh vantage point on China's (relatively) recent past. Accounts of the two, three, or four centuries preceding 1800 as constituting China's early modernity are generally concerned first and foremost with challenging, through the elaboration of various resonances and commonalities, the prevailing view that the Chinese historical experience is fundamentally different from that of Europe. Such accounts remind us that the same period is characterized in both contexts by increasing commercial prosperity, imperial expansion, and a flowering of popular fiction in the vernacular. The increasing use of this nomenclature has prompted lively debates over whether such comparisons are valid and whether a period designation that emerged in a European context as a more capacious and cosmopolitan alternative to the traditional Renaissance could ever be appropriately applied to the study of Chinese history. Participants in these debates have generally taken for granted that China's recent modernization has followed a different trajectory than Europe's, and that its impetus cannot be convincingly traced back to developments in the late Ming and early Qing, whatever resemblances such developments might seem to bear to proto-modern developments in contemporary Europe. One crucial question these debates have not taken up, however, and which the present chapter will seek to address, is whether and in what ways the designation of Chinese literature of this period as early modern might usefully refract received perspectives on the category of "modern Chinese literature." The suggestion in what follows will be that even if twentieth-century literary developments in China cannot be said to follow in a linear, let alone teleological, progression from those of the seventeenth or eighteenth century, designating this earlier period as early modern can still provide a useful heuristic for rethinking the relationship of the modern to its pasts in terms less rigidly confined by presumptions of radical alterity.

By referring to the designation *early modern* as a heuristic, I mean to stress its practical utility as an idea to think with, rather than its suitability as an historical descriptor. Failing to maintain this distinction between the provisional and the deterministic leads us too often into sterile terminological disputes. Applying a label to an historical period is, after all, merely a convenient strategy for creating a category under which otherwise disparate historical facts, concepts, and developments might be grouped together and understood more clearly in relation to each other and to knowledge about contiguous periods. While this categorizing function of period names is obviously essential to the business of historical scholarship, as cultural historians we get into trouble when we mistake invented categories for empirical realities and descend into debates over whether or not the early Qing was "early modern," as if "early modernity" were a fixed and determinate characteristic that might be definitively discerned, like steam engines or smallpox inoculation, in some periods and not in others. If we can agree that the purpose of literary history is to generate insightful and compelling narratives about a textual heritage, then we can, perhaps, bracket questions of the suitability of the *early modern* label for a particular moment in China's literary past and ask instead what work it might do for us in our ongoing efforts to reach a fuller understanding of that time.

While the term *early modern* appeared in print as early as 1869 and entered mainstream historical scholarship in the 1940s, it only rose to its current prominence beginning in the 1970s through the work of Natalie Zemon Davis, Peter Burke, and others. In European history, it is generally taken to span roughly the period from the Protestant Reformation in the early sixteenth century through the French Revolution in the late eighteenth. In contrast with the competing term *Renaissance*, which is associated with European cultural phenomena inspired by the reemergence of classical traditions, "early modernity" evokes a more global perspective, in its attention to voyages of discovery and expanding trade networks, as well as a more forward-looking if not teleological one, with its implicit interest in narratives of progress and genealogies of particular hallmarks of modernity.[3]

Both the globalist and progressivist orientations of the early modern rubric have proven attractive, since the early 1980s, to historians of the Ming and Qing dynasties committed to contesting some of the entrenched legacies of early-twentieth-century Sinology. Attending to China's participation in the world systems of transregional trade has helped to complicate the persistent thesis of xenophobic isolationism that long served to buttress accounts of the decisive exceptionalism of Europe's Age of Discovery. And a renewed emphasis on the internal dynamics of historical change in China has dislodged the old Hegelian diagnosis of eternal stasis and the accompanying view of China's modernization in the twentieth century as solely a belated and grudging response to the impact of Western arms and ideas.[4] While the majority of these early revisionist works, perhaps not surprisingly, focused on historical developments in those areas—such as science, economics, and politics—that might be deemed most congenial to the early modern China paradigm, one of the very first major works to introduce the concept, Paul Ropp's *Dissent in Early Modern China:* Ju-lin wai-shih *and Ch'ing Social Criticism,* grounded its analysis in the "strikingly modern" characteristics of a work of eighteenth-century vernacular literature, to which we'll return below.[5]

For Ropp and his successors, the concept of early modern China is fundamentally comparative, in that it is based on the elaboration of features in late-imperial Chinese society that are recognizably modern or proto-modern from the vantage point of European history. The list of similarities and parallels between Europe and China that emerge from this body of scholarship is a long one, including rapid population growth, sustained economic expansion, commercialization, and urbanization. These are seen to contribute to a broad range of superstructural developments including technological innovation, the emergence of new financial institutions, the blurring of class distinctions, the emergence of a public sphere, the commoditization of knowledge, and, in the literary domain, the development of increasingly naturalistic and secular modes of storytelling. Above all, it is perhaps the pervasiveness of a sense of dynamism, of rapid and unsettling change and creative responses to change across a variety of social sectors, that emerges as the most essential common core of the early modern period through these comparisons. Their cumulative effect, in any event, has been to rehabilitate late-imperial Chinese history as a contrastive foil for theories of European modernity, while simultaneously integrating it more fully into emerging narratives of world history.[6]

While this approach has steadily gained currency, it also has its critics, who claim, first, that the term *early modern* introduces a problematic teleology that seems to presume a singular trajectory of modernization and therefore to shift attention yet again from the particularities of the Chinese experience in this period to the puzzle of China's failure to pursue it. If China was arguably early modern at the height of Qing prosperity in the eighteenth century, why did it not turn the corner into full-bore modernization in the nineteenth? And in the absence of this takeoff, it might be added, how can the term *early modern* retain any logical validity? Second, critics argue that while the early modern paradigm is generally allied with a China-centered historiography intended to dislodge the old Eurocentric assumptions concerning Chinese historical stasis and lack, its deployment of what is essentially a European yardstick for assessing degrees of proto-modernity repositions Europe as the definitive standard for comparison and the normative model for the emergence of modernization. Just as it did for Weber, then, European history becomes a master narrative alongside which other national or regional histories invariably come up short. Third, the term *early modern* and the comparisons it invites are often decried as being too broad and therefore reductive. Both early modern China and its European counterpart are rendered, for the sake of an academic exercise, into an undifferentiated mass, obscuring salient differences in the quest to establish basic commensurability, an especially unwelcome result at a moment when the dominant historiographic trends tend to favor the excavation of the local and particular over the delineation of macro-scale generalizations.[7]

For example, Dorothy Ko explicitly distances herself from comparative objectives in the introduction to her influential book *Teachers of the Inner Chambers: Women and Culture in Seventeenth-Century China:*

Many of the social trends and institutions discussed in this book do bear a superficial resemblance to counterparts in early modern Europe: rising female literacy
rates, the emergence of the woman writer, the growing importance of urban readers
and theatergoers as consumers of culture, a general retreat into the private world of
domesticity and sentimentality—to name the more salient examples. These superficial resemblances, however, mask the more substantive differences in social structure, political institutions, and historical dynamics. . . . Without detracting from
the importance of comparative history, I contend that the paucity of our present
knowledge about the nature of social change in seventeenth-century China does not
allow for meaningful comparisons.[8]

Alongside those China scholars who object to the *early modern* rubric for largely
theoretical or methodological reasons are others who are willing to entertain it as
a working hypothesis only to find that it comes up short on empirical grounds. In
important essays published since 2000, On-Cho Ng, Jack Goldstone, and Lynn Struve
each review particular aspects of seventeenth- or eighteenth-century Chinese intellectual history within the broad comparative framework suggested by the concept of a
global early modernity and conclude that the appearance of broad similarities between
the Chinese and European cases breaks down on closer examination. Ng asks whether
Qing thought demonstrates an affinity with European early modernity in marking
a substantial departure from that of the previous period, specifically with respect to
understandings of "the nature of knowledge, the sense of the past, and the claim of the
ultimate ground for ethico-moral values." While he finds evidence of certain resemblances, he maintains that Chinese intellectuals did not face a crisis of authority comparable to that which defined so much of the contemporary European experience, and
that Chinese developments in each of the selected areas did not correspond in any
substantive way with those in contemporary Europe.[9] Jack Goldstone takes this argument one step further in insisting not only on the uniqueness of the Enlightenment's
epistemological crisis, but also on its explanatory force in accounting for Europe's subsequent modernization: "The history of the 'great divergence,' properly understood,
is thus a history built on a great disengagement of the West from the dominance of
its core classical traditions, and the birth of a new model of society . . . . which had no
counterpart outside of Europe."[10] Lynn Struve draws on a remarkable archive of seventeenth-century memoirs to press further on the second of Ng's categories, historical
consciousness, and to ask whether Chinese writers confronted with a rapidly changing
society displayed the awareness of a radical disjuncture with the past characteristic of
so many early modern European textual developments. She finds, in short, that they
did not, and that these memoirs display no "discourse of progress or lack thereof."[11]

All of these critiques, theoretical and empirical, serve as powerful reminders of the
limits on the scalability of historical concepts and the potential dangers of overly facile
comparison. They go a long way, as well, toward explaining why explicitly comparative
macrohistorical work on this period is still relatively rare. Taken together, however,
they do raise the question, suggested by Ko's introduction, of what, exactly, constitutes
meaningful, or valid, or worthwhile comparison. The question is a crucial one here,

given that the majority of scholarship that invokes the idea of early modern China does so with the express or underlying purpose of pointing out resemblances or differences between particular features of pre-twentieth-century Chinese and European societies. Is a comparison meaningful only when the two objects compared are found to be identical? Obviously not. Does it become meaningful, then, only when there is a predominance of similar over dissimilar features? Or does the meaningfulness of a comparison arise, perhaps, not from the qualities of the historical objects being compared as much as from the insight produced by their juxtaposition?

This last possibility returns us to the difference between the denominative and heuristic value of the concept of the early modern introduced above. I would argue that most critiques of the concept's application in the Chinese context principally target its denominative use. All three of the major theoretical objections I have outlined above and all three of the more recent empirical studies take as their starting point a reading of the term *early modern* in the revisionist scholarship as entailing a claim something like the following: "Chinese society in (say) the seventeenth century, or certain characteristics or products of that society, can rightfully be called 'early modern.'" And all of the objections the critics raise rightfully foreground certain problems with such a view. These objections gain less traction, however, if we read the concept instead as a strategic and provisional gesture intended to generate fresh understandings, rather than to establish definitive claims about the past. From this vantage point, our original claim might become something more like "Chinese society in the seventeenth century—or certain characteristics or products of that society—can be usefully juxtaposed with non-Chinese counterparts for the purpose of illuminating or foregrounding potentially unrecognized features of one or both contexts." Such features might take the form of similarities or differences. What matters most, presumably, is not which way the preponderance of findings go but that the comparison enables the production of new findings in the first place. In this case, the designation *early modern* serves as little more than a convenient, neutral marker of historical contemporaneity and a framework for setting up particular comparative explorations. Because it does not, in this reading, make or imply any truth-claim about the past, it is much less vulnerable than its denominative variant to charges of being teleological, Eurocentric, or reductionist.

Why then, one might ask, retain the *early modern* concept at all? And why privilege synchronic comparisons in this period over broad Eurasian comparisons in earlier periods or even nonsynchronic comparisons? What sets the early modern case apart, I would argue, is simply that the confluence of a significant number of broad historical parallels over these several centuries between the two ends of the Eurasian land mass creates the necessary conditions for productive analogy, where analogy is understood as a provisional comparison between two concepts that exhibit a certain degree of similarity for the purpose of generating further insight about one or both objects. To serve this purpose, an analogy does not require, obviously, strict equivalence between all aspects of both objects, nor even between most of them. If I notice certain similarities between current sectarian conflicts among Muslims in the Middle East and those among Christians in early modern Europe, the analogy might well enhance my understanding of one or both contexts, and will likely do so even if I recognize the many substantial differences between them. Obvious differences can, in fact, serve to amplify the generative power of analogy, as they do in the case of metaphor, which is nothing more than a rhetorically productive analogy between two radically unlike objects. The abundance of evidence that seventeenth- or eighteenth-century China exhibits significant differences from contemporary Europe makes it difficult to sustain a claim that Chinese society in this period possessed all or most of the attributes we associate with European early modernity. Such evidence of variation has less consequence, however, for the project of global or transcultural early modernity understood not as a series of historical claims, but as the basis and framework for a series of potentially revealing analogical thought experiments. Such a heuristic understanding of our term, then, might invite a revision of Ko's repudiation of comparison along these lines: "Many of the social trends and institutions discussed in recent scholarship on seventeenth- and eighteenth-century China bear a striking resemblance to counterparts in early modern Europe. While these resemblances exist alongside substantive differences, the inevitable gaps in our present knowledge about seventeenth-century China and Europe require us to leverage such comparisons for the new insights on both societies they may provide." Comparison is, above all, a tool for generating new knowledge. The most meaningful comparisons, then, and indeed the only worthwhile ones, are those that most usefully address gaps in what we know.

Most of the scholarship that has taken up the category of "early modern China" within an intercultural framework has focused on historical rather than literary comparisons. And indeed, while explicitly comparative methodologies characterize the cutting edge of world historical scholarship, they feel almost retrograde within a literary context. The stuff of literature (and, perhaps more importantly, of literary scholarship) seems somehow too singular, too subjective, too distinctively individual, too idiosyncratic— in short, too incomparable—to submit to the abstraction and even aggregation that a program of systematic comparison would appear to require. Contrastive comparisons went out with Herder and the flattening teleologies of *Volksgeist*; the conformative variety seems tainted by the quasi-mystical quest for universals in early-twentieth-century approaches to folklore morphology and the collective unconscious.[12]

Given the reflexive discomfort these legacies of intellectual history now entail, it is useful to recall that prior to the twentieth century, the most distant and presumably inassimilable of literary traditions was very often understood in the West through the elaboration of a remarkably precise and extensive schema of one-on-one correspondences with European works. It is often said that Goethe inaugurated the age of world literature in a conversation with Johann Eckermann in January 1827. It is less frequently remembered that the occasion of his declaration was a conversation about a Chinese novel that he had just read in translation, or that his pronouncement was followed, in the subsequent seventy-five years, by the observation of an apparently endless series of parallels and convergences between Chinese and Western literary traditions.[13] Given the contemporary currency of a paradigm that stressed the radical alterity of China in other domains, nineteenth-century European students of Chinese literature were repeatedly surprised to find that the literary productions of East and West were actually quite similar in many respects. Commentators noted resemblances among genres, so that Chinese plays were described as commensurable with Greek dramas, Confucian moral maxims with Biblical aphorisms, and Chinese novels with the realist fictions of Richardson or Fielding, set as they were in a recognizable everyday world populated with ordinary, middle-class characters speaking ordinary, vernacular language. Individual writers and works from the Chinese and European tradition were regularly lined up for comparison, so that Confucius 孔子 appeared as a counterpart to Aristotle, Zhuangzi 莊子 as the Chinese Parmenides, Sima Qian 司馬遷 as a Han dynasty Herodotus, and the Kangxi dictionary as a precursor to Webster's unabridged. China's Tang dynasty, widely held to be the golden age of poetry, was equated with the Augustan age in England, with Du Fu 杜甫 compared to Dryden and Li Bai 李白 being China's answer to Alexander Pope.[14]

More recently, it has not been uncommon for Western scholars of Chinese literature to point out incidental parallels between particular works or genres in the two traditions for the purpose of providing familiar points of reference for non-Chinese readers. The self-conscious ironic wit of the seventeenth-century iconoclast writer Li Yu 李漁, for example, might be compared, in passing, to that of Oscar Wilde or Bernard Shaw, or Tang Xianzu's 湯顯祖 romantic tragedy *The Peony Pavilion* (牡丹亭) to the roughly contemporaneous *Romeo and Juliet*. It is rare, however, for such comparisons to be sustained, and not uncommon for their potential usefulness beyond a mere benchmarking function to be dismissed out of hand.

Why should this be? After all, the juxtaposition of early modern China and England would seem largely justified in historical terms. In both China and England, widespread rebellions in the 1630s led first to civil war and eventually to a dynastic revolution in the 1640s, which was followed in turn, in both locations, by a period of imperial consolidation and expansion through the eighteenth century. Historians of both countries date to this period a dramatic increase in commercial activity, the proliferation and growth of urban trade centers, the wide circulation and conspicuous consumption of new classes of luxury goods, and a notable fascination among the elite with the imitation of foreign arts and architecture, so that we find the Chinese Pagoda at Kew Gardens being erected, for example, within a few years of the European-inspired pleasure palaces at Yuanmingyuan. This expansion of commerce was predictably linked in both contexts to increasing social mobility and corresponding anxieties over social promiscuity, debates on the moral effects of luxury, and the reification of taste as a means of adjudicating competing forms of consumption for the purpose of class differentiation. While causal connections become difficult to discern when it comes to matters of personal belief, it is striking to note as well that an increasingly humanist orientation in religion and philosophy led, in both China and England, to a greater emphasis on personal responsibility for self-cultivation through individual interpretation of canonical texts and the careful scrutiny and recording of one's own behavior.

This pattern of broad resonances extends even to the literary domain. Both China and England witnessed during this period a dramatic expansion in commercial publishing. New audiences gave rise to new genres, and we find in both contexts a flourishing of newspapers, travel accounts, conduct guides, and manuals of taste, as well as novel experiments in autobiographical writing, occasional essays, and poetry by women. Vernacular fictions, increasingly concerned with depicting, in widely accessible language, the lives of ordinary people in ordinary settings, proliferated in both places, spawning similar sets of subgenres along the way, including fictions in the amatory, criminal, sentimental, domestic, and pornographic modes.

The novel comes into its own as a dominant and increasingly legitimate popular form at roughly the same time in China and England through an appeal to audiences who apparently shared some comparable tastes and desires. Similar breakthroughs in the use of social realism as a narrative strategy are ascribed to the pseudonymous Lanling Xiaoxiao Sheng 蘭陵笑笑生, author of *The Plum in the Golden Vase* (金瓶梅; pub. 1610) and Daniel Defoe, writing approximately a century later. *The Dream of the Red Chamber* (紅樓夢) was composed in the mid-eighteenth century and first printed in the 1790s, making it contemporary with the similarly elaborate and psychologically astute feminocentric fictions of Samuel Richardson and Jane Austen. Increasingly vocal social criticism found an outlet in the new genre of the satirical-realist novel, whose most important early Chinese exemplar, *The Scholars* (儒林外史) by Wu Jingzi 吳敬梓, was completed in 1750, within two decades of the similarly barbed *Joseph Andrews* by Henry Fielding (1742), *Vicar of Wakefield* by Oliver Goldsmith (1761), and *Humphrey Clinker* by Tobias Smollett (1766).

The coemergence of a strong satirical tradition in vernacular fiction seems particularly noteworthy, given the degree to which, as a narrative mode, satire responds both to the most local, contingent particularities of language and custom and to broader social trends. The resonances between the visions of early modern Chinese and English satirists at both these levels are striking. Bustling urban centers, associated with conspicuous consumption and the dislocation of traditional norms, provide a common backdrop for the action, and one often set in contrast with a utopian rural world that has been left behind. Ambivalence toward the metropolis hinges on the competing attractions of wealth and of respite from the degrading exertions involved in its pursuit. A sustained fascination with the minutiae of trade, financial transactions, and capital accumulation signals the expanding symbolic significance of money, while changing attitudes toward commercial activity are revealed in the explicit elaboration of a new merchant ethos founded on the sanctity of contracts. Wealth increasingly displaces lineage as the critical determinant of social status, leading to expanded social mobility and the deterioration of traditional social hierarchies.

The contemplation of this brave new world produces in writers in both locations an attitude of ironic detachment and, indeed, refines ironic expression into a newly dominant rhetorical mode. Readerly identification with characters is forestalled by ridicule of follies displayed in often exaggerated terms and heightened through the regular invocation of the scatological and sexual grotesque, an essentially conservative device that seems often implicitly to reaffirm orthodox moralities through a contrast with modern scenes of decay. Hypocrisy, pretension, arrogance, sensual indulgence, and blinding social ambition are among the personal vices most commonly condemned; implicit throughout is a broader condemnation of the society and the recent social changes that encourage them. The development of social realism—an increasingly microscopic attention to the banalities of the everyday existence of relatively ordinary characters—goes hand in hand, in both contexts, with that of social criticism, reaching a culmination in the great comic novels of the mid-eighteenth century.[15]

All of which is to suggest that we are contending here with an instance of literary historical convergence that is, at the very least, sufficient to ground provisional analogies, if not denominative historical claims. But how might such a comparative literary analysis invoking the rubric of "early modern China" most constructively be pursued? What are the conditions for the effective use of "early modern" as a heuristic and the avoidance of the most common pitfalls of literary historical comparison? I will outline in what follows what I take to be four important components of such a procedure, illustrating each with reference to the possibility of theorizing early modern satire within a post-Eurocentric frame.

Cross-cultural literary comparison has often suffered from an excessively taxonomical approach. The exercise too often devolves into a kind of cultural morphology, a ponderous matching game based on checklists of features. The game has two possible outcomes, each as predictable as it is deadening to further enquiry. Whether the focus is on specific tropes or texts or more broadly imagined genres or poetic modalities, the aim is to demonstrate that the objects on both sides of the comparison are either essentially similar or essentially different. Recent work by respectable comparatists thinking across the China-Europe divide seems notably susceptible to the obvious allure of conclusions of both types, and the advocates of each feed off the rhetorical excesses of the other. The reader is ultimately left with a dispiriting choice between a bland humanistic universalism on one hand, and a selection of quasi-nationalist exceptionalisms on the other, a situation which presumably goes some way toward accounting for the reluctance of other scholars to take up the game.

The fundamental problem here is not the comparative impulse itself, but the questions it sets out to address. To begin with what is essentially a quantitative goal—the assessment of the degree to which two cultural objects are similar or distinct—is to limit oneself a priori to a narrow range of essentially quantitative outcomes: one can demonstrate, with more or less nuance and sophistication, that corresponding sets of defining characteristics match up neatly or that they don't. A vastly more expansive range of possible outcomes would come into view, I would suggest, if we were to replace the taxonomist's playbook with the poet's, and to shift our focus away from evaluating degrees of resemblance towards harvesting the fruits of productive analogy. One doesn't ask the poet to demonstrate the truth of the resemblance asserted by a metaphor. One asks the poet, rather, to posit such a resemblance as something like a logical premise from which other forms of understanding will naturally follow. The most promising comparative approach to the study of a transregional early modernity would likewise posit a certain kind of similarity as a premise, and proceed from there to explore the chasmic spaces opened and illuminated by what might best be termed an intercultural metaphor.

The immediate reaction of many literary historians to a sustained comparison between satirical fictions in early modern England and China would most likely be either to contest the accuracy of asserted parallels by pointing to the innumerable differences between the forms of satire employed, say, by Henry Fielding and Wu Jingzi, or else to claim that satire is, if not a literary universal, at least so commonplace that the observation of resemblances is not a particularly noteworthy one. From an analogical standpoint, it should be clear that these two kinds of responses would not be entirely germane, in that they proceed from a shared assumption that the ultimate objective of comparative analysis is an assessment of degrees of resemblance. To escape the stifling grip of this assumption requires putting aside the impulse to assess the legitimacy of a comparison as a truth claim in itself in order to assess, instead, the reactions it can potentially catalyze as a hermeneutic prompt. How might the vaunted tradition of eighteenth-century English satire appear when refracted through a suggestive analogy with a Chinese counterpart—or vice versa? What recessed features of an overly familiar object might a robust structural analogy bring precipitously into view? The satirist, perhaps above all other writers, appreciates the purging and redemptive powers of self-alienation. There is surely a poetic justice, then, in pursuing the alienation of that craft through a reconfigured metaphorics of comparison.

Juxtaposing two representative works of eighteenth-century satirical fiction will help to illustrate the productiveness of this approach. As suggested above, Fielding's *Joseph Andrews* and Wu Jingzi's *The Scholars* emerged within an eight-year period from contexts—literary and historical—that present enough obvious resemblances to justify an analogical thought experiment. The most significant of these include, again, increasing commercialization, the progressive erosion of social boundaries between merchant classes and traditional elites, the growing popularity and legitimacy of vernacular fiction, and the rising prominence of realism and subjectivism in fictional writing. Claims for all these trends are repeated so frequently in monocultural studies of seventeenth- and eighteenth-century China and England as to render them nearly clichés. Considerably less common is the claim that the close alignment of such developments itself might be worthy of note or sufficient to license a more sustained elaboration of the transcultural category that they suggest.

Such an elaboration might proceed in any number of directions, and I will only sketch out a few of these to illustrate each of the more general methodological suggestions I am offering here. To begin, we might observe the disruptive effects of our posited analogy on the familiar logic of monocultural genealogies as an explanatory paradigm within literary history. The accepted lineage for a work like *Joseph Andrews* is variegated and complex. As a realist novel, it descends from antecedent developments in natural philosophy, theory of mind, journalism, and Puritan self-examination, among others. As a work of satirical fiction, it claims *Don Quixote* and *Gulliver's Travels* among its forebears, and draws self-consciously on the mock-heroic techniques perfected by Pope and his Augustan contemporaries.[16] As an exemplar of the narrative and moral self-consciousness that heralds the emergence of modern subjectivity, it arises out of a long historical process of progressive interiorization that, in Charles Taylor's influential account, encompasses Augustine, Descartes, and Locke.[17] The argument implicit in the powerful impulse to identify literary and philosophical antecedents for Fielding's work is that genealogy is destiny, or that at least it has substantial explanatory force. Whether Fielding is seen to rework the tradition he inherits or to struggle against it, he remains a product of these varied English and European lineages. Our understanding of the provenance of *Joseph Andrews* gives considerable causal weight to contemporary socio-logical developments as well, of course, but this does little to shake the conviction that everything we need to know to account for and interpret a work like Fielding's we can glean from the study of its local cultural contexts, broadly understood. And the same holds for Wu Jingzi and *The Scholars*.

An analogical juxtaposition of the two works challenges the self-sufficiency of autochthonous literary history. If pathbreaking works of satirical fiction are emerging from discrete contexts that reveal similar clusters of shaping forces, then any origin story that attends exclusively to local developments and lineages is plainly insufficient to account for the larger pattern being observed or for the place of an individual work within that pattern. The characters of Joseph Andrews and Parson Adams might rec-ognize Don Quixote and Sancho Panza as their great-grandfathers, but we are obliged, by their simultaneous repositioning within a trans-Eurasian frame, to acknowledge as their brothers the paragons of integrity and simple virtue that Wu Jingzi introduces in the first and final chapters of *The Scholars*. The structural parallels between the open-ings of the two novels are striking, as are the similarities in the way the incorruptibil-ity of their heroes so prominently flaunted in their opening scenes functions as a foil for the satirical critiques that follow. The peasant artist and autodidact Wang Mian improbably declines the honor of a wealthy local official's patronage on the grounds of a principled rejection of his corrupt and tyrannical ways. Joseph Andrews draws on an equally surprising reserve of moral integrity in rejecting the sexual advances of his wealthy and attractive employer, Lady Booby. In both cases, the hero's upright stance occasions a violent response from his slighted would-be benefactor and his casting out into a symbolic exile, a movement which simultaneously orients the moral compass of the work and provides the reader with a marginalized vantage point within the work from which to reflect on subsequent events.

As intriguing as such parallels might appear in themselves, they serve in the context of the present methodological experiment merely to flesh out the analogical structure posited at the outset. The real payoff from the analogy arises from the insight into the character and structural function of Joseph and Wang Mian afforded by the recognition of their fraternity. Having established a common category that encompasses them both, the reader is afforded a perspective on each that is inaccessible, even unimaginable, from within the silo of monocultural literary history. The newfound affinity between the two characters and texts prompts me, in rereading the famous opening chapters of *Joseph Andrews*, to put aside a response overly conditioned by my familiarity with the scene's allusions to *Pamela* and the sexual innuendo of Restoration comedy in order to perceive with far greater clarity, for example, the scene's implicit commentary on the nature of power relations and the social dynamics of patronage. The metaphorical affordance that invites me to read Joseph as a talented Chinese peasant or Lady Booby as a proud and hot-tempered Ming dynasty magistrate foregrounds for me, with an efficacy unique to metaphor, the political drama entailed by his choice and the vindictiveness of her response.

If the first requirement of the proposed method for rethinking early modern satire is to establish as a premise a fertile cross-cultural analogy, the second is to jettison the notion of satire altogether. And, of course, not just satire. To the extent that we are serious about embracing a postnational reconfiguration of literary study, it will prove increasingly necessary to downgrade the rather exalted category of genre or mode in favor of the category of function. Established formal distinctions among types of literary writing, or even between the literary and nonliterary, tend not to travel well. They typically emerge within the context of a particular tradition and reflect the local history of formal innovation within that tradition. In their concern with the nuances of the structure of a particular work, they tend, moreover, to privilege its purely aesthetic dimension over other manifest social functions in the arenas of ritual, for example, politics, healing, warfare, courtship, history, religion, or commerce. Given the relatively late invention of the concept of literature in most societies, insisting that "world literature," of whatever theoretical denomination, conform to the categories of its idiosyncratically European instantiation seems narrow-minded at best. Rather than asking at the outset, then, what a particular work *is* (a novel or a history, an epic or a prose poem, a satire or a slightly off-key sentimental effusion), in the domain of world literature—and, for the sake of my argument, in its constitutive comparative methodologies—we would be better served by asking what it *does*, and what it has done for or to listeners and readers in its previous incarnations.

While genre can, for a writer, clearly take on a prescriptive function and serve to shape literary production as much as to describe it, within literary scholarship its predominant role is descriptive. A genre is, above all, a taxonomical definition of a literary form that takes the form of a list of characteristic features, the presence of some minimum combination of which is deemed necessary to qualify a work as a member of the designated class. As such, it constitutes in strictly formal terms an arbitrary assemblage of descriptors that would admit, in principle, of endless possibilities of recombination. Genres, as a result, provide an extraordinarily useful conceptual apparatus for mapping vast terrains of literary production and tracing the evolution of distinctive modes of writing. Their shortcoming as a set of rubrics for cross-cultural work is that their definitional boundaries tend to follow the contours of the particular literary landscape in which they emerged. Our awareness of the feature sets that constitute the epic, the sonnet, and the novel is deeply saturated by our simultaneous awareness of the historical contexts under which they flourished. As a result, there is often an understandable resistance to the very idea of, say, an autochthonous Chinese instantiation of these forms, just as there would be to a modern Kansas poet's claim to having produced a twenty-first-century epic. When the possibility of Chinese counterparts is admitted, the resulting comparisons have too often faulted Chinese writers for producing works that fail to display, or to display with sufficient panache, those features that are understood to be constitutive of the genre.

The problem, in other words, lies in the reification of an arbitrary designation, the misrecognition of a useful heuristic for an empirical reality. A shift in emphasis from genre to function sidesteps this problem. Genre encourages us to view literature in its nominative aspect. Within Western metaphysics, nominatives, and especially the more abstract ones, tend to have a built-in rigidity and stasis. Once a novel, always a novel: a reassuringly stable but stultifying outlook. Function, on the contrary, evokes the transitive—and consequently transformative and transient—power of the literary. The transience and unpredictability of literary function renders it largely useless as the basis for a classificatory scheme. But the suppleness such features imply, the responsiveness to contextual variation, and the provisionality of outcomes perfectly complement a comparative procedure premised on analogy. In considering literature across two or more contexts that are not even technically similar, let alone congruent, the cumbersome and at this stage rather hypertrophied apparatus of genre is likely only to foreshorten our enquiry, revealing, as it must, discrepancies and failures, and ultimately obscuring from view far more than it reveals. More promising by far is a close, almost ethnographic attentiveness to the lives and behaviors of literary object as agents within a system of social relations, as it is only with reference to what historical subjects and their literary productions are observed to do rather than are imagined to be that a comparative method can produce meaningful insights on the past.

What, then, is the social function of satire? In the most general terms, it tends to exaggerate, caricature, mock, ridicule, send up, laugh at, or parody—all in order to expose, rail against, condemn, provoke, reform, or remonstrate. To this list of connotations, we might add that the Chinese term for satire, *fengci* (諷刺), could be translated literally as "language used to prick" (the second character combines two elements meaning "thorn" and "knife"). If we specify further a focus on satirical fiction, we observe that this characteristic pricking action is achieved through and alongside thoroughgoing efforts to describe a recognizable world, tell an engaging story in a common language, and encourage readerly identification with relatively ordinary characters. The payoff from the shift from a nominative paradigm of genre to a transitive paradigm of function is not the resulting catalog of verbs, however, but rather the invitation to consider the motives and the implications of the actions denoted by these verbs on a given social stage. What are the contours of a situation to which "pricking" might be a common, even predictable response? What does the bearer of the thorn set out to achieve with the prick, and why? What is the problem, whether contingent or structural, to which a well-aimed ironic jab is the obvious solution?

Posing the question in this way enables us to pursue the implications of the suggestive analogy that commensurative comparison makes available. Once we become attuned to the possibility of a structural resonance between two literary contexts and to the role of literary works as a more or less predictable functional response to a generalizable set of circumstances, we are much better positioned both to think beyond the silos of national literary history, to recognize meaningful patterns across these histories in time and space, and thereby to distinguish and disaggregate the contingent and determinate aspects of that history. The formal innovations of a Swift or a Fielding, a Li Yu or a Wu Jingzi, the wit and raillery, the remonstrance partaking of both nostalgia and common sense, surely appear in a different light once we consider them, by way of a structural analogy, as emerging in response to a comparable set of conditions: a moment of profound social transformation occasioned by newfound commercial wealth, mobility, and commoditization.

Both *The Scholars* and *Joseph Andrews* respond to these changing circumstances through a rhetoric of ridicule. The objects of their pricking barbs are so closely aligned as to be almost interchangeable: characters displaying boastfulness, arrogance, vanity, or a love of luxury are repeatedly taken down by episodes of burlesque physical humor that alternate with only slightly more subtle ironic jabs. Both works invite us to laugh at the self-absorption of men with an excessive fondness for fine clothing and at the time-wasting vanity of ladies of quality. Both invite disdain for the strutting haughtiness of the mighty and for the sordidness of the pathways they've taken to power. They share a common delight in unmasking affectations of every kind, and the frequency of these unmaskings might suggest that the circumstance of eroding social boundaries characterizing the worlds from which they arose entails both more opportunities for social climbers and more resentment at their opportunism than is the case in more stable times. Beyond condemning hypocrisy and pride, however, and enabling cathartic laughter at the expense of the powerful, the satirical thorns that fill the pages of both works produce a heightened awareness of a particular ideal in opposition to which these foibles can be most clearly discerned. In both cases, this ideal is consistently associated with values of simplicity, naturalness, and spontaneity, and in both cases, it emerges most clearly in the many episodes that parody false knowledge or feigned erudition on the part of doctors, scribblers, and pseudointellectuals of all stripes.

The value of such a comparison derives not from the enumeration of parallels, but rather from the deployment as a fresh heuristic of the transcultural category that they serve to elaborate and reinforce. Read individually, these two exemplars of mid-eighteenth-century satirical fiction can provide insight chiefly into local social contexts, local literary lineages, the literary talents of a particular author, and perhaps, if we're feeling magnanimous, certain universals of the human condition. Read analogically, they enable the recognition of patterns and the construction of interpretive models at a scale between the particular and the universal allowing us to consider, for example, the possibility of structural relationships between social mobility and the quest for authenticity, or between luxury consumption and the critique of false learning, or, perhaps most importantly, between the readerly self-examination and self-reform required by satire and the progressive interiorization of ethical judgment widely held to be a hallmark of modernity. I will pursue some of these possibilities further below, but I hope that even this brief sketch will have helped to illustrate how shifting the emphasis in our comparison from the formal features of satire understood as a mode or genre to the effects that thorn-prick rhetoric produces as a response to particular conditions nudges us beyond the temptations of merely quantitative or taxonomic comparison to entertain the possibilities of a transcultural literary early modernity as an interpretive device.

My use of Fielding and Wu Jingzi as examples here, however, may be misleading. While there is clearly some place for pursuing the implications of a broader analogical comparison through the pairing of particular authors, in general terms its goals will best be served by a perspective at one further remove that focuses at least as much on trajectories as on individual writers and works. This third requirement of analogical comparison is logically entailed by the second, the functional emphasis of which foregrounds a temporal dimension largely absent from the framework of genre. Unlike nouns, which tend to sit around and grow fat if they don't slip into timelessness altogether, verbs metabolize: they respond and engage and transform, and thereby become the engine and indeed the very precondition of temporal perception. To imagine literature as a form of agency, then, is to imagine it as a dialectical process that unfolds over time, and that therefore can be perceived only as a succession of stages and events and never as a fully realized object, complete and sufficient in itself. Individual pairings of literary gestures and motifs remain important: one would surely want to attend, say, to the striking proliferation of grotesquely deformed women and harebrained academicians in the early modern satirical fictions of both China and England, though these would serve primarily to bring into focus the larger trend lines required to recognize and account for analogical literary transformations over time. They might help us to understand, for example, why and how it is that irony emerges simultaneously as a dominant rhetorical mode in both early modern contexts, how it conditions the emergence of new forms of realistic narration, and how it evolves, again in both contexts, from a hard-edged, violent, and caustic gesture to a more subtle, aestheticized, and domesticated one.

Like the shift to function, this emphasis on temporality preserves the distinctiveness of the local while lifting the silos that too often condition its apprehension. Analogy, it bears repeating, not only avoids the flattening effect of stricter models of resemblance, it requires difference and distance in order to achieve the cognitive leverage that is its raison d'être. That is, there is no question of reducing one satirical tradition to a variant of the other, precisely because the proposed method depends a priori on the presumption of alterity to achieve its interpretive potential. At the same time, this gesture exposes the pandemic myopia that occasions every attempt to certify Swift or Fielding as the purebred literary progeny of Horace, Juvenal, Shakespeare, and Dryden, or the works of Wu Jingzi as, in a direct or straightforward way, occasioned by the precedents of Pu Songling 蒲松齡 and Feng Menglong 馮夢龍. The process and product of literary history are both contingent and uncannily reverberant, a paradox that at once authorizes and underwrites a more expansive account of its worldliness.

What fresh perspectives on literary historical continuity and succession might be brought into view through our focus on *Joseph Andrews* and *The Scholars*? A suggestive comparative analysis of early modern novelistic traditions in China and Europe by Andrew Plaks offers several compelling starting points. In the course of an argument that the emergence of the novel in these two spheres was closely synchronized with respect to broader cultural changes in the two societies, he suggests that Northrop Frye's model of gradual descent in the Western narrative tradition from a concern with larger-than-life kings and warriors down to a faithful and often caricatured depiction of familiar human experience applies equally well to the trajectory outlined by the "four masterworks" of the Chinese novelistic tradition. This observation leads in turn to the striking claim that "the paradigmatic use of irony as its primary rhetorical mode for exploring the labyrinth of autonomous identity and defining the intrinsic limitations of self-realization" is "perhaps the most significant area of literary convergence between the Chinese and the European novel."[18] The progressive devolution of the literary hero and concomitant evolution of ironic and satirical narration are amply exemplified in our two novels, with their thoroughgoing delight in ridiculing painfully "real" and recognizable characters. The true payoff, though, in recognizing these works as representatives of analogical processes lies in their usefulness in demarcating the category of early modern identity formation to which Frye's formulation alludes. Both narratives, as noted above, produce and legitimize the position of an innocent and simple-hearted outsider as a necessary foil to the pretense and affectation that uniformly characterize their objects of ridicule. If we can accept, for the sake of argument, the general claim that certain shared social conditions of early modernity tend to produce a literary interest in affectation, and that this interest is associated in turn with an exploration of the ideal of authenticity that it so brazenly flouts, we can then reposition our exemplary texts in relation to a transcultural early modern moment that encompasses, in varying configurations, both of these concerns.

On the Chinese side, the debts of eighteenth-century literary satirists like Wu Jingzi to the philosophical elaboration of an ethics of authenticity by Wang Yangming 王陽明, Li Zhi 李贄, and the Taizhou School have been persuasively established. And indeed, a character like Wang Mian in the opening chapter of *The Scholars* can readily be seen to embody the virtues of genuineness, spontaneity, and naturalness embraced by such writers in his artistic practice, rejection of external sources of authority, and steadfast adherence to his own intuitions about correct behavior.[19] By this account, the concern with genuine feeling as the basis of a discipline of self-examination and self-rectification characteristic of much radical thought of the late Ming is one component of a broader cultural phenomenon that also encompasses the literary satires of the seventeenth and eighteenth centuries. The conspicuous florescence, in early modern writings, of a rhetoric of ridicule and an ethics of authentic sentiment would appear to be two mutually constitutive and mutually reinforcing developments with respect to norms of moral reasoning and self-reflection in a period of relatively rapid social change.

Such a model reveals unexpected continuities if we apply it, as the structure of our analogy licenses us to do, to English literary history of the late seventeenth and eighteenth centuries. The best-established master narrative about this period, which we've inherited from the Romantic poets themselves, is that poetic Romanticism and the cult of sensibility on which it drew marked a decisive break from the Augustan poetics of the Restoration and early eighteenth century. Where the Augustans—poets like Pope and Swift—had embraced a neoclassical aesthetic of poise and balance and a deeply satirical moral vision, the Romantics, led by Wordsworth, explicitly repudiated the elitism and the stylized artifice of their predecessors, advocating instead a poetic technique dedicated to "the spontaneous overflow of powerful feelings" as experienced by ordinary people and captured in the language of ordinary speech.[20] This paradigm of rupture applies less neatly to fiction of the period, and Fielding's work in particular can be seen to embody both of these impulses. But placing *Joseph Andrews* alongside *The Scholars* and, provisionally, within a Chinese historical frame, potentially foregrounds a broader continuity between the seemingly antithetical literary projects that dominated the beginning and end of the eighteenth century in England. Recognizing an intellectual lineage between the Taizhou School's philosophers of authenticity and Wu Jingzi's groundbreaking *fengci* fiction and entertaining the possibility that this connection can be viewed as a characteristic of a transcultural early modern phenomenon allows us to bracket the familiar dichotomy that structures our view of eighteenth-century English literary history and to discern an analogous link between Wordsworth's Taizhou-style individualism and Pope's *fengci* wit. The chronology of the development of the schools of sentiment and satire appears reversed in the English case—from a Chinese vantage point, Wordsworth really ought to have written a century or two before Pope—but it is precisely the disruption of a familiar perspective this reversal entails that enables us to question the paradigm of radical discontinuity on which the Romantics founded their remarkably resilient conception of modernity.

The fourth and final requirement of the proposed method of early modern comparison is, as this analysis begins to suggest, that it adopt—in a selective, provisional, and unabashedly provocative way—analytical terms, categories, and points of reference as the basis for the deliberate alienation and reconceptualization of all that is well known, and often too well known, in the target literary and cultural context. Comparative projects frequently struggle with issues of terminology. Parts of the above discussion have blithely invoked terms like *novel, fiction,* and *satire* on the implicit premise that, while of European lineage, they're sufficiently supple, when deployed in an explicitly comparative context, to facilitate a certain kind of relatively abstract analysis. One potentially attractive approach to remedying such an uncritical one-sidedness in the deployment of such terms is to set out explicitly to redefine them with respect to multiple literary traditions. The English term *novel*, for example, might be stretched out and reconfigured so as to accommodate a much wider, cross-cultural range of extended prose narrations than its implicit English referents currently allow. More attractive still, however, is the possibility of bracketing—as one reflexively brackets many a stale cliché—the vastly over-determined English word altogether, in order to reconsider the field of early modern English—or even European—prose fictions as an idiosyncratic subset of *xiaoshuo* (小說; literally "small speech"), which is a category which historically encompassed not only Chinese novels but also short stories, occasional essays, and a variety of other forms, and which, accordingly, has a sufficiently unfamiliar lineage, teleology, and associational valence to achieve a genuinely productive degree of alienation. The origins of *fengci*, likewise, in the ancient and endlessly elaborated practice of seeking out the songs and laments of the common people for the purposes of political remonstration, might well provide a usefully unfamiliar paradigm for reconsidering the relations between writers and rulers in England's Age of Satire.

Henry Fielding's leading role in conventional accounts of the rise of the novel notwithstanding, *Joseph Andrews* might be more usefully described as *xiaoshuo* than as a novel. Its wavering adherence to verisimilitude, its persistent eruptions of narrative self-consciousness, and its interpellation of a variety of seemingly ill-matched genres— romance, Latin verse, sermon, mock epic, children's story, and literary criticism—fit the considerably more capacious and less prescriptive category of *xiaoshuo* much more comfortably than any category of *novel* that might be extrapolated from the standard exemplars of Austen, Dickens, or Hardy. Such a provisional reclassification makes immediately apparent two limitations of the *novel* category: its role, first, in buttressing the conceptual silo of Eurocentrism, and second, in imposing a teleological template on early modern fiction that arguably overdetermines the perspective from which modern readers approach it. To read *Joseph Andrews* through *The Scholars* as a kindred *xiaoshuo* brings into play a very different set of narrative expectations and a degree of openness to a literary experiment conditioned at least as much by the globalizing forces of early modernity as by any preestablished genre ideal.

The roots of the term *fengci* evoke a long history in China of intellectuals holding themselves responsible for the moral rectitude of their leaders and the state. Whereas in English, political satire is a subclass of a rhetorical device that more typically takes the foibles of individuals and categories of people as the target of ridicule, in Chinese, all satire potentially bears a political subtext owing to its roots in the traditionally accepted duty of political remonstrance. Certainly such a distinction is borne out in a comparison of the two books we've been considering here. Whereas the intention behind Fielding's send-ups of foolish pride comes across as primarily comic, Wu Jingzi's unrelenting mockery of the learning, aspirations, and values of the late Ming literati class reads as a sustained cry of alarm at the degradation of the social institution—the examination system—he recognizes as most determinative of the fortunes of the ruling dynasty. Embracing this difference as a variation within a larger analogical equation provides traction for a reading of Fielding through the conventions of *fengci*—or vice versa. Fielding doesn't take aim at political institutions. He is, though, unrelenting in his association of affectation and its associated vices with power, elevated social standing, and every imaginable form of hierarchy. There is no equivalent in Fielding's world of an imperial examination on which to pin the source of all this human folly. The comparison does suggest, however, the possibility of remapping the moral failing of pride as he depicts it in the text from a religious canvas onto a sociopolitical one, a gesture which might well reveal a degree of structural dysfunction every bit as severe and ubiquitous as that lamented by Wu Jingzi's occasional clear-eyed heroes.

I have attended at such length here to problems of comparative methodology because the designation of Ming-Qing literature as early modern necessarily implies a comparative framework, and because comparisons of the usual taxonomic variety lead predictably to dead ends. Provided we understand the designation *early modern* not as a deterministic claim but as a provisional heuristic, it can helpfully resituate our readings of the Chinese literature of the period in relation to three distinct con-texts the term itself brings into play. Early modernity as a world system character-ized, among other things, by expanding trade networks and silver flows breaks down the silos of nation-bound literary history and the illusion of literary trends as purely autochthonous developments. As analogical scaffolding, it invites selective and strate-gic intercultural cross-readings with other locations in the early modern world. And as an anticipatory historical marker, it encourages a reevaluation of the genealogy of modern Chinese literature more closely attuned to a past always already situated within world-historical time. When Ba Jin's character Qin laments the literary preferences of the "old-fashioned scholars" at her school, she has no way of knowing that the politi-cal execution in 1931 of the leftist writer Rou Shi 柔石, author of "A Slave Mother" (為奴隸的母親) and *February* (二月), would inspire a belated eulogy by Lu Xun 魯迅 in which he would compare his fallen comrade favorably, in his brusque manner and uncompromising dedication to his beliefs, to Fang Xiaoru 方孝孺, a Ming writer who died as a martyr of imperial remonstrance and who was later anthologized in the same *Selected Ancient Chinese Essays* (古文觀止) that Qin had dismissed as hopelessly old-fashioned. Nor would she have known that Wang Zengqi 汪曾祺, one of the leading writers of the immediate post-Mao era, would openly acknowledge his debt to Gui Youguang 歸有光, another "ancient" Confucian included in the same anthology, for inspiring his seemingly "modern" commitment to writing about the common man.[21] Modern Chinese literature is, above all, a relational category. But those pasts with which it appears to be in conversation are of course never fixed or constant, and have increasingly been brought into focus, in recent decades, through new relational lenses themselves.

NOTES

1. Ba Jin, *The Family*, trans. Sidney Shapiro (Honolulu: University Press of the Pacific, 2001), 7 [translation revised].
2. David Der-wei Wang, in *Fin-de-siècle Splendor: Repressed Modernities of Late Qing Fiction, 1849–1911* (Stanford: Stanford University Press, 1997), documents the continuing currency of the dualistic paradigm as well as its inadequacy in accounting for the incipi-ent modernities to be found in late-nineteenth-century Chinese literature.
3. A helpfully probing history of the term is provided in Phil Wittington, *Society in Early Modern England: The Vernacular Origins of Some Powerful Ideas* (Cambridge: Polity Press, 2010).
4. See Wang, *Fin-de-siècle Splendor*; and Paul A. Cohen, *Discovering History in China: American Historical Writing on the Recent Chinese Past* (New York: Columbia University Press, 1984).
5. Paul S. Ropp, *Dissent in Early Modern China: Ju-lin wai-shi and Ch'ing Social Criticism* (Ann Arbor: University of Michigan Press, 1981), 3. Examples of other scholarly works from the same period espousing the early modern China paradigm include Jonathan Porter, "The Scientific Community in Early Modern China," *ISIS* 73.4 (1982): 529–544,

and William T. Rowe, *Hankow: Commerce and Society in a Chinese City, 1769–1889* (Stanford: Stanford University Press, 1984).

6. For a valuable survey of this scholarship, see Soren Clausen, "'Early Modern China': A Preliminary Postmortem," Working Paper 84–00 (Centre for Cultural Research, University of Aarhus, 2000): 1–39. For a collection of more recent comparative scholarship that explicitly theorizes the problem of the "early modern" category, see David Porter, ed., *Comparative Early Modernities* (London: Palgrave, 2012).

7. Clausen, "Early Modern China," 22–39.

8. Dorothy Ko, *Teachers of the Inner Chambers: Women and Culture in Seventeenth-Century China* (Stanford: Stanford University Press, 1994), 24–25.

9. On-Cho Ng, "The Epochal Concept of 'Early Modernity' and the Intellectual History of Late Imperial China," *Journal of World History* 14.1 (2003): 41–42.

10. Jack A. Goldstone, "Divergence in Cultural Trajectories: The Power of the Traditional within the Early Modern," *Comparative Early Modernities*, ed. David Porter (New York: Palgrave, 2012), 190.

11. Lynn A. Struve, "Chimerical Early Modernity: The Case of 'Conquest-Generation' Memoirs," *The Qing Formation in World Historical Time*, ed. Lynn A. Struve (Cambridge: Harvard University Press, 2004), 369.

12. For a rich and productive sampling of recent arguments considering the pros, cons, affordances, and challenges of (mostly literary) comparison, see Rita Felski and Susan Friedman, eds., *Comparison: Theories, Approaches, Uses* (Baltimore: Johns Hopkins University Press, 2013).

13. David Damrosch, *What is World Literature?* (Princeton: Princeton University Press, 2003), 10–11.

14. See, for example, John Francis Davis, *The Chinese: A General Description of China and its Inhabitants*, 3 vols. (London: Charles Knight, 1845), 259–276.

15. Andrew H. Plaks has developed this idea in a number of works, including "After the Fall: *Hsing-shi yin-yuan chuan* and the Seventeenth-Century Chinese Novel," *Harvard Journal of Asiatic Studies* 45.2 (December 1985): 543–580, and "The Novel in Premodern China," in *The Novel, Volume 1: History, Geography, and Culture*, ed. Franco Moretti (Princeton: Princeton University Press, 2007), 181–213.

16. Ronald Paulson's *Satire and the Novel in Eighteenth-Century England* (New Haven: Yale University Press, 1967) and J. Paul Hunter's *Before Novels: The Cultural Contexts of Eighteenth-Century English Fiction* (New York: Norton, 1990) still offer useful starting points for exploring these genealogies.

17. Charles Taylor, *Sources of the Self: The Making of the Modern Identity* (Cambridge: Harvard University Press, 1989), 127–176.

18. Andrew H. Plaks, "The Novel in Premodern China," 186, 202, 211.

19. See especially Ropp, *Dissent*, 39–40 and 217–221, as well as Wm. Theodore de Bary, "Individualism and Humanitarianism in Late Ming Thought," in *Self and Society in Ming Thought*, ed. Wm. Theodore de Bary (New York: Columbia University Press, 1970), 145–248, and Pauline Lee, *Li Zhi, Confucianism, and the Virtue of Desire* (Albany: SUNY Press, 2012).

20. William Wordsworth, "Preface," *Lyrical Ballads*, ed. Michael Gamer and Dahlia Porter (Peterborough, ON: Broadview, 2008), 175.

21. Gloria Davies, *Lu Xun's Revolution* (Cambridge: Harvard University Press, 2013), 289; Carolyn Fitzgerald, *Fragmenting Modernisms: Chinese Wartime Literature, Art, and Film, 1937–49* (Boston: Brill, 2013), 148.

WORKS CITED

Ba Jin. *The Family*. Trans. Sidney Shapiro. Honolulu: University Press of the Pacific, 2001.

Clausen, Soren. "'Early Modern China': A Preliminary Postmortem." Working Paper 84–00 (Centre for Cultural Research, University of Aarhus, 2000): 1–39.

Cohen, Paul A. *Discovering History in China: American Historical Writing on the Recent Chinese Past*. New York: Columbia University Press, 1984.

Damrosch, David. *What is World Literature?* Princeton: Princeton University Press, 2003.

Davies, Gloria Davies. *Lu Xun's Revolution*. Cambridge: Harvard University Press, 2013.

Davis, John Francis. *The Chinese: A General Description of China and its Inhabitants*, 3 vols. London: Charles Knight, 1845.

de Bary, William Theodore. "Individualism and Humanitarianism in Late Ming Thought." In *Self and Society in Ming Thought*. Ed. William Theodore de Bary. New York: Columbia University Press, 1970. 145–248.

Felski, Rita, and Susan Friedman, eds. *Comparison: Theories, Approaches, Uses*. Baltimore: Johns Hopkins University Press, 2013.

Fitzgerald, Carolyn. *Fragmenting Modernisms: Chinese Wartime Literature, Art, and Film, 1937–49*. Boston: Brill, 2013.

Goldstone, Jack A. "Divergence in Cultural Trajectories: The Power of the Traditional within the Early Modern." In *Comparative Early Modernities*. Ed. David Porter. New York: Palgrave, 2012. 165–192.

Hunter, J. Paul. *Before Novels: The Cultural Contexts of Eighteenth-Century English Fiction*. New York: Norton, 1990.

Lee, Pauline. *Li Zhi, Confucianism, and the Virtue of Desire*. Albany: State University of New York Press, 2012.

Ko, Dorothy. *Teachers of the Inner Chambers: Women and Culture in Seventeenth-Century China*. Stanford: Stanford University Press, 1994.

Ng, On-Cho. "The Epochal Concept of 'Early Modernity' and the Intellectual History of Late Imperial China." *Journal of World History* 14.1 (2003): 37–61.

Paulson, Ronald. *Satire and the Novel in Eighteenth-Century England*. New Haven: Yale University Press, 1967.

Plaks, Andrew H. "After the Fall: *Hsing-shi yin-yuan chuan* and the Seventeenth-Century Chinese Novel." *Harvard Journal of Asiatic Studies* 45.2 (December 1985): 543–580.

Plaks, Andrew H. "The Novel in Premodern China." In *The Novel, Volume 1: History, Geography, and Culture*. Ed. Franco Moretti. Princeton: Princeton University Press, 2007. 181–213.

Porter, David, ed. *Comparative Early Modernities*. London: Palgrave, 2012.

Porter, Jonathan. "The Scientific Community in Early Modern China." *ISIS* 73.4 (1982): 529–544.

Ropp, Paul S. *Dissent in Early Modern China: Ju-lin wai-shi and Ch'ing Social Criticism*. Ann Arbor: The University of Michigan Press, 1981.

Rowe, William T. *Hankow: Commerce and Society in a Chinese City, 1769–1889*. Stanford: Stanford University Press, 1984.

Struve, Lynn A. "Chimerical Early Modernity: The Case of 'Conquest-Generation' Memoirs." In *The Qing Formation in World Historical Time*. Ed. Lynn A. Struve. Cambridge: Harvard University Press, 2004. 335–372.

Taylor, Charles Taylor. *Sources of the Self: The Making of the Modern Identity.* Cambridge: Harvard University Press, 1989.

Wang, David Der-wei. *Fin-de-siècle Splendor: Repressed Modernities of Late Qing Fiction, 1849–1911.* Stanford: Stanford University Press, 1997.

Wittington, Phil. *Society in Early Modern England: The Vernacular Origins of Some Powerful Ideas.* Cambridge: Polity Press, 2010.

BORDERS AND BORDERLANDS NARRATIVES IN COLD WAR CHINA

XIAOJUE WANG

IN 1956, the *Hong Kong Commercial Daily* (香港商報) began serializing *The Sword Stained with Royal Blood* (碧血劍), a landmark early work of the New School martial arts fiction, one of the most widely read forms of modern Chinese literature in Hong Kong, Singapore, and other Sinophone communities in Southeast Asia, and later Taiwan and eventually Mainland China.[1] It was authored by Jin Yong 金庸 (pen name of Louis Cha 查良鏞), who had recently relocated from Mainland China to the British Crown colony of Hong Kong. Set during the Ming-Qing dynastic change, the novel tells the adventures of the young knight-errant Yuan Chengzhi, who joins forces with the peasant rebel Li Zicheng 李自成 to overthrow the corrupt Ming court and avenge the death of his father, the Ming general Yuan Chonghuan 袁崇煥, who defeated Nurhaci and was later wrongly executed by the Chongzhen 崇禎 Emperor. As a consequence, the Ming empire collapses and falls to the Manchus, and the peasant army turns out to be no less corrupt and brutal than the previous regime. The story ends with Yuan abandoning all hope in the Chinese mainland and sailing off with his comrades to an island close to Brunei in the southern seas.

Given the political circumstances of the time and Hong Kong's position between the Nationalists in Taiwan and the Communists on the mainland, Yuan's departure for the maritime region surrounding China has often been read as an allusion to the Nationalist retreat to Taiwan, which itself evokes the historical precedent of the Ming general Zheng Chenggong's 鄭成功 taking over of Taiwan as a base to restore the Ming dynasty that fell to the Manchu rule. Yuan's journey to the southern seas is also reminiscent of another heroic tale, *Sequel to the Water Margin* (水滸後傳), written by the Ming loyalist Chen Chen 陳忱 shortly after the Ming-Qing transition, which describes Li Jun's expedition in the southern seas. Leading a cohort of surviving bandits of the Mountain Liang, Li established a utopian kingdom in Siam underpinned by

Confucian ethics and rites after the Song dynasty lost the northern Chinese mainland to the Jurchen.[2] In Jin Yong's *Royal Blood*, however, Yuan's island experience remains undepicted. The novel stops with Yuan leaving the Chinese mainland and does not follow through with his explorations of the world beyond China's borders, which has led some scholars to suggest that the novel's lack of a utopian imagination located overseas betrays Jin Yong's Sinocentric cultural view.[3] John Christopher Hamm, for instance, argues that New School martial arts fiction is more interested in "a story of China proper, the middle kingdom, the unassailable center of cultural authority."[4] Providing no narrative of Yuan's life on the southern isle, Jin Yong's literary imaginations are more or less bounded by a notion of cultural China. However, given Yuan's disillusionment with political authority, be it the Ming dynasty, the rebel force of Li Zicheng, or the Manchu conquerors, his maritime adventure might rather involve migration, land reclamation, and settlement than an anti-Manchu mission in Brunei. After all, unlike the Ming official Zheng Chenggong or the reincarnated Mountain Liang heroes in Chen Chen's loyalist imagination, Yuan represents a hero in the world of Rivers and Lakes (*jianghu* 江湖), which is always already situated in the borderland of the orthodox sociopolitical system. Turning away from the collapsing margins of a past polity, the New School martial arts fiction marks a departure from rather than an inheritance of a loyalist literature that is predicated on the political legitimacy of a lost regime.

Although he evades a substitute political discourse in *Royal Blood*, since Yuan's frontier isle remains unspecified, Jin Yong's own literary practice significantly shaped the cultural landscape in Hong Kong, a new Cold War frontier between the two antagonist Chinese regimes across the Taiwan Strait. When martial arts fiction was censored in both the PRC and Taiwan, the New School martial arts novelists in Hong Kong reinvented the chivalric narrative tradition and turned this peripheral colony into a major site of creative cultural production. Probing dynastic crises or political transitions, these martial arts imaginations explore ambiguous or alternative cultural identities and historical consciousness along geopolitical fissures or borders, and project an ideal Chinese culture into a place beyond the borders of China proper.

Jin Yong is certainly not alone in imagining China within and beyond the nation's borders at the conjunction of the Great Divide. During the Cold War era, there are many literary writings that emplot borders, border-crossers, and borderlands experiences—a body of literature I call borderlands narratives. This chapter examines the borderlands narratives of Cold War China and offers an introduction to the diversity and dynamics of Cold War Sinophone writings. In the current scholarship, these works have been positioned within conventional discursive frameworks that emphasize nationalism, Communism, or anti-Communism. My reading, however, seeks to move beyond the reliance on existing categories and place them in dialogue with one another. In this way, we may observe how literary styles establish connections across China and beyond.

In recent years, studies of the cultural Cold War have gradually moved away from a focus on cultural production from the United States and the Soviet Union, and instead started to examine transnational literary trends. Adam Piette has critiqued the predominant trend in English-language criticism to treat Cold War–era cultural production as an exclusively Euro-American phenomenon and has urged scholars to look beyond the US–Soviet framework,[5] while Andrew Hammond has similarly proposed a global Cold War literature as a critical category, emphasizing that the "recognition of the global reach of the Cold War needs to be central to any study of the period's cultural production."[6] The 1949 divide in China and the formation of the Cold War order in Asia substantially affected Chinese literary topography.

This mid-twentieth-century geopolitical transformation resulted in the reconfiguration of multiple, disparate Chinese cultural zones. Consequently, in the post-1949 era one cannot address Chinese literature and culture without first unpacking the notions of *China* and *Chinese*. The Cold War geopolitics led to Asian decolonization, Chinese migration, socialist internationalism, and a consolidated anti-Communist Free China, and thus conditioned a notion of Chinese literature that cannot be restricted by the territorial boundaries of the People's Republic of China (PRC), the Republic of China (ROC), or the Chinese diaspora. The Cold War constitutes a critical stage for the formation of a transnational, multivalent Chinese-language cultural landscape that leads to the emergence of a global Sinophone literature. How should we attend to the diverse and dynamic literary practices in a network of heterogeneous, interconnected sites within and outside the Chinese mainland, traversing the conventional restrictions of national literature? How should we consider Chinese-language cultural productions of the Cold War era beyond the binary discursive framework in place during the Cold War that pitted communism against capitalism and the PRC against the Nationalist Taiwan?

Cold War borderlands literature is concerned with not only physical borders but also figurative ones. The great Chinese divide and the complex Cold War dynamics in East Asia entailed new or compounded long-existing dividing lines, borders, boundaries, and frontiers extending from Sino-Soviet to Sino–Southeast Asian borderlands, from the Taiwan Strait to the disputed islands and waters in the South China sea. Cold War borderlands literature thematizes the jagged borders of China, with its unstable frontiers and nondemarcated territories, thus unveiling the volatile nature of the nation-state, the empire, or any other political entity as well as challenging the notion of a homogenous Chinese culture and identity. By exploring connections between different geopolitical regions, these borderlands narratives illustrate convoluted cultural identities that complicate both the dichotomous ideology of the Cold War period and the myth of a monolithic China.

These works trace not only literal borders but also imaginative, metaphorical ones that are not identifiable as lines or contours on a map. These are borders produced along the lines of ethnicity, race, gender, as well as language, emotion, and existential angst. This body of literature is also concerned with such borders and borderland experiences. In *Borderlands/La Frontera*, the pioneer border theorist Gloria Anzaldúa distinguishes between the concepts of borders and borderlands: "Borders are set up to define the places that are safe and unsafe, to distinguish us from them. A border is a dividing line, a narrow strip along a steep edge. A borderland is a vague and undetermined place created by the emotional residue of an unnatural boundary. It is in a constant state of transition."[7] Although situated in different geopolitical circumstances,

Anzaldúa's notion of borderlands as a transitional, residual state is helpful in my analysis of Chinese Cold War literature. In the body of writings that I call *borderlands narratives*, the authors portray a borderland state in both temporal and spatial terms. Such borderland experiences of the protagonists condition the emergence of new, shifting forms of identity that disregard geopolitical boundaries. Although often written from within a distinctive ideological bloc, these literary imaginations do not necessarily fit in the prevailing Cold War assumption. Rather, they reveal the complex alignment, and lack thereof, of cultural identity and political ideology, and therefore open up new perspectives for reading Chinese or Sinophone literature of the Cold War.

Below, I read Lu Ling's 路翎 "'Battle' of the Lowlands" (窪地上的"戰役") in conjunction with Eileen Chang's 張愛玲 *Love in the Redland* (赤地之戀).[8] Both works are set in Chinese-Korean border regions and address issues of China–Korea contact from the perspective of romantic love during the Korean War period. Although from opposing ideological stances, both stories wind up converting the military battlefield into a site of personal emotional crisis, and the foreign land into the other space that is out of sync with dominant ideologies. I will then read Deng Kebao's 鄧克保 (Bo Yang 柏楊) *Alien Lands* (異域), which tells the story of a Kuomintang (KMT) force that continued to fight on in the borderlands of southwestern China, Burma, Laos, and Thailand long after the government had retreated to Taiwan.[9] *Alien Lands* has been regarded as a war fiction or anticommunist fiction. My reading, however, positions it at the intersection of aesthetic imagination and ethnographic accounts, war reportage and cultural encounters, border crossing and land reclamation. Although informed by ideological dictates of the KMT, the PRC cultural propaganda bureaus, or in Eileen Chang's case by the United States Information Agency (USIA) in Hong Kong, these three works explore border-crossing experiences in national, cultural, or existential terms, and further complicate the jagged boundaries of China and identity politics. I treat these borderlands narratives as a cross-cultural, intra-Asian site that is not always compatible with the Cold War geopolitical discourses. As my reading will show, the border-crossers in these works embody a subjectivity that cannot be fully integrated into the framework of nation-state, diaspora, or Cold War ideology in general.

THE LOWLAND, THE REDLAND, AND THE SPACE OF CRISIS

Both Lu Ling's "'Battle' of the Lowlands" and Eileen Chang's *Love in the Redland* emplot the Korean War. The Korean War was the inaugural hot war in the Cold War era. Regional wars, civil wars, proxy wars, and other forms of armed conflicts continued during the Cold War era on Chinese borders and other regions in Asia. Therefore, the Cold War, with its connotations of zero armed conflicts in the context of the US–Soviet stand-off, is by no means "cold" in the Second and Third worlds.

In 1954 Lu Ling (1923–1994) published the short story, " 'Battle' of the Lowlands," in the leading literary journal of the fledgling socialist China, *People's Literature* (人民文學). It tells a tragic love story between a Chinese People's Volunteer (CPV) soldier and a Korean girl in a northern Korean village during the Korean War. While the Korean girl, Kim Shenji, dreams of marriage and a life of happiness, the Chinese soldier Wang Yinghong is prohibited from responding to her love due to military regulations. The forbidden romance ends with Yinghong choosing to go to a decisive battle and dying a heroic death.

Rising to literary fame in the 1940s, Lu Ling was the most talented writer of the leftist July School (七月派). When he published his first novella "Hungry Guo Su'e" (飢餓的郭素娥; 1942), he was only twenty years old. Known for his distinctive representation of the "primitive life force" (原始的強力) and his incisive exploration of the spiritual wound of modern China, he was regarded as the genuine disciple of Hu Feng 胡風, whose theory of "subjective fighting spirit" (主觀戰鬥精神) urged writers to mobilize their own life forces to fathom the inner world of those who had been wounded or humiliated so as to seek means of emancipation. Lu Ling's magnum opus, the two-volume *Children of the Rich* (財主的兒女們; 1945 and 1948)—which is more than 1,300 pages long and was acclaimed by Hu as "the greatest cultural event in modern Chinese literary history"—presents an ambitious exploration of the cultural, psychological, and social changes of modern China.[10] Tracing Jiang Chunzu's perilous exile from Shanghai to the immense inland during the anti-Japanese war, the novel charts this young man's restless spiritual battles between clashing ideas, including the tensions between solitary subjectivity and the masses, romantic love and lust, traditional and modern values, and individual *ressentiment* and ideological contradictions. In his discussion of Hu Feng and Lu Ling's introspective examination of modern Chinese subjectivity, Kirk Denton considers Lu Xun 魯迅 as their forerunner: "he who is tempted by external attractions will take an inward turn, engaging metaphysical meditation, calling on self-reflection and lyrical feeling, doing away with materialistic limitations, and inhabiting the domain of the innate mind."[11] Lu Ling's scrutiny of the wounded subjectivity at its most vulnerable and obscure is conspicuously at odds with Mao Zedong's 毛澤東 notion that the individual should, for the sake of a larger social goal, subordinate himself to the national and socialist collectivity, which would foresee the predicament confronting him in socialist China.

In December 1952, Lu volunteered to join a writers' delegation to visit the Korean War front, where he stayed until the Korean Armistice Agreement was signed in July 1953. After returning to China, he published a set of writings dramatizing Korean War experiences, including the controversial " 'Battle' of the Lowlands." Despite their initial passionate reception among general readers, these writings soon provoked vehement attacks by mainstream writers and critics of the young Chinese republic for betraying a counterrevolutionary nature, promoting capitalist humanism, and distorting reality, particularly that of the Chinese–Korean relationship. In 1955, he was arrested as a member of the Hu Feng clique and was incarcerated. When he was finally released in 1980, he was a schizophrenic old man.

The main points of controversy revolve around the violation, in Lu Ling's "Lowlands," of the pure friendship between Chinese soldiers and the Korean people and the sacred code of international solidarity. For the PRC, the Korean War was waged in a foreign country; therefore, the question of how to adjust the relationship between the Chinese troops and the Korean people was critical to guaranteeing military victory. In the 1950 order to the Chinese People's Volunteers (CPV), Mao Zedong stipulated:

> While in Korea, the Chinese People's Volunteers must show fraternal feelings and respect for the people, the People's Army, the Democratic Government, the Workers' Party and the other democratic parties of Korea as well as for Comrade Kim Il Sung, the leader of the Korean people, and strictly observe military and political discipline. This is a most important political basis for ensuring the fulfillment of your military task.[12]

In his article written for the sixtieth anniversary of the signing of the Korean Armistice Agreement, Wang Hui 汪暉 observes that the Maoist notion of "people's war" employed during Chinese revolutions prior to 1949 was changed into that of international war upon China's entry into the Korean War. However, the core issue of the people's war—what Wang Hui calls "the interpenetration and entanglements of military and everyday life matters"—was still a significant part of the CPV's operations in the Korean Peninsula.[13] The Maoist "fish-in-water" relationship between the army and the people during the people's war was changed into the fraternal feelings between Chinese soldiers and the Korean people, which constituted the foundation of socialist solidarity.

In his discussion of the aesthetic strategies adopted by early PRC films on the Korean War, Ban Wang notes that the heightened moral imperative of "an ethics of international altruism" converts the horrendous battle scene into a sublime, triumphant act, and the soldiers into "the most lovely, or lovable" people.[14] Among literary works on the Korean War of the 1950s, Wei Wei's 魏巍 essay "Who Are the Most Lovable People?" (誰是最可愛的人) is a case in point that successfully transforms the macabre war scenes into a lyrical piece of moral edification. The bulk of the article depicts appalling scenes of war violence: soldiers' body parts on the battleground, corpses twisted in grotesque postures, weapons splattered with brain tissue, and so forth. These meticulous, naturalistic details are overshadowed by a moralistic emphasis on patriotism, heroism, and socialist internationalism culminating in the most lyrical lines of Korean War literature:

> Dear friends, when you are taking the first train in the morning to the factory, when you are carrying your hoes and rakes on your way to the fields, when you are drinking your first cup of soymilk, when you are taking your backpack to go to school, when you are sitting down quietly at your desk to plan a day's work, when you are feeding a piece of apple to your child's open mouth, when you are taking a leisurely stroll with your wife, do you realize you are in a state of happiness?[15]

However, this lovable person in the Third-World international arena is prohibited from engaging in private, romantic love, particularly interracial or interethnic love. Whereas scenes of Chinese soldiers risking their lives to rescue Korean civilians abound in literary and cinematic narratives of the time, romantic liaisons between soldiers and Korean women are rarely touched upon. This China–Korea solidarity is marked by a relationship of stoic kinship. Not surprisingly, in a representative article of condemnation, Ba Jin 巴金, the veteran May Fourth New Culturist, accused Lu Ling of contaminating the pure, innocent feeling between China and Korea, which should be "like that between brother and sister, or between son and mother."[16] The overemphasis on the blood relationship in the rhetoric of "Chinese and Korean's are one family" betrays an anxiety of transgressing the incest taboo. Wei Wei, the author of the macabre yet lyrical essay praising the most lovable people, censured Lu's story as a malicious rewriting of the traditional tragic romance of Liang Shanbo and Zhu Yingtai, a love story ending in the death of the young couple whose relationship was hindered by Yingtai's "feudalist" father, who did not approve of Shanbo's poor family background. Wei vehemently argued that Lu Ling cast the sacred military discipline in analogy to the viciously obstinate Mr. Zhu, Yingtai's father, the epitome of feudalist ideology, thus repackaging the classical love story on the battlefield.[17]

"'Battle' of the Lowlands" unfolds in a small Korean village where a reconnaissance squad is undergoing military training. The soldiers live with a Korean family composed of an elderly mother and a daughter. They help the Korean mother and daughter with burdensome chores like carrying water, chopping wood, and fixing the roof, while the mother and the daughter cook for the squad and help do their laundry. During the everyday interactions, the girl, Kim Shenji, falls in love with Wang Yinghong, though the latter, obsessed with his military adventure, is unaware of Shenji's love. It isn't until Yinghong's lieutenant, Wang Shun, warns him of the potential violation of the voluntary army's discipline that Yinghong starts to realize the girl's feelings for him, after which he begins to wonder whether or not he should continue doing daily chores for her family. Meanwhile, Shenji, now envisioning Yinghong as her future husband rather than a "foreigner," starts to resist his helping with the chore of carrying water, for collecting and carrying water are women's responsibilities in Korea. Thus, in addition to military regulations, the relationship is further complicated by language barriers and different cultural codes. Interestingly, the two young people never communicate their feelings face to face. In the most intimate scene, it is the mother of the Korean girl who expresses, in Korean and by way of her motherly embrace, the inclusion of the young Chinese soldier into her family. The soldier, who understands little Korean, is mesmerized by the tender, low voice and recalls the night when his own mother saw him off to war.

These sites of personal intimacy are inextricably bound up with the larger themes of patriotism and socialist internationalism. Notwithstanding its harshly attacked depiction of private emotions, the story itself was squarely set within the political ideology of the Resisting America, Aiding Korea (抗美援朝) campaign. The literary and cinematic works on the Korean War of the 1950s and 1960s promoted international socialist solidarity underlined by Chinese nationalist sentiments and generated the sense of an Asian united front against imperialist Western powers. This notion of a united Asia differed from that of the Greater East Asia Co-Prosperity Sphere promoted by Japanese imperialism as an Eastern competitor to Western modernization. Instead it was grounded in the socialist discourse of class consciousness and class struggle. As Kwai-cheung Lo argues, "For China, Asia constituted a new meaning of socialism that expressed and defined social relationships within China and China's relationship to the region and to the world."[18]

Whereas the dominant rhetoric promoted the treatment of Koreans as siblings, it by no means ignored their ethnic difference with Chinese. On the contrary, this distinction was constantly highlighted in the literary and cinematic works produced at the time. Lu Ling's "Lowlands" is no exception. When the squad is assigned to the war front to collect information, the village holds a party to send them off. Shenji, who is an activist in the village performance troupe, sings and dances in her beautiful pink silk dress and plays the role of the wife of a soldier of the Korean People's Army. Although Yinghong is preoccupied with the upcoming mission, his initial war experience, he is mesmerized by Shenji's feminine beauty.

Here, masculine heroism is reinforced by the cross-ethnic male gaze at the female body dressed in outlandish, ethnic clothes. How should one address this ethnographic exhibitionism that abounded in Korean War cultural productions? Frantz Fanon begins his article "Algeria Unveiled" by calling our attention to the political and cultural significance of clothes in human civilization: "The way people clothe themselves, together with the traditions of dress and finery that costume implies, constitutes the most distinctive form of a society's uniqueness, that is to say the one that is the most immediately perceptible."[19] In responding to the French colonial administration's decision to unveil Algerian women, Fanon alerts us to the intricate duplicity of this apparently nonviolent enterprise: as it championed the liberation of the Algerian woman from the bondage of patriarchal tradition, it also opened her to the Western sexual fantasy or, even worse, authorized sexual violence against her: "the evocation of this freedom given to the sadism of the conqueror, to his eroticism, creates faults, fertile gaps through which both dreamlike forms of behavior and, on certain occasions, criminal acts can emerge."[20] In the anticolonial socialist solidarity spelled out in the Resisting America, Aiding Korea campaign, an inverted type of power coercion is at play: by "veiling" Korean women in their traditional costumes, the Chinese socialist regime envisioned the Korean nation as vulnerable and weak, waiting to be protected and saved. In the literary and cinematic productions of the time, Korean women are frequently depicted in colorful, traditional ethnic dresses, singing and dancing, objectified as an ethnographic spectacle. Not unlike the colonial removal of the veil, the confinement of a minor nation within the boundaries of the gendered and sexualized customs betrays the double-edged socialist hegemony: it identifies Korea as China's socialist sibling while confirming Korea's ethnic difference and its historical relation to China as a secondary state.[21]

As Yinghong gradually comes to experience a "strange, sweet yet uneasy feeling," the young scout yearns more fervently for the opportunity to participate in a military mission: "He would now, on behalf of his mother, and on behalf of that girl, fight for his country, for world peace"—as if it were the only solution for this impossible love relationship.[22] In the final reconnaissance mission, when dispatched to his spot to wait for the appearance of the enemy, Yinghong is overwhelmed by the unbearable intensity at the moment of absolute stillness and solitude: "His thoughts started to get away from him. Such a silence, such an absolute standstill . . . he had never before experienced this. He even felt himself engulfed and paralyzed by this deep stillness so much so that he would never be able to stand up again."[23] In a hallucinatory state, he sees the gentle face of his mother, and then the Korean girl dancing in the role of the soldier's wife. This inward existential experience of the self is reminiscent of Lu Ling's unruly neurotic protagonists of the 1940s, perpetually trapped in arduous psychological struggles for an unequivocal subjectivity. After the platoon successfully captures an American officer, they proceed to retreat. To protect their team members as they transport the captive back for military information, the platoon leader Wang Shun and Yinghong stay behind to provide cover. After Yinghong is seriously injured and surrounded by American soldiers, he decides to sacrifice himself to protect Wang Shun, whom he deeply admires. Shenji's dancing figure appears one more time in his hallucination. This time, she dances for Chairman Mao and his mother at the foot of the Tiananmen Gate Tower in Beijing. In the besieged lowland of the final battle, the swirling female figure elicits Yinghong's last vigor and strength, ready to sacrifice his life—what could be more politically dubious yet fascinating? As the platoon leader delivers to Shenji the blood-soaked handkerchief embroidered with the couple's names, a token of love that Yinghong kept in the inner pocket of his uniform close to his heart, the forbidden love is thus sanctioned and sublimated over the martyred body. What the author could not have expected was that such a sublimation of individual love in the face of political goals would not spare him the accusation of transgressing beyond the cross-ethnic romantic and sexual boundary.

Displacing the military lowland with a libidinal site of intense desires, Lu Ling's border-crossing narrative betrays its most individualistic moment. Having skirted the interethnic edges in terms of culture, desire, or romantic subjectivity, Lu, along with his unruly characters, was ruthlessly purged.

The rupture between the political and the personal found a most unexpected echo in an anticommunist fiction written on the other side of the Cold War division, which also dramatizes the Korean War. The same year that Lu Ling's story was published in Beijing, Eileen Chang (1920–1995) finished her novel *Love in the Redland* during her sojourn in the British colony Hong Kong. Lu Ling's and Chang's war stories form a fascinating dialogue from the opposite ends of the Cold War iron curtain. Emplotting the destructive force of war as a trope for romance, passion, and desire, both of these literary imaginations spill over the political boundaries predicated by clear-cut ideological positions. By displacing political conviction with libidinal vigor, both writers unconsciously subverted the dominant political discourse even as they believed that they remained within the established boundaries. In a way, the Korean battlefield becomes the alien land in the hearts of their troubled characters, a heterotopia deviating from emotional or ethnic norms as well as communist and anticommunist political doctrines. To cross the China–Korea border to this imaginative "other space" amounts to the peril of staring into the heart of darkness full of passions and betrayals—political as well as romantic—and of probing the unfathomable human psychological borderland.

Like Lu Ling, Eileen Chang established her literary fame in the 1940s. While Lu Ling followed the nationwide migration to the vast inner China, Chang spent the wartime in the fallen city of Shanghai and in Hong Kong under Japanese occupation. Focusing on characters from declining aristocratic families stranded in the modern transition, Chang's early works established an aesthetic of everyday life marked by a pervasive mood of desolation. Because her writings shied away from the predominant topics of revolution and national salvation, she was sidelined and subsequently erased from official literary histories in the postwar period. Shortly after the founding of the People's Republic of China, Chang left Shanghai for Hong Kong and eventually for the United States, where she led a reclusive life until her death in 1995.

During her sojourn in Hong Kong from 1953 to 1955, Chang wrote two political novels with the sponsorship of the USIA: *Rice-Sprout Song* (秧歌) and *Love in the Redland*.[24] Even as these two Cold War novels explore human desire and frailty in the face of historical atrocities, they nevertheless bear the clear imprint of anticommunist propaganda fiction and are firmly entrenched in the cultural Cold War against Chinese communism.

Despite the strong endorsement by the cultural propaganda machinery, these two novels were never successful—either politically or commercially. They were not popular in Free China either. Despite its anticommunist theme, *Love in the Redland* could not even pass the KMT censorship during the martial law period, let alone compete with prevalent tendentious works such as Chen Jiying's 陳紀瀅 *Fool in the Reeds* (荻村傳, 1951), which was translated into English in 1959 by none other than Eileen Chang.

Love in the Redland narrates the love story of a young couple, Liu Quan and Huang Juan, to illustrate political and emotional disillusionment during a time of historical turbulence, from the land reform through the Three-Antis Movement to the Korean War in socialist China. As recent college graduates, Liu Quan and Huang Juan witness the brutality of the land reform movement. After Liu Quan is reassigned to Shanghai, he becomes involved in a political conspiracy and is sent to jail. Huang Juan consents to become the mistress of a powerful communist cadre in exchange for Liu's release. Devastated and disillusioned, Liu volunteers to fight in the Korean War. While the first part of the novel is set in a rural area during the land reform period, Shanghai— the capitalist and Westernized city par excellence—takes center stage in the rest of the novel. During socialist construction, this former commercial and cosmopolitan city was turned into a ghost town, with the lurking specters of Shanghai petty urbanites stranded in a liminal state of uncertainty.

The most intriguing twist comes at the end of the story. Exhausted in both political and romantic battles in the nightmarish city of Shanghai, Liu chooses to join the

People's Volunteer Army and to be deployed to the Korean War front. Personal crisis and emotional agony wound up in a political commitment, as if ideological infatuation could serve as a panacea for psychological malaise: "He only felt that he would no longer survive on the Chinese mainland; he couldn't even breathe. All he wanted was to go away—the farther, the better. He was not afraid of suffering on the battlefield, of getting injured, handicapped, or killed. It was as if the pain in his heart could only be covered by a larger pain."[25] Crossing the China-Korea border in the morning mist, Liu feels relief: "he was now in a foreign country, after all. He thought that the junction of time and space was intriguing. Sometimes, time functioned like space. The distance of ten thousand miles was like that of five or ten years. The past was now like a haze" (222–223).

In a fierce battle, Liu is seriously injured. Lying on the open ground with heaps of corpses, mutilated bodies, and limbs, next to the corpse of a young soldier with a rotting face, Liu is forsaken in an absolute stillness. *Love in the Redland* was often criticized for its lack of the artistic finery that marked Chang's other writings. Unlike Lu Ling, Chang did not have firsthand experience of the Korean War. In an interview, she said she received a synopsis of the war and raw materials from the USIA office in Hong Kong. Her depiction of gruesome war savagery might not read as graphic and vivid as that by Wei Wei in his "Who Are the Most Lovable People," which Chang sarcastically referred to through the character of Liu Quan. However, rather than dwelling on war brutality, Chang probed her character's psyche, from fear to resentment, and from megalomania to neurosis. For her, the domain of human subjectivity—confronting love, lust, and desire—is no less treacherous than war itself.

Liu Quan is captured and sent to an internment camp. Shortly after the signing of the armistice, he and his fellow prisoners of war are given the choice to be repatriated to Free China—which is to say, Taiwan. To everyone's surprise, however, he rejects the offer and opts instead to return to Mainland China:

> He would like to go back to the mainland, to leave the captives here behind and join the other group of captives. As long as one man like him remained among them, the Communists would never feel comforted.
>
> He didn't entertain hope to see Huang Juan again. But his life was exchanged by her happiness; so he always thought that he should be responsible to her by taking best advantage of his life. Except for that, he couldn't think of a better way to spend his life. (253)

For Liu, the only way to repay Huang Juan for her sacrifice of love and innocence is to serve as a secret agent resisting communism from within. In order to embattle his existential despair and subjectivity in crisis, Liu paradoxically chooses to become an agent of infiltration, a profession that relies on the very dissolution of a constant identity. How seriously can such a commitment be taken? Given Liu's suspicious political resume, one would hardly foresee a bright future for his covert anticommunist operation. The boundary between the personal and the political is once again blurred.

Just like his determination to go to the war front to ease his psychological pain, Liu's return to Red China constitutes yet another selfish, personal leap under the cloak of a national cause.

C. T. Hsia contended that this is a book about personal and political betrayal.[26] Shuang Shen argues that the theme of betrayal provides Chang a platform to deal with her own unsettling diasporic experiences after leaving China: "Writing about betrayal allows her to describe the complex contextualization of the diasporic subject vis-à-vis multiple nation-states in the context of the Cold War."[27] Rather than being predicated on the dichotomous rhetoric of betrayal and loyalty, Chang's writings expose the arbitrary nature of political conviction, polarization, and antagonism that marked the capricious nature of the Cold War climate. In that sense, Eileen Chang's and Lu Ling's stories of love unto death on the Korean battlefield explore the intricate edges of ethics, emotions, and politics at moments of historical contingencies and existential crisis. For Wang Yinghong and Liu Quan, being a reconnaissance scout or an undercover agent— fluid, hybrid identities based on a shifting sense of self—is at the core of their lives. Deeply embroiled in the politics of proxy war, Lu's and Chang's protagonists have to live with a proxy identity that they are unable to transcend. Walking a fine line between loyalty and betrayal, the national and the personal, their borderline experiences marked their service in the hot war zone of the Cold War and shaped their border-crossing existence.

ALIEN LANDS, BORDERLANDS, AND OTHER SPACES

Whereas the Korean War experiences of border-crossing, both physical and metaphorical, center on the intrinsic entanglement of romance and politics, the next war fiction I read, situated in the southwestern border area that straddles the undemarcated borders between China and Burma, deals with political abandonment and existential trials, and ultimately teases out the essential corporeality and finitude of human existence.

In 1960, Taipei's *Independent Evening News* (自立晚報) started to serialize a report about a stateless army in the jungles of the borderlands between China's Yunnan Province and Burma, titled *Fighting in Alien Lands for Eleven Years* (血戰異域十一年). It was enthusiastically welcomed by readers, most of whom were recent émigrés having retreated to Taiwan with the Nationalist government, and was published as a monograph a year later under the new title *Alien Lands*. The protagonist and first-person narrator of *Alien Lands*, Deng Kebao, bears the same name as the text's author, though, as it turns out, the reportage is actually a fictional work by Bo Yang, who used the pseudonym Deng Kebao and claimed that this story was based on actual interviews with evacuated refugee soldiers from the Lone Army. The work depicts the experiences of the Nationalist Eighth Field Army that fought on in the borderlands of southwestern China, Burma, Laos, and Thailand long after the government had retreated to Taiwan. It begins with the loss of Yunnan province to the Chinese Communists in 1949, followed by the exodus of the remaining Nationalist troops, their families, and local civilians across the border between Burma and China. In addition to the siege and military attacks by the Chinese communist army, local Burmese troops, and indigenous tribes, this Lone Army also faced adverse conditions, including starvation, disease, hostile weather, and betrayal from within their own ranks. Every time they pulled together to forge a semblance of life, new conflicts were right around the corner.

Under such harsh conditions, the ill-equipped forces still managed to fight their way back into Chinese territory twice and eventually formed an anticommunist coalition beyond the Chinese borders to contain the spread of communism in Southeast Asia. The newly independent state of Burma, already feeling vulnerable with the People's Republic of China to its north and American-supported Thailand to the southeast, considered the remnant Nationalist troops a menace to its national security. In 1953 and 1954, under international pressure, a large portion of the Lone Army was directed to evacuate to Taiwan. A group of soldiers and officers refused to follow the evacuation order and were forced into the jungles of the Thai-Burmese border. As the international power system changed in the 1970s, with the PRC replacing the KMT in the United Nations and the reconfiguration of America's Asian strategy, this remnant of former KMT troops in Burma and Northern Thailand lost their strategic importance, and turned from anticommunist warriors into stateless refugees.[28] In a meticulous and relentless manner, *Alien Lands* describes numerous brutal and desperate battles as well as the deprivation and suffering of these people fighting for survival in the ruthless jungle of fear, treachery, and political conspiracy. The story ends at the critical conjuncture in 1954, when the protagonist and his family refuse to retreat to Taiwan and follow a small body of forces into the mountainous jungles.

I read *Alien Lands* at the intersection of aesthetic imagination and historical account, war reportage, and borderland exploration. Bo Yang's depictions of China's southwest border regions with their hybrid ethnic minority cultures place the work in a genealogy of Han Chinese accounts of China's borderland. Such works often adopt the form of local gazetteers and personal miscellaneous notes, which—through the long course of dynastic history, particularly during the Ming and Qing—have been marked by a combination of the central court's Confucian agenda of sinicization, anecdotal records of local ethnic cultures, and a reflexive look at Chinese civilization itself. In studies of China's imperial frontiers, where political rivals competed for resources and dominance, scholars on Chinese history have explored active cultural and economic exchanges and syncretism in borderlands communities.[29] The vast border regions, though politically contested and often undemarcated, provided contact zones of cultural fluidity and hybridity. In his study of the changing political and cultural institutions on the Yunnan frontier during the Qing, Charles Patterson Giersch argues that the central court's policy of one-directional hegemonic sinicization was often not put into action on the southwestern borders. Instead, vibrant movements of acculturation and syncretism occurred on all local levels between indigenous tribes, the Qing court, Siam, and Burmese regimes.[30]

Alien Lands can also to be placed in dialogue with a group of writings on the Chinese Expeditionary Army in the 1940s. In 1942, when Japan landed troops in Burma, a Chinese military expedition force was dispatched to protect the Burma Road. Among the volunteers was Mu Dan 穆旦, who later became a renowned poet of the Nine Leaves Group. Defeated and besieged, the expeditionary force was forced into the Yeren Shan (Wildmen Mountain), the tropical jungle sprawling more than two hundred miles along the border between China and Burma. Fifty thousand soldiers died as a result of disease, starvation, torrential rains, poisonous snakes, insects, and wild beasts. Five months later, Mu Dan emerged out of the jungle in India as one of few survivors. He narrated his "journey of death" in a poem pervaded by macabre imagery, "The Jungle's Apparition: To the Skulls on the Rivers of the Hukwang Valley" (森林之魅：祭胡康河上的白骨; 1945). Written as a dialogue between the man and the jungle, this is the only poem he composed about his war experience. The wrenching, nightmarish experiences in the Burmese rainforest were recorded by General Du Yuming 杜聿明 (1904–1981), the commander of the Expeditionary Army for whom Mu Dan served as an interpreter, in his war report *A Brief Account of the Chinese Expeditionary Army Fighting against Japan in Burma* (中國遠征軍入緬對日作戰述略; 1961), and by Sun Kegang 孫克剛 (1911–1967) in his war reportage *Quelling the Bandits in Burma* (緬甸蕩寇誌; 1946).[31]

Bo Yang's literary imagination filled *Alien Lands* with gripping depictions of fierce battles, flames of war, and ghastly scenes of human suffering, death, and violence. However, it is the contemplation of the irrationality and incomprehensibility of war atrocities that renders the novel a compelling work compared with conventional war fiction. It reminds us that war experiences were both a material and an existential condition. The notion of "alien lands" denotes not merely the lost KMT government in Mainland China or the foreign Burmese and later Thai states but also the extremity of human struggle for survival in the extreme conditions of the tropical rain forests. Scenes of corporeal mutilation, disembodiment, and deprivation are reminiscent of Mu Dan's verses some ten years earlier when he personified the jungle as "unfurling my mammoth green leaves, my teeth" and addressing the human being: "Welcome, come and strip yourself of blood and flesh."[32] Compared with the immense capacity and infinite threat of the jungle, human beings appear powerless. The vulnerability and finitude of human life renders any political ideology meaningless.

Alien Lands is no conventional anticommunist fiction that preaches ideological propaganda. The original goal of the Lone Army was to establish an anticommunist foundation along the border regions. The Southwest borderlands and Southeast Asia generally could be constructed as a crucial site for restoring the lost Chinese mainland and for reclaiming the lost legitimate polity. In this light, the Lone Army can be regarded as in a loyalist (遺民) tradition that can be traced back to China's long dynastic history. Severed from the geographical or historical legitimacy of a former dynasty, these loyalists enacted the political and cultural orthodoxy of a toppled state by refusing to serve the new court. The novel includes many moments when historical narratives of loyalist tradition are evoked to support the Lone Army mentally at times of deepest despair. David Der-wei Wang reminds us in his conception of post-loyalism in the context of modern Taiwan history that the loyalists derived their meaning from the "crumbling margins of legitimacy and subjectivity."[33] In this light, being loyalist leftovers of a severed past is both a historical and an existential condition.

However, the novel's reflections on the materiality and finitude of human existence and the state of complete abandonment by political authorities ultimately destabilized its overarching nationalistic, anticommunist theme. When the KMT government, now settled in Taiwan—an island that represented the geographical and political entity of China—issued the evacuation order demanding the Lone Army to "return" to its homeland, more than half of the troops determined to remain in the border region. By refusing to go to Taiwan, a "home" they had never visited, were they trying to preserve the base for an anticommunist coalition? Were they so dedicated to the diehard anticommunist mission that they would rather stay in the primitive tropical jungles? By not joining the regular army in Taiwan, they opted to give up their citizenship in the Republic of China. Now stateless, whose nationalistic cause were they fighting? Which political or cultural legitimacy were they preserving and restoring? When these loyalists were not holding any political legitimacy, orthodox national identity and delineations were complicated. As a text alien to political or historical genealogies, the novel helps us to rethink the inadequacy of national frameworks for considering the political or personal experiences of these military refugees or other exilic subjects who were stranded in border regions across conventional political entities.

Alien Lands constantly appeals to destiny and transcendental immanence to explicate the state of failure, suffering, and human tragedy. Nation or ethnicity is not the only basis for identity politics in this novel. This story of an army without a country is more concerned with the self-positioning of Chinese people in the era of war, geographical divide, and family loss, dispersal, and uprootedness, which all destroyed the very foundation of human existence and subjectivity. In this light, the novel offers an articulation of a Chinese consciousness beyond the restrictions of geopolitical boundaries. Its most compelling element is not its depiction of wrenching war atrocities and their aftermath, nor the sense of orphanhood and abandonment by the Nationalist government, but rather the troop's final desperate determination to pursue self-exile into the primitive jungles outside human civilization. In a poignant way, the Lone Army endeavored to preserve a sense of Chineseness that is cut off from any nation state, and from the Nationalist or communist political authority. Its mission was to reclaim land in the jungle so as to assert a sense of virtue, history, and cultural belonging. In the undemarcated border areas between China, Burma, and Thailand, these military refugees preserved the language, customs, values, and cultural essentials of Chinese civilization. And yet the purpose of the Lone Army's land reclamation and resettlement in the border region was not that of sinicization as championed by the previous Chinese empire. It also did not follow the route of cultural nationalism as a "scattering of seeds and flowers, planting of spiritual roots," as it was conceived and promoted by the new Confucianist Tang Junyi 唐君毅 during his diasporic years in Cold War Hong Kong. Rather, the Lone Army's endeavor can be viewed as a heterotopia that resonates with the classical "Peach Blossom Spring" (桃花源) ideal. A topos in Chinese literary imagination, Tao Qian's 陶潛 (365?–427) "Peach Blossom Spring" evokes a state of statelessness, "with no idea of the Han dynasty, not to mention the Wei and Jin dynasties," where people live a simple life, remote from political turmoil.[34] What could exemplify in a more suitable yet tragic way the endeavor of being Chinese, being human, and setting down roots in an alien land?

These literary works from different locales in Cold War Asia portray borderlands and border-crossing experiences in political, psychological, ethical, and cultural terms, and explore divergent cultural identities and alternative spaces that arise from these experiences. All three stories thematize a form of space: *di* (地) or *yu* (域), which denotes terrain, territory, land, place, or *topos*. These notions do not only point to nation, state, and ideological blocs, they also evoke alternative, other spaces, or what Michel Foucault calls heterotopias, which are characterized by their contesting and deviating from the established order and structure of a human society. While utopias, as perfected or inverted forms of human societies, are "fundamentally unreal spaces," heterotopias are real phenomena to be found in every civilization.[35] Situated at the Chinese-Korean or Sino-Southeast Asian borders or on the verge of emotional or existential borderlands, these Cold War heterotopias disrupt and complicate the prevailing national or ideological views. These other spaces are demarcated by borders and boundaries occasioned by historical, ethical, linguistic, and cultural tensions. In these other spaces, we see predominant systems and hierarchies loosening up, we see conventional geopolitical boundaries made permeable or being transgressed, and we witness the emergence of ambiguous subjectivities.

To read Cold War Chinese-language literature within the context of borders and borderlands allows us to examine the interstices and ambivalent subject positions within and outside conventional geopolitical topographies, thus positioning these literary productions and human experiences beyond the restrictions of national or ideological delineation. It also helps us rethink the discourse of center versus margins. As my reading reveals, borders and heterotopias are located at unexpected sites, sometimes at the very center, of our culture and civilization. They are not margins; rather, they are fissures and sites of openings, inhabited by multivalent forms of cultural identity. These borderlands narratives are concerned with new subject positions rather than charting new centers and margins and perpetuating the divide between both.

Through the comparative reading of borderlands imaginations, I have sought to explore new perspectives to examine Cold War Chinese-language literature. The Cold War may be considered a taxonomical category with which to examine Chinese-language cultural productions of this new international epoch. Here, the Cold War does not refer to a category of historical periodization or geopolitical demarcation, but to a global configuration of confrontations and interactions, connections and intersections in both geopolitical and geopoetic terms. This convoluted constellation necessitates a comparative investigation of Chinese literature produced in disparate regions in Asia and beyond, across the boundaries between nation-states, as well as a delinking of Chinese literature from the national literature model. If Cold War Chinese literature can be said to exist as a taxonomical category, it lies in exactly the cross-regional, global currents facilitated by the international geopolitical conflicts that we call the Cold War.

Recent theoretical reflections on global Sinophone literature—in particular, Jing Tsu and David Wang's discussion of "global Chinese literature" and Shu-mei Shih's "Sinophone articulations"—bespeak the enduring Cold War posterity in the field of Chinese literary studies.[36] This category of global China or the Sinophone challenges a vision of Chinese culture as homogeneous and monolithic. Shu-mei Shih, for instance, describes the Sinophone as "a network of places of cultural production outside China and on the margins of China and Chineseness where a historical process of heterogenizing and localizing of continental Chinese culture has been taking place for several centuries."[37] The Cold War marks a key moment in the historical processes, a moment that reshuffled and further complicated the intricate Sinophone network of cultural practices and imaginations. Rescuing Cold War Sinophone writings from the conventional frameworks that emphasize themes of nationalism, communism, or anticommunism, we will be able to compare Chinese-language literature across various localized and interrelated regions in Asia and tease out their convergent or divergent thematic and aesthetic concerns. Such a comparative study fractures the bipolar antagonism of two Chinese governments into multiple notions of China and Chineseness.

NOTES

1. Jin Yong 金庸, *Bixue jian* 碧血劍 [The sword stained with royal blood] (Beijing: Beijing sanlian shudian, 1994), abbreviated as *Royal Blood* hereafter.
2. Chen Chen 陳忱, *Shuihu houzhuan* 水滸後傳 [Sequel to *The Water Margin*, 1664] (Beijing: Zhonghua shuju, 2004). For a study of the theme of utopia in this novel, see Luo Shuiyu 駱水玉, "Shuihu houzhuan: Jiuming yimin Chen Chen de haiwai qiankun" 《水滸後傳》: 舊明遺民陳忱的海外乾坤 [Sequel to *The Water Margin*: Ming loyalist Chen Chen's overseas kingdom], *Hanxue yanjiu* 漢學研究 [Sinological studies] 19.1 (2001): 219–248; for a detailed study of the fiction and Chen's life, see Ellen Widmer, *The Margins of Utopia:* Shui-hu hou-chuan *and the Literature of Ming Loyalism* (Cambridge, MA: Harvard University Asia Center, 1987).
3. See, for instance, Weijie Song 宋偉杰, *Cong yule xingwei dao wutuobang chongdong: Jin Yong xiaoshuo zai jiedu* 從娛樂行為到烏托邦衝動: 金庸小說再解讀 [From entertainment activity to utopian impulse: Rereading Jin Yong's fiction] (Nanjing: Jiangsu renmin chubanshe, 1999), chap. 4.
4. John C. Hamm, *Paper Swordsmen: Jin Yong and the Modern Chinese Martial Arts Novel* (Honolulu: University of Hawaii Press, 2005), 74.
5. Adam Piette, *The Literary Cold War: 1945 to Vietnam* (Edinburgh: Edinburgh University Press, 2009).
6. Andrew Hammond, *Global Cold War Literature* (London and New York: Routledge, 2012), 2.

7. Gloria Anzaldúa, *Borderlands/La Frontera: The New Mestiza* (San Francisco: Spinsters/ Aunt Lute, 1987), 7. In North American scholarship, border theory focuses on US-Mexico border studies and draws heavily on social science, particularly ethnography and anthropology. Border theorists such as Anzaldúa and Renato Rosaldo not only explore experiences of separation, migration, and violence across borders but also highlight borderlands as a zone of creative cultural production and a potential site of multiculturalism. See, for instance, Renato Rosaldo, *Culture and Truth: The Remaking of Social Analysis* (Boston: Beacon, 1993). Later, scholars such as David E. Johnson and Alejandro Lugo expanded the ideas of border and borderlands to examine multiple borders—geographical, cultural, and psychic—to define the Americas and American identity. See *Border Theory: The Limits of Cultural Politics*, ed. Scott J. Michaelsen and David E. Johnson (Minneapolis: University of Minnesota Press, 1997). Although I draw on concepts of border and borderlands from North American border studies, my discussion of Chinese borderlands narratives is squarely situated in the geohistorical moment of Cold War Asia, which I view not merely as a moment of antagonism and segregation but also as one of connection and contiguity.

8. Lu Ling 路翎. "Wadi shang de 'zhanyi'" 窪地上的"戰役" ["Battle" of the lowlands]. *Renmin wenxue* 人民文學 [People's literature] 3 (1954): 1–21; Eileen Chang, *Chidi zhilian* 赤地之戀 [Love in the redland] (Taipei: Huangguan chubanshe, 1991).

9. Deng Kebao 鄧克保 (Bo Yang 柏楊), *Yi yu* 異域 [Alien lands] (Taipei: Hsing-kuang chubanshe, 1961).

10. Hu Feng 胡風, "Xu" 序 [Preface] (1945), in Lu Ling, *Caizhu de ernümen* 財主的兒女們 [Children of the rich] (Hefei: Anhui wenyi chubanshe, 1995), 1.

11. Kirk Denton, *The Problematic of Self in Modern Chinese Literature: Hu Feng and Lu Ling* (Stanford: Stanford University Press, 1998), 44–45.

12. Mao Zedong, *Selected Works of Mao Tsetung*, Vol. 1 (Beijing: Foreign Language Press, 1977).

13. Wang Hui 汪暉, "Ershi shiji Zhongguo lishi shiye xia de kangmei yuanchao zhanzheng" 二十世紀中國歷史視野下的抗美援朝戰爭 [The war of resisting America and aiding Korea from the perspective of twentieth-century Chinese history]. *Wenhua zongheng* 文化縱橫 [Cultural horizon] 6 (2013): 78–100.

14. Ban Wang, "Art, Politics, and Internationalism: Korean War Films in Chinese Cinema," in *The Oxford Handbook of Chinese Cinemas*, ed. Carlos Rojas and Eileen Chow (New York: Oxford University Press, 2013), 250–268.

15. Wei Wei 魏巍, "Shui shi zui keai de ren?" 誰是最可愛的人 [Who are the most lovable people?], *Renmin ribao* 人民日報 [People's daily], April 11, 1951.

16. Ba Jin 巴金, "Tan 'Wadishang de zhanyi' de fandongxing" 談《窪地上的"戰役"》的 反動性 [On the counterrevolutionary nature of "Battle of the Lowlands"], *Renmin wenxue* 人民文學 [People's literature] 8 (1955): 1–7.

17. Wei Wei, "Jilü—jieji sixiang de shijinshi: Tan Lu Ling de xiaoshuo 'wadishang de zhanyi'" 紀律——階級思想的試金石：談路翎的小說《窪地上的"戰役"》 [Disciplines—the criterion of class consciousness: On Lu Ling's story "Battle of the lowlands"], *Jiefangjun wenyi* 解放軍文藝 [Literature and art of the People's Liberation Army] 3 (1955): 15.

18. Kwai-cheung Lo, "The Idea of Asia(nism) and Trans-Asian Products," in *The Oxford Handbook of Chinese Cinemas*, ed. Carlos Rojas and Eileen Chow (New York: Oxford University Press, 2013), 558.

19. Frantz Fanon, "Algeria Unveiled," in *A Dying Colonialism* (New York: Grove Press, 1965), 35.

20. Fanon, "Algeria Unveiled," 45.

21. For a discussion of how the public image of Korea was transformed from the derogatory "Gaoli bangzi" (高麗棒子, literally "Korean yokel") into "Amani" (阿媽尼, or Omani) during the war mobilization in socialist China in early 1950s, see Zhao Ma, "Culturing the Korean War: Popular Entertainment, Political Propaganda, and the Making of Revolutionary Citizenship in Early 1950s China," a public lecture, at Capital Normal University, Beijing (December 11, 2012).

22. Lu Ling, "'Battle' of the Lowlands," *Renmin wenxue* 3 (1954): 10–11.

23. Lu Ling, "'Battle' of the Lowlands," 12.

24. Eileen Chang is a bilingual writer. *Rice Sprout Song* was first written in English in 1954, followed by a Chinese version entitled *Yang ge*. *Chidi zhilian* was first written in Chinese in 1954 and rewritten in English, titled *Naked Earth,* in 1955 and 1956 in America. The Chinese edition was published in October 1954 by the USIA-sponsored Tianfeng publishing house, while the English one failed to find a publisher in America and was published in 1956 by Youlian 友聯 [Union] Press of Hong Kong. *Naked Earth* is not a direct English translation of *Chidi zhilian*. The discussion in this chapter is based on the Chinese version, and therefore *Love in the Redland* is used as the English title to avoid confusion with *Naked Earth,* the title of Chang's original version. On the main differences between the two versions, see Gao Quanzhi 高全之, "Kaichuang fangru dajiang lai" 開窗放入大江來 [Opening the window and letting in the river], in *Zhang Ailing xue: Piping, kaozheng, gouchen* 張愛玲學：批評, 考證,鈎沉 [Studies on Eileen Chang: Criticism, textual analysis, and exploration of lost materials] (Taipei: Yifang, 2003), 219–236.

25. Eileen Chang, *Love in the Redland,* 222. Subsequent citations of this work are given parenthetically in the text.

26. C. T. Hsia, "Eileen Chang," in *A History of Modern Chinese Fiction 1917–1957,* 3rd ed. (Bloomington: Indiana University Press, 1999), 427–431.

27. Shuang Shen, "Betrayal, Impersonation, and Bilingualism: Eileen Chang's Self-Translation," in *Eileen Chang: Romancing Languages, Cultures and Genres,* ed. Kam Louie (Hong Kong: Hong Kong University Press, 2012), 92–93.

28. For some studies of the Lone Army and its social and cultural lives in Burma and Thailand, see, for instance, Wen-Chin Chang, "Beyond the Military: The Complex Migration and Resettlement of the KMT Yunnanese Chinese in Northern Thailand," PhD diss., K.U. Leuven, Belgium, 1999; Qin Yihui 覃怡輝, *Jinsanjiao guojun xieleishi 1950–1981* 金三角國軍血淚史 [The tragic history of the KMT troops in the Golden Triangle, 1950–1981] (Taipei: Linking Press, 2009); and Shu-min Huang, *Reproducing Chinese Culture in Diaspora: Sustainable Agriculture and Petrified Culture in Northern Thailand* (Lanham, MD: Lexington Books, 2010)

29. See, for instance, Piper Rae Gaubatz's *Beyond the Great Wall: Urban Form and Transformation on the Chinese Frontiers* (Stanford: Stanford University Press, 1996); Peter C. Perdue, "Boundaries, Maps, and Movement: Chinese, Russian, and Mongolian Empires in Early Modern Central Eurasia," *International History Review* 20.2 (1998): 263–286, and *China Marches West: The Qing Conquest of Central Asia* (Cambridge: Harvard University Asia Center, 2005).

30. Charles Patterson Giersch, *Asian Borderlands: The Transformation of Qing China's Yunnan Frontier* (Cambridge: Harvard University Asia Center, 2006). See also *Chinese Circulations: Capital, Commodities, and Networks in Southeast Asia,* ed. Eric Tagliacozzo

and Wen-chin Chang, with a foreword by Wang Gungwu (Durham: Duke University Press, 2011).

31. Du Yuming 杜聿明, *Zhongguo yuanzhengjun rumian duiri zuozhan shulüe* 中國遠征軍入緬對日作戰述略 [A brief account of the Chinese Expeditionary Army fighting against Japan in Burma], in *Zhonghua wenshi ziliao wenku* [A compilation of cultural and historical materials of China], vol. 4 (Beijing: Wenshi ziliao chubanshe, 1996). Sun Kegang 孫克剛, *Miandian dangkou zhi* 緬甸蕩寇誌 [Quelling the bandits in Burma] (Shanghai: Shanghai guoji tushu, 1946). Sun was the nephew of the famous KMT general Sun Liren, and was a survivor of the Chinese Expeditionary Army.

32. Mu Dan 穆旦, "Senlin zhi mei: Ji Hukang he shang de baigu" 森林之魅: 祭胡康河上的白骨 [The jungle's apparition: To the skulls on the rivers of the Hukwang Valley], in *Mu Dan zixuanji* 穆旦自選集 [Selected works of Mu Dan] (Tianjin: Tianjin renmin chubanshe, 2012), 129–130.

33. David Der-wei Wang, "Post-Loyalism," in *Sinophone Studies: A Critical Reader*, ed. Shu-mei Shih, Chien-hsin Tsai, and Brian Bernards (New York: Columbia University Press, 2013), 93–116.

34. Tao Qian 陶潛, "Taohua yuan ji bing shi" 桃花源記並詩 [The record of Peach Blossom Spring and the poem], in *Tao Yuanming ji jiaojian* 陶淵明集校箋 [Annotations of Tao Yuanming's works], ed. Gong Bin 龔斌 (Shanghai: Shanghai guji chubanshe, 1999), 402.

35. Michel Foucault, "Of Other Spaces," *Diacritics* 16 (Spring 1986): 24.

36. See Jing Tsu and David Der-wei Wang, eds., *Global Chinese Literature: Critical Essays* (Leiden: Brill, 2010), and Shu-mei Shih, *Visuality and Identity: Sinophone Articulation across the Pacific* (Berkeley: University of California Press, 2007).

37. Shu-mei Shih, *Visuality and Identity*, 4.

Works Cited

Anzaldúa, Gloria. *Borderlands/La Frontera: The New Mestiza*. San Francisco: Spinsters/Aunt Lute, 1987.

Ba Jin 巴金. "Tan 'Wadishang de zhanyi' de fandongxing" 談《窪地上的"戰役"》的反動性 [On the counter-revolutionary nature of "Battle of the Lowlands"]. *Renmin wenxue* 人民文學 [People's literature] 8 (1955): 1–7.

Bo Yang 柏楊. *Yi yu* 異域 [Alien lands]. Taipei: Hsing-kuang chubanshe, 1961.

Chang, Eileen 張愛玲. *Chidi zhilian* 赤地之戀 [Love in the Redland]. Taipei: Huangguan chubanshe, 1991.

Chen Chen 陳忱. *Shuihu houzhuan* 水滸後傳 [Sequel to the Water Margin]. Beijing: Zhonghua shuju, 2004.

Denton, Kirk. *The Problematic of Self in Modern Chinese Literature: Hu Feng and Lu Ling*. Stanford: Stanford University Press, 1998.

Du Yuming 杜聿明. *Zhongguo yuanzhengjun rumian duiri zuozhan shulüe* 中國遠征軍入緬對日作戰述略 [A brief account of the Chinese Expeditionary Army fighting against Japan in Burma]. In *Zhonghua wenshi ziliao wenku* [A compilation of cultural and historical materials of China], vol. 4. Beijing: Wenshi ziliao chubanshe, 1996.

Fanon, Frantz. "Algeria Unveiled." In *A Dying Colonialism*. New York: Grove Press, 1965. 35–67.

Foucault, Michel. "Of Other Spaces." *Diacritics* 16 (Spring 1986): 22–27.

Gaubatz, Piper Rae. *Beyond the Great Wall: Urban Form and Transformation on the Chinese Frontiers*. Stanford: Stanford University Press, 1996.

Giersch, Charles Patterson. *Asian Borderlands: The Transformation of Qing China's Yunnan Frontier*. Cambridge: Harvard University Asia Center, 2006.

Hamm, John C. *Paper Swordsmen: Jin Yong and the Modern Chinese Martial Arts Novel*. Honolulu: University of Hawai'i Press, 2005,

Hammond, Andrew. *Global Cold War Literature*. London and New York: Routledge, 2012.

Hsia, Chih-tsing. *A History of Modern Chinese Fiction 1917–1957*, 3rd ed. Bloomington: Indiana University Press, 1999.

Hu Feng 胡風. "Xu" 序 [Preface]. 1945. In Lu Ling. *Caizhu de ernümen* 財主的兒女們 [Children of the rich]. Hefei: Anhui wenyi chubanshe, 1995. 1–6.

Jin Yong 金庸. *Bixue jian* 碧血劍 [The sword stained with royal blood]. Beijing: Beijing san-lian shudian, 1994.

Lo, Kwai-cheung. "The Idea of Asia(nism) and Trans-Asian Products." In *The Oxford Handbook of Chinese Cinemas*. Ed. Carlos Rojas and Eileen Chow. New York: Oxford University Press, 2013. 548–565.

Lu Ling 路翎. "Wadi shang de 'zhanyi'" 窪地上的"戰役" ["Battle" of the lowlands]. *Renmin wenxue* 人民文學 [People's literature] 3 (1954): 1–21.

Mao Zedong. *Selected Works of Mao Tsetung*, Vol. 1. Beijing: Foreign Language Press, 1977.

Michaelsen, Scott J., and David E. Johnson, ed. *Border Theory: The Limits of Cultural Politics*. Minneapolis: University of Minnesota Press, 1997.

Mu Dan 穆旦. "Senlin zhi mei: Ji Hukang he shang de baigu" 森林之魅： 祭胡康河上的白骨 [The jungle's apparition: To the skulls on the rivers of the Hukwang Valley]. In *Mu Dan zixuanji* 穆旦自選集 [Selected works of Mu Dan]. Tianjin: Tianjin renmin chubanshe, 2012. 129–131.

Perdue, Peter C. "Boundaries, Maps, and Movement: Chinese, Russian, and Mongolian Empires in Early Modern Central Eurasia." *International History Review* 20.2 (1998): 263–286.

Piette, Adam. *The Literary Cold War: 1945 to Vietnam*. Edinburgh: Edinburgh University Press, 2009.

Rosaldo, Renato. *Culture and Truth: The Remaking of Social Analysis*. Boston: Beacon, 1993.

Shen, Shuang. "Betrayal, Impersonation, and Bilingualism: Eileen Chang's Self-Translation." In *Eileen Chang: Romancing Languages, Cultures and Genres*. Ed. Kam Louie. Hong Kong: Hong Kong University Press, 2012. 91–112.

Shih, Shu-mei. *Visuality and Identity: Sinophone Articulation across the Pacific*. Berkeley: University of California Press, 2007.

Song Weijie 宋偉杰. *Cong yule xingwei dao wutuobang chongdong: Jin Yong xiaoshuo zai jiedu* 從娛樂行為到烏托邦衝動：金庸小說再解讀 [From entertainment activity to utopian impulse: Rereading Jin Yong's fiction]. Nanjing: Jiangsu renmin chubanshe, 1999.

Sun Kegang 孫克剛. *Miandian dangkou zhi* 緬甸蕩寇誌 [Quelling the bandits in Burma]. Shanghai: Shanghai guoji tushu, 1946.

Tagliacozzo, Eric, and Wen-chin Chang, ed. *Chinese Circulations: Capital, Commodities, and Networks in Southeast Asia*. Durham: Duke University Press, 2011.

Tao Qian 陶潛. "Taohua yuan ji bing shi" 桃花源記並詩 [The record of Peach Blossom Spring and the poem]. In Gong Bin 龔斌, ed. and annotation, *Tao Yuanming ji jiaojian* 陶淵明集校箋 [Annotations of Tao Yuanming's works]. Shanghai: Shanghai guji chuban-she, 1999. 402.

Tsu, Jing, and David Der-wei Wang, ed. *Global Chinese Literature: Critical Essays*. Leiden: Brill, 2010.

Wang, Ban. "Art, Politics, and Internationalism: Korean War Films in Chinese Cinema." In *The Oxford Handbook of Chinese Cinemas*. Ed. Carlos Rojas and Eileen Chow. New York: Oxford University Press, 2013. 250–268.

Wang, David Der-wei. "Post-Loyalism." In *Sinophone Studies: A Critical Reader*. Ed. Shumei Shih, Chien-hsin Tsai, and Brian Bernards. New York: Columbia University Press, 2013. 93–116.

Wang Hui 汪暉. "Ershi shiji Zhongguo lishi shiye xia de kangmei yuanchao zhanzheng" 二十世紀中國歷史視野下的抗美援朝戰爭 [The war of resisting America and aiding Korea from the perspective of twentieth-century Chinese history]. *Wenhua zongheng* 文化縱橫 [Cultural horizon] 6 (2013): 78–100.

Wei Wei 魏巍. "Shui shi zui keai de ren?" 誰是最可愛的人 [Who are the most lovable people]. *Renmin ribao* 人民日報 [People's daily], April 11, 1951.

Wei Wei 魏巍. "Jilü—jieji sixiang de shijinshi: tan Lu Ling de xiaoshuo 'wadishang de zhanyi'" 紀律——階級思想的試金石：談路翎的小說《窪地上的"戰役"》 [Disciplines—the criterion of class consciousness: On Lu Ling's story "Battle of the lowlands"]. *Jiefangjun wenyi* 解放軍文藝 [Literature and art of the People's Liberation Army] 3 (1955): 15.

CHAPTER 2.3

....

HAO RAN AND
THE CULTURAL
REVOLUTION

....

XIAOFEI TIAN

A godly thorough reformation,
Which always must be carried on,
And still be doing, never done. . . .

(Samuel Butler, *Hudibras*)

A young wife in bed: alone, sleepless, tormented by longing for her husband on a moonlit night. This is a classic trope in the Chinese literary tradition, one of the most evocative motifs appearing in countless premodern poems and stories and possessing an immense cultural resonance. Then, in a story whose third, and final, version was written in "Beijing of the red month of May of 1957," we see just such a young bride lying in bed alone and experiencing "misery for the first time in her life." It turns out, however, that instead of being tortured by desire for her absent husband, she is thinking about her backward father-in-law.[1] Fifteen years later, during the Chinese Revolution era, the author Hao Ran 浩然 (1932–2008), then already a famous writer, revealed that the real-life archetype for the heroine of his story was a girl who had had clashes with her parents; but feeling that a woman's conflict with her parents-in-law could become more "easily intensified and representative," he had changed "father and daughter" to "father-in-law and daughter-in-law."[2] In the same essay, Hao Ran claims that his stories are not "written into being," but "revised into being."[3]

In many ways, the act of revision on the part of the paradigmatic socialist peasant writer Hao Ran—whether it is the problematic repackaging of a classic theme or the rewriting of a text to make it more correct—presents an allegory of the central issue to be discussed in this chapter: cultural revolution.

Cultural Revolution and the
Treachery of the Literary Language

In its narrow sense, the term *cultural revolution* refers to the Great Proletarian Cultural Revolution (1966–1976), a politically motivated mass movement that was launched by Chairman Mao Zedong. One of its essential purposes, as indicated by its name, was to revolutionize Chinese culture. If, however, we look beyond the term's immediate association, we find that cultural revolution is a recurrent theme in modern Chinese literary and social history; and, as scholars have suggested, the roots of the Great Proletariat Cultural Revolution must be examined "in the context of certain tendencies in Chinese cultural and social developments in the twentieth century."[4] We could identify at least three important moments before the 1966 dateline that form an intellectually coherent narrative of the cultural revolution of modern China. The first two are obvious: the New Culture movement in the early twentieth century, which advocated a break with the cultural past to mold a new, modern China, and then the year 1942, when Mao delivered his famous talks at the Yan'an Forum on Literature and Arts from the Communist Party's headquarters in Yan'an, Shaanxi.[5] In these talks, Mao formulated an ideological guideline for the development of literature and the arts in a socialist regime: they must serve the workers, the peasants, and the soldiers, and be subjected to the political interests of the Party.[6]

The third moment in the narrative of continuous cultural revolution in modern China, as a follow-up to the Yan'an talks, is less obvious but no less crucial than the first two: 1958 was the year of the Great Leap Forward, a socioeconomic campaign to vastly accelerate the nation's industrial and agricultural production. In a parallel move, Mao also launched a Great Leap Forward in cultural production that same year: poems—referred to as "folk songs" (*min'ge* 民歌)—were produced in massive quantity. Over 200,000 poems were reportedly composed in one shire by its 267 "poetry-writing units."[7] Written on posters, blackboards, walls, and wooden or bamboo plaques, as well as orally composed in public poetry competitions, verses proliferated from city streets to farming fields. They were pared down and selected into a slim volume titled *Red Flag Ballads* (紅旗歌謠), edited by none other than the cultural luminaries of the People's Republic, Guo Moruo 郭沫若 (1892–1978) and Zhou Yang 周揚 (1908–1989). With its three hundred poems divided into four sections, respectively entitled "Odes to the Party" and "Agricultural, Industrial, and Military Songs," the anthology turns out to be a socialist recreation of the *Book of Odes* (詩經), China's earliest and most canonical poetry collection, supposedly pared down to about three hundred from three thousand poems and edited by Confucius himself. To further drive the parallel home, the editors in the preface of *Red Flag Ballads* explicitly refer to the anthology as "the new 'Airs of the Domains' [國風, the first section of the *Book of Odes*] of the new socialist age." And yet, compared to the *Red Flag Ballads*, "even the *Three Hundred Poems* [a traditional reference to the *Book of Odes*] are outshone."[8] The same year also saw the publication of Mao's nineteen poems in English translation by Beijing's Foreign Language Press; the number nineteen, like three hundred, bears a special significance because of the canonical group of poems traditionally referred to as the "Nineteen Old Poems," which, along with the *Book of Odes*, stands at the fountainhead of classical Chinese poetry. The year 1958 was one of astronomical production figures and magic numbers.

The poems of the "Airs" section of the *Book of Odes* were supposed to have been popular songs sung by the common folk, serving as symptoms and signs of the people's moods. If the king gets to hear the distressed songs and is wise, he reforms the government. One legend about the origin of the "Airs" is that the Zhou kings sent officials to villages to collect songs in order to learn the people's concerns, an unmistakable antecedent for *Red Flag Ballads*. The immense cultural resonance again emerges in Chen Kaige's 陳凱歌 1984 film *Yellow Earth* (黃土地), which opens with a Communist soldier collecting local songs on the barren plateau of northern Shaanxi, the birthplace of the communist revolution as well as the old Zhou heartland.

The poems of *Red Flag Ballads*—in glaring contrast to the "Airs," which mostly sing of a world gone wrong—are all joyful. With the people so happy, there is no need for the government to reform, and the moral education implicit in this volume is directed at a different target altogether. In the words of its editors, *Red Flag Ballads* is intended to enlighten "our writers and poets"—the traditional scholar elite, known today as the intelligentsia—for "the new folk songs will produce a greater and greater influence on the development of modern poetry."[9] Mao was intent on transformation: the common folk into a self-conscious, progressive proletariat, and the intellectuals into humbled members of the laboring masses. Ironically, he chose to begin with "teaching through poetry," the ancient Confucian method of bringing about social change.

No writer embodies the transformed and transformative common folk better than Liang Jinguang 梁金廣 (1932–2008), better known as Hao Ran, the socialist writer laureate par excellence, whose fiction primarily focuses on rural life in north China in the socialist construction period. Hao Ran, who published his first short story in 1956, is best known for his novels *Bright Sunny Skies* (艷陽天) and *The Golden Road* (金光大道); both sold millions of copies and were made into movies in the 1970s, turning him into a household name and the most eminent writer during the Great Proletarian Cultural Revolution period. Growing up in rural poverty and orphaned at a young age, Hao Ran only received three and a half years of schooling, probably less formal education than any other prominent modern writer. He was not only saved from destitution by the Communist Party, but also owed his literary stardom entirely to opportunities created by the new socialist regime.[10]

An antithesis of the traditional Chinese cultural elite, Hao Ran epitomizes the cultural revolution of modern China, because he wrote from within the peasants as a peasant himself, not a gentleman observer standing on the outside looking in. For centuries, the Chinese elite had romanticized and glamorized farmers, extolling their freedom from the pressures of public life constraining a scholar-official, or sympathizing with their sufferings in hard times; but the farmers were always objects of a distant gaze and never talked back—until Hao Ran. Quite aware of his unique place in the Chinese literary tradition, Hao Ran justifiably refers to his story of success as a "miracle," and to himself as "a representative of the peasants marching toward culture."[11]

A product of Mao's cultural revolution and its living embodiment, Hao Ran the peasant writer carried on the revolution by, to use an old Chinese metaphor, "tilling with his pen" (筆耕). His writings exemplify the complex modes of meaning production in China's socialist literature. Although it is frequently described as no more than revolutionary propaganda serving the state ideology, socialist literature, especially from the early years of the People's Republic, is essentially performative: instead of being merely representational or reflective of a preexisting "socialist reality," it attempts to found a new social order by proclaiming it, and is thus constitutive of the socialist reality. And yet, as J. Hillis Miller put it, "[all] performatives are to some degree out of the control of the one who speaks them."[12] The creative participation of readers figures prominently in meaning production. In her book on Cultural Revolution culture, Barbara Mittler stresses the diverse interpretations to which Cultural Revolution propaganda art has been subjected by the Chinese people. Pointing out that "Cultural Revolution (and perhaps all) propaganda was received and experienced in many different, and often contradictory, ways by individuals from different generations and backgrounds," she rightly balances the agency of artists with that of audiences.[13]

While the author's intention and the reader's interpretation can and do frequently clash with each other, the text itself may also prove protean and uncontainable. This chapter wishes to call attention to a particularly intriguing aspect of socialist verbal art: the treacherous working of literary language. The socialist writer may yearn for newness in terms of literary expressions and moral values, but just as Mao employed the old Confucian program to achieve his cultural revolution, the very medium used to express the new socialist ideal, with its tropes, imageries, and cultural habits, is burdened by history—tainted, so to speak, by the very past it vows to cast off. With language functioning as an impediment to the author's intended meaning, sense is constantly threatened by its own dissolution not in senselessness but in perversion. If we can no longer uphold the distinction between form and content in our post-Saussure age, we have to study the content of form and examine how form can complicate the message of even the most blatantly straightforward revolutionary propaganda. "The New Bride" (新媳婦), Hao Ran's story that features the sleepless young wife on a moonlit late summer night, presents an illuminating case in point.

CHUJIA 出嫁 AND CHUJIA 出家

Included in Hao Ran's first story collection, *Magpies on the Branch* (喜鵲登枝), published in 1958, "The New Bride" was singled out for praise by two notable contemporary critics, Ye Shengtao 葉聖陶 (1894–1988) and Ba Ren 巴人 (i.e., Wang Renshu 王任叔, 1901–1972).[14] The story is set in a village in the Bohai Bay region, which encompasses a large part of Hebei Province. A young woman, Bian Huirong, causes a disturbance in the sleepy village on her wedding night by refusing to conform to the old practice of "roughhousing in the nuptial chamber" (*nao dongfang* 鬧洞房). Her unconventionality does not stop there: the day after her wedding, she begins working in the fields, and the task she tackles—breaking up manure for use as fertilizer—is none too delicate and not the sort of work considered appropriate for a new bride. Later, when it turns out that female laborers, despite handling an equal amount of work, are granted fewer work credits than the male laborers, Huirong is the one who protests to the head of the production team and ultimately sets things right. She is much admired by the young people in the village and endorsed by the director of the agricultural co-op, but predictably comes into conflict with the elders of her family, especially her conservative father-in-law, Liang the Elder. The conflict culminates in a public confrontation when she angrily denounces a young "middle peasant" (中農), Huang Quanbao, for his selfish behavior at a village meeting, and defies her father-in-law, who is trying to shut her up and drag her home. After some trials and tribulations, the bride eventually wins the middle peasant over and also becomes reconciled with her father-in-law. The end of the story features a happy family reunion, as the bridegroom, a Youth League cadre working and living away from home at the county headquarters, comes back to the village for a visit after his month-long absence.

The new bride is clearly intended to be a representative of the Socialist New Woman in both body and spirit. In keeping with the stereotypical physical attributes of the "ideal socialist hero," she is strong and muscular, "with a large build and two thick arms, full of strength from head to toe."[15] She is public-minded, as demonstrated by her criticism of the selfish middle peasant. Most importantly, she resists traditional gender roles: she does not submit meekly to the roughhousing practice on the wedding night; instead of staying at home and helping her mother-in-law with housework, she decides to go and work at the co-op together with her father-in-law; and she vocally insists on women's rights by demanding "equal work and equal pay." Nevertheless, underneath all the newness of the new bride, there is something old and familiar. We recognize the stereotype of a shrew.

There is no shortage of shrew stories from premodern China, either in historical accounts or as literary representation, a fact that has been well demonstrated by Yenna Wu.[16] One shrew text is especially pertinent, because its female protagonist is a problematic new bride whose unconventional behavior on her wedding night gets her in much trouble. This is the anonymous vernacular story "An Account of the Sharp-tongued Li Cuilian" (快嘴李翠蓮記), from the sixteenth-century story collection *Stories from the Qingpingshan Hall* (清平山堂話本), compiled by Hong Pian 洪楩.[17]

In many ways, Li Cuilian the shrew is comparable to Bian Huirong the socialist heroine. Her most prominent feature is her apparent perfection in everything she is and does. Pretty, competent, and hard-working, she seems to be an ideal wife but for one fact: she has a brain, she has a temper, and, worst of all, she is a talker. She has something to say on just about everything, and she always speaks in verse. Within three days of her wedding, she drives her in-laws completely insane. Her husband is forced to divorce her and send her back to her native home. Since her own family blames her bitterly for what has happened, Li Cuilian makes a decision: "Not tolerated by either my husband's family or my own, I will just cut off my hair and become a nun!" She even declines her brother and sister-in-law's offer to accompany her to the convent of her choice, saying: "Once I leave my secular home, every place is my home—not just Clear Voice Temple."[18] A story of *chujia* 出嫁 ("getting married") ends with *chujia* 出家 ("leaving home," which is to say, entering a religious order), as Li renounces all family relationships and the social constraints imposed on her through such relationships.

Like Li Cuilian, Bian Huirong is portrayed as a near-perfect young woman: she is pretty according to the 1950s socialist standard, competent, and hard-working. In her mother-in-law's words, she would have made "a wonderfully lovable daughter-in-law" if only she had been "more obedient and had had a mild temperament."[19] Instead, she talks back, she reasons, and her "two pretty eyes" can turn into "sharp knives."[20] The most striking correspondence between the two brides is what transpires on the wedding day. After Li Cuilian swears at the matchmaker and roundly scolds the astrologer during the ceremony, the newly married couple is finally seated in their nuptial chamber and the astrologer begins to perform a ritual known as the "scattering of grains around bed-curtains." The verses he chants apparently offend Cuilian's sensibilities, and the new bride promptly jumps up, grabs a rolling pin, deals the astrologer two blows, and drives him out with a cursing doggerel. At this point the groom is roused to anger, citing tradition to rebuke Cuilian. To this Cuilian speaks another doggerel in reply, threatening to throw him out along with the astrologer.

A remarkably similar incident opens Hao Ran's story: on the wedding night, other brides would keep their heads down and not say a word when the wedding guests begin their roughhousing, but Bian Huirong jumps off her *kang* bed as soon as the male guests crowd into her room, cheerily greeting everybody with a smile:

> "Please, everyone, come in quickly. Are you all here to congratulate us on our marriage? Wonderful! We are all fellow members of the same co-op now. We will live together and work together. I am a newcomer and I don't know anything. From now on, I hope you will all watch out for me and help me. Please have a seat, please do!"[21]

The articulate new bride, devoid of any maidenly reserve and bashfulness, puts all the men to shame. After she has a fiery exchange with Huang Quanbao, the most unruly of the male guests, everybody beats a fast retreat. It is not the groom but the groom's father who complains, and a female neighbor and kin, Auntie Liang, tries to gently rebuke the new bride by citing tradition: "Roughhousing in the nuptial chamber is an old custom of many, many years." The bride retorts, "Not all old customs are still useful."[22]

Nevertheless, Bian Huirong does not represent a simple socialist repackaging of the premodern problem girl, for the differences between the two heroines are equally salient. The modern bride is, on one hand, keenly aware of the importance of female empowerment, and, on the other hand, much more family-oriented than her premodern counterpart. While Li Cuilian discovers "freedom and ease" (自在) in a Buddhist convent, for the socialist new woman "leaving home" is out of the question, not just because entering a religious order is no longer a viable solution in a socialist society, but because of the changed context of "home." [23]

A Family Woman

Like many heroes and heroines of Cultural Revolution novels and short stories, Bian Huirong is an orphan, whose parents, as is typical of the genre, have died a martyr's death for the revolution.[24] She has grown up with her brother and sister-in-law, who notably are both Party members. Thus, the Party is her symbolic parent. After she gets married, she finds herself a member of two new families: the larger family of the agricultural co-op, and a smaller family constituted primarily of her parents-in-law. Her husband, who works and lives away from her, is only marginally in the picture.

The traditional family hierarchy of a patriarchal society, with the senior male reigning as the head of the family, never falters in this fictional universe. A striking conversation between father and son about the future of the bride takes place in the middle of the story. Liang the Elder, who is upset with his progressive daughter-in-law, tells his son He'nan: "When you go back to work, take your wife with you. Out of sight, out of mind." To this the son replies, "Let her stay home with you for a month. After a month I will be back for a vacation. By that time, as long as you can bear to part with her, I will take her away to live outside."[25] The discussion in no way involves Bian Huirong herself. She is a passive object being negotiated and decided upon between the men in the family. A similar conversation is repeated at the end of the story, but with a twist. While the new bride is cooking family dinner with her mother-in-law in the kitchen, the son informs the father that he plans to take his wife with him. The father, who has changed his attitude toward Bian Huirong by now, protests:

> "It isn't easy for a young couple to make a life together outside. How can we elders set our mind at ease about this? You are not all that far away; why cannot you just come home and visit her when you have a chance?"
>
> He'nan said, "Well, it's really not a problem for us; it's just for you and Ma who are getting on there. . . ."
>
> Liang the Elder glanced at his son, not quite able to put his finger on his feelings. He said in a soft voice, "Me and your Ma, well, since you are so often away, how can we manage without someone like her by our side?"[26]

This is the end of the story, and Liang the Elder literally has the last word. For all her sturdy physique and independent spirit, the new bride is a pawn, loved and fought over by father and son. She herself is complicit in the male game of power. The day after her wedding, her mother-in-law tries to give her guidance in dealing with household matters; the bride replies, much to her mother-in-law's chagrin: "After He'nan is gone, Dad and I will go and join in the work at the co-op. You can stay at home and take care of these things."[27] Though standing up for her own liberation from the old way of life, she is clearly not troubled by the structure of gendered division of labor per se, with women doing housework inside and men working outside; the only difference is that she as a young woman wants to join the men and leave the older woman to do the housework.

Older women are represented by two familiar types in this story: the noisy and bossy type embodied by Auntie Liang, and the nice, quiet, and submissive type like Mother Liang. They are basically treated as backward and inconsequential. While being an older male earns one a position of authority, either in public or in private, being an older female signifies an almost total loss of value in family and society. Though also women, Mother Liang and Auntie Liang are clearly not in the same league as Bian Huirong or Cuiying, the young female vice head of the production team. Indeed, both Mother Liang and Auntie Liang are referred to only by their status earned through marriage, while the younger female characters are the ones being allowed the dignity and individuality of having a personal name. A dialogue in the story indicates that naming is a conscious authorial choice: when Cuiying addresses the bride as "Big Sister-in-law," the bride immediately puts a stop to it, saying, "Don't call me that. My name is Bian Huirong." "Oh I see," Cuiying says, "Comrade Bian Huirong!"[28] Having a name, as opposed to being known in kinship terms, signifies having an identity and a position in society. Gender equality is, however, complicated by age.

Whether in her immediate family or in the larger family of the agricultural co-op, the structure of male authority never changes. The director of the co-op and the head of the production team are both male, and Liang the Elder is the head of a subdivision of the production team. Only when he is sick does the bride get to stand in for him for a day. On the outside, the bride constantly appeals to the authority of the co-op director in all of her difficult situations; on the inside, she desperately seeks her father-in-law's approval. In fact, when we look closely, we are not so sure that the bride has ever broken through to the real outside. Her husband, He'nan, works as a cadre in the Communist Youth League at the county level; he and his father both refer to the county seat as "outside" (外邊). Despite being active outside her immediate household and the traditional "inner quarters," Bian Huirong has never been on the real "outside." She is relegated to a perpetual *nei* 內, "inside," and hierarchical layers are mapped on gendered spatial division and on local space.

At the end of the day, the bride is just a meek daughter-in-law and an acquiescent wife. The family reunion at the end is more about her reconciliation with her father-in-law than about her brief reunion with her husband. The socialist new woman is much more politically correct than the sixteenth-century heroine when measured by a neo-Confucian standard, which has been the dominant moral standard in society since late imperial times. The latter subverts the family and social order by opting out of it altogether.

The Subtext of Incest and Adultery

Bian Huirong's filial piety nevertheless finds expression in strange ways. Section Four of the story opens with the following passage:

> It was a late summer night, cool, quiet. The moon that was sinking in the western sky gilded the leaves of the white pear tree on the east side. The half-ripe pears hanging on the branches were as shiny and beautiful as if carved out in dark green jade. The cassia tree blossoming outside of her window eagerly sent forth a sweet scent.
>
> Bian Huirong softly opened the half-closed door of her room and went to bed without bothering to turn on the lamp. Her heart felt as if it were filled with a pile of jumbled iron wires: frustrated, and aching. With what happened today, she tasted misery for the first time in her life.[29]

This is the scene that I describe at the beginning of this chapter. The young bride sleepless in bed is dwelling on her earlier confrontation with her father-in-law with regret. The narrative language setting the atmosphere is unmistakably lyrical and romantic: the moon, the tree bearing fruits, and the aromatic cassia blossoms are all hackneyed poetic images that can evoke sensibilities far more fitting for lovers. Pear (*li* 梨) puns with "separation" (*li* 離), and seems particularly relatable to Bian Huirong's situation, whose husband has left for his job in the county seat just a few days after their wedding. The most remarkable image is that of the "jumbled iron wires," *luan tiesi* 亂鐵絲 (literally, "tangled iron threads"), filling the bride's heart. *Si* 絲 ("silk" or "silk threads") is commonly used as a pun for *si* 思 ("longing") in traditional love songs, and "tangled silk threads" (*luansi* 亂絲) is the famous metaphor in the song lyric attributed to the lyricist Li Yu 李煜 (937–978) to the tune title "The Pleasure of Meeting":

> 無言獨上西樓, 月如鉤, 寂寞梧桐深院鎖清秋。
> 剪不斷, 理還亂, 是離愁。別有一番滋味在心頭。

> Without a word I climbed the western tower,
> the moon was like a hook.
> The silent yard stretched deep
>   through chestnut trees,
> enclosing autumn, cool and clear.

> You can cut it, but never cut it through,
> Get it set,
>   then it's a mess again—
> that's the sadness of being apart.
> It has a flavor all its own
>   in the human heart.[30]

One need not wonder about Han Ran's level of classical learning, since the lines, "You can cut it, but never cut it through,/Get it set, then it's a mess again," have practically acquired the status of a proverb in the Chinese language, and Hao Ran had been a passionate reader of China's classical novels as well as an avid traditional opera fan.[31] The punchline is well known: the very thing that resists cutting and severing is ironically the "sadness of being apart," figured here as tangled threads/longing. By transforming "silk threads" into "iron threads," Hao Ran gives an age-old image a modern twist.

What we have here are two discourses that are uncomfortably juxtaposed. The "tangled iron threads" in Bian Huirong's heart with regard to her father-in-law are as discordant to the romantic setting as the moon, the cassia, and the pears are to a story with a socialist message. Hao Ran is trying to write a simple story of binary opposition: progressiveness versus conservatism, public-mindedness versus selfishness; but the story is problematized by the nuances of a literary language out of his control. The built-in cultural meaning of the images he employs brings a troubling dimension of repressed sexuality to the fore.

As the story moves on, the story's title, "Xin xifu," takes on an unexpected sense of ambiguity. *Xifu*, a northern Chinese colloquial expression for wife, is also the term indicating daughter-in-law. Obviously Bian Huirong is both, but she seems much more invested in the latter role. Indeed, she so successfully repairs her relation with her father-in-law that he no longer wants to part with her. At the end of the story, when the son suggests taking Bian Huirong to the county seat to live with him, Liang the Elder is "not quite able to put his fingers on his feelings" (心裏不知啥味, or literally, "not knowing the flavor in his heart"). On one hand, this phrase echoes a sentence that describes how the newlywed couple feels upon seeing each other after their month-long separation: "They both had this feeling in their hearts that they could not quite articulate" (心裏都有一股說不出來的滋味);[32] on the other hand, it evokes the last line of Li Yu's song lyric: "It has a flavor all its own in the human heart" (別有一番滋味在心頭). The "sadness of being apart," never articulated between the separated young couple, is displaced to a doting father-in-law. Whether these textual echoes are deliberate is beside the point. Rather, what deserve note are the negative terms adopted by the author—not knowing (*buzhi* 不知), and unable to articulate (*shuobuchulai* 說不出來): besides slyly constituting the narrator's comments on the limits of conscious knowledge and language, the negations simultaneously broach and suppress illicit desire (it is important to note that not only is incestuous passion forbidden, but romantic love is likewise inappropriate in the socialist discourse). Ultimately, a linguistic approximation to incest forms part of the reading pleasure, and the verbal furtiveness replicates the very form of the taboo romance itself.

The absence of the bridegroom through most of the story is also underscored by the young wife's intense interaction with the other backward male character, Huang Quanbao, who clashes with her on her wedding night. Just like Liang the Elder, Huang Quanbao becomes incapacitated in the course of the story largely thanks to his conflict with Bian Huirong. Each instance of incapacitation is designed as an act of poetic justice, with the backward males punished and the progressive bride empowered, since she is put in the position of taking care of the disabled males. In each case, however, Bian Huirong is placed in close physical proximity to the men in a compromising manner. When her father-in-law is sick, she rushes into his room in the middle of the night to feel his forehead before she has a chance to button up her blouse. When Huang Quanbao pierces his foot on a broken willow branch in the field, she places his bleeding foot in her lap, tears off a large part of her blouse, and bandages his foot with it, as "blood saturated her pants and sullied both of her hands."[33] It is perhaps inevitable that blood should flow in a story about a bride, but the blood that might have been appropriate for the wedding night is displaced to a public setting tinted with socialist pastoralism and charged with erotic tension.

The demasculinization of the two backward male characters is completed by their tears of gratitude and repentance, as they are moved by Bian Huirong's selflessness and magnanimity. A great deal of bodily fluid—sweat, tears, and blood—flows in the story, although none comes from the bride herself, who is portrayed as a superwoman. After walking five or six miles to get a doctor for her father-in-law in the middle of the night, she works in the field all day, and at the end of the day carries the immobilized Huang Quanbao on her back all the way home. Hers is a body devoid of weakness or desire, the idealized body of a "new" member of the new society.

When the story was reprinted in a 1973 selection of Hao Ran's stories, *Songs of Spring* (春歌集), Hao Ran revised it heavily. Many of the revisions try to repress, but instead only serve to highlight, the sexual tension and gender stereotyping in the original story. In depicting the custom of "roughhousing in the nuptial chamber," the original version states that sometimes wedding guests would even "rip off the new bride's clothes, or spray pepper powder in her nostrils."[34] In the revised version the guests are said to "spray pepper powder in the new bride's nostrils, or pour cold water over the new bride's head."[35] The sexual violence inherent in the phrase, *bo yifu* 剥衣服 (rip off clothes), as opposed to the more neutral *tuo yifu* 脱衣服 (take off clothes), and the speculative nakedness of *this* bride, Bian Huirong, are edited out, although they resurface in the bride's voluntary stripping of her blouse to dress the wound of Huang Quanbao's foot.

Many more revisions occur in the "foot cutting" episode. The original version of the episode contains the following words: "Women are often afraid of blood. Several women here were all stunned: some covered their eyes, and some were so scared that they ran away."[36] The revised version merely states: "Several women were all stunned by the blood and did not know what to do."[37] The simplicity of the statement accentuates Bian Huirong's courage and resourcefulness without disparaging the other women or generalizing about the perceived female weakness in general. Finally, the description "blood stained her pants and sullied both of her hands" is revised to read "blood flew onto Bian Huirong's pants and made a large red blot." The avoidance of the mention of hands seems to be an attempt to downplay the physicality of Bian Huirong's tending of Huang Quanbao. Earlier, as they work side by side in the field, she is said to be "chatting and laughing with him like nothing had happened [between them];" the revised version deletes "with him."[38] The deletion, another attempt to distance Bian Huirong from Huang Quanbao, tones down a classic example of "unresolved sexual tension" between a male and female character. The makeover, effected by Hao Ran during the Cultural

Revolution era, of his early short stories published between 1958 and 1960 is a conscious act of suppression that exposes rather than conceals.[39]

CODA

Earlier scholars have noted Hao Ran's recycling of techniques and motifs from traditional Chinese drama and fiction.[40] Michael Egan even goes so far as to argue that a sense of cultural and literary familiarity about Hao Ran's fiction is what makes *Bright Sunny Skies* successful, as opposed to his later work *The Golden Road*, which he sees as impoverished because it is largely deprived of "references to traditional culture."[41] In this chapter, I have attempted to take the discussion in a different direction by stressing how the socialist content of Hao Ran's fiction is infinitely complicated by the literary tropes and images he uses. On a surface level, revolution sublimates and normalizes every wayward impulse; on an underlying level, however, every wayward impulse continues to seek gratification without ever bothering to justify itself because it is always already disguised under the normalizing discourse of the revolution. There is a gray area where these two levels of reading negotiate with each other and produce a special form of covert pleasure. At least one reader talks about having had sexual fantasies about the new bride during his sent-down years in the countryside, though he complains that Hao Ran's writing was "too clean" for him to use the story as an actual aid for masturbation.[42]

The Cultural Revolution movement represents a mass quest for transparency, which, in a totalitarian regime, makes control possible and easy. People were classified and labeled as "Black Five Categories" or "Red Five Categories," and their identities were marked by physical signs during struggle sessions, such as dunce caps, plaques hung around the neck with one's name and class identity, or the more lasting "yin-yang haircut" (a haircut that shaves half of the head). More broadly, transparency was sought through "exposure" (*jiefa* 揭發, *jielu* 揭露, or *baolu* 暴露), whether the uncovering of a "hidden class enemy" or public self-examination and self-critique. When Hao Ran revised his early stories during the Cultural Revolution era, he was aiming to make the stories more straightforward and transparent as revolutionary propaganda. As he put it, he felt that his literary language in those early stories "lacked precision, was interspersed with many obscure dialect words and slang, and even contained some naturalistic elements that hurt the images of the characters."[43] He revised and excised, only to highlight what he desired to suppress.

The more serious impediment to Hao Ran's attempt to simplify his stories is the fact that, by its very nature, language resists the obsessive quest for transparency. Even in a story as straightforward as "The New Bride," the opacity of language resists the writer's attempt to sing a simple ode to the socialist new woman. In the Greek myth about Oedipus and the Sphinx, the lack of transparency in language drives people to despair and death and creates a horror; Oedipus brought back transparency by solving the Sphinx's riddle, which destroyed the horror embodied in the Sphinx. Agamben argues that the Sphinx was not asking people to solve a riddle but was merely proposing a mode of speech. Oedipus' sin was therefore not incest, but destroying that mode of speech and inaugurating a breach between signifier and signified.[44] In this regard, Hao Ran's real achievement as a writer lies in his reestablishment, perhaps completely contrary to his intention, of a mode of speech wrought with ambiguity and double meanings. The sublimation of an incestuous impulse by resorting to a progressive socialist discourse both eliminates the need for committing the act of incest and paradoxically gives room for the impulse to continue to exist. It is a cultural revolution that "always must be carried on,/And still be doing, never done."

NOTES

Epigraph from Reginald Brimley Johnson, *The Poetical Works of Samuel Butler: A Revised Edition with Memoir and Notes*, vol. 1. (London: George Bell & Sons, 1893), 10.

1. Hao Ran, *Xique deng zhi* 喜鵲登枝 [Magpies on a branch] (Beijing: Zuojia chubanshe, 1958), 21 and 16.

2. Hao Ran, "*Chunge ji* bianxuan suoyi" 春歌集編選瑣憶 [Miscellaneous memories of the selection and compilation of *Songs of Spring*], in *Hao Ran yanjiu zhuanji* 浩然研究專集 [Special collection of Hao Ran studies], ed. Sun Dayou 孫達祐 and Liang Chunshui 梁春水 (Tianjin: Baihua wenyi chubanshe, 1994), 100.

3. Hao Ran, "Miscellaneous Memories," 110.

4. Paul Clark, *The Chinese Cultural Revolution: A History* (Cambridge: Cambridge University Press), 5.

5. See Rana Mitter, *A Bitter Revolution: China's Struggle with the Modern World* (Oxford: Oxford University Press, 2004), 230; also Barbara Mittler, *A Continuous Revolution: Making Sense of Cultural Revolution Culture* (Cambridge: Harvard University Asia Center, 2012), 30–31.

6. See Mao, "Talks at the Yan'an Forum on Literature and Art," trans. Bonnie McDougal, in *Reading in Modern Chinese Literary Thought*, ed. Kirk Denton (Stanford, CA: Stanford University Press, 1996), 458–484.

7. Tian Ying 天鷹, *Yijiuwuba nian Zhongguo min'ge yundong* 1958年中國民歌運動 [China's Folk Song Movement of 1958] (Shanghai: Shanghai wenyi chubanshe, [1959] 1978), 30–31 and 51.

8. *Hongqi geyao* 紅旗歌謠 [Red flag ballads], ed. Guo Moruo 郭沫若 and Zhou Yang 周揚 (Beijing: Hongqi zazhishe, 1958), 2.

9. *Red Flag Ballads*, 3.

10. Hao Ran, *Hao Ran koushu zizhuan* 浩然口述自傳 [Oral autobiography by Hao Ran], ed. Zheng Shi 鄭實 (Tianjin: Tianjin renmin chubanshe, 2008), 111–160.

11. Hao Ran, *Oral Autobiography*, 303–304. See also Richard King, *Milestones on a Golden Road: Writing for Chinese Socialism, 1945–80* (Vancouver: UBC Press, 2013), 114–115.

12. J. Hillis Miller, *Illustration* (Cambridge: Harvard University Press, 1992), 55.

13. Mittler, *A Continuous Revolution*, 16.

14. Ye Shengtao 葉聖陶, "Xin nongcun de xin miaomao: Du *Xique dengzhi*" 新農村的新面貌: 讀喜鵲登枝 [The new face of the new countryside: Upon reading

Magpies on a Branch], *Dushu* 讀書 [Reading] 14 (1958): 23. Ba Ren 巴人, "Lue tan *Xique dengzhi ji qita*" 略談喜鵲登枝及其他 [A brief discussion of *Magpies on a Branch* and others]. *Renmin wenxue* 人民文學 [People's literature] 11 (1959): 117.

15. Lan Yang, "The Ideal Socialist Hero: Literary Conventions in Cultural Revolution Novels," in *China's Great Proletarian Cultural Revolution: Master Narratives and Post-Mao Counternarratives*, ed. Woei Lien Chong (Lanham, MD: Rowman and Littlefield, 2002), 192–193. Hao Ran, *Magpies on a Branch*, 5.

16. Yenna Wu, *The Chinese Virago: A Literary Theme* (Cambridge: Harvard University Asia Center, 1995).

17. The story is rendered simply as "The Shrew" in H. C. Chang's English translation. H.C. Chang, *Chinese Literature: Popular Fiction and Drama* (Edinburgh: Edinburgh University Press, 1973), 32–55.

18. Hong Pian 洪楩, ed., *Qingpingshan tang huaben* 清平山堂話本 [Stories of the Qingpingshan Hall] (Shanghai: Gudian wenxue chubanshe, 1957), 66.

19. Hao Ran, *Magpies on a Branch*, 5.

20. Hao Ran, *Magpies on a Branch*, 14.

21. Hao Ran, *Magpies on a Branch*, 2–3.

22. Hao Ran, *Magpies on a Branch*, 4.

23. Hong Pian, *Stories of the Qingpingshan Hall*, 66.

24. Yang, "The Ideal Socialist Hero," 191. See also Pollard, "The Short Story in the Cultural Revolution," 104.

25. Hao Ran, *Magpies on a Branch*, 11.

26. Hao Ran, *Magpies on a Branch*, 21.

27. Hao Ran, *Magpies on a Branch*, 6.

28. Hao Ran, *Magpies on a Branch*, 7.

29. Hao Ran, *Magpies on a Branch*, 15–16.

30. Translated by Stephen Owen, in *An Anthology of Chinese Literature: Beginnings to 1911* (New York: W. W. Norton, 1996), 569.

31. By his own account, Hao Ran's first literary education consists of oral storytelling tradition, live theater performance, classical vernacular novels, and, among other things, *chantefables* and opera play scripts. Hao Ran, *Oral Autobiography*, 25–26, 47–57.

32. Hao Ran, *Magpies on a Branch*, 20.

33. Hao Ran, *Magpies on a Branch*, 18.

34. Hao Ran, *Magpies on a Branch*, 2.

35. Hao Ran, *Chun ge ji* 春歌集 [Songs of spring] (Tianjin: Tianjin renmin chubanshe, 1973), 23.

36. Hao Ran, *Magpies on a Branch*, 18.

37. Hao Ran, *Songs of Spring*, 38.

38. Hao Ran, *Magpies on a Branch*, 17. Hao Ran, *Songs of Spring*, 37.

39. For an extensive discussion of the politics of Hao Ran's revision of his early short stories, see Xiaofei Tian, "Castration for the People: The Politics of Revision and the Structure of Violence in Hao Ran's Short Stories," in "The Making and Remaking of China's 'Red Classics': Politics, Aesthetics and Mass Culture in Literary Icons of Socialism and Their Contemporary Remakes," ed. Li Li Peters and Rosie Robert, work in progress.

40. See Cyril Birch, "Continuity and Change in Chinese Fiction," in *Modern Chinese Literature in the May Fourth Era*, ed. Merle Goldman (Cambridge: Harvard University Press, 1977), 397–400. See also Michael Egan, "A Notable Sermon: The Subtext of Hao Ran's Fiction,"

in *Popular Chinese Literature and Performing Arts in the People's Republic of China: 1949–1979*, ed. Bonnie McDougal (Berkeley: University of California Press, 1984), 227–231.

41.   Egan, "A Notable Sermon," 233.

42.   Liu Xueyan 劉學顏, *Ai wu zhu* 愛無助 [Love is helpless] (Nanchang, Jiangxi: Baihuazhou wenyi chubanshe, 2011), 153.

43.   Hao Ran, "Miscellaneous Memories," 107.

44.   Giorgio Agamben, *Stanzas: Word and Phantasm in Western Culture*, trans. Ronald L. Martinez (Minneapolis: University of Minnesota Press, 1993), 135–139.

Works Cited

Agamben, Giorgio. *Stanzas: Word and Phantasm in Western Culture*. Trans. Ronald L. Martinez. Minneapolis: University of Minnesota Press, 1993.

Ba Ren 巴人. "Lüe tan *Xique dengzhi* ji qita" 略談喜鵲登枝及其他 [Brief discussion of *Magpies on a Branch* and other topics] *Renmin wenxue* 人民文學 [People's literature] 11 (1959): 115–120.

Birch, Cyril. "Continuity and Change in Chinese Fiction." In *Modern Chinese Literature in the May Fourth Era*. Ed. Merle Goldman. Cambridge: Harvard University Press, 1977. 385–404.

Chang, H. C. *Chinese Literature: Popular Fiction and Drama*. Edinburgh: Edinburgh University Press, 1973.

Clark, Paul. *The Chinese Cultural Revolution: A History*. Cambridge: Cambridge University Press, 2008.

Egan, Michael. "A Notable Sermon: The Subtext of Hao Ran's Fiction." In *Popular Chinese Literature and Performing Arts in the People's Republic of China: 1949–1979*. Ed. Bonnie McDougal. Berkeley: University of California Press, 1984. 224–243.

Guo Moruo 郭沫若 and Zhou Yang 周揚, ed. *Hongqi geyao* 紅旗歌謠 [Red flag ballads]. Beijing: Hongqi zazhishe, 1958.

Hao Ran 浩然. *Chun ge ji* 春歌集 [Songs of spring]. Tianjin: Tianjin renmin chubanshe, 1973.

Hao Ran 浩然. "*Chunge ji* bianxuan suoyi" 春歌集編選瑣憶 [Miscellaneous memories of the selection and compilation of *Songs of Spring*]. In *Hao Ran yanjiu zhuanji* 浩然研究專集 [Special collection of Hao Ran studies]. Ed. Sun Dayou 孫達祐 and Liang Chunshui 梁春水. Tianjin: Baihua wenyi chubanshe, 1994. 93–111.

Hao Ran 浩然. *Hao Ran koushu zizhuan* 浩然口述自傳 [Hao Ran's oral autobiography]. Ed. Zheng Shi 鄭實. Tianjin: Tianjin renmin chubanshe, 2008.

Hao Ran 浩然. *Xique dengzhi* 喜鵲登枝 [Magpies on a branch]. Beijing: Zuojia chubanshe, 1958.

Hong Pian 洪楩, ed., *Qingpingshan tang huaben* 清平山堂話本 [Stories of the Qingpingshan Hall]. Shanghai: Gudian wenxue chubanshe, 1957.

King, Richard. *Milestones on a Golden Road: Writing for Chinese Socialism, 1945–80*. Vancouver: UBC Press, 2013.

Liu Xueyan 劉學顏. *Ai wu zhu* 愛無助 [Love is helpless]. Nanchang, Jiangxi: Baihuazhou wenyi chubanshe, 2011.

Mao Zedong. *Nineteen Poems*. Beijing: Foreign Language Press, 1958.

Mao Zedong. "Talks at the Yan'an Forum on Literature and Art." Trans. Bonnie McDougal. In *Reading in Modern Chinese Literary Thought*. Ed. Kirk Denton. Stanford: Stanford University Press, 1996. 458–484.

Miller, J. Hillis. *Illustration*. Cambridge: Harvard University Press, 1992.

Mitter, Rana. *A Bitter Revolution: China's Struggle with the Modern World*. Oxford: Oxford University Press, 2004.

Mittler, Barbara. *A Continuous Revolution: Making Sense of Cultural Revolution Culture*. Cambridge: Harvard University Asia Center, 2012.

Owen, Stephen, ed. and trans. *An Anthology of Chinese Literature: Beginnings to 1911*. New York: W. W. Norton, 1996.

Pollard, D. E. "The Short Story in the Cultural Revolution." *China Quarterly* 73 (1978): 99–121.

Tian Ying 天鷹. *Yijiuwuba nian Zhongguo min'ge yundong* 1958 年中國民歌運動 [China's Folk Song Movement of 1958]. Shanghai: Shanghai wenyi chubanshe, [1959] 1978.

Wu, Yenna. *The Chinese Virago: A Literary Theme*. Cambridge: Harvard Asia Center, 1995.

Yang, Lan. "The Ideal Socialist Hero: Literary Conventions in Cultural Revolution Novels." In *China's Great Proletarian Cultural Revolution: Master Narratives and Post-Mao Counternarratives*. Ed. Woei Lien Chong. Lanham, MD: Rowman and Littlefield, 2002. 185–211.

Ye Shengtao 葉聖陶. "Xin nongcun de xin miaomao: Du *Xique dengzhi*" 新農村的新面貌: 讀喜鵲登枝 [The new face of the new countryside: upon reading *Magpies on a Branch*]. *Dushu* 讀書 [Reading] 14 (1958): 23–24.

CHAPTER 2.4

....

AT THE BORDERS OF CHINESE LITERATURE

Poetic Exchange in
the Nineteenth-Century Sinosphere

....

MATTHEW FRALEIGH

ON June 3, 1951, more than one hundred poets spent the day composing classical Sinitic verse at Osaka's Tenmangū shrine. Representing several Sinitic poetry societies based in Kyoto, Kobe, Nara, and other nearby Japanese cities, the participants first composed extemporaneously on "Hearing a cuckoo" (聽杜鵑), a topic revealed to them as the event commenced. In keeping with one popular practice of social versification employed since the Tang, the poets drew lots for this opening round to determine the rhyme groups that they would use to compose their poems, with the codified categories of rhyme likewise being rooted in Tang precedent. After lunch, the assembled poets took part in a second, competitive round on the topic of "Early summer pastorale" (初夏田園), with a single rhyme group stipulated for all participants to use and multiple prizes awarded both for those who completed their poems fastest and for those whose work was judged the best. While this particular event took place in postwar Japan, the highly conventional nature of the topics, the specific forms of poems composed (Tang-era *jintishi* 近體詩, literally "recent-style poetry"), the rhyme categories used, and even the ways in which these rhyme categories were assigned meant that traditionally educated Sinospheric intellectuals from roughly any point in the past millennium or more would have had little difficulty in following the day's festivities, comprehending the poems it yielded, and contributing their own. In fact, among those taking part in this poetic gathering at the Osaka shrine were more than a dozen Chinese and Korean members of Kobe's Kanzan Ginsha (觀山吟社) Sinitic verse society.

Written according to the grammar of Literary Sinitic and conforming to the rhythmic and prosodic regulations of classical Sinitic poetry, the works composed that day by the Japanese, Chinese, and Korean individuals would have exhibited an extremely high, if not always complete, degree of intraregional intelligibility. It would be a challenge to find any telltale signs of authorial nationality, for example, in the diction of the following verse, judged to be the best presented on the topic "Early summer pastorale":

微雨晴來麥氣清
水風陣陣午涼生
詩人也愛田家趣
時聽池蛙閣閣聲

Once the light rains clear, the wheat is freshly fragrant;
Wind gusts over the water, bringing cool to the noon hour.
A poet also delights in the charms of rural dwelling—
Listening to the occasional croak-croak of pond frogs.

The rhyme characters of this quatrain—those ending the first, second, and fourth lines (*qing, sheng,* and *sheng* in modern Mandarin pronunciation)—are all part of the traditional rhyme group *geng* (庚), the category that was designated for all participants to use in their compositions during the competitive round. Likewise, the above quatrain observes the most fundamental guidelines governing the variation of level and deflected tones within each line and also between lines. These qualities unmistakably confirm that consideration of rhyme, tone, and rhythm—features of poetic works that we tend to associate with orality—was an indispensable component of the compositional process for all taking part, even for those (presumably the majority) with little or no competence in spoken Chinese.

   Yet while the Chinese, Korean, and Japanese participants all plainly attended to these aural aspects as they produced their poems, the modes of oral performance most common in their respective cultural contexts were not identical. The pronunciation of individual characters as well as the reading strategies employed in the recitation of Literary Sinitic texts have of course varied widely historically and geographically, both within China and throughout the Sinosphere. A single written text such as the above quatrain could for this reason be vocalized in multiple ways, and it was in this domain of oral performance that such differences in intraregional practice were exhibited most clearly. Reporting on the Osaka gathering, a contemporary Japanese magazine for enthusiasts of Sinitic verse noted that "each of the extemporaneous compositions was recited in the three national languages" of the participants, which "heightened interest all the more."[1] That each of the composed poems could be recited trilingually surely served to affirm the participants' shared engagement with a transnational literary tradition even as it reminded them of the region's discrete nations, cultures, and languages.

   What did the above verse, written by Japanese poet Hirose Roshū 広瀬芦洲, sound like when recited in Japan's "national language"? The answer is not entirely clear. The Japanese magazine's report on the day's festivities merely prints the Sinitic text of Roshū's winning poem, giving no indication whatsoever of how it might actually have been vocalized in Japanese. In all likelihood, however, it would have been recited using the *kundoku* (訓讀) approach of "reading with a gloss." In this method of "vernacular reading," the Literary Sinitic text is transformed into a distinct (and usually highly Sinified) register of Japanese, a sort of "translationese" that preserves as closely as possible the diction and structure of the written text while construing it in accord with Japanese syntax and with the necessary grammatical particles and inflections. A typical *kundoku* rendition of Roshū's quatrain might go as follows:

微雨晴來麥氣清	微雨 晴れ來りて麥氣清し	(*biu hare kitarite bakki kiyoshi*)
水風陣陣午涼生	水風 陣陣として午涼生ず	(*suifū jinjin toshite goryō shōzu*)
詩人也愛田家趣	詩人也た田家の趣きを愛し	(*shijin mata denka no omomuki o aishi*)
時聽池蛙閣閣聲	時に聽く 池蛙閣閣の聲を	(*toki ni kiku chia kakukaku no koe o*)

But this is just one possibility. Given the verb-final nature of Japanese syntax, it would also be perfectly reasonable, for example, to relocate the verb 聽 (*kiku*) to the end of the fourth line, following its object, just as the verb in the third line, 愛 (*aisu*), has been placed at the end of that line, following its object. These are mainly matters of preference; a mid-sentence verb may create a slight sense of anastrophe in Japanese, but the effect is stylistic rather than semantic.

This phenomenon of "vernacular reading" was not unique to Japan; early on in the course of their encounters with Chinese texts, many cultures on the peripheries of Chinese civilization developed a host of approaches for making Literary Sinitic texts intelligible in their local languages.[2] Recent research has in fact pointed to similarities between East Asian vernacular reading practices and those developed within the European context; far from being an exception, John Whitman argues that "vernacular reading—reading a text written in the script, orthography, lexicon and grammar of a more prestigious 'cosmopolitan' language out loud in the vernacular language—has been a standard and widespread process throughout the history of written languages."[3] In the Japanese case, the pioneers of writing in the archipelago, very likely influenced by practices conveyed by scribes with ties to the Korean peninsula, developed over the centuries the apparatus of *kundoku* as a means to render Literary Sinitic texts more accessible to speakers of Japanese. Systems of "gloss marks" called *kunten* (訓點) were developed to annotate Literary Sinitic texts and thereby indicate how they might be read through *kundoku*, but so widespread was this reading method that a highly trained Japanese reader of Literary Sinitic might not require gloss marks at all in order to make an "on the fly" construal of the text in Japanese by means of *kundoku*. The crucial point is that whether or not the Japanese reader made use of written annotations, the original Sinitic text remained intact and in view. Though *kundoku* differs in some important ways from the processes we typically associate with the term "translation," inasmuch as it operates at the interface of two languages, it is useful to think of *kundoku* as a form of translation in which the "target text" does not replace the "source text," but merely supplements it; indeed, the target text (the oral pronunciation) may never be written down.[4]

The prevalence of *kundoku* as a means of engaging with Literary Sinitic texts and the ever-present possibility of transforming any Literary Sinitic text into a distinct register of Japanese by means of *kundoku* creates an ambiguity in the minds of some as to whether texts written in Literary Sinitic by Japanese should properly be considered Literary Sinitic at all. If in fact the Japanese authors of these ostensibly Literary Sinitic texts would conventionally have vocalized them using some form of "vernacular reading," the argument goes, then shouldn't this uninscribed Japanese vocalization that surely lurks behind the deceptively Chinese surface of the text be the principal object of our attention? It is important to bear in mind, however, that the process of *kundoku*, while systematic, is anything but mechanical. Fundamentally, it is an interpretive act. Techniques of *kundoku* and preferences for the resulting vocalization varied widely over time, but the broad trend over the centuries was toward a more "source-oriented" approach to rendering the Literary Sinitic text: one that more closely follows the original syntax, endeavors to gloss all characters in the original, and uses more Sinoxenic readings than indigenous Japanese equivalents (that is to say one that favors the conventional Japanese phonetic approximation of a word's Chinese pronunciation, such as *chia* for 池蛙, rather than the vernacular Japanese *ike no kaeru*).

Such synchronic and diachronic variations in approaches to *kundoku* are one reason that scholarly editions offering *kundokubun* (訓讀文; "text interpreted in the vernacular") glosses of Japanese Sinitic poets' texts often do not agree on how they ought to be vocalized, even in those cases when they fully concur about the meaning of a given passage. In the absence of any *kundokubun* gloss for Roshū's winning quatrain from the competition at Osaka's Tenmangū shrine, I offered my own rendition, but to appreciate the diverse range of possibilities within the *kundoku* approach, let us examine a verse from that shrine's namesake, Sugawara no Michizane 菅原道真 (845–903), early Heian Japan's most celebrated Sinitic poet. One of Michizane's best known quatrains is the following, which he wrote in exile near the end of his life:

離家三四月
落淚百千行
萬事皆如夢
時時仰彼蒼

Since leaving home, three or four months;
I shed tears, a hundred or a thousand lines.
Myriad things are all like a dream;
Constantly I look up at blue Heaven.

Consider the first couplet. One preeminent Japanese scholar of early Heian texts, presumably attempting to reconstruct a highly Japanized rendition that would be more in keeping with the "target-oriented" approach to *kundoku* that prevailed in Michizane's time, renders these lines: 家を離れて三四月　落つる淚は百千行 "*ie o hanarete mitsuki yotsuki / otsuru namida wa momotsura chitsura.*"[5] But another equally illustrious

Japanese scholar instead suggests a sparer, syntactically unrearranged, all-Sinoxenic reading: 離家 三四月 落涙 百千行 "*rika san shi gatsu / rakurui hyakusenkō.*"[6] In some cases manuscripts contain gloss marks that can help us work out a plausible vocalization in line with what we have been able to reconstruct about contemporary *kundoku* styles, but a great many Sinitic texts by Japanese circulated with no gloss marks whatsoever (such as we saw with Roshū's winning quatrain from 1951). Even if some gloss marks are present in a text, it is not always clear who added them and when, and they almost never record a full phonetic transcription, all of which means that a conjecture about vocalization can only ever be one possible rendition among many. The two scholars' readings of Michizane's couplet that I have quoted could hardly be more dissimilar from one another, and other scholars have proposed any number of additional possibilities.[7] While these various reconstructions are definitely worthwhile contributions to our historical understanding of how a text might have been orally recited in a particular context, we must not delude ourselves into thinking that if we could only pinpoint the correct *kundoku* gloss we would thereby have fully grasped what the Japanese Sinitic poet was *really* trying to write. Even if we could reliably reconstruct how a Japanese author of a given Sinitic text vocalized it, this would only be part of the picture; such knowledge would shed important light on the text's performance, but would also shift our attention away from features of the written text that were unmistakably central to its composition. For example, Michizane was clearly attentive to grammatical parallelism when he wrote this couplet, yet that feature disappears if we follow the first scholar's proposed reading (which distorts the shared verb-object structure of the first two words of each line, reading them as object-verb in the first line and verb-object in the second). Obviously Michizane was conscious of rhyme as well, completing the poem with the fourth line's 蒼 (J. *sō*; C. *cang*) to rhyme with the second line's 行 (J. *kō*; C. *hang*). Yet this feature of the text, undeniably integral to its composition, also disappears in conventional *kundoku* renditions because they make the verb 仰 terminal and thus bury the rhyme character 蒼; the first scholar reads this line *oriori ka no sō o aogu* and the second reads it *jiji hisō o aogu*.

Let me be clear; I am not suggesting that any of these *kundoku* renditions is mistaken, nor am I suggesting that *kundoku* deserves no consideration. It is of course important to think about the range of performative possibilities latent in or implied by the poetic text, but we should always bear in mind the fact that just as *kundoku* operates to supplement rather than replace the original text, the vocalization it produces is an extratextual or at least paratextual feature of the Sinitic text. A phonocentric privileging of the conjectured vocalization can cause us to overlook significant features of the poem as a written text. The account of the gathering at the Osaka shrine in 1951 reminds us that even as Japan's Sinitic poets enjoyed the sonorous recitation of their Sinitic verses through *kundoku*, it was the coherent written form of these Sinitic texts that enabled their broader circulation.

As in other Sinospheric nations, the number of Japanese poets composing in classical Sinitic forms was on the decline when the Osaka gathering took place in the early postwar period, but circumstances could not have been more markedly different a hundred years earlier. Though standard narratives of Japanese literary history have been somewhat slow to embrace the fact, the nineteenth century was unquestionably the peak of Sinitic expression in Japan in terms of the sheer number of active composers, the volume of their publications, their comprehensive geographic spread, and their unprecedented social and gender diversity. Many critics have further argued that Sinitic literature in Japan also reached its qualitative zenith during this period, when figures such as Rai San'yō 頼山陽 (1780–1832) and Mori Kainan 森槐南 (1863–1911) were at their most prolific.[8] Indeed, both San'yō and Kainan are among the three Japanese Sinitic poets arrayed among their Chinese contemporaries in Wu Kaisheng's 吳闓生 1924 *Anthology of Forty Poets from the Late Qing* (晚清四十家詩鈔).

At the same time, however, the last decade of the nineteenth century also saw the status of Sinitic genres change radically in Japan as newly imported frameworks of literary history premised on monolingualism and phonocentrism redefined the production of Sinitic texts as a practice external to "national literature," a change symbolically marked by a shift in the very terminology by which Sinitic genres were identified. For example, whereas *shi* (詩) had long been used in Japanese to refer specifically to Literary Sinitic poetry, the term came to be used as the default translation for "poetry" in general around this time, prompting the neologism *kanshi* (漢詩; "Han poetry") to be adopted to specify Sinitic poetry (whether produced by Chinese, Japanese, or other Sinospheric poets). A series of parallel shifts in curricular structures and instructional content meant that well-educated Japanese in coming generations increasingly acquired Sinitic compositional ability only through their own independent initiative. Nevertheless, in the decades after these changes irrevocably marginalized Sinitic expression within the Japanese literary context, a number of national and regional Sinitic poetry societies remained active. The magazine from which I quoted Roshū's poem is but one of several journals devoted to the enterprise that continued to be published through the middle of the twentieth century. While the number of practicing Sinitic poets in present-day Japan is admittedly very small, there remain forums that publish their work even now.

The 1875 anthology *A Euphonious Meiji Collection* (*Meiji kōinshū* 明治好音集), which assembles over two hundred poems (in both Sinitic and Japanese forms) composed since the 1868 Meiji Restoration, offers a glimpse of the Japanese literary world before these dramatic transformations took place. Compiled by Okabe Keigorō 岡部啓五郎, the collection vividly captures how large the Sinitic literary tradition still loomed in the early Meiji literary landscape and how textually mediated interaction between its Japanese practitioners and their Sinospheric counterparts had come to be increasingly commonplace. The anthology features the compositions of a wide array of Japanese poets, including members of the imperial household, prominent statesmen and military figures, oppositional journalists, noted scholars, and many lesser-known individuals from the public at large: a diversity of voices that Japan's newly founded newspapers and other periodical commercial media were now regularly bringing together on the printed page. While Japanese people are by far the primary composers of the poems in this collection, *Meiji kōinshū* also features several works by Chinese and Koreans, including both residents of Japan and others whom Japanese encountered abroad. In its inclusion of these poems, *Meiji kōinshū* reminds us that Literary Sinitic long endured as a vital expressive medium outside of China and that it also served as an important mode of exchange among traditionally educated Sinospheric individuals even as Japan, China, and Korea were engaged in the difficult process of reconfiguring their relations through new paradigms of nationhood.

The first poem attributed to a Chinese person in Okabe's collection was written in the wake of Japan's 1874 punitive expedition against indigenous groups in southern Taiwan, a conflict that laid bare the irresolvable tensions between the traditional Sinocentric order and new models of sovereignty premised on the nation-state. The two events that precipitated the 1874 conflict had occurred a few years earlier, when several dozen shipwrecked seafarers from the Ryukyus and subsequently some from the Japanese mainland had been murdered by Taiwanese indigenes. Japan's efforts to seek redress for what it saw as its subjects' wrongful deaths in these two incidents were complicated by the ambiguous status of the majority of the victims, for the Ryukyus were then "dually affiliated" with both the fledgling Meiji state and the Qing dynasty. At the same time, when the Qing disavowed responsibility for the Taiwanese indigenes' actions by arguing that these southern groups dwelt "beyond the pale" (化外; C. *huawai*) of Qing cultural suasion, they furnished Japan with grounds to marshal new frameworks of "international law" in order to mount the counterargument that the Qing must therefore have no sovereignty over southern Taiwan. Japan launched its punitive expedition in April 1874, and after its decisive victory in battle against the Mudan 牡丹 (J. Botan) indigenous group in early June, hostilities soon came to a halt. Negotiations with the Qing over reparations, however, would drag on for many more months.

It was not long after the surrender of the Mudan and the "complete pacification" of Taiwan had been announced that Ou Hunan 歐湖南, reportedly a "Qing man from Jiangsu who resides in Yokohama," wrote the quatrain that would eventually find its way into Okabe's collection of Meiji verse. In it, Ou expresses skepticism about what Japan had achieved in waging the Taiwan Expedition, alluding to the contentious debate over sending forces to chastise Korea that had roiled the Japanese government the previous year:

日本方今事太艱
征韓議罷討臺灣
國力耗衰爲何事
惟見奏勳擒女蠻

In Japan of late, affairs grow quite distressing;
Just as debate about "attacking Korea" concludes, they strike Taiwan.
For what do they exhaust and deplete their national strength?
All we see from their "meritorious service": the capture of a barbarian girl.[9]

Ou Hunan refers in the last line to one of the Taiwan Expedition's most sensational events: Japanese forces' removal of a twelve-year-old aboriginal girl from her village and the Meiji government's short-lived efforts to "educate" her in Japan.[10] This poem first appeared in *Shinbun zasshi*, a Tokyo periodical patronized by the Meiji government that was then publishing every other day and that had reported the girl's arrival in Tokyo just a few weeks earlier.[11] Ou's quatrain was reprinted in other Japanese media and soon prompted numerous Japanese poets to contribute their own responsive quatrains that duplicated his rhyme characters: 艱 (C. *jian*; J. *kan*), 灣 (C. *wan*; J. *wan*), and 蠻 (C. *man*; J. *ban*).

Okabe's anthology *A Euphonious Meiji Collection* directs our attention to these interactive and intraregional dimensions of Sinitic literary production in early Meiji, for in addition to Ou Hunan's original poem, it also reproduces a series of eight quatrains that the Sinological scholar Ōtsuki Bankei 大槻磐渓 (1801–1878) composed in response and which he published in other Tokyo newspapers that summer.[12] In a prefatory note, Bankei explains that upon seeing a number of "my countrymen" offer matched-rhyme compositions in response to "the poem on Taiwan by the Qing man Ou Hunan," he has felt an "unbearable itch" to join the conversation. One of his quatrains reads:

> 國事多端天步艱
> 遠征何暇問臺灣
> 縱是取爲吾屬島
> 不成一事牡丹蠻

> National affairs entangle us and the times bring adversity;
> A distant campaign—what leisure do we have to consider Taiwan?
> Even were we to take possession of the island,
> It would come to nothing: the Mudan barbarians.

In another quatrain from the series, Bankei echoes the suggestion of futility apparent above; he alludes to a Fan Chengda 范成大 poem (which in turn draws upon an allegorical passage in the Taoist classic *Zhuangzi* 莊子) to suggest that the stakes of the conflict are so low that they cannot justify the loss of human life. In yet another poem from the same series, however, Bankei expresses his sympathy for the plight of the shipwrecked sailors and his puzzlement as to why the Qing opposed the acculturation of those who had been responsible for their slaughter.

Near the end of his anthology, Okabe includes Ou Hunan's response to the spirited exchange of Sinitic poems that his quatrain on the Taiwan Expedition had unleashed in Tokyo's newspapers. Following the precedent that he had established in his first contribution, Ou Hunan duplicated his own original rhyme characters in a second quatrain:

> 男兒報國豈辭艱
> 愧我潛身橫港灣
> 寸丹遙獻邊防策
> 要護南陲十八蕃

> A man serves his country—how can he refuse the challenge?
> In shame, I hide myself along the bay at Yokohama port.
> Though meager, I offer from afar my loyalty to defend the periphery;
> And protect the eighteen tribes of the southern frontier.[13]

The phrase *eighteen tribes* designates southern Taiwan's indigenous population, of which the Mudan were part. Ou's poem is dated August 10, 1874, suggesting that rather than the already-concluded military conflict between Japanese forces and Taiwanese indigenes, the focus of his attention was probably the tense negotiations between Japanese and Qing officials that brought the two nations close to the brink of war in the summer of 1874.[14] In the lengthy prose preface to his second quatrain, Ou Hunan identified himself as "a shoemaker long resident in Yokohama" and acknowledged the many quatrains that Japanese poets had written in response to his original verse.[15]

The Japanese who wrote Sinitic poems matching Ou Hunan's rhymes used the opportunity to articulate diverse views about the Taiwanese Expedition and the larger questions it raised. As the examples we have seen by Bankei and Ou Hunan himself both suggest, even a single poet might give voice to various perspectives on the crisis, ranging from fervent nationalism to cool indifference. Another common reaction to the Taiwan Expedition was disappointment that a trivial dispute should have divided potential allies. Consider the following quatrain by Narushima Ryūhoku 成島柳北 (1837–1884), written around the time the protracted negotiations between Japan and the Qing at last approached a settlement:

> 予室翹翹知不知
> 風風雨雨太淒其
> 雙禽何事少長策
> 爭啄牡丹花一枝

> My house is all to pieces, do you not see?
> Winds and rains so cold and desolate.
> What can they intend—two birds lacking long-term plans,
> Vying to peck at a single sprig of peony?[16]

The first couplet draws upon diction from a *Book of Odes* (詩經) ode in which a beleaguered small bird pleas with a fierce kite-owl for mercy. In the second couplet, Ryūhoku extends this ornithological metaphor for the Sino-Japanese conflict with a pun on the name of the Mudan indigenes, an ethnonym written with characters that also signify the peony flower. The implicit kinship that this poem proposes in comparing Japan and China to "two birds" becomes more overt in the second of Ryūhoku's two quatrains, which begins:

> 弟兄何意漫交兵
> 知是東洋氣運更

> Why should brothers recklessly battle each other?
> Know that this is a moment on which the fate of the East turns.

Ryūhoku's final quatrain in the series elaborates on the broader geopolitical concern that the above couplet identifies, concluding with the following:

不知蚌鷸孰收利
今日江頭漁父多

Who knows whether the clam or the snipe will reap the rewards,
But along the river today there are many fishermen.

In alluding to the famous *Strategies of the Warring States* (戰國策) parable of a clam and a snipe stubbornly locked in conflict with one another when a passing fisherman seizes them both, Ryūhoku points out the more ominous threat posed by Western powers seeking to expand their presence in East Asia.

As this profusion of poetry in a broad range of early Meiji newspapers indicates, Literary Sinitic texts were clearly an important part of Japanese public discourse about the Taiwan Expedition. Ou Hunan's initial quatrain, the numerous quatrains that Japanese poets wrote matching its rhymes, and Ou's subsequent response to these show how Sinitic poetry functioned at this time as a vital literary practice that transcended national borders, enabling dialogue among individuals who may have had no spoken language in common but nevertheless shared competence in a written language and familiarity with its canonical texts.[17] One of the most consistent refrains in the Sinitic poetic exchanges and brush-talks published in early Meiji newspapers was a gesture to this bond through phrases that cast participants as those with a "shared written language" (同文; C. *tongwen*, J. *dōbun*) or as fellow members of "this culture of ours" (斯文; C. *siwen*, J. *shibun*).[18] Clearly, Meiji Japanese Sinitic poets were aware of Chinese and other Sinospheric individuals as potential readers and participants in their Sinitic poetic discourse even during this early stage, and Ou Hunan was not alone in taking part. The following year, for example, Luo Xuegu 羅雪谷, a Guangzhou painter and calligrapher resident in Tokyo, wrote in to the *Chōya shinbun* (朝野新聞 [The nation]) to explain that he had read the poetry exchanges of the scholars Nakamura Keiu 中村敬宇 (1832–1891) and Ōtsuki Bankei in the newspaper's pages (mentioning in particular an installment featuring poems that touched on the Taiwan Expedition), and had felt moved to offer his own set of verses that matched their rhymes.[19]

In some ways, such textually mediated interaction between Japanese and other Sinospheric individuals was nothing new. After all, one of Japan's oldest anthologies of Sinitic verse, the early-ninth-century *Collection of Literary Masterpieces* (*Bunka shūreishū* 文華秀麗集), preserves Sinitic poems exchanged between Japanese officials and emissaries from the northeast Asian state of Parhae.[20] During Japan's early modern period (1603–1867), the Tokugawa shogunate's restrictions on overseas travel and its close regulation of contacts with the outside world meant that occasions when Japanese scholars could interact in person with other Sinospheric individuals were quite rare, but they were by no means nonexistent. The Sinitic poetry collections of several seventeenth-century Japanese poets preserve their exchanges with Ming refugees such as Chen Yuanyun 陳元贇 (1578–1671) and Zhu Shunshui 朱舜水 (1600–1682), and the Ōbaku 黄檗 (C. Huangbo) Zen sect, founded by Chinese monk émigrés in the mid-seventeenth century, was another important channel of such interaction. Yet another opportunity came through the periodic visits of embassies from Chosŏn Korea to Japan, and the shogunate was careful to appoint men who were particularly accomplished in Sinitic prose and poetry to take part in these diplomatic meetings. Similarly, those Japanese who had occasion to visit Nagasaki often made a point of touring the district where Chinese merchants dwelt, and brush-talk exchanges of Sinitic prose and poetry with these individuals are one common feature of the travelogues and other texts they wrote to commemorate their journeys.[21] By the mid-nineteenth century, as the Tokugawa era entered its final years, such opportunities began to increase slowly with the arrival of Qing émigrés to Japan's newly opened ports. Likewise, the diaries of the Japanese officials who served on the several shogunal overseas missions in the 1860s show that when they visited Shanghai or Hong Kong, many engaged in brush-talks with local Chinese, sought to have their Sinitic poetry evaluated by them, or solicited their calligraphy.[22]

Yet the Meiji scene was different for many reasons, not least of which was its vastly greater scale. The number of Sinospheric visitors to Japan increased dramatically in these years, especially after the 1878 establishment of a Qing permanent legation in Tokyo.[23] Moreover, whereas highly educated individuals had been somewhat exceptional among the earlier visitors (many of whom made their living as merchants), the early Meiji period saw numerous statesmen, scholars, and other individuals who had attained distinction in traditional learning and literary arts come to Japan. In addition, the flourishing Meiji media landscape also facilitated forms of literary interaction that were qualitatively different from those common in the early modern period. The publication of exchanges of Sinitic poetry and prose in Japan's newspapers and magazines opened them up to a nearly unbounded potential readership, making it possible for individuals not present at an initial interaction to nevertheless insinuate themselves long after the fact. Conversely, the rapid publication schedule of periodical media and the penetration of the modern postal system meant that even geographically dispersed individuals could engage in exchanges that approached synchronicity with individuals whom they might never meet face to face.[24]

While opportunities to exploit these dimensions of the Meiji media landscape proliferated greatly with the presence of many literarily inclined statesmen among the Qing diplomatic corps, the basic framework was already in place in 1874 when Ye Songshi 葉松石 (1839–1903) arrived in Tokyo from Zhejiang to take up a post as Chinese instructor at Tokyo School of Foreign Languages.[25] His poetry frequently appeared in various print media such as the major daily newspaper *Chōya shinbun*, and when he returned to China in 1876, the Sinitic poetry and prose journal *Shinbunshi* (新文詩 New prose and poetry) even compiled a special issue in his honor.[26] Ye Songshi's published exchanges with Bankei, Keiu, and countless other Japanese literary figures often showcased a certain easygoing camaraderie. Consider a somewhat jocular set of four-teen rhymed couplets Ye sent to Bankei, which begins:

> 我來日本歲已再
> 此間方物何所愛
> 寶刀舞妓磐溪翁
> 惟斯三者繫心胸

> It is already the second year since I came to Japan;
> What do I cherish among the local offerings?
> Treasured swords, dancing girls, and Old Bankei;
> It is these three alone that capture my heart.

In addition to Ye Songshi's numerous avowals in this poem of the appreciation for wine and women that he shares with Bankei, he also plays upon the name of the latter's studio, Hall of Fondness for Antiquity (Aikodō 愛古堂) to suggest another bond between them:

> 翁是今人愛古人
> 古心古貌最清真

> You, Sir, are a man of the present, but also a man "fond of antiquity";
> Sharing the mind of the ancients and a venerable air, you are pure and
>   genuine.

Bankei's published response duplicated the rhymes of Ye's twenty-eight lines, including this match of the above couplet, which similarly highlights their shared link to a textual tradition:

> 幸是異域同文人
> 情話憑筆見天真

> Fortunate that you, though in a foreign land, are one who shares the
>   written word;
> In telling our feelings we rely upon the brush, revealing our true natures.[27]

When Ye Songshi toured western Japan on the eve of his return to China in 1876, Bankei published a series of matched-rhyme poems in the Chōya shinbun that imagined from afar his friend's enjoyment of Kyoto's attractions:

> 羨汝東山携妓去
> 祇園清水醉歌行

> I envy you venturing off to Eastern Hill with geisha in hand;
> Tipsily singing as you stroll through Gion and Kiyomizu.[28]

In this couplet from one of the five quatrains he composed, Bankei allusively super-imposes onto Ye Songshi the figure of Xie An 謝安 (320–385), the Jin literatus famed for tarrying with courtesans on Eastern Hill (東山): a particularly apt gesture given that one of the major scenic sites Songshi visited in Kyoto was the identically named Higashiyama (東山).

As these recurrent references to antiquity and the written word as well as allu-sive invocations of canonical precedents suggest, the textual interactions between Ye Songshi and his Japanese counterparts were stages on which they performed their membership in a common tradition (though as the polysemy of 東山 shows, even an established reference could be invested with a particular local significance). While the participants themselves and the print media that carried their exchanges tended to emphasize the commensurability of those taking part, occasionally their discrepancies instead became the focus of attention. Consider how Ye Songshi's status as a foreign national was taken up by a Japanese writer in the latter's scathing 1875 critique of those Japanese intellectuals who refused to use the solar calendar, which had been adopted by Japan over two years earlier. The spirited essayist allowed that while benighted residents of rural Japan might be forgiven for sticking to their old customs, for an educated man to flout the officially promulgated calendar of his nation, dismissing it merely because it was of Western provenance, made him nothing but a "peculiar scoundrel." To clarify his point, the author of the piece adduced as evidence "a qua-train that the Qing man Ye Songshi wrote in our country on New Year's Eve by the old calendar":

近來東國行西法
二月寒梅未着花
我愛山家無曆日
歲時依舊學中華

These days, the Eastern Land adopts Western ways;
In their "second month," the "cold plums" still show no blossoms.
Fond of my mountain retreat, I need no calendar;
For years and seasons I continue to follow the Central Efflorescence.[29]

In the eyes of the essayist, "For a Chinese person to say something like this because he is maintaining his own country's calendrical methods is perfectly reasonable, but our country has already reformed its practice to the new calendar." In quoting and assessing the propriety of this poem, the Japanese essay affirms a broader transnational textuality that Ye Songshi and the Sinitic poets of Japan shared while at the same time using the poem itself to highlight the cultural and political distinctions between the two nations. A similar tension between these intraregional and local frames marks the structure of *Quatrains by Tokyo's Men of Talent* (*Tōkyō saijin zekku* 東京才人絶句), an important early Meiji anthology of Sinitic poetry that Mori Shuntō 森春濤 (1819–1889), who was emerging as a leading Sinitic poet in Tokyo at the time, published the same year. The main text comprises quatrains by 160 Japanese poets, followed by an appended selection of fifteen quatrains by Ye Songshi situating him as both part of and yet somehow separate from the other poets in the collection.[30]

As these examples attest, apart from his teaching duties, Ye Songshi was an extraordinarily energetic contributor to the Sinitic poetry scene in early Meiji Japan. After returning to China, he published *Collected Farewell Songs from Japan* (*Fusang lichang ji* 扶桑驪唱集), a collection containing several of his own poems alongside the poems that more than forty Japanese literary figures presented to him upon his departure.[31] When Ye Songshi returned to live in Japan a second time in the 1880s, he was again welcomed enthusiastically by Japanese literary figures. Almost all of the poets whose work is featured in *Collected Farewell Songs from Japan* were individuals whom Ye had met during his first stay in Japan, the majority of compositions taking the form of matched-rhyme responses to Ye Songshi's own poems and many of them presented to him at farewell banquets convened in his honor. However, a few of the poems Ye Songshi ultimately included only came to his attention much later, including some printed in the *Chōya shinbun* from poets he had never met.[32] As these published responses echoing the rhymes of Ye's original quatrains from his time in Kyoto multiplied over time, the effect was a crescendo. One of the last Japanese poets to contribute to this 1876 sequence specifically references the poems that "Masters Bankei, Keiu, and Ryūhoku" addressed to "Qing visitor Ye Songshi" in the heading to his series and then goes on to weave into one of his five quatrains the names of three additional Japanese poets whose exchanges with Ye Songshi in Kyoto had also been published by the newspaper.[33]

Quoting a phrase from the *Analects* at the opening to one of his quatrains, this final contributor made an important observation. He wrote that Ye Songshi and his Japanese counterparts "forged their friendship through shared cultivation and learning" (以文會友).[34] That this cultivation was founded upon a shared textuality is implicit in the word *wen* (文), which can refer to various forms of cultivation but might be interpreted more narrowly to refer to familiarity with certain foundational texts, including of course the *Analects* itself. Mastery of the written language of Literary Sinitic was the essential basis of these encounters, because with very rare exceptions, the Japanese individuals who exchanged Sinitic poetry with Ye Songshi had absolutely no facility with spoken Chinese. They had learned to read Literary Sinitic through the *kundoku* approach, and most would have employed it when they recited their own poetic compositions aloud.[35] Yet like all Sinitic poets in Japan, they were also attentive to rhythmic and structural features of the Sinitic text that *kundoku* conceals; their focus on end-rhyme, for example, is the manifest starting point of the responsive compositions that we have seen.[36] While the modes by which Ye Songshi and his Japanese counterparts would have orally recited Sinitic texts surely differed, this gap seems to have been of relatively little interest to them (even though Ye Songshi himself was employed to teach modern spoken Chinese). Rather, what is repeatedly demonstrated and often self-reflexively emphasized in their interactions is their shared status as creators of written Sinitic texts.

To be sure, some Japanese Sinitic poets of earlier eras had enthusiastically pursued the study of spoken Chinese and had enjoyed reciting their compositions in this manner.[37] In addition to those Japanese in the ancient and medieval periods who studied Chinese pronunciation in formal educational settings or who had the opportunity to acquire such oral proficiency through travel to China, some early modern scholars, such as Ogyū Sorai 荻生徂徠 (1666–1728), made a point of reading Sinitic texts using Chinese pronunciation rather than through the *kundoku* approach. Nevertheless, recitation of Sinitic texts in Chinese pronunciation remained an exceptional practice in Japan into the modern period. Consider the following report on the activities of Japanese students at Higashi Honganji's Shanghai Annex, an outpost that the major Japanese Buddhist temple had founded in 1876 as part of its wide-ranging efforts to undertake missionary activity on the Asian continent as well as to provide pastoral services to overseas Japanese. The Japanese priests who were sent to study at the Shanghai Annex were chosen for the competence in Literary Sinitic they had acquired in Japan, but as a letter sent to the *Chōya shinbun* shows, they were now learning to recite their compositions using their new skills in spoken Chinese:

> Those who score highest [on tests of Sinitic poetry and prose] have their work evaluated by Sun Airen. Last month there were some who had every word of their composition endorsed with praising circles or emphasis marks. Of course, the prose and poetry lessons are conducted using Chinese pronunciation. Thus when they recite their poems in the Chinese pronunciation, it produces a certain unusual charm.[38]

Clearly this was an unfamiliar and novel mode of articulation for the students. After quoting some of the winning poems along with Shanghai instructor Sun Airen's laudatory comments, the head of the *Chōya*, Narushima Ryūhoku, offered this:

> Ziyu [i.e., Mencius] said: "A man's surroundings transform his air just as the food he eats changes his body." It only makes sense. Now when I read the poems of the Honganji students in China, their air and tone are naturally different from those of our country's people. We ought to raise to the west a flag of surrender![39]

As one who continued writing Sinitic poetry to the very end of his life, Ryūhoku was of course being hyperbolic in proposing "surrender," but however facetious his metaphor of competition was, it also directs our attention to the fact that he, like most Japanese Sinitic poets, saw himself as engaged in the same enterprise as his Chinese counterparts.

Ryūhoku's newspaper also published many essays that are, by contrast, bitingly dismissive of the literary abilities of some less-educated Qing émigrés to Japan and ruthlessly scornful of the misplaced obsequiousness with which some Japanese related to them. Yet these essays in fact conversely demonstrate the same point: that Japanese Sinitic poets saw themselves as members of a broader tradition they shared with eminent figures from the Chinese past:

Recently a kind of curious practice has become popular in literati and poetic circles. Mr. A asks a Tang man fresh off the boat to correct his poems. Mr. B entreats the Qing embassy to provide some brushwork for framing. . . . If a Qing visitor drools we treat it like pearls or jade. If a Tang man farts, we wonder if it is orchid or musk. He has only to write a piece of prose and we will revere it as the equal of Han Yu or Liu Zongyuan without considering at all whether it is fine or poor. He has only to brush a single character and we treasure it as a direct transmission from Yan Zhenqing or Ouyang Xun. . . . How would anyone know that many of them are migrant merchants if not failed students? . . . I am not saying that the Chinese are not deserving of respect. But to think that just because someone is Chinese that means he is a great scholar or a worthy sage or a literary master . . . is laughable![40]

Rather than nationality, the essayist argues, it was one's cultivation and mastery of literary arts that demonstrated a meaningful bond to a shared tradition, and these were of course practices at which Japanese Sinitic poets could also excel. An essay published in the newspaper the following year extends this critique of the "servility" of some Japanese literati in the face of Chinese nationals by lauding Japan's own Sinitic poets and scholars:

In recent years, men from China possessing a smattering of knowledge of the written word come creeping in like snakes in early spring, and whenever the young lords of literati society see one, they race to have their [Sinitic] poetry and prose corrected, or request a preface or a colophon. They copy out in advance their own best works and then present these, saying, "Oh, Living [Su] Dongpo! Latter-day Master who Does as He Pleases [i.e., Lu You]! Patriarch of the main house! Please condescend to enlighten me with your august teaching!"[41]

While the Chinese are quick to lavish praise on the Sinitic works the Japanese show them, the essayist continues, an eminent Japanese teacher of Sinitic poetry and prose would dismiss these compositions out of hand, a discrepancy the essayist attributes to the Chinese émigrés lack of education and literary skill:

They are amateurs, and if one were to compare them to our great masters, it is like weighing a paper lantern against a temple bell. If you think I am making reckless remarks, then just take a careful read of the poetry and prose that they write. You will not be impressed. But people are awestruck by their nation's name, quailing when they see their bewhiskered appearance and hear their Chinese pronunciation. This is what is called servility.

The defensive vehemence of these remarks perhaps reveals a certain anxiety or ambivalence that some Japanese Sinitic poets no doubt felt. Yet we should also take note of the fact that the argument is clearly not couched in terms that posit the independence or distinction of Japanese Sinitic literary arts from the broader Sinospheric tradition.

In both essays, the author unmistakably believes himself qualified to assess the poetic and calligraphic abilities of the Qing émigrés, and as the enumeration of several Tang and Song luminaries in these two pieces shows, the implicit standards are framed as rooted in Chinese precedent rather than deriving from some independent Japanese set of criteria.

If this essayist was underwhelmed by the literary skills of some of the great many Qing émigrés to Japan during these years, his critique was no blanket condemnation. Following in the steps of Ye Songshi, a number of Qing poets were beginning to become prominent participants in contemporary Japanese Sinitic poetry circles at precisely this time. Most notable were those affiliated with the first Qing legation, the staff of which included such eminent poets as Secretary Huang Zunxian 黃遵憲 (1848–1905). In fact, the very next day after the first of the above two essays appeared in the *Chōya shinbun*, the same newspaper published the poem Vice Minister Zhang Sigui 張斯桂 (1816–1888) had written on observing a hot-air balloon demonstration at the Japanese Army training school, a work that would be published in China's *Shun Pao* (申報) newspaper the following year.[42] While in this case the Japanese newspaper published the Qing diplomat's Sinitic poem first, the reverse was often true as well; a lengthy series of quatrains that Zhang Sigui wrote about Japan's distinct material culture, unfamiliar customs, and notable sites was first published in *Xunhuan ribao* (循環日報) and *Shun Pao* before being reprinted a month later in the *Chōya shinbun*.[43] The appearance of the same poems at roughly the same time in both Japanese and Chinese newspapers reminds us of the transnational textuality that bound Qing poets like Zhang Sigui with Sinitic poets in Japan. At the same time, however, Zhang's quatrains also pointed out Japan's local linguistic and cultural specificity within this broader frame. In this series, Zhang has conspicuous fun incorporating many terms (of both Sinitic and Japanese provenance) that would have seemed unusual or even unrecognizable to his Chinese readers, providing brief notes to explain to them that 料理 means "fine cuisine," for example, and that 玉子 means "a chicken's egg."

One of the most celebrated Qing intellectuals to visit Japan in early Meiji was the pioneering journalist Wang Tao 王韜 (1828–1897). Even prior to his visit, Wang Tao had written about Japan in several essays, quoting from Japanese Sinitic texts that he had read in Hong Kong, and he had also made the acquaintance of several Japanese who passed through the colonial port.[44] Shortly after Wang's 1873 *Chronicle of the Franco-Prussian War* (普法戰記) had been published, it came to the attention of Japanese journalist Kurimoto Joun 栗本鋤雲 (1822–1897). Joun was so impressed that he began making arrangements for it to be published in Japan, though ultimately the Japanese Army preempted him by publishing a colloquial Japanese translation of the text just as Joun's *kunten* version (an edition featuring Wang Tao's original text with gloss marks) was nearing completion. Undeterred, Joun soon began working with his former collaborators on the publication project and several other Japanese intellectuals to invite Wang to make a visit. Wang was delighted to accept the invitation, and in the course of his several months in Japan during the summer of 1879, he saw its major ports, toured the countryside, became a connoisseur of Tokyo nightlife, and attended a truly staggering number of parties.

Wang spoke no Japanese, but this in no way hindered him from having extensive conversations about any number of topics with Japanese literary figures. A great many of these written interactions were printed simultaneously in Kurimoto Joun's *Yūbin hōchi shinbun* (郵便報知新聞, Postal Dispatch News) and they can also be traced through Wang's own account *Japan Travelogue* (扶桑遊記), published almost immediately after he completed his journey. With very rare exception, interpreters seem to have been absent from these gatherings. All indications are that the interaction was principally textual, and thus it is not surprising that Wang frequently uses terms such as *wenshi* (文士; "literary gentleman") to describe the Japanese whom he meets. He offers high praise in the travelogue for the eminent Japanese historian and traditional scholar Shigeno Yasutsugu 重野安繹 (1827–1910), for example, praising his Sinitic prose style.[45] And he was particularly pleased to meet the Sinologue Masuda Gakuyō 増田岳陽 (1825–1899), who had written a comprehensive history of the Qing dynasty two years earlier that made reference to Wang Tao himself. Gakuyō had written his text in Literary Sinitic at a time when sources were scarce and, needless to say, no dynastic history was available. Before leaving Japan, Wang Tao purchased several hundred copies of the text with the intention of selling them in China.[46]

Wang Tao's travelogue, first published in Japan, is part of the large body of modern East Asian Sinitic texts that do not fit easily into frameworks premised upon "national literature." There is no question that Wang Tao is a major figure of modern Chinese letters and his text is unambiguously a canonical work, included in major anthologies of Chinese texts. Yet Wang's published travelogue, edited by Joun, contains well over one hundred Sinitic verses composed by Japanese he encountered in the course of his travels. In quoting Sinitic verses that he received by Japanese individuals, and in writing his own poems in response, Wang draws no distinction in the travelogue between the Sinitic poems by Japanese poets and those written by the Chinese diplomats and expatriates he also encountered during his travels. Before reaching Tokyo, for example, Wang spent a few days in western Japan, where he met with Qing émigré Wu Hantao 吳瀚濤 and Kobe consular official Liao Shuxian 廖樞仙. Both of these men presented poetry to Wang, which he records in his travelogue along with the matched-rhyme responses he subsequently composed for both men.[47] Precisely the same mode of interaction characterizes his meetings with dozens of Japanese literati in Yokohama and Tokyo. At one early gathering, some twenty Japanese present poems to him, and Wang's travelogue records the poem he writes for the occasion along with the matched-rhyme response that the poet Ono Kozan 小野湖山 (1814–1910) spontaneously composes in return.[48] Similarly, when Wang's travelogue recounts his visit to the Kōrakuen 後樂園, a garden in Tokyo designed by Ming refugee Zhu Shunsui 朱舜水 (1600–1682), it includes the "old style" poems that Wang himself, as well as Huang Zunxian and

Japanese Sinological scholar Kametani Seiken 亀谷省軒 (1838–1913), composed about the history of the site.[49]

In this way, the text directs our attention to the realm of transnational literary interaction that shared mastery of Literary Sinitic texts and textual practices made possible for modern East Asian intellectuals. While I have focused in this chapter on poetic interactions between nineteenth-century Chinese and Japanese, Sinitic poetry was of course a vibrant medium of exchange between Japanese as well. Consider Wang Tao's experience encountering a stele outside Chōmeiji Temple's gates one day when he was out strolling along the Sumida River. This site was famous for the beautiful cherry blossoms that bloomed on its banks, a spring-time sight commemorated in the poems inscribed on the stele that was erected there in 1870. Though the stele is no longer extant, having been destroyed in the Great Kantō earthquake of 1923, it originally contained Sinitic octaves composed by four poets, including Ōnuma Chinzan 大沼枕山 (1818–1891), who was arguably the most prominent poet in Tokyo at the start of the Meiji era. Upon visiting the temple grounds, Wang Tao takes the time to respond poetically to each of the four Sinitic verses inscribed on the stele, composing verses that match the rhymes of the four octaves and recording them in his travelogue.[50] Wang's response to the Sinitic verse by Chinzan that he saw before him is completely analogous to that of a Japanese contemporary, Ōtsuki Bankei, whose encounter a few years earlier with Chinzan's poem on the Sumida River bank stele had prompted him also to write an octave that duplicated Chinzan's original rhyme characters.[51] Bankei and Wang Tao would have vocalized Chinzan's octave in mutually unintelligible ways, but their shared participation in a broader transregional textuality made it possible for them to leave behind comparable traces of their encounters with this written work.

When Chinzan and the other three poets initially wrote their poems on the blossoms and when Bankei wrote his rhymed response, they took part in a practice that has consistently formed an essential part of Japanese literary expression from the inception of literacy in the seventh century through the modern period. Even as a full range of vernacular forms developed and thrived in Japan, Sinitic poetic and prose genres continued to flourish, stimulating and in turn being stimulated by Japanese-language works. In approaching Japan's vast body of Sinitic literature, it is important for us to be mindful of its local specificity: considering the nature of the Sinitic texts (of both Chinese and Japanese provenance) that were canonized in Japan as exemplary models, the forms of composition that became dominant, the methods by which Japanese producers of Sinitic texts attained their proficiency, and the various ways in which Sinitic texts were appreciated and recited. At the same time, however, we must balance such attentiveness to the particularities of Japan's Sinitic literary tradition with a recognition that the composition of Sinitic texts was an important means by which Japanese authors could insinuate themselves into a broader literary enterprise, one with a long history in Japan but that also extended beyond its borders.

NOTES

1. *Gayū* 雅友 [Friends in elegance] 2 (June 1951), 14.

2. Kin Bunkyō 金文京, *Kanbun to higashi Ajia: Kundoku no bunkaken* 漢文と東アジア：訓読の文化圏 [Literary Sinitic and East Asia: The cultural sphere of vernacular reading] (Tokyo: Iwanami shoten, 2010), chap. 2.

3. John Whitman, "The Ubiquity of the Gloss," *Scripta* 3 (2011), 95–121, quotation at 95. See also John Whitman et al., "Toward an International Vocabulary for Research on Vernacular Readings of Chinese Texts (漢文訓讀 Hanwen Xundu)," *Scripta* 2 (2010): 61–83.

4. For a useful outline of distinctions between *kanbun kundoku* and prototypical translation, see Judy Wakabayashi, "The Reconceptionization of Translation from Chinese in 18th-Century Japan," in *Translation and Cultural Change: Studies in History, Norms, and Image Projection,* ed. Eva Hung (Philadelphia: John Benjamins, 2005), 119–146. Noting that whereas translation can take place between two spoken languages, *kundoku* requires a written source, Saitō Mareshi 齋藤希史 has argued that *kundoku* should be understood in terms of vocalization rather than translation; see his *Kanji sekai no chihei: Watakushitachi ni totte moji to wa nanika* 漢字世界の地平：私たちにとって文字とは何か [The horizon of the Sinographic world: What does writing mean for us?] (Tokyo: Shinchōsha, 2014), chap. 3. While *kundoku* can be profitably understood either way, I think the fundamentally interpretive aspects of the practice as well as its essentially interlingual nature are clearest when we conceive of it as a type of translation.

5. Kawaguchi Hisao 川口久雄, ed., *Sugawara no Michizane* 菅原道真, *Kanke bunsō, Kanke kōshū* 菅家文草・菅家後集 [Literary drafts of the Sugawara house; Later collection of the Sugawara house], vol. 72 of *Nihon koten bungaku taikei* 日本古典文學大系 [Collection of classical Japanese literature] (Tokyo: Iwanami shoten, 1966), 477. The more target-oriented nature of *kundoku* styles in Michizane's time is in part explained by the fact that recitation of Sinitic verse in Chinese pronunciation was still a common practice.

6. Kojima Noriyuki 小島憲之 and Yamamoto Tokurō 山本登朗, eds., *Sugawara no Michizane* 菅原道真 [Sugawara no Michizane], vol. 1 of *Nihon kanshijin senshū* 日本漢詩人選集 [Anthology of Japanese Sinitic poets] (Tokyo: Kenbun shuppan, 1998), 141.

7. Another authoritative edition offers "*ie o hanarete san shi gatsu/rakurui hyakusenkō*"; see Sugano Hiroyuki 菅野禮行 and Tokuda Takeshi 德田武, eds., *Nihon kanshishū* 日本漢詩集 [Collection of Japanese Sinitic verse], vol. 86 of *Shinpen Nihon koten bungaku zenshū* 新編日本古典文学全集 [New complete collection of classical Japanese literature] (Tokyo: Shōgakukan, 2002), 153. Still another scholar suggests "*ie o hanarete san shi gatsu/namida o otosu hyakusenkō*"; see Igarashi Chikara 五十嵐力, *Heianchō bungakushi* 平安朝文学史 [A history of Heian-era literature], vols. 3–4 of *Nihon bungaku zenshi* 日本文学全史 [A complete history of Japanese literature] (Tokyo: Tōkyōdō, 1939), 3: 126.

8. Observing that "The Tokugawa was without doubt the high point of Chinese poetry in Japan," the eminent Sinologist Yoshikawa Kōjirō 吉川幸次郎 identifies the late Tokugawa poet San'yō as the period's finest; see his "Chinese Poetry in Japan: Influence and Reaction," *Journal of World History* 2.4 (1955): 883–894, quotation at 892. Iritani Sensuke 入谷仙介, while sharing Yoshikawa's high regard for San'yō, states that the later

figure Kainan achieved the "ultimate" of Japanese Sinitic poetic expression; see his *Kindai bungaku toshiteno Meiji kanshi* 近代文学としての明治漢詩 [Meiji Sinitic poetry as modern literature] (Tokyo: Kenbun shuppan, 1989), 21.

9. Okabe Keigorō 岡部啓五郎, ed., *Meiji kōinshū* 明治好音集 [A euphonious Meiji collection] (Tokyo: Heibonsha, 2009 [1875]), 15a.

10. The capture of the Taiwanese aboriginal girl and her experiences in Japan were the subject of much interest in the Meiji press; see Matthew Fraleigh, "Transplanting the Flower of Civilization: The 'Peony Girl' and Japan's 1874 Expedition to Taiwan," *International Journal of Asian Studies* 9.2 (2012): 177–209. For a discussion of Japanese reportage on the Taiwan Expedition, see Matthew Fraleigh, "Japan's First War Reporter: Kishida Ginkō and the Taiwan Expedition," *Japanese Studies* 30.1 (2010): 43–66.

11. *Shinbun zasshi* 新聞雑誌 277 (July 18, 1874), 7b. The full run of *Shinbun zasshi* is reprinted as vols. 49–66 of *Tōkyō Akebono shinbun* 東京曙新聞 (Tokyo: Kashiwa shobō, 2004–2009). Ou Hunan's poem appears on 64:150. The coverage of the girl's arrival in Japan appears in *Shinbun zasshi* 267 (28 June 1874), 7a–b; rpt. vol. 63, 415–416.

12. Okabe, 19b–20b. Bankei's series of eight quatrains appears in *Chōya shinbun*, September 29, 1874. Four of these had originally appeared in the *Yūbin hōchi shinbun*, August 20, 1874.

13. Okabe, 35a–b. Ou Hunan's response appeared in *Shinbun zasshi* 302 (September 8, 1874), 6a–b; rpt. vol. 65, 55–56.

14. See Leonard H. D. Gordon, *Confrontation Over Taiwan: Nineteenth-Century China and the Powers* (Lanham, MD: Rowman and Littlefield, 2007), 108–112.

15. Certainly the Japanese press and the poets who responded to his verse seem to have taken Ou Hunan at his word, but we cannot rule out the possibility that a Japanese was the actual author of these poems attributed to "Ou Hunan."

16. *Chōya shinbun* November 4, 1874. I have incorporated phrases from Arthur Waley's translation of the ode (Mao no. 155); see Arthur Waley, *The Book of Songs* (New York: Grove, 1987 [1937]), 235.

17. *Meiji kōinshū* includes, for example, Sinitic poems composed by three Korean individuals to Japanese diplomat Moriyama Shigeru 森山茂 (1842–1919), as well as several poems addressed by Qing officials to another diplomat, Tanabe Taichi 田辺太一 (1831–1915), who took part in negotiations with the Qing after the Taiwan Expedition; see Okabe, 16a–17a, 28b–29a.

18. Richard John Lynn discusses the use of the term *siwen* in contemporary exchanges in "'This Culture of Ours' and Huang Zunxian's Literary Experiences in Japan (1877–82)," *Chinese Literature: Essays, Articles, Reviews (CLEAR)* 19 (1997): 113–138, and "Huang Zunxian and His Association with Meiji Era Japanese Literati (Bunjin): The Formation of the Early Meiji Canon of Kanshi," *Japan Review* 15 (2003): 101–125. On the complex ways in which the *dōbun* rhetoric was invoked through the mid-twentieth century, see Satō Kazuki 佐藤一樹, "'Same Language Same Race': The Dilemma of *Kanbun* in Modern Japan," in Frank Dikötter, ed., *The Construction of Racial Identities in China and Japan: Historical and Contemporary Perspectives* (Honolulu: University of Hawai'i Press, 1997), 118–135.

19. See *Chōya shinbun*, December 9–10, 1875. In a brief prose preface, Luo explains that he had read the poetic exchanges between Bankei and Keiu in the November 27, 1875 *Chōya shinbun*. Known particularly for his *zhihua* (finger-painting), Luo Xuegu resided in Japan for six or seven years; see Tsuruta Takeyoshi 鶴田武良, "Raihaku gajin kenkyū: Ra

Sekkoku to Ko Tetsubai" 来舶画人研究—羅雪谷と胡鉄梅 [Research on immigrant painters: Luo Xuegu and Hu Tiemei], *Bijutsu kenkyū* 美術研究 [Research in the arts] 324 (1983): 61–67.

20. While only one side of the exchange is preserved, Japan's oldest extant collection of Sinitic verse, the *Kaifūsō* 懷風藻, contains poems composed by Japanese participants at banquets held to fête Sillan emissaries around 723; see H. Mack Horton, "Literary Diplomacy in Early Nara: Prince Nagaya and the Verses for Envoys from Silla in *Kaifūsō*," in *China and Beyond in the Mediaeval Period: Cultural Crossings and Inter-Regional Connections,* ed. Dorothy C. Wong and Gustav Heldt, (Amherst, NY: Cambria, 2014), 261–277.

21. The diary of Nagakubo Sekisui 長久保赤水 (1717–1801), *Nagasaki kōeki nikki* 長崎行役日記 [Diary of official travel to Nagasaki], is one example; his poetry exchanges with Qing residents of Nagasaki are gathered in *Shinsa shōwashū* 清槎唱和集 [Collection of poetic exchanges with Qing visitors]. Several other such exchanges are discussed in Ueno Hideto 上野日出刀, *Nagasaki ni asonda kanshijin* 長崎に遊んだ漢詩人 [Sinitic poets who traveled to Nagasaki] (Fukuoka: Chūgoku Shoten, 1989).

22. During his 1862 visit to Hong Kong, Ichikawa Seiryū was able to obtain the calligraphy not only of several Chinese residents but of an unexpected member of the Sinosphere, James Legge, who echoed phrasing in *Analects* XII:5 when he presented Seiryū with the inscription "The world under Heaven is a single family; all men in the four seas are brothers" 天下爲一家四海皆兄弟. See Ichikawa Wataru 市川渡 (Seiryū 清流), "Biyō ōkō manroku" 尾蠅歐行漫録 [A leisurely record of a journey to Europe like a fly on a horse's tail], rpt. in Nihon Shiseki Kyōkai 日本史籍協会, ed., *Kengai shisetsu nikki sanshū* 遣外使節日記纂輯 [Compilation of overseas embassies' diaries] (Tokyo: Tokyo University Press, 1971), II: 249–562; this passage occurs on pp. 280–281. For a recent examination of Japanese travelers' brushtalks with residents of Shanghai in 1862, see Joshua Fogel's *Maiden Voyage: The Senzaimaru and the Creation of Modern Sino-Japanese Relations* (Berkeley: University of California Press, 2014), esp. chaps. 3–6.

23. For further discussion of the specificity of Meiji-era Literary Sinitic exchanges between Japanese and Qing intellectuals, see Atsuko Sakaki, "Waves From Opposing Shores: Exchanges in a Classical Language in the Age of Nationalism," in *Sino-Japanese Transculturation: From the Late Nineteenth Century to the End of the Pacific War,* ed. Richard King, Cody Poulton, and Katsuhiko Endō (Lanham, MD: Lexington Books, 2012), 33–43, and Gōyama Rintarō 合山林太郎, *Bakumatsu, Meijiki no Kanbungaku no kenkyū* 幕末.明治期の漢文学の研究 [Research in Sinitic literature of the late Tokugawa and Meiji period] (Osaka: Izumi shoin, 2014). 214–235.

24. To be sure, even prior to the advent of a more efficient and reliable postal system, there were some exceptional cases in which earlier Japanese Sinitic poets engaged with Qing individuals whom they never met. Letters transmitted by intermediaries permitted Rai San'yō and his student Ema Saikō 江馬細香 (1787–1861) to exchange poetry with the literarily inclined Qing merchant Jiang Yunge 江芸閣, a frequent visitor to Nagasaki; see Robert James Tuck, "The Poetry of Dialogue: Kanshi, Haiku and Media in Meiji Japan, 1870–1900" (PhD diss., Columbia University, 2012), 47–55.

25. On Ye Songshi's activities in Japan see Chen Jie 陳捷, *Meiji zenki Nitchū gakujutsu kōryū no kenkyū: Shinkoku Chūnichi Kōshikan no bunka katsudō* 明治前期日中学術交流の研究: 清国駐日公使館の文化活動 [Research on Sino-Japanese academic exchange in the

early Meiji period: The cultural activities of the Qing Embassy in Japan] (Tokyo: Kyūko shoin, 2003), 14–30.

26. See *Shinbunshi besshū* 5 (1876).

27. *Chōya shinbun*, May 30, 1875. In the preface to a brushtalk with Ye Songshi that Bankei published in the May 28 *Chōya*, he describes Ye Songshi, whom he first met a year earlier, as a "stylish and elegant scholar good at poetry and prose."

28. *Chōya shinbun*, September 3, 1876.

29. Ye Songshi's quatrain appears in the *Chōya shinbun*, May 20, 1875. It is followed by his "authorial annotation" reading: "Japan has changed its regulations to use the Western calendar. It is already the fifth day of the second month. But there are people in the countryside who still use the 'seasons of Xia'" (自註日本制改洋曆已二月初五日矣然鄉民仍有行夏之時者). Ye Songshi alludes here to *Analects* XV.11.

30. Ye Songshi's poems appear in Mori Shuntō 森春濤, *Tōkyō saijin zekku* 東京才人絕句 [Quatrains by Tokyo's men of talent] (Tokyo: Nukada Shōzaburō, 1875), II: 46a–47b.

31. A Nanjing publisher printed *Fusang lichang ji* in 1891, but the main text seems to have been completed around the autumn of 1876, just after Ye returned to China. Rpt. in Wang Baoping 王寶平, ed., *Zhong Ri shiwen jiaoliu ji* 中日詩文交流集 [Collection of Sino-Japanese exchanges in poetry and prose] (Shanghai: Shanghai guji chubanshe, 2004), 125–147.

32. Ye Songshi's *Fusang Li chang ji* includes a note recounting how a Japanese man visited him in Shanghai not long after his return, presenting several poems addressed to him that had appeared in the *Chōya*; see Wang Baoping, 143–144. Among these is a series of five by Mizukoshi Kōnan 水越耕南 (1849–1933), whom Ye Songshi had never met; Kōnan's poems originally appeared in *Chōya shinbun*, September 20, 1876.

33. The December 9, 1876 *Chōya shinbun* contains two sets of five quatrains submitted by readers in response to Ye Songshi's Kyoto poems; I refer to the second of these, by a poet calling himself Heiha shōshi 萍波小史. His third quatrain contains the names of Okamoto Kōseki 岡本黄石 (1811–1898), Kusakabe Suiu 日下部翠雨 (Meikaku 鳴鶴, 1838–1922), and Gōyama Hōyō 神山鳳陽 (1824–1889). In his preface, Heiha shōshi humbly states that after the work of such predecessors, his contribution can only be "a dog's tail attached to a sable coat."

34. The poet alludes to *Analects* XII.24, which D. C. Lau translates: "A gentlemen makes friends through being cultivated" (君子以文會友); see *The Analects* (Harmondsworth, UK: Penguin, 1979), 117.

35. When Japanese print media published these exchanges, they tended to add *kunten* "gloss marks" (to the poems of both Ye Songshi and the Japanese poets), thereby making them accessible to those less familiar with reading Literary Sinitic. Poems and brushtalks exchanged directly between participants did not have these markings of course.

36. These rhyme categories were codified in the early Tang and reflect medieval pronunciation. Japanese poets availed themselves of many of the same rhyme dictionaries and reference tools that their counterparts elsewhere in the Sinosphere used. Yet even without recourse to such materials and with no knowledge of spoken Chinese, a Japanese can still often perceive a poem's rhyme and rhythm simply by pronouncing its constituent characters using their Sinoxenic readings (*on'yomi*), the same unarranged all-Sinitic approach used by one scholar to construe Michizane's first couplet: *ri ka san shi gatsu/raku rui hyaku sen kō* 離家三四月 落淚百千行.

37. The mastery of contemporary Middle Chinese pronunciation was an important part of the curriculum at the State Academy during Japan's early Heian period, and Sinitic poems were often recited using such phonetic approaches in formal contexts. From the tenth century onward, however, *kundoku* approaches to recitation became increasingly dominant. For a detailed discussion of Sinitic literary practice in Japan during this period of transition, see Brian Robert Steininger, "Poetic Ministers: Literacy and Bureaucracy in the Tenth-Century State Academy" (PhD diss., Yale University, 2010), especially chaps. 1 and 2.

38. *Chōya shinbun*, December 22, 1876. The phrase translated "unusual charm" is *okashiki fūchi*; while *fūchi* (風致) is an unambiguously positive term meaning "elegance" or "charm," the adjective *okashi* has a broader range—it can mean "delightful," "interesting," or "charming," but can also mean "funny" (either in the sense of "weird" or in the sense of "humorous"). Given the pairing with *fūchi*, however, I think that these last senses are unlikely.

39. Ryūhoku alludes here to *Mencius* VIIA.36; see D. C. Lau, *Mencius* (Harmondsworth, UK: Penguin, 1970), 190.

40. "Ryūkō no ki" 流行ノ奇, *Chōya shinbun*, August 7, 1878.

41. *Chōya shinbun*, February 5, 1879.

42. Zhang Sigui's poem appears in *Chōya shinbun*, August 8, 1878; *Shun Pao* printed a revised version on April 9, 1879.

43. Nineteen quatrains from Zhang Sigui's *Shidong shilu* 使東詩録 [A poetic record of a mission to the East] appear in *Shun Pao* 2131 (April 7, 1879); these were reprinted in three installments in the *Chōya shinbun* on May 18, 24, and 28, 1879. An annotation in the first installments indicates that the Japanese newspaper had obtained the poems from their appearance in *Xunhuan ribao* (which often shared content with *Shun Pao*).

44. Wang Tao's travelogue is *Fusang youji/Fūsō yūki* 扶桑遊記 [Japan travelogue], ed. Kurimoto Joun 栗本鋤雲 (Tokyo: Hōchisha shuppan, 1880), 3 vols. Secondary scholarship on his travels in Japan includes Tang Quan 唐権, *Umi o koeta tsuyagoto: Nitchū bunka kōryū hishi* 海を越えた艶ごと：日中文化交流秘史 [Amorous affairs that crossed the sea: A secret history of Sino-Japanese cultural exchange] (Tokyo: Shin'yōsha, 2005), 285–304; Paul Cohen, *Between Tradition and Modernity: Wang T'ao and Reform in Late Ch'ing China* (Cambridge: Harvard University Press, 1974), 99–109; and Ihara *Takushū* 伊原澤周, *Nihon to Chūgoku ni okeru Seiyō bunka sesshuron* 日本と中國における西洋文化攝取論 [A study of the reception of Western culture in Japan and China] (Tokyo: Kyūko shoin, 1999), 120–143.

45. See the entry for io3.28 (May 18, which Wang incorrectly dates May 17) in Wang Tao, I: 17a.

46. Masuda Gakuyō's history is titled *Shinshi ran'yō/Qingshi lanyao* (清史攬要) (Tokyo, 1877); see Chen Jie, "Research on Sino-Japanese Academic Exchange," 174–182.

47. For the exchange with Wu Hantao, see the entry for io3.22 (May 12, 1879); Wang Tao, I: 12a–13a. The exchange with Liao Shuxian occurs over the course of the following two days; see Wang Tao, I: 13a–14b.

48. See the entry for io3.25 (May 15, 1879); Wang Tao, I: 15a–b.

49. See the entry for 04.05 (May 25, 1879); Wang Tao, I: 25a–28b.

50. See the entry for 04.03 (May 23, 1879); Wang Tao, I: 21a–22a.

51. Ōtsuki Bankei 大槻磐渓, *Aikodō mankō* 愛古堂漫稿 [Casual drafts from the Hall of Fondness for Antiquity] ([Tokyo]: [s.n.], 1874), 7a.

Works Cited

Chen Jie 陳捷. *Meiji zenki Nitchū gakujutsu kōryū no kenkyū: Shinkoku Chūnichi Kōshikan no bunka katsudō* 明治前期日中学術交流の研究: 清国駐日公使館の文化活動 [Research on Sino-Japanese academic exchange in the early Meiji period: The cultural activities of the Qing Embassy in Japan]. Tokyo: Kyūko shoin, 2003.

Cohen, Paul. *Between Tradition and Modernity: Wang T'ao and Reform in Late Ch'ing China.* Cambridge: Harvard University Press, 1974.

Fogel, Joshua. *Maiden Voyage: The Senzaimaru and the Creation of Modern Sino-Japanese Relations.* Berkeley: University of California Press, 2014.

Fraleigh, Matthew. "Japan's First War Reporter: Kishida Ginkō and the Taiwan Expedition." *Japanese Studies* 30.1 (2010): 43–66.

Fraleigh, Matthew. "Transplanting the Flower of Civilization: the 'Peony Girl' and Japan's 1874 Expedition to Taiwan." *International Journal of Asian Studies* 9.2 (2012): 177–209.

Gordon, Leonard H. D. *Confrontation over Taiwan: Nineteenth-Century China and the Powers.* Lanham, MD: Rowman and Littlefield, 2007.

Gōyama Rintarō 合山林太郎. *Bakumatsu, Meijiki no Kanbungaku no kenkyū* 幕末明治期の漢文学の研究 [Research in Sinitic literature of the late Tokugawa and Meiji period]. Osaka: Izumi shoin, 2014.

Horton, H. Mack. "Literary Diplomacy in Early Nara: Prince Nagaya and the Verses for Envoys from Silla in *Kaifūsō.*" In *China and Beyond in the Mediaeval Period: Cultural Crossings and Inter-Regional Connections.* Ed. Dorothy C. Wong and Gustav Heldt. Amherst, NY: Cambria, 2014. 261–277.

Ichikawa Wataru 市川渡 (Seiryū 清流). "Biyō ōkō manroku" 尾蠅歐行漫録 [A leisurely record of a journey to Europe like a fly on a horse's tail]. Rpt. in *Kengai shisetsu nikki sanshū* 遣外使節日記纂輯 [Compilation of overseas embassies' diaries]. Ed. Nihon Shiseki Kyōkai 日本史籍協会. Tokyo: Tokyo University Press, 1971. II: 249–562. [Original work ca. 1863.]

Igarashi Chikara 五十嵐力. *Heianchō bungakushi* 平安朝文学史 [A history of Heian-era literature]. Vols. 3–4 of *Nihon bungaku zenshi* 日本文学全史 [A complete history of Japanese literature]. Tokyo: Tōkyōdō, 1939.

Ihara Takushū 伊原澤周. *Nihon to Chūgoku ni okeru Seiyō bunka sesshuron* 日本と中國における西洋文化攝取論 [A study of the reception of Western culture in Japan and China]. Tokyo: Kyūko shoin, 1999.

Iritani Sensuke 入谷仙介. *Kindai bungaku toshiteno Meiji kanshi* 近代文学としての明治漢詩 [Meiji Sinitic poetry as modern literature]. Tokyo: Kenbun Shuppan, 1989.

Kawaguchi Hisao 川口久雄, ed. Sugawara no Michizane 菅原道真. *Kanke bunsō, Kanke kōshū* 菅家文草・菅家後集 [Literary drafts of the Sugawara house; Later collection of the Sugawara house]. Vol. 72 of *Nihon koten bungaku taikei* 日本古典文學大系 [Collection of classical Japanese literature]. Tokyo: Iwanami shoten, 1966.

Kin Bunkyō 金文京. *Kanbun to higashi Ajia: Kundoku no bunkaken* 漢文と東アジア: 訓読の文化圏 [Literary Sinitic and East Asia: The cultural sphere of vernacular reading]. Tokyo: Iwanami shoten, 2010.

Kojima Noriyuki 小島憲之 and Yamamoto Tokurō 山本登朗. *Sugawara no Michizane* 菅原道真 [Sugawara no Michizane]. Vol. 1 of *Nihon kanshijin senshū* 日本漢詩人選集 [Anthology of Japanese Sinitic poets]. Tokyo: Kenbun shuppan, 1998.

Lau, D. C. *Mencius.* Harmondsworth, UK: Penguin, 1970.

Lau, D. C. *The Analects.* Harmondsworth, UK: Penguin, 1979.

Lynn, Richard John. "Huang Zunxian and His Association with Meiji Era Japanese Literati (*Bunjin*): The Formation of the Early Meiji Canon of Kanshi." *Japan Review* 15 (2003): 101–125.

Lynn, Richard John. "'This Culture of Ours' and Huang Zunxian's Literary Experiences in Japan (1877–82)." *Chinese Literature: Essays, Articles, Reviews (CLEAR)* 19 (1997): 113–138.

Mori Shuntō 森春濤. *Tōkyō Saijin zekku* 東京才人絶句 [Quatrains by Tokyo's men of talent]. Tokyo: Nukada Shōzaburō, 1875.

Okabe Keigorō 岡部啓五郎, ed. *Meiji kōinshū* 明治好音集 [A euphonious Meiji collection]. Tokyo: Ōta Kin'emon, 1875. Rpt. Tokyo: Heibonsha, 2009.

Ōtsuki Bankei 大槻磐渓. *Aikodō mankō* 愛古堂漫稿 [Casual drafts from the Hall of Fondness for Antiquity]. [Tokyo]: [s.n.], 1874.

Saitō Mareshi 齋藤希史. *Kanji sekai no chihei: Watakushitachi ni totte moji to wa nanika* 漢字世界の地平: 私たちにとって文字とは何か [The horizon of the Sinographic world: What does writing mean for us?]. Tokyo: Shinchōsha, 2014.

Sakaki, Atsuko. "Waves from Opposing Shores: Exchanges in a Classical Language in the Age of Nationalism." In *Sino-Japanese Transculturation: From the Late Nineteenth Century to the End of the Pacific War.* Ed. Richard King, Cody Poulton, and Katsuhiko Endō. Lanham, MD: Lexington Books, 2012. 33–43.

Satō Kazuki 佐藤一樹. "'Same Language Same Race': The Dilemma of *Kanbun* in Modern Japan." In *The Construction of Racial Identities in China and Japan: Historical and Contemporary Perspectives.* Ed. Frank Dikötter. Honolulu: University of Hawai'i Press, 1997. 118–135.

Steininger, Brian Robert. "Poetic Ministers: Literacy and Bureaucracy in the Tenth-Century State Academy." PhD diss. Yale University, 2010.

Sugano Hiroyuki 菅野禮行 and Tokuda Takeshi 徳田武, eds. *Nihon kanshishū* 日本漢詩集 [Collection of Japanese Sinitic verse]. Vol. 86 of *Shinpen Nihon koten bungaku zenshū* 新編日本古典文学全集 [New complete collection of classical Japanese literature]. Tokyo: Shōgakukan, 2002.

Tang Quan 唐権. *Umi o koeta tsuyagoto: Nitchū bunka kōryū hishi* 海を越えた艶ごと: 日中文化交流秘史 [Amorous affairs that crossed the sea: A secret history of Sino-Japanese cultural exchange]. Tokyo: Shin'yōsha, 2005.

Tsuruta Takeyoshi 鶴田武良. "Raihaku gajin kenkyū: Ra Sekkoku to Ko Tetsubai" 来舶画人研究—羅雪谷と胡鉄梅 [Research on immigrant painters: Luo Xuegu and Hu Tiemei]. *Bijutsu kenkyū* 美術研究 [Research in the arts] 324 (1983): 61–67.

Tuck, Robert James. "The Poetry of Dialogue: Kanshi, Haiku and Media in Meiji Japan, 1870–1900." PhD diss. Columbia University, 2012.

Ueno Hideto 上野日出刀. *Nagasaki ni asonda kanshijin* 長崎に遊んだ漢詩人 [Sinitic poets who traveled to Nagasaki]. Fukuoka: Chūgoku Shoten, 1989.

Wakabayashi, Judy. "The Reconceptionization of Translation from Chinese in 18th-Century Japan." In *Translation and Cultural Change: Studies in History, Norms, and Image Projection.* Ed. Eva Hung. Philadelphia: John Benjamins, 2005. 119–146.

Waley, Arthur. *The Book of Songs.* New York: Grove, 1987.

Wang Baoping 王寶平, ed. *Zhong Ri shiwen jiaoliu ji* 中日詩文交流集 [Collection of Sino-Japanese exchanges in poetry and prose]. Shanghai: Shanghai guji chubanshe, 2004.

Wang Tao 王韜. *Fusang youji/Fūsō yūki* 扶桑遊記 [Japan travelogue]. Ed. Kurimoto Joun 栗本鋤雲. Tokyo: Hōchisha shuppan, 1880. 3 vols.

Whitman, John. "The Ubiquity of the Gloss." *Scripta* 3 (2011): 95–121.

Whitman, John, Miyoung Oh, Jinho Park, Valerio Luigi Alberizzi, Masayuki Tsukimoto, Teiji Kosukegawa, and Tomokazu Takada. "Toward an International Vocabulary for Research on Vernacular Readings of Chinese Texts (漢文訓讀 Hanwen Xundu)." *Scripta* 2 (2010): 61–83.

Wu Kaisheng 吳闓生. *Wan Qing sishijia shichao* 晚清四十家詩鈔 [Anthology of 40 poets from the late Qing]. Taibei: Taiwan Zhonghua shu ju, 1970 [1924].

Yoshikawa Kōjirō 吉川幸次郎. "Chinese Poetry in Japan: Influence and Reaction." *Journal of World History* 2.4 (1955): 883–894.

CHAPTER 2.5

....

SENSE OF PLACE AND URBAN IMAGES

Reading Hong Kong in Hong Kong Poetry

....

KWOK-KOU LEONARD CHAN

A poem on Hong Kong, written in the 1920s, opens as follows:

> LAMP-BESTARR'D, and with the star-shine gleaming
> From her midnight canopy or dreaming
>   Mirror'd in her fragrant, fair lagoon:
> All her streets ablaze with sheen and shimmer:
> All her fire-fly shipping-lights a-glimmer,
>   Flitting, flashing, curving past Kowloon:[1]

Titled "Hong Kong," this poem by Sir Cecil Clementi (1875–1947), governor of Hong Kong from 1925 to 1930, describes the view of a hilly city at night, lit up and enlivened by street lamps, household lights, and the stars. The poem exudes a warm and tranquil atmosphere, with its repetition of images of light, such as "household glow," which "cheers and blesses/ Weary men and guides them home to rest," and the "Milky Way" that showers the earth with "Danaë's golden dower." Underscored by a sense of romanticism, the poem portrays the colony in an idyllic light.

This poem was composed in November 1925, shortly after Clementi assumed his duties as governor. Proficient in both Mandarin and Cantonese, Clementi had profound knowledge of traditional Chinese culture, and apparently a strong personal affection for the place under his governance.[2] Despite the peaceful ambience of the poem, Hong Kong was in great turmoil at that time. Clementi arrived at the height of an interminable, crippling strike, which constituted a severe blow to the colony's economy and people's livelihood. The effect of the strike gradually waned in late 1926, but Hong Kong still faced many challenges, including a perennial water shortage.[3] If we attempt to connect the poem with the daily reality at that time, we can say that canopied under the glittering sky was a young immigrant community, struggling with housing congestion, high rent, poor sanitation, a highly stratified social structure, and other problems.[4] People's daily living stands in stark contrast to the glittering lights in the poem, which are symbols of serenity and prosperity.

Since its early years, Hong Kong has been known for its spectacular night view, created by a unique geographical landscape and urban structure. In 1887, Governor Sir William des Voeux (1834–1909) applauded the city's illuminations, saying they made a scene "which could hardly be equalled outside of fairyland."[5] It is easy to imagine Clementi being fascinated by the view. At the same time, the poem, described by Minford as "Kiplingesque," has a clear subtext of imperialism:[6]

> Grandly here the Master Builder's power
> Crowns the work of England in Cathay.

The colonial undertone brings to mind Said's interpretation of Orientalism: the West as male gender dominance, or patriarchy, and the Oriental as its Other, a silent, attractive female.[7] A capable and determined colonial administrator, Clementi was "a no-nonsense, fire-eating imperialist of the old school,"[8] and Spurr's comment on his governorship, namely that "the thoughtful, learned Governor left Hong Kong a better place to live with," is an understated summary of the work he did there.[9] But Clementi's Hong Kong rhapsody is more an imaginary construction than a reflection of the real urban condition. It is a romanticized picture of Hong Kong, with little relevance to local people's lives at that time.

EARLY HONG KONG IN POETRY: POETS IN THE THIRTIES

Clementi's poem adopts a panoramic bird's-eye perspective, a narrative point of view that highlights the distance between the narrator and the narrative subject.[10] It took more time for poetic voices that resonated more strongly with local people's visions to emerge. In the late 1920s and 1930s, Hong Kong's cultural fabric underwent noticeable changes. The influence of the New Culture Movement in mainland China became more and more manifest, and the local literary scene was much enriched by activities of the "South-bound" writers—mainland writers who came to Hong Kong in fear of political instability at home. The many newly launched—albeit mostly short-lived—literary magazines provided more chances of publication. The art of poetry thrived, and the city of Hong Kong became a favorite object of poetic contemplation.

Many poets active in the thirties wrote about Hong Kong, for example, Ou Waiou 鷗外鷗 (1911–1995), Liu Muxia 柳木下 (1914–1993), Liu Huozi 劉火子 (1911–1990), and Li Yuzhong 李育中 (1911–2013). Ou Waiou's *Poems of Ou Waiou* (鷗外鷗之詩,

1985) includes a group of works subtitled "Hong Kong Album" (香港照像冊). The works depict the city from multiple perspectives. "The Big Horse Race" (大賽馬; 1939) satirizes Hong Kong people's obsession with money and their spiritual emptiness—an observation that still holds currency today; and "Walls of the Naval Port Singapore" (軍港星加坡的牆; 1943) is a somber account of the city's colonial background and its precarious political situation in the face of Japanese attack.[11] Liu Muxia presents Hong Kong in a different light. "Skyscraper" (大廈; 1938) offers an anthropomorphic description of a tall modern building. The narrator, a country boy, is astounded by the scale of the building, and he imagines the innumerable windows to be eyes and orifices through which "the skyscraper sees and breathes."[12] Near the end of the poem, he poses a question to the "windows":

> 窗子, 你望著什麼呢?
> (是我的家鄉嗎)
> 這是牠的回答:
> ——紐約和倫敦...

> Windows, what might you be looking at?
> (Is it my home town?)
> This is their answer:
> —New York and London . . .

Hong Kong's cityscape saw a dramatic change in the 1930s, with the completion in 1935 of the old Hong Kong Bank Building, the first high-rise in Hong Kong. This was a precursor of the many skyscrapers and ultra-skyscrapers that would later become symbolic of the city.[13] Liu's poem reflects the city's growing affluence and Westernized spirit, in a simple style and language befitting a country boy. With a tinge of sentimentalism, the imaginary dialogue at the end of the work hints at the fact that the city's development into a capitalist metropolis is a one-way journey and there will be no return to the past.

The underside of a society undergoing rapid industrialization and urbanization is a recurrent theme of poetic works written in the thirties. Liu Huozi explores social inequality in his "In the City, at Noon" (都市的午景; 1934). Framed by temporal imagery and the antithetical notions of heaven and hell, this carefully crafted work presents the contrastive lifestyles of the rich and the poor with a surrealistic touch. Citroën cars, cafés, tiffin, and jazz are used to describe how affluent white-collar workers enjoy their lunch break; they are set in contrast with the humble way poor machine workers take their meager, unpalatable meals. Li Yuzhong's "North Point, the City of Victoria" (維多利亞市北角; 1934) has a strong ecological emphasis. It describes the damage to land and environment wrought by industrial civilization, using motifs such as motor noise and coal smoke.

Whereas poets of the thirties started to contemplate Hong Kong with a critical eye, Hong Kong had been considered a pied-à-terre, a place of only temporary sojourn, by many of its inhabitants in the early years. For example, among the four early poets introduced, Liu Muxia was born in Guangdong and came to Hong Kong in his twenties; the other three, although born and raised in Hong Kong, all spent a great portion of their adult life in China to pursue their careers and other goals. It was in later years that, following the city's growth, a stronger sense of rootedness emerged in the community, and people's growing attachment to the city was transposed into a distinct "sense of place" in local poetry. In his discussion of space and place, Tuan Yi-Fu describes place as what space becomes when "we get to know it better and endow it with value."[14] If people make places out of space, they are also defined by the places they create or, as Edward Relph succinctly puts it, "people are their place and a place is its people."[15] Focusing on the concept of "topophilia," a neologism used to describe humankind's emotional ties with their material environment,[16] the remainder of this chapter analyzes how Hong Kong poets construct an identity for themselves and their place by finding expression for their urban experience. The core of my discussion focuses on North Point and Nathan Road—two of the busiest districts in Hong Kong—and their position within the poetic imagination. Emphasis will be put on the myriad images used by the poets to present the multilayered landscape and cacophony of the streets and the joy and pathos of living in a complex urban city. Paying particular attention to poetry's sociohistorical function as a construction site of cultural memory, the discussion looks into the feeling of topophilia toward specific places, as well as the sociocultural critique of the poems, which gives rise to an antithetical feeling of topophobia.

URBAN IMAGES 1: NORTH POINT, AS A SITE OF MEMORY

North Point is a commercial and residential district on the northern tip of Hong Kong Island with a long history of urban development. In the late 1940s, a large number of mainland Chinese came to Hong Kong, including many from Shanghai and the nearby provinces of Ningbo and Nanjing. These immigrants, who shared similar languages and cultural habits, often congregated in North Point. By the 1950s, the place had become a haven for the Shanghainese, creating a cultural aura so unique that it earned the sobriquet of "Little Shanghai." In more recent decades, with old Shanghainese families moving away and more Fujianese immigrants coming in, the place gradually came to be known as "Little Fujian." The Fujianese immigrant group still has a strong presence, but with new urban developments the district has become home to a people of diverse provincial and ethnic origins. In short, it is a reflection of Hong Kong as a place profoundly characterized by myriad cultures.[17]

The hub of the district is King's Road, a long, bustling road lined with shops, restaurants, commercial centers, and residential buildings on both sides. One of Hong Kong's oldest urban symbols, the tram, runs on this road. This old means of transport is a recurring motif in local literary works. Ma Lang 馬朗 (his original name is Ma Boliang 馬博良, b. 1933), a poet who came to Hong Kong from Shanghai in the early 1950s, wrote "A Night in North Point" (北角之夜; 1957). This lyrical poem opens with a man seeing the last night tram passing through. The sight takes him back to a world he was familiar with, a flamboyant world of wine, dancing girls, and songs. It is worth mentioning here that the tram is a symbol of urbanity not only in Hong Kong but also in Shanghai; it was a major means of transportation in both cities. This urban symbol thus links the two cities together, unfolding a shifting, fluid world where different times and places are woven together. The poem foregrounds a sensation of drunkenness, with descriptions such as "Hence [I] fall into a kind of drunkenness of the amethyst" (於是陷入一種紫水晶裡的沉醉) and "creeks of mint wine" (薄荷酒的溪流).[18] The surreal allusions help create an effect where everything seems both real and illusory.

The tram also captured the imagination of Leung Ping-kwan 梁秉鈞 (also known by his pen name, Yesi 也斯, 1949–2013), such as in his poem "Freezing Night: Tram Depot" (寒夜・電車廠; 1974). Leung was a prominent poet, essayist, and short story writer, as well as a university professor and photographer. Born in Guangzhou, he grew up in a village in Aberdeen, at the southern part of Hong Kong Island, then moved at the age of ten to North Point, where the city streets captured his imagination and fostered in him a lifelong interest in urban culture.[19] As with other local writers such as Xi Xi 西西 (b. 1938), Wong Bik-wan 黃碧雲 (b. 1961), and Dung Kai-cheung 董啟章 (b. 1967), Leung's Hong Kong–oriented works question the identity of this (post)colonial city which thrives on a symbiotic relationship between old and new, local and foreign, East and West. Leung wrote his first set of poems on Hong Kong streets and places in the 1970s, and they were collected in his first poetry collection, *Thunder and Cicada Songs* (雷聲與蟬鳴; 1978 [2009]). "At the North Point Car Ferry" (北角汽車渡海碼頭; 1974) is perhaps the best known and most critically acclaimed of his early works.

The North Point Ferry is located in Harbor Parade, a relatively subdued area slightly away from the clamorous King's Road. The opening of Leung's poem provides readers with cues with respect to its temporal and spatial dimension:

寒意深入我們的骨骼
整天在多塵的路上
推開奔馳的窗
只見城市的萬木無聲
一個下午做許多徒勞的差使
在柏油的街道找尋泥土[20]

The chill was through to the bone.
Bussing all day along dusty streets,
in a window slid wide open,
one knew the muteness of the lines of trees.
On an afternoon of numerous dull errands
one hardly saw the earth at all, just concrete.

The poem is set in a city in winter, and is narrated through the perspective of a person taking a long bus ride. This short stanza demonstrates several characteristics of Leung's poetry: a preference for sites and images that are quotidian rather than extraordinary; a detached and observant tone; the use of plain, simple language; and the mix of a strong sense of urbanity with the subtle sensitivity of pastoral poems, an effect created by incorporating poetic signs which are familiar images in Chinese classical poems, for example "chill" and "muteness of the lines of trees."

The second stanza is full of images of smoke and fire. The narrator describes his companion's eyes as being as "black as coal." "Fine smoke" pervades the air and a fire breaks out at a tire factory across the harbor, emitting "plumes of black smoke" and "rolling black clouds," followed by a description of "oil slicks" and the smell of "smoke and burned rubber." Ackbar Abbas's observation that these dark images "turn the familiar sights of Hong Kong into a postapocalyptic landscape" might be an exaggeration, but these images do point to the precariousness of urban living.[21] The instability of the concrete-covered city is further highlighted by the metaphor of buildings' wavering reflections on water:

親近海的肌膚
油污上有彩虹
高樓投影在上面
巍峨晃蕩不定

Up close to the body of the sea
her rainbows were oilslicks.
The images of the skyscrapers
were staggering giants on the waves.

By the 1970s, Hong Kong had grown into a modern commercial city. But the "staggering giants" seem to suggest that the city's success might not have a solid foundation. Thriving under a political reality of a "borrowed place, borrowed time," the city's development had a single focus on material progress; its economic achievements were not matched by solid sociocultural foundations.[22] The wavering reflections also hint at the anxiety and confusion in the minds of the urban dwellers, who face a fast-changing and increasingly complex material and social environment. As Leung explains, the images work on two levels: "[the poem] tries to simultaneously portray the inner and outer space, using 'floods and black clouds' to hint at the city's anguish, 'staggering giants on waves' to depict the illusive growth of property and prosperity that one presently faces and the unpredictability of the future."[23]

Although not structured around a binary opposition between the old and the new, the urban and the rural, the poem evokes a sense of longing for the good old days, when the city was not so polluted and covered in concrete. A line in the third stanza reads: "The suns of our good old songs go out, one by one" (我們歌唱的白日將一一熄去). The urban images in the work expose the underlying tension of society, culminating in the end in a symbol of the city's uncertain future:

逼窄的天橋的庇蔭下
來自各方的車子在這裏待渡

In the narrow shelter of the flyover,
cars and their people waited a turn to go over.

Leung states that the ending is intended to characterize the situation of Hong Kong, where "everybody is waiting in place to cross, not knowing what the future holds."[24] This sense of uncertainty can be explained in relation to the city's rapid urbanization, and specifically the psychological stress brought by the disappearance of the old and the familiar. It can also be interpreted in light of colonialism, which made marginality a feature not only of the city's geographical existence but of its cultural and political identity. People in Hong Kong feel a strong sense of insecurity and are highly conscious of the unknowable future, because the city in which they live is, in Leung's description, "always at the edge of things and between places."[25] In many situations, marginality can be understood as a built-in weakness. The city's vulnerability became most apparent in the 1980s and 1990s, when the powerful political "centers" held negotiations over its fate. The long and torturous process that decided Hong Kong's future disrupted, and in many cases drastically changed, many of its people's lives.

But notwithstanding the vague sense of insecurity, this poem filled with bleak images does not end with overwhelming pessimism. "Waiting" is often accompanied by emotions such as agitation, anxiousness, and perhaps also worries over the outcome of the wait, but it also implies hope. "Waited a turn to go over" is the English rendering of *daidu* (待渡) in the Chinese version. The Chinese expression is a combination of two verbs: *dai* (待), "to wait," and *du* (渡), "to cross." Yet *du* also has a more profound meaning. Aside from its literal meaning of passing through a certain area, it is often used metaphorically to refer to going through a difficult period, or enduring hardship. When used in a Buddhist context, it hints at the possibility of enlightenment and transcendence after suffering. If we take the ending, which foregrounds possibilities and does not negate hope, as an oblique allusion to the city's situation, the poet's vision is not an entirely despairing one.

This vision can be contemplated in relation to Rey Chow's study of Leung's poetry as colonial literature. Inherent in colonialism, Chow argues, is an inferior political status, appropriation, and exploitation, but this system can be turned into a more positive condition, "a form of opportunity, in which the daily experience of oppression is synchronized with a self-conscious search for freedom in alternative forms."[26] Whether in a geographical or political sense, marginality prompts one to "develop a bi- or multicultural consciousness."[27] Leung's literary career involves a longtime practice of what he calls "negotiations of cultures," and he often finds himself "criticizing one culture from the perspective of another."[28] This strong sensitivity to cultures leads to a characteristic Chow sees in his works: an "insistence on an openness."[29] Leung's poetic journey is, in this light, "a self-conscious search for freedom," a search that highlights the importance of "openness" in contrast to colonialism's cultural centrality and superiority.[30] One can observe that Leung's attitude toward the condition of colonialism is a pragmatic one. His poetic allusions to Hong Kong have very little to do with the theoretical implications or ideological consequences of the system. They focus more on how culturally and humanistically rich conditions can be best achieved within a historically determined context.

The North Point Pier is no longer the same place as before. The passenger ferry is still in service, but the car ferry has been out of use for a long time, having ceased to be an important means of transport in the 1970s, with the Cross-Harbor Tunnel and Mass Transit Railway coming into operation. Leung had indeed written the poem knowing that the car ferry would soon disappear.[31] Capturing the place in its days of vitality and vigor, Leung's poetic narrative situates the relatively unnoticed pier as a site of social memory, a place with a historical dimension that reflects the vicissitudes of the city's growth.

Urban Images 2: The Past and Present of Nathan Road

Nathan Road is a main road in Kowloon. Running from south to north, it starts from its junction with Salisbury Road in Tsimshatsui and ends at its interjection with Boundary Street in Sham Shui Po. It was originally named Robinson Road, after Sir William Robinson (Hong Kong governor 1891–1898), but was renamed in 1909 after Sir Matthew Nathan (Hong Kong governor 1904–1907). Once a quiet, tree-lined boulevard, its streetscape has been drastically transformed since the 1950s by rapid redevelopment. Nowadays, this teeming road packed with buildings is a densely populated area, a bustling business district, as well as a focal point where people visit for the diverse range of entertainment it provides.

This noisy, messy, lively place has appeared in many literary works. For instance, Nathan Road, more specifically the Nathan Hotel, is an important setting in émigré writer Cao Juren's 曹聚仁 (1900–1972) *The Hotel* (酒店; 1954), a novel about the lives of Chinese immigrants in the city in the 1950s. Many Hong Kong writers have drawn inspiration from the place; examples are Shu Xiangcheng's 舒巷城 (1921–1999) poem "Tsimshatsui" (尖沙咀; year unknown) or Hua Gai's 華蓋 (birth year unknown) essay "Lyricism in Nathan Road" (彌敦道抒情; 1964). A more recent poetic work on the area is "Nathan Road" (彌敦道; 2001), written by Yip Fai 葉輝 (b. 1952). Yip is an experienced journalist as well as a poet, essayist, short novel writer, and literary critic. His poem tells the story of a man who tries to revisit his past by going back to Nathan Road, where he spent his younger days, but ends up disoriented by an alien streetscape. It begins with the man's failed effort to search for the train station:

走遍尖沙咀他找不到火車站
天空旋轉如墓, 他們圍繞如牆
聽他細說黑白的彌敦道
倒流著伊斯曼的一九六一
不舍晝夜的逝水年華

Walking around Tsimshatsui all day and still he can't find the station.
The sky spins like a tombstone and they surround him like a wall,
listening to him describe a black-and-white Nathan Road,
rolling back to an Eastman-Kodak 1961
the months and years flowing away day and night.[32]

The protagonist is unable to find the station because it was torn down in the late 1970s.[33] At a loss and apparently physically exhausted, he tells the people who surround him his story. His recollections conjure up past sites and events, turning the bygone, a "black-and-white Nathan Road," into a series of vivid scenes, or, using the extra-diegetic narrator's metaphor, an "Eastman-Kodak 1961."

The poem's protagonist, an apprentice tailor in the Nathan Road area in 1961, looks back on his past life that involved his boss and "Auntie," a seamstress whom he secretly admired. Even though his life was harsh and simple, marked by minor and major tragedies such as his boss's death and Auntie's marriage to another man, it also had its pleasures. For example, he would get up late at night to sew clothes for Auntie's doll, and once he had dinner with Auntie and then the two lined up at a theater to get movie tickets. This subtle romance between the apprentice tailor and Auntie forms the core of the narration. But the main focus of the poem is not unrequited love but irreversible time. The poem abounds with place names closely related to local people's daily living: buildings that are both residential and commercial (Mirador Mansion, Alhambra Building), restaurants (King of King, Cherikoff, King Wah), and theaters (Gala Theatre, Princess Theatre, Yaumati Theatre). Many of these places, for example the Gala Theatre, the Princess Theatre, and King Wah Restaurant, have long disappeared. Mirador Mansion and Alhambra Building still exist, but over the years the gigantic buildings have changed from symbols of Nathan Road's modernity to marks of its past. The narrator also mentions Mongkok Pier, where Auntie went to deliver her work, and which fell into disuse in the early 1970s. The topography of the old man's memory map is drastically different from the present-day Nathan Road, showing that the spatial and temporal dimensions of human experience are inextricably linked. Hence, the poet describes the place by using a temporal concept: "Nathan Road is as long as a lifetime."

This strong sense of time, conveyed through spatial description, is further emphasized by the metaphor of the river, a familiar metaphor for the unidirectional flow of time. The poet conceives Nathan Road as a place divisible into two parts: areas "down the coast" and "up the coast." The young tailor works "down the coast" at Mirador Mansion in Tsimshatsui, an upscale district for tourists and shoppers. "Up the coast" is where the tailor lives and Auntie works, and it mainly refers to Sham Shui Po and Mongkok, places traditionally considered to be less affluent. The poem provides a description of the harshness of common people's lives in the 1960s. For example, the apprentice "did 400 hours of unskilled work" before he was finally given half a day off. Yet the hardship is not described with bitterness. The poem paints the image of a young man who is not well off, but who is content with a simple life because he is emotionally supported by the companionship of Auntie and the master-disciple relationship he has with his boss. The old man laments the disappearance of the old world, a world in which traditional values prevail and provide a basis for one's social identity. The changed streetscape reflects an enervated socio-ethical structure, one that has been eroded by modern commodity culture and overwhelming materialism.

The old man's reaction to the streetscape of the new millennium is a dramatic presentation of the disconcerting effect of modernization on the human mind. In a sociological study of the impact of modernization on human consciousness, Peter Berger and his coauthors offer a detailed analysis of how technological and economic development increases feelings of nervousness, frustration, and alienation. Modernization and its institutions have an effect of splintering traditional ways of thought and kinship patterns. People's identity is destabilized, and as a result, urban dwellers are prone to feel a sense of rootlessness and impermanence. Echoing Heidegger's claim that "homelessness is becoming a world fate,"[34] Berger et al. state that "*modern man has suffered from a deepening condition of 'homelessness.'*"[35] The old man's confusion epitomizes this condition. It is an especially poignant case because the changes in the streetscape of Nathan Road also point to the homogenizing effect of globalization. Many old theaters and restaurants mentioned in the poem have been converted into glass-walled shopping malls lined with shops of omnipresent brands. The massive power of capitalist expansion further weakens the old "sense of place" and, consequently, deepens the mental condition of "homelessness."

We have seen that place and time are inseparably linked in the poem. The temporal dimension of the work foregrounds another important theme: the power of memory. Despite the confusion, there is a touch of warmth in the poem, created by the old man's fond attachment to his past. With a nearly Proustian intensity, the old man's memory evokes past joys and pains, giving him a sense of personal history, which in turn makes it possible for him to reconnect with the old "sense of place." Nostalgia turns into a constructive force that calms and soothes the mind. The poem posits memory as a palliative, a mental process that can attenuate the devastating effect of the disappearance of sense of place and the condition of homelessness. In a remarkably Bergsonian manner, the poet sees memory as a mechanism of the mind through which the past can be revived. Yip writes about memory in a later article: "Memory is a deeper, more complex phenomenon. It implicates 'internalization' and 'fortification', the symbiosis of all elements in our past lives. The past is connected with one's 'present state' in memory, and through this it is regenerated."[36] "Nathan Road" is a poetic manifestation of this belief that memory can be empowering and productive. For the old man, the past generated by memory is far more intense and visceral than the present of the poem, the year 2001.

Hence Yip's poem has a strong lyrical element. It shows how by lyricizing memory, or the landscape of the past, one can recover lost sensations and feelings, and in so doing, rebuild a sense of familiarity in a rapidly changing environment. In this sense, memory is efficacious for relieving urban pressures, but it is nonetheless not curative. Through memory the poem's protagonist managed to connect his past with an alienated present, yet he is still disoriented, since the place is no longer recognizable. The first stanza of the poem suggests a physical breakdown—"the sky spins like a tombstone and they [the bystanders] surround him like a wall" (天空旋轉如墓, 他們圍繞如牆)—and in the penultimate stanza "the policeman helps him into the ambulance" (警察先生送 他上了救護車). One can notice that toward the end of the poem the man's memory becomes even more scattered and disjointed. The movie *West Side Story* (1961) suddenly comes to his mind, and the poem closes with his insistence that he has to get off at a bakery to buy lotus-seed cake for Auntie. This suggests mental confusion, an inability to distinguish between past and present.

The poem explores place and identity, using buildings, neon lights, restaurants, theaters, and other urban images of Nathan Road in the past. Together, the nostalgic symbols paint an old streetscape. They recreate the ambience and essence of a bygone era, a world with a different sense of value compared with the present. As a physical manifestation of time, the poem highlights memory's function of easing the mind in the stressful and chaotic urban environment. Although confused and fragmentary, memory at least connects the old man with the external world; it saves him from becoming a rootless and deracinated man in a place which was once home to him. The poem exhibits two contradictory feelings. The old man's loyalty to his past suggests a deep emotional attachment to the place, or topophilia. On the other hand, his inability to reconcile himself with the present, his physical exhaustion and confused perceptions, suggest an antithetical feeling that we can call topophobia. The two contrastive feelings seem to aptly sum up modern urban life, which is often a bittersweet experience full of paradoxes and opposites.

The old man's disillusionment can be understood more generally as representing the vague unease that people feel who live in a society that has lost contact with its past. In a material-centered culture, the past is considered useless and irrelevant; the old has to make way for the new and changes have to be fast, so as to maximize profits and catch up with the latest trend or technology. Little thought is given to how the past can be preserved or strengthened to reinforce the present, or to how it can be used for building a strong, distinctive, and consistent cultural identity. T. S. Eliot wrote that it is "historical sense," "a sense of the timeless as well as of the temporal and of the timeless and of the temporal together," that situates a writer within a literary tradition.[37] The same can be said for places. A sense of tradition can only be achieved through an understanding of the dynamic relationship between past and present. Development essentially means replacing the old with the new; it entails destruction and creation. Tuan Yi-Fu's remark that "all creative effort—including the making of an omelet—is preceded by destruction" is certainly true.[38] But urban development without due consideration for cultural continuity has a negative effect. As Yip Fai's poem demonstrates, this impairs people's sense of topophilia and increases a feeling of topophobia. Whereas changes and development are part of nature and should be embraced rather than feared or shunned, history is strewn with examples of damage done by changes motivated or propelled by material profits, bureaucratic complacency, or a blind faith in technology. In the case of Hong Kong, many old sites with historico-cultural and aesthetic value have been torn down. These demolitions demonstrate a failure to recognize the sociocultural implications involved in the dilemma between revival and removal of historic sites. It is interesting that in recent years Hong Kong youths have taken a more active role in protests against the destruction of historical relics.[39] Their enthusiasm for the preservation of past relics can be attributed to a variety of factors, but it is certainly at least partly motivated by the younger generation's fear of losing the connection with their past, and their awareness of the fact that the erosion of collective memory will eventually leave a void that negatively impacts the formation of their social and cultural identity.

CONCLUSION: IN RESPONSE TO CECIL CLEMENTI

Another work by Leung Ping-kwan can be cited as a further example of how Hong Kong poetry has been used as a medium of sociocultural critique, and of the extent to which the genre reflects the city's history of changes when seen diachronically. In 1997, the handover year, Leung wrote "In Response to Cecil Clementi" (悼逝去的—和金文泰香港詩). It opens as follows:

> 我從山腳下仰望已經看不見星空
> 太燦爛了日本電器廣告牌一重重
>
> I gaze from the foot of the mountain
> and espy
> not a single firefly
> steaming by,
> not a single star
> gleaming in the sky,
> no fairy lights on an earthly paradise,
> But a special Economic Zone
> lit up in a blaze of Japanese neon
> dazzling the eye.[40]

The poem's title was originally "In Response to General Jin" (悼逝去的—和金制軍香港詩). "General Jin" is the name Lu Xun 魯迅 (1881–1936) used to ridicule Sir Cecil Clementi in an essay written shortly after his lecture trip to Hong Kong in 1927, in which he mocks the former governor's efforts to promote traditional Chinese culture in the colony. Leung later changed the title to refer instead to Cecil Clementi, because, as he explains, he had learned more about Clementi and did not completely agree with Lu Xun's view.[41] By contrasting Hong Kong's night view in the 1920s and near the end of the past millennium, the poem challenges Clementi's romantic vision that framed Hong Kong as "a perfect meeting place of East and West."[42] It also touches on the cultural pressures and ambiguity colonialism entails:

費盡思量勉強步和你異鄉的韻律
多年來你的言語總令我結結巴巴

See how hard I have to try
to squeeze myself into your foreign rhyme!
For years I've had to stammer like this
in your borrowed tongue!

The narrator cannot decide if it is "indifference" or "a strange nostalgia" that he feels now that the colonial era is near its end. Neither is he particularly enthusiastic about the impending changes. Describing the city's people as "cultural waifs," the poem expresses an ambivalent attitude toward the city's past—ambivalent because of a silent understanding that the city's prosperity has owed much to a political system that is morally reprehensible. The ambivalence in this poem, and in Leung's many other poems that touch upon Hong Kong's colonial background, points at the deeply ironic core of Hong Kong as a success story of East meeting West.

Whereas all of the poems discussed in this chapter are centered upon Hong Kong, each in its own way, many of them contain a nostalgic element. Nostalgia, as David Lowenthal notes, is a "sociological complaint," "an increasingly pervasive ailment" of the modern age.[43] But nostalgia does not necessarily mean indulgence in a romanticized past or an unwillingness to face the present. As argued by Leo Spitzer, when critically tempered, nostalgic discourse can assume the function of "a potential anchor for personal and group stability and identity."[44] Irrespective of whether they focus on colonial experience or the trauma of modernity, the cityscapes invoked in the poems analyzed above provide clues as to how a collective identity is gradually formed. They offer an imaginative yet reality-based account of the city's development history, a poetic description of the way time's flow manifests itself as a changing sense of place.

NOTES

1. Cecil Clementi, *A Journal in Song* (Oxford: Blackwell, 1928), 85. All quotations of the poem are taken from this edition.
2. Clementi and his wife left Hong Kong in 1930 with sadness, saying "I would gladly have stayed here rather than anywhere else in the world." Quoted in Frank Welsh, *A History of Hong Kong* (London: Harper Collins, 1993), 390. Also, according to his descendants, Clementi always said that the happiest years of his life were spent in Hong Kong. See May Holdsworth, *Foreign Devils: Expatriates in Hong Kong* (Oxford: Oxford University Press, 2002), 38.
3. Zhang Lianxing 張連興, *Xianggang ershiba zongdu* 香港二十八總督 [The twenty-eight British governors of Hong Kong] (Beijing: Zhaohua chubanshe, 2007), 224.

4. David Faure gives an interesting account of common people's lives in early Hong Kong. See "The Common People in Hong Kong History: Their Livelihood and Aspirations until the 1930s," in *Colonial Hong Kong and Modern China: Interaction and Reintegration*, ed. Lee Pui-tak (Hong Kong: Hong Kong University Press, 2005), 9–38.

5. Quoted in Austin Coates, *A Mountain of Lights: The Story of the Hong Kong Electric Company* (London: Heinemann, 1977), 3.

6. John Minford, "Foreword: 'PK,'" in *Islands and Continents: Short Stories by Leung Ping-kwan*, ed. John Minford (Hong Kong: Hong Kong University Press, 2007), xiii.

7. See Edward Said, "Orientalism Reconsidered," in *Reflections on Exile and Other Essays* (Cambridge: Harvard University Press, 2000), 202 and 212.

8. Peter Wesley-Smith, *Clementi, Customs, and Consuls and Cables: Some Issues in Hong Kong-China Relations* (Hong Kong: s.n., 1973), 3.

9. Russell Spurr, *Excellency: The Governors of Hong Kong* (Hong Kong: FormAsia, 1995), 156.

10. Because of the distance and the sense of detachment the bird's-eye view implies, it is often used in literary works and films related to colonialism. For example, E. M. Forster's *A Passage to India* (1924) opens with a panoramic vision of Chandrapore. Henry King's *Love is a Many-Splendored Thing* (1955), a filmic adaptation of Eurasian novelist Han Suyin's *A Many-Splendored Thing* (1952), a love story set in Hong Kong in the late 1940s, begins with a bird's-eye shot of the colony's landscape.

11. See Ou Waiou 鷗外鷗, *Ou Waiou zhi shi* 鷗外鷗之詩 [Poems of Ou Waiou] (Guangzhou: Hua Cheng chubanshe, 1985), 12–15 and 44–45.

12. Liu Muxia 柳木下, *Haitian ji* 海天集 [The sea and the sky], 18–19; translated by Eva Hung in *To Pierce the Material Screen: An Anthology of 20th-Century Hong Kong Literature*, vol. 2, ed. Eva Hung (Hong Kong: Research Centre for Translation, The Chinese University of Hong Kong, 2008), 51. All Chinese and English quotations of the poem are taken from the same sources.

13. Norman Owen et al., *The Heritage of Hong Kong: Its History, Architecture & Culture* (Hong Kong: FormAsia, 1999), 47.

14. Tuan Yi-Fu, *Space and Place* (Minneapolis: University of Minnesota Press, 1977), 6.

15. Edward Relph, *Place and Placelessness* (London: Pion Limited, 1976), 34.

16. Humanistic geographer Tuan Yi-Fu has expanded the concept in such works as *Space and Place* and *Topophilia* (New York: Columbia University Press, 1990).

17. See Jason Wordie, *Streets: Exploring Hong Kong Island* (Hong Kong: Hong Kong University Press, 2002), 184–186.

18. Ma Boliang 馬博良 (Ma Lang 馬朗), "Beijiao zhi ye" 北角之夜 [A night in North Point], in *Fenqin de langzi* 焚琴的浪子 / *Ronald Mar's Poems: The Prodigals Who Burn Lyres* (Hong Kong: Maisui chuban youxian gongsi, 2011). The phrases are my own translations.

19. See Gordon T. Osing, "An Interview with Leung Ping-kwan," in *City at the End of Time: Poems by Leung Ping-kwan* 形象香港: 梁秉鈞詩選 (Hong Kong: Hong Kong University Press, 2012), 212.

20. Leung Ping-kwan 梁秉鈞, "At the North Point Car Ferry" (北角汽車渡海碼頭; 1974), trans. Gordon T. Osing and Leung Ping-kwan. Both the Chinese original and English translation are taken from *City at the End of Time: Poems by Leung Ping-kwan*, 80–81. All quotations of the poem are taken from the same edition.

21. Ackbar Abbas, *Hong Kong: Culture and the Politics of Disappearance* (Hong Kong: Hong Kong University Press, 1997), 131.

22. Richard Hughes uses this phrase as part of the title of a book on Hong Kong he wrote in 1968. Since then it has become a popular phrase people use to describe Hong Kong. Hughes

got the inspiration from an article in *Life* (1959) entitled "Hong Kong's Ten-Year Miracle," written by Han Suyin. See Richard Hughes, *Borrowed Place, Borrowed Time: Hong Kong, and Its Many Faces* (London: Andre Deutsch, 1968), "Acknowledgement," n.p.

23. Leung Ping-kwan, "Urban Poetry of Hong Kong," in *Hong Kong Culture & Urban Literature*, ed. Leung Ping-kwan, Amanda Hsu, and Lee Hoi-lam (Hong Kong: Hong Kong Story Association, 2009), 74.

24. Leung Ping-kwan, "Urban Poetry of Hong Kong," 74.

25. This is a line from Leung's poem "Images of Hong Kong" (形象香港). Both the Chinese original and English translation are taken from Leung Ping-kwan, *City at the End of Time*, 88, 89.

26. Rey Chow, "Things, Common/Places, Passages of the Port City: On Hong Kong and Hong Kong Author Leung Ping-kwan," in *Ethics after Idealism: Theory, Culture, Ethnicity, Reading* (Bloomington and Indianapolis: Indiana University Press, 1998), 186.

27. Rey Chow, "Things, Common/Places, Passages of the Port City," 187.

28. Leung Ping-kwan, *City at the End of Time*, 174.

29. Rey Chow, "Things, Common/Places, Passages of the Port City," 187.

30. Rey Chow, "Things, Common/Places, Passages of the Port City," 187.

31. Leung told this to Japanese scholar Yamota Inuhiko when the two visited the pier. See Yesi and Yamota Inuhiko, *Shouwang Xianggang: Xianggang-Dongjing wangfu shujian* 守望香港: 香港－東京往復書簡 [Watching Hong Kong: Letters between Hong Kong and Tokyo], trans. Han Yanli 韓燕麗 (Hong Kong: Oxford University Press, 2013), 81.

32. Yip Fai 葉輝, "Nathan Road" 彌敦道, trans. Brendan O'Kane. Both the Chinese original and English translation are taken from *Nathan Road* 彌敦道 (Hong Kong: The Chinese University Press, 2011), 16–19. All quotations of the poem quoted in this chapter are taken from the same edition.

33. The train station was moved to Hung Hom in the 1970s. The Clock Tower, the only remnant of the Kowloon Station on the Kowloon-Canton Railway, still stands on the old site as a landmark of the city.

34. Quoted in Edward Relph, *Place and Placelessness*, 143.

35. Peter L. Berger, Brigitte Berger, and Hansfried Kellner, *The Homeless Mind* (New York: Random House, 1973), 77.

36. Yip Fai 葉輝, "Shu Xiangcheng shi de xiaoshi meixue" 舒巷城詩的消失美學 [The aesthetics of disappearance in Shu Xiangcheng's poetry], in *Shihua: Shiyuan yu shijiao* 詩話: 詩緣與詩教 [Notes on poetry: Poetic affinity and didacticism] (Hong Kong: Maisui chuban youxian gongsi, 2008), 95–99. This is my own translation.

37. T. S. Eliot, "Tradition and the Individual Talent," *Selected Essays* (London: Faber and Faber, 1951), 14.

38. Tuan Yi-Fu, *Space and Place*, 197.

39. For example, many young people participated in the movements against the demolition of the old Star Ferry Pier in 2006 and of Queen's Pier in 2007. More recently, among those who actively support the preservation of historical relics found in the areas covered in the Guangzhou-Shenzhen-Hong Kong Express Rail Link project, many are of a younger generation.

40. Leung Ping-kwan 梁秉鈞, "In Response to General Jin" 悼逝去的——和金制軍香港詩. Translation by John Minford. Both the Chinese original and English translation are taken from *Fly Heads and Bird Claws* 蠅頭與鳥爪: 梁秉鈞詩集 (Hong Kong: MCCM Creations, 2012), 103–104. All quotations of the poem are taken from the same source.

41. See Leung Ping-kwan, "Guan yu 'dao shiqu de—he Jin zhijun xianggang shi'" 關於〈悼逝去的—和金制軍香港詩〉 [About "In response to General Jin"], in *Huxi shikan* 呼吸詩刊 [Huxi poetry] 4 (January 1998): 68. Leung has also talked about this poem and his views on Clementi in "Writing across Borders: Hong Kong's 1950s and the Present," in *Diasporic Histories: Cultural Archives of Chinese Transnationalism*, ed. Andrea Riemenschnitter and Deborah L. Madsen (Hong Kong: Hong Kong University Press, 2009), 31; "Xianggang wenxue yu wenhua: bentu, Zhongguo, shijie" 香港文學與文化: 本土、中國、世界 [Hong Kong literature and culture: The local, China, and the world], in *Renwen Xianggang: Xianggang fazhan jingyan de quanxin zongjie* 人文香港: 香港發展經驗的全新總結 [Humanistic Hong Kong: A new summary of Hong Kong's development experience], ed. Hung Ching-tin 洪清田 (Hong Kong: Zhonghua shuju, 2012), 60–62.

42. Leung Ping-kwan, "Writing across Borders: Hong Kong's 1950s and the Present," 21.

43. David Lowenthal, "Past Time, Present Place: Landscape and Memory," *Geographical Review* 65 (January 1975): 2.

44. Leo Spitzer, "Back Through the Future: Nostalgic Memory and Critical Memory in a Refuge from Nazism," in *Acts of Memory: Cultural Recall in the Present*, ed. Mieke Bal, Jonathan Crewe, and Leo Spitzer (Hanover and London: Dartmouth College and University Press of New England, 1999), 101.

WORKS CITED

Abbas, M. Ackbar. *Hong Kong: Culture and the Politics of Disappearance*. Hong Kong: Hong Kong University Press, 1997.

Berger, Peter L., Brigitte Berger, and Hansfried Kellner. *The Homeless Mind*. New York: Random House, 1973.

Cao Juren 曹聚仁. *Jiudian* 酒店 [The hotel]. Hong Kong: Joint Publishing, 1999.

Chow, Rey. "Things, Common/Places, Passages of the Port City: On Hong Kong and Hong Kong Author Leung Ping-kwan." In *Ethics after Idealism: Theory, Culture, Ethnicity, Reading*. Bloomington and Indianapolis: Indiana University Press, 1998. 168–188.

Clementi, Cecil. *A Journal in Song*. Oxford: Blackwell, 1928.

Coates, Austin. *A Mountain of Lights: The Story of the Hong Kong Electric Company*. London: Heinemann, 1977.

Eliot, Thomas Stearns. "Tradition and the Individual Talent." In *Selected Essays*. London: Faber and Faber, 1951. 13–22.

Faure, David. "The Common People in Hong Kong History: Their Livelihood and Aspirations until the 1930s." In *Colonial Hong Kong and Modern China: Interaction and Reintegration*. Ed. Lee Pui-tak. Hong Kong: Hong Kong University Press, 2005. 9–38.

Forster, Edward Morgan. *A Passage to India*. London: Arnold, 1945.

Han Suyin. *A Many-Splendored Thing*. Boston: Little, Brown, 1952.

Holdsworth, May. *Foreign Devils: Expatriates in Hong Kong*. Oxford: Oxford University Press, 2002.

Hua Gai 華蓋. "Midun dao shuqing" 彌敦道抒情 [Lyricism on Nathan Road]. *Zhongguo xuesheng zhoubao* 中國學生週報 [The Chinese students' weekly] 639, October 16, 1964.

Hughes, Richard. *Borrowed Place, Borrowed Time: Hong Kong, and Its Many Faces*. London: Andre Deutsch, 1968.

Hung, Eva. *To Pierce the Material Screen: An Anthology of 20th-Century Hong Kong Literature*, Vol. II. Hong Kong: Research Centre for Translation, The Chinese University of Hong Kong, 2008.

Leung Ping-kwan 梁秉鈞. *City at the End of Time: Poems by Leung Ping-kwan* 形象香港: 梁秉鈞詩選. Hong Kong: Hong Kong University Press, 2012.

Leung Ping-kwan 梁秉鈞. *Fly Heads and Bird Claws* 蠅頭與鳥爪: 梁秉鈞詩集. Hong Kong: MCCM Creations, 2012.

Leung Ping-kwan 梁秉鈞. *Leisheng yu chanming* 雷聲與蟬鳴 [Thunder and cicada songs]. Hong Kong: Wenhua gongfang, 2009.

Leung Ping-kwan 梁秉鈞. "Writing across Borders: Hong Kong's 1950s and the Present." In *Diasporic Histories: Cultural Archives of Chinese Transnationalism*. Ed. Andrea Riemenschnitter and Deborah L. Madsen. Hong Kong: Hong Kong University Press, 2009. 23–42.

Leung Ping-kwan 梁秉鈞. "Urban Poetry of Hong Kong." In *Hong Kong Culture & Urban Literature*. Ed. Leung Ping-kwan, Amanda Hsu, and Lee Hoi-lam. Hong Kong: Hong Kong Story Association, 2009. 60–82.

Leung Ping-kwan 梁秉鈞. *Islands and Continents: Short Stories by Leung Ping-kwan*. Ed. John Minford with Brian Holton and Agnes Hung-chong Chan. Hong Kong: Hong Kong University Press, 2007.

Leung Ping-kwan 梁秉鈞. "Guan yu 'dao shiqu de—he Jin zhijun xianggang shi' " 關於〈悼逝去的—和金制軍香港詩〉[About "In Response to General Jin"]. *Huxi shikan* 呼吸詩刊 [Huxi poetry] 4 (January 1998): 67–69.

Liu Muxia 柳木下. *Haitian ji* 海天集 [The sea and the sky]. Hong Kong: Shanghai Bookstore, 1957.

Lowenthal, David. "Past Time, Present Place: Landscape and Memory." *Geographical Review* 65 (January 1975): 1–36.

Ma Boliang 馬博良 (Ma Lang 馬朗). *Fenqin de langzi* 焚琴的浪子 / *Ronald Mar's Poems: The Prodigals Who Burn Lyres*. Hong Kong: Maisui chuban youxian gongsi, 2011.

Minford, John. "Foreword: 'PK.'" In *Islands and Continents: Short Stories by Leung Ping-kwan*." Ed. John Minford. Hong Kong: Hong Kong University Press, 2007. vii–xviii.

Ou Waiou 鷗外鷗. *Ou Waiou zhi shi* 鷗外鷗之詩 [Poems of Ou Waiou]. Guangzhou: Hua Cheng chubanshe, 1985.

Owen, Norman, et al. *The Heritage of Hong Kong: Its History, Architecture & Culture*. Hong Kong: FormAsia, 1999.

Relph, Edward. *Place and Placelessness*. London: Pion Limited, 1976.

Said, Edward W. "Orientalism Reconsidered." In *Reflections on Exile and Other Essays*. Cambridge: Harvard University Press, 2000. 198–215.

Shu Xiangcheng 舒巷城. "Tsimshatsui" 尖沙咀. In *Dushi Shichao* 都市詩鈔 [A collection of urban poetry]. Hong Kong: Arcadia Press, 2004. 98–101.

Spitzer, Leo. "Back Through the Future: Nostalgic Memory and Critical Memory in a Refuge from Nazism." In *Acts of Memory: Cultural Recall in the Present*. Ed. Bal Mieke, Jonathan Crewe, and Leo Spitzer. Hanover, NH: University Press of New England, 1999. 87–104.

Spurr, Russell. *Excellency: The Governors of Hong Kong*. Hong Kong: FormAsia, 1995.

Tuan, Yi-Fu. *Space and Place*. Minneapolis: University of Minnesota Press, 1977.

Tuan, Yi-Fu. *Topophilia*. New York: Columbia University Press, 1990.

Welsh, Frank. *A History of Hong Kong*. London: Harper Collins, 1993.

Wesley-Smith, Peter. *Clementi, Customs, and Consuls and Cables: Some Issues in Hong Kong-China Relations*. Hong Kong: s.n., 1973.

Wordie, Jason. *Streets: Exploring Hong Kong Island*. Hong Kong: Hong Kong University Press, 2002.

Yesi 也斯 (Leung Ping-kwan 梁秉鈞). "Xianggang wenxue yu wenhua: Bentu, Zhongguo, shijie" 香港文學與文化: 本土、中國、世界 [Hong Kong literature and culture: The local, China, and the world]. In *Renwen Xianggang: Xianggang fazhan jingyan de quanxin zongjie* 人文香港: 香港發展經驗的全新總結 [Humanistic Hong Kong: A new summary of Hong Kong's development experience]. Ed. Hung Ching-tin 洪清田. Hong Kong: Zhonghua shuju, 2012. 43–62.

Yesi 也斯 (Leung Ping-kwan 梁秉鈞) and Yamota Inuhiko. *Shouwang Xianggang: Xianggang—Dongjing wangfu shujian* 守望香港: 香港—東京往復書簡 [Watching Hong Kong: Letters between Hong Kong and Tokyo]. Trans. Han Yanli 韓燕麗. Hong Kong: Oxford University Press, 2013.

Yip Fai 葉輝. *Nathan Road* 彌敦道. Hong Kong: The Chinese University Press, 2011.

Yip Fai 葉輝. *Jingjing shiji: Zai ri yu ye de jiafeng li* 鯨鯨詩集: 在日與夜的夾縫裏 [Jing Jing's poems: In the gap between day and night]. Hong Kong: Wenhua gongfang, 2009.

Yip Fai 葉輝. "Shu Xiangcheng shi de xiaoshi meixue" 舒巷城詩的消失美學 [The aesthetics of disappearance in Shu Xiangcheng's poetry]. In *Shihua: Shiyuan yu shijiao* 詩話: 詩緣與詩教 [Notes on poetry: Poetic affinity and didacticism]. Hong Kong: Maisui chuban youxian gongsi, 2008. 95–99.

Zhang Lianxing 張連興. *Xianggang ershiba zongdu* 香港二十八總督 [The twenty-eight British governors of Hong Kong]. Beijing: Zhaohua chubanshe, 2007.

CHAPTER 2.6

....

WARTIME TAIWAN

Epitome of an East Asian Modality of the
Modern Literary Institution?

....

SUNG-SHENG YVONNE CHANG

... as I was reading my fellow historians, it became clear that the encounter of Western forms and local reality did indeed produce everywhere
a structural compromise—as the law predicted—but also, the compromise itself was taking rather different forms. At times, especially in the
second half of the nineteenth century and in Asia, it tended to be very
unstable ...

(Franco Moretti, *Distant Reading*)

NOTABLE among recent attempts at building a nonexclusivist framework for studying
world literature is the world-system approach of Franco Moretti and Pascale Casanova.
It appears, however, that for Casanova, only a select few East Asian writers, such as
Nobel Prize winners Kawabata Yasunari 川端康成 and Gao Xingjian 高行健, may
be admitted to the "international marketplace" of literature. This conclusion makes
sense, to be sure, provided that we accept her basic assumption about the existence of
a "Greenwich Meridian" of modern world literature, which serves as an "absolute point
of reference unconditionally recognized by all contestants."[1] Unlike Casanova, Moretti
does not immediately dismiss authors consigned to "dominated regions." Tracking the
global diffusion of a modern European literary form, the novel, that has reached different regions of the world in the past centuries, he takes special note of the fact that this
literary encounter essentially entailed "a compromise between a western formal influence (usually French or English) and local materials."[2] That the initial phase of Asia's
adaptation of "western forms" in the second half of the nineteenth century appeared to
be especially "unstable" may well be explained by the latter's relatively late arrival, by
the wide distance between the two large civilizational blocs of Asia and the West, and
by the sheer magnitude of the region's premodern aesthetic traditions against which
these Western forms were competing.

After the initial encounter and beginning at slightly different times, however, intellectuals in different parts of East Asia launched a "high culture quest" that included an attempt to integrate and adapt the imported category of "literature." They did so with the same self-consciousness and earnestness displayed during their attempts to integrate such other modern institutions as the nation-state, capitalism, mass literacy, Western-style education, Western-style judicial systems, and so forth. And it is for this reason that we propose a methodology that applies such sociologically oriented theories as Peter Bürger's notion of the institution of art, which treats aesthetic concepts and creative practices as a subsystem of society, and Pierre Bourdieu's concept of the field of cultural production to the examination of modern East Asian literary processes in the wake of the region's encounter with the hegemonic West.[3]

Over the past two decades, postcolonial and multiculturalist discourses have effectively discredited claims for the universal validity of Eurocentric literary views and evaluative criteria. Progress toward expanding the scope of literary inquiries to include the non-West, however, has been fairly uneven. Compared to literature from the former Western colonies, such as the Anglophone and Francophone regions, literature from modern East Asia has received significantly less attention. This is caused, in my view, not only by a knowledge deficit, in terms of empirical facts, but also by a lack of systematic examination of the distinctive dynamics, internal cross-currents, and shared patterns of modern literary development within the region, and a sociologically oriented structural approach promises to fruitfully address this issue.

Before proceeding, it is necessary to call attention to two fundamental features of the East Asian encounter with the modern literary institution. First, the literary movement in East Asia was fundamentally a second-order phenomenon, in that it coincided with the rise and spread of modernism in the Euro-American region, which was itself a late phase of what Bürger calls the evolving bourgeois institution of art.[4] The concurrent East Asian and Euro-American literary movements both spanned a large geographical space supporting a civilizational bloc, but what distinguished them is that the East Asian one was a derivative phenomenon modeled on Euro-American notions of modern literature, which had reached a point of intensified formal self-awareness under the influence of its modernist movement.

The second feature of the encounter also has to do with the temporal aspect. Establishing a modern literary institution in their local settings while already being actors on the world stage, individual East Asian societies went through compressed timetables, and moreover the process was frequently disrupted in violent ways. Thrust into the modern world by imperialist and colonial forces, East Asian societies suffered from incessant wars, revolutions, and regime changes over a relatively brief timespan, which often entailed drastic reorientations in the governing laws of cultural fields. Nothing better exemplifies the type of events that disrupted and redirected literary developments in modern East Asia than those created by the mid-twentieth-century political upheavals. China and North Korea introduced the socialist paradigm and reconstituted their cultural institutions across the board. In the Free World bloc, new regimes in Japan, South Korea, and Taiwan re-established a capitalist mode of cultural production while also vigorously denouncing important elements of the dominant ideology and associated aesthetics advocated by their predecessors in the prewar period. In addition to the sea changes that occurred in the mid-twentieth century across the globe, other momentous events—including the Sino-Japanese War, the Japanese *kominka* (皇民化) campaign, the Allied occupation of postwar Japan, the Chinese Cultural Revolution, the martial law period in Taiwan, and the Hong Kong Handover—also effected definitive and far-reaching changes in the evolutionary trajectories of local literary institutions.

In order to get the big picture, the proposed methodology shifts the focus from product to process, from disconnected facts to evolutionary patterns, and from emblems of national literature to structural affinities in the literary histories of modern East Asia's member societies. As long as one still gauges literature by what individual artists manage to achieve, as Casanova does, rather than investigating collective processes, it is hard to avoid the mistake of applying ostensibly universal criteria to East Asian literary agents and, often, finding them lacking. The main sections of this chapter, "Wartime Taiwan's Restructured Literary Field" and "The All Important Aesthetic Issues," will explore several typical features of latecomers to the world literary system by means of a case study.[5] For instance, these latecomers are frequently subject to political interventions resulting in paradigmatic shifts in cultural production, including drastic restructuring of the literary field through a new set of principles of inclusion and exclusion. Rather than focusing on violence against arbitrarily excluded literary agents, it is time to also more systematically investigate the structural forces that enable cultural production in the new period. Also, the field, restructured by extrinsically and arbitrarily motivated forces, nonetheless assumes structural qualities essential to its normative model, and as a result the political power dynamics are mediated by aesthetic positions, albeit emphatically in a sociohistorically inflected manner. Moreover, the competing aesthetic positions within the field inevitably register influences from literary models of the hegemonic West, and therefore it is imperative for scholars to carefully trace the multilayered genealogies of these positions. Another notable feature deserving attention is that, as a majority of East Asian cultural fields in reality enjoy a rather low degree of autonomy, their participants must deploy different kinds of coping strategies to fend off immediate pressures, and as a result develop certain types of habitus. The situation becomes even more strained when society enters a state of emergency, and even a minimum degree of cultural normalcy can no longer be maintained.

In sum, we concur with recent discourses on world literature that East Asia has partaken in the overarching process of the global spread and local entrenchment of Western-originated "modern literature" over the past hundred and fifty years or so. In practice, however, more systematic examination of the actual configurations of this process in the region must be done to pave the way for a genuinely nonexclusivist study of world literature. This chapter's investigation of literature in wartime Taiwan is conceived with the assumption that if we can substantiate the generalizations stated above through case studies drawn from different periods of modern East Asian literary history, we may come one step closer to portraying the special modalities of local literary institutions that the region has seen in the last century. Such studies may also bear witness to the fact that the "structural compromise" envisioned by Moretti has occurred beyond the literary form per se, with effects permeating various aspects of literary production on a colossal scale.

CURRENT REVISIONIST DISCOURSES
IN THREE CHINESE SOCIETIES

In the post–Cold War era, cultural production and consumption in most East Asian societies increasingly resemble those of advanced capitalist societies. Recently, however, we have witnessed a perplexing phenomenon, in that there appears to be a conservative turn among the intellectual elites in three Chinese societies, especially among intellectuals with a progressive bent, as they begin earnestly to call for a return to the cultural legacies of a previous "dark age": the New Left in China harks back to the socialist legacy of the Mao period, while separatists in Taiwan and Hong Kong reference cultural formations that originated under Japanese or British colonial rule.[6] As a literary historian, one cannot but be intrigued by the fact that, their widely divergent political agendas notwithstanding, these voices seek to invoke a bygone period in which collective efforts at building a locally based modern literary institution were made, though eventually thwarted.

This revisionist trend is partly a product of the contemporary ideological landscape, a reaction against the menaces brought about by neoliberal globalization and the highly commercialized mainstream culture it fosters. Also, the postcolonial discourse of the past three decades has provided felicitous idioms for scholarly reassertion of the subject positions of native literary agents who were intricately caught in an inherently unfair game. Finally, the prominent localist thrust may be seen as a reaction to emergent social anxieties, generated in each of these three societies by the identification of a new Other: for the PRC this was the United States, and for Taiwan and Hong Kong it was the rising China. What concerns us most as literary historians, however, is a somewhat different question: why is it that rehabilitations of segments of literary history that were formerly perceived as aberrant are now playing such a pivotal role?

My tentative answer to this question is that the incomplete evolutionary trajectories of local literary institutions bear witness to the possibility of an authentic indigenous form of modern culture, thus fueling hope of its fuller realization under more favorable circumstances.[7] This line of thought immediately harks back to a cluster of long-standing epochal themes, such as the recurring Westernization debates in China and the Overcoming Modernity debates in Japan. In parts of the world that entered modernity belatedly, little choice was available besides building modern institutions with resources drawn from models imported from the West. This process is inherently

Janus-faced, as the emulation of the fruits of advanced civilizational development is psychologically intertwined with the involuntary submission to imperialist and colonialist domination. This is the shared intellectual backdrop between the revisionist scholarship summarized above and the approach I adopt here. At the same time, however, this approach underscores the special nature of the adopted category of "literature" as a social institution, which bears imprints of the modern society's steady movement toward greater differentiation, specialization, and professionalization. To accurately comprehend the modality of its entrenchment in East Asia, we are obliged to conduct a more nuanced and detailed analysis that distinguishes the literary field from society as a whole, and the findings may both reinforce and contradict arguments formulated in current revisionist scholarship.

The remainder of this chapter will examine the literary scene in the last years of colonial Taiwan, with close reference to several representative works of revisionist scholarship. In doing so, I hope to tease out some distinctive features that characterize the local entrenchment of the modern literary institution at variance with more general cultural phenomena, thus mapping out a discipline-specific methodology that simultaneously illuminates the complex issue of revisionist localism.

The works I am referring to here have been published within the past two decades by scholars such as Zhou Wanyao 周婉窈, Chen Peifeng 陳培豐, Liu Shuqin 柳書琴, Fujii Shozo 藤井省三, and Wu Ruiren 吳叡人.[8] While they differ in subject matter and theoretical framework, these studies have all geared their arguments toward two main objectives. First, they seek to offer proof of individual or collective agency exercised by Taiwanese under Japanese rule. Because colonial rule sometimes took a hegemonic form and at other times was patently coercive, the question of authenticity, whether the colonial subject was true to him or herself despite external pressures and influences, becomes crucial to this line of inquiry. Second, they attempt to delve into the problem of "modern civilization" (近代文明), which featured centrally in colonial discourse. This, in turn, is seen from two different angles, that of the Taiwanese people's attitudes toward Japanese-mediated modernization and that of objective "modern" conditions attained in the colony.

In a sense, these endeavors may be seen as a decolonizing enterprise that was supposed to have taken place after 1945, but was delayed by the postwar Nationalist rule of Taiwan. In particular, during the four-decade-long martial law period, the officially sanctioned Sinocentrism went hand in hand with a suppression of historical knowledge of the fifty years during which Taiwan had been governed by Japan. For this reason, when scholarly reflection on the Japanese colonization was belatedly launched in the 1990s, the immediate task was to rectify the bias harbored by the general population against the colonial period. An across-the-board stigmatization, reinforced by prolonged censorship of public articulation of collective memories, had put the authenticity of individual experiences of Japanese colonization under suspicion. Problems surrounding the Taiwanese people's agency under Japanese rule naturally feature prominently in all these scholarly endeavors. And yet, as Chen Peifeng has demonstrated in *The Different Intentions behind the Semblance* of *"Douka": Language Policy, Modernization and Identity in Taiwan under Japanese Rule* (「同化」的同床異夢：日治時期臺灣的語言政策、近代化與認同; 2006), issues related to the "modernity problematic" are perhaps even more fundamental.[9] Chen's study examines the enthusiastic local response to the colonial government's promise of "modern civilization" as part of the *douka* (同化) process (which Chen has convincingly distinguished from Western colonial assimilation programs), and how Taiwanese writers had no qualms about assimilating Western-originated aesthetic resources through the Japanese. Intense negotiations took place, not as a self-conscious resistance to the colonial order but rather through interpositional struggles within the literary field, which in turn were complexly mediated through internal laws that governed its functioning.

Among other sources, the following case study draws heavily from the diaries of Lü Heruo 呂赫若 (1915–1950). Lü was a member of the second generation of colonial Taiwanese writers, which is to say those born roughly between 1905 and 1920, whose creative careers reached maturity during wartime. Born to a family of landowning gentry in central Taiwan, Lü attended Taizhong Normal School from age fifteen to twenty, and as soon as he finished six years of obligatory primary-school teaching, went to Tokyo to study music in 1940. Through his voice teacher, the well-known music educator Nagasaka Yoshiko 長坂好子 (1891–1970), Lü joined the Tokyo Takarazuka Theater Company (or Toho Opera Troupe; 東京宝塚劇場) as a chorus singer. Nonetheless, eking out a meager existence for a family of six in wartime Japan wasn't easy. Afflicted with a lung disease, Lü finally decided to take his pregnant wife and four children back to Taiwan in May 1942.

Over the next three years, before relocating to the countryside in December 1944 during the bombings of Taipei, Lü held various office jobs, performed as a singer, actively engaged in cultural activities, and became a passionately dedicated writer whose fiction earned praise from his peers as well as the recognition of esteemed Japanese critics. The life he led in this period was perhaps similar to that of writers in many twentieth-century urban centers, being packed with salon-style gatherings, drinking parties, and conversations centered on contemporary cultural affairs and the publication of their works, often through coterie journals they themselves put together. Joining Zhang Wenhuan 張文環 (1909–1978), an energetic leader in the field who had returned to Taiwan after a decade in Tokyo, Lü quickly became a core member of *Taiwan Literature* (臺灣文學), which Zhang had founded in 1941.

In the tumultuous years following the retrocession of Taiwan to the ROC, culminating in the February 28 Incident, Lü joined the communist underground and died near the revolutionary base of Luku after fleeing from Taipei in fear of being arrested. He has been celebrated in the post–martial law period as a victim of the White Terror. His preserved diaries from 1942 to 1944 coincided with the so-called golden age of colonial Taiwanese literature.[10] The meticulous accounts of his daily activities in the literary circle and records of his private thoughts and feelings are extremely valuable sources for our examination.

WARTIME TAIWAN'S RESTRUCTURED
LITERARY FIELD

The first half of the case study proposes that, despite their ostensibly arbitrary genesis, literary fields produced by drastic political changes in modern East Asia nonetheless may assume a semblance of normalcy in their structural constitution as an effect of their normative models. As a result, the extrinsically motivated power dynamics are still complexly and obligatorily mediated through the field's internal laws, especially those governing interpositional competition. This crucial process of *mediation*, mandated by the perfunctory normalcy of the field, is often overlooked by revisionist scholarly discourses, as these approaches tend to make no clear distinction between the literary field and the society at large.

When literary scholars first encountered the previously taboo category of Taiwanese literature—held suspicious during the martial law period for its alleged separatist implications—in the early 1990s, many were intrigued by the sudden surge of literary activity at the height of the Pacific War, between 1941 and the end of 1943, which also saw the intensification of war mobilization programs. This short period of time witnessed the production of impressive literary works, vibrant critical exchanges, and factional skirmishes in private and public venues that reached unprecedented levels of professionalism and sophistication. It may not be an exaggeration to say that the evolution of a local institution of modern literature that had begun in the mid-1920s reached maturity in these few years.

Most scholars dealing recently with literature from this period have focused on its sensitive political implications, as the label *kominka literature* suggests: namely, collaboration with or submission to coercive mobilization. In *The Different Intentions*, however, Chen Peifeng uses literary works from this period in a different way.[11] When Chen's book, an excellent study of the dynamic negotiations between colonial authority and the Taiwanese with respect to national language education throughout the fifty-year colonial period, reaches the 1940s, Chen abruptly switches from empirical documentation to the analysis of literary texts. The justification he gives is that as the *kominka* campaign intensified, most other forms of expression were suppressed. Here, Chen takes advantage of the inherent thematic indeterminacy and polysemous linguistic registers of literary works to conduct a diagnostic reading of the effects of the Japanese *douka* during this late stage of its enforcement. The Japanese language and many aspects of the Japanese lifestyle had not only encroached upon the daily lives of authors and other members of the Taiwanese educated class, they also performed a rich array of symbolic and indexical functions for their users.

Our inquiry takes a completely different angle. Evidence suggests that the context within which these writers engaged in creative and social activities strongly resembled a "normal" literary field in bourgeois society, with its publishing channels, interpersonal networks, and consecrating agencies. There was, however, the patent incongruity between this self-regulating field and the tumultuous historical context. To what extent did the literary field function according to its internal governing laws, and how were external forces refracted through these laws?

As commonly seen in East Asia's compressed, crisis-ridden course of modernization, some extrinsically motived policies resulted in a drastic restructuring of Taiwan's literary field in the early 1940s, not unlike the situation at other critical junctures, such as China's entrance into a socialist period in 1949, its return to the bourgeois mode of literary production in the early 1980s, or the Nationalist retreat to Taiwan. Scholars have convincingly argued that the revitalization of cultural activities in Taiwan in the early 1940s was an ironic spinoff of the Japanese war propaganda effort, which emphasized the role of local culture.[12] It dramatically reversed the low morale and productivity in Taiwan's literary circles that had prevailed since the banning of Chinese-language newspaper columns in February 1937. This artificially engineered field of cultural production quickly acquired a life of its own, driven by mechanisms internal to the field's structural operation. That Taiwan in the 1940s was subject to the double constraints of colonial subjugation and wartime mobilization only makes this contrived normality more salient.

If we look at Chen Peifeng's comprehensive treatment of how Japanese colonizers implemented the *douka* policies in Taiwan, there are many examples of similar unintended consequences.[13] Over the five decades of Japanese colonial rule, the idealistic vision of the Japanese educator Isawa Shūji 伊澤修二 (1851–1917), who established the national language education bureau in Taiwan, underwent numerous modifications and was repeatedly undermined by bureaucratically minded administrators who sought to preserve the basic interests of colonial domination as well as being constrained by financial and other pragmatic matters. Isawa's vision nonetheless set the parameters for later policies, because it built into the institution an ideology of linguistic nationalism and became a structural factor with which all successors were forced to reckon. One may easily find a connection between the European origin of the linguistic nationalism of Ueda Kazutoshi 上田萬年 (1867–1937), which Isawa inherited, and the Herderian approach to local culture that informed the Japanese war effort in the early 1940s. This point unquestionably reinforces the notion of far-reaching, though often unpredictable, influences of East Asian intellectuals' assimilation of Western high culture. What also deserves special attention is the significant role institutions played. The war assistance policies channeled symbolic and material resources into local cultural organizations, which were instrumental in giving birth to the literary revival, though their significance went beyond the original political design.

What were the structural factors built into the new cultural field at its genesis? What role did they play in shaping the vibrant literary culture that ensued? Can we talk about this literary culture not in narrowly defined political terms, but rather in terms of the evolution of a locally based modern institution of literature? As observed in every incidence of politically engendered restructuring of the cultural field, the immediate effect was felt in the field's membership qualifications, often resulting in violence against cohorts of former members of the field through exclusion or unfavorable changes in the rules of the game. In Taiwan, the establishment of a monolingual Japanese policy starting in 1937 altered the criteria determining who could become viable members of the literary field. Older generations of writers, especially those active in the May Fourth–inspired Chinese vernacular literary movement, saw a sudden devaluation of their cultural capital.[14] For other reasons, the left-wing writers, the backbone of Taiwan's literary activities during the 1930s, were also marginalized.[15] In their place, second-generation colonial Taiwanese who had received a complete Japanese-language education and ethnic Japanese residents (including those born in Taiwan) became privileged players. Given the aggressive *douka* practice, there was little doubt that the Japanese language would eventually replace Chinese and become the dominant linguistic medium of literary creation. This process, however, was artificially accelerated.

The circle in which Lü Heruo moved after returning to Taiwan included not only colleagues and business patrons (such as Zhang Wenhuan and Wang Jingquan 王井泉 [1905–1965] of *Taiwanese Literature*), but also fellow writers (such as Wu Yongfu 巫永福 [1913–2008], Long Yingzong 龍瑛宗 [1911–1999], Yang Yunping 楊雲萍 [1906–2000], Yang Kui 楊逵 [1905–1985], and Ye Shitao 葉石濤 [1925–2008]), a literary critic (Huang Deshi 黃得時 [1909–1999]), as well as painters (Li Shiqiao 李石樵 [1908–1995] and Yang Sanlang 楊三郎] 1907–1995]), a musician (Lü Quansheng 呂泉生 [1916–2008]), theater people (Song Feiwo 宋非我 [1916–1992] and Lin Boqiu 林博秋 [1920–1998]), and other elites (Chen Yisong 陳逸松 [1907–1999], Huang Qirui 黃啟瑞 [1910–1976], and Gu Zhenfu 辜振甫 [1917–2005]), among others. Nearly all those included in this cursory inventory belonged to a similar age cohort (a notable exception being the younger protégé of Nishigawa Mitsuru 西川滿 (1908–1999), Ye Shitao, which explains his role as a foe rather than friend in the diary), and many had studied in Japan. This group is precisely the artistically oriented counterpart of the middle-class consumers of Japanese-language magazines that Fujii Shozo, a well-known scholar in post–martial-law Taiwanese literary studies, sees as forming the breeding ground of a burgeoning sense of "Taiwanese consciousness."

Reacting to the resistance model hailed by the pioneering study of literature in Japan's former colonies by Ozaki Hotsuki 尾崎秀樹 (1928–1999), and drawing from Benedict Anderson and Jürgen Habermas, Fujii connects the reading public of Japanese magazines in Taiwan during the war period with the proto-nationalism of "Taiwanese consciousness."[16] The primary basis of this collective identity, he suggests, was their proficiency in Japanese, as the Japanese literacy rate reached 57 percent in 1941.[17] As the Pacific War increased their contact with their Asian neighbors, the Taiwanese developed a new model of Self/Other relations through their superior language skills, resulting in another example of the unintended consequences of the Japanese colonizers' attempts to promote a "national language."[18] What concerns us here is the fact that, focusing on literary reception and collective identity, Fujii does not draw a clear distinction between the literary field and the larger society. He thus misses the opportunity to explore the effects of the monopolizing use of Japanese as a literary medium on writers, and that of commenting on the status of the literary field as a whole.

The most significant effects of these Japanese policies involved the arbitrary redrawing of the boundaries of the literary field, as well as the recalibration of the value of the cultural capital of different cohorts of players. Nonetheless, it is important to recognize that as soon as the Japanese language became the common currency of literary commerce, it came to assume the function of an equalizer. Although Taiwanese literati outnumbered Japanese, the latter nevertheless possessed greater cultural and symbolic capital. At the same time, despite the disparity within the hierarchically structured colonial society, participants in the literature game had to play by the same rules, were given access to the same circulation channels, and were evaluated within the same system of consecration. This dramatically increased the degree of integration between writers and critics from the colonizing and the colonized classes, resulting in alliances and partisanships across racial lines. This was borne out by a series of developments in the field between 1941 and 1943.

After returning from Japan, Zhang Wenhuan joined the journal *Literary Taiwan* (文藝臺灣), led by Nishigawa Mitsuru. He found the journal's penchant for romantic exoticism disagreeable, however, and therefore in 1941, he and Uchiyama Atsumu 中山侑 (1909–1959), a Taiwan-born Japanese, left to found a rival journal, *Taiwan Literature*. Following the announcement of the winners of the First Taiwanese Culture Prize in February 1943, Kudo Yoshimi 工藤好美 (1898–1992), a literature professor at Taipei Imperial University, published an article praising the realistic style of Zhang Wenhuan's story "Night Monkeys" (夜猿) while obliquely taking issue with the novel *A Settlers' Village in the South* (南方移民村), authored by his colleague Hamada Hayao 濱田隼雄 (1909–1973).[19] The latter article triggered the well-known "*kuso* realism" (糞寫實主義) debate (literally, "shit realism") of 1943. Best known among the resulting fiery exchanges were Nishigawa's attack on the realist style of Zhang Wenhuan and Lü Heruo, and Yang Kui's vigorous rebuttal from the viewpoint of Proletarian Literature. A notable exception to the largely racially aligned partisanship between *Literary Taiwan* and *Taiwan Literature* was Ye Shitao, Nishigawa's young protégé, who penned a rejoinder in support of his mentor's tirade against "realism."[20]

Factional struggles and the development of partisanship are sure signs of maturation in a cultural field as it reaches a higher degree of diversification and pluralization in terms of its aesthetic positions. More symptomatic of the consolidation of a new, relatively autonomous cultural field is when its members begin to engage in efforts at self-legitimation. The appearance in May 1941 of the article "The Past, Present, and Future of Taiwanese Literature" (臺灣の文學的過現未) by Shimada Kinji 島田謹二 (1901–1993), a specialist in French literature at Taipei Imperial University, is a case in point. The article situated Taiwanese literature within the context of the Japanese empire with the label *waidi* (外地; literally "overseas territories," which is to say the colonies) as opposed to *neidi* (內地; literally "the interior," referring to Japan proper). A couple of years later, clearly in reply to Shimada, Huang Deshi published the essay "Outline of Taiwanese Literature" (臺灣文學史序說), offering an entirely different view of Taiwanese literary history.[21]

Wu Ruiren's comparison of the two different historiographical approaches in a 2009 article traces their theoretical underpinnings to European sources of inspiration: Shimada appealed to nineteenth-century European notion of realism as high art, while Huang appealed to the influential French theorist Hippolyte Taine's sociological positivistic concepts of national literary history. Like many scholars in Taiwan, Wu is not primarily interested in the genealogy of these concepts, but rather in the positions the authors of the articles occupied within the sociopolitical structure of the colony. Citing Kyoko Hashimoto 橋本恭子, Wu mentions in a footnote that although Shimada had been living in Taiwan for over ten years by the time he wrote the article, he had had little contact with local Taiwanese, the only exception being his student-friend Huang Deshi. [22] In Wu's view, strictly speaking, Shimada's account was therefore merely a history of "Japanese-language literature written in Taiwan," addressed primarily to his fellow Japanese readers.[23] This line of argument is undoubtedly justified, though if viewed from the angle of what Bourdieu calls a space of position-takings, as long as the article exerted a visible impact it must be deemed a valid and meaningful position-taking act *within* the field.[24] The particular nature of this exchange is significant in that it served as a clear index of the maturation of the literary field. When members of a field begin to engage in struggles for the right to define and control the legitimate discourse of their own activities, the field may be said to have reached a certain degree of self-awareness.

The preceding discussion suggests that in the early 1940s, Taiwan's newly restructured literary field quickly assumed a semblance of relative autonomy as characterized by the "normal" cultural field in a bourgeois society.[25] As has been commonly observed, modern East Asian cultural fields are often too intimately embedded in the general field of power, to the point that it becomes difficult for the cultural field's internal laws to maintain their integrity. What remain insufficiently explored, however, are the intermediaries that serve to connect these two apparently incongruous conditions. In 1940s Taiwan, what constituted the mechanisms through which the extrinsically motived power dynamics exerted their impact on individual literary agents, as well as on the status of the literary institution as a whole?

With the exclusion from the field of their immediate Taiwanese predecessors, the second generation of colonial Taiwanese writers, who were now the main productive force in the literary field, sought mentorship from certain senior Japanese critics and scholars, who also played the critical role of consecrating agents. According to Lü Heruo's diaries, he paid several visits to Kudo Yoshimi 工藤好美 (1898–1992), a literature professor at Taipei Imperial University, to seek advice on artistic matters, and he was also on friendly terms with another member of the literature faculty there, Takita Teiji 瀧田貞治 (1901–1946). Years later, in his afterword to Lü's published diaries (2004), Lü's son made a point of mentioning that Lü's literary reputation was consolidated after receiving a positive review by renowned Japanese writer and poet Jun Takami 高見順 (1907–1965).[26]

This, however, is not the whole picture. In contrast to the above-mentioned mentor-mentee relationships, there was strong antagonism between these rising Taiwanese writers and their Japanese counterparts such as Nishigawa Mitsuru and Hamada Hayao.

The *kuso* realism debate of 1943, indisputably a pivotal moment in colonial Taiwanese literary history, is a case in point. The majority of scholars on the subject have focused on the contention between the colonizers and the colonized, represented by *Literary Taiwan* and *Taiwan Literature*, led by Japanese and Taiwanese writers respectively, at a time of intensified *kominka* campaign and wartime mobilization.[27] At first sight, these views appear to confirm Bourdieu's contention that a cultural field's external forces only exert their impact through refraction by the field's internal governing laws, given that nearly all these scholars have underscored the assumption that the charged power relations were *mediated* through a rivalry between the aesthetic positions of romanticized exoticism versus nativist realism.[28] Following the thrust of the revisionist, localist discourse, these scholars have either explicitly or implicitly prioritized the colonizer-versus-colonized conflict surfacing under the pressure of the war to the extent that the complex phenomenon of mediation is treated as a matter of course.[29] It is precisely our contention, however, that without prying open the complex process of aesthetic mediation, it is impossible to have an accurate understanding of the interpositional struggles of the restructured literary field. Rather than focusing on the roles of literary agents as members of society, which is undeniably important to our understanding their places in the literary field's space of positions, we instead maintain that the aesthetic issues, issues pertaining to Bourdieu's "space of position-taking," occupy an even more central place within literary scholarship.[30]

The All-Important Aesthetic Issues

The second half of the case study focuses on aesthetic issues, and stresses the peculiar role played by artistic beliefs imported from the modern West, in particular the high-culture vision of "autonomous art" as described by Peter Bürger.[31] Insofar as shared artistic beliefs help underpin the structural coherence of the literary community, the multilayered genealogies of aesthetic resources that shape such beliefs in literary agents of modern East Asia ought to be seriously studied along with sociopolitically determined positional alliances. Ultimately, however, inherent discrepancies between the internal drive of imported models of literary institution and local historical realities inevitably produce compromises, as exemplified by the coping strategies adopted by writers in wartime Taiwan's politically subjugated literary field.

Let us begin with the problematic relations between textual models, such as those designated by the fluid term *realism*, and aesthetic conceptions, which generate beliefs in the literary agents in regard to the basic nature and function of literature. For instance, how is Yang Kui's leftist aesthetic ideology different from that of Lü Heruo and Zhang Wenhuan, whose realistic works he defended with such persuasiveness during the *kuso* realism debate? What is the relationship between the realism subscribed to by Lü and Zhang and that which was upheld by Shimada, who found works produced by local Taiwanese writers lacking in a categorical sense?

Lü Heruo's diaries offer solid evidence that the aesthetic conceptions to which he subscribed can be traced directly to those developed in Western bourgeois society. First, it should be noted that during the *kuso* realism debate, Lü Heruo, whose work was a target of Nishigawa's denigrating remarks, expressed his irritation in his diaries in an interesting way. Rather than defending realism, as did Yang Kui, Lü instead attributed Nishigawa's act of aggression to the latter's lack of real talent in creative writing—a condemnation that undercut the legitimacy of the criticism by denying Nishigawa's role as a competent player of the game.[32] This and dozens of other remarks on literature-related subjects in Lü's diaries illustrate his vocational vision. The assumption of shared criteria of excellence places a strong emphasis on the importance of peer recognition. Whereas mentions of formal attributes of literary works clearly were associated with the textual model of realism—which holds that literary works should be a truthful representation of the reality of life, the importance of structure in literary composition, and so forth— the normative qualities of a realist style were equated with ideals of literary excellence. Lü viewed literature as a self-sustaining and self-validating realm of activity, with its own principles of evaluation and dictates derived from its intrinsic logic. He portrayed his own literary pursuit as a quest for ideals that transcend mundane interests, defy short-term rewards, and demand relentless, persevering, and unsparing efforts at mastering and perfecting a set of skills specific to the art of literary writing.[33] The only utility that art might serve—according to Lü and his friend Zhang Wenhuan—was that it promised to elevate the cultural level of Taiwan society. This function, moreover, was built on the premise of universal standards. After reading works by Lao She 老舍, for instance, Lü was so impressed he declared that, from that point on, he would take Chinese literature as his model for writing novels, and Japanese and Western literature as his model for writing short stories. The international endeavor of creative writing was envisioned in a highly professional sense, a "republic of letters" (to borrow Pascale Casanova's phrase) based on a set of global criteria dictated by the genre rather than the author's place of origin.

These notions of art exhibit quintessential characteristics of Bürger's concept of the institution of art, the "autonomous status" of which was the evolutionary result of Western bourgeois society over several centuries;[34] they are also reminiscent of the habitus of artists who occupy the autonomous pole in Bourdieu's field of cultural production (adherence to the art-for-art's-sake principle; artistic production targeted at a subfield of the "restricted-scale," which is to say other producers), who accept the delayed reward and longer compensation cycle, and uphold a cultural elitism that is built into the hierarchized consecration system.[35] Significantly, they are at odds with the leftist vision of literature as a vehicle for proletarian revolution, as subscribed to by Yang Kui, but fraught with echoes of Shimada's conceptions of realism, which were embedded in the same tradition of European high culture. One may suggest that, despite the fact that Shimada, an advocate of *waidi* literature, and Lü and Zhang, representatives of the resistant localism, all occupied opposing positions in the literary field of the early 1940s, a more careful mapping of the aesthetic genealogies tells a story of aesthetic kinship.

Incidentally, Wu Ruiren's cogent analysis of the divergent historiographies laid out by Shimada and Huang Deshi drives home the distinctions between literary scholarship and other types of revisionist discourse. Wu points out an important contradiction in Shimada's argument: his advocacy of genuinely *realistic* writing is bound to give birth to a localist subject-position, which potentially will subvert the imperialist order that frames the notion of *waidi* literature. It is precisely against this dilemma that Wu sees in Huang's adaptation of Taine's ideas a creative solution: Huang redefines the localist Taiwanese culture as fundamentally pluralistic, constantly reincarnating itself through the incessant process of indigenization, of becoming Taiwanese, which finds echoes in contemporary theories of the fluid and multifaceted process of identity formation. Focusing on ties between the realistic mode of literary depiction and identification with local subjects, Wu expresses his perplexity over Shimada's use of W. B. Yeats as an example of realism achieved by writers of *waidi* literature, on the grounds that Yeats was well known for his subversive stance toward British domination. Shimada's alleged oversight largely depends on the assumption of a logical connection between the literary mode of realism and a resistant political position. A literary historian, however, is more likely to be intrigued by the discovery that the term *realism*, as it appeared in Shimada's article, served a dual function—simultaneously referring to a textual model and indexing a culminating aesthetic achievement. Insofar as they were conceived within the Western-originated aesthetic frame of autonomous art, the artists' empirical life must be separated out from their aesthetic products and the ideals they embodied. Lurking behind Shimada's article was an earnest call for the Japanese to achieve a high standard of literary achievement, and the normative qualities of realism stood for that ideal for its author as well as for writers like Lü and Zhang. In other words, they were products of disparate, yet congruent, literary genealogies. Decades later, modernism would replace the emblematic function of realism. In spite of their divergent textual models and the artistic procedures they entailed, the roles these concepts played in modern East Asian writers' quest for high culture were strikingly similar.

The revitalized literary field in wartime Taiwan was constituted by a new corps of writers occupying different positions, and yet there was something else that was essential to its structural coherence, which was a shared belief in aesthetic values. The fact that Japanese now became the sole legitimate linguistic medium of creative writing meant that it also served as a vehicle for Taiwanese writers to gain access to a set of Western-originated normative concepts of art. At this stage of literary evolution, such aesthetic visions were embodied through specific textual models—particularly realism—which to some extent replaced earlier literary paradigms inspired by May Fourth Enlightenment and leftist ideology.

We have seen how Lü and Zhang devoted their Tokyo years to reading literary works—Lü's diaries mention works of French, German, British, and American as well as Japanese and Chinese origin—and to immersion in a modern aesthetic tradition with clearly conceived goals of cultivating sophisticated taste and mastering skills of creative writing that would qualify them as writers. The notion of writers as artists, along with the aforementioned presuppositions about the nature of art, was an essential part of the imported category of literature in modern East Asia. Aside from the rich prestige associated with returned students from abroad in those days, the fact that Lü, Zhang, Wu Yongfu, and Weng Nao 翁鬧, among others, developed a literary habitus by internalizing a set of beliefs shared by people like Shimada and Kudo Yoshimi should be seen as a significant reason for their emergence as leading authors in the newly con-structed literary field.

If we accept these propositions, then it makes sense to shift our attention from the literary works' reflective and political function, and instead consider how they were shaped in the first place. Indeed, to chart the convoluted genealogies of literary genres, schools, and other types of influence and to ascertain which lineages may have crossed borders are among the most daunting tasks faced by literary historians of modern East Asia. The large number of debates and polemics found in its literary histories are driven not only by nativist and traditionalist reactions to Western-originated influences, but also intermix and become conjoined at different levels and locations, as shadows, extensions, or "proxy wars" that rippled out from their places of origin (think of the many versions of the left-versus-right debate). Japanese literary scholar Tarumi Chie 垂水千惠 has suggested that the *kuso* realism debate was an extension of a Japanese literary polemic between the Japanese Romantic School and the People's Bookstore.[36] In her acclaimed study *The Path of Thorns: Literary Activities and Cultural Resistance of Taiwanese Students in Japan* (荊棘之道：台灣旅日青年的文學活動與文化抗爭), Liu Shuqing draws a connection between artist-poet-leftist activist Wang Baiyuan 王白淵 (1902–1965), who went to Tokyo to study art in 1921, and another Taiwanese student who studied literature in Japan in the 1930s, Zhang Wenhuan.[37] According to Liu, the link between them was the short-lived Taiwanese Art Research Club and the journal *Formosa* (福爾摩沙; 1932–1934), which attracted police action because of its members' involvement in leftist activities, affecting the careers of both Wang and Zhang. Wang went to Tokyo as a gifted, sensitive, and starry-eyed youth from the col-ony in search of models of modern civilization, only to be awakened to the ugly truth of colonialism and imperialism, the twin ills of modernity, which turned his pilgrim-age into a tortuous journey of leftist colonial resistance. Liu argues for the potency of Wang's moderate leftist legacy carried over by Zhang up to the 1940s, when he returned to Taiwan and emerged as a leader among Taiwanese writers.

With a wealth of empirical data, Liu has opened up an extremely fruitful direction for studies of colonial Taiwanese literature, which, by examining the trajectories of a succession of positions taken by key literary agents (writers), aims at substantiating claims of literary genealogy that had previously been vaguely assumed. A Bourdieuian approach could also complement the insights of Liu and other scholars by calling atten-tion to the "genealogies of aesthetic resources." More specifically, shifting attention from a "space of positions" to a "space of concrete manifestations of acts of position-taking" may allow us to track the trajectories along which aesthetic resources traveled via textual models of realism, proletarian literature, romantic exoticism, and so forth, as well as artistic conceptions pertaining to the function of art. Severed from the social context of their places of origin, the Western-originated aesthetic resources traveled

through East Asia via circuitous routes, and the way they participated in new relationships in local cultural production could not always be determined by a known set of
relations between the literary agents, which is to say between Japanese colonizer and
colonized Taiwanese (Zhang, Lü, and Shimada), or by alliances formed in debates or
polemics (Lü and Yang Kui). We should be able to pry open the leftism-resistance-real-
ism trio that has mostly been taken for granted in existing scholarship and study the
case of wartime Taiwan within a larger regional context, as the multilayered genealogies of aesthetic positions are a defining feature of the second-order literary project
of East Asia's building its own institution of modern literature via borrowed aesthetic
resources. To varying degrees, all modern East Asian literary histories face issues pertaining to the precarious status of artistic autonomy in a politically subjugated cultural
field and the coping strategies of writers. In an artificially engineered, quasi-autonomous cultural field flanked by menacing political threats, participating members are
constantly navigating a tug-of-war between political and cultural legitimacy. Rather
than dismissing such fields as aberrant, it is more useful to analyze their special mode
of existence and the particular mechanisms deployed by writers to sustain their functioning. Otherwise, it would be difficult to account for the impressive literary accom-
plishments achieved in Taiwan under martial law and in Maoist China, when cultural
activities were constrained by politically imposed parameters that delimited the per-
missible scope of artistic expression.

Works by Zhou Wanyao and Liu Shuqin on Taiwanese cultural activities during the
period of Japanese war mobilization have a significant bearing on this line of inquiry.
Departing from a commonly adopted strategy of exonerating cultural agents who had
been stigmatized as collaborators by interpreting their work as surreptitious forms
of resistance or even as deliberate acts of appropriation, Zhou and Liu instead stress
the biopolitical dimension of lived experience. Zhou's oral history project, based on
interviews with older Taiwanese who had lived through the period, clearly aims at
foregrounding the discrepancies between the sensory and material nature of personal
memories and the prefabricated interpretive schemas sprung from larger sociopolitical realities. This point is underscored by her book title's reference to a military song
popular in the 1940s, "Marching to the Sea" (Umi Yukaba), which was etched in the
memories of those who lived through that period. Zhou's examination of the middle-
school textbooks that featured Japanese historical figures as models of a universal
code of behavior (such as honesty) or culturally specific virtues (such as loyalty to the
emperor) share the same thesis: ideological indoctrination and war propaganda do not
function solely through the ideational content of the messages, but also through registers of a sensory and material nature that came to shape notions of self and identity of
Taiwan's so-called lost generation.

Just as Zhou's work assumed a landmark status in rectifying the pervasive bias
toward the war period, Liu's sympathetic study of Zhang Wenhuan's participation in
the *kominka* war mobilization activities as a member of the colonial government's
propaganda task force is significant in that it tips the balance of the post–martial law
kominka controversy and helps to promote a discourse that stresses Zhang's role as

a leader of localist literary resistance. How does Liu's account succeed in offsetting Zhang's well-documented activities of assisting in the war effort? To be sure, these were involuntary acts of compliance, and yet they inevitably undermine any positive image of Zhang's role. What is more, whereas Zhou studies the structure of feeling of the period by focusing on the war generation of average Taiwanese, whose formative years coincided with a period in which school textbooks turned toward promoting Japanese nationalism and who were immersed in the fascist euphoria of patriotism at a more impressionable age, Liu's work deals with writers who were in their thirties and presumably more mature.

In a sense, Liu's meticulous account of Zhang's daily engagements in networking, giving speeches, writing media columns, and making trips to local communities as a government-enlisted mobilizing agent offer a vivid portrayal of the workings of an extremely common coping mechanism of people who suffer political subjugation of any sort—namely to bracket judgmental responses to uncontrollable factors that impinge upon one's life so as to ensure its normal function, despite the restrictions. The diaries of Lü Heruo also offered classic examples. Whereas Lü is best known today as a leftist martyr of the White Terror, his political activism did not begin until after the war. During wartime, although Lü was not specifically recruited to provide high-profile public services like Zhang, as a celebrity and government employee he regularly sang on public occasions and participated in cultural activities that were part of the war propaganda program. Yet it was evident that he regarded these as unwelcome nuisances to be put up with, along with other mundane necessities of life, in order to be able to dedicate his heart and soul to fiction writing. He was obviously annoyed by the tedious work involved in the assignments and was more than ready to dismiss them, but occasionally he was also pleased by an inspired performance he or other people were able to deliver. Asked by his friend Zhang Wenhuan to attend the notorious Writers' Congress of Greater East Asia, Lü declined, because he had no desire to revisit Tokyo. An ambivalently worded diary entry seems to imply he had an appointment with a government censor, possibly having to do with publishing matters—if true, Lü's eminently business-as-usual attitude about it is noteworthy. Another notable incident was the exasperation Lü expressed after receiving a Volunteer Soldier recruiting notice sent to his office; he found it too blatant, unbefitting a civilized country, which made him sound like a liberal living in the modern West.

Details of such coping mechanisms undoubtedly strike a universalist tone, and acknowledgement of this universality helps us to come to terms with the realities of quasi-autonomous cultural fields. In such fields, intrusive forces from external fields of power (especially the political field) can be bracketed and dismissed by writers for the sake of maintaining a semblance of normalcy in the field, which in turn sustains its productive functions. However, there is always a challenge, in that the boundary between political legitimacy and cultural legitimacy threatens to become blurred, especially when the society enters a state of exception—either in times of emergency, such as war or enemy occupation, or in times of ultranationalist or ultraleftist ideological dominance, such as the *kominka* period or the Cultural Revolution—during which it becomes difficult to maintain even the bare bones of normality, and when the political and cultural fields collapse into one. Under such unusual circumstances, when individuals are subjected to the effects of the pervasive "structure of feeling" of the time, politically derived legitimacy principles often acquire a personal dimension and infiltrate individual writers' vocational visions. Examples abound in different historical periods, in East Asia and elsewhere. In our case, when Lü went to Taipei Imperial University to seek advice from Kudo Yoshimi and came back with doubts about whether it was indeed time for him to write literary works that "benefit our time," he was not submitting to any tangible pressure or coercion, or compromising his integrity for external motives (such as fame or recognition). Yet the dubious ending of "Clear Autumn" (清秋), the title story of Lü's collection published in 1944, suggests that in the end he made compromises. In "Clear Autumn," a young Taiwanese man who recently graduated from medical school in Japan returns to Taiwan and wavers between the pursuit of progressive ideals and a practical career as a doctor in his rural hometown; the latter choice would have the added benefit of allowing him to fulfill his filial duties. The decision is made *for* him through a deus ex machina, in that two people who had stood in the way of his opening a clinic are suddenly recruited to join the war in the South, a mission described as profoundly uplifting. A subplot of the story also highlights the tantalizing excitement that the protagonist's younger brother feels about his new assignment by the pharmaceutical company to a post in the South. That the South, as the site of Japan's newly acquired colonies and of dangerous battles in an imperialist war on the brink of defeat, stands for such unequivocally positive qualities as adventure, hope, promise, patriotism, and the opportunity to fulfill progressive ideals and youthful ambitions is obviously the result of an act of will on the author's part. Critics who apply aesthetic standards to which Lü himself earnestly subscribed are likely to interpret this ending as a structural flaw. For us, it is an exemplary dilemma faced by writers caught in the precarious situation of the "cultural legitimacy principle" who are losing the battle in times of emergency.

RECAPITULATIONS

Bourdieu argues that the field of cultural production is governed by its own functioning laws and that, historically speaking, cultural fields in Western capitalist societies of the last two centuries have moved toward greater autonomy.[38] Bürger maintains that the institution of art in bourgeois society since around 1800 has increasingly assumed an autonomous status.[39] Drawing from these theories and enlarging the scope of a world-literary phenomenon described by Moretti as "a compromise between a western formal influence (usually French or English) and local materials," this chapter has explored some special modalities found in East Asian societies as they built their own modern literary institutions, following established Western models, which had arrived around the second half of the nineteenth century.[40] As a result of its relatively late start, the East Asian modernization process is compressed, and the course by which various modern institutions—including the institution of literature—are entrenched in local settings is frequently disrupted by external forces, reoriented into drastically different paradigms, and typically fraught with supposedly aberrant structural elements. Using a special literary phenomenon in wartime Taiwan as material for a case study, and in dialogue with some recent scholarship on the Japanese colonization of the island, this chapter argues that these seemingly deviant traits are in fact quite common in the cultural history of modern East Asia. This hypothesis, of course, may only be validated if we apply the sociologically oriented analytical schemes employed here to other periods of East Asian literary history that appear to exhibit some structural affinities, such as Korea's colonial period, martial-law Taiwan, China's socialist era, Shanghai under Japanese occupation, and Japan under Allied occupation.

NOTES

1. Pascale Casanova, *The World Republic of Letters*, trans. M. B. DeBevoise (Cambridge: Harvard University Press, 2004), 87.
2. Moretti, *Distant Reading* (London: Verso, 2013), 50.
3. Ideas of Peter Bürger adopted in this chapter are mostly taken from *Theory of the Avant-garde* (Minneapolis: University of Minnesota Press, 1984) and *The Institutions of Art*, coauthored with Christa Bürger (Lincoln: University of Nebraska Press, 1992). Applications of Pierre Bourdieu's concepts are primarily based on essays collected in *The Field of Cultural Production: Essays on Art and Literature* (New York: Columbia University Press, 1993).
4. Bürger and Bürger, *The Institutions of Art*.
5. For a general discussion of cultural developments in modern East Asia as exemplified by the case of Taiwan, see Sung-sheng Yvonne Chang, "Literary Taiwan in East Asian Context," in *The Columbia Sourcebook of Literary Taiwan* (New York: Columbia University Press, 2014), 1–36.
6. Such revisionist discourses are to be emphatically distinguished from the postwar controversies of the right-wing stigmatization of "wartime collaboration" and the left-wing critiques of militarism.
7. Over the *longue durée*, all imported cultures become indigenized under normal circumstances and over extended periods of time. In the parts of the world that have belatedly entered modernity, however, the modern institutions that had already been substantially shaped by the hegemonic Western culture have had to be assimilated under unfavorable circumstances, lacking sufficient time and stability.
8. All of these works are solidly grounded in meticulous archive-based research and supported by cogent theoretical arguments. Fujii is a Japanese national and a professor of Chinese literature at Tokyo University. Zhou, Chen, and Wu all work at Academia Sinica in Taipei, Taiwan. Zhou is a Yale-trained historian; Chen got his PhD from Tokyo University, where he studied under Wakabayashi Masahiro 若林正丈, Japan's leading scholar of modern Taiwan; and Wu got his doctoral degree in political science from the University of Chicago. Liu got her PhD in Chinese literature at National Tsing Hua University in Hsinchu, Taiwan, and has studied with such pioneers of colonial Taiwanese literary studies as Lin Ruiming 林瑞明 and Chen Wanyi 陳萬益. Slightly

before or concurrent with the appearance of critical scholarship like theirs, some important groundwork was done, consisting of large-scale translation projects, led by such
scholars as Chen Wanyi and Huang Yingzhe 黃英哲, that rendered primary sources
of Taiwanese literature from the colonial period available in Chinese. A particularly
valuable source of reference for the present study is Huang's edited volume, *Rizhi shiqi
Taiwan wenyi pinglun ji: Zazhi bian* 日治時期臺灣文藝評論集: 雜誌篇 [Major texts
of Taiwanese literary criticism: The Japanese colonial period, 1912–1945: Periodicals]
(Tainan: Guojia Taiwan wenxue guan, 2006).

9. Chen Peifeng 陳培豐, *"Tonghua" de tong chuang yi meng: Rizhi shiqi Taiwan de yuyan zhengce,
   jindaihua yu rentong* 「同化」的同床異夢: 日治時期臺灣的語 言政策、近代化與認同
   [The different intentions behind the semblance of "douka": The language policy, modernization and identity in Taiwan during the period of Japanese rule] (Taipei: Maitian, 2006).

10. After Lü's death, his family burned all his manuscripts due to the chilling political climate
    of the 1950s. They later explained that they only saved the diaries because they contained
    the birth information of his children. These diaries only resurfaced after the lifting of
    martial law and were translated into Chinese and published in the early 2000s.

11. Chen Peifeng, *"Tonghua" de tong chuang yi meng.*

12. Scholars have specifically pointed out links between the revitalization of Taiwan's cultural
    scene and the establishment of the Imperial Rule Assistance Association (大政翼贊會/
    大政翼贊会), which was created by Prime Minister Fumimaro Konoe on October 12,
    1940, and evolved into a ruling political party. The Association was instrumental in
    Japan's total war effort.

13. Chen Peifeng, *"Tonghua" de tong chuang yi meng.*

14. The ability to write in modern Chinese vernacular was an acquired skill for Taiwanese,
    whose mother tongue was often a different variety of Chinese, but it was obviously easier
    for those old enough to have attended the *shufang* (書房), an equivalent of *sishu* (私塾),
    or private tutorial classes for gentry-class children to prepare them for the Civil Service
    Examination.

15. The traditionalist literati by this time were not merely marginalized, but excluded from
    the modern literary institution.

16. Ozaki Hotsuki was a Japanese literary critic who was born in Taiwan and repatriated to
    Japan after the war. His work in the 1960s on literature in Japan's former colonies was
    among the earliest postwar studies of Taiwanese colonial literature. See Ozaki Hotsuki
    尾崎秀樹, *Jiu zhimindi wenxue de yanjiu* 舊殖民地文學的研究 [A study of literature of
    Japan's former colonies] (Taipei: Renjian, 2004 [1971]).

17. See Fujii Shozo 藤井省三, *Taiwan wenxue zhe yi bainian* 台灣文學這一百年 [The last
    hundred years of Taiwanese literature], trans. Zhang Jilin 張季琳 (Taipei: Yifang, 2004),
    46. While this number was convincingly challenged by Zhou Wanyao as somewhat
    inflated, the claim that members of an expanded educated class derived a sense of supe-
    riority from their Japanese-language proficiency seems tenable.

18. This emphatically included Chinese, as in one example given by Fujii featuring the
    superior linguistic skills of the Taiwanese recruited to serve as interpreters during the
    Pacific War.

19. Huang Huizhen 黃惠禎, *Zouyi pipan jingshen de duanjie: Siling niandai Yang Kui
    wenxue yu sixiang de lishi yanjiu* 左翼批判精神的鍛接: 四〇年代楊逵文學與思想
    的歷史研究 [The forging of leftist critique: Research on the writing and thought of Yang
    Kui during the 1940s] (Taipei: Xiuwei: 2009), 165.

20. Ye would later emerge as a prominent figure and a converted "realist" in postwar and especially post-martial-law Taiwan's literary scene.

21. See Huang Deshi 黃得時, "Taiwan wenxue shi xushuo" 臺灣文學史序說 [Preface to a history of Taiwanese literature], in *Riben tongzhi qi Taiwan wenxue wenyi pinglunji* 日本統治期台灣文學台文藝文評論集 [Criticism on Taiwanese literature under Japanese rule], ed. Nakajima Toshio 中島利郎, He Yuangong 河原功, and Shimomura Sakujiro 下村作次郎 (Tokyo: Lüyin shufang, 2001), 86–95.

22. Wu Ruiren 吳叡人, "Chongceng tuzhehua xia de lishi yishi: Rizhi houqi Huang Deshi yu Shimada Kinji de Taiwan wenxue shilun de chubu bijiao fenxi" 重層土著化下的歷史意識：日治後期黃得時與島田謹二的台灣文學史論的初步比較分析 [Historical consciousness of multilayered indigenization: A preliminary comparative analysis of the literary history discourses of Huang Te-shih and Shimada Kinji]. In *Taiwan shi yanjiu* 臺灣史研究 [Research on Taiwanese history] 6.3 (September 2009): 147.

23. See Wu Ruiren, *Historical Consciousness*, 138.

24. According to Bourdieu, literary agents who occupy available positions in a cultural field are both empowered and restrained by these positions, in the sense that the assets and properties associated with the positions serve to orient their aesthetic choices and position-taking strategies. See Bourdieu, *The Field of Cultural Production*.

25. Here literature, as a modern social institution, is conceived as embedded in a subsystem of modernity, the institution of the market. See Anthony Giddens, *The Consequences of Modernity* (Stanford: Stanford University Press, 1991).

26. See Lü Heruo 呂赫若, *Lü Heruo riji: (1942–1944 nian) Zhongyi ben* 呂赫若日記：(一九四二–一九四四年) 中譯本 [Lü Heruo's diary: (1922–1944) Chinese translation], trans. Zhong Ruifang 鍾瑞芳 (Tainan: Guojia Taiwan wenxue guan, 2004), 477.

27. Huang Huizhen, *The Forging of Leftist Critique*, 150.

28. Bourdieu, *The Field of Cultural Production*.

29. Even Fujii Shozo, who interprets the "*kuso* realism" debate as a lively interaction among members of the field made possible by a thriving modern literary publishing industry, stresses the receptive rather than the productive side, ultimately in support of the agency thematic.

30. Bourdieu, *The Field of Cultural Production*.

31. Bürger, Peter. *Theory of the Avant-garde*.

32. See Lü Heruo, *Lü Heruo's Diary*, 339.

33. For instance, Lü's diaries repeatedly mentions the pains associated with writing: "One ought to pursue literature at the cost of excruciating pains" (338); "I must write in large quality, with great diligence" (343).

34. Bürger and Bürger, *The Institutions of Art*.

35. Bourdieu, *The Field of Cultural Production*.

36. Huang Huizhen points out that, according to Tarumi Chie, the debate about *kuso* realism is to be seen as a continuation of the debate between Japanese romanticism and the People's Bookstore; see *The Forging of a Leftist Critique*, 164–165. See also Tarumi Chie 垂水千惠, "Kuso Realism lunzheng zhi beijing: Yu *Renmin wenku* pipan zhi guanxi wei zhongxin" 「糞 realism」論爭之背景——與《人民文庫》批判之關係為中心 [The background for the debate about shit realism: The criticism of *The People's Bookstore*], in *Yuelang qianxing de yidai: Ye Shitao ji qi tong shidai zuojia wenxue guoji xueshu yantaohui lunwenji* 越浪前行的一代：葉石濤及其同時代作家文學國際學術研討會論文集 [A generation of overcoming hardship: An international conference on Ye Shitao and his contemporaries], ed. Zheng Jiongming 鄭炯明 (Kaohsiung: Chunhui, 2002), 31–50.

37. Liu Shuqin 柳書琴, *Jingji zhi dao: Taiwan lu Ri qingnian de wenxue huodong yu wen-hua kangzheng* 荊棘之道：臺灣旅日青年的文學活動與文化抗爭 [The path of thorns: Literary activities and cultural resistance of Taiwanese students in Japan] (Tapei: Lianjing, 2009).
38. Bourdieu, *The Field of Cultural Production*.
39. Bürger, *Theory of the Avant-garde*.
40. Moretti, *Distant Reading*, 50.

WORKS CITED

Bourdieu, Pierre. *The Field of Cultural Production: Essays on Art and Literature.* New York: Columbia University Press, 1993.

Bürger, Peter. *Theory of the Avant-garde.* Minneapolis: University of Minnesota Press, 1984.

Bürger, Peter, and Christa Bürger. *The Institutions of Art.* Trans. Loren Kruger. Lincoln: University of Nebraska Press, 1992.

Casanova, Pascale. *The World Republic of Letters.* Trans. M. B. DeBevoise. Cambridge: Harvard University Press, 2004.

Chang, Sung-sheng Yvonne. "Literary Taiwan in East Asian Context." In *The Columbia Sourcebook of Literary Taiwan.* New York: Columbia University Press, 2014. 1–36.

Chang, Sung-sheng Yvonne. "Taiwanese New Literature and the Colonial Context: A Historical Survey." In *Taiwan: A New History.* Ed. Murray Rubinstein. Armonk, NY: M. E. Sharpe, 1999. 261–274.

Chen Peifeng 陳培豐. *"Tonghua" de tong chuang yi meng: Rizhi shiqi Taiwan de yuyan zhengce, jindaihua yu rentong* 「同化」的同床異夢：日治時期臺灣的語言政策、近代化與認同 [The different intentions behind the semblance of "douka": The language policy, modernization and identity in Taiwan during the period of Japanese rule]. Taipei: Maitian, 2006.

Fujii Shozo 藤井省三. *Taiwan wenxue zhe yi bainian* 台灣文學這一百年 [The last hundred years of Taiwanese literature]. Trans. Zhang Jilin 張季琳. Taipei: Yifang, 2004.

Giddens, Anthony. *The Consequences of Modernity.* Stanford: Stanford University Press, 1991.

Huang Deshi 黃得時. "Taiwan wenxue shi xushuo" 臺灣文學史序說 [Preface to a history of Taiwanese literature]. In *Riben tongzhi qi Taiwan wenxue wenyi pinglunji* 日本統治期台灣文學台文藝文評論集 [Criticism on Taiwanese literature under Japanese rule]. Ed. Nakajima Toshio 中島利郎, He Yuangong 河原功, and Shimomura Sakujiro 下村作次郎. Tokyo: Lüyin shufang, 2001. 86–95. First published in *Taiwan wenxue* 臺灣文學 [Taiwanese literature] 3.3 (July 31, 1943).

Huang Huizhen 黃惠禎. *Zouyi pipan jingshen de duanjie: Siling niandai Yang Kui wenxue yu sixiang de lishi yanjiu* 左翼批判精神的鍛接：四〇年代楊逵文學與思想的歷史研究 [The forging of leftist critique: Research on the writing and thought of Yang Kui during the 1940s]. Taipei: Xiuwei: 2009.

Huang Yingzhe 黃英哲, ed. *Rizhi shiqi Taiwan wenyi pinglun ji: Zazhi bian* 日治時期臺灣文藝評論集: 雜誌篇 [Major texts of Taiwanese literary criticism: The Japanese colonial period, 1912–1945: Periodicals]. Tainan: Guojia Taiwan wenxue guan, 2006.

Liu Shuqin 柳書琴. *Jingji zhi dao: Taiwan lu Ri qingnian de wenxue huodong yu wenhua kang-zheng* 荊棘之道：臺灣旅日青年的文學活動與文化抗爭 [The path of thorns: Literary activities and cultural resistance of Taiwanese students in Japan]. Tapei: Lianjing, 2009.

Lü Heruo 呂赫若. *Lü Heruo riji: (1942–1944 nian) Zhongyi ben* 呂赫若日記：（一九四二-一九四四年)中譯本 [Lü Heruo's diary: (1922–1944) Chinese translation]. Trans. Zhong Ruifang 鍾瑞芳. Tainan: Guoli Taiwan wenxue guan, 2004.

Moretti, Franco. *Distant Reading*. London: Verso, 2013.

Ozaki Hotsuki 尾崎秀樹. *Jiu zhimindi wenxue de yanjiu* 舊殖民地文學的研究 [A study of literature of Japan's former colonies]. Taipei: Renjian, 2004 [1971].

Shimada Kinji 島田謹二. "Taiwan no wenxue de guo xian wei" 臺灣の文學的過現未 [The past, present, and future of Taiwan literature]. In *Rizhi shiqi Taiwan wenyi pinglun ji: Zazhi bian* 日治時期臺灣文藝評論集. 雜誌篇 [Major texts of Taiwanese literary criticism: The Japanese colonial period, 1912–1945: Periodicals]. Ed. Huang Yingzhe 黃英哲. Tainan: Guojia Taiwan wenxue guan, 2006. 97–116. First published in *Wenyi Taiwan* 文藝臺灣 [Literary Taiwan] 2.2 (May 20, 1941).

Tarumi Chie 垂水千惠. "Kuso Realism lunzheng zhi beijing: Yu *Renmin wenku* pipan zhi guanxi wei zhongxin" 「糞 realism」論爭之背景——與《人民文庫》批判之關係為中心 [The background for the debate about shit realism: The criticism of *The People's Bookstore*]. In *Yuelang qianxing de yidai: Ye Shitao ji qi tong shidai zuojia wenxue guoji xueshu yantaohui lunwenji* 越浪前行的一代：葉石濤及其同時代作家文學國際學術研討會論文集 [A generation of overcoming hardship: An international conference on Ye Shitao and his contemporaries]. Ed. Zheng Jiongming 鄭炯明. Kaohsiung: Chunhui, 2002. 31–50.

Wu Ruiren 吳叡人. "Chongceng tuzhehua xia de lishi yishi: Rizhi houqi Huang Deshi yu Shimada Kinji de Taiwan wenxue shilun de chubu bijiao fenxi" 重層土著化下的歷史意識：日治後期黃得時與島田謹二的台灣文學史論的初步比較分析 [Historical consciousness of multilayered indigenization: A preliminary comparative analysis of the literary history discourses of Huang Te-shih and Shimada Kinji]. In *Taiwan shi yanjiu* 臺灣史研究 [Research on Taiwanese history] 6.3 (September 2009): 133–163.

Zhou Wanyao 周婉窈. *Haixing xi de niandai: Riben zhimin tongzhi moqi Taiwan shi lunji* 海行兮的年代：日本殖民統治末期臺灣史論集 [The era of "marching to the sea": Essays on Taiwanese history toward the end of Japanese colonial rule]. Taipei: Yunchen wenhu, 2002.

CHAPTER 2.7

....

SONG OF EXILE, FOUR-WAY VOICE

The Blood-and-Sweat Writings of Southeast Asian Migrants in Taiwan

....

CHANG CHENG AND LIAO YUN-CHANG

ORIGINALLY a journalist in her home country Vietnam, Phạm Thảo Vân 范草雲 went to Russia to find work, and subsequently moved to Taiwan. She has definite leadership qualities, and in 2006, when she was working as a household assistant for a Taipei Municipal community, while taking her elderly clients out for walks every afternoon she coordinated with other Vietnamese workers to establish the Thảo Vân Dance Troupe. The troupe was frequently invited to perform at multicultural events organized by the Taipei municipal government, and in this way the Vietnamese workers were able to earn some extra money.

In 2006, the cover of the inaugural issue of the multilingual migrant newspaper *Four-Way Voice* (*Sifang Bao*, 四方報)—of which one of us, Chang, was the co-founding editor—featured a photograph of the troupe performing in Taipei's 228 Peace Memorial Park.[1] When Phạm Thảo Vân saw the image, she sent the newspaper a handwritten letter in beautiful Vietnamese script, asking:

> Why is it that, here in Taiwan where there are so many people from Vietnam, we do not have a newspaper that we can call our own? Sometimes I go to various bookstores looking for Vietnamese-language newspapers and periodicals, but always return empty-handed. A handful of Vietnamese newspapers and magazines are sometimes passed around between friends, but they are all tattered and the print is faded. Whenever I see these familiar Vietnamese words, however, I always feel a keen sense of joy, as though I had a close friend by my side. Today, the appearance of *Four-Way Voice* is like a dream come true. A voice belonging to the Vietnamese people has finally been born.

Pham's letter captures in miniature a set of questions concerning the status of migrant literature in contemporary Taiwan, and also of migrant literature in general.

The Southeast Asian migrants who began to arrive in Taiwan in ever-greater numbers around 1990 often live in an environment where they are linguistically isolated, but they nevertheless use their blood, sweat, and tears to write about their daily labor, which goes unnoticed by mainstream society. For instance, between September of 2006 and 2013, the *Four-Way Voice* received more than 18,000 handwritten letters and pictures, most of which were from Vietnamese migrants living and working in Taiwan. Meanwhile, other Taiwan media outlets that use Southeast Asian languages, such as the Central Broadcasting Station, the Tagalog journal *The Migrants*, and the Indonesian language journals *Intai* and *Indo Suara*, also received countless letters from their readers. These letters function as an invaluable historical record that Taiwan's Chinese-language sources are unable to replicate, and therefore should definitely be included in the category of Taiwan literature.

According to recent census figures, in 2014 there were about 23 million people living in Taiwan, including about 500,000 migrant workers and another 200,000 marriage migrants from Southeast Asia. Does what these migrants write in non-Chinese languages (including Vietnamese, Thai, Indonesian, Cambodian, and Filipino) count as Taiwan literature? Chen Fangming 陳芳明, a professor of Taiwan literature at National Chengchi University, has proposed that "irrespective of an author's ethnicity, as long as their work expresses emotions or memories associated with this territory of Taiwan, it should count as Taiwan literature."[2] We agree, and would classify Taiwan literature as including all literature having a connection to the territory of Taiwan and its people. By this definition, the rubric of Taiwan literature would definitely include writings by migrants from Southeast Asia living and working in Taiwan. More generally, all literary works capable of enriching Taiwan literature should be similarly welcomed—even ones written in languages that may be unfamiliar to mainstream Taiwan society.

MIGRANTS IN TAIWAN

In the initial decades following World War II, Taiwan was a net source of out-migration, but as its economy began to expand it developed a large demand for additional labor, and therefore in 1989 the government approved a new regulation regarding foreign migrants. Around this time, lower-class Taiwan men began encountering difficulties in finding spouses, and transnational marriages became increasingly common. Most of the world's prosperous regions have encountered a similar phenomenon, and other Sinophone societies, including not only Mainland China but also Hong Kong, Macao, Singapore, and Malaysia, have large migrant populations. However, national, linguistic, racial, gender, and class differences, together with rapidly established transnational marriages and mutually suspicious relations between employees and employers, often make it difficult for these migrants to obtain social acceptance and recognition in their new communities. Taiwan's government has not responded in a timely fashion to this growing phenomenon, and consequently the basic needs of its migrant community have not been met.

At present, most of Taiwan's Southeast Asian population consists of foreign students, marriage migrants, and migrant workers, but the willingness of these migrants to "speak" in native-language media such as *Four-Way Voice* is contingent on a number of factors. Out of the 18,000 letters *Four-Way Voice* received between 2006 and 2013, for instance, very few were from foreign students and less than 10 percent were from marriage migrants; the vast majority were from migrant workers, particularly household domestics and caregivers.

To begin with, most of the foreign students in Taiwan either come from relatively well-off families or are on school fellowships. Their Chinese and English is relatively good, and since virtually all of them can use the Internet it is not difficult for them to stay in touch with their home countries. Moreover, there is an obvious social gap between the foreign students and other migrant groups in Taiwan, and therefore they rarely associate with one another. The reason so few of the letters were from foreign students, accordingly, is that these students have many sources of information at their disposal, such as student associations and foreign student websites, and therefore they don't need a foreign-language periodical like *Four-Way Voice*.

The vast majority of the roughly 200,000 Southeast Asian marriage migrants currently in Taiwan are women. Serving as wives, mothers, and daughters-in-law in Taiwanese households, these women are under intense pressure to quickly integrate into Taiwan society. At the same time, because of expectations placed on these "Taiwanese daughters-in-law" and their next generation of "new Taiwanese sons," the Taiwan government and various local organizations have established literacy and "lifestyle adjustment" classes to help these women learn Chinese and adapt to their new environment. In 2005, the Taiwan government raised 3 billion New Taiwan Dollars (NTD) to establish a support and counseling fund for foreign spouses. Given this combination of pressure and support, these marriage migrants' ability to speak and understand Chinese is usually not an issue, though their ability to read and write depends on the individual.

As for why comparatively few of the letters are from marriage migrants, there are two possible reasons. First, after marriage migrants enter Taiwanese households, they are recognized (and they view themselves) as Taiwanese citizens; and second, marriage migrants in Taiwanese households rarely have "a room of their own," and therefore if they want to read and write in a language that the rest of the family is unable to understand, they risk being regarded as "other." Furthermore, marriage migrants who *regard themselves* as Taiwan citizens will often refuse to read or write in their native language, making them unlikely to read or contribute to native-language publications like *Four-Way Voice*.

The largest immigrant group in Taiwan, meanwhile, consists of the roughly half a million foreign blue-collar workers—including not only caregivers and domestic workers but construction workers, manufacturing workers, and workers in the fishing industry. Workers in the construction or the fishing industry generally do not need to use Chinese in their job, and they typically work with other migrants with whom they can interact in their native language. As a result, their Chinese-language ability is usually fairly weak, and in some work environments where there is a high proportion of foreign workers, the employer or the employment agency provides the workers with newspapers, magazines, and even cable TV in their native language, which in turn further decreases their need to learn Chinese. At the same time, however, given that most of these migrant workers are employed in professions where they work closely with large numbers of other immigrants from the same region, they are less motivated to turn to publications like *Four-Way Voice* in search of a virtual community.

More than 80 percent of the contributors to *Four-Way Voice*, meanwhile, are caregivers or domestic workers. Because they live with their employers in an environment in which the dominant language and culture is foreign (for them) but in which they spend virtually all their time caring for others and are generally not able to communicate over the Internet, letter-writing is the most convenient and economical medium through which to express themselves. Unlike marriage migrants, foreign domestic workers are not regarded as members of the families of their employers, and therefore both they and their employers "regard them (the migrant workers) as foreign 'others', and not as Taiwan citizens who may later become like them." One result of this situation, however, is that these domestics are relatively free to continue using their native language, and many of them become active readers of and contributors to native-language periodicals like *Four-Way Voice*.

The importance of these sorts of native-language periodicals for migrant workers can be observed from the following letter submitted to *Four-Way Voice* by a domestic named Nguyễn Thị Oanh 阮氏鶯:

> Today, a friend gave me a copy of *Four-Way Voice*, and I can't describe how delighted I was. I carefully read every page, and was deeply moved by those friendly words and sincere emotions. I tried not to cry, but tears nevertheless streamed down my face. I really did cry, but these were actually tears of joy. From now on, I will have another companion, and will have more energy to overcome the challenges and adversity I may face, and which will also support me as I complete the remainder of my journey, heading toward a bright future.[3]

This group of long-silenced migrant workers discovered in *Four-Way Voice* a stage on which they could express themselves. It was as if we had succeeded in opening up a small window, but soon found ourselves nearly inundated by a mountain of letters.

The paper on which these letters were written often revealed as much as the text of the letters themselves. The migrants often used whatever they had on hand, including calendar paper, hospital medical record forms, children's parent-teacher contact books, and even obituary notices—all of which functioned as evidence of their labor and also as an index of their work environment. The newspaper's editorial office, meanwhile, took each letter received and coded, scanned, and saved it, sometimes selecting an appropriate passage to post in the current issue. Out of these submissions, those that were deemed appropriate for Taiwan readers were then translated for the Chinese-language edition of the newspaper.

These submissions could be grouped into a few broad categories, including longing for one's family and hometown, lamenting being poor, being in love, complaining about bad employers, and expressing gratitude for good ones. There were also many long autobiographical narratives, though very few of these made the reader feel truly happy. For instance, the autobiographical essay "Wandering for Eight Years" (流亡八年) narrates a series of unfortunate events. The author, Ah Zhu 阿珠, describes how, after a romantic breakup in Vietnam, she became a marriage migrant in Taiwan. Her first marriage was to a Taiwan man who already had three sons, and he initially treated her rather well, though upon learning that she was pregnant his attitude abruptly changed:

> Before my husband married me, he had a forty-year-old girlfriend who had two daughters. This woman wasn't interested in marrying him, and instead merely wanted to maintain a romantic relationship. Eventually they had a fight, whereupon the man went to Vietnam and married me.
>
> After the other woman discovered that the man had married me, she wept for a long time. When my husband learned that I was pregnant with a son, he decided to get back together with the other woman and refused to give me anything.[4]

However, a marriage migrant living away from her home country typically doesn't have many choices, and therefore must simply endure what comes:

> Although we were sleeping in the same bed, my husband wouldn't even touch me, and if I touched him he would curse me. As time passed, I felt increasingly lonely at home, and the park was my close friend. Sitting on the park bench, watching the tree leaves slowly blow around, I reminisced about life in Vietnam....
>
> At the time, I constantly thought about getting divorced, but I had already embarrassed my family to the point that they couldn't even lift their heads—wasn't that enough? It would be simply too embarrassing if I were to return home pregnant only shortly after having gotten married. So, I ultimately dismissed the possibility of divorce, and instead resolved to simply endure my fate.

In the end, Ah Zhu and her husband agreed to separate, whereupon Ah Zhu embarked on a life of exile. During that period, she worked in a restaurant, sold betel nuts, and worked as a hostess in a bar. She met many other men who fell in love with her, only to abandon her as soon as they ran into difficulty. For a long time she was involved with a gang member with violent tendencies:

> During that period, I was continually beaten. From that day forward, he constantly followed me, and whenever he thought he was in the right, he would beat me. He wouldn't let me talk to customers, either men or women. If they were young women, he would

claim that they were lesbians, or else would suspect that they were trying to help me leave him. But every time he beat me, he would allow me to go wherever I wanted, or else would buy me clothes and give me money—all so that I would forgive him.

When Ah Zhu sent her manuscript to *Four-Way Voice*, she explained that she was working part-time in a massage parlor and in a karaoke hall. By that point, she had already earned enough money to retrieve her son from her former husband and send him to a Vietnamese school in Taipei. At the end of her letter, she wrote, "I hope everyone will forgive me. Because of my environment, I have no choice but to be like this. I hope that God will take pity on me, and allow me to have a normal life."

PUBLISHING WRITINGS BY MIGRANTS

When the former journalist Phạm Thảo Vân's letter was published in the second issue (October 2006) of the journal, it was enthusiastically received, and she followed up with a poem she received from her son, who was still in Vietnam. Titled "When Mother is Away" (Mẹ vắng nhà) the poem illustrated the unseen burden and sense of homesickness that all migrant workers in Taiwan must face:

Mẹ vắng nhà một năm
Chín mươi ngày có lẻ
Con tưởng chừng thế kỷ
Không thấy bong mẹ hiền

Mơi ơi, mẹ có biết
Khi mẹ gửi tiền về
Bố nhận mà bố khóc
Thương mẹ nơi xứ xa
Ngày đêm làm vất vả
Lo cho người ở nhà
Bố đã mua xe máy
Mười tám triệu hai trăm
Ngày ngày bố đi làm
Trông oai ghê mẹ ạ
Còn lại biểu bà nội
Xây ngõ, sửa cầu ao
Chẳng còn sợ mưa rào
Ông bà đi trơn ngã
Biểu bà ngoại hai triệu
Làm vốn nuôi đàn gà
Bốn trăm con mẹ ạ
Bố mua máy vi tính
Nối mạng in tơ nét

Để bố thưởng cho con
Vì con được giải nhì
Cuộc thi toán thành phố
Bây giờ mỗi chủ nhật
Con lại mở chương trình

Cũng chạy sang nghe nhờ
Còn bà ngoại nghe rồi
Cứ bảo con dặn mẹ
Đừng có nghe kẻ xấu
Bỏ trốn ra ngoài làm
Như cô Liễu làng mình
Mới sang có sáu tháng
Đã tham tiền bỏ trốn
Giờ bị trục xuất về
Già đình nợ đầm đìa
Toàn cãi nhau mẹ ạ

Chúc các cô, các chú
Chúc các mẹ, các dì
Luôn vui vẻ khỏe mạnh
Con lại chờ chủ nhật
Nghe tin tức mẹ hiền
Đang ở nơi xứ xa.

Mother, you left home a year and three months ago, but it feels like a century.
Father holds the money you send home, with tears streaming down his face.
With this money,
Father bought a motorcycle, and he looks very handsome riding it to work;
We also repaired our doors and windows, and repaired the road, so that grandmother
and grandfather could walk more easily.
We also sent my maternal grandmother four hundred chicks, which she could sell after
they grow up.
I earned good grades in math, and was ranked second in the city.
Father bought me a computer, and encouraged me to go online.
Dearest mother, please take good care of yourself,
We all miss you very much.
Your mother hopes you won't be like this other woman from our village,
Who ran away after only working for half a year,
But after returning to Vietnam she owed a lot of money,
And had no way of paying it back, and as a result,
Her family argued continuously about money every day.

Dearest mother,
I hope you and the other uncles and aunties
Are all working well in Taiwan.
Mother, we really miss you!

Phạm's son detailed the benefits his family derived from the money that Phạm earned while working abroad, and urged his mother not to run away from her employer.

At the time, Phạm, in addition to caring for an elderly Taiwanese lady, also had to clean her employer's two houses while cooking and washing for ten other families. Her employer, however, wanted to replace her with another domestic who would be even more docile and obedient. Phạm could not afford to lose her job, because her entire family back in Vietnam was relying on her monthly salary of ten thousand NTD, and furthermore she had not yet repaid the several thousand US dollars she had borrowed in order to come to Taiwan in the first place.

Foreign blue-collar workers in Taiwan are subject to many legal restrictions, and it is extremely difficult for them to formally change jobs. Eventually, Phạm left her employer, thereby permitting her to move about Taiwan more freely. She used a fluid and beautiful writing style to describe her fellow Vietnamese migrant workers, and even interviewed several illegal organizations that sought to lure Vietnamese female migrants into the sex trade. Phạm, who was involved in social groups for Vietnamese migrant workers, frequently visited fellow Vietnamese who had been injured, and also helped with fundraising. During the 2014 controversy between China and Vietnam over a Chinese oil rig in a disputed area of the South China Sea, she even organized a demonstration in Taipei that attracted more than a thousand people. Afterwards, when Vietnamese protesters looted a Taiwanese factory in Vietnam, she convened a small press conference to tearfully apologize on their behalf.

As an "escaped migrant," Phạm Thảo Vân was still able to appear in public, but had to maintain a greater degree of vigilance. In order to avoid arrest, for instance, she usually travelled by taxi, which permitted her to go directly to her destination. At the slightest warning, she would change jobs, but even then there have been several times that she has only narrowly avoided being caught. This sort of tense existence has left her with perforated eardrums and chronic migraines. She once used a friend's fake ID to see the doctor, and the doctor told her that she could not fly in this condition. She told us with a smile that even if the police were to arrest her, they would not be able to put her on a plane back to Vietnam.

From Phạm's writings—which have been published in bilingual versions in *Four-Way Voice* and can be found on Facebook—we see the true predicament of Southeast Asian migrant workers in Taiwan. There are tens of thousands of these migrants, all of whom are caught between their home country and this foreign land. Some quietly endure their predicament, while others, like Phạm, choose to struggle to improve their lot.

After Phạm fled her employer, we created a new section of *Four-Way Voice* devoted to letters from these "escaped migrants." After we opened this new section, "Flight," our editorial office was flooded with new letters and pictures, testifying to untold amounts of hardship and humiliation. The editorial office struggled to translate these letters into Chinese for the benefit of Taiwan readers unfamiliar with the circumstances of these escaped migrants, and particularly the employers from whom the migrants were fleeing in the first place. In this way, we hoped to offer readers a chance to better understand these hardworking foreigners struggling to survive while hiding in plain sight.

The reason these migrant workers were willing to leave their jobs and became "escaped migrants" lacking legal protection was usually poor work conditions and their inability to receive their wages on time. For instance, the anonymous author of an essay titled "Diary of a Slave" writes,

> Grandma [the elderly woman cared for by the essay's author] and I had to live in a tiny second-floor room, which was only large enough for Grandma's bed, meaning that I had to sleep in the hallway that the family used to reach the bathroom. Therefore, I slept on the floor with the bathroom at my head and Grandma's toilet chair at my feet.
>
> Grandma frequently had to use the bathroom, and I would always have to help her. Each time I lay down again, someone else in the family would need to use the restroom, and they would simply step over me. To save money, they wouldn't flush the toilet, and the stench would get so bad that I would have to flush it myself. When my boss's wife (Grandma's daughter-in-law) heard me flush, she would come over and stop me, saying, "We only flush once every third time someone uses the toilet." Rich people can be incredibly stingy!

In another essay titled "Forced to Flee," a migrant by the name of Vũ Thị Chính 武氏正 explains why her unnamed friend decided to run away:

> Eventually, "H" was sexually violated by her evil boss. She didn't know what to do, and didn't dare tell anyone. Moreover her boss subsequently warned her that if she told anyone he would send her back to her home country. "H" wanted to ask her placement agency for help, but not only did they not help her, they even urged her not to anger her boss. When "H" asked to change jobs, they warned her that if she had too many demands they would simply send her home.
>
> After that, whenever "H"'s boss tried to violate her, she would resist, so eventually he called her placement agency and lodged a complaint about her, asking them to send her home. In the end, "H" had no choice but to run away. . . . Moreover, "H"'s boss called mine and told him to watch me carefully, because otherwise I might run away as well.

This is not to say, of course, that all escaped migrants have a "reasonable" basis for running away, but we also shouldn't automatically view them as criminals. In order to permit more Taiwanese to see them, and so that these firsthand accounts by escaped migrants might permit people from different backgrounds, different classes, and different social positions to better understand one another, *Four-Way Voice* coordinated with *China Times* to edit and publish some of these letters in both Chinese and Vietnamese, and the result was a book titled *Flight: Our Beautiful Island, Their Prison* (逃：我們的寶島, 他們的牢).[5]

After the publication of *Flight*, divorce emerged as a contentious topic in Taiwan, with many locals accusing Southeast Asian women of marrying Taiwanese men for money, and then getting divorced as soon as they had secured their citizenship. On the other hand, given that many marriages between people of similar ethnicities and cultural backgrounds frequently end in divorce, is it at all surprising that the marriages between people from different nations, different cultures, and different languages may sometimes also result in misunderstandings? The following year, the editorial office of *Four-Way Voice* edited a number of letters from marriage migrants and also added some interviews with reporters and social workers, in coordination with the *China Times* publication office, as a volume titled *Separation: Our Purchases, Their Lives* (離: 我們的買賣, 她們的一生).[6]

Printed in attractive paperback editions and available in both Vietnamese-language and Chinese-language editions, these two volumes represent an extension of the *Four-Way Voice* project—functioning not only to recognize and validate these literary writings by foreign workers in Taiwan, but also to make them more widely available.

WRITING COMPETITIONS

In 2001, when Ma Ying-Jeou 馬英九 was still mayor of Taipei, he and the director of Taipei's Labor Department, Cheng Tsun-chi 鄭村棋, established a poetry and essay competition for migrant workers. The competition was called "Taipei, Please Listen to Me!" (台北, 請聽我說!); it included separate divisions for poetry and prose, with the prose submissions, either essays or short stories, needing to be under a thousand characters. The winner of each division would receive a prize of ten thousand NTD, and the winning submissions would be published in a volume.

Cheng Tsun-chi, who previously worked as a labor activist, believed that this strategy of "using culture as a tactic" was a productive way of using government resources in order to try to improve the public perception of foreign workers and help establish their subjectivity.[7] After the mayor and the Labor Department director were replaced, the competition was renamed "Taipei, Listen to Me Again" (台北, 請再聽我說) and it continues to be held annually. In 2014, the office in charge of administering the competition changed its name to the Taipei City Foreign and Disabled Labor Office, and the director Chen Hui-chi 陳惠琪 observed that "in addition to allowing our foreign worker friends to use poetry and prose to record their state of mind working in Taiwan and to help relieve their feelings of homesickness and work pressures, [this event] can also help Taipei residents to understand them better, to respect different voices, and increase the mutual understanding between Taipei residents and these foreign workers."

In its inaugural year, the competition received 216 poems written in English, Indonesian, Filipino, and Thai. Because the jurors could not read all the poems in their original languages, the selection process had to proceed in two stages, wherein all of the submissions written in Thai, Indonesian, Vietnamese, and Filipino were first subjected to a preliminary review by Greater China–based specialists in these Southeast Asian languages, who ultimately selected forty poems. After these works were translated into Chinese, the resulting texts were evaluated by a panel of five judges, including Director Cheng Tsun-chi and Taiwan poets and authors.

Cheng Tsun-chi reported being astounded by the high quality of the submissions, and remarked that

> most [of the poems] described the experience of working and the process of adapt-ing to life in a foreign land. From this, it was clear how strongly foreign workers in Taiwan feel about their work and their foreign work environment! This made me wonder what sorts of tools local workers could use to represent themselves, and what they would choose to express. Would they, like the foreign works, also use poetry to express their feelings about their work environment?[8]

The winner of the competition the first year was a twenty-seven-year-old high school graduate from Indonesia who was working in Taipei as a domestic caregiver. Her prize-winning entry, *Lakon Hidup* (Life is a Play), used the figure of a puppet to represent her life and position as a migrant worker:

> Like a script for a puppet play
> We are mere puppets,
> Our laughter and tears
> Are but a story that has already been written,
> That has already been scripted in a very lively and tumultuous manner.
> A puppet
> Has no choice but to follow its fate as directed by the puppeteer
> And perform a preassigned character
> If this were but a fraud,
> What would the puppet do?
> Anything it performed would be meaningless.[9]

The author explained: "For me, writing poetry is a means of communication that I can use to express my thoughts and feelings. This kind of writing has already become a habit for me, and when I am feeling depressed or homesick I'll often take up a pen and write a poem—to express my inner feelings."[10]

When one of the judges, the poet Chang Hsiang-hua 張香華, observed that in the most recent set of submissions the contributors "did not complain as much about their employers as compared to previous years' contributors," Lucie Cheng 成露茜 (the co-founder of *Four-Way Voice*) replied, "I'm afraid that treating these submissions as though they were mere media reports is simply too optimistic." Instead, Cheng agreed with another juror, Chung Ch'iao 鍾喬, who observed that "the poetry and essays written by these foreign workers may be considered a type of 'literature of the oppressed,' and it is only from this sort of aesthetic perspective that we can truly grasp the life impressions that the authors are communicating through their writings."[11]

In 2013, in the thirteenth installment of the Poetry and Literary Competition, the mayor of Taipei, Hau Lung-pin 郝龍斌, offered a preface titled "A deeply inclusive international metropolis," in which he wrote:

> Our foreign laborer friends have crossed oceans to come to work in Taiwan, where they strive from dawn to dusk to meet and interact with us. You could say that

Taiwan is their second home, and therefore in order to help Taipei residents better understand these foreign friends, we decided that in 2001 we would create an annual migrant laborer literary competition. We are currently hosting the thirteenth installment of the competition, and each year we have more submissions than before. Reading these prize-winning works, I sincerely believe that poetry and prose are like true friends who can express their feelings to one another."

In his preface, Hau Lung-pin quoted from two prize-winning works. One of these was a poem titled "Overseas Song" (Senandung Tanah Ranta/海外歌唱) by an Indonesian worker who won the first-place award of the poetry category of that year's competition:

> Di luar negeri ada ratus-ribuan saudara sebangsa Cuma tahu nama,
> tetapi tidak dapat bertemu
> Dan juga berita mereka
> Seperti mencari jarum halus di dalam tumpukkan jerami
> Berjuang selalu dapat balikkan kenyakinan yang berlawanan
> Kami tidak sendirian
> Dengan kekuatan sendiri menjadi pahlawan sesungguhnya
>
> Overseas, there are millions of compatriots
> So many that I can only know their names, and have no way of meeting them all
> Even finding basic information about them
> Is like looking for a needle in a haystack
> However, they use poetry and prose to encourage themselves as well as everyone else
> Struggles always challenge one's faith,
> But we are not lonely
> But rather rely on ourselves to be true heroes.

The other was a poem titled "Thank you Taiwan" (Salamat Taiwan/謝謝台灣/) by an Indonesian worker who was awarded the second-place prize in the poetry competition:

> saat saya meninggalkan negara saya kekuatan dan kesabaran adalah
>   satu-satunya barang yang ku miliki
> . . .
> terima kasih Taiwan, engkau jadikan aku anggota keluargamu
> Bantuan engkau adalah takdir terhadap impian masa depanku tidak karena
>   ini menjadi sia-sia
> Terima kasih Taiwan, engkau tarik aku dari kemiskinan
>
> When I left my homeland,
> Strength and endurance were the only things that I possessed
> . . .
> Thank you Taiwan; you have treated me like family
> Your aid is preordained, and as a result my dreams for the future have not been in vain.
> Thank you, Taiwan; you have pulled me up from poverty.

Although this sort of officially sponsored competition cannot help but feature some official-sounding essays praising contemporary Taiwan, we believe that the recognition and financial reward this sort of competition is able to offer migrant authors for their submissions play a considerable role in helping validate the existence of this sort of writing.[12]

THE 2014 TAIWAN LITERATURE AWARD
FOR MIGRANTS

As a result of the publication of the volumes *Flight* and *Separation*, a volunteer at *Four-Way Voice*, Lin Xiuzhen 林秀貞, and the author Huang Tangmu 黃湯姆 came to recognize the power of migrant literature, and in 2013 they proposed that we establish a literature prize for migrant authors.[13] From a literary perspective, it was hoped that migrant writings could help enrich Taiwan literature, while from the perspective of the migrants themselves, it was hoped that this platform would permit them to tell their stories and showcase their talent.

The resulting prize, the Taiwan Literature Award for Migrants, was awarded for the first time in 2014. Submissions were first screened by experts in the Southeast Asian languages in which they were written, and then the shortlisted works were translated into Chinese to be evaluated by a panel of experts, including the Taiwan literature scholar Chen Fangming, the Malaysian Chinese author Ng Kim Chew 黃錦樹, and the avant-garde Taiwanese author Lo Yi-chun 駱以軍. Unlike the "Please Listen to Me" competition, which regarded the migrant writings as "a positive way to express one's feelings" (as Taipei mayor Hau Lung-pin put it) and which sought primarily to increase the mutual understanding between migrants and Taiwan residents, the Taiwan Literature Award sought instead to affirm the legitimacy and future prospects of migrant literature. As the award's own multilingual webpage puts it, the objective of the award "is to encourage, and record the history that is happening now. Through the literary productions of immigrants, migrant workers, we will see stories of living in foreign lands (migrant workers), the feeling of having two homelands (immigrants), and having parents of two nationalities (second-generation of new inhabitants), open before our eyes."[14]

Some of the most interesting submissions were fictional stories. For instance, one of the Honorable Mention awardees, Erin Sumarsini, was recognized for her Indonesian-language work "The Story of Ye Feng and Carlos" (Kisah Ye Feng dan Carlos), in which she adopts the perspective of a domestic worker to describe the close affection between a boy with Down Syndrome and his household's pet dog. This perfectly paced story recounts in moving detail how the boy would take the old dog out for a walk, but unspoken is the implicit question that haunts this essay: does the status of a foreign domestic in this household even rise to that of a pet dog?

The author of the submission that won the first-place prize, which was titled "Dream of a Foreign Land" (Giấc mơ nơi xứ người), had come to Taiwan to find work because her family back in the Philippines was very poor, and in Taiwan she fell in love with a migrant worker who had come from Vietnam under similar circumstances. But when the young man returned to Vietnam, he betrayed her and got together with the author's best friend. At the same time, the author encountered problems at work and was afraid that she might be sent home. Responsible for paying her family's debts, and also feeling resentment toward her former lover, the author impulsively decided to marry a Taiwanese man. After the marriage, however, this man began treating her very coldly. He forbade her from going out to work, but also wouldn't give her any spending money, saying, "I'm already providing you with food and a place to live, and you have electricity and water. What do you need money for?"

Commenting on this essay, juror Lo Yi-chun remarked that the author maintains a very calm and resigned attitude toward her fate. "She is very well-behaved, and accepts her hardship. She deceives her mother, telling her that everything is going fine. Feeling homesick and betrayed, as soon as she escapes one nightmare she finds herself in an even more terrifying one. Reading her story, every pain follicle of my being was distressed, and particularly the last line of her essay gave me goose bumps." He was referring to the author's use of a Vietnamese saying to describe a young woman's inability to control her fate: "a girl's body is like a river ferry, and who knows where the river will run clear and when it will be muddy" (Đời người con gái như mười hai bến nước, biết bến nào đục bến nào trong).

The winning author, whose pen name is Hương Cỏ May 芒草香, describes her reaction upon learning she had won as follows: "When I received the telephone call, notifying me that I was one of the finalists, I was excited and very moved. I cried, not because of the enormous monetary prize, but rather because I knew that someone had been moved by my writing. My only hope was someone might look after and protect me and the other women who have come here from my homeland, so that we might thereby feel less homesick, and experience less suffering as a result of being away from home." However, she was not willing to reveal her true name, because her relationship with her Taiwanese husband's family was not good, and she was about to get divorced.

The Significance of Migrant Literature

When various different literary forms compete with one another, it is inherently difficult to evaluate them by the same standards. However, for us the Migrant Literature Prize was merely a means to an end. On one hand, the competition was intended to provide a means by which we could help migrants gain some recognition for their writing, while on the other hand it would encourage these migrants to use their writing in order to offer their "evaluations" of Taiwan itself.

Yes, that is correct. In the end, the object of this exercise is Taiwan itself.

The essays by migrant authors in native-language publications like *Four-Way Voice*, together with the prize-winning submissions to the "Please Listen to Me" competition and the Migrant Literature Award, all permit these lower-class foreign migrant workers to recount their feelings and experiences, and thereby have the potential to offer Taiwan's residents a more truthful and intimate "evaluation."

(translated by Carlos Rojas)

Notes

1. *Sifang bao* 四方紙 [Four-way voice] is a monthly published under the auspices of Shih Hsin University's *Lihpao Daily*. The journal, which released its inaugural issue in September of 2006, is published primarily in Southeast Asian languages, and secondarily in Chinese. The inaugural issue appeared only in a Vietnamese edition and a Thai edition, but in 2011 the journal added Indonesian, Cambodian, and Filipino editions.

2. Chen Fangming 陳芳明, "Wo de wenxue guixiang lu" 我的文學歸鄉路 [My literary path back to my homeland], lecture given in 2011, archived at http://newsblog.chinatimes.com/openbook/archive/27907.

3. *Four-Way Voice* (December 2006).

4. This essay was later reprinted in the volume *Li: Women de maimai, tamen de yisheng* 離：我們的買賣, 她們的一生 [Separation: Our purchases, their lives] (Taipei: Shibao chubanshe, 2013).

5. *Tao: Women di baodao, tamen de lao* 逃：我們的寶島, 他們的牢 [Flight: Our beautiful island, their prison] (Taipei: Shibao chubanshe, 2013).

6. Both *Separation* and *Flight* were published simultaneously in separate Vietnamese-language and Chinese-language editions.

7. See Wu Yongyi 吳永毅, "Wu *Home* kegui: Gongsi fanzhuan yu waiji jialao suo-shou zhi shikong paichi de ge'an yanjiu" 無 *Home* 可歸：公私反轉與外籍家勞所受之時空排斥的個案研究 [No *Home* to return to: Inversions of public and private, and a case study of the spatial-temporal exclusions endured by foreign domestics], *Taiwan shehui yanjiu jikan* 台灣社會研究季刊 [Taiwan society studies quarterly] 66 (June 2007): 1–74.

8. Taipei City Labor Department, 2002, 37.

9. Taipei City Labor Bureau, "Taibei, qing ting wo shuo!" 台北,請聽我說! [Taipei, listen to me!], 2002, 34.

10. Taipei City Labor Bureau, "Taipei, Listen to Me!" 34.

11. Taipei City Labor Bureau, "Taipei, Listen to Me!" 52.

12. The full text of these two poems and other winning entries can be found at: "Qing zai ting wo shuo!" 請再聽我說! [Please listen to me again], Taipei City Labor Bureau, December 2013.

13. At the time the prize was established, one of us (Chang Cheng) was serving as the editor-in-chief of *Four-Way Voice*, while the other (Liao Yun-Cheng) was the acting deputy editor-in-chief of *Lihpao Daily*.

14. 2015 Taiwan Literature Award for Migrants, home page (available in multiple languages). http://2014tlam-en.blogspot.tw.

Works Cited

Li: Women de maimai, tamen de yisheng 離：我們的買賣，她們的一生 [Separation: Our purchases, their lives]. Taipei: Shibao chubanshe, 2013.

Tao: Women de baodao, tamen de lao 逃：我們的寶島，他們的牢 [Flight: Our beautiful island, their prison]. Taipei: Shibao chubanshe, 2013.

Wu Yongyi 吳永毅, "Wu *Home* kegui: Gongsi fanzhuan yu waiji jialao suoshou zhi shikong paichi de ge'an yanjiu" 無 Home 可歸：公私反轉與外籍家勞所受之時空排斥的個案研究 [No *Home* to return to: Inversions of public and private, and a case study of the spatial-temporal exclusions endured by foreign domestics]. *Taiwan shehui yanjiu jikan* 台灣社會研究季刊 [Taiwan society studies quarterly] 66 (June 2007): 1–74.

CHAPTER 2.8

....

WHERE THE "TRANS-PACIFIC" MEETS CHINESE LITERATURE

....

SHUANG SHEN

ONE day in July of 1952, Eileen Chang 張愛玲 crossed the border between Mainland China and Hong Kong and stepped into a new life of exile that would take her further and further from Shanghai, a city that had defined and inspired her literary productivity in the decade prior to this departure. A decade later, Chang recounted this experience of departure in a dreamy English-language essay titled "A Return to the Frontier," which was ostensibly a travelogue recording her "homecoming" to Taiwan and Hong Kong, these being the only Chinese worlds accessible to her despite her reluctance to consider them as her real home.[1] The essay, in its meandering movement through past and present, illusion and reality, departure and return, begs the question of just where those boundaries lie, and which (indeed whose) reality the narrator could accept. Acutely aware that, like thousands of refugees who left the newly established People's Republic of China in the mid-twentieth century, Chang and her cohort were essentially voting with their feet in favor of the so-called free capitalist world, Chang nonetheless could not see a future for herself or people like her in this new world. Thus, in contrast to the expectations of Max Ascoli, the editor of *The Reporter*, where Chang's essay was published, the work functions poorly as an organ of anticommunist propaganda.[2]

For the contemporary critic, Chang's essay raises the question of how we might reconceptualize Chinese literature and the sphere of the trans-Pacific once we stop viewing the mid-twentieth-century Chinese immigrant solely as a political icon, a seamless illustration of the Manichean logic of the Cold War. To borrow from the provocative title of Chang's essay, we may ask what new frontiers are opened up if we return to a literary figure such as Chang, not in a way that reinforces the centrality of her already canonized body of work written in Shanghai, but by focusing instead on her more ambiguous and ambivalent journeys across the Pacific and considering the various destinations where she and her works ultimately landed.

Chang and other migrant Chinese writers are generally considered from the perspective of either Chinese diasporic literature or Sinophone literature, both of which cover a variety of meanings and critical positions. The fields of Chinese diaspora studies and Sinophone studies currently revolve around specific concerns, such as the relationship between the diaspora and the homeland or the interaction between dominant and minority cultural formations. While these critical considerations are important, the common impetus behind these inquiries, which is to say the need and desire to go beyond a narrowly defined "China" and the conventional boundaries of Chinese studies as an area-studies discipline, has ironically restricted this discussion about what Jing Tsu and David Der-wei Wang have characterized as the historical "interaction between the production of literatures and moving agents" in the Chinese diaspora.[3] I propose, on the contrary, to perceive Chinese migrant writers and Chinese literature's trans-Pacific journeys in broader terms as a historical scene of "worlding"—drawing inspiration for this term from contemporary discussions of world literature, postcolonial studies, and transnational cultural studies. The focus on worlding, through relinking Chinese diasporic literature with world history, can more effectively orient our attention toward the "new social relations" created in the "malleable space" of the diaspora, as Tsu and Wang beckon us to do in their discussion of global Chinese literature.[4]

Worlding does not refer just to the circulation of literary texts beyond national borders (circulation being a crucial aspect of "world literature," as defined by David Damrosch), nor is the term to be taken as a synonym of *migration* and *diaspora*, or of Arjun Appadurai's postnational "scapes" ("mediascape," "ideoscape," "technoscape," and so forth). While *worlding* bears intricate connections with transborder movement and globalization, the word, given its deep-rooted antipositivist connotations derived from Heidegger's postmodernist ontology, leads not to a simple acceptance of an objective description of the world or globalization as factual but to an interrogation of this description. In her postcolonialist reading of *Jane Eyre, Wide Sargasso Sea*, and *Frankenstein*, Gayatri Spivak unpacks the imperialist ideology of "the worlding of the Third World" and critiques how metropolitan feminist narratives naturalize and legitimate colonialism through the erasure of the colonized woman.[5] In recent discussions of world literature, Djelal Kadir proposes that we consider the *world* in *world literature* as a verb in order to cast a critical perspective upon the conjunction between globalization and the current "upsurge of a discourse of/on world literature."[6] Kadir writes:

> In pursuing this examination, it might be apposite to the discussion of world literature and globalization to take the word "world" as verb, and to read globalization not as boundless sweep but as bounding circumscription. *To world* and *to globalize*, then, would have to be parsed in light of their subject agencies and their object predicates. World and globalization, thus, would be imputable actions, rather than anonymous phenomena. The virtue of imputability resides in the prospect of being able to trace responsibility and consequence, not as mechanical cause and effect

necessarily, but as motivation and outcome in an object relation of subject agency as it affects a phenomenon and makes it a/the world.[7]

These discussions have given a poststructuralist edge to Heidegger's philosophical term, enabling us to engage critically with positivist world constructions in our socio-economic life and intellectual inquiries by taking into account the position of these constructions in the real world.

Inspired by these discussions, I suggest that we should not understand the trans-Pacific turn of Chinese literary studies as yet another expansion of the territory of Chinese literature by refashioning it as "world literature" or "transnational" literature, as if the prestige or value associated with the concepts prefaced with *world* or *trans-* were indisputable. Rather, our attention should be devoted to the examination of the relationship between this broadly defined Chinese literature and the trans-Pacific world(s) it makes, as well as that between the literature and the real worlds of the Pacific societies it touches. Contemporary diaspora studies and Sinophone literary studies have defined their agendas based on critical concerns with particular modes of worlding that reflect contemporary power dynamics in the Pacific region. These discussions, however, have not exhausted all possible angles with which one might engage with Chinese diasporic literature, which is actually more multifaceted and unruly than has been acknowledged by diaspora studies and Sinophone studies as they are currently practiced. The worlding of Chinese literature is historical and continuous, highly dependent upon specific global configurations at particular moments of history. To look into the worlding of Chinese literature in the trans-Pacific context means mobilizing the broader Pacific as a source of energy to redraw the cartography of Chinese literature while interrogating the relationship between politics and literature in this space. Since this worlding posits the Chinese world as one among many in the larger Pacific context while situating Chinese literature in close proximity to other literatures, it makes the entire Pacific what Kadir calls the "object predicate" of our intellectual inquiry and the "responsibility and consequence" of scholars situated in a specific area studies discipline—namely, Chinese studies.[8] To the extent that this consideration of the trans-Pacific worlding of Chinese literature delves into the fundamental question of literature and politics in the Pacific context, its concerns are broader than either Chinese diaspora studies or Sinophone studies.

Chinese literature's trans-Pacific worlding during the Cold War period, epitomized by the symbolic event of Chang's departure from Mainland China, can be perceived as a particularly significant moment in Chinese literary history. The reconfiguration of the Chinese cultural landscape and the Chinese diaspora by global and regional geopolitics at this historical moment has left an indelible imprint on contemporary history and culture. The Cold War presents unique challenges to the current endeavors to reach beyond the nation-state and reestablish regional ties in the Pacific. This chapter will thus return to this historical moment as a case study to tease out some key concerns of the trans-Pacific worlding of Chinese literature. But we must first start with a better understanding of the history of the Pacific and trans-Pacific as regional ideational constructions.

THE *PACIFIC* AND THE *TRANS-PACIFIC* AS CONCEPTS

Before rushing to enlarge the map of modern Chinese literature, we must confront the process of mapping itself and the history of regionalist conceptualizations, which are themselves, as Michelle Keown and Stuart Murray argue, "products of ideology, with their boundaries shifting in response to changing geopolitical dynamics."[9] As Arif Dirlik argues, "there is no Pacific region that is an 'objective' given, but only a competing set of ideational constructs that project upon a certain location on the globe the imperatives of interest, power, or vision of these historically produced relationships."[10] In contemporary sociohistorical investigations of the concept of the Pacific, the United States is frequently cited as a powerful force that defines the Pacific along with many trans-Pacific initiatives. "The Pacific region, *as* a region, is a EuroAmerican invention," argues Arif Dirlik. "The Pacific, as it assumed conceptual form, did so as a periphery to an expanding EuroAmerican world economy, which structured the incipient region in accordance with its own economic and political logic."[11] Similarly, for Naoki Sakai and Hyon Joo Yoo, "the trans-Pacific marks the realpolitik and metaphoric territorialization of Asia in an American-centered global capital[ist] and military-political system."[12] Bruce Cummings dates the current interest in the Pacific and the rise of the Pacific Rim to the modernization and globalization in Asia after the 1970s, arguing that:

> "Pacific Rim" was a construct of the mid-1970s for revaluing East and Southeast Asia, as Westerners (mostly Americans) recognized and defined it, in ways that highlighted some parts and excluded (or occluded) others. The centerpiece of this construct was Japan, a newly risen sun among advanced industrial countries. . . . Organized into the region were "miracle" economies in Japan, South Korea, Taiwan, Hong Kong, Malaysia, and Singapore, with honorable mention for Thailand, the Philippines, Indonesia, and post-Mao (but pre-Tiananmen) China.[13]

The term *Pacific Rim*, Cummings adds, "invoked a newborn 'community' that anyone, socialist or not, could join . . . as long as they were capitalist. Rimspeakers of course continued to look with curiosity if not disdain upon anyone who did not privilege the market."[14] These discussions suggest that regional concepts such as the *Pacific*, the *Pacific Rim*, or the *Asia Pacific* are not simple spatial configurations. Rather, the sociopolitical forces that occasioned a particular regional discourse constitute a powerful agent that also determines who belongs or does not belong to this region.

If concepts such as *Pacific* or *Asia Pacific* retain such close connections with US domination in the region and the recent history of global expansion of capitalism in Asia, what is the possibility of conceptualizing, as Rob Wilson and Dirlik propose, the "Asia/Pacific" as a "new regional conceptualization" above and beyond this same history? Indeed, how does the trans-Pacific negotiate this history of political domination and capitalist expansion that defined this region as a region? How can we expect that the identifications of the so-called "fluid, furious, and dislocational 'transnationalization' of public space and local culture" would undo the boundaries revolving around the "country/island/state" of area studies?[15]

As soon as we move beyond the United States as the exclusive perspective from which to view the Pacific, the bilateral model of comparison, the pattern Spivak describes as "my country or region over against 'the West,'" is replaced by the more urgent question of what the Pacific or trans-Pacific means for Asia.[16] Kuan-Hsing Chen, a cultural studies scholar from Taiwan, rightly argues that a simple and blanket opposition to the West does not automatically restore the "agency and subjectivity" of Asia.[17] Chen states:

> If Asia is to have analytical value, it does indeed have to be placed within the frame of world history, but if world history is understood as Euro-American imperialism and capitalist expansion, the agency and subjectivity of Asia are stripped away. . . . If the legitimacy of the discourse on Asia is discounted, we are left with the old binary opposition between the East and the West, which erases Asia's rich multiplicity and heterogeneity.[18]

What Chen's insistence on seeing Asia in terms of "multiplicity and heterogeneity" leads to is the recognition that the trans-Pacific cannot be a singular perspective. If the Pacific means different things for different locations in the region, then transnational imaginations of interregional connections would necessarily differ from one location to the next. The intellectual payoff of conceptualizing the trans-Pacific along an East-West axis has to be rather different from other forms of trans-Pacific comparisons and conjunctions, such as the critical project of "other Asias" that Spivak invites us to imagine.

Trying to come to terms with why there is a lack of regional consciousness among the Chinese intelligentsia, Sun Ge, a Japan Studies scholar from China, delves into the difficulties with the worlding of Japanese and American regionalist thinking in China. While Sakai and Yoo may prefer to define a "trans-Pacific imagination" by anchoring it upon "the complicity of the old and the new empires, the new alliance of Japan and the United States," whether this perspective can work equally well for Chinese intellectuals is still an open question.[19] Sun's cautionary note about deploying a regional perspective as "an abstract framework" and substituting that for what Sun calls the "plentitude of history" serves as an antidote against placing the regional above the local.[20]

By referring to the "plenitude of history," Sun draws attention to the twentieth-century history of wars, specifically the Asia Pacific war and the Cold War, which served as both catalysts for building strategic regional alliances and as roadblocks for the development of regional consciousness in China and other societies affected by these wars. How to develop regional perspectives without replicating the dominant region-alist discourses that have sought to unite the region for the purpose of war depends to a large extent on how well the wounds of the war are healed. Yet as Sun and Chen both suggest, the dominance of hegemonic geopolitical regional thinking in the Pacific has made East Asia linger in a continuous state of war. Chen specifically draws atten-tion to the Cold War, which interrupted the process of decolonization for East and Southeast Asia, making it impossible for these societies with repeated histories of colo-nization to come to terms with the colonial legacy. The Cold War can be considered, in Pheng Cheah's terms, as a moment of "normative world-making," a historical pro-cess of "spiritually and materially shaping and making the world through the prescrip-tion of normative ends."[21] The Cold War as a normative global structure significantly complicated the power dynamics in multiple Chinese societies and contributed to the separation of different Chinese worlds in the post–World War II period. Thus, as Chen proposes, we must "de–Cold War" in order to seriously consider the prospect of "a Great Reconciliation" between Taiwan and Mainland China, as well as among the for-mer warring states in Asia.[22]

Yet, according to Cheah, the world has not been properly contained or exhausted by the "normative world making" of dominant global structures in the form of the Cold War, globalism, capitalism, or imperialism. Following Heidegger, Cheah distinguishes between two concepts of the "world": "the vulgar concept of the world . . . as the sum total of objects in space" and "the world as something created by communication and discursive exchange among human subjects." Cheah writes, "For Heidegger, a world is precisely what cannot be represented on a map. Cartography reduces the world to a spatial object. In contradistinction, worlding is a force that subtends and exceeds all human calculations that reduce the world as a temporal structure to the sum of objects in space. Imperialist cartography is such a calculation in the sphere of geopolitical economy."[23] In light of these observations, we could ask whether revisiting the history of the Cold War—a moment of imperialist "calculation" that rearranged the Chinese worlds while redrawing their boundaries—would paradoxically enable us to uncover a world that "exceeds" the normative structures of dominant world making.

Sun Ge's attempt to reaffirm the role of history in shaping regional consciousness is commendable precisely because it draws our attention to the sociopolitical origin of geographical concepts such as that of the region. Yet she has ignored the possible artic-ulation between the realm of experience and that of intellectual thought, often medi-ated by cultural or literary forms. In fact, her assessment that in contemporary China "the region [of] East Asia is more or less limited to the experiential dimension, and has not entered the realm of ontological investigation" may have inadvertently identified just the site from which regionalist consciousness can be excavated.[24]

Recent work in East Asian cultural studies, Chinese diaspora studies, and Sinophone studies presents a convincing argument about why literature offers an equally viable if not better repository (compared to intellectual thought) for East Asian regional consciousness.[25] Yet questions remain as to not only how one reads a region out of literature, but also what objectives we hope to accomplish with regionalist readings of literature. These questions would return us to the issue of *worlding*, which, as Kadir defines the term, is a matter of tracing "responsibility and consequence" and delineating the "motivation and outcome" of an imaginary construction of the world.[26] What does a regionalist imagination do for Chinese literature, and vice versa?

To answer this question, I turn to the literature of the Cold War, a category that for me not only refers to the literature created in the 1950s and 1960s in the shadow of the Cold War but also includes remembrances of the earlier Asia Pacific War, to search for new approaches to reading both Chineseness and literature, which would take us beyond the familiar Chinese communities and reposition them in the wider Pacific.[27] Since the war proves to be a common yet divisive experience for many Asian societies and for Chinese people living in ideologically oppositional worlds, the regional perspectives that emerge from this "war literature" serve not so much to unite the Pacific region or unify disparate Chinese worlds, but rather to shed light on trans-Pacific connections as a historical construction so as to enable us to reflect on why certain regional links are remembered and others forgotten in a contemporary context.

Chinese literature's participation in the Cold War is generally subsumed under the model of the two competing nation-states across the Taiwan Strait, the PRC and the ROC. Yet in an article on mid-twentieth-century war narratives, David Der-wei Wang complicates this nationalist conception of literary history by drawing attention to Chinese writers in the 1950s and the 1960s who were interested in representing various wars in different parts of Asia, not just the Chinese Civil War. Wang states that

> even if we were to construct a China-centered discussion about narratives in the times of the "Great Divide," our realm of concern has to go beyond the Mainland and Taiwan. ... It is only when we integrate the Nationalist-communist conflict into a narrative of world history that we can fully understand the lasting effect of the "Great Divide" and the complexity of mid-twentieth-century war narratives."[28]

Wang proceeds to analyze two distinct sets of war narratives: narratives that have been canonized as a result of their depictions of national wars, and those that have been marginalized on account of their depictions of forgotten or forgettable wars. The narratives in the second group were often penned by diasporic writers. These narratives, like their authors, have lived a life of dispersal and exile, some having found a second home in other national literatures seemingly unconnected with the world of Chinese literature. The object of a trans-Pacific inquiry into these narratives would serve not so much to recover individual marginalized writers or their works, bringing them back to the pantheon of Chinese literary history, but rather to underscore the rich variety of midcentury diasporic literature, whose significance and politics far exceeded any unified discourse of Chineseness. The conceptualization of diaspora from a singular perspective of "nostalgia for the homeland" would be a gross reduction of the complex embeddedness of these works in multiple national histories and world history.

If we take this broadly defined Chinese war literature as a repository of regional imagination, we still need to come to terms with what Wang has called the "'China-centered discussion of . . . the 'Great Divide.'" Spivak's proposal of critical regionalism can be of help here, particularly in terms of her emphasis on a critical perspective toward one's native language and identity. Spivak states:

> "Asia" is not a place, yet the name is laden with history and cultural politics. It cannot produce a naturalized homogeneous "identity." The name "Pacific" has the same salutary absence of a naturalized homogeneous identity that can be immediately connected to it. It can therefore serve to set limits to mere identitarianism in any one of the politico-geographical entities, "from Taiwan to New Zealand," with Hawaii, the Marquesas, and the Easter Islands on its eastern edge, as "Asia" can contain ours.[29]

Adopting *Asia* as "a place-holder in the iteration of a citation," Spivak proposes a regionalist perspective that thinks of Asia as "one continent in its plurality, rather than reduce it only to our own regional identity."[30] To achieve this, it is necessary for us to stop "think[ing] of our own corner as exemplary of our continent." Rather, we should employ the humanistic methodology of close reading, "entering through friendship with the language(s)," to uncover the historical and pretheoretical connections among Asian cultures.[31] To read Chinese literature in a trans-Pacific context, I propose that we must approach the term *Chinese* in the same way that Spivak understands the term *Asia*. In *Other Asias*, Spivak faults some recent "Sinocentric world-system theories" for "generally equating dominant economic systems with cultural formations," yet Sinocentrism does not need to be the only anchor or outcome for Chinese literary or cultural studies conducted at a regional or global scale.[32] There isn't a singular or unified version of Chineseness even in Mainland China; thus, uncovering the "multiplicity and heterogeneity" (Kuan-Hsing Chen's phrase) in *Chineseness* is as necessary as "pluraliz[ing] Asia."[33] Trans-Pacific Chinese literature can be the basis and starting point for a critical regionalist imagination of Asia. The term *Chinese* understood beyond the limits of the nation-state should be able to "name the critical position" from which global or regional connections will be investigated from historical perspectives.[34]

C.Y. LEE AND JIN ZHIMANG: A COMPARATIVE EXERCISE

I will illustrate a trans-Pacific reading of Chinese literature by looking at two novels, both of which present the experience of the migrant Chinese as a site of regional imagination of the Pacific. These narratives—one written in English and the other in Chinese; one situated in North America, the other in Asia—do not cover the Pacific rim or bear the same identity markers as works of Chinese literature. In fact, we would not go very far if we merely attempted to cite these narratives of outliers from a more conventional understanding of the category of Chinese literature. Instead, it would be more productive to use these narratives to tap into the trans-Pacific as a site of knowledge production, and explore what the term means both for cultural agents with different political orientations situated at different locations of the Pacific and for Chinese literature as a history and an academic discipline.

These two narratives are implicated in the politics and ideology of the Cold War, but they do not fit neatly into the specific national cultures in which they are situated. By juxtaposing these two narratives, I hope to show that the trans-Pacific, as an arena of intense power struggles, was not dominated exclusively by the Cold War superpowers. Interregional alliances were constructed in a multidirectional manner, not neatly arranged according to the North-South or East-West axes with which we are familiar today. The Cold War standoff of opposing ideological camps not only did not stop all kinds of movement, physical and virtual; it actively shaped flows of people and cultural articulations across national borders. As Asian American historians have shown, the demographics of Chinese immigration to the United States and the identity of Chinese Americans were affected by the US Cold War policies in complex ways.[35]

From a disciplinary perspective, putting these two narratives together allows us to reflect on the institutional production of trans-Pacific knowledge. The two narratives highlight the difference and conjunction between North America–based ethnic studies and area studies. The two fields represent different versions of trans-Pacific studies: one puts pressure on the concept of *America* and attempts to address the problems raised by that of *America's Pacific*, while the other is more concerned with the notions of *Asia's* or *China's Pacific*. Yet the two texts demonstrate that our knowledge of the Pacific would greatly benefit if the two disciplinary inquiries were brought together more closely. From a historical perspective, they bear witness to complex entanglements of power and history between Euro-America and Asia, East and Southeast Asia. They also demonstrate how native languages and local epistemological frameworks in one location of the Pacific produce the histories of other places. With regard to trans-Pacific studies from within Asian American studies, we can ask whether there is room to consider the Asian side of the Pacific with as much complexity and heterogeneity as the US side, and with regard to Sinophone studies we may consider the possibility of other critical approaches that are not focused on Sinitic languages.

The first case is C. Y. Lee, a writer most famous for his 1957 novel *Flower Drum Song*, which was later adapted into a Broadway musical by Rodgers and Hammerstein. The musical is generally read in Asian American studies as a symptomatic text that preaches assimilation and multiculturalism at a moment when the Chinese Exclusion Act had just been repealed and Asian immigrants were beginning to be absorbed into the national body.[36] What intrigues me is that in both Rodgers and Hammerstein's musical and most Asian American criticism, there is a conscious or unconscious translation of *Asia's Pacific* into *America's Pacific*. In Lee's novel, the main characters Mei Li and her father had just arrived in San Francisco from Los Angeles, and "they had come with General White, a retired army general who had lived in China for more than twenty years, and would have died there, as he had hoped, if the Communists had not driven him out."[37] Here we find the references to the Nationalist Party's defeat in the Mainland and the consequent exile of many KMT-affiliated personnel and their families. In Rodgers and Hammerstein's play, however, this reference to Chinese history has disappeared. Mei Li and her father are depicted as illegal stowaways on a boat docked in San Francisco, as if where they came from no longer mattered. In a discussion of the Broadway production, Anne Cheng draws attention to Mei Li's use of the term *wetback* in reference to her illegal status. Mei Li has just learned this term from a Western B, movie she was watching on TV the night before, and this term references not just illegal Mexican aliens, but also the history of Chinese exclusion.[38] According to Cheng, the use of this phrase brings back the shadow of the exclusion era, at the very moment when the exclusion had been repealed, and reveals that "national identity . . . is legislated through loss."[39]

The translation of Mei Li's story into an American story of immigration does not mean that Asia's Pacific has completely disappeared from Lee's works. In *Lover's Point*, which Lee published a year after the commercial success of *Flower Drum Song*, we witness a different kind of entanglement between Asian history and American history, one that revolves around the traumatic memories of the Asia Pacific War and the post–World War II recovery. Due to this thematic focus, Lee's Anglophone novel invites interesting and meaningful comparisons with Sinophone literature from the same period, together constructing a postwar memory culture of a trans-Pacific scope. In particular, one is reminded of popular novels by Xu Su 徐速, such as *The Star, the Moon, and the Sun* (星星月亮太陽) and *The Girl Called Sakurako* (櫻子姑娘), or films such as *The Star of Hong Kong* (香港之星), *Hong Kong Nights* (香港之夜), and *Hong Kong, Tokyo, Hawaii* (香港、東京、夏威夷), which were collaboratively produced by the Singapore-based Sinophone film studio MP&GI and the Japanese Toho film studio. While these works of Chinese literature and film are situated on opposite shores of the Pacific and separated by linguistic difference, many of them depict interracial romance set against the backdrop of the war.[40] In *The Girl Called Sakurako*, Xu Su tells a tragic love story between Yingzi, the daughter of a Japanese commander, and Wu Hansheng, a hardcore Chinese nationalist and a guerrilla fighter whose name means "the voice of the Han people." This romance, which is doomed to end tragically in the reality of the Sino-Japanese War, turns out to be only a repetition of an earlier episode of Yingzi's family history, when her mother was forced to leave her Chinese lover in a period of growing tension between the two countries. Yingzi thus epitomizes the complex historical Sino-Japanese relationship earlier in the twentieth century.

Like *The Girl Called Sakurako*, *Lover's Point* also features an interracial romance between a Chinese immigrant and a Japanese war bride. This detail alludes to the collective Chinese memory of the Asia Pacific war, but unlike Xu's novel, this Sino-Japanese theme is explored from a vantage point firmly situated in the novel's contemporary moment—America during the Cold War period. Both novels posit transgressive romantic relationships as an occasion to articulate Chinese diasporic sentiments, the sense of non-belonging and abandonment by the nation state.

Lover's Point situates the Chinese immigrant not just in the United States but in the trans-Pacific history of US geopolitical advancement in Asia. It connects the typical immigrant topos of Chinatown with strategic sites in a US geopolitical mapping, such as the military language school where the protagonist Chiang Fu teaches Chinese. The novel opens in Monterey, California, where Chiang Fu, a part-time Chinese teacher at the Army Language School, meets and falls in love with Aika, a Japanese war bride abandoned by her American husband Mike after her arrival in the United States. After Chiang loses his job at the Army school, he goes to San Francisco to work as a personal secretary for Mr. Yee, a rich bachelor desperately trying to find himself a mail-order bride from Hong Kong. Yet the narrative shows a wide array of Chineseness that exceeds the category of the "ethnic" as defined from a North American perspective. Chiang recognizes that he "had no roots in a new country and did not belong to any society, not even the Chinese society, which was Cantonese. He was as foreign to the Cantonese [as they] were to him; they even had to depend on the English language to communicate."[41]

The Cold War is a driving force behind this story, for it not only shaped the power relations between Asian countries and the United States, it also directly impacted Chiang's personal life. Chiang finds in his love for Aika a more eroticized and less threatening replacement of his emotionally estranged wife, who has remained in China. In the novel, we are told that Chiang receives a letter from his cousin in China, who accuses America of preventing Chinese students from returning to their homeland, but "Chiang couldn't help chuckling. Mr. Liu had once shown him a letter from his nephew in Peiping. The wording was exactly the same."[42] Yet Chiang's righteous denunciation of China is closely related to his psychology of abandonment: " 'Sometimes I wonder if Mao Tse-tung really wants us to go back,' Chiang said. 'Perhaps he just makes up all this for propaganda purposes.' "[43] These reflections delineate a psychological structure that parallels personal with national love, in a way that resonates strongly with Yu Dafu's 郁達夫 1921 short story "Sinking" (沈淪). The dramatization of the psychology of the modern man in "Sinking" takes place in Japan via a series of romantic relationships between a Chinese student with Japanese women, while Lee's *Lover's Point* shifts the locus to the United States, reminding us that the China-Japan connection is perhaps best understood not as a bilateral relationship between two nation states but as a triangulated relationship between the United States, Japan, and China.

Lee's novel manages and barely holds together a variety of themes that are simultaneously ethnic (Asian American), national (American), and trans-Pacific (both East-West and inter-Asian). It taps into the novel's contemporary moment—the global Cold War—but comes to terms with this new historical moment by drawing upon what Sun Ge has calls the "plenitude of history." In the fictional space of the novel, Chiang not only faces the legacy of the Sino-Japanese conflict—what one character half-jokingly calls the "three hundred years of enmity [between Chinese and Japanese]"—but also positions himself in a new international configuration signified by his competition with an American man over the feelings of a Japanese woman. Chiang as an immigrant subject, although placeless in national terms, embodies complex international power relations in the Pacific. The novel is similarly placeless in Asian American, American, and Chinese literatures, and belongs only to the fluctuating space of the trans-Pacific, where international conflicts and geopolitical maneuvers constantly shape identities both local and regional.

Much as trans-Pacific journeys in the Cold War period did not just involve non-leftist writers, their destinations did not have to be the United States. The biography of the Malaysian Chinese communist writer Jin Zhimang 金枝芒 charts a trans-Pacific terrain no less ambitious than that of nonleftist writers such as C. Y. Lee and Eileen Chang. Jin's migration to Malaysia in the 1930s has to be contextualized in the larger histories of Chinese migration to the South Seas region and the transnational political movements against Japanese imperialism in the Chinese diaspora. As a cultural worker and a revolutionary, Jin participated in major political movements, including the War of Resistance against Japan, the decolonization of Malaya, and the guerilla warfare that communist fighters waged against the Malayan government in the 1950s. Jin returned to China in 1960 as a liaison between the Malayan Communist Party and the Chinese Communist Party and never went back to Malaysia before his death in the 1980s. Jin Zhimang's case can be considered an example of what Pheng Cheah calls "revolutionary cosmopolitanism," which stemmed from "*huaqiao* [overseas Chinese] spectralization," or the formation of a collective consciousness revolving around a "fervent patriotism" toward China.[44] Cheah argues that "this patriotism was not necessarily a form of chauvinism, and it played a part in the stimulation of indigenous nationalism, and, later, communism and socialism in Southeast Asia."[45] The progressive politics of the overseas Chinese had a strong presence in Malaysian Sinophone literary history, for as the Chinese Malaysian writer Ng Kim Chew 黃錦樹 tells us, the literature of "Southbound writers" (南來作家) from Mainland China developed along two trajectories in Malaya: a literature of exile and one of local place. Within the second category, "[the] sense of place is molded by the material conditions of geographical, historical, and social differences and established by the need for a literature that identifies with local consciousness, which, when it was under the influence of the prewar trend of left-wing literature, took the path of realism (just as in Taiwan's nativist literature [鄉土文學])."[46] Given Jin's enthusiastic advocacy for "local themes" and "local voice," which he expressed in a series of articles about Sinophone Malaysian literature in the 1940s, Jin would fit more easily into the aforementioned second trajectory of Sinophone Malaysian literature as described by Ng.

Yet the local should be viewed as an enigma and problematic for leftist writers such as Jin. In Jin's Chinese-language novel *Hunger* (飢餓), we need to understand the meaning of *local* in terms not only of the "geographical, historical, and social differences" between Malayan Chinese communities and China, but also of the political condition of Malaya's communist movement in the 1950s. Here, the "local" is figured as the dwelling of the guerilla fighters, enclosed spaces in the forests with policed boundaries. It is these metaphors that prompt Ng to observe in this novel a repetitive movement of encampment and breakthrough. History tells us that in the early 1950s, the British general Harold Briggs devised a number of strategies in order to defeat the communist guerrilla fighters in Malaya by cutting them off from their sources of supply in Malaya's rural population. Under Briggs's Plan, a significant percentage of the rural Chinese in Malaysia were forcibly relocated to guarded camps called New Villages to cut off communism from its mass and material base. Consistent with this history, the novel contains many scenes of guerrilla fighters breaking through the fences in order to obtain food and local peasants trying to smuggle food to the guerrilla. The work can thus be read in the context of this significant episode of local history.

If the local refers to the communist struggles in Malaya that Jin Zhimang tries to represent, then it is besieged in another sense. Given the author's close connections with the Chinese Communist Party and his residence in China for over two decades, the neglect by the Chinese authorities toward this manuscript signifies a nontranslation between local communist struggles and the international scene of world revolution. The marginalization of the book in China couldn't have been due to the novel's subject matter or political position, but it may have something to do with the work's depiction of a crisis in the communist movement rather than its success—the situation that communist revolutionary workers have lost their connection with the masses, the workers and peasants without whose support the communist movement cannot survive. This political rumination over the ability of communism to survive in a state of rootlessness and disconnection, along with its picture of a local movement under challenge and duress, could have been an unwelcome message for the Chinese Communist Party.

Jin's text features an oversized human body, dislocated from its surroundings, for political and social reasons. The body looks large because it is bloated due to overconsumption of indigestible roots and leaves:

> In the faint light of early evening appears a round belly the size of a football, its skin stretched thin till it is almost transparent. Refracted by the light, the belly seems covered with a web of intricately woven vanes, each trying to push out of the skin and clearly distinguishable by its particular shades of darkness.[47]

According to Ng Kim Chew, details such as these expose the writer's dedication to aesthetic realism, a taller order than the demands of communist propaganda. This evaluation reveals Ng's criticism of the "local place" school of Sinophone Malaysian literature. Ng writes:

> Both the nativist literature and literary realism espoused in Taiwan and Malaysia tend to consider themselves closer to reality, yet underestimate the importance of cultural capital. Consequently, they underestimate the complexity of the domain of representation (the craft of language and literature) to the extent that the impoverishment of language and technique is construed as one of the manifestations of

nativism (本土性) or its unique characteristic. A corollary operation is an attempt to revise the criteria for universal value in literature, reorienting it toward the regional standard of "reflecting reality" (反映現實), "nativism" (本土性), "local identity" (在地認同), which takes precedence over literariness.[48]

However, instead of perceiving aesthetics as antagonistic or naturally superior to propaganda, we may think of both realism and propaganda as requiring aesthetic mediation. Jin's novel suggests that representing the local place is never something as simple as "reflecting reality," since what constitutes a reality already involves aesthetic and political judgment. Ng points out some intriguing exclusions and lapses in Jin's depiction of the communist movement. For instance, interethnic perspectives are completely missing, since there is not a single non-Chinese character in this novel. In this apparently ahistorical move of overprivileging Chinese presence in Malaya's communist movement, Jin's text reminds us that the local life in Malaya produced by literature cannot do without ideological and aesthetic choices. Given Jin's revolutionary work in a transnational setting, we shouldn't forget the nonlocal frameworks of representation that also shaped Jin's Malayan narrative. The text underwent several rounds of editing while Jin was in China. Although we cannot assess precisely to what extent these revisions contributed to Jin's allegedly Sinocentric perspective, it is clear that Jin's novel, despite its local subject matter, extends beyond Malaysia, in terms of both meaning and significance.

CONCLUSION

Situated in different political positions in Cold War geopolitics, C. Y. Lee and Jin Zhimang demonstrate the various ways in which the trans-Pacific mattered for the ethnic Chinese subject and for the aesthetics and politics of Chinese literature. As Michelle Keown and Stuart Murray argue, the Pacific "has necessarily been conceived of in terms of absence and presence."[49] These narratives demonstrate that attention to the trans-Pacific in any specific moment yields more complex narratives of local identity and regional imagination than blanket valorization of postnationalism or border-crossing. A trans-Pacific turn in Chinese literature cannot be a matter of simply enlarging the scale of analysis in celebration of "scale jumping" and transgression. In fact, both novels, in their engagement with Cold War political powers, construct well-defined regional centers and reinforce the boundaries around ideologically informed regional structures. In this respect, the two novels are undeniably products of history.

If we want to consider Lee's English-language narrative about a homeless Chinese refugee and Jin's Sinophone portrayal of a Chinese migrant's political activities in Malaya as literary works belonging to the same category—whether Chinese diasporic literature, Sinophone literature, or simply Chinese literature—we need to not just enlarge our scope of attention to the trans-Pacific, but recognize that all of these intellectual categories are closely connected to the historical crossings across the Pacific. It is by examining the historical embeddedness of trans-Pacific narratives that we come to terms with their use or abuse in the contemporary context.

NOTES

1. "A Return to the Frontier," *The Reporter,* March 28, 1963.
2. Ascoli himself defined the agenda of *The Reporter* as "every inch anti-Communist"; see Martin K. Doudna, *Concerned about the Planet: The Reporter Magazine and American Liberalism, 1949–1968* (Westport, CT: Greenwood Press, 1977), 94.
3. Jing Tsu and David Der-wei Wang, "Introduction: Global Chinese Literature," in *Global Chinese Literature*, ed. Jing Tsu and David Der-wei Wang (Leiden: Brill, 2010), 3.
4. Tsu and Wang, "Introduction," 3.
5. See Gayatri Spivak, "Three Women's Texts and a Critique of Imperialism," *Critical Inquiry* 12.1 (Autumn 1985): 243–261.
6. Djelal Kadir, "To World, To Globalize—Comparative Literature's Crossroads," *Comparative Literature Studies* 41.1 (2004): 2.
7. Kadir, "To World," 2.
8. Kadir, "To World," 7.
9. Michelle Keown and Stuart Murray, "Our Sea of Islands: Globalization, Regionalism, and (Trans)Nationalism in the Pacific," in *The Oxford Handbook of Postcolonial Studies*, ed. Graham Huggan (Oxford: Oxford University Press, 2013), 609.
10. Arif Dirlik, "The Asia-Pacific Idea: Reality and Representation in the Invention of a Regional Structure," in *What Is in a Rim: Critical Perspectives on the Pacific Region Idea*, ed. Arif Dirlik (Lanham, MD: Rowman & Littlefield, 1998), 15–16.
11. Dirlik, "The Asia-Pacific Idea," 22, 24.
12. Naoki Sakai and Hyon Joo Yoo, "Introduction: The Trans-Pacific Imagination: Rethinking Boundary, Culture and Society," in *The Trans-Pacific Imagination—Rethinking Boundary, Culture and Society*, ed. Naoki Sakai and Hyon Joo Yoo (Singapore: World Scientific, 2012), viii.
13. Bruce Cummings, "Rimspeak; or, The Discourse of the 'Pacific Rim,'" in *What Is in a Rim: Critical Perspectives on the Pacific Region Idea*, ed. Arif Dirlik (Lanham, MD: Rowman & Littlefield, 1998), 55.
14. Cummings, "Rimspeak," 56.
15. Arif Dirlik, "Introduction: Asia/Pacific as Space of Cultural Production," in *Asia/Pacific as Space of Cultural Production*, ed. Rob Wilson and Arif Dirlik (Durham: Duke University Press, 1995), 12.
16. Gayatri Chakravorty Spivak, *Other Asias* (Malden, MA: Blackwell, 2008), 214.
17. Chen Kuan-Hsing, *Asia as Method: Toward Deimperialization* (Durham: Duke University Press, 2010), 205.
18. Chen, *Asia as Method*, 205.
19. Sakai and Yoo, "Introduction," 6.
20. Sun Ge, "Reconceptualizing 'East Asia' in the Post-Cold War Era," in *The Trans-Pacific Imagination: Rethinking Boundary, Culture and Society*, ed. Naoki Sakai and Hyon Joo Yoo (Singapore: World Scientific, 2012), 273.

21. Pheng Cheah, "World against Globe: Toward a Normative Conception of World Literature," *New Literary History* 45.3 (Summer 2014): 323.

22. Chap. 3, "De-Cold War: The Im/possibility of 'Great Reconciliation,'" in Chen Kuan-Hsing, *Asia as Method: Toward Deimperialization*.

23. Cheah, "World against Globe," 322.

24. Sun Ge, "Reconceptualizing 'East Asia' in the Post-Cold War Era," 54.

25. Karen Thornber's *Empire of Texts in Motion: Chinese, Korean, and Taiwanese Transculturations of Japanese Literature* and Margaret Hillenbrand's *Literature, Modernity, and the Practice of Resistance: Japanese and Taiwanese Fiction, 1960–1990* are examples of recent work on inter-Asia cultural flows and regional consciousness in East Asia.

26. Kadir, "To World," 7

27. The periodization of the Cold War in Asia demands a different consideration from the situation of the United States. In most works of Chinese literature of the mid-twentieth century, the Cold War is presented as a continuation of the Chinese Civil War, and even of the Asia Pacific War.

28. David Der-wei Wang 王德威, "Zhanzheng xushi yu xushi zhanzheng: Yan'an, Jinmeng, yiji yiwai" 戰爭敘事與敘事戰爭: 延安, 金門, 及其以外 [War narratives narrating war: Yan'an, Jinmen, and beyond] (unpublished manuscript).

29. Spivak, *Other Asias*, 9–10.

30. Spivak, *Other Asias*, 214.

31. Spivak, *Other Asias*, 8, 226.

32. Spivak, *Other Asias*, 219.

33. Spivak, *Other Asias*, 8.

34. Spivak, *Other Asias*, 235.

35. Asian American historians such as Madeline Hsu have studied the impact of the Cold War on Chinese immigrant population and communities in the United States.

36. For criticism of the Broadway production *Flower Drum Song*, see Anne Anlin Cheng, *The Melancholy of Race: Psychoanalysis, Assimilation, and Hidden Grief* (New York: Oxford University Press, 2001) and Gina Marchetti, *Romance and the "Yellow Peril": Race, Sex, and Discursive Strategies in Hollywood Fiction* (Berkeley: University of California Press, 1993).

37. C. Y. Lee, *Flower Drum Song* (New York: Penguin, 2002), 133.

38. Cheng, *The Melancholy of Race*, 43–44.

39. Cheng, *The Melancholy of Race*, 44.

40. For a discussion of the representation of the Asia Pacific War in Hong Kong films during the Cold War period, see Mai Lang 麥浪, "Lengzhan fenwei xia de Xianggang yuyan: Dianmao yu Dongbao de 'Xianggang' xilie" 冷戰氛圍下的香港寓言: 電懋與東寶的「香港」系列 [A Hong Kong allegory in the context of the Cold War: The "Hong Kong" trilogy of MP&GI and Toho], in *Lengzhan yu Xianggang dianying* 冷戰與香港電影 [Cold War and Hong Kong film], ed. Huang Ailing and Li Peide (Hong Kong: Xianggang Dianying Ziliao Guan, 2009), 191–208.

41. C. Y. Lee, *Lover's Point* (New York: Farrar, Straus and Cudany, 1958), 235.

42. Lee, *Lover's Point*, 217

43. Lee, *Lover's Point*, 152.

44. Pheng Cheah, *Inhuman Conditions: On Cosmopolitanism and Human Rights* (Cambridge: Harvard University Press, 2006), 134.

45. Cheah, *Inhuman Conditions*, 134.

46. Ng Kim Chew, "Minor Sinophone Literature: Diasporic Modernity's Incomplete Journey," in *Global Chinese Literature*, ed. Jing Tsu and David Der-wei Wang (Leiden: Brill, 2010), 17.

47. Jin Zhimang 金枝芒, *Jie* 饑餓 [Hunger] (Kuala Lumpur: Penerbitan Abad Dua Pulua Satu, 2008), 154.
48. Ng Kim Chew, "Minor Sinophone Literature: Diasporic Modernity's Incomplete Journey," 17.
49. Michelle Keown and Stuart Murray, "Our Sea of Islands: Globalization, Regionalism, and (Trans)Nationalism in the Pacific," 607.

Works Cited

Chang, Eileen 張愛玲. "A Return to the Frontier." In Chang, *Chongfan biancheng* 重返邊城 [A return to the frontier]. Taipei: Huangguan Chubanshe, 2008. (Originally published in *The Reporter*, March 28, 1963.)

Cheah, Pheng. "World against Globe: Toward a Normative Conception of World Literature." *New Literary History* 45.3 (Summer 2014): 303–329.

Cheah, Pheng. *Inhuman Conditions: On Cosmopolitanism and Human Rights.* Cambridge: Harvard University Press, 2006.

Chen, Kuan-Hsing. *Asia as Method: Toward Deimperialization.* Durham: Duke University Press, 2010.

Cheng, Anne Anlin. *The Melancholy of Race: Psychoanalysis, Assimilation, and Hidden Grief.* New York: Oxford University Press, 2001.

Cummings, Bruce. "Rimspeak; or, The Discourse of the 'Pacific Rim.'" In *What Is in a Rim: Critical Perspectives on the Pacific Region Idea.* Ed. Arif Dirlik. Lanham, MD: Rowman & Littlefield, 1998. 53–72.

Dirlik, Arif. "Introduction: Pacific Contradictions." In *What Is in a Rim: Critical Perspectives on the Pacific Region Idea.* Ed. Arif Dirlik. Lanham, MD: Rowman & Littlefield, 1998. 3–14.

Dirlik, Arif. "The Asia-Pacific Idea: Reality and Representation in the Invention of a Regional Structure." In *What Is in a Rim: Critical Perspectives on the Pacific Region Idea.* Ed. Arif Dirlik. Lanham, MD: Rowman & Littlefield, 1998. 15–36.

Doudna, Martin K. *Concerned about the Planet: The Reporter Magazine and American Liberalism, 1949–1968.* Westport, CT: Greenwood Press, 1977.

Jin, Zhimang 金枝芒. *Jie* 饑餓 [Hunger]. Kuala Lumpur: Penerbitan Abad Dua Pulua Satu, 2008.

Kadir, Djelal. "To World, To Globalize—Comparative Literature's Crossroads." *Comparative Literature Studies* 41.1 (2004): 1–9.

Keown, Michelle, and Stuart Murray. "Our Sea of Islands: Globalization, Regionalism, and (Trans)Nationalism in the Pacific." In *The Oxford Handbook of Postcolonial Studies.* Ed. Graham Huggan. Oxford: Oxford University Press, 2013. 607–627.

Lee, C. Y. *Flower Drum Song.* New York: Penguin, 2002.

Lee, C. Y. *Lover's Point.* New York: Farrar, Straus and Cudany, 1958.

Lowe, Lisa. "The Trans-Pacific Migrant and Area Studies." In *The Trans-Pacific Imagination: Rethinking Boundary, Culture and Society.* Ed. Naoki Sakai and Hyon Joo Yoo. Singapore: World Scientific, 2012. 61–74.

Marchetti, Gina. *Romance and the 'Yellow Peril': Race, Sex, and Discursive Strategies in Hollywood Fiction.* Berkeley: University of California Press, 1993.

Mai Lang 麥浪. "Lengzhan fenwei xia de Xianggang yuyan: Dianmao yu Dongbao de 'Xianggang' xilie" 冷戰氛圍下的香港寓言：電懋與東寶的 「香港」 系列 [A Hong Kong allegory in the context of the Cold War: The "Hong Kong" trilogy of MP&GI and

Toho]. In *Lengzhan yu Xianggang dianying* 冷戰與香港電影 [Cold War and Hong Kong film]. Ed. Huang Ailing and Li Peide. Hong Kong: Xianggang Dianying Ziliao Guan, 2009. 191–208.

Ng Kim Chew 黃錦樹. "Zuihou de zhanyi: Lun Jin Zhimang de 'Ji'e'" 最後的戰役：論金枝芒的「饑餓」 [The last battle: On the novel *Ji'e* by Jin Zhimang]. *Sinchew News*, March 14, 2010, retrieved from http://news.sinchew.com.my/node/152694?tid=15.

Ng Kim Chew 黃錦樹. "Minor Sinophone Literature: Diasporic Modernity's Incomplete Journey." In *Global Chinese Literature*. Ed. Jing Tsu and David Der-wei Wang. Leiden: Brill, 2010. 15–28.

Sakai, Naoki, and Hyon Joo Yoo. "Introduction: The Trans-Pacific Imagination: Rethinking Boundary, Culture and Society." In *The Trans-Pacific Imagination—Rethinking Boundary, Culture and Society*. Ed. Naoki Sakai and Hyon Joo Yoo. Singapore: World Scientific, 2012. 1–44.

Sun, Ge. "Reconceptualizing "East Asia" in the Post-Cold War Era." In *The Trans-Pacific Imagination: Rethinking Boundary, Culture and Society*. Ed. Naoki Sakai and Hyon Joo Yoo. Singapore: World Scientific, 2012. 253–278.

Shih, Shu-mei. "Comparison as Relation." In *Comparison: Theories, Approaches, Uses*. Ed. Rita Felski and Susan Stanford Friedman. Baltimore: The Johns Hopkins University Press, 2013. 79–98.

Spivak, Gayatri Chakravorty. *Other Asias*. Malden, MA: Blackwell, 2008.

Spivak, Gayatri Chakravorty. "Three Women's Texts and a Critique of Imperialism." *Critical Inquiry* 12.1 (Autumn 1985): 243–261.

Tsu, Jing, and David Der-wei Wang. "Introduction: Global Chinese Literature." In *Global Chinese Literature*. Ed. Jing Tsu and David Der-wei Wang. Leiden: Brill, 2010. 1–14.

Xu Su 徐速. *Xingxing yueliang taiyang* 星星月亮太陽 [The star, the moon, the sun]. Xianggang: Gaoyuan chubanshe, 1953.

Xu Su 徐速. *Yingzi guniang* 櫻子姑娘 [The girl called Sakurako]. Beijing: Zhongguo Youyi Chuban Gusi, 1985.

Wang, David Der-wei 王德威. "Zhanzheng xushi yu xushi zhanzheng: Yan'an, Jinmeng, yiji Yi Wei" 戰爭敘事與敘事戰爭：延安, 金門, 及其以外 [War narratives narrating war: Yan'an, Jinmen, and beyond]. Unpublished manuscript. Presented at the international conference on "The Era of the Great Divide" at Aichi University, Nagoya, August 4–6, 2013.

Wilson, Rob, and Arif Dirlik. "Introduction: Asia/Pacific as Space of Cultural Production." In *Asia/Pacific as Space of Cultural Production*. Ed. Rob Wilson and Arif Dirlik. Durham, NC: Duke University Press, 1995. 1–16.

XIAOLU GUO AND THE CONTEMPORARY CHINESE ANGLOPHONE NOVEL

BELINDA KONG

IN a 2008 essay titled "Fragments of My Life," Xiaolu Guo 郭小橹 contemplates an ID card she has carried with her for over thirty years, from the village of Shitang to Beijing, from China to England. It reads, "Chinese, Hui Minority, Peasant Household." She goes on to remark wryly,

> I've never understood what is Hui and why I am a peasant. The only thing I know is that my family came from a rural Hui Muslim background, while most Chinese are Han Majority . . . I have been all right with that ID card. I learnt to speak Mandarin at schools and in Beijing, and I eat pork too. . . . But why Hui? Why peasant? We never had one piece of land to grow rice or anything. We lived in a fishing village. . . . If I belong to the Hui People, Muslims, of Turkish and Persian background, then why don't we live in the western part of China?[1]

Traveling through the Northwest provinces in the 1990s on film projects, Guo was eager to meet fellow Huis in Xinjiang but failed to do so. Two years later in Qinghai, surrounded by ethnic minorities, she no longer cared about root-seeking and wanted only to be a "world citizen." A decade later still, a world traveler now in a "rich and dead village in England," she was prepared to identify herself as someone "from China," but an Englishwoman mistook her for "the girl from Hong Kong who visited here last year" and, by way of apology, added, "You know, all Chinese look the same to us." Finally, looking at a map of China in English, in "decayed Europe" now, she muses:

> That is confusing—when you read your own country's map in a foreign language, you are not sure any more where those places are supposed to be. I don't really find the China with its cities and towns, all I see are those borders: Mongolia, Kazakhstan, Uzbekistan, Turkmenistan, Afghanistan, Pakistan, India, Burma, Nepal, Cambodia,

Laos, Vietnam, and many other countries lost in the South China Sea and the Pacific Ocean. And on that map I'm still trying to find out why I am a Hui and why I am a peasant and why I am a Chinese.[2]

What begins as an ironic self-distancing from the imposed label of *Hui* quickly becomes a narrative of missed and rejected opportunities for ethnic identification. *Hui* is that which Guo is supposed to embody but somehow manages to never coincide with, whether in China or England, in Chinese or English. As a descendant of a minority group, she could not even locate herself at the correct margins. If the Communist Party first imposed this out-of-place classification on her, England too wants to see in her another variety of colonial cosmopolitanism, or else an undifferentiated racial otherness. Europe follows suit by legitimating her place of origin only to dislodge it onto a foreign language—unqualifiedly Chinese at last, but on a map with no recognizable home country, only borders. Caught through the decades between these not so dissimilarly alienating forms of biogovernance, Guo may feign confusion about her identity, but she understands all too well the power of a state and its language to fabricate, prefix, and contain what she is.

While Guo strategically invokes the category of *Hui* in this essay to ironize her identification with Chineseness within the PRC, when facing the Western media she does not insist on her Hui difference but readily assumes the label of *Chinese* in order to speak out against prevailing clichés about China. In an interview in early 2014, she is asked: "you're quoted as saying 'there's strong self-censorship inside every artist.' In context, I presume you mean Chinese artists. How much of that self-censorship stays with you after leaving China?" To this question that reflexively equates *Chinese* with censorship, Guo responds tartly:

> Self-censorship happens not only in China, or Iran or ex-Soviet places. It can happen anywhere. If an artist penetrates a certain taboo or a certain power through their work, he or she will face this problem. I'm always saying that commercial censorship is our foremost censorship globally today. Why do we still pretend we are free?[3]

Neither playing apologist for communist China nor complacently allying with the liberal West, Guo attributes censorship to democratic as much as authoritarian states. In doing so, she shrewdly shifts the terms of analysis from a geopolitical dichotomy to comparable modes of governance. If the two sites differ, it is in the mechanisms of their respective censorship regime.

This critical bifocality typifies Guo's public avowals. Not one given to eulogy or defense of either the PRC or the West, she is much more apprehensive about the operations of sovereign power that extend across both sites. With customary provocativeness, she has declared, "People always think there is a culture clash between China and other countries—a culture shock. I don't believe in culture shock."[4] Instead, she draws attention to commonalities in governmental power and professes a distrust in states of whatever stripe: "I couldn't trust any state. I can't believe anything's freer in one state or another—it's just degrees. . . . If I changed, [it's because] I discovered the body of the state is impenetrable."[5]

In Guo's fictions, too, we can chart an argumentative arc from culture and language to biopower and geopower—what Sheldon Lu calls "geobiopower"—as the predominant concerns of the new millennium.[6] For Guo, the task of the contemporary Chinese Anglophone novel is to pose the relation between China and the West as above all a political, rather than merely cultural or linguistic, problem. Her first novel in English, *A Concise Chinese-English Dictionary for Lovers* (2007), is often considered an exploration of cultural and linguistic difference, but I would contend that it can be more fruitfully examined within biopolitical and geopolitical perspectives. In turn, this can yield a rethinking of the politics of the Anglophone novel. Beyond the geopolitics of language, Guo's third novel in English, *UFO in Her Eyes* (2009), provides a new conceptual framework for contemporary Chinese literature through its conjunction of totalitarianism, biopower, and capitalism. While much post-9/11 Anglophone writing highlights the body politics of the security state, recent literature from China instead tends to spotlight the body in biocapital—that is, the increasing entanglement of the state regulation of bodies with capitalist goals.[7] My chapter, then, focuses on Guo's Anglophone writing as a kind of double prism: to illuminate what she brings to conceptions of *Anglophone* on one hand and those of *Chinese* on the other. She is a particularly apt figure to discuss in this context, for we can perceive in her fictions a rich cross-fertilizing of the postmillennial anxieties of both the Anglophone and the Chinese novel. Ultimately, Guo intimates that China's and the West's governance regimes may not be so distinct in our time, and may potentially overlap in a not too distant future.

RETHINKING THE ANGLOPHONE

At first sight, Guo may appear as a paragon of global literary success. Born in a fishing village in Zhejiang in 1973, she studied at the Beijing Film Academy in the 1990s and left China in 2002 on a film scholarship for London, where she now lives as a British citizen. Before becoming an author in English, she had already published two novels and several essay collections in Chinese, and she continues to produce films in both languages as an independent filmmaker. While she has numerous translators, she also self-translates. She rewrote and translated her first novel in Chinese, *Fenfang de sanshiqi du er* (芬芳的三十七度二; 2000), into English as *20 Fragments of a Ravenous Youth* (2008).[8] And though *UFO in Her Eyes* currently has no Chinese novelistic counterpart, Guo spent two years adapting it into the film *Santouniaocun jishilu* (三頭鳥村記事錄; 2011), or *Records of Three-Headed Bird Village*.[9] She is thus a cultural producer and self-translator across languages and media.

Given this prolific bilingual oeuvre, it may be easy to forget the institutional conditions that precipitated Guo's Anglophone career in the first place. As she underscores in an interview, however, her decision to begin writing in English stemmed first and foremost from linguistic inequities and institutional disempowerment: "When I came to the U.K. ten years ago, everyone told me I couldn't send my books directly to publishing houses—that I had to go through a literary agent. So I did, and then I found out the agents couldn't provide a translator or read my Chinese. There was—there still is—a big shortage of good Chinese-English literary translators. So for two years in London, I was stuck waiting, not writing, with several Chinese books I couldn't get translated."[10] While her decision to write in English turned out to be creatively "liberating," allowing her to experiment with new narrative forms, Guo nonetheless emphasizes the tremendous imbalance in commercial power between English and Chinese in the British publishing industry. As a literary language, the latter is not only dependent and marginal but economically unviable for the immigrant writer. Guo here echoes other Anglophone Chinese writers before her who have faced a similar predicament, such as Ha Jin, who often speaks of his adoption of English as a matter of physical and spiritual "survival."[11]

Yet Guo departs from her peers in a significant respect: she does not appeal to the dichotomy between Chinese as a language of repression and English as a language of freedom. In the past dozen years, this binary has become a commonplace in the Anglophone West, expressed earnestly at first by some diaspora writers as they tackle subjects censored by the PRC government such as the Tiananmen Massacre, but subsequently reiterated and enshrined into literary dogma by media outlets. Ha Jin has been a particularly staunch voice in this regard, eschewing Chinese as a language "polluted by revolutionary movements and political jargon" while embracing English as the language that "preserve[s] the integrity of [his] work" and grants him a more universal "literary citizenship."[12] In more gendered terms, female writers such as Anchee Min, Annie Wang, and Yiyun Li have also variously referred to English as their escape route from self-censorship in Chinese, whether political, cultural, or emotional.[13] Though they are not wrong to lament the pressures of communist censorship, these writers rarely go on to elaborate on the limits of writing in English or to weigh the relative constraints of an Anglophone book market. However nuanced in context, their comments have the unfortunate effect of polarizing English and Chinese and elevating the former as a vehicle of emancipation from the latter's oppression. This discourse has contributed too, perhaps, to the escalation of the recent debate over Mo Yan's 莫言 Nobel Prize and the question of whether the "disease" of Maoist language lingers in all contemporary Chinese literature.[14]

In this context, Guo represents an important voice that redefines the relation of English to Chinese. Recognizing the tenacity of a kind of phonic Orientalism, she refuses to pit one language against the other. As we have seen, she not only implicates the Anglophone as a site of "commercial censorship" but deems it even more powerful, because more insidious, than the communist one. Where the PRC government acts overtly and censors by suppression and exclusion, the Western publishing industry operates furtively, by way of an exclusive inclusion. At the 2014 Jaipur Literature Festival, Guo clarified this point with the controversial claim that "English American literature . . . is overrated, massively overrated." Most Anglophone writers, she observed, tend to fall back on commercially popular forms of realism and "let the lazy, easy traditional narrative—which is controlled by the publishing industry—roll all over the readers and dominate the market"; as a result, "readers and cinemagoers have been trained to read and watch very mainstream stuff. It's like being given sleeping pills. It sends people to a non-reflective sleep state."[15] So, even as she concedes that writing in English makes her *feel* freer, she distrusts this freedom as the "easiest and laziest" choice on her part, premised as it is on the psychic conditioning of a market that numbs creativity and forecloses criticism. Guo neatly captures here Pascale Casanova's caustic critique of the Anglo-American book market's linguistic insularity and devaluing of literary translations, as well as the US-led corporatization of publishing industries everywhere that starves out avant-garde writing while mass-producing formulaic versions of "world fiction."[16] Moreover, as I will analyze below, her description dovetails with Luciana Parisi and Steven Goodman's concept of "mnemonic control"—a mode of capitalist biopower that programs "the feelings, movements, and becomings of bodies, tapping into their virtuality by investing preemptively in futurity."[17] The contemporary Anglophone novel, then, may be a potent site of biocapitalist power.

Guo's provocations train our eye on the institutional and geopolitical dimensions of literary language use and, more pointedly, on English's dominance in the production and reproduction of world literature. As she puts it, "we are too much living in an English-speaking world."[18] That English is a language of global power is of course not a new insight. What Guo's views push against, though, is a prevailing paradigm in literary criticism that, explicitly or implicitly, treats English as a privileged site of heterogeneity, polyglossia, or translingualism. Not surprisingly, this paradigm itself arose as a response to empire. Perhaps most notable in this critical genealogy is Homi Bhabha's notion of hybridity, which plants within colonial power the seeds of its own deconstruction, activated when colonized subjects subversively mimic the language of domination and turn the eye of power back upon itself.[19] After and alongside Bhabha, numerous critics have proposed analogous theories of the interstices of language and culture, in-between spaces where multiplicity can surface. Ironically, because of its status as a former language of empire and the current lingua franca of globalization, English has become the most hospitable target for these articulations. In the process, the Anglophone novel has undergone a strangely utopian rehabilitation: no longer reductively aligned with empire or power, it is now read for its hybrid, translingual, or polyphonic qualities, as the very site where cross-cultural differences become discernible and contests of power are felicitously laid bare.

This is the framework through which Guo's writing has primarily been read. Of her fictions, *A Concise Chinese-English Dictionary for Lovers* is the most amenable to this perspective, and critics have thus far focused exclusively on this text in her oeuvre. Narrated in the voice of twenty-three-year-old Zhuang Xiao Qiao, who goes by Z because no one in England can pronounce her name, the novel takes the form of Z's diary and performatively records her struggles with English over the course of her one-year stay in London. As the months progress, the entries grow ever less ungrammatical and more complex. In the prologue, Z bemoans in fragmented English: "As

I far away from China, I asking me why I coming to West. Why I must to study English like parents wish? Why I must to get diploma from West?"[20] By the epilogue, though, Z is able to reflect back on the past year's experiences in fluent and lyrical prose. She memorializes the moment of double consciousness when she was first seen by her English lover and felt irrevocably altered by a gaze she later internalizes: "When I first saw you, I felt I saw another me, a me against me, a me which I contradicted all the time. And now I cannot forget you and I cannot stop loving you because you are a part of me."[21]

By assuming Z's evolving voice and portraying her as an eager learner of English in the Western metropolis, and by playing up the unequal power relations between Chinese and English via the two main characters, Guo readily invites postcolonial evaluations on the politics of language here. Yet critics have gone further with their terms of analysis by reading *Dictionary* as an affirmation of feminist "bi-lingual" writing,[22] a reflection of "transcultural" and "translingual" border-crossing,[23] a "translational novel" about London as a city of "polyglossia" and a "complex contact zone,"[24] or a critique of "fluidity" discourses of globalization.[25] Despite their different emphases, what unites these readings is a tacit validation of the Anglophone novel as doing positive cross-cultural work in our time—by revealing existing plurality within English or showing it at its seams, by hybridizing and creolizing English from within, or even by exposing the violence and domination of English vis-à-vis other languages. On this paradigm, the Anglophone novel offers a sufficiently rich discourse of hybridity, heterogeneity, and inequality to narrate its encounters with linguistic others and to perform an internal critique of its own hegemony; at its most complex and sophisticated, exemplified by writing such as Guo's, the Anglophone novel serves as a platform for the most ethical of textual practices.

If we take seriously Guo's assessment of the Anglophone publishing industry as an institution of biocapitalist censorship, however, an opposite interpretation emerges. Instead of bearing out ideas of hybridity, polyglossia, and translingualism, *Dictionary* can equally be read as a narrative of these ideas' inadequacy and failure. Along this reading, the novel is not an attempt to illustrate a translingual or translational process by which both Chinese and English become transmuted, nor does it epitomize the effort to destabilize the authority of English from within. On the contrary, Z's progress in English can be interpreted as a process of biopolitical discipline, whereby the Chinese migrant gradually gets absorbed into a dominant, proper, and publishable English. That this process is tied to the global capitalist power of English is part of the novel's premise, since Z is sent to England not by her own wishes but on the orders of her wealth-aspiring parents. Moreover, the novel's linguistic universe is far from one in which a concert of different Englishes coexists. In Z's relationship with her English lover, for example, change arguably occurs on both sides, but linguistic change is heavily one-sided. While she accrues ever more complicated English, he never learns even elementary Chinese, nor does his English become mixed or creolized with hers. At most, he feels depleted by Z's constant questioning, her "stealing" of his language, as though he is becoming "slower and slower" in speech and "losing [his] words."[26] Still, in this satire of the Englishman's cultural insularity and anxiety, Guo does not hold up the possibility of his learning Chinese as necessarily a desirable or ethical act, since he would be doing so squarely within the Anglophone center, without the need to ever let go of the primacy of English.

By contrast, Chinese eventually disappears from the text—even after Z returns to China. Early on, she would occasionally translate between Chinese and English, whether by inscribing Chinese proverbs and expressions or cataloging objects in both languages. In addition, midway through the novel, she abruptly abandons English to write two entire chapters in Chinese, in which she vents her long-held frustrations with the English language as much as her English lover. Titled "nonsense" and "freedom," as if to self-referentially mark the polar status of Chinese to English for her at this point, these chapters bespeak Z's desperate desire to escape from the prison-house of English. Ironically, on their facing pages the chapters are translated for the reader into standard colloquial English, as if by the hand of an invisible editor who denies Z her attempt at linguistic flight. For instance, the "nonsense" chapter begins:

> 我真他媽地厭倦了這樣說英文,這樣寫英文。我厭倦了這樣學英文。我感到全身緊縛, 如同牢獄。我害怕從此變成一個小心翼翼的人, 沒有自信的人。因為我完全不能做我自己, 我變得如此渺小, 而與我無關的這個英語文化變得如此巨大。我被它驅使, 我被它強暴, 我被它消滅。我真想徹底忘記這些單詞, 拼法, 時態。我真想說回我天生的語言, 可是, 我天生的語言它是真正的天生的嗎?我仍然記得小時候學漢語有同樣的苦功和痛楚。[27]

On the facing page, this passage is translated into a level of English that Z has yet to attain:

> *I am sick of speaking English like this. I am sick of writing English like this. I feel as if I am being tied up, as if I am living in a prison. I am scared that I have become a person who is always very aware of talking, speaking, and I have become a person without confidence, because I can't be me. I have become small, so tiny, while the English culture surrounding me becomes enormous. It swallows me, and it rapes me. I wish I could just go back to my own language now. But is my own native language simple enough? I still remember the pain of studying Chinese characters when I was a child at school.[28]*

This bilingual chapter is much discussed by Guo's critics, but their interpretations differ in emphasis depending on which edition they are working with. In the first British edition by Chatto & Windus and in subsequent Vintage editions from London, the English passage is tagged with the line "Editor's translation" in boldface, but in the first US edition by Nan A. Talese as well as in the Anchor paperback reprints and Wheeler large-print editions, this tagline is removed, leaving the source of translation even more ambiguous.[29] While we do not know for certain whether Guo herself is Z's "translator" here and whether the "editor" is merely a textual device, the silent emendation made by some real-life editor during the course of the novel's publication history ironically bears out Guo's theme of secret editorial intervention.

Furthermore, as Eunju Hwang points out, the bilingual reader will note that Z's "stormy Chinese," prefaced with the swear words *tamade* (他媽地), becomes sanitized in the English version.[30] Hence, even as Z ends the chapter by equating English with Chinese as both difficult and painful forms of communication, the text itself is quick to contain her momentary bilingual impulse by reinstating her into a proper, bowdlerized English. After the chapter on "freedom," Chinese characters appear in the text only once more, in a passing reference to "China, '中國,'"[31] but even this invocation of the nation fails to safeguard its language. In the epilogue, Z is back in Beijing, but her diary has become wholly monolingual. She is advised by friends and family to capitalize on her new facility with English, and though she feels alienated from their mercenary attitude, she continues her self-narration in her most perfected English yet. Without the need for a disciplining editor now, she voluntarily pays homage to England as the country where she "became an adult" and "grew into a woman."[32] By implication, English's ideological grip now stretches into China's own capital, heralding the disappearance of the bilingual writer.

Thus reframed, *Dictionary* may be interpreted as a warning against over-rehabilitating the Anglophone novel. To invest this genre with too valorizing a set of ethical functions may risk buttressing the resilience and capaciousness of English in co-opting other languages. Even when writers strive to enact a politics of maximal inclusion within English, they may simultaneously advance a geopolitics of assimilation and erasure beyond English. For Guo, the Anglophone novel may well be a mechanism by which English comes to consume what Talal Asad calls "weaker" languages under the guise of internal diversity.[33] She does not militate against using English tout court as a language of fiction, as Ngugi wa Thiong'o has done[34]—Chinese, after all, is not the same as Gikuyu in its decolonizing capacity as a native tongue—but neither does she settle for a narrative patchwork of "all the Englishes" she knows, à la Amy Tan.[35] Rather, she advocates for a more honest and critical appraisal of the Anglophone novel's biocapitalist conditions and geopolitical limits. In this sense, she is not merely cautioning against overgeneral or reductive uses of hybridity as an analytical term.[36] She goes further to question the very belief that hybrid textual practices are ever geopolitically disruptive, especially if Anglophone writers are granted ever greater license to stay within the confines of a now recuperated and robustly expanded English.

By bringing this skeptical perspective to conceptions of the Anglophone, Guo stresses what it does *not* bring to conceptions of Chineseness: a radically deessentializing hermeneutics or textual politics. If one formulation of "Anglophone Chinese diasporic literature" tends to position the Anglophone in the role of introducing "difference and hybridity" or "splitting and subjunctification" into Chinese identity, Guo would agree that for a Chinese migrant to enter into English is for her to actively "question . . . what it means to be Chinese outside of China," as Emma Teng suggests, as well as to be "excluded from being a 'native speaker' or from having a claim to the written literary tradition" as a racial and linguistic other, as Dorothy Wang argues.[37] Yet, Guo would go on to add that to write in English is also to gain passage into a realm of geopolitical power—what Amitav Ghosh calls the "anglophone empire." Writing during the months of the US invasion of Baghdad, Ghosh argues that the phrase *new American empire* is a misnomer, for the Iraq War is "neither new nor purely American." Instead, it is dominated by the coalition of "America, Britain, and Australia—three English-speaking countries whose allegiances are rooted not just in a shared culture and common institutions but in a shared history of territorial expansion."[38] In the post-9/11 world, English is not just one nation's colonial instrument but a geopolitical unifier, the matrix for exceptional deployments of power. To write within this latter-day Anglophone empire is to be surrounded by its discourses of antiterrorism, military intervention, and the security state. In an era when Western governments lead the charge in adopting emergency measures and intervening in human life by suspending citizen rights domestically as much as launching preemptive attacks abroad, concerns over sovereignty, biopower, and geopolitics have come sharply to the fore in Anglophone discourses. In turn, recent theories of the Anglophone novel have come to foreground these issues. Longstanding postcolonial preoccupations with cultural difference and language hierarchies are not so much superseded as recast within these frameworks, just as the novel itself is now reconceived as the forum for negotiating everyday ethics in crisis states or imagining alternative modes of governmentality.[39] Arguably, it is this heightened alert to geopower and biopower that the Anglophone novel can most usefully import into our reading of contemporary Chinese literature. Not by accident, it also provides the key to decoding Guo's most resonant novel in this context.

Conceptualizing "Chinese"

Perhaps the most striking, and also most inexplicable, element in *UFO in Her Eyes* is its connection to September 11. On this date in the novel's speculative future China of 2012, in the fictional Hunan village of Silver Hill, a peasant woman allegedly sights a UFO and saves the life of the "alien" who drops from it into the local rice fields. This event triggers the suspicion of the village chief, who dutifully reports it to the town bureau and on up the chain of command, until agents arrive from the provincial government as well as Beijing to investigate the case. The narrative unfolds over the next three years, in the form of "national security and intelligence agency" files, compiled mostly from interview transcripts but also village meeting records and correspondence between the agents and their superiors. As it turns out, the foreign body that fell from the sky was a New Yorker who claims to have been bitten by a snake while hiking in the Hunan mountains. In gratitude to the peasant woman Kwok Yun for rescuing him, he writes a $2,000 check to the village, thereby catapulting it into a capitalist frenzy. Within a few years, with additional funding from the provincial government, Silver Hill is transformed from one of the poorest areas in the country into a UFO theme park and modern factory town, complete with its own Five Year Plan, shopping mall, sports center, and, by novel's end, smog pollution and worker riots. While some residents, like the village chief, gush about Silver Hill eventually "liv[ing] up to its name and becom[ing] a place where you will truly find silver on the streets . . . a launch pad for the future of China"—a veritable Gold Mountain, now materializing on home turf—others are embittered by their displacement from old ways of life, variously resorting to self-isolation, migration, even suicide, as rural bodies unassimilable by China's emerging capital.[40]

Through this dystopic parable of one village's modernization, Guo adamantly spotlights the social and human costs of the PRC's so-called economic miracle. In this literary endeavor, she is not unique. Much recent Chinese literature is concerned with exposing the underside of China's rapid development, whether in rural or urban settings, for peasants or intellectuals, migrants or entrepreneurs. This preoccupation cuts across national and linguistic lines, uniting diverse writers within the mainland with many who have left for the Anglophone West, and Chinese- with English-language productions. Numerous examples from the past dozen years can be cited, from Chan Koonchung's 陳冠中 *The Fat Years* (盛世: 中國二〇一三年; 2009), Yan Lianke's 閻連科 *Dream of Ding Village* (丁庄夢; 2006), Murong Xuecun's 慕容雪村 *Leave Me Alone: A Novel of Chengdu* (成都, 今夜請將我遺忘; 2002), and Liao Yiwu's 廖亦武 *Corpse Walker* (中國底層訪談錄; 2001), all written in the PRC, to diasporic fictions that circulate mainly in English such as Yiyun Li's 李翊雲 *Kinder Than Solitude* (2014), Ma Jian's 馬建 *The Dark Road* (2013), and Geling Yan's 嚴歌苓 *The Banquet Bug* (2006). *UFO in Her Eyes* joins their ranks as another instance of the Chinese Anglophone novel.

In this context, the marker *Chinese* is not anchored in the use of a Sinitic language, nor does it refer simply to a text's national setting or an author's identity and biography. In Guo's case, these factors are certainly relevant and operate to set up what we might dub, following Michel Foucault, her "Chinese author function," the ways her name and work circulate discursively. Yet I would propose a more specific conceptual nexus that characterizes the contemporary Chinese novel. Like many of the writers cited above, Guo insists that China today must be understood not as merely another chapter in the inevitable spread of global capital but as a case of totalitarianism's endurance in this very era. As her novel's epigraph of Milan Kundera suggests, Silver Hill's transformation needs to be grasped in relation to a "totalitarian society . . . [whose] power, as it grows ever more opaque, requires the lives of citizens to be entirely transparent."[41] So-called post-socialist or post-totalitarian PRC state power, far from being curtailed by economic reform, is in fact entirely compatible with and flourishes hand-in-hand with capitalism. Indeed, totalitarian power may well be more pervasive, if also more opaque, than ever before. And increasingly, it is entangled with the communist state's management of biological life as a vehicle of economic gain. Time and again, writers zero in on the body as a new vital object of political control as well as state profit, from the laboring body of the migrant worker to the reproductive body of the woman, from the diseased body of the AIDS-infected peasant to the dissident body of the political prisoner. The contemporary Chinese novel is therefore an especially fertile site for examining issues of biocapital. For a literature that is putatively mired in communist censorship, this is no small irony—especially when juxtaposed against an Anglophone commercial market that broadcasts its freedom but everywhere hides its own biocapitalist censorship effects.

From this angle, Guo and other Chinese Anglophone writers of biocapitalist fictions present a useful complication to Shu-mei Shih's model of the Sinophone. In Shih's formulation, the Sinophone encompasses the many "Sinitic-language communities and cultures outside China as well as the ethnic minority communities and cultures within China" that have emerged largely as a legacy of China's historical colonialisms.[42] Moreover, the Sinophone is necessarily an idea "in the process of disappearance," for "when local concerns voiced in local languages gradually supersede pre-immigration concerns for immigrants and their descendents through generations," the Sinophone loses "its raison d'être."[43] For Shih, Guo might have qualified as a Sinophone writer when she was a Hui inside the PRC, but once she started writing in English abroad she ceased to be Sinophone in the strict sense, though she could, like Ha Jin, play a role in indexing the Sinophone at its vanishing point.[44] Yet, as we have seen, Guo did not stop writing in Chinese because she overcame her nostalgia for China and acculturated into the practices of Britain, nor has she stopped producing films in Chinese, in and about China, concurrently with her Anglophone fictions. She may belong to a very small class of immigrant bilingual cultural producers, but her case highlights the nonequivalence between language use and geographical allegiance or political orientation. Sinophone and Anglophone are not mutually exclusive existential categories with a unilateral vector toward localization, nor is language inevitably the horizon of disappearance or emergence for specific kinds of subjectivity, a telltale marker of an author's conversion from one kind of being into another. Returning to the lexicon of the state, Guo would maintain instead that "language is a passport, [a] dubious, dangerous passport."[45] And as with that geopolitical document, whether one is allowed safe passage depends more on the political institutions in power than on the individual supplicant.

It is Guo's persistent attention to geopower and governance that gives meaningful context to her repeated invocations of September 11 in *UFO in Her Eyes*. The book opens with the date 09-11-2012, the final interviews take place on 09-11-2015, and the American hiker's zip code is 11901 (an encryption of 11-09-2001). Beyond the play with numbers, a host of other details recall the historical 9/11, including the references to New York, the conjured image of a falling man, the narrative device of China's own NSA files, and of course, the titular trope of an unidentified flying object. While these signs of September 11 are ubiquitous, their meanings are less obvious. Does Guo want to intimate that capitalist development for rural China is akin to 9/11 for America, that modernization is a form of terrorism? Conversely, can 9/11 serve as a metaphor for globalization, the forcing open of one's world by the penetration of another's? Does 9/11 function figuratively or causally here? That is, is Guo implying that rural China now undergoes its own belated version of catastrophic rupture, or is she insinuating a stronger claim about the wide reach of America as the global hub of traumatic sightings and reproducible terror, à la Jacques Derrida's "empire of the fable"?[46] In short, which target is Guo's dark satire aimed at? For a novel that can confine itself solely to China, that does not need to implicate America or terrorism for its critique, the exact link between PRC biocapitalism and the US terrorist attack is rather elusive.

Precisely for this reason, I would venture that it is more important for Guo to stage these questions than to answer them definitively. By doing so, she constructs the contemporary Chinese Anglophone novel as a site for cross-examining the evolving concerns of the Anglophone with the Chinese novel, and for working out the open-ended political relation between the West and the PRC. On one hand, where much post-9/11 Anglophone writing presses us to consider geopolitics beyond individual states, she accordingly raises the specter of 9/11 for her narrative of China. On the other, she showcases the significance of China for any global analysis of biopolitics, since she is keenly aware, as Susan Greenhalgh and Edwin Winckler demonstrate, that biological life has been a "central object of power" in the PRC since its founding.[47] With its state-directed market economy, the PRC offers a particularly sharp illustration of the intersection of capital and biopower, constituting a contemporaneous but non-Western model of life politics in the new millennium. Its representation in the Chinese Anglophone novel shifts the terms of globalization from deterritorialized networks of capital and data, however celebratorily or critically conceived, to geobiopower, the different modes by which states in both hemispheres govern territorialized life in our time. Guo is careful, however, to avoid positioning China as simply a biopolitical precursor to the post-9/11 West, for such a view would grant China a place in global history only to entrench it more deeply in an Orientalist tradition of the despotic East. By emphasizing the West's complicity in bolstering totalitarian biocapitalism, *UFO* compels us to imagine a near future when the West and the PRC draw ever closer.

Without depicting any geography beyond the Hunan countryside, Guo locates the story of Silver Hill within the space of capital's global circulation, so that her characters are seen as casualties of not just PRC state agendas but also US neoliberal power. As the village chief explains to Kwok Yun via a cosmological analogy at one point, Silver Hill is a planet and the town government is its sun: "Just as the earth receives warmth from circling the sun, so Silver Hill has to circle around the government so we can get financial support, otherwise we would die amidst our tea bushes." When a puzzled Yun then asks who the sun circles around, the chief, flustered by this "political question," nonetheless replies: "We Chinese used to be our own sun.... And now, we are attracted to ... no, it's more than attraction, we are actually circling around ... the USA.... America is the sun for the Chinese government."[48] This capitalist cosmology unfolds concretely on the ground when the New Yorker falls miraculously out of the sky and becomes Silver Hill's benefactor. He is at once a catalyzing agent of development and a spokesperson for neoliberalism. When he sends his letter of thanks to Silver Hill a few months later—a letter written in English that no one in the village can read except for the school headmaster—he expresses his gratitude to Yun for saving his life but issues his $2,000 check not to her but to the local authorities, to "help fund [the] village school and any children in need."[49] His mandate for American money's use in uplifting Third-World children from poverty and ignorance bypasses his supposed female savior while vesting economic power in those already endowed with cultural and political power, such as the headmaster and the local party chief. This gesture of long-distance and selective benevolence parallels the communist government's own procedure for improving Silver Hill by literally bulldozing over its inhabitants, as US and PRC interests now intertwine.

Beyond neoliberal capital, America serves another crucial function in Guo's novel: as trigger and emblem for the modern security state. This is the most evocative dimension of the text's September 11 references. By juxtaposing New York and Silver Hill, Guo comes very close to suggesting that the post-9/11 US security state and the post-socialist Chinese one are mirror revivals of totalitarianism in our time. Both countries may have democratic trappings such as market economies and cultural pluralism, but they coincide above all in the ubiquity of their surveillance apparatus. If one hallmark of totalitarian power is its abolishing of the boundary between public and private, then nothing ought to lie outside of the state's eyes, nothing will go unseen. The second an unknown object appears in one locale to any individual, however fringe or insignificant, the state must step in to interrogate and identify. Narratively, then, the UFO is the consummate metaphor for totalitarianism's intolerable blind spot, and the UFO witness is the state's last frontier of security. Still, Guo optimistically hints at the nontotality of this gaze. By the novel's end, Yun and the communist state are locked in stalemate. While the latter deftly capitalizes on the UFO sighting as a national event and co-opts Silver Hill into its modernization program, Yun's memory remains in excess of these biocapitalist schemes. We glean from the government's own transcripts that she in fact did not see a UFO on September 11, that she had never heard of the word until the village chief interpellated the object for her, and that her memory is "completely different" from the monument erected by the authorities, "not round and flat, not even white."[50] The hyperreal of capitalism does not utterly replace memory and experience, after all. Even if Yun comes to be classified as a "State Witness 人証" and joins "the group of dissidents, criminals and notable citizens who are under permanent surveillance," we deduce it is this very structure of power that has changed her from pliant attestant to defiant subject, someone who by novel's end dares to address the government agents with mockery and exasperation: "What do you want to know now? Have you not investigated my whole life already?"[51]

Even more intriguingly, Guo hints that, in the post-9/11 world of international surveillance, the limit of one totalitarian state's gaze is precisely another's. Since the novel is constructed as records of the PRC government, what we never learn—such as the real identity of the flying object or of the American hiker—signals the boundaries of state intelligence. Indeed, not only did Yun not see an alien ship, she fainted prior to the American's alleged fall and discovered his body in the rice fields only afterward. The gaps in her account play off of the novel's September 11 references to raise the possibility that the New Yorker, too, may serve his own security state. Operating within a wider compass, he parachutes from the center of terrorist attacks into the most remote and trivial of global hinterlands. Eerily, he descends unseen and departs unheard. Except for the anonymous village children who help Yun carry his body into her house, no one in Silver Hill recalls encountering him, and he mysteriously disappears without a trace that very afternoon, somehow managing to evade all communist monitors on his return journey. In an age when mutual accusations of cyberspying have become the norm in Sino-US relations, Guo's enigmatic American readily assumes an aura of espionage, less an interpretive aporia than the signifier of an intelligence black hole, in the geopolitical landscape of terror and its far-flung counterassaults.[52]

Guo's imagining of geography is therefore geopolitically synchronic. In the novel's surrealist world map, China and America may appear at first to follow the concentric layout of empire, of colony to metropole or planet to sun, along the village chief's metaphor. On this cartography, the periphery receives news of the center's catastrophe eleven years late, to the day. But at the same time, the two sites are geopolitically superimposed—so that a body from one can fall through the decade into the other's future in just one instant. For Guo, then, to think in terms of geobiopower is to remap the local and global in terms of biosovereignty, to connect distant points of state power and plot them as coordinates on a common grid. In globalization, individuals may move across linguistic and national boundaries, but ultimately they remain as bodies within intractable biopolitical regimes.

If the most curious feature of the novel is its connection to September 11, the most curious aspect of this connection is its orientation toward the future. While 9/11 has prompted much reflection on history and its fallout in the present, Guo directs our eye to the event's potential bearing on futurity, and more ominously, its vanquishing of futurity altogether. The ironic question on Kwok Yun's tee-shirt—"Is This The Future?" written in English and illegible to her—menaces us with the prospect that the future has already arrived, though it may not be legible as such, and that alternative futures will henceforth be foreclosed.[53] What is nightmarish about Silver Hill's fate is not what may yet come but what may now never come to pass. This narrative experimentation with time is intimately tied to an imagining of totalitarianism, for as Maria Nikolajeva points out, totalitarian fictions frequently entail the depiction of "heterochronia, a multitude of times," as well as a summoning of the idea of total time, absolute omnipotence over time itself.[54] Yet most frightening, perhaps, is totalitarianism's potential to possess the future. As Hannah Arendt asserts, totalitarian terror "rules supreme" when it claims "the total explanation of the past, the total knowledge of the present, and the reliable prediction of the future," effectively confiscating the possibility of "natality"— that "supreme capacity of man" to inaugurate new beginnings and that "politically . . . is identical with man's freedom."[55] In exactly this way, as Guo is well aware, the speculative genre of dystopia has traditionally served as a potent instrument of critique of totalitarian states.

But unlike classic dystopic novels of the far future, *UFO* sets itself in a near future, heightening our sense of the quickly collapsing boundary between present and future. Indeed, the novel's projected years are so close to Guo's moment of writing that its time frame is already partly our past, or else a rapidly receding present. From the perspective of social change, it is not difficult to embed this sense of condensed, fast time within the dynamics of China's development, because the speed with which the country is hurling itself into a calculated future has already created landscapes pregnant with their virtual selves of tomorrow. Fortuitously, recent biopolitical theorists have suggested a similar link between neoliberal capitalism and futurity. As noted, Luciana Parisi and Steve Goodman broach the concept of "mnemonic control" to describe the operations of "affective capitalism," on which "hyperbranded environments of consumption" control not just the brain but the body, not just cognition but affect, and not just actual thoughts and feelings but future ones: "Possessed by seductive brand entities, you flip into autopilot, are abducted from the present, are carried off by an array of prehensions outside chronological time into a past not lived, a future not sensed."[56] Mnemonic control is thus "power over futurity, which is seen as the power to foreclose an uncertain, indeterminate future by producing it in the present."[57] Extrapolating from this, we might say that the near future is the tense par excellence of a biocapitalist milieu, where the present is lived not independent of but as an annexed territory of an already predetermined next moment. Targeting the near future, biocapital forecloses even the far future that classic totalitarianism afforded. In turn, the near future dystopia may well be biocapital's paradigmatic genre, as the mechanics of the totalitarian state now combine, revitalized, with the machinery of capitalism. Among Chinese biocapitalist fictions, Chan Koonchung's *The Fat Years*, also a near-future dystopic novel published in 2009 and set in 2013 China, fits Parisi and Goodman's theory most neatly.[58]

But *UFO* is not that novel, and Silver Hill is not that mnemonically controlled future. Toward the novel's end, Kwok Yun, despite her material improvement as the new wife of the headmaster and a soon-to-be urban resident, is not the only character whose desires fail to align with the state's. The local fish farmer drowns himself in his carp pond, the rice farmer curses the authorities for burying his rice fields, and the former butcher goes on a shooting spree at a construction site, killing one government agent, all amid proliferating riots and protests by newly arrived migrant workers. Guo, it would seem, reserves capitalism's affective bioengineering for the Anglophone book market and its commercial censorship. Rather than reprogrammed docile consumers, she portrays a turbulent countryside rocked by agitation and cloaked in fear. Silver Hill's biocapitalist modernity approximates instead a neoliberal temporality where "the near future lean[s] even nearer, spilling into the present, filling the present with fear, speculation, anxiety, and, perhaps beneath all this, a generalized and heightened sense of expectancy of what has not yet come."[59] So it is precisely in the time of "the very near future" that the village chief foresees Silver Hill living up to its name.[60] As the chief intuits, the near future will be neoliberalism's first battleground and prized trophy, to be waged and won—or defeated and annulled—only on the edges of global prosperity. If one cannot empty this time of fear, speculation, and anxiety and fill the void with silver, then "security forces [must] come down here and ensure safety, so that the building work can continue."[61] But this mobilizing of security forces resaturates the present with trepidation and foreboding, conjuring once again the specter of September 11. Not incidentally, Guo's novel resonates most loudly with post-9/11 theories of preemptive state power.

In recent years, critics of the US security state have articulated models of biopolitics and time that hauntingly resurrect earlier theories of totalitarianism. Brian

Massumi, for one, trenchantly argues that post-9/11 America has inaugurated a regime of "national enterprise emergency," where neoconservative and neoliberal forces work in concert to produce "preemptive power."[62] For Massumi, the Bush administration successfully constructed a threats discourse so that the uncertain prospect of a terrorist attack—which can strike at any moment, anywhere—is now blended into and made indistinguishable from a wide array of potential dangers, from climate change and natural disasters to epidemics and domestic crime. In this atmosphere of the omnithreat, an actual and verified terrorist attack is no longer needed for the marshaling of sovereign power or the rolling out of national troops. Instead, since every threat is now potentially contiguous with terrorism, the declaration of national emergency and martial law has become the de facto reaction to a host of crises: "In a crisis-prone environment, threat is endemic, uncertainty is everywhere; a negative can never be proven. The on-all-the-time, everywhere-on-the-ready military response operatively annexes the civilian sphere to the conduct of war. Civilian life falls onto a continuum with war, permanently potentially premilitarized, a pole on the spectrum."[63] As François Debrix and Alexander Barder likewise point out, if there is a distinction to be made between security's "geopolitics of territorial sovereignty" and its "biopolitics of species life," the two mechanisms of power are nevertheless equally oppressive and bloody.[64] For Massumi, in this situation, preemptive power becomes the norm. Its temporal scope encompasses not just existing life but a "potential more of life to come." In anticipation of already interpellated future attacks, preemptive power aims to "hijack" the very potential of futurity as its prototerritory.[65] If biocapitalism seeks to engineer the future through cognitive and affective controls over individuals' bodies and minds, the security state seeks to destroy the proto-future of the threat even before it comes into being. Indeed, as Doug Davis contends, the US government has long appropriated the narrative tropes of speculative science fiction, particularly stories of mass destruction, to justify preemptive strikes from at least the atomic bomb onward. "The irony of defense planning in the war on terror," he notes, "is that its strategic thinking is based upon speculative catastrophic events that do not exist, that are so terrible they must never exist"—except "*as a story about our future*."[66] The rhetoric of national defense is hence a kind of science fiction, what he calls "strategic fiction."

Massumi's and Davis's post-9/11 America mirrors Guo's 2015 China, but hers is a near future that parades the ever-tightening partnership between preemptive and biocapitalist power, in both the PRC and the West. Caught in its own September 11 time loop, Silver Hill by the novel's end is gridlocked between internal terror and permanent surveillance, escalating riots and emergency counterstrikes, random eruptions of civil violence and ever more militarized executions of five-year plans. The line between security and development, surveillance and profit is increasingly blurred, as are the distinctions between foreign and domestic threat, actual attack and possible protest, state criminal and state hero. Before 9/11, totalitarian and capitalist frameworks might have sufficed to explain Guo's experiments with time. In the postmillennial decades, however, these frameworks have accreted an additional layer of resonance, for China as much as the Anglophone empire. When terror is no longer localized as a group-specific massacre at home or an explosion abroad but has become generalized as a fearful present suffused with already speculated futures—for Hunan peasants as much as New York cosmopolitans, Boston Marathon runners as much as air travelers between Kuala Lumpur and Beijing—any account of futurity in writing would seem impoverished without an acknowledgment of this new global configuration of terror-oriented experience on one hand and the crisis-oriented state's preemptive power structure on the other. Thus, Guo warns, we must look for bodies that fall, not just in the here and now but possibly through time and across continents, to safeguard the future that may soon be lost everywhere.

NOTES

1. Xiaolu Guo, "Fragments of My Life," *Independent*, May 10, 2008, retrieved September 16, 2014, from http://www.independent.co.uk/news/world/asia/writer-xiaolu-guo-fragments-of-my-life-823519.html.
2. Xiaolu Guo, "Fragments of My Life."
3. Xiaolu Guo, "Why Do We Still Pretend We Are Free?" interview by Reed Colley, *Guernica*, January 30, 2014, retrieved September 16, 2014, from http://www.guernicamag.com/daily/xiaolu-guo-why-do-we-still-pretend-we-are-free/.
4. Xiaolu Guo, "I don't think English society cares about the Chinese at all," interview by Geoffrey Macnab, *Guardian*, March 3, 2010, retrieved September 16, 2014, from http://www.theguardian.com/film/2010/mar/03/she-a-chinese-xiaolu-guo.
5. Xiaolu Guo, "Growing up in a communist society with limited freedom, you're a spiky, angry rat," interview by Maya Jaggi, *Guardian*, May 31, 2014, retrieved September 16, 2014, from http://www.theguardian.com/books/2014/may/30/xiaolu-guo-communist-china-interview.
6. Sheldon H. Lu, *Chinese Modernity and Global Biopolitics: Studies in Literature and Visual Culture* (Honolulu: University of Hawai'i Press, 2007), 7.
7. For formulations of biocapital and related concepts, see Kaushik Sunder Rajan, *Biocapital: The Constitution of Postgenomic Life* (Durham: Duke University Press, 2006); Nikolas Rose, *The Politics of Life Itself: Biomedicine, Power, and Subjectivity in the Twenty-First Century* (Princeton: Princeton University Press, 2006); Stefan Helmreich, "Species of Biocapital," *Science as Culture* 17.4 (2008): 463–478; and Aihwa Ong, "Introduction: An Analytics of Biotechnology and Ethics at Multiple Scales," in *Asian Biotech: Ethics and Communities of Fate*, ed. Aihwa Ong and Nancy N. Chen (Durham: Duke University Press, 2010), 1–51.
8. *20 Fragments of a Ravenous Youth* has in turn been back-translated into Chinese as *Qingchun, jibuzeshi* (青春, 飢不擇食; 2009) in Taiwan and *Taotie qingchun de ershi ge shunjian* (饕餮青春的二十個瞬間; 2010) in Mainland China.
9. Guo states in an interview: "The film is much more developed than the novel. I wrote the novel within two months in Paris, but then it took me two more years to write the script, talk to producers and go on locations scout." See Clare Pennington, "Author Guo Xiaolu on UFOs, Modern China and What Comes Next," *BlouinArtinfo*, March 28, 2013, retrieved September 16, 2014, from http://encn.blouinartinfo.com/news/story/883897/author-guo-xiaolu-on-ufos-modern-china-and-what-comes-next.
10. Xiaolu Guo, "Why Do We Still Pretend We Are Free?"

11. Ha Jin, "The Language of Betrayal," in *The Migrant as Writer* (Chicago: University of Chicago Press, 2008), 32.

12. Ha Jin, "Exiled to English," *New York Times*, May 31, 2009.

13. See "Anchee Min," *Steven Barclay Agency*, 2014, retrieved September 16, 2014, from http://barclayagency.com/min.html; Annie Wang, "A Conversation with Annie Wang," *Bold Type* 6.01 (2002), retrieved September 16, 2014, from https://www.randomhouse.com/boldtype/0602/wang/interview.html; and Yiyun Li, "A Conversation with Yiyun Li on *A Thousand Years of Good Prayers*," *Yiyunli.com*, 2014, retrieved September 16, 2014, from http://www.yiyunli.com/1000YearsQA.php.

14. See Anna Sun, "The Diseased Language of Mo Yan," *Kenyon Review Online* (Fall 2012), retrieved September 16, 2014, from http://www.kenyonreview.org/kr-online-issue/2012-fall/selections/anna-sun-656342/. For responses to Sun's article, see Perry Link, "Does This Writer Deserve the Prize?" *New York Review of Books*, December 6, 2012, retrieved September 16, 2014, from http://www.nybooks.com/articles/archives/2012/dec/06/mo-yan-nobel-prize/; Charles Laughlin, "What Mo Yan's Detractors Get Wrong," *ChinaFile*, December 11, 2012, retrieved September 16, 2014, from http://www.chinafile.com/what-mo-yans-detractors-get-wrong; and Perry Link, "Politics and the Chinese Language: What Mo Yan's Defenders Get Wrong," *ChinaFile*, December 27, 2012, retrieved September 16, 2014, from http://asiasociety.org/blog/asia/politics-and-chinese-language-what-mo-yans-defenders-get-wrong.

15. Xiaolu Guo, "Why Do We Still Pretend We Are Free?"

16. Pascale Casanova, "From Internationalism to Globalization," in *The World Republic of Letters*, trans. M. B. DeBevoise (Cambridge: Harvard University Press, 2004), 164–172.

17. Luciana Parisi and Steve Goodman, "Mnemonic Control," in *Beyond Biopolitics: Essays on the Governance of Life and Death*, ed. Patricia Ticineto Clough and Craig Willse (Durham: Duke University Press, 2011), 164.

18. Xiaolu Guo, "Savidge Reads Grills . . . Xiaolu Guo," interview by Simon Savidge, *Savidge Reads*, January 27, 2010, retrieved September 16, 2014, from http://savidgereads.wordpress.com/2010/01/27/savidge-reads-grills-xiaolu-guo/.

19. Homi Bhabha, *The Location of Culture* (New York: Routledge, 1994).

20. Xiaolu Guo, *A Concise Chinese-English Dictionary for Lovers* (New York: Anchor Books, 2007), 4. Unless otherwise noted, all references to the novel are to this edition.

21. Xiaolu Guo, *A Concise Chinese-English Dictionary for Lovers*, 279.

22. See Susie Thomas, "'With your tongue down my throat': Hanan al-Shaykh's *Only in London* and Xiaolu Guo's *A Concise Chinese-English Dictionary for Lovers*," *Literary London: Interdisciplinary Studies in the Representation of London* 5.2 (2007): n. pag, retrieved September 16, 2014, from http://literarylondon.org/london-journal/september2007/thomas.html.

23. See Eunju Hwang, "Love and Shame: Transcultural Communication and Its Failure in Xiaolu Guo's *A Concise Chinese-English Dictionary for Lovers*," *ARIEL* 43.4 (2012): 69–95; and Ulla Rahbek, "When Z Lost Her Reference: Language, Culture and Identity in Xiaolu Guo's *A Concise Chinese-English Dictionary for Lovers*," *Otherness: Essays and Studies* 3.1 (2012): 1–12.

24. See Rachael Gilmour, "Living Between Languages: The Politics of Translation in Leila Aboulela's *Minaret* and Xiaolu Guo's *A Concise Chinese-English Dictionary for Lovers*," *Journal of Commonwealth Literature* 47.2 (2012): 207–227. Among Guo's critics, Gilmour is the most meticulous in embedding *Dictionary* within a theoretical lineage but also the most exemplary of the utopian approach to the Anglophone novel.

25. See Angelia Poon, "Becoming a Global Subject: Language and the Body in Xiaolu Guo's *A Concise Chinese-English Dictionary for Lovers*," *Transnational Literature* 6.1 (2013): 1–9.

26. Xiaolu Guo, *A Concise Chinese-English Dictionary for Lovers*, 14 and 141.

27. Xiaolu Guo, *A Concise Chinese-English Dictionary for Lovers*, 142.

28. Xiaolu Guo, *A Concise Chinese-English Dictionary for Lovers*, 143, italics in original. Interestingly, in the bilingual Chinese-English edition of the novel, the order of the passages is flipped, giving the impression that Z composes both the "nonsense" and "freedom" chapters in English; the original Chinese passages are allotted to the facing pages, as if in translation. See Xiaolu Guo, *Lianren ban zhong ying cidian* 戀人版中英詞典 [Lovers' edition of Chinese-English dictionary], trans. Guo Pinjie 郭品潔 (Taipei: Dakuai wenhua, 2008), 133, 144. Though beyond my chapter's scope, also of note is this bilingual edition's translation of Z's English into fully grammatical Chinese throughout the novel, thus erasing the effect of a language learner's evolving voice.

29. Xiaolu Guo, *A Concise Chinese-English Dictionary for Lovers* (London: Chatto & Windus, 2007), 180; *A Concise Chinese-English Dictionary for Lovers* (London: Vintage, 2007), 180; *A Concise Chinese-English Dictionary for Lovers* (New York: Nan A. Talese, 2007), 143; *A Concise Chinese-English Dictionary for Lovers* (New York: Anchor, 2007), 143; and *A Concise Chinese-English Dictionary for Lovers* (Detroit: Wheeler Publishing, 2007), 212. In a previous draft of her article, in a passage that unfortunately did not make its way into print, Eunju Hwang details these textual variances in different editions of Guo's novel. As she further reports to me in an e-mail, the French Buchet/Chastel edition and the South Korean Minumsa edition both contain the tagline to "editor's translation." The Taiwanese Chinese-English bilingual edition, however, does not.

30. Eunju Hwang, "Love and Shame," 81.

31. Xiaolu Guo, *A Concise Chinese-English Dictionary for Lovers*, 202.

32. Xiaolu Guo, *A Concise Chinese-English Dictionary for Lovers*, 282.

33. Talal Asad, "The Concept of Cultural Translation in British Social Anthropology," in *Writing Culture: The Poetics and Politics of Ethnography*, ed. James Clifford and George E. Marcus (Berkeley: University of California Press, 1986), 157–158.

34. See Ngũgĩ wa Thiong'o, *Decolonising the Mind: The Politics of Language in African Literature* (Portsmouth, NH: Heinemann, 1986), 157.

35. Amy Tan, "Mother Tongue," *Threepenny Review* 43 (1990): 8.

36. For this critique, see Steven Yao, "Taxonomizing Hybridity," *Textual Practice* 17.2 (2003): 357–378.

37. Emma J. Teng, "What's 'Chinese' in Chinese Diasporic Literature?" in *Contested Modernities in Chinese Literature*, ed. Charles A. Laughlin (New York: Palgrave Macmillan, 2005), 75, 65; and Dorothy Wang, "Does Anglophone Chinese Diasporic Avant-garde Writing Exist?" *Journal of the Association for the Study of Australian Literature* 12.2 (2012): 14 and 12.

38. Amitav Ghosh, "Imperial Temptations," in *Incendiary Circumstances: A Chronicle of the Turmoil of Our Times* (Boston: Houghton Mifflin, 2005), 28.

39. See Arne De Boever, *States of Exception in the Contemporary Novel* (New York: Continuum, 2012), and *Narrative Care: Biopolitics and the Novel* (New York: Bloomsbury, 2013); and John Marx, *Geopolitics and the Anglophone Novel, 1890-2011* (Cambridge: Cambridge University Press, 2012).

40. Xiaolu Guo, *UFO in Her Eyes* (London: Chatto & Windus, 2009), 185.

41. Quoted as epigraph in Xiaolu Guo, *UFO in Her Eyes*.

42. Shu-mei Shih, "Introduction: What is Sinophone Studies?" in *Sinophone Studies: A Critical Reader*, ed. Shu-mei Shih, Chien-hsin Tsai, and Brian Bernards (New York: Columbia University Press, 2011), 12.

43. Shu-mei Shih, *Visuality and Identity: Sinophone Articulations across the Pacific* (Berkeley: University of California Press, 2007), 31–32.

44. See Shu-mei Shih, *Visuality and Identity*, 179; and Chien-hsin Tsai, "Issues and Controversies," in *Sinophone Studies: A Critical Reader*, ed. Shu-mei Shih, Chien-hsin Tsai, and Brian Bernards (New York: Columbia University Press, 2011), 22.

45. Quoted in Alison Flood, "Writers Attack 'Overrated' Anglo-American Literature at Jaipur Festival," *Guardian*, January 20, 2014, retrieved September 16, 2014, from http://www.theguardian.com/books/2014/jan/20/writers-attack-overrated-american-literature-jaipur-festival.

46. See Hilary Thompson, "Before After: Amitav Ghosh's Pre-1856 Cosmopolis as Post-9/11 Lost Object," in *The City after 9/11: Literature, Film, Culture*, ed. Keith Wilhite (Madison, NJ: Fairleigh Dickinson University Press, forthcoming).

47. Susan Greenhalgh and Edwin A. Winckler, *Governing China's Population: From Leninist to Neoliberal Biopolitics* (Stanford: Stanford University Press, 2005), 1. For biopolitics and China, see also Susan Greenhalgh, "The Chinese Biopolitical: Facing the Twenty-first Century," New Genetics and Society 28.3 (2009): 205–222, and *Cultivating Global Citizens: Population in the Rise of China* (Cambridge: Harvard University Press, 2010); and Brian Salter and Catherine Waldby, eds., "Biopolitics in China," *East Asian Science, Technology and Society* 5.3 (2011): 287–357.

48. Xiaolu Guo, *UFO in Her Eyes*, 70–71.

49. Xiaolu Guo, *UFO in Her Eyes*, 81.

50. Xiaolu Guo, *UFO in Her Eyes*, 191.

51. Xiaolu Guo, *UFO in Her Eyes*, 194 and 189.

52. In its implicit portrayal of China and the United States as mirror security states in our time, *UFO* anticipates the much more explicit equation of PRC with British biopower in Guo's next novel, *I Am China* (2014).

53. Xiaolu Guo, *UFO in Her Eyes*, 80.

54. Maria Nikolajeva, "Time and Totalitarianism," *Journal of the Fantastic in the Arts* 20.2 (2009): 186.

55. Hannah Arendt, *Totalitarianism: Part Three of* The Origins of Totalitarianism (New York: Harcourt, 1968), 177 and 168.

56. Luciana Parisi and Steve Goodman, "Mnemonic Control," 163–164.

57. Luciana Parisi and Steve Goodman, "Mnemonic Control," 167.

58. Chan Koonchung 陳冠中, *Shengshi: Zhongguo erlingyisan nian* 盛世：中國二〇一三年 [Age of Prosperity: China 2013] (Hong Kong: Niujin daxue chubanshe, 2009); translated by Michael S. Duke as *The Fat Years* (London: Doubleday, 2011).

59. Patricia Ticineto Clough and Craig Willse, "Beyond Biopolitics: The Governance of Life and Death," in *Beyond Biopolitics: Essays on the Governance of Life and Death*, ed. Patricia Ticineto Clough and Craig Willse (Durham: Duke University Press, 2011), 2.

60. Xiaolu Guo, *UFO in Her Eyes*, 185.

61. Xiaolu Guo, *UFO in Her Eyes*, 184.

62. Brian Massumi, "National Enterprise Emergency: Steps Toward an Ecology of Powers," in *Beyond Biopolitics: Essays on the Governance of Life and Death*, ed. Patricia Ticineto Clough and Craig Willse (Durham: Duke University Press, 2011), 30.

63. Brian Massumi, "National Enterprise Emergency," 20–21.

64. François Debrix and Alexander Barder, *Beyond Biopolitics: Theory, Violence, and Horror in World Politics* (New York: Routledge, 2012), 10.

65. Brian Massumi, "National Enterprise Emergency," 30–31.

66. Doug Davis, "Science Fiction Narratives of Mass Destruction and the Politics of National Security," in *New Boundaries in Political Science Fiction*, ed. Donald M. Hassler and Clyde Wilcox (Columbia: University of South Carolina Press, 2008), 148.

WORKS CITED

"Anchee Min." *Steven Barclay Agency*, 2014. Retrieved September 16, 2014, from http://barclayagency.com/min.html.

Arendt, Hannah. *Totalitarianism: Part Three of* The Origins of Totalitarianism. New York: Harcourt, 1968.

Asad, Talal. "The Concept of Cultural Translation in British Social Anthropology." In *Writing Culture: The Poetics and Politics of Ethnography*. Ed. James Clifford and George E. Marcus. Berkeley: University of California Press, 1986. 141–164.

Bhabha, Homi. *The Location of Culture*. New York: Routledge, 1994.

Casanova, Pascale. "From Internationalism to Globalization." In *The World Republic of Letters*. Trans. M. B. DeBevoise. Cambridge: Harvard University Press, 2004. 164–172.

Chan Koonchung 陳冠中. *Shengshi: Zhongguo erlingyisan nian* 盛世:中國二〇一三年 [Age of prosperity: China 2013]. Hong Kong: Niujin daxue chubanshe, 2009.

Clough, Patricia Ticineto, and Craig Willse. "Beyond Biopolitics: The Governance of Life and Death." In *Beyond Biopolitics: Essays on the Governance of Life and Death*. Ed. Patricia Ticineto Clough and Craig Willse. Durham: Duke University Press, 2011. 1–16.

Davis, Doug. "Science Fiction Narratives of Mass Destruction and the Politics of National Security." In *New Boundaries in Political Science Fiction*. Ed. Donald M. Hassler and Clyde Wilcox. Columbia: University of South Carolina Press, 2008. 145–156.

De Boever, Arne. *Narrative Care: Biopolitics and the Novel*. New York: Bloomsbury, 2013.

De Boever, Arne. *States of Exception in the Contemporary Novel*. New York: Continuum, 2012.

Debrix, François, and Alexander D. Barder. *Beyond Biopolitics: Theory, Violence, and Horror in World Politics*. New York: Routledge, 2012.

Flood, Alison. "Writers Attack 'Overrated' Anglo-American Literature at Jaipur Festival." *Guardian*, January 20, 2014. Retrieved September 16, 2014, from http://www.theguardian.com/books/2014/jan/20/writers-attack-overrated-american-literature-jaipur-festival.

Ghosh, Amitav. "Imperial Temptations." In *Incendiary Circumstances: A Chronicle of the Turmoil of Our Times*. Boston: Houghton Mifflin, 2005. 26–31.

Gilmour, Rachael. "Living Between Languages: The Politics of Translation in Leila Aboulela's *Minaret* and Xiaolu Guo's *A Concise Chinese-English Dictionary for Lovers*." *Journal of Commonwealth Literature* 47.2 (2012): 207–227.

Greenhalgh, Susan. "The Chinese Biopolitical: Facing the Twenty-first Century." *New Genetics and Society* 28.3 (2009): 205–222.

Greenhalgh, Susan. *Cultivating Global Citizens: Population in the Rise of China*. Cambridge: Harvard University Press, 2010.

Greenhalgh, Susan, and Edwin A. Winckler. *Governing China's Population: From Leninist to Neoliberal Biopolitics*. Stanford: Stanford University Press, 2005.

Guo, Xiaolu 郭小橹. *20 Fragments of a Ravenous Youth*. London: Chatto & Windus, 2008.

Guo, Xiaolu 郭小橹. *A Concise Chinese-English Dictionary for Lovers*. New York: Anchor Books, 2007.

Guo Xiaolu 郭小橹. *Fenfang de sanshiqi du er* 芬芳的三十七度二 [Fenfang's 37.2 degrees]. Xian: Shanxi renmin chubanshe, 2000.

Guo, Xiaolu 郭小橹. "Fragments of My Life." *Independent*, May 10, 2008. Retrieved September 16, 2014, from http://www.independent.co.uk/news/world/asia/writer-xiaolu-guo-fragments-of-my-life-823519.html.

Guo, Xiaolu 郭小橹. "Growing up in a communist society with limited freedom, you're a spiky, angry rat." Interview by Maya Jaggi. *Guardian*, May 31, 2014. Retrieved September 16, 2014, from http://www.theguardian.com/books/2014/may/30/xiaolu-guo-communist-china-interview.

Guo, Xiaolu 郭小橹. *I Am China*. London: Chatto & Windus, 2014.

Guo, Xiaolu 郭小橹. "I don't think English society cares about the Chinese at all." Interview by Geoffrey Macnab. *Guardian*, March 3, 2010. Retrieved September 16, 2014, from http://www.theguardian.com/film/2010/mar/03/she-a-chinese-xiaolu-guo.

Guo Xiaolu 郭小橹. *Lianren ban zhong ying cidian* 戀人版中英詞典 [Lovers' edition of Chinese-English dictionary]. Trans. Guo Pinjie 郭品潔. Taipei: Dakuai wenhua, 2008.

Guo Xiaolu 郭小橹. *Qingchun, jibuzeshi* 青春, 飢不擇食 [Youth, beggars can't be choosers]. Trans. Guo Pinjie 郭品潔. Taipei: Dakuai wenhua, 2009.

Guo, Xiaolu 郭小橹. "Savidge Reads Grills … Xiaolu Guo." Interview by Simon Savidge. *Savidge Reads*, January 27, 2010. Retrieved September 16, 2014, from http://savidgereads.wordpress.com/2010/01/27/savidge-reads-grills-xiaolu-guo/.

Guo Xiaolu 郭小橹. *Taotie qingchun de ershi ge shunjian* 饕餮青春的二十個瞬間 [Twenty moments of a gluttonous youth]. Trans. Liao Ying 繆莹. Beijing: Xinxing chubanshe, 2010.

Guo, Xiaolu 郭小橹. *UFO in Her Eyes*. London: Chatto & Windus, 2009.

Guo, Xiaolu 郭小橹. "Why Do We Still Pretend We Are Free?" Interview by Reed Colley. *Guernica*, January 30, 2014. Retrieved September 16, 2014, from http://www.guernicamag.com/daily/xiaolu-guo-why-do-we-still-pretend-we-are-free/.

Helmreich, Stefan. "Species of Biocapital." *Science as Culture* 17.4 (2008): 463–478.

Hwang, Eunju. "Love and Shame: Transcultural Communication and Its Failure in Xiaolu Guo's *A Concise Chinese-English Dictionary for Lovers*." *ARIEL* 43.4 (2012): 69–95.

Hwang, Eunju. "Re: Xiaolu Guo Question." Message to Belinda Kong. October 29, 2014. E-mail.

Jin, Ha. "Exiled to English." *New York Times*, May 31, 2009.

Jin, Ha. "The Language of Betrayal." *The Migrant as Writer*. Chicago: University of Chicago Press, 2008. 31–60.

Laughlin, Charles. "What Mo Yan's Detractors Get Wrong." *ChinaFile*, December 11, 2012. Retrieved September 16, 2014, from http://www.chinafile.com/what-mo-yans-detractors-get-wrong.

Li, Yiyun. "A Conversation with Yiyun Li on *A Thousand Years of Good Prayers*." *Yiyunli.com*, 2014. Retrieved September 16, 2014, from http://www.yiyunli.com/1000YearsQA.php.

Link, Perry. "Does This Writer Deserve the Prize?" *New York Review of Books*, December 6, 2012. Retrieved September 16, 2014, from http://www.nybooks.com/articles/archives/2012/dec/06/mo-yan-nobel-prize/.

Link, Perry. "Politics and the Chinese Language: What Mo Yan's Defenders Get Wrong." *ChinaFile*, December 27, 2012. Retrieved September 16, 2014, from http://asiasociety.org/blog/asia/politics-and-chinese-language-what-mo-yans-defenders-get-wrong.

Lu, Sheldon H. *Chinese Modernity and Global Biopolitics: Studies in Literature and Visual Culture*. Honolulu: University of Hawai'i Press, 2007.

Marx, John. *Geopolitics and the Anglophone Novel, 1890–2011*. Cambridge: Cambridge University Press, 2012.

Massumi, Brian. "National Enterprise Emergency: Steps Toward an Ecology of Powers." In *Beyond Biopolitics: Essays on the Governance of Life and Death*. Ed. Patricia Ticineto Clough and Craig Willse. Durham: Duke University Press, 2011. 19–45.

Nikolajeva, Maria. "Time and Totalitarianism." *Journal of the Fantastic in the Arts* 20.2 (2009): 184–192.

Ngũgĩ wa Thiong'o. *Decolonising the Mind: The Politics of Language in African Literature*. Portsmouth, NH: Heinemann, 1986.

Ong, Aihwa. "Introduction: An Analytics of Biotechnology and Ethics at Multiple Scales." In *Asian Biotech: Ethics and Communities of Fate*. Ed. Aihwa Ong and Nancy N. Chen. Durham: Duke University Press, 2010. 1–51.

Parisi, Luciana, and Steve Goodman. "Mnemonic Control." In *Beyond Biopolitics: Essays on the Governance of Life and Death*. Ed. Patricia Ticineto Clough and Craig Willse. Durham: Duke University Press, 2011. 163–176.

Pennington, Clare. "Author Guo Xiaolu on UFOs, Modern China and What Comes Next." *BlouinArtinfo*, March 28, 2013. Retrieved September 16, 2014, from http://encn.blouinartinfo.com/news/story/883897/author-guo-xiaolu-on-ufos-modern-china-and-what-comes-next.

Poon, Angelia. "Becoming a Global Subject: Language and the Body in Xiaolu Guo's *A Concise Chinese-English Dictionary for Lovers*." *Transnational Literature* 6.1 (2013): 1–9.

Rahbek, Ulla. "When Z Lost Her Reference: Language, Culture and Identity in Xiaolu Guo's *A Concise Chinese-English Dictionary for Lovers*." *Otherness: Essays and Studies* 3.1 (2012): 1–12.

Rose, Nikolas. *The Politics of Life Itself: Biomedicine, Power, and Subjectivity in the Twenty-First Century*. Princeton: Princeton University Press, 2006.

Salter, Brian, and Catherine Waldby, eds. "Biopolitics in China." *East Asian Science, Technology and Society* 5.3 (2011): 287–357.

Shih, Shu-mei. "Introduction: What is Sinophone Studies?" In *Sinophone Studies: A Critical Reader*. Ed. Shu-mei Shih, Chien-hsin Tsai, and Brian Bernards. New York: Columbia University Press, 2011. 1–16.

Shih, Shu-mei. *Visuality and Identity: Sinophone Articulations across the Pacific*. Berkeley: University of California Press, 2007.

Sun, Anna. "The Diseased Language of Mo Yan." *Kenyon Review Online* (Fall 2012). Retrieved September 16, 2014, from http://www.kenyonreview.org/kr-online-issue/2012-fall/selections/anna-sun-656342/.

Sunder Rajan, Kaushik. *Biocapital: The Constitution of Postgenomic Life*. Durham: Duke University Press, 2006.

Tan, Amy. "Mother Tongue." *Threepenny Review* 43 (1990): 7–8.

Teng, Emma J. "What's 'Chinese' in Chinese Diasporic Literature?" In *Contested Modernities in Chinese Literature*. Ed. Charles A. Laughlin. New York: Palgrave Macmillan, 2005. 61–79.

Thomas, Susie. "'With your tongue down my throat': Hanan al-Shaykh's *Only in London* and Xiaolu Guo's *A Concise Chinese-English Dictionary for Lovers*." *Literary London: Interdisciplinary Studies in the Representation of London* 5.2 (2007): n. pag. Retrieved September 16, 2014, from http://literarylondon.org/london-journal/september2007/thomas.html.

Thompson, Hilary. "Before After: Amitav Ghosh's Pre-1856 Cosmopolis as Post-9/11 Lost Object." In *The City after 9/11: Literature, Film, Culture*. Ed. Keith Wilhite. Madison, NJ: Fairleigh Dickinson University Press, forthcoming.

Tsai, Chien-hsin. "Issues and Controversies." In *Sinophone Studies: A Critical Reader*. Ed. Shu-mei Shih, Chien-hsin Tsai, and Brian Bernards. New York: Columbia University Press, 2011. 17–24.

Wang, Annie. "A Conversation with Annie Wang." *Bold Type* 6.01 (2002). Retrieved September 16, 2014, from https://www.randomhouse.com/boldtype/0602/wang/interview.html.

Wang, Dorothy. "Does Anglophone Chinese Diasporic Avant-garde Writing Exist?" *Journal of the Association for the Study of Australian Literature* 12.2 (2012): 1–17.

Yao, Steven. "Taxonomizing Hybridity." *Textual Practice* 17.2 (2003): 357–378.

....

POET OF THE LATE
SUMMER CORN
Aku Wuwu and Contemporary Yi Poetry

....

MARK BENDER

SLOUCHING within a well-padded sofa, in the midst of a sedate Chengdu teahouse, and partially obscured by the steam from a fresh glass of bitter buckwheat tea, poet Aku Wuwu 阿庫烏霧, otherwise known by his Chinese moniker Luo Qingchun 羅慶春, started speaking about his childhood:

> My mother told me that at the most difficult point of her labor, there in our mountain home, she beheld the apparition of an elder with white locks and a pale visage laughing as he stood before her. At the moment of my birth the vision subsided. Later, by this story, people of the village understood that mine was the path of a learned person, and not that of a farmer. . . . The date of my birth is the year of the dragon. On my identity card it reads May 10, 1964. But in fact, the real date is unknown. My mother only said that I was born after the cutting of the late summer corn.[1]

This anecdote, delivered in the midst of a long day of cotranslation of his work, instantly added another layer of context to the puzzle of Aku Wuwu's bifurcated corpus of poetry and his stance as a "cultural hybrid" (文化混血). Visions, such as the omen of success brought by the laughter of the pale, white-haired elder, seem to be a source of inspiration for some of Aku's most powerful poetry. The fact that there is no written record of his birth amidst drying corn cobs and patchwork potato fields attests to the position he holds as a contemporary ethnic minority poet linked directly to a traditional life-world that has changed dramatically within his own lifetime. The poem, one of several we were translating that week spent in Chengdu teahouses, was written in a script conveying the sounds of the Nuosu (諾蘇) dialect of the Yi (彝) language, his "mother tongue" (*muyu* 母語). The lines, which he spoke word by word as we sought for equivalents in English, were an immanent expression of individual perception bubbling up from a

deep pool of tradition and personal experience into the glaring lights of a present bifurcated between rural and urban, minority and majority, national and global. Another
set of poems, more personal and less evocative of Yi culture, is composed in Mandarin
Chinese, which for Aku is an adopted language, a "second mother tongue" (*di'er muyu*
第二母語). The use of Mandarin makes for easy engagement with the major flow of
literature in China today. The process and challenges of translating these poems are
somewhat different, though they still require cultural knowledge and an emotional
connection with the writing. Some of the poems, both Nuosu and Chinese, have made
their way into Aku's emotionally charged public readings, while an increasing number have been translated by this author and others into other languages, particularly
English. However, until very recently the Nuosu and Chinese poems were wholly separate collections, with the Nuosu poems remaining untranslated and hermetically sealed
in a script that even few Nuosu can read easily.

The anecdote of the pale-faced elder also alludes to Aku Wuwu's birth into a society
that was still adjusting to massive social changes, including the late-1950s destruction
of the traditional hierarchical society that for centuries had been headed by an elite
class of lords who held sway over the lives of several classes of serfs and slaves. Though
Aku's birthdate is not known, his birthplace is a hamlet in Mianning county, located
in the rugged hills of the Liangshan Yi Autonomous Prefecture in southern Sichuan
province.[2] Raised under sometimes difficult circumstances by his widowed mother
and elder sisters, Aku spoke Nuosu dialect exclusively until age seven. His childhood school was ensconced in a canyon hung with a chain-link bridge that connects
the banks of the roaring Yalong River. Each day he walked four hours along rough
mountain trails to school and then back, receiving four hours of schooling midday,
and his first sentence in Chinese was "Long live Chairman Mao!" (*Mao Zhuxi wansui*
毛主席萬歲). His name in Yi romanization is Apkup Vytvy (the "p" and "t" designate
linguistic tones and are otherwise silent), which is written ꀊꈌꃴꃷ in the modern Yi
syllabary.[3] According to Wen Peihong 文培紅, a professor of American ethnic literature at Southwest University for Nationalities (*Xinan minzu daxue* 西南民族大學
or SWUN) in Chengdu, the name Aku Wuwu was given to him by a Han "educated
youth" (*zhiqing* 知青) who was sent from Chengdu to Liangshan to "learn from the
peasants" during the Cultural Revolution (1966–1976). The educated youth decided
that this Mandarinized version of his name was more easily pronounceable, and
consequently it became the poet's nom de plume.[4] Later, Aku was given an official
Mandarin name, Luo Qingchun, and although he now goes by that name in professional circles, he has never forgotten his roots deep in the mountains and rivers of
Liangshan. This bifurcated, dual identity projects into the body of works, whether
written in Nuosu or Chinese.

Although the Cultural Revolution was a disaster for the nation, it had real benefits
for rural students like Aku Wuwu by creating opportunities to expand their horizons
and options. Upon completing high school in Xichang, the prefectural capital, Aku was
able to enroll as an undergraduate at SWUN, where he and a number of other southwestern ethnic minority poets have studied. It was during these early years at SWUN

that Aku came in contact with the reviving literary scene in China and caught the wave of foreign writing being introduced into the country by the early 1980s, much of it in the form of translations. The university was the initial seedbed for the later flourishing of Aku's bilingual corpus of writing in which he would explore issues of ethnic, social, and linguistic identity through groundbreaking efforts in writing poetry in his native "mother tongue" of Nuosu and in the equally challenging medium of his "second mother tongue," Standard Chinese.

THE SOUL CALLER

Aku's best-known poem, "Calling Back the Soul of Zhyge Alu" (*Ax lu yyr kup* ꀊꇐꈪꈨ), is a call to cultural and spiritual revival among the Yi people.[5] Known in Mandarin as "Zhaohun" (招魂) ("Soul calling"), the poem invokes the spirit of a mythic Yi culture hero who, like the Han Chinese hero Hou Yi 后羿 and the Miao 苗 (Hmong) hero Hsang Sa, saves the world from immanent destruction by shooting down extra suns that are scorching the earth. The poem mimics rites conducted by Yi ritualists to "call back" the wandering souls of the afflicted, especially children, in a type of ritual that was once common in south and southwest China. Aku wrote the poem in Nuosu dialect while studying in Beijing in 1986. His earliest audiences were small groups of native Nuosu speakers in the capital. Over time, he performed in a variety of urban and rural venues, including academic conferences and rural middle schools. Since 2007, he has recited portions of the poem in multicultural bookstore events in Chengdu, appearing with other ethnic minority poets and local Han poets. He has also appeared onstage with Amo Niuniu (literally "mother's youngest daughter"), a folksinger group comprised of three middle-aged Nuosu women. In the Liangshan Mountains, the group has performed for large gatherings at folk festivals and made special appearances in rural schools. The lines below, which mention "Father" (*Abbo*) and "Mother" (*Amo*), typify the power of his performed poetry, which is punctuated by gestures, gesticulations, and paralinguistic explosions, often eliciting strong emotional responses in audiences.[6] There is also mention of an object of material culture—a lidded wooden bowl—that holds ritual significance to the Nuosu. As will be seen, such imagery is a key component of his verse.

> The rice *Abbo* and *Amo* have prepared is steaming—
> The rising steam has no soul.
> In the four directions all is sunlit—
> The sun's rays have become icicles.
> Every heart is becoming a wooden compote
> Searching in every direction: east, west, north, south.
> Screaming,
>   Crying,
>   Shouting—

Calling back the soul.
O la, come back!
O la, come back!
Whether in the Yi areas,
Come back!
Whether in the Han areas,
Come back!

ꀀꆈꌠꉙ
ꀕꆏꉘꈎꌷꐕꂿ
ꆿꌠꃆꌦ
ꀋꀨꏮꌺꃀꉻꂷ
ꃅꆪꎆꆧ

ꌺꊪꀻꏦꌠꎆꀉꑳ
ꃀꇰꌅꈜꃅꄤ
ꉙꀕꀑꇬ
ꀄꈬꆧ
ꁷꃀꆧ
ꄮꃀꆧ
ꋊꑘꄷꎆꐭ

ꉚ...ꆹ! ꉚ...ꆹ!
ꆏꃆꇈꆏ
ꑸꃅꇈꆏ

lip yi shy vut jox
ap bbo ax mo zza nyi hxo pox
zza sot lu ap nyi
nip mu ly ke xyx ca jjiex luo wu
xyx ca zzup wu shop

hxie mop ma nex kur mut zzyr jjip ge vex
bbux ddur bbu jji yyx o yyx hmy
jox vo qip ge vex
gurx zhyr wu mu
guox ggie wu mu
dox ssi wu mu
yyr kut hla xie lix ge vex

ox. . . la! ox. . . la!
nip mu jjox nyi la
shuo ggot jjox nyi la

As is the case with many ethnic minority writers in East Asia, if not worldwide, Aku is part of a generation of individuals raised in traditional cultures and caught in the dynamics of rapid social change.[7] Though presently living an urban lifestyle, he retains both cultural and linguistic fluency with the Yi tradition. His work exhibits an interest in what American poet Gary Snyder has called "the old ways," yet conveys a realization that the influences of the majority culture are pervasive and irreversible.[8] He promotes the recognition of the value of traditional folk culture, especially oral tradition and material folk arts, and the use of the "mother tongue" in both daily life and literature. In his words, ethnic minority writers today are unavoidably cultural hybrids who must write in Chinese to gain footing in the literary world. Yet, despite the obstacles, Aku is a strong advocate of "mother tongue literature" (*muyu wenxue* 母語文學) written in the Nuosu script. "Mother tongue" means not only the level of language, but the ways of thinking and cultural perceptions that are inherent in language use. Writing in a mother tongue is also a buttress against acculturalization and a means to maintain cultural identity that is at the deepest level connected to the wellspring of his being. Even in his works in Chinese, it is important to him to utilize Nuosu folk ideas and patterns of thinking. On the other hand, Chinese as a medium of poetic expression is enriched by voices from outside the linguistic and cultural mainstream.[9]

Aku sees his poetic works as "textbooks" that, whether written in his first or second mother tongue, may help foster appreciation of traditional culture among young people in both urban and rural areas.[10] His voice as a cultural hybrid is the contemporary voice of an ethnic minority individual speaking within a diverse nation. Although readily categorized as an indigenous writer working in an indigenous language, Aku prefers to self-identify as a mother-tongue writer, since the term *indigenous* is complicated, difficult to calibrate in a country with a long and complex history of internal migration and cultural mixing. The idea of a "mother tongue" gives primacy to Aku's claim to being an authentic voice for both his own poetic vision and his vision for the spiritual welfare of his people. At the same time, he views his Chinese language poetry, written in his "second mother tongue," as an acknowledgment that his own life, like the lives of his fellow Yi, is inextricably entwined with the dominant linguistic register of China, and by extension with mainstream Chinese life. In another anecdote, Aku relates how this dichotomy of self-expression crystallized in front of him one morning at breakfast. He suddenly noticed that his son was responding to his questions posed in Nuosu by speaking in Chinese. This caused him to reflect on the situation in which most ethnic poets writing in China today use Mandarin as a poetic medium, yet still write what is considered as ethnic poetry. This theme of bilingualism and biculturalism has become an important aspect of Aku's critical writing and poetry.

Although Aku has vigorously promoted writing in the Nuosu dialect of Yi—and now has a following of younger poets writing both in Yi and Chinese—the intended audience for this Yi language poetry is less clear. While literacy in a modern Nuosu script was actively promoted from the late 1970s to the 1990s, as the market reforms transform rural areas and many young people are drawn to urban areas for employment the knowledge of Mandarin takes on a more practical value. Though the Yi script is taught in some rural primary and middle schools in Liangshan prefecture today and there have been attempts to popularize the script in various media, relatively few Nuosu read with the fluency needed to appreciate literary works, or have the ability to utilize the modern Yi script as a medium for literary creation.

ETHNIC MINORITY WRITING
IN SOUTHWEST CHINA

One of the most dramatic reorganizations of China in the post-1949 period has been the extensive identification and legitimization of what are presently fifty-six *minzu* (民族)—a term meaning roughly "ethnic group." In imperial times and under the Nationalists in the early twentieth century, there was official recognition of different ethnic groups within China's borders, but these categorizations tended to be rather broad. Under the influence of the Soviet Union in the 1940s and 1950s, scholars and officials in New China created a system by which the diverse peoples of the nation-state were identified and classified by a combination of traits that could include language group, customs, history, livelihood, and so forth.[11] Most people identified as ethnic minorities (*shaoshu minzu* 少數民族) lived in newly created "autonomous" areas of varying sizes located along the country's inland borders. The majority ethnic group, making up over 91 percent of the population, is called the Han (漢); the nation's official language, Mandarin, is based on a northern dialect of Chinese and is referred to as *Hanyu* (漢語; or literally, "Han language"). Since 1949, Mandarin has become a second language for most ethnic minority people in China and Han speakers of local Chinese dialects.

The legacy of these ethnic policy decisions is evident in China's internal politics and economic development, and has ramifications for other spheres of life, including the arts and literature. Since the 1950s, and again after the social disruptions of the 1960s and 1970s, voices from a growing number of ethnic minority writers and artists from around the nation have been heard in local, regional, national, and international venues. Earlier works carried the stamp of the political needs and currents of the day. Since the early 1980s, more diverse opportunities for education and expression have fostered the rise of a cohort of younger writers who experiment with new styles and content matter.

One region of great creative activity is multiethnic southwest China, which has produced writers from several ethnic groups. Those with international reputations include the ethnically Tibetan (藏) authors Zhaxi Dawa 扎西達娃, Alai 阿來, and Dondrup Gyel 端智嘉.[12] In Yunnan province, home to twenty-eight official ethnic groups, many writers from the Hani (哈尼), Jingpo (景頗), Wa (佤), Bai (白), Dai (傣), and other groups are active, particularly in local literary scenes.[13] Beginning in the early 1980s, a comparatively large number of poets of the Yi ethnic group, whose traditional home is southern Sichuan, Yunnan, and western Guizhou, emerged on local and national literary scenes.[14] Among the Yi poets, a large percentage are members of the ethnic subgroup known as the Nuosu, affiliated with the geographical regions of the Greater and Lesser Liangshan Mountains in southern Sichuan and northern Yunnan province.[15]

WRITTEN AND ORAL TRADITIONS
OF YI LITERATURE

Numbering around nine million, the Yi are one of China's largest official groups, though customs and language vary quite widely among the dozens of local subgroups. While most Yi live in upland communities in central and southern Yunnan province, the Nuosu areas of southern Sichuan and northwest Yunnan are the most culturally conservative in terms of language and culture. Therefore, in approaching contemporary Yi poetry it is important to understand an individual poet's geographical roots and subgroup affiliation. By far the largest percentage of Yi poets are members of the Nuosu subgroup. That said, all of the Yi speak languages in the Tibeto-Burman family and have for centuries been herders and agriculturalists in the uplands of the southwest. The last 100 years have brought unrelenting changes to the Yi areas, and new contexts have emerged since 1949 for interaction between the Yi and other ethnic groups.

Traditional Yi written literature has a long history that is intertwined with rich oral and written traditions of myth, ritual, epic, legend, poetry, stories, and folk knowledge associated with various communities of people now known as Yi in parts of southwest China. Many ritual and literary works were written in the ancient script, which is native to southwest China. The syllabic script is very different from the scripts used for Chinese, Sanskrit, and Burmese, the *dongba* (東巴) pictographic writing of the Naxi (納西) ethnic group, or other regional writing systems. The surviving texts were written and used mostly by priests known as *bimo*, who conducted rituals for individual, family, and community welfare and were important tradition-bearers of local lore and genealogies. Existing examples of traditional Yi writing, in the form of scrolls or bound pages, date back to the Ming dynasty, though evidence suggests that some of the texts themselves date back even earlier. The local variants of the script are not completely intelligible to *bimo* across the Yi areas. In the 1970s, a modern Yi script called the Liangshan Standard Yi Script was developed and is in limited use today in the Yi regions of Sichuan and part of northwest Yunnan. The 819 standardized graphs represent the sounds of Nuosu pronunciation in Xide county and are based on elements of the traditional script system.[16]

Verse was the standard medium of writing, with five-syllable lines being the most common. Subject matter included chants used in rituals by the *bimo* to call back the wandering souls of the sick or guide the souls of the dead to the land of the ancestors, family and community protection rites, divination, and genealogies. Yi literature has many epics narrating the creation of the earth, sky, waters, landscapes, and forms of life, including humans. Epics like the Nuosu *Book of Origins* (*Hne wo tep yy* ꊿꄷꅉ) are rich in imagery of the environment and traditional Yi life. Such texts, like numerous local folk song traditions and folk stories, have informed the works of many contemporary Yi poets; these include bridal laments featuring young women, like "Mother's Daughter" (*Ax mo hnix sse* 𐒥𐒦𐒦) and the tragic story of a runaway bride, "Gamo Anyo" (*Ga mop at nyop* 𐒥𐒦𐒦).

There is also a traditional body of critical writings on the appreciation of texts written in ancient Yi based on oral traditions. Written in verse, these critical writings include short treatises on the writing of histories, poetry, songs, stories, and rituals. The best known were composed by a high-ranking *bimo* named Jushezhe 舉奢哲 and a female *bimo* (a true rarity) named Amaini 阿買妮.[17] According to Yi genealogies, both figures may have lived over one thousand years ago, very likely in western Guizhou. Their works on poetry emphasize the proper use of rhyme and the sound value of words, as well as repetition, parallelism, antithesis, and parataxis (the juxtaposition of dissimilar elements). Certain observations reveal that when these critical writings refer to written texts, they are also suggesting ways such texts are voiced in oral performances, a dynamic between the written and spoken word that is still relevant in the study of contemporary Yi literature, which consists of poetry, short stories, and the occasional novel written by Yi authors. Amaini writes in particular about a common format for poems and folk songs called the "three-part poem" (三段詩), which begins with an image of the sky or a mountaintop, followed by descending images of a mountainside or valley, and finally a focus on human inhabitants, often the courting activities of young lovers. It is important to understand, however, that the local traditions of Yi writing were not universally known throughout the ethnic communities classified since 1949 under the category of Yi. Moreover, it is only in very recent years that the local traditions of oral and written lore from the various Yi areas have been made available to scholars and writers, often as translations into Mandarin.

THE LIANGSHAN SCHOOL OF CONTEMPORARY YI POETRY

As noted, most contemporary Yi poets belong to the Nuosu subgroup of the Yi ethnic group and hail from areas in southern Sichuan and northwest Yunnan provinces. As a whole, these Nuosu poets can be considered the Liangshan school of modern Yi poetry, the name derived from the Liangshan Mountains of southern Sichuan and the eponymous Liangshan Yi Autonomous Prefecture and smaller autonomous areas in the region.[18] A number of the Nuosu poets live in major cities such as Chengdu and Beijing, where they are employed in government offices, national think tanks like the Chinese Academy of Social Sciences, and universities. Some grew up in deeply rural settings and spoke only Yi as children, while others were raised in county or prefectural seats (such as Xichang, the capital of Liangshan prefecture), or in larger cities in environments where Mandarin was a common tongue and educational opportunities were more readily available. These differences in background also mean a different engagement with Yi culture, which in turn impacts the use of imagery and folk ideas in the poetry. Although since the early twentieth century all Yi poets have written in modern poetic registers strongly influenced by currents in the development of modern Chinese literature (and its foreign influences), their writings as a whole exhibit a number of characteristics that in some ways echo content in works of many minority poets in China, and sometimes certain Han poets writing from the margins.

Like most ethnic writers in China, Yi poets in southwest China, with few exceptions, are Sinophone poets, in that they write primarily in Mandarin.[19] Borrowing a phrase from the indigenous Khasi poet Kynpham Sing Nongkynrih from Northeast India (where many ethnic minority poets write in English), Mandarin is the "language of interaction" for poetry in China.[20] This common medium is used by ethnic minority writers for a variety of reasons. Many writers either do not have linguistic competency in the ancestral tongue or find it more useful to use Mandarin to further their careers and reach larger audiences. Aku Wuwu is unusual among the Liangshan poets in that for decades he has resolutely written in both Yi and Mandarin. Influenced by Aku's long-term interest in "mother tongue" writing, a number of younger Yi poets have recently begun to compose some of their work in modern Yi script, and some established poets are having poems originally written in Chinese recast in Yi.

The Liangshan School has its roots in the works of several modern Yi poets active in the first decades of New China, including Wuqi Lada 吳琪拉達 (of Guizhou and Sichuan) and Tipu Zhibu 替樸支不 (of Guangxi), who began publishing poems in Chinese in the 1950s and combined modern styles of poetry with folk themes. These early works were written in the framework and discourse of Socialist agendas of the day. The Cultural Revolution promoted aggressive policies toward ethnic minority groups and their literatures, hindering further development. After the decade of turbulence, a new generation of Yi poets emerged on China's regional and national literary scenes, at a moment when diverse experimental voices were blossoming all over China. The new poets were variously stimulated by mainstream poetic currents of the late 1970s and early 1980s, especially the "Misty" or "Obscure" (*menglong* 朦朧) poets and the "seeking roots" (*xungen* 尋根) poets, who had a nostalgic interest in tradition and local rural culture, and the growing influx of works by foreign writers, usually in Chinese translation. Yet these Yi poets also brought with them unique cultural perspectives and poetic traditions.

The first Yi poet to gain national attention in the post–Cultural Revolution era both for his work and his status as a minority writer was Jidi Majia 吉狄馬加, who grew up in the Butuo area of Liangshan prefecture and attended SWUN in Chengdu. By the early 2000s, Jidi was the temporary head of the Chinese Writers' Association, and he has recently held high-level government offices in Qinghai province, where he has used his influence to host several major international poetry gatherings at Lake Qinghai. Jidi's work is a mix of poems on ethnic and personal themes, some of which incorporate imagery from his travels in Europe and elsewhere. His work has been influenced by the nativist writings of South American poets such as Pablo Neruda, Octavio Paz, and Gabriela Mistral. Evocative, lyrical, and mellifluous, Jidi's work inspired a generation of young Yi writers who saw him as a model of success.[21]

The majority of the Liangshan poets today write within a "literary micro-environment" centered in Liangshan prefecture, with several members living in Chengdu and elsewhere.[22] These poets, who all emerged in the 1980s and 1990s, include the late Ma Deqing 馬德清, Luowu Laqie 倮伍拉且, Bamo Qubumo 巴莫曲布嫫, Asu Yue'er 阿蘇越爾, Eni Mushasijia 俄尼牧莎斯加, and Sha Ma 沙馬, followed by the somewhat younger poets Lu Juan 魯娟 and Asuo Layi 阿索拉毅. Their writing tends to concern local and personal themes and, with a few exceptions, is little affected by avant-garde movements. One member of the group is Fa Xing 發星, who though technically a Han, grew up in the Liangshan region and writes on Nuosu themes. Besides single-authored collections published by a variety of local and national publishing houses, works of the Liangshan poets (and critical articles about them) appear in journals such as the local *Liangshan Literature* (涼山文學) and the national *Nationalities Literature* (民族文學) as well as general poetry journals. Unofficial journals, such as *Yi Wind* (彝風), have been printed at private expense, and a number of the poets have online blogs. Conferences, large and small, are regularly held on Yi studies, and many poets participate in these events as academics and sometimes as performing poets. Several informal gathering spots have been popular with ethnic poets and artists in Beijing and Chengdu, including a restaurant in Beijing founded by members of China's first successful ethnic rock group, the Nuosu band Mountain Eagle (山鷹組合), founded in 1990. In Chengdu, the Native Tongue Bar, active from 2004 to 2012, was known for its hip ethnic "Beat" feel. The bar was the site of numerous poetry readings and concerts patronized by members of various ethnic backgrounds in the Chengdu art and literature scene.[23] In recent years, major urban bookstores and mainstream poetry bars in Chengdu have also become occasional venues for multiethnic poetry readings. Within this milieu of Liangshan poets, Aku Wuwu stands out as a gifted maverick for his interest in and use of the modern Yi script as a medium for written poetry.

Aside from modernist literary influences, the strong tradition of Yi verbal art and vernacular culture has in varying degrees impacted the writings of most poets in the Liangshan poetry school. Among these cultural influences are oral folk songs, narrative poems, proverbs, chants, rituals, festivals, customs, and corollaries of the narrative and lyrical forms in written literary texts. The Nuosu poets often evoke images of traditional lifestyles (which continue in some form or another in rural areas) and imagery of the natural or pastoral world that is being affected by rapid social change.[24] Popular images are rural folk doing various activities such as hunting, weaving, singing, dancing, drinking, and other pursuits that resonate with constructions of Yi identity. Unique items of material culture are especially prevalent and include images of felt cloaks, turbans, lacquered wooden bowls and eating utensils, silver ornaments, tiny brass mouth harps, sweet and bitter buckwheat cakes, bony chunks of meat, potatoes, native vegetables, and embroidery needles made of water deer teeth. Tigers, eagles, musk deer, rhododendron flowers, mountains, forests, rivers, and lightning are typical of the poetic imagery drawn from nature. Many poems exhibit a sometimes ambivalent stress on ethnic pride and promote a unique sense of "Nuosuness." Such longing for expressions of ethnic identity as tangible tradition also manifests itself in urban versions of folk festivals such as the highly commercialized summer Torch Festival in Xichang, which draws large numbers of Yi people from all over. Such festivals, and other public displays evidence the revival, creation, and recreation of traditions since the 1980s, including a wide variety of "traditional" folk dances, music, and elaborate costumes. Thus, items of tradition in many manifestations are readily available to inform the written works of the Liangshan School poets and act as correlative presences in the poems. This factor is key in understanding the work of Aku Wuwu.

CULTURAL HYBRID AS COSMOGRAPHER

Positioning himself as a cultural hybrid, a poet of differential identities that play out in the medium of his verses, Aku Wuwu faces the contemporary world as a seer into the past, present, and future. Dream, ecstatic channeling, sweet whispering, sensuous lyricism, and primal roaring—displayed in poems with titles like "Calling Back the Soul of Zhyge Alu," "Grass Effigy" (草偶, or *Ry bbur* ⵏⵅ), and "Red Sea" (紅海, or *Shur hni* ⵇⵣ)—are key aspects of his means of communication, inscribed in print and made immanent in performance. Aku began writing in the mid-1980s in the wake of Jidi Majia's creative casting of Yi culture in the poetic medium of Chinese. His bilingual/bicultural repertoire of poems and prose poems forces his diverse readers (and auditors) to engage with his notions of the bicultural positioning of modern ethnic minority writers. To date, he has published six volumes of poetry, including two collections of Yi poems, *Winter River* (冬天的河流, or *Cux wa yyp mop* ⵏⵉⵐⵣ; 1994) and *Tiger Tracks* (虎跡, or *Lat jjup* ⵃⵊ; 1998), together with four collections in Mandarin, *Out of the Land of Sorcerers* (走出巫界; 1995), *Selected Poems of Aku Wuwu* (阿庫烏霧詩歌選; 2004), a volume focused on his initial trip to the Mississippi River basin, titled *Appeal of the Mississippi River* (密西西比河的傾訴; 2008), and a collection of prose-poems titled *Hybrid Age* (混血時代; 2015). Aku's 2010 volume of short, lyrical essays entitled *The Wizard's Voice* (神巫的祝咒) describes aspects of Nuosu folk and ritual culture that can often serve as footnotes to his poems.[25] Outstanding among his theoretical works, in which he explains his ideas of cultural hybridity and second mother tongue, is a collection of essays titled *Spirit to Spirit: Discussions of Contemporary Ethnic Minority Poetry in Chinese* (靈與靈的對話: 中國當代少數民族漢語詩論; 2001).[26]

Aku describes portions of his work as "literary anthropology" (文學人類學), though a better English equivalent that embodies the character of his work would be "ethnographic literature," in the sense of a literature that records and utilizes high-context details of human life within particular situations. Another term that could describe his work is *cosmographic*, a concept revived from the works of anthropologist Franz Boas by eco-critic Joni Adamson.[27] A cosmographer looks at the plurality and diversity of the cosmos, each part with its own valuable story. Thus, not only is the human universe a subject of inquiry, so too are endless life- and geo-forms making up what eco-critics like Adamson call the "pluriverse." Aku's work often includes not only humans but also animals, plants, ghost, and natural forces that are sometimes transformative and shape-shifting. Moreover, as a type of cosmopolitical eco-ethnography, his work (and that of other Yi poets) often touches on the dynamics of humans within both human-manipulated environments and what is left of the natural world. [28]

On one hand, Aku's conception of his poems as textbooks of tradition leans toward the ancient Chinese idea that literature is didactic, but on the other hand it encompasses a knowledge of tradition within a creative dynamic that invites creative responses from readers and listeners. His poetry is often visceral, juxtaposing imagery and sonic elements in presentations that are at once wholly open to interpretation by readers of any background, but are often coded with referents that conjure elements of myth, ritual, and custom that hold the potential for meaning making for readers who are in the contexts of Yi life-worlds. Although Aku is open to anyone experiencing his verse, he offers poems that also communicate layers of specialized knowledge to specialized audiences.

Relevant here is epic scholar John Miles Foley's idea of "traditional referentiality" which suggests that many images in traditional oral and oral-connected literary texts have "metonymic" functions that conjure knowledge embedded in the web of culture.[29] Thus, an image of a flower may have an aesthetic appeal—sometimes very powerful—to any listener or reader, but may also offer the potential for evoking culturally specific knowledge and meaning. Regarded from this perspective, Aku's work is like the story-cloths embroidered by Hmong immigrants to the United States in the late 1970s that feature aspects of traditional upland lifestyles in Southeast Asia, the patchwork *arpilleras* created by women in the Chilean Andes, or the family quilts from Appalachia that may elicit aesthetic responses from consumers remote from the sites and life-worlds of production, but may also have very deep and specific meanings for the individual, family, or folk group that produced them. [30]

That a large amount of Aku's imagery is drawn from his interactions with Yi ritualists, craftspeople, and rural folk is not accidental. Indeed this medium of imagery represents a set of cultural nodes that Aku wishes to highlight as beacons for carrying on in some fashion viable aspects of traditional Yi culture into the emergent contemporary. For Aku and other Yi poets, this context is the contemporary world of the Yi ethnic group, which ranges from upland pastoral and wild landscapes to urban ones, within the dynamic social changes wrought by a modernizing China. Aku's rural background gives him a ready store of experience and folk knowledge, which has been bolstered by more academic studies of tradition, including a study of practices of the female Nuosu shamans known as *monyi*. His extensive contacts throughout the Liangshan mountains and frequent trips to the area keep him in close touch with local cultural developments.

Dozens of poems in Aku's *Appeal of the Mississippi*, written in Chinese, deal with encounters with American Indian writers, poets, tribal leaders, and others in several Native American communities during his early trips to the United States, beginning in 2005. In 2014, Aku traveled to Japan to recite with indigenous Ainu poets and oral

tradition-bearers. The indigenous poets Aku met on his travels share certain characteristics with ethnic minority writers in China, despite obvious differences in sociocultural and historical situations, particularly in the areas of language loss and the
effects of displacement from land-based economies to urban-based industry on local
culture.

Whether his poems are written in Mandarin or the modern Yi syllabary, certain
patterns emerge in Aku's poetic technique. In both languages, dream, ritual, oral tradition, traditional customs, material culture, and his own unique ways of seeing the
world are utilized in the creation of structures of meaning. That said, his Nuosu language poems tend to invoke much more "thick" ethnographic content and deeper
culturally referential imagery.[31] Several poems written in Chinese about his North
American experiences use imagery from Native American myth and folklore, especially stories from the northwest and Great Lakes cultures, which would be unfamiliar to many current US residents. For example, a poem called "The Land on Sea
Turtle" (海龜托起的大地) combines references to both Yi mythology and Native
American myth:

> In my ancestors' creation epic
> there is a record of a great flood.
> The kind-hearted *Jjut mu ssep nyop*
> gained the attention of Heaven with a wisp of smoke,
> proving once again that human reproduction
> is the intent of Nature.
>
> In the legends of Indians in North America,
> the unsettled land under their feet
> slowly formed on the back of a turtle from the depths of the vast sea,
> with the assistance of birds.
> Only by using your deepest sense of conscience to incessantly press
> against every inch of spiritful land
> can you receive true motherly love. (May 2005)

> 我祖先的史詩裡
> 有洪水漫天地的記載
> 善良的居木熱牛
> 借助佑護神的暗示
> 以一束銀針似的青煙
> 再次證明:人類的繁衍
> 純屬自然的旨意
>
> 北美印第安人傳說
> 他們腳下喧囂的大地
> 是在眾鳥的協助下
> 於汪洋深處
> 由一隻海龜的脊背
> 慢慢延伸而成

不斷用生命的良知
去貼近每一片靈性的土地
你才可能獲得
真正的母愛

Here, Aku borrows imagery from a Nuosu creation myth in the *Hnewo tepyy*, or *Book of Origins*, which describes how the youngest of three brothers manages to survive a great flood and restart human civilization; his fire-making activities arouse the attention of the Sky God, who eventually sends his youngest daughter to earth to marry the young man and repopulate the earth. The links between earth and sky are facilitated by birds. In the succeeding lines, Aku refers to the Iroquoian myths of Turtle Island, also invoking the assistance of birds. The linkage between the myth worlds is that of the pervasiveness of spirits in the respective lands and the relations to the land that echo in juxtaposition as "trans-indigenous" with other native cultures in different parts of the globe.[32] The reference to American Indian myth is a result of Aku's readings of a number of texts translated into Chinese and conversations with Native American acquaintances on his journeys.[33]

An example of Aku's cosmographically rich Nuosu poems is "Grass Effigy," which centers on an effigy of woven grass produced by *bimo* to ward off harmful ghosts, which is called *ry bbur* in Nuosu (草偶 in Chinese).[34] The art of crafting these effigies is still passed down within lines of *bimo* today, and they are often seen in rituals in both rural and urban settings, or wherever a *bimo* is invited to doctor. The effigy represents one of a vast horde of harmful ghosts that inflict an assortment of afflictions upon traditional Nuosu; during the ritual the ghost is placated with sacrifices of chickens, pigs, goats, or even larger farmyard creatures, and is eventually sent away. Afterward, the effigy is hung in the mountains to decay. The poem begins with a reference to the makers and conductors of grass effigies and rituals, noting they are "more numerous than ant eggs beneath stone slabs." The poem then offers images of pine tree seedlings being dispersed across rugged hills that have been devastated by clear-cutting. The forests seem like "bunches of spiders carrying their eggs" or "married women in the fields/Carrying their children as they plant the crops." Yet over time these "pine tree children" become mulch, as the years and seasons turn, greening the devastated forests. The imagery then shifts to an anecdote about a middle-aged Yi women who, after the completion of a grass-effigy ritual to purify her household, is annoyed by the hissing of unseasoned sticks in her home's fireplace, and rashly extinguishes them in a wooden trough used for pig slop. In the realm of sympathetic magic, this act of disrespect is reciprocated when her brother slips off a mountain path to his death. The poem then shifts to the following description:

> The red-footed grasses
> Are cut and regrow,
> Cut and regrow.
> The grass effigies in the pine forests,

The old are followed by the new,
The old are followed by the new.
In the past were the Twelve Sons of Snow and
The red-footed grasses were among those sons of snow.
But not many people still remember this.
Now ant eggs have become stars in the sky,
Becoming the old bear's most lovely ornaments.

ꂷꑋꀯꑘꊪꑘꌦ.
ꑊꑌꈝꇅꀒ.
ꄹꀕꂷꑌꃑ,
ꂷꑋꈓꂷꇅꑄ,
ꑵꒉꈐꇰꌸꌋꅔ.
ꐗꄮꈐꑴꋪ,
ꑭꋚꃘꋆꑌꇮꃀ.

Ryp ddu xy hni yyt dde nix dde xi.
Te juo ry bbur shyt ddur li zot qip.
A hlex vo nre sse ku jox,
Ryp ddu xy hni vo nre sse nge su,
Co shut a hnat go shut su ap jjo.
Bbut vup qip ww jyx sse jjip,
Wo mox ndit fu ndit hne kax nze ww.

    Embedded in the text are references to Nuosu traditional myth and cosmology. In the proclamation of the cyclic passage of the ages marked by destruction and regrowth—in the metonym of grass—the poet evokes lines from the *Book of Origins*, in which various grasses are among the twelve sons (offspring) or tribes of snow.[35] These twelve categories of living beings include those without blood and those with blood. The former category of the folk taxonomy includes six species of trees and grasses, while the latter category includes animals such as frogs, snakes, birds, bears, monkeys, and humans. But as the poet notes, this knowledge, as is the immanent knowledge behind the making and use of effigies, is being lost in the rapidly altering landscapes of the present—a world that is increasingly less part of collective memory. Active bearers of such knowledge are increasingly joining the ancestors, who like the bears, have left the ecosystems of Liangshan for the other world.
    A dream-like quality pervades much of Aku's work, possibly the legacy of the laughing, pale-faced elder of his mother's dream and the pool of Nuosu tradition that includes the frequent passing between the numinous and material worlds, a dynamic with its "own reasons, logic, and coherence."[36] The twisted course of some poems may be attributed to the course of creation, which the poet has described as a bursting forth of poetry from a state of reverie. In a suite of poems published in English translation as "Four Trees and Three Seas," drawn from his Nuosu language collection *Tiger Tracks*, a dreamlike quality is pervasive.[37] In the poem "Red Sea," dream and reality commingle as the individual voice dissolves into the whole of existence:

Now that the red sea cannot be seen by eyes,
and now that it is untouchable by hands,
it is only there in dreams.
When a sleepless, unsettled, endlessly
roaming spirit appears—
it seems to come from the shores of the red sea,
and when leaving goes in the direction of that sea.

When waking you discover that all
the rosy red fruits have become a red sea.
The fiery red fireplace has become a red sea.
The vibrant red thoughts in people's hearts have become a red sea.
The place you are at has become a red sea.
The place I am at has become a red sea.

ꈌꑘ, ꆈꌠꏂꌠꉜ,
ꆈꌠꏂꌠꉜ,
ꀕꇉꉪꌹ,
ꄷꀕꄻꃀꆈꊙꉻꃆ,
ꆏꈌꆏꀠꀕꆆꈐꈎꄹ,
ꊙꈌꆏꀠꀕꋜꀕꎃꐚꈎꆆꑘꉜ.

ꆏꈌꆆꑞ,
ꌧꋏꋠꐎꂷꆆꈩꑘꆏꈌꑘ;
ꇬꑝꇬꈎꆆꈩꑘꆏꈌꑘ;
ꊿꐎꉻꃀꉷꇖꆆꑘꀕꈩꑘꆏꈌꑘ;
ꆅꈌꆅꇁꆆꈌꑘ,
ꉪꈌꉪꇁꆆꈌꑘ.

shur hni, nyuo mo ap hxit ggup jjux,
lot yu ap hxit ggup jjux,
iet muop go ax di,
yyr di hlax di it ap dda nyi ap dda max su,
lax nyi shur hni xip ma xy nzix la sux mu jjip,
bbox nyi shur hni xip ma jox hxep da bbo sux mu jjip go shex.

it jjip la mox ne,
syr zza qi ma hnix go wu su nyi shur hni jjip;
lip yi ga kux hnix lo wu su nyi shur hni jjip;
vo co hxie mop ngop lu hnix zhyrx wu su nyi shur hni jjip;
nit ggup nit lep nyi shur hni,
ngat ggup ngat lep nyi shur hni.

After publishing several volumes of poetry and prose poems Chinese between 2005 and 2012, Aku revisited his Nuosu poetry in 2014, composing in a new style he describes as "genealogical poetry." Innovatively, Aku seeks to break the typical conventions of the contemporary free verse in which most Yi poetry is cast and injects aspects of style that are in some ways throwbacks to ancient Yi literature, in particular the recitation of clan genealogies. The first intellectual task of young Nuosu boys is learning the family genealogy, which typically spans twenty or thirty generations. Aku's first poem to utilize this repurposed poetic tradition is "Genealogy and History" (*Co cyt: jju cyt* ꆈꌠ:ꆈꌠ in Nuosu, and 人譜歷史 in Chinese). The 209-line poem is a genealogy of Aku's patrilineal line consisting of twenty-four sections of nine lines in which the line length varies from eight to thirteen Yi graphs, in some instances a series of four or five graphs that echo the format of many traditional songs and written texts. *Cyt* is the traditional Nuosu term for a genealogy (both oral and written), which serves a crucial function in Yi rituals.

Like the "eco-genealogies" that comprise the great creation epic *Book of Origins*, the family genealogy that Aku first memorized from oral tradition as a boy begins with the creation of the cosmos, referencing the sky, seas, stars, sun, and moon, and the stirring of life on earth.[38] The genealogy then unfolds generation by generation, noting each of Aku's male ancestors, down to himself and his son, in a manner similar to the latter part of *Book of Origins*, which outlines the migrations of the ancient Yi tribes. Several sections reference *bimo* ritualists far back in Aku's patrilineal line. The text is rife with references to folk knowledge, reflecting a familiarity with a vast range of Yi traditional literature and folklore, including ancient heroes, *bimo*, crafts, customs, codes of conduct, ecological knowledge, and history, all related in a quasi-traditional style and available as metonymic referents to traditional Yi culture. This example from Part 7 indexes a key Nuosu ritual as it plays on the dynamics of acculturation by employing the term *Shuo* ꎭ, a Nuosu word for Han people:

> The conducting of the *Nipmu* ritual to send off the ancestral
>   tablet is done by Nuosu people, residing in the Yi areas,
> Those Nuosu who do not do the ancestral send-off
>   ritual have changed into *Shuo*.

> ꆀꃅꌠꆀꌡ, ꆀꌡꆀꃅꋥ.
> ꆀꌡꆀꀋꃅ, ꆀꐩꎭꐪꁧ.

> nip mu su nip sse, nip sse nip mu zzur.
> nip sse nip ap mu, nip qot shuo jjip bbo.

The final section of the poem is iconoclastic in that unlike the traditional patrilineal genealogies in which women's lines are not mentioned (as they "marry out" of the family), the content is an attempt at gender parity that highlights the essential value of the female principle in the cycle of life. Since female names have not come down in Aku's traditional genealogy, it is the logic straddling the line between Nuosu dreamtime and Aku's contemporary vantage point that positions the genders:

> Because Mother is the root; Mother produces seeds; Father
>   is a flower; Father is fruit,
> Because Mother is black earth; mother is the womb of all
>   living beings; Father is a producer of things; Father is
>   produced by things.

ꀊꈌꀊꈌꄷꑌꐎꑌꈚꐎꒉ
ꀊꈌꑟꀊꈌꀕꑌꐎꑌꑳꆈꒌꒉ

mop li njip mop li zhep pat li vie pat li ma nge jjip hne
mop li za nuo mop li pat yi pat li zzur lu ddur lu nge jjip hne

Continual innovation is characteristic of Aku Wuwu's poetic production, which is not "poetry from the head," as some contemporary Burmese poetry is described, but a holistic poetry of the heart, mind, dream, and soul.[39] Aku envisions himself as a conduit between past, present, and future; shamanist, yet intellectual; cross-cultural and transnational, yet indigenous; seeking, and sometimes finding, meaning in the cosmos at large. This quest is materialized in poems written in two tongues. One is the unique mother tongue of his birth, a medium rich in referential power and in which he communicates most naturally his inner being. The other is his adopted tongue, a more transparent medium which opens doors to opportunity and exposure within China. Via translation, both are mediums that reach beyond the local to join national and international poetic conversations while contributing to the project of writing the ethnic minority voices of China.

NOTES

1. Personal communication.
2. Mark Bender, "The Spirit of Zhyge Alu: The Nuosu Poetry of Aku Wuwu," in *Blood Ties: Writing Across Chinese Borders*, ed. Frank Stewart, Karen Gernant, and Chen Ziping, *Manoa: A Pacific Journal of International Writing* 17.1 (2005): 113–118.
3. In the Liangshan Standard Yi Syllabary popularized in the 1970s, 819 graphs were modified from traditional written characters to form a modern syllabary based on sounds in standard Northern Yi dialect. Subsequently a form of romanization was also created. In the romanization the letters x, t, and p are added to discrete syllables to represent, respectively, the high, higher, and falling tones of the four tones of Northern Yi (a level tone is unmarked). A word such as *bimo*, accordingly, would be written as "*bimox* ꊪꂷ," with the addition of the tone marker. However, certain Yi words such as *bimo, monyi* (female shaman), and proper names are often written in English without the tone markers. In a few instances in this chapter, names of Yi persons hailing from other dialect areas (which do not have commonly used romanization systems) are represented in Chinese characters and *pinyin* romanization.
4. Wen Peihong 文培紅, "Xiaoshi zhong de jianshou: Fang Yizu muyu shiren Aku Wuwu" 消逝中的堅守:訪彝族母語詩人阿庫烏霧 [Persistence in vanishing: An Interview with Yi mother tongue poet Aku Wuwu], *Zhongguo minzu bao* 中國民族報 [Journal of Chinese ethnicities] 1 (June 2007): 9. An English version of the interview appears in Aku Wuwu's *Coyote Traces: Aku Wuwu's Poetic Sojurn in America*, trans. Wen Peihong and Mark Bender (Beijing: Minzu chubanshe and Columbus, OH: Foreign Languages Publications, 2015).
5. The poem, along with three others about his mother, his grandfather, and life in the mountains, was published in a special 2005 edition of *Manoa: A Pacific Journal of*

International Writing titled *Blood Ties: Writing across Chinese Borders*, 123–330, issued by the University of Hawai'i. Aku's featured poems were all translated from Nuosu language by Mark Bender, Aku, and a young Nuosu teacher and student of comparative literature named Jjiepa Ayi ꁌꄖꀙ. The translation work included a trip to Aku's home area in Liangshan, oral performances of the poems, and several weeks of interaction between the participants as the project proceeded line by line. Although two of Aku's Chinese-language poems were published in the 2004 volume entitled *The Poem Behind the Poem: Translating Asian Poetry* (edited by Frank Stewart), the poems in *Blood Ties* were the first translations of modern Nuosu language poetry to be published outside China in a foreign language. Following that publication, a journal associated with the People's Poetry Gathering requested a submission of a Nuosu-language poem that included the original-language text. As a result, a translation of Aku's poem "The Sacred Yyrx yyr Grass" was published in 2006 in *Rattapallax 13*, in a special section edited by Catherine Fletcher titled "Endangered Languages." This was the first publication of a Nuosu-language poem in translation with its original language version in a foreign journal. During a 2005 visit to the Department of East Asian Languages at The Ohio State University, Aku recorded performances of select Nuosu and Chinese language poems with performance poet Kate Polak, which were issued in a combination book/CD multilanguage format by the Foreign Languages Publications at Ohio State University (Aku and Bender, ed. 2006). The Oregon-based journal of poetry and translation *Basalt* has featured two of Aku's poems that include the original Yi graphs, see Aku Wuwu, "Washing the Sun" (Hxo bbu yyx ci), trans. Mark Bender and Aku Wuwu, *Basalt* 3.1 (2008): 11. A poem translated from Nuosu, entitled "Soul of the Felt Cloak," also appeared in an issue of *Manoa* edited by the eco-authors Barry Lopez and Frank Stewart; see *Gates of Reconciliation: Literature and the Ethical Imagination*, ed. Frank Stewart and Barry Lopez, *Manoa: A Pacific Journal of International Writing* 20.1 (2008): 93–95. A reprint of a translation of "Tiger Tracks" was selected for inclusion in *Language for a New Century: Contemporary Poetry from the Middle East, Asia, and Beyond*, ed. Tina Chang and Nathalie Handal (New York: W.W. Norton, 2008), 40. In 2011, the online journal *Cha* published a suite of poems drawn from Aku's Nuosu work *Tiger Tracks* (*Lat jjup*) called "Three Seas and Four Trees." Other publications in English have followed, most notably *Coyote Traces: Aku Wuwu's Poetic Sojourn in America*, published in a bilingual format (Chinese and English) in 2015.

6. Aku Wuwu, "Four Poems," trans. Mark Bender, Aku Wuwu, and Jjiepa Ayi, *Blood Ties: Writing Across Chinese Borders*, ed. Frank Stewart, Karen Gernant, and Chen Ziping, *Manoa: A Pacific Journal of International Writing* 17.1 (2005): 119–130.

7. Mark Bender, Ethnographic Poetry in North-East India and Southwest China, *Rocky Mountain Review*, Special Issue (2012). 107–129. Retrieved September 16, 2014 from http://www.rmmla.org/ereview/SI2012/Bender.pdf.

8. Gary Snyder, *The Old Ways* (San Francisco: City Lights Books, 1977).

9. Luo Qingchun 羅慶春, *Ling yu lingde duihua Zhongguo dangdai shaoshu minzu Hanyu shilun* 靈與靈的對話:中國當代少數民族漢語詩論 [Spirit to spirit: Discussions of contemporary ethnic minority poetry in Chinese] (Hong Kong: Tianma tushu youxian gongsi, 2001), 52–56.

10. Luo Qingchun, *Ling yu lingde duihua*, 51–53.

11. Thomas S. Mullaney, *Coming to Terms with the Nation: Ethnic Classification in Modern China* (Berkeley: University of California Press, 2011).

12. Lauran R. Hartley and Patricia Schiaffini-Vedani, eds., *Modern Tibetan Literature and Social Change* (Durham: Duke University Press, 2008), xx–xxi.

13. Mark Bender, "The Cry of the Silver Pheasant: Contemporary Ethnic Poetry in Sichuan and Yunnan," *Chinese Literature Today* 2.2 (2012): 68–74.

14. Li Hongran 李鴻然. *Zhongguo dangdai shaoshu minzu wenxue shilun* 中國當代少數民族文學史論(上) [Discussions of the history of contemporary Chinese ethnic minority literature, vol. 1] (Kunming: Yunnan jiaoyu chubanshe, 2003).

15. Stevan Harrell, *Ways of Being Ethnic in Southwest China* (Seattle: University of Washington Press, 2002), 81–103.

16. David Bradley, "Language Policy for the Yi." *Perspectives on the Yi in Southwest China,* ed. Stevan Harrell (Seattle: University of Washington Press, 2001), 195–213.

17. Bamo Qubumo 巴莫曲布嫫, *Yingling yu shi hun: Yizu gudai jingji shixue yanjiu* 鷹靈與詩魂: 彝族古代經籍詩學研究 [Golden eagle spirit and poetic soul: A study of Yi nationality poetics] (Beijing: Zhongguo shehui kexue yuan chubanshe, 2001).

18. Mark Bender, "Dying Hunters, Poison Plants, and Mute Slaves: Nature and Tradition in Contemporary Nuosu Yi Poetry," *Asian Highlands Perspectives* 1 (2009): 117–158.

19. Hartley and Schiaffini-Vedani, eds., *Modern Tibetan Literature and Social Change.*

20. Bender, "Ethnographic Poetry in North-East India and Southwest China," 109.

21. Jidi Majia 吉狄馬加, *Rhapsody in Black, Poems by Jidi Majia,* trans. Denis Mair (Norman: University of Oklahoma Press, 2014).

22. Bender, "Dying Hunters, Poison Plants, and Mute Slaves," 120–121.

23. Bender, "The Cry of the Silver Pheasant," 68–69.

24. Bender, "Dying Hunters, Poison Plants, and Mute Slaves," 124–125.

25. Aku Wuwu 阿庫烏霧, *Shenwu de zhuzhou: Aku Wuwu renleixue sanwenji* 神巫的祝咒:阿庫烏霧人類學散文集 [The wizard's voice: An anthology of Aku Wuwu's ethnographic prose] (Beijing: Zhongguo xiju chubanshe, 2010).

26. Aku has also edited three collections of poems, short stories, and prose poems by several dozen young Yi writers, most of whom are graduates of the Yi studies program at SWUN. One volume, *Children of the "Book of Lessons"* (*Hmat mu tep yy* ꉐꫭꋒꒉ), issued in 2012, is completely in Nuosu. Since 2001, Aku has organized the Golden Sands River Yi Literature Conference on Yi literature.

27. Joni Adamson, "Environmental Justice, Cosmopolitics, and Climate Change," in *Literature and the Environment,* ed. Louise Wrestling (Cambridge: Cambridge University Press, 2013), 169–183.

28. Greg Garrard, *Ecocriticism,* 2nd ed. (New York: Routledge, 2011), 86–89; Joni Adamson, "Indigenous Literatures, Multinaturalism, and Avatar: The Emergence of Indigenous Cosmopolitics," *American Literary History,* Special Issue on "Sustainability in America" 24.1 (Spring 2012): 143–167.

29. John Miles Foley, *The Singer of Tales in Performance* (Bloomington: Indiana University Press, 1995), 42–47.

30. Joan Newlon Radner, *Feminist Messages: Coding in Women's Folk Culture* (Urbana: University of Illinois Press, 1993), vii.

31. Clifford Geertz, "Thick Description: Towards an Interpretive Theory of Culture," in *The Interpretation of Cultures: Selected Essays* (New York: Basic Books, 1973), 5–6.

32. Chadwick Allen, *Transindigenous: Methodologies for Global Native Literary Studies* (Minneapolis: University of Minnesota Press, 2012), xiv–xix. See also Mark Bender,

"*Ogimawkwe Mitigwaki* and 'Axlu yyr kut': Native Tongues in Literatures of Cultural Transition," *Sino-Platonic Papers* 220 (2012): 1–28.

33. Critics Wen Jin and Liu Daxian have explored these themes in reference to Aku's interfacing with Native American cultures in Wen Jin and Liu Daxian, "Double Writing: Aku Wuwu and the Epistemology of Chinese Writing in the Americas," *Amerasia Journal* 38.2 (2012): 45–63.

34. Aku Wuwu, "Grass Effigy," trans. Mark Bender, *Chinese Literature Today* 4.1 (2014): 74–75.

35. Mark Bender, "Tribes of Snow: Animals and Plants in the Nuosu *Book of Origins*," *Asian Ethnology* 67.1 (2008): 5–42.

36. Michael Pomedli, *Living with Animals: Ojibwe Spirit Powers* (Toronto: University of Toronto Press, 2014), xii–xiv.

37. Aku Wuwu, "Four Trees and Three Seas," trans. Mark Bender, *Cha: An Asian Literary Journal* 14 (July 2011). Retrieved September 16, 2014 from http://www.asiancha.com/content/view/890/299/.

38. Mark Bender, "Landscapes and Life-forms in Cosmographic Epics from Southwest China," in *Tòv Aziïn Tyyl'* II [Central Asian epics II], ed. A. Alimaa (Ulaanbaatar, Mongolia: Mongol Ulsyn Zasgiïn Gazar, Soël, Sport, Ajalal Jyychlalyn Jam, 2013), 238–252.

39. James Byrne and Ko Ko Thett, eds., *Bones Will Crow: An Anthology of Burmese Poetry* (DeKalb, IL: Northern Illinois University Press, 2013), 147.

Works Cited

Allen, Chadwick. *Transindigenous: Methodologies for Global Native Literary Studies.* Minneapolis: University of Minnesota Press, 2012.

Adamson, Joni. "Environmental Justice, Cosmopolitics, and Climate Change." *Literature and the Environment.* Ed. Louise Wrestling. Cambridge: Cambridge University Press, 2013. 169–183.

Adamson, Joni. "Indigenous Literatures, Multinaturalism, and Avatar: The Emergence of Indigenous Cosmopolitics." *American Literary History* (ALH). Special Issue: Sustainability in America. 24.1 (Spring 2012): 143–167.

Aku Wuwu 阿庫烏霧. *Hunxue shidai* 混血時代 [Hybrid age]. Beijing: Zuojia chubanshe, 2015.

Aku Wuwu 阿庫烏霧. *Coyote Traces: Aku Wuwu's Poetic Sojourn in America.* Trans. Wen Peihong and Mark Bender. Beijing: Minzu chubanshe and Columbus, OH: Foreign Languages Publications, 2015.

Aku Wuwu 阿庫烏霧. "Grass Effigy." Trans. Mark Bender. *Chinese Literature Today.* 4.1 (2014): 74–75.

Aku Wuwu 阿庫烏霧. "Four Trees and Three Seas." Trans. Mark Bender. *Cha: An Asian Literary Journal.* July, 14, 2011. Retrieved September 16, 2014 from http://www.asiancha.com/content/view/890/299/.

Aku Wuwu 阿庫烏霧. *Shenwu de zhuzhou: Aku Wuwu renleixue sanwenji* 神巫的祝咒: 阿庫烏霧人類學散文集 [The wizard's voice: An anthology of Aku Wuwu's ethnographic prose]. Beijing: Zhongguo xiju chubanshe, 2010.

Aku Wuwu 阿庫烏霧. *Mixixibi he de qing su* 密西西比河的傾訴 [Appeal of the Mississippi River]. Beijing: Zuojia chubanshe, 2008.

Aku Wuwu 阿庫烏霧. "Tiger Skins." Trans. Mark Bender, Aku Wuwu, and Jjiepa Ayi. In *Language for a New Century: Contemporary Poetry from the Middle East, Asia, and Beyond.* Ed. Tina Chang and Nathalie Handal. New York: W.W. Norton, 2008. 40.

Aku Wuwu 阿庫烏霧. "Soul of the Felt Cloak." Trans. Mark Bender and Aku Wuwu. In *Gates of Reconciliation: Literature and the Ethical Imagination.* Ed. Frank Stewart and Barry Lopez. *Manoa: A Pacific Journal of International Writing* 20.1 (2008): 93–95.

Aku Wuwu 阿庫烏霧. "Washing the Sun" (Hxo bbu yyx ci). Trans. Mark Bender and Aku Wuwu. *Basalt* 3.1 (2008): 11.

Aku Wuwu 阿庫烏霧. "The Sacred Yyrx Yyr Grass." Trans. Mark Bender, Aku Wuwu, Jjiepa Ayi, and Jiri Motie. In *Rattapallax* 13. Ed. Catherine Fletcher. New York: Ratapallax Press, 2006. 59.

Aku Wuwu 阿庫烏霧. "Four Poems." Trans. Mark Bender, Aku Wuwu, and Jjiepa Ayi. In *Blood Ties: Writing Across Chinese Borders.* Ed. Frank Stewart, Karen Gernant, and Chen Ziping. *Manoa: A Pacific Journal of International Writing* 17.1 (2005): 119–130.

Aku Wuwu 阿庫烏霧. *Aku Wuwu shige xuan* 阿庫烏霧詩歌選 [Selected poems of Aku Wuwu]. Chengdu: Sichuan minzu chubanshe, 2004.

Aku Wuwu and Mark Bender, eds. *Tiger Traces: Selected Nuosu and Chinese Poetry of Aku Wuwu.* Columbus, OH: Foreign Language Publications, 2006. (Book comes with audio CD.)

Bamo, Qubumo 巴莫曲布嫫. *Yingling yu shi hun: Yizu gudai jingji shixue yanjiu* 鷹靈與詩魂:彝族古代經籍詩學研究 [Golden eagle spirit and poetic soul: A study of Yi nationality poetics]. Beijing: Zhongguo shehui kexue yuan chubanshe, 2001.

Bender, Mark. "Landscapes and Life-forms in Cosmographic Epics from Southwest China." In *Tòv Aziïn Tyyl'* II [Central Asian epics II]. Ed. A. Alimaa. Ulaanbaatar, Mongolia: Mongol Ulsyn Zasgiïn Gazar, Soël, Sport, Ajalal Jyychlalyn Jam, 2013. 238–252.

Bender, Mark. Ethnographic Poetry in North-East India and Southwest China. *Rocky Mountain Review*, Special Issue (2012): 107–129. Retrieved September 16, 2014 from http://www.rmmla.org/ereview/SI2012/Bender.pdf.

Bender, Mark. "The Cry of the Silver Pheasant: Contemporary Ethnic Poetry in Sichuan and Yunnan." *Chinese Literature Today* 2.2 (2012): 68–74.

Bender, Mark. "Ogimawkwe Mitigwaki and 'Axlu yyr kut': Native Tongues in Literatures of Cultural Transition." *Sino-Platonic Papers* 220 (2012): 1–28. Retrieved September 16, 2014 from http://sino-platonic.org/complete/spp220_native_tongues.pdf.

Bender, Mark. "Dying Hunters, Poison Plants, and Mute Slaves: Nature and Tradition in Contemporary Nuosu Yi Poetry." *Asian Highlands Perspectives* 1 (2009): 117–158.

Bender, Mark. "Tribes of Snow: Animals and Plants in the Nuosu *Book of Origins*." *Asian Ethnology* 67.1 (2008): 5–42.

Bender, Mark. "The Spirit of Zhyge Alu: The Nuosu Poetry of Aku Wuwu." In *Blood Ties: Writing Across Chinese Borders.* Ed. Frank Stewart, Karen Gernant, and Chen Ziping. *Manoa: A Pacific Journal of International Writing* 17.1 (2005): 113–118.

Bradley, David. "Language Policy for the Yi." *Perspectives on the Yi in Southwest China.* Ed. Stevan Harrell. Seattle: University of Washington Press, 2001. 195–213.

Byrne, James, and Ko Ko Thett, eds. *Bones Will Crow: An Anthology of Burmese Poetry.* DeKalb: Northern Illinois University Press, 2013.

Dangdai daliangshan Yizu xiandai shixuan, 1980–2000 當代大涼山彝族現代詩選 [The Daliangshan Yis Contemporary Poetry Anthology, 1980–2000]. Beijing: Zhongguo wenlian chubanshe, 2002.

Dayton, David. "Big Country, Subtle Voices: Three Ethnic Poets from China's Southwest." MA thesis, University of Sydney, Sydney, Australia, 2006. Retrieved September 16, 2014 from http://ses.library.usyd.edu.au/bitstream/2123/1630/5/01frontDayton.pdf.

Foley, John Miles. *The Singer of Tales in Performance*. Bloomington: Indiana University Press, 1995.

Garrard, Greg. *Ecocriticism*. 2nd ed. New York: Routledge, 2011.

Geertz, Clifford. "Thick Description: Towards an Interpretive Theory of Culture." In *The Interpretation of Cultures: Selected Essays*. New York: Basic Books, 1973. 3–30.

Harrell, Stevan. *Ways of Being Ethnic in Southwest China*. Seattle: University of Washington Press, 2002.

Hartley, Lauran R., and Patricia Schiaffini-Vedani, eds. *Modern Tibetan Literature and Social Change*. Durham: Duke University Press, 2008.

Jidi Majia. *Rhapsody in Black, Poems by Jidi Majia*. Trans. Denis Mair. Norman: University of Oklahoma Press, 2014.

Li Hongran 李鴻然. *Zhongguo dangdai shaoshu minzu wenxue shilun* 中國當代少數民族文學史論 (上) [Discussions of the history of contemporary Chinese ethnic minority literature, Vol. 1]. Kunming: Yunnan jiaoyu chubanshe, 2003.

Luo Qingchun 羅慶春. *Ling yu lingde duihua—Zhongguo dangdai shaoshu minzu Hanyu shilun* 靈與靈的對話: 中國當代少數民族漢語詩論 [Spirit to spirit: Discussions of contemporary ethnic minority poetry in Chinese]. Hong Kong: Tianma tushu youxian gongsi, 2001.

Mullaney, Thomas S. *Coming to Terms with the Nation: Ethnic Classification in Modern China*. Berkeley: University of California Press, 2011.

Radner, Joan Newlon. *Feminist Messages: Coding in Women's Folk Culture*. Urbana: University of Illinois Press, 1993.

Pomedli, Michael. *Living with Animals: Ojibwe Spirit Powers*. Toronto: University of Toronto Press, 2014.

Snyder, Gary. *The Old Ways*. San Francisco: City Lights Books, 1977.

Vytvy ꀀꑷ. *Cux wa yyp mop* ꊿꆈꃆ [Winter River]. Chengdu: Sichuan minzu chubanshe, 1994.

Vytvy ꀀꑷ. *Lat jjup* ꆿꐜ [Tiger Tracks]. Chengdu: Sichuan minzu chubanshe, 1998.

Wen Jin and Liu Daxian. "Double Writing: Aku Wuwu and the Epistemology of Chinese Writing in the Americas." *Amerasia Journal* 38.2 (2012): 45–63.

Wen Peihong 文培紅. "Xiaoshi zhong de jianshou: Fang Yizu muyu shiren Aku Wuwu" 消逝中的堅守: 訪彝族母語詩人阿庫烏霧 [Persistence in vanishing: An interview with Yi mother tongue poet Aku Wuwu]. *Zhongguo Minzu bao* 中國民族報 [Journal of Chinese ethnicities], June 1 (2007): 9.

LITERARY TRANSLATION AND MODERN CHINESE LITERATURE

JI JIN

IN March of 1920, China's first collection of poetry in the modern vernacular, Hu Shi's 胡適 (1891–1926) *Experiments* (嘗試集), was published by Shanghai's East-Asia Library and was enthusiastically received. Hu Shi sought to free his poetry from the fetters of traditional poetic forms, to break with tradition, and to craft an entirely new type of poetry in free verse in the modern vernacular out of a metamorphosis of traditional verse. With this work, Hu Shi paved the way for a new generation of poetic writing in Chinese, but his daring innovation featured an element of translation. For instance, the poem "Uncontainable!" (關不住了!) was not Hu Shi's own creation but rather was a translation of "Over the Roofs" by the US poet Sara Teasdale (1884–1933):

> 我說：“我把我的心收起，
> 像人家把門關了，
> 叫愛情生生的餓死，
> 也許不再和我為難了” 。
>
> 但是屋頂上吹來，
> 一陣陣五月的濕風，
> 更有那街心琴調，
> 一陣陣的吹到房中。
>
> 一屋裡都是太陽光，
> 這時候愛情有點醉了，
> 他說：“我是關不住的，
> 我要把你的心打碎了!”[1]

I said, "I have shut my heart,
As one shuts an open door,

That Love may starve therein
And trouble me no more."

But over the roofs there came
The wet new wind of May,
And a tune blew up from the curb
Where the street-pianos play.

My room was white with the sun
And Love cried out in me,
"I am strong, I will break your heart
Unless you set me free."[2]

From a contemporary perspective, to include a translated work in this sort of volume might well appear unimaginable, though those familiar with late Qing literature know that this kind of phenomenon was actually quite common. When we look back at the development of Chinese literature from the late Qing onward, we see that literary translation occupied a prominent position. In fact, literary translation and the development of modern Chinese literature were closely connected. Since literary translations constituted a large portion of the Chinese literary works published in the modern era, when the production and consumption of translated literature flourished, the impact of literary translations on the modernization of modern Chinese literature cannot be overestimated. In fact, the link between literary translations and modern Chinese literature became a special condition for modern literature, as literary translation encouraged and propitiated the development of modern Chinese literature.

The earliest and arguably most important literary translations were, of course, the novels translated by Lin Shu 林紓 (1852–1924). Since Lin Shu had no knowledge of foreign languages and had to rely on oral translations by others, his process of translation involved a considerable amount of creation. Frequently, Lin Shu's understanding of a text even emerged from a misreading of the original text, which became the basis for rewriting and embellishment, yet this was precisely what led to the birth of the genre of literature in translation. Qian Zhongshu 錢鍾書 (1910–1998) described how

when Lin Shu was of the opinion that the original text was not sufficiently beautiful, he added a bit here and embellished a bit there, and thus rendered a text's language more concrete, made its scenes more lively, and added literary flourish to its descriptions. We cannot but think of the instances in Sima Qian's 司馬遷 *Records of the Historian* (史記)—which Lin Shu worshipped—in which past accounts were polished and embellished. . . . When he [Lin Shu] came across literary infelicities or deficits of the original in the process of translation, he had to usurp the writer's pen and emend these.[3]

One of Lin Shu's most important achievements was bringing foreign works into the fold of China's cultural tradition, since he effected a Westernization of the language of Chinese modern literature, thereby crafting a language that resembled the original and yet was also quite different from it.

We could even claim that Lin Shu's literary translations are actually an integral part of Chinese literature, and in fact many other writers began writing literature under the influence of Lin Shu's translations. Lin Shu's translation of Alexandre Dumas fils's *The Lady of the Camellias* (*La dame aux camélias*; Chinese title: 巴黎茶花女遺事) and other novels into literary Chinese profoundly influenced the changes in narrative structure, perspective, and genre of modern Chinese fiction. For instance, Su Manshu's 蘇曼殊 (1884–1918) *The Lone Swan* (斷鴻零雁記) and Xu Zhenya's 徐枕亞 (1889–1937) *Jade Pear Spirit* (玉梨魂) and *The Snow Crane's Tears* (雪鴻淚史) were directly influenced by Lin Shu's rendition of *The Lady of the Camellias*. Translators like Lin Shu contributed to a situation in which translation became creation, thus linking early translations into literary Chinese and novels composed in literary Chinese and shaping the distinctive textual form of literary translations.

What was true for texts translated into literary Chinese was equally true for those translated into the modern vernacular, the earliest of which was Edward Bulwer Lytton's (1803–1873) *Night and Morning* (Chinese title: 昕夕閑談), though it would be more apt to call this a rewriting rather than a straight translation.[4] In 1902, Liang Qichao 梁啟超 (1873–1929) and his collaborators translated Jules Verne's (1828–1905) *Two Years' Vacation* (*Deux ans de vacances*, Chinese title: 兩年假期) into vernacular Chinese and published it in the journal *New Citizen* (新民叢報) that Liang had founded. Afterward, *The New Novel* (新小說) and other journals published translations of numerous novels into modern vernacular Chinese, and in 1906 the first association of translators, the Society for Translation and Communication, was founded in Shanghai.[5]

The translations produced during what Patrick Hanan has called the "second period of translating fiction into modern Chinese" beginning in 1902 also contained many additions and deletions, as well as instances of rewriting.[6] For instance, when Zhou Guisheng 周桂笙 (1873–1936) translated Fortuné du Boisgobey's (1821–1891) *In the Serpent's Coil* (*Margot la balafrée*, Chinese title: 毒蛇圈), he added a long passage describing how the female protagonist Camille (Chinese name 妙兒) missed her father Tiburce Gerfaut (Chinese name 鐵瑞福). In the afterword, editor Wu Jianren 吳趼人 explained:

> The passage in which Camille misses her father does not appear in the original. Since the text earlier describes Gerfaut's profound longing for his daughter time and again in such intensity, I think that not mentioning Camille's longing for her father, so as to balance kindness and filiality, would inevitably constitute a shortcoming. . . . It was very expedient of the translator to insert this passage. Even though the original work lacks this passage, I know that Camille cannot but have felt this way, and therefore even though the passage may be fabricated, it is not at all superfluous.[7]

All of these works, irrespective of whether they were translated into literary Chinese or the modern vernacular, focused on the power of the narrator, on changes in the structure of chapters, and on new content, and thus systematically opened the way for the creation of a new literature in modern Chinese. It can be said without exaggeration that modern Chinese fiction was a new literary genre that emerged thanks to the influence of translated novels. Lu Xun's 魯迅 (1881–1936) "Diary of a Madman" (狂人日記),

published in the journal *New Youth* (新青年) in May 1918, symbolized the "official" birth of modern narrative by way of its innovative literary form, but it also drew on the influences that Lu Xun had received from translated literature, including Nikolai Gogol's (1809–1852) "Diary of a Madman," Fyodor Dostoyevsky's (1821–1881) descriptions of mental illness, and Mikhail Artsybashev's (1878–1927) psychological analyses. Whether it was through their description of interiority, their narrative perspective, or their temporal structure, these translations all contributed to the complete renewal of modern narrative.

The flourishing of literature in translation after the late Qing went hand in hand with the development of modern Chinese literature and became an important practice of modern literature. Literature in translation constituted a completely new means of modern creation and expression, and was no longer merely an instrument for the transfer from one language into another. After several decades of development, the earlier practice of translation in which rendition into another language was coupled with rewriting and adaptation gradually disappeared, replaced by translations that were more faithful to the originals. These literary works in translation became the object of study, imitation, and reference for modern writers. Apart from a minority of writers able to read foreign literature in the original, Chinese authors mostly accessed these works through translations, which implied an inherent connection between translation and the production of modern literature that became increasingly important.

TRANSLATIONS IN THE CONTEMPORARY PERIOD

The success of many writers has its origin in the study of and reference to literature in translation. For instance, the narrative style of avant-garde writer Ge Fei 格非 in the late 1980s shifted from realism to a more reflexive mode of writing. Even though this emerged partly from Ge Fei's own experiences, the influence of writers like Jorge Luis Borges (1899–1986), Gabriel García Márquez (1927–2014), and other non-Chinese writers whose work Ge Fei read in translation had an equally strong impact on him. Under the influence of literature in translation, Ge Fei, Yu Hua 余華, Su Tong 蘇童, and other young avant-garde writers were able to break with established modes of writing and develop their individual styles, which provided an alternative experience in a time of ideological rupture and was key in China's process of literary renewal and transformation.

Ge Fei's early writings and Borges's stories show similar literary structures, especially their interest in metatextual conceits. Borges often drew on his vast erudition and used other books and historical records as models for his stories, offering modern rewritings of earlier texts such as the Bible to endow his new stories with complex layers and to craft complex metatextual structures. In this respect, Ge Fei's stories "Greenish Yellow"

(青黃) and "Ye Lang's Journey" (夜郎之行) follow the spirit of Borges's "Tlön, Uqbar, Orbis Tertius" and "The Immortal" (El inmortal). "Greenish Yellow" narrates the process of researching a term, *greenish yellow*, that appears in the fictive *History of Chinese Courtesans*. On one hand, the visit of the first-person narrator to Mai Village to do research drives the work's plot; on the other, content from *History of Chinese Courtesans* is inserted in this plotline. What makes this even more distinctly unreal is that the text inserts the narrator's deductions about the fictional plot into the story itself. Therefore, the story of the term *greenish yellow* in *History of Chinese Courtesans*, the story's own narrative, together with the narrative within the narrative intersect repeatedly, and consequently the reality of *greenish yellow* becomes ever more indistinct through constant repetition. After oscillating between reality and fiction, the story concludes by having the narrator return to the library and find a dictionary entry that specifies that *greenish yellow* is actually the name of a plant—a perennial of the Scrophulariales family. This resembles the way in which research about Tlön in Borges's story is inspired by the aphorism "mirrors and copulation are abominable, for they multiply the number of mankind," which triggers the discovery of the imaginary world of Tlön in which being is secondary to thought.[8] Since all things rely on thought for their existence, Tlön's existence influences reality: "Contact with Tlön, the *habit* of Tlön, has disintegrated this world. Spellbound by Tlön's rigor, humanity has forgotten, and continues to forget, that it is the rigor of chess masters, not of angels."[9]

These narratives often skillfully use realistic detail as an entry point into their texts. For instance, the fascination with the term *greenish yellow* in "Greenish Yellow" is attributed to a specific page of the fictitious *History of Chinese Courtesans*, just as the appearance of the world of Tlön follows a character's consultation of *The Anglo-American Cyclopaedia*, in a process that mixes reality and fiction. This gives the reader a bewildering sense of the real, only to take a turn toward the fictional by way of rapidly presenting something that is difficult to ascertain, so that reality is purely the point of emergence of a fictional story and conceptual reflection. As a result, reality and fiction become intricately fused.

The similarity between "Ye Lang's Journey" and "The Immortal" lies in the pursuit and abandonment of an ideal world. This illusionary structure uses the narrator's journey as plot line and serves as background for the historical content of a book, resulting in a series of twists and turns, and ultimately in flight. The creatively powerful insertion of the plot between historical records creates the hallucinatory effect of a dialogue between reality and history. In the postscript to "The Immortal," Borges writes: "*As the end approaches . . . there are no longer any images from memory—there are only words.*"[10] Similarly, Ge Fei writes at the beginning of "Ye Lang's Journey": "Afterwards Ye Lang's journey has been proven to be incorrect, since Ye Lang had already disappeared from the records and from the imaginary."[11] Both confessions are quite similar. Borges's story uses a rewriting of the last volume of Alexander Pope's draft of the translation of the *Iliad* to reveal how the text within the text has infiltrated history and leads to the search for the city and the river of the immortals, while Ge Fei's text reveals that the story's plot is fictional, based on the traditional story of "Yelang's city," in order to turn reality into a literary construct that enters a story derived from history. In both Borges's and Ge Fei's texts, an imaginary world blurs the limit between history and reality as the narratives oscillate between reality and fiction, thereby endowing their texts with a special quality.

While Ge Fei's relationship with Borges's works is one of emulation and citation, other writers have adopted an original writing style through a dialogue with literature in translation. This does not necessarily entail a rejection of literature in translation, but rather points to a more sophisticated reception. For a truly accomplished writer, the study and emulation of literature in translation by no means constitutes an obstacle; instead, it may reveal a broader artistic and spiritual space. For instance, Han Shaogong's 韓少功 Dictionary of Maqiao (馬橋詞典) and its use of the form of the dictionary novel may have been influenced by Milan Kundera (b. 1929), who composed a dictionary of his own works in The Art of the Novel (L'art du roman, 1986), or by Milorad Pavic's (1929–2009) Dictionary of the Khazars (Hazarski rečnik, 1984), but these translated works only provided Han Shaogong with creative inspiration. Han's success lies in how he pushes the form of the dictionary novel to its extreme in order to craft an entire aesthetic world. The novel uses the local dialect of Maqiao in order to recount Maqiao's history, geography, people, and customs, as well as explanations of the author's persona in the form of stories and integrates them into the structure of a dictionary novel. What is even more remarkable is that Han Shaogong uses a local dialect that had long been ignored in order to subvert the popular vernacular, and shows that a world full of meaning lies behind the culture of the people. From this he crafts an entirely new space for language and literary art for Chinese literature. Han Shaogong manages to surpass his predecessors Kundera and Pavic and create new artistic meaning.

No matter whether authors such as Ge Fei and Han Shaogong use literature in translation as an object of imitation or as a model to be contested, the close attention to literature in translation elucidates the complex link between translated literature and Chinese literature. The flourishing and development of modern literature cannot be separated from a contemporary engagement with literature in translation, which has already become an important literary practice on a par with the production of Chinese literature. And yet, in light of the enormous amount of literary translations in the modern era, we cannot but ask how we might integrate the history of literary translations and their continued influence into the narrative of the history of modern Chinese literature. How can we rethink the dialectical relation between literature in translation and modern Chinese literature, as well as the possibility of literature and literary creation from the broader perspective of world literature? These are key questions that a discussion of literary translation and modern literature has to address.

LITERARY HISTORY

In the 1920s and 1930s, a group of early critics of China's new literature included literary translations in their purview of a narrative of literary history. For instance, Chen

Zizhan's 陳子展 (1898–1990) *A History of the Chinese Literature of the Past Thirty Years* (最近三十年中國文學史), Zhu Ziqing's 朱自清 (1898–1948) *An Outline of Research on New Chinese Literature* (中國新文學研究綱要), Wang Zhefu's 王哲甫 *A History of China's New Literature Movement* (中國新文學運動史), Guo Zhenyi's 郭箴一 *A History of the Chinese Novel* (中國小說史), and others all dedicate chapters specifically to the discussion of literature in translation. But afterwards, the role of literature in translation in the development of Chinese literature rarely received thorough consideration in literary histories. Since the 1980s, even though projects with a systemic objective, such as Huang Xiuyi's 黃修已 *A History of Chinese Literature in the Twentieth Century* (20世紀中國文學史) and Chen Sihe's 陳思和 *A Complete View of New Chinese Literature* (中國新文學整體觀), began to pay more attention to the formative influence and creative changes in Chinese literature caused by foreign cultures and literatures, the unique discursive contribution of literature in translation rarely enters into the framework of research on literary history. In discussions of Chinese literature, literature in translation is usually treated merely as foreign literature and is thereby accorded a secondary status.

Only after the 1990s did scholars like Xie Tianzhen 謝天振 begin to push for the consideration of literature in translation as part of modern Chinese literature and to view it as a distinctive literary practice that was as important as the production of literature. Xie Tianzhen emphasized that literature in translation must be considered part of modern Chinese literature, arguing that "literary translation is a form of literary production, as well as a form of existence for a work of literature. From this vantage point, literary translation and literature in translation have their own aesthetic value."[12]

The independent aesthetic value of literature in translation derives from its combination of alterity and indigeneity. On one hand, literature in translation is the translation of literary works of authors from foreign countries, and in this respect it provides a new perspective on the production of Chinese literature and enriches the creation of Chinese writers. This kind of alterity provides the basis for research on the link between Chinese and foreign literatures. Most contemporary comparative literature approaches focusing on the relationship between Chinese and foreign literatures trace the influences of foreign literary works on Chinese literature and are thus based on the paradigm of alterity. It is also this alterity that makes literature in translation appear foreign on readers' bookshelves, and encourages us to overlook the translator who gives them a second life.

On the other hand, traditional translation theory often focuses on the question whether it is possible to transmit the original faithfully; this kind of pursuit of faithfulness in translation, however, ignores the role of literature in translation as a distinctive literary practice, while the existence of translation errors and of retranslation underscores the indigenous quality of translated literature. It is a basic fact that the language of literature in translation is that of its host culture, and its words and phrases reveal the erudition and literary knowledge of the translator. In the process of translation, retranslations and mistranslations are unavoidable, and the linguistic changes of the host culture, differences in the status of translators, and adjustments in the objectives of translation all mean that literature in translation undergoes changes in order to facilitate its reception. Literature in translation is a kind of creative, transcultural betrayal. After being translated, a literary work no longer belongs only to its original literary world, since it has become fused with a new cultural horizon and has thereby become part of another linguistic and literary world. Once we view literature in translation as a part of Chinese literature, we will gain new insight into the relationship between Chinese and foreign literatures.

How literature in translation finds a balance between alterity and indigeneity is the best test of a translator's powers of literary expression and of cultural understanding. The extraordinary power of translation lies in its ability to express the essence of another culture as well as that of its host culture. In the age of globalization, world literature has already become an imaginary commons by means of global circulation, translation, and dissemination, and every translator and translated work plays an important role in this process. As Itamar Even-Zohar writes, "I conceive of translated literature not only as an integral system within any literary polysystem, but as a most active system within it."[13] I would like to call for more of what Walter Benjamin terms "real translation": "A real translation is transparent; it does not cover the original, does not block its light, but allows the pure language, as though reinforced by its own medium, to shine upon the original all the more fully."[14] In these "real" literary translations, different literatures and cultures collide, enter into exchange, and mutually support each other, continually renewing each other's concept of literature and aesthetic modes and enriching the discursive realm of world literature. Of course, translated literature is the most active part in the multicultural polysystem of literature, and serves to negotiate between different cultures and incessantly imports new elements into a culture. Cultural translation introduces an element of alterity and, at the same time, continually deconstructs the hegemony of the dominant culture and promotes the fusion of different cultures.

World literature is evolving into an expression of cultural globalization and aesthetic reality. Given that modern Chinese literature is part of world literature, what kind of challenge does translated literature face? What kind of change can literature in translation and modern literature elucidate? On one hand, modern Chinese literature is itself already part of world literature, and in a way, Chinese literature has already become "world literature's Chinese literature." On the other hand, as long as the world remains a virtual Tower of Babel, translated literature will continue to have meaning and value, exerting its influence on the spirit of modern Chinese literature and its forms of expression.

In the discourse of world literature, every literature needs to maintain and develop its distinctive aesthetic character through interactions with others. Following the spread of economic globalization, information technology, international capital, and mass media, we face a period of cultural relativism and symbiosis. In this context, all literatures have their raison d'être, and we have even less means to transcend the total structure of world literature and to insist on singing only to our own tune. Instead, contemporary Chinese literature will always subsist and develop within the context and discursive realm of world literature, it will always be an inescapable other. In fact, the literatures of different countries are foreign to one another, but they collectively constitute the imaginary commons of world literature. Therefore, we can even less afford to overlook the presence and value of literature in translation, since it is precisely by means of translation that Chinese literature can become even more strongly a part of world literature.

Accordingly, if we regard literature in translation as part of modern Chinese literature, we should not limit our inquiry into modern literature to the internal, homogeneous dimension of modern literary creation, but should pay attention to modern Chinese literature's multiplicity and heterogeneity. Through the intervention of translators and through a change in language, what was once foreign literature is no longer located outside of Chinese literature, and instead has become a corpus of texts filled with the subjectivity and creativity of translators who use Chinese as their means of expression. Furthermore, translated texts have maintained mutually beneficial links with Chinese literary creation and have become a part of modern Chinese literature. Of course, to treat translated texts as a part of Chinese literature also implies the othering of Chinese literature itself, challenges the "Chineseness" of Chinese literature, and changes the status of Chinese literature. As a result, Chinese literature is no longer a hermetically closed, self-sufficient system, but has been endowed with a global dimension. If this is the age of world literature, therein lies the hope for Chinese literature.

(translated by Andrea Bachner)

Notes

Portions of this essay have been previously published in the following Chinese-language articles: "Hui zhi bu qu de 'tazhe'" 揮之不去的 "他者" [The unerasable "other"], *Zhong Shan* 鐘山 6 (1999): 203–206; "Zuojiamen de zuojia: Borges ji qi zai Zhongguo de yingxiang" 作家們的作家——博爾赫斯及其在中國的影響 [The writer of writers: Borges's influence in China], *Dangdai zuojia pinglung* 當代作家評論 [Criticism on contemporary writers] 3 (2000): 102–109; "Wenben lüxing de ditu: Cong *Zhongguo xiandai fanyi wenxue shi* tanqi" 文本旅行的地圖——從《中國現代翻譯文學史》談起 [Mapping textual circulation: A discussion of *A History of Modern Chinese Literary Translations*], *Zhongguo bijiao wenxue* 中國比較文學 [Comparative literature in China] 3 (2008): 118–122; "Zuowei shijie wenxue de Zhongguo wenxue" 作為世界文學的中國文學 [Chinese literature as world literature], *Zhongguo bijiao wenxue* 中國比較文學 [Comparative literature in China] 1 (2014): 27–36.

1. Hu Shi 胡適. "Guan bu zhu le!" 關不住了! [Uncontainable!], in *Changshi ji* 嘗試集 [Experiments] (Beijing: Renmin wenxue chubanshe, 1984), 44.
2. Sara Teasdale, "Over the Roofs," *Poetry* 3.6 (March 1914): 200.
3. Qian Zhongshu 錢鍾書, "Lin Shu de fanyi" 林紓的翻譯 [Lin Shu's translations], in *Qi zhui ji* 七綴集 [Seven pieces patched together] (Shanghai: Shanghai guji chubanshe, 1996), 85–86.
4. Patrick Hanan 韓南, "Baihua fanyi xiaoshuo de di'er ge jieduan" 白話翻譯小說的第二個階段 [The second phase of translations of novels into modern Chinese], in *Hanan Zhongguo xiaoshuo lun ji* 韓南中國小說論集 [A collection of Patrick Hanan's writings on Chinese novels] (Beijing: Beijing daxue chubanshe, 2008), 321.

5. See Hanan, "The Second Phase of Translations of Novels into Modern Chinese," 322.
6. See Hanan, "The Second Phase of Translations of Novels into Modern Chinese."
7. Fortuné du Boisgobey, *Margot la balafrée*, trans. Zhou Guisheng 周桂笙 as *Du she quan* 毒蛇圈 [In the serpent's coil] (Changsha: Yuelu Shushe, 1991), 87.
8. Jorge Luis Borges, "Tlön, Uqbar, Orbis Tertius," in *Collected Fictions*, trans. Andrew Hurley (New York: Penguin, 1998), 68–81, quotation at 68.
9. Borges, "Tlön, Uqbar, Orbis Tertius," 81.
10. Jorge Luis Borges, "The Immortal," in *Collected Fictions*, trans. Andrew Hurley (New York: Penguin, 1998), 183–195, quotation at 195.
11. Ge Fei 格非, *Ge Fei wenji: Shu yu shi; Yelang zhi xing* 格非文集：樹與石; 夜郎之行 [Works by Ge Fei: The tree and the stone; Yelang's journey] (Nanjing: Jiangsu wenyi chubanshe, 1996), 257.
12. See Xie Tianzhen 謝天振, *Yijiexue: Bijiao wenxue yu fanyi yanjiu xin shihe* 譯介學：比較文學與翻譯研究新視野 [Translation studies: New perspectives on comparative literature and research on translation] (Shanghai: Fudan daxue chubanshe, 2011), 113.
13. Itamar Even-Zohar, "The Position of Translated Literature within the Literary Polysystem," *Poetics Today* 11.1 (1990): 45–51, quotation at 46.
14. Walter Benjamin, "The Task of the Translator," in *Illuminations*, trans. Harry Zohn, ed. Hannah Arendt (Glasgow: Fontana/Collins, 1970), 69–82, quotation at 79.

Works Cited

Benjamin, Walter. "The Task of the Translator." *Illuminations*. Trans. Harry Zohn, ed. Hannah Arendt. Glasgow: Fontana/Collins, 1970. 69–82.
du Boisgobey, Fortuné. *Margot la balafrée*. Trans. Zhou Guisheng 周桂笙 as *Du she quan* 毒蛇圈 [In the serpent's coil]. Changsha: Yuelu shushe, 1991.
Borges, Jorge Luis. *Collected Fictions*. Trans. Andrew Hurley. New York: Penguin, 1998.
Even-Zohar, Itamar. "The Position of Translated Literature within the Literary Polysystem." *Poetics Today* 11.1 (1990): 45–51.
Hanan, Patrick 韓南. "Baihua fanyi xiaoshuo de di'er ge jieduan" 白話翻譯小說的第二個階段 [The second phase of translations of novels into modern Chinese]. In *Hanan Zhongguo xiaoshuo lun ji* 韓南中國小說論集 [A collection of Patrick Hanan's writings on Chinese novels]. Beijing: Beijing daxue chubanshe, 2008. 321.
Hu Shi 胡適. "Guan bu zhu le!" 關不住了! [Uncontainable!]. In *Changshi ji* 嘗試集 [Experiments]. Beijing: Renmin wenxue chubanshe, 1984. 44.
Qian Zhonghu 錢鍾書. "Lin Shu de fanyi" 林紓的翻譯 [Lin Shu's translations]. In *Qi zhui ji* 七綴集 [Seven pieces patched together]. Shanghai: Shanghai guji chubanshe, 1996. 85–86.
Teasdale, Sara. "Over the Roofs." *Poetry* 3.6 (March 1914): 200.
Xie Tianzhen 謝天振. *Yijiexue: Bijiao wenxue yu fanyi yanjiu xin shihe* 譯介學：比較文學與翻譯研究新視野 [Translation studies: New perspectives on comparative literature and research on translation]. Shanghai: Fudan daxue chubanshe, 2011.

GENRE IN MODERN CHINESE FICTION

Righteous Heroes of Modern Times

CHRIS HAMM

CHINESE martial arts achieved global recognition with the international success of Hong Kong martial arts cinema at the beginning of the 1970s. Spearheading the genre's entry onto the world stage were the films of actor and martial artist Bruce Lee 李小龍. In *Fist of Fury* (精武門, 1972; also released in the United States under the title *The Chinese Connection*), Lee plays Chen Zhen, a fictional disciple of the historical martial artist Huo Yuanjia 霍元甲 (1868–1910). Chen Zhen avenges his master's death at the hands of the perfidious Japanese in the treaty port city of Shanghai, then pays for his vigilante justice by facing an impromptu international firing squad. In the film's final sequence he charges his executioners with a flying kick and a defiant battle cry, whereupon the camera suddenly freezes, suspending him in mid-air as shots ring out and the soundtrack music swells. The image uncannily prefigures both Lee's sudden death at the apex of his career and the deathlessness of his cinematic legacy. Sequels, imitations, parodies, remakes, and reinterpretations have kept the Bruce Lee mystique, the stories of Huo Yuanjia and Chen Zhen, and the genre of martial arts cinema alive through the present day.

Lee's films marked not only a local cinematic genre's appearance before global audiences but the transformation of the genre itself, as the fledgling Golden Harvest studio moved to differentiate itself from the dominant Shaw Brothers by turning from swordplay costume dramas to the revenge-driven sagas of unarmed combat that came to be known as the *kung fu* (sub)genre. Genre is not a property of a given film but a system of relationships between films (or works in other media). As such, it survives, and indeed exists, only through the tension between "repetition and difference."[1] A given work belongs to a genre to the extent that it reproduces, inherits, or carries on what are perceived to be established conventions. In reproducing these conventions, the work declares its allegiance to a regime of generic verisimilitude that is distinct from the regime of cultural verisimilitude that passes for reality at any given time and place.[2] At the same time, a genre work succeeds (in the senses both of succession and of success) in part by varying or violating the material that it inherits. The tension at the heart of the genre system is figured within *Fist of Fury* in the relationship between Chen Zhen and his martyred master. By avenging Huo Yuanjia, Chen Zhen proves himself his successor, yet in order to achieve his vengeance, he must reject the master's teachings—repeatedly invoked by his fellow students—of patience, humility, and self-control. Chen Zhen is and is not Huo Yuanjia, just as the kung fu film is and is not the swordplay film that preceded it. The logic of transmission and succession echoes the logic of genre; genre is a form of transmission.

While *Fist of Fury* can claim a pivotal position in the history of martial arts cinema, it occupies a place in at least two other traditions as well: a specific tradition of narratives of the deeds and career of Huo Yuanjia that began to emerge soon after his death, and a much broader tradition of Chinese narratives of martial prowess and spirit, circulated through both written literature and the performing arts. Chinese martial arts film was born from the interaction between cinema (including early Hollywood action genres) and the most distinctive of Chinese fictional genres, "martial arts fiction" (*wuxia xiaoshuo* 武俠小說). The production conventionally identified as the wellspring of Chinese martial arts film, Mingxing Film Company's *Burning of Red Lotus Temple* (火燒紅蓮寺; 1928–1931), was an adaptation of a portion of the novel *Marvelous Gallants of the Rivers and Lakes* (江湖奇俠傳, serialized beginning in 1923) by Xiang Kairan 向愷然 (1890–1957), writing under the penname Pingjiang Buxiaosheng 平江不肖生. Xiang Kairan, regarded as the "father of martial arts fiction," is credited with shaping the genre and igniting public fervor for it through two novels that began serialization in the same year: *Marvelous Gallants* and *Righteous Heroes of Modern Times* (近代俠義英雄傳). And the narrative of *Righteous Heroes* is structured around Xiang Kairan's elaboration of the nascent legend of Huo Yuanjia.

This chapter explores the place of genre in modern Chinese fiction through a reading of *Righteous Heroes of Modern Times*. Although the novel is rightly considered one of the foundational works of modern martial arts fiction, my focus here is not so much on the ways in which it contributed to the genre's narrative, thematic, and rhetorical conventions as on the ways in which it engages the question of genre itself. The novel's narrative centers on the question of the transmission of China's martial arts. The text establishes connections and parallels between the transmission of the martial arts and the transmission of narrative—both the transitivity of the narrative act per se and the transmission of particular bodies of narrative material. The tale it tells of the martial arts involves a transformation, a modernization, of the mode of transmission. In its consideration of its own narrativity, the text identifies elements of a similar transformation. At the same time, it declares allegiance to a regime of generic rather than cultural verisimilitude.

The negotiation of boundaries between "serious" and "popular" culture, as well as the significance of genre allegiance as a marker of nonserious literature, involved unusually high stakes in China in the early 1920s. Writers associated with the New

Culture and May Fourth movements who promoted European-inspired realism portrayed their iconoclasm not as a mere maneuver within the literary field but as part of a broader struggle for cultural identity and national survival. They represented the literary others against whom they differentiated themselves as stubbornly standing on the wrong side of a historical line dividing art from self-indulgence, the international from the indigenous, and the new from the old. Their success in controlling contemporary discourse, and the subsequent enshrinement of their views in literary historiography, shaped perceptions of martial arts fiction and other popular genres for most of the twentieth century.

THE LEGEND OF HUO YUANJIA

At the heart of the Huo Yuanjia legend is a tale of nationalistic martyrdom. Huo, a champion of China's martial arts, is struck down by foul play at the hands of the Japanese. In many later tellings this fate is the tragic coda to a series of stirring triumphs over foreign challengers—Russian, American, European, and finally Japanese. In Xiang Kairan's 1923 novel, however—and this accords with what we can reconstruct of the historical record—Huo Yuanjia never actually engages in physical contest with a Western opponent. Instead of triumph, the novel offers frustration: Huo seeks in vain, over the course of eighty-four chapters, to measure Chinese martial arts against the West.

His efforts begin when a Russian strongman appears in Tianjin and insults the Chinese as a nation of weaklings who know nothing of modern physical culture. Huo challenges him to a match, but the Russian responds with an invitation to a friendly exchange; Huo insists on either a retraction or a fight with no holds barred, and the Russian deems it wisest to simply decamp. Huo's moral victory (if it can be called that) neither demonstrates the actual efficacy of the Chinese martial arts nor answers the Russian's troubling charges about China's backwardness. His countrymen's backwardness is in fact the next challenge Huo must face, as he first deflects an invitation to ally himself with the "divine" martial arts of the Boxer rebels, then defends a group of Chinese Christian converts against the Boxers' ravages. These deeds spread Huo's fame across the land, and when, some time later, the strongman O'Brien appears in Shanghai, Huo again feels called upon to personally vindicate his nation's arts against Western insult. He travels south to Shanghai and enters into protracted negotiations with O'Brien's agent. Frustrated by the delays, Huo tries to arrange an ancillary match with a pair of American fighters, one black and one white, but these plans too founder in wrangling over technicalities. In an attempt to garner publicity and support, Huo erects a public challenge stage, a *leitai* (擂台), in Shanghai's Zhang Gardens. His sole challenger, however, is a fellow Chinese, and Huo's reluctant victory over his countryman embroils him in the very struggles for reputation and cycles of vengeance that the *leitai* had sought to transcend. The long-sought bout with O'Brien finally falls through when O'Brien and his agent skip town. At this point a Japanese doctor from whom Huo has sought treatment pressures him into a "friendly" match against Japanese martial artists. Huo prevails, but after further treatment from the doctor falls into convulsions and dies.

Although Huo vanquishes Chinese and Japanese opponents, his attempts to match himself in physical contest against Western champions encounter only frustration and delay. From another perspective, however, these frustrations and delays are the very spaces in which a different order of struggle takes shape: a struggle not to vanquish a foreign fighter, but to articulate the role and identity of the Chinese martial arts in a modernizing transnational world. And an essential element of this latter struggle is a transformation of the means by which the martial arts are transmitted from one generation to the next.

TRADITION AND TRANSMISSION

In 1923, the year in which *Righteous Heroes* began serialization, Xiang Kairan contributed to *A Record of the Words and Deeds of the Boxing Masters* (拳師言行錄), a collection of classical-language anecdotes and biographies from the world of the martial arts.[3] *Words and Deeds* organizes its material into eight thematic categories, of which the first is "Taking Disciples" (授徒) and the second "Seeking a Teacher" (訪師). Although technical skill, physical prowess, courage, and moral integrity are all elements of the martial arts, the foundation of the enterprise, as the anthology's prioritization makes clear, is the problem of tradition. The word *tradition* here does not designate a static body of knowledge and practice, martial or otherwise. It refers rather to the institutions, relationships, and media by which practice and knowledge are passed from one human being to another, one generation to another, and thereby kept alive.

Righteous Heroes thematizes tradition in this sense from the very outset of Huo Yuanjia's story, which foregrounds tensions in the patrilineal transmission of an inheritance. The particular inheritance in question is the "Trackless Art" (迷蹤藝), a system of martial arts practiced by members of the Huo clan of Jinghai county in Tianjin. It is unclear, notes the narrator, whether the art's name refers to its mysterious origins or to its foes' inability to grasp its subtleties; in either case, though, the name indexes the art's inaccessibility, and thus the weight of the Huo clan's proprietary claim. So jealously guarded is the art that even the clan's own female members, destined to marry out of the family, are forbidden to learn it. But the young Huo Yuanjia is excluded from the transmission as well; he is so weak and sickly that his father fears he will discredit the family name. Huo Yuanjia spies on his brothers' training and practices in secret. When a challenger bests the family's champion, it is Huo Yuanjia who steps forward, prevails, and is embraced by his father as a rightful successor.

In this almost Arthurian fable of birthright, a rightful heir languishes unrecognized until the revelation of hidden worth vindicates his succession. Both the protagonist and the clan to which he succeeds enjoy the fruits of his triumph. At the same time, though, the story raises questions about the logic of the patrilineal transmission. Do certain standards of fitness attenuate the presumption of patrilineal inheritance, and if they do, what validity can the system of patrimony still claim? Although the text does not frame the issues in precisely these terms, it pointedly follows the story of Huo Yuanjia's triumph with an excursus on the viciousness of the martial world—the enmity engendered by secrecy and the obsession with reputation, and the cruelty of the conventions for dueling. The chapter commentary targets even more explicitly the damage inflicted on China's cultural heritage by the practice of restricted transmission: "Under these circumstances, can we even hope to see the arts progress? The Huo family's 'Trackless Art'—not transmitted to those of other surnames, kept private rather than public—shares the common defect of the realm of the arts, and this is why the author has taken pains to point it out."[4]

With support from his now proud father, Huo Yuanjia goes into Tianjin city to open an herb store. Aspirants seek him out, attracted by his renown, and he accepts one as his disciple. Although he respects clan rules by not teaching the restricted "Trackless Art," this acceptance of an outsider marks the first step toward a new model of transmission. And here in the treaty port of Tianjin, he encounters a new order of challenge: not from a rival from the martial world, contesting standing and reputation within that familiar milieu, but from a foreigner, the Russian strongman, whose very presence assigns the arts Huo champions a new and broader dimension of significance.

The central issue raised by the encounter is that of the role of the Chinese martial arts in a multinational and modernizing world. The theater in which the strongman performs epitomizes this world as manifested in the treaty port city of Tianjin. The theater is cosmopolitan, a space in which Chinese and foreigners intermingle, though with clearly established distinctions and hierarchies. It is a commodified space, in which access to economic resources serves as a prerequisite for participation and as an index of status. And it is a space that employs modes and media of communication distinct from the networks of reputation and private affiliation that inform the traditional world of the martial arts: handbills, newspapers, public speech, and performance. Within this space and employing these media, the Russian invokes a discursive framework that defines modern physical culture as linked with science and the nationalist project in both its racial and civic aspects:

> "The science of physical education concerns the strength of the race and the prosperity of the nation. How can it be that there is not a single organization in the entire country devoted to its study and improvement? Because of my wish to let the Chinese know the value of physical education, I will display my skills in Tianjin for a week, then proceed to Beijing, Shanghai, and other locales to perform. I earnestly welcome China's strongmen and experts in physical education to come forward and join me in this study." (15:1, 180)

Huo's very involvement with the Russian implies an admission of the validity of the discursive terms of engagement articulated here. And as the episode concludes with the

Russian's capitulation to Huo's immediate demands, Huo's mastery of this new discourse of the national body remains conflicted and incomplete. It remains unclear how Huo will coordinate his passion for these new ideals with his continuing allegiance to the social and discursive structures within which his inheritance is embedded. Similarly, it remains unclear whether the Chinese martial arts as a practice are a valid candidate for integration into the modern system of physical education. Huo can only fret over the unrealized possibilities of which he has now been made aware: "Although I drove him off in a rage, what he said on stage today actually spoke right to China's greatest defect. If I weren't tied up at present with these trivial matters of business, I would truly like to step up and devote all my efforts to promoting China's martial arts. What good does it do for me, one single man, to be strong?" (15:1, 190–191)

The narrative arc of the novel's second half recapitulates the incident of the Russian strongman. A foreign athlete insults the Chinese people, prompting Huo Yuanjia to issue a challenge; negotiations ensue, leading in the end not to a match but only to the foreign champion's withdrawal. In this instance, though, the tale is writ much larger, extending, with complications and digressions, over some forty chapters. The challenge to O'Brien takes Huo from Tianjin to Shanghai, where he finds himself increasingly embroiled in the commercial, legal, social, and media practices of life in the modern metropolis. Even when the long-anticipated match with O'Brien has come to naught, the irrevocable complications of Huo Yuanjia's experiences in Shanghai propel him toward a new model for the social role and context of the martial arts—and at the same time toward a premature and inglorious death.

The opening of the O'Brien episode defines several of the elements that will shape ensuing events: Huo Yuanjia's fervor to answer any challenge to Chinese honor, his unpreparedness to deal with the unfamiliar contexts and practices within which these challenges appear, and the crucial role of his associate Nong Jingsun—a cosmopolitan businessman, fluent in English and on good terms with the foreign community—in mediating between Huo and an alien world. When Nong first walks in brandishing a newspaper, Huo can't even be bothered to read O'Brien's advertisement because of the foreign words with which the text is sprinkled. But no sooner has Nong summarized the insulting challenge than Huo, jumping to his feet in indignation, vows to travel to Shanghai to confront the foreigner. In Shanghai, Nong's assistance proves indispensable, since the proposed match with O'Brien must be arranged with reference not to the traditions of the martial world, but rather to the legal and economic protocols of a transnational capitalist system. Nong explains to Huo that O'Brien represents the interests of his sponsors and investors, not his own personal honor. Arranging the match requires negotiating with his agent, Wolin, over details of licensing, wagers, date and venue, a contract, lawyers, and financial guarantors. The first round of negotiations with Wolin marks only the beginning of a tortuous and ultimately fruitless process.

Over the course of his sojourn in Shanghai, both Huo Yuanjia's aims and the means by which he seeks to realize them undergo a transformation. What begins as a determination to personally answer O'Brien's challenge gradually shifts to the broader project of promoting the martial arts as a tool for building the strength of the Chinese people.

This shift, in turn, posits a fundamental change in the way the martial arts are transmitted and in the kinds of communities the process of transmission creates. Or, to put it another way, the desire to repurpose the martial arts toward the creation of a different kind of community requires a new practice of transmission.

Earlier episodes have laid the groundwork for these changes. We have seen how Huo's own education reveals contradictions in the received mode of master-to-disciple transmission, how Huo tests the limits of the traditional model by accepting a disciple from outside his clan, and how the Russian strongman's challenge first stirs Huo's ambition to promote the martial arts. O'Brien's new challenge and the ensuing negotiations in Shanghai engage Huo and Nong in renewed discussion of these issues. But the first move towards attempting a new strategy occurs when Huo, returning to Tianjin in search of support, is rebuffed by his family. His father and elder brother see a public match against an unknown foreigner as an unwarranted risk, and are anxious about the financial obligations Huo is incurring. It is at this point, as the tension between Huo's heritage and his ambitions becomes acute, that Nong proposes to erect a *leitai* in Shanghai's Zhang Gardens.

Nong's *leitai* restages the Russian strongman's appearance in the Tianjin theater, but with Huo Yuanjia at the center of the stage. It is not merely an expansion of Huo's Shanghai venture beyond the original aim of a match against O'Brien, but also a reimagining of the challenge platform as previously known in the martial world and (as several characters point out) in the pages of fiction. It departs from tradition first of all in being a commercial venture. When Huo demurs at the idea of selling tickets, Nong explains that this procedure will relieve the Huo clan's financial difficulties, is necessary to defray the expenses of the O'Brien match, and accords with international norms for sporting competitions. The new *leitai*'s second and even more fundamental innovation is in its purpose. Martial artists customarily opened a *leitai* in order to establish a reputation or for other purely personal ends. Huo's *leitai*, however, is intended not to aggrandize Huo himself but rather to attract champions from all over China in order to present a unified response to foreign arrogance and aggression. And in order to achieve this end, it will make use of the new media of communication and their hub in the metropolis of Shanghai. "The notion is both original and apt," opines a supporter, Peng Shubai, when he first hears the plan:

> "If you were to try it in any of the provinces of China's interior, you wouldn't necessarily be able to call many people together. But Shanghai is where China and the West meet, with transport by land and sea to the four corners of the world. We just have to put together a few advertisements in various languages, and publish them in the newspapers, both Chinese and foreign. Within a few weeks, not just the whole nation, but everyone in the whole world will know about it!" (64: 4, 158)

Nong Jingsun promotes the *leitai* through networking, advertisements, and press conferences, and it eventually opens with great ceremony. On the first day, a single challenger appears, a hot-headed youngster named Zhao whose insistence on matching himself against Huo leads only to a humiliating defeat. Enthusiastic press coverage of the bout brings crowds to the venue over the following days, but discourages challengers. As the days drag on without further event, the crowds fade, promotion proves fruitless, Huo's purse is drained, and the *leitai* closes. Nong Jingsun has misread the readiness of the martial community, and of the public, to embrace his new vision. The *leitai*'s failure to break the mold of tradition is underscored by the sequel, when the defeated Zhao's master, Zhang Wenda, opens his own *leitai* to challenge Huo, driven by the old imperatives of factional rivalry and revenge.

Even as the *leitai* fails, however, it opens another avenue for the realization of a new form for the martial arts. On the day when Huo receives the news that O'Brien has forfeited their match, Nong brings him a proposition from figures in Shanghai's education circles who wish to establish a school promoting physical education through the Chinese martial arts. The project vindicates the *leitai* by opening an opportunity that will benefit the whole nation. "Up until now," Nong explains,

> "those in education circles have generally been obsessed with a superstitious faith in Western learning. Anything foreign was good, and anything native to China, no matter what it might be, was uniformly rejected. In this day and age, when foreign physical education holds sway, who would dare mention promoting the Chinese martial arts? The credit for bringing the education world to its senses, and making them take the initiative to promote the martial arts, is entirely due to the *leitai*." (77: 6, 35)

Plans for the school are finalized at a banquet held by its sponsors in honor of Huo's victory over Zhang Wenda. Huo insists that there is no glory to be claimed from fighting his own countrymen, and laments that he was not born in an age when his martial skills might have served the nation on the field of battle. He announces, though, that he is prepared to serve as instructor at the school. While the clan elders will not change the rule that forbids teaching their Trackless Art to outsiders, they have announced that Huo Yuanjia will not be punished for any violations, and is free to proceed as he sees fit. A new body for the martial arts—the Jingwu Athletic Association (精武體育會), a civic organization that members of China's modern urban society may freely join—is born. In order to serve as a tool for strengthening the nation, the Chinese martial arts have moved from master-disciple transmission to public dissemination, from patriliny to democracy. It is this transformation of the mode of transmission that is consecrated by Huo Yuanjia's martyrdom.

TRANSMISSION AND NARRATION

Huo Yuanjia's democratization of martial arts instruction is taken up in many later versions of his story. It is a theme that lends itself to treatment in a variety of modes, including the antitraditional, the populist, and the nationalistic. What is striking about Xiang Kairan's novel is its exploration of the resonances between transmission in the martial arts on one hand and the mediality of narration on the other.

If my discussion so far has given the impression that the bulk of the novel is concerned with the adventures of Huo Yuanjia, then I have misrepresented the work. Huo Yuanjia's story does provide the framework, structural and thematic, of the novel as a whole, but it is a framework that is attenuated to an extreme degree by the inclusion of anecdotes, tales, and minibiographies of dozens of martial artists and other colorful figures. At the point in the tale where Huo, in Shanghai, first encounters Peng Shubai, the narrator breaks off to introduce Peng's uncle, Peng Jizhou, an official in Shaanxi, and to tell the tale of his dealings with the bandit Hu Jiu. At the start of the fifty-first chapter, the narrator directly addresses the question of the novel's design:

> I've already told how Peng Jizhou, with his constable Zhu Youjie, called upon Hu Jiu by night and then returned to his *yamen*. Now, as I resume my account, I need only explain what was behind this whole affair, and then get back to the main story (正文) of how Peng Shubai aided Huo Yuanjia in setting up his *leitai* in Shanghai. Most of my readers are undoubtedly thinking that since I'm telling the tale of Huo Yuanjia, I should just go right ahead and write it, plain and straight, without endlessly breaking off into nodes and branches, tossing the main story off to one side and blithely haring off after these extraneous anecdotes, time and again, to my readers' exasperation. You must understand, dearest readers, that although in composing this *Tale of Righteous Heroes* I have not made Huo Yuanjia the central character throughout the entire text, yet all the many and various matters that arise invariably derive from the thread of Huo Yuanjia. And if I were to simply write out the events of Huo Yuanjia's entire life in some three or five chapters, then wouldn't I have to take each one of these related tales and write it up as a short story, starting from scratch over and over again? If I wrote it in this manner, not only would I find it uninteresting as a writer, but I dare say you too, dearest readers, would feel that it was fairly dull. (51: 3, 154)

While this apologia features a certain defensiveness, it also presumes and cultivates a readerly interest in the formal aspects of fiction. It lays bare the narrative's machinations, inviting the reader to savor the author-narrator's skills. And it prioritizes the pleasures of this aesthetic negotiation over the exigencies of the matter ostensibly at hand—the matter of our righteous hero Huo Yuanjia. One could argue that many of the interpolated stories reinforce certain themes of the primary narrative—the trials and limitations of master-disciple transmission, for instance, or the challenges of life in the modern metropolis. One could also argue that the frustration they create by delaying the flow of the primary narrative reproduces on the level of readerly experience the frustration that bedevils the protagonist in his desire to prove himself against a foreign challenger. But the text itself, in the voices of both narrator and commentator, makes clear that the digressions are meant to be entertaining in their own right, and, further, that their obfuscation of the primary narrative itself constitutes a form of pleasure. The author-narrator, no less than his protagonist, is a master of the "trackless art."

Of the text's concrete strategies for elaborating and delaying the narrative, two in particular stand out. One is the technique familiar from traditional fiction going back at least to *The Water Margin* (水滸傳), whereby one character's encounter with another within the diegesis provides the pretext for a change of narrative direction. In *Righteous Heroes*, many of the links between one character and the next either begin from or lead to the relationship between master and disciple. The introduction of a certain figure occasions an account of his martial training and thus of his master's career, or a chance encounter between two martial artists leads to the establishment of a master-disciple relationship. In such cases, the handing off of the narrative thread from one character to the next directly replicates the networks of transmission that constitute the world of the traditional martial arts. This handing-off is conducted by the text's extradiegetic narrator, who employs traditional Chinese fiction's rhetorical simulation of the interaction between a storyteller and his audience, and often (as in the example above) explicitly draws attention to his own manipulation of the narrative and the readerly pleasure it supposedly affords.

A second mechanism for introducing digressive material is intradiegetic narration. The pleasures of digressive storytelling are modeled for the reader by characters within the novel who tell stories to other characters; the characters within the stories they tell take a similar delight in storytelling, creating multiple levels of nesting narration. The first and most prominent of the intradiegetic narrators is none other than Huo Yuanjia himself. After the incident with the Russian strongman, Huo is approached by the son of an old acquaintance who urges him to join the antiforeign Boxer movement. Huo makes his excuses to the misguided youth, then regales Nong Jingsun with tales of the father's exploits: "In any case we've got time on our hands today, and since I've gotten this far in the tale, I might as well tell you the amusing story of what happened to him in Caozhou" (16: 1, 207). Nong for his part, as Huo's interlocutor, provides a diegetic echo and instantiation of the audience typically implied in the narrator's address to the reader:

> When Nong Jinsun heard this, he couldn't help but interrupt to ask, "So just who was it that they mistook him for? Why did they need to mobilize such a crowd of troops to come and capture him?" Would you like to know how Huo Yuanjia responded? You'll hear all about it in the seventeenth chapter! (16: 1, 212)

The narrator's use of the traditional storyteller's voice contributes to the blurring of the boundaries between his own address to his readership and the intradiegetic tale-telling that animates the networks of the martial world. But the novel's narrator claims another role as well: that of a personalized author, the historical Xiang Kairan. In a later passage the historicized author-narrator directly addresses the composition of the novel and his motives in writing:

> In the 15th year of the Republic [1926], I, Buxiaosheng, had brought this *Tale of Righteous Heroes* as far as the 65th chapter, when matters led me to depart Shanghai,

and I was unable to continue writing. That was now five whole years ago, and I had already made up my mind to simply abandon the book there at the halfway point. Writing fiction was in my case entirely for the sake of making a living. I am not a military man, capable of drilling troops or fighting battles, and so I can't obtain a position in the military world; nor am I a politician either, fond of flapping my lips and drumming my tongue, and so I can't busy myself in the world of politics; much less do I have any particular scientific knowledge or specialized technical skills that would allow me to scrape together a bowl of rice in the worlds of education or busi-'ness. Utterly unskilled, with no means to make a living, all I knew to do was to pick up my feeble brush and scratch out a few works of irrelevant fiction, thereby trick-ing a bit of rice into my bowl. Five years ago, unexpectedly, Providence stretched out its hand, and I was able to obtain an itinerant position in the interior. I could give up writing fiction without having to starve, and so was quite happy to set this feeble brush of mine aside. I had always imagined that those who bought and read these trivial tales did so in any event only to pass the time, and it made no real difference whether this book was completed or not. Contrary to my expectations, a good num-ber of readers wrote letters to inquire, directly or indirectly, and went on to urge me to bring the novel to completion.

In the course of my travels through the provinces of Henan and Zhili over the last few years, I have seen and heard various matters similar in character to those found in the previous eight sections of this book. What's more, as it so happens, I have lost that itinerant position, and must resume my old profession. It seems to me that rather than starting from scratch and leaving the book's readers disappointed, it would be better to first complete the present work; and thus, once more, I take my feeble brush in hand, and write as follows. . . . (66: 4, 200–201)

The storyteller spinning tales for his listeners is at the same time the professional writer crafting a product for the market. The resultant author-narrator is a persona that accepts and utilizes the commodified mediation facilitated by new technologies and institutions for the dissemination of fiction. The transformation of the narrator inevitably implies a transformation of the audience as well. On the other end of an exchange initiated by the narrativized author and mediated through the publishing industry stands neither the classical-language anecdote's posited audience of inti-mates nor traditional vernacular fiction's imagined marketplace crowd, but a reading and buying public democratized by commerce and unrestricted by temporal and geo-graphic particularities.

In recognizing and invoking in this manner the author-audience relationships made possible by mass-mediated print culture, *Righteous Heroes* shares ground with other fiction of the late Qing and early Republic.[5] What distinguishes the novel from other texts is the way in which it figures these relationships diegetically, in its representation of the changing mediatory structures of the martial arts. The community of consumers of the modern fictional text—its public—is structurally and functionally analogous to the community of practitioners of the martial arts as mediated through mass publica-tion and open-membership organizations; the public the novel's Huo Yuanjia seeks to address through a new dissemination of the martial arts echoes the public the novelist

Xiang Kairan addresses as an author of mass-market fiction. The point is not that Huo Yuanjia serves as a projection of an authorial persona (a plausible but reductionist reading) but rather that the text's perception of modernity as a transformation of mediality—a transformation of the mode of transmission, and of the relationships and communities the mode of transmission requires and enables—encompasses equally both the martial arts and the art of fiction.

Yet even while suggesting parallels between the transmission of narrative and the transmission of the martial arts, and a parallel modernization of the two processes of transmission, the text excludes the possibility that fiction might bear responsibilities on the order of those that the martial arts are expected to shoulder. The text, in the voices of both narrator and commentator, unequivocally endorses Huo Yuanjia's project of serving the nation and its people by democratizing the transmission of the martial arts. This endorsement mirrors, as best we can tell, the views of the historical author; Xiang Kairan began penning guides to the martial arts before he ever wrote fiction, and his writings in this vein were but one aspect of a lifetime of practice, instruction, promotion, and administrative service in martial arts organizations.[6] Authorship as such, however, and in particular the writing of fiction, receives no such vote of confidence. The passage above presents the profession of author as an expedient rather than a vocation, and pointedly contrasts the production of "irrelevant fiction" (不相干的小說) with professions (the military, politics, education, business) associated at the time with service to the modernizing nation.

A little less than a year before *Righteous Heroes* began serialization, Mao Dun 茅盾, drawing lines to distinguish the "new literature" associated with the New Culture and May Fourth movements from the "old literature" of China's past and its regressive descendants, characterized "old school fiction" (舊派小說) as concerned with "entertainment" (遊戲), "leisure" (消遣), and "commercialism" (金錢主義).[7] The passage above suggests that Xiang Kairan would not be inclined to contest the characterization of the fiction he and others practiced as a nugatory pleasure with potential commercial value. What he *would* object to, presumably, is the premise that makes Mao Dun's characterization a condemnation: the premise that fiction is properly a form of "literature" (文學) with responsibilities to "art" (藝術) that allow for no "disloyalty" (不忠誠) of the sort that entertainment, commerce, and leisure entail. For Xiang Kairan and his peers in the "old school," "fiction" (*xiaoshuo* 小說) remains "small talk" (*xiao shuo* in a more literal sense), with that term's twin connotations of peripherality and social exchange. In particular, the discourse of social exchange is evident in the text's staging of narrator-audience relationships, while peripherality implies a subsidiary relationship to lived experience and issues of import, though by no means a complete divorce.

The first chapter of *Righteous Heroes* frames the novel as an encyclopedic footnote to the story of Tan Sitong 譚嗣同 and the martyrs of 1898. This device reproduces the long-established understanding of *xiaoshuo* as "unofficial history" (外史)—a status that allows fiction to approach matters of recognized significance from intimate or unorthodox angles, and at the same time gives it license to bend the rules of facticity that apply to official historiography. This understanding allows Xiang Kairan to use fiction to reflect on the role of martial arts in the crisis of Chinese modernity, but disallows both the power to "convey the Way" (文以載道), traditionally credited to more consecrated forms of literary activity, and the potential to transform consciousness and social relations championed by the advocates of a New Literature.

CONCLUSION

As noted earlier, Xiang Kairan's novels are recognized as pioneering the parameters for the new genre of martial arts fiction. In the years following the appearance of *Righteous Heroes* and *Marvelous Gallants*, the formal and thematic conventions of the genre coalesced, in part on the basis of the possibilities sketched out by these two works.[8] While the elaboration and reinforcement of genre characteristics allowed for considerable variation, including the articulation of distinctive subgenres and signature authorial styles, it also involved a closing off of possibilities and a habituation of martial arts–related material to the confines—one might almost say the ghetto—of genre literature. Over the course of the twentieth century, there are instances of authors working outside the genre who draw on similar material—Lao She's 老舍 1934 "Soul-Slaying Spear" (斷魂槍) is perhaps the best-known example—and of authors working within the genre but widely perceived as having transcended its confines and reentered a more expansive literary terrain (most famously Jin Yong 金庸). The position occupied by Xiang Kairan's works is unique. While contributing foundational elements to the nascent genre, they also carry a wealth of material and possibilities beyond those that will become reified as the genre's defining characteristics, and they avoid the glassy-eyed lack of irony that marks much of the subsequent development of martial arts material in both the romantic *wuxia* (武俠) and national-chauvinistic kung fu or *gongfu* (功夫) substrains.

But the value of Xiang Kairan's work in understanding the role of genre in modern Chinese fiction is not limited to his novels' fundamental contributions to the genre of *wuxia xiaoshuo*. *Righteous Heroes'* exploration of the parallels between the transmission of the martial arts and the transmission of narrative offers a metaphoric reflection on genre itself. Precisely because questions of tradition and genealogy are so central to the world of the martial arts, the novel's representation of this world enacts and thematizes changes in the literary field. It portrays the Chinese martial arts in a moment of crisis, challenged by a body of foreign practice and seeking a response that balances transformation against the maintenance of identity. The parallel in the literary realm is not so much the thematic and formal (sub)genre of martial arts fiction itself as the metagenre of traditional narrative practice as a whole. It would be a mistake to uncritically reproduce or reify the New Literature critics' delineation of the contours of "old school fiction," just as it would be simplistic to denude the distinctions they sought to establish of their historic specificities and reduce them to no more than another case of generic versus cultural verisimilitude. It is nonetheless necessary to recognize that the explicit commitment to "repetition" or inheritance as the foundation of "difference" or transformation that Xiang Kairan here exemplifies, in narrative practice as well as in content, plays into the hands of the iconoclasts whose European-inspired models of literary realism dominated Chinese fiction for much of the twentieth century. In light of the status to which genre fiction was to be relegated, it is fitting that Huo Yuanjia's apparent triumph in modernizing the Chinese martial arts is accompanied by the modernizer's death—a death marked, what's more, not with the bang that ushered Bruce Lee into immortality, but with an ignominious whimper.

Notes

1. Stephen Neale, *Genre* (London: BFI, 1980), 13.
2. Steve Neale, "Questions of Genre," *Screen* 31.1 (Spring 1990): 46–48.
3. Jiang Xiahun 姜俠魂, ed., *Quanshi yanxing lu* 拳師言行錄 [A record of the words and deeds of the boxing masters] (Shanghai: Zhenmin bianjishe, 1923; reproduced Taipei: Yiwen chuban youxian gongsi, 2003). *Words and Deeds* was also included as the "Anecdotes Section" ("Yishi lei" 軼事類) of the more comprehensive martial arts compendium *Panorama of the National Arts* (*Guoji daguan* 國技大觀), published in the same year.
4. Pingjiang Buxiaosheng 平江不肖生, *Jindai xiayi yingxiong zhuan* 近代俠義英雄傳 [Righteous heroes of modern times] (Taipei: Shijie shuju, 2003). Translations from the text are my own. Citations refer to the five-volume 2003 edition by chapter, volume, and page number. For instance, this passage corresponds to chapter 5, volume 1, page 60, noted as 5:1, 60. Commentary at the end of each chapter, composed by Shi Jiqun 施濟群, was present both in the original serialization of the novel and in early monograph editions; the 2003 edition rightly includes it as an integral component of the text.
5. See Patrick Hanan, "The Narrator's Voice Before the 'Fiction Revolution,'" in *Chinese Fiction of the Nineteenth and Early Twentieth Centuries* (New York: Columbia University Press, 2004), 9–32; also Alexander Des Forges, "From Source Texts to 'Reality Observed': The Creation of the 'Author' in Nineteenth-Century Chinese Vernacular Fiction," *Chinese Literature: Essays, Articles, Reviews* 22 (December 2000).
6. For Xiang Kairan's life and career, see Xu Sinian 徐斯年 and Xiang Xiaoguang 向曉光, "Pingjiang Buxiaosheng Xiang Kairan nianbiao" 平江不肖生向愷然年表 (Chronological table of Pingjiang Buxiaosheng Xiang Kairan), *Xinan daxue xuebao (shehui kexue ban)* 西南大學學報(社會科學版) [Journal of Southwest University (Social Sciences Edition)] 38.6 (November 2012), and Roland Altenburger, "Xiang Kairan," in *Dictionary of Literary Biography 328: Chinese Fiction Writers, 1900–1949*, ed. Thomas Moran (Detroit: Thomson Gale, 2006).
7. "Ziranzhuyi yu Zhongguo xiandai xiaoshuo" 自然主義與中國現代小說 [Naturalism and modern Chinese fiction], in *Xiaoshuo yuebao* 小說月報 [The short story magazine] 13.7 (July 10, 1922).
8. Xu Sinian 徐斯年 surveys his contributions to the genre in "Xiang Kairan de 'xiandai wuxia chuanqi huayu'" 向愷然的"現代武俠傳奇話語" [Xiang Kairan's "discourse of modern martial arts romanticism"], *Zhongguo xiandai wenxue yanjiu congkan* 中國現代文學研究叢刊 [Modern Chinese Literature Studies] 4 (2012).

Works Cited

Altenburger, Roland. "Xiang Kairan." In *Dictionary of Literary Biography 328: Chinese Fiction Writers, 1900–1949*. Ed. Thomas Moran. Detroit: Thomson Gale, 2006. 235–240.

Des Forges, Alexander. "From Source Texts to 'Reality Observed': The Creation of the 'Author' in Nineteenth-Century Chinese Vernacular Fiction." *Chinese Literature: Essays, Articles, Reviews* 22 (December 2000): 67–84.

Hanan, Patrick. "The Narrator's Voice Before the 'Fiction Revolution.'" In *Chinese Fiction of the Nineteenth and Early Twentieth Centuries*. New York: Columbia University Press, 2004. 9–32.

Jiang Xiahun 姜俠魂, ed. *Quanshi yanxing lu* 拳師言行錄 [A record of the words and deeds of the boxing masters]. Taipei: Yiwen chuban youxian gongsi, 2003 (reproduction of 1923 edition).

Mao Dun 茅盾. "Ziranzhuyi yu Zhongguo xiandai xiaoshuo" 自然主義與中國現代小說 [Naturalism and modern Chinese fiction]. *Xiaoshuo yuebao* 小說月報 [The short story magazine] 小說月報 13.7 (July 10, 1922). 1–12.

Neale, Stephen. *Genre*. London: British Film Institute, 1980.

Neale, Steve. "Questions of Genre." *Screen* 31.1 (Spring 1990): 45–66.

Pingjiang Buxiaosheng 平江不肖生. *Jindai xiayi yingxiong zhuan* 近代俠義英雄傳 [Righteous heroes of modern times]. 5 vols. Taipei: Shijie shuju, 2003.

Xu Sinian 徐斯年 and Xiang Xiaoguang 向曉光. "Pingjiang Buxiaosheng Xiang Kairan nianbiao" 平江不肖生向愷然年表 [Chronological table for Pingjiang Buxiaosheng Xiang Kairan]. *Xinan daxue xuebao (shehui kexue ban)* 西南大學學報(社會科學版) [Journal of Southwest University (social sciences edition)] 38.6 (November 2012): 95–109.

Xu Sinian 徐斯年. "Xiang Kairan de 'xiandai wuxia chuanqi huayu'" 向愷然的"現代武俠傳奇話語" [Xiang Kairan's "discourse of modern martial arts romanticism"]. *Zhongguo xiandai wenxue yanjiu congkan* 中國現代文學研究叢刊 [Modern Chinese literature studies] 4 (2012): 88–97.

REPRESENTATIONS OF THE INVISIBLE

Chinese Science Fiction in the Twenty-First Century

MINGWEI SONG

> I see the abyss in the sky; I see the nothingness in all eyes.
> 於天上看見深淵。於一切眼中看見無所有
>
> (Lu Xun, "Inscriptions on the Tomb")

IN 2010, when a new wave of Chinese science fiction (sf) began to attract attention from literary scholars and critics, Fei Dao 飛氘 (b. 1983), a young writer belonging to this new wave, described the genre as a "lonely hidden army" (寂寞的伏兵). He was addressing an audience attending a major conference on Chinese literature of the first decade of the twenty-first century, among whom he believed few even knew that sf had entered a new age of dynamism and glory in China.[1] "Science fiction has been like a lonely hidden army in contemporary Chinese literature," Fei Dao said, "who laid low in the wilderness where nobody really cared to look at them. One day, when the opportunity is ripe, some valiant generals will perhaps unexpectedly rush out and change the heaven and earth. But it is also very likely that they will remain forever hidden and unknown, without anyone listening to them, and they will eventually perish without ever seeing daylight."[2] Fei Dao imagined the future history of sf as if it were itself a science fiction story: many years later, after this army has been lost to oblivion, people will excavate some mysterious weapons from where the army had once been hidden, but they will have no clue about who invented the weapons or used them.[3]

Comparing science fiction to a "lonely hidden army" is a revealing way of characterizing the genre's marginalized status in the Chinese literary canon. Despite a promising beginning during the final decade of the Qing, the genre remained nearly invisible in China during most of the twentieth century, except for a few short-lived booms that took place in Hong Kong's Cold War years, Taiwan's 1970s and 1980s, and China's early Reform Era. It was not until the beginning of the twenty-first century that the genre underwent a new revival in the PRC, first emerging on the Internet and then quickly spreading to the book market and mass media. Critical attention to the recent boom of the genre has begun recently, focusing in particular on three writers: Wang Jinkang 王晉康 (b. 1948), Liu Cixin 劉慈欣 (b. 1963), and Han Song 韓松 (b. 1965), who are known as Chinese sf's "Big Three." Time will tell whether these authors will in fact transform the sf literary landscape, but their writings have certainly energized and complicated contemporary China's literary scene.

And yet, Fei Dao's metaphor also speaks to the unique strength of the genre, particularly the dynamics of its textuality enabled by its unconventional and subversive nature. Sf is portrayed as an army that has maneuvered to be placed in the wilderness to launch an ambush, suggesting a potential conflict with the "visible," or conventionally established order of the mainstream. Sf is therefore not merely a marginalized genre, but also a literary force positioned to oppose or contend with the "center." I have dubbed this recent boom of Chinese sf the "new wave" to underscore its cutting-edge literary experiment and subversive cultural and political significance.[4] The new wave of Chinese sf, like its Anglo-American counterpart, represents a new attempt to "find a language and a social perspective for science fiction that is as adventurous and progressive as its technological visions."[5] In other words, the new generation of Chinese sf authors has to reinvent the genre with a new literary self-consciousness and a new social awareness, and to represent the complexity, ambiguity, and uncertainties of both the fantasy and reality of China's changes, or the world's, in their own ways that transgress the mainstream literary realism and official political discourse.

Concerning literary representation, there can also be a more intricate "hidden" meaning in Fei Dao's works, pertaining to the poetics of the new wave of Chinese sf. Imagining sf as a set of mysterious weapons to be excavated as archaeological artifacts that will awe future generations can be viewed as evoking a vision that actually characterizes our own time. At present, these weapons, and the entire army, remain out of sight, and only in the future—or in a science fictional imagination—may they come to represent what was, or *is*, "invisible." Fei Dao's metaphorical representation of the genre invites us to speculate whether there is an invisible component of contemporary reality that can only be represented in science fiction. As will be discussed below through an analysis of works by Han Song, this transformation of an "invisible" present-time reality to a science fictional representation creates the political meaningfulness and poetic suggestiveness of the new wave of Chinese science fiction, while in Liu Cixin's stories and novels the representation of the "invisible" takes a sublime turn, which energizes the genre as an imaginary realm opening up to possibilities and perceptions beyond what is conventionally known as "reality."

My discussion of Chinese sf in this chapter centers on the representation of the invisible: sf as an invisible genre; the new wave sf's representation of the "invisible" reality of China, and the invisible body and universe in Liu Cixin's alternative vision of what literary imagination can achieve. The chapter ends with a coda featuring a brief discussion of the invisible "posthumans" among China's migrant workers, as featured in Chen Qiufan's 陳楸帆 (b. 1981) novel *The Waste Tide* (荒潮; 2013).

The Phenomenon of *Santi* and the Dark Side of SF

Liu Cixin's novel *The Three-Body Problem* (三體) and its two sequels, *The Dark Forest* (黑暗森林) and *Death's End* (死神永生), were published in China between 2006 and 2010 and constitute a trilogy known as *The Three-Body Trilogy* (三體三部曲) to fans, but referred to by Liu himself as *Remembrance of Earth's Past* (地球往事). For many Chinese readers, *Santi* is synonymous with sf—not only because of its role in show-casing the genre's revival in China, but also because it has supposedly redefined the aesthetics of Chinese science fiction. Some critics have expressed reservations about the claim that *The Three-Body Problem* "has singlehandedly lifted Chinese science fiction to a world-class level,"[6] but it may be fair to say that Liu Cixin's role in shaping the new wave of Chinese sf is equivalent to Jin Yong's 金庸 role in shaping a new tradition of martial arts romance. Although *The Three-Body Trilogy* has helped make Chinese sf a burgeoning new field in contemporary Chinese literature, however, singling out Liu Cixin ignores some larger trends of the genre—including its ongoing transformation into a new wave with darker and more sophisticated aesthetics.

This darker side of sf is reflected in the genre's long history as a marginalized part of modern Chinese literature. The genre almost never enjoyed a continuous, uninterrupted development until its most recent revival, and its short booms alternated with long periods of dormancy. Each time the genre was revived, a new generation of science fiction writers had to reinvent the genre, giving Chinese sf multiple points of origin as well as a fragmented tradition.

Early Chinese science fiction first prevailed among late Qing reformers who invested it with a strong utopian sentiment.[7] It lost its momentum when mainstream modern Chinese literature was conceptualized almost completely in terms of realism after the May Fourth period. Science fiction was pushed out of the Republican literary canon as a part of the "repressed modernities" that did not survive modern Chinese literature's paradigm shift.[8] It nearly disappeared for several decades, with only a small number of works emerging between the late Qing and the 1950s, including Lao She's 老舍 dystopian novel *The Cat Country* (貓城記; 1932).

Under the socialist regime, science fiction was reinstated as a subgenre of children's literature and tasked with spreading scientific knowledge and correct ideology. Political teleology and determinism did not leave much room for visions beyond the known and familiar, which sabotaged the genre's dynamism. During the 1970s and 1980s, writers in Taiwan began to reanimate the genre by incorporating dystopian visions and social criticism, while PRC writers also tried experiments with the genre conventions so that they could engage political reflections—though the latter immediately met with harsh criticism in the Party-led campaign against spiritual pollution.[9] An entire generation of Chinese science fiction writers was silenced by political criticism and institutional punishment when all the sf magazines of the Reform Era were shut down in the early 1980s, with the sole exception of the Chengdu-based *Science Literature* (科學文藝), which was later renamed *Science Fiction World* (科幻世界) and became the base for the genre's third revival.

The genre's most recent revival began in the late 1990s, and was made possible when the Internet became a new platform for literary creation. New authors of science fiction emerged first as online writers, created an increasingly large fandom among young netizens, and later gained recognition from mainstream media. It is difficult to characterize the recent revival of the genre by simply comparing it to its earlier booms in China, or to American sf's Golden Age or the British New Wave. Contemporary Chinese science fiction has consolidated and reinvented a variety of generic conventions, cultural elements, and political visions—ranging from space opera to cyberpunk fiction, from utopianism to posthumanism, and from parodied visions of China's rise to deconstructions of the myth of national development. In a peculiar way, over the past decade Chinese sf has simultaneously entered its Golden Age and generated a "new wave" subversion of the genre. Like *The Three-Body Trilogy*, Chinese sf reenergizes the narrative conventions of the space opera through showcasing the most splendid image of the universe and space war across light-years, but it also reveals the complexities and problematics of a posthuman moral dilemma that darkens its own splendor.

Although the genre has previously enjoyed short-lived booms, the artistic sophistication and political ambivalence that characterize the current new wave are unprecedented. As I have discussed elsewhere, it was in 1989 that a new paradigm of science fictional imagination began to emerge and complicate the genre's cultural dynamics, and the first work of the new wave was no other than Liu Cixin's political cyberpunk novel *China 2185* (中國 2185), which was drafted in the spring of 1989 but remains unpublished.[10] The importance of 1989 is highlighted by Liu Cixin himself when he reminisces how he first conceived *The Era of the Supernova* (超新星紀元), his first published science fiction novel, on the night of June 3, 1989, when he was left alone in a hotel room in Beijing. He mentions a nightmare he had on that restless night, featuring bayonets, troops, children, war, the dying sun, and an explosive supernova.[11] *China 2185* dramatizes a cybernetic uprising in which Mao is resurrected, and *The Era of the Supernova* presents an apocalyptical vision of the anarchic future ruled by children playing a war game.

China 2185 was later circulated on the Internet, and *The Era of the Supernova* was published, after the author's vigorous revisions, in 2003, when Chinese science fiction had been resurrected from its own downfall across the 1980s and 1990s.[12] The trend called the new wave in Chinese sf grew out of the post-1989 political culture, and it has not only resurrected the genre but has also subverted its own conventions, which had been dominated by political utopianism and technological optimism throughout nearly the entire twentieth century.

Contemporary Chinese science fiction has prevailed at a time when the Chinese government dreams a "Chinese dream" (中國夢), but the new wave has also unleashed a nightmarish unconscious. The new wave has a dark and subversive side that speaks either to the "invisible" dimensions of reality or simply the impossibility of representing a certain "reality" dictated by the discourse of the national "dream." Representing the impossibilities and uncertainties, as well as imagining a future history and larger space beyond the known and visible in scientific and political terms, has made sf a distinctive literary genre that cuts sharply into the popular imagination and intellectual thinking of those who are even faintly aware of the alterity. On its most radical side, the new wave of Chinese sf has been thriving on an avant-garde cultural spirit that encourages the audience to think beyond the conventional ways of perceiving reality and challenge the commonly accepted ideas about what constitutes the existence and self-identity of a person surrounded by technologies of self, society, and governance.

The works of both Han Song and Liu Cixin have fundamentally shaped the new wave, though the styles of these two authors could hardly be more dissimilar. Liu is considered an author of "hard science fiction,"[13] with lucid speculations on seemingly plausible changes of physical laws, while Han writes more allegorical works, full of uncanny and sometimes inexplicable images that are aimed at illuminating reality's dark underbelly. Both authors, however, have enriched the style of the new wave through their own approaches to representing the invisible.

Technologies of Dreaming

Han Song began writing science fiction stories in the 1980s, helping pioneer the new wave and resurrect the genre. By profession, Han Song is a senior journalist working for China's Xinhua News Agency, and in his spare time he writes dark science fiction stories and novels. For his allegorical depictions of nightmarish scenes, Han Song's style has been called Kafkaesque.[14] His science fictional imagination is an audacious effort to peer beneath the surface reality of everyday life in contemporary China. The deep truth of reality is presented in a way that may appear incredible in a work of conventional realism, but is explained technologically through science fiction—with technology carrying a political meaning as well as serving as a textual strategy. In many of his short stories and novels, an invisible technology controls people's mind and dictates their dreaming, but at the same time the representation of this hidden reality is enabled by the technology of dreamlike science fictional imagination.

In Han Song's "The Fear of Seeing" (看的恐懼), a short story published in 2002, a baby is born with ten eyes in its forehead.[15] The parents are worried, but also curious about what the baby sees, how it perceives the world, and how it dreams. A computer scientist helps connect the infant's brain to a device that projects its visual perception onto a screen. What the parents see on the screen, however, is not the familiar scene of the bedroom where the baby is, but instead "something grey, misty, enormous, and continuous that covers the entire screen and does not dissipate."[16] After a long period of troubling research, the scientist comes to the conclusion that the baby, with its special vision, actually sees the "truth" of the world, which is indeed formless, illusive, and chaotic. But then the parents begin to wonder whether the reality that we all see is a false image of the world. The recently bought apartment, the furniture, the job, life in general—are they all an illusion? Then who engineers the ordinary sight we take for granted as reality? The story also betrays the uneasy realism of the science fictional imagination: do we all need ten eyes on our forehead in order to see the invisible truth of our reality? The text itself, as an sf story, is built upon a speculation of turning science fiction into a truth-claiming technology.

In the same year that "The Fear of Seeing" was published in *Science Fiction World*, Han Song wrote "My Fatherland Does Not Dream" (我的祖國不做夢), which has never been published.[17] The latter story showcases the nightmarish side of China's economic boom: the entire Chinese population "sleepwalks" at night, unconsciously participating in the creation of the country's economic miracle and helping realize the nation's dream of wealth and power. The word Han Song uses for *sleepwalk* is *mengyou* (夢遊), which literally means "dream-walk," and he emphasizes that citizens do not remember their dreams when they wake up each morning. They do not "see" the actual nocturnal life they are living, and instead the entire dream-walking population lives blindly and aimlessly.

The nocturnal activities, however, make everyone feel so tired that they have to take the "un-sleeping pills" (去困靈) manufactured by a state-owned arsenal (which used to manufacture tanks and cannons) to stay awake during the daytime. A young Chinese journalist feels puzzled by the prevailing daytime exhaustion, and with the help of an American agent (who is later arrested on charges of espionage), he discovers the dark secret of Beijing's sleepwalking population. He witnesses his wife, neighbors, and every resident in the community walking like zombies in the streets and boarding buses that transport them to factories, companies, arsenals, research laboratories, and shopping malls, where they work, research, and consume like crazy. There are sleepwalking teachers teaching sleepwalking students, and sleepwalking "city monitors" surveil sleepwalking political dissidents.

The young journalist Xiao Ji also discovers that every night his wife is transported to a hotel room to provide special service to an old man, who is actually not sleepwalking. Xiao Ji confronts the old man, whom he recognizes as a national leader he had seen on TV, but the old man gives Xiao Ji a lecture about the national policies on sleepwalking. It turns out that the Chinese government has invented a marvelous technology of manipulating people's sleep and sleepwalking through secretly sending "communal microwaves" (社區微波) to the residents. Sleepwalking proves to be an efficient way of sustaining China's rapid economic development. It enables the sleeping citizens to be better organized to work, consume, and socialize harmoniously, creating a new nation of disciplined and devoted citizens.

The old man proudly tells Xiao Ji, "Sleepwalking has awakened 1.3 billion Chinese people," which sounds like an ironic reprisal of Lu Xun's 魯迅 famous call for enlightenment intellectuals to awaken China's sleeping population. The entire nation is now going back to sleep, or worse, sleepwalking; restless, senseless, and dreamless, they are deprived of the right to see reality, not to mention dreaming an alternative. Han Song's story was written ten years before the Chinese government began to promote the "Chinese dream"—a collective dream for the entire nation. In the story, sleepwalkers act out the uncanny unconscious of the Chinese dream dictated by the very few "sleepless" national leaders on a "committee of darkness" (黑暗委員會). The sleepwalking population turns the Chinese dream into a reality that they do not see, living in a dream that is not theirs.

Through representing the invisible, Han Song opens up a new space for the poetics of sf as a literary representation that, as the above two stories exemplify, illuminates the invisible dimensions of reality by representing ordinary life by way of a strategy of estrangement. Both "The Fear of Seeing" and "My Fatherland Does Not Dream" showcase the new wave style. On one hand, they point to the technological mechanism of the power in governing and administrating the ordinary life of Chinese people and their sense of reality, which renders sf an allegory that illuminates the deeper truth of China's reality. The fear of seeing the truth of the world and the secret technologies of sleepwalking or dreaming may both be metaphorically interpreted with meaningful references to China's current political culture. On the other hand, the narrative, as a dreamlike fantasy or a twisted representation of reality, contains a self-reflective strategy of displaying its own technologies of dreaming—reflecting both the conspiracy of controlling people's minds and an interpretative approach to making this conspiracy representable in the dreamlike sf textuality. In this way, Han Song's sf storytelling is self-consciously relating its textuality to its implied message about social reality.

With respect to Han Song, I agree with sf theorist Seo-young Chu's revision of Darko Suvin's definition of sf as a literary genre representing "cognitive estrangement."[18] While most scholars believe that sf achieves the effect of cognitive estrangement through "an imaginative framework," Chu instead conceptualizes "science fiction as a mimetic discourse whose objects of representation are nonimaginary yet cognitively estranging."[19] Contrary to the common belief that sf is the opposite of realism, Chu argues that the language of sf operates as a representation of reality with high-intensity mimesis, which presents the metaphorical, the figurative, and the poetic as the literal.

Han Song often observes that "China's reality is more science fictional than science fiction," implying that what he writes is not merely metaphorical, figurative, or poetic, but sheds light on reality itself.[20] At the same time, it is arguably only science fiction that can represent this reality, which would otherwise remain unrepresentable. Through Han Song's writings, sf and China's reality are not only metaphorically but also metonymically related through the textual fabrication of China's reality as scientific speculations that illuminate the truth of the otherwise invisible reality. In this situation, the reality depicted in science fiction is more mimetic than any conventional version of realism allows. Reality, or the deep truth of reality, is absent in mainstream realism, and is only representable in the discourse of science fiction, which decides its subversive nature as a genre that defies the "fear of seeing."

Han Song speculates on the intertwined fates of the nation and the sf genre: "China has become the world's second largest economy in 2011, but that's largely based on cheap labor. We do not have Hawking or Jobs. Is it related to [the lack of] sf?"[21] He actually laments general readers' lack of interest in sf, which speaks to a lack of imagination. Like Liang Qichao 梁啟超 a century earlier, Han Song sees in sf a magical power that could inspire a nation: "Science fiction is unpredictable, so its newness in literature is particularly precious. Science fiction is a sort of literature that dreams, and it is itself a utopia. It is not wild conjecture, but an imagination based on a certain reality . . . it's so fortunate for me to encounter sf in such a special epoch, because I can therefore dream of more worlds."[22]

In other words, sf also represents a vision beyond the limited possibilities that "reality" offers. In Han Song's sf stories and novels, imagination and dreaming transgress the restricted areas of popular imagination and intellectual thinking of an epoch that is obsessed with certain dreams. "My Fatherland Does Not Dream" is perhaps the most obvious illustration of sf's relatedness to the dream (or "un-dream") of the epoch, itself both an evocation and a subversion of the official discourse on the Chinese dream even prior to the emergence of this concept. In many of Han Song's other writings, notably in his novels, the representation itself can evolve into a puzzle with multiple layers of allegories and symbols, which turn the "cognitive estrangement" of reality into an elusive suggestion of the alternative vision that is mysteriously unattainable, unfathomable, and transcendentally nihilistic, as shown in one of his most famous novels, *Subway* (地鐵; 2010).

Subway begins with a surreal moment against the backdrop of mundane daily life. An ordinary government clerk takes the subway home every night, but one evening the train appears different. It keeps running in the dark space beneath the city without stopping at any stations, and the passengers all appear to have fallen asleep (or died)—sitting motionless, breathless, and with beastly expressions. A character known as Old Wang attempts to wake the passenger sitting across the aisle, "but he does not seem willing to wake up. [Old Wang] hesitates for a moment before trying to touch him. When his hand reaches the body of that passenger, it goes through it without meeting any resistance. He reaches a territory that is absolute nothingness. He has lived more than half a century, but nothing has prepared him for this."[23]

Han Song's uncanny narrative turns an ordinary daily experience into a surreal adventure. It unfolds in the underground space of Beijing's subway system, the construction of which began during the Cultural Revolution—initially to serve as a military bunker to prepare the capital for nuclear wars. Since the beginning of the Reform Era, the subway—together with all sorts of rail transport, including the recent high-speed rail system and maglev—has become a symbol of China's rapid high-speed development. In the preface to his novel, Han Song describes China's obsession with speed on rail: "This nation built the Great Wall, and it has now built the largest railway system in the world, unrivaled in terms of speed, length, intensity, and advancement. . . . The subway has become a focal point of contemporary Chinese people's emotion, desire, value, and destiny, which is also rendered as a special symbol for urban civilization."[24]

The subway runs beneath the surface of the city and invisibly changes the structure of time-space and people's daily experience. In his story, Han Song presents the truth that is invisible to those taking the Beijing subway. The first subway line in Beijing was a circuit in which a train could theoretically run forever. Old Wang sits on the train that has now turned into a nightmare. As the only passenger staying awake, he sees mysterious dwarves silently pack the sleeping passengers into green bottles and take them into the darkness of the lower underground. The train finally stops, and he gets off, but when he later tries to tell other people what he has seen, he realizes that this experience is completely unbelievable. The misty narrative of Han Song's *Subway* never reveals the truth behind Old Wang's experience, but the secrecy of the invisible and irrational forces lying beneath surface reality makes life itself a puzzle. Old Wang lives his life as usual on the surface, but reality has actually become a strange time-space that drives him crazy, until one day he is also—without any explanation provided in the narrative—packed into a green bottle. The surreal invades the reality that has now become unreliable and unaccountable.

Subway actually consists of five individual novellas connected by the common theme of the subway. The first novella, "The Last Train" (末班), presents the strange experience of Old Wang. The second, "Thrilling Mutation" (驚變), depicts another train that never stops as the passengers gradually evolve into different inhuman species who finally arrive at a platform light years away, which is being dreamed by an "indescribable brain."[25] The third, "Symbols" (符號), describes a group of people exploring the mysterious underground system that has been reduced to ruins in the near future; after a series of adventures and reflections, they reach the conclusion that those subway accidents are disastrous byproducts of a "cosmopolitanization" (宇宙化) project that the government, which is actually an interplanetary company, is experimenting with. The fourth, "Paradise" (天堂), describes an apocalyptic future where posthuman survivors, who have lived in the ruins of the subway for millions of years, come back to the "paradise" on the ground; it has, however, already been taken over by rats, which evolved and replaced humankind as the masters of the planet. In the last novella, "Ruins" (廢墟), the offspring of humankind, now living on a small planet, send a boy and a girl back to Earth to solve the mystery of the demise of human civilization, but they become lost in the labyrinth of subway ruins, where the boy, before his death, eventually realizes that "nothing really exists."[26]

Han Song's writing style in *Subway* is marked by ambiguity and multivalent symbolism, which adds to the difficulty of understanding even the basic storyline. What really transpires in the subway system remains a mystery to all the characters in the novel. The truth may remain forever elusive, making the reality appear even more surreal. However, the sensation of living in an explicable, nightmarish experience, as the five novellas reveal, testifies to Han Song's comparison of the Chinese reality to science fiction. The science fictional textuality itself makes literal the allegorical illumination of what "reality" is—or what it is not. The opening of "Symbols" reads:

> Xiao Wu is running like crazy on the street. Many objects fly in his direction.
> Some of those flying objects look like bees, but they are actually flying micro-monitors, with nanoradars connected to the supercomputers owned by the companies collecting the market data.

Electronic waves also jump at him like tuna fish. The visible light is black, which is the basic color of the city. The day looks like night. All the lights in the city are manmade, including the invisible synthesized lights—UV and Alpha-Gamma Rays—whose frequencies are owned by the medical insurance companies to treat the sexual impotence of the residents.

The dark red rain, which is colored by industrial poisons, also pours down on him. The rain never stops, which is the mainstream art form of the city. Under the rain that corrupts everything, strange flowers and weird grass flourish vibrantly on the streets covered by spit, waste paper, and semen. Those are genetically reengineered tropical plants.

Small cars move slowly, like little ghosts. Because of the shortage of gas, and also because the ethanol cars, electric cars, and biological cars are not very economical, people put a coal stove on the backseat, which lasts all year long and can be used to generate energy and light. The stove emits sulfur dioxide, which is transformed into dark biological light.

Humans live as if at the bottom of the ocean. The rich people put fake fish gills into their faces, which make them look like they have contracted measles but actually protect them from the poisonous air.

The city is called S city, where an experiment is being carried out.[27]

Xiao Wu does not know where he was born. He does not know why, but his memory is completely gone.[28]

The character Xiao Wu is a stranger, like the eponymous protagonist of Jia Zhangke's 賈樟柯 film by the same name, who is lost in his own hometown. "S city" in *Subway* perhaps refers to Shanghai, where Han Song worked for many years, but the novel itself explains that the "S" comes from the city's motto: "Submit, Sustain, Survive, Succumb." At the same time, the name may also be borrowed from Lu Xun's fictional "S town," which Lu Xun used as a stand-in for the entire country. The science fictional discourse on novel gadgets and imaginary environments may also invite speculations on China's technological progress, together with its ethical and environmental effects. The protagonist's amnesia is another indicator of the cultural symptoms of China's post-1989 period.

However, the novel's strengths arguably lie in its labyrinthine narrative and stylish language. Han Song is the closest to an avant-garde experimental novelist among the new wave authors of sf. In the last three parts of *Subway*, he sometimes completely discards the coherence of narrative to foreground waves of sensations that correspond to a wide range of absurd, ridiculous feelings that may or may not come from the experience of living in contemporary Chinese society. The textual disorientation is perhaps even more telling than any message the work is attempting to convey. The text reads like a literary pastiche of imaginary news reports painted with dark humor and hysterical exaggeration to such an extent that it goes beyond displaying the absurdity of the familiar.

If we take *Subway* as a text that speaks to its own textuality instead of some outer reality, we may realize that beneath the surreal details of the absurd plot, Han Song reveals the eternal void, the inexplicable absence of anything meaningful, or the absolute nothingness that transcends time and space, and devours the "Chinese dream" or the even more grandiose project of "cosmopolitanization." All the surface prosperity and its ruinous shadows, the rise and decline of civilizations, the pursuit of "truth" across time and space, and the carefully crafted symbols and signs are presented within a self-contained, self-referential textual space in a profoundly nihilist manner. As a science fictional text, *Subway* may have subverted its own purpose of grasping reality at last. Or reality is itself surreal, beyond recognition, and transformed into a hellish negative of the image of reality, as Lu Xun says: "I see the abyss in the sky; I see the nothingness in all eyes."[29]

UNSEEN BODIES AND HIDDEN DIMENSIONS

Liu Cixin approaches the invisible from a different dimension. Compared with Han Song's nightmarish gaze into the abysmal darkness of an invisible "reality" or even the nothingness behind that reality, Liu Cixin's vision is more sublime, full of dazzling details and plausible speculations about concrete world systems that he creates and depicts as if they were real. Han Song and Liu Cixin are said to represent "soft" and "hard" science fiction, respectively.[30] If the former mainly concentrates on reflections on social reality and the power of technology, the latter is more directly concerned with technology itself. A computer scientist by training, Liu Cixin confesses to being a technologist and committed to scientism,[31] but he also compares writing science fiction to a creation process in which an sf writer should "create and depict a world like God."[32] His sf stories and novels are mostly about constructing world systems that are beyond the familiar and yet, supposedly, based on scientifically plausible changes of physical rules.

For Liu Cixin, science fiction is like a scientific experiment. The possible changes of physical laws motivate the plot development, and his task is to concretize these possibilities to make them appear plausible. For example, in his novella "Mountain" (山), Liu imagines a bubble world at the center of a rocky planet, in which some metallic intelligent creatures evolve into a civilization. Their "sky" is solid rock, and their world is an enclosed space. What if there were a Copernicus living among them who dared to propose that the bubble they inhabit is not, in fact, the center of the universe? What if their Columbus dared to sail to the other side of the solid sky? Liu Cixin presents an epic story about this alien civilization that overcomes all sorts of difficulties and eventually comes to the surface of their planet to see the infinite sky full of stars.[33]

"Mountain" illustrates how Liu Cixin makes visible a world that closes itself within an invisible planetary core. His speculations focus on the strenuous effort to bring the invisible to the surface—a process that turns imaginative possibilities into scientifically plausible reality. For Liu Cixin, such a story is not intended to be an allegory of a national experience, and it can even be said that there is a touch of political apathy in most of his works, which, unlike Han Song's, show tendencies of transcending China's contemporary political reality and looking beyond the horizon of our own time for a technological utopia of the future humankind or posthumanity. Although *China 2185* is full of political references, Liu Cixin also invests its narrative with a strong scientism that experiments with cybernetic constructions of governance, and also points to a posthuman future decided by technological progress.

The creations of the world systems can take place on both macro and micro levels. Liu's 1999 short story "The Village Schoolteacher" (鄉村教師) connects the fate of some Chinese students in a poverty-stricken rural area to an intergalactic war that has been raging for twenty millennia,[34] and in "Micro-era" (微紀元), which he also composed in 1999, humanity has evolved into microbe-like creatures adapted to the deteriorating environment of the Earth torched by an explosive sun.[35] The common characteristic of these two worlds is their invisibility, as the advanced beings engaging in the intergalactic war are never depicted directly, and the micro-humans' world is only revealed through a special computer program that produces a virtual reality.

An absence of visibility is also found in *The Three-Body Trilogy*, which doesn't actually focus on bodies. A central character of the third volume, who later becomes a nearly messiah-like figure to help humans survive, is rendered literally bodiless, in the sense that only his brain is sent into deep space. Whether the alien species that captures his brain will be able to reproduce his body remains a mystery throughout most of the narrative. Even when he finally reappears, supposedly with a body, the other central character, his lover, does not get to see him when an accident separates them forever.

The "body" in the three-body problem—which is an actual mathematical puzzle— also remains unseen. In particular, Liu Cixin imagines a star system that has a lone planet orbiting three stars, but because of the mutual gravitational attractions, the orbit of the planet is unpredictable and chaotic. The civilization that develops on that planet has a completely different view of the world, which is chaotic and unpredictable, and the civilization's clash with humanity drives the trilogy's main plot. But the physical appearance of so-called Trisolarans, the alien species living on that planet, is never described.[36] Instead, the unseen bodies are replaced by humanoid self-images in a virtual reality game called "Three Body," in which human players, through incarnations in real historical figures like King Wen of Zhou, Mozi, the First Emperor, Copernicus, Newton, and von Neumann, gradually come to grasp the reality confronting the Trisolarans, the truth of the lawlessness and formlessness of their world. At the end of the first volume, two small intelligent particles known as sophons are sent by Trisolarans to Earth to spy on human civilization. Sophons are invisible to humans, but when their dimensionality is increased they may grow into three dimensions, unfold both inside and outside of any space in six dimensions, or even become completely unobservable in eleven dimensions.[37]

Through the contact with alien species and human diasporas across the galaxies, some characters in the novel approach the truth of the universe, which has multiple hidden dimensions beyond human perception. In the final volume of the trilogy, when the first human spaceship leaves the solar system, it encounters a mysterious four-dimensional "bubble" within which space appears timeless and beyond measure:

This depth was not a matter of distance: it was bound up in every point in space. Guan Yifan's exclamation later became a classic quote:

"A bottomless abyss exists in every inch."

The experience of high-dimensional spatial sense was a spiritual baptism. In one moment, concepts like freedom, openness, profundity, and infinity all gained brand-new meanings.[38]

This passage recalls Liu Cixin's description of his response to Arthur C. Clarke's *2001: A Space Odyssey*:

I went out to look at the sky after closing the book. Everything around me suddenly disappeared. The ground under my feet turned into a smooth flat geometric plane that extended limitlessly to the beyond. I stood alone under the splendid starry sky, confronting the enormous mystery that the human mind could not understand. From then on, the starry sky has completely changed in my eyes, a sensation like when one leaves a pond to see the ocean.[39]

What Liu is describing here is, in effect, the Kantian sublime: infinite, formless, boundless, overwhelming, with a magnitude beyond the human ability to grasp. By the end of *The Three-Body Trilogy*, human survivors have begun to piece together a paradise-like image of the original universe, which is said to have eleven dimensions and which is timeless and endless. However, it is not a paradise, because it also gives birth to intelligence. The eleven-dimensional universe exists for only an instant, when the highest intelligence born in that universe quickly invents a very dangerous weapon that lowers the number of dimensions in order to wipe out other species in higher dimensions. In fact, the three-dimensional universe known to humans is the ruin of the ancient space wars.

On the astronomical scale, the unfathomable magnitude of the universe transcends good and evil. For *The Three-Body Trilogy*—which asks whether the morally self-aware humans could survive in a fiercely hostile and immoral world—the sublime dimension of the universe presents a gateway to transcendence. The climax of the novel involves the collapse of our solar system. A mysterious higher intelligence that patrols the universe passes by our solar system and the neighboring Trisolaran system, and accidentally discovers the civilizations that had developed in this remote area of the galaxy. The alien throws an extraordinarily thin sheet into the solar system, but this turns out to be an invincible weapon that destroys every intelligent species that might potentially become a rival of its owners. Called "dual vector foil," this sheet changes the structure of the space-time continuum, reducing the three-dimensional solar system to two dimensions. The entire solar system begins to fall into an infinitely large, flat picture: planet by planet, object by object, molecule by molecule, the Sun, Jupiter, Saturn, Venus, Mars, the Earth, and all humanity turn two-dimensional.[40]

At this moment, humans directly observe the hostility and rivalry among intelligent existences populating the universe. For the surviving characters in the novel, this marks the beginning of humanity's apprenticeship with an intelligent maturity that matches the sophistication of the universe itself. The universe is a fearsome, abysmal place. Humanity seeks survival and tries to sustain itself in a war that it has virtually no chance of winning.

This moment illustrates Liu Cixin's attempts to render the sublime visible. The entire process of the solar system's two-dimensionalization is displayed with dazzlingly concrete details—each drop of water is depicted as though it were as large and complex as an enormous two-dimensional ocean. Liu Cixin depicts this imagined and miraculous catastrophe directly, straightforwardly, and precisely as if it were real. Three survivors stationed on Pluto observe this reality, awed by the moon-size snowflakes that are the two-dimensional water molecules. The two-dimensional imaginary of the solar system provides a thrilling moment that concretizes sublime invisibility.

This is a telling moment in Liu Cixin's writing, which may be compared to the "dual vector foil." The two-dimensional picture epitomizes Liu Cixin's artistic approach to sf: a sublime world image is created out of precise details. His work speaks directly to the infinity of the universe, but he also seeks to transform the invisible and infinite into a plausible physical reality. By the end of the trilogy, he enlivens his work with a wondrous sensation that lifts science fiction from determinism or national allegory (or whatever is rooted in certainty) into a transcendental imaginary realm that opens up to possibilities and perceptions beyond ordinary reality. Yet he also renders the sublime visible, as the very magnetic force of science fiction.

CODA: THE POSTHUMAN REVELATION OF THE NEW MILLENNIUM

Between Liu Cixin's sublime speculations and Han Song's nightmares, there is a middle ground of Chinese sf that has been explored by younger writers like Chen Qiufan, whose first novel *The Waste Tide* combines realism with allegory to present the hybridity of humans and machines in the posthuman image of a cyborg who, living anonymously in the lowest depths of society, is awakened to a new self-identity and class-consciousness.

Actually, Liu Cixin and Han Song also presented posthuman images in their stories and novels. In Liu Cixin's "Micro-era," for instance, the micro-humans have no memories and therefore are not able to carry on the heritage of humanity itself, while in Han Song's "Symbols," Xiao Wu cries out with the last breath of his life: "Children, save me!", inverting the famous last sentence of Lu Xun's "Diary of a Madman": "Save the children!" But the future posthuman "children" will not save him; instead "the shameless laughter of the infants bursts out from the void, crushes onto the invisible shores, and generates lascivious echoes."[41] This image of posthuman "children" characterizes another important aspect of the new wave of Chinese sf, which uses an image of posthumanity to mark a point of difference.

This point of difference, as represented in the monstrosity, alienness, heterotopia, transgendered or trans-species beings, and intercybernetic consciousness, poses questions about what is human, or posthuman, in an age of new technological, ecological, and political possibilities.[42] The vision of a posthuman existence challenges the conventions of identity, race, gender, class, and other social constructs of the self. Like the android replicants in Ridley Scott's *Blade Runner*, these posthumans are virtually indistinguishable from ordinary humans, but at the same time invite a reexamination of how we understand humanity itself. Posthumanity can also be interpreted as a subversive representation of the human conditions in the context of China's pursuit of power and wealth, a nightmarish counterpart to the "Chinese dream." In this regard, Chen Qiufan's *The Waste Tide* represents an effort to create a new posthuman subjectivity born out of speculations about China's future.

The Waste Tide presents grotesque images of China's invisible masses of migrant workers and the invisible posthuman beings among them. The novel depicts a near-future version of China with a focus on a southern city that thrives on the recycling of imported electronic waste, including corrupted hardware that contains artificial intelligence. This fictional future world is actually based on Chen Qiufan's home city of Shantou, Guangdong—an area that has seen rapid economic development during the Reform Era. One of Shantou area's most populous towns, Guiyu, is indeed the world's largest electronic waste site, where hundreds of millions of discarded electronic devices are dumped each year. This electronic waste is processed by migrant workers and has caused significant environmental damage and human health problems.[43]

In *The Waste Tide*, Guiyu (貴嶼; literally "treasure island") is renamed Guiyu (硅嶼; literally "silicon island"), but it also acquires an additional homophonic meaning of "*guiyu*" (鬼域, literally "the ghostly domain") on account of its inhuman conditions. Local corruption, combined with transnational capitalism, produces a dark picture of China's near future. Millions of migrant workers live under deadly electronic pollution, and they are turned into waste humans, like the waste products they work on. These waste people—who are ignored and mistreated by the locals—lead a miserable and invisible life without any means of defending their own rights.

In Chen Qiufan's work, Xiaomi, a teenage girl who lives anonymously like a ghost, turns into a superhuman cyborg, which in turn triggers a revolution in Guiyu, where the natural is no longer separable from the cybernetic posthumanity. Exposed to hazardous electronic wastes dumped from the most advanced Western laboratories, where artificial intelligence was cultivated, Xiaomi, who was constantly bullied and harassed by the locals, evolves into the very first member of a new species that gains self-consciousness.[44]

The most remarkable portion of the novel focuses on the intense inner struggle that takes place between Xiaomi's human conscience and the monstrous cybernetics of her posthuman counterpart. Called Xiaomi 0 and Xiaomi 1, respectively, the character's split personalities may point to the schizophrenic nature of the posthuman conditions created by the complex global mutations of political economy. Her rapid development of a superhuman power and a yearning for revenge on humanity indicate the paradoxical combination of a posthuman belief in technological magnificence and a profound questioning of the practical limits of that same technology.

The main achievement of *The Waste Tide* is that it opens up a journey to interiority for the new wave of Chinese sf. In contrast to Han Song's focus on invisible social reality and Liu Cixin's fascination with the sublimity of the universe, Chen Qiufan's novel points out a new direction for Chinese sf. If there is a posthuman revelation of *The Waste Tide*, it may anticipate a new millennium that sees a new class-consciousness for the invisible masses, a new technology of self that absorbs technology, and a self-conscious representation of the posthuman identity in the rising new wave that, like the waste tide, sweeps the invisible terra known as China's science fictional shadow.

NOTES

Epigraph from Lu Xun 魯迅, "Mujiewen" 墓碣文 [Inscriptions on the tomb], in *Lu Xun quanji* 魯迅全集 [Complete works of Lu Xun]. Beijing: Renmin wenxue chubanshe, 2005, vol. 2, 207.

1. In June 2010, the science fiction writers Han Song and Fei Dao were invited to attend a conference on twenty-first-century Chinese literature held in Shanghai, which was considered the first important occasion for sf to receive attention from scholars and critics of contemporary Chinese literature. Han Song wrote an account of his experience attending the conference, which was widely circulated in the online community of sf fans. See Han Song 韩松, "Wei kehuan er huozhe: Canjia xin shiji shinian wenxue guoji yantaohui" 為科幻而活著——參加"新世紀十年文學"國際研討會 [To live for science fiction: Notes on the international conference on "the literature of the first decade of the twenty-first century"], in *2010 niandu Zhongguo zuijia kehuan xiaoshuo ji* 2010 年度中國最佳科幻小說集 [The best Chinese science fiction 2010], ed. Wu Yan 吳岩 and Guo Kai 郭凱 (Chengdu: Sichuan renmin chubanshe, 2011), 306–312. After the conference, several influential Chinese-language literary magazines and academic journals, such as *Shanghai wenxue* 上海文學, *Nanfang wentan* 南方文壇, *Shanghai wenhua* 上海文化, *Dushu* 讀書, and *Dangdai zuojia pinglun* 當代作家評論, all published articles or even special features on Chinese science fiction during 2010–2011.

2. Fei Dao 飛氘, "Jimo de fubing: Xinshiji kehuan xiaoshuo zhong de Zhongguo xingxiang" 寂寞的伏兵: 新世紀科幻小說中的中國形象 [The lonely hidden army: The image of China in the science fiction of the new century], in *2010 niandu Zhongguo zuijia kehuan xiaoshuo ji*, 317. All translations in this chapter are my own unless otherwise noted.

3. Fei Dao, "Jimo de fubing," 317.

4. Mingwei Song, "After 1989: The New Wave of Chinese Science Fiction," *China Perspectives* 1 (2015): 8.

5. Robert Scholes and Eric S. Rabkin, *Science Fiction: History, Science, Vision* (Oxford: Oxford University Press, 1977), 88.

6. Yan Feng 嚴鋒, "Guangrong yu mengxiang" 光榮與夢想 [Glory and dream], in Liu Cixin 劉慈欣, *Liulang diqiu* 流浪地球 [The wandering earth] (Wuhan: Changjiang wenyi chubanshe, 2008), 3.

7. For research on late Qing science fiction, see David Der-wei Wang, *Fin-de-siècle Splendor: Repressed Modernities of Late Qing Fiction, 1849–1911* (Stanford: Stanford

University Press, 1997), 252–312; Nathaniel Isaacson, "Chinese Science Fiction and Colonial Modernities" (PhD diss., UCLA, 2011).

8. David Der-wei Wang discusses science fiction or science fantasy as one of the literary genres representing the repressed modernities in *Fin-de-siècle Splendor*.

9. For research on Chinese science fiction during the early Reform Era, see Rudolf Wagner, "Lobby Literature: The Archaeology and Present Functions of Science Fiction in the People's Republic of China," in *After Mao: Chinese Literature and Society, 1978–1981*, ed. Jeffrey Kinkley (Cambridge: Harvard University Press, 1985), 17–62. The works of several writers from this generation were translated into English and anthologized in Wu Dingbo and Patrick Murphy's collection *Science Fiction from China* (New York: Praeger, 1989).

10. I have identified *China 2185* as the origin of the new wave in an article on Liu Cixin. See Song Mingwei 宋明煒, "Tanxingzhe yu mianbiezhe: Liu Cixin de kehuanshijie" 彈星者與面壁者：劉慈欣的科幻世界 [Star pluckers and wall facers: The science fiction of Liu Cixin], *Shanghai wenhua* 上海文化 [Shanghai culture] 3 (2011): 17–30.

11. Liu Cixin, "Diyidai kehuanmi de huiyi" 第一代科幻迷的回憶 [The memories of the first-generation sf fans], in Liu Cixin, *Liu Cixin tan kehuan* 劉慈欣談科幻 [Liu Cixin on science fiction] (Wuhan: Hubei kexue jishu chubanshe, 2014), 134–135.

12. The text is available on kehuan.net.cn.

13. Kunkun 困困, "Reng youren yangwang xingkong" 仍有人仰望星空 [Someone still looks up to sky], in *2011 niandu Zhongguo zuijia kehuan xiaoshuo ji* 2011年度中國最佳科幻小說集 [The best Chinese science fiction 2011], ed. Wu Yan and Guo Kai (Chengdu: Sichuan renmin chubanshe, 2012), 403.

14. The blurb printed on the cover of his 2011 novel *Ditie* 地鐵 [Subway] reads: "Kafka stuck in an electronic prison."

15. The story was first published in *Kehuan shijie* 科幻世界 [Science fiction world] 2002.7 and later included in Han Song, *Kan de kongju* 看的恐懼 [The fear of seeing] (Beijing: Remin youdian chubanshe, 2012), 67–85.

16. Han Song, *Kan de kongju*, 77.

17. The story was last accessed on douban.com (December 28, 2014) http://www.douban.com/note/167116945/. For this chapter, I have referred to a manuscript the author sent to me.

18. For Darko Suvin's definition of sf, see Darko Suvin, *Metamorphoses of Science Fiction: On the Poetics and History of a Literary Genre* (New Haven: Yale University Press, 1979), 3–15. For Chu's argument, see Seo-young Chu, *Do Metaphors Dream of Literal Sleep? A Science-Fictional Theory of Representation* (Cambridge: Harvard University Press, 2010), 3–15.

19. Chu, *Do Metaphors Dream of Literal Sleep?*, 3.

20. Han Song, "Dangxia Zhongguo kehuan de xianshi jiaolü" 當下中國科幻的現實焦慮 [Anxieties about reality in current Chinese science fiction], *Nanfang wentan* 南方文壇 [Southern culture forum] 6 (2010): 30.

21. Han Song, *Kan de kongju*, 388.

22. Han Song, *Yuzhou mubei* 宇宙墓碑 [Tombs of the universe] (Shanghai: Shanghai renmin chubanshe, 2014), 378.

23. Han Song, *Ditie* 地鐵 [Subway] (Shanghai: Shanghai renmin chubanshe, 2011), 17.

24. Han Song, *Subway*, 9 and 11.

25. Han Song, *Subway*, 90.

26. Han Song, *Subway*, 293.

27. The experiment is later revealed as the government's "cosmopolitanization" project.

28. Han Song, *Subway*, 93–94.

29. Lu Xun 魯迅, "Mujiewen" 墓碣文 [Inscriptions on the tomb], in *Lu Xun quanji* 魯迅全集 [Complete works of Lu Xun] (Beijing: Renmin wenxue chubanshe, 2005), vol. 2, 207.

30. Kunkun, "Reng youren yangwang xingkong," in *2011 niandu Zhongguo zuijia kehuan xiaoshuo ji*, 403.

31. Liu Cixin, "Weishenme renlei hai zhide zhengjiu" 為什麼人類還值得拯救 [Why are humans still worthy of rescuing], in *Liu Cixin tan kehuan*, 34–42.

32. Liu Cixin, "Cong dahai jian yidishui" 從大海見一滴水 [Seeing a drop of water in the ocean], in *Liu Cixin tan kehuan*, 46.

33. Liu Cixin, "Shan" 山 [Mountain], in Liu Cixin, *Weijiyuan* 微紀元 [Micro-era] (Shenyang: Shenyang chubanshe, 2010), 225–258.

34. Liu Cixin, "The Village Schoolteacher," trans. Christopher Elford and Jiang Chenxin, *Renditions* 77/78 (2012): 114–143.

35. Liu Cixin, "Weijiyuan," in *Weijiyuan*, 85–108.

36. "The Trisolaran data contained no descriptions of the biological appearance of Trisolarans," observes the narrator in the first volume of the trilogy. Liu Cixin, *The Three-Body Problem*, trans. Ken Liu (New York: Tor, 2014), 347.

37. Liu Cixin, *The Three-Body Problem*, 374–378.

38. Liu Cixin, *Sishen yongsheng* 死神永生 [Death's end] (Chongqing: Chongqing chubanshe, 2010), 196–197. The translation is Ken Liu's, quoted from the unpublished manuscript of his translation, *Death's End* (New York: Tor, forthcoming).

39. Liu Cixin, "SF jiao—lun kehuan xiaoshuo dui yuzhou de miaoxie" SF 教—論科幻小說對宇宙的描寫 [The cult of SF: On depictions of the universe in science fiction], in *Liu Cixin tan kehuan*, 88.

40. Liu Cixin, *Death's End*, 433–460.

41. Han Song, *Subway*, 199.

42. For discussions on the philosophical, political, and cultural meanings of posthumanity, see H. Katherine Hayles, *How We Became Posthuman: Virtual Bodies in Cybernetics, Literature, and Informatics* (Chicago: University of Chicago Press, 1999), and Rosi Braidotti, *The Posthuman* (Cambridge: Polity Press, 2013).

43. For more information on the electronic pollution in Guiyu, see Jim Puckett and Ted Smith, eds., "Exporting Harm: The High-Tech Trashing of Asia," 2002, available at http://www.ban.org/E-waste/technotrashfinalcomp.pdf.

44. Chen Qiufan 陳楸帆, *Huangchao* 荒潮 [The waste tide] (Wuhan: Changjiang wenyi chubanshe, 2013), 103–109.

WORKS CITED

Braidotti, Rosi. *The Posthuman*. Cambridge, UK: Polity Press, 2013.

Chen Qiufan 陳楸帆. *Huangchao* 荒潮 [The waste tide]. Wuhan: Changjiang wenyi chubanshe, 2013.

Chu, Seo-young. *Do Metaphors Dream of Literal Sleep? A Science-Fictional Theory of Representation*. Cambridge: Harvard University Press, 2010.

Fei Dao 飛氘. "Jimo de fubing: Xinshiji kehuan xiaoshuo zhong de Zhongguo xingxiang" 寂寞的伏兵: 新世紀科幻小說中的中國形象 [The lonely hidden army: The image of China in the science fiction of the new century]. In *2010 niandu Zhongguo zuijia kehuan xiaoshuo ji* 2010 年度中國最佳科幻小說集 [The best Chinese science fiction 2010]. Ed. Wu Yan 吳岩 and Guo Kai 郭凱. Chengdu: Sichuan renmin chubanshe, 2011. 313–317.

Han Song 韓松. "Dangxia Zhongguo kehuan de xianshi jiaolü" 當下中國科幻的現實焦慮 [Anxieties about reality in current Chinese science fiction]. *Nanfang wentan* 南方文壇 [Southern culture forum]. 6 (2010): 28–30.

Han Song 韓松. "Wei kehuan er huozhe: Canjia xin shiji shinian wenxue guoji yantaohui" 為科幻而活著——參加"新世紀十年文學"國際研討會 [To live for science fiction: Notes on the international conference on "the literature of the first decade of the twenty-first century"]. In *2010 niandu Zhongguo zuijia kehuan xiaoshuo ji* 2010 年度中國最佳科幻小說集 [The best Chinese science fiction 2010]. Ed. Wu Yan 吳岩 and Guo Kai 郭凱. Chengdu: Sichuan renmin chubanshe, 2011. 306–312.

Han Song 韓松. *Ditie* 地鐵 [Subway]. Shanghai: Shanghai renmin chubanshe, 2011.

Han Song 韓松. *Kan de kongju* 看的恐懼 [The fear of seeing]. Beijing: Remin youdian chubanshe, 2012.

Han Song 韓松. *Yuzhou mubei* 宇宙墓碑 [Tombs of the universe]. Shanghai: Shanghai renmin chubanshe, 2014.

Han Song 韓松. "Wo de zuguo buzuomeng" 我的祖國不做夢 [My fatherland does not dream]. Unpublished manuscript.

Hayles, H. Katherine. *How We Became Posthuman: Virtual Bodies in Cybernetics, Literature, and Informatics.* Chicago: University of Chicago Press, 1999.

Isaacson, Nathaniel. "Chinese Science Fiction and Colonial Modernities." PhD diss., UCLA, 2011.

Kinkley, Jeffrey ed. *After Mao: Chinese Literature and Society, 1978–1981.* Cambridge: Harvard University Press, 1985.

Kunkun 困困. "Reng youren yangwang xingkong" 仍有人仰望星空 [Someone still looks up to sky]. In *2011 niandu Zhongguo zuijia kehuan xiaoshuo ji* 2011 年度中國最佳科幻小說集 [The best Chinese science fiction 2011]. Ed. Wu Yan 吳岩 and Guo Kai 郭凱. Chengdu: Sichuan renmin chubanshe, 2012. 397–412.

Liu Cixin 劉慈欣. *Liulang diqiu* 流浪地球 [The wandering earth]. Wuhan: Changjiang wenyi chubanshe, 2008.

Liu Cixin 劉慈欣. *Weijiyuan* 微紀元 [Micro-era]. Shenyang: Shenyang chubanshe, 2010.

Liu Cixin 劉慈欣. "Weijiyuan." In *Weijiyuan.* Shenyang: Shenyang chubanshe, 2010. 85–108.

Liu Cixin 劉慈欣. "Shan" 山 [Mountain]. In *Weijiyuan.* Shenyang: Shenyang chubanshe, 2010. 225–258.

Liu Cixin 劉慈欣. *Sishen yongsheng* 死神永生 [Death's end]. Chongqing: Chongqing chubanshe, 2010.

Liu Cixin 劉慈欣. *Liu Cixin tan kehuan* 劉慈欣談科幻 [Liu Cixin on science fiction]. Wuhan: Hubei kexue jishu chubanshe, 2014.

Liu Cixin 劉慈欣. "Weishenme renlei hai zhide zhengjiu" 為什麼人類還值得拯救 [Why are humans still worthy of rescuing]. In *Liu Cixin tan kehuan.* Wuhan: Hubei kexue jishu chubanshe. 34–42.

Liu Cixin 劉慈欣. "Cong dahai jian yidishui" 從大海見一滴水 [Seeing a drop of water in the ocean]. In *Liu Cixin tan kehuan.* Wuhan: Hubei kexue jishu chubanshe. 45–54.

Liu Cixin 劉慈欣. "SF jiao—lun kehuan xiaoshuo dui yuzhou de miaoxie" SF 教—論科幻小說對宇宙的描寫 [The cult of SF: On depictions of the universe in science fiction]. In *Liu Cixin tan kehuan.* Wuhan: Hubei kexue jishu chubanshe. 86–89.

Liu Cixin 劉慈欣. "Diyidai kehuanmi de huiyi" 第一代科幻迷的回憶 [The memories of the first-generation sf fans]. In *Liu Cixin tan kehuan*. Wuhan: Hubei kexue jishu chubanshe. 134–139.

Liu Cixin 劉慈欣. "The Village Schoolteacher." Trans. Christopher Elford and Jiang Chenxin. *Renditions* 77/78 (2012): 114–143.

Liu Cixin 劉慈欣. *The Three-Body Problem*. Trans. Ken Liu. New York: Tor, 2014.

Lu Xun 魯迅. "Mujiewen" 墓碣文 [Inscriptions on the tomb]. In *Lu Xun quanji* 魯迅全集 [Complete works of Lu Xun]. Beijing: Renmin wenxue chubanshe, 2005. Vol. 2, 207–208.

Puckett, Jim, and Ted Smith, eds. "Exporting Harm: The High-Tech Trashing of Asia." 2002. http://www.ban.org/E-waste/technotrashfinalcomp.pdf.

Scholes, Robert, and Eric S. Rabkin. *Science Fiction: History, Science, Vision*. Oxford: Oxford University Press, 1977.

Song Mingwei 宋明煒. "Tanxingzhe yu mianbiezhe: Liu Cixin de kehuanshijie" 彈星者與面壁者：劉慈欣的科幻世界 [Star pluckers and wall facers: The science fiction of Liu Cixin]. *Shanghai wenhua* 上海文化 [Shanghai culture] 3 (2011): 17–30.

Song, Mingwei. "After 1989: The New Wave of Chinese Science Fiction." *China Perspectives* 1 (2015): 7–13.

Suvin, Darko. *Metamorphoses of Science Fiction: On the Poetics and History of a Literary Genre*. New Haven: Yale University Press, 1979.

Wagner, Rudolf. "Lobby Literature: The Archaeology and Present Functions of Science Fiction in the People's Republic of China." In *After Mao: Chinese Literature and Society, 1978–1981*. Ed. Jeffrey Kinkley. Cambridge: Harvard University Press, 1985. 17–62.

Wang, David Der-wei. *Fin-de-siècle Splendor: Repressed Modernities of Late Qing Fiction, 1849–1911*. Stanford: Stanford University Press, 1997.

Wu Dingbo and Patrick Murphy, eds. *Science Fiction from China*. New York: Praeger, 1989.

Wu Yan 吳岩 and Guo Kai 郭凱, eds. *2010 niandu Zhongguo zuijia kehuan xiaoshuo ji* 2010 年度中國最佳科幻小說集 [The best Chinese science fiction 2010]. Chengdu: Sichuan renmin chubanshe, 2011.

Wu Yan 吳岩 and Guo Kai 郭凱, eds. *2011 niandu Zhongguo zuijia kehuan xiaoshuo ji* 2011 年度中國最佳科幻小說集 [The best Chinese science fiction 2011]. Chengdu: Sichuan renmin chubanshe, 2012.

Yan Feng 嚴鋒. "Guangrong yu mengxiang" 光榮與夢想 [Glory and dream]. In *Liulang diqiu* 流浪地球 [The wandering earth]. By Liu Cixin. Wuhan: Changjiang wenyi chubanshe, 2008. 1–6.

LEUNG PING-KWAN

Shuqing *and Reveries of Space*

REY CHOW

IN the Chinese language, few flavors are linked to as extensive a network of associations as the taste of bitterness. A glance at the typical dictionary entries under the character 苦 (*ku*; meaning "bitter") yields a list, usually far from exhaustive, of idioms and usages carrying manual, psychological, medicinal, legal, religious, political, and strategic connotations. So numerous and so expansive are such connotations that the list begins to feel a bit like the classifications given in Jorge Luis Borges's fantastical Chinese encyclopedia. How can so many different categories of meaning all have to do with *ku*? Is *ku* perhaps one of the greatest abstractions under the Chinese sun, precisely because everyone takes it for granted that he or she already knows what it is?

In this exploratory spirit, let me begin my discussion of Leung Ping-kwan 梁秉鈞 (pen name Yesi 也斯, 1949–2013) by reading a poem that I consider to be one of his finest: "Bittermelon" (給苦瓜的頌詩; 1988–1989). The original and the English translation go as follows:

> 給苦瓜的頌詩
>
> 等你從反覆的天氣裏恢復過來
> 其他都不重要了
> 人家不喜歡你皺眉的樣子
> 我卻不會從你臉上尋找平坦的風景
> 度過的歲月都摺疊起來
> 並沒有消失
> 老去的瓜
> 我知道你心裏也有
> 柔軟鮮明的事物
>
> 疲倦地垂下
> 也許不過是暫時憩息
> 不一定高歌才是慷慨

把苦澀藏在心中
是因為看到太多虛假的陽光
太多雷電的傷害
太多陰晴未定的日子?
我佩服你的沉默
把苦味留給自己

在田畦甜膩的合唱裏
堅持另一種口味
你想為人間消除邪熱
解脫勞乏, 你的言語是晦澀的
卻令我們清心明目
重新細細咀嚼這個世界
在這些不安定的日子裏還有誰呢?
不隨風擺動, 不討好的瓜沉默面對
這個蜂蝶亂飛, 花草雜生的世界

Bittermelon

Wait until this moody weather is over—
that's all that matters.
Some can't stand your lined face
but I don't look for an empty landscape there.
All the past gathers in your furrows;
nothing ever really goes away.
Old Bittermelon, inside
I know your heart,
the tender, gamboge fruit.

You're not worn-out or beaten-down,
you're just resting.
The loudest song's not necessarily passionate;
the bitterest pain stays in the heart.
Is it because you've seen lots of false sunlight,
too much thunder and lightning, hurt and hurting,
too many indifferent and temperamental days?
Your silence is much to be admired;
you keep the bitter taste to yourself.

In the rows of flowery, tiresome singing
you persist in your own key.
You'd like to heal this bad fever of a world.
Your haunting song would like to soothe our weariness,
open the heart and freshen the eye,
give us the world to chew on again.
In these shaken times, who more than you holds
in the wind, our bittermelon, steadily facing
worlds of confused bees and butterflies and a garden gone wild.[1]

Although there are notable discrepancies between the original and the translation, important features of Leung's work are readily apparent in this exemplary ode. The first is the choice, characteristic of all of Leung's poetic musings, of an ordinary object, in this case a gourd, commonly used by Chinese cooks during the summer. What this object conjures are, of course, all those associations about *ku* to which I allude at the beginning, from pain, misery, and hard labor to tragic history, penal servitude, and asceticism. The simplicity of Leung's choice is thus deceptive. This ordinary object provokes nothing short of a meditation on collectively shared values, in particular what may count as suffering, how to cope with it, and how to represent it.

The bittermelon is physically unattractive. Different from fruits and vegetables with smooth, colorful surfaces, its dull green, furrowed exterior rather reminds one of a frowning face and tends not to be well liked ("人家不喜歡你皺眉的樣子," "Some can't stand your lined face"). Having introduced this object-protagonist, the poet—or the lyrical voice—proceeds not only to describe it from without but also to give it an interiority. What are the possible thoughts and sentiments of a bittermelon?—the reader is invited to imagine. Key to this interiority is the melon's unostentatious nature, its manner of keeping the taste of bitterness to itself ("把苦澀藏在心中," "the bitterest pain stays in the heart"; "把苦味留給自己," "you keep the bitter taste to yourself").

Noteworthy here is a subtle conceptualization of space through a reference to folding: "度過的歲月都摺疊起來/並沒有消失," "All the past gathers in your furrows/nothing ever really goes away."[2] The times lived through—and the experience accumulated—are, the poet tells us, folded and layered together in ways that are not lost. Through these folds and layers, the melon turns into a site of reflexivity, so that the poet can, despite the melon's age ("老去的瓜," "Old Bittermelon"), intuit in its heart a tender and bright side of things ("我知道你心裏也有/柔軟鮮明的事物," "I know your heart,/the tender, gamboge fruit").

The fold, to wit, serves as that delicate line of demarcation between the inside and the outside, allowing for a series of contrasts to emerge between two very different orders of things. Leung brings attention to these contrasts throughout the poem, juxtaposing external phenomena with what is internal or imperceptible: the melon's surface and seeming fatigue, the loudest song, the elements (sunlight, thunder, lightning, wind, and changeful weather), a "flowery, tiresome" chorus, butterflies and bees busily fluttering about, and a garden gone wild are carefully pitted against the melon's quiet composure. From this latter perspective, the poet writes, the melon, refusing to please ("不討好的瓜"), insists on a different kind of flavor ("堅持另一種口味"). Wishing to relieve the human world of excess heat and physical exhaustion ("你想為人間消除邪熱/解脫勞乏"), it speaks an obscure and difficult language ("你的言語是晦澀的"). Nonetheless, this language is exactly what helps clear our minds and brighten our vision, and enables us to savor the world anew ("卻令我們清心明目/重新細細咀嚼這個世界").[3]

In a skillfully compressed composition, Leung succeeds not only in portraying a quotidian object overladen with unexamined commonsensical assumptions but also in transforming it, as it were, from the inside out. Through the remarkable detail of the fold and its chain of associations—interiority, memory, temporality, preservation, and redemption—the bittermelon turns into what may be called, after Michel Foucault, a heterotopia, an other space, in which a new kind of truth about bitterness, and with it a different notion of potency, comes to the fore.

In a writing career that spanned nearly half a century, from the mid-1960s to the early 2010s, Leung (who was a professor of Chinese and Comparative Literature at the University of Hong Kong and then at Lingnan University, Hong Kong) produced many volumes of poems, essays, short stories, novels, and newspaper columns, as well as literary, film, and cultural criticism. His enviable versatility was evident in the numerous experiments he undertook in different genres and in the easy moves he made between artistic creativity and scholarly study. As was characteristic of his love for the arts, Leung also collaborated with photographers, visual artists, musicians, choreographers, fashion designers, translators, and academics in various multimedia projects. It seems fair to say that Leung proved with his work how intellectual preoccupations did not have to be segregated from the rest of society, but on the contrary should be deeply connected with it. Furthermore, instead of declaring that connection in purely theoretical formulations, he demonstrated time and again the rich possibilities of partnership, indeed of active collaboration, that lie between the two realms.[4]

A recurrent theme of Leung's writings—one that only a few of his readers have, to my knowledge, explored to date—is an investment in the literary and artistic mode he refers to as *shuqing* (抒情).[5] Although a conventional translation of this term is "lyrical" or "lyricism," what Leung means by it considerably exceeds the meanings of these English words. In what follows, I'd like to offer some observations about the connotations and implications of this, his beloved mode, especially as it is imbricated with his approaches to space.

As can be seen in my brief discussion of the ode to the bittermelon, Leung has a distinctive manner of depicting the everyday world.[6] Be the subject matter a utensil, a repast, a museum exhibit, a musical or dance performance, a visit to an unknown town or country, or an encounter with old friends or strangers, Leung seldom simply describes; more often, he attempts to discover, through intimate ruminations, the singularities of each entity or phenomenon he comes upon.[7] This keen pursuit of the material world—filled with things and their sensuous attributes—is, as he tells us in the essay "Notes on the Thing Poem" (關於詠物詩的筆記), traceable to the Chinese poetic genre known as "thing poem" or *yongwushi* (詠物詩).[8] If this immense curiosity about the material world has its roots in Leung's familiarity with classical Chinese poetry and poetics, it is also reworked through his erudition in a host of other literatures, including the works of modern poets from Rainer Maria Rilke, Ezra Pound, and T. S. Eliot to W. H. Auden and Pablo Neruda, modern fiction writers such as Virginia Woolf, Shen Congwen 沈從文, Fei Ming 廢名, and Wang Zengqi 汪曾祺, and contemporary literary critics such as Jaroslav Průšek, Ralph Freedman, Paul de Man, and many others. Even more critically, no discussion of Leung's work would suffice without a consideration of the influence exerted on his imagination by cinema. During his lifetime, Leung was a film enthusiast, well versed in different national cinemas and film directors throughout the twentieth century. In his poems and narratives, Leung made copious use of the cinematographic sense of capture and montage to produce novel extensions and contractions of space—whether space is understood in a geographical, architectural, phenomenological, psychological, or interpersonal sense. As well, he experimented with a mode of fiction writing that consciously adopts cinematic techniques of narrating, imaging, and editing (see for instance the posthumously published short story "Transmigration of the Soul of Someone who Drowned" [淹水者的超道]).[9]

The first significant quality that marks Leung's writing as a whole is hence a heightened sense of formal aesthetics. If poetry, as mediated by linguistic differentiations, specializes in reflections through time, cinematography's visualizing techniques, such as zooms close-ups, long takes, tracking shots, and the like, facilitate experiments with space. When Leung writes about things as surprising as the face and taste of a bittermelon, the patterns on leaves, the shades of seaweed, or the flavors of a pomegranate, his pen or writing is also serving as a camera lens, an instrument for revealing an endless series of what the German Jewish cultural critic Walter Benjamin, in his discussion of photography and film, named the *optical unconscious*. As can be seen even in a relatively short piece such as "Bittermelon," however, as well as purely formal innovations, Leung insists on the significance of emotion. This is most obvious in the sensorial-technical vocabulary he invokes to describe modern Chinese lyrical fiction, for instance in the essay "Modern Chinese Lyrical Fiction" (中國現代抒情小說), with terms such as *symbolism* (意象), *atmosphere* (氣氛), *tone* (語調), *condensation* (濃縮), *ellipsis* (省略), *skipping* (跳躍), *implicitness* (含蓄), *self-restraint* (收斂), and *lightness of touch* (豁淡自然).[10] Leung considers these, which amount to a repertoire of literary practices of minimalization and compression, essential to the production of undramatic, indirect, and understated effects. What he seeks to articulate by the category *shuqing* is, in sum, the combination of a poetic and cinematographic formalism, on one hand, and on the other, a type of emotion-cum-practice of (self-)restraint and (self-)discipline. Contrary to a more popularized sense of free or liberalized expression, *shuqing* for Leung is, much like the folds and layers he notices on the bittermelon, a style of reflexivity, an inward-turning vision in which the self as such becomes objectified—or thing-ified—through a controlled act of composition and, in that process, merged with the external world.[11]

How does this conception of the lyrical mode, to which Leung repeatedly returns in his many discussions of fiction and film,[12] inform Leung's relationship with Hong Kong, his hometown, where literary and cultural production has always led a marginal existence? How does Leung navigate and negotiate between his fondness for *shuqing* and what seem to be the crude, because overdetermined, geopolitical factors shaping virtually all contemporary discussions of Hong Kong, factors such as British colonialism, Euro-American Orientalism, commercialism, overcrowding and scarcity of resources, fraught and antagonistic relations with Mainland China, and so forth? If lyricism for some creative authors means immersion in a subjective universe, isolated and sometimes hermetically sealed from the rest of society, Leung's pursuit of *shuqing* is decidedly different.

To see this, we can turn to some remarks he made during an interview conducted near the end of his life. When discussing the frustrating matter of the lack of official support for writers in Hong Kong, Leung raised a hypothetical question: "Should things improve someday, enough to produce a professional writer, who can live within his own circle, enjoy beneficial terms, ignore practical issues, write in a vacuum and receive praise for it, and have no need to face hardships—would work written under such conditions be better?" His succinct and astute answer: "I doubt it."[13] This willingness to see that there is another side to even an intractable situation—one that afflicted his entire career—gives Leung's work its admirably resilient quality. Even as he spoke against the systemic indifference to writers in Hong Kong, he understood that writing is not something that will automatically get better simply by having official sponsorship. His own work is an excellent case in point of how artistic integrity is about creating spaces where virtually no space and no nurturance can be found.

The attractive sense of stillness found in many of his poems, then, stems much less from a poetic consciousness's aloofness than from an engagement with unexpected shades and insights embedded in the most negligible of objects. What seems like stillness is really the poetic consciousness's way of stepping aside to allow an other to emerge. Such stepping aside—a small gesture perhaps, but also one that involves a not-so-small politics of handling interpersonal and intersubjective space—brings about the movement Leung calls *you* (遊), a journeying-through that is not only physical but also mental and spiritual.[14] Whereas other writers may associate lyricism with fleeting sensations, Leung's *shuqing* is rather about lingering. Instead of fetishizing, as some tend to do, the phenomenon of disappearance, his poetic consciousness hangs around patiently to allow objects and scenes an opportunity to come into view and speak for themselves.[15] This is why in Leung's work the lyrical voice is seldom solitary. More typically, Leung invents dialogues among different imagined voices: not only clogs, furniture, buildings, streets, statues, piers, birds, trees, ghosts, and mountain goblins but even the obnoxious real estate developer, that leading culprit of Hong Kong's staggering disparities in wealth and deteriorating environmental conditions, has a voice and a place in his universe. An excerpt from the late, fairy tale–like prose poem "Land" (土地; 2011), together with its English translation, reads as follows:

土地

政府又再賣地了。許多腦滿腸肥的地產商都出席, 不斷舉手出價,
　　牌子此起彼落。
　....
勝利的地產商 ... 來到綠樹環繞的湖邊, 看着眼前的湖水,
　　盤算把它填平來蓋高層盒子。
山林裡的精靈感覺到外來者不懷好意的計劃。其中一個現身了,
　　是不到兩呎的小矮人, 留着長長的白鬍子:
"不, 你不能動這湖 ..."
成功的地產商看一眼這湖, 但他眼中只有白花花的銀子, 其他什麼都看不見了!
　　他一口回絕: "不!"
他往手上的地圖打了個大交义, 寫下 "填平!" 兩字。

Land

The government was once again selling land. There they all were, the
round-faced, big-bellied estate agents, again and again raising a hand to
bid, one card going up as another came down. . . .
The victorious estate agent . . .
. . . reached the shore of the tree-lined lake. Looking
across the stretch of water he started to plan how he'd have it filled up
and have high-rise blocks erected in its place.
The forest spirits sensed that the plans the stranger was harbouring
boded no good. One of them appeared before him. He was a dwarf, no
more than two foot tall, and with a very long white beard.
"Don't do it, you mustn't touch the lake. . ."
The successful estate agent glanced at the lake, but all he saw was shining
white silver, and nothing else. He flatly refused:
"No!"
He made a big cross in the map he was holding in his hand and added
the two words: "Fill up."[16]

Not surprisingly, we find in many poems the interesting insertion of the second-person pronoun, *ni* (你), a "you" with whom the poet, in the form of *wo* (我) or "I," conducts an imaginary conversation. With this simple address and opening, a poem becomes the setting for a relationship unfolding between the poet and his object (so that, for instance, we hear him talking directly to the bittermelon, complimenting it on its reticence: "Your silence is much to be admired"/"我佩服你的沉默"). Whereas for a modern European poet such as Charles Baudelaire the encounters in urban spaces (such as mid-nineteenth-century Paris) confirmed the increasing ephemerality, harshness, and lack of reciprocity of relationships (be these relationships among strangers or between human beings and things), for Leung, the point is rather that there is always another position, perspective, and angle on the world to be entertained besides one's own. As he puts it in the poem on a flame tree ("The Flame Tree" [鳳凰木]): "You don't want me to see you in a fixed way" and "I don't want you to see me in a fixed way"/ "你不要我用既定的眼光看你"; 我不要你用既定的眼光看我").[17]

While this relationship with another being—the core to Leung's lyrical mode— is marked frequently in the poems by the use of the second-person pronoun, it is expressed through another grammatical connector in his book titles. The conjunctions *he* (和) and *yu* (與), meaning "and," "together with," "alongside," and so forth, in these book titles are, for the attentive reader, something of a signature: *Islands and Continents* (島和大陸), *Thunder and Cicada Songs* (雷聲與蟬鳴), *The Book and the City* (書與城市), *Postcolonial Affairs of Food and of the Heart* (後殖民食物與愛情), *The Visible and the Invisible* (顯與隱), and *Fly Heads and Bird Claws* (蠅頭與鳥爪), to name just a few.[18] Even when it is not explicitly mentioned, the copular is reiterated as a wish through Leung's attention to issues of marginality, exile, diaspora, and post-coloniality, which he approaches in ways that are at once sensorially and linguistically concrete, giving to migrant populations and transient phenomena an innovative set of spatial accommodations. In the repeated move of adding, of making room for others, what begins as a formal experiment—such as the proliferation of new spaces through unusual visual perspectives on ordinary objects—gives way to something utopian: a democratic ethos, the capaciousness of which is best summed up in the spatial-moral term Leung often uses in relation to *shuqing: kuanrong* (寬容; tolerant, lenient, generous; literally "spaciously accommodating"). If *shuqing* has to do with restraining and controlling oneself, *kuanrong* is rather about letting the other be, letting the other take up space around and within oneself.

Leung's relationship to Hong Kong should, ultimately, be understood in terms of this mutuality between an aesthetics and an ethics he underscores through the myriad imaginary dimensions—what I will term *reveries of space*—running through his work. Encapsulated not only in the form of photographic images but also in its incessant demolitions and reconstructions, its mobile and rigid class distinctions, its relentless speeds, and its ubiquitous commodities, the city of Hong Kong, exasperating in so many ways, also inspires, paradoxically, an enduring feeling of tenderness and attachment that can only be called love. The grasp of this dialectical bondage between the lyrical and the urban distinguishes Leung's work from that of many of his fellow Chinese-language writers, for whom lyricism often remains a vehicle of transcendent yearnings, reserved for revolution, the nation, the people, the ancestral landscape, and similarly lofty topics. Insofar as intellectuals in the People's Republic of China, as elsewhere, are increasingly confronted in the global era with the brutal material consequences of rapid urbanization, they may, in due course, come to recognize the prescience of Leung's thoroughly immanent visions.

In Leung's reveries of space, senses, things, and relationships are typically brought into play in such ways as to become a gathering, both in the sense of an artistic collection and in the sense of a community in formation. How to gather all possible senses, things, people, and their stories, and pass them on to future generations? Among the memorable images Leung has given us, one seems to me an eminently apt symbol of both the lure and the challenge posed by such a transmission. Interweaving Leung's favorite themes of historical rootedness (and uprooting), chance, metamorphosis, hybridization, and involuntary cohabitation, the image, invoked in the essay "The Strange Big Banyan Tree" (古怪的大榕樹; 1987), is that of a weird-looking banyan tree, found on a street in Hong Kong. Imagining a gathering of storytellers and listeners across generations, Leung addresses his readers in such a way as to guide them, ever so gently and thoughtfully, toward his deepest concerns. How to listen? How to write? How to live with our objects, our memories, and all our others, day in and day out? Let me conclude with an excerpt of his remarks:

> 古怪的大榕樹也許我們的現實本身是荒謬而不貫徹的呢! 我抬頭看見: 我們找到的也是一棵古怪的大榕樹呢, 不僅因為它根葉繁密, 而是因為它的枝幹間夾纏着磚牆, 還依稀有門框的形跡, 彷彿可以開門住進樹裡面去。原來那本來是長在屋旁的榕樹, 日本人來的時候, 屋裡人跑光了, 樹毫無阻攔地恣意生長, 把屋子都壓扁了, 樹把屋子吞到肚裡, 長成這樹不像樹, 屋不像屋的東西。坐

在這樹下聽故事，過去習慣聽故事的氣氛和關係不同了。若說故事是虛構的，聽故事的人會發覺，本身所處的背景也不穩定，所見的符號也不貫徹，訊息大概也不同了。

我們站在這樣一棵大樹下，怎樣開始說我們的故事呢？...

在這樣的情況下，一向被認為是中國現代小說主流的寫實主義，不免顯得侷促，難以說盡心志與世界之間的種種複雜關連，唯有依賴其他各種方法補充。我自己對中外抒情小說的嘗試十分嚮往...

Perhaps our reality itself is absurd and disjointed! I look up: what we find is a weird-looking, big banyan tree. Weird, not only because it is lush with (aerial) roots and leaves but also because its branches and trunks are all entangled with the brick wall, and still bearing faint traces of a door frame, as though we could open the door right there and go live inside. Turns out that the tree used to grow next to the house. When the Japanese came, the inhabitants fled; unobstructed, the tree grew liberally, crushing and leveling the house. The tree swallowed the house, ending up in the form of this thing that looked like a tree and yet is not a tree, that looked like a house and yet is not a house. As we sit under this tree listening to stories, past customs of storytelling are changing. If the stories are fictional, those listening will notice that their own circumstances, too, are unstable . . .

As we stand under this big tree, how do we begin to tell our stories? . . .

Under these circumstances, the realism that is usually considered the mainstream of modern Chinese fiction seems rather limited, as it cannot fully articulate the complex relations between our feelings and thoughts and the world outside. We can only supplement it with other methods. For my part, I greatly cherish the experiments with the lyrical novel, Chinese and Western . . .[19]

NOTES

1. "Bittermelon," trans. Gordon T. Osing, in *City at the End of Time*, ed. and intro. Esther M. K. Cheung (Hong Kong: Hong Kong University Press, 2012), 146–147.

2. For this reason, I would have translated these lines in a more literal manner than Gordon T. Osing so as to preserve the mention of folding from the Chinese text. Such a translation would read: "the times lived through are all folded up in layers; nothing is lost."

3. This reference to the clearing of minds and brightening of vision is, of course, culturally specific and borders on the untranslatable. The reference is derived from the Chinese custom of attributing to bittermelons the medicinal benefit of cooling the body. Hence bittermelon's other, more preferred, name (as typically listed on restaurant menus, for instance): *lianggua* or cool melon.

4. For summaries of Leung's life and work, see Andrea Riemenschnitter, "Preface," trans. Helen Wallimann, in Leung Ping-kwan, *Sichtbares und Verborgenes: Gedichte/The Visible and the Invisible: Poems/Xian yu yin: Shi ji* 顯與隱：詩集, ed. Andrea Riemenschnitter (Hong Kong: MCCM Creations, 2012), 12–19; Zheng Zhengheng 鄭政恆, "Yesi: Zai renjian xiezuo" 也斯：在人間寫作 [Yesi: Writing in the human realm], *Ming Bao* 明報 [Ming bao daily], January 11, 2013; Mary Shuk-han Wong 黃淑嫻, Amanda Hsu Yuk-kwan 許旭筠,

et al., eds., *Gaobie renjian ziwei (Yesi jinian tekan)* 告別人間滋味(也斯紀念特刊)/ *Farewell, Flavors of the Floating World in Commemoration of Yesi* (Hong Kong: Lingnan University, 2013); and Mary Wong and Betty Ng, eds., *Huikan Yesi* 回看也斯/*Leung Ping Kwan (1949-2013), A Retrospective* (Hong Kong: Leisure and Cultural Services Department, 2014).

5. For examples of the exploration of the lyrical in Leung's work, see Chen Huiying 陳惠英, "Shuqing xiaoshuo yu shiyan (jiexuan)" 抒情小說與試驗 (節選) [Lyrical fiction and experiment], in *Yesi zuopin pinglun ji* 也斯作品評論集 [Criticism on Yesi], ed. Chen Suyi 陳素怡 (Hong Kong: Xianggang wenxuepinglun, 2011), 149–156, and Huang Jinghui 黃勁輝, "Zhongxi shuqing: Yesi *Jianzhi* zhong qishiniandai zhimin Xianggang de dushi xiandai qinggan" 中西抒情: 也斯《剪紙》中七十年代殖民香港的都市現代情感 [The lyrical between China and the West: Modern urban feeling and colonial Hong Kong in the 1970s in Yesi's Papercuttings], in *Wenxue pinglun* 文學評論 [Hong Kong literature study] 14 (June 2011): 19–32.

6. See also Rey Chow, "Things, Common/Places, Passages of the Port City: On Hong Kong and Hong Kong Author Leung Ping-kwan," in *Ethics after Idealism* (Bloomington: Indiana University Press, 1998), 168–188.

7. See the list of Leung's works in the Works Cited section.

8. *Liang Bingjun juan* 梁秉鈞卷 [Works by Leung Ping-kwan], ed. Ji Si 集思 (Hong Kong: Sanlian, 1989), 171–172.

9. Leung Ping-kwan et al. *Dianying xiaoshuo* 電影小說 [Film novels] (Hong Kong: Wenhua gongfang, 2014), 24–96.

10. Leung's notions of lyricism and modernity, influenced by literary critics such as Paul de Man and Ralph Freedman, are part of his studies of a number of modern Chinese authors such as Fei Ming, Shen Congwen, Wang Zengqi, and others.

11. *Liang Bingjun juan*, 325–342; see also Huang Jinghui 黃勁輝 and Mary Shuk-han Wong 黃淑嫻, "Zhongai dianying de shiren xiaoshuojia" 鍾愛電影的詩人小說家 [A poet and novelist in love with cinema], *Bai jia wenxue zazhi* 百家文學雜誌 [Park literary magazine] 11 (December 2010): 10–26; and Huang and Wong, "Dianying he wenxue chuangzuo de duitan" 電影和文學創作的對談 [Dialogues on film and literary creation], *Bai jia wenxue zazhi* 百家文學雜誌 [Park literary magazine] 12 (June 2011): 57–64.

12. For related interest, see Leung's discussion of *shuqing* in the context of Chinese cinema in "Shuqing, xiandai yu lishi—cong *Xiao cheng zhi chun* dao *Ruan Lingyu*" 抒情, 現代與歷史—從《小城之春》 到《阮玲玉》 [The lyrical, modernity and history—from *Spring in a Small Town* to *Ruan Lingyu*, aka *Centre Stage*], in *Wenxue yu biaoyan yishu: Di sanjie xiandangdai wenxue yantaohui lunwenji* 文學與表演藝術: 第三屆現當代文學研討會論文集 [Literature and performative art: The third conference on research in modern and contemporary literature], ed. Chen Bingliang 陳炳良 (Hong Kong: Lingnan University Department of Chinese, 1994), 72–95.

13. Huang Jinghui 黃勁輝 and Mary Shuk-han Wong 黃淑嫻, "Zhong'ai dianying de shiren xiaoshuojia" 鍾愛電影的詩人小說家 [A poet and novelist in love with cinema], *Bai jia wenxue zazhi* 百家文學雜誌 [Park literary magazine] 11 (December 2010): 21, my translation.

14. *Liang Bingjun juan*, 71–128; *Amblings*, trans. Kit Kelen et al. (Macao: ASM, 2010).

15. For a helpful discussion of this point, see Douglas Kerr, "Leung Ping-Kwan's *Amblings*: A Review of the Right-Hand Pages," *Cha: An Asian Literary Journal* 15 (November 2012), retrieved February 3, 2015 from http://www.asiancha.com/content/view/1007/314/.

16. Translated by Helen Wallimann, in *Sichtbares und Verborgenes*, 72–73.

17. *Liang Bingjun juan*, 138–139; *City at the End of Time*, trans. Gordon T. Osing and Leung Ping-kwan, ed. Esther M. K. Cheung (Hong Kong: Hong Kong University Press, 2012), 142–145.

18. See also Ye Hui 葉輝. "'Yu' de 'zhongjian shixue'—Chongdu qingnian Yesi de sanwen" 「與」的「中間」詩學——重讀青年也斯的散文 [The study of poetic copulas and interstices—Rereading Yesi's early essays], *Wenxue pinglun* 文學評論 [Hong Kong literature study] 14 (June 2011): 13–18.

19. *Yesi de Xianggang* 也斯的香港 [Yesi's Hong Kong] (Hong Kong: Sanlian, 2005), 49–50, my translation.

WORKS CITED

Chen Huiying 陳惠英. "Shuqing xiaoshuo yu shiyan (jiexuan)" 抒情小說與試驗 (節選) [Lyrical fiction and experiment]. In *Yesi zuopin pinglun ji* 也斯作品評論集 [Criticism on Yesi]. Ed. Chen Suyi 陳素怡. Hong Kong: Xianggang wenxuepinglun, 2011. 149–156.

Chow, Rey. "Things, Common/Places, Passages of the Port City: On Hong Kong and Hong Kong Author Leung Ping-kwan." In *Ethics after Idealism*. Bloomington: Indiana University Press, 1998. 168–188.

Huang Jinghui 黃勁輝. "Zhongxi shuqing: Yesi *Jianzhi* zhong qishiniandai zhimin Xianggang de dushi xiandai qinggan" 中西抒情：也斯《剪紙》中七十年代殖民香港的都市現代情感 [The lyrical between China and the West: Modern urban feeling and colonial Hong Kong in the 1970s in Yesi's Papercuttings]. *Wenxue pinglun* 文學評論 [Hong Kong literature study] 14 (June 2011): 19–32.

Huang Jinghui 黃勁輝 and Mary Shuk-han Wong 黃淑嫻. "Zhong'ai dianying de shiren xiaoshuojia" 鍾愛電影的詩人小說家 [A poet and novelist in love with cinema]. *Bai jia wenxue zazhi* 百家文學雜誌 [Park literary magazine] 11 (December 2010): 10–26.

Huang Jinghui 黃勁輝 and Mary Shuk-han Wong 黃淑嫻. "Dianying he wenxue chuangzuo de duitan" 電影和文學創作的對談 [Dialogues on film and literary creation]. *Bai jia wenxue zazhi* 百家文學雜誌 [Park literary magazine] 12 (June 2011): 57–64.

Kerr, Douglas. "Leung Ping-Kwan's *Amblings*: A Review of the Right-Hand Pages." *Cha: An Asian Literary Journal* 15 (November 2012). Retrieved February 3, 2015 from http://www.asiancha.com/content/view/1007/314/.

Leung Ping-kwan 梁秉鈞. *Amblings*. Trans. Kit Kelen et al. Macao: ASM, 2010.

Leung Ping-kwan 梁秉鈞. *City at the End of Time*. Trans. Gordon T. Osing and Leung Ping-kwan. Ed. Esther M. K. Cheung. Hong Kong: Hong Kong University Press, 2012.

Leung Ping-kwan 梁秉鈞. *Dao he dalu* 島和大陸 [Islands and continents]. Hong Kong: Wah Hon Publishing, 1987.

Leung Ping-kwan 梁秉鈞. *Fly Heads and Bird Claws/Yingtou yu liaozhua* 蠅頭與鳥爪. Trans. Brian Holton et al. Ed. Christopher Mattison. MCCM Creations, 2013.

Leung Ping-kwan 梁秉鈞. *Houzhimin shiwu yu aiqing* 後殖民食物與愛情/*Postcolonial Affairs of Food and the Heart*. Hong Kong: Oxford University Press, 2009.

Leung Ping-kwan 梁秉鈞. *Islands and Continents*. Ed. John Minford et al. Hong Kong: Hong Kong University Press, 2007.

Leung Ping-kwan 梁秉鈞. *Leisheng yu chanming* 雷聲與蟬鳴 [Thunder and cicada songs]. Hong Kong: Damuzhi banyuekan, 1979.

Leung Ping-kwan 梁秉鈞. *Liang Bingjun juan* 梁秉鈞卷 [Works by Leung Ping-kwan]. Ed. Ji Si 集思. Hong Kong: Sanlian, 1989.

Leung Ping-kwan 梁秉鈞. *Shu yu chengshi* 書與城市 [The book and the city]. Hong Kong: Xiangjiang, 1985.

Leung Ping-kwan 梁秉鈞. "Shuqing, xiandai yu lishi—cong *Xiao cheng zhi chun* dao *Ruan Lingyu*" 抒情，現代與歷史—從《小城之春》到《阮玲玉》 [The lyrical, modernity and history—from *Spring in a Small Town* to *Ruan Lingyu*, aka *Centre Stage*]. In *Wenxue yu biaoyan yishu: Di sanjie xiandangdai wenxue yantaohui lunwenji* 文學與表演藝術: 第三屆現當代文學研討會論文集 [Literature and performative art: The third conference on research in modern and contemporary literature]. Ed. Chen Bingliang 陳炳良. Hong Kong: Lingnan University Department of Chinese, 1994. 72–95.

Leung Ping-kwan 梁秉鈞. *Sichtbares und Verborgenes: Gedichte/The Visible and the Invisible: Poems/Xian yu yin: Shi ji* 顯與隱：詩輯. Ed. Andrea Riemenschnitter. Hong Kong: MCCM Creations, 2012.

Leung Ping-kwan 梁秉鈞. *Travelling with a Bitter Melon*. Ed. Martha P. Y. Cheung. Hong Kong: Asia 2000, 2002.

Leung Ping-kwan 梁秉鈞. *Yesi de Xianggang* 也斯的香港 [Yesi's Hong Kong]. Hong Kong: Sanlian, 2005.

Leung Ping-kwan 梁秉鈞et al. *Dianying xiaoshuo* 電影小說 [Film novels]. Hong Kong: Wenhua gongfang, 2014.

Riemenschnitter, Andrea. "Preface." Trans. Helen Wallimann. In Leung Ping-kwan. *Sichtbares und Verborgenes*. 12–19.

Wong, Mary Shuk-han 黃淑嫻, Amanda Hsu Yuk-kwan 許旭筠, et al., eds. *Gaobie renjian ziwei (Yesi jinian tekan)* 告別人間滋味(也斯紀念特刊)/*Farewell, Flavors of the Floating World in Commemoration of Yesi*. Hong Kong: Lingnan University, 2013.

Wong, Mary, and Betty Ng, eds. *Huikan Yesi* 回看也斯/*Leung Ping Kwan (1949–2013), A Retrospective*. Hong Kong: Leisure and Cultural Services Department, 2014.

Ye Hui 葉輝. "'Yu' de 'zhongjian shixue'—Chongdu qingnian Yesi de sanwen" 「與」的「中間」詩學——重讀青年也斯的散文 [The study of poetic copulas and interstices—Rereading Yesi's early essays]. *Wenxue pinglun* 文學評論 [Hong Kong literature study] 14 (June 2011): 13–18.

Zheng Zhengheng 鄭政恆. "Yesi: Zai renjian xiezuo" 也斯：在人間寫作 [Yesi: Writing in the human realm]. *Ming Bao* 明報 [Ming bao daily], January 11, 2013.

GENRE OCCLUDES THE CREATION OF GENRE

Bing Xin, Tagore, and Prose Poetry

NICK ADMUSSEN

MUCH contemporary Chinese prose poetry has a strong generic identity. Romantic, expressive, impressionistic, and abstract, its genre is palpable in the reading of the poem—individual pieces feel similar. This similarity, though, is neither derived from nor identical to works that have been named as prose poetry, or *sanwenshi* 散文詩. Prose poems of the Republican era, when the term *sanwenshi* was first used, were typified by experimentation, generic hybridity, formal lawlessness, and a shared mistrust of strict aesthetic categories.[1] The creative work that readers, editors, and authors called prose poetry before 1949 was varied to the extent that it makes more sense to consider it not as a genre but as an appellation, a particular way of describing many different kinds of work that range from unrhymed verse to short stage plays.[2] These pieces shared a generic name—prose poetry—but were produced with vastly different writing practices. Genre histories, however, largely focus on the history of the name rather than the origin and nature of prose poetic writing practice: this chapter attempts to assess that tradition, and ask how and why contemporary prose poetry looks and sounds the way it does.

Beginning in 1957 with the publication of Ke Lan's 柯藍 *Short Flute of Morning Mist* (早霞短笛), contemporary prose poetry grew from roots in the humanist but ultimately Party-loyal socialism of the Hundred Flowers Period. After Deng liberalized, and arguably humanized, the politics of the Mao period, prose poetry became quite widespread, appearing in a monthly newspaper (now defunct) and two magazines (still extant) devoted exclusively to prose poetry, as well as countless literary magazines, anthologies, and individual collections.[3] The authors and editors of these poems were linked personally and politically by institutions like the China Prose Poetry Study Group (中國散文詩學會), as well as a host of regional organizations. The success of this group of people in the world of publishing and the similarity of their creative work dominate the way in which readers of Chinese prose poetry today encounter the term *prose poetry*. The appellation as it was used in the 1920s is now seen through the lens of the contemporary genre, as an anticipation of a type of literature with which it shares surprisingly little.

The most important difference between the two periods, perhaps, is that rather than pushing back against strict metrical poetics, prose poetry in China today investigates and intervenes in the practice of prose from a position on the boundaries of prose writing itself. By borrowing the sonic and visual qualities of prose, prose poetry allows its readers to identify and question their assumptions about prose, about its objectivity, its transparency, and its relationship to plain speech. Writing that looks like prose but refuses to do the work that we expect from prose reveals that our reliance on prose forms is a matter of convention and expectation rather than an inherent formal function. By making those conventions and expectations visible, prose poetry also opens the grounds for their manipulation and transformation. To name prose poetry as a genre unto itself, on the other hand, to visualize it as the product of a separate tribe of authors who inherit the appellation from their May Fourth forebears, is to miss the way in which prose poetry plays across the boundaries of prose and poetry. This genre gestures outward as an intervention rather than inward toward self-definition: to read those outward acts, we must look past concepts of genre that center around categories and boundaries, and look instead at prose poetry as an evolving and transforming set of performances.

The existence of a widespread generic categorization called *prose poetry* can make it difficult to see or understand the many ways in which the practice arose; visualizing the categorization as a kind of territory instructs us to look for the founding and occupation of the category itself, rather than the noncategorical or transcategorical qualities that prose poems share with other kinds of literature. This is most sharply the case with the interventions made in prose poetry by the translations of Bing Xin 冰心. Her versions of poems by Rabindranath Tagore (1861–1941), a world-famous Bengali poet and the first non-European winner of the Nobel Prize for Literature, were deeply influential; many contemporary Chinese prose poems look like these translations. They were not, however, influential in a categorical way. Because they were translations and because of their unique provenance, their appearance as literary products did not result in generic boundaries being drawn or redrawn around them: the pieces were easily categorized as being outside Chinese prose poetry. What was influential was instead the *work* that the translation of Tagore's poems represented, the interventions Bing Xin's translations made into poetry and prose, and the ideologies that both shaped and were shaped by her particular version of the work of translation.

Describing his early career, during which he wrote mainly prose poetry, Liu Zaifu 劉再復 says: "I was willing to accept an innocent self, so I liked poetry, I liked Tagore, I liked Mozart, I liked Bing Xin."[4] Wolfgang Kubin argues that "many a modern Chinese poet is nothing more than a translated Tagore," and identifies Bing Xin as the foremost example.[5] The record of literary interactions further shows that behind many prose poetry careers, there lies the implicit or explicit presence of Bing Xin. She was tangentially involved in the funding and organization of the *Prose Poetry Newspaper* (散文詩報), appears repeatedly in histories and analyses of the genre, and had lifelong relationships with leaders of early prose poetry like Guo Feng 郭風.[6] Bing Xin was not, however, a prose poet in the style or manner of the *Prose Poetry Newspaper*, Guo Feng, or Liu Zaifu: her own short prose, mainly published in the 1920s, was often editorially identified, and self-identified, as fiction or essays.[7] Her poetry, albeit highly influenced by Tagore, lies somewhere between his shortest verse and Japanese haiku, and has substantial differences from contemporary prose poetry. Her foundational influence on contemporary prose poetry comes instead from her 1955 translation of Tagore's *Gitanjali*, which she titled *Jitanjiali* (吉檀迦利). Published only two years before Ke Lan's seminal collection, Bing Xin's translation does, in fact, explicitly call the pieces *poetry* even though they take the shape of prose, and she later calls them prose poems.[8] This is an inversion of her earlier May Fourth–era practice, which was more likely to categorize texts with poetic qualities as some type of prose, whether *xiaopin* (小品), *meiwen* (美文), or *xiaoshuo* (小說).[9] This change in name is doubtlessly motivated by the nature of the text Bing Xin is translating: one literal translation of *Gitanjali* is "song offerings," and Bing Xin chooses to gloss the Bengali title as *xian shi* (獻詩), "poems offered up."[10]

But Bing Xin was not translating Tagore's Bengali poetry into Chinese prose; instead, she was translating English prose renditions of Bengali poetry into Chinese prose. Able to work only in English and Chinese, she produced her translations from the English version of *Gitanjali*, which Tagore had based upon poems from several of his collections, and which he wrote aboard a ship en route to his first visit to England.[11] The English *Gitanjali* and the Bengali poems on which it is based have important differences. The first is the particular deployment of the lyric; the Bengali poems were conceptualized and often circulated as songs as well as texts, and their rhythmic and rhyming structure reflects the roots of Bengali verse in traditions of oral performance and music.[12] The English prose versions are arguably metrical and rhythmic, as well, but for the English reader—and especially, perhaps, for the Chinese reader of English— that music is muted, distanced.[13] Amit Chaudhuri points out that "as a Bengali poet, Tagore's instinct was to simplify" his verse, and bring it close to the vernacular—but that what he produced in English was instead full of "thees and thous" enabled in part by Tagore's early education at Christian schools, and benefiting perhaps from British associations between the literature of the Orient and antique, classical wisdom.[14] *Gitanjali* in English was partially produced through the logics of translation, but must also be seen as an independent creation for a new literary context. The mixture of terminology in Mary Ellis Gibson's *Indian Angles* is telling. She writes, "Though Tagore's poetry combined the influences of English romantic poetics, Bengali folk traditions, and Vaishnava poetry, his self-translations of these poems were clearly written with an expectation of the London market."[15] Gibson suggests that *Gitanjali*, even though it is a self-translation of Tagore's own poems, is to be contrasted with his own Bengali originals. *Gitanjali*'s roots in the British market give the collection something new, something not simply "translated" but "written" in a process comparable to the composition of an original poem.

The creative dimension of Tagore's self-translative praxis is intimately linked to his ideologies about art, language, and translation. At a dinner in Beijing, he addressed a group of scholars with the following: "Languages are jealous. They do not give up their best treasures to those who try to deal with them through an intermediary belonging to an alien rival. You have to court them in person and dance attendance on them."[16] Visible throughout Tagore's discussions of art is an insistence that art is irreducible, that it is an experience and not a product; like all the other parts of reality, "we know it, not because we can think of it, but because we directly feel it."[17] Discussing the translation of his poems into Chinese (albeit before Bing Xin produced her own), he says, "Man cannot reach the shrine, if he does not make the pilgrimage. So, you must not hope to find anything true from my own language in translation."[18] For Tagore, art must necessarily be human-centered and practiced by hand; it cannot be artificially or automatically transmitted outside of its relationship to the language and voice of a speaker. Tagore therefore writes his own English versions of his Bengali poems, bringing them to English readers as an individually authored literary experience.

In producing her translation of *Gitanjali*, however, Bing Xin was acting explicitly as a translator and as an intermediary; she was obviating the need for Chinese readers to "make the pilgrimage" into English or Bengali. But she did not believe, as Tagore did, that it was impossible to find "anything true" from the English version in her translation. Introducing a collection of her translations, she wrote that the best poems she translated "were written [by Tagore and Gibran] in English, and have not undergone translation by others from Bengali or Arabic. I start my translations from the word 'trust' (*xin* 信) and I can take responsibility for them myself. I have never dared to retranslate a translation!"[19] Even in the same breath as Bing Xin admits that translation can degrade the desirability of a literary work, and elides the fact that Tagore's *Gitanjali* was in fact a self-translation, she claims the central importance of faithfulness and trustworthiness in her own translations. Bing Xin's discussion of *xin* is brief—she is no theorist—but it does reveal a great deal about the principles under which she translated Tagore. Her concept of *xin* requires a writer to take the position that there is a content to poetry that can be separated from its language and reproduced in other idioms. Bing Xin's defense of her own work shows, though, that such a reproduction is prone to anxiety-producing errors and losses. A bad translator—or a retranslator of a prior translation—can produce impurities or inventions that distance the result from the original. This is why the sense of *xin* as faithfulness, prescription to the ideal of the original, is matched by a sense of the term as trustworthiness. A good translator cannot necessarily avoid losses—Bing Xin's translations are quite different from Tagore's English *Gitanjali*—but limits them, as we shall see, to the parts of the poem that are of secondary or tertiary importance, and can be relied upon to make those decisions on behalf of the reader. Bing Xin's protestation that she refuses to take part in retranslation is intended to convince us that her motive is to correctly and appropriately take down the English pieces into Chinese; it also recommends her translation by eliding the complex, hybridized transformation that the poems have already gone through in Tagore's hands.

Bing Xin's concept of *xin* is more than just practical; its many valences reinforce Lydia Liu's instruction to read methodologies of translation as fundamentally ideological, context-driven, and historicized.[20] Once we read her translation methodology in this way, we can see not just a practical opposition between Tagore and Bing Xin, but a broad political and aesthetic difference as well. During a celebrated conversation with Albert Einstein, Tagore expressed his lifelong belief in human subjectivity: "This world is a human world—the scientific view of it is also that of the scientific man,"[21] and nothing comes to us save through "an organ of thoughts which is human."[22] This view was not antimodern; rather, it was an attempt to force open a space inside the modern in which to independently and meaningfully pursue non-European cultural practices alongside Eurocentric scientific modernity.[23] To put people at the center of science and modernity is to make Einstein, for example, into someone who can be spoken to instead of simply listened to and obeyed. As Chaudhuri puts it, "Tagore's poetry, especially his songs . . . speak of an old world that is lost but is being transformed into something new."[24] The goal is not to wind modernity back to the premodern, but to draw from the premodern—in a way that occasionally satisfies Orientalist notions of the exotic ahistorical—in order to create a contemporary, vernacular Bengali poetry that can serve as the basis for a new and independent regional culture. This is evident in the way he writes traditional, devotional-style poetry in which the old gods have been replaced by a "religion of man."[25] Translation fights Tagore's attempt to found this culture by mechanically reproducing the meaning, but not the experience, of the text, separating the art from its human author. Translation holds the promise of finding something true in art without making "the pilgrimage" that connects the reader to the author in language.

Bing Xin's position is quite different. To her, it is the reproduction that is emphasized, and whatever she takes to be irrecoverable and nonconvertible ends up being abandoned: "I only dare to translate prose poems or fiction, I don't dare translate poetry. I've always thought that poetry is a literary form whose musicality is particularly strong."[26] Discussing *Stars* (星) and *Spring Water* (春水), her Tagore-influenced collections of 1921 and 1922, she writes that they "are not poetry. At least at that age, I hadn't set my sights on the composition of poetry. I didn't understand modern poetry, I didn't trust it, and I didn't dare try it. I felt like poetry's heart was in its content and not its form."[27] Her position on the possibility of writing original modern poetry subsequently changed, but her distinction between musical, untranslatable verse and content-oriented, portable prose never did. For her, rhyme and meter were untranslatable, musical, and ineffable, while prose content was separable, reproducible, and usable. This is why *xin* translation can only take place in the world of prose. In an essay called "On Prose" (關於散文), Bing Xin opens by writing "Prose is the literary form that I love most,"[28] and continues to enumerate the best things about prose: its flexibility and its freedom. Prose flourished after 1949, she writes, because "all of the new people and new experiences appearing all over the country influenced and encouraged a great many writers."[29] The diversity and novelty of those experiences and identities, the advent of modernity, needed a transparent medium with no restrictions: prose. For Bing Xin, belief in a unitary and universal modern world that can be conceptualized by humanity—whether or not it has been conceptualized, and whether it is described in the language of physics, psychology, or literature—must be spoken and shared through precise translation, a transparent and trustworthy medium that does not alter the unity of the world it describes. The desirability of that modernity motivates the abandonment of experiences that are unspeakable in its idiom. To Tagore, unitary and objective modernity is impossible, in part because it requires a language of science that is not a subjective language of "scientific man." Bing Xin translates as if that modernity were possible with the right technique, as if language truly could produce a trustworthy, anxiety-free reproduction of the core content of experience.

To be clear, Bing Xin never wrote anything formal that disagreed with Tagore's philosophy. Instead, she embraced it. One of her earliest published writings is a letter to "the Indian Philosopher Tagore," in which she praises his syncretism and his natural aesthetics as the expression of beliefs she has long held, but has been unable to elucidate.[30] When a poem in *Gitanjali* addresses the ineffable and speaks from the human to the transcendent, Bing Xin translates those concepts—indeed, one feels that she is attracted to their sublime enormity. *Gitanjali* #102 reads, "I put my tales of you into lasting songs. The secret gushes out from my heart. They come and ask me, 'Tell me all your meanings.' I know not how to answer them. I say, 'Ah, who knows what they mean!' "[31] In *Stars*, Bing Xin engages in similar gestures to the inexpressible:

> 無限的神秘
>   何處尋它？
> 微笑之後
>   言語之前
> 便是無限的神秘了。

> Limitless mystery,
>   where can it be found?
> After the smile,
>   before language,
> that is the limitless mystery.[32]

What is displayed here is not Bing Xin insisting on the theoretical existence of a translatable, trustworthy language that does not transform the truths it contains; quite the opposite. It is the implicit ideology of her method of translation that transforms *Gitanjali* into *Jitanjiali*, and prose poetry in China arises in part from her particular, hybrid mix of a subjective, human-centered ideology inherited from Tagore, transmitted in a form that she believed to be objective, transparent, inhuman, and therefore "free."

Tracking the translation of the poems, step by step, gives a sense of what Bing Xin's practice does to the art she translates. In lieu of the Bengali, here is the first stanza of Joe Winter's contemporary English translation of poem #22 from Tagore's Bengali *Gitanjali* (poem #3 in his English rendition), which has been translated with a certain level of sensitivity to the original's meter and rhyme:

> Maestro your song is such as to astound.
> Dumbstruck I only listen to the sound.
> Its melody-light fits the world as a cover;
> through the heavens its air is carried over;
> bursting through rock a tumultuous river
> streams out to make a melody of the ground.[33]

This version retains Tagore's six-line stanza from the original Bengali, for which he was particularly well known,[34] and it also keeps the Bengali version's pentameter—itself imported from English verse—and its AABBBA rhyme scheme.[35] The language of the Bengali as well as of Winter's version above is vernacular and rhythmic, and in quite a different diction from Tagore's version of the stanza in the English *Gitanjali*:

> I know not how thou singest, my master! I ever listen in silent amazement.
> The light of thy music illumines the world. The life breath of thy
>   music runs from sky to sky. The holy stream of thy music breaks through
> all stony obstacles and rushes on.[36]

Tagore's English version is in unrhymed prose, but is strongly rhythmic at the same time. Likely due to Tagore's reproduction and transformation of Bengali verse meters, the excerpt can be divided into three phrase-groups, all of roughly equal and balanced length: ten syllables/eleven syllables, eleven syllables/twelve syllables, and twenty syllables.[37] The inversion here is telling: in the Bengali poem, Tagore uses a traditional English meter, and in the English poem, he imports a Bengali meter. Present in this practice, at some level, is a sense of necessary cultural difference deployed alongside the attempt to bridge that difference. As mentioned above, the ritual and devotional quality of rhyme has been replaced by Biblical diction, and the occasional use of formal inversions that were already archaic by the early twentieth century: I *ever listen*, I *know not*. One wonders if Tagore would have written new rhymes had he been able to do so. He accepted that English was a barrier to *Gitanjali*, once telling his niece "[that] I cannot write English is such a patent fact that I never had even the vanity to feel ashamed of it."[38] The diction in question, however, immediately recognizable in the British market Tagore was addressing, does much to identify the poem as something declaimed and offered rather than simply written to be scanned. Bing Xin's version of the paragraph appears below, with an English version that attempts to be tonally and lexically faithful to her translation rather than Tagore's original:

> 我不知道你怎樣地唱, 我的主人! 我總在驚奇地靜聽。
> 你的音樂的光輝照亮了世界。你的音樂的氣息透徹諸天。你的音樂的聖泉
> 沖過一切阻礙的岩石, 向前奔湧。[39]

I don't know how you sing, my master! I am always listening quietly, in amazement. The light of your music illuminates the world. The breath of your music pierces the sky. The holy well of your music collides with all the rocks that impede it, and rushes forward.

Bing Xin's version lacks any "faithful" interaction with the Bengali or English rhythms, it chooses a modern vernacular free of intentional grammatical inversions or archaic language, and it does not create any replacement for these qualities. Unlike Tagore's English and Bengali meters, his participation in the Bengali musical tradition, and his archaic English speech, Bing Xin's translation declines to use or adapt classical Chinese rhythms or language—an understandable decision for a poet who was so committed to the May Fourth project of cutting out imperial, premodern Chinese culture at the root. Without traditional meters or language, there is little that identifies this piece as a song. More fundamentally, the fact that the lyricized qualities of the originals can be suppressed under an ideology of *xin* faithfulness amounts to the assessment that traditional, regional prosody is a transient and disposable by-product of a poem, something that is not inextricably linked to its most important content. This matches cultural attitudes common after the May Fourth movement. Reformers in the early Republican era argued that traditional Chinese culture is premodern, and contemporary transnational culture is modern; old verse forms are vessels for weak, inhumane traditional culture, and new verse forms can produce healthy, empowered citizens. Instead of advocating for this transition, though, Bing Xin is producing an epistemological structure that ensures it. Bing Xin is quite clear, in her translator's preface, that the music of the Bengali *Gitanjali* and the "delicate poetic feeling" of the English version are both untranslatable, and have therefore been abandoned.[40] When Bing Xin claims that prose is "free," she means that it is free from convention and free from the past: it is free of the untranslatable and contingent music of tradition and locality. What poetry means is separable from that music, and can be rendered in prose.[41] This philosophy of translation is particular to her praxis, as we know that other translators draw different lines between the translatable and the untranslatable. For example, Bing Xin's contemporary, poet Bian Zhilin 卞之琳, explicitly claims that translating content without regard for metrical and musical "flavor" is not *xin* or faithful.[42] Her philosophy is also subtractive, in that objectivity is reached by the negation and elimination of successive subjectivities.[43]

Due to its impact on Chinese letters, though, it seems clear that the Chinese version of *Gitanjali* represented powerful, positive novelty for its readers. Although *xin* as a translation philosophy might have been subtractive, what resulted from it was something new. The subjectivities and particularities that remain in the poems become powerfully important: because *xin* promises the rendering of objective, core material across languages, the particular shape of the medium in which core material is expressed comes to be interpreted as an indivisible part of that material. This is visible in the way in which foreignness, and foreign linguistic structures, are rendered in Bing Xin's translation. Although Bing Xin eschews the recreation of archaic inversions and King James grammar, her version of *Gitanjali* does tend to reproduce vernacular English syntax.

For instance, in the first sentence of poem #3, above, she reproduces the English and Bengali clause order by putting *my master* after the rest of the sentence. Chinese, with its topic-comment heritage, more commonly would place the object of address before the sentence's main clause. Similarly, when Bing Xin translates ejaculatory particles like *ah* or *oh*, she inserts them into the position they hold in Tagore's English version, even when their position in Chinese would normally appear in a different part of the sentence.[44] None of these linguistic predilections is absolute, and modern Chinese sentences are flexible enough to accept multiple syntactical orders, but the effect is one of gentle alienation, the palpable sense of foreignness in the Chinese-language translations. This makes sense as a product of modernity and *xin* ideology: the transparent language that can render our objective reality is yet to be invented. It cannot be handed down from the ancients, because that would insinuate it had been used and then forgotten or rejected. The new objective forms must therefore have an alien or undiscovered quality to them, and this justifies the use of structures from unfamiliar languages, especially those that are considered more modern, more effective, or more flexible.[45]

Prose poetry today retains these ideologies, both in structure and spirit; a major vessel for their dissemination is imitation of Bing Xin's translation of Tagore. Unlike other genres, prose poetry never does entirely nativize into an unremarkably Chinese undertaking. While other types of short lyric prose take traditional Chinese names (*meiwen, sanwen, xiaopin*), and individual pieces are shunted from one genre to another by editors and publishers, prose poetry as a genre retains its otherness even down to its unwieldy three-character generic name *sanwenshi*. This matches, in a way, the implicit position the translations take with regard to the vernacular: they claim to reflect Chinese speech, and they do reflect it in some ways, but they also transform it. They do so by working from the assumption that classical Chinese idioms and structures are *not* vernacular—even though they make up a measurable part of daily Chinese speech—and that structures from foreign languages can and should be treated as vernaculars, even when they are archaic or affected.[46] These assumptions are an ideal ("we should have a language in which daily speech has no reference to premodern language or literature") expressed as the definition of an almost ontological category ("the vernacular is the language of actual use; it is the opposite of the classical and the traditional").

Interest in the vernacular is just one of the ways in which Bing Xin echoes Tagore's work, however; another centers around the concept of the *simple*. In her introduction to her translation of *Gitanjali*, Bing Xin says that Tagore has written the "most simple and most beautiful" of all Bengali poems, and claims that they are composed in "the people's own lively and simple language."[47] Later, she goes so far as to call Tagore "innocent" (*tianzhen,* 天真).[48] This attitude is reflected in her translations of his poetry, where she consistently opts for a Chinese rendition that can be read with ease. In English, *Gitanjali* #28 begins, "Obstinate are the trammels," which is translated as "羅網是堅韌的" ("the nets are resilient").[49] The difference between the two is more than the archaic and rarefied diction of the English; in the English version, there is a slight mismatch between *obstinate*, which generally refers to living beings, and *trammels*, which is an abstract noun, and as a result the juxtaposition defamiliarizes them both. In the corresponding Chinese version, the words *luowang* (羅網; "nets") and *jian-ren* (堅靭; "resilient") fit together more comfortably. What this increased simplicity and straightforwardness reinforces is one of the basic and often-imitated qualities of both the English and Chinese versions of *Gitanjali*: the constant and seemingly effortless motion from the most concrete language to the most abstract.

Consider the next poem, #29: "He whom I enclose with my name is weeping in the dungeon. I am ever busy building this wall all around; and as this wall goes up into the sky day by day I lose sight of my true being in its dark shadow."[50] Part of the appeal of the poem is that it invites the reader to visualize a familiar image, like a wall under construction whose shadow grows longer as it gets taller, and to see that image equated with nearly unimaginable abstractions. What is a "true being"? What is it to "enclose" someone with a "name"? To call these mysterious concatenations simple, as Bing Xin does, is to represent them as basic elements of experience, as if one was being asked to describe the contents of a drawer that contained a pen, a piece of paper, and eternal love. Song forms and elaborate diction bind the concrete and the abstract in language, they produce a new artificially literary occasion in which abstract and concrete experiences can coexist; to simplify that language, to boil it down even further toward the quotidian as Bing Xin does, is to intensify the reality of the abstract and equate it even more strongly with the concrete. Her translation of #29 therefore begins "被我用我的名字囚禁起來的那個人, 在監牢中哭泣" ("The person whom I have captured with my name weeps in prison").[51] In the Chinese, the sense of the fictive and imaginative is less strong: from the dramatic "dungeon" to the physical conundrum of "enclosure" to the literary diction of "he whom," the English version feels more like an invented maxim or parable rather than a realist description. Bing Xin's version in fact reinforces the poem's underlying juxtaposition of the tangible and the intangible, a practice that becomes crucially important to 1950s poets tasked with writing romantic realist art that is required to be both unremittingly ideological and wholly concrete.

The juxtaposition of the tangible and intangible in Bing Xin's translations is metonymic for the intervention into literary art and literary genre that her translations represent. Tagore's poems are intended to produce, among other things, material traces of the unspeakable divine; Bing Xin's translations attempt to produce a prose account or version of his work that faithfully retains some particular traces of his poetry, itself already transformed by a prior passage into prose. Her belief about what the original poetry does—and especially what can be retained across languages and styles—makes his poetry, his prose, and her prose *visible* as media, even at the moment when she claims that her translation is based in reproductive *xin* transparency. The first sentences of her introduction to her translation read: "This book *Gitanjali* is a poetry collection by the Indian poet Rabindranath Tagore. *Gitanjali* is an Indian word that means 'poems offered up.'"[52] Like the enclosure made from the human name in poem #29, the rendering of these poems into prose is a conundrum that defamiliarizes both prose and poetry. Even as the translation quietly claims the power of prose—that it can be used to render poetry—it also makes prose visible as a form in a way that contradicts assumptions about its ability to transparently render diverse experience without trans-formation or loss. If prose is the standard objective, why must we specify it or defend it? This moment of the defamiliarized visibility of prose as an instrument is vastly differ-ent from the way that Tagore produced the English *Gitanjali*, which retained musicality and orality, and did not make epistemological or categorical claims that the English versions were faithful to the Bengali originals. For Tagore, the two sets of works were related pieces, using slightly different techniques to pursue overlapping but measurably distinct goals.

Bing Xin's conundrum is also substantially different from the existence of an inde-pendent genre called *prose poetry* that is understood to mix qualities from each con-stituent genre; it is instead the uneasy claim that poetry has become prose, a claim that the finished work contains something central to poetry that can be and has been refined and then transported into other terms, other genres. The name *prose poetry* and the sense of a stable category that it provides prevent us from seeing the verbal, procedural negotiation with poetry by prose (and vice versa) in which Bing Xin's translation, and the prose poetry it influenced, engage. *Prose poetry* is often interpreted as designating simply a subcategory of poetry that uses prose methods;[53] such a definition is ill suited to carry the idea that an individual piece, like Bing Xin's *Gitanjali*, is directed outside its own genre, serving as a commentary on other types of poetry, or indeed other types of prose. This is evident in the fact that later works called *prose poetry* engage in multiple types of interventions and transformations both into poetry and into prose. There exist lyricizations and subjectifications of prose forms—for instance, the *Prose Poetry Newspaper* once advocated for and published a "reportage-style" prose poetry that borrowed its structure from the prose genre of reportage literature.[54] There are also poems that carry out Bing Xin's implication that prose more faithfully recreates real experience, and that poems about the realities of socialist life should be in prose. For example, the work of socialist-era prose poets features a great deal of detailed description of agriculture, industry, travel, and other quotidian events. Still other poems make similarly quotidian experiences seem, by the poetic manner of their description, highly lyrical and subjective, and tightly centered around the poem's speaker, as is true of a great deal of the prose poetry of Liu Zaifu.[55] We know that avant-garde, experimental, or even simply novel work inside a genre has the power to transform it. However, we rarely consider genres as projects whose force is directed outside their genre, and it is even rarer to conceptualize genre prac-tices as side effects of other literary practices like translation, even though we know that many genres—including the sonnet, the villanelle, and Chinese regulated verse—have transnational influences and roots.[56] To name a genre and draw a circle around certain works invariably entails breaking connections between those works and others to which they are related. As one moves back in time towards the genesis of a genre, the number of crucial interactions between works inside a genre and works outside a genre swells until it is difficult to say much with certainty about the genre's origins.

Prose poetry is an especially critical field of inquiry for the understanding of generic origins because it is so resolutely textual and modern. Its early history has practically no oral component, was rarely performed or read live, and has been elaborately documented. Rather than relying on records accumulated by later practitioners or viewers of the genre, we can observe and read influential works of the proto-genre as well. Reading before a genre's origin encourages us to historicize genre and visualize it not as a successful or failed ontological category, but as a bundled set of practices— among which acts of generic naming (announcing that one is writing in a genre, or being told that one is doing so) hold equal importance with compositional methodologies, ideological preferences, and the challenges of communication.[57] Other approaches arise because the language of genre as it is sometimes understood today participates in the same intellectual lineage of the objective modern that is implied by Bing Xin's belief in faithful translation: we assert, then test, then sometimes deny the possibility that there is a transparent metalanguage outside literary practice that can appropriately or reliably divide works into categories. To treat the question of genre in this way, regardless of the outcome of the debate, is to focus on particular qualities of literary pieces that serve to distinguish or connect groups of works with the expectation that these distinguishing factors will then be the crucial or central quality of writing in genres. When we instead rephrase the question to ask what people are *doing* when they claim to be reading or writing prose poetry, we begin a conversation that allows genres to overlap and affect one another, that allows them to speak and listen outside themselves in a historicized, contingent, contradictory way. This matches the contingencies and historical shifts we see in the corpus of modern and contemporary Chinese prose poetry.

Bing Xin's translation of *Gitanjali* rests precisely within the zone of exclusion generated by the tradition of genre studies. Because it is a translation, her work is not comfortably Chinese; because it is of a work from 1913, it is not comfortably contemporary; and because it accrues the qualities of prose poetry during the process of translation itself, it is hard to identify the book as a straightforward exemplar of the genre. And yet it is this work—by which I refer both to the poems of *Jitanjiali* as well as the work of translation that Bing Xin performed to produce them—that provoked contemporary Chinese prose poets and helped establish the contemporary genre. Critic Che Zhenxian 車鎮憲 elides the influence of translation, assuming the translations collapse into the originals, but is straightforward about its result: "Tagore's prose poetry created a deep and persistent influence among Chinese writers, particularly his praise-songs to life, nature, and love. Even more, his boiling passions, rich imagination, and profound philosophy directly forged generation after generation of Chinese poets and writers."[58] To envision genre as a category rather than a kind of performance would be to relegate these influences to an extrageneric, supplementary role; worse, it would prevent us from reading and understanding the intricate ideological and practical process that brought Tagore's original Bengali poems to the generative border of Chinese prose poetry, a process that powerfully colors the life of *Gitanjali* in Chinese letters. If we instead choose to understand prose poetry as a performance, Bing Xin's translations can rightly be seen as a crucial part of the vocabulary of gesture through which prose poetry addresses and transforms both poetry and prose.

Notes

1. Its first use in 1918 was a half-mistaken effort at translation by Liu Bannong. See Michel Hockx, *Questions of Style: Literary Societies and Literary Journals in Modern China, 1911–1937* (Leiden: Brill, 1993).

2. By *unrhymed verse*, I am referring to the way Guo Moruo 郭沫若 uses the phrase in his introduction to *The Sorrows of Young Werther*. See Kirk Denton, ed. *Modern Chinese Literary Thought: Writings on Literature, 1893–1945* (Stanford: Stanford University Press, 1996), 204–205. By *short stage-play*, I mean Lu Xun's "The Passer-By," in *Wild Grass*, trans. Gladys Yang and Yang Xianyi (Beijing: Waiwen chubanshe, 2000). A more comprehensive discussion of the early period of Chinese prose poetry and a rationale for its separation from later prose poetry appears in Nick Admussen, "Trading Metaphors: Chinese Prose Poetry and the Reperiodization of the Twentieth Century," *Modern Chinese Literature and Culture* 22.2 (Fall 2010): 88–129.

3. The newspaper was *Sanwenshi bao* 散文詩報 from Zhuhai, Guangdong. The magazines are *Sanwenshi* 散文詩 in Yiyang, Hunan, and *Sanwenshi de shijie* 散文詩的世界 in Chengdu, Sichuan. Two of the largest anthologies are Feng Yi 馮藝, ed., *Zhongguo sanwenshi daxi* 中國散文詩大系 [Compendium of Chinese prose poetry] (Nanning: Guangxi minzu chubanshe, 1992) and Wang Fuming 王幅明, ed., *Zhongguo sanwenshi jiushinian* 中國散文詩90年 (1918–2007) [Ninety years of prose poetry (1918–2007)] (Zhengzhou: Henan Wenyi Chubanshe, 2008), but there are also yearly "best of" compilations, as well as many individual anthologies. Single-author collections of the 1980s are too numerous to name.

4. Liu Zaifu 劉再復, *Yuanyou suiyue* 遠遊歲月 [My wandering years] (Hong Kong: Cosmos Books, 1994), 77.

5. Wolfgang Kubin, "Stray Birds: Tagore and the Genesis of Modern Chinese Poetry," *Asian and African Studies* 18.2 (2009): 43.

6. Ke Lan's visit to Bing Xin is mentioned in Zhongguo Sanwenshi Xuehui, eds., *Yongyuan de Ke Lan* 永遠的柯藍 [Ke Lan forever] (Guangzhou: Huacheng Chubanshe, 2007), 96. An example of Bing Xin's working relationship with Guo Feng appears in Bing Xin 冰心, *Bing Xin quanji* 冰心全集 [The complete works of Bing Xin], vol. 7 (Fujian: Haixia Wenyi Chubanshe, 1994), 63.

7. Admussen, "Trading Metaphors," 95.

8. She calls the pieces "poetry" in Bing Xin, *Complete Works*, vol. 4, 142. She calls them "prose poems" in 1983; see Bing Xin, *Complete Works*, vol. 7, 408.

9. For the interplay of these forms, see Charles Laughlin, *The Literature of Leisure and Chinese Modernity* (Honolulu: University of Hawai'i, 2008).

10. Bing Xin, *Complete Works*, vol. 4, 141.

11. Bing Xin, *Complete Works*, vol. 7, 407.

12. Rabindranath Tagore, *Song Offerings*, trans. Joe Winter (London: Anvil Press, 2000), 15–16.

13. See Amulyadhan Mukhopadhyay, *Studies in Rabindranath's Prosody and Bengali Prose-Verse* (Calcutta: Rabindra Bharatai University, 1999), 62–64. He argues that some poems in *Gitanjali* are in gently transposed Bengali meters and are fundamentally quantitative (counting phrase length rather than accentual patterns). He points out that these rhythms are rare in English, and perhaps this is why readers at the time remarked on the poems' beauty without analyzing their rhythm. This is borne out by searches for performances of the poems: those in Bengali are set to music, and those in English are generally read and

not sung—except when the English performances are by people from Bengal, in which case they are sometimes musical arrangements of the English poems.

14. Amit Chaudhuri, *On Tagore: Reading the Poet Today* (New Delhi: Penguin Group, 2012), 10–11.

15. Mary Ellis Gibson, *Indian Angles: English Verse in Colonial India from Jones to Tagore* (Athens: Ohio University Press, 2011), 255.

16. Rabindranath Tagore, *Talks in China* (Calcutta: Arunoday Art Press, n.d.), 66.

17. Rabindranath Tagore, *A Tagore Reader* (New York: Macmillan, 1961), 257.

18. Tagore, *Talks*, 68.

19. Bing Xin 冰心, "Xu" 序 [Preface], *Bing Xin zhuyi xuanji* 冰心著譯選集 [Selected writings and translations of Bing Xin], vol. 1. (Fujian: Haixia wenyi chubanshe, 1986), 1–2.

20. Lydia Liu, *Translingual Practice: Literature, National Culture, and Translated Modernity—China, 1900–1937* (Stanford: Stanford University Press, 1995), 3.

21. David L Gosling, *Science and the Indian Tradition: When Einstein Met Tagore* (New York: Routledge, 2007), 141.

22. Gosling, *Science and the Indian Tradition*, 162.

23. My particular understanding of the modern here comes in part from Eric Hayot, *On Literary Worlds* (Oxford: Oxford University Press, 2013), 115, where he typifies the modern period as the period in which the existence of a single, unitary, objective world was theorized, then reified. Tagore responded throughout his career to the assumption that such a modern world must be based on European ideas and cultures. His desire to valorize "Eastern" culture made him particularly popular in China; see Zheng Zhenduo's attitude in Stephen N. Hay, *Asian Ideas of East and West: Tagore and His Critics in Japan, China and India* (Cambridge: Harvard University Press, 1970), 193.

24. Chaudhuri, *On Tagore*, 36.

25. Chaudhuri, *On Tagore*, 8–9. It's also visible in the fact that the English *Gitanjali* is really a new kind of transnational writing, one that straddles languages and tradition in a way particular to modern Indian literature. Cf. Kubin, "Stray Birds," 42.

26. Bing Xin, *Complete Works*, vol. 7, 408.

27. Bing Xin 冰心, "Xu" 序 [Preface] *Bing Xin shiji* 冰心詩集 [Collected poems of Bing Xin] (Shanghai: Kaiming shudian, 1949), 9–10.

28. Bing Xin, *Selected Writings*, vol. 1, 543.

29. Bing Xin, *Selected Writings*, vol. 1, 544.

30. Bing Xin, *Selected Writings*, vol. 1, 33.

31. Rabindranath Tagore, *Gitanjali* (New York: Scribner, 1997), 120.

32. Bing Xin, *Selected Writings*, vol. 2, 205.

33. Tagore, *Song Offerings*, 49.

34. Mukhopadhyay, "The Rhythm of Bengali Prose," 45.

35. This particular form, which Mukhopadhyay calls rhymed blank verse, could also be read as a kind of iambic pentameter; for a discussion of Tagore's use and adaptation of Western meters and prosodic elements, including the sonnet, see Mukhopadhyay, "The Rhythm of Bengali Prose," 59–73. My warmest thanks to my colleague Sreemati Mukherjee for supplying much-needed expertise concerning the sounds of the Bengali original.

36. Tagore, *Gitanjali*, 19.

37. This rhythmic analysis is adapted from Mukhopadhyay, *Studies in Rabindranath's Prosody and Bengali Prose-Verse*, 62–64. The rest of poem #22 is loosely based on eight-syllable meters.

38. Chaudhuri, *On Tagore*, 88.

39. Bing Xin, *Complete Works*, vol. 4, 143.

40. Bing Xin, *Complete Works*, vol. 4, 142.

41. In a 1920 essay on translation, Bing Xin says that the target language of translation should be "common" (通俗) in order to be understood by the widest audience: this also asserts that literature is reducible, that nothing of particular value is lost by simply relating the content of a literary work. Bing Xin, "Yishu de wojian" 譯書的我見 [My views on translated books], *Yanda jikan* 燕大季刊 [Yanjing university quarterly] 1.3 (September 1920), n.p., accessed at http://www.bingxin.org/databank/zp/zw/ysd.htm.

42. Leo Tak-Hung Chan, ed. *Twentieth Century Chinese Translation Theory* (Philadelphia: John Benjamins, 2004), 75.

43. Ironically, this kind of thinking is also at play in the critical community's head-scratchingly insistent practice of reading and sometimes dismissing Bing Xin's prose exclusively through the lens of her gender. For a summary of this practice, see Wendy Larson, "The End of 'Funü Wenxue': Women's Literature from 1925 to 1935," *Modern Chinese Literature* 4.1/2 (Spring/Fall 1988): 46–47. To the critics Larsen describes, Bing Xin's femininity is figured as a supplement, a grease on the lens that tints her vision, and her gender must be suppressed in order for her to be a vessel for true realist fiction.

44. Examples appear in poems #9 and #39.

45. Lu Xun reflects this belief in a 1931 letter to Qu Qiubai: "Neither Chinese speech nor writing is precise enough in its manner of expression. . . . To cure this ailment, I believe we have to do it the hard way and seek to render thought in wayward syntactical structures. What is old and foreign (coming from other provinces, regions and countries) can finally be embraced as our own. . . . For an example, Europeanized syntax is most common in the writings of the Japanese. . . ." Collected in Chan, *Twentieth Century Chinese Translation Theory*, 159. This is notable not just because Lu Xun looks to Europe as a font of desirable linguistic qualities, but because it is *syntax* that he believes can make the desired change, rather than rhythm, diction, vocabulary, or any number of other linguistic qualities.

46. For the persistence of classical rhythm in modern Chinese, see Perry Link, *An Anatomy of Chinese: Rhythm, Metaphor, Politics* (Cambridge: Harvard University Press, 2013), 21–112.

47. Bing Xin, *Complete Works*, vol. 4, 141–142.

48. Bing Xin, *Complete Works*, vol. 7, 408.

49. Tagore, *Gitanjali*, 44; Bing Xin, *Complete Works*, vol. 4, 153.

50. Tagore, *Gitanjali*, 45.

51. Bing Xin, *Complete Works*, vol. 4, 153.

52. Bing Xin, *Complete Works*, vol. 4, 141.

53. Wang Guangming and Teng Gu, for example, both define prose poetry as "poems written using prose," or "用散文寫的詩." See Wang Guangming 王光明, *Sanwenshi de shijie* 散文詩的世界 [The world of prose poetry] (Wuhan: Changjiang wenyi chubanshe, 1987), 27–28.

54. See, for example, *Sanwenshi bao* 散文詩報 [Prose poetry newspaper] no. 10, 1987, n.p.

55. Liu Zaifu 劉再復, *Liu Zaifu sanwenshi heji* 劉再復散文詩合集 [A combined anthology of Liu Zaifu's prose poetry] (Beijing: Huaxia chubanshe, 1988).

56. For the latter, see Victor H. Mair and Tsu-lin Mei, "The Sanskrit Origins of Recent-Style Prosody," *Harvard Journal of Asiatic Studies* 51.2 (December 1991): 375–470.

57. Here I follow and adapt concepts from Ralph Cohen, "History and Genre," *New Literary History* 17.2 (Winter 1986): 203–218.

58. Che Zhenxian 車鎮憲, *Zhongguo xiandai sanwenshi de chansheng fazhan jiqi dui xiaoshuo de yingxiang* 中國現代散文詩的產生發展及其對小說文體的影響 [The development of modern Chinese prose poetry and its influence on fiction] (Beijing: Zuojia Chubanshe, 1999), 90–91.

Works Cited

Admussen, Nick. "Trading Metaphors: Chinese Prose Poetry and the Reperiodization of the Twentieth Century." *Modern Chinese Literature and Culture* 22.2 (Fall 2010): 88–129.

Bing Xin 冰心. *Bing Xin quanji* 冰心全集 [The complete works of Bing Xin], vol. 7. Fujian: Haixia wenyi chubanshe, 1994.

Bing Xin 冰心. *Bing Xin shiji* 冰心詩集 [Collected poems of Bing Xin]. Shanghai: Kaiming Shudian, 1949.

Bing Xin 冰心. *Bing Xin zhuyi xuanji* 冰心著譯選集 [Selected writings and translations of Bing Xin]. Fujian: Haixia wenyi chubanshe, 1986.

Bing Xin 冰心. "Yishu de wojian" 譯書的我見 [My views on translated books], *Yanda jikan* 燕大季刊 [Yanjing University quarterly] 1.3 (September 1920) [n.p.], accessed at http://www.bingxin.org/databank/zp/zw/ysd.htm.

Chan, Leo Tak-Hung, ed. *Twentieth Century Chinese Translation Theory*. Philadelphia: John Benjamins, 2004.

Chaudhuri, Amit. *On Tagore: Reading the Poet Today*. New Delhi: Penguin Group, 2012.

Che Zhenxian 車鎮憲. *Zhongguo xiandai sanwenshi de chansheng fazhan jiqi dui xiaoshuo de yingxiang* 中國現代散文詩的產生發展及其對小說文體的影響 [The development of modern Chinese prose poetry and its influence on fiction]. Beijing: Zuojia Chubanshe, 1999.

Cohen, Ralph. "History and Genre." *New Literary History* 17.2 (Winter 1986): 203–218.

Denton, Kirk, ed. *Modern Chinese Literary Thought: Writings on Literature, 1893–1945*. Stanford: Stanford University Press, 1996.

Feng Yi 馮藝, ed. *Zhongguo sanwenshi daxi* 中國散文詩大系 [Compendium of Chinese prose poetry]. Nanning: Guangxi minzu chubanshe, 1992.

Gibson, Mary Ellis. *Indian Angles: English Verse in Colonial India from Jones to Tagore*. Athens: Ohio University Press, 2011.

Gosling, David L. *Science and the Indian Tradition: When Einstein Met Tagore*. New York: Routledge, 2007.

Hay, Stephen N. *Asian Ideas of East and West: Tagore and His Critics in Japan, China and India*. Cambridge: Harvard University Press, 1970.

Hayot, Eric. *On Literary Worlds*. Oxford: Oxford University Press, 2013.

Hockx, Michel. *Questions of Style: Literary Societies and Literary Journals in Modern China, 1911–1937*. Leiden: Brill, 1993.

Kubin, Wolfgang. "Stray Birds: Tagore and the Genesis of Modern Chinese Poetry." *Asian and African Studies* 18.2 (2009): 40–50.

Larson, Wendy. "The End of 'Funü Wenxue': Women's Literature from 1925 to 1935." *Modern Chinese Literature* 4.1/2 (Spring/Fall 1988): 46–47.

Laughlin, Charles. *The Literature of Leisure and Chinese Modernity*. Honolulu: University of Hawai'i, 2008.

Link, Perry. *An Anatomy of Chinese: Rhythm, Metaphor, Politics*. Cambridge: Harvard University Press, 2013.

Liu, Lydia. *Translingual Practice: Literature, National Culture, and Translated Modernity—China, 1900–1937*. Stanford: Stanford University Press, 1995.

Liu Zaifu 劉再復. *Liu Zaifu sanwenshi heji* 劉再復散文詩合集 [A combined anthology of Liu Zaifu's prose poetry]. Beijing: Huaxia chubanshe, 1988.

Liu Zaifu 劉再復. *Yuanyou suiyue* 遠遊歲月 [My wandering years]. Hong Kong: Cosmos Books, 1994.

Lu Xun. *Wild Grass*, trans. Gladys Yang and Yang Xianyi. Beijing: Waiwen chubanshe, 2000.

Mair, Victor H., and Tsu-lin Mei. "The Sanskrit Origins of Recent-Style Prosody." *Harvard Journal of Asiatic Studies* 51.2 (December 1991): 375–470.

Mukhopadhyay, Amulyadhan. *Studies in Rabindranath's Prosody and Bengali Prose-Verse*. Calcutta: Rabindra Bharati University, 1999.

Tagore, Rabindranath. *Gitanjali*. New York: Scribner, 1997.

Tagore, Rabindranath. *Song Offerings*. Trans. Joe Winter. London: Anvil Press, 2000.

Tagore, Rabindranath. *A Tagore Reader*. New York: Macmillan, 1961.

Tagore, Rabindranath. *Talks in China*. Calcutta: Arunoday Art Press, n.d.

Wang Guangming 王光明. *Sanwenshi de shijie* 散文詩的世界 [The world of prose poetry]. Wuhan: Changjiang Wenyi Chubanshe, 1987.

Zhongguo Sanwenshi Xuehui 中國散文詩學會, eds. *Yongyuan de Ke Lan* 永遠的柯藍 [Ke Lan forever]. Guangzhou: Huacheng Chubanshe, 2007.

PART III

METHODOLOGY

....

CHINESE LITERARY THOUGHT IN MODERN TIMES

Three Encounters

....

DAVID DER-WEI WANG

> Judging by the goings-on of the contemporary intellectual circle, we have
> been used to selecting Chinese subjects [for literary study] in terms of
> Western concepts. For good or ill, this has become an inevitable tendency.[1]

THUS Zhu Ziqing 朱自清 (1898–1948) wrote in his review of Guo Shaoyu's 郭紹虞
(1893–1984) *The History of Chinese Literary Criticism, Volume 1* (中國文學批評史
上卷). Neither Guo Shaoyu's nor Zhu Ziqing's scholarship draws much attention any
more. But Zhu's remarks regarding Western impacts on Chinese literary studies bear
an uncanny relevance to our field today, because, more than ever before, "we have been
used to selecting Chinese subjects [for literary study] in terms of Western concepts."

"Theory" has become an integral part of modern Chinese literary and cultural studies since the last decades of the twentieth century, such that we have taken it for granted
that we may conduct research with recourse to theories ranging from New Criticism to
deconstruction, and from psychoanalysis to Marxism.[2] Theory has changed the paradigm of contemporary Chinese literary studies, bringing a methodological rigor and
critical vision neither Zhu Ziqing nor Guo Shaoyu could have imagined in their day.
Meanwhile, theory has generated no less discontent when it betrays its assumption of
universal applicability or hegemonic, Orientalist claims.

To be clear, I do not object to the theoretical underpinning of modern Chinese literary and cultural studies. Quite the contrary, echoing Zhu Ziqing's observation, I contend that the field of modern Chinese literature and literary studies presupposes the
implementation of "Western concepts" and theoretical engagements. It will be recalled
that "literature" as we understand it today was not made into a curricular subject in
the humanities program until 1902, after the Japanese and German models, and that

"modern literature" did not become a discipline till the late 1920s, as a result of the contestation between indigenous and foreign discourses.

What I am proposing is that we should seek to reengage theory, enacting "the mobility of ideas across time and space, which draws attention to the ways in which contexts both transform and are transformed by its movement."[3] I argue that the "mobility" of theory inherent in the current theoretical paradigm has not taken us far enough in exploring new terrains. This is where Zhu Ziqing, Guo Shaoyu, and many other scholars of their time may still have something to teach us. Contrary to the conventional perception that the May Fourth era was a period of total antitraditionalism, intellectuals at the time appeared to have been radical comparativists when analyzing modern, foreign importations as well as traditional legacies. For example, his indebtedness to Nietzsche and Stirner aside, Lu Xun 魯迅 expresses his modernist angst by revisiting the abysmal pathos of both Qu Yuan 屈原 (340–278 BC) and Tao Qian 陶潛 (395–427).[4] Wang Guowei 王國維 (1877–1927) strives to cope with his existential crisis in terms of not only Kant's and Schopenhauer's philosophy but also the "mental vista" (*jingjie* 境界) originating with Buddhist thought. In the leftist camp, where Qu Qiubai 瞿秋白 (1899–1935) demonstrated a strong penchant for lyricism traceable to the *Classic of Poetry* (詩經) despite his commitment to Lunacharsky and Plekhanov, Hu Feng's 胡風 (1902–1985) avant-garde "subjective fighting spirit" (主觀的戰鬥精神) is said to carry the imprint of both the Mencian thought of the Mind and György Lukács's Hegelian/Marxian revolutionism.

I describe these Chinese intellectuals' critical dialogics in terms of *wenlun* (文論), which I translate as *literary thought*, following critics such as Marián Gálik, Stephen Owen, and Kirk Denton.[5] As Stephen Owen observes, *literary thought* refers to "a group of diverse texts, which in turn belong to distinct genres," which tries to "explain the role literature plays in [a] civilization and to describe literature and literary works in terms that have resonance in other areas of intellectual and social life."[6] Unlike literary theory (as used in this chapter), which assumes more rigorous rules of intellectual exercise and rhetorical protocol, literary thought instead finds its articulation contingent on various occasions and cultural and intellectual reverberations.

To be sure, the phrase *literary thought* has its limitations. With its lofty connotation, it does not fully account for the social occasions and material conditions that inform the exercise of the writings under discussion, nor does it speak to the generic hybridity and historical contingency underlying these writings. Still, my point is that, despite the rise of Western-style literary discourse after the May Fourth era, literary thought continued to play a significant role in modern China, affecting "the author, text, world, reader nexus," in the form of "letters, prefaces, speeches . . . polemical essays,"[7] as well as fictitional creations.

I propose that we triangulate the paradigm of modern Chinese literary and cultural studies by bringing literary thought to bear on theoretical engagement on one hand and textual studies on the other. Above all, the tradition of Chinese literary thought has taught us that, insofar as *wen* (文) means pattern, sign, demeanor, artistic inscription, and cultural upbringing, *wenxue* (文學), or "literature," is an art of registering, and being registered by, the incessant metamorphosis of forms, thoughts, and attitudes over times and spaces. To that end, I introduce in the following three cases for discussion, each of which touches on a key concept of Chinese literary thought—the dictum of *shi yan zhi* (詩言志; "poetry is that which expresses what is intently on the mind"), the trope of *xing* (興; "affective evocation"), and the dialogic of *shishi* (詩史; "poetry as history")—while speaking to issues that concern contemporary theory. Needless to say, in the given scope of this chapter, my discussion will be preliminary, and my purpose lies in raising questions for further inquiries.

SHI (詩) AND ITS NEGATIVE DIALECTIC

In February and March of 1908, an essay titled "The Power of Mara Poetry" (摩羅詩力說) and published under the name Lingfei 令飛 appeared serially in *Henan* (河南), an overseas Chinese student magazine based in Tokyo. The essay deplored the degenerate condition of China and called for a "spiritual warrior" who would be able to "disturb people's minds," and who was said to be best embodied by a poet. The essay's author identified Qu Yuan, the legendary Chinese poet who allegedly wrote *Songs of the South* (楚辭), as the paragon for "giving voice to what his forebears feared to say."[8] Still, influenced by Nietzsche and Stirner, he considered that Qu Yuan's poetic defiance was weak. By contrast, for Lingfei, Lord Byron, with his recalcitrant passion and heroic deeds, personifies the true model of the modern poet, the Mara Poet.

Lingfei was the pen name of Zhou Shuren 周樹人 (1881–1936), who later came to be known as Lu Xun 魯迅 and is celebrated as the founding father of modern Chinese literature. Seeing China as emaciated by feudalistic traditions and ossified thoughts, Lu Xun considered poetry, and by extension, literature, the desired form of agency with which to enliven Chinese humanity and therefore elevate its capacity to engage the modern world:

> Every mind harbors poetry; the poet makes the poem, but it is not his alone, for once it is read the mind will grasp it . . . and all things animate raise their heads as though witness to dawn, giving scope to its beauty, force, and nobility.[9]

Lu Xun's call for a new literature as the way to reinvigorate China resonated with many other reform-minded intellectuals of his time. Liang Qichao 梁啟超, a forerunner of late Qing political reform, proclaimed that Chinese modernization hinged on "poetry revolution" as early as 1899. While these intellectuals were pursuing radical change in China, the way they conceptualized the symbiotic relationship between political and literary reforms suggests a traditional connection. Although the young Lu Xun hailed Byron as the model "spiritual warrior" for Chinese to emulate, he nevertheless couched his argument in terms strongly reminiscent of the canon of *shijiao* (詩教), or "cultivation through poetry." Poetry in premodern China meant not just a literary genre but rather a cultural repository, one that informs all values, from interpersonal articulation to political protocol, from affective expression to epistemological contemplation. Arguably the most famous statement about the nature of poetry, the "Great Preface to the *Classic of Poetry*" (詩大序), contends:

> The poem is that to which what is intently on the mind (*zhi* 志) goes. In the mind (*xin* 心) it is "being intent" (*zhi* 志); coming out in language (*yan* 言), it is a poem. . . . The affections (*qing* 情) are stirred within and take on form (*xing* 形) in words (*yan*). If words alone are inadequate, we speak them out in sighs. If sighing is inadequate, we sing them. If singing them is inadequate, unconsciously our hands dance them and our feet tap them.[10]

Lu Xun's provocation subverts as much as it sustains the validity of such a statement. He called attention to the poet's "Satanic power" to transgress and demolish the status quo, thus giving his poetic vision a negative, even demonic, thrust. Lu Xun likened such a demonic power to that of Mara, the fiendish deity of the Sanskrit tradition, the Devil. With its exotic, mysterious origin and its capacity for total negation, the naming of Mara cuts against the grain of what one can associate with Chinese poetic culture in general and poetic subjectivity in particular. More importantly, time-honored concepts such as *zhi* and *qing* are not denigrated in toto, as one might have expected. Instead, they are called on to serve a purpose completely out of tune with the exegetic tradition. Thus with regard to the dictum that poetry cultivates *zhi* and *qing*, teaching one "not to stray" (*siwuxie* 思無邪), Lu Xun retorts, if poetry is supposed to "express one's free will," "to force one not to stray [in composing poetry] is to curb one's free will. How can there be a promise of liberty under whips and halters?"[11]

Lu Xun's radical hermeneutics strikes us in that it brings novel ideas to engage the tradition, only to bring about its own implosion. In this regard, his counterpart is none other than Liang Qichao, who promoted fiction, a genre traditionally associated with uncultivated tastes, as the most powerful avenue for political reform. In this proposal, for which Liang claims he found inspiration in Japan and the West, Liang paradoxically suggests that fiction is simultaneously a genre that has poisoned Chinese society for centuries, but is also that which may serve as a miraculous potion to cure the contemporary ills of that same society.

It will be remembered that Plato drove poets out of the Republic for fear that their works would weaken the morale of the citizens of his ideal state. In the case of early modern Chinese critics, a similar argument leads to a rather different conclusion. Lu Xun welcomes Mara to help transform traditional poetry, in the hope that the devilish utterance can give rise to a robust Chinese sound. Liang Qichao celebrates poisonous fiction, asserting that its incredible power will first cleanse it of its own poisonous nature and then be administered to revive the audience it had earlier poisoned. Both seem to function as examples of the Derridian notion of the *pharmakon*, but a more pertinent association is perhaps the old Chinese medical concept of *yidu gongdu* (以毒攻毒; "using a poison to cure a poison").[12] Regardless, one must observe the negative dialectics arising from their treatises and contemplate its impact on modern Chinese literary discourse, and the aporia arising therefrom.

The year 1908 did not witness only the advent of the Mara Poet. In November, Wang Guowei published his *Remarks on Song Lyrics and the Human Condition* (人間詞話). Having consummated his passion for Western philosophers from Kant to Schopenhauer, Wang seeks to resuscitate in his work both the format and argument of Chinese poetics, along the lines of lyrical evocation as represented by Yan Yu 嚴羽 (1191–1241), Wang Fuzhi 王夫之 (1619–1692), and Wang Shizhen 王世禎 (1634–1711). Nevertheless, despite his effort to recapitulate premodern poetics, the way Wang Guowei engages with notions such as subjectivity and objectivity, idealism and realism, indicates his eclecticism in light of Western aesthetics. At his most polemical, Wang Guowei invoked Nietzsche's dictum "the best literature is that which is written in blood" as his criterion for evaluating song lyrics.[13]

Wang Guowei's pursuit results in his own theory of a "mental vista" (*jingjie* 境界), a state of awakening that is prompted by, but not limited to, the experience of poetic composition. This "mental vista" is subjective and aesthetically evocative, but it also resonates with the "arch-lyrical occasion" in literature as in history. Although carrying Buddhist connotations, *mental vista* registers Wang's idiosyncratic reflection on history. Having witnessed a succession of political crises in the Qing, Wang was haunted by a pessimistic outlook on Chinese civilization, such that he took *ci*—the song lyric, a unique genre of Chinese poetry known for its delicate mood and exquisite imagery—as not a confirmation of but a farewell to his cherished cultural legacy.

According to Wang, precisely because of their immersion in a most delicate form of poetry, *ci* poets are more sensitive than their poetic peers to the threat of cultural vandalism in a time of brutal reforms and spurious modernization. Wang's work unfailingly conveys an elegiac intent, which, together with his exquisite linguistic performance, evokes the tension of self-indulgence and self-denial—perhaps the "modern" malaise of exhausted melancholia.

The virtual dialogue between Lu Xun and Wang Guowei makes 1908 a year of much significance for the fashioning of modern Chinese literary thought in modern times. Critics have described Lu Xun and Wang Guowei in antagonistic terms, such as formalist aesthetics versus volitional articulation, or cultural nostalgia versus revolutionary yearning. This contrastive reading is an oversimplification. Both Lu Xun and Wang Guowei, each in his own way, were seeking to answer the question how a poetic subjectivity can help illuminate historical circumstances. Whereas Lu Xun's Mara Poet strikes with his fiendishly seductive power to provoke and destroy, Wang Guowei's melancholy song lyricist doggedly seeks a mindscape through which to reconcile poetic sentiment and historical contingency. Both brought Western discourse to bear on the Chinese context, and both pondered the tenability of their agendas vis-à-vis a time which appeared anything but poetic.

Of the two, Lu Xun has no doubt commanded more attention thanks to the moral urgency and polemical intensity of his treatise. His Mara Poet would undergo multiple incarnations in the early modern period, from the romantic iconoclast of the May

Fourth era to the leftist warrior during the revolutionary era. Lu Xun passed away in October of 1936, and was quickly deified by Mao Zedong and his propagandists; meanwhile, his Mara Poet assumed, as it were, a new identity, becoming either a righteous Communist Party cadre-writer or a Maoist fanatic. It may not be an exaggeration to say that the cult of Mara-turned-Mao culminated in the Cultural Revolution, when the whole nation was bedeviled by an anarchist craze and defiant impulse—a poetic and political carnival of the most dangerous kind.

It would take a few more decades for us to reappreciate the fact that Lu Xun was never a naive instigator of revolution, and that his Mara Poet proved Janus-faced from the outset. True, Lu Xun sought to upset traditional literature by having recourse to Mara's "devilish voice," but he was always wary of the ominous potential inherent in this voice. Such an awareness led him to engage not only with social and political evils but also with the "stratagem of unnamable entities" (無物之陣)—the amorphous existence of nihilism—permeating the world as well as his own mind. As he makes his poetic subjectivity a self-cannibalistic corpse in "Epitaph" ("Mujiewen" [墓碣文]; 1925), Lu Xun provides a polemic of poetic subjectivity against itself:

> I tore out my heart to eat it, wanting to know the true taste. But the pain was so agonizing, how could I tell its taste? . . .
> When the pain subsided, I savored the heart slowly. But since by then it was stale, how could I know its true taste?[14]

Not unlike Lu Xun, Wang Guowei underwent his own trial in deliberating the function of literature and the poet's role in modern times. He ended up consumed by the melancholy bent of his ideal song lyricist. On June 2, 1927, Wang drowned himself in a pond of the Imperial Garden in Beijing. His brief will states: "After fifty years of living in this world, the only thing yet to happen to me is death; having been through such historical turmoil, nothing further can stain my integrity."[15]

Wang's death has been attributed to, among other causes, domestic and psychological turbulence, his immersion in Schopenhauer's philosophy, and his eschatological vision. Above all, as a political conservative, Wang is said to have ended his life out of loyalism to the Qing. However, Chen Yinke 陳寅恪 (1890–1969), Wang's friend and a renowned historian, describes his drowning as consummating "the thought of freedom, and the spirit of independence."[16] To take Chen's point one step further, one may argue that Wang's "freedom" and "independence" make sense not as a political belief but as a poetic pursuit, a "mental vista," as he discusses in *Remarks on Song Lyrics and the Human Condition*. For at the beginning of the Chinese modern age, Wang had already discerned the modern as something more than the staged realization of enlightenment and revolution. Faced with the drastic incompatibilities between public and private claims, he asserted his freedom and independence negatively, in a willful act of self-annihilation. Thus his suicide paradoxically testified to the emergence of a new, post-traditional Chinese subjectivity.

XING (興): FROM EVOCATION
TO REVOLUTION

In the vocabulary of premodern Chinese poetics, *xing* is arguably the concept that has drawn the most attention. Etymologically, *xing* refers to a range of affective responses such as, among others, being evocative, creative, uplifting, and jubilant. The word *xing* is said to be derived from the practice of mood related to the rituals of divination in ancient times; it became associated with the motivation of literary creativity in classics such as *The Analects* (論語) and *The Rites of Zhou* (周禮). Confucius is said to have recommend *xing* as the primary virtue of learning poetry, followed by *guan* (觀; "contemplation/observation"), *qun* (群; "collectivity"), and *yuan* (怨; "expression of dissent and pathos").[17] *Xing* is supposed to be channeled through poetry so as to attain the state of "benevolence" (*ren* 仁).

Critics have pointed out how *xing* has given rise to a literary culture that is substantially different from its Western counterpart. In contrast with the Western discourse of mimesis, which is derived from the dialectic of representation, *xing*, as Owen explains, is "an image whose primary function is not signification but, rather, the stirring of a particular affection or mood: [*xing*] does not 'refer to' that mood; it generates it."[18] *Xing* continuously drew intellectual attention among both modernists and traditionalists in the modern age. In 1934, Liang Zongdai 梁宗岱 (1903–1983) published a collection of essays titled *Xiangzheng zhuyi* (象徵主義; "symbolism"), arguably the first serious theoretical engagement with Symbolist poetry. Trained in France, Liang was an admirer of Baudelaire and Mallarmé; he was particularly known for his apprenticeship with Paul Valéry. For Liang, poetry is the most exquisite configuration of language, sound, and imagery, free of all objective references to scenes, narrative, reasoning, and sentiments. With Valéry as his example, he passionately proposes that poetry is a "pure form, and that pure poetry is nothing but a 'poeticization of the soul as it is.'"[19]

The search for a pure form of poetry—especially in the spirit of French symbolism—had been a significant trend since the early twenties. What makes Liang Zongdai's poetics peculiar is the way he juxtaposes symbolism and traditional Chinese poetics, making some of the most provocative statements regarding Chinese-Western comparative literature in the early days of that field. Liang makes a bold observation by likening symbolism to *xing*, as evinced in the *Classic of Poetry*. Referring to the definition in *The Literary Mind and the Carving of Dragons* (文心雕龍), "*Xing* rouses . . . that which rouses the affections depends on something subtle for the sake of reflective consideration,"[20] Liang contends that "by 'something minute' [*wei* 微], [*xing*] intimates the subtle relationship between two things which may look irrelevant to each other on the surface yet can be mutually implicated. Feeling can be generated by 'referring to something minute and subtle that evokes the associative consideration of the other.'"[21] Through the resonance between the poetic mind and things in the world,

Liang calls forth the "visionary state" (*lingjing* 靈境), which he contends is not unlike the Baudelairean "correspondence."[22]

At almost the same time, Wen Yiduo 聞一多 (1899–1946) took a different approach to understanding this same concept of *xing*. Like Liang Zongdai, Wen considers *xing* a vibrant, creative thrust that motivates the beginning of the (cosmic, natural, human, and poetic) world. But they part ways in identifying the source of the "creative thrust." Whereas Liang aligns *xing* with the ever-generative power of lyric consciousness, Wen finds in it the primordial demonstration of social bonds. Inspired by modern disciplines such as anthropology, mythological studies, and social psychology, Wen argues that *xing* functioned as not a mysterious source of affection but a tangible "structure of feeling," to use Raymond Williams's terminology, informed by the conceptual framework, value system, and behavioral pattern of a society. Intriguingly enough, Wen Yiduo also invoked the concepts of *symbol* and *symbolism* as a way to explain the transitive power of *xing*. For him, *xing* points to the encryption and sedimentation of the collective (un-)conscious in the face of natural and social stimuli and challenges. While *xing* finds its demonstration in ritualistic practices, it calls for a more subtle semiotic system through which to sustain its transitive power. Wen calls such a process *xiangzheng shouyan* (象徵瘦言; "using symbols or puns"). That is, by evoking an image, a scene, a poetic trope, or a historical circumstance, *xing* presents itself like an esoteric password through which the latent knowledge of a society surfaces and the hidden "structure of feeling" becomes intelligible. As such, *xing* becomes a politically charged rhetorical game, ever pointing to the return of that which is being repressed, and oppressed, in a society.

We can now better see the tension between Liang Zongdai and Wen Yiduo in thinking of *xing* and symbolism. By reassessing *xing* in terms of symbolism, Liang tries to bring Chinese poetics up to date, and his goal is to tease out the quintessential element of modern Chinese sensibility which he believed had been plagued by social agitations and callousness. On the other hand, the way Wen Yiduo juxtaposes *xing* with symbol refers not to an immanent trope, as is the case of Liang Zongdai, but a linguistic artifice with which to negotiate the totem and taboo of a society. Wen thus endows his *xing* with a communitarian implication unavailable in Liang's treatise. At its most political, Wen's endeavor amounts to nothing less than calling forth an "imagined community" of its own kind. This imagined community relies on not the geopolitical spread of print capitalism, as Benedict Anderson would have it, but the mythopoetic retrieval of totemism.

Nevertheless, if one reads Liang's and Wen's works more carefully, one finds that they were both advancing a project involving how to broach Chinese modernity. At a time when China was seen, and felt, as trapped in a continuum of crises, it may not be a coincidence for the two modernists to find in *xing* a "symbol" with which to elucidate the murky status quo. Etymologically, *xing* means to create from naught something affectively uplifting. Thus, whereas Liang Zongdai yearned for a "visionary state," Wen Yiduo sought to develop his own genealogy of Chinese civilization. As discussed above, however, *xing* in traditional Chinese literary thought lies outside the Western scope of metaphor. Liang was attracted to the formal intricacy and semantic obscurity in both *xing* and symbol,[23] but he overlooked the factor that *xing* "is not how a word is 'carried over' from its 'proper' sense to a new one, but rather how the presentation of some phenomenon . . . in words is mysteriously able to stir . . . a response or evoke a mood."[24] Likewise, Wen's discovery in *xing* of the embryonic form of Chinese civilization risks streamlining that which is supposed to be evocative rather than anthropologically verifiable. Insofar as both Liang and Wen were poets in their own right, perhaps their projects bespoke as much their poetic conjuration as their academic pursuit: through *xing*, they were searching for—or even inventing—a "secret password" to the "visionary state" of modern China.

It was not only in the hands of the modernists that *xing* underwent a redefinition; the concept also took a more radical dimension when traditionalists strove to reinterpret it. For instance, Ma Yifu 馬一浮 (1883–1967) and Hu Lancheng 胡蘭成 (1906–1981) each developed a theory of *xing* during the Second Sino-Japanese War and the Chinese Civil War, respectively. Ma was one of the most respected neo-Confucianists in the Republican era, while Hu was a flamboyant literatus-turned-collaborator during wartime. In particular, Hu was notorious for his clandestine marriage with Eileen Chang 張愛玲 (1920–1995), the most talented woman writer in twentieth-century China. Although Ma and Hu could not have been further apart in background, upbringing, and intellectual inclination, they nevertheless both found in *xing* a way through which to confront the challenges befalling modern China.

Ma Yifu joined the exodus to the hinterland after the Second Sino-Japanese War broke out, vowing to carry on Confucian teaching and learning regardless of the atrocious circumstances. The two Confucian virtues he strove to promote were *xing* and *ren*. Whereas *xing* emotes feeling through poetic evocation, bringing the pristine vitality of life force back to the world, *ren* facilitates the substance of such a pursuit, offering the goal of the harmonious union of heaven and humanity. Ma's agenda is best summarized by his poetic couplet:

> Although the world is engulfed in battles,
> My heart remains attached to the rite and music.
> 天下雖干戈, 吾心仍禮樂 [25]

To withstand cultural vandalism and spiritual bankruptcy, Ma calls for restoring the Six Arts (*liuyi* 六藝, namely rites, music, archery, charioteering, calligraphy, and mathematics) of ancient China. Moreover, he considers history as nothing but a repository of feeling, crystallized by poetry. By yoking the metaphorical and metaphysical claims of poetry, Ma imagines a "history" that transcends temporalities at the evocation of *xing*. In sharp contrast with the prevalent calls to arms, Ma found hope for China in a total aestheticization of politics and history.[26]

Although Ma Yifu's promotion of *xing* appeared to be the opposite of the revolutionary discourse of his time, it touches on a mythopoetic dimension that may equally serve as the motivation of revolution. Such a call for *xing* in relation to revolution found its most peculiar manifestation in Hu Lancheng's work. Hu maintained close ties to the neo-Confucianists throughout his career, and he allegedly admired Ma the most.[27] In Hu's exegesis, *xing* is further radicalized in the direction of mysticism. As a force of genesis or creation, *xing* suggests neither divine will nor human artifice; it is said to arise where the somatic and the semiotic, the natural and the figurative, meet. The ultimate realization of *xing* in history is none other than revolution.

Take for example Hu's *China Through Time* (山河歲月; 1954). By upholding the inventive, spontaneous force of *xing*, Hu challenges the linear progression of time and the master narrative of telos that characterize traditional historiography. He ascribes the agency of *xing* to popular society, as opposed to the ruling class and elite that dominated traditional history. He contends that it is the commoners who lend each historical moment a lively form, which is best represented by folksongs, popular customs, and local festivities in accordance with the seasonal cycle (*jie* 節). The popular form is not always associated with peaceful everyday life, however. *Xing* is also said to be an impulse among the people for drastic change whenever life becomes unbearable; hence the eruption of popular uprisings.

With elements such as poetic creativity, folk culture, and popular uprising well integrated into his vision, Hu Lancheng is ready to move on to discuss the meaning of modernity. He argues that China has been faced with an unprecedented crisis since the advent of Western civilization after the Opium War, a fact that makes recalling *xing* poetics-cum-politics all the more urgent. For Hu, the modern incarnation of *xing* is revolution: "The essence of Chinese revolution is *xing*."[28] Revolution is both a military undertaking *and* a festive celebration; it is even said to have given rise to the "jubilant air and exciting mood."[29]

Insofar as Hu Lancheng associates *xing* with the festive and revolutionary impulse of popular society, his treatise, particularly the part on the politics of local theaters and festivities, may remind us of Mikhail Bakhtin's (1895–1975) theorization of the carnival.[30] To be sure, Bakhtin was working in a different political environment—the Stalinist regime in the 1940s—and his intellectual training was completely different from Hu's. Critics have discussed the ambivalent undercurrent of Bakhtin's carnival: it is framed by a preordained calendar and spatial terrain, and therefore susceptible to authoritarian containment; on the other hand, it always entertains an impulse for excess that may lead to a violent denial of *any* kind of order. By contrast, Hu Lancheng's Chinese festivity may initially appear much more benign, if only because it lacks the kind of Dionysian urge inherent in the Bakhtinian paradigm. Bakhtin proposes an organic cycle of degeneration and rebirth, a bodily principle that defies abstractions, and a sphere of polyphony.[31] Hu Lancheng plays out the antithesis of such a model. Hu's festivity aims at transcending time and body in the name of *xing*; instead of polyphony, unison rules. Above all, Hu intended his revolutionary festivity to be not a deviation from but a return to the desired orthodoxy: the Sage Kingship.

In the final analysis, Hu's *xing* discourse harbors a menacing agenda, in that he makes violence an integral ingredient in his lyrical take on popular society. Before the Sage Kingship is restored, military measures must be on call, while violence and atrocity are virtually guaranteed as given. Accordingly, Hu cannot avoid the fact that his vision of *xing* tacitly reaffirms the brutal conditions of history even as it seeks to evade or transcend them. Indeed, it is little surprise he should suggest: "Even if Mao Zedong and his cohorts have killed millions of people, I won't blink my eyes for a moment. It is the way of the human not to kill the innocent; but it is the Way of Heaven to kill the innocent. I cannot be more benevolent than Mao Zedong."[32]

SHISHI (詩史) AND POESIS
IN THE AFTERMATH OF HISTORY

In December of 1938, Feng Zhi 馮至 (1905–1993) and his family arrived in Kunming, Yunnan, after a long journey to flee the Japanese invasion. Before the outbreak of the Second Sino-Japanese War the year before, Feng had already enjoyed a reputation as both "the best lyricist of modern China," in Lu Xun's words, and a first-rate scholar of German literature, including Goethe and Rilke. But Feng Zhi found his kindred spirit in Du Fu 杜甫, "the sage of Chinese poetry." Feng Zhi had quoted Du Fu's line "Standing alone in desolation, I sing poems all by myself" (獨立蒼茫自詠詩) as the epigraph of his collection *Northern Journey* (北遊; 1929).[33] But it was the hardship of the westward journey to the hinterland that made him truly understand the suffering Du Fu underwent during the An Lushan Rebellion (755–763). Feng wrote the following quatrain:

> While a refugee with my wife and daughter,
> I finally realize the truthfulness of Du Fu's every word;
> Unable to appreciate the blood and tears permeating his poems,
> I had led a deluded life over a peaceful decade.[34]

> 攜妻抱女流離日,
> 始信少陵字字真;
> 未解詩中盡血淚,
> 十年佯作太平人。

Written in the form of the seven-character quatrain, the poem was a far cry from the modernist form for which Feng Zhi had otherwise been popular. It nevertheless testified to his determination to emulate the Tang poet's engagement with "poetry *as* history" (*shishi* 詩史).

Shishi has been a canonical term in Chinese poetics since the eighth century, thanks to Du Fu's works that chronicled individual fates vis-à-vis dynastic cataclysm. The ninth-century Tang literatus Meng Qi 孟棨 famously observed, "When a poetic incantation is occasioned by an event, it is precisely where deep feelings concentrate" (觸事興詠, 尤所鍾情).[35] Meng Qi considers both the circumstantial and emotive functions of *qing*, thus articulating the reciprocal relationship between historical experience and poetic mind. Meng Qi's engagement with poetry as history points to one important factor of poetic manifestation since ancient times: "the process of [poetic] manifestation must begin in the external world, which has priority without primacy. As latent pattern follows its innate disposition to become manifest, passing from world to mind to literature, a theory of sympathetic resonance is involved."[36] Accordingly, when Du Fu is recognized as the arch-practitioner of "poetry as history," this refers not merely to the poet's historiographical and mimetic capacity, but also to his vision, which makes his poetic mind resonate with historical and cosmic turbulences.

The deliberation and practice of "poetry as history" reached a climax in the late Ming and early Qing, coinciding with dynastic cataclysms. When the Ming loyalist Huang Zongxi 黃宗羲 declares "Where history collapses, poetry arises" (史亡而後詩作), he is soliciting lyrical evocation not only as a testimony to dynastic catastrophe but also as a re-vision of both historical consciousness and poetic mind.[37] Notwithstanding its antitraditional claims, modern Chinese literature intensified rather than doing away with the *shishi* discourse, as evinced by Feng Zhi's poetry and poetics. The devastations of wartime life compelled Feng Zhi to contemplate a series of questions regarding the cycle of life and death, the necessity of change, and the burden of making choices and commitments in life. Rilke and Goethe loomed large in his works,[38] but it was Du Fu who inspired Feng Zhi when pondering the role a poet plays in the face of historical catastrophe. The result is a collection of twenty-seven sonnets titled *Sonnets* (十四行詩; 1942), arguably the best of Feng's oeuvre. Through an imaginary dialogue with Du Fu, Feng Zhi presented his own vision of poetry as history:

> You endure starvation in a deserted village,
> Thought about the dead filling up the trenches,
> But you sang the elegies incessantly
> for the fall of human magnificence.
>
> Warriors die, were wounded on battlefields,
> Meteors fall at sky's end,
> Ten thousand horses disappeared with the floating clouds
> and your life was the sacrifice for them.[39]

> 你在荒村裏忍受饑腸，
> 你常常想到死填溝壑
> 你却不斷地唱著哀歌
> 爲了人間壯美的淪亡：
>
> 戰場上健兒的死傷，
> 天邊有明星的隕落，
> 萬匹馬隨著浮雲消没...
> 你一生是他們的祭享。

Feng Zhi continued to work on Du Fu in the postwar years, while he underwent a drastic ideological metamorphosis as he was drawn to communism and became a supporter of revolution. When his volume *A Biography of Du Fu* (杜甫傳) was published in 1952, it revealed that he had developed a new understanding of poetry as history. In Feng's portrait, Du Fu is viewed as the "people's artist" of the Tang dynasty, sympathizing with the misery of the people and anticipating the rise of a proletarian revolution. In the same year, he dedicated a poem to Mao Zedong, "My Thanks to Chairman Mao" (感謝毛主席):

> You make the mountains and rivers
> Look so beautiful, lucid
> You make everyone regain their youth
> You make me, an intellectual,
> Have conscience again . . .
> You give birth to us anew
> You are our benefactor forever.[40]

> 你讓祖國的山川
> 變得這樣美麗、清新,
> 你讓人人都恢復了青春,
> 你讓我, 一個知識分子,
> 又有了良心。
> . . .
> 你是我們再生的父母,
> 你是我們永久的恩人。

I am not suggesting that Feng Zhi's worship of Mao was disingenuous, but rather I argue that after the Liberation, poets such as Feng Zhi felt compelled to express their "thanks" *because of* their conviction in the refreshed power of poetry as history in the new regime. In historical hindsight, however, a poem such as "My Thanks" indicates the "exegetical bonding"—the technology of the self as a mutual examination through discursive exercises—sanctioned by the Party, rather than proclaiming the subtlety of poetry as history. As a result, Feng cast for himself an image that could not be farther away from that of Du Fu.[41]

Poetry as history in the socialist era was not necessarily transformed into a mere exercise of Maoist eulogy, as is the case of Feng Zhi. In 1954, Chen Yinke (1890–1967) circulated in private a long essay titled "On *Love in Two Lives*" (論再生緣). Arguably the most erudite historian in modern China, Chen Yinke was teaching at Sun Yat-sen University at the time, suffering from both a dire eye ailment and the ever-stricter ideological control. He took nevertheless a great interest in *Love in Two Lives*, such that he considered it comparable to Du Fu's poetry as history.[42]

Love in Two Lives is a prosimetric (*tanci* 彈詞) narrative about the adventures of a young woman named Meng Lijun in the guise of a man, her struggle against fate, and her dedication to her beloved. The author was Chen Duansheng 陳端生 (1751–ca. 1796), a woman about whom we know little. Chen composed the first sixteen chapters of *Love in Two Lives* before she turned twenty; then her writing came to a stop after her husband was exiled to Xinjiang. She resumed writing twelve years later, but passed away before she was able to finish the work.

Throughout his career as a historian, Chen had sought to elucidate Chinese cultural values regardless of barbarian invasions and dynastic contingencies, and he opened up the space for debate over personal integrity versus political power. His choice to study a prosimetric narrative, often associated with folk culture and with plebian and feminine connotations, in his late years was peculiar, leading one to ponder his motivation. In his study, Chen Yinke first undertakes a meticulous research of Chen Duansheng's life and times. He breaks with the scholarly style of his early works, introducing his own experience of war, devastation, and above all, his own poems, with his reading of Chen Duansheng. He makes three observations: that Chen and her heroine demonstrate a defiant attitude toward the ethical strictures and social boundaries of their time, that she manages to compose a story which surpasses all its antecedents in structure as well as vision, and that she masters the conventions of full-length seven-character metric narrative so skillfully that she competes well with not only Du Fu but also the singers of Western epics.[43]

Thanks to Chen Yinke's efforts, Guo Moruo 郭沫若 (1892–1978) also found a great appeal in *Love in Two Lives*. He praised the rhetorical accomplishment of the narrative, likening it to the novels of Stendhal and Balzac, and celebrating Chen Duansheng's antitraditional bearing over Du Fu's. Guo was a leftist ideologue, and his criticism sidestepped some of the most poignant points in Chen Yinke's reading.[44] At a time when history became a formulaic mandate and poetry a propaganda tool, however, what is at stake in his efforts to inscribe poetry as history? In what sense can a prosimetric narrative by an obscure woman be brought to compare with Du Fu, the arch-poet as historian? Above all, what are Chen Yinke's conceptual ground and critical strategy in engaging with poetry as history?

In his reading of *Love in Two Lives*, Chen Yinke takes pains to applaud the "freedom, self-respect, independence" of Chen Duansheng's thinking.[45] His description brings to mind the famous elegy he wrote to commemorate Wang Guowei's self-drowning in 1927: Wang's suicide had demonstrated "the spirit of independence, the freedom of thought." As discussed above, despite the widespread perception at the time that Wang had committed suicide for the fallen Qing dynasty, Chen found in the poet's self-annihilation a gesture not of obsolete loyalism but of willful cultural restorationism. In other words, through his seemingly anachronistic sense of loyalism, Wang acted out his vehement critique of Chinese modernity in crisis.

When Chen Yinke invoked a similar statement to describe Chen Duansheng's work, twenty-three years after his elegy in memory of Wang Guowei, he was enacting another process of encryption. Like Wang Guowei, Chen was not worrying about the transition of political power so much as the collapse of Chinese cultural heritage in the wake of the Communist Revolution. But unlike Wang Guowei, who took his own life at its most intense moment of crisis, Chen chose to survive historical change as a prolonged process of self-elegy. Such a decision made Chen's "literary turn" all the more complex. Through his meticulous study of Chen Duansheng and her prosimetric narrative, Chen Yinke transgressed the boundaries of time, gender, genre, and discipline, bringing Chen Duansheng, Wang Guowei and himself together into the communion of defiant (literary) souls vis-à-vis historical strictures.

Chen Yinke's approach may risk the charge of intentional or affective fallacy by the standard of Western criticism. However, in view of the fact that literature or *wenxue* stands for not so much a representational system of signs as an interactive process of manifestation in life as in art, Chen's endeavor calls for a different kind of understanding. It brings to mind the famous statement in *Mencius* regarding poetry and its interaction with the world:

> If befriending the good *shi* [士 "intellectual"] of the whole world is not enough, then one may go on further to consider the ancients. Yet is it acceptable to recite their poems and read their books without knowing what kind of persons they were? Therefore one considers the age in which they lived.[46]

Here the key concept is *zhiren lunshi* (知人論世), or "to know the person—the poet or the intellectual—by considering the age in which he lived." Much exegesis has been undertaken regarding the meaning of this Mencius phrase. For our purposes, suffice it to say that poetry (literature) points to a special way of engaging with the human condition and the text, in that "one knows the other through the text, but the text is comprehensible only by knowing the other."[47] One may refer to such an approach in terms of the hermeneutical "fusion of horizons" or the neohistoricist "circulation" of textual poetics and politics. In the given context, however, Chen may well have considered poetry (literature) the pivot that sets in motion the intersubjective process of reading the person as well as reading the world.

Accordingly, *Love in Two Lives* is not supposed to have been treated as a "fictional" account. Rather, Chen would have read it as a factual account of an experience in historical time, a human consciousness encountering, interpreting, and responding to the world.[48] It is a unique form of history, one that tells of the fantasies and frustrations that registered the time Chen Duansheng and her heroine lived through—a "history of the heart" (*xinshi* 心史)—and this history has left its own imprint on Chen's heart.

By juxtaposing Feng Zhi's and Chen Yinke's engagement with poetry as history, we come to realize that the canon of *shishi* was not outdated in the New Era; rather it simply underwent various forms of reinterpretation. Feng Zhi had striven to emulate Du Fu, only to make his *Biography of Du Fu* one of the least poetic accounts of his idol. On the other hand, it would take years for readers to realize the rich allegorical power Chen Yingke saw at work in *Love in Two Lives*. In the 1960s, Chen wrote *Biography of Liu Rushi* (柳如是別傳), excavating the romance between the late Ming courtesan Liu Rushi and her two patrons, Chen Zilong 陳子龍 and Qian Qianyi 錢謙益, respectively. As with Chen Duansheng, Chen Yinke sought here to rescue another late imperial talented woman from oblivion, if with more empathy with the choices and dilemmas of those enduring the toll of political disorder. Thus Chen wrote to express not only his nostalgia for the "free spirits" of bygone ages, but his re-vision of the generic—even gendered—attributes of poetry as history.

I have described three exemplary subjects drawn from modern Chinese literary thought: the poetics of *shi yanzhi*, the figure of *xing*, and the polemics of poetry as history. My description is by no means an exhaustive summary of the roots and ramifications of these concepts, nor does it suggest a coherent, causal linkage between the premodern legacy and its modern appropriations. Instead, I argue that before theory became the methodological paradigm of Chinese literary and cultural studies, a rich and contested discourse of literary thought had already been in the making, derived from, and reacting to, both traditional Chinese literary discourse and modern Western theoretical practice. We are in a better position than ever to engage with this rich tradition so as to buttress our exercise of literary theory. To conclude, we return to another quote by Zhu Ziqing, from his review of Luo Genze's 羅根澤 (1900–1960) and Zhu Dongru's 朱東潤 (1898–1988) *A History of Literary Criticism* (中國文學批評史, 1946):

> We are at the beginning of a new era of literary criticism, an era that engages us to assess all values anew. In order to assess all values anew, we need to recognize the values in the tradition, as well as the standards by which we undertake our assessment   Such a critical engagement will not only illuminate the past, but also interpret the present and point to the path to the future.[49]

Notes

1. Zhu Ziqing 朱自清, "Ping Guo Shaoyu Zhongguo wenxue pipingshi shangjuan" 評郭紹虞《中國文學批評史》上卷 [A review of a history of Chinese literary criticism by Guo Shaoyu, volume 1]. In *Zhu Ziqing gudian wenxue lunwenji* 朱自清古典文學論文集 [Zhu Ziqing's criticism on classical Chinese literature] (Shanghai: Shanghai guji chubanshe, 1981), 539.
2. By *theory* I mean a systematic discourse of literary studies that prevailed in Anglo-American as well as continental academia in the second half of the twentieth century. As a cultural institution, a pedagogical methodology, and a cultural capital, theory draws on a wide range of conceptual and pragmatic frameworks of knowledge other than aesthetically defined literature. For a reflection on and critique of theory, its historical context, and its strength and limitations, see Murray Krieger, *The Institution of Theory* (Baltimore: Johns Hopkins University Press, 1994); and Michael Pane and John Scad, eds., *Life after Theory* (London: Continuum, 2003). There have been a series of critiques of theory from a Sinophone and comparative-literary perspective in recent years; see, for instance, Rey Chow, *The Age of the World Target: Self-referentiality in War, Theory, and Comparative Work* (Durham: Duke University Press, 2006), and Terry Eagleton, *After Theory* (London: Basic Books, 2003). For an effort to redefine theory in light of ethnic studies, see Françoise Lionnet and Shu-mei Shih, "Introduction," in Françoise Lionnet and Shu-mei Shih, eds., *The Creolization of Theory* (Durham: Duke University Press, 2011), 1–33.
3. Leigh Jenco, introduction to the edited volume "Chinese Thought as Global Theory: Diversifying Knowledge Production in the Social Sciences and Humanities" (unpublished manuscript).

4. For a recent study of Lu Xun's dialogical relationship with the Chinese tradition, see Eileen Cheng, *Literary Remains: Death, Trauma, and Lu Xun's Refusal to Mourn* (Honolulu: University of Hawai'i Press, 2013), particularly chap. 2.

5. Marián Gálik, "The Comparative Aspects of the Genesis of Modern Chinese Literary Criticism," in *The Chinese Text: Studies in Comparative Literature*, ed. Ying-hsiung Chou (Hong Kong: Chinese University Press, 1986), 177–190; Stephen Owen, *Readings in Chinese Literary Thought* (Cambridge: Harvard Yenching Institute Monograph Series, 1992); Kirk Denton, *Modern Chinese Literary Thought: Writings on Literature, 1893–1945* (Stanford: Stanford University Press, 1996).

6. Owen, *Readings*, 3.

7. Denton, *Modern Chinese Literary Thought*, 19.

8. Lu Xun, "Moluo shilishuo" 摩羅詩力說 [On the theory of Mara poetry], in *Lu Xun quanji* 魯迅全集 [Complete works of Lu Xun] (Beijing: Renmin wenxue chubanshe, 1980), vol. 1, 69.

9. Denton, *Modern Chinese Literary Thought*, 102.

10. Owen's translation in *Readings*, 39–43. Here and below, Chinese transliterations have been changed to *pinyin*, and Chinese characters have been added.

11. Denton, *Modern Chinese Literary Thought*, 102.

12. Jacques Derrida, "Plato's Pharmacy," in *Dissemination*, trans. Barbara Johnson (Chicago: University of Chicago Press, 1981), 67–186.

13. Wang Guowei, *Renjian cihua* 人間詞話 [Remarks on song lyrics and the human condition] (Chengdu: Sichuan renmin chubanshe, 1981), 21.

14. Lu Xun (Lu Hsun), *Wild Grass*, trans. Gladys and Xianyi Yang (Beijing: Foreign Language Press, 1974), 18.

15. For a succinct analysis of Wang Guowei's will, see Ye Jiaying 葉嘉瑩, *Wang Guowei ji qi wenxue piping* 王國維及其文學批評 [Wang Guowei and his literary criticism] (Taipei: Guiguan chuban gongsi, 1978), chap. 2.

16. Chen Yinke 陳寅恪, "Haining Wang xiansheng zhi beiming" 海寧王先生之碑銘 [Epitaph in commemoration of Mr. Wang Guowei], in *Qinghua jiushinian meiwenxuan* 清華九十年美文選 [Selected prose on Tsing-hua University] (Beijing: Tsinghua daxue chubanshe, 2001), 208.

17. D. C. Lau's translation, *The Analects* (New York: Penguin, 1968), 145.

18. Owen, *Readings in Chinese Literary Thought*, 46.

19. Liang Zongdai 梁宗岱, "Xiangzheng zhuyi" 象徵主義 [Symbolism], in *Shi yu zhen* 詩與真 [Poetry and truth] (Beijing: Zhongyang bianyi chubanshe, 2006), 87.

20. Liang Zongdai, "Xiangzheng zhuyi," 71. Liu Xie, *Wenxin diaolong*, "興者, 起也。……起情者, 依微以擬議." *Wenxin diaolong jiaozhu*, 文心雕龍校注 [Annotated *Wenxin diaolong*] (Taipei: Heluo tushu chubanshe, 1976), 240.

21. Liang Zongdai, "Xiangzheng zhuyi," 71.

22. Liang Zongdai, "Xiangzheng zhuyi," 75.

23. Liang Zongdai, "Xiangzheng zhuyi," 85–86.

24. Owen, *Readings in Chinese Literary Thought*, 257–258. See also Chen Taisheng's 陳太勝 comment, in *Xiangzheng zhuyi yu zhongguo xiandai shixue* 象徵主義與中國現代詩學 [Symbolism and Chinese modernist poetics] (Beijing: Beijing daxue chubanshe, 2005), chap. 4.

25. Ma Yifu, "Jiaoju shuhuai jiande zhuyou jianwen" 郊居述懷兼答諸友見問 [An expression of life in rural seclusion in response to friends' concerns], retrieved December 26, 2015, from http://www.booksloverhk.com/poetrecent49_ma_fung.htm.

26. Quixotic as he might sound, Ma entertains a vision of rejuvenation tantamount to an ontological shake-up. He takes it as a poet's moral imperative to unveil the obscure façade of reality. He could serve as an imaginary interlocutor with Heidegger, who was contemplating almost at the same time the revelatory power of poetry in a totally different epistemological context.

27. Ng Kim Chew 黃錦樹 has pointed out that Hu benefited directly from Ma's theory of *ren* and *xing* with regard to national crisis. "Hu Lancheng yu xinrujia: Zhaiwu guanxi, hufa zhaohun yu liyue gexin xinjiuan" 胡蘭成與新儒家——債務關係、護法招魂與禮樂革命新舊案 [Hu Lancheng and the neo-Confucians: Relationship of indebtedness, guarding the orthodoxy and calling for the dead, and the new and old projects of revolution through ritual and music], in *Wen yu hun yu ti: Lun xiandai zhongguoxing* 文與魂與體:論現代中國性 [Literature, soul, and body: On Chinese modernity] (Taipei: Ryefield, 2006), 155–185.

28. Hu Lancheng 胡蘭成, *Zhongguo de liyue fengjing* 中國的禮樂風景 [The vista of Chinese ritual and music] (Taipei: Yuanliu chubanshe, 1991), 157.

29. Hu Lancheng, *Shanhe suiyue* 山河歲月 [China through time] (Taipei: Yuanliu chubanshe, 1991), 243.

30. Mikhail Bakhtin, *Rabelais and His World*, trans. Helene Iswolsky (Cambridge: MIT Press, 1968).

31. See my discussion in *Fin-de-siècle Splendor: Repressed Modernities of Late Qing Fiction, 1849–1911* (Stanford: Stanford University Press, 1997), chap. 4.

32. Hu Lancheng, *Jinsheng jinshi* 今生今世 [This life, this world] (Taipei: Yuanliu chubanshe, 1991), 628. See Ng Kim Chew's succinct discussion in "Hu Lancheng yu xinrujia," 155–185.

33. Du Fu, "Leyouyuan ge" 樂遊園歌 [Song of leyou garden], in Chouzhaoao 仇兆鰲, *Dushi xiangzhu* 杜詩詳注 [Du Fu's poetry with complete annotations] (Beijing: Zhonghua shuju, 1979), vol. 2, 103.

34. Feng Zhi, "Zhu caotang chuangkan" 祝草堂創刊 [For the inauguration of "caotang"], in *Feng Zhi quanji* 馮至全集 [Complete works of Feng Zhi] (Shijiazhuang: Hebei jiaoyu chubanshe, 1998), vol. 4, 226.

35. See Zhang Hui 張暉, *Zhongguo shishi chuantong* 中國詩史傳統 [The tradition of poetry as history in China] (Beijing: Sanlian shudian, 2012).

36. Owen, *Traditional Chinese Poetry and Poetics: Omen of the World* (Madison: University of Wisconsin Press, 1986), 21.

37. As Zhang Hui cautions, nevertheless, the early Qing also witnessed a philological and evidential turn of the notion of *shishi*; that is, poets and scholars tended to treat poetry merely as a testimony to or even factual account of historical experience. "Zhongguo shishi chuantong" 中國詩史傳統 [The tradition of poetry as history in China], *Dushu* 讀書 [Reading] 9 (2012): 151–158.

38. Feng was a great admirer of Rilke. For him, Rilke "never indulges in narcissistic whims or aloof, circuitous symbols"; he "watches the multitude of things in the world with love and pure feeling," and his poetry is a crystallized form of "experience" rather than mere emotions. Meanwhile, Feng Zhi welcomes Goethe's wholesome, robust attitude toward life and its continued transformation. He celebrates its kinetic potential as a way to energize the Rilkean "solitude and endurance." He stresses Goethe's notion of *Entsagen*—a resolution to renounce that which is apparently pleasing and indispensable to life—which he believes complements Rilke's resistance to the routines of life and idées fixes. See my

discussion in *The Lyrical in Epic Time: Chinese Intellectuals and Artists through the 1949 Crisis* (New York: Columbia University Press, 2015), chap. 3.

39. Feng Zhi, "Sonnet 12," translated by Dominique Cheung, in *Feng Chih* (Boston: Twayne, 1979), 82.

40. Feng Zhi, "Ganxie Mao zhuxi" 感謝毛主席 [My thanks to Chairman Mao), *Feng Zhi Quanji*, vol. 2, 50–52.

41. I am referring to David Apter and Tony Saich's argument in *Revolutionary Discourse in Mao's Republic* (Cambridge: Harvard University Press, 1994), 263.

42. For a general account of Chen Yinke and his essay on Zaishengyuan, see Wang Rongzu 汪榮祖, *Shijia Chen Yinke* 史家陳寅恪 [Chen Yinke the historian] (Taipei: Lingking, 1984), chap. 13.

43. Chen Yinke 陳寅恪, *Hanliutang ji* 寒柳堂集 [A volume of cold willow studio] (Beijing, Sanlian shudian, 2009), 64–71.

44. Guo Moruo 郭沫若, *Guo Moruo gudian wenxue lunwenji* 郭沫若古典文學論文集 [Guo Moruo's criticism on classical Chinese literature] (Shanghai: Shanghai guji chubanshe, 1985), 876–930.

45. Chen Yinke, *Hanliutang ji*, 67.

46. Owen, *Readings in Chinese Literary Thought*, 34.

47. Owen, *Readings in Chinese Literary Thought*, 35.

48. Owen, *Traditional Poetry and Poetics*, 15.

49. Zhu Ziqing, "Shiwenping de fazhan" 詩文評的發展 [The development of criticism on poetry and prose], *Dushu tongxun* 讀書通訊 [Newsletter on reading] 113 (1946): 14–17.

Works Cited

Apter, David, and Tony Saich. *Revolutionary Discourse in Mao's Republic*. Cambridge: Harvard University Press, 1994.

Bakhtin, Mikhail. *Rabelais and His World*. Trans. Helene Iswolsky. Cambridge: MIT Press, 1968.

Chen Taisheng 陳太勝. *Xiangzheng zhuyi yu zhongguo xiandai shixue* 象徵主義與中國現代詩學 [Symbolism and Chinese modernist poetics]. Beijing: Beijing daxue chubanshe, 2005.

Chen Yinke 陳寅恪. "Haining Wang xiansheng zhi beiming" 海寧王先生之碑銘 [Epitaph in commemoration of Mr. Wang Guowei]. In *Qinghua jiushinian meiwenxuan* 清華九十年美文選 [Selected prose on Tsing-hua University]. Beijing: Qinghua daxue chubanshe, 2001. 208.

Chen Yinke. *Hanliutang ji* 寒柳堂集 [A volume of cold willow studio]. Beijing, Sanlian shudian, 2009.

Cheng, Eileen. *Literary Remains: Death, Trauma, and Lu Xun's Refusal to Mourn*. Honolulu: University of Hawai'i Press, 2013.

Chow, Rey. *The Age of the World Target: Self-referentiality, in War, Theory, and Comparative Work*. Durham: Duke University Press, 2006.

Confucius. *The Analects*. Trans. D. C. Lau. New York: Penguin, 1968.

Denton, Kirk. *Modern Chinese Literary Thought: Writings on Literature, 1893–1945*. Stanford: Stanford University Press, 1996.

Derrida, Jacques. "Plato's Pharmacy." In *Dissemination*. Trans. Barbara Johnson. Chicago: University of Chicago Press, 1981. 67–186.

Du Fu 杜甫. "Leyouyuan ge" 樂遊園歌 [Song of leyou garden]. In Chouzhaoao 仇兆鰲. *Dushi xiangzhu* 杜詩詳注 [Du Fu's poetry with complete annotations]. Beijing: Zhonghua shuju, 1979, vol. 2, 103.

Eagleton, Terry. *After Theory*. London: Basic Books, 2003.

Feng Zhi 馮至. "Ganxie Mao zhuxi" 感謝毛主席 [My thanks to Chairman Mao]. In *Feng Zhi quanji* 馮至全集 [Complete works of Feng Zhi]. Shijiazhuang: Hebei jiaoyu chubanshe, 1998, vol. 2, 50–52.

Feng Zhi 馮至. "Sonnet 12." Trans. Dominique Cheung. In *Feng Chih*. Boston: Twayne, 1979. 82.

Feng Zhi 馮至. "Zhu caotang chuangkan" 祝草堂創刊 [For the inauguration of "caotang"]. In *Feng Zhi quanji* 馮至全集 [Complete works of Feng Zhi]. Shijiazhuang: Hebei jiaoyu chubanshe, 1998, vol. 4, 226.

Gálik, Marián. "The Comparative Aspects of the Genesis of Modern Chinese Literary Criticism." In *The Chinese Text: Studies in Comparative Literature*. Ed. Ying-hsiung Chou. Hong Kong: Chinese University Press, 1986. 177–190.

Guo Moruo 郭沫若. *Guo Moruo gudian wenxue lunwenji* 郭沫若古典文學論文集 [Guo Moruo's criticism on classical Chinese literature]. Shanghai: Shanghai guji chubanshe, 1985.

Hu Lancheng 胡蘭成. *Jinsheng jinshi* 今生今世 [This life, this world]. Taipei: Yuanliu chubanshe, 1991.

Hu Lancheng 胡蘭成. *Shanhe suiyue* 山河歲月 [China through time]. Taipei: Yuanliu chubanshe, 1991.

Hu Lancheng 胡蘭成. *Zhongguo de liyue fengjing* 中國的禮樂風景 [The vista of Chinese ritual and music]. Taipei: Yuanliu chubanshe, 1991.

Jenco, Leigh. "Introduction." In *Chinese Thought as Global Theory: Diversifying Knowledge Production in the Social Sciences and Humanities* (unpublished manuscript).

Krieger, Murray. *The Institution of Theory*. Baltimore: Johns Hopkins University Press, 1994.

Liang Zongdai 梁宗岱. "Xiangzheng zhuyi" 象徵主義 [Symbolism]. In *Shi yu zhen* 詩與真 [Poetry and truth]. Beijing: Zhongyang bianyi chubanshe, 2006. 67–89.

Lionnet, Françoise and Shu-mei Shih. "Introduction." In *The Creolization of Theory*. Ed. Françoise Lionnet and Shu-mei Shih. Durham: Duke University Press, 2011. 1–33.

Liu Xie 劉勰. *Wenxin diaolong jiaozhu* 文心雕龍校注 [Annotated *Wenxin diaolong*]. Taipei: Heluo tushu chubanshe, 1976.

Lu Xun 魯迅. "Moluo shilishuo" 摩羅詩力說 [On the theory of Mara poetry]. In *Lu Xun quanji* 魯迅全集 [Complete works of Lu Xun]. Beijing: Renmin wenxue chubanshe, 1980, vol. 1, 69.

Lu Xun (Lu Hsun). *Wild Grass*. Trans. Gladys and Xianyi Yang. Beijing: Foreign Language Press, 1974.

Ma Yifu 馬一浮. "Jiaoju shuhuai jiande zhuyou jianwen" 郊居述懷兼答諸友見問 [An expression of life in rural seclusion in response to friends' concerns], retrieved December 26, 2015, from http://www.booksloverhk.com/poetrecent49_ma_fung.htm.

Ng Kim Chew 黃錦樹. "Hu Lancheng yu xinrujia: Zhaiwu guanxi, hufa zhaohun yu liyue gexin xinjiuan" 胡蘭成與新儒家——債務關係、護法招魂與禮樂革命新舊案 [Hu Lancheng and the neo-Confucians: Relationship of indebtedness, guarding the orthodoxy and calling for the dead, and the new and old projects of revolution through ritual and music]. In *Wen yu hun yu ti: Lun xiandai zhongguoxing* 文與魂與體:論現代中國性 [Literature, soul, and body: On Chinese modernity]. Taipei: Ryefield, 2006. 155–185.

Owen, Stephen. *Readings in Chinese Literary Thought*. Cambridge: Harvard Yenching Institute Monograph Series, 1992.

Owen, Stephen. *Traditional Chinese Poetry and Poetics: Omen of the World*. Madison: University of Wisconsin Press, 1986.

Pane, Michael and John Scad, eds. *Life after Theory*. London: Continuum, 2003.

Wang, David Der-wei. *Fin-de-siècle Splendor: Repressed Modernities of Late Qing Fiction, 1849–1911*. Stanford: Stanford University Press, 1997.

Wang, David Der-wei. *The Lyrical in Epic Time: Chinese Intellectuals and Artists through the 1949 Crisis*. New York: Columbia University Press, 2015.

Wang Guowei 王國維. *Renjian cihua* 人間詞話 [Remarks on song lyrics and the human condition]. Chengdu: Sichuan renmin chubanshe, 1981.

Wang Rongzu 汪榮祖. *Shijia Chen Yinke* 史家陳寅恪 [Chen Yinke the historian]. Taipei: Lingking, 1984.

Ye Jiaying 葉嘉瑩. *Wang Guowei ji qi wenxue piping* 王國維及其文學批評 [Wang Guowei and his literary criticism]. Taipei: Guiguan chuban gongsi, 1978.

Zhang Hui 張暉. *Zhongguo shishi chuantong* 中國詩史傳統 [The tradition of poetry as history in China]. Beijing: Sanlian shudian, 2012.

Zhang Hui. "Zhongguo shishi chuantong" 中國詩史傳統 [The tradition of poetry as history in China]. *Dushu* 讀書 [Reading] 9 (2012): 151–158.

Zhu Ziqing 朱自清. "Ping Guo Shaoyu Zhongguo wenxue pipingshi shangjuan" 評郭紹虞《中國文學批評史》上卷 [A review of a history of Chinese literary criticism by Guo Shaoyu, volume 1]. In *Zhu Ziqing gudian wenxue lunwenji* 朱自清古典文學論文集 [Zhu Ziqing's criticism on classical Chinese literature]. Shanghai: Shanghai guji chubanshe, 1981. 539.

Zhu Ziqing 朱自清. "Shiwenping de fazhan" 詩文評的發展 [The development of criticism on poetry and prose]. *Dushu tongxun* 讀書通訊 [Newsletter on reading] 113 (1946): 14–17.

CHAPTER 3.2

GAO XINGJIAN

The Triumph of the Modern Zhuangzi

JIANMEI LIU

FLEEING is an action that Gao Xingjian 高行健 has frequently taken throughout his life. In 1983, after his play *Bus Stop* (車站) was banned, he was diagnosed with lung cancer. He made a quick decision to flee Beijing for the remote forest regions of Sichuan province, and then roamed along the Yangtze River—a journey that inspired his famous novel *Soul Mountain* (靈山; 1990). In 1987, he traveled to Germany as a visiting artist and later decided not to return to China; he eventually settled in Paris. His self-exile made his 2000 Nobel Prize in Literature controversial in mainland China, where most of his works remain banned.

The first Chinese Nobel Prize laureate in Literature, Gao Xingjian occupies a singular position in the history of Chinese modernist drama. In 1981, at a time when most Chinese were still unfamiliar with Western absurdist drama, he published *A Preliminary Discussion of the Art of Modern Fiction* (現代小說技巧初探), a pioneering theoretical book that introduced Western modernism to China and helped writers go beyond the dominant mode of realism at the time. During this same period, Gao initiated the birth of avant-garde theater in China, leaving an innovative legacy of experimental dramas such as *Alarm Signal* (絕對信號; 1982), *Bus Stop* (1983), *Wild Man* (野人; 1985), and *The Other Shore* (彼岸; 1986). Although he could have stayed in China, he instead chose a life of exile and settled in Paris, an action that can be described as a form of self-salvation. Composed in exile, his writings have transgressed the geopolitical boundaries of nation/state, providing a unique mode of diasporic and Sinophone articulation that maintains distance from the political center, searching for inner space and freedom, and advocating a universal set of values for mankind.

Gao Xingjian's winning the Nobel Prize in 2000 caused a protracted debate in China about the politics of the Nobel Prize as well as his diasporic writing. Those who denigrated Gao Xingjian's work complained of the Nobel Prize's anticommunism and criticized Gao's decision to flee his home country. The polemic at hand involved his French citizenship, which gave the Chinese government a chance to deny him as the first Chinese writer to win the coveted prize. Regardless of his citizenship, however, Gao won the prize based on his Chinese-language writing, which combined Western modernist narratology and traditional Chinese philosophies. By defining writing as an escape, a challenge to the ruling ideological paradigm of the moment as well as existing conditions, Gao proclaims that only through escape can he find his true self as well as the real meaning of literature. The act of fleeing or seeking self-exile, which can be defined as both political protest and aesthetic adventure, has therefore become one of the central themes in Gao's work. By associating escape and freedom closely together—"regarding freedom as the first essential for creative work, and escape as the only way of securing freedom"[1]—Gao Xingjian has explored an aesthetics that is based on freedom as contained in *Zhuangzi* (莊子) and Chan (Zen) Buddhist texts. Defining his own writing as "cold literature," he says, "Cold literature is literature that entails fleeing in order to exist, it is literature that refuses to be strangled by society in its quest for spiritual salvation. If a race cannot accommodate this sort of non-utilitarian literature it is not merely a misfortune for the writer but a tragedy for that race."[2] In *Soul Mountain*, the protagonist escapes from the political center to a more marginal culture and a primeval forest. In Gao's play *Flight* (逃亡; 1990), the middle-aged protagonist wants to abandon revolution as well as the hell of the self, which is the shadow in his heart. "Being alive means being always on the run. We are running away either from political persecution or from other people, and we also run away from ourselves. Once we are awakened, we will find that is exactly the self that we cannot run away from. Such is the tragedy of modern man."[3] In Gao's play *Snow in August* (八月雪; 1997), the Sixth Patriarch Huineng runs away from various kinds of authorities, refusing to be the world's savior or others' idol, but advocating "self-salvation" from which to pursue the "total freedom" that comes from one's heart. Considering fleeing as a path toward freedom, Gao Xingjian's literary encounter with the modern and the past involved a sustained embrace of Zhuangzi's and Chan Buddhist thinking.

This chapter focuses on Gao Xingjian's novel *Soul Mountain* and his two poems "As Free as a Bird" (逍遙如鳥) and "Roaming Spirit and Metaphysical Thinking" (遊神與玄思). By reading Gao's work through Zhuangzi's spirit, I try to open up a new perspective from which to examine the thematic and philosophical connections between the aesthetics of Gao's self-exile and Zhuangzi's notion of absolute spiritual freedom. I argue that Gao's works not only captivate the philosophical tenets of Zhuangzi and Chan Buddhism, they simultaneously reinterpret them. Even if Gao's works are all about "pure aestheticism," they are still strictly censored in the PRC. In this way, apparently apolitical themes that pervade Gao's works, reminiscent of Zhuangzi's notion of spiritual transcendence, the escape from or rejection of the political, and the ideal of self-salvation, become profoundly political, since they turn into a powerful gesture of resistance against political hegemony.

Soul Mountain: The Symbol
of Inner Freedom

Begun in 1982 in China and completed in 1989 in France, Gao Xingjian's famous novel *Soul Mountain* can be read as a book about fleeing as well as searching for the meaning of life. In other words, the physical roaming becomes a figure for a spiritual quest. By way of its experimental style, the novel restages the narrator's experience of the world, replacing the character's name with personal pronouns and replacing the story line with a description of the protagonist's psychological rhythm. Though Gao Xingjian was well known for his assimilation of Western modernist writing techniques, in this novel he delved into the origins of nonmainstream Chinese cultures that have been marginalized by the dominant Confucian culture, including the reclusive culture of Chinese intellectuals, the nature-centered culture of Daoism, the wisdom-seeking culture of Chan Buddhism, and lost folk cultures. The similarities among these four cultures lie in their common unofficial or marginal status, their refusal of tyranny, their longing for freedom, their emphasis on the individual life, and their struggle against mainstream cultural concepts. The notion of individual spiritual liberation that made all four cultural traditions so important to Gao Xingjian is most strongly expressed in Zhuangzi's thought.

Like Wang Zengqi 汪曾祺, Han Shaogong 韓少功, and Ah Cheng 阿城, in *Soul Mountain* Gao Xingjian regards nature as his central concern, but he includes not only outer nature, such as mountains, rivers, and trees, but also inner nature, meaning the cosmos of the human psyche. The theme of "natural ecological protection" that appeared as early as the 1980s in Gao's drama *Wild Man* continues to pervade the text of *Soul Mountain*. Reading *Soul Mountain* as an excavation of Daoist ecology or as nature-oriented or environmental literature, Thomas Moran points out that this novel "joins other fictions of the 1980s in tallying the costs to the imagination of the reality of disappearing primeval forest."[4] By elaborating the journey of the protagonist "I" in the forest, Gao vehemently criticizes modern men's plunder and ravage of nature. For instance, during his journey, the narrator "I" observes that the primeval forest has been gradually swallowed and wiped out by the greediness of human beings. He is critical of the government's Three Gorges Dam, because he believes it will destroy the ecology of the Yangzi River. Facing the deeply wounded forest, the protagonist sighs: "Zhuangzi said as early as two thousand years ago, the useful trees die early for being cut, the useless trees are luckier. Yet the contemporary people are greedier than the ancient men. Huxley's theory of evolution is also doubtful."[5] Facing such vast destruction, Gao Xingjian feels he has no way to stop contemporary China's tide of "development" or humans' greedy nature, and consequently realizes there is no way to save the world. What one can do is seek self-salvation, as he says in his essay collection *Without Isms*:

> In saving the nation and saving the people, if the individual is not saved first, then ultimately it will all be a lie, or at least empty talk. The most important thing is for an

individual to save himself. In such a big nation and country, if the individual cannot save himself, then how can the nation and the country be saved? So nothing is more immediate than self-salvation.[6]

Abandoning the notion of "nation-salvation" that prevailed for the whole twentieth century, Gao Xingjian undertakes his own self-salvation not only through his outer natural travel but also through his inner natural travel. *Soul Mountain* is in fact an inner *Journey to the West* (西遊記). The main protagonist in the novel, a persona of the author, has been divided into three pronominal figures: "you," "I," and "he." Alternating between first-, second-, and third-person voices, the novel is partly autobiographical and partly imaginary narrative with no plot, combining both physical travel and mind travel. Although the critic Jian Ming doesn't use "outer travel" and "inner travel" to describe *Soul Mountain*, he gives a clear and interesting observation of the protagonist's two different kinds of journeys:

> Gao Xingjian's *Soul Mountain* (*Lingshan* 靈山) features a tripartite protagonist's life voyage that unfolds in two structurally parallel journeys; namely, the I-narrator's travel along the Yangtze River valley, and the you-narrator's highly symbolic spiritual journey in search of Lingshan. On their respective journeys, the I-narrator endeavors to find an "authentic life" (*shishi zaizai de shenghuo* 實實在在的生活) and ponders on life's meaning in the real world, while the you-narrator probes life's ultimate goal in an allegorical tale—his search for the fictitious, metaphoric Lingshan.[7]

The process of the author's searching for the soul mountain is the process of his finding inner relief, of breaking the fetters imposed by external powers as well as the bonds of internal desire and hindrances, and returning to spiritual freedom. When the protagonist is seen in the hustle and bustle of city streets, he resembles a spiritual prisoner, whereas when he travels to a remote and undeveloped region or the primeval forest, he gains considerable freedom and enjoyment.

Manifesting an extraordinary power and freedom of invention, *Soul Mountain* can be read as a journey to the innermost landscape as well as a journey in search of a soul mountain, or a spiritual home, that is unencumbered with political, economic, and ethical limitations. By mixing anecdotal plots, lyrical meditations, fantastical dreams, and enigmatic memories, the novel unfolds a cosmic vision of human existence presented by certain recurring motifs such as death, darkness, solitude, wandering, the mountain, love, and sex. But what does this *soul mountain* mean, and does the protagonist eventually succeed in finding it? At the end of the novel we find a frog's twinkling eyes—an ending without any answer, because the author wants readers to meditate and comprehend by themselves. However, Gao Xingjian later explains in his literary theoretical book *Aesthetics and Creation*: "The frog appearing in the snow in *Soul Mountain* constructs an image, and this sort of enlightenment is similar to a Chan Buddhist realm."[8] What we can understand is that a soul mountain is not something located outside oneself, but rather the free spirit that inhabits one's heart. This soul mountain can be interpreted as a mountain of Chan Buddhism or a mountain of freedom. Most importantly, it symbolizes the absolute spiritual freedom that Zhuangzi advocates. According to Liu Zaifu 劉再復,

> A soul mountain is a kind of glimmer inside one's heart. It could be as vast as the universe, or it could also be as tiny as a glimmer in the heart. Everything is determined by this kind of unquenchable glow, and the most difficult thing for people is maintaining this glimmer through countless trials and hardships. The glimmer represents the conscience of brightness and life that hasn't been contaminated by mundane fame and profit. Once we secure such a glimmer, we will have found a soul mountain.[9]

Likewise, we can also view a soul mountain as consisting of a state of inner awakening. Once we arrive at a stage of enlightenment, of freedom, we may find our soul mountain, but without such enlightenment we can never find it. In other words, freedom is self-given rather than given by others.

The path toward a soul mountain depends on self-searching rather than other people's guidance. In chapter 76 of *Soul Mountain*, the protagonist asks an elderly man wearing a long gown and carrying a staff where soul mountain is:

"Venerable elder, can you tell me the location of soul mountain?"

"Where have you come from?" the old man asks instead.

He says from Wuyizhen.

"Wuyizhen?" The old man ruminates for a while. "It's on the other side of the river."

He says he has just come from that other side of the river. Can he have taken the wrong road? The old man cocks an eyebrow and says, "The road is not wrong, it is the traveler who is wrong."

"Venerable elder, what you are saying is absolutely correct." But what he is asking is whether soul mountain is on this side of the river.

"If I say it's on that side of the river then it's on that side of the river." The old man is annoyed.

. . .

The old man closes his eyes to concentrate.

"Venerable elder, didn't you say it is on the other side of the river?" He has to ask again. "But I've already come to this side of the river—"

"Then it's on that side of the river," the old man crossly interjects.

"And if I use Wuyizhen to get my bearings?"

"Then it's still on that side of the river."

"But I have already come to this side of the river from Wuyizhen, so when you say that side of the river, shouldn't it be this side of the river?"

"Don't you want to go to soul mountain?"

"Precisely."

"Then it's on that side of the river."

"Venerable elder, surely you're talking metaphysics?"

The old man says in all earnestness, "Aren't you asking the way?"
He says he is.
"Then I've already told you."[10]

The dialogue between the "he" and the elder sounds a little metaphysical, but it is not deliberately mystifying; instead, it allows readers to comprehend what lies beyond the mysterious and abstruse. It can be seen as an attempt to formulate an answer: don't ask others for directions, because the path toward a soul mountain is right in your heart. Does "the other side of the river" mean this shore or the other shore? The elderly man doesn't provide a direct answer, and instead leaves it up to the traveler. In fact, through the elderly man's language of Chan Buddhism, the author is trying to tell us that a soul mountain is neither on this shore nor on the other shore, nor can it be guided by others. Just as freedom comes from one's own consciousness, a soul mountain is only accessible through one's awakening. In other words, Buddha doesn't live inside the forest and temples but in one's uncontaminated heart.

In chapter 64, Gao Xingjian writes:

It was like that, the night wind was coming from all directions, he was standing in an empty square and he heard a rustling noise, he couldn't make out whether it was the wind or the sound of his heart, he suddenly felt he had discarded all responsibilities, had attained liberation, he was at last free, this freedom in fact came from himself, he could begin everything all over again, like a naked baby, thrown into the wash-basin, kicking his little legs, crying without restraint to let the world hear his voice.[11]

Gao's interpretation of freedom stems from his understanding of Chan Buddhism, which holds the view that Buddha nature is within oneself. One should rely on oneself rather than any power external to the self to overcome the obstruction of delusion, confusion, and worries derived from the mundane world. According to the Sixth Patriarch of Chan, Huineng, "Good friends, *bodhi* is the wisdom of *prajñā*. People of this world possess it fundamentally and naturally. It is only because your minds are deluded that you are unable to become enlightened yourselves."[12] The choice for obtaining Buddha nature, or freedom, primarily depends on the choice of the individual's awareness of the need of freedom. Regarding Huineng as a great thinker, Gao Xingjian has adopted Chan's notion of self-salvation—relying on oneself to gain inner freedom—and resurrected it in the contemporary time. This also bears on the complex interweaving of Gao's literary concepts, as he writes: "The freedom of writing is neither given by God, nor could be bought; instead, it derived from your inner necessity   It is better to say freedom is in your heart than to say Buddha is in your heart. Whether to use it or not is totally up to you."[13] Gao Xingjian never specifies what he meant by a soul mountain, but his conception of it is clear from his description. The truth of *Soul Mountain* is to open the gates of the heart, inviting in Buddha as well as freedom. This kind of awakening that transcends all the obstacles set by mundane value systems also comes closest to Zhuangzi's spirit, which highlights absolute freedom by soaring beyond the boundaries of social and political relations.

As Free as a Bird:
The Modern Expression
of "Free and Easy Wandering"

The spirit of individual emancipation manifested in Zhuangzi's "Free and Easy Wandering" (逍遙遊) chapter, which transgresses all of the boundaries and limits of "little knowledge" (小知), permeates Gao Xingjian's novels *Soul Mountain* and *One Man's Bible* (一個人的聖經), as well as many of his plays, such as *Snow in August*. But here, instead of discussing his novels and plays, I will focus on his poetry. Gao's 2009 poem "As Free as a Bird" (逍遙如鳥) is a modern version of Zhuangzi's "Free and Easy Wandering," and the title indicates a connection with the roaming spirit of Zhuangzi's giant mythical bird, the Peng (or "roc"). According to Zhang Yinde, "The poem must be called a direct reference to and rewriting of *Zhuangzi*'s fable of the roc. Gao Xingjian uses a terse modern language poem to change the artistic concept of the roc beating its wings and leaping into the air to roam a proverbial thousand miles, while at the same time pointing out the importance of the theme of 'roaming' in his works."[14] Indeed, in this poem, by transforming seemingly negative life choices such as escaping, exile, and self-marginalization into a positive free spirit, Gao Xingjian's "As Free as a Bird" exemplifies Zhuangzi's spirit, which celebrates the ultimate free and unfettered state. At the beginning of this poem, Gao writes:

你若是鳥
僅僅是只鳥
迎風即起
率性而飛
眼睜睜俯視
暗中混沌的人世
飛越泥沼
於煩惱之上
聽風展翼
這夜行毫無目的
自在而消遙

if you are a bird
nothing more than a bird
you rise with the wind
you fly as you please
with your eyes wide open
you look at the world below
this big mass of chaos
you fly across the muddy swamp
above all the troubles
at ease and carefree[15]

Drawing on a romantic and visionary quality similar to that found in Zhuangzi's "Free and Easy Wandering," Gao Xingjian's description here mirrors the original introduction of the Peng in the *Zhuangzi*: "When the Peng travels to the South Ocean, the wake it thrashes on the water is three thousand miles long, it mounts spiralling on the whirlwind ninety thousand miles high, and is gone six months before it is out of breath."[16] The free flight of Gao's bird undoubtedly reflects Zhuangzi's spiritual liberation, realizing a sense of freedom that lies in "purposelessness" (無目的), which transcends the utilitarian pursuit of material gain, social expectation, and even life and death. Not only has Gao Xingjian put down the burdens he carried from the past, he also refuses to create any new illusions and utopian fantasies or fit himself into various ideological frameworks in reality. Once he drops all those burdens, putting down all kinds of complaints, scruples, and hatreds, he feels that freedom can be found everywhere.

As Gao Xingjian pointed out in an essay titled "Freedom and Literature," an individual's freedom is completely confined by various living conditions. Besides political pressure and social regulations, there are still all kinds of economic and ethical restrictions as well as psychological wonders. If an individual's freedom is subjected to political authorities and isms such as Marxism-Leninism, Maoism, and various forms of nationalism in the twentieth century, then in the globalized age an individual is inevitably turned into a consumerist animal, which is another form of the disappearance of the individual. These modern dilemmas, sometimes more sometimes less, are unavoidable. Freedom is never an inherent right and cannot be granted by anyone.[17]

Facing such existential dilemmas of modern man, Gao takes Zhuangzi's Peng to heart and makes it his own, equating fleeing, self-exile, and marginality with freedom. He was especially drawn to the notion of the Peng freeing itself from all sorts of restrictions imposed by politics, society, the economy, ethics, and emotion, and doing whatever he wants to cross clouds and fog, glimmers and morning rays, mountains and lakes, sea and desert, day and night, flying freely between sky and land, absorbing all the beautiful things into its eyes—a free image that reaches the "ultimate joy" (至樂) of outer traveling.

In Gao's poem, the Peng's outward traveling soon transforms into Gao's own inner journey—an open expression of the poet's own emotions, his own soulful experience.

偌大一隻慧眼
引導你前去
未知之境
憑這目光
你便如鳥
從冥想中升騰
消解詞語的困頓
想像都難抵以抵達
那模糊依稀之處
霎時間在眼前
——浮現

> a pair of big intelligent eyes
> guides you to move forward
> into an unknown state
> because of this vision
> you are just like a bird
> rising from meditation
> solving the problem of words
> reaching the state where even imagination can hardly arrive
> ambiguous and blurred
> but instantly being unfolded at present[18]

A kind of spiritual enjoyment (or the joy of meditation) appears to have been spread over the interior landscape of the poet's soul, casting light on his self-reflection. The pair of big intelligent eyes refers to "the third eye," which Gao Xingjian defines as the artist's ability to observe himself retrospectively,[19] leading the travel itself into the innermost and infinite universe of an individual. With this pair of big intelligent eyes, the poet is capable of escaping from the hell of self, delving into the depth of the spiritual realm.

In his "Free and Easy Wandering" chapter, Zhuangzi talks about "spiritual travel" (*shenyou* 神遊), as well as "depending on something" (*youdai* 有待) and "depending on nothing" (*wudai* 無待):

> Or that [Liezi] now, he journeyed with the winds for his chariot, a fine sight it must have been, and did not come back for fifteen days. (Even so, there was something he failed to plant in his own soil.) The former of them, in the hope of bringing blessings to the world, failed to break clean away; the latter, even if he did save himself the trouble of going on foot, still depended on something to carry his weight. As for the man who rides a true course between heaven and earth, with the changes of the Six Energies for his chariot, to travel into the infinite, is there anything that he depends on?[20]

Liezi remains at the stage of *youdai*—relying on something, because he needs to depend on the power outside, waiting for the wind from the right direction in order to fly. In this sense, he hasn't reached the true sense of freedom and isn't able to keep the initiative in his own hands. To achieve the stage of *wudai*—depending on nothing—one has to take the right path of the developing rules of heaven and earth, following the changing of the six *qis*, going with the flow of nature. The "perfect," "true," "divine" person of the "Free and Easy Wandering" chapter is capable of reaching the state of *wudai*. In "As Free as a Bird," Gao Xingjian starts from the bird's outer travel, which has to depend on the wind, and proceeds to the narrator's inner travel, which depends on nothing and travels freely, even to the place that words cannot describe and that even the imagination cannot reach. By borrowing the language of Chan Buddhism, he shows the inner spiritual travel springing from meditation, with no limits or boundaries.

明晃晃一片光亮
空如同滿
令永恒與瞬間交融

時光透明
而若干陰影與裂痕
從中涌現某種遺忘

a light brightening and dazzling
emptiness is exactly the fullness
eternity and the instant melt together
time becomes transparent
yet a kind of oblivion
sprung up from shadow and scar[21]

Through meditation as well as aesthetic creation, the narrator/author accesses the state of depending on nothing, in which time and space lose their meaning, eternity and the moment are interwoven, and "forgetfulness" can be actualized.

It is certain that this forgetfulness is in accord with Zhuangzi's concept of "I am losing myself" (吾喪我) and "sitting and forgetting" (坐忘), which, as Li Zehou 李澤厚 said, "emphasizes the unity of humans with nature (heaven, earth, and all things), rather than the rejection of nature."[22] According to Qian Mu, "Losing oneself is equivalent to sitting and forgetting, which means losing one's cognition in that there results in no separation between the subject and the object; therefore one begins to approach the big connection (*datong* 大同) and travel between heaven and earth. This is the highest state of Zhuangzi's ideal life."[23] In "As Free as a Bird," it is through "forgetting" that the poet discovers the resonances between his own inborn nature and external objects, and therefore can see or sense "a light of brightness" and "transparency" in his heart, gaining the highest state of humans and heaven, becoming oneness.

However, after pushing Zhuangzi's ideal state to the extreme, Gao Xingjian writes the following lines, which describe the poet's persona as falling short of the ideal of freedom:

你重又暗中徘徊
清楚的只是
你畢竟不是鳥
也解不脫
這無所不在
總糾纏不息
日常的紛擾

again you secretively wander,
what you are certain of is that
after all, you are not the bird and
have no way to get rid of
the omnipresent and forever entangling
conflicts and worries in daily life[24]

These lines reveal an interesting shift of Gao Xingjian's emphasis vis-à-vis Zhuangzi's famous "Free and Easy Wandering" chapter. Although both texts underscore the individual's free spirit, Gao Xingjian pays more attention to the individual's existential dilemmas and conflicts with society—a true situation of human existence that is contrasting the gestures of "wandering" and "flying." Therefore, in addition to his identification with Zhuangzi's notion of individual spiritual liberation, Gao Xingjian has a second, equally significant, motivation for accentuating the reality in which human beings have to live, within complicated and entangling social and political relations in which one is doomed to lose one's freedom. In such "an omnipresent and forever entangling daily life," a Peng's wings are bound to reality, and it can hardly soar up to the sky. Gao's courage to face the truth of reality makes him highlight two points. First, Zhuangzi's free spirit doesn't exist in the real world, but only in the field of spiritual and aesthetic creation, especially literary creation. Second, even within spiritual and aesthetic creation, one must accept that human beings are normal and weak, and only by doing so can one create concrete, real individuals instead of abstract concepts about people in literature.

Gao Xingjian attempts to insert a certain kind of "clear consciousness" into Zhuangzi's romantic spirit of limitless freedom. It is precisely because of this that the distinction between Zhuangzi and Gao Xingjian is relatively easy to draw. While Zhuangzi advocates a kind of ideal personality—the "perfect," "true," "divine" person—Gao Xingjian emphasizes the "normal heart" (平常心) as well as weakness, a kind of thought that is obviously influenced by Chan Buddhism.

Guided by Chan Buddhism, Gao Xingjian expresses bewilderment at any kind of illusions about an ideal "perfect," "true," and "divine" person. He insists that writers and poets should realize their role, giving up illusions of playing the role of "hero," "fighter," or "savior," "the incarnation of justice," "the conscience of society," or "superman."[25] For Gao, it is only through discarding those illusions that one can truly gain freedom. Clearly, by adopting Chan Buddhism's tenet of "the normal heart," Gao attains a new level of richness and understands the premise of achieving limitless freedom, which entails setting aside illusionary notions of superman and saint.

Here we need to note that Zhuangzi's philosophy and Chan Buddhism share many similarities. As Li Zehou observers, "both are anticonventional; both nullify distinctions between self and things, subject and object, life and death; both repudiate knowledge, stressing instead awakening, closeness with nature, and transcendence."[26] Zhuangzi's concept of "forgetting the self" is similar to Chan Buddhism's "breaking through the obsession of self" (破我執); Zhuangzi's shattering of our ordinary perspectives on the world—his deconstruction of truth, knowledge, and language as something final, absolute, and unchangeable—is equivalent to Chan Buddhism's "breaking through the obsession of rules" (破法執). Yet there are distinctions between the two schools, as Li Zehou explains:

> First, Zhuangzi's "On the Equality of Things" (齊物論) is still based on theoretical and logical interpretations of relativism, but Zen Buddhism is based on instinct and epiphany. Second, Zhuangzi tries to establish the ideal personality, such as the "perfect," "true," and "divine" person, but Zen Buddhism talks about a certain kind of mythical spiritual experience.[27]

For me, there is a stark distinction between Zhuangzi's pursuit of an ideal personality and Chan Buddhism's advocacy of the "normal heart," because the former is almost impossible for normal people to attain, whereas the latter can be accomplished by returning to ordinary daily life to comprehend the true and metaphysical meaning of existence. By seeking a completely enlightened state of mind inside "the normal heart," Chan Buddhism has provided another path toward spiritual liberation.

Gao's espousal of "the normal heart" of Chan Buddhism sheds light on why even if he refers to Zhuangzi's figure of the soaring Peng bird as a metaphor for spiritual freedom, he is also persistent in criticizing Nietzsche. His central criticism of Nietzsche is that establishing the subjective spirit of the self doesn't necessarily entail self-expansion, self-craziness, or regarding the self as the savior of the world:

> The superman claimed by Nietzsche has left a deep mark on the arts of the twenti-
> eth century. Once an artist believes he is a superman, he starts to become paranoid.
> That kind of infinite self-expansion is transformed into blind and uncontrollable
> violence, from which the artistic revolutionaries are burgeoning. However, artists
> are in fact as weak as normal people; they cannot undertake the great destiny of sav-
> ing mankind, nor can they rescue the world.[28]

By identifying with the notion of "a weak person" (脆弱人), Gao Xingjian diverges from the pattern of participating in society and saving the country established by Lu Xun 鲁迅 and other mainstream Chinese writers. During the twentieth century, Chinese writers were frequently called upon to play roles such as that of national savior or to take on historical or political responsibilities. Yet, through the lens of Chan Buddhism, Gao Xingjian comes to question Lu Xun's concept of "spiritual warrior." In his play *Snow in August*, Gao tells a story of the Sixth Patriarch of Chan Buddhism, Huineng, who liberated himself from fame and power as well as various kinds of power relations and vexing issues and therefore obtained limitless freedom. This drama corresponds to Zhuangzi's spirit presented in the "Easy and Free Wandering" chapter but is rooted in the idea of the normal heart. Similarly, by accepting Huineng's notion of "the normal heart," Gao is no longer concerned about fulfilling any social responsibility or pursuing a transcendent ideal personality; instead he seeks a spiritual path to eternal freedom. Therefore his definition of a writer is quite different from that of Lu Xun, who encour-aged Chinese writers to plunge into national affairs. For Gao, only through forsaking the utopian idea of changing the world as well as being the world's savior can a writer rediscover the real sense of freedom. What is important is not to be a fighter, a flag-bearer, or a drummer, but to face squarely one's own weakness as a human being and confront the limitations of self. Correspondingly, we shouldn't exaggerate literature's social function, regarding it as an instrument to change the world; instead, for Gao Xingjian, it is quite sufficient that literature is able to witness humanity, history, and the existential condition of human beings.

Since the true sense of freedom exists in the field of spiritual and aesthetic creation rather than in reality, it is crucial for writers and poets to create a place where they can put their heart, where the big Peng bird can rest after it roams freely. As Zhang Yinde points out, "such a state of resting coexists with roaming freely all over the world, supplementing each other."[29] Toward the end of "As Free as a Bird," the narrator finds a resting place, "a harbor of refuge" that is neither heaven nor hell but rather a piece of pure land, a sacred place, a final destiny, and a place where one can entirely escape from all the vexing issues of reality and rediscover the peaceful heart. Facing the weakness of life, the narrator who once roamed as free as a bird still possesses dignity as a human being:

> 你可曾見過
> 一隻老鳥
> 衰弱不堪
> 惶恐不安
> 淒淒慘慘
> 哀怨
> 哭泣
> 乞求
> 苟延殘喘?

> have you ever seen a bird
> who is frail and debilitated
> who is struck by panic
> who is sad and full of complaints
> crying and begging
> lingering on in a feeble existence?[30]

After finding "a harbor of refuge," a hidden place, the narrator just wants to be a weak person. It is precisely because of this clear consciousness of self-reflection, self-awareness, and self-transcendence that he is facing death calmly and with dignity:

> 是鳥都找好
> 隱匿之地
> 垂危之際
> 靜靜等侯
> 生命消逝
> 這聖地莫不
> 也是你的歸宿
> 又在何處?

> as long as he was a bird, he would find
> a hidden place
> silently waiting for
> the disappearance of life
> doesn't this sacred place
> also belong to your destiny
> where is it?[31]

With a normal heart, the poet who is like a bird has obtained the true sense of freedom, which includes not only the freedom of life but also the freedom of death. No kind of outward power, not even God's hand, can move him any longer. In this sense, this free person can calmly face worldly affairs, which are ever-changing, and can calmly face life and death.

Roaming Spirit and Metaphysical Thinking: A Free Subject's Unrestrained Gallop Through Life

In another poem, "Roaming Spirit and Metaphysical Thinking" (遊神與玄思), Gao Xingjian again refuses to be attuned to postmodern trends and tempos but safeguards an aesthetic conception and a spiritual enlightenment that are packed with Zhuangzian and Chan Buddhism-style awakening instead. As in *Soul Mountain*, in which the personal pronouns *you, I*, and *he* all refer to the same person, Gao Xingjian in this poem uses the personal pronouns *you* and *I* to refer to different facets of the same protagonist. The slight difference is that in this poem, "you" is the main protagonist, while "I" is featured as another self to question and mock this "you." This protagonist's journey is one of self-reflection and self-salvation, and it is a journey in which he grants himself a limitless freedom.

At the beginning of the poem, "you" resembles the protagonist in *Soul Mountain*, who thinks he is close to the God of death, but later discovers that God has spared him and allowed him to regain his life and freedom. Such an experience has surprisingly given him a brand-new vision of the world:

> 如今, 你離蒼天很近
> 離人寰甚遠
> 方才贏得這份清明
> 啊, 偌大的自在!
>
> 你俯視人世
> 芸芸眾生
> 紛紛擾擾
> 一片混沌
> 竄來竄去
> 全然不知
> 那隱形的大手
> 時不時暗中撥弄

> now since you are so close to the sky,
> yet so far away from the crowd,
> you then have won this quietness
> Ah, such limitless freedom!

> you look down at all the living creatures
> who are among the fury and the chaos
> hurrying here and there
> completely without knowing
> that invisible big hand
> is secretively handling them.[32]

The gesture of "looking down" is similar to the gesture of a bird that is flying in the sky, distant from other living creatures in the mundane world. In contrast to other creatures, whose fate is manipulated by invisible hands, the protagonist has won quietness and limitless freedom by taking the position of a bird.

Since he has gained such freedom, the protagonist is no longer obsessed with the kinds of reasons and concepts that had fettered him before, but can freely choose his own path:

> 要知道
> 你好不容易從泥沼爬出來
> 何必去清理身後那攤污泥
> 且讓爛泥歸泥沼
> 身後的呱噪去鼓噪
> 只要生命未到盡頭
> 儘管一步一步
> 走自己的路
>
> you should know
> it takes a lot of effort for you to climb out of the swamp
> why bother to go back to clean the mud behind you
> just let mud go back to morass
> just let the hullabaloo behind you belong to uproar
> as long as life hasn't ended
> why not just walk your own road
> step by step[33]

In real life, Gao Xingjian chose to leave China, where freedom of speech was not allowed. Choosing a life of exile, he is finding his own path by exploring how an individual life unfolds when it detaches itself from the center of politics and embarks on a journey of self-discovery and self-assertion. This poem's self-reflexivity creates a different state of consciousness that establishes "exile" as a key concept. In fact, in Gao's system of thought "exile" is always momentous. For him, human beings live not only in various kinds of spiritual prisons of society but also in the prison created by the self; therefore, although it is challenging to escape from prisons built by others, it is even more arduous to escape from the self-built prison. As Gao Xingjian once observed,

> When the individual is confronted by the all-engulfing fanatical tides of the times, whether it is the violent revolution of communism or wars initiated by fascism,

the only escape is to flee, and this must be recognized before disaster is upon him. To flee is thus to save oneself, and even more difficult to flee are the dark shadows of the inner mind of the self, and if one lacks sufficient awareness of the self, one will undoubtedly first be buried in the hell of the self, and right until death not see the light.[34]

It is certain that Gao Xianjing interpreted the reclusive way of keeping distance from the mundane world advocated by Zhuangzi and Chan Buddhism as his own manner of exile. In other words, he upholds the banner of exile due to his aspiration for limitless freedom. Gao Xingjian's play *Flight* expresses the same point of view, that one not only needs to flee from political persecution from the outside world but also needs to flee from the inner hell of the self. Realizing that it is impossible to find freedom in the field of reality, such as politics, economics, ethics, and human relations, he regards *exile* as a kind of light that dispels the shadows of reality. By bestowing positive meaning upon exile, he is able to come to terms with power and knowledge, which sometimes alienate human beings.

After transforming the negative connotations of *exile* into positive ones, Gao Xingjian in "Roaming Spirit and Metaphysical Thinking" is searching for a Garden of Eden, in which one can restore a pure heart and wander freely in the spiritual world. Replacing the hell made by others as well as the self-made hell, this Garden of Eden is established specifically for spiritual creation, a place to shine even after exile—this is Gao Xingjian's way of self-salvation. He writes:

> 你不妨再造
> 一個失重的自然
> 心中的伊甸園
> 可以任你優游
> 由你盡興
>
> why don't you rebuild
> a nature that has zero gravity
> a Garden of Eden in your heart
> that allows you to travel freely
> and thoroughly enjoy yourself?[35]

To rebuild nature, a Garden of Eden in one's heart, means to create an inner universe within oneself. If rebuilding an outer nature is impossible, to rebuild an inner nature is by all means practical and feasible. This kind of rebuilding is not a delusion about changing the world into a utopia, as the Communist Party propagandizes, but rather a free spiritual and aesthetic creation that doesn't need to be shaped to fit the political, social, and ideological exigencies of totalitarianism, revolution, and nation.

In his article "Freedom and Literature," Gao Xingjian posed this question: "The conflict between the dilemmas of survival and the free will is the perennial topic of literature: how the individual transcends his environment and is not controlled by it."[36] Just as for Zhuangzi, the primary concern for Gao is the question of anti-alienation of the individual. Interestingly, the answer he has provided is simple but decisive:

> The tragedy and comedy and even the absurdity of the struggle, can only be dealt with aesthetically, but writers through the ages from ancient Greek plays down to the modern novels pioneered by Kafka have in fact succeeded. Some things are achievable by humans, while others are not, and while humans cannot defy fate they are able to aesthetically transform experiences and feelings into literary and art works that can even be transmitted to later generations, and in so doing transcend both the dilemmas of reality and the times. Therefore it is only in the realm of the purely spiritual that humankind can possess an abundance of freedom.[37]

Indeed, the literary field is supposed to be the area with the most freedom, because it offers the possibility of some form of re-creation. Once writers and poets get rid of outward illusions, refusing to be superman-like madmen, declining all kinds of utopian ideas, they will be able to enter the inner Garden of Eden and fully enjoy the freedom of creation and recreation. Therefore, the center of the protagonist's spiritual roaming and metaphysical thinking is the aesthetic spirit:

不如回到性靈所在
重建內心的造化
率性畫上個園圈
再後退一步
將生存轉化爲關注
睜開另一隻慧眼
把對象作爲審美

why don't you come back to the place where spirit is
rebuild the inner world
draw a circle capriciously
then take one step back
turn surviving into care
open the other eye of wisdom
regard the object as aesthetics[38]

Ironically, this kind of aesthetic spirit has been sanctioned by a long modern Chinese literary tradition idealizing literature as an instrument for nation building. Liu Zaifu once pointed out, "Gao Xingjian is the one who is most capable of staying in the literary state, differentiated from the state as a political instrument or as a commercial product, and transgressing various kinds of relations of gain and loss."[39] It is true that only literature can allow writers and poets a real sense of freedom; therefore, the essential spirit of literature is congruent with Zhuangzi's great roaming spirit, definitely detached from political concerns and economic rules. By pointing out that literature is a path toward the Peng bird's freedom, a path that can be taken and that writers should feel proud of, Gao's pure literary spirit most closely approximates Zhuangzi's spirit of art, defined by Xu Fuguan 徐復觀 as the highest art.[40]

In "Roaming Spirit and Metaphysical Thinking," Gao Xingjian presents himself as "a traveler," "a player," "a man of leisure," and "a hidden man," a definition that is related to his aesthetic of exile as well as his life state of limitless freedom. It also allows him to challenge the traditional role of writers, who must undertake heavy social and national responsibilities.

你一個游人
無牽無挂
沒有家人
沒有故鄉
無所謂祖國
滿世界游蕩

你沒有家族
更無門第
也無身份
孑然一身
倒更像人

你如風無形
無聲如影
無所不在
你
僅僅是一個指稱
一旦提及
霎時面對面
便在鏡子裏邊

啊你
一個優人
嘻嘻哈哈
調笑這世界
游戲人生
全不當真

哦,你
一個悠人
悠哉游哉
無所事事
一無執著
無可無不可

嘿,你
好一個幽人
在社會邊緣
人際之間
那種種計較
概不沾邊

ah you, a traveler
without a tie in the world
no family
no hometown
no so-called motherland
roams all over the world

you have no clan
no social status
no identity
just one person
yet more like a human

you are like wind without shape
shadow without sound
staying everywhere

you is only a pronoun
once mentioned
face to face in an instant
you are inside the mirror

ah, you
a player
laughing and joking
mocking this world
treating life as merely a game
without taking it seriously

oh, you
a leisure man
free from constraint, free in traveling
doing nothing
persisting in nothing
either having or not having

hey, you
what a hidden man
on the periphery of society
aloof from any kind of calculated human relations[41]

    The common characteristic found in the preceding figures for the "traveler" (*youren* 游人), "artist" (*youren* 優人), "man of leisure" (*youren* 悠人), and "hidden man" (*youren* 幽人) is a homophonic allusion to "wandering" (*you* 遊). Traveling around the world, fooling around, wandering free from constraints, or loitering on the margins of society, these figures all represent a special kind of person in modern society who can best represent Zhuangzi's spirit in the "Free and Easy Wandering" chapter. Simultaneously, the action of *you* also denotes and emphasizes the attitude of playfulness. Drawing comparisons between *Zhuangzi* and Erasmus's *In Praise of Folly*, Victor Mair argues that the striking resemblance between these two works is a playful attitude toward life, an attitude that transcends "an overemphasis on earnest reasoning." He adds, "The playful human being reacts naturally to whatever circumstances present themselves. He does not proffer answers to unasked questions nor offer solutions to hypothetical problems."[42] In his interpretation of the *Inner Chapters*, which is about free and easy wandering, Michael Crandell also suggests that wandering (*you* 遊) refers to the kind of free-spiritedness that "allows one to shift back and forth between various perspectives and opinions without the friction of conflict and emotional upset."[43] Indeed, through wandering in free-spiritedness, one can put fame, gain, and wisdom behind and completely enter the artistic state.

According to Xu Fuguan, "Zhuangzi's so-called 'perfect man,' 'true man,' and 'divine man' are all capable of wandering. The one who can wander is actually the one who demonstrates the spirit of art. He is also a person who becomes artistic in his heart. The word '*you*' runs through the whole book of *Zhuangzi* precisely for this reason."[44] Therefore, "the traveler," "the player," "the man of leisure," and "the hidden man" with whom Gao Xingjian identified are all distant from society and the mundane world, without hometown or family, on the edge of society, are "useless" (*wuyong*) yet free, playing around, wandering around, mocking the world—this is the position of Zhuangzi's artistic spirit that Xu Fuguan interprets. Only by acknowledging such a position can the inner spirit of art fly high.

Toward the end of this poem, there is an interesting dialogue between the "I," who is characterized as a "passenger" and as a feeble person waiting for his time of death to leave the world, and the "you," who is able to gain "instant eternity" while wandering freely inside literature and art. "You are eternal, but I am only a passenger."[45] No doubt both "you" and "I" refer to different facets of the same quasi-autobiographical poet. The image of the narrator "you" is intimately and essentially free, assuring us that the literary state can satisfy the most excessive demands by imagination and has a transcendental value. Even if the narrator "I" is already more than seventy years old and his physical body is declining, the narrator "you" can travel easily between life and death. This kind of "traveling" exemplifies the spirit of art that is upheld by Gao Xingjian as an everlasting aesthetics and the beauty of the soul. Like Zhuangzi's Peng allegory, Gao's traveling will also be sustained as an inspiring and eternal fable and metaphor. At the end of this poem, Gao reemphasizes the importance of the aesthetics of roaming:

在這世上游蕩
又像一個隱喻
或一則寓言

wandering in the world
it is also like a metaphor, or a fable[46]

Such wandering without any purpose, which can lead to the purest spirit of art, immune to any commercial or political manipulation, is precisely the modern version of Zhuangzi's Peng allegory. From "returning to nature" to "rebuilding nature," from exile to reconstruction, Gao Xingjian has found a way to differentiate himself from Wang Zengqi, Ah Cheng, and Han Shaogong; moreover, he has surpassed Nietzsche as well as the postmodernists, who were less concerned with self-salvation.

Although Gao Xingjian is known for being the first Chinese writer to bring absurdist drama as well as the dimension of modernism to China, he is actually a multidimensional writer and artist, being not only a successful novelist but also a successful dramatist, drama director, film director, painter, critic, and poet. After fleeing from the communist totalitarian state of China, he has gained freedom and devoted himself to the realm of spiritual and aesthetic creation and innovation, allowing his multifaceted talent to shine. It is not surprising that his writings still cannot be openly published in mainland China, even if what he insists upon is nothing but the freedom of aesthetic and artistic pursuit. What distinguishes Gao Xingjian from others is his political and aesthetic understanding of fleeing, from which he has fully gained the freedom to write, to innovate, and to produce. As he said, "I believe that even if politics and society are touched upon in literary creation, it is better to 'flee' than to 'participate,' because this would deflect social pressures from oneself and also cleanse oneself spiritually."[47] Compared to other Chinese writers such as Mo Yan 莫言, who dwells on local culture and the spirit of the native land, Gao Xingjian represents a trend of inner reflection and inner searching usually seen in highly educated intellectuals who have been influenced by Western existentialism, Zhuangzi's philosophy, and Chan Buddhism. His gestures of fleeing, self-exile, wandering—all part of diasporic writing—allow him to embrace the universal values of humanity. Even if some of his dramas, such as *Snow in August* and *The Story of the Classics of Mountains and Seas*, contain significant Chinese elements, he still persistently transcends national boundaries and expresses universal themes and subject matter.

Since freedom is perhaps the most important keyword for understanding Gao Xingjian and his oeuvre, his case propels us to ponder the relationship between individual freedom and literature. In the context of modern Chinese literature, the identity and meaning of individual life and self-fulfillment are usually entangled with and inseparable from freedom in a collective, political sense. However, while political emancipation in the national independence or social reform movement has become a fundamental and dominant theme for modern fictional discourse, individuality and the pursuit of independent life have gradually been pushed aside and never completely realized, except during the short period of the May Fourth movement and the new period of literature after the Cultural Revolution. The emphasis on collective responsibility always seems to reveal an unbearable lack of individual rights. Even a writer choosing a private life (a garden of one's own) in order to stay out of the struggles between the left and the right cannot be tolerated when mainstream Chinese literature expresses the drive for a grand heroic or collective life. It is exactly because the frustrated desire to reclaim individuality had been constantly misremembered that many modern Chinese writers strove to conjure the spirit of Zhuangzi. Among them, Gao clearly is one of the firmest writers to affirm and embrace Zhuangzi's spirit of individual freedom and liberation as well as pure aesthetic attitude. Yet, ironically, such a pure aesthetic stance, which is all about detachment from politics, is regarded as a resistance against political ideology in mainland China. Inevitably tinged with political meanings, Gao Xingjian's fleeing and self-exile closely associated with his literary works have represented the most compelling case of the interplay between literature and individual freedom at the end of the twentieth century.

Notes

1. Lin Gang, "Toward an Aesthetics of Freedom," in Michael Lackner and Nikola Chardonnens, eds., *Polyphony Embodied: Freedom and Fate in Gao Xingjian's Writings* (Berlin/Boston: De Gruyter, 2014), 121.
2. Gao Xingjian, *Cold Literature: Selected Works by Gao Xingjian*, trans. Gilbert C. F. Fong and Mabel Lee (Hong Kong: The Chinese University Press, 2005), 24.
3. Gao Xingjian, *Meiyou zhuyi* 沒有主義 [Without isms] (Hong Kong: Tiandi tushu youxian gongsi, 2000), 20.
4. Thomas Moran, "Lost in the Woods: Nature in *Soul Mountain*," *Modern Chinese Literature and Culture* 14.2 (Fall 2002): 219.
5. Gao Xingjian, *Lingshan* 靈山 [Soul mountain] (Hong Kong: Tiandi tushu, 2000), 349.
6. Gao Xingjian, *Without Isms*, 21.
7. Ming Jian, "Life's Unattainable Goal and Actualized Meaning: Existential Anxiety and Zen Tranquility in Gao Xingjian's *Soul Mountain*," *Chinese Literature Essays, Articles, Reviews* 31 (2009): 97–98.
8. Gao Xingjian, *Aesthetics and Creation*, trans. by Mabel Lee (New York: Cambria Press, 2012), 38.
9. Liu Zaifu, *Gao Xingjian lun* 高行健論 [On Gao Xingjian] (Taibei: Lianjing chuban, 2004), 173.
10. Gao Xingjian, *Soul Mountain*, trans. Mabel Lee (Sydney: HarperPerennial, 2000), 525–526; translation modified.
11. Gao Xingjian, *Soul Mountain*, 450.
12. John R. McRae, ed. and trans., *The Platform Sutra of the Sixth Patriarch* (Berkeley: Numata Center for Buddhist Translation and Research, 2000), 22.
13. Gao Xingjian, *Without Isms*, 351.
14. Zhang Yinde, "Gao Xingjian Carefree: *Of Mountains and Seas* and *Carefree as a Bird*," in Lackner and Chardonnens, *Polyphony Embodied*, 143.
15. Gao Xingjian, *Youshen yu xuansi: Gao Xingjian shige ji* 遊神與玄思：高行健詩歌集 [Roaming spirit and metaphysical thinking: A collection of Gao Xingjian's poetry] (Taibei: Lianjing chuban, 2012), 23–26.
16. A. C. Graham, *Zhuangzi: The Inner Chapters* (London: Unwin Paperbacks, 1986), 43. Transliteration of Chinese revised to conform to *pinyin* conventions.
17. See Gao Xingjian, "Freedom and Literature," in Lackner and Chardonnens, *Polyphony Embodied*, 11–17.
18. Gao Xingjian, *Roaming Spirit and Metaphysical Thinking*, 26–28.
19. Gao Xingjian, *Cold Literature: Selected Works by Gao Xingjian*, trans. Gilbert C. F. Fong and Mabel Lee, 21.
20. Graham, *Zhuangzi: The Inner Chapters*, 44.
21. Gao Xingjian, *Roaming Spirit and Metaphysical Thinking*, 26–28.

22. Li Zehou, *The Chinese Aesthetic Tradition*, trans. Maija Bell Samei (Honolulu: University of Hawai'i Press, 2010), 84.

23. Qian Mu, *Zhuanglao tongbian* 莊老統編 [The complete arguments of Zhuangzi and Laozi] (Beijing: Sanlian shudian, 2002), 287.

24. Gao Xingjian, *Roaming Spirit and Metaphysical Thinking*, 28–29.

25. Gao Xingjian, *Cold Literature: Selected Works by Gao Xingjian*, trans. Gilbert C. F. Fong and Mabel Lee, 3, 11, 39.

26. Li Zehou, *The Chinese Aesthetic Tradition*, 167.

27. Li Zehou 李澤後, *Zhongguo gudai sixiang shilun* 中國古代思想史論 [A theory of Chinese ancient thought] (Tianjin: Tianjin shehui kexueyuan chubanshe, 2003), 202.

28. Gao Xingjian, *Ling yizhong meixue* 另一種美學 [Another kind of aesthetics] (Taibei: Lianjing chuban, 2001), 10.

29. Zhang Yinde, "Gao Xingjian Carefree."

30. Gao Xingjian, *Roaming Spirit and Metaphysical Thinking*, 30–31.

31. Gao Xingjian, *Roaming Spirit and Metaphysical Thinking*, 31–32.

32. Gao Xingjian, *Roaming Spirit and Metaphysical Thinking*, 90–91.

33. Gao Xingjian, *Roaming Spirit and Metaphysical Thinking*, 96–97.

34. Gao Xingjian, "Freedom and Literature," 16.

35. Gao Xingjian, *Roaming Spirit and Metaphysical Thinking*, 97.

36. Gao Xingjian, "Freedom and Literature," 13.

37. Gao Xingjian, "Freedom and Literature," 13–14.

38. Gao Xingjian, *Roaming Spirit and Metaphysical Thinking*, 112.

39. Liu Zaifu, *On Gao Xingjian*, 40.

40. According to Xu Fuguan 徐復觀, "The heart that Zhuangzi masters is exactly the subject of the spirit of art. Originally Zhuangzi didn't mean our modern sense of art, but what came from his heart is naturally the spirit of art, which naturally succeeds a life of art and from here succeeds to the highest art." Xu Fuguan, *Zhongguo yishu jingshen* 中國藝術精神 [The Chinese spirit of art] (Shanghai: Huadong shifang daxue chuban she, 2001), 42.

41. Gao Xingjian, *Roaming Spirit and Metaphysical Thinking*, 123–126.

42. Victor H. Mair, "Chuang-tzu and Erasmus: Kindred Wits," in *Experimental Essays on Chuang-Tzu*, ed. Victor H. Mair (Honolulu: University of Hawai'i, 1983), 98.

43. Michael Crandell, "'Play' in the Inner Chapters," in *Experimental Essays on Chuang-Tzu*, 114.

44. Xu Fuguan, *The Chinese Spirit of Art*, 38.

45. Gao Xingjian, *Roaming Spirit and Metaphysical Thinking*, 126–128.

46. Gao Xingjian, *Roaming Spirit and Metaphysical Thinking*, 131–132.

47. Gao Xingjian, *Cold Literature*, 8.

Works Cited

Gao Xingjian 高行健. *Lingshan* 靈山 [Soul mountain]. Hong Kong: Tiandi tushu, 2000.

Gao Xingjian 高行健. *Ling yizhong meixue* 另一種美學 [Another kind of aesthetics]. Taibei: Lianjing chuban, 2001. 10.

Gao Xingjian 高行健. *Meiyou zhuyi* 沒有主義 [Without isms]. Hong Kong: Tiandi tushu youxian gongsi, 2000.

Gao Xingjian 高行健. *Cold Literature: Selected Works by Gao Xingjian*. Trans. Gilbert C. F. Fong and Mabel Lee. Hong Kong: The Chinese University Press, 2005.

Gao Xingjian 高行健. *Aesthetics and Creation*. Trans. by Mabel Lee. New York: Cambria Press, 2012.

Gao Xingjian 高行健. *Youshen yu Xuansi—Gao Xingjian shiji* 遊神與玄思–高行健詩集 [Roaming spirit and metaphysical thinking: A collection of Gao Xingjian's poetry]. Taibei: Lianjing chuban, 2012.

Graham, A. C. *Zhuangzi: The Inner Chapters*. London: Unwin Paperbacks, 1986.

Lackner, Michael, and Nikola Chardonnens, eds. *Freedom and Fate in Gao Xingjian's Writings*. Berlin/Boston: De Gruyter, 2014.

Li Zehou. *The Chinese Aesthetic Tradition*. Trans. Maija Bell Samei. Honolulu: University of Hawai'i Press, 2010.

Li Zehou 李澤厚. *Zhongguo gudai sixiang shilun* 中國古代思想史論 [A theory of Chinese ancient thought]. Tianjin: Tianjin shehui kexueyuan chubanshe, 2003.

Liu Zaifu 劉再復. *Gao Xingjian lun* 高行健論 [On Gao Xingjian]. Taibei: Lianjing chuban, 2004.

McRae, John R., ed. and trans. *The Platform Sutra of the Sixth Patriarch*. Berkeley: Numata Center for Buddhist Translation and Research, 2000.

Ming Jian. "Life's Unattainable Goal and Actualized Meaning: Existential Anxiety and Zen Tranquility in Gao Xingjian's *Soul Mountain*." *Chinese Literature Essays, Articles, Reviews* 31 (2009): 97–98.

Moran, Thomas. "Lost in the Woods: Nature in *Soul Mountain*." *Modern Chinese Literature and Culture* 14.2 (Fall 2002): 219.

Qian Mu 錢穆. *Zhuanglao tongbian* 莊老統編 [The complete arguments of Zhuangzi and Laozi]. Beijing: Sanlian shudian, 2002.

Zhang Yinde. "Gao Xingjian Carefree: *Of Mountains and Seas* and *Carefree as a Bird*." In *Polyphony Embodied: Freedom and Fate in Gao Xingjian's Writings*. Ed. Michael Lackner and Nikola Chardonnens. Berlin/Boston: De Gruyter, 2014. 139–148.

CHAPTER 3.3

....

HISTORIOGRAPHY
IN THE CHINESE
TWENTIETH CENTURY

....

HAUN SAUSSY AND GE ZHAOGUANG

ON January 19, 1929, Liang Qichao 梁啟超 (b. 1873) passed away in Beijing. That year, the newly founded Nanjing journal *Historical Studies* (史學雜誌) published in its very first number an essay by the noted historian Miao Fenglin 繆鳳林 pointing out that though Liang's writings had touched on a great number of different fields, from beginning to end "history was the center of his preoccupations." Miao's essay enumerated the fields to which Liang had contributed—history of ideas, political history, history of scholarship, economic history—and added that "in a multiplicity of fields, with a variety of points of view, he was able to inaugurate countless areas of historical study."[1]

Liang Qichao's passing coincided with a new turn in the trend he had initiated in the last years of the Qing dynasty. With his *Commentaries on Chinese History* (中國史敘論; 1901) and *New Historical Studies* (新史學; 1902), Liang had indeed inaugurated a modernist, critical turn in traditional Chinese historiography. Over the following three decades, "new historical studies" developed into a full-blown movement and began to undergo further transformations. By the time of Liang's death in 1929, three major new approaches were disputing among themselves the terrain of Chinese historical studies—namely, the continuation of the modernist historiographical movement (scientism), the attempt to establish historiography as the basis of national identity (nationalism), and the pursuit of a materialist explanation of history (Marxism).

As to the first approach, the early years of the Republic were the time at which a modernist historiography grounded on scientific inquiry became dominant. In 1929, the remains of the *Homo erectus* specimen known as Peking Man were discovered in the Zhoukoudian cave system outside Beijing, archeologists began excavating the Shang dynasty ruins near Anyang, and the recently established Academia Sinica research institute for historical linguistics relocated to Beiping (Beijing). Furthermore, the institute's original eight departments were regrouped into Historical Studies (under the direction of Chen Yinke 陳寅恪), Linguistics (under the direction of Y. R. Chao 趙元任), and Archaeology and Anthropology (under the direction of Li Ji 李濟). It was from this year that Chinese academia adopted the institutional forms of modern historical scholarship.

As to the second approach, it was also during this period that nationalist historiography became a major current of thought—not only as a result of the ongoing national crisis, but also as a result of actions taken by the Nationalist government. On the very day that Liang Qichao passed away, the *Republican Daily* (民國日報) began serializing Hu Hanmin's 胡漢民 long report titled "Only Through Nationalism Can One Speak of Cosmopolitanism" (有民族主義才可以講世界主義), symbolizing China's shift from a pursuit of one-world policies of international integration to a pursuit of nationalism. A powerful national consciousness influenced historical studies (a salient example was the rebuttal of the notion that the population and culture of China had originated in Western Asia, taken to deny China's distinctiveness). It was also in that same year that the government banned the *Middle School Textbook in Modern Chinese History* (現代初中本國史教科書) edited by Gu Jiegang 顧頡剛 (1893–1980) and Wang Zhonglin 王鐘麟 (1884–1966).[2] Given that Gu had adopted a "skeptical" perspective in rewriting ancient Chinese history that led him to question the historical existence of the so-called "Three Sovereigns and Five Emperors," some readers felt that if this work were adopted as a textbook it would compromise students' sense of national pride and their ability to identify with their ethnic and national heritage.[3] After 1929, with the onset of Japan's invasion of China (1931–1945), historical studies aimed at affirming the unity of the Chinese people and national recognition became the new trend.

As to the third approach, it was also in this same period that Marxism and its attendant historical vision began to enter China, ultimately becoming one of the country's most influential modes of historical analysis. Many influential social debates at the time—including debates on the system of landholding, taxation, social organization, historical periodization, and so forth—were profoundly influenced by Marxist texts imported from Germany, Japan, and the Soviet Union. In September of 1929, for instance, Guo Moruo 郭沫若 (1892–1978) wrote the preface to his *Studies in Ancient Chinese Society* (中國古代社會研究)—although the book itself would not be completed until later—in which he affirmed that he was adopting Engels's views on the origins of the family, private property, and the state, clearly revealing the degree to which Marxism had already begun to influence Chinese historiography.

These three new historiographic trends that emerged around 1929 collectively transformed twentieth-century Chinese historiography, drawing it progressively farther away from traditional historical approaches. However, it should be emphasized that these transformations were merely extensions of the challenges to traditional historiography that Liang Qichao had initiated in his *Commentaries on Chinese History* and *New Historical Studies*. Thus, when we consider twentieth-century Chinese historiography, we must start from Liang Qichao's initial critiques of traditional Chinese historical studies.

What did Liang Qichao initiate? To answer this question, we should look at the state of history-writing in China before 1900. For centuries, the purpose and organizing principle of history-writing in China had been clear: history was the reservoir of examples and lessons, and it formed, along with the Classics and their commentaries, the basis of preparation for the civil service examinations. Beginning with the Han, every successive dynasty left behind an officially recognized history largely composed of extracts from the archives. For any situation that the imperial court or one of its subordinate managers might encounter, a precedent could always be found that would guide the choice of appropriate responses. This expectation of the exemplary value of history—the use of the past as a "comprehensive mirror to be applied in the service of governing" (資治通鑑), to quote from the title of the most famous summary history—shaped the content of traditional histories and the ways they were read.[4] To write a good answer to a policy question or a text-interpretation question, the examinee had to be versed in the details of the dynastic histories, and, if given one case, needed to be ready to provide concordant and contrasting instances. A counterexample from the Ming dynasty only confirms this set of aims for history-writing: the verdicts on famous figures of the past pronounced by the heterodox scholar Li Zhi 李贄 (1527–1602) were seen as scandalous, because to take them seriously would have required adopting new standards of right and wrong, and thus different policy objectives.[5]

With the demise of the examination system and the old-style civil service, historians in China were indeed confronted by such new standards and objectives. It could no longer be taken as axiomatic that a good policy was one that acted to preserve the reigning dynasty in conformity with the rules laid down by antique sages. Those who wrote history or argued about how it should be written took their models from abroad and now thought of Chinese history as a subset of world history, using analogies from ancient Egypt, Rome, Persia, the European Middle Ages, and other domains that dynastic history had never found of the slightest relevance. They posed the problems of Chinese history—and the paramount problem of the survival of the Chinese nation—in frameworks drawn sometimes from relatively neglected Chinese sources, but more often in terms of commercial or Darwinian competition.[6] The New Text Confucianism of Kang Youwei 康有為 (1858–1927) read history in the light of the *Gongyang* and *Guliang* commentaries to the *Spring and Autumn Annals* (春秋公羊傳, 穀梁傳), drawing from them an imperative of periodic institutional change, and Kang's later periodical *Buren* (不忍) illustrated this with chronologies of past empires. Kang's outline of a future world government, *Datong shu* (大同書; drafted starting in 1902, partially published in 1913 and 1919, first printed as a whole in 1935), extended the same principles to the surface of the entire globe.[7] Its version of history is indeed a "classicism": in it the most radical change (for instance, sexual and racial equality and universal democracy) is imagined only as a return to the constant rule.

For Kang Youwei's most distinguished follower, Liang Qichao, such utopian nostalgia stood outside of the possible subjects of history-writing. Rather than imagining a world reformed in the idealized image of predynastic China, Liang wrote about a China subjected to change from without and forced into debilitating compromises. This external pressure forced the writing of history to adopt far-reaching changes in structure and orientation, many of which Liang was the first to express and promote.

The Expansion and Compression
of History

During the first half of the twentieth century—which is to say, during the period lead-ing up to 1949—Chinese historiography underwent a number of transformations. Four aspects of these are worthy of note: namely, historical compression, spatial expansion, increase of historical sources, and the growing complexity of historical questions.

What is historical compression? It is the dwindling away of the supernatural ele-ment in traditional perspectives on Chinese prehistory. Through a process of historical research and excavation, Chinese historians demonstrated that many canonical views on Chinese prehistory were nothing more than legends, or even deliberate fabrica-tions. The accumulation of such insights led toward historical skepticism; that is to say, they ultimately compressed the legendary period of Chinese history. Alternatively, they sought to apply evidentiary methods to historical legends, and in this way used material evidence to rewrite accepted historical narratives and exclude from history the long-lived myths and legends pertaining to the period of the Three Sovereigns and the Five Emperors. This is what is meant by the modernization of learning or the scien-tific reform of academic inquiry: refusing to use legend or myth in the place of actual history. On the other hand, this is also a revolutionary necessity, in that following the collapse of Confucian orthodoxy, the historical system of legitimation that relied on the precedent of the legendary sovereigns Yao, Shun, and Yu was destroyed, as was the myth of an ideological genealogy that had developed out of Confucianism. The result was a reconstruction of history that put modern China on a new historical trajectory.

From Kang Youwei to Gu Jiegang's *Debates on Ancient History* (古史辯; 1926–1941), Chinese historiography gradually established a new tradition.[8] It should be noted that this process we are calling historical compression—namely, the modern historical ten-dency to expel legendary and mythical qualities from history—can also be found in Japan and Korea. In Japan, it has traditionally been believed that the Japanese people are descended from the sun goddess, suggesting a history that is just as long as that of the Chinese. However, from Shiratori Kurakichi 白鳥庫吉 (1865–1942) to Tsuda Sōkichi 津田左右吉 (1873–1961), Japanese historians have rejected this mythical account. At the same time, Koreans have been challenging a mythical history of their own. Korea actually has two mythical systems, one of which contends that the legend-ary sage Gija 箕子 from China's late Shang dynasty is the ancestor of the Korean people. However, during later periods, Koreans—out of a sense of national pride and in order to reinvent their own history—were no longer willing to speak of Gija, and instead focused on a figure named Tangun 檀君, who was said to have lived during roughly the same period as China's legendary Three Sovereigns. However, Shiratori Kurakichi and another Japanese historian of Korea Imanishi Ryū 今西龍, each of whom published a study titled "An Investigation of Tangun" (檀君考), both indicated that Tangun was initially derived not from an origin myth for the Korean people but rather from a set of myths and shamanistic rituals associated with a local deity from the Pyongyang area. Tangun began to be claimed as the common ancestor of all Koreans as a nationalistic gesture following the thirteenth-century Mongol invasion of the Korean peninsula.[9] So it can be seen that during the late nineteenth and early twentieth centuries, countries throughout East Asia initiated movements to put aside legend and mythology.

"Spatial expansion" is the expansion of the geographic purview of Chinese historical inquiry, so that it is no longer limited to a linear system extending from the time of the Three Sovereigns and Five Emperors up to the present—in other words, it no longer frames history within the confines of ethnically Han China. The modernity of this expansion derives from the fact that it was in the modern period that European Sinologists, in a series of exploratory and colonial exercises, undertook considerable research into various regions along China's periphery, including what is now Xinjiang, Tibet, India, Central Asia, and Southeast Asia (Burma and Vietnam). The linguistic and religious backgrounds of this extended region were very complex and their respective cultural backgrounds were different, and out of this encounter developed the broad academic tradition now known as Orientalism. The Sinologists include figures such as Paul Pelliot (1878–1945) and his advisor Édouard Chavannes (1865–1918), who, apart from translating Sima Qian's 司馬遷 *Records of the Historian* (史記), also inherited and extended Europe's Orientalist tradition, focusing on the history of East-West contact in geographic areas outside of Han China, including Central Asia, South Asia, and Southeast Asia.[10] A similar trend of envisioning China from its borderlands can also be observed among China scholars from Japan. Japanese scholars such as Shiratori Kurakichi, Naitō Torajirō 内藤湖南 (1866–1934), and Naka Michiyo 那珂通世 (1851–1908) shared an interest not only in Han China but also in geographic areas corresponding to other ethnic groups such as the Manchus (Manchuria), Mongolians (Mongolia), Hui (Xinjiang and Central Asia), Tibetans (Tibet), and Koreans (Korea). In academic terms, these scholars were following trends in early-twentieth-century Western historiography, though on a political level their research is also closely connected to Japanese efforts to strategically divide up the territory of China.

A number of colonial and imperial factors underpinned these academic trends. Nonetheless, these foreign historians also helped catalyze a number of new directions in international scholarship on China, particularly with respect to research on the history, geography, and culture of non-Han territories located along China's periphery. In order to study these regions, it was necessary to understand a variety of languages, religions, and histories. In China, where the traditional approach up until the Qing dynasty had been one of "using China to explain China," whereby canonical Chinese-language texts such as the "Four Books and Five Classics," the twenty-four orthodox dynastic histories, and the *Comprehensive Mirror For Governing* (資治通鑑) were used to explain Chinese tradition, this came as an innovation. By the late Qing, however, a significant shift was already underway, as China found itself confronting external pressure and internal instability. This helped encourage a scholarly interest in the geography and history of northwestern regions of Xinjiang and Central Asia. From this point on, Chinese scholarship gradually underwent a profound transformation, as scholars found it increasingly necessary to familiarize themselves with Western scholarly trends and perspectives. By the late Qing, these new trends had already yielded significant results, including Ke Shaomin's 柯劭忞 (1850–1933) compilation of the *New Yuan History* (新元史), Shen Cengzhi's 沈曾植 (1850–1922) compilation of the *Annotated Secret History of the Yuan* (元秘史箋注), and Tu Ji's 屠寄 (1850–1922) compilation of the *Record of Mongol History* (蒙兀兒史記). However, Chinese of the time did not have a particularly strong motive for pursuing this topic, and consequently these transformations in academic research did not translate into Chinese social movements. Awareness of the importance of the borderlands for explaining Chinese history was slight, and therefore these questions remained merely academic. In Japan, it was another story, as such academic issues had a pragmatic appeal. But by the 1920s and 1930s, the situation underwent a fundamental transformation as Chinese historians energetically began studying border regions and minority languages and dialects, as well as religions and cultures.

The increase of historical sources is an indirect effect of "historical compression." Many texts that had previously been viewed as authentic now came under critique and suspicion, and therefore could no longer be used as sources of history. Moreover, because of the process of spatial expansion, documents from Han-ethnicity China were no longer sufficient. In particular, due to a shift in historical perspectives, greater attention was brought to historical narratives, as attention gradually shifted from emperors and princes and the cyclical rise and fall of dynasties to considerations of society and communities; consequently, historians no longer focused only on traditional texts.

In addition, during the first half of the twentieth century, European historians such as Paul Pelliot, Marcel Granet (1884–1940), Henri Maspero (1883–1945), Sylvain Lévi (1863–1935), and Bernhard Karlgren (1889–1978), together with Japanese historians such as Shiratori Kurakichi, Naitō Torajirō, Fujita Toyohachi 藤田丰八 (1869–1929), Kano Naoki 狩野直喜 (1868–1947), Ichimura Sanjirō 市村瓚次郎 (1864–1947), and Kuwabara Jitsuzō 桑原騭藏 (1870–1931) had a profound influence on historical studies in China. Chinese scholars had no choice but to develop a sense of scholarly competition. However, in what respect could Chinese scholarship surpass the work of these Japanese and Western scholars? As it happens, it was precisely during this period that several pivotal historical discoveries were made whose significance gradually came to be recognized, as a result of which Chinese scholars were able not only to rival the achievements of these foreign scholars but even to surpass them.

Wang Guowei succinctly summarized these pivotal advances in a lecture that he gave in 1925 at Tsinghua University, in which he pointed to the discovery of the Shang dynasty oracle bones, the bamboo inscriptions from Dunhuang and the Western territories, the Six Dynasties and Tang dynasty documents from the Mogao Caves and the Dunhuang Library Cave, and the files from the Imperial Cabinet Repository, together with records of the alien peoples who had resided on Chinese territory in the past.[11] The historical texts that were uncovered through these discoveries played an enormous role in the pivotal transformation that Chinese historiography underwent in the 1920s and 1930s, and they linked up closely with the new perspectives, new methodologies, and new problematics that began to emerge during this period.

The increasing complexity of historical questions is a matter of new perspectives and methods as well. As Liang Qichao observed, previous Chinese historians had recorded factual events but did not subject them to a process of analysis and interpretation, and furthermore they primarily focused on official dynastic history. By the twentieth century, however, prodded by the transformation of the Chinese nation-state and under the influence of Japanese and Western scholarship, Chinese historians gradually came to recognize that it would be necessary to attend not only to traditional topics such as politics, economics, and institutions, but also to a number of new questions that had emerged during the nation's transition from a traditional imperium into a modern nation-state, such as Chinese-foreign relations, nationalism, religion, border regions, recognition, center and periphery, stimulus and response, revolution and reform, social stages and historical periodization, general history and distinctive experience, and so forth—questions never encountered in several thousand years of Chinese history-writing. Accordingly, historical studies in modern East Asia and China increasingly required the formulation of new positions, perspectives, methodologies, and theories. Thus, the selection of historical materials, the techniques of historical narration, the choice of historical point of view, and the standards of historical critique all underwent vast changes.

Liang Qichao, it should be recognized, was the first to announce these transformations in Chinese historiography.

Liang's judgments on earlier Chinese history-writing were severe. In *Commentaries on Chinese History* and *New Historical Studies*, he presented a critique of previous history-writing together with a set of criteria for the contemporary study of history.[12] External critique played an essential enabling role. Liang examined recent works of European history and distilled their differences from dynastic history as it had traditionally been composed in China. In the previous century or so, European history had shifted from recording facts to explaining causes; it had gone from providing a record of the royal line to accounting for "the movement and evolution of the whole human race." It was time for Chinese historians to adopt a similar mission. "The study of history," Liang said, "is the broadest and the most penetrating kind of study. It is the mirror of the nation and the wellspring of patriotism. Contemporary European nationalism arose from history-writing. Historians can claim credit for half of the rise in civilizational level among the nations of the world."[13] Liang's words of advice to historians, like his views on popular fiction, responded to the late Qing crisis. They posited a new type of bicultural intellectual as the agent of China's regeneration.

Liang Qichao's fundamental recommendations for historiography can be brought under four headings: (1) Chinese historical scholarship should shift from narrating historical events to analyzing causal relations (in this respect, Liang was influenced by evolutionary theory); (2) Chinese historical scholarship should shift from a reign-by-reign approach to a focus on the history of popular movements and social life (including intellectual achievements, industrial production, artistic creation, religion, and politics); (3) historical studies should attend to the world, nations, and peoples, and should no longer limit themselves to the traditional confines of Han China but should reevaluate China against a broader background; (4) Chinese historical scholarship should position itself within a broader geographical and ethnic framework and no longer focus exclusively on Han China and its dynastic regimes.

CRITICAL OR EDIFYING HISTORY?

After 1919, the May Fourth movement's historiography sought to "organize the national past" (整理國故), in the words of a slogan taken up by Hu Shi 胡適 (1891–1962). The aim was to reassess Chinese history "critically, objectively and systematically," to quote Cai Yuanpei 蔡元培 (1868–1940), prefacing Hu's 1919 *A History of Ancient Chinese Philosophy* (中國古代哲學史). The forum in which this enterprise was most conspicuously pursued was the series *Debates on Ancient History* (古史辯), published in seven volumes over the period 1926–1941. In this series, classical texts were sifted for their likely provenance, their most plausible interpretation, and their reliability as sources for history. Under the chief editorship of Gu Jiegang, scholars such as Hu Shi, Qian Xuantong 錢玄同 (1887–1939), Fu Sinian 傅斯年 (1896–1950), and others proposed new analyses and datings of the *Book of Odes* (詩經), the *Book of Changes* (易經), the *Book of Documents* (書經), and other works that had traditionally been considered authoritative. Among these scholars' methodological hypotheses is the idea that the earlier the date claimed for a text or a tradition, the more it is probable that it post-dates texts for which a more recent date is asserted. The reason is that in a competition for authority, latecomers had to resort to more exorbitant claims of historical priority for their ideas, invoking not events in recent memory but Yao, Shun, Yu, and the Yellow Emperor as their witnesses. Thus the lore surrounding the sage-kings of antiquity was redefined as a residual decoration from the philosophical polemics of the Warring States and Han periods. By casting aside these myths and by showing that the Classics were products of a centuries-long "stratification" of diverse ideas, Gu hoped to destroy the persistent fictions of a "golden age" in antiquity and of a "single origin for the Han people." Both patterns had been essential to traditional historiography and both seemed unpromising as core beliefs of a modern republic; nevertheless, politics would keep them in circulation.

New sources for Chinese history abounded in the interwar years. The excavations at Anyang uncovered thousands of oracle-bone inscriptions and other artifacts that gave new reality to the Shang dynasty (traditional dates 1766–1122 BCE). The manuscripts extracted from the Silk Road caves of Dunhuang gave historians vivid insights into the mixing of languages, peoples, and beliefs between the Six Dynasties and the Tang. The imperial archives, now opened for research, allowed for new understandings of the Ming and Qing. Fu Sinian proclaimed that "history is source history." This attitude took institutional form in the Institute of History and Philology (founded 1928), which Fu directed at Academia Sinica and later at National Taiwan University, where Fu became president.

Restricting the scope of history-writing to the examination of sources was a sound strategy for avoiding trouble in an ideologically polarized time. In 1923 Gu Jiegang published a history textbook for high schools, omitting the "three sovereigns" of remote antiquity as belonging to legend rather than to history. In a controversy stirred up by the Guomindang's chief ideologue Dai Jitao 戴季陶 (1891–1949), the textbook was suppressed for "endangering the foundations of the state." "The one thing that has enabled the Chinese to stand together," Dai pronounced, "is the common belief that all Chinese share the same ancestor." Gu dismissed such mythmaking and held that the nation would be better supported by rationality, but *raison d'état* carried the day and in 1929 the book was withdrawn.[14] Some years later, in the midst of the war with Japan, Qian Mu 錢穆 (1895–1990) began his *Outline of Our National History* (國史大綱) with the following "Principles to be Acquired Before Reading the Present Work":

1. It is evident that every nation, especially one that has attained a high intellectual level, must be aware of its own past.
2. By "must be aware of its own past" is meant particularly a feeling of pride and respect (溫情與敬意) for that past.
3. Pride and respect for one's own past must at least preclude a quarrelsome nihilism, as it must at least preclude the sense that the present generation stands on the pinnacle of history, such that we project all our own crimes and weaknesses on the ancients.
4. It is evident that only insofar as a nation possesses the conditions enumerated above does that nation have the hope of progressing into the future.[15]

Qian Mu's requirement of a preliminary "pride and respect" recalls, in a mild collegial tone, the motives for Dai Jitao's suppression of a book that might have deprived citizens of their belief in a common ancestor. It suggests the putting aside, under emergency conditions, of the iconoclastic program—the "quarrelsome nihilism"—of the 1920s. But it must also be recognized that some Japanese historians at the time were in fact arguing that there was no such thing as the Chinese nation. Indeed, starting in the Meiji period (1868–1912), Japanese scholars had delved into the history, culture, and geography of Korea, Manchuria, and Mongolia with the aim of detaching these areas from the sphere of Chinese history. Furthermore, they put forth the thesis that China was not a (modern) nation for the reason that from ancient times onward it had lacked firm national boundaries. Yano Jin'ichi 矢野仁一 (1872–1970), for example, contended that *China* was simply a name for the zone south of the Great Wall that happened to be inhabited by the Han.[16] In particular, after the Mukden Incident of September 18, 1931 and the establishment of the Manchukuo state in the following year, Japanese historians accentuated their explanation of "China" in these terms. One countereffect of this polemic was to spur Chinese historians to concentrate on questions of nation and race and to form narratives of the unitary character of China and of the "Chinese nation." Fu Sinian, in this spirit, hastened to write a history of Manchuria as a rebuttal of the Japanese colonists' contention that their occupation was a restoration of the status quo.[17]

HISTORY GUIDED BY CLASS STRUGGLE

In the second half of the twentieth century, after the Chinese Communist Party had won power, Chinese historiography, being constrained and influenced by ideology, underwent massive changes. The newly dominant Marxist historiography assumed a worldwide framework and integrated Chinese history into its categories. In 1928, with his *Studies in Ancient Chinese Society*, Guo Moruo had begun the operation of correlating the eras of ancient Chinese history with the sequence of modes of production and class conflict laid out by Marx and Engels.[18] After 1949, owing to the influence of theories of class struggle, according to which the oppressed classes are the motor of history, and of the five stages of historical progress (primitive society, slave society, feudal society, capitalist society, and socialist society), five problems attracted the attention of historians: namely the periodization of ancient Chinese history, the feudal system of land ownership, the sprouts of capitalism, peasant rebellions, and the formation of the Chinese nation. The Marxist model was avowedly a general one, and Chinese experience figured in it only as a specific case, but inconsistencies between different historians' applications of the model led to historiographical controversies.[19] In these debates, often keyed to statements by Stalin or Mao, previously influential historians such as Hu Shi and Fu Sinian (both of whom were excoriated for having fled to Taiwan), Gu Jiegang (now denounced as a "rightist"), and Chen Yinke (marginalized and under suspicion) were no longer heard. Until the 1980s, the *History of China* (中國通史) edited by Bai Shouyi 白壽彝 with the assistance of Guo Moruo and others, the *Annotations to the History of China* (中國通史簡編) and the *History of China in the Modern Period* (中國近代史) edited by Fan Wenlan 范文蘭 (1893–1969), and the *Outline of the History of China* (中國史綱要) edited by Jian Bozan 翦伯贊 (1898–1968) were considered authoritative works of history.[20] Although these authors occasionally differed in their presentation of specific problems, they concurred ideologically and politically, as they did in the form of their writing of history and in their analysis of documents. In addition to this guidance from within the historical profession, successive political campaigns—including the Hundred Flowers, Anti-Rightist, Cultural Revolution, and Criticize Confucius and Lin Biao campaigns—narrowed history-writing in the People's Republic to a small set of options.

After 1949, historical scholarship in mainland China came to display a very obvious ideological tendency. Following Soviet theoretical models, this scholarship contended that humanity must transition through five historical stages (namely, that of primitive society, slave society, feudalism, capitalism, and finally socialism and communism), and Chinese historical scholarship demonstrated that China had also progressed through these five stages. Furthermore, this historical perspective views historical movement as being located in slaves' resistance to their masters, peasants' resistance to landowners, and workers' resistance to capitalists. In addition, this approach locates one of the forces of social development in the tension between old relations of production and the

continuous increase in productivity. As a result, in the debates over research methodologies that emerged in mainland Chinese historical circles during this period, a few
scholars who still followed historiographic trends from the first half of the century
insisted that one should ground one's conclusions on a careful examination of historical documents, archeological remains, and broad investigations. However, there were
also some scholars who, driven by politics and ideology, believed that one should have
"discourse drive history," that is, the use of a set of predetermined concepts and theories
to demonstrate how excavated historical artifacts prove the necessity of a set of underlying historical "rules" or "truths." Although the first set of (evidentiary) attitudes were
certainly not fully eliminated, the second set of (ideological) attitudes obviously had an
enormous influence. As a result the so-called "five golden flowers" emerged in Chinese
historical scholarship—which is to say, five hot research topics: (1) the origins of the
Han people, (2) historical periodization, (3) peasant uprisings, (4) the germ of capitalism, and (5) the administration of feudal land.

From Class Struggle
to Economic Competition

After the 1980s, as the Mao era closed and was succeeded by the Deng era, the historical
profession in China underwent important changes, which can be summarized in three
points. First, historians put aside the ideologically fraught questions of prior years, and
areas of history that had previously been neglected, such as cultural history, the history
of social life, and intellectual history, took on central importance. Second, new theories of history from the West replaced the Marxist-Leninist-Stalinist dogma that had
dominated the previous few decades, so that the field of history became more diversified. And third, certain areas of research yielded new results that set new standards,
chiefly in the areas of cultural, intellectual, and social history. Breaking with the style
of research that attended only to the elite stratum and to philosophical currents in the
abstract, at a great distance from the contexts of history and society, historians based
their investigations on broader historical documentation, on archaeological materials,
and on anthropological reports, thus enriching the field with new and varied content.

The transition from traditional to modern China was such a complex subject that the
modern and contemporary period of Chinese history was a site of particularly impressive
innovations. Problems such as the nature of modernization and modernity, the theory
of (Western) impact and (Eastern) response, the Great Divergence between China and
Europe, and conflicts internal to the different countries of East Asia inspired historical
discussion. Additionally, the exploration of new source materials (including the archives
of the Ming and Qing dynasties, as well as archives relating to China held in Western
countries, Korea, and Japan) brought unprecedented depth and breadth to historical
research. In the field of modern Chinese history, a truly international dialogue has arisen,

with the result that certain problems have become generally recognized as discussion topics for worldwide history: among them, systems of tribute and infeodation; the difference between empire and nation; comparisons between the Chinese and European economies; colonization, migration and trade; and inter-Asian relations. The officially sanctioned "opening" of China after 1978 inspired historians to reengage with world history, the plotline of which was often either economic exchange or technological diffusion.[21] In short, history in contemporary China is a field endowed with considerable programmatic and analytic powers; although historians are no longer officials of an imperial court, what they have to say about the definition and the fate of "China" is still taken seriously.

NOTES

1. See Miao Fenglin 繆鳳林, "Jingdao Liang Zhuoru xiansheng" 敬悼梁卓如先生 [Obituary for Liang Qichao], *Xueheng* 學衡 [Critical review] 617 (January 1929): 7. On Liang and his influence, see Q. Edward Wang, *Inventing China Through History: The May Fourth Approach to Historiography* (Albany: SUNY Press, 2001).

2. Gu Jiegang 顧頡剛 and Wang Zhonglin 王鐘麟, *Xiandai chuzhong benguoshi jiaocaishu* 現代初中本國史教科書 [Middle school textbook in modern Chinese history] (Shanghai: Shangwu, 1923).

3. Cao Boyan 曹伯言, ed., *Hu Shi riji* 胡適日記 [Hu Shi's journals], vol. 5 (Hefei: Anhui jiaoyu chubanshe, 2001), 380–382.

4. Sima Guang 司馬光, ed., *Zizhi tongjian* 資治通鑑 [Comprehensive mirror for governing], first published 1084, 20 vols. (Beijing: Zhonghua shuju, 1956).

5. See the 1601 memorial in accusation of Li by Zhang Wenda 張問達 in Gu Yanwu 顧炎武, *Rizhi lu* 日知錄 [Daily acquisition of knowledge] (Shanghai: Shangwu, 1947), 18/28b–29b.

6. See Peter Zarrow, "The Rise of Confucian Radicalism," in *China in War and Revolution, 1895–1949* (New York: Routledge, 2006), 12–30, and James Reeve Pusey, *China and Charles Darwin* (Cambridge: Harvard East Asia Monographs, 1983). Xia Zengyou 夏曾佑 (1861–1924) exemplified evolutionist history in a textbook published in 1904, more broadly circulated after 1933 under the title *Zhongguo gudaishi* 中國古代史 [A history of ancient China] (Shijiazhuang: Hebei jiaoyu, 2000).

7. See Kang, *Datong shu* 大同書 (Shanghai: Zhonghua, 1935), trans. Laurence G. Thompson as *Ta T'ung Shu: The One-World Philosophy of K'ang Yu-wei* (London: Allen & Unwin, 1958).

8. See Wang Fansen 王汎森, *Gushibian yundong de xingqi* 古史辯運動的興起 [The origins of the Ancient History Debate movement] (Taipei: Yunchen chubanshe, 1987).

9. Imanishi Ryū 今西龍, "An Examination of Tangun" 檀君考, originally published in 1929 and reprinted in Imanishi, *Studies in Ancient Korean History* 朝鮮古史の研究 (Tokyo: Kokusho, 1970).

10. See Ikeda On 池田温, "Chavannes" 沙畹, in Takata Tokio 高田时雄, ed., *The Genealogy of East Asian Research in Europe* 東亞學の係普「欧米篇」(Tokyo: Taishukan, 1996), 104–113.

11. Wang Guowei 王國維, *Zuijin resanshinian zhong Zhongguo fajian zhi xin xuewen* 最近二三十年中中國發現之新學問 [New Chinese scholarly trends from the past twenty or thirty years], in *Wang Guowei yishu* 王國維遺書 [The posthumous works of Wang Guowei], vol. 5 (Shanghai: Shanghai guji, 1983), 65–69.

12. See Xu Guansan 許冠三, *Xin shixue jiushi nian* 新史學九十年 [The New Historiography after ninety years] (Changsha: Yuelin, 2003).

13. Liang Qichao, "Zhongguo zhi jiu shi" 中國之舊史 [China's old histories], part one of "Xin shixue" 新史學 [On New Historiography]. *Yinbing shi wenji* 飲冰室文集 [Collected writings from the ice-drinker's studio], vol. 1 (Beijing Zhonghua shuju, 1989), 1–3.

14. On this episode, see Shen Songqiao 沈松僑, "Shaohuan chenmo de wangzhe: Kuayue guozulishi de jiexian" 召喚沈默的亡者：跨越國族歷史的界線 [Calling out the silent dead: Transgressing the boundaries of national history], *Sixiang* 思想 [Thought] 2 (2006): 75–92, especially 79–80; and James Leibold, "Competing Narratives of Racial Unity in Republican China: From the Yellow Emperor to Peking Man," *Modern China* 32 (2006): 181–220.

15. Qian Mu 錢穆, *Guoshi dagang* 國史大綱 [Outline of our national history] [1940] (Taipei: Shangwu, 1975), 1.

16. Yano Jin'ichi 矢野仁一, *Kindai Shina shi* 近代支那史 [Modern Chinese history] (Kyoto: Kōbundō, 1926); *Manshūkoku rekishi* 滿洲國歷史 [The history of Manchukuo] (Tokyo: Meguro, 1933), partially translated as *Historical Backgrounds of Manchuria: Manchuria Was Not an Integral Part of China* (Tokyo: League of Nations Association of Japan, 1933).

17. Fu Sinian, *Dongbei shigang* 東北史綱 [An outline of the history of northeast China] [1932] (Shanghai: Shanghai guji, 2012).

18. Guo Moruo 郭沫若, *Zhongguo gudai shehui yanjiu* 中國古代社會研究 [Research on ancient Chinese society] (Shanghai: Zhongya, 1928).

19. See Timothy Brook and Gregory Blue, eds., *China and Historical Capitalism: Genealogies of Sinological Knowledge* (Cambridge: Cambridge University Press, 2002).

20. Bai Shouyi 白壽彝, ed., *Zhongguo tongshi* 中國通史 [History of China], 22 vols. (Shanghai: Shanghai renmin chubanshe, 1989–1999); Fan Wenlan 范文蘭, *Zhongguo tongshi jian bian* 中國通史簡編 [Annotations to the History of China] (Beijing: Renmin chubanshe, 1964); Jian Bozan 翦伯贊, *Zhongguo shi gangyao* 中國史綱要 [Outline of the history of China] (Beijing: Remin chubanshe, 1962).

21. See Luo Xu, "Confronting the Walls: Efforts at Reconstructing World History in China at the Turn of the Twenty-First Century," in Roger Des Forges, Haun Saussy, and Thomas Burkman, eds., *Chinese Walls in Time and Space* (Ithaca: Cornell University East Asia Series, 2010), 329–365.

Works Cited

Bai Shouyi 白壽彝, ed. *Zhongguo tongshi* 中國通史 [History of China], 22 vols. Shanghai: Shanghai renmin chubanshe, 1989–1999.

Brook, Timothy, and Gregory Blue, eds. *China and Historical Capitalism: Genealogies of Sinological Knowledge.* Cambridge: Cambridge University Press, 2002.

Cao Boyan 曹伯言, ed. *Hu Shi riji* 胡適日記 [Hu Shi's journals], vol. 5. Hefei: Anhui jiaoyu chubanshe, 2001. 380–382.

Fan Wenlan 范文蘭. *Zhongguo tongshi jian bian* 中國通史簡編 [Annotations to the history of China]. Beijing: Renmin chubanshe, 1964.

Fu Sinian 傅斯年. *Dongbei shigang* 東北史綱 [An outline of the history of northeast China] [1932]. Shanghai: Shanghai guji, 2012.

Guo Moruo 郭沫若. *Zhongguo gudai shehui yanjiu* 中國古代社會研究 [Research on the societies of ancient China]. Shanghai: Zhongya, 1928.

Gu Jiegang 顧頡剛 and Wang Zhonglin 王鐘麟. *Xiandai chuzhong benguoshi jiaocaishu* 現代初中本國史教科書 [Middle school textbook in modern Chinese history]. Shanghai: Shangwu, 1923.

Gu Yanwu 顧炎武. *Rizhi lu* 日知錄 [Daily acquisition of knowledge]. Shanghai: Shangwu, 1947.

Jian Bozan 翦伯贊. *Zhongguo shi gangyao* 中國史綱要 [Outline of the history of China]. Beijing: Remin chubanshe, 1962.

Ikeda On 池田温. "Chavannes" 沙畹. In 東亞學の係普「欧米篇」[The genealogy of East Asian research in Europe]. Ed. Takata Tokio 高田时雄. Tokyo: Taishukan, 1996. 104–113.

Imanishi Ryū 今西龍. 檀君考 [An examination of Tangun] [1929]. In 朝鮮古史の研究 [Studies in ancient Korean history]. Tokyo: Kokusho, 1970.

Kang Youwei 康有為. *Datong shu* 大同書. Shanghai: Zhonghua, 1935.

Kang Youwei 康有為. *Ta T'ung Shu: The One-World Philosophy of K'ang Yu-wei*. Trans. Laurence G. Thompson. London: Allen & Unwin, 1958.

Leibold, James. "Competing Narratives of Racial Unity in Republican China: From the Yellow Emperor to Peking Man." *Modern China* 32 (2006): 181–220.

Liang Qichao 梁啟超. "Xin shixue" 新史學 [On New Historiography]. In *Yinbing shi wenji* 飲冰室文集 [Collected writings from the ice-drinker's studio], vol. 1. Beijing: Zhonghua shuju, 1989. 1–32.

Miao Fenglin 繆鳳林. "Jingdao Liang Zhuoru xiansheng" 敬悼梁卓如先生 [Obituary for Liang Qichao]. *Xueheng* 學衡 [Critical review] 617 (January 1929): 7.

Pusey, James Reeve. *China and Charles Darwin*. Cambridge: Harvard East Asia Monographs, 1983.

Qian Mu 錢穆. *Guoshi dagang* 國史大綱 [Outline of our national history] [1940]. Taipei: shangwu, 1975.

Shen Songqiao 沈松僑. "Shaohuan chenmo de wangzhe: Kuayue guozulishi de jiexian" 召喚沈默的亡者：跨越國族歷史的界線 [Calling out the silent dead: Transgressing the boundaries of national history]. *Sixiang* 思想 [Thought] 2 (2006): 75–92.

Sima Guang 司馬光, ed. *Zizhi tongjian* 資治通鑑 [Comprehensive mirror for governing], 20 vols. Beijing: Zhonghua shuju, 1956.

Wang Fansen 王汎森. *Gushibian yundong de xingqi* 古史辯運動的興起 [The origins of the Ancient History Debate movement]. Taipei: Yunchen chubanshe, 1987.

Wang, Q. Edward. *Inventing China Through History: The May Fourth Approach to Historiography*. Albany: State University of New York Press, 2001.

Wang Guowei 王國維. *Zuijin resanshinian zhong Zhongguo fajian zhi xin xuewen* 最近二三十年中中國發現之新學問 [New Chinese scholarly trends from the past twenty or thirty years]. In *Wang Guowei yishu* 王國維遺書 [The posthumous works of Wang Guowei], vol. 5. Shanghai: Shanghai guji, 1983. 65–69.

Xia Zengyou 夏曾佑. *Zhongguo gudaishi* 中國古代史 [A history of ancient China]. Shijiazhuang: Hebei jiaoyu, 2000.

Xu Guansan 許冠三. *Xin shixue jiushi nian* 新史學九十年 [The New Historiography after ninety years]. Changsha: Yuelin, 2003.

Xu, Luo. "Confronting the Walls: Efforts at Reconstructing World History in China at the Turn of the Twenty-First Century." In *Chinese Walls in Time and Space*. Ed. Roger Des Forges, Haun Saussy, and Thomas Burkman. Ithaca: Cornell University East Asia Series, 2010. 329–365.

Yano Jin'ichi 矢野仁一. *Kindai Shina shi* 近代支那史 [Modern Chinese history]. Kyoto: Kôbundô, 1926.

Yano Jin'ichi 矢野仁一. *Manshûkoku rekishi* 滿洲國歷史 [The history of Manchukuo]. Tokyo: Meguro, 1933.

Yano, Jin'ichi 矢野仁一. *Historical Backgrounds of Manchuria: Manchuria Was Not an Integral Part of China*. Partial translation of *Manshûkoku rekishi*. Tokyo: League of Nations Association of Japan, 1933.

Zarrow, Peter. "The Rise of Confucian Radicalism." *China in War and Revolution, 1895–1949*. New York: Routledge, 2006. 12–30.

CHAPTER 3.4

....

STRUCTURE AND RUPTURE IN LITERARY HISTORY AND HISTORIOGRAPHY

....

YINGJIN ZHANG

WE are confronted with a peculiar divergence of literary historiography in Chinese and English scholarship: whereas Chinese scholarship of modern Chinese literature boasts of an impressive array of literary histories that confidently trace over a century of literary development, scholarship in English has deliberately stayed away from any large-scale historiographic work and has instead preferred to focus on specific authors, groups, decades, and subjects.[1] I suggest that paradigm shifts in North American academia since the 1980s have consolidated a sense of vanished totality, which has encouraged deconstructive, postmodern work marked by heterogeneity and fragmentation and has cultivated a habit of searching for alterity and discontinuity. In contrast, Chinese scholars have operated with the renewed confidence that, after decades of the superimposed uniformity and homogeneity of socialist thinking, they are empowered to engage in a series of projects on rewriting literary history and reimagining a different globality that promises simultaneously to reconnect with literary tradition and modernity.

In addition to tracking the divergence of a centripetal mindset in China and a centrifugal one in North America, I consider a number of innovative ventures in the history of Euro-American literatures and their implications for Chinese literary historiography. By bringing divergent trends in China and Euro-America together in a comparative perspective, I hope to explore alternative visions and practices of literary history (international, cross-regional, and translocal) that may be obscured by an exclusive emphasis on a vanished totality or reimagined globality. Crucial to a reexamination of issues in literary historiography is the shifted subjectivity of the literary historian: we must reevaluate subject positions abandoned, authorized, denied, or appropriated in different localities of cultural, ideological, and academic productions.

Literary History: Between the Extrinsic and the Intrinsic Approach

In a succinct overview of the development of literary history as an academic discipline in the West over the last three hundred years, Lee Patterson perceives a cyclical pattern of movement from an extrinsic history of literature (an approach emphasizing the relation of literature, as a collection of writings, to history, as a series of events) to an intrinsic one (an account of literature as a whole or of specific modes, genres, or forms), and then back from the intrinsic to the extrinsic again.[2] Patterson points out two apparent weaknesses in nineteenth-century literary historicism: first, its reliance on a mechanistic cause-and-effect mode of explanation and its attendant belief in the objectivity and reliability of its own positivist methodology; and second, its formulation of zeitgeist (the spirit of the time) as an overriding concept that would explain, in homogeneous and even monolithic terms, the emergence of patriotic nationalism and cultural identity in the literary imagination. Recruited to promote nation-building through university education, literary history was upgraded to an eminent status among academic disciplines, and national literature was studied almost exclusively in relation to dominant external factors such as geography, racial/national identity, and historical period.[3] "For in enumerating them," declared Hippolyte Taine in 1863, "we traverse the *complete* circle of the agencies; and when we have considered race, circumstance, and epoch . . . , we have exhausted not only the *whole* of the actual causes, but also the *whole* of the possible causes of motive."[4]

From the mid-1910s to the late 1920s, formalist theorists like Roman Jakobson challenged the extrinsic approach by reformulating literature as a self-referential, self-sufficient artwork intricately constructed according to immanent rules of structure. In its effort to create a "science of literature," Russian Formalists defined literature as "a kind of writing primarily concerned with neither reference to the world nor communication with an audience but rather with the conventions—the forms—of writing itself."[5] American New Criticism developed similar views of literature in the 1940s and 1950s, concentrating on textual—rather than social and historical—mechanisms in the production of meaning and interpretation. The inherent ahistoricity of this type of intrinsic scholarship is evident in such formalist notions as the "dynamics of literary forms" and is embodied in a series of literary histories that address issues of literary pattern, category, mode, genre, imagery, symbolism, style, myth, and so on.

The rise of structuralism in the 1960s and its transformation into poststructuralism since the 1970s fundamentally changed the ontological status of literature. The "linguistic turn" initiated by Ferdinand de Saussure brought new attention to discursive practices of literature, and literature is now placed in a position analogous to other forms of "writing" such as history (by Hayden White), philosophy (by Jacques Derrida), and the physical sciences (by Thomas Kuhn). Moreover, interrogations by Marxist scholars like Raymond Williams and feminist criticism since the 1970s have revealed many hidden ideological functions literature performs all the time, engendering a "cultural turn" in historical scholarship. For example, as Patterson observes, while legitimizing and preserving certain kinds of writing to be highly aesthetic, "the concept of 'literature' has been used to stigmatize writings by the culturally marginalized and politically repressed—women, blacks, gays, and members of the Third World, among others"—or to dismiss the significance of new academic initiatives and interests, including film studies, gender studies, and cultural studies.[6] Ironically, it is precisely these new initiatives and interests that have developed rapidly and have in turn helped to transform literary scholarship since the 1980s.

By now it is hardly an exaggeration to claim that literature as a privileged discipline has been dethroned in the humanities, the author as a great mind or genius has been pronounced "dead" (by Roland Barthes and Michel Foucault), and the kind of literary history as conceived and practiced prior to the rise of poststructuralism has disintegrated at its most fundamental level in North America. Although new—and in many ways revisionist or even *interventionist*—histories of women's literature, black literature, literature of other racial minorities (for instance, Asian Americans, Hispanic Americans, and Native Americans), and queer literature have appeared in greater numbers recently, and although New Historicism and anthropological approaches to literary history, as noted by Patterson, have brought fruitful results over the past decade, the fact remains that, at least in theoretical terms, literary history is now more than ever considered an almost "impossible" intellectual enterprise.

David Perkins poses a straightforward question as an eye-catching title for his 1992 book—*Is Literary History Possible?*—and presents this paradox: "we cannot write literary history with intellectual conviction, but we must read it."[7] A self-acclaimed "skeptical" and "relativizing historian," Perkins does not hide his elitist attitude and mixed feelings: on one hand he deplores the disintegration of narrative literary history, and on the other hand he feels reluctant to accept recent revisionist histories because they do little but "promote feelings of identity and solidarity within the group by emphasizing continuities with the situation of members of the group in the past."[8] Upon closer scrutiny, Perkins's paradox arises not so much from the object of literary history as from his particular kind of definition and expectation of this intellectual practice: "literary history cannot surrender the ideal of objective knowledge of the past. Though the ideal cannot be achieved, we must pursue it, for without it the otherness of the past would entirely deliquesce in endless subjective and ideological reappropriations."[9] The ideological function of literary historiography is clearly foregrounded in this articulation of an unattainable ideal that one must pursue anyway.

Perkins is by no means the first to broach the impossibility thesis. As early as 1949, René Wellek had asked, "Is it possible to write literary history, that is, to write that which will be both literary and a history?"[10] Wellek's answer was negative by 1973, for he was dissatisfied with "the mixture of biography, bibliography, anthology, information on themes and metrical forms, sources, attempts at characterization and evaluation sandwiched into background chapters on political, social, and intellectual history which is called 'literary history.' "[11] "The fall of literary history" has had a long trajectory in North America since then.[12] Two publications bearing the title "Is Literary History Obsolete?" appeared in 1965 and 1970, respectively.[13] After tracing the decline of literary history during the 1970s and 1980s, Robert Johnston conceded in 1992 that comprehensive literary history constitutes an "impossible genre."[14]

Vanished Totality: Fragments Reintegrated into a Larger Context

The challenge to literary history has found support in much recent Euro-American theorization, where totality is regarded as an impossible object and hence undesirable in literary or cultural historiography. Writing in German, Hans Ulrich Gumbrecht questions two formulations of the historical totality: first, the German Romantic belief that "it was the genius of the great writers in whose discourse . . . one could hope to attain, once and for all, in its 'totality,' that national character of which the national history was taken to be the articulation"; second, Georg Lukács's Marxian hypothesis that "it is the principle of exemplification proper to 'great,' 'realist' art which makes possible the 'objective knowing of the totality of a historical situation and the laws of history underlying it.' "[15] In the wake of poststructuralist thought, the ground for "laws of history" in literature and culture has been proven untenable; literature no longer functions as the unproblematic depository of "objective" knowledge of national history and national character, and literary history has relapsed into the status of "fragment of a vanished totality."[16] Writing in French, Roger Chartier draws on Foucault's insight on treating "the procedures of discourse in their discontinuity and their specificity" and promotes "the study of circumscribed and unconnected bodies of material with no pretence to global history."[17] For Chartier, "[cultural] history has lost is ambition to be all-embracing, to be sure, but it has perhaps gained an unprecedented attention to the texts."[18]

Fredric Jameson announced in 1984 that "the principal contribution that contemporary historiography has made is to insist on history as a series of breaks rather than as a continuity."[19] Concepts of discontinuity and fragmentation point to a new vision of vanished totality, which informed two innovative works of new literary history in the late 1980s. In terms of organization, *The Columbia Literary History of the United States* edited by Emory Elliott (1988) and *A New History of French Literature* edited by Denis Hollier (1989) appear more like encyclopedias than histories, for both strive not to construct a linear, causality-plotted account of the development of literature but to identify symptomatic fragments such as events, moments, and disruptions in history— not necessarily restricted to the literary sphere alone—that are noteworthy in their own rights and constituent of a diachronic or synchronic structure of meaning visible only in a larger, extraliterary context.

As a matter of fact, Elliott already anticipated a distinctive feature of this sort of encyclopedic history to be "modestly postmodern: it acknowledges diversity, complexity, and contradiction by making them structural principles, and it forgoes closure as well as consensus."[20] The diversity of literary subjects and critical voices is facilitated by seventy-four contributors, whose essays are divided into five parts, each coordinated by an associate editor and each containing several multiauthored chapters. In contrast to "modern" architecture that stresses streamlined uniformity and utilitarian functionality, Elliot employs a different architectural metaphor to describe encyclopedic history: "Designed to be explored like a library or an art gallery, this book is composed of corridors to be entered through many portals intended to give the reader the paradoxical experience of seeing both the harmony and the discontinuity of materials."[21] Apart from conventional sections on such key writers as Nathaniel Hawthorne, Mark Twain, and William Faulkner, the encyclopedic format allows Elliott's history to offer chapters on literary diversities in 1865–1910 (covering new immigrants and the New Woman) as well as on comparative literary cultures in 1910–1945 (covering Afro-American literature, Mexican American literature, Asian American literature, and women writers between the wars).

Similarly, Hollier's history aims to furnish a "panorama of literature in its cultural context—music, painting, politics, and monuments public and private."[22] True to this panoramic view of literary history through an interdisciplinary lens, Hollier's book contains an essay on film, but it is not a traditional survey of a national cinema but a close-up look at a specific month. In "1954, January: On Certain Tendencies of the French Cinema," Dudley Andrew elaborates the ramifications of an otherwise insignificant event: *Cahiers du cinéma* published François Truffaut's vitriolic manifesto against French cinema. Andrew situates Truffaut's revolt against the postwar tradition of *cinéma de qualité*, which thrived on "quality" adaptations of famous French novels, and he further discusses the ways Truffaut's "tendency" contributed to the rise of "the *auteur* policy" and "a specifically cinematic *écriture*" subsequently known as French new wave cinema.[23]

Interdisciplinarity is, admittedly, only one of many innovative features in Hollier's history, which consists of 199 essays, each of which is written by an individual contributor and is cued to a date and an event. "The juxtaposition of these events is designed to produce an effect of heterogeneity and to dispute the traditional orderliness of most histories of literature."[24] Specifically, traditional classification schemes by authors and periods have undergone "a fragmentation," and the book has instead "focused on nodal points, coincidences, returns, resurgences."[25] Perhaps more than Elliott's history, Hollier's foregrounds those fragments from literary and cultural realms that would enable the reader to appreciate literature from a fresh perspective and reconceptualize literary history as a *procedural* rather than conclusive project. To quote Malcolm Bowie's endorsement, Hollier's book is "a history that is now self-aware, discontinuous, and suspicious of its own procedures."[26] Precisely due to what Jonathan Arac describes as its "self-consciously postmodern organization," Marshall Brown praises Hollier's book to be "the most current and most advanced exemplar of a nonconvulsive, nonirruptive, linguistically sensitive literary history."[27] In varying degrees, Hollier's scheme has captured the "nonsimultaneity of the simultaneous" in cultural history.[28]

Undoubtedly, much of the conceptualization of discontinuity and fragmentation as structural principles in new literary historiography reflects the deconstructive and postmodern tendencies in North American academia during the 1980s and 1990s. Given their deliberate avoidance of consecutiveness and coherence, Perkins classifies Elliott's and Hollier's books under the "encyclopedic" form of literary history and labels them "postmodern" in a negative sense: "Encyclopedic form is intellectually deficient. . . . Because it aspires to reflect the past in its multiplicity and heterogeneity, it does not organize the past, and in this sense, it is not history."[29] Dismissive of fragmentation and nonlinearity, Perkins's criticism is misplaced because encyclopedic history does organize the past, albeit in an intellectually challenging way that decisively disavows the hitherto unproblematized conviction in totality.

Ironically, a criticism of encyclopedic history similar to Perkins's was expressed as early as 1976, when Gerald Mast asserted that "a truly *encyclopedic* history of the cinema would not be a history at all but an encyclopedia."[30] I find Mast's assertion ironic because, contrary to Perkins, Mast's objection derives from a suspicion of the very idea of historical totality. In film studies, such a totality is embodied in what Jean Mitry envisions as a "proper" history of the cinema, which, in Richard Abel's summary, is "simultaneously, a history of its industry, its technologies, its systems of expressions (or, more precisely, its systems of signification) and aesthetic structures, all bound together by the forces of the economic, psychological and cultural order."[31] Instead of the unattainable idea of totality in film historiography, Mast would gladly settle for less: "The history of the cinema will never be written; we shall simply have to be satisfied with histories of the cinema."[32]

Compared with Mast's reluctant abandonment of totality in film historiography, Elliot's and Hollier's works represent a strategic challenge to the conventions of literary history, a challenge symptomatic of postmodern scholarship in general. Their preference for fragmentation, discontinuity, and heterogeneity dovetails with a general move in contemporary historiography across academic disciplines: namely, the move from global history to sectorial or fragmentary history, from monumental history to diagrammatic history, from historicist history to structural history, and from documental history to conjectural history. Just as "the unilateral idea of causality" is eliminated in postmodern historiography, "the idea of totality seems to be left aside, substituted by the ideas of plurality, fragmentation, and absence of center."[33]

ALTERNATIVE VISIONS: MODERN CHINESE LITERATURE IN NORTH AMERICA

A relatively new academic field, modern Chinese literature studies in North America has been fashioned by a succession of intellectual trends ranging from New Criticism to postmodernism and cultural studies. As a result, it has cultivated visions alternative to the academic production in the People's Republic of China (PRC) from the 1950s onward. One major difference between North America and the PRC is the peculiar divergence in literary historiography: compared with 119 literary histories of "modern Chinese literature" (1919–1949) published in the PRC from 1951 to 2007, there is only one such work in English, written by C. T. Hsia, limited to the genre of fiction and issued as early as 1961.[34] In retrospect, it is significant that the North American field would abandon Hsia's inaugural effort and has stayed away from a general history of modern Chinese literature for over half a century, although the forthcoming publication of David Der-wei Wang's new literary history of modern China, modeled after Hollier's, will fill this longstanding gap.[35]

In my view, a tacit consensus on the vanished totality came to be widely accepted in the field by the early 1990s, and it has fundamentally undermined the conviction that had informed Hsia's scholarship in the 1960s and many scholars in the 1970s and 1980s. At the height of the Cold War, Hsia unambiguously expressed his opposition to the PRC formulation—"my main intention has been to contradict rather than affirm the Communist view of modern Chinese fiction"—although he did it by drawing on his doctoral training in New Criticism at Yale University during the 1950s.[36] Fighting against the "intentional fallacy" he saw as typical of Marxist literary criticism, Hsia argued that "literature is to be judged not by its intentions but by its actual performance: its intelligence and wisdom, its sensibility and style."[37]

Hsia was obviously confident in the possibility of literary historiography, as he sought to contradict Marxist ideological criticism with a New Critical aesthetic and to engage in "remaking the canon" in modern Chinese fiction by "dwell[ing] on his own insights and idiosyncrasies in an authoritative style."[38] Commending Hsia's history as "groundbreaking," "monumental," and "canonical," David Wang identifies "a paradigm shift" in Hsia's work and argues that "all subsequent Chinese literary theories cannot succeed until they have absorbed Hsia's paradigm and translated it into their own."[39] A profound irony, however, is that historically the paradigms informing Hsia's own scholarship—New Criticism from North America as well as F. R. Leavis's "Great Tradition" and Matthew Arnold's "disinterestedness" from Great Britain—had been abandoned by literary scholars in Euro-America by the early 1980s. As Terry Eagleton asked in 1983, "how many students of literature today read them?"[40]

Although Hsia's belief in literary "integrity" based on a universal concept of humanity has been dismissed as indefensible in an academic climate in favor of diversity and heterogeneity, his history contains a methodological emphasis on individual authors that would be followed by North American scholars. In this sense, his 1961 history is arguably more important as *author studies* than as historical scholarship: out of nineteen chapters, Hsia devoted ten to individual authors (Lu Xun 魯迅, Mao Dun 茅盾, Lao She 老舍, Shen Congwen 沈從文, Zhang Tianyi 張天翼, Ba Jin 巴金, Wu Zuxiang 吳組緗, Eileen Chang 張愛玲, Qian Zhongshu 錢鍾書, and Shi Tuo 師陀), with other chapters focused on groups of writers in different periods. Not surprisingly, Hsia's "author-centered approach to literary history" was taken up by subsequent scholars.[41] Leo Ou-fan Lee launched his career in 1973 with a book on the "romantic" generation of Chinese writers and consolidated his reputation with a monograph on Lu Xun in 1987.[42] In 1980, Edward Gunn used the term "unwelcome muse" to recover a group of authors from Beijing and Shanghai who had been marginalized by PRC literary historiography.[43] In 1992, David Wang addressed complications and contradictions in fictional realism by moving from Lu Xun as a pioneer to Mao Dun, Lao She, and Shen Congwen, describing each author as blazing his own path.[44] During the 1980s, other scholars devoted book-length studies to individual authors, such as Ding Ling 丁玲, Mao Dun, Qian Zhongshu, and Shen Congwen, but this author-centered approach has quickly lost traction since the 1990s.

Apart from author studies, North American scholars still pay attention to literary schools and groups of writers. Perry Link adopted a sociological approach to examine the rise of print culture and the popular urban fiction of mandarin ducks and butterflies in the late Qing and early Republican eras.[45] Michel Hockx investigated questions of style related to modern Chinese literary societies and literary journals in the field of cultural production.[46] Studies on decades and periods represent another organizational scheme close to the practice of literary historiography. David Wang pushed the beginning of modern Chinese literature to the late Qing period by highlighting incipient modernities in the literary field that would be repressed by May Fourth discourse.[47] Xudong Zhang measured the cultural fever of the 1980s by exploring different modes of modernism in post-Mao China and followed with another book on postsocialism and the changing cultural politics of the 1990s.[48]

Although the majority of English books on modern Chinese published since the late twentieth and early twenty-first centuries do not fall into the category of literary historiography, they have nonetheless reshaped the landscape of Chinese literary history in one way or another. A number of books on women and women's literature seek to restore the centrality of women's contribution to modern Chinese literature, and new research on gender, sexuality, and love has significantly enriched the field. In fact, many scholars have typically chosen a historical framework for their exploration of particular themes and subjects, such as configurations of the city, imbrications of aesthetics and politics, articulations of Chinese modernity, complications of history and memory, and representations of trauma and pain. Typically, by now, their texts often include cinema and the visual arts, and often feature cultural productions from Hong Kong and Taiwan.[49]

On one hand, we may regard recent monographs from North America as constituting a variety of fragments that have chipped away the previous edifice of uniformity and homogeneity; as such, these monographs have captured fragments of a vanished totality, fragments whose disjuncture with literature and history calls for reintegration or renarrativization into literary history as construed in a larger framework.[50] On the other hand, there is no denying that the lack of a comprehensive history of modern Chinese literature in English is both conspicuous and puzzling. A prevalent consensus

on the vanished totality may account for such a lack, but Euro-American national literatures have yielded literary histories of various sorts in an equally inhospitable academic
environment. As Robert E. Spiller declared in 1948, "each generation should produce at
least one literary history of the United States, for each generation must define the past
in its own terms."[51] Chinese literary scholars writing in English may claim depths of
research upon disavowing comprehensiveness, but how many of them can declare that
they really have no need to consult any literary history written in Chinese? This situation compels us to face the paradox presented by Perkins, which may be modified to fit
our situation: we cannot write literary history with intellectual conviction in English,
but we must read it in Chinese.[52]

RE-IMAGINED GLOBALITY: LITERARY HISTORIOGRAPHY IN THE PRC

Contrary to their theoretically minded counterparts in North America, scholars in
the PRC tend to believe firmly not only in historical totality but also in its ultimate
representability. To be sure, the institutionalization of modern Chinese literature in
the PRC took a trajectory radically different from that in North America, and the conventional PRC division of the field into early modern (*jindai* 近代), modern (*xiandai*
現代), and contemporary (*dangdai* 當代) foregrounds the dependency of literary history on a restrictive political periodization, with the May Fourth movement of 1919
and the founding of the PRC in 1949 as two monumental dates. The mandatory alignment of literary history with political history was instituted as early as 1951 in Wang
Yao's 王瑤 book, where "the history of modern Chinese literature is charted as one
of progressive movement toward the direction (or *telos*) legitimated by Mao Zedong
毛澤東 in the canon-setting 'Yan'an Talk' in 1942."[53] To correct Wang's ideologically
problematic "bourgeois" or "petty-bourgeois" position when it comes to treating
individual writers, Ding Yi's 丁易 1955 history conformed with a narrow political
interpretation and unequivocally labeled writers as revolutionary, progressive, and
bourgeois. Modern Chinese literature was redefined *instrumentally* as "operating
under proletarian leadership and the united front, serving the popular masses, and
fighting against imperialism, feudalism, and bureaucratic capitalism."[54] The "totality"
of such a political vision in literary historiography would entail a relentless exclusion
of writers whose works do not live up to the communist expectation or fall outside its
charted course of progress. As late as 1979, Tang Tao's 唐弢 three-volume history still
defines modern Chinese literature as an "integral part of the people's revolutionary
cause under the leadership of the proletariat," where "literary struggles are subordinate to political struggles."[55]

By the time the first wave of "rewriting literary history" (重寫文學史) hit the
PRC in the late 1980s, a renewed commitment to historical totality had empowered

a younger generation to reintroduce writers and works previously marginalized or excluded from official history.[56] To a certain extent, the ensuing process of canon revision was reminiscent of Hsia's search for an alternative canon in his 1961 book, which had a remarkable afterlife when it was translated into Chinese in 1979.[57] But the PRC projects of rewriting literary history were larger in scope than any such attempts in North America, and they were motivated by a restored sense of historical totality (as then-missing puzzle pieces were rediscovered one by one) and a self-appointed mission of historical rectification (so that unjust political verdicts could be relinquished or renegotiated).

A reimagined globality quickly emerged to inform new initiatives in literary historiography, and Chen Sihe's 陳思和 trajectory is symptomatic of this growing field. From his 1987 book on the total view of new literature, which concentrates on May Fourth enlightenment discourse and its subsequent transformation, and which necessarily marginalizes popular literature and the literature from the occupied areas, to his 1993 work on the tradition-saturated "folk sphere" (*minjian* 民間), doubly separated from the official and the intellectual sphere, Chen has proposed a comprehensive vision of modern Chinese literature not just in its own totality but also in a *globality* that includes, intranationally, its persistent immersion in regional folk traditions and, internationally, its steady integration into world literature.[58] This reimagined globality has enabled him from 1999 onward to excavate the "clandestine writings" (*qianzai xiezuo* 潛在寫作)—works written without public knowledge but published years later when the repressive political environment changed—of the socialist period.[59] Since 2000, Chen has questioned the unidirectional influence model in comparative literature and recommended a vision whereby twentieth-century Chinese literature is seen to contribute to world literature on an equal basis with other national literatures.[60] Moreover, Chen has been able to incorporate his theoretical hypotheses into a popular textbook history on contemporary Chinese literature, positing that after successive periods of "common names" (*gongming* 共名), when intellectuals were mobilized and moved in the direction of a given zeitgeist, Chinese culture has entered a period of "no name" (*wuming* 無名) since the 1990s, when widespread polyphony and polyvalence have frustrated the efforts of competing terms (e.g., *new condition, postmodern*) to specify the period with any consensus.[61]

By a 2009 estimate, Chen Sihe's textbook was one of seventy-two histories of contemporary (i.e., post-1949) Chinese literature published in the PRC between 1960 and October 2008.[62] As illustrated in Chen's case, the proliferation of literary histories since the 1980s has occurred in part for pedagogical reasons, because the rapid expansion of institutions of higher and continued education has created a huge market for textbooks catering to students at various levels.[63] Contrary to the typical solitary work model in the North American China field, collaborative research is the norm in the PRC, where government funding encourages multiyear, multi-institution megaprojects and where universities compete with one another in sponsoring their own versions of literary history. The foundational conviction in totality and globality is evident in Yang Yi's 楊義 ambitious recent goal to include ethnic minority and other regional literatures: "to investigate, in its totality (整體性), the general features of Chinese national literature and its life span through a few millennia and to strengthen and deepen the understanding of the collective consciousness (共同體意識) of the Chinese nation."[64] Like Taine and Lukács, Yang treats literary history as a reliable means of locating and reconstructing national character and historical consciousness, of creating discursive continuities and conferring cultural legitimacy to the nation. Obviously, cultural nationalism constitutes the core foundation for imagining totality in and through literary history.

As expected, some PRC scholars have recently challenged the prevalent consensus on totality and the reimagined globality on theoretical, methodological, and even pedagogical grounds. Gao Yuanbao 郜元寶 blames the practice of "colossal, comprehensive" (大而全) historiography for blurring the line between grand history and literary history, pushing the latter to the brink of paralysis or collapse. He highlights the obvious disjuncture and incompatibility between literary and social developments and envisions a "bottom-up"—not "top-down"—approach to literary history that favors detailed, disparate, yet oftentimes intertwining "literary stories" (文學故事).[65] Cheng Guangwei 程光煒 similarly grapples with dissatisfaction with a totalizing literary history and calls for interventions by way of "defamiliarization" (陌生化). Through years of high school and college education, historical narratives of modern Chinese literature are all too familiar to most PRC scholars, who have been "disciplined" for too long and are too sympathetic with authors and texts they study to successfully "rethink" literary history.[66] Furthermore, citing the example of Qian Zhongshu, an erudite scholar of Chinese and Western literatures, who is skeptical of grand theory and prefers scrutinizing "fragments of civilization" (文明的碎片), Chen Pingyuan 陳平原 encourages scholars to peep through the "interstices" (縫隙) at specific questions conducive to "the reflection, interrogation, and reconstruction of the picture of literary history already familiar to the world."[67] While entertaining a scenario of "if there were no literary history," Chen lists such positive consequences as "disjointed and untotalizable" (不成體統) knowledge, idiosyncratic and fragmented scholarship, and distrust of norms and consensus.[68]

What is intriguing in Chen Pingyuan's hypothesis is his identification with parallel trends of questioning totality and globality in traditional Chinese scholarship and postmodern Western scholarship. Obviously, Chen is cognizant that the current status of literary history in the PRC is unlikely to change due to its superimposed ideological function in education and its lucrative profits in textbook publishing. Nonetheless, I take his hypothetical scenario, along with Gao Yuanbao's and Cheng Guangwei's separate proposals, as part of a growing voice in the PRC that calls for new ways of reconceptualizing literary history.

SHIFTED SUBJECTIVITY: TOWARD
COMPARATIVE LITERARY HISTORY

To return to North America, I suggest that one alternative vision of literary historiography is embodied in the recent theory and practice of comparative literary history. Interestingly, despite poststructuralist and postmodern work in North America since the late twentieth century literary historiography has not disappeared. Back in 1984, Lawrence Lipking had almost abandoned literary history as "a shifty and awkward and devious kind of work, [for] perfection is not to be expected of it."[69] By 1995, however, he was glad to see that "good literary histories still bumble on" and "the impossibility of writing them does not stop scholars from trying and often succeeding."[70]

Sure enough, the general consensus on the vanished totality has not prevented scholars from exploring other ways of *rethinking* literary history. Drawing insights from Fernand Braudel's historical methodology in the respected French *Annales* tradition, Mario J. Valdés and Linda Hutcheon conceive of a new "comparative literary history" that "would not only try to keep in the foreground this dialectic hermeneutic movement between past and present, but would try to . . . study literature in contexts beyond the aesthetic and formal, taking into account relevant political, anthropological, economic, geographic, historical, demographic, and sociological research in articulating the contexts of a community's literature."[71] Reminiscent—in its ambitious scope—of Mitry's "proper" history of the cinema referenced above, comparative literary history is defined "as a collaborative interdisciplinary study of production and reception of literature in specific social and cultural contexts" and, Valdés continues, "[t]he nation need no longer be the model."[72]

Originally launched as a set of multiauthored, multivolume histories sponsored by the International Comparative Literature Association (ICLA) in 1993 and further funded by the Social Sciences and Humanities Research Council of Canada from 1996 to 2001, the large-scale collaborative research was designated the Literary History Project and administered by the University of Toronto. Initially, it comprised three separate comparative literary histories, one concentrated on Latin America, another on the African diaspora, and the third on Eastern and Central Europe.[73] For the three-volume Latin American project, which involved 242 collaborators from twenty-two countries across three continents and took ten years to complete, Valdés defines its aim as "multiplicity, not totality—perspectival insight, not empyrean oversight."[74] He renounces "[a] not uncommon reductive illusion . . . that the 'classics' of literature are the works of genius that somehow exist beyond time and rise above lived life to the point of separating authors from their community."[75] Like Elliot's and Hollier's encyclopedic models, comparative literary history seeks to "construct a history without closure, one that can be entered through many points and can unfold through many coherent, informed, and focused narrative lines."[76]

The opportunity proffered by comparative literary history, in Linda Hutcheon's judgment, consists in "shift[ing] the emphasis of the study of literary production and reception away from the nation-state and therefore away from the usual national his-torical models based on single ethnicity and single language"—in short, away from "the limitations of that nineteenth-century teleological (but also linear, causal, sequen-tial) narrative of literary history."[77] The resulting comparative, transnational vision demands that the new model be "flexible, untotalizing (untotalizable, perhaps), and capacious enough to deal with ... the heterogeneous effect on historical perception brought about by electronic technology and the mass media," as well as by the massive migration and diasporic life characteristic of our current era of globalization.[78] For Hutcheon, a genuinely comparative project succeeds in capturing what recent decades of cultural criticism have described by the Bakhtinian term *dialogic*: "associations of hybridity, flexibility, a willingness to engage conflicts at issue without seeking resolu-tion, a resistance to closure, a distrust of single responses, and a keen sense of the 'oth-erness' of a past that is nonetheless not alien."[79]

In theory, therefore, the dialogic is more than a simple dialogue. Since "the basic premise of the dialogues is the other's response," Valdés declares that "the reading of history is never a dialogue"; because individual voices that have spoken in the past are lost, historians and "readers are invited to engage in a dialogue with each other"—a dialogue about the past, or more precisely "about the various ways we can (re)construct it and about the various possibilities in recuperating lost voices."[80] The concept of the dialogic therefore forsakes the false objectivity of positivism and grants subjectivity to both the historian and the reader. The past and the present are placed in a dynamic, intersubjective, and dialogic structure, and totality and fragments are reconsidered in a dialectic relationship: "The phenomena that a history of literary culture brings out of the intersubjective totality of human experience can only be constituted through traces of documents, circumstances surrounding their authors, and past readings."[81] This emphasis on intersubjective dialogue is reminiscent of Elliott's radical assertion that "there is no past except what can be construed from these documents as they are filtered through the perceptions and special interests of the historian who is using them."[82]

In practice, however, Valdés and his collaborators on East-Central European literatures—especially Marcel Cornis-Pope and John Neubauer—have worked out a nodal scheme for comparative literary history. On one hand, they reject the traditional model of organicism, whereby a national literature is narrated as a linear development from its perceived origins through growth to either a predestined decay or an escha-tological fulfillment. On the other hand, they also avoid the postmodern encyclopedic form as represented by Hollier's book, which actually has dropped the word *history* from the title of its expanded French edition.[83] For Cornis-Pope and Neubauer, national histories are crucial to East-Central Europe (a transnational region with perhaps the greatest cultural diversity in the world), and they must be brought into a dialogue with one another in a comparative framework. Methodologically, this is done through a conceptualization of a node as "the starting point for multiple derivations," "a point in a network at which the multiple lines of development come together."[84] As such, a node functions as a hub of the network where a dynamic process is in place, simultaneously, to facilitate a centrifugal dissemination of the cultural imaginary produced in the area and to provide centripetal attraction, drawing creative individuals and cultural institutions into interaction.

True to its vision of multiplicity, the four-volume *History of the Literary Cultures of East-Central Europe* (2004–2007) maps the two centuries of literary production in the region five times, each time from a different nodal point. First, it highlights temporal nodes and selects eight significant dates or date clusters in political history that stand out in literary history. Second, it revisits conventional concepts of literary history—genre, movement, and period—as literary nodes, tracing them as transformative rather than transhistorical categories and situating them in relation to multimedia constructions, such as opera and cinema. Third, it delineates topographical nodes (e.g., cities, border areas) and contextualizes their roles in multicultural production and the formation of a hybrid identity. Fourth, it examines institutional nodes like publishing houses, censorship organizations, theaters, academies, and evaluates their national and transnational aspirations. Finally, it studies figurative nodes from imaginary or historical repertoires and treats them as subjects constructed through writing, reading, canonization, or suppression. These nodes do not function in isolation but interact with one another in dialectic relationships.

With its organization around nodal points, Cornis-Pope and Neubauer's history "consists of a great many *microhistories*, i.e., of localized, perspectival, and situated stories that cannot be easily read as symbols or synecdoches of an overarching organic system."[85] This nonorganic, nontotalizing mode is at its most innovative when it presents temporal nodes in reverse chronological order: it starts with 1989, a pivotal year in recent world history, and leaps backward through 1956/1968, 1948, 1945, 1918, 1867/1878/1881, and 1848 to 1776/1789. Reversing the order of temporal nodes intensifies the sense of historical disjuncture emphasized in the project's subtitle and frustrates any attempt to ascribe inevitable laws to history. It further foregrounds the historians' shifted subjectivity by highlighting a presentist position and makes the recognition of historical contingency a structuring principle: "The focus on different nodes makes all of them contingent."[86] As a result, different histories—micro as well as macro—compete with and complement each other, and their multivocal, polylocal coexistence within a set of narratives subverts the foundational myth of a singular evolutionary history and the godlike omniscient narrator who spoon-feeds the reader.

The antimonolithic thrust of comparative literary history brings us to the prestigious subjectivity Valdés grants to the historian and the reader, or more precisely, *the historian as reader*: "The unity of the history is in the reader who reads as an explorer."[87] As a risk-taking reader, the historian is expected to question the pre-given consensus on the totality or globality of literary history and proactively set out to mine diverse textual traces in the interstices and interplay of historical conjunctures and disjunctures for a new understanding of both literature and history. Two routes to such narrative interstices and interplays is found in Sacvan Bercovitch's road map for his eight-volume *Cambridge History of American Literature* (1994–1996): "One way leads through the discovery of difference: the interruptions and discontinuities through which literary history unfolds. Another way leads through the acknowledgement of connection: the shared anxieties, interests, and aspirations that underlie our perception of those conflicts and so impose a certain cohesion (professional, intellectual, and generational) upon difference itself."[88] Like Valdés, Bercovitch foregrounds the historian's subjectivity in both discovering difference and recognizing connection. By adopting "a strategy of multivocal description," Bercovitch's megaproject in American literary history "unfolds through a polyphony of large-scale narratives."[89]

CONCLUSION: INTERSTICES AND INTERPLAY IN MODERN CHINESE LITERARY HISTORY

Bercovitch's terms *multivocal* and *polyphony* suggest the relevance of musical metaphors to the current rethinking of literary history. Indeed, in an attempt at "the musicalization of literary history," Brown urges us to "rethink literary history in sym-phonic guise, as a sounding together in temporally ordered form of the disparate voices and strands of utterance claiming our attention from the past."[90] Like Bercovitch and Valdés, Brown shores up the subjectivity of the historian who is attentive to historical voices. "Between the Scylla of the trivially anecdotal (though not all anecdotes are trivial) and the Charybdis of totalizing systems (though not all systems are rigidly hegemonic)," he predicts, "histories sensitive to swerve and nuance . . . can recover the marks of expression before they congeal, for better or worse, into configured signs of the times."[91] As emblematic of postmodern scholarship, Brown's rethinking invests in the interstitial or liminal regions between past and present, object and subject, literature and history, but he does it without giving up altogether on the possibility of a system of signification—musical, temporal, or otherwise.

As a matter of fact, the idea of *system* is on top of the agenda for comparative literary history, which "examines literature as a process of cultural communication within one language area or among a number of them without attempting to minimize cultural diversity."[92] The concept of literary culture as *communication* system distinguishes Valdés's model from two mutually contrasting practices: on one hand, "monumental literary history" offers a "parade of genius and masterpieces" and "decontextualizes literature by presenting ideas, styles of writing, and creativity in isolation from the social reality"; on the other hand, "antiquarian literary history . . . values everything that can be assembled from the past abandoning the critical sense of the present."[93] Contrary to the dominance of a static view of literature in both monumental literary history and antiquarian literary history, Valdés envisages a dynamic system of dialectic interplay at different levels of engagement:

> Literary history cannot be merely deconstructive of past authority or reconstructive of an ideological paradigm of the present. The hermeneutic foundation of literary history is both interactive with the assemblage of constituted events of the past and dialogically engaged in the present. In effect, the literary history we propose is a

dialectic of two historicities—the constituted past event and the historian's performance that has reconstituted the event, and a second dialectic engagement with other historians, past, present, and future.[94]

In sum, comparative literary history is characterized firstly by its endeavor to move beyond both the postmodern impulse to deconstruct the totality vested in monumental literary history and the noncommittal habit of assembling available documents from the past in antiquarian literary history; secondly by its theorization of literary culture as thriving in the interstices and interplay of nodal points in a dynamic communication system that involves production, regulation, dissemination, and reception; and thirdly by its call for collaborative research modeled after the sciences and social sciences. Understood in this way, comparative literary history has much to offer to the historiography of modern Chinese literature, both in North American and in the PRC. For scholars in North America, the longstanding lack of a general history of modern Chinese literature in English, which is currently being filled by David Wang's project, deserves serious intervention, for the pretext of a vanished totality itself does not suffice to explain the lack of critical engagement with issues of literary historiography.

For scholars in the PRC, the model of comparative literary history provides much food for thought. Simply because the majority of existing Chinese textbooks fall in the category of either monumental literary history or antiquarian literary history, it is a daunting challenge to explore alternative ways of reenvisioning modern Chinese literary history. First, in theoretical terms, it is time to rethink the legitimacy of the monolithic grand history based on an organic, evolutionary, or even teleological model of causal, linear, or sequential narration. By way of a "defamiliarization" of the current consensus (per Cheng Guangwei's call), one may discover examples of difference—or even dissent—in a wide array of "interstices" (Chen Pingyuan's term) and disjunctures that have punctuated the history of modern Chinese literature all along. What Stephen Greenblatt posits as the "need for rupture" is provocative in the Chinese context as well:

> To write cultural history we need more a sharp awareness of accidental judgments than a theory of the organic; more an account of purposes mistook than a narrative of gradual emergence; more a chronicle of carnal, bloody, and unnatural acts than a story of inevitable progress from traceable origins. We need to understand colonization, exile, emigration, wandering, contamination, and unexpected consequences, along with the fierce compulsions of greed, longing, and restlessness, for it is these disruptive forces that principally shape the history and diffusion of languages, and not a rooted sense of cultural legitimacy. Language is the slipperiest of human creations; like its speakers, it does not respect borders, and like the imagination, it cannot ultimately be predicated or controlled.[95]

Modern Chinese literature has been ravaged by disruptive forces unpredictable and ultimately delegitimized by any laws of history or internal principles of literary form. Retrieving history from the interstices of prohibited expressions and lost voices (e.g.,

Chen Sihe's "clandestine writings") will go a long way to undermine the national myth of homogeneity and singularity and to add to the polyphony—cacophony as well as symphony—in modern Chinese literature.

Second, in methodological terms, in line with Greenblatt's reminder that language does not respect borders, comparative literary history encourages border-crossing investigations—polylocal, cross-regional, transnational, interdisciplinary. Modern Chinese literature abounds in such border-crossing activities, from its inaugural act of crossing the linguistic border from *wenyan* 文言 (classical Chinese) to *baihua* 白話 (modern vernacular) to many of its writers' frequent travels between the rural and the urban area, between the south and the north, between the hinterland and the coast, between China and Japan, Europe, America, and other places. A reexamination of modern Chinese literature in its dialectic interplay between various temporal, topographical, institutional, literary, and figurative nodes will yield a history rich in diversity, hybridity, and contingency, a history that cannot be adequately yoked to reflect an unchanging national character or to chart a superimposed teleological destiny.

Third, in narrative terms, comparative literary history cultivates a multilayered model of flexible, multivocal, but effective communication between the historian, the text, and the reader. Valdés defines "effective literary history" as "an open system of inquiry that takes up numerous closed systems and contextualizes them."[96] For this new dialogic system to remain open, it must on one hand resist the discourse of totalization whereby literature is appropriated to illustrate a historical consciousness in the past or an ideological paradigm of the present, and on the other hand search for localized, situated "microhistories" that are routinely excluded from traditional literary history. In a sense, these microhistories function like Gao Yuanbao's "literary stories" in that both seek to trace diverse, digressive, or crisscrossing routes and points of connection without hiding contentions and contradictions among them.

Given the centripetal force in Chinese culture and the entrenched national—if not always nationalist—models in literary historiography, it is too early to expect any major paradigm shift in PRC scholarship. Taiwan scholars, however, have drawn on theories of postmodernism and postcolonialism in rewriting Taiwan literary history, especially regarding its pre-1945 period of Japanese colonization.[97] In North America, scholars have likewise moved beyond the national literature paradigm to investigate what Greenblatt delineates as "colonization, exile, emigration, wandering, contamination" (cited earlier), mostly in connection with various forms of Chinese writings across borders. One such centrifugal imperative is envisioned in Shu-mei Shih's exclusion of mainland China in her new concept of the Sinophone, and her inclusion of "the margins of China and Chineseness" is intended "to give space for minoritized and colonized voices within China, be they Tibetan, Mongolian or Uyghur."[98] Here, Shih's inclusion of ethnic minorities works in the opposite direction of Yang Yi's totalizing project of Chineseness, as her Sinophone is an interventionist, counterhegemonic practice that negotiates its way through cracks and fissures of existing paradigms (e.g., Chinese studies, diaspora studies) in search of cohesion beyond its apparent difference. Nonetheless, due to its ideological preference for exclusion on territorial grounds, the Sinophone may not gain as much currency as "global Chinese literature," because the latter keeps its spatiality open as it remaps the world of literature that is, for better or worse, still Chinese.[99]

I conclude my deliberation on the structure and rupture in literary history and historiography with two important lessons Valdés reminds us of by referring to the *Annales* School of historiography: "(1) that history is, not unlike a geologically mature meandering river, a discontinuous process of starts and stops of major ruptures and of constant returns; (2) that historical facts become events when they are contextualized."[100] For the first lesson, we may revisit the Yellow River: in spite of its awe-inspiring image of rushing waters through central China, how many times in history did the river change its course and how many deserted, dried-up riverbeds were left behind and glossed over in literature? For the second lesson, we may consider how obscure anecdotes have become alive in Greenblatt's scholarship. Given a second life by what is known as New Historicism, these anecdotes or microhistories excavate traces of forgotten memories and lost voices by recontextualization, by reestablishing unexpected yet plausible connections, and they open up a new entryway to literary history and enable the reader to rethink and reexperience a familiar history again and anew, in a manner that is fundamentally opposed to the totalization of grand, "Hegelian" historiography.[101]

NOTES

1. I use the English phrase *modern Chinese literature* to cover the periods of what in Chinese would be referred to as *xiandai wenxue* 現代文學 ("modern literature") and *dangdai wenxue* 當代文學 ("contemporary literature") as well as the later part of *jindai wenxue* 近代文學 ("early modern," i.e., late Qing literature from the 1850s onward). However, I retain the term *contemporary* (i.e., post-1949) when referring to titles in Chinese publications.
2. See Lee Patterson, "Literary History," in *Critical Terms for Literary Study*, eds. Frank Lentricchia and Thomas McLaughlin (Chicago: University of Chicago Press, 1989), 250–262.
3. Much of Linda Hutcheon's critique of the nationalist model of literary history applies to mainland China; see her chapter in *Rethinking Literary History: A Dialogue on Theory*, eds. Linda Hutcheon and Mario J. Valdés (New York: Oxford University Press, 2002), 14–24.
4. Hippolyte Taine, "History of English Literature: Introduction," in *Critical Theory Since Plato*, ed. Hazard Adams (Fort Worth: Harcourt Brace Jovanovich, 1992), 610, emphases added.
5. Patterson, "Literary History," 253.
6. Patterson, "Literary History," 258.
7. David Perkins, *Is Literary History Possible?* (Baltimore: Johns Hopkins University Press, 1992), 17.
8. Perkins, *Is Literary History Possible?*, 137, 176.
9. Perkins, *Is Literary History Possible?*, 185.
10. In René Wellek and Austin Warren, *Theory of Literature* (New York: Harcourt, 1949), 263.

11. René Wellek, *The Attack on Literature and Other Essays* (Chapel Hill: University Press of North Carolina, 1982), 66.

12. Wellek, *The Attack*, 64.

13. See *The Third Dimension: Studies in Literary History*, ed. Robert E. Spiller (New York: Macmillan, 1965), 3–14; special issue of *New Literary History* 2.1 (1970): 1–193.

14. Robert Johnston, "The Impossible Genre: Reading Comprehensive Literary History," *PMLA* 107.1 (1992): 26–37.

15. Hans Ulrich Gumbrecht, "History of Literature—Fragment of a Vanished Totality?," trans. Peter Heath, *New Literary History* 16.3 (1985): 470.

16. Gumbrecht, "History," 478.

17. Roger Chartier, *Cultural History: Between Practices and Representations*, trans. Lydia G. Cochrane (Cambridge, UK: Polity Press, 1988), 10–11.

18. Chartier, *Cultural History*, 11.

19. In *Rewriting Literary History*, Tak-Wai Wong and Ackbar Abbas, eds. (Hong Kong: Hong Kong University Press, 1984), 347.

20. Emory Elliott, ed., *Columbia Literary History of the United States* (New York: Columbia University Press, 1988), xiii.

21. Elliott, *Columbia Literary History*, xiii.

22. Denis Hollier, ed., *A New History of French Literature* (Cambridge: Harvard University Press, 1989), front cover.

23. In Hollier, *A New History*, 993–1000.

24. Hollier, *A New History*, xix.

25. Hollier, *A New History*, xx.

26. Hollier, *A New History*, back cover.

27. See Arac in *The Uses of Literary History*, ed. Marshall Brown (Durham: Duke University Press, 1995), 24; Marshall Brown, "Introduction: Contemplating the Theory of Literary History," *PMLA* 107.1 (1992): 23. The impact of Hollier's book is evident in two subsequent volumes: David E. Wellbery, ed., *A New History of German Literature* (Cambridge: Harvard University Press, 2004); Greil Marcus and Werner Sollors, eds., *A New Literary History of America* (Cambridge: Harvard University Press, 2009).

28. Gumbrecht, "History," 479.

29. Perkins, *Is Literary History Possible?*, 60.

30. Gerald Mast, "Film History and Film Histories," *Quarterly Review of Film Studies* 1.3 (1976): 297.

31. Richard Abel, "Don't Know Much About History; or the (In)Vested Interests of Doing Cinema History," *Film History* 6.1 (1994): 110–115.

32. Mast, "Film History," 298.

33. Jenaro Talens and Santos Zunzunegui, "Toward a True History of Cinema: Film History as Narration," *Boundary 2* 24.1 (1997): 28–29.

34. See Zhang Quan 張泉, "Xianyou Zhongguo wenxueshi de pinggu wenti" 現有中國文學史的評估問題 [Issues in the evaluation of existing histories of Chinese literature], *Wenyi zhengming* 文藝爭鳴 [Contentions] 2008.3: 54.

35. As of 2014, the only exception is a reference book, Bonnie McDougall and Louie Kam, *The Literature of China in the Twentieth Century* (New York: Columbia University Press, 1997), but the situation will change with the long-anticipated volume David Derwei Wang, ed., *New Literary History of Modern China* (Cambridge: Harvard University Press, 2016).

36. C. T. Hsia, *A History of Modern Chinese Fiction*, 1st ed. (New Haven: Yale University Press, 1961), 498.

37. Hsia, *A History*, 506.

38. See David Der-wei Wang, "Introduction," in C. T. Hsia, *A History of Modern Chinese Fiction*, 3rd ed. (Bloomington: Indiana University Press, 1999), ix and xxi.

39. Wang, "Introduction," viii, xv, and xxxii–xxxiii.

40. Terry Eagleton, *Literary Theory: An Introduction* (Oxford: Basil Blackwell, 1983), 199.

41. Yingjin Zhang, "Modern Chinese Literature as Institution: Canon and Literary History," in *The Columbia Companion to Modern East Asian Literature*, ed. Joshua Mostow (New York: Columbia University Press, 2003), 329.

42. Leo Ou-fan Lee, *The Romantic Generation of Modern Chinese Writers* (Cambridge: Harvard University Press, 1973); Leo Ou-Fan Lee, *Voices from the Iron House: A Study of Lu Xun* (Bloomington: Indiana University Press, 1987).

43. Edward M. Gunn, *Unwelcome Muse: Chinese Literature in Shanghai and Peking* (New York: Columbia University Press, 1980).

44. David Der-Wei Wang, *Fictional Realism in Twentieth-Century China: Mao Dun, Lao She, Shen Congwen* (New York: Columbia University Press, 1992).

45. Perry Link, *Mandarin Ducks and Butterflies: Popular Fiction in Early Twentieth-Century Chinese Cities* (Berkeley: University of California Press, 1981).

46. Michel Hockx, *Questions of Style: Literary Societies and Literary Journals in Modern China, 1911–1937* (Leiden: Brill, 2003).

47. David Der-wei Wang, *Fin-de-siècle Splendor: Repressed Modernities of Late Qing Fiction, 1849–1911* (Stanford: Stanford University Press, 1997).

48. Xudong Zhang, *Chinese Modernism in the Era of Reforms: Cultural Fever, Avant-garde Fiction, and the New Chinese Cinema* (Durham: Duke University Press, 1997); Xudong Zhang, *Postsocialism and Cultural Politics: China in the Last Decade of the Twentieth Century* (Durham: Duke University Press, 2008).

49. For a survey of English scholarship on modern Chinese literature, see Yingjin Zhang's "General Introduction," *A Companion to Modern Chinese Literature*, ed. Yingjin Zhang (London: Wiley-Blackwell, 2016), 1–37.

50. This was accomplished to a certain extent by Kirk Denton, who edited the 329-page section on modern Chinese literature in the *Columbia Companion*, ed. Mostow, 287–616.

51. Quoted in Elliott, *Columbia Literary History*, xi.

52. There might be an elitist mindset at work in North America, as scholars are "disciplined" to privilege "theory" and brush aside "empirical" work such as literary history and encyclopedias, thereby duplicating a global division of labor which assigns the non-West a "low" status of primary research, always in need of "catching up" with "high" intellectual theorization from the West.

53. Yingjin Zhang, "The Institutionalization of Modern Literary History in China, 1922–1980," *Modern China* 20.3 (1994): 359. See also Wang Yao 王瑤, *Zhongguo xin wenxue shigao* 中國新文學史稿 [A draft history of new Chinese literature] (Shanghai: Shanghai wenyi chubanshe, 1982; first published 1951), 1: 19.

54. Ding Yi 丁易, *Zhongguo xiandai wenxue shilüe* 中國現代文學史略 [A brief history of modern Chinese literature] (Beijing: Zuojia chubanshe, 1955), 4. Its English edition appeared in 1959, two years before Hsia's history.

55. Tang Tao 唐弢, ed., *Zhongguo xiandai wenxue shi* 中國現代文學史 [A history of modern Chinese literature] (Beijing: Renmin wenxue chubanshe, 1979), vol. 1, 9 and 13.

56. The project of "rewriting literary history" was launched in 1988 by *Shanghai wenxue* 上海文學 (Shanghai literature), where Chen Sihe 陳思和 and Wang Xiaoming 王曉明 coedited a section on the topic for a year and a half. The overseas magazine *Jintian* 今天 [Today] continued the discussion in a section of the same title from 1991 to 2001.

57. C. T. Xia 夏志清, *Zhongguo xiandai xiaoshuo shi* 中國現代小說史 [A history of modern Chinese fiction], trans. Liu Shaoming 劉紹銘 et al. (Hong Kong: Youlian chubanshe, 1979).

58. See Chen Sihe 陳思和, *Zhongguo xin wenxue zhengti guan* 中國新文學整體觀 [A total view of new literature in China] (Shanghai: Shanghai wenyi chubanshe, 1987); Chen Sihe, "Minjian de fuchen: Dui kangzhan dao wenge wenxueshi de yige chanshixing jieshi" 民間的浮沉: 對抗戰到文革文學史的一個闡釋性解釋 [The rise and fall of the folk sphere: A tentative explication of the literary history from the war of resistance to the Cultural Revolution], *Shanghai wenxue* 1994.1: 68–80.

59. Chen Sihe, "Shilun dangdai wenxueshi (1949–1976) de 'qianzai xiezuo'" 試論當代文學史 (1949–1976) 的 "潛在寫作" [A preliminary study of "clandestine writings" in contemporary literature, 1949–1976], *Wenxue pinglun* 文學評論 [Literary review] 1999.6: 104–113.

60. Chen Sihe, "Mantan wenxueshi lilun de tansuo he chuangxin" 漫談文學史理論的探索和創新 [Thoughts on explorations and innovations in the theory of literary history], *Wenyi zhengming* 2007.9: 54–61.

61. Chen Sihe, ed., *Zhongguo dangdai wenxueshi jiaocheng* 中國當代文學史教程 [A textbook history of contemporary Chinese literature], 2nd ed. (Shanghai: Fudan daxue chubanshe, 2005). By December 2008, this book had sold 175,000 copies.

62. See Xu Zidong 許子東, "Xiezuo shijian yu wenxueshi xianchang" 寫作時間與文學史現場 [The present time of historiography and the past scene of literary history], in Chinese Department, ed., *"Wusi" yu Zhongguo xiandangdai wenxue guoji xueshu yantaohui* "五四" 與中國現當代文學國際學術研討會 [An international conference on the "May Fourth" and modern Chinese literature] (Beijing: Peking University, April 2009), 135.

63. One source estimates that 1,600 titles of Chinese literary histories were produced around the world from 1880 to 1994, while another identifies 2,885 books related to Chinese literary history around 2000; see Zhang Quan, "Xianyou Zhongguo," 54–55. By 2006, there were reportedly twenty million college students in China; see Chen Sihe, "Mantan," 52.

64. Quoted in Zhang Quan, "Xianyou Zhongguo," 56.

65. Gao Yuanbao 郜元寶, "Meiyou 'wenxue gushi' de wenxueshi: zenyang jiangshu Zhongguo xiandai wenxueshi" 沒有"文學故事"的文學史: 怎樣講述中國現代文學史 [Literary history without "literary stories": how to narrate modern Chinese literature], *Nanfang wentan* 南方文壇 [Southern literary forum] 2008.4: 13–19.

66. Cheng Guangwei 程光煒, "Wenxueshi yanjiu de 'moshenghua'" 文學史 "陌生化" ["Defamilarization" of the study of literary history], *Wenyi zhengming* 2008.3: 33–41.

67. Chen Pingyuan 陳平原, "Chongjian 'wenxueshi'" 重建 "文學史" [Reconstructing "literary history"], *Xiandai Zhongguo* 現代中國 [Modern China] 12 (April 2009): 226–228.

68. Chen Pingyuan, "Jiaru meiyou 'wenxueshi'" 假如沒有 "文學史" [If there were no "literary history"], *Dushu* 讀書 [Reading] 2009.1: 69–75.

69. In *The Uses*, ed. Brown, 12.

70. In *The Uses*, ed. Brown, 12.

71. Mario J. Valdés and Linda Hutcheon, "Rethinking Literary History—Comparatively" (American Council of Learned Societies Occasional Paper, no. 27, 1994), 2–3.

72. Mario J. Valdés and Djelal Kadir, eds., *Literary Cultures of Latin America: A Comparative History* (New York: Oxford University Press, 2004), 1: xix.

73. Valdés and Hutcheon, "Rethinking," 7–10. The African diaspora project, originally coordinated by Biodun Jeyifo and Henry Louis Gates, Jr., apparently did not materialize. For ICLA sponsorship, see front matters in Marcel Cornis-Pope and John Neubauer, eds., *History of the Literary Cultures of East-Central Europe: Junctures and Disjunctures in the 19th and 20th Centuries*, 4 vols. (Amsterdam: John Benjamins, 2004–2010). See also Mario J. Valdés and Djelal Kadir, eds., *Literary Cultures of Latin America: A Comparative History*, 3 vols. (New York: Oxford University Press, 2004).

74. Linda Hutcheon, Djelal Kadir, and Mario J. Valdés, "Collaborative Historiography: A Comparative Literary History of Latin America" (American Council of Learned Societies Occasional Paper, no. 35, 1996), 2.

75. Hutcheon, Kadir, and Valdés, "Collaborative Historiography," 4.

76. Hutcheon, Kadir, and Valdés, "Collaborative Historiography," 5.

77. In *Rethinking*, eds. Hutcheon and Valdés, 8, 30.

78. In *Rethinking*, eds. Hutcheon and Valdés, 26.

79. In *Rethinking*, eds. Hutcheon and Valdés, 30.

80. In *History*, eds. Cornis-Pope and Neubauer, 1: xv.

81. In *History*, eds. Cornis-Pope and Neubauer, 1: xvi.

82. Elliott, *Columbia Literary History*, xvii.

83. Denis Hollier, ed., *De la littérature française* (Paris: Bordas, 1993).

84. In *History*, eds. Cornis-Pope and Neubauer, 1: xiv.

85. In *History*, eds. Cornis-Pope and Neubauer, 1: 18.

86. In *History*, eds. Cornis-Pope and Neubauer, 1: 34.

87. In *History*, eds. Cornis-Pope and Neubauer, 1: xvi.

88. Sacvan Bercovitch, ed., *The Cambridge History of American Literature*, Vol. 1, 1590–1820 (New York: Cambridge University Press, 1994), 4.

89. Bercovitch, *Cambridge*, 4–5.

90. In *Rethinking*, eds. Hutcheon and Valdés, 140, 143.

91. In *Rethinking*, eds. Hutcheon and Valdés, 143.

92. In *Rethinking*, eds. Hutcheon and Valdés, 75.

93. In *Rethinking*, eds. Hutcheon and Valdés, 74.

94. In *Rethinking*, eds. Hutcheon and Valdés, 93.

95. In *Rethinking*, eds. Hutcheon and Valdés, 61.

96. In *Rethinking*, eds. Hutcheon and Valdés, 69.

97. See, for instance, Tee Kim Tong 張錦忠 and Ng Kim Chew 黃錦樹, eds., *Chongxie Taiwan wenxue shi* 重寫臺灣文學史 [Rewriting Taiwanese literary history] (Taipei: Maitian, 2007).

98. Shu-mei Shih, "Foreword: The Sinophone as History and the Sinophone as Theory," *Journal of Chinese Cinemas* 6.1 (2012): 5. See also Shu-mei Shih, *Visuality and Identity: Sinophone Articulations across the Pacific* (Berkeley: University of California Press, 2007), 4.

99. See Jing Tsu and David Der-wei Wang, eds., *Global Chinese Literature: Critical Essays* (Leiden: Brill, 2010).

100. In *History*, eds. Cornis-Pope and Neubauer, 1: xiii.

101. See Catherine Gallagher, "Counterhistory and the Anecdote," in *Practicing New Historicism*, eds. Catherine Gallagher and Stephen Greenblatt (Chicago: University of Chicago Press, 2000), 49–74.

WORKS CITED

Abel, Richard. "Don't Know Much About History; or the (In)Vested Interests of Doing Cinema History." *Film History* 6.1 (1994): 110–115.

Bercovitch, Sacvan, ed. *The Cambridge History of American Literature.* Vol. 1, 1590–1820. New York: Cambridge University Press, 1994.

Brown, Marshall. "Introduction: Contemplating the Theory of Literary History." *PMLA* 107.1 (1992): 13–25.

Brown, Marshall, ed. *The Uses of Literary History.* Durham: Duke University Press, 1995.

Chartier, Roger. *Cultural History: Between Practices and Representations.* Trans. Lydia G. Cochrane. Cambridge, UK: Polity Press, 1988.

Chen Pingyuan 陳平原. "Chongjian 'wenxueshi'" 重建"文學史" [Reconstructing "literary history"]. *Xiandai Zhongguo* 現代中國 [Modern China] 12 (April 2009): 226–228.

Chen Pingyuan 陳平原. "Jiaru meiyou 'wenxueshi'" 假如沒有"文學史" [If there were no "literary history"]. *Dushu* 讀書 [Reading] 2009.1: 69–75.

Chen Sihe 陳思和. *Zhongguo xin wenxue zhengti guan* 中國新文學整體觀 [A total view of new literature in China]. Shanghai: Shanghai wenyi chubanshe, 1987.

Chen Sihe 陳思和. "Minjian de fuchen: Dui kangzhan dao wenge wenxueshi de yige chan-shixing jieshi" 民間的浮沉: 對抗戰到文革文學史的一個闡釋性解釋 [The rise and fall of the folk sphere: A tentative explication of the literary history from the war of resistance to the Cultural Revolution]. *Shanghai wenxue* 上海文學 [Shanghai literature] 1994.1: 68–80.

Chen Sihe 陳思和. "Shilun dangdai wenxueshi (1949–1976) de 'qianzai xiezuo'" 試論當代文學史 (1949–1976) 的"潛在寫作" [A preliminary study of "clandestine writings" in contemporary literature, 1949–1976]. *Wenxue pinglun* 文學評論 [Literary review] 1999.6: 104–113.

Chen Sihe 陳思和, ed. *Zhongguo dangdai wenxueshi jiaocheng* 中國當代文學史教程 [A textbook history of contemporary Chinese literature]. 2nd ed. Shanghai: Fudan daxue chubanshe, 2005.

Chen Sihe 陳思和. "Mantan wenxueshi lilun de tansuo he chuangxin" 漫談文學史理論的探索和創新 [Thoughts on explorations and innovations in the theory of literary history]. *Wenyi zhengming* 文藝爭鳴 [Contentions] 2007.9: 54–61.

Cheng Guangwei 程光煒. "Wenxueshi yanjiu de 'moshenghua'" 文學史的"陌生化" ["Defamilarization" of the study of literary history]. *Wenyi zhengming* 2008.3: 33–41.

Cornis-Pope, Marcel, and John Neubauer, eds. *History of the Literary Cultures of East-Central Europe: Junctures and Disjunctures in the 19th and 20th Centuries.* 4 vols. Amsterdam: John Benjamins, 2004–2010.

Ding Yi 丁易. *Zhongguo xiandai wenxue shilüe* 中國現代文學史略 [A brief history of modern Chinese literature]. Beijing: Zuojia chubanshe, 1955.

Eagleton, Terry. *Literary Theory: An Introduction.* Oxford: Basil Blackwell, 1983.

Elliott, Emory, ed. *Columbia Literary History of the United States.* New York: Columbia University Press, 1988.

Gallagher, Catherine. "Counterhistory and the Anecdote." *Practicing New Historicism.* Ed. Catherine Gallagher and Stephen Greenblatt. Chicago: University of Chicago Press, 2000. 49–74.

Gao Yuanbao 郜元寶. "Meiyou 'wenxue gushi' de wenxueshi: Zenyang jiangshu Zhongguo xiandai wenxueshi" 沒有"文學故事" 的文學史: 怎樣講述中國現代文學史 [Literary history without "literary stories": How to narrate modern Chinese literature]. *Nanfang wentan* 南方文壇 [Southern literary forum] 2008.4: 13–19.

Gumbrecht, Hans Ulrich. "History of Literature—Fragment of a Vanished Totality?" Trans. Peter Heath. *New Literary History* 16.3 (1985): 467–479.

Gunn, Edward M. *Unwelcome Muse: Chinese Literature in Shanghai and Peking*. New York: Columbia University Press, 1980.

Hockx, Michel. *Questions of Style: Literary Societies and Literary Journals in Modern China, 1911–1937*. Leiden: Brill, 2003.

Hollier, Denis, ed. *A New History of French Literature*. Cambridge: Harvard University Press, 1989.

Hollier, Denis, ed. *De la littérature française*. Paris: Bordas, 1993.

Hsia, C. T. *A History of Modern Chinese Fiction*. 1st ed. New Haven: Yale University Press, 1961.

Hsia, C. T. 夏志清. *Zhongguo xiandai xiaoshuo shi* 中國現代小說史 [A history of modern Chinese fiction]. Trans. Liu Shaoming 劉紹銘 et al. Hong Kong: Youlian chubanshe, 1979.

Hutcheon, Linda, Djelal Kadir, and Mario J. Valdés. "Collaborative Historiography: A Comparative Literary History of Latin America." American Council of Learned Societies Occasional Paper no. 35, 1996.

Hutcheon, Linda, and Mario J. Valdés, eds. *Rethinking Literary History: A Dialogue on Theory*. New York: Oxford University Press, 2002.

"Is Literary History Obsolete?" Special issue, *New Literary History* 2.1 (1970): 1–193.

Johnstone, Robert. "The Impossible Genre: Reading Comprehensive Literary History." *PMLA* 107.1 (1992): 26–37.

Lee, Leo Ou-fan. *The Romantic Generation of Modern Chinese Writers*. Cambridge: Harvard University Press, 1973.

Lee, Leo Ou-fan. *Voices from the Iron House: A Study of Lu Xun*. Bloomington: Indiana University Press, 1987.

Link, Perry. *Mandarin Ducks and Butterflies: Popular Fiction in Early Twentieth-Century Chinese Cities*. Berkeley: University of California Press, 1981.

Marcus, Greil, and Werner Sollors, eds. *A New Literary History of America*. Cambridge: Harvard University Press, 2009.

Mast, Gerald. "Film History and Film Histories." *Quarterly Review of Film Studies* 1.3 (1976): 297–314.

McDougall, Bonnie, and Louie Kam. *The Literature of China in the Twentieth Century*. New York: Columbia University Press, 1997.

Patterson, Lee. "Literary History." In *Critical Terms for Literary Study*. Ed. Frank Lentricchia and Thomas McLaughlin. Chicago: University of Chicago Press, 1989. 250–262.

Perkins, David, ed. *Theoretical Issues in Literary History*. Cambridge: Harvard University Press, 1991.

Perkins, David. *Is Literary History Possible?* Baltimore: Johns Hopkins University Press, 1992.

Shih, Shu-mei. *Visuality and Identity: Sinophone Articulations across the Pacific*. Berkeley: University of California Press, 2007.

Shih, Shu-mei. "Foreword: The Sinophone as History and the Sinophone as Theory." *Journal of Chinese Cinemas* 6.1 (2012): 5–7.

Spiller, Robert E. *The Third Dimension: Studies in Literary History*. New York: Macmillan, 1965. 3–14.

Taine, Hippolyte. "History of English Literature: Introduction." In *Critical Theory Since Plato*. Ed. Hazard Adams. Fort Worth, TX: Harcourt Brace Jovanovich, 1992. 609–620.

Talens, Jenaro, and Santos Zunzunegui. "Toward a True History of Cinema: Film History as Narration." *Boundary 2* 24.1 (1997): 1–34.

Tang Tao 唐弢, ed. *Zhongguo xiandai wenxue shi* 中國現代文學史 [A history of modern Chinese literature]. Beijing: Renmin wenxue chubanshe, 1979–1980.

Tsu, Jing, and David Der-wei Wang, eds. *Global Chinese Literature: Critical Essays*. Leiden: Brill, 2010.

Valdés, Mario J., and Linda Hutcheon. "Rethinking Literary History—Comparatively." American Council of Learned Societies Occasional Paper no. 27, 1994.

Valdés, Mario J., and Djelal Kadir, eds. *Literary Cultures of Latin America: A Comparative History*. 3 vols. New York: Oxford University Press, 2004.

Wang, David Der-Wei. *Fictional Realism in Twentieth-Century China: Mao Dun, Lao She, Shen Congwen*. New York: Columbia University Press, 1992.

Wang, David Der-wei. *Fin-de-siècle Splendor: Repressed Modernities of Late Qing Fiction, 1849–1911*. Stanford: Stanford University Press, 1997.

Wang, David Der-wei. "Introduction." In C. T. Hsia, *A History of Modern Chinese Fiction*. 3rd ed. Bloomington: Indiana University Press, 1999. vii–xxxv.

Wang, David Der-wei, ed. *New Literary History of Modern China*. Cambridge: Harvard University Press, 2016.

Wang Yao 王瑤. *Zhongguo xin wenxue shigao* 中國新文學史稿 [A draft history of new Chinese literature]. 2 vols. Shanghai: Shanghai wenyi chubanshe, 1982 [1951].

Wellek, René. *The Attack on Literature and Other Essays*. Chapel Hill: University Press of North Carolina, 1982.

Wellek, René, and Austin Warren. *Theory of Literature*. New York: Harcourt, 1949.

Wellbery, David E., ed. *A New History of German Literature*. Cambridge: Harvard University Press, 2004.

Wong, Tak-Wai, and Ackbar Abbas, eds. *Rewriting Literary History*. Hong Kong: Hong Kong University Press, 1984.

Xu Zidong 許子東. "Xiezuo shijian yu wenxueshi xianchang" 寫作時間與文學史現場 [The present time of historiography and the past scene of literary history]. In *"Wusi" yu Zhongguo xiandangdai wenxue guoji xueshu yantaohui* "五四" 與中國現當代文學國際學術研討會 [An international conference on "May Fourth" and modern Chinese literature]. Ed. Chinese Department, Peking University, April 2009.

Tee Kim Tong 張錦忠 and Ng Kim Chew 黃錦樹, eds. *Chongxie Taiwan wenxue shi* 重寫臺灣文學史 [Rewriting Taiwanese literary history]. Taipei: Maitian, 2007.

Zhang Quan 張泉. "Xianyou Zhongguo wenxueshi de pinggu wenti" 現有中國文學史的 評估問題 [Issues in the evaluation of existing histories of Chinese literature]. *Wenyi zheng-ming* 2008.3: 54–56.

Zhang, Xudong. *Chinese Modernism in the Era of Reforms: Cultural Fever, Avant-garde Fiction, and the New Chinese Cinema*. Durham: Duke University Press, 1997.

Zhang, Xudong. *Postsocialism and Cultural Politics: China in the Last Decade of the Twentieth Century*. Durham: Duke University Press, 2008.

Zhang, Yingjin. "The Institutionalization of Modern Literary History in China, 1922–1980." *Modern China* 20.3 (1994): 347–377.

Zhang, Yingjin. "Modern Chinese Literature as Institution: Canon and Literary History." In *The Columbia Companion to Modern East Asian Literature*. Ed. Joshua Mostow. New York: Columbia University Press, 2003. 324–332.

Zhang, Yingjin, ed. *A Companion to Modern Chinese Literature*. London: Wiley-Blackwell, 2016.

....

READING LU XUN'S EARLY ESSAYS IN RELATION TO MARXISM

....

VIREN MURTHY

Lu Xun has often been called the father of modern Chinese literature, and there have been different ways of interpreting his work in relation to Marxism and modernity. Following the Yan'an period, the Chinese Communist Party canonized Lu Xun as a Marxist, and in this case Marxism was understood as a type of modernization theory. This initiated a narrative that claimed that Lu Xun started out as a somewhat bourgeois or even a liberal writer in his early period, but after his famous prose poem collection *Wild Grass* (野草) he became a Marxist. However, in postwar Japan and since the 1980s in China, Europe and the United States, scholars began to read Lu Xun as an existential critic of modernity, and in this way affirmed more of a continuity between his earlier and later works.[1] This perspective on Lu Xun has since been developed by critics such as Wang Hui and Leo Ou-fan Lee, who have emphasized his connections with German philosophers such as Friedrich Nietzsche and Max Stirner.[2] In other words, Lu Xun has been torn out of the older Marxist framework and placed in a more romantic antimodern perspective. The romantic anticapitalist or antimodern reading of Lu Xun shatters the earlier Marxist categories of feudal and bourgeois thought and poses anew the question of how to use a Marxist framework to understand a figure such as Lu Xun. This chapter attempts to bring Marxist theory in dialogue with Lu Xun's work, by focusing on his early writings and reading them in relation to theorists such as Moishe Postone, Jacques Bidet, Karatani Kojin, and Michel Henry. Through a close reading of Lu Xun's texts we can examine debates within the Marxist tradition, especially about issues related to global capitalism and the possibilities of a socialist future in countries on the periphery of the world-system. In this way, Lu Xun and Marxist theory can illuminate one another.

The two Lu Xun essays we will analyze below, "On the Refutation of Malevolent Voices" (破惡聲論) and "Concerning Imbalanced Cultural Development" (文化偏至論), were both published in 1908, in a Chinese student-run journal from Tokyo called *Henan* (河南). Lu Xun wrote them in classical Chinese about four years after he arrived in Japan to study medicine. By this point he had already decided to study literature after realizing that the Chinese people's spirits, rather than their bodies, needed to be radically transformed. The essays were composed during what some would call a transitional period in Lu Xun's career before his famous story collection *Outcry* (呐喊), and consequently they are not usually categorized as literature, but rather as philosophy or social criticism. Indeed, during this time Lu Xun was involved in a variety of scholarly activities, including studying the classics with his famous teacher, Zhang Taiyan 章太炎, and these essays are clearly influenced by the latter's philosophical interests.[3]

It is precisely the eclectic nature of these texts that makes them interesting from the standpoint of Marxism. The essays gesture at something that haunts modernity, which will be a theme throughout Lu Xun's later writings. Lu Xun encourages readers to question modernity by discussing how people have lost their individuality in larger processes of society. From the perspective of Marxist theory, this poses the question of how to grasp individual creative activity in relation to social processes such as capital. In the chapter on large-scale machinery in volume 1 of *Capital*, Marx explains how with the advent of machines, the human being becomes a mere appendage to the machine. But there is another side to this phenomenon. Lu Xun posits a romantic vision of the self that resists the mechanistic tendencies of modernity—this is precisely the side that haunts modernity. A key question that emerges is how to theorize and historicize this haunting, which is not only significant for an understanding of Lu Xun and modern Chinese literature, but also represents a larger global problematic. Lu Xun and his image in revolutionary China, along with the transnational afterlife of revolutionary China, are comprehensible only from a global theoretical perspective.

Lu Xun's work, accordingly, poses a larger methodological question about how to read literary or philosophical texts. Put simply, his work forces us to become clear about the methodological grounds that legitimate our use of theory to interpret a given text. A common assumption in both intellectual history and literature is that we need to put writings in context. With respect to Lu Xun's early texts, this would mean reading his work in light of other works from the late Qing and Meiji period. In addition, one could also look at the authors that Lu Xun himself read at the time, such as Nietzsche and Stirner. From this perspective one could ask: how does Marx come into the picture?

We find a potential answer to this question in Peter Gordon's recent questioning of the contextualist thesis, in which he observes:

> Intellectual history is by definition not merely a description of perceptible objects but an inquiry into meaning. From this basic premise intellectual historians have recognized their own hermeneutic implication in the meanings they study, and they have developed sophisticated theories so as to explain the way that any access to past meaning must of necessity involve the historian in an act of interpretation rather than objectivistic description. . . . This is because the holistic definition of a context

encourages us to believe that a context is an objective thing that can be identified in a purely descriptive and noninterpretative fashion.[4]

Gordon objects to the Cambridge School intellectual historians, such as Quentin Skinner, who claimed that in order to understand a text one must place that text in relation to a larger discursive context. Gordon contends that identifying context is no simple matter. He charges intellectual historians with a type of naive objectivism, in that they hope to be able to read context as if it were transparent. Gordon's point is that historicists risk reducing texts to contexts and fail to realize that certain ideas might go beyond their so-called contexts and possess a certain redemptive value for later generations.

The idea of redemptive value is intimately connected to a process of haunting. The basic idea is that texts signify beyond immediate discursive contexts; there is some-thing beyond the meaning presented on the page. Gordon relates this redemptive ges-ture to Hegel and stresses negativity as a counter against reification. This will be an important part of our reading of Lu Xun. Gordon cites the following passage from Theodor Adorno and Max Horkheimer's *Dialectic of Enlightenment* to make his point:

> The actual is validated, knowledge confines itself to repeating it, thought makes itself mere tautology. The more completely the machinery of thought subjugates existence, the more blindly it is satisfied with reproducing it. Enlightenment thereby regresses to the mythology it has never been able to escape. For mythology had reflected in its forms the essence of the existing order—cyclical motion, fate, domi-nation of the world as truth—and had renounced hope.[5]

Adorno and Horkheimer here describe a problem—namely, the opposition between an increasingly mechanized world and the voices that haunt it, which cannot be reduced to textual context and instead require the historian to draw from a theoretical universe beyond mere textual connections. Marxism can provide an approach to determine con-text in this larger sense, not as transparent and merely referring to discourse, but as dynamic and having a significance beyond itself.

The dynamic ground for Lu Xun's world—and the methodological ground for read-ing Lu Xun—is not only China, but rather the complex and contradictory world of global capitalism. Capitalism provides a transnational context that is not merely discur-sive; it forms the conditions for the possibility of the production of ideas. Consequently, Marxism becomes crucial from two related perspectives. First, Marxism shares with many romantic critiques of modernity, including those advanced by Lu Xun, Stirner, and Nietzsche, an animosity toward the alienation associated with capitalist modernity. Second, and perhaps more importantly, Marxists constantly attempt to outline meth-ods of understanding the contradictions inherent in capitalism and show how the logic of capitalism is related to the production of ideology. Neither of these perspectives is dependent on relations of influence. However, the second perspective illuminates the conditions that make influence and comparison meaningful. Put simply, it is precisely global capitalist modernity that enables various forms of discourse, including literary production.

Lu Xun, the Late Qing, and Marxist Problematics

Scholars of late Qing and early Republican literature and thought, especially those working from a Marxist perspective, often assert that during the late Qing, China entered modernity because of its antagonistic contact with global capitalism and imperialism. Scholars such as David Der-wei Wang, Theodore Huters, and Wang Hui have turned to the late Qing as a locus of modernity and antimodernity in different senses of the word. In this section, I seek to theorize the gestures Lu Xun makes against modernity in his early essays in relation to the global context of late Qing China and late Meiji Japan.

From the perspective of intellectual history, late Qing reformers and revolutionaries all embarked on a path toward modernity, but at the same time they expounded critiques of aspects of modernity, including capitalism, and especially the state. I have written about Zhang Taiyan's early critique of collective domination, which we will see continues in Lu Xun's early work.[6] In Lu Xun's context, individuality is intimately connected to a type of life force and vitalism that confronts alienated forms of human subjectivity, such as the state and capital. We can connect this opposition to transformations that originate in Europe but take on a new meaning in late Qing and early republican China. Specifically, while the concept of individuality was originally associated with the promotion of capitalism, by the late nineteenth century individuality had come to entail a certain resistance to capitalism and rationalization. The concepts of life and vitalism are perhaps even more clearly connected to a type of romantic resistance to capitalist modernity.

A brief look at the historical context of Lu Xun's early writings reveals the importance of concepts of life and individuality. It is well known that Lu Xun's early connection to literature was mediated by the nation and nationalism.[7] This was of course during the Russo-Japanese War, a period of heightened nationalism in Japan and the period of New Government policies in China. So, on one hand, there is no doubt that Lu Xun was thinking about how to make China powerful and wealthy. However, on the other hand, during the late Meiji period, intellectuals increasingly mobilized against modernity from different perspectives. Since their countries were located on the periphery of the global capitalist system of nation-states, both Chinese and Japanese intellectuals experienced the connections between capitalism and imperialism. In addition, by the early twentieth century, Meiji Japan had already progressed along the path to industrialization. For example, between 1890 and 1900 manufacture more than doubled as society and production became increasingly mechanized. As a result, intellectuals increasingly perceived the problems of capitalism, including rampant income inequality and the general commodification of life. In response, many Japanese intellectuals shifted away from discourses extolling enlightenment and industrialization à la Fukuzawa Yukichi and began to develop philosophical critiques of the mechanization associated with industrial capitalism through recourse to concepts such as individual consciousness and the heart, both of which are connected to vital activity and life. One of the pioneers of this trend was the Meiji poet Kitamura Tōkoku 北村透谷, but we know that Lu Xun was influenced by others who could loosely be associated with movements that stressed consciousness and individuality, including Saitō Nonohito and Anesaki Masaharu.[8]

Here we see the enlightenment and capitalist modernity confronted by another side that continues to haunt it. This other side is often characterized by that which cannot be subsumed by capital and is embodied in concepts such as life, voice, and religion/superstition. From this latter perspective, modernity is haunted because of the alienation at its core, which makes that which is alienated return in different forms. The haunting can also be understood as the return of that which is different in order to destabilize the homogeneity connected to a mechanization that turns people into cogs in a machine.

Lu Xun explicitly connects this domination and mechanization to domination by groups. The following passage from "On a Refutation" suggests how he perceived this relationship.

> However, if everyone leans in the same direction and ten thousand mouths sing the same tune, this singing cannot come from the heart, it is mere chiming in with others, like the meshing of gears in a machine. Such a chorus is more disturbing to the ear than the groaning of trees or the clamorous cries of certain birds, because it emphasizes the profound silence in the background.[9]

We will examine this essay in greater detail in the next section. The majority of this text expresses an antimodern impulse. This particular portion of the text, however, offers us an entry point to understand the logic of capitalist modernity. Lu Xun describes a situation in which life or the heart-mind confronts machines, and this discussion leaves us with the question of how to understand his work with respect to Marxism, especially with respect to the second analytical perspective concerned with grasping the structural dynamic of capital. The connection at first sight is extremely clear: Lu Xun invokes an image that recalls Max Weber's idea of cogs in the machine. Behind such a process, however, is what Marx describes as a situation in which the "conditions of work employ the worker." Marx writes:

> Even the lightening of the labor becomes an instrument of torture, since the machine does not free the worker from the work, but rather deprives the work itself of all content. Every kind of capitalist production, in so far as it is not only a labor process but also capital's process of valorization, has this in common, but it is not the worker who employs the conditions of his work, but rather the reverse, the condition of work employ the worker. However, it is only with the coming of machinery that this

inversion [*Verkehrung*] first acquires a technical and palpable reality. Owing to its conversion into an automaton, the instrument of labor confronts the worker during the labor process in the shape of capital, dead labor, which dominates and soaks up living labor-power. The separation of the intellectual faculties of the production process from manual labor, and the transformation of those faculties into powers exercised by capital over labor, is, as we have already shown, finally completed by large-scale industry erected on the foundation of machinery. The special skill of each individual machine operator, who has now been deprived of all significance, vanishes as an infinitesimal quantity in the face of the science, the gigantic natural forces, and the mass of social labor embodied in the system of machinery, which together with those three forces, constitutes the power of the 'master'.[10]

This passage occurs late in *Capital*, in the chapter on large-scale machinery, which appears after the introduction of relative surplus value and industrialization. The idea of work deprived of all content is already contained in capitalism insofar as it stresses "abstract labor" as opposed to labor connected to the production of specific use-values. However, this type of process comes to culmination and becomes "palpable" when machines subordinate living labor to dead labor. Machines were introduced to accelerate the production of surplus-value, but in the capitalist system they have the effect of making the worker into a mere appendage of the machine, thus undercutting the worker's autonomy. In particular, the deskilling of the workforce, "the separation of intellectual faculties of the production process from manual labor," results in workers using their minds less; their actions become merely physical, mechanical, chiming in with the whole system of production, which becomes a type of collective domination.

In "Concerning Imbalanced Cultural Development," published a few months before "A Refutation" and in the same journal, Lu Xun deals with the theme of mechanization and argues that a certain liberation of subjectivity was at the root of the development of material culture, but then this culture eclipsed the subjectivity that was its condition of possibility. This shows both the emergence of the individual and the possibility of a new type of community, but also the alienation of both individuals and community:

> As these fetters were removed and thought was liberated, every aspect of society was affected. Discoveries in metaphysics were coupled with inventions in the realm of the natural sciences.
>
> From those inceptions, still more new things arose—the age of discovery, mechanization, science, technology, and commerce was at hand. None of this could have been conceivable without the lifting of constraints and the liberation of the human mind.[11]

Lu Xun's understanding of the emergence of industrial capitalism follows Weber's description in *The Protestant Ethic and the Spirit of Capitalism*, which had been published two or three years earlier. While Lu Xun probably was unaware of this text, the confluence of such ideas again suggests that Lu Xun was trying to make sense of a larger global structural and discursive dynamic. Although Lu Xun does not focus on religion, like Weber he places the emphasis on a type of subjectivity and practice, along with the liberation of the individual from traditional religious fetters. Lu Xun also claims that such liberation paradoxically leads to a type of enslavement to material goods and to material progress:

> To cite the most obvious advances, we need only look toward the manifold increases in textile and steel production, mining, and other industries, the applications of which have been numerous in warfare, manufacture, and transport. With the harnessing of steam and electric power, the whole state of affairs in the world was suddenly altered in a way greatly expedient to all human undertakings. Having partaken of these benefits, one's faith in them is naturally strengthened to a point where they become the very criteria upon which everything, be it spiritual or material, is judged.[12]

In this passage, we return to the problem of being cogs in the machine, where organization, as expressed in warfare, industries, and transport, comes to dominate life. From the standpoint of production, increasing mechanization and technology are linked to the production of relative surplus value or the acceleration of the production of profits. But Lu Xun contends that the effects of mechanization are not limited to the sphere of production. As he mentions above, "every aspect of society was affected," including subjectivity. Science and technology became the ultimate standards, and consequently they subsumed life. One of the effects of this scientism would be the eclipse of ethics, the replacement of what Kant would call understanding (*Verstand*) for reason (*Vernunft*). Understanding in this context can focus on specific problems, including the pursuit of individual interests. We get a sense of this in the above passage with the phrase "having partaken of these benefits." In short, "pursuing benefits" refers to the understanding, given that this involves an immediate gratification of one's desires or narrow objectives. However, what is lacking is Kant's sense of reason or the ability to think about fundamental issues such as the constitution of community or politics.

In particular, Lu Xun suggests that the repeated consumption of commodities turns people into passive subjects ready to receive and reproduce idle chatter. As a result, they cease to use their spiritual faculties and do not attempt to imagine other possibilities for the social and political world. In other words, the process of consumption can mirror the separation of intellectual faculties in the realm of production. Moreover, one tends to forget the role of subjectivity in the process of material productivity and thus obliterate the human dimension of history. To some extent, Lu Xun is here adumbrating what Wang Hui has called "depoliticized politics."[13] The emphasis on consumption and material goods appears to be apolitical, but it has the political effect of creating passive subjects without imagination, bereft of life force and subordinate to the mechanization of life. Lu Xun emphasizes that it is only through this awakening that people would resist this subordination to dead labor and posit a different type of future community.

Before examining Lu Xun's own attempt to get beyond the politics of depoliticization, we need to consider the historical context in which he wrote in relation to

Marxist theory. One could argue that the history of the development of science in both China and Japan is intimately connected to attempts to produce relative surplus value. In other words, once the working day is relatively stable, firms attempt to increase profits by accelerating the rate of production through new technologies. This process was more successful in the cities than in rural areas. The Self-Strengthening Movement, which began in major cities of China in the 1860s, aimed precisely at increasing technological mediation.[14] Lu Xun was perhaps pointing to the flipside of some of the successes of the Self-Strengthening Movement as they were continued into other reform movements and the New Government Policies of the early twentieth century. Lu Xun also emphasized a corollary to the process of production, which we could call the crisis of the rise in material culture during the nineteenth century.

However, both these movements are complex, and how we understand either the Self-Strengthening Movement or the New Government Policies will depend on the type of Marxism we employ. According to the Hegelian-Marxist perspective, Marx illustrates two movements that undercut particularity, namely the predominance of abstraction and the pervasive force of the collective in the form of the factory. In the same vein, Marx describes capitalism as having two sides—on one hand, the anarchy of the market, and on the other, the despotism of the factory.[15] The preceding passage from Lu Xun highlights the domination of the collective, but at the same time poses larger questions of how we are to understand the above tendencies in relation to history. Below, I contrast the Hegelian Marxist paradigm to a couple of other Marxists who question the nature of the totality of capital.

Hegelian Marxists have argued that capital operates like Hegel's *Geist* and therefore encompasses both individual and collective sides. In other words, as the logic of capital unfolds, it encompasses both individual sides, as in market exchange, and collective sides, connected to the organization of the factory. The question here concerns how we should understand these two sides that we see in capital in relation to other structures of modernity. Should we follow Georg Lukács and Moishe Postone and see the state and other institutions as merely expressions of one side of the commodity form and capitalism, namely the collective, despotic side?[16]

The stakes of accepting such an interpretation are high, not only for the study of Europe but also for the study of countries on the periphery of the world system, such as late Qing China. Specifically, the preceding universal framework would allow us to interpret late Qing thought and literature as expressing the logic of the commodity form. I have previously employed this strategy in my analysis of Zhang Taiyan, but here I would like to complicate this paradigm further by drawing on recent interpretations of Marxism by Jacques Bidet, Karatani Kojin, and Michel Henry. These works bring out two issues: the relation between labor/life and capital and the imbrication of state or organization and capital.

With respect to the first issue, the passage from *Capital* cited above might appear to suggest that capital has completely subsumed labor. After all, Marx refers to capital's use of technological mediation to produce relative surplus value as the real subsumption of labor into capital. However, this does not imply that labor is subsumed by capitalism without residue. Capitalism takes earlier forms of labor or production and uses them in order to create surplus value. This is the meaning of Marx's use of the concept of inversion (*Verkehrung*).[17] We should realize, however, that inversion is not the same as sublation (*Aufhebung*). In other words, even after the inversion, labor as a basic activity remains something that the worker does, and this accounts for the experience of being inverted. This allows for the possibility of resistance from the standpoint of life and the individual.

We will return to Lu Xun's use of life below, but Marxist theory can also shed light on that which dominates labor and life, namely the machine and in particular the relationship between machine and community. Lu Xun uses the phrase "like cogs in a machine" (*ruo jiqikuo* 若機器栝), and if we follow the Hegelian interpretation, we could conclude that the formation of community in a global capitalist world is part of the same logic as that of the machine in the factory. However, by using the word *ruo*, Lu Xun refers to a likeness, which also allows for difference. On one hand, this difference suggests the problem associated with *Verkehrung*, namely that the individual becomes like a cog in the machine but is not subsumed in the machine. This is what allows the space for Lu Xun to reflect on other possibilities for the individual and, in particular, resistance. But another issue emerges here: namely, the nature of the machine in relation to communities. In the above citation from Marx, the machine represents a part in the process of capital, but in the passage from Lu Xun, we are dealing with a type of community, which appears like a machine. Consequently, before proceeding further we must ask about the relationship between modern forms of community, such as nation, state, and capital.

Karatani Kojin has argued that although capitalism requires the nation-state to exist, the nation and the state work on different principles from capital; they need to be considered as "agents on their own."[18] Karatani decided to leave the texts of Marx to develop his theory, but Bidet returns to *Capital* and reconstructs it in such a way as to bring out the implications of the state. Marx begins his analysis of capitalist society by examining commodity exchange and also production for the market, but he soon points out that even the simplest commodity exchange requires legal presuppositions and even forms of community. In Chapter 2 of *Capital*, Marx explains what must exist in order for exchange to take place: "The guardians [of commodities] must therefore recognize each other as owners of private property. This juridical relation, whose form is the contract, whether as part of a developed legal system or not, is a relation between two wills which mirrors the economic relation."[19] Exchange on the market presupposes some type of legal structure, which cannot itself be completely reducible to the market. More precisely, one of the key elements of capitalism, namely money, is bound up by the state from its inception. Marx explains that money presupposes the collective act of a society and the backing of the state, given that "only the action of society can turn a particular commodity into the universal equivalent."[20] Not only that, but even after this initial constitution, the circulation of money is inextricably connected to the actions of the state; the role of the Chinese state in controlling currency in recent years provides a particular instance of this general principle.

Examining these early chapters of *Capital*, Bidet contends that capitalist modernity has two sides, namely market and organization. These two poles of modernity imply one another and are often analogous, but they do not have the same logic. The market becomes the foundation for the transformation of money into capital, which implies the split of society into workers and capitalists. However, the state, which is essential for upholding the class relations of the capitalist market along with its logic, cannot be reduced to this logic. For this reason, the twentieth century saw numerous struggles over the role of the state in capitalism and different state formations associated with capitalism. Organization, of which the state is one major component, is often associated with hierarchies based on what Foucault would call knowledge-power.

This vision of the two poles of modern capitalist domination goes some distance in helping us to conceptualize the late Qing and the Meiji in the context of global capitalism, especially because it was precisely the Qing state that promoted quasi-market relations and industrialization during the late nineteenth and early twentieth century. However, there are other dimensions to the story. The preceding citation from Marx describes a situation after money is turned into capital and the capitalist market itself represents a tension. Specifically, commodity exchange presupposes free and equal subjects who enter into contracts. Bidet calls this presupposition of equality and liberty the "meta-structure of capital,"[21] which is connected to another haunting. This is because as money turns into capital, the presuppositions of exchange turn into their opposite. Free and equal subjects enter into exchanges that produce class relations of inequality. In this case, however, those who are on the unequal side of the relationship will constantly have recourse to the principles of the metastructure in order to struggle for equality and freedom. In short, the metastructure will constantly haunt capitalist relations.

In *État-Monde*, Bidet claims that such a haunting only takes place on the local level and that there is no metastructure on the global level, namely the level of the world-system.[22] However, Lu Xun and other late Qing thinkers writing about the uneven world-system of nation-states would suggest that there is a related but different haunting that goes on at the level of the nation-state. Bidet is of course correct to note that, although dominated by flows of capital and migration, the world-system, which we could also call the global capitalist system of nation-states, does not have an overarching state to control it. Thus there is no guarantee of freedom and equality as is the case in liberal states that institute citizenship. However, the global market is still not governed by a state of nature. There are international contracts and laws that save it from falling into complete anarchy, and consequently the world-system is in a state between order and lawlessness, which is the context for imperialist aggression, an important concern for Chinese intellectuals throughout the twentieth century and in the late Qing in particular. The critique of imperialism itself was based on notions of sovereignty and an ideal of equality among nation-states or a vision of global equality and freedom beyond nation-states, which we can see in thinkers such as Zhang Taiyan and Kang Youwei 康有為, as well as in Lu Xun's essays. In Lu Xun's case, we see a double haunting. On one hand, life haunts the global capitalist system of nation-states in the form of an anti-imperialist nationalism; this has been underscored by Jameson and others.[23] On the other hand, Lu Xun's concept of life and voice also haunts the alienation embedded in capitalism and the nation-state and yearns for another type of community on both global and domestic levels.

Lu Xun's "On the Refutation of Malevolent Voices"

The bulk of Lu Xun's essay concerns resistance to modern structures and the global system from the standpoint of life and the nation. Lu Xun's own rethinking of the notions of life, heart, and voice in relation to the nation must be understood in the context of global inequality, but we shall see that he affirms the internal dimension of the heart in a way that is critical of most spatial embodiments, including the nation-state. This goes against those who use the concept of the nation as their standpoint of critique, such as the early Liang Qichao 梁啟超. Lu Xun affirms concepts such as the heart and voice, both of which suggest a life force opposed to an alienated humanity, idle chatter, and institutionalized groups.

From the above discussion we can see that there are many institutions that embody this idle chatter, including ones in market, state, and global systems. But the above analysis has not come to grips with that which escapes the above forms of objectification. In other words, one must here not only theorize forms of objective mediation, such as market, organization, and world-system, but also that which these mediations constantly try to incorporate but cannot fully subsume—namely, life itself. We can see this idea of something that cannot be completely subsumed especially clearly in Lu Xun's early writings, such as "On the Refutation of Malevolent Voices."

Lu Xun's early writings deal with the above problematic in terms of groups and organization. He resists groups, both national and transnational, from the standpoint of the individual, and more specifically from the heart, which is something like a non-rational ontological source. "On the Refutation of Malevolent Voices" refers to differences in voices based on whether they stem from the heart-mind or from some external source. In short, malevolent voices are bereft of heart-mind or life and are abstractly imposed from the outside. When one implements an abstract ideal without regard for particulars, one homogenizes and eradicates differences. The heart-mind becomes the locus of difference, but the scope of this locus is not fixed. It is linked to the individual, but it can also be the source of a new type of nationality.[24] Lu Xun connects the fate of the nation with a specific type of voice that could clear the way for something new to appear.

> Corroded at the core and wavering spiritually, our previously "glorious nation" (華國) seems destined to wither away of its own accord amid the throes of

internecine quarrelling among the heirs to our civilization. Yet throughout the empire not a word is spoken against this, idle chatter reigns, and all channels are blocked.[25]

Note that the beginning of this passage invokes a certain temporality of loss: a once glorious nation is in the process of self-destruction. With respect to China, the immediate context of this essay is of course the movements leading to the 1911 Revolution, the New Government Policies of the Qing dynasty, and the general sense of crisis surrounding the late Qing. Indeed, these factors encouraged thinkers during the early twentieth century to constantly ponder the question of national survival. The problem concerns a lack of unity. But against this, Lu Xun points to a past that is fundamentally futural. Through this past one is supposed to speak out against the present, through a nation that emerges against nationalist imperialism—that is, resists the unequal system of nation-states. Through this negative trope, namely the absence of speech, Lu Xun urges readers to speak out against the injustices of the world. At this point, Lu Xun alludes to something like a metastructure, namely a language that transcends the present and points toward a better world. However, all channels are blocked because of an inability to hear or see beyond the present. About a century after this essay was published, today we can see an analogous situation, namely an inability to think of radically new possibilities with respect to capitalism. To some extent, Lu Xun points precisely to a type of apathy toward political presents and futures, which would perhaps overlap with his famous slide-show experience and his later *Outcry*. However, by partially drawing on the Japanese romantic tradition, along with the ideas of Zhang Taiyan, and grounding nationalism in the heart-mind, Lu Xun initiates a logic that goes inward and beyond the contemporary nation.

While such a logic of resistance is inspired by the heart-and-mind, it begins with language. Lu Xun underscores that language is twofold, in that it harbors the possibility of critique but at the same time can also reenforce existing structures. He suggests that what he calls "idle chatter" serves precisely to reproduce the structures of power. *Idle chatter* is a translation of *jimo* (寂漠), which is usually translated as "loneliness," though it can also be rendered as "silence." But Wang Hui explains that it represents a type of voice that is disembodied from the heart and subjectivity; in other words, it is an alienated voice.[26] Focusing on the modern context of Lu's writings, I take a certain interpretive license and translate *jimo* as "idle chatter" in order to echo the English translation of the term *Gerede* in Heidegger's *Being and Time*. For Heidegger, *Gerede* refers to a state in which

discoursing has lost its primary relationship-of-Being towards the entity talked about, or else has never achieved such a relationship, it does not communicate in such a way as to let this entity be appropriated in a primordial manner, but communicates rather by following the route of *gossiping* and *passing the word along*. . . Idle talk is constituted by just such gossiping and passing the world along—a process by which its initial lack of grounds to stand on (*Bodenstandslosigkeit*) becomes aggravated to complete groundlessness (*völlige Bodenlosigkeit*). The groundlessness of idle talk is no obstacle to its becoming public; instead it encourages this. Idle talk is the possibility of understanding everything without previously making the thing one's own. If this were done, idle talk would founder; and it already guards against such a danger. Idle talk is something which anyone can rake up; it not only releases one from the task of genuinely understanding, but develops an undifferentiated kind of intelligibility, for which nothing is closed off any longer.[27]

While this is not the place to go into a full discussion of Heidegger's concept of *Gerede*, like Lu Xun's concept of *jimo* it expresses a loss of self, of not making something one's own. Moreover, Heidegger's concept of language also opens out to something beyond the merely human, namely Being, or a primordial ground, which haunts idle chatter. When this ground is blocked and one is separated from it, there is an undifferentiated type of intelligibility, which we could associate with the exchange value side of the commodity form, money, mechanization and modern bureaucracies. Because there is no differentiation, the content of idle chatter says nothing definitive. Idle talk represents a kind of abstraction that is mistaken for the concrete. In other words, it is a variant of what Georg Lukács calls reification—or that which presents itself immediately as the ground, but on further reflection turns out to be merely a surface or superficial phenomenon. Lu Xun opposes a discourse about the larger structural calamities of the nation to this idle chatter.

Lu Xun argues that to counter this blockage and idle chatter, one must have recourse to a special kind of voice that is intimately connected to subjectivity and the heart.

As I have not yet abandoned hope for the promise of the future, I remain eager to hear the voices from the hearts (*xinsheng* 心聲) of all thinking men and earnestly entreat them to share with me their illuminating thoughts (內曜).

For such illuminating thoughts can provide the wherewithal to smash through darkness, while voices from the heart may well prove our deliverance from falsehood and chicanery.

Such voices function in society like the roar of spring thunder stirring the plants into bud, like the first light of dawn heralding the passing of the night.[28]

The beginning of this passage invokes a sense of futurity with the concepts of hope and a promise, both of which are connected to voices from the heart. These voices are linked to the emotive side of the human being and can break through the idle chatter of superficial language that does not come from the heart. Moreover, just as Heidegger contrasts idle chatter with a kind of speech that stems from existence, Lu Xun opposes *jimo* to a voice intimately connected to something that emerges within. This voice is connected to illuminating thoughts that come from within and then can be shared. So hope for something beyond is connected to language, interior light, and communication, which constantly haunts superficial language. This type of communicative practice provides hope to transcend the falsehood and chicanery of society or groups (*renqun* 人群). Voices from the heart and idle chatter are connected to two types of society, the former based on the sincere communication of an inner light and the latter based on trickery. But the hope associated with the first is also connected to another type of transcendence, namely that of nature. It is almost as if nature helps the inner voice. It is thus in a type of limbo between independence and dependence on something nonspecifiable. Lu Xun describes this nonspecifiable something with metaphors of thunder and dawn, which again foreshadow a new future. The sage serves as a catalyst for these insurmountable forces.

The sage embodies nature and consequently can communicate from a transcendent perspective. Lu Xun believes that the speech of a sage derives its resoluteness from a link to this nonspecifiable something, which he again compares to the power of nature:

> His [the sage's] speech is full and cannot be stopped, because of the sheer forcefulness which illuminates his heart and because these words stir in his mind like the great waves of a mighty ocean.[29]

Notice that here it is almost as if words displace the subjectivity of the individual; in particular, the individual responds to something that stirs like great waves, and this represents a movement that begins with interiority. If this movement stopped at interiority, Lu Xun would be open to the charge of relativism that Irving Babbitt and others levy against Romanticism. However, Lu Xun posits a relationship between interiority and something else that moves one to act and speak. This something is precisely that which haunts and will be expressed in voice and life. It is precisely the relationship between voice and something that stirs it that both breaks down the simple barrier between inner and outer and, at the same time, gives voice its integrity. This resolute integrity gives voice the power to break free from the idle chatter of the group and posit a different type of community in the future.

The voice and the heart represent a type of life force that brings together opposites such as the objective world of nature and subjective emotions. Gao Yuanbao 郜元寶 underscores the importance of the concept of life in Lu Xun's writings.[30] Gao emphasizes the link between Lu Xun's uses of the "heart" and some notion of life. On this point, perhaps the Marxist who is most helpful is Michel Henry, who explicitly theorizes life as something that is excluded by and haunts the reifications of capital and the general homogenizing effects of modern life.

The sage represents precisely an attempt to regain this particular life, which is being abolished by the two faces of modernity: market and organization. This is possible because, as in Bidet's discussion of *Verkehrung*, homogenization or subsumption is never complete. As Henry writes in *I am the Truth*:

> Behind all these so-called "economic" and "social" activities, what is acting ... is the transcendental ego, whose every power is given to itself in the givenness to itself of this ego, such that this fundamental I Can alone is capable of walking, lifting, striking—of accomplishing each of the acts implicated in each form of labor.[31]

Henry describes a relation of that which is concealed or behind, the transcendental self and its actions. The sage represents something like this transcendence, but Lu Xun does not quite describe a transcendental ego, if transcendence is understood in a Christian context. Rather, as we saw above, the sage's subjectivity is grounded in nature. Lu Xun's early essays confront superficial exteriority and its political forms with precisely this type of interior feeling of life, the givenness of a fundamental connection to nature. Lu Xun's recourse to life is linked to a type of existential transformation toward oneself that resists the various structures imposed upon it.

Through this existential transformation, and by overcoming the alienations of modernity, the heart-life also allows the possibility of connecting the individual with the social. The heart-life plays the role of an ontological-natural source that is at once individual and social. Lu Xun discusses the way in which voices from the heart move people:

> Consequently, once his voice arises, it will revive the whole world, and that strength could well prove greater than any other natural force, stirring the human world and startling it into an awakening. This awakening will mark the beginning of our rise out of the present situation. Only when one speaks from the heart does the self return to itself (朕歸於我), and then one can begin to have an individual identity; only when each person possesses an individual identity will the community (*qun* 群) approach a total awakening.[32]

In Lu Xun's view, the voice of this person, the sage, is a type of historical force. Note that earlier in this text, Lu Xun uses terms such as all "under heaven" (*tianxia* 天下)[33] and the "human world" (*renjianshi* 人間世),[34] which suggests that in addition to awakening the nation, he refers to a world-historical beginning of larger spatial scope. The awaking is also a temporal category, which Lu Xun indicates with the concept of quanyu (權輿), literally "beginning" or the sprouting of something new. Rather than specific geographical boundaries, Lu Xun seeks to highlight the principles of the beginning of a new community. Moreover, this community can emerge only when the self returns to itself and speaks from the heart rather than being lost in idle chatter. Notice that only when each individual returns to itself will the community approach total awakening. Here we see the relationship between the voice of the heart and a type of community associated with the metastructure, namely the ideal of a community of free and equal individuals.

CONCLUSION: GHOSTLY FUTURES AND RELIGIOUS PRESENTS

We have seen that Lu Xun does not grasp the possibility of a new future as stemming directly from the path that history was taking at his time. Concepts such as *heart* and *voice* go against modernity and mechanization. Lu Xun's *heart* and *voice* have a strange liminal status—as voices continue to haunt the present seeking redemption. One could argue that in Lu Xun's later writings and especially in his literature, this haunting becomes more explicit, with his various references to ghosts, the heart, and the life of the dead. On this point, Lu Xun seems close to Walter Benjamin, who invokes an anti-modern messianic power that moves toward socialism. Lu Xun's voices from the heart provide a transcendental perspective, but combined with normativity, which gives such voices direction. These voices are not blind.

Perhaps because Lu Xun's concepts of voice and heart are both human and transcendent, we see him constantly interrogate religion and ghosts. Lu Xun's affirmations of both religion and ghosts are connected to an existential acknowledgment of popular culture and everyday life, emphasizing the plight of those who are excluded from society. Like Zhang Taiyan, Lu Xun was influenced by Anesaki Masaharu's *Introduction to Religion (Shūkyōgaku gairon)*, but, unlike Zhang, Lu Xun relies on a more general concept of religion as seeking a type of transcendence. Religion represents the desire to go beyond the material world, a desire which is bound with the quest for a different type of future. By focusing on subjective desire, he understands superstition and religion in opposition to objective movements, such as those driven by the universal principle, progress, and civilization. During the later 1910s, Lu Xun followed twentieth-century Chinese intellectuals in championing the goals of enlightenment and science, which ran counter to superstition, but he constantly returned to issues related to superstition, such as ghosts.

A full discussion of the role of ghosts and religion in Lu Xun goes beyond the scope of this conclusion, but the importance of the trope of ghosts grows as Lu Xun becomes increasingly aware of the difficult relation between resistance and history. At this point, the position of the sage is replaced by the figure of the ghost, which embodies both life and death—it is in-between. There are a number of historical reasons for Lu Xun's shift in perspective, including the failure of a series of movements such as the 100 Days Reform, the Boxer Rebellion, and even the 1911 Revolution. In his works during these periods, there is also a strange sense of total domination by the both world-system and various power structures in the domestic sphere.

In this context, Lu Xun observes in "On a Refutation" that "Our gentry, at a time when the country is on the decline, have become spiritually blocked and interested only in petty gain. Though they are alive physically, they are dead spiritually."[35] Recall that this spiritual death is one of the reasons that Lu Xun allegedly switched from medicine to literature. Note that here again the problem is focusing on one's own petty gain and this becomes tantamount to being dead. Given that the living are dead and incapable of transcending petty desires, it might follow that the hope lies in the dead, who might actually be more living. After all, in the opening passage of this essay, he speaks of "our great nation," which of course includes people of the past, who are no longer physically here. In this essay, Lu Xun does not explicitly invoke the figure of the ghost, though he does make a comment that goes against later Enlightenment intellectuals' views on superstition: "Thus the most urgent task before us today is to rid ourselves of this hypocritical gentry; 'superstition' itself may remain!"[36]

Superstition and religion both refer to the modes of transcendence, but perhaps the most common aspect of superstition informing transcendence is seen in the concept of ghosts, which is also pervasive in popular culture. According to a purely scientific view, there are no ghosts and all that we need be concerned with is our present. The belief in ghosts implies a debt that we owe to those who have suffered in the past and seek redemption long after they are dead. This is the fundamental temporal dimension of ghosts. We see this clearly in Lu Xun's famous 1918 short story, "Diary of a Madman" (狂人日記), in which children appear connected in some way to the oppression of the past—the thousands of years of cannibalism and the various people who were eaten in the past. In this context, we can understand Lu Xun's recurrent fascination with the figure of the ghost, understood as a revenant that claims justice and constantly trumps intellectuals who are complacent with conventional paradigms. A well-known example of such a reference to ghosts in Lu Xun's work can be found near the beginning of his 1924 short story, "A New Year's Sacrifice" (祝福), in which a servant woman known as Xiang Lin's wife asks the narrator, "After a person dies, does he turn into a ghost?"[37] The narrator finds himself at a loss when faced with these questions, because they point to aspects of life and hope beyond abstract or codified knowledge. Moreover, such sensibilities are linked to practices of the common people, such as Xianglin's wife, who represent various oppressions in society that go unnoticed or unnamed. These unnamed and unrecorded injustices serve to haunt the present world and potentially push it beyond a world of structural domination, which often uses the metastructures of freedom and equality to legitimate domination. It is precisely that haunting that brings such ideals back to contemporary society, and consequently ghosts—including Lu Xun's own ghost—suggest a way to redeem past lives in an alternate future.

NOTES

1. Perhaps the most famous among Japanese scholars of Lu Xun is Takeuchi Yoshimi, whose 1944 book established a new paradigm for Lu Xun studies in Japan: Takeuchi Yoshimi, *Rojin* 魯迅 [Lu Xun] (Tokyo: Noma Sawako, 2003). I have analyzed Takeuchi's essay in "The 1911 Revolution and the Politics of Failure: Takeuchi Yoshimi and Global Capitalist Modernity," *Frontiers of Literary Studies in China* 6.1 (2012): 19–38.
2. See Wang Hui 汪暉, *Fankang juewang: Lu Xun jiqi wenxue shijie* 反抗絕望：魯迅及其文學世界 [Resisting despair: Lu Xun and his literary world], rev. ed. (Beijing: Sanlian shudian, 2008). Leo Ou-fan Lee, *Voices from the Iron House: A Study of Lu Xun* (Bloomington: Indiana University Press, 1987).
3. For more on the historical background of Lu Xun's work during this time, see Wang Hui's essay on the text "Voices of Good and Evil: What is Enlightenment? Towards a Rereading of Lu Xun's 'Towards a Refutation of Malevolent Voices,'" trans. Ted Huters and Yangyang Zong, *boundary 2* 38.2 (2011): 67–123.
4. Peter Gordon, "Contextualism and Criticism in the History of Ideas," in *Rethinking Modern European Intellectual History*, ed. Darrin M. McMohan and Samuel Moyn (Oxford: Oxford University Press, 2014), 43.
5. Theodore W. Adorno and Max Horkheimer, *Dialectic of Enlightenment*, trans. Edmund Jephcott (Stanford: Stanford University Press, 2002), 20. Gordon, "Contextualism and Criticism," 48.

6. Viren Murthy, *The Political Philosophy of Zhang Taiyan: The Resistance of Consciousness* (Leiden: Brill, 2011), chap. 5.

7. The now classic and controversial essay that tackles this issue from a theoretical perspective is Fredric Jameson's "Third-World Literature in the Era of Multinational Capital," *Social Text* 15 (Autumn 1986): 65–88.

8. See Suzuku Sadami 鈴木貞美, *Seimei de yomu nihon no kindai: Taishō seimei shugi no danjō to tenkai* 生命で読む日本の近代：大正生命主義の誕生と展開 [Reading Japanese modernity as life: The birth and development of Taisho vitalism] (Tokyo: NHK, 1995). On Lu Xun and Saito Nonohito and Anesaki Masaharu, see Nakajima Osafumi 中島長文, *Fukurō no koe: Rojin no kindai* 梟の声：魯迅の近代 [The cry of an owl: Lu Xun's modernity] (Tokyo, Heibonsha, 2006). Indeed, this is also the period when Japanese intellectuals refashioned Buddhism in light of German idealism in ways that overlapped with the way in which Zhang Taiyan, one of Lu Xun's teachers, was rethinking Buddhism.

9. Lu Xun, "Po esheng lun" 破惡聲論 [On the refutation of malevolent voices], in Lu Xun, *Lu Xun quanji* 魯迅年全集 [The complete works of Lu Xun], vol. 8, (Beijing: Renmin wenxue, 2005), 26. I would like to thank Jon Kowalis for sharing his translation of this and other early essays with me. I basically follow Kowalis's translations while making minor changes.

10. Karl Marx, *Capital*, vol. 1 (London: Penguin, 1990), 548–549. Translation amended.

11. Lu Xun 魯迅, "Wenhua pianzhi lun" 文化偏至論 [Concerning imbalanced cultural development], in *Lu Xun quanji*, vol. 1, 48.

12. Lu Xun, "Concerning Imbalanced Cultural Development," 49.

13. See Wang Hui, "Depoliticized Politics from East to West," in *The End of Revolution: China and the Limits of Modernity* (London: Verso, 2009), 3–19.

14. Benjamin Elman, "National Warfare and the Refraction of China's Self-strengthening Reforms into Failure," *Modern Asian Studies* 38.2 (2004): 283–326.

15. Marx, *Capital*, vol. 1, 477.

16. Georg Lukács, *History and Class-Consciousness: Studies in Marxist Dialectics*, trans. Rodney Livingsten (Cambridge: MIT Press, 1971). Moishe Postone, *Time, Labor and Social Domination: A Reinterpretation of Marx's Critical Theory* (Cambridge: Cambridge University Press, 1993).

17. Jacques Bidet, "Le néoliberalisme comme régime et comme subjectivité: Marx et Foucault recyclés l'un par l'autre" [Neoliberalism as regime and as subjectivity: Marx and Foucault recycled by one another] (unpublished manuscript, 2014), 28.

18. Karatani Kojin, *The Structure of World-History* (Durham: Duke University Press, 2014), xv.

19. Marx, *Capital*, vol. 1, 178.

20. Marx, *Capital*, vol. 1, 180.

21. Jacques Bidet, *État-Monde* (Paris: PUF, 2011), chap. 2 passim.

22. Bidet, *État-Monde*, 146.

23. Frederic Jameson, "Third-World Literature in the Era of Multinational Capital."

24. Wang Hui has pointed out that this idea of voices is also connected to late Qing issues related to language reform. In short, both the reformers and the anarchists proposed to unify language. In his famous speech to the exchange students in Tokyo written in 1906, immediately after his release from jail, Zhang proposed to develop the national essence through reviving "language and writings," "traditional political systems," and "events

about historical characters." Against both reformers such as Kang Youwei and anarchists such as Wu Zhihui 吳稚暉, Zhang stresses national particularity related to the Chinese language. See Wang Hui, "Voices of Good and Evil: What is Enlightenment?" 77.

25. Lu Xun, "A Refutation", 25.

26. Wang Hui, "Voices of Good and Evil: What is Enlightenment?" 87.

27. Martin Heidegger, *Being and Time*, trans. John Macquerrie and Edward Robinson (New York: Harper and Row, 1962), 212–213; *Sein und Zeit* (Tübingen: Max Niemeyer, 1984), 168–169.

28. Lu Xun, "A Refutation," 25.

29. Lu Xun, "A Refutation," 25–26.

30. Gao Yuanbao, *Lu Xun liu jiang* 魯迅六講 [Six lectures on Lu Xun] (Beijing: Beijing chubanshe, 2007). See chap. 1.

31. Michel Henry, *I am the Truth: Towards a Philosophy of Christianity*, trans. Susan Emanuel (Stanford: Stanford University Press, 2003), 244. Cited in Clayton Crockett, "Truth of Life: Michel Henry on Marx," in *Words of Life: New Theological Turns in French Phenomenology*, ed. Bruce Ellis Benson and Norman Wirzba (New York: Fordham University Press, 2010), 173.

32. Lu Xun, "A Refutation," 26.

33. Lu Xun, "A Refutation," 25.

34. Lu Xun, "A Refutation," 26.

35. Lu Xun, "A Refutation," 30.

36. Lu Xun, "A Refutation," 30.

37. Lu Xun, "A New Years Sacrifice," in *Lu Xun Selected Stories*, trans. Yang Hsien-yi and Gladys Yang (London: W. W. Norton, 1977), 125–143, quotation at 127.

WORKS CITED

Bidet, Jacques. "Le néoliberalisme comme régime et comme subjectivité: Marx et Foucault recyclés l'un par l'autre" [Neoliberalism as regime and as subjectivity: Marx and Foucault recycled by one another]. Unpublished manuscript, 2014.

Bidet, Jacques. *État-Monde: Libéralisme, socialisme et communisme à l'échelle mondiale*. Paris: PUF, 2011.

Elman, Benjamin. "National Warfare and the Refraction of China's Self-strengthening Reforms into Failure." *Modern Asian Studies* 38.2 (2004): 283–326.

Gao Yuanbao 郜元寶. *Lu Xun liu jiang* 魯迅六講 [Six lectures on Lu Xun]. Beijing: Beijing chubanshe, 2007.

Heidegger, Martin. *Being and Time*. Trans. John Macquerrie and Edward Robinson. New York: Harper and Row, 1962.

Heidegger, Martin. *Sein und Zeit*. Tübingen: Max Niemeyer, 1984.

Henry, Michel. *I am the Truth: Towards a Philosophy of Christianity*. Trans. Susan Emanuel. Stanford: Stanford University Press, 2003. 244.

Jameson, Fredric. "Third-World Literature in the Era of Multinational Capital." *Social Text* 15 (Autumn 1986): 65–88.

Lee, Leo Ou-fan. *Voices from the Iron House: A Study of Lu Xun*. Bloomington: Indiana University Press, 1987.

Lu Xun 鲁迅. "Po esheng lun" 破惡聲論 [On the refutation of malevolent voices]. In *Lu Xun quanji* 鲁迅年全集 [The complete works of Lu Xun], vol. 8. Beijing: Renmin wenxue, 2005. 25–40.

Lu Xun 鲁迅. "Wenhua pianzhi lun" 文化偏至論" [Concerning imbalanced cultural development]. In *Lu Xun quanji*, vol. 1. 45–65.

Lu Xun. "A New Years Sacrifice." In *Lu Xun Selected Stories*. Trans. Yang Hsien-yi and Gladys Yang. London: W. W. Norton, 1977. 125–143

Lukács, Georg. *History and Class-Consciousness: Studies in Marxist Dialectics*. Trans. Rodney Livingsten. Cambridge: MIT Press, 1971.

Karatani Kojin. *The Structure of World-History*. Durham: Duke University Press, 2014.

Marx, Karl. *Capital*, vol. 1. London: Penguin, 1990.

Murthy, Viren. *The Political Philosophy of Zhang Taiyan: The Resistance of Consciousness*. Leiden: Brill, 2011.

Murthy, Viren. "The 1911 Revolution and the Politics of Failure: Takeuchi Yoshimi and Global Capitalist Modernity." *Frontiers of Literary Studies in China* 6.1 (2012): 19–38.

Nakajima Osafumi 中島長文. *Fukurō no koe: Rojin no kindai* 梟の声：魯迅の近代 [The cry of an owl: Lu Xun's modernity]. Tokyo, Heibonsha, 2006.

Postone, Moishe. *Time, Labor and Social Domination: A Reinterpretation of Marx's Critical Theory*. Cambridge: Cambridge University Press, 1993.

Suzuku Sadami 鈴木貞美. *Seimei de yomu nihon no kindai: Taishō seimei shugi no danjō to tenkai* 生命で読む日本の近代：大正生命主義の誕生と展開 [Reading Japanese modernity as life: The birth and development of Taisho vitalism]. Tokyo: NHK, 1995.

Wang Hui 汪暉. *Fankang juewang: Lu Xun de wenxue shijie* 反抗絕望：魯迅的文學世界 [Resisting despair: Lu Xun and his literary world]. Rev. ed. Beijing: Sanlian shudian, 2008.

Wang Hui. "Depoliticized Politics from East to West." In *The End of Revolution: China and the Limits of Modernity*, by Wang Hui. London: Verso, 2009. 3–19.

Wang Hui. "Voices of Good and Evil: What is Enlightenment? Towards a Rereading of Lu Xun's 'Towards a Refutation of Malevolent Voices.'" Trans. Ted Huters and Yangyang Zong. *boundary 2* 38.2 (2011): 67–123.

CHAPTER 3.6

INTUITION, REPETITION, AND REVOLUTION

Six Moments in the Life of Ah Q

WANG HUI

> But in the end, as though my thoughts were possessed by a ghost, I always came back to the idea of writing the story of Ah Q.
>
> (Lu Xun, *The True Story of Ah Q*)

THE True Story of Ah Q (阿 Q 正傳), one of Lu Xun's 魯迅 most influential works, opens with a preface in which the narrator describes how he came to write a biography of the work's eponymous—yet at the same time nameless—protagonist. The preface begins:

> For several years now I have been meaning to write the true story of Ah Q. But at the same time I felt some trepidation, which goes to show that I am not one of those who achieve glory by writing. An immortal pen has always been required to record the deeds of an immortal man, who becomes known to posterity through his writing even as his writing becomes known to posterity through the man—until finally it is not clear who is making what and what is making whom. But in the end, as though my thoughts were possessed by a ghost, I always return to the idea of writing the story of Ah Q.[1]

Curiously, there has been virtually no commentary from Chinese scholars on the phrase "as though my thoughts were possessed by a ghost" (仿佛思想裡有鬼似的). For Chinese readers, the phrase simply means that the narrator (or the author) was not fully in control of himself when he wrote this novella about Ah Q. When the work was translated into Japanese, however, translators discovered that the phrase presented some difficulties. Lu Xun scholar Takeuchi Yoshimi 竹内好 was the first to point this out, and a debate ensued between Japanese scholars over how the phrase should be rendered: whether to follow the Chinese reading and treat it as an abstract expression, or to translate the phrase more literally, as suggesting that a ghost had in fact entered the narrator's thoughts.

The preface goes on to explain that the narrator doesn't even know the name of the person whose biography he is preparing to write, and instead just knows that his given name is pronounced "Gui" (or "Quei," as it is rendered in the story). The narrator suggests several Chinese characters that match this pronunciation, but doesn't mention that another such homonym is the Chinese word for *ghost, gui* (鬼). Read along these lines, accordingly, the opening paragraph might suggest that the novella is a product of the narrator's thoughts' having been haunted by the ghost that is Ah Q himself.

Ah Q is famous for his "spiritual victory method" (精神勝利法)—his ability to transform apparent defeat and humiliation into a symbolic victory by renarrativizing the event in question in a way that is more favorable to him. A form of Nietzschean *ressentiment*, this strategy seeks to transform objective weakness into a form of symbolic strength, but in a way that often appears patently absurd to everyone but Ah Q himself. To the extent that Ah Q's trademark gesture represents an attempt to transform failure into a symbolic victory, however, I am interested in moments in the text where Ah Q's symbolic victories are themselves short-circuited by failure.

DOES AH Q REALLY WANT TO BE A REVOLUTIONARY?

The True Story of Ah Q—which was serialized in the literary supplement of the Beijing newspaper *Morning Post* (晨報副刊) between December 4, 1921 and February 12, 1922—opens at an indeterminate point in the late imperial period, but by the end of the work it has become clear that the story overlaps with the 1911 Revolution that helped bring down the Qing dynasty. In fact, Ah Q himself ends up trying to join forces with the revolutionaries who enter the region. Given that Ah Q has traditionally been viewed as a symbol of the sickness of traditional China's national character, his eventual relationship with the progressive cause of the 1911 Revolution has presented a challenge for many critics.

In 1926, for instance, Zheng Zhenduo 鄭振鐸 published an influential critique of *The True Story of Ah Q*, in which he addressed the issue of Ah Q's becoming a revolutionary:

> When I first read [the novella] in the *Morning News*, I did not agree with it, nor do I agree with it now. The author seems to have concluded this story too hastily. Not wanting to continue writing, he simply gave Ah Q a "Grand Finale." Surely, even the author himself, when he started the story, could not have guessed that a man like Ah

Q would eventually want to be a revolutionary and would come to such an end. Ah Q, it seems, must have had a dual personality.[2]

Lu Xun acknowledged Zheng Zhenduo's criticism, but responded with a detailed discussion of the origins of the work, in which he addresses the question of its treatment of revolution:

> To my mind, as long as there was no revolution in China, Ah Q would not have become a revolutionary; but once there was one, he did. This was the only fate possible for my Ah Q and I would not say he has a dual personality. The first year of the Republic has gone, never to return; but the next time there are reforms, I believe there will still be revolutionaries like Ah Q. I only wish that, as people say, I had written about a period in the past, but I fear what I saw was not the past but the future—even as much as twenty to thirty years from now. Actually this reflects no discredit to the revolutionaries. Ah Q, after all, did roll up his queue with a chopstick.[3]

Lu Xun believes that depicting Ah Q as a revolutionary does not "discredit" the revolutionary movement, and that Ah Q's revolution is neither a premodern revolution nor a precursor of modernity, but rather it represents the destiny of the Chinese people. Therefore, the key to understanding *The True Story of Ah Q* is to try to understand why the souls of these silent people contain the potential for revolution.

But how should we understand this potential? First, if Ah Q is simply an expression of China's national character, this would suggest that the revolution is not internal—because it is impossible to discover the inevitability of revolution through Ah Q's method of seeking spiritual victory. If the people's souls do not contain this sort of potential, then Ah Q does indeed have two distinct personalities, and scholars have been unable to find any proof of this "internal element" within the text itself. In 1930 Wang Qiaonan 王橋南 (1896 –?) adapted *The True Story of Ah Q* into a film script titled *Women and Bread* (女人與麵包) and asked Lu Xun for his opinion. Lu Xun responded that he felt the novella "lacks key elements for being adapted for theater or film, because as soon as it is acted out, it can only create comic effects. When I wrote Ah Q, my objective was indeed neither to amuse nor to pity. Also I doubt that the 'stars' of the time would be able to portray the scenes in question."[4] Lu Xun suggested that Wang Qiaonan's interpretation was a misreading of the text, and Lu Xun's dissatisfaction derives from the fact that this type of interpretation continues to view Ah Q's personality as one-dimensional.

Second, on the surface Ah Q's revolution appears to be just a repetition of old patterns and customs, but if that were all, what would it mean? This requires an explanation of Lu Xun's understanding of the relationship between repetition and revolution. In his response to Zheng Zhenduo, Lu Xun emphasizes that Ah Q's revolution occurred in China and yielded the "first year of the Republic." That Ah Q's revolution differs from all previous movements is due not to Ah Q's motivation but rather to the revolutionary event itself. The revolution occurred as a form of repetition, yet also contains an element of uniqueness. Otherwise, why would Lu Xun say that the first year of the Republic "has gone, never to return"? The first year of the Republic was a unique historical moment, but by raising both the issue of reform and the repetitive nature of revolution, Lu Xun is pointing to the similarly repetitive nature of Ah Q's revolution itself. Every repetition has a unique element that is distinct from that which precedes it, and this element is produced by a process of repetition and difference. Therefore, if we want to understand Ah Q's revolution, we must first examine the relationship between his actions and the status of the revolution as an "event."

While most commentators have been primarily concerned with Ah Q's method of spiritual victory, I will focus instead on the method's occasional failures. To this end, I will examine six moments in Ah Q's life when Ah Q loses self-control. Although each of these moments is mentioned only in passing, they are nevertheless crucial for our understanding of the relationship between Ah Q and revolution. These moments might seem at first to be a few repetitive incidents, but they are actually substantially different from one another, which is to say that there is change within the repetition. These changes, moreover, cannot be understood simply by considering Ah Q's motivations or a particular timeline, and instead they must be interpreted as responses to specific aspects of his environment.

THE TRUE STORY AS GENEALOGY OF OFFICIAL HISTORY

It is somewhat ironic that Lu Xun chose to structure *The True Story of Ah Q* as a biography, given that Lu Xun actually loathed those who wrote biographies. For instance, when Li Jiye 李霽野 (1904–1997) wrote to him in 1936 suggesting that Lu Xun should either write an autobiography or else assist his wife Xu Guangping 許廣平 (1898–1968) in writing a biography for him, Lu Xun replied:

> I will not write an autobiography, nor am I that keen on having others write my biography. My life is far too ordinary, and if this were sufficient for a biography, then China would instantly have 400 million such biographies, filling the libraries to bursting point. I have quite a few small thoughts and ideas that disappear at a moment's notice. No doubt it seems regrettable, but in actual fact they are nothing more than trivial things.[5]

This passage emphasizes Lu Xun's view of the ephemerality of his own writing, and resembles the explanation of the "true story" in the preface to *The True Story of Ah Q*, in which the narrator emphasizes that he is not seeking to "achieve glory by writing," and later notes that he perceives his writing as being merely "ephemeral."

So why would Lu Xun want to write his novella in the form of a "true story"? In the preface, the narrator observes that "there are many types of biographies: official biographies, autobiographies, unauthorized biographies, legends, supplementary biographies, family histories, sketches," but he notes that none of these was particularly suited for Ah Q. Therefore, he observes, "I took the last two words from the expression 'enough of this digression, and back to the true story' (閑話休題言歸正傳) and used this as my title." Here, the term *true story* (*zhengzhuan* 正傳) connotes the precise opposite of *official history* (*zhengshi* 正史) and its corresponding genealogy.

A paradigmatic example of this sort of official history can be found in Sima Qian's 司馬遷 *Records of the Historian* (史記), which opens with a section labelled "Basic Annals" (本級) and which contains the "Biographies of the Five Emperors." Discussions of philosophers such as Laozi 老子, Mozi 墨子, Mencius 孟子, Xunzi 荀子, and Zhuangzi 莊子, meanwhile, all appear in the section labelled "Ranked Biographies" (列傳). In fact, of the early philosophers, only Confucius was granted the honor of being included in the section labelled "Hereditary Houses" (世家), which contains histories of Chinese kingdoms and dynastic lines. By the logic of this sort of genealogical structure, accordingly, Ah Q should not have been qualified to have a biography at all, nor should the pseudonymous author of *The True Story of Ah Q* have been qualified to write it (the novella was published under the pseudonym Ba Ren, which is derived from the phrase *xiali baren* [下里巴人], meaning "popular literature or art"). Lu Xun's use of the "true story" format to write a biography of Ah Q, like his decision to publish it under the penname Ba Ren, obviously does not conform to the traditional understanding of the biographical genre. Placing this true story in the context of other biographies—whether individual, imperial, or feudal—reveals a genealogy either outside or beneath a conventional genealogy of the Chinese people.

Not only does the concept of a true story reflect a genealogical perspective that has traditionally been excluded from official history, the character *zheng* (正; meaning "orthodox" or "true") in the phrase *zhengzhuan* ("true story") similarly challenges the notion of official history (*zhengshi*) itself. Just as Nietzsche found the roots of morality in evil and Feuerbach found the roots of God in man, Marx found the roots of humanity in social relations. In this respect, the study of genealogy is itself potentially revolutionary. The root of the genealogical system represented by feudal, imperial, and ranked biographies can be found in this paradoxically unorthodox genre of the "true story" or "orthodox biography" (*zhengzhuan*). Without this genre of the true story, in other words, we would be unable to understand the origins of official history. Having biographies implies having feudal and imperial biographies, but it also suggests that there is a much larger genealogical system that has been excluded from this official genealogical system. Without this genre of the true story that focuses on those *without* social distinction, the orthodox social order would not be possible; and yet as soon as these sorts of true stories emerge, the official history is presented with a potential crisis.

In this respect, there is a natural connection between revolution and this genre of the true story that focuses on that which has been excluded from official history. If an insignificant author (Ba Ren) can compose a biography of an even more insignificant figure (Ah Q), the result can only take the form of a "true story." Given that this true story was in fact written and published in the newspaper for all to read, it constituted a revolutionary act that subverted the genealogy of official history. In principle, the publication of this sort of true story pointed to the existence of an alternative genealogy outside the official one, as a result of which that which appears nonexistent is revealed to be merely suppressed.

A general rule of writing a biography is that the author should at least know the subject's surname—but Ah Q has no known surname. For a while he was called *Zhao*, until a character known as Old Man Zhao demanded: "How could you be named Zhao!—Do you think you are worthy of the name Zhao?" (513/68). No one is sure how to write Ah Q's given name either. Everyone called him "Ah Gui" (or "Ah Quei," in the romanization that Lu Xun used in his story) but the narrator notes that no one knew which Chinese character should be used to write it. Moreover, the narrator concludes that "after his death no one mentioned Ah Quei again; for he was obviously not one of those whose name is 'preserved on bamboo tablets and silk'" (514/68).

Not only does Ah Q have no name, he also has no identifiable past. The story discusses the question of Ah Q's hometown, noting that although he lived in Weizhuang, he also lived in other places and could not be counted as a Weizhuang native. In Weizhuang, he resides in the Tutelary God's Temple, but this is not his real home; he does odd jobs for others, but does not have a stable job. With no real name, no known past, no social status, no home, and no job, he lacks all the preconditions for a conventional biography. In the eyes of official histories, wouldn't someone like this essentially not exist? Does not transforming something nonexistent into something that exists effectively threaten the status of those historical figures who do have a name and past?

One of the more notable characteristics of Lu Xun's writing is his use of strategic interjections to link the present with the past, and the text's diegesis with the larger environment within which the text is positioned. The scholar Wang Yao 王瑤 compared this practice to playing the part of the "second clown" in Mulian Opera, which has a role in the plot but can also turn to and engage directly with the audience.[6] For instance, the narrator of the preface explains that the Q in Ah Q's name is a foreign letter, and that

> there is nothing to be done but to use the Western alphabet, writing the name according to the English spelling as Ah Quei and abbreviating it to Ah Q. This is equivalent to blindly following the magazine *New Youth*, and I am thoroughly ashamed of myself; but given that even such a learned man as Mr. Zhao's son could not solve my problem, what else can I do? (514/69)

In this way, the narrator ironically interjects into the story the *New Youth* (新青年) vernacular language movement debate over names and how they are established. But why did the vernacular language movement precipitate such a debate in the first place? Precisely because of the intimate relationship between language and names, the vernacular language movement touches on the question of how names match up with their referents, together with the closely related question of social order. Ah Q, meanwhile, has no name, no past, and he can only be referred to by the letter Q—but if a foreign letter can become a part of the Chinese language, does this not suggest that the soul of the Chinese people also contains an alien element?

Lu Xun's attitude toward the progressive goals promoted by *New Youth* was not entirely favorable, in that he frequently saw the old within the new, conservatism within radicalism, and regression within reform. Examples of this can be found in the emphasis on positivist historical research as deployed in both the Rearranging the National Heritage movement and the New Culture Movement. Lu Xun directs his criticism at the trend that uses scientific methodology to "rearrange the national heritage" and recount history. In the preface to *True Story of Ah Q*, the narrator remarks:

> My only consolation is the fact that the character *Ah* (阿) is absolutely correct. This is definitely not a result of false analogy, and will certainly stand the test of scholarly criticism. As for the other problems, it is not for an unlearned person such as myself to solve them, and I can only hope that disciples of Dr. Hu Shi, who has such "a passion for history and antiquities," may be able to throw new light on them. I am afraid, however, that by then my *True Story of Ah Q* will have long since slid into oblivion. (515/70)

Having no name and no status, Q was born from "nothingness," and if we apply Hu Shi's 胡適 positivism to Ah Q, we find that there is no way to prove his existence. Therefore, in a sense he is someone who does not even exist. But here, the alien culture represented by the foreign letter has again been subverted. This paragraph alludes to Lu Xun's opposition to Hu Shi, to the Debates on Ancient History, and to modern positivist historiography. Early-twentieth-century positivist historiography rejected as mere legends traditional accounts of the earliest periods of Chinese history, and consequently the movement had a distinct antitraditional flavor. However, like the logic of official history, this positivist historiography also excluded all the characters, achievements, and stories that had been passed down orally, on the grounds that they could not be proven and were therefore outside of the category of formal history.

Modern historiography in China emerged at a time when "true stories" were once again being rejected, as the modern historical order was established through a process of systematic exclusion. From the point of view of official or positivist history, had it not been for the fact that the author was "possessed by a ghost," then *The True Story of Ah Q* would never have been written. It is not only because he has no name that Ah Q cannot enter official history, but also because this history was only established through a process of matching names with realities. In this respect, *The True Story of Ah Q* represents not just a subversion of the structural foundation of official history, but also a rejection of modern positivist history and the genealogy of its knowledge production.

The First and Second Moments of the Failure of Ah Q's Spiritual Victory—"The Bitterness of Defeat" and "Standing at a Loss"

Conventional interpretations hold Ah Q to be an allegorical character who embodies certain qualities that Lu Xun associates with the Chinese people. In other words, although Ah Q is not a real person, he is nevertheless real to the extent that we consider him a character type. The text contains many vivid descriptions of Ah Q's cowardice and method of seeking spiritual victory, which are presented as representations of the Chinese people's so-called evil nature (劣根性). Is it possible, however, to find a few moments where Ah Q might have some sense of self-awareness?

Lu Xun wanted to depict the soul of the Chinese people, but he also wanted to express Ah Q's potential for revolution. If the text contained no depictions of Ah Q's individual existence, then it would be impossible to ascertain his revolutionary potential. These sorts of moments may also be seen as symptoms of the collective transformation of the Chinese people, but they must first appear as the individual, affective response of an actual person. Ah Q is someone who never thinks, and instead lives in a fantasy world and is constantly spinning stories about himself, others, and society as a whole. He has many moments of apparent self-consciousness, but no actual self. As a result, these moments cannot be found at the level of his consciousness, but rather they are located at the level of his unconscious and his basic instincts. It is only in these instances where he momentarily loses control that can we can catch a glimpse of Ah Q's implications for the possibility of revolution.

The May Fourth reformers hoped to use new culture to raise people's self-awareness, since in their view the nature of the Chinese people was grounded in their lack of self-consciousness. The Confucian classics established rules for how people should act, and consequently when people feel pain they simply create a narrative to rationalize it. In *True Story of Ah Q*, however, Lu Xun incorporated some fleeting elements involving instincts and desires that had previously been concealed within this Confucian order. I contend that Ah Q contains several moments of self-awakening. By this, I do not necessarily mean revolutionary awakening, but rather the protagonist's instinctive awareness of his unfavorable situation. At which moments do we find the strongest congruence between Ah Q's self-expression and his objective circumstances?

A good example of the paradoxes inherent in Ah Q's spiritual victory method can be found in a sequence described at the beginning of the second chapter:

> The people of Weizhuang only made use of his services or treated him as a laughing-stock, without ever paying the slightest attention to his background. Ah Q himself remained silent on this subject, except that when quarrelling with someone Ah Q

might glance at him and say, "We used to be much better off than you! Who do you think you are, anyway?" (515/71)

When Ah Q attempts to imagine himself as a perfect man, however, the narrator notes the shiny ringworm scars on his scalp, which is a topic that Ah Q treats as taboo. So, just as Chinese emperors often prohibited the use of characters found in their given names, Ah Q similarly tries to render taboo words related to his condition. When others use these words anyway, Ah Q responds dismissively, saying, "You don't even deserve . . ."

Such a refusal to admit defeat recurs at the end of chapter 2, in a description of how Ah Q for once happens to win at gambling. He then proceeds to pick a fight, in which he is beaten up and has his silver pieces confiscated by his opponent. Under normal circumstances, Ah Q would simply have tried to explain the event away, but in this case he feels a flash of unhappiness:

> So white and glittering a pile of silver! It had all been his . . . but now it had disappeared. He was not comforted by the thought that this was tantamount to being robbed by his own son, nor was he comforted by thinking of himself as a lowly insect. This time he really tasted the bitterness of defeat. (519/74–75)

China has rarely celebrated the figure of the defeated hero, and in this passage Lu Xun tacitly criticizes the Chinese for not understanding defeat. At this point, Ah Q suddenly feels a vague sense of defeat, which the narrative describes as simply a flash of unhappiness. This moment is merely fleeting, however, as Ah Q quickly finds a way of transforming this setback into a symbolic victory. Nevertheless, Lu Xun notes that when he was writing this particular chapter he found himself becoming increasingly serious, and I propose that his shift in attitude was closely grounded in Ah Q's feeling of defeat.

In chapter 3, there is another scene in which Ah Q can no longer claim a spiritual victory after defeat. When a character named Whiskers Wang physically beats Ah Q, Ah Q tries to claim this as a sort of symbolic victory but fails:

> As best Ah Q could remember, this was the first humiliation of his life. He had always scoffed at Whiskers Wang on account of his ugly bewhiskered cheeks, but he had never been scoffed at, much less beaten, by him. But now, against all expectations, Whiskers Wang had in fact beaten him. Perhaps what they said in the market place was really true: "The emperor has abolished the official examinations, so that scholars who have passed them are no longer in demand." As a result, the Zhao family must have lost prestige. Was this why everyone was treating him contemptuously?
> Ah Q just stood there at a loss. (521/77–78)

Ah Q attempts to claim a symbolic victory by placing himself within the same hierarchical order that Whisker Wang is in the process of challenging, but even as he concocts stories such as that "the emperor has abolished the official examinations" and "the Zhao family must have lost prestige," there is still that moment when he simply "stood there at a loss" (無可適從的站著). The narrative does not specify what precisely Ah

Q is thinking, but rather it focuses on this moment when he loses the ability to spin a new yarn to rationalize his defeat. Like the moment discussed above, when Ah Q first "tasted the bitterness of defeat," we find here another instance in which he tacitly acknowledges defeat, and where his perplexity represents a transition point in which he seems to recognize his fate.

This recognition, however, is merely fleeting. Afterwards, Ah Q is beaten by a local with foreign pretensions, known as the Bogus Foreign Devil (假洋鬼子), and although this technically qualifies as Ah Q's second humiliating incident, he is nevertheless able to shrug it off as though it never happened. Therefore, throughout this chapter there is only this one sentence—"Ah Q stood there at a loss"—that breaks through Ah Q's account of himself and establishes a relationship between him and his environment. While the rest of the chapter emphasizes how Ah Q's self-account remains completely cut off from reality, this one sentence allows us to realize that Ah Q is not a simple character type, but rather a human being who is still developing.

THE THIRD AND FOURTH MOMENTS—SEX AND HUNGER, AND THE BREAKTHROUGH OF AH Q'S SURVIVAL INSTINCT

While chapter 3 concludes with Ah Q taking pleasure in bullying a young nun in a local tavern, the following chapter makes a clean break with this narrative and instead follows Ah Q's instinct. His "victory" of having bullied the nun has unanticipated consequences, in that he subsequently begins thinking obsessively about women. The joy he feels after bullying the nun challenges his former belief in the strict segregation of the sexes, to the point that upon seeing the Zhao family's maid he begs her to sleep with him, then throws himself at her feet. Even after the maid flees the scene, Ah Q continues kneeling there, "only dimly aware that something was wrong."

In the latter half of this section, the narrator describes Ah Q's virtual amnesia but declines to defend him. It is also in this chapter that the word *rebel* (造反) appears for the first time, when the bailiff lectures Ah Q: "You can't even keep your hands off the Zhao family servants, you rebel! You've made me lose sleep, damn you!" (528/ 84–85). Ah Q is being called a rebel for trying to fondle one of his master's maids, as his sexual desire challenges the existing hierarchical order. Ah Q's act of rebellion, however, is completely unconscious—he suddenly finds himself kneeling before the maid, unaware of the words coming out of his own mouth.

At the end of the chapter, we find another moment where Ah Q's spiritual victory suffers an unexpected defeat. Suddenly, Ah Q finds himself with neither the desire nor the ability to concoct his own stories, and the narrative reverts to a flat style that represents the end of rhetoric, and suggests that reality begins to expose itself. In this scene, Ah Q apologizes to the Zhao family and returns to the Tutelary

God's Temple where he lives. Then, we are told, "he began to feel that something was wrong" (528/85–86).

Several potential explanations are offered for what Ah Q feels is "wrong" (有些古怪). For instance, at this point he happens to be naked from the waist up, and furthermore all of the women in Weizhuang have suddenly begun acting shy around him. There is also, however, a deeper explanation for what is wrong, which is rooted in Ah Q's new-found sensitivity to his external environment:

> First, the tavern refused him credit; second, the old man in charge of the Tutelary God's Temple made some uncalled-for remarks, as if he wanted Ah Q to leave; and third, for many days—he couldn't remember exactly how many—not a soul had come to hire him. He could put up with being refused credit, and he could simply ignore the old man at the temple who was urging him to leave; but when no one came to hire him, Ah Q had no choice but to depart. (531/86)

Ah Q's feeling that something is wrong comes from a sense that things have left their usual patterns, and it bears a direct connection to a response to his instinct and physical nature. It is not Ah Q's consciousness, but rather his instinct, intuition, and physical urges that make this a crucial moment. Clearly, something is starting to develop—but what?

While in chapters 2 through 4 the narrative maintains a basically objective point of view, beginning with chapter 5 a more subjective perspective begins to emerge. At the same time, even in the earlier descriptions of his "taste of defeat" in the second chapter, his "standing at a loss" in the third, and his "dimly aware something was wrong" in the fourth, we find the seeds for what will become an important shift in narrative perspective that I would describe as a process of subjectivization. In each of these earlier scenes Ah Q is described from the perspective of an outside observer, and even when the topic turns to his sexual desires, there is still no discernible subjective angle. Chapter 5, however, is still narrated from an outside perspective, but nevertheless begins to incorporate some subjective elements as well, to the point that at times these subjective elements even begin to replace Ah Q's viewpoint. We can say that these narratives represent the perspective of both the omniscient observer *and* of Ah Q himself. Bitter cold, sexual frustration, and acute hunger are all difficult to narrate purely from the point of view of an outside observer, yet they also cannot be narrated entirely from Ah Q's own point of view, since he lacks the ability to express his own feelings.

We may observe this transition in the following passage, which describes Ah Q's search for food:

> As he walked along the road "in search of food" he saw the familiar tavern and the familiar steamed bread, but he passed them without pausing. This was not what he was looking for, although he himself did not know what precisely he was looking for.
>
>   Since Weizhuang was not a big place, he soon left it behind. Most of the country outside the village consisted of paddy fields, green as far as the eye could see with the tender shoots of young rice, dotted here and there with round, black, moving objects, which were peasants cultivating the fields. But blind to the delights of

country life, Ah Q simply went on his way, for he knew intuitively that this was far removed from his "search for food." (531/88–89)

Although Ah Q does not know what he himself wants, we nevertheless see this sequence partially from his perspective. Notably, he does not stop to enjoy the pastoral scene in front of him, because he instinctively realizes that it is far removed from his search for food. It is only after this that the narrative reverts back to a more objective mode, with the observation that Ah Q finally arrives at the Convent of Quiet Self-improvement.

There are two points in this description that merit consideration. The first concerns the depiction of the landscape and the expression of Ah Q's emotions. Ah Q is a man who lives under the double weight of his "method of spiritual victory" and his instinct for survival, and neither scenery nor emotions are of any interest to him. But in this description of his search for food, the scenery carries distinct emotional connotations. The idyllic scenery stands in contrast to the hermetically sealed nature of Ah Q's inner world, and is also connected to the momentary loss of his desire for food. The familiar tavern with familiar steamed rolls becomes part of the scene, just like the paddy fields and shoots of young rice and the farmers. Ah Q's mode of emotional expression bears a direct relation to the first appearance of scenery as an objective world. Without this moment, there would be no scenery.

The second point is the appearance in this passage of the neologism *zhijue* (直覺; "intuition"). Given that Ah Q's awakening is grounded in his defeat, hunger, cold, and sexual frustration, his awareness of his situation comes from intuition, and it is precisely on account of this connection between intuition and self-awareness that Ah Q reflects that he is "searching for something else; though what that something was, he actually couldn't say." This is not written from Ah Q's perspective, rather it is Lu Xun composing "representations of human life in China as I experienced it," and thereby endowing Ah Q with a sense of dignity.[7] This dignity begins with Ah Q's realization that he himself is not entirely certain what he is seeking.

THE FIFTH MOMENT—REVOLUTIONARY INSTINCT AND BOREDOM

In *The True Story of Ah Q*, the concept of *intuition* represents a perception of one's own situation prior to analysis or reasoning, and hence without Ah Q's trademark spiritual victory method. The latter is a product of analysis and reasoning, but it is nonetheless incapable of overcoming his intuition, since intuition is characterized by immediacy, speed, individuality, and belief. An intuitive judgment is typically made instantly. We could also argue that Ah Q's revolution is the result of an intuitive decision produced by a moment of intuitive enlightenment, while his perception of his own death is similarly a product of his intuitive imagination. Thus, on one hand intuition produces moments when Ah Q is able to break through his spiritual victory method, while on the other hand his spiritual victory method remains a powerful weapon with which to resist his intuitive judgment, so that his own intuition remains at the level of the unconscious. The key to understanding Ah Q is the relation between intuition and the spiritual victories, and although he has a tendency to overcome his intuition by means of his spiritual victories, intuition still dominates his actions at critical moments.

When Ah Q resolves to go to the city, for instance, this decision derives from his intuition that "there is nothing to be had" in Weizhuang. However, what precisely pushes Ah Q to leave Weizhuang? On one hand, he is driven by anxiety precipitated by a feeling of hunger, cold, and sexual frustration, which convinces him that Weizhuang can no longer support him.[8] On the other hand, might we say that lurking behind Ah Q's intuitive decision to leave is an awareness of the ongoing revolution? We are told that "Ah Q had long known of revolutionaries, and this year had seen revolutionaries being decapitated with his own eyes," and at the moment "it had occurred to him that the revolutionaries were rebels and that a rebellion would make things difficult for him." Could this mean that Ah Q's decision to go to the city also implies an intuitive recognition of the revolutionary events unfolding there?

In theory, entering the city is an event that could have enabled Ah Q to enter official history. In order for this to happen, however, he would have had to already be a man of social status, but Ah Q has no status, and therefore his entering the city cannot count as an event. Nevertheless, when Ah Q returns to Weizhuang, he is perceived as having become rich, and therefore everyone in town views him with "suspicion mingled with respect" (533/91). Later, this suspicious respect develops into deference when Ah Q tells the townspeople about executions of the revolutionaries. For the townspeople, the execution of the revolutionaries is a way of maintaining the social order, and it is here that Ah Q has the best possibility of entering official history—in exploiting the violent power of this order, as well as in winning the greatest appreciation from the men and women of Weizhuang. Unfortunately, Ah Q's fairy tale–like return to Weizhuang ultimately comes to nothing when it is revealed that he actually did not strike it rich in the city, but instead is merely a petty thief.

Chapter 6 is written from the perspective of Weizhuang society, but in chapter 7 there is another shift in narration when the provincial candidate's boat arrives at Weizhuang, which the townspeople perceive as an indication that the revolutionaries will soon enter the city. This occurs on the evening of the fourteenth day of the ninth lunar month of the third year of the Xuantong reign period, which corresponds to November 4, 1911, in the Gregorian calendar, which also happened to be the day that Hangzhou was occupied by nationalist forces and Lu Xun's hometown of Shaoxing was declared "recovered" in the 1911 Revolution.[9] Here, Lu Xun combines annals-style historical facts with the "true story" genre he adopts for the novella as a whole. We do not know anything about Ah Q's ancestry, but the place, time, and setting of the narrative are nevertheless set within the context of revolutionary history. Marxist critics view *The True Story of Ah Q* as an allegorical commentary on the

Xinhai revolution, but to the extent that the novella is an allegory, it is an allegory not just of the nation or of the revolution, but also of the transformation of the national character.

Initially, Ah Q shares the same perspective as the townspeople, in that he sees the revolutionaries as rebels and believes that a rebellion would make things difficult for him. The result is that Ah Q holds a deep loathing for the revolution, but even here Ah Q's intuition is revived once again:

> Who could have guessed they could so frighten a successful provincial candidate renowned for thirty miles around? Consequently, Ah Q could not help feeling rather "entranced," and the terror of the villagers only added to his delight.
>   "Revolution is perhaps not a bad thing," he thought. "Finish off the whole lot of them ... damn them! ... I would like to go over to the revolutionaries myself." (538–539/97)

There are two potential explanations for Ah Q's reaction. First, he may sense that Weizhuang is no longer able to accommodate his needs, and second, he perceives that what happened in the city could frighten even a successful provincial candidate. Despite his depleted finances, Ah Q has some more wine and "suddenly, in a curious way, he felt as if the revolutionaries were he, and all the people in Weizhuang were his captives. Unable to contain himself for joy, he could not help shouting, 'Rebellion! Rebellion!'" (538–539/97).

After Ah Q returns to the Tutelary God's Temple, there is a description of how he fantasizes about the fear and reverence with which he will be received by the other villagers, then about the riches he will get from other people's houses. But Ah Q had not anticipated that Mr. Zhao and Mr. Qian, two of Weizhuang's elites, would have already pledged to join the revolutionaries. Ah Q's temporary break from the Weizhuang order has already vanished, and now he realigns with it, as he speculates that perhaps the other townspeople didn't realize he had joined the revolutionaries. Ah Q may have an instinctual desire for revolution, but he has no revolutionary consciousness. It is only when his instinct urges him that he is able to acknowledge his own defeats and helplessness, but each time he comes to his senses he tacitly reaffirms the existing social order.

If we compare chapters 5 and 7, we can see certain parallels in the two sets of narrative shifts. In chapter 5, the narrative is full of bitter hardship and moves from an objective to a subjective perspective, while in chapter 7, as the revolution is already underway and Ah Q is determined to become a revolutionary, the narrative perspective similarly shifts from an objective to a subjective perspective. It is precisely this latter shift, moreover, that permits Lu Xun to hint at the self-denial of the revolution: Ah Q's own revolution is rooted in an instinctive revolution, but as soon as his instinct is transformed into consciousness, the latter can only result in a return to the old order of Weizhuang. The reason for the revolution's failure lies in the temporary nature of Ah Q's instinct, as well as the inevitability that this instinct will undergo changes.

From this angle, we can begin examining some of the deeper meanings in chapter 8, by which time the Xinhai Revolution has been temporarily aborted and Weizhuang has, by and large, reverted back to its former order. Although the revolutionaries had arrived, their "coming" in the end had not made a great deal of difference.[10] Ah Q knew only two revolutionaries, one being the revolutionary whose execution he observes upon entering the city, and the second being the Bogus Foreign Devil who sometimes uses the foreign language promoted by *New Youth*. I propose that the fifth pivotal moment in Ah Q's life occurs when the Bogus Foreign Devil forbids Ah Q to join the revolution:

> Ah Q put up his hands to protect his head, and without knowing what he was doing fled through the gate; but this time the Bogus Foreign Devil did not give chase. After running more than sixty steps Ah Q slowed down, and began to feel very upset, because if the Bogus Foreign Devil would not allow him to be a revolutionary, there was no other way open to him. In the future he could never hope to have men in white helmets and white armor come to call on him. All his ambition, aims, hope, and future had been blasted at one stroke. (545/105)

This episode marks a critical turning point, wherein Ah Q begins to feel upset and realizes that "there was no other way open to him," and only a road of "boredom" (無聊) lay before him:

> Never before had he felt so bored. Even coiling his pigtail on his head now struck him as pointless and ridiculous. As a form of revenge he was very tempted to let his queue down, but in the end he did not do so. He wandered around till evening, when after drinking two bowls of wine on credit he began to feel in better spirits, and in his mind's eye he once again saw fragmentary visions of white helmets and white armor. (545–546/105).

Ah Q feels that his coiled queue is meaningless, but letting it down is equally meaningless. As a result of having been forbidden to join the revolution, Ah Q comes to feel that life has lost its meaning. But the resulting boredom far exceeds the level of individual experience, and extends to the entire event—including a suspicion of the revolution and all the change it may bring.

In Lu Xun's famous "Preface" to *Call to Arms* (〈吶喊〉自序), there is an emphasis on "loneliness" and "boredom." Lu Xun writes, "For although recalling the past may make you happy, it may sometimes also make you lonely, and there is no point in clinging in spirit to lonely bygone days. However, my trouble is that I cannot forget completely, and these stories have resulted from what I have been unable to erase from my memory."[11] But where can we find the origin of this loneliness? It originates in boredom. After describing the failure of the journal *New Life* (新生) that Lu Xun and his partners tried to launch during this period, Lu Xun immediately spoke of "boredom":

> The unprecedented sense of boredom that I subsequently came to feel began at this time. Initially, I did not really understand anything. Later I felt if someone's

proposals were met with approval, this should encourage him; if they met with opposition, this should make him fight back; but the real tragedy for him was to lift up his voice among the living and meet with no response, neither approval nor opposition, just as if he were left helpless in a boundless desert. So I began to feel lonely.[12]

Boredom is not a direct recognition of defeat, but a profound suspicion of the insignificance of everything one has done and has experienced. The sense of loneliness that produced *A Call to Arms* is premised on boredom. Boredom nullifies any meaning—and the resulting call to arms is an expression of a wish to resist. Loneliness is a motivation for creativity, while boredom is a foundation of loneliness. Hence the negativity of boredom bears the potential for creativity.

For Ah Q, meanwhile, this sense of boredom appears only in a flash, and thinking quickly ruins its potential:

The more Ah Q thought of it the angrier he grew, until he was in a towering rage. "So no rebellion for me, only for you, eh?" he fumed, nodding furiously. "Damn you, you Bogus Foreign Devil—all right, *be* a rebel! That's a crime for which you get your head chopped off. I'll turn informer, then see you dragged to town to have your head cut off—your whole family executed. . . . To hell with you!" (547/ 107)

Ah Q returns to thinking and relying on the order of Weizhuang, without allowing the sense of boredom to linger or infiltrate his actions. Boredom was his instinctual attempt to mark himself off from the order of Weizhuang, but in this instant he dispels this sense of boredom and his thinking reemerges. Ah Q's death confirms his realization that to rebel is a crime punishable by decapitation. He dies at the hands of the revolution by which he was so entranced, as a result of not being able to let his sense of boredom linger on.

That Ah Q dies in the postrevolutionary order is perhaps a coincidence. But still it was likely—just as a high Qing official such as Li Yuanhong 黎元洪 could be dragged in by the revolutionaries to become a "Leader of the Revolution," Ah Q could become a "big general." Those who mistakenly stumble into revolution might be able to win honor, and may appear as "elites" (好漢) and receive acclaim in the press. On the other hand, Ah Q might instead become a doormat for those elites who are winning prizes, earning money, and making a name for themselves. What difference is there between these elites and Ah Q? None. The only difference in fact lies in the plotting of each official history: they conceal what should be concealed and reveal what should be revealed. Some people slip into the annals of official history accidentally, while others enter openly under the badge of being elites. The divergent fates of Ah Q and of these elites is a common phenomenon in times of revolution. Lu Xun is therefore less focused on whether Ah Q finally surrendered to the revolutionaries, and instead his question is: what new qualities were born in Ah Q during his revolution?

The Sixth Moment—Death and the Grand Finale

The sixth and final moment of an apparent failure of Ah Q's trademark symbolic victories can be found in a famous passage in chapter 9. After the Zhao family is robbed, Ah Q is secretly pleased, but he could hardly have anticipated that four days later he would be seized in the middle of the night by a group of police and militia and taken to the city. He is violently interrogated, after which he is told he must sign a document, which is presumably his "confession." Terrified because he does not even know how to write his own name, Ah Q picks up a writing brush for the first time in his life and attempts to draw a circle in lieu of a signature, but is mortified by his inability to even draw a good circle.

Ah Q's response, however, falls under the category of thought rather than instinct. His inability to resist his instinctive reactions emerges clearly when he looks again at the crowd:

> At that instant his thoughts swirled like a whirlwind. Four years earlier, at the foot of the mountain, he had met a hungry wolf that had followed him for a distance, wanting to devour him. He had nearly died of fright, but luckily he happened to have a knife in his hand, which gave him the courage to get back to Weizhuang. (551–552/112)

In this scene, Ah Q's hallucinations created by his sense of insecurity rapidly transform into psychological anxiety. This scene marks another pivotal shift from an objective to a quasi-subjective point of view:

> He had never forgotten that wolf's eyes, fierce yet cowardly, gleaming like two will-o'-the-wisps, as if boring into him from a distance. Now he saw eyes more terrible even than the wolf's: dull yet penetrating eyes that, having devoured his words, still seemed eager to devour something beyond his flesh and blood. And these eyes kept following him at a set distance.
> These eyes seemed to have merged into one, biting into his soul.
> "Help, help!"
> But Ah Q never uttered these words. All had turned black before his eyes, there was a buzzing in his ears, and he felt as if his whole body were being scattered like so much dust. (551–552/112)

In comparison with Ah Q's previous sense of boredom, this new feeling of terror grants him the ability to break out of something, to distinguish between his body and soul. While the self created by his spiritual victories was a cheerful one, the "soul" mentioned here is one that has suffered deep pain. Where does the anguished soul come from in this passage? It is in those eyes that Ah Q's method of spiritual victory is annulled by his fear of death, and with this Ah Q can for the first time comprehend the pain wrought upon a twisted soul.

Some readers approaching the story from a realistic perspective have asked how a simple villager could have had such a complicated set of responses to the fear of being eaten, to the wolf's eyes, and to the wolf itself. Zhang Xudong, meanwhile, sees the allegorical structure of *The True Story of Ah Q* as essentially modernist.[13] It is, however, perhaps not useful to try to differentiate rigorously between realism and modernism, given that Lu Xun's realistic narratives often contain allegorical structures, or sophisticated rhetorical devices and dark allusions, thus conflating the limits between subjective or objective, realist or abstract, and descriptive or allusive narration.

These six moments in Ah Q's life offer insight into the possible failure of his spiritual victory method. These reflections on Ah Q's instinct and intuition are also explorations into whether transcending an external worldly perspective can yield a new consciousness. Ah Q's sense of defeat, his feeling of not knowing what to do, his sense of boredom, fear, and momentary loss even of the self—all this can help us understand whether or not Ah Q became a revolutionary. The six moments in *The True Story of Ah Q* are also instances of Ah Q's figurative awakening, though in each case they only last a split second.

But why do these moments occur at all, and what possibilities do they contain? What is the logic behind their fleeting appearance and prompt repression? When rereading the preface and the reasons why Ah Q cannot enter official history with a new understanding of these moments of failure, we can come to a new understanding of the novella as a whole. Rather than say that the *True Story of Ah Q* outlines how Ah Q's spiritual victory method works, it would perhaps be more accurate to say that the work illustrates a series of instances when this method fails. These moments of failure function as prophecies for the countless Chinese who will eventually participate in the revolution. They will participate in the revolution, and perhaps even lay down their lives for it, but the change produced by the revolution is captured by those momentary transformations in Ah Q's life. It is through just these six moments that Ah Q as a living being is engraved into the depths of emptiness, like a ghost that has entered our thoughts and which is impossible to exorcise.

These ghosts are the traces of a past life.

(translated by Natasha Gentz and Carlos Rojas)

NOTES

1. Lu Xun 鲁迅, *Ah Q zhengzhuan* 阿Q正傳 [The true story of Ah Q], in *Lu Xun quanji* 鲁迅全集 [Complete works of Lu Xun], vol. 1 (Beijing: Renmin wenxue chubanshe, 2005). A translation of this work, Lu Hsun, *The True Story of Ah Q*, can be found in *Call to Arms*, ed. Yang Xianyi and Gladys Yang (Beijing: Foreign Language Press, 1981). The English translations used in this chapter have all been extensively revised. Citations from this text will be indicated parenthetically in the main text, with the page number of the Chinese edition followed by the corresponding page number in the English translation.
2. Xi Di 西諦 (Zheng Zhenduo 鄭振鐸), "Nahan" 吶喊 [Call to Arms], *Wenxue zhoubao* 文學週報 [Literature monthly] 251 (November 21, 1926): 50.

3. Lu Xun, "*Ah Q zhengzhuan* de chengyin" 〈阿Q正傳〉的成因 [How *The True Story of Ah Q* was written], in *Complete Works of Lu Xun*, vol. 3, 217.

4. Lu Xun, "Zhi Wang Qiaonan" 致王乔南 [To Wang Qiaonan], in *Complete Works of Lu Xun*, vol. 12, 245.

5. Lu Xun, "Zhi Li Qiye" 致李霽野 [To Li Qiye] (May 8, 1936), in *Complete Works of Lu Xun*, vol. 14, 95.

6. Wang Yao 王瑤, "*Gushi xinbian* sanlun" 〈故事新編〉散論 [Essays on *Old Stories Retold*], in Wang Yao, *Lu Xun zuopin lunji* 魯迅作品論集 [Collected essays on Lu Xun's works] (Beijing: Renmin wenxue chubanshe, 1984).

7. Lu Xun, "Ewen yiben *Ah Q zhengzhuan* xu ji zhuzhe zixu chuanlue" 俄文譯本〈阿Q正傳〉序及著者自敘傳略 [Preface and author's commentary to the Russian translation of *The True Story of Ah Q*], in *Complete Works of Lu Xun*, vol. 7, 84.

8. Freud has distinguished three types of anxiety: objective, spiritual, and moral anxiety. Though they might appear to be unrelated, in fact they permeate, transform, and impact each other. See Sigmund Freud, "New Introductory Lectures on Psychoanalysis," in *Standard Edition of the Complete Psychological Works of Sigmund Freud*, ed. and trans. James Strachey, vol. 22 (London: Hogarth Press, 1964), 1–184 (originally published in 1933).

9. See the explanatory footnote on pp. 557–558 of the Chinese text and on p. 96 of the English translation.

10. This expression appears in Lu Xun, "Refeng wushiliu 'laile'" 熱風五十六 '來了' [Hot wind 56, 'Coming']" (May 1919), *Complete Works of Lu Xun*, vol. 1, 363–364. Refuting the saying "Extremism is coming," Lu Xun writes: "Regardless which ism, I have never heard that what has thrown China into disorder, all the chaos from the past until today, is because of some ism. 'Extremism' won't be coming, there is no need to be frightened about it. Only if 'coming' will be coming should one be frightened." After giving an example, he continues: "When the Republic was founded, I was living in a small county town which had long put up the white flag already. One day I suddenly saw numerous men and women fleeing in complete disorder, town people fled to the village and village people to the town. Upon asking them what had happened, they responded: 'They say it is coming.' Hence we can see that all they feared was the 'coming,' like myself. At that time there was only 'majority-ism', 'no-extremism'!" *Complete Works of Lu Xun*, vol. 1, 363–364.

11. Lu Xun, "*Na Han* zixu" 〈吶喊〉自序 [Preface to *Call to Arms*], in *Complete Works of Lu Xun*, vol. 1, 437.

12. Lu Xun, "Preface to *Call to Arms*," 437

13. Zhang Xudong 張旭東, "Zhongguo xiandaizhuyi qiyuan de 'ming' 'yan' zhi bian: chongdu *Ah Q zhengzhuan*" 中國現代主義起源的 "名" "言" 之辯：重讀〈阿Q正傳〉 [A dialectics of 'name' and 'voice' in relation to the origin of Chinese modernism—Rereading *The True Story of Ah Q*], *Lu Xun yanjiu yuekan* 魯迅研究月刊 [Lu Xun studies monthly] 1 (2009): 4–5.

WORKS CITED

Freud, Sigmund. "New Introductory Lectures on Psychoanalysis." In *Standard Edition of the Complete Psychological Works of Sigmund Freud*. Ed. and trans. James Strachey, vol. 22. London: Hogarth Press, 1964. 1–184 (originally published in 1933).

Lu Xun 魯迅. *Ah Q zhengzhuan* 阿Q正傳 [The true story of Ah Q]. In *Lu Xun quanji* 魯迅全集 [Complete works of Lu Xun], vol. 1. Beijing: Renmin wenxue chubanshe, 2005.

Lu Xun 魯迅. "Ah Q zhengzhuan de chengyin" 〈阿Q正傳〉的成因 [How *The True Story of Ah Q* was written]. In *Complete Works of Lu Xun*, vol. 3. 217.

Lu Xun魯迅. "Ewen yiben *Ah Q zhengzhuan* xu ji zhuzhe zixu chuanlue" 俄文譯本〈阿Q正傳〉序及著者自敘傳略 [Preface and author's commentary to the Russian translation of *The True Story of Ah Q*]. In *Complete Works of Lu Xun*, vol. 7. 84.

Lu Xun 魯迅. "*Na Han* zixu"《吶喊》自序 [Preface to *Call to Arms*]. In *Complete Works of Lu Xun*, vol. 1. 437.

Lu Xun 魯迅. "Zhi Wang Qiaonan" 致王乔南 [To Wang Qiaonan]. In *Complete Works of Lu Xun*, vol. 12. 245.

Lu Xun 魯迅. "Zhi Li Qiye" 致李霽野 [To Li Qiye] (May 8, 1936). In *Complete Works of Lu Xun*, vol. 14. 95.

Lu Hsun. *The True Story of Ah Q*. In *Call to Arms*. Ed. Yang Xianyi and Gladys Yang. Beijing: Foreign Language Press, 1981.

Wang Yao 王瑤. "*Gushi xinbian* sanlun"《故事新編》散論 [Essays on *Old Stories Retold*]. In Wang Yao, *Lu Xun zuopin lunji* 魯迅作品論集 [Collected essays on Lu Xun's works]. Beijing: Renmin wenxue chubanshe, 1984.

Xi Di 西諦 (Zheng Zhenduo 鄭振鐸). "Nahan" 吶喊 [Call to arms]. In *Wenxue zhoubao* 文學週報 [Literature monthly] 251 (November 21, 1926).

Zhang Xudong 張旭東. "Zhongguo Xiandaizhuyi qiyuan de 'ming' 'yan' zhi bian: chongdu *Ah Q zhengzhuan*" 中國現代主義起源的"名""言"之辯：重讀〈阿Q正傳〉 [A dialectics of 'name' and 'voice' in relation to the origin of Chinese modernism—Rereading *The True Story of Ah Q*]. *Lu Xun yanjiu yuekan* 魯迅研究月刊 [Lu Xun studies monthly] 1 (2009): 4–5.

....

FROM SHAME TO FREEDOM
Undoing Spectral Identity in Li Ang's Seeing Ghosts

....

CHAOYANG LIAO

> Unlike guilt, shame does not seek to penetrate surfaces or tear away veils;
> rather, it seeks comfort in them, hides itself in them as in a safe haven.
> Our relationships to the surface change in shame ... we become fasci-
> nated with its maze-like intricacies, its richness and profundity.
>
> (Joan Copjec, "May '68, The Emotional Month")

> But when one has understood by seeing fully that things are empty, one is
> no longer deluded. Ignorance ceases, and the twelve spokes [of the wheel]
> come to a halt.
>
> (Nārgārjuna, "Seventy Verses on Emptiness")

LACAN famously made the claim that the Japanese are "unanalyzable." This claim is
based mainly on the use of Chinese characters in Japanese. The characters are accompanied by a foreign sound system (*on yomi*) but can also be read "exegetically" with native
sounds (*kun yomi*). This presence of a foreign language within the native one compels
constant translations between speech and character, disturbs relations between signifier and signified, and, Lacan points out, produces a subjectivity supported by identification with "a constellated heaven" rather than the "unary trait" (*trait unaire*).[1]

Lacan takes the term *unary trait* from Freud's term *einziger Zug*, defining it as the
"factor of consistency through which something is distinguished from what surrounds
it."[2] Thus the oneness of such a trait consists not in the unity of the whole, but in the
counting of a partial "stroke" or "trait" as a point of structural consistency, a minimal
support for meaning even when meaning is not known. If the unconscious thinks in
a way "foreign to us as a restaurant menu written in an unknown language," the menu
can still be read in some way as a menu because of this minimal support.[3] For Lacan,
the Japanese are collectively unanalyzable because in their experience foreign language
menus have become daily fare, and menus are no longer identifiable as menus.

Lacan's act of intercultural reading is puzzling in more than one way. Karatani Kōjin is prompted to comment that Lacan is "half-joking."[4] Most importantly, Lacan's gesture is embarrassing in that it borders on a reductive representation of otherness, but is also interesting in inflecting the analyst's silence into what amounts to a profession of incompetence in face of the unknowability of a foreign world. The importance of the analyst's silence in clinical work as a minimal support for discourse, even in "analyz-able" cases, should remind us of the possibility that there is more to explore behind the seeming hole of knowledge in unanalyzability.

Here we are dealing with a peculiar feature of psychoanalytic theory as a general "method": theory is posed as a weak form of knowledge, constantly mindful of limits imposed by the new. Psychoanalysis is an interpretive activity distinguished by its stress on the pursuit of "truth" in experiential singularity. Like all interpretive activities, it produces and employs generalities of knowledge, but, in both clinical and nonclinical practice, such generalities tend to lose importance when they have served their pur-pose, that is, when they have caused to emerge determinations specific to the history and situation of the particular subject of analysis. This is why the analyst's position is said to be characterized by a "way of humility," a mindfulness of its own "place of the abject" where dignity is maintained by an ability to efface one's ego.[5] Thus Lacan refers to some of the analyst's generalities as a "weak logic" that is just "strong enough" for the purpose of conveying its sense of incompleteness to those who need to be made aware of it.[6] Such active self-doubting may seem to confirm suspicions about the efficacy of psychoanalytic theory when removed from its original cultural context, but in fact points to a different plane where cultural contexts may enter a certain form of dialogic translatability.

Kazushige Shingu explains the need for the unary trait (for analyzability) by appeal-ing to writing as the production of "fixation points" facilitating the arrival of truth in analysis.[7] Here "fixation" refers to the emergence, not the immutability, of oneness or consistency. As meaning is produced in communicative acts when a variety of formally possible interpretations are crystallized into a contextually appropriate reading, so is subjective truth intimated when seemingly random associations fix themselves, as if writing themselves into a "point" of understanding and, reflexively, of writing itself. The Japanese writing system, modeled on floating foreignness rather than punctual crystallization, resists the anchoring of fixation points: "Writing itself falls to the status of a signifier among other signifiers."[8] In technical terms, such writing, constantly dis-tracted from the structuring of unary traits, does not take well to the formation of the master signifier (S_1), but is spread across the anonymous store of all signifiers (S_2). S_1 and S_2 are two initial positions in the four "discourses" or types of social ties elaborated by Lacan in his *Seminar XVII* (1969–1970).[9] Presumably, when the distinction between these positions is blurred, the discourses themselves, including the analyst's discourse, become less effective as explanatory schemas.

On the other hand, recent discussions of the four discourses reveal how receptive psychoanalytic theory can be to the possibility that as times change, the conditions of analyzability also change, possibly accompanied by a decline in the importance of the unary trait itself in the West. The theory of discourses itself seems to be partly an attempt to address a post-Freudian weakening of the classical form of the master's discourse, recalling what Lacan "predicted" in the 1930s as "the decline of the paternal imago."[10] Several commentators have pointed to shifts between Lacan's times and ours, often described as a further veering toward the "society of enjoyment" or "the demise of symbolic efficiency."[11] This further veering makes it necessary to reconsider how the discourses work precisely, or if the fourfold scheme is in need of modification, not least because its formulation was deeply embedded in the aftermath of the agitations of 1968.[12]

In light of this constant effort to be attentive to historical specificity, the unanalyzability of the Japanese may be regarded as an expression of the cautionary modesty of psychoanalytical knowledge when cultural difference demands a reworking of its templates.[13] The mention of unanalyzability, of course, may seem to imply a closure, a prolonged resistance to amelioration, but such fixing of the unanalyzable points precisely to the spectrality of established knowledge constantly criticized by Lacan as trapped in the fantasy of the coinciding of knowledge and power and haunted by "the threatening spectre of the knowledge that we have not acquired."[14] It is more in keeping with the spirit of psychoanalysis to read unanalyzability as an opening up of knowledge to the unknown, a minimal affirming of the latter's translatability.

The "threatening spectre" of the unknown is a reflection of the spectrality of knowledge itself, a general perceptual failure created by "our own delight in the spectres of epistemological value and plenitude."[15] Psychoanalytic theory claims to offer some access to the "real," to forces that shape our conscious life but remain hidden from "delighting" established knowledge. These forces are more "real" in the same way as the Zen master considers ignorance, or knowledge of ignorance, as what matters in knowledge.[16] Such knowledge in ignorance inevitably partakes of the spectrality of established knowledge; it does not deny the usefulness of practical knowledge, nor can it "prove" itself objectively as a better or truer account of reality. It can only follow a "weak logic," a half-saying of truth that, without leaving knowledge (qua uncertainty) behind, introduces some substance into the spectrality of both the known and the unknown. As will be shown below, the unary trait becomes in an important sense the mediating term between naive fixation predicated on spectral knowledge and a broader openness to the half-truths of contextual determination, departing from the former but also giving a certain solidity of truth to the latter.

GHOST "SUPPOSED TO KNOW"

Psychoanalysis spectralizes knowledge by haunting it with forces from the unknown, but becomes spectral itself when faced with floating foreignness. This reflexivity points to affinities between psychoanalysis and a certain type of ghost story. In the following, I will outline a reading of *Seeing Ghosts* (看得見的鬼), Li Ang's 李昂 collection of "creative" ghost stories, to show how these stories depict the foreignness of the experiential world of new ghosts, employing the gaps of knowledge introduced by such foreignness to display a degree of unanalyzability in the sense of a constellating of knowledge and discourse with the unknown, at the expense of punctual fixation.[17]

To see the relevance of the psychoanalytic mode of knowledge/ignorance for our understanding of *Seeing Ghosts*, one has to proceed in a rather circuitous way. We may begin with the fact that, out of all the details of *The Tibetan Book of the Dead*, Li Ang refers to the seeing of colored lights in two passages in the first story, "The Ghost of Savage Wives' End." Yuezhen/Yuezhu 月珍/月珠, the titular ghost of the story, is a Babuza woman, a plains aborigine of mixed blood who, because of ethnic circumstances, practiced prostitution when alive.[18] She has been wrongfully tortured to death in prison by a Chinese subprefect, then locked within hardened salt piled on her distorted body by people who pitied her. After a very long time, she regains consciousness and begins to move, fighting to gain free space inch by inch from the salt. When she can move her head, she looks at her own feet to assure herself that she still has a body. At some point she recalls hearing about lights guiding the dead to the other world, but decides that she "has not been guided by these," that is, by radiant lights in five colors: blue, white, yellow, red, and green in the known order.[19] After another long period of time and having been freed from the salt and then "lived" through many events, her abused body is completely healed and ready for liberation. She is about to depart from this world when she actually sees the lights, first white, then yellow, then red, then green and blue.[20]

The order of the lights when they are mentioned for the first time repeats that of the five lights in Tibetan *bardo* teaching. As presented in *The Tibetan Book of the Dead*, *bardo* means a middle or liminal state, especially that between life and rebirth experienced by the deceased. The five guiding lights occur on the first five days of the *bardo* of reality, a fourteen-day period following the *bardo* of the moment of death and preceding the *bardo* of seeking rebirth.[21] But why are lights that appear later in the story ordered differently? Here as elsewhere throughout *Seeing Ghosts*, Li Ang is following a strategy of "half-citing," referring to elements of known social and cultural history without treating them as an anonymous store of fixed facts (S_2). The reordering of colors brings to bear the specificity of the ghost's positioning in the east within the ordering scheme of the five stories (on ghosts of the east, the north, the center, the south, and the west of the nation, in that order). The plan of the cardinal directions with a center is itself a reference to the mandalas of deities given in *The Tibetan Book of the Dead*, where, again, the ordering is different, beginning with the center and proceeding to the east, the south, the west, and the north. Thus, the different ordering of *Seeing Ghosts* would seem to explain why the ghost of the east, with her unique place at the beginning, should see the light of the east first, rather than that of the center.

An important corollary of the invoking of *bardo* liberation in the first story is that the staple wisdom of the east in *bardo* teaching, the Great Round Mirror Wisdom, implicitly becomes an important element of the story.[22] The mirror foregrounds the passivity of visual experience, appropriately echoing the incapacitated "mental body"

726   METHOD: PSYCHOANALYSIS

of the deceased in the second *bardo* phase, who are confused by the new world they have been thrown into, in the same way as a baby "must accustom itself after birth to our world."[23] Furthermore, in order to understand in some sense or act on what is seen, the deceased can rely on their training when alive, but usually also need living guides beside their bodies reciting messages of *bardo* teaching (not unlike subtitles attached to images), confirming that the *bardo* by itself is very much a state of seeing or hearing but not knowing.

In *Seeing Ghosts*, Yuezhen/Yuezhu's tutelage after freeing herself from the salt sets up a pattern to be followed by other stories. She acts with the passive receptivity of a learner, reflective of a modesty not unlike that of the psychoanalyst reviewed above. For example, she abandons her plans for revenge on the subprefect when she finds that power has changed hands and the subprefect's office is now abandoned and dilapidated. She decides to act no further when she sees the new Japanese masters destroy a mummified body that may have been that of the subprefect. Overhearing the living explain why the Japanese do it, she reaches some kind of understanding, but pays no attention to what does not concern her, that is, how the "Han settlers or sinicized natives" are being oppressed by the Japanese.[24]

There is no ethical choice here; the situation changes simply because the ghost has been encased in the salt for too long. But the blind course of events becomes a sort of mirror, reflecting the stilling of anger (the target emotion of the Mirror Wisdom) in her: she now thinks of revenge only out of a sense of symbolic duty, acting timidly and cautiously because she does not know very well how to proceed or even how to find her way around town. Later on (now "hundreds of years" after she died), she becomes a local deity "without her knowing why." It all began when, after the February 28 uprising in 1947, a few people who escaped to Japan reported having seen the likeness of an "ethereal" woman leading them away from the pursuing party. But the ghost herself seems to have nothing to do with the incident: "Indeed, it might have been just the fog which confused the pursuers."[25] One misrecognition leads to another, and people begin to read hopeful lottery numbers into details on her body or in her acts. She now becomes, in Lacanian parlance, a spirit "supposed to know," but in fact remains silent, doing nothing except mirroring back people's fantasies and desires.

MODESTY AND SHAME

At the end of the last session of *Seminar XVII*, Lacan told students at the University of Paris at Vincennes that they had come to the seminar to be made ashamed: "it is because I happen to make you ashamed, not too much, but just enough."[26] Lacan inflects the sense of shame here by using *honte* (felt shame) instead of *pudeur* (modesty or capacity for shame), but still maintains a sense of the other side of the feeling of shame by "half-saying": the shame should be "not too much, but just enough."[27] This quantitative mediation of a qualitative distinction allows Lacan to maintain a sense of *pudeur* even when referring to *honte*. This mediation is important for the reading of the first story of *Seeing Ghosts* because in this story, the mirror-like modesty of a spirit "supposed to know" unfolds in the context of the wrongful humiliation and excessive shaming imposed by the subprefect on Yuezhen/Yuezhu. How these two elements come together will determine the meaning of the protagonist's liberation at the end.

At the beginning of a series of descriptions leading up to the seeing of the *bardo* lights, the ghost starts to dance in front of her own little shrine, inspired by a strip dance she watched earlier that night. The strip dance is intended to please Lord of the Rock, a local deity, and is performed by a plain-looking woman with an aging body. The strip dancer does it for money, but is terrified when the music keeps repeating itself and for a long time she is unable to stop the dance. In addition, she feels a great number of spectators watching her when there is, other than the ghost herself, only one man actually present: the man who hired her to perform for the Lord to repay some favor. The interest of the strip dance is purely monetary and has nothing to do with shame, but shame seems to be evoked when the dancer reports that something has been trying to "enter" her, and she has to keep "wiggling and waggling wildly" to keep herself away from the "thing."[28]

Here quantification (unexpected length of time and number of spectators) provides a support for a sense of excess and, in response, the emergence of shame as "the experience of limitation," of the limiting of an "infinity that haunts any interiorization."[29] In Lacan's half-shaming of the students, quantification works as a regulator introducing the restraint of an analyst's position to turn felt *honte* into a possibility of training in *pudeur*. In Li Ang's compassionate shaming of the dancer, quantification works as a mirror, eliciting from the scene of the dance an evasion of the piercing gaze, here essentially a mirror-like field of the Other. The dance reveals that there can be a real sense of modesty behind the seeming shamelessness of a monetary transaction.

Following Eve Sedgwick's interpretation of her felt shame after the September 11 attacks whenever she sees the void previously occupied by the Twin Towers, Joan Copjec stresses that shame "is not caused by prohibition or repression." Rather, it comes from a disturbed field of reflexivity:

> My look is deflected or disarmed, not by any (negative) judgment, but in response to the rupturing of an interpersonal bridge, the interruption of the comforting circuit of recognition by which my look sends back to me an image that confirms my identity.[30]

In this sense, shame should be distinguished from guilt. In contrast to guilt, which is a secondary "effect on the Subject of an Other that judges," shame is "primary" in the sense of being "related to an Other prior to the Other that judges," an Other "that only sees or lets be seen."[31] Clearly, the dancer in the story resists the "thing" not out of moral prohibition or repression, for which she obviously does not care too much. Her shame is more primitive.

Also, the strip dancer continues a separate thread of characters figuring, in contrast to the guiltlessness of the ghost, shamelessness. In the beginning there is, of course, the subprefect, who shamelessly abuses his power to "make an example" of a native woman who dares to challenge the Chinese by trying to reclaim ancestral land rights. The second case is the seekers of lottery fortunes who subject themselves impudently to the dream of commanding total knowledge. These two cases are accompanied by two cases of collective shame: first, there are the anonymous and ethnically indistinct onlookers who are so shamed by Yuezhen/Yuezhu's unsightly body as to want to restore their "circuit of recognition" by piling salt on it after dark. Later on, when word begins to spread about the ghost's beneficence, there are those who know things about respect for the spiritual enough to take action to place the refound body in a shrine and cover her with clothing (or, alternatively, an urn) and a veil.

The resolution of this tension between individual shamelessness and collective shame begins to take shape with the strip dancer's situation, where there is a reversal into the more traditional mingling of individual shame and collective or nonhuman lust (the Lord as an "obscene Other" positioned in authority). The ghost's dance then effects a rebuilding of the "interpersonal bridge" by the further reversal of imposed shame into a modest refutation of shamelessness, ending with the ghost's act of merging with and disappearing into the five colored lights. That is, while the ghost's dance replicates the strip dancer's nudity and gestures (or acts) of autoeroticism, it is not based on shame-lessness but on the renunciation of a shameless world. Within the causality of the sto-ryline, this renunciation effects a deflecting of the forced rupturing of interpersonal identification, a mirroring of the uncanny void back to banal social linkage itself. This amounts to a shaming of imposed shame for its impotent dependence on the façade of comforting but spectral knowledge, in both colonial history and capitalistic modernity.

Shameful Flesh and Dreamed Awakening

The shaming of imposed shame maintains the ruptured state of the social circuit of reflexivity and makes use of it. Here we are leaving the world of the analyst's modesty and moving to that of the act. Shame based on established knowledge is yielding to shame based on knowledge as ignorance, but points beyond ignorance to a different worlding. This dimension may have come from the tradition of *bardo* teaching which prefers bold intensification rather than tactful restraint, always giving the deceased a choice between two lights but preferring the radiant lights of the beyond over the weaker, visually more comforting lights that accompany the strong but less attractive ones but would lead straight to the sufferings of rebirth. Deleuzians would call this radiant but frightening world beyond the world of the impersonal, a "second world" that can appear to us only through gaps in the framing knowledge of our first world, but can intimate the possibility of a radical perspective in which "meaningful change can only occur by changing the existing frame or structure."[32]

But perhaps by following *bardo* teaching, Li Ang is offering something a bit more modest and a bit closer to Lacanian theory. This becomes immediately clear when the text chooses to use a lowly strip dance as sisterly preparation for the ghost's final awakening. In fact, the ghost looks at the scars on the "wounds of shame" on her deformed body "for the first time in hundreds of years" after seeing the unattractive body of the strip dancer.[33] The latter, therefore, functions as a mirror image that triggers a dormant ability in the ghost's perceptual body. This other body enables the ghost to initiate her imminent enlightenment, just as a pigeon or a migratory locust has to depend on exposure to "an image akin to its own" to mature in ability or in behavior.[34]

As a human case, however, the ghost's singularity departs not only from examples of ethology, but from the famous misrecognition of the integrity of the body attributed to the mirror phase of the human baby. The ghost's enlightenment instances, rather, a dispersal of the body, not a disappearing but a deeper abiding with the unknown, not as or not simply as an alternative world but as a source of tonal singularization that despectralizes established knowledge by adding a sense of the real to it, not all the way but "just enough" to blur the distinction between the real and the spectral. To borrow Soto Zen master Dōgen's formulation, even when the ghost leaves the world, her story continues to "speak of a dream from within a dream," that is, from the position of the unconscious embedded within the world of spectral knowledge: "The dream state and the awakened state—each is an appearing of the real (*jissō* 實相). They are beyond large and small, beyond superior and inferior."[35]

Such singularization rules out a fixed body of revealed knowledge in favor of a split discourse straddling the dream state and the awakened state. In general, this is a peculiar feature of Buddhism where "sacred" authority is attained rather than revealed, which tends to lead to a humbling aporetic duality:

> there must be a persistence of conceptuality if an enlightened one is to act compassionately and teach others of the way to freedom from suffering. The problem then is to reconcile the conception-free nature of enlightenment that lies beyond knowledge with the conceptual activity required for and in post-enlightenment teaching that conveys knowledge of enlightenment to others.[36]

The ghost, of course, has no intention to linger in spectral conceptuality, but the story of her attaining freedom participates in the general effectivity of the liberatory discourse of Buddhism, and quite naturally points to the same kind of split discourse in other cases of enlightenment, each with a singular inflection of the general pattern.

The splitting is clearly displayed in the ghost's shedding of (spectral) shame described in the final dance, which takes the form of placing shame in spectrality, returning it to its true status as arbitrarily imposed signifiers. This spectral shame is visually present (seen) in two forms, both proud work done by the subprefect: two giant breasts each filled with ten mangled lumps of flesh moved from lower parts of the ghost's former body, and then ten artificial, mouth-shaped vaginas (technically vulvae) sculpted out of the ten cuts on the lower body from which flesh has been gouged for the breast job. As the ghost caresses her giant breasts, presumably shrunken now into something smaller, the foreign lumps of flesh inside them are "ejected" one by one, returning the breasts to their original, uncrowded state. Then the ghost starts to play with her one true orifice, her biological vaginal opening, and as her pleasure mounts, one after another of the artificial copies "fall off" or "fly away" from her body. As these *man*-made flesh-parts fall on the salty ground in front of the shrine, the text observes, they dutifully arrange themselves into their intended positions, becoming deflected empty signifiers, spectral reminders of the ghost's shamed body, now single-mindedly bearing witness to the unerasable wrongdoings of the powerful.[37]

At the same time, this undoing of shame is described with an uncanny insistence on numbers. The text counts the wounds and pieces of flesh with great interest, almost echoing the interest of the fortune seekers who endlessly debate whether the reported count of ten vaginas is inclusive or exclusive of the original one. In other words, the text prepares for the ghost's liberation with a movement in the opposite direction, toward "conceptuality" or spectral knowledge, so much so that one can almost perceive a shaming celebration of "double ten" (ten cuts on each breast doubled by ten vaginas) as imposed signifiers of national birth.[38] A sense of the real emerges when the insistence on numbers leads to a despectralization of the One: when the ten artificial vaginas are removed, *one* natural vagina remains, now recognized as one's very own source of pleasure, part of the "original root and fountain" of the body as "one's own place."[39] This is not a simple return to narcissism and spectral identity but is infused with a sense of the wholeness of the interpersonal or, more precisely, the inter-being, without which "one's own place" would be confronted with a void on the "other side," a breaking of the mirror, a relapse into shame.

Similarly, the erotic pleasure the ghost obtains from her own body is not an indication that she is not free from craving, for her desire is not a desire encased within the fixed conceptualization of a self. Rather, the ghost has to identify with, to literally imitate and *be* the strip dancer, without shame, and reveal that there is buddhahood in the lowly world of fleshly desire. This reversal of direction partakes of the buddhas' desire and compassion to remain in the world and teach their achievement to other beings, that is, to maintain an inter-being "circuit of recognition," comforting not in the sense of following established practices of social discourse but in the real sense of a hopefulness that liberation is still possible in a shameless world.

It is to be expected that Li Ang would be criticized as politically suspect for her otherworldly outlook in this story. Darryl Sterk, for example, is unimpressed by what appears as escapism:

> One might have expected more from Li Ang than an orgasmic ghost dance that ends all-too-easily in spiritual transcendence, in happiness outside history. ... The final freedom of the aboriginal maiden comes too easily, and suggests the continued

national exclusion of the aborigines, the national failure to include them ethically or ethnically into the Taiwanese nation.[40]

In addition to the complexities involved in referring to a "Taiwanese nation" here, one has to remember that justice and fairness mean nothing without respect for singularized affective lives. From a psychoanalytic perspective, nominal inclusion and symbolic equality are based on beliefs in the possible fullness of ethical knowledge and therefore on a discourse enmeshed in spectrality. Li Ang foresaw precisely this kind of criticism by beginning with a story of shame and modesty.

KNOWLEDGE AS EROS

Yuezhen/Yuezhu, of course, leaves the human world, but her story remains. In the mandala-like scheme of *Seeing Ghosts*, her story is only the opening story. The insistence on the desire to remain in the world, to continue the narration, is as real as her disappearance. In the Afterword to *Seeing Ghosts*, Li Ang comments on the mandala-like arrangement of the five stories:

> As stories of the four main ghosts are completed, a way of ordering them suggests itself. In this scheme, parts of the "ghost country" follow the order of ghosts of the east, of the north, of the center, of the south, and of the west; this is different from the convention of referring to the east first, followed by the west, the south, the north, and the center, and naturally there is allegorical significance in this.[41]

Li Ang, as usual, does not spell out this "allegorical significance," and she mentions only the habit of referring to directions in everyday Chinese. My reading, however, suggests that we may also bring the conventional ordering of *bardo* teaching to bear on Li Ang's stories.

In *The Tibetan Book of the Dead*, the five parts of the mandala are not differentiated by superiority but only ordered in terms of time. There is a general movement from this life to the next, and the better prepared or disposed the deceased are, the sooner they attain liberation from rebirth. As time progresses, the hope of liberation becomes, in principle, dimmer and dimmer for the unprepared. Li Ang, of course, is not adopting this scheme in a simple way, so there are substantial differences between her pseudo-mandala and the Tibetan model. It is easy, nevertheless, to find a progression here too, at least a partial one, again not in terms of merit or superiority, but in terms of a compassionate return to the world.

On this account, the ghost of the first story begins the series by immediately achieving liberation, but she cannot simply remain in its isolated self-enjoyment, which would again lead to a disruptive void on the "other side" and a relapse into shame. There are two ways to open up the "happiness outside history" and allow human time to be affected by happiness. The conventional way consists in turning shame into guilt, appealing to an authority in the settling of accounts and the restoring of equilibrium whenever it is disturbed. The psychoanalytic way consists in adopting shame as pointing to the interconnectivity of singularities, a basis for a rebuilt symbolic world mindful of the unknown.

The conventional solution is clearly figured in the second story, the story of the north, in which a vengeful ghost is sent back to China following the intervention of local shamans and deities to restore a balance of interests. A female shaman, reportedly descended from Babuza witches, is possessed by the ghost and, disclosing the ghost's story in a series of theatrical performances, acts out a rape that converts the dances of the first story into public show. Eventually, female communication and embodied intensity yield to hierarchical authority, and a male deity, originally from China, has to forcefully deliver a verdict to stop the haunting. In sum, the deviance of the subprefect of the first story is corrected by restoring the integrity of administrative authority, from out of this world if necessary. The spectrality of this solution is indicated by the fourth story, the story of the south, where countless unvindicated victims, collectively called Cousin of the Screwpines (Lintou Jie 林投姐), return as ghosts to haunt the living. This is the shortest story among the five, presumably because it covers well-trodden ground, being included to pay homage to innumerable traditional stories of female ghosts.[42]

Without denying the partial effectivity of a masculine elaboration of ethical knowledge, a different solution is offered in the other stories, that is, stories of the horizontal axis. Here the first story is continued by the third (ghost of the center) and the fifth (ghost of the west). I cannot discuss these stories fully, but will sketch a few important themes connecting the three stories.

We have seen how, in the first story, the shedding of the spectral many leads to the emergence of the one true orifice. This One is echoed by a shift in the narrator's naming of the protagonists. Typically, a protagonist begins as a cluster of multiple names bearing alternate storylines in a way resembling hypertextual writing. Except for the Cousin of the Screwpines, however, each cluster of hypertextual ghosts gradually merge into one as their separation from the world of the living deepens, eventually dropping this-worldly appellations, being called now generically "the ghost" or "the female ghost" (女子鬼魂). This folding of the multiple into one is the external reflection of the shedding of shameful signifiers in the first story, and indicates that the stories are intended as paths leading to knowledge in the presymbolic unknown, figured as the world of the dead who have no signifiers to count with.

In the story of the center, this experience of the presymbolic undergoes a fully elaborated process of tutelage in multiple forms of knowledge. The titular ghost Yuehong/Yuxuan 月紅/月玄(璇), having killed herself after a shaming incident to protect her virginal reputation, begins to learn the pleasures of sex by reading old books hidden in the family library, by watching people of the lower classes do "it," and by comparing the two. After some time, she is able to upload herself, as it were, into the bodies of living lovers. Eventually she expands this tutelage in eros by learning to collect and organize historical information gathered from overheard conversations, then writing it down on buildings around Sky Blind Street (不見天), the central business hub of the town. In the climactic scene, when the covers of the street are ordered by the Japanese authorities to be demolished, the ghost removes her clothes and initiates a coital act in which she enlarges her body to embrace and "enter" the covered street.

Here the coinciding of knowledge and eros follows the model set up by the erotic dance of the first story, but this time, the liberation occurs somewhere closer to the human world, since the ghost, by refusing to leave, is apparently going to die a second death, to be extinguished when the old street goes down as if she were living. The text insists on the fact that the fatal coitus cannot be explained by a balanced consideration of interests: the ghost could have easily left the place and found shelter elsewhere, after which, presumably, she could restore the historical records from her memory.[43] In other words, the ghost enters liberation by extinction as a chosen act of honor and commitment, of fidelity to the fact that, for her, knowledge and eros have become one. The records are done not for neutral transmission of knowledge but as fleshly work, the inseparable outgrowth of her experiential body.[44] Similarly, Sky Blind Street is not simply a shelter from light but a place in which she grew up (and grew dead) and with which she fell in love. In this way, the pursuit of knowledge is inflected into the heroics of singular love, the foregrounding of a *sinthome* as the real heart of her symptomatic act of writing.

In Lacanian psychoanalysis, *sinthome*, an old spelling of *symptôme* (symptom) picked up from Rabelais by Lacan in the mid-1970s, refers to a symptomatic formation beyond analysis, a point of unanalyzability. In this new understanding of the symptom, analysis ends when the subject can live with or even enjoy or make use of the *sinthome* after troubling symptoms are dissolved. A *sinthome* cannot be interpreted as a set of messages from the unconscious, but consists in a "ciphering" that involves consciousness in a singular way as reciprocally imbricated in the unconscious.[45] In other words, the *sinthome* instances a knotting or "constellating" of the conscious and the unconscious, a coming to terms with floating foreignness.

In the sense of becoming such a *sinthome*, the ghost of the center foregoes the discourse of awakening but continues the mode of dreaming "from within a dream," of the straddling of the dream state and the awakened state, or the symptom and the cure. By refusing to leave Sky Blind Street, the ghost enacts a deeper refusal to yield on her desire as her *sinthome*, now removed from the world of analyzable discourses but made intelligible for inhabitants of the world of spectral knowledge by the eroticized offering of a new, sharable world of *jouissance*.

RETURNING TO THE UNARY TRAIT

When Yuehong/Yuexuan's writings are destroyed as Sky Blind Street goes down, their singularity undergoes a change. The text specifically describes the ghost's initial decision to forego the well-ordered, blocky regular script and undertake this work in the "one brush" or "one stroke" (*yibi* 一笔) cursive style, thus invoking the unary trait as the beginning of singular writing.[46] We have seen how the third story doubles this unary trait, a means of technical or stylistic fixation, with the more complex *sinthome* of the singular individual. Without denying fixation, the *sinthome* links the unary trait to the void or hole of signification, producing, at the limits of analyzability, a general sense of the translatability of the unknown.

Here the unary trait appears as a figure of the unwritten that remains after the erasure of the ghost historian's writings, a "littoral" trace, evoked by a lost oneness, that marks a hole in sense and knowledge. In Lacan's usage, the "littoral" refers to the shores or limits of the "streaming" of signifiers, thus also the trace or "trait" of singularity in significa-tion. Lacan compares this oneness of the littoral to the "singularity of the hand" that "crushes the universal" in Asian calligraphy, felt even by "a novice" in reading Chinese such as Lacan.[47] The littoral allows such singularity to retain a sense of presence after its erasure, allowing a piece of one's *jouissance* to be registered in psychic reality, "a trace of something that is primary and exceeds all the significations in play."[48] To feel the cursives of history, therefore, one does not need an account of the details of historical happenings: the diverse messages of this historical littering are necessarily subsumed in the oneness of a "letter," a singular fixing of the void into something beyond erasure.

In this sense, when writing is important enough, its erasure cannot but leave a hole in established knowledge, a cohering not only of the reality of its unknown, as evoked by the orifice of *jouissance* in the first story, but of the reality of the "edge of the hole" out-lined by the letter as littoral.[49] In much the same way, an ideogram in Chinese attains full singularity in expression as a non-arbitrary signifier only when the visual likeness it is originally based on is left behind. Such littoral writing "does not copy the signifier, but its language effects (*effets de langue*), what is forged from it by who speaks it."[50]

As the stories move from the center to the west on the horizontal axis, the littoral explicitly shifts back to its natural instance, the unary trait, but not without giving it a new sense. Appropriately, the discourse of the center, featuring Wisdom of the Sphere of Modes in *The Tibetan Book of the Dead*, also yields to the discourse of the west with its Wisdom of Fine Discriminations.[51] Yuechang/Yue'e 月嫦/月娥, the "traveling ghost" of the fifth and last story, having been murdered by her unfaithful Chinese husband, is the only one among the wronged protagonists who manages to complete an act of revenge. Her ability to make useful "discriminations" has been predicated on a sense of modest respect: as a tactful woman, she knows how to solve problems, to go *one more* step forward in her plan of revenge and also beyond. On the other hand, she also knows that, having become a symptom herself (because of her husband), she is a unary trait, that *one more* that is *no more than one*.[52] With the help of a geomancer who assumes great risk in interfering with fate, she crosses the strait and lands in China in pursuit of her husband. She then thanks and bids farewell to the geomancer, knowing that she has to do the rest by herself if she is to complete herself as "one stroke."

The story of the traveling ghost, however, does not end in the ghost's physical disappearance or extinction as in the earlier stories. By staying in the ghosts' world indefinitely, Yuechang/Yue'e is positioned closer to rebirth, not rebirth into the next life but a turning of afterlife into a shadow world fully inclusive of the world of the living. This is a long process lasting until the age of airplanes; and the text devotes a great deal of space to describing how, in order to facilitate the formation of the ghost's new world, a new kind of modesty is shown on the part of the living when they are faced with the world of spirits. Here respect for the unknown is no longer based on the authority of deities or the mediation of shamans. Rather, folk belief is traced to a more primitive moment, that of the discrimination of objects seen under the light of the unary trait.

Thus, in the beginning, a black umbrella is used by the geomancer to hide and protect the ghost while traveling. After her revenge, the ghost continues to use the black umbrella as a good hiding place, but begins to regard it as the place of her "primal life" (*benming* 本命).[53] Eventually, since she is always holding it whenever she is seen during the night, the umbrella becomes part of her "classic image."[54] She now engages in countless voyages for the pleasure of movement, and, since she is supposed to know if she would be safe on a ship, sailors recognize the umbrella as not only indicative of her presence but of a safe voyage. Some even deliberately prepare similar umbrellas as a way to lure her on board.

Thus the umbrella becomes a "fixation point," a "trait," not just a convenient hiding place. It allows the ghost to accumulate experience and knowledge by always making *one more* trip or taking up *one more* form of travel. On the other hand, its repetition also gives her a place among the living as a signifier in the symbolic system, a way to always appear *one more* time as "a ghost" or "that ghost." We have seen that the same productiveness led to shameless searches for supposed knowledge (of lottery numbers) in the first story. Here, on the contrary, people cannot turn the ghost into a deity because she insists on abiding in playful movement as a means without end, making voyages without leaving the ship on arrival, appearing to the living without making use of their belief, and attending rites of deliverance just for fun.

The ghost's free play is figured in her pronouncing at various points that she is the ocean, the mainland, and the island. These identifications follow from her free movement, which begins with her ability to connect herself to the minimal umbrella. The text gives a very precise account of this breaking, indeed littoralizing of claustrophobic space: after using the umbrella for the practical purpose of revenge and as a means of continuing to "live," she has to learn the ability to enter and leave the umbrella by using a mantra the geomancer taught her. This entering and leaving of the minimal space within the umbrella, in a sense also the minimal distinction or "discrimination" between *fort* and *da*, constitutes the initial mindfulness of the littoral, the beginning of a unary trait that will be extended to cover all her later trips and movements.

The unary trait is the support of proliferating signifiers, but it is itself devoid of signification. The unique insight of psychoanalytic theory shows this emptiness and this purposelessness as not only a way to relate to one's *jouissance* but an opening onto the unknown, an ignorance that enables knowledge. Repetition introduced by the unary trait reveals knowledge as both a "means of *jouissance*" and a "loss of *jouissance*," a meeting with limits and an evoking of the beyond.[55]

The story of the traveling ghost gives an appropriate ending to the national allegory, proposed in the Preface, bearing on Taiwan's future as a "ghost country."[56] Here the soteriology of the *sinthome* yields to but also repeats itself in the productivity of the political, exploring the possibilities of a free subject, free not only from shame and oppression but also from the complacency of spectral knowledge. With its constant reminders that the productivity of the unary trait comes from the translatability between the limits of sense and the void of ignorance, such a form of identity can be clearly distinguished from one based on the master signifier (S_1) or on assumed full knowledge (S_2).

FROM TRANSGRESSION TO MODESTY

Considering Li Ang's notoriety for aggressive verbalizations of all aspects of the sexual act in her works, it is not surprising that transgression and subversion are proposed as the focus of the stories of *Seeing Ghosts*.[57] Indeed, Li Ang herself refers to feminist Ueno Chizuko's comment on women virtually becoming ghosts if they dare to "transgress."[58] One may focus on how the text scrutinizes the female body and point to a "carnival of carnality" in which great vitality is released to blast away the walls of decorous conduct and the imperfections of the physical body.[59] Or one may call attention to larger issues such as the need to "overturn" the "binary oppositions" and the ineradicable violence of colonial writing.[60] Indeed, one can easily argue that different kinds of transgression are allegorical reflections of each other, evoking a general sense of converging lines of reading without much room for variation.

It is true that transgression often informs women's acts in *Seeing Ghosts* and in Li's many other works, insofar as these women seem to enjoy acting in such a way as to break common gender expectations. More generally, transgression also provides a frame for the usual understanding of the author's career as one characterized by transgressive or subversive writing. Thus David Der-wei Wang describes Li Ang as one who "uses the rash words and invective that spew [i.e., should have spewed] from our mouths to reveal thoughts and fears we are ashamed to mention."[61] Wang is actually referring to the shame incurred when one confronts an "unspeakable world of sex," but would probably not object when Eric Lin, quoting Wang's comment to explain *Seeing Ghosts*, shifts effortlessly from thoughts and inhibitions about sex to transgressive thinking and knowing in general. Thus the state of sexual inhibition is easily conflated with the state of cognitive deprivation: "isn't Li's use of 'rash words and invective' to discuss historical issues a means to make us see our tendency to avoid looking squarely at this island's turbid past?"[62]

Such metaphorical association of knowledge with eros captures some of the driving impulses at work in Li Ang's works. In general, however, it is not clear how the affective side of the association would work out: what would be the equivalent of a "shameless" knowing of sexual pleasure when it is reflected in thought and knowledge? One wonders, indeed, if such allegorizing readings might foster a readerly desire for the cognitive taming of the sensual, or satisfy a social need for making bad women useful for the public (as a teacher of the values of transgression). What we have seen in *Seeing Ghosts* points precisely to the opposite: knowledge and social discourse can, without blame, be made useful for those bad women who desire to clear their bad names and to vindicate their goodness.

In *Seeing Ghosts*, transgression comes mainly from negative characters, such as the subprefect who abuses his power and shames his imperial mandate, or the husband who murders his wife after embezzling funds from their family business. The transgression of sexual decorum on the part of the women, if present at all, pales beside such literal assaults on life and civility. Subversion, likewise, comes mostly from casting doubt on the images of good male roles and the model stories of the male world; such subversion may not be very effective since it can always be argued that the deviating characters or cases are only exceptions. Again, we may always fall back on Li Ang's writing itself to find some good old transgression, but largely limited to the now routinized violation of verbal decorum, or the kind of technical half-subverting attested when, for example, Li Ang refers to her ordering of the cardinal directions as "subverting" conventional usage and to her stories as "creative," namely not constrained by the conventional ghost story.

Among the main protagonists, none can be said to have subverted anything important, unless one wishes to cite the kind of unforgiving sexual propriety that has led one of our protagonists to suicide. Such propriety, with a variation addressed specifically to writing women, is no doubt still subscribed to by many in Taiwan today, but no longer articulated with an affective intensity that answers to the domain of shame and guilt behind the façade of the master signifier. As demonstrated above, Li Ang has moved ahead to target something far less spectral than, and closer to the roots of, such moral knowledge. Forms of spectral knowledge come and go, but the roots animating them are common, for example, to the oppressors of the Qing dynasty and to the modern fortune seekers of the first story of *Seeing Ghosts*. Such roots are still subject to change, but, not being part of the work of signifiers, cannot be transgressed. Li Ang's move might easily be overlooked if we forget the great affective weight laid down in the first story, that is, the weight of shame and humiliation. A ghost bearing such affective weight would ponder revenge, but would not think immediately of transgressing public values.

The distinction lies no doubt in the distance of public discourse from embodied affectivity residing in the real. From a psychoanalytic point of view, legitimation of transgression by way of knowledge and truth, of courage in "knowing thyself" or "being your own master," is part of an inherited discourse of modernity that Lacan has described as the "modernized master's discourse."[63] The spectrality of such mastery is revealed by its forgetting of the impossibility of full knowledge. Transgression, in this context, pertains to the question of guilt, of a reading of how one is judged. By contrast, *Seeing Ghosts* begins with the more primitive question of shame, of the affectivity of seeing, as expounded in psychoanalysis:

> guilt is the effect on the subject of an Other that judges, thus of an Other that contains the values that the subject has supposedly transgressed. One would also claim that shame is related to an Other prior to the Other that judges, that it is

a primordial Other, not one that judges but instead one that only sees or lets be seen.[64]

Thus we may note that, when Wang mentions the feeling of being "ashamed," the context of verbal transgression clearly points to the judging of shame rather than shame per se: first one lives peacefully in shame, then, upon reading Li Ang, one is made to doubt if the reading makes one feel guilty of shamelessness, or, alternatively, if one should feel guilty of having been too ashamed. Similarly, it would be more plausible to describe the act of "looking squarely" at history as guiltless rather than free from shame, since cognitive taboos are supported by a judging Other.

It is certainly true that Li Ang's authorial act, here as elsewhere, is transgressive in placing itself provocatively in guilt. Post–martial law Taiwan, however, is very much a "society of enjoyment." When shamelessness has become the norm, transgression is becoming less and less effective as a way of provocation, for "even before we can assert our individuality through our resistance to the Norm, the Norm enjoins us in advance to resist, to violate, to go further and further."[65] Yang Tsui 楊翠 is perhaps more to the point in describing *Seeing Ghosts* as a personal project in self-cultivation and in the working through of pathology.[66] But one has to go one step further and see that such working through has to be reflected into, to interface with, the interpersonal and the political, especially when the pathology itself comes from social determinations. In a world filled with threats of sacrificial violence and landscapes of horror and fear, liberation has to be liberation both from and of such a world.[67]

Modesty, as a mode of knowledge, allows the unary trait, the "littoral" line, to mediate between this cacophony and the spectral self, to inject the lack of harmony into the latter, not to further its spectrality but to produce some substance by giving form to the void and to ignorance, pointing to a higher oneness defined by the limits of sense and making possible both a ciphering of the cacophony in the spectral self and a tarrying with the readability of spectrality from within spectrality. This is why we may need to take Li Ang more seriously than as an unruly transgressor at large in permissive times. Using insights from psychoanalytic theory but aiming at their ghostlier hesitations rather than the standard paths of "analyzability," I have described Li Ang's project, also a ghostly project, as one that problematizes shame and places self-knowledge in modesty. Beyond *Seeing Ghosts*, there may be a larger movement, not exactly a movement from a "dark" to a "bright" Li Ang, but one from transgression to a profounder thinking of modesty, from a politics of liberation to one of the translatability of foreignness.[68] Such translatability may yet prove to be indispensable for imagining rebirth within the *bardo* state of our contemporary life.

NOTES

Epigraphs are taken from Joan Copjec, "May '68, The Emotional Month," in *Lacan: The Silent Partners*, ed. Slavoj Žižek (London: Verso, 2006), 111, and Nārgārjuna, "Seventy

Verses on Emptiness," trans. Chr. Lindtner, in *Master of Wisdom: Writings of the Buddhist Master Nārgārjuna*, trans. Chr. Lindtner, rev. ed. (Berkeley: Dharma Publishing, 1997), 115.

1. Jacques Lacan, "Lituraterre," trans. Dany Nobus, *Continental Philosophy Review* 46 (2013): 333; see also Lacan's Seminar of 12 May 1971 in "On a Discourse That Might Not Be a Semblance, The Seminar of Jacques Lacan, Book XVIII," trans. Cormac Gallapher, unpublished typescript, VII, 17.

2. Jacques Lacan, "Identification: The Seminar of Jacques Lacan, Book IX (1961–1962)," trans. Cormac Gallapher, unpublished typescript, V, 1.

3. The quote comes from Dany Nobus and Malcolm Quinn, *Knowing Nothing, Staying Stupid: Elements for a Psychoanalytic Epistemology* (London: Routledge, 2005), 109.

4. Karatani Kōjin 柄谷行人, "Nihon seishin bunseki—Akutagawa Ryūnosuke 'Kamigami no bishō'" 日本精神分析—芥川龍之介『神神の微笑』 [Psychoanalysis in Japan: On Akutagawa Ryūnosuke's "The Smile of the Gods"], in *Nihon seishin bunseki* 日本精神分析 [Psychoanalysis in Japan] (Tokyo: Bungei shunjū, 2002), 76.

5. Éric Laurent, "Symptom and Discourse," in *Jacques Lacan and the Other Side of Psychoanalysis: Reflections on* Seminar XVII, ed. Justin Clemens and Russell Grigg (Durham: Duke University Press, 2006), 251.

6. Jacques Lacan, *The Other Side of Psychoanalysis: The Seminar of Jacques Lacan, Book XVII*, trans. Russell Grigg, ed. Jacques Alain Miller (New York: W. W. Norton, 2007), 207.

7. Kazushige Shingu, "Freud, Lacan and Japan," in *Perversion and Modern Japan: Psychoanalysis, Literature, Culture*, ed. Nina Cornyetz and J. Keith Vincent (London: Routledge, 2010), 265–266. The term "unary trait" (*einziger Zug*) comes from Freud, but is also linked by Lacan to "one stroke" (*yihua* 一畫) in Shitao's 石濤 theory of painting; see Èric Laurent, "The Purloined Letter and the Tao of Psychoanalysis," in *The Later Lacan: An Introduction*, ed. Véronique Voruz and Bogdan Wolf (Albany: State University of New York Press, 2007), 40–41.

8. Shingu, "Freud," 266.

9. Lacan, *Other Side*. For introductory accounts of the four discourses see Slavoj Žižek, "Four Discourses, Four Subjects," in *Cogito and the Unconscious*, ed. Slavoj Žižek (Durham: Duke University Press, 1998), 74–81; Alexandre Leupin, *Lacan Today: Psychoanalysis, Science, Religion* (New York: Other Press, 2004), chap. 3. The unary trait is linked to the signifier as "the simplest form of mark, which properly speaking is the origin of the signifier." Lacan, *Other Side*, 46.

10. Adrian Johnston, "Lacanian Theory Has Legs: Structures Marching in the Streets," *South Atlantic Review* 72.2 (2007): 102.

11. This is a constant theme in Slavoj Žižek's work. See, for example, *The Ticklish Subject: The Absent Centre of Political Ontology* (London: Verso, 1999), 322–334. See also Todd McGowan, *The End of Satisfaction? Jacques Lacan and the Emerging Society of Enjoyment* (Albany: State University of New York Press, 2004). Despite its early date, the revisionary work of late Lacan continues for many to offer prognostic insights. Juliet Flower MacCannell, for one, thinks it "is of extreme importance to us today"; see "The Real Imaginary: Lacan's Joyce," *S: Journal of the Jan Van Eyck Circle for Lacanian Ideology Critique* 1 (2008): 57.

12. For examples of "historicizing" readers, see Jacques-Alain Miller, "On Shame," and Slavoj Žižek, "*Objet a* in Social Links," in *Jacques Lacan and the Other Side of Psychoanalysis: Reflections on* Seminar XVII, ed. Justin Clemens and Russell Grigg, 11–28 and 107–128. Taking a cue from Lacan's 1972 proposal of a fifth discourse, that of the

capitalist, Levi R. Bryant argues that this fifth discourse is actually the first member of a second set of four discourses, and that this second quartet is actually what animates Žižek's reading of Lacan's original scheme. Bryant lists four more sets as not yet used but logically possible variations; see his "Žižek's New Universe of Discourse: Politics and the Discourse of the Capitalist," *International Journal of Žižek Studies* 2.4 (2008). For an explicit attempt to refute this historicizing "vogue," see Nobus and Quinn, *Knowing Nothing*, 118–137.

13. This is the point made by Dany Nobus in his "Illiterature," in *Re-inventing the Symptom: Essays on the Final Lacan*, ed. Luke Thurston (New York: Other Press, 2002), 36.

14. Nobus and Quinn, *Knowing Nothing*, 2.

15. Nobus and Quinn, *Knowing Nothing*, 119–120.

16. Lacan himself compared the analyst with the Zen master. See Nobus and Quinn, *Knowing Nothing*, 31–32.

17. The Chinese title of *Seeing Ghosts, Kandejian de gui* (看得見的鬼), is usually translated as "Visible Ghosts," but "Seeing Ghosts" is preferred here. This rendering can be found in an early review from Taiwan; see Eric Lin, "*Seeing Ghosts*," trans. Scott Williams, *Taiwan Panorama* 29.6 (2004), retrieved July 2, 2014 from http://www.taiwan-panorama.com/en/show_issue.php?id=2004693061ooe.txt. As Yenna Wu points out, the title can be read in two ways: "ghosts that can be seen," and "ghosts that can see"; Yenna Wu, "(Dis)Embodied Subversion: The Mountain-Pass Ghost in Li Ang's *Visible Ghosts* (*Kandejian de gui*)," in *Li Ang's Visionary Challenges to Gender, Sex, and Politics*, ed. Yenna Wu (Lanham, MD: Lexington Books, 2014), 149. For reasons that will become obvious in the following, the second reading is of paramount importance. Indeed, some acts performed by the ghosts imply their invisibility. In spite of numerous reported sightings, for example, the ghost of the second story is directly seen and heard only through a medium.

18. The protagonists of *Seeing Ghosts* are typically given double or multiple names, implicitly and sometimes explicitly accompanied by alternate storylines. This naming device will be discussed below.

19. Li Ang 李昂, *Kandejian de gui* 看得見的鬼 [Seeing ghosts] (Taipei: Lianhe wenxue, 2004), 21. This text is referred to throughout as *Seeing Ghosts*. Unless otherwise noted, all translations from this text are mine.

20. Li Ang, *Seeing Ghosts*, 42.

21. W. Y. Evans-Wentz, ed., *The Tibetan Book of the Dead*, trans. W. Y. Evans-Wentz, 3rd ed. (London: Oxford University Press, 1960), 101–118.

22. Evans-Wentz, *Tibetan Book*, 109–110, renders this wisdom as "Mirror-like Wisdom." The original term in Sanskrit, *ādarśa jñāna*, is usually rendered as *dayuanjing zhi* 大圓鏡智 in Chinese texts. For a brief account of the five wisdoms in Indian Buddhism, see Priya Ananda and Ajith Prasad, "Models of Personality in Buddhist Psychology," in *Foundations of Indian Psychology*, vol. 1: *Theories and Concepts*, ed. R. M. Matthijs Cornelissen, Girishwar Misra, and Suneet Varma (New Delhi: Dorling Kindersley India, 2011), 162–165.

23. Evans-Wentz, *Tibetan Book*, 105n.

24. Li Ang, *Seeing Ghosts*, 25.

25. Li Ang, *Seeing Ghosts*, 28.

26. Lacan, *Other Side*, 192–193.

27. For a discussion of Lacan's usage of *honte* and *pudeur*, both often translated into English as "shame," see Adrian Johnston and Catherine Malabou, *Self and Emotional Life: Philosophy, Psychoanalysis, and Neuroscience* (New York: Columbia University Press, 2013), 157–161.

28. Li Ang, *Seeing Ghosts*, 37.

29. Simon Critchley and Jamieson Webster, *The Hamlet Doctrine* (London: Verso, 2013), 229.

30. Joan Copjec, "The Descent into Shame," *Studio Art Magazine* 168 (2007), in *Studio Art Magazine: Texts, Abstracts, Excerpts*, retrieved July 8, 2014 from http:// holyfly.com/studio/pdf/friezeP1-82.pdf, 62.

31. Jacques-Alain Miller, "On Shame," in *Jacques Lacan and the Other Side of Psychoanalysis: Reflections on* Seminar XVII, ed. Justin Clemens and Russell Grigg, 13.

32. N. Robert Glass, "The *Tibetan Book of the Dead*: Deleuze and the Positivity of the Second Light," in *Deleuze and Religion*, ed. Mary Bryden (London: Routledge, 2001), 66 and 72–73.

33. Li Ang, *Seeing Ghosts*, 40.

34. These are examples of the "formative effects" of gestalt images given in Jacques Lacan, "The Mirror Image as Formative of the I Function as Revealed in Psychoanalytic Experience," in *Écrits: The First Complete Edition in English*, trans. Bruce Fink (New York: Norton, 2006), 77.

35. Hubert Nearman, trans., *Shōbōgenzō: The Treasure House of the Eye of the True Teaching, a Trainee's Translation of Great Master Dōgen's Spiritual Masterpiece* (Mount Shasta, CA: Shasta Abbey Press, 2007), 508. Translation modified.

36. Chakravarthi Ram-Prasad, *Indian Philosophy and the Consequences of Knowledge: Themes in Ethics, Metaphysics and Soteriology* (Aldershot, UK: Ashgate, 2007), 149.

37. Li Ang, *Seeing Ghosts*, 40–42.

38. There are ten cuts on *each* breast which shoot out lumps of flesh, then ten cuts on the lower body which fall off. Li Ang seems to have lost count of these body parts, or to wish to make some point, mentioning only "twenty cuts" in all "from around the body." See Li Ang, *Seeing Ghosts*, 31–32 and 41–42.

39. Li Ang, *Seeing Ghosts*, 40.

40. Darryl Cameron Sterk, "The Return of the Vanishing Formosan: Disturbing the Discourse of National Domestication as the Literary Fate of the Aboriginal Maiden in Postwar Taiwanese Film and Fiction," PhD diss. (University of Toronto, 2009). Sterk seems to have softened his position a bit recently, now also referring to freedom from "the shackles of history"; see Darryl Sterk, "The Spirit of Deer Town and the Redemption of Li Ang's Uncanny Literary Home," *Chinese Literature Today* 2.1 (2011): 27.

41. Li Ang, *Seeing Ghosts*, 238–239.

42. Li Ang, *Seeing Ghosts*, 239.

43. Li Ang, *Seeing Ghosts*, 139.

44. The ghost writes with her whole body: "As if the blood, and everything contained in it, has entered her body, lodged in her circulatory vessels, becoming permanent inscriptions of memory. Thus the female ghost does nothing more than raise her hand . . . and words come out of the end of the giant bamboo or shell ginger twig, spontaneously forming blood-hued script"; in this way "every word and every sentence is connected to her heart and her blood; all are from her soul." Li Ang, *Seeing Ghosts*, 123 and 127.

45. See Èric Laurent, "Three Enigmas: Meaning, Signification, Jouissance," in *The Later Lacan*, ed. Voruz and Wolf, 125–126; and Jacques-Alain Miller, "Joyce with Lacan," in *The Literary Lacan: From Literature to Lituraterre and Beyond*, ed. Santanu Biswas (Calcutta: Seagull Books, 2012), 4.

46. Li Ang, *Seeing Ghosts*, 117.

47. Lacan, "Lituraterre," 331.

48. Laurent, "Purloined Letter," 33. Laurent also discusses Lacan's interest in Chinese culture as shown in his reference to calligraphy here; see 37 and 40–45.

49. Lacan, "Lituraterre," 329.

50. Lacan, "Lituraterre," 332 (translator's brackets).

51. The Wisdom of the Sphere of Modes (*dharmadhātu jñāna*) and the Wisdom of Fine Discriminations (*Pratyavekṣaṇā jñāna*) are usually called in Chinese texts *fajie zhi* 法界智 and *miaoguancha zhi* 妙觀察智. See Evans-Wentz, *Tibetan Book*, 106–107; Ananda and Prasad, "Models of Personality," 164–165.

52. For an explication of Lacan's distinction of "one more" and "not more than one," see Laurent, "Purloined Letter," 37–38.

53. Li Ang, *Seeing Ghosts*, 215–216.

54. Li Ang, *Seeing Ghosts*, 224, 227, and 235.

55. Lacan, *Other Side*, 48.

56. Li Ang, *Seeing Ghosts*, 7–8.

57. See, for example, Yenna Wu, "(Dis)Embodied Subversion," 145–146; Chia-Rong Wu, "Encountering Spectral Traces: Ghost Narratives in Chinese America and Taiwan," PhD diss. (University of Illinois at Urbana-Champaign, 2010), 160. Fan Mingru 范銘如, "Lingyan xiang-kan: Dangdai Taiwan xiaoshuo de gui/difang" 另眼相看：當代台灣小說的鬼/地方 [Seeing with other eyes: Ghosts/ghostly places in contemporary Taiwanese fiction], *Taiwan wenxue yanjiu xuebao* 台灣文學研究學報 [Journal of Taiwan literary studies] 2 (2006): 124–129, also stresses the transgressing or "overcoming" of spatial regimentation in all the stories.

58. Quoted in Yenna Wu, "(Dis)Embodied Subversion," 146.

59. Hao Yu-hsiang 郝譽翔, "Guisheng jiujiu de guozu yuyan: Li Ang, *Kandejian de gui*" 鬼聲啾啾的國族寓言：李昂《看得見的鬼》 [A national allegory of howling ghosts: Li Ang's *Seeing Ghosts*], in *Da xugou shidai: Dangdai Taiwan wenxue guangpu* 大虛構時代：當代台灣文學光譜 [Age of the great illusion: The literary spectrum of contemporary Taiwan] (Taipei: Lianhe wenxue, 2008), 212; Yenna Wu, "(Dis)Embodied Subversion," 151.

60. Chien Yu-yen 簡玉妍, "Lun Li Ang, *Kandejian de gui*, de houzhimin lunshu" 論李昂《看得見的鬼》的後殖民論述 [On postcolonial discourse in Li Ang's *Seeing Ghosts*], *Zhanghua wenxian* 彰化文獻 [Zhanghua review] 15 (2010): 143–145.

61. David Der-wei Wang 王德威, "Xulun: Xing, chouwen, yu meixue zhengzhi" 序論：性、醜聞、與美學政治 [Introduction: Sex, scandal, and the politics of aesthetics], in Li Ang 李昂, *Beigang xianglu renren cha* 北港香爐人人插 [All sticks are welcome in the censer of Beigang] (Taipei: Maitian, 1997), 12; quoted in Lin, "*Seeing Ghosts*."

62. Wang, "Xulun," 12; Lin, "*Seeing Ghosts*."

63. Lacan, *Other Side*, 35.

64. Miller, "On Shame," 13.

65. Slavoj Žižek, *The Puppet and the Dwarf: The Perverse Core of Christianity* (Cambridge: MIT Press, 2003), 56.

66. Yang Tsui 楊翠, "Mojie yu guiguo jiaofeng zhi yu: Lun Song Zelai, *Xuese bianfu jianglin de chengshi*, yu Li Ang, *Kandejian de gui*, zhong de zhengzhi yu xingbie" 魔界與鬼國交鋒之域：論宋澤萊《血色蝙蝠降臨的城市》與李昂《看得見的鬼》中的政治與性別 [In the contest zone between the demons and the ghosts: On politics and gender in Song Zelai's *City Where the Blood-Red Bat Descended* and Li Ang's *Seeing Ghosts*], in *Zhanghua wenxue da lunshu* 彰化文學大論述 [The great pursuit of Zhanghua literature], ed. Lin Ming-teh 林明德 et al. (Taipei, Wunan, 2007), 454.

67. For a reading of such threats and landscapes in Li Ang's "sinister regionalism" see Chen Wei Lin 陳惠齡, "Lun Li Ang xiaoshuo zhong Lucheng xiangtu de yizhi shuxie"

論李昂小說中鹿城鄉土的異質書寫 [The heterogeneous writing of Deer Town local lore in Li Ang's fiction], *Danjiang zhongwen xuebao* 淡江中文學報 [Tamkang journal of Chinese literature] 24 (2011): 131–162.

68. The dark and bright versions of Li Ang are explained in Li Ang, "Dark Li Ang versus Bright Li Ang: A Self-Interview," *Chinese Literature Today* 2.1 (2011): 14–23.

WORKS CITED

Ananda, Priya, and Ajith Prasad. "Models of Personality in Buddhist Psychology." In *Foundations of Indian Psychology*. Vol. 1: *Theories and Concepts*. Ed. R. M. Matthijs Cornelissen, Girishwar Misra, and Suneet Varma. New Delhi: Dorling Kindersley India, 2011. 146–169.

Bryant, Levi R. "Žižek's New Universe of Discourse: Politics and the Discourse of the Capitalist." *International Journal of Žižek Studies* 2.4 (2008). Retrieved June 18, 2014 from http://zizekstudies.org/index.php/ijzs/article/view/163.

Chen Wei Lin 陳惠齡. "Lun Li Ang xiaoshuo zhong Lucheng xiangtu de yizhi shuxie" 論李昂小說中鹿城鄉土的異質書寫 [The heterogeneous writing of Deer Town local lore in Li Ang's fiction]. *Danjiang zhongwen xuebao* 淡江中文學報 [Tamkang journal of Chinese literature] 24 (2011): 131–162.

Chien Yu-yen 簡玉妍. "Lun Li Ang, *Kandejian de gui*, de houzhimin lunshu" 論李昂《看得見的鬼》的後殖民論述 [On postcolonial discourse in Li Ang's *Seeing Ghosts*]. *Zhanghua wenxian* 彰化文獻 [Zhanghua review] 15 (2010): 132–146.

Copjec, Joan. "May '68, The Emotional Month." In *Lacan: The Silent Partners*. Ed. Slavoj Žižek. London: Verso, 2006. 90–114.

Copjec, Joan. "The Descent into Shame." *Studio Art Magazine* 168 (2007). *Studio Art Magazine: Texts, Abstracts, Excerpts*. Retrieved July 8, 2014 from http://holyfly.com/studio/pdf/friezeP1-82.pdf. 59–80.

Critchley, Simon, and Jamieson Webster. *The Hamlet Doctrine*. London: Verso, 2013.

Evans-Wentz, W. Y., ed. *The Tibetan Book of the Dead*. Trans. W. Y. Evans-Wentz. 3rd ed. London: Oxford University Press, 1960.

Fan Mingru 范銘如. "Lingyan xiangkan: Dangdai Taiwan xiaoshuo de gui/difang" 另眼相看：當代台灣小說的鬼/地方 [Seeing with other eyes: Ghosts/ghostly places in contemporary Taiwanese fiction]. *Taiwan wenxue yanjiu xuebao* 台灣文學研究學報 [Journal of Taiwan literary studies] 2 (2006): 115–130.

Glass, N. Robert. "*The Tibetan Book of the Dead*: Deleuze and the Positivity of the Second Light." In *Deleuze and Religion*. Ed. Mary Bryden. London: Routledge, 2001. 65–75.

Hao Yu-hsiang 郝譽翔. "Guisheng jiujiu de guozu yuyan: Li Ang, *Kandejian de gui*" 鬼聲啾啾的國族寓言：李昂《看得見的鬼》 [A national allegory of howling ghosts: Li Ang's *Seeing Ghosts*]. *Da xugou shidai: Dangdai Taiwan wenxue guangpu* 大虛構時代：當代台灣文學光譜 [Age of the great illusion: The literary spectrum of contemporary Taiwan]. Taipei: Lianhe wenxue, 2008. 211–213.

Johnston, Adrian. "Lacanian Theory Has Legs: Structures Marching in the Streets." *South Atlantic Review* 72.2 (2007): 99–105.

Johnston, Adrian, and Catherine Malabou. *Self and Emotional Life: Philosophy, Psychoanalysis, and Neuroscience*. New York: Columbia University Press, 2013.

Karatani Kōjin 柄谷行人. "Nihon seishin bunseki: Akutagawa Ryūnosuke 'Kamigami no bishō'" 日本精神分析—芥川龍之介『神神の微笑』 [Psychoanalysis in Japan: On

Akutagawa Ryūnosuke's "The Smile of the Gods"]. In *Nihon seishin bunseki* 日本精神分析 [Psychoanalysis in Japan]. Tokyo: Bungei shunjū, 2002. 55–105.

Lacan, Jacques. "On a Discourse That Might Not Be a Semblance: The Seminar of Jacques Lacan, Book XVIII." Trans. Cormac Gallapher. Unpublished typescript.

Lacan, Jacques. "Identification: The Seminar of Jacques Lacan, Book IX (1961–1962)." Trans. Cormac Gallapher. Unpublished typescript.

Lacan, Jacques. "The Mirror Image as Formative of the I Function as Revealed in Psychoanalytic Experience." In *Écrits: The First Complete Edition in English*. Trans. Bruce Fink. New York: Norton, 2006. 75–81.

Lacan, Jacques. *The Other Side of Psychoanalysis: The Seminar of Jacques Lacan, Book XVII*. Trans. Russell Grigg. Ed. Jacques Alain Miller. New York: W. W. Norton, 2007.

Lacan, Jacques. "Lituraterre." Trans. Dany Nobus. *Continental Philosophy Review* 46 (2013): 327–334.

Laurent, Éric. "Symptom and Discourse." In *Jacques Lacan and the Other Side of Psychoanalysis: Reflections on* Seminar XVII. Ed. Justin Clemens and Russell Grigg. Durham: Duke University Press, 2006. 229–253.

Laurent, Éric. "The Purloined Letter and the Tao of Psychoanalysis." In *The Later Lacan: An Introduction*. Ed. Véronique Voruz and Bogdan Wolf. Albany: State University of New York Press, 2007. 25–52.

Laurent, Éric. "Three Enigmas: Meaning, Signification, Jouissance." In *The Later Lacan: An Introduction*. Ed. Véronique Voruz and Bogdan Wolf. Albany: State University of New York Press, 2007. 116–127.

Leupin, Alexandre. *Lacan Today: Psychoanalysis, Science, Religion*. New York: Other Press, 2004.

Li Ang 李昂. *Kandejian de gui* 看得見的鬼 [Seeing ghosts]. Taipei: Lianhe wenxue, 2004.

Li Ang. "Dark Li Ang versus Bright Li Ang: A Self-Interview." *Chinese Literature Today* 2.1 (2011): 14–23.

Lin, Eric. "*Seeing Ghosts*." Trans. Scott Williams. *Taiwan Panorama* 29.6 (2004). Retrieved July 2, 2014 from http://www.taiwan-panorama.com/en/show_issue.php?id=200469306100e.txt.

MacCannell, Juliet Flower. "The Real Imaginary: Lacan's Joyce." *S: Journal of the Jan Van Eyck Circle for Lacanian Ideology Critique* 1 (2008): 46–57.

McGowan, Todd. *The End of Dissatisfaction? Jacques Lacan and the Emerging Society of Enjoyment*. Albany: State University of New York Press, 2004.

Miller, Jacques-Alain. "On Shame." In *Jacques Lacan and the Other Side of Psychoanalysis: Reflections on* Seminar XVII. Ed. Justin Clemens and Russell Grigg. Durham: Duke University Press, 2006. 11–28.

Miller, Jacques-Alain. "Joyce with Lacan." In *The Literary Lacan: From Literature to Lituraterre and Beyond*. Ed. Santanu Biswas. Calcutta: Seagull Books, 2012. 1–7.

Nārgārjuna. "Seventy Verses on Emptiness." Trans. Chr. Lindtner. In *Master of Wisdom: Writings of the Buddhist Master Nārgārjuna*. Trans. Chr. Lindtner. Rev. ed. Berkeley: Dharma Publishing, 1997. 94–119.

Nearman, Hubert, trans. *Shōbōgenzō: The Treasure House of the Eye of the True Teaching, a Trainee's Translation of Great Master Dōgen's Spiritual Masterpiece*. Mount Shasta, CA: Shasta Abbey Press, 2007.

Nobus, Dany. "Illiterature." *Re-inventing the Symptom: Essays on the Final Lacan*. Ed. Luke Thurston. New York: Other Press, 2002. 19–43.

Nobus, Dany, and Malcolm Quinn. *Knowing Nothing, Staying Stupid: Elements for a Psychoanalytic Epistemology.* London: Routledge, 2005.

Ram-Prasad, Chakravarthi. *Indian Philosophy and the Consequences of Knowledge: Themes in Ethics, Metaphysics and Soteriology.* Aldershot, UK: Ashgate, 2007.

Shingu, Kazushige. "Freud, Lacan and Japan." In *Perversion and Modern Japan: Psychoanalysis, Literature, Culture.* Ed. Nina Cornyetz and J. Keith Vincent. London: Routledge, 2010. 261–271.

Sterk, Darryl Cameron. "The Return of the Vanishing Formosan: Disturbing the Discourse of National Domestication as the Literary Fate of the Aboriginal Maiden in Postwar Taiwanese Film and Fiction." PhD diss., University of Toronto, 2009.

Sterk, Darryl Cameron. "The Spirit of Deer Town and the Redemption of Li Ang's Uncanny Literary Home." *Chinese Literature Today* 2.1 (2011): 24–30.

Wang, David Der-wei 王德威. "Xulun: Xing, chouwen, yu meixue zhengzhi" 序論: 性、醜聞、與美學政治 [Introduction: Sex, scandal, and the politics of aesthetics]. In Li Ang 李昂, *Beigang xianglu renren cha* 北港香爐人人插 [All sticks are welcome in the censer of Beigang]. Taipei: Maitian, 1997. 9–42.

Wu, Chia-Rong. "Encountering Spectral Traces: Ghost Narratives in Chinese America and Taiwan." PhD diss., University of Illinois at Urbana-Champaign, 2010.

Wu, Yenna. "(Dis)Embodied Subversion: The Mountain-Pass Ghost in Li Ang's *Visible Ghosts* (*Kandejian de gui*)." In *Li Ang's Visionary Challenges to Gender, Sex, and Politics.* Ed. Yenna Wu. Lanham, MD: Lexington Books, 2014. 145–165.

Yang Tsui 楊翠. "Mojie yu guiguo jiaofeng zhi yu: Lun Song Zelai, *Xuese bianfu jianglin de chengshi* yu Li Ang, *Kandejian de gui* zhong de zhengzhi yu xingbie." 魔界與鬼國交鋒之域：論宋澤萊《血色蝙蝠降臨的城市》與李昂《看得見的鬼》中的政治與性別 [In the contest zone between the demons and the ghosts: On politics and gender in Song Zelai's *City Where the Blood-Red Bat Descended* and Li Ang's *Seeing Ghosts*]. In *Zhanghua wenxue da lunshu* 彰化文學大論述 [The great pursuit of Zhanghua literature]. Ed. Lin Ming-teh 林明德 et al. Taipei: Wunan, 2007. 444–479.

Žižek, Slavoj. "Four Discourses, Four Subjects." In *Cogito and the Unconscious.* Ed. Slavoj Žižek. Durham: Duke University Press, 1998. 74–113.

Žižek, Slavoj. *The Ticklish Subject: The Absent Centre of Political Ontology.* London: Verso, 1999.

Žižek, Slavoj. *The Puppet and the Dwarf: The Perverse Core of Christianity.* Cambridge: MIT Press, 2003.

Žižek, Slavoj. "*Objet a* in Social Links." In *Jacques Lacan and the Other Side of Psychoanalysis: Reflections on Seminar XVII.* Ed. Justin Clemens and Russell Grigg. Durham: Duke University Press, 2006. 107–128.

CHAPTER 3.8

....

PASSION AND POLITICS
IN REVOLUTION

A Psychoanalytical Reading of Ding Ling

....

BAN WANG

IN an episode of Ding Ling's 丁玲 novella *Shanghai, Spring 1930* (1930 年春上海), activist and labor organizer Wang Wei is dating Mary. He loves Mary but disproves of her consumer habits, her vanity, and her bourgeois, extravagant lifestyle. He hopes that love between them will triumph over their differences and that her inclinations will someday be reconciled with his devotion to a broader horizon of revolutionary activity. One night in his reverie over Mary, literally a sleeping beauty, Wang Wei fantasizes that Mary will become sympathetic to his outlook and even join him: "Besides being in love, they could discuss many important questions, such as the world economy, politics, and how to liberate the laboring masses."[1] Instead of wanting to be an extravagantly dressed lady, Mary would prefer a coat of homespun cloth, which would "highlight her distinctive qualities even more" and radiate a different style of beauty. She would be strong, healthy, and slightly masculine but still retain "her original, seductive beauty" (149–150). Wang Wei falls in love with this dream image and wants to kiss her.

But love and revolution do not come together as bedfellows in this story. The lovers' parting of ways takes the most dramatic form, as Wang Wei plunges into revolution and participates in a street demonstration. When arrested by the police, he sees Mary walking, elegant and sated, shopping bags in hand, out of a glamorous department store.

This scenario concerns the familiar themes of love and revolution, sex and social commitment.[2] Critics argue that private love is forever at odds with political, collective movement. Wang Wei's dream of a beautiful woman devoted to politics will mar the elegant beauty of a modern lady à la Madame Bovary. Flamboyant, sexy, and beautiful, Mary in her seductive femininity symbolizes the new modern woman often associated with Shanghai—a classic femme fatale, ubiquitous in Ding Ling's early fiction. She embodies a new female personality that is, in Tani Barlow's words, "a bundle of

emotional conditions" and "fundamentally sexual" (27). In this view it is only natural that private, feminine desire and individual pursuits of sensuous gratification are
incompatible with political passion and hostile to the abstract, collective agenda.

In criticism of modern Chinese literature, the portrayal of a sexually promiscuous
woman with a libertarian lifestyle is frequently approached through the lens of psychoanalysis. Deploying the concepts of sex, the unconscious, repression, and desire,
this approach received much attention and became popular in China in the 1920s and
1930s.[3] It also resurfaced as one of the favored critical methodologies in the 1980s as
China moved toward a period of ideological relaxation. Rather than discuss the fate of
psychoanalytical criticism, however, I attempt to follow Wang Wei's dream by showing
how love as a form of libidinal life force or passion can have access to broader social
horizons. Mary likes Wang Wei not simply out of love but also because of a "boundless
new hope for life and an energy she had never experienced before" (148). But psychoanalytical criticism tends to treat love, desire, or fictional portrayals of psychic interiority
as merely sexed, private, or irrational in contradistinction with socially accepted sets of
norms. On the other hand, the criticism keeps the wide social and political world at bay
as a realm where private inner life, the unconscious, emotion, and libidinal energy do
not belong. It is not that individuals committed to politics and revolution have no mind
of their own, but that they seem to have a different moral and emotional makeup: they
appear inauthentic, unreal, and deluded, acting under externally imposed imperatives
and false consciousness. Their behavior and action, though passionate and exuberant,
do not originate from the bottom of their heart and are shorn of roots in libidinal life
and the unconscious. The politically committed are ideologues or fanatics, soaring to
spiritual or superhuman heights.

This binary implies a limited understanding of psychoanalysis and overlooks the
radical and socially transformative potential of this historically evolving discourse. By
addressing the sex-centered mode in psychoanalytical criticism and by tracing certain fraught moments in Ding Ling's fiction, I suggest that private love can be an integral part of collective solidarity, that unconscious drives can propel the impulse for
social change, and that libidinal energy can fuel political passion and collective action.
Following radical critics like Marcuse and Castoriadis, who enlist psychoanalysis for
a socially transformative agenda, I call the process whereby libidinal energy translates
into political passion "positive sublimation." By clarifying this term in Chinese psychocultural studies and analyzing Ding Ling's fiction, I will challenge the rigid separation
of libidinal life from social commitment, love from politics, and the individual from
the collective.

SEX, SPIRIT, AND POLITICS

In her book *From Ah Q to Lei Feng: Freud and Revolutionary Spirit in 20th Century
China*, Wendy Larson argues with rich evidence and insight that it is ill-advised to

apply the concept of sexuality to the analysis of the revolutionary personality and that sex cannot be the basis of revolutionary subject formation. Fascinated with the surge of episodes of sexual expression and libidinal abandon in works like Jiang Wen's 姜文 1995 film *In the Heat of the Sun* (陽光燦爛的日子) and sexually explicit fiction by Wang Xiaobo 王小波, Larson began her psychocultural study of Chinese literature and film by enquiring into the relevance of European-American psychoanalytical discourse to Chinese literary criticism. She intended to question the privileging of sex as the key to modern subjectivity crystalized in the term "sexual modernity."[4] But as she went on, Larson ran into difficulties: although the works she examined abound in sexual representation, her research compelled her to look for a different concept of the mind in revolutionary discourse. Demystifying the narrow development of Freudian psychoanalysis and deploring the misguided use of sex as pivotal to modern subjectivity, Larson argues against the prevalent notion that sexual revolution may lead to political revolution. Pitting the revolutionary discourse of the mind against the Freudian, sexual psyche (or a certain brand of gentrified, conservative, but hegemonic Freudianism), Larson posits a revolutionary formation of the subject that is "socially developed but informed by a passionate spring of emotion and intellect."[5] In sum, she argues that sex-based subjectivity is inadequate to our understanding of the formative experience of the revolutionary subject.

Against the sex-centered analysis of Chinese culture based on such terms as sexuality, repressed desire, and sublimation, Larson has shown that mental life in revolutionary China is not driven by the sublimation of libidinal drives. Rather, the forging of the revolutionary subject is a spiritual process based on the Leninist principle of reflection and consciousness modeling. The individual is subject to a rigorous process of ideology and pedagogy and by means of spiritualization is elevated into ethical positions, Party imperatives, and correct political attitude. But this spiritualization is not self-directed, self-running, and spontaneous; it is an orientation and ceaseless reorientation in relation to the powers that be. Revolutionary discourse, in short, is a mind-shaping machinery that manufactures revolutionary subjects. While it may be spiritually inspired and emotionally resonant, the individual's mental life is bereft of any reference to sexual and libidinal undercurrents, of any inwardness and feelings. To such a high-minded formation, therefore, the concept of sex—the major interpretative key in psychoanalytical criticism in the West—is wrongly applied.

Larson is correct in critiquing a version of psychoanalytical criticism marked by a sex-centered hermeneutics and therapy procedure. But the individualized notion of sex—indeed a misguided approach to culture and politics—reflects a degeneration of the metapsychological understanding of sexuality as libido, life force, passion, and affect to a narrow cluster of terms like *genital sex, Oedipus complex, desire, family romance*, or *repressed unconscious*. This narrowing down did not only occur in Chinese criticism but also became paradigmatic in the West, as psychoanalysis became more orthodox and sex was valorized as the key element in popular culture in the postwar decades. This sex-centered interpretation cuts off the inner, subjective life from its objective correlatives, from its interplay with and active role in regards to culture, morality, and politics. Yet if we recall the broad notion of sexuality as Eros and libidinal energy, the term sexuality should encompass those primary undercurrents not fully contained by cultural constraints. Against the rational ego, these primary strata are imbedded in and derived from childhood memory, past injuries, traumas, attachments, kin relations, and ancient history. As I will argue, in certain circumstances strata of libidinal life force may be unleashed to flow and overspill the boundaries of norms and institutions, not only as a disruptive but also as a vital force for change.

Larson's analysis confirms the ritualistic formation of the revolutionary subject delineated by David Apter and Tony Saich. In their influential book *Revolutionary Discourse in Mao's Republic,* Apter and Saich analyze the way in which politics intertwines with the ritual of fostering emotion and passion in the revolutionary era in Yan'an. Taking issue with the analysis of Chinese politics through the economic, rational model, they enquire into how the quasi-religious, revolutionary discourse generates passion, purpose, and meaning. By investigating pedagogy, ideological campaigns, thought transformation, and mass mobilization, they give a sociological account of how "the discourse community was reformed and generated sufficient power to change the course of Chinese history."[6] Set up in contrast to the modern, rational subject of economic interest, this discourse-power nexus worked to mobilize the revolutionary masses, whose passion and energy are pivotal to what they call "inversionary" politics in the emancipatory movements of national independence and class liberation. In times of peace and economic reform, the rational, interest-obsessed individual is the norm. Rather than a parade of passion and energy, the economic, interest-driven image of the individual sees politics instrumentally as a process that "objectifies private and individual wants and desires in the form of social needs and priority according to a distributive schedule and alternative possibility" (4). Premised on the individual person as a rational agent engaged in calculation and choice, this type of subjectivity presupposes the primacy of ego over libido and of the rational individual over the irrational and primary psychic undercurrents. Individuals are supposed to know full well what they want, and political groups struggle against each other with clearly designated goals for power, advantage, and interest.

Instead of the calculating individual, Apter and Saich attend to the emotional aspect in the way "proto-religious features of social formation intertwine with secular theory of politics" (3). Political power is generated not by means of interest calculation but by the use of "interior languages, symbols, and interpretive networks" (2). Through their study of the Chinese Revolution, Apter and Saich describe scenes of dramatic mobilization of the poorly educated peasants and make a case for popular pedagogy and empowerment that fired up the imagination and instilled faith. This "logocentric" politics is preoccupied with "projections made on the basis of some doctrinal definition of necessity that specifies its own rules and theoretical principles and for which it provides its own logic" (4). Its power rests on the ritualistic, discursive, emotional setting that persuades individuals to communicate their private stories and personal sentiments to the collectivity—a form of "collective individualism" (4). The logocentric model acknowledges the role of inspirational discourse as well as its symbolic expressions.

Although they touch on emotion and quasi-religious ethos, Apter and Saich pay excessive attention to logic and discursive features in their emphasis on cognition and interpretation, which recalls Larson's spiritualization of Leninist principles. It is true that emotional elements are present in rituals and inspirational discourse, but they do not plumb the psychic, libidinal undercurrents that may drive these outward manifestations. By deploying a language of body and interiority, Apter and Saich allow suggestive psychoanalytical elements to emerge. They speak of "the body as a point of visceral departure for a larger and more theatrical frame," of ideological processes that are "symbolically dense and loaded with interior meanings," and of the retrieval of the past in projection of a future both mythical and logical (5). There are also redemptive and transformative elements, such as the "oracular vision" and "exegetical persuasiveness" in the charismatic figure of Mao and the storytelling rituals in revolutionary discourse (4). For all these evocative hints, however, further psychoanalysis in relation to the social is needed to illuminate the libidinal depths of revolutionary politics.

Although Lucian Pye's influential study *The Spirit of Chinese Politics* recalls Larson's use of spirit, it is a spirited denial of any spirit in Chinese politics, a deficiency Pye traces to the Confucian tradition. To Pye the interplay of psychic and libidinal force between individual, society, and state is to be read as always antagonistic. He sees political dynamism between psyche and culture, internal and external, as occurring in "the elbow room between the realms of conformity at the top and of spontaneity beneath the surface." "Conformity and rebellion have indeed been the lifeblood of modern Chinese politics," Pye states categorically.[7] The underground seething of discontent and subversion is matched by totalitarian rule. The relationship between the individual and sociopolitical norms is portrayed as a perpetual, clandestine cat-and-mouse struggle between the state on one hand and dissenting writers on the other. The moral norms, state imperatives, and dominant discourse inflict endless stricture and pain on innocent individuals. To write about stirrings of the mind is to write about the pain and suffering of mental repression and political censorship. In this picture, writing literature is either a gesture of resistance or a descent into despair. Any voice that calls for change within the social order tends to be deemed complicit with the Party-state. This total control of the mind entails an image of the psyche as a mere social robot, hollowed out by external norms.

What the above three views have in common is that they plot the formation of subjectivity as a mere product of discourse and doctrine. Premised on a rigid divide between the individual and the social, this picture of a top-down hegemony seems so total and penetrating that it hollows out the emotional core of psychic inwardness and constructs the modern subject entirely on the doctrinal and ideological basis.

POSITIVE SUBLIMATION AND PSYCHO-
SOCIAL TRANSFORMATION

In his essay "Group Psychology and the Analysis of the Ego," Freud writes that individual psychoanalysis is "concerned with the individual man and explores the paths by which he seeks to find satisfaction for his instinctual impulses; but only rarely is individual psychology in a position to disregard the relations of this individual to others."[8] Rather than sex-obsessed hermeneutics, the radical edge of psychoanalysis insists that individual psychology is at the same time social psychology. The concept of sublimation, as Norman Brown writes, constitutes the link between the psyche and human culture, between the individual and the social. The fruitful paradox of the concept asserts "a connection between higher culture activities and the infantile irrational prototypes, between pure mental constructs and sexuality."[9]

Psychoanalytical criticism today, however, tends to posit a negative notion of sublimation in the link between the individual and the social. Hegemonic discourse and institutions, often dubbed the "symbolic order," are portrayed as a straitjacket alienating and repressing the individual. To live up to the symbolic order and to fit into the norms is to delude, deceive, and alienate our true, inner nature as human beings. The social norms are seen as a distorting mirror, causing misrecognition and bordering on tyranny. Little attempt has been made to articulate hope for socio-psychic change beyond the status quo and the entrenched power relations. Psychoanalytical criticism finds in deconstruction a close ally, and their united front engages in an anarchistic and negative agenda: demystifying, dismantling, deconstructing, and demythologizing.

In contrast to the sex-centered school, a left-leaning current of psychoanalysis has been a source of hope through its articulation of the libidinal, subjective potential for cultural revival and social change. In Freud's time, the psychoanalysis establishment splintered, with some left-leaning groups seeking to deploy the new knowledge for social welfare and offering mental counseling for the poor and underprivileged. In her book *Freud's Free Clinics: Psychoanalysis and Social Justice, 1918–1938*, Elizabeth Ann Danto depicts several groups of psychoanalysts who sought to bring new concepts of the human mind into the service of social as well as psychic change. Coinciding with Ding Ling's transition from individualistic works to political fiction, these doctors, in the spirit of Vienna's social democracy, provided free council and treatment for the disadvantaged and the urban working class.[10] The most significant event in this history of radical psychoanalysis is the Frankfurt School's program to align psychoanalysis with Marxist historical materialism. Through such psychosocial "Freudian revisionists" as Herbert Marcuse, Norman Brown, Erich Fromm,[11] and more recently Fredric Jameson and Cornelius Castoriadis, radical psychoanalysis taps into psychic depths and libidinal drives to articulate hope for social and political change. In the social movements of the 1960s, works by Marcuse, Brown, and Fromm inspired vibrant activism, raised consciousness, and fueled critiques of capitalist alienation. The marriage of Marx and Freud has been a critical device against the culture industry and the military-industrial complex, and a source of hope for the disadvantaged, the repressed, and the disenfranchised.

Of these psychoanalytical critics, Marcuse and Castoriadis are most relevant to our analysis of the concept of sublimation and the emotional roots of revolutionary culture. Marcuse articulates an expanded notion of sexuality and projects a nonrepressive order by means of artistic utopianism and collective solidarity. This may take place "if the sex instincts can, by virtue of their own dynamic and under changed existential and social conditions, generate lasting erotic relations among mature individuals."[12]

For Marcuse, the organization of libido by the socially acceptable morality under capitalist production has turned sexuality qua life force into narrowly defined sexual relations between men and women. Sexuality loses its broad meaning as libidinal energy and is harnessed to material labor in order to procure food and daily necessities. The pressure to labor and survive channels the libido into the narrow confines of genital sex and childbearing, which are also related to the production of society; these strictures "perpetuate the desexualization of the body" (182) so that the body is subject to the demands of socially useful performance.

Insisting that this truncated sexuality is a historical construct, not a biological and natural fact, Marcuse finds in Freud an account of the historical vicissitudes of the libidinal drives. The checkered career of the instincts means there has been struggle and challenge derived from the potential of instinctual life for its own free development independent of civilizational constraints. This latent potential manifests itself in fantasy, dreams, and aesthetic experience. It not only entails a critique of the culturally dominant reality principle, but also heralds a future governed by a new reality principle that speaks the language of the pleasure principle. Here, artistic activity offers a prospect whereby libido becomes sublimated—not in the sense of being passively framed into the social order but rather in that it is forged into the beautiful forms of the self's own making. This is the aesthetic, idealistic scenario of love's labor inherent in the model of positive sublimation.

Driven by the pleasure principle, fantasy has been dismissed as useless and unreal. But fantasy keeps alive in a submerged way the structure and the tendencies of the subject prior to its organization by the reality principle, "prior to its becoming an 'individual' set off against other individuals." Committed to the id, fantasy in art preserves "the memory of the subhistorical past when the life of the individual was the life of the genus, the image of the immediate unity between the universal and the particular under the rule of the pleasure principle" (129).

In Freud's account, the ego works to strategize and to cope with the outside world for the purpose of self-preservation and survival. The fully socialized ego functions smoothly under the aegis of the reality principle. The sex instinct, on the other hand, denotes autoerotic love: love of one's own body and objects like oneself. While he remained ambiguous about this, Freud sometimes suggested that the sex instinct underlies and informs the ego instinct, and may select any object-choice as its love object. This thought usurps ego domination and the primacy of genital sex by pointing to the fact that the pleasure principle secretly uses the reality principle as a "detour" for its own fulfillment.[13] This ambiguity means that sexuality does not have to be confined to genital sex and will find other outlets for its own release and satisfaction. By engaging with other venues, such as work, communal bonds, emotional ties, and human relations, sexuality resexualizes these outward cultural frames and social relations.

In Brown's reading, the sexualization of the world constitutes the unity of the individual with the world. The ultimate aim of the sex drive is always outward: it is to become one with the world, resexualize the desexualized body, and infuse the arid world with erotic hues and auras. Implicit in Freud's remarks on the sex instinct, wrote Brown, is the suggestion that "there is only one loving relationship to objects in the world, a relation of being-one-with-the world which, though closer to Freud's narcissistic relation (identification), is also at the root of his other category of possessive love (object-choice)."[14] Speaking of this expanded self-love as a love of objects, Marcuse notes that the rational ego is "shaken and replaced by the notion of an undifferentiated, unified libido prior to the division into ego and external objects."[15] This, in the footsteps of Freud's self-critique, challenges the Freudian orthodoxy that the ego dominates the id: the rational subject dominates the libidinous undercurrents.

Following up on this critique of ego domination, Marxist psychoanalytical critic Cornelius Castoriadis reverses the position of ego and id, not by having the id overflow and usurp the ego (which would result in madness or libidinal abandon) but by enabling the id to energize and empower the ego. The rational subject is thus placed in touch with its roots in libidinal processes. The orthodox Freudian formulation is the famous "*Wo Es war, soll Ich werden*" (Where That was, I should/ought to become). *That* stands here for the id, and by purging and repressing unsocial instinctive drives the ego comes into being—in accord with social norms and morality. According to Castoriadis, if psychoanalysis were about the conquest of the ego where the id used to be, if it only studied a process of the self rising up from the ruins of the id, it would be an impossible and monstrous project. Such a project is indeed monstrous because "there can be no human being whose Unconscious is conquered by the Conscious, whose drives are fully permeated and controlled by rational considerations, who has stopped fantasizing and dreaming." The unconscious remains the strongest impetus in making us human, Castoriadis pronounces. What prevents us from becoming social robots—completely rationalized egos—is that "uncontrolled and uncontrollable continuous surge of creative radical imagination in and through the flux of representations, affects, and desires." So, he insists, Freud's statement should be changed to "*Wo Ich bin, soll auch Es auftauchen*" ("Where I [Ego] am [is], That [Id] should/ought also to emerge").[16]

Castoriadis insists on translating Freud's *werden* in the above formula as "become." This is because altering the ego's dominance over the id is an uphill, transformative process, one of "taking in the contents of the Unconscious."[17] Castoriadis's reversal sets off positive from negative sublimation. Negative sublimation privileges the socialized, rational ego that rules over libidinal life, even though it is historically contingent, a "vicissitude which has been forced upon the instincts entirely by civilization."[18] As a renunciation of instinct and as a psychic façade, negative sublimation sees civilization, with all its technologies, agendas, spiritualization, and socialization, as something superimposed onto the instinctual strata. Civilization impedes and sidetracks the instincts' natural needs for pleasure and satisfaction in order to meet the imperious demands of sociocultural reality and economic production. Through this opposition between culture and psyche, negative sublimation is most often associated with a negative series of psychic functions: repression, defense, myth, illusion, deflection, protection, fantasy, and pathology. These terms are part of the ego's defensive mechanism against the irruptive tendencies from within the psychic topography.

In contrast, positive sublimation articulates a congenial process of channeling and reorganizing libido. In its vision the aim of the instincts is changed and the blocking of libido by heavy-handed social norms gives way to libidinal discharge in seeking pleasure. At the heart of this account is the major shift in psychoanalysis that Marcuse, Brown, and Castoriadis have noted above: the absorption of the ego instinct into a broader theory of libido, the channeling of the self into a subset of an all-encompassing libido.

Positive sublimation is epitomized by the artist's creation with an eye to a reenchanted, resexualized, transformed reality. Haunted by a longing for erotic interconnectedness with things and other people; driven by a yearning for the mother's body, for primal happiness, and ancient memory, the engaged artist does not simply build castles in the air for aesthetic purposes but is bent on changing and reshaping the repressive reality. By rejecting conformism inherent in negative sublimation, the artist imagines utopian play-space within practical reality. In this light, psychoanalysis moves from the therapeutic to the social, from the inside to the outside. The sublimatory process is, as Castoriadis puts it, "rather a practical/poetical activity where both participants are agents and where the patient is the main agent of the development of his own self-activity."[19] As we will see in Ding Ling's work, the patient provides the cure from her own inner resources. Positive sublimation is both poetic and active, utopian and worldly, for its aim is "the appearance of another being" and its "object is human autonomy."[20] Less constrained by the symbolic order and the repressive system, the artists are creators of symbols, not brokers of symbolic capital, nor prisoners indentured to an external repressive structure based on profit. Positive sublimation proffers an image of the powerful, libido-driven, passionate human subject.

Negative sublimation fits the self into the established norms, rules, and identification, as well as the reality principle. In contrast, positive sublimation projects a trajectory of libidinal development in conjunction with cultural rejuvenation. It seeks a unified, re-assured self while forging emotional ties. In sociopolitical terms, positive sublimation envisages the becoming of an individual as a member of an emotionally connected and vibrant community. In this process, the individual's private passions are not repressed and shunned or "spiritualized" into quasi-religious rhetoric. Rather, individual passion is enhanced and given flesh and blood as an intense form of libidinal upsurge. When many individuals converge in this way, the political experience is one of the becoming of a political group, class, and community. This is made possible by tapping into libidinal energy, by releasing frustration, and by giving expression to the deepest yearnings inherent in the group's memory. Revolutionary movements, as Apter and Saich observe, are symptomatic outbursts of long-standing grievances and frustrations against corrupt, unjust social conditions. Radical politics elaborates these psychic grievances into compelling forms of truth, and transforms events and experience into narratives and inspirational texts.[21]

POLITICAL PASSION IN DING LING'S FICTION

Positive sublimation envisages a proactive link of the individual to culture, of inner life to outer reality. Instead of being repressed by the cultural norms, the individual and groups, driven by the pleasure principle, strive to create a nonrepressive reality. The mind in request of autonomy and freedom strives ceaselessly to transfer libidinal undercurrents in a proactive direction and into impassioned world-changing projects. In contrast to social repression, positive sublimation asserts a more active agency of the individual in relation to collectivity and envisages a fluid interaction between individualism and politics. If national politics expresses the wills of and empowers individuals, the individual's passion and autonomy must flow and converge into a passionate politics of social change. As Slavoj Žižek puts it, one can enjoy one's nation as one's self. [22]

Ding Ling's work and life have generated much controversy, which centers principally on the link of the individual to politics. Literary critics in favor of individualism tend to dote on Ding Ling's earlier self-centered writings and eschew her later works that address weighty political issues of war, military life, and rural reform. For them, Ding Ling's career seems to be filled with outrageous paradoxes. Ding Ling began as a staunchly individualistic writer who pursued self-fulfillment and self-realization with brilliant modernist originality, only to abandon it by identifying with revolutionary causes and the Party. In this chapter I examine Ding Ling's works in the light of the individual's proactive link to politics. In the national crisis of the 1930s, Ding Ling's fiction underwent a shift from self-centered to politicized work. This transition challenges the conventional image of political culture that engulfs individuals and eradicates autonomy.

Ding Ling's earlier works are indeed marked by an outpouring of untrammeled libido. Her novella *Miss Sophia's Diary* (莎菲女士的日記; 1927) features a female protagonist marked by libidinal aggressiveness. Miss Sophia is an individualist with a knack for manipulating her friends and lovers. Suffused with aggressive, unrestrained sexual impulses, Miss Sophia embodies the new wave of sexual promiscuity and instinctual release that came to enjoy increasing cultural cachet in the era of the iconoclastic, antitraditional May Fourth Culture. Yet Miss Sophia's libido-drenched fantasy and daydreams seem doomed, and her every attempt to make relations fit her narcissistic desire invariably fails. The disintegration of the self in her psychic trouble is a testament to the rise and fall of the May Fourth individual. Mentally emancipated from traditional norms, this individual becomes acutely aware of her sexual independence and vigorously claims autonomy in shaping her own life. Yet this awakened sense of self-determination remains an illusion and often turns into suicidal despair.

The paradox of Ding Ling's transition from the individual to the collective goes away if we consider her work as a change over time. Written in the transitional years when Ding Ling was becoming involved in the leftist organizations, the novella *Shanghai, Spring 1930* begins with a quandary of private despair and sexual frustration and moves on to narrate in Sophia-like Meilin a quest for an outlet and release of her pent-up energy. After a period marked by a routine heterosexual relation with the egocentric writer Zibin, Meilin finds herself a caged bird, trapped in a comfortable yet suffocating lifestyle. The narcissistic, romantic writings by her lover, which she used to admire, lose their meaning in the face of the turbulent social and political circumstances. In the Shanghai of spring 1930, the spectacle of inequality and exploitation stares her in the face. "Pot-bellied businessmen and blood-sucking devils wizened and shriveled from overwork on their abacuses were going full tilt in the careening money market, investing and manipulating to increase their exploitation of the laboring masses and to swell their astronomical wealth."[23] The colonial subjugation of the Chinese nation as well as the misery of the urban working class gives rise to discontent and to an urge to break out of bourgeois confinement. For Meilin, withdrawing into a self-indulgent cocoon and turning a blind eye to social ills seem repugnant. The narrow confines of her sexual life, arrested and truncated, block libidinal energy.

Although she is drawn to the workers' movement, Meilin knows little about its political-economic character. But intuitively, she senses that social engagement opens up a wider field for her potential and a space for her passion and energy. It is where she can invest her passion and fantasy, get up and act; where she can even engage in literary activity. "Action had become an instinctual need. She wanted to be with the masses, to try to understand society, and to work for it" (133). Increasingly she feels that "the role of wife, the role of lover, did not satisfy her" (133). Engaging with the workers in the social movement, Meilin realizes that politics also needs its symbolic counterpart in literature and speech, which provides a venue for her literary talent. Meilin's experience with the collectivity is one of emotional connection and solidarity. Far from draining her emotional life and curbing her desire, she enthuses over the activists' meetings, becoming excited and eager to shake hands with everybody, and associating with worker activists as comrades.

In terms of sexuality, Meilin's growing admiration for the male activist underlines her identification with the collective. This sexual love writ large finds a fuller expression in Part II of *Shanghai, Spring 1930*. In contrast to the split between Wang Wei and Mary mentioned at the beginning of this chapter, this part offers a glimpse of how love may merge into revolution. Parallel to the story of Wang Wei and Mary runs a budding romance between Feng Fei, Wang's friend and secretary of a labor organization, and a female bus ticket-seller. Feng encounters the ticket-seller on his bus rides and takes a liking to her. What attracts him about this young woman is not only her conventional feminine charms. Educated and capable, the ticket-seller seems to display a "clear understanding of politics" as well as "class consciousness" (142). During his frequent bus trips, Feng's respect for the woman grows and his love increases. After a casual conversation, they immediately feel like old acquaintances. Affection does not run merely along ideological lines, to be sure. The woman, "whose face had that healthy color that came not from makeup, but from working with a will and high spirits" (142), exudes an innocent beauty. She becomes more attractive also because Feng is able to conjure up images of her class background and "a glorious, gripping history" (142) behind her. This history may be her identity as a member of the working class in a struggle to improve her social condition.

As they participate in political activities, affection between the ticket-seller and Feng blossoms into a love aligned with passion. As the leader of the movement, Wang Wei, in the midst of protesting crowds, feels that the mobilized workers and citizens move like "a surge of roaring waves toppling the mountains and churning up the city in its raging flames" (169). Yet what he sees in the blossoming of love and intimacy between the ticket-seller and Feng Fei goes hand in hand with the surge of popular, political energy around him. In the midst of demonstrations, Wang catches a moment that merges intimate love and collective solidarity. With his lover's hand clasped tightly in his, Feng is ecstatic and is beaming with pride. This "extraordinary" display of love and emotion moves Wang Wei so much that his hidden dream of the idealized revolutionary Mary springs to his mind: "Ah, his former dream has now been realized by Feng Fei! That woman was a true revolutionary" (169). And her female beauty is equal to that of Mary. In this vignette, love grows and blossoms in the midst of surging activism and political involvement. Love is transferred to collective solidarity and bound up with political passion. But that does not take away from personal love and female beauty. Rather, political involvement enhances affection and beauty. This scenario is typical of a narrative that involves love and revolution.

I have previously written about the similar libido-drenched moment in the collective gathering. Although the collective spectacle may seem to engulf the individual into an amorphous crowd, it stages a scene of the individual's rebirth, the dissolution of her helplessness, and the upsurge of her private emotion flowing into political passion. Instead of the individual being sublimated in the negative sense into a nameless, abstract ideological position, he or she joins the collective that unites disparate individuals as its members, bolsters their pride and dignity, and gives them access to "an intensely shared emotional ambience and enjoyment." This is an instance of positive sublimation.[24]

Much criticism of Ding Ling's writing career faults her for succumbing to political authorities and becoming a Party writer. While this criticism is partially valid, the perspective of positive sublimation allows us to discern a more proactive, inner drive in the journey from the individual to the collective. The much-discussed story "In the Hospital" (在醫院中) exemplifies this proactive link between psychic life and outer reality. The protagonist Lu Ping, an energetic, independent woman—a thinly veiled reference to Ding Ling in her early years—makes a series of career decisions that are compromises between individual desire and external authority. Though uninterested in pediatrics and passionate about literature, she nevertheless obeys her father's order and completes four years of medical education at a modern university in Shanghai. The outbreak of the Anti-Japanese War gives her an opportunity to invest her libidinal energy in military activity, and she uses her medical knowledge to serve the national defense. In a military hospital in Shanghai she acts as a mother, girlfriend, and sister to the wounded soldiers. Although no romantic relation ensues, she embraces the emotional connectedness and community. Her decision to move to Yan'an and enroll in the Resistance University continues this broadening of her libidinal energy into collective activity and revolutionary causes. She believes that being a political worker is a role cut out for her, because its pedagogical mission requires literary and rhetoric skills. Yet when the Party assigns her to a medical post in a field hospital in the base area, she obeys, with much frustration. From this point on, the story focuses on how the individual is in conflict with the collective. Lu Ping applies herself diligently to the daily business and improvement of the hospital, is underappreciated and misunderstood, wavers between self-love and collective demands, and suffers from alienation and neglect. The story traces the unfolding of her anguish and despair but also portrays the defeat and victory of her struggle to invest professional work with political passion.

Negative libido, manifest in sadistic innuendos and power struggles reminiscent of *Miss Sophia's Diary,* underlines Lu Ping's relations with hostile coworkers and poisons the atmosphere. Though a cultivated, nice young girl of a gentry family, Lu Ping is not immune to aggression. She finds herself trapped in emotional alienation and swallowed by hateful gossip and accusations. The collective environment presents a morass, a closed-in space for the venting of primal, egoistic aggressiveness in the midst of what is supposed to be an inspiring, revolutionary organization.

Lu Ping attempts to mitigate alienation by associating with her friends. They hang out as a literary and emotional group and meet often to discuss shared interest in literature. The literary, emotional bonds are then transferred to more disciplinary work. In her relation with Dr. Chang, she wants to learn surgical techniques from him in an impending operation so that she can work as a surgeon on the battlefront. The night before the operation, she is concerned about the chilly temperature of the operation room and the well-being of the patient. An empathetic reflection of herself, uncared for and neglected, her thoughts turn to her past under maternal care and she luxuriates in the warm affective images of her home and community. But this self-indulgence quickly dissolves into her caring and thinking about the patient. She writes a letter requesting supplies for heating up the operation room. During the operation, when she and her friends become sick due to excessive gas from the stove, Lu Ping is left in the cold at the steps outside the operation room, neglected by virtually everybody. This blow shakes her faith in the revolution: "The revolution was for all mankind. Why then, were even the closest comrades so lacking in love?"[25]

With doubts about revolution and rage against injustice, Lu Ping is mounting a counterattack, a negative libidinal outburst. She "could assail others and bring them down" (290). At the moment a soldier without feet comes onto the scene and gives her advice. He advises her about how to proceed within this very imperfect revolutionary system. His teaching and personal example save her from sinking into "petty bourgeois mentality." A victim of medical incompetence, this soldier has lost both of his feet due to the doctor's errors. Yet he clearly makes a distinction between the dire consequences of the revolutionary organization and its broader meaning for its individual members. Educated in the Soviet Union and an editor of books for the masses, he overcomes his despair after his amputation and gets involved further in the liberation movement. He educates Lu Ping about the backwardness of the medical profession and the real conditions, but also makes her aware of the supportive environment and sympathetic colleagues she had ignored. Encouraged by the generosity of the patient's spirit, Lu Ping overcomes her bitterness and is ready to return to the collective cause once again.

"In the Hospital" has been seen as a rebuke of the Communist Party and collectivism by venting petty bourgeois, liberalist sentiments. In the Yan'an rectification campaign that compelled urban writers and intellectuals to purge bourgeois thoughts, Ding Ling came under criticism for such writings. Huang Ziping 黃子平 reads Lu Ping's mental symptoms as signs of the sick body of a bourgeois character, which is cured by the "social hygiene" of ideology.[26] Huang's view accords with the scenario of negative sublimation whereby unsocial, "sickly" thoughts and feelings are purged through political therapy and ideological tempering in order for the individual to build up a "virtuous" character under the dictate of the collective norms.

Sickness and its cure is a motif in Lu Xun's 魯迅 early writings and threads through modern Chinese literature. Frustrated by his father's sick body and then by the sick spirits of his countrymen, Lu Xun embarked on a project of engaged literature in order to cure the diseased soul of the Chinese nation. Lu Xun's writing is intended to expose sickness and suffering so as to call attention to possible cures. Yet Huang Ziping sees "In the Hospital" as an ironic reversal of this sickness-cure nexus: Lu Ping, the classical literary youth of May Fourth Culture, tries to cure the "sick," inefficient hospital. Yet her intervention, engagement, and passion for what she sees as a diseased organization turns out to be diagnosed as her own sickness, which is to be cured by ideological hygiene.[27] The literary analogy to Lu Xun is apparent. Lu Ping's literary ambition goes into her cure of the social ills and is evident in her different career pursuits. Her interest in public speech and rhetoric, her association with the small literary circle in the hospital, and her effort to educate the patients and staff about culture—all this points to literature as a proactive, passionate means for change. Her father makes her study medicine against her interest, but to her medicine is meaningless without political import. And her real passion for literature and rhetoric moves her closer to politics. Yet Lu Ping's literary-political attempt to "cure" the sick conditions of the hospital boomerangs back on herself.

Viewed in light of the individual's proactive link to the collective, I would argue that Lu Ping's story follows Lu Xun's motif of searching for a cure for social and cultural pathologies. The story can be read not as a petty bourgeois sickness healed by official ideological therapy, but rather as an attempt to reform sick conditions and pathological mentalities. True, the staff and administrators of the hospital are part of the revolutionary body, but they are mired in traditional, regressive mentalities and habits, wallowing in egoism, selfishness, patriarchal relations, and unscientific practices. These are pathologies that await revolutionary solutions. As Castoriadis notes, the patient also participates in the healing process as an active "agent of the development of his own self-activity."[28]. This reflects the positive sublimation of the individual to collective commitment. The May Fourth literary youth begins as a rebel alienated from and critical of the social body, "drawing blood for the purposes of an objective diagnosis." But in the national crisis, the rebel finds a place within the body and turns into "a white blood cell fighting for the survival not of the self but of the larger organization."[29] The deficiencies and flaws of the hospital are like cancerous cells plaguing the collective body and are to be cured by an effort of self-reform. Thus, rather than signs of petty bourgeois weaknesses unfit for the revolution, Lu Ping's reform efforts work like white blood cells—a restless revolutionary drive infused with passion and frustration. The point is to create a healthy environment and to make the hospital a truly functioning revolutionary organization.

Literary scholar He Guimei 賀桂梅 comments on the sickness-cure nexus by characterizing this story in terms of a constant drive to revitalize an ossified revolutionary establishment.[30] For He, Lu Ping epitomizes the critical voice against a flawed, stagnant system. Building on He's suggestions, I argue that Lu Ping's attempted "cure" is not to negate the collective agenda, not to acquiesce to the system, but to make a proactive move to heal and transform the revolutionary body. The cure is attempted in hopes that the revolutionary ideal and system will be reconciled, the revolutionary form truly at one with its content. The story testifies to the scenario of positive sublimation, whereby inner drives engage with external social constraints, not to come under their yoke but to spill over and change their contour.

Lu Ping's personality echoes the militant struggle-happy passion that Ding Ling describes in her essay "Struggle is Enjoyment" (戰鬥是享受), where she writes about her excitement at observing a group of people risking their lives to salvage useful material from the torrents of a river:

> They are enjoying the ultimate pleasure, the apex of triumph and joy, which are lost on those who stand by on the riverbank. Those bystanders uninvolved in the struggle, safe from the terrifying waves and torrents; those who never have a chance to wrest a victory of life from the brink of death will never comprehend such a joy. Only in constant struggle does one experience the meaning of living and have a genuine sense of life existence. Only in struggle does one feel youthful fire burning within oneself and experience brightness and pleasure. [31]

Here, Ding Ling internalizes revolutionary striving into a militant spirit and extolls the passionate intensity of a collective endeavor. To constantly strive to go beyond ordinary routines to seek "power and heat" constitutes the revolutionary spirit. This philosophy of life places the individual in perpetual tension and conflict with her environment: she grapples with the existing conditions of life not to adapt or conform but to transform.

The revolutionary spirit, as a drive to critique and transcend reality, challenges the conventional divide between the individual and society, which sees the individual's commitment to the collective as signs of eradication of her autonomy. This view is mistaken in that it equates an evolving collective with the established reality. To equate the existing revolutionary system with its driving spirit ignores the fact that the established system easily lapses and corrupts and needs to be constantly jumpstarted with its own driving spirit and vitality. In Ding Ling's case, the revolutionary drive fuels a vigilant critique of the reality so as to project a richer, more fulfilling reality. But the revolutionary regime, being institutionalized, bureaucratic, ossified, or mired in regressive ideas and mentalities, is often at loggerheads with professed revolutionary ideals.

In this sense, the passionate revolutionary spirit is an inner push upward within the congealed revolutionary system, taking on a transformative, not confirmative, role against the system. In Ding Ling as much as in Lu Ping, we see a proactive link of the individual to the collective. Rather than negating or being cured by the revolution, Lu Ping carries on the revolutionary spirit more vigorously and radically than her colleagues and superiors. Instead of yielding to the system, she sees the true nature of what a modern revolution seeks to achieve yet is falling short of its goal. So the proactive drive is, in He Guimei's apt words, a "revolution within a revolution."[32]

Lu Ping's development from a self-absorbed personality seeking public venues tells a story of how she is tempered along the lines of positive sublimation. Through trial and error, she has learned from the soldier without feet that engaging collective politics is the way to reform it and that retreat is not an option. But the process of bringing the revolutionary body up to its own ideals is a patient, uphill battle. It is a process that reorients libidinal passion toward a broader arena of action in the anti-imperialist war and the battle for national independence. Lu Ping's criticisms regarding the deficiency of the hospital and the moral lapses of her coworkers and bureaucratic, incompetent leaders are meant to suggest the yawning gap between revolutionary spirit and actual conditions, not the outright negation of the collective agenda, much less the shirking of her political responsibility.

To conclude, positive sublimation shows not only the ways libidinal energy may find a public path to work itself out, but also how the revolutionary subject, driven by passion and guided by the spirit, seeks to transform the social environment by tapping into hidden dreams, both collective and individual. The lesson of "In the Hospital" lies not in the tempering of the petty bourgeois mentality into revolutionary virtue. The rigid divide between self and collective, inner life and social norms, the individual and society is to be transcended. By identifying herself with the man without feet and becoming ever more involved in the collective cause, Lu Ping seeks to change her world, the world of her identification and belonging that has hurt and wronged her. By engaging with and merging into the public world of collective struggle, Lu Ping matures and her deepest ambition finds an expansive space to play itself out.

NOTES

1. Tani Barlow, ed. *I Myself Am a Woman: Selected Writings of Ding Ling* (Boston: Beacon Press, 1989), 149. Further references to Ding Ling's works will be in parentheses in the text.

2. Jianmei Liu, *Revolution Plus Love: Literary History, Women's Bodies, and Thematic Repetition in Twentieth-Century Chinese Fiction* (Honolulu: University of Hawai'i Press, 2003).

3. Ning Wang, "Freudianism and Twentieth-Century Chinese Literature," in *The Reception and Rendition of Freud in China*, ed. Tao Jiang and Philip Ivanhoe (London and New York: Routledge, 2013), 3–23.

4. Wendy Larson, *From Ah Q to Lei Feng: Freud and Revolutionary Spirit in Twentieth Century China* (Stanford: Stanford University Press, 2009), 2.

5. Larson, *From Ah Q to Lei Feng*, 4.

6. David Apter and Tony Saich, *Revolutionary Discourse in Mao's Republic* (Cambridge: Harvard University Press, 1994), 2. Further references will be provided in parentheses in the text.

7. Lucian W. Pye, *The Spirit of Chinese Politics*, New Edition (Cambridge: Harvard University Press, 1992), "Preface" and ix–x.

8. Sigmund Freud, *The Standard Edition of the Complete Psychological Works of Sigmund Freud*, ed. James Strachey (London: Hogarth Press, 1953), 3765.

9. Norman Brown, *Life Against Death: The Psychoanalytical Meaning of History*, 2nd ed. (Hanover: Wesleyan University Press, 1959), 135.

10. Elizabeth Ann Danto, *Freud's Free Clinics: Psychoanalysis and Social Justice: 1918–1938* (New York: Columbia University Press, 2005).

11. Martin Jay, *The Dialectical Imagination: A History of the Frankfurt School and the Institute of Social Research, 1923–1950* (Boston: Little, Brown, 1973), 86–112.

12. Herbert Marcuse, *Eros and Civilization: A Philosophical Inquiry into Freud* (New York: Vintage Books, 1962), 182. Further references will be provided in parentheses in the text.

13. Brown, *Life Against Death*, 40–45. Marcuse, *Eros and Civilization*, 29–31.

14. Brown, *Life Against Death*, 42.

15. Marcuse, *Eros and Civilization*, 152.

16. Cornelius Castoriadis, *World in Fragments: Writings on Politics, Society, and Psychoanalysis, and the Imagination* (Stanford: Stanford University Press, 1997), 127–128.

17. Castoriadis, *World in Fragments*, 128.

18. Sigmund Freud, *Civilization and Its Discontents*, ed. and trans. James Strachey (New York: Norton, 1961), 44.

19. Castoriadis, *World in Fragments*, 129.

20. Castoriadis, *World in Fragments*, 129.

21. Apter and Saich, *Revolutionary Discourse in Mao's Republic*, 5.

22. Slavoj Žižek, *Tarrying with the Negative: Kant, Hegel, and the Critique of Ideology* (Durham: Duke University Press, 1993), 200.

23. Tani Barlow, 128. Further references to Ding Ling's works will be provided in parentheses in the text.

24. See Ban Wang, *The Sublime Figure of History: Aesthetics and Politics in Twentieth Century China* (Stanford: Stanford University Press, 1997), 136. In Larson's reference to my analysis of sublimation in this book, the concept is understood in terms of negative sublimation, see Larson, *From Ah Q to Lei Feng*, 66. Rereading my own work while writing this chapter, I feel my explanation of the concept in that book is ambiguous. My text suggests that sublimation in revolutionary discourse could play out either negatively or positively. This chapter aims in part to clarify the ambiguity and to highlight the positive, proactive potential of sublimation in order to understand transformative political passion.

25. Ding Ling, "In the Hospital," in *Modern Chinese Stories and Novellas: 1919–1949*, ed. Joseph Lau, C. T. Hsia, and Leo Lee (New York: Columbia University Press, 1981), 290. Further references to this story will be provided in parentheses in the text.
26. Huang Ziping 黃子平, "Bing de yinyu yu wenxue shengchan" 病的隱喻與文學生產 [Sickness as metaphor and the production of literature], in *Piping kongjian de kaichuang* 批評空間的開創 [Opening critical space], ed. Wang Xiaoming 王曉明 (Shanghai: Dongfang chubanshe, 1998), 318–323.
27. Huang Ziping, "Sickness as Metaphor," 318–319.
28. Castoriadis, *World in Fragments*, 129.
29. This is Marston Anderson's interpretation of the rebellious individual's social responsibility based on Hu Shi's 胡適 metaphor of the rebel as white blood cell. See Anderson's comment on Hu Shi in his *Limits of Realism: Chinese Fiction in the Revolutionary Period* (Berkeley and Los Angeles: University of California Press, 1990), 35.
30. He Guimei 賀桂梅, "Zhishi fenzi, nüxing yu geming" 知識份子、女性與革命 [Intelligentsia, women, and revolution], in *Dangdai zuojia pinglun* 當代作家評論 [Review of contemporary writers] 3 (2004): 112–127.
31. Quoted in He Guimei, "Intelligentsia, Women, and Revolution," 115.
32. He Guimei, "Intelligentsia, Women, and Revolution," 115.

Works Cited

Anderson, Marston. *Limits of Realism: Chinese Fiction in the Revolutionary Period*. Berkeley and Los Angeles: University of California Press, 1990.

Apter, David, and Tony Saich. *Revolutionary Discourse in Mao's Republic*. Cambridge: Harvard University Press, 1994.

Barlow, Tani, ed. *I Myself Am a Woman: Selected Writings of Ding Ling*. Boston: Beacon Press, 1989.

Brown, Norman. *Life Against Death: The Psychoanalytical Meaning of History*. 2nd ed. Hanover, NH: Wesleyan University Press, 1959.

Castoriadis, Cornelius. *World in Fragments: Writings on Politics, Society, and Psychoanalysis, and the Imagination*. Stanford: Stanford University Press, 1997.

Danto, Elizabeth Ann. *Freud's Free Clinics: Psychoanalysis and Social Justice: 1918–1938*. New York: Columbia University Press, 2005.

Freud, Sigmund. *Civilization and Its Discontents*. Ed. and trans. James Strachey. New York: Norton, 1961.

Freud, Sigmund. *The Standard Edition of the Complete Psychological Works of Sigmund Freud*. Ed. James Strachey. London: Hogarth Press, 1953.

He Guimei 賀桂梅. "Zhishi fenzi, nüxing yu geming" 知識份子、女性與革命 [Intelligentsia, women, and revolution]. *Dangdai zuojia pinglun* 當代作家評論 [Review of contemporary writers] 3 (2004): 112–127.

Huang Ziping 黃子平. "Bing de yinyu yu wenxue shengchan" 病的隱喻與文學生產 [Sickness as metaphor and the production of literature]. In *Piping kongjian de kaichuang* 批評空間的開創 [Opening critical space]. Ed.Wang Xiaoming 王曉明. Shanghai: Dongfang chubanshe, 1998. 317–333.

Jay, Martin. *The Dialectical Imagination: A History of the Frankfurt School and the Institute of Social Research, 1923–1950*. Boston: Little, Brown, 1973.

Larson, Wendy. *From Ah Q to Lei Feng: Freud and Revolutionary Spirit in Twentieth Century China*. Stanford: Stanford University Press, 2009.

Lau, Joseph, C. T. Hsia, and Leo Lee, eds. *Modern Chinese Stories and Novellas: 1919–1949*. New York: Columbia University Press, 1981.

Marcuse, Herbert. *Eros and Civilization: A Philosophical Inquiry into Freud*. New York: Vintage Books, 1962.

Pye, Lucian W. *The Spirit of Chinese Politics*. New ed. Cambridge: Harvard University Press, 1992.

Wang, Ban. *The Sublime Figure of History: Aesthetics and Politics in Twentieth Century China*. Stanford: Stanford University Press, 1997.

Wang, Ning. "Freudianism and Twentieth-Century Chinese Literature." In *The Reception and Rendition of Freud in China*. Ed. Tao Jiang and Philip Ivanhoe. London and New York: Routledge, 2013. 3–23.

Žižek, Slavoj. *Tarrying with the Negative: Kant, Hegel, and the Critique of Ideology*. Durham: Duke University Press, 1993.

EILEEN CHANG AND THE GENIUS ART OF FAILURE

TZE-LAN DEBORAH SANG

EILEEN Chang 張愛玲, one of the most acclaimed twentieth-century Chinese writers, was ironically obsessed with failure almost from the beginning of her literary career. In "My Dream of Being a Genius" (天才夢; 1939)—an essay Chang wrote while still a first-year student at the University of Hong Kong—she famously opens with these lines:

> I am an odd girl. Viewed as a genius since I was little, I have had no objective in life besides developing my extraordinary gifts. Yet, when my childhood fantasies gradually faded, I discovered that I have nothing except the dream of being a genius. All I possess is a genius's peculiarities and shortcomings. The world may forgive Wagner's eccentricities and madness, but they will not forgive mine.[1]

Intense self-doubt permeates this self-sketch. Chang expresses an acute anxiety about having been misguided in fancying herself a genius, and the worry that she is only an imposter. Even more unsettling, she discovers in herself many of the eccentricities and lunacies of a genius but few of a genius's redeeming qualities. Worse than a fraud, she is a misfit.

Continuing to expound on this negative self-image, Chang's essay nevertheless turns into a subtle accusation, a voicing of suppressed anger at someone else. It becomes evident that Chang's sense of failure is a direct product of her mother's normative expectations. Describing her childhood, Chang highlights her own literary talent, portraying herself as a precocious writer who wrote her first fictional work at the age of seven, though no amount of talent could protect her from feeling like a failure as she grew older, because what was expected of her was not literary accomplishment. She writes:

> At school my development was given free rein, and my self-confidence grew. Things changed when I was sixteen, when my mother returned from France and scrutinized me—her daughter—whom she hadn't seen for years.

"I regret having taken fastidious care of you when you had typhoid," she told me. "I'd rather see you die than see you live and torture yourself."

I discovered that I could not peel apples, and it was only after making prodigious efforts that I finally learned how to mend socks. I was afraid of going to the hair salon, of greeting houseguests, and of trying on newly tailored clothes that the dressmaker brought me. Many people tried to teach me how to knit, to no avail. After living in a house for two years, I was still at a loss when someone asked me where the doorbell was. I rode in a rickshaw to a hospital daily to take shots, but after three months I still did not recognize the street. In short, in the practical world, I was good for nothing.

My mother gave me two years to learn to adapt to the environment. She taught me how to cook, how to do laundry by using detergent, how to walk with the right posture, how to take a hint by observing someone's eyes. She taught me to pull the window curtains after turning on the lights, and how to study my facial expression in the mirror. She told me to avoid telling jokes unless I had a sure talent for humor.

When it comes to the commonsense useful for interacting with others, I show shocking stupidity. My two-year plan was a failed experiment. My mother's grave warning did not influence me in any way other than knocking my thinking off balance.

It is not that I cannot appreciate any part of the art of life at all. . . . When there is no interaction between people, I am filled with the joy of life. But I cannot overcome the small irritations that gnaw at me, even for one day. Life is a gorgeous robe, infested with fleas.[2]

In this dramatic staging of her self, Chang describes in no uncertain terms the trauma of normative femininity. As a cerebral girl who is single-mindedly interested in writing and drawing, she is subjected to gender policing by her mother, who takes definite steps to bring Chang into line with conventional bourgeois femininity. Of paramount importance in her mother's eyes are social grace and domestic skills. She teaches Chang to cook, launder, sew, knit, and, above all, make herself pleasant and unobtrusive in social interactions. Tragically, Chang fails to meet her mother's expectations. What is worse, she suffers lasting emotional damage from her mother's criticisms as she loses her blissful childhood confidence in her own abilities. She can no longer think in an unselfconscious manner, because now she realizes that there is an entirely different set of expectations—represented by her mother—that judges her every move. A harsh superego now keeps constant watch over her, ever vigilant about the gap between her and an idealized standard. Trauma and failure are now inextricably intertwined.

"My Dream of Being a Genius" foreshadows the fascination with failure that constitutes one of the central characteristics of Chang's writings. The essay is telling even if readers cannot take it as an undistorted self-portrait or unadulterated truth. In Chang's retrospective account of how she composed "My Dream," the essay is presented as an unsuccessful exercise that falls short of truthful self-expression. According to Chang, the text was constrained by arbitrary circumstances and exigencies, and she originally wrote it in order to enter it into a composition contest organized by the West Wind Press in Shanghai. She struggled to stay under the specified word limit, which she claims had the effect of curtailing the truthfulness of the content.[3] The piece, in other words, is a condensed and therefore oversimplified account, and contains, one suspects, certain exaggerations for dramatic effect. Compromised though it may be, I contend that it introduces certain motifs that recur in Chang's later writings. The essay is a prefiguration—not because it can be taken as an accurate reflection of Chang's self-image, but rather because it is a textual performance that creates a narrative of trauma and constructs a central character haunted by failure as a traumatic aftershock.

Failure is a prominent theme in many of Chang's works, though it appears in many guises. Although failure is fascinating precisely because of its unpredictability—one can fall short of or deviate from the definition of success in such a multiplicity of ways that it is difficult to generalize—it is worth noting that it is often through failure and a panoply of emotions of loss, shame, resentment, self-doubt, envy, and feelings of backwardness, entrapment, and unrequited love that Chang calls into question gender and sexual norms. For instance, in Chang's posthumously published auto-biographical novel *Small Reunions* (小團圓), the protagonist Jiuli's sense of failure, like that of the narrator of "My Dream," comes from her interactions with an overly critical mother. Failure to conform to the behavioral standards prescribed by the mother effectively problematizes—or even subverts—bourgeois heteronormative ideals.[4] Chang exposes the glorified images of bourgeois femininity and masculinity as unattainable. What is more, through descriptions of failed relationships, Chang interrogates the mythology of heterosexual romance. The negative emotions attendant on failure, then, may be interpreted as performing a productive function insofar as they gesture toward, if not directly open up, the possibilities of alternative gender and sexual futures.

In another twist, Chang's fascination with failure manifests itself as a repeated exploration of the failings of the modern girl, an exploration that implicitly responds to the discourse on the shortcomings of the modern girl that ran rampant in the Chinese media throughout the 1930s and 1940s. Provocatively, by closely examining the modern girl's vanity, materialism, and hunger for love, Chang does not so much condemn the decadence of the modern girl (as some of her contemporaries were wont to do in their commentaries) as explore the social conditions that may have contributed to her weaknesses and frailties. The failings of the modern girl, in other words, open up questions about social determinism as well as individual freedom and responsibility. To a significant extent, Chang's depictions of the modern girl's failings may even be interpreted as indictments of structural gender inequalities, in that such systemic issues are shown to have played a major role in shaping and deforming the modern girl's character. The modern girl is a product of her times, and is thus a sign and a symptom.

Many of the heroines in Chang's most popular stories and novellas are steeped in failure. To name just a few: Ge Weilong in "Aloeswood Incense, the First Brazier" (沈香屑：第一爐香), Cao Qiqiao and Jiang Chang'an in "The Golden Cangue" (金鎖記), Wu Cuiyuan in "Sealed Off" (封鎖), Yin Baoyan in "Yin Baoyan Visits My Flat, Bringing a Bouquet" (殷寶灩送花樓會), and Gu Manzhen and Gu Manlu in *The Affinity of Half a Lifetime* (半生緣). Some of these characters, like Ge Weilong, Cao

Qiqiao, and Yin Baoyan, get entangled in hurtful relationships because of their emotionality, irrationality, and vanity. Others, such as Wu Cuiyuan and Gu Manzhen, strive to be self-reliant educated professionals and yet either receive insincere, vacuous validation of their vocational achievements from family and society or are struck down by conservative patriarchal forces.

Without going into detail about all the permutations of failure in these texts, here I will examine just one example. In "Aloeswood Incense: The First Brazier," Weilong is a middle-school student whose family has temporarily relocated to Hong Kong due to the threat of war in Shanghai. Now that her family, of modest means, is planning to return to Shanghai, she seeks financial help and guardianship from her aunt Madame Liang—a middle-aged, well-connected widow who has inherited a substantial fortune—to remain in Hong Kong in order to complete her studies. Upon making contact with her aunt, she discovers that her aunt has an insatiable appetite for men's affection and has been using young pretty women that she employs as domestic servants to bait men. The aunt, seeing socialite material in Weilong, showers her with an expensive wardrobe the moment Weilong moves into her mansion. Weilong senses imminent danger and yet, under the illusion that she can draw boundaries to protect herself, decides to stay. After countless parties in which she gets introduced to Hong Kong's socialites, Weilong falls in love with George, a playboy of mixed race. When she discovers that he is carrying on an affair with her maid even as he is becoming intimate with her, she contemplates leaving Hong Kong to be reunited with her family in Shanghai, yet finds it difficult to extricate herself from the life to which she is now accustomed. As she lies in bed recovering from a bad case of the flu and pneumonia, a tangle of thoughts plagues her mind:

> Weilong was smitten with doubt—could she have fallen ill on purpose? Was she unconsciously unwilling to go home, seeking to delay her return? It was easy enough to say that she'd go back, become a new person, start a new life, and so on; but she no longer was the simple girl she'd once been. Go to school, then go out and get a job: perhaps this wasn't the best path for someone like her—pretty, but without much ability. Of course she'd have to get married. A new life meant a new man. A new man? She'd lost all her self-confidence because of George; she couldn't cope with other people now. The minute George had stopped loving her, she was in his power. She knew very well that he was only an ordinary playboy, that there was nothing especially terrifying about him—the terrifying thing was the passion, raging and wild beyond words, that he inspired in her.[5]

After considerable self-torment and a strong dose of pragmatic advice from Madame Liang, Weilong eventually decides to stay and, moreover, to entice George into marriage by making it understood that she would financially support him with the money she would earn from involvements with other men. Partly because of her infatuation with George and partly because of the hypnotizing power of a life of luxury, she willingly becomes a pawn, busy all day hooking men for Madame Liang and getting money for George. The story ends with a moment of painful realization as she and George go to Wanchai to enjoy the Chinese New Year's market. Mingling with the crowd, she notices brightly rouged prostitutes and inebriated sailors:

> Along came a gang of sailors, drunk and throwing firecrackers in every direction. When they saw Weilong, they started to aim at her, and the firecrackers raced like meteors toward the moon. Weilong was so scared she turned and ran. George found their car, and pushed her toward it; they got in, started the engine, and left Wanchai.
> "Those drunken mudfish," George said with a smile. "What do they take you for?"
> "But how am I any different from those girls?"
> Steering with one hand, George reached out with the other to cover her mouth. "Talk such nonsense again and—"
> "Yes, yes! I was wrong. I admit it," Weilong apologized. "How could there not be any difference between us? They don't have a choice—I do it willingly!"[6]

A sharp pain shoots through Weilong's consciousness as she realizes that what she is doing is but a glamorized form of prostitution. In a moment of rare candor, she and George come close to speaking the naked truth. And yet, she has by now deviated too far from her original plan of educating herself and finding someone who would love her back. There is no return; her life is pure abjection.

In many ways, Weilong is the proverbial modern girl with glaring moral failings and deficiencies decried by countless Chinese social commenters in the 1930s and 1940s.[7] She is corruptible, has little resistance to the lure of money and glamor, is overly needy of love and attention, is deluded about the extent to which she can enjoy sexual freedom without psychological and moral compunctions, and is oblivious to nobler issues such as the need for social reforms or the urgency of strengthening the nation against impending crises. Yet, through nuanced delineation of Weilong's feelings and thought processes, Chang makes her human rather than a caricature. Chang gives us insight into Weilong's psyche, so much so that few readers can withhold their empathy from this character. Does society really leave much choice to a young woman like Weilong, who is attractive but has no special skills and talent? Isn't her choice to stay in an upper-class social circle by turning herself into a high-priced commodity supremely understandable on some level, given the fact that the alternative would be to find a job with meager pay upon graduation and to marry someone she does not necessarily love in exchange for a modicum of financial security? By presenting the options that Weilong faces and weighs in her contemporary context, Chang goes beyond the question of individual free will and responsibility and instead gestures toward structural issues such as male economic dominance.

Beyond the texts with pronounced cases of failure mentioned above, even in a story like "Love in a Fallen City" (傾城之戀), which at first blush seems to be about a woman's successful escape from her stiflingly conservative family, the heroine Bai Liusu's victory is in fact bittersweet—she succeeds in luring Fan Liuyuan into marriage only with the help of the Japanese siege of Hong Kong. Moreover, now that they are married, he begins to reserve his witty jokes for flirting with other women. Liusu's victory, in other words, is contingent on circumstance, as is their love. It is a conditional and precarious love—a love with blemishes. In the final analysis, Liusu—as someone economically and psychologically dependent on Liuyuan—has merely escaped from one patriarchal household to enter another. She is still far from the self-determining modern woman living happily ever after with her true love that modern fairy tales would like us to believe in.[8]

But perhaps the most spectacular failure is none other than that suffered by Wang Jiazhi in "Lust, Caution" (色·戒). Inspired by a real incident, the technically brilliant story that Chang labored over for twenty years features an intricate narrative structure, incorporating multiple layers of carefully arranged metaphors and ironies.[9] The story's main action consists of former college student Wang Jiazhi's attempt to lure the intelligence chief Mr. Yi into a death trap. Temporally, the assassination attempt is sandwiched between two scenes in which witty yet insipid conversations take place around a mahjong table among the wives of the officials of the Nanjing collaborationist regime supported by the occupying Japanese. Here, mahjong does not signify a domestic space far removed from the world of political intrigue as much as it functions as a trope for politics. Intense psychological drama takes place just beneath the surface of raucous merriment, and through a juxtaposition of surface events and hidden psychological drama Chang draws a suggestive parallel between gambling and Jiazhi's act of taking chances with her own life, since it is indeed risky business for her to act as a bait in the assassination plot, a dangerous move that can lead as easily to irrevocable loss as to victory. Moreover, by framing the political assassination plot with the mahjong scenes, Chang draws another comparison between the mahjong players' frivolous competition and the deadly political rivalry between the leaders of the KMT (Chinese Nationalist Party), Chiang Kai-shek 蔣介石 and Wang Jingwei 汪精衛.

Apart from the metaphor of gambling and strategy, another extended metaphor that runs through the story involves the trope of playacting. Jiazhi, a former amateur actress in college, regards her role in the assassination plot as a stage performance. The theatricality of the whole episode is foreshadowed by the very first lines of the story, which describe Jiazhi's beauty as accentuated, rather than compromised, by the harsh, artificial light that shines on the mahjong table. She is, in other words, well suited to the spotlight and the stage. Later, in the middle of the story, before a full flashback to Jiazhi's student life in Guangzhou and Hong Kong begins, Chang makes the comparison between her actions and playacting even more explicit when she writes: "[Jiazhi] had, in a past life, been an actress; and here she was, still playing a part, but in a drama too secret to make her famous."[10] Then, before the story's climax and denouement, the narrator's description of Jiazhi's state of mind again turns to acting: "Her stage fright always evaporated once the curtain was up."[11]

After leading Mr. Yi to a jewelry shop where he is to be killed by her coconspirators, Jiazhi abandons the assassination scheme. This is how Chang describes the critical moment:

> He was an old hand at this: taking his paramours shopping, ministering to their whims, retreating into the background while they made their choices. But there was, she noted again, no cynicism in his smile just then; only sadness. He sat in silhouette

against the lamp, seemingly sunk into an attitude of tenderly affectionate contemplation, his downcast eyelashes tinged the dull cream of moths' wings as they rested on his gaunt face.

He really loves me, she thought. Inside, she felt a raw tremor of shock—then a vague sense of loss.

It was too late.[12]

Thinking that Yi really loves her, at this crucial moment Jiazhi abandons the assassination plot for which she has sacrificed so much. Haiyan Lee has provided a philosophical reading, through a Levinasian lens, of the moment in which Jiazhi gazes into Yi's face, interpreting Jiazhi's decision to let Yi go as the self's ethical, transcendent response to the other.[13] Although her reading is thought-provoking, I want to emphasize here that Jiazhi's recognition of the expression on Yi's face as love is a classic case of misrecognition, for at that very moment, Yi is thinking no more than the fact that he has his power and position to thank for the great fortune of enjoying the favor of such a beautiful woman. His thoughts are more self-congratulatory than amorous. Jiazhi, likewise, is more motivated by the euphoria of receiving attention than by an altruistic ethical impulse.

Jiazhi tends to indulge in theatrical illusion, and is reluctant to exit her role in the attic of the jeweler's shop. Indeed, when she sees the six-carat diamond ring presented to her by the jeweler, "she [registers] a tinge of regret that it [is] to be no more than a prop in the short, penultimate scene of the drama unfolding around it."[14] She wants the illusion to continue, and her love for the mirage overpowers her political convictions. This is her tragic flaw.

Though published in the 1970s, this story harks back to the public debate over the modern girl that raged in Chinese cities in the 1930s and 1940s. In that debate, Chinese reformist intellectuals tried to distinguish between authentically modern and pseudo-modern women. They criticized modern women's preoccupation with Western fashion as superficial trappings. They denounced the decadent and hedonistic modern woman and attempted to define the real modern woman as intent on reform and committed to the greater good.[15] Although some scholars believe the debate peaked around 1934, just after Chiang Kai-shek launched the New Life Movement, in reality it continued through the Sino-Japanese War and into the 1940s. In some ways, Jiazhi is the quintessential failed modern girl attacked by Chinese reformist intellectuals during the 1930s and 1940s—one who fetishizes love (and its material tokens, such as diamonds) and is not sufficiently committed to political principles or the exigencies of national salvation. In this belated or deferred response to the modern girl debate, completed in the 1970s, Chang is both registering a criticism of the modern girl's failings and revealing to us that there is no easy distinction between success and failure. After a two-year period of slow becoming, Jiazhi finally succeeds in inhabiting the role of the glamorous and amorous modern girl precisely at the very moment that she is executed—thus physically destroyed—by the secret police by Yi's order. It is her death that seals her fate as his possession, like the ghost of a tiger's prey forever belonging to the tiger. It is a gruesome vision of love, in which Jiazhi's identity as a lover is secured through her physical annihilation. The individualistic modern girl, then, succeeds in arriving at a state of being precisely at the moment of her political and corporeal failure. It is through this ironic double vision of failure that Chang challenges both the idealized heterosexual romance and mandatory love for the nation.

Chang's writings explore many forms of failure. On one hand, failure is revealed as the direct consequence—the traumatic aftershock—of not being able to conform to the harsh expectations of normative bourgeois femininity. On the other hand, failure is exposed as the product of normative bourgeois femininity. The modern girl—icon of the most desirable bourgeois femininity—in the process of becoming a sexually captivating temptress and a glittering consumer, all too frequently foregoes commitments to her own intellectual growth, as well as to societal improvement and national salvation. In other words, embodying the quintessence of modern bourgeois femininity, the modern girl is perceived as being prone to moral, intellectual, and political failings. Refreshingly, however, Chang does not simplistically condemn these modern girls, and instead she delves into their psychological processes, bringing to light their full humanity and compelling the reader to consider the social, economic, and political forces that have shaped them. In this respect Chang differs significantly from many social commentators during the 1930s–1940s, who inveighed against the decadence of the modern girl and neglected systemic male domination as a reality that confronted the modern girl at every turn.

CODA

Chang has been something of a favorite with critics as they try to theorize a female literature in Chinese, whether conceptualizing female writing as grounded in the female body or else making the opposite move of delinking it from biology. In a pioneering study from 1988, for instance, Yvonne Chang identifies Eileen Chang as having exerted a strong influence on a host of young women writers who came into their own in Taiwan between the mid-1970s and 1980s. She discerns a pronounced tendency toward lyrical sentimentalization that is shared by the followers of Eileen Chang in Taiwan, including Yuan Qiongqiong 袁瓊瓊, Chu T'ien-wen 朱天文, and others.[16] Similarly fascinated with the question of literary lineage, David Der-wei Wang has constructed a genealogy that extends both backwards and forwards in time and expands out spatially. He views Eileen Chang as a writer who best exemplifies the confluence of the multiple strands of Shanghai literature, from late Qing courtesan novels to May Fourth Romanticist literature, 1930s leftist literature, and 1930s modernist literature.[17] For Wang, Chang epitomizes the rich tradition of the Shanghai school (海派) in modern fiction. She has become a fountainhead of inspiration for numerous writers in Taiwan and Hong Kong since the 1960s and also some mainland Chinese writers since the 1980s. Significantly, the genealogy that Wang constructs crosses gender lines, and in this manner he reimagines modern Chinese literary history by giving a woman writer paradigmatic significance.

Adopting a different approach to female writing, Rey Chow has famously argued that Eileen Chang's style is characterized by an attention to detail that one might call feminine. For Chow, this feminine detail signifies an inherent resistance to the grand narratives of history, which typically revolve around the nation. According to Chow, "detail" is distinctly feminine and can be defined as "the sensuous, trivial, and superfluous textual presences that exist in an ambiguous relation with some larger 'vision' such as reform and revolution."[18] It is through a meticulous magnification of the sensuous and the seemingly frivolous that Chang registers her departure from dominant political ideologies, as well as her disagreement with the naive and overgeneralizing theses about "humanity" that pervade the Chinese rhetoric about modernity.

Taking the question of female writing in yet another direction, Nicole Huang has linked Eileen Chang to other women writers active in 1940s Shanghai, emphasizing their roles as public intellectuals who shaped and mediated popular culture in Shanghai under Japanese occupation (from December 3, 1941 to August 15, 1945). Focusing on Chang's informal essays rather than her fiction, Huang argues that "the meticulous descriptions of clothes, food, furniture, and all types of spatial forms, such as mansions, apartments, elevators, bedrooms, bathrooms, kitchens, balconies, streets, shops, cafés, movie theaters, and vegetable markets . . . can be read as cultural commentaries of the time." According to Huang, the "fascination of women writers with 'irrelevant' details was a direct response to the era in which they lived."[19] She maintains that "the domestic was extended into the public realm" when "domestic issues were discussed in every major media space," thus blurring the boundaries between public and private.[20] To push this argument further, we might say that in a time of war and occupation, attention to the domestic and the seemingly trivial was nothing less than a strategy for women writers to enter into public culture. They actively constructed a meaningful universe based on everyday, quotidian experiences precisely because they were faced with the constant threats of censorship and destruction.

That Chang's work lends itself to such diverse forms of feminist inquiry is a testament to its polysemy and complexity. Besides these diverse approaches to female writing that have taken Eileen Chang as a prime example, scholars interested in gender representation as both a consequence and a manifestation of Chinese modernity have also gravitated toward Chang's works, and almost all of Chang's major stories and novels have been analyzed at great length in terms of the gender politics of representation, with topics running the gamut from female subjectivity to female fetishism, woman as fetish, mother-daughter relationships, male psychology, the war between the sexes, the female body and the nation, and same-sex desire.[21] It is in the spirit of exploring the gender politics of representation that I have considered the theme of failure in Chang's works in this chapter. Failure, as deviation from the norm, provides an opening for a critique of the yardsticks for success. It is through failure that reflections on the legitimacy and suitability of certain definitions of success are set in motion. It is also in failure that alternatives to the idealized standard can be embodied and articulated.

Practicing the art of failure, Chang succeeds in undoing received assumptions about what is respectable, desirable, and good. Even if her explicit intention is not to subvert gender and sexual norms, her insistence on exploring what lies outside the narrowly defined realm of perfection makes her work inspiring even today. Particularly provocative are her studies of the modern girl's romantic, moral, and political failures. By withholding judgment, she allows us to see into the deepest recesses of the modern girl's psyche, to recognize her humanity, including her naïveté and even innocence. Chang shines a bright light on the ways in which the much-maligned modern girl is hostage to a male-dominated economic and political order.

NOTES

1. Eileen Chang 張愛玲, "Tiancai meng" 天才夢 [My dream of being a genius], in *Zhangkan* 張看 [Zhang looks] (Taipei: Huangguan, 1991), 240. All translations are mine unless otherwise noted.

2. Chang, *Zhangkan*, 242.

3. Chang, *Zhangkan*, 245

4. For feminist and queer theorizations of failure, see Judith Butler, *Gender Trouble: Feminism and the Subversion of Identity* (New York: Routledge, 1990); Judith Halberstam, *The Queer Art of Failure* (Durham: Duke University Press, 2011). For discussions on failure and identity in Chinese literature and film, see Jing Tsu, *Failure, Nationalism, and Literature: The Making of Modern Chinese Identity, 1895–1937* (Stanford: Stanford University Press, 2004); Brian Bergen-Aurand, Mary Mazzilli, and Wai-siam Hee, eds., *Transnational Chinese Cinemas, Embodiment, Corporeality, and the Ethics of Failure* (Los Angeles: Bridge21 Publications, 2014).

5. Eileen Chang, *Love in a Fallen City*, trans. Karen S. Kinsbury (New York: New York Review of Books, 2007), 68–69.

6. Chang, *Love in a Fallen City*, 76.

7. For criticisms of superficial modern girls, see, for instance, Cheng Zhi 承志, "Modeng xiaojie" 摩登小姐 [Modern girls], *Modeng zhoubao* 摩登週報 [Modern weekly] 1.4 (1932): 5; Meng Sigen 孟斯根, "Zhongguo 'modeng' nüzi de weiji" 中國「摩登」女子的危機 [The crisis of China's "modern" girls], *Huanian* 華年 [Magnificent years] 2.6 (1933): 7–10; Shi Guang 世光, "Xianweijing xia de modeng nüzi" 顯微鏡下的摩登女子 [The modern girl under the microscope], *Shizhao yuebao* 時兆月報 [Shizhao monthly] 30.3 (1935): 6–7; Nan Xi 南兮, "Gudao funü de modeng bing" 孤島婦女的摩登病 [Women's malaise of being modern in orphan-island Shanghai], *Xiandai jiating* 現代家庭 [Modern family] 4.5 (1940): 30. For a defense of modern girls who are gold diggers, see Lin Yutang 林語堂, "Modeng nüzi bian" 摩登女子辯 [A defense of modern girls], *Lunyu* 論語 [The Analects bimonthly] 67 (1935): 6–8. For commentaries that attempt to salvage the word *modeng* (modern) by disassociating it from the perceived connotations of decadence and hedonism, see Tian Nan 天南, "Modeng bu tuifei" 摩登不頹廢 [Being modern is not the same as decadent], *Shiri tan* 十日談 [Decameron] 11 (1933): 4; Tian Nan 天南, "Modeng jiuguo lun" 摩登救國論 [Being modern can save the country], *Shiri tan* 十日談 [Decameron] 9 (1933): 3; Yang Tiannan 楊天南 [most likely the same as Tian Nan], "Modeng wuzui lun" 摩登無罪論 [Being modern is not a crime], *Shiri tan* 十日談

[Decameron] 7 (1933): 4; Zhang Kebiao 章克標, "Tichang modenghua" 提倡摩登化 [To promote modernization], *Hua'an* 華安 [China's peace] 2.3 (1934): 13.

8. The issue of failure appears also in some of Chang's works written after leaving Shanghai, such as "Stale Mates" (五四遺事), "My Classmates from Youth Are Far From Lowly" (同學少年都不賤), and so forth. At the end of Chang's writing career, at least two of her last creative fiction works, "Lust, Caution" and the Chinese autobiographical novel *Small Reunions*, also extensively explore failure (although failure is less prominent in the English counterparts of *Small Reunions*—*The Fall of the Pagoda* and *The Book of Change*); see below.

9. Chang mentions that the story was based on some "material" she had obtained, which vaguely implies that it was inspired by a real incident; see Eileen Chang 張愛玲, "Wangran ji" 惘然記 [Lingering regrets], in *Zhang Ailing diancang quanji* 張愛玲典藏全集 [Special edition of Eileen Chang's works], vol. 9 (Taipei: Huangguan, 2001), 208. Since the story's adaptation as a film by Ang Lee 李安, there has been wide speculation that it is loosely based on the KMT underground agent Zheng Pingru's attempt to lure and assassinate the collaborationist intelligence chief Ding Mocun in 1939. On the Zheng Pingru incident, see Luo Jiurong 羅久蓉, "Lishi zhenshi yu wenxue xiangxiang: Cong yige nü jiandie zhi si kan jindai Zhongguo de xingbie yu guozu lunshu" 歷史真實與文學想像：從一個女間諜之死看近代中國的性別與國族論述 [Historical reality and literary imagination: Gender and the discourse of the nation in the death of a female spy], *Jindai Zhongguo funüshi yanjiu* 近代中國婦女史研究 [Research on women in modern Chinese history] 11 (2003): 47–98; for an excellent study comparing the Zheng incident and Eileen Chang's story "Lust, Caution," see Guo Yuwen 郭玉雯, "Zhang Ailing Sejie tanxi—jianji xiangguan zhi lishi jizai yu Li An de gaibian dianying" 張愛玲〈色戒〉探析——兼及相關之歷史記載與李安的改編電影 [A Study of Eileen Chang's 'Lust, Caution'—mentioning also the relevant historical records and Ang Lee's screen version of the story], *Taiwan wenxue yanjiu jikan* 台灣文學研究集刊 [NTU studies in Taiwan literature] 4 (2007): 41–76.

10. Eileen Chang, *Lust, Caution*, translated by Julia Lovell (New York: Anchor Books, 2007), 20.

11. Chang, *Lust, Caution*, 29.

12. Chang, *Lust, Caution*, 40.

13. Haiyan Lee, "Enemy Under My Skin: Eileen Chang's *Lust, Caution* and the Politics of Transcendence," *PMLA* 125.3 (2010): 640–656.

14. Chang, *Lust, Caution*, 40.

15. For related discussions, see Louise Edwards, "Policing the Modern Woman in Republican China," *Modern China* 26.2 (2000): 115–147; Tze-lan D. Sang, "Failed Modern Girls in Early-Twentieth-Century China," in *Performing "Nation": Gender Politics in Literature, Theater and the Visual Arts of China and Japan, 1880–1940*, ed. Catherine Yeh, Doris Croissant, and Joshua Mostow (Leiden: Brill Academic Publishers, 2008), 179–202.

16. Sung-sheng Yvonne Chang, "Yuan Qiongqiong and the Rage for Eileen Chang among Taiwan's Feminine Writers," *Modern Chinese Literature* 4.1–2 (1988): 203.

17. David Der-wei Wang 王德威, "Cong haipai dao Zhangpai: Zhang Ailing xiaoshuo de yuanyuan yu chuancheng" 從海派到張派：張愛玲小說的淵源與傳承 [From "Shanghai style" to "Chang style": The origin and legacy of Eileen Chang's narrative], in *Ruhe xiandai, zenyang wenxue* 如何現代怎樣文學 [The making of the modern, the making of literature] (Taipei: Maitian, 1998), 325.

18. Rey Chow, *Woman and Chinese Modernity: The Politics of Reading between West and East* (Minneapolis: University of Minnesota Press, 1991), 85.

19. Nicole Huang, *Women, War, Domesticity: Shanghai Literature and Popular Culture of the 1940s* (Leiden: Brill, 2005), 38.

20. Huang, *Women, War, Domesticity*, 39. On Chang's departure from grand narratives, see also Leo Ou-fan Lee, *Shanghai Modern* (Cambridge: Harvard University Press, 1999).

21. To name just a few: Shui Jing has analyzed the portrait of a lady in "Aloeswood Incense, the First Brazier" and masculinity in "Red Rose, White Rose"; see Shui Jing 水晶, *Zhang Ailing de xiaoshuo yishu* 張愛玲的小說藝術 [The Art of Eileen Chang's fiction] (Taipei: Dadi, 1973), 99–107, 109–142. David Wang has looked at the figure of the hungry woman in Chang's *The Rice Sprout Song* and other writers' works, arguing that in modern Chinese literature, we see that "national hunger has been imagined in feminine terms, owing, perhaps, to women's somatic vulnerability during natural and man-made famines, or to women's conventional role in the semiotics of conventional victimology." David Der-wei Wang, "Three Hungry Women," *boundary* 2 25.3 (1998): 48. See also the essays under "Part Two: Gender Politics," in Yang Ze 楊澤, ed., *Yuedu Zhang Ailing: Zhang Ailing guoji yantaohui lunwenji* 閱讀張愛玲：張愛玲國際研討會論文集 [Reading Eileen Chang: Essays from the international conference on Eileen Chang] (Taipei: Maitian, 1999), 161–275, and "Part Four: Woman, Body, and Image," in Lin Xingqian 林幸謙, ed., *Zhang Ailing: Wenxue, dianying, wutai* 張愛玲：文學·電影·舞台 [Eileen Chang: literature, film, and the stage] (Hong Kong: Oxford University Press, 2007).

Works Cited

Bergen-Aurand, Brian, Mary Mazzilli, and Wai-siam Hee, eds. *Transnational Chinese Cinemas, Embodiment, Corporeality, and the Ethics of Failure.* Los Angeles: Bridge21 Publications, 2014.

Butler, Judith. *Gender Trouble: Feminism and the Subversion of Identity.* New York: Routledge, 1990.

Chang, Sung-sheng Yvonne. "Yuan Qiongqiong and the Rage for Eileen Chang among Taiwan's Feminine Writers." *Modern Chinese Literature* 4.1–2 (1988): 201–224.

Cheng Zhi 承志. "Modeng xiaojie" 摩登小姐 [Modern girls]. *Modeng zhoubao* 摩登週報 [Modern weekly] 1.4 (1932): 5.

Chow, Rey. *Woman and Chinese Modernity: The Politics of Reading between West and East.* Minneapolis: University of Minnesota Press, 1991.

Edwards, Louise. "Policing the Modern Woman in Republican China." *Modern China* 26.2 (2000): 115–147.

Guo Yuwen 郭玉雯. "Zhang Ailing Sejie tanxi—jianji xiangguan zhi lishi jizai yu Li An de gaibian dianying" 張愛玲〈色戒〉探析——兼及相關之歷史記載與李安的改編電影 [A study of Eileen Chang's 'Lust, Caution'—mentioning also the relevant historical records and Ang Lee's screen version of the story]. *Taiwan wenxue yanjiu jikan* 台灣文學研究集刊 [NTU studies in Taiwan literature]. 4 (2007): 41–76.

Halberstam, Judith. *The Queer Art of Failure.* Durham: Duke University Press, 2011.

Huang, Nicole. *Women, War, Domesticity: Shanghai Literature and Popular Culture of the 1940s.* Leiden: Brill, 2005.

Lee, Haiyan. "Enemy Under My Skin: Eileen Chang's *Lust, Caution* and the Politics of Transcendence." *PMLA* 125.3 (2010): 640–656.

Lee, Leo Ou-fan. *Shanghai Modern*. Cambridge: Harvard University Press, 1999.

Lin Xingqian 林幸謙, ed. *Zhang Ailing: Wenxue, dianying, wutai* 張愛玲：文學·電影·舞台 [Eileen Chang: Literature, film, and the stage]. Hong Kong: Oxford University Press, 2007.

Lin Yutang 林語堂. "Modeng nüzi bian" 摩登女子辯 [A defense of modern girls]. *Lunyu* 論語 [The Analects bimonthly] 67 (1935): 6–8.

Luo Jiurong 羅久蓉. "Lishi zhenshi yu wenxue xiangxiang: Cong yige nü jiandie zhi si kan jindai Zhongguo de xingbie yu guozu lunshu" 歷史真實與文學想像：從一個女間諜之死看近代中國的性別與國族論述 [Historical reality and literary imagination: Gender and the discourse of the nation in the death of a female spy], *Jindai Zhongguo funüshi yanjiu* 近代中國婦女史研究 [Research on women in modern Chinese history] 11 (2003): 47–98.

Meng Sigen 孟斯根. "Zhongguo 'modeng' nüzi de weiji" 中國「摩登」女子的危機 [The crisis of China's "modern" girls]. *Huanian* 華年 [Magnificent years] 2.6 (1933): 7–10.

Nan Xi 南兮. "Gudao funü de modeng bing" 孤島婦女的摩登病 [Women's malaise of being modern in orphan-island Shanghai]. *Xiandai jiating* 現代家庭 [Modern family] 4.5 (1940): 30.

Sang, Tze-lan D. "Failed Modern Girls in Early-Twentieth-Century China." In *Performing "Nation": Gender Politics in Literature, Theater and the Visual Arts of China and Japan, 1880–1940*. Ed. Catherine Yeh, Doris Croissant, and Joshua Mostow. Leiden: Brill Academic Publishers, 2008. 179–202.

Shi Guang 世光. "Xianweijing xia de modeng nüzi" 顯微鏡下的摩登女子 [The modern girl under the microscope]. *Shizhao yuebao* 時兆月報 [Shizhao monthly] 30.3 (1935): 6–7.

Shui Jing 水晶. *Zhang Ailing de xiaoshuo yishu* 張愛玲的小說藝術 [The art of Eileen Chang's fiction]. Taipei: Dadi, 1973.

Tian Nan 天南. "Modeng bu tuifei" 摩登不頹廢 [Being modern is not the same as decadent]. *Shiri tan* 十日談 [Decameron] 11 (1933): 4.

Tian Nan 天南. "Modeng jiuguo lun" 摩登救國論 [Modernity can save the country]. *Shiri tan* 十日談 [Decameron] 9 (1933): 3.

Tsu, Jing. *Failure, Nationalism, and Literature: The Making of Modern Chinese Identity, 1895–1937*. Stanford: Stanford University Press, 2004.

Wang, David Der-wei 王德威. "Cong haipai dao Zhangpai: Zhang Ailing xiaoshuo de yuanyuan yu chuancheng" 從海派到張派：張愛玲小說的淵源與傳承 [From "Shanghai style" to "Chang style": The origin and legacy of Eileen Chang's narrative]. In *Ruhe xiandai, zenyang wenxue* 如何現代怎樣文學 [The making of the modern, the making of literature]. Taipei: Maitian, 1998. 319–335.

Wang, David Der-wei 王德威. "Three Hungry Women." *boundary 2* 25.3 (1998): 47–76.

Yang Tiannan 楊天南. "Modeng wuzui lun" 摩登無罪論 [Being modern is not a crime]. *Shiri tan* 十日談 [Decameron] 7 (1933): 4.

Yang Ze 楊澤, ed. *Yuedu Zhang Ailing: Zhang Ailing guoji yantaohui lunwenji* 閱讀張愛玲：張愛玲國際研討會論文集 [Reading Eileen Chang: Essays from the international conference on Eileen Chang]. Taipei: Maitian, 1999. 161–275.

Zhang Ailing 張愛玲 (Eileen Chang). *Love in a Fallen City*. Trans. Karen S. Kinsbury. New York: New York Review of Books, 2007.

Zhang Ailing 張愛玲 (Eileen Chang). *Lust, Caution*. Trans. Julia Lovell. New York: Anchor Books, 2007.

Zhang Ailing 張愛玲 (Eileen Chang). "Wangran ji" 惘然記 [Lingering regrets]. In *Zhang Ailing diancang quanji* 張愛玲典藏全集 [Special edition of Eileen Chang's works], vol. 9. Taipei: Huangguan, 2001. 3–5.

Zhang Ailing 張愛玲 (Eileen Chang). "Tiancai meng" 天才夢 [My dream of being a genius]. *Zhangkan* 張看 [Zhang looks]. Taipei: Huangguan, 1991. 239–242.

Zhang Kebiao 章克標. "Tichang modenghua" 提倡摩登化 [To promote modernization], *Hua'an* 華安 [China's peace] 2.3 (1934): 13.

CHAPTER 3.10

....

FROM EXILE TO QUEER
HOMECOMING

Chen Xue's A Wife's Diary

....

E. K. TAN

> In the evening, as we bid goodbye before going home, I hugged mother
> as if we had never hugged before. Sis said she also wanted a hug and
> embraced mother. When Breakfaster gave mother a hug, she gently
> said: "Come home often with Yaling." It was as if she said: "Bring her
> home more often!"
>
> (Chen Xue and Breakfaster, *A Wife's Diary*)

IN her diary novel *A Wife's Diary* (人妻日記; 2012), Taiwanese lesbian writer Chen
Xue 陳雪—writing in the voice of a character known as Chen Yaling 陳雅玲, which
is also Chen Xue's real name—details her first Chinese New Year family reunion in
rural Taichung. After almost a decade of not participating in this yearly tradition,
her homecoming means more than just a simple trip to spend time with her parents
and siblings. This is her first homecoming trip with her lesbian partner, known as
Breakfaster 早餐人. She sees this as her trip back to her maternal family (回娘家)—a
common practice in Sinophone cultures whereby the married daughter returns to
her maternal family home for a visit with her new family. After much anticipation
and worrying, this queer homecoming turns out to be pleasant and heartwarming,
despite some moments of awkwardness. The day after the reunion dinner, the entire
family gathers to participate in one of the most popular social activities in Taiwan:
karaoke. Chen's father, a man of few words, is the one who initiates the activity. After
setting up the stereo system, he watches his children and Breakfaster sing. Contented,
he speaks more than usual. Chen's mother, in a much more direct manner with her
attentiveness to Breakfaster, and with her almost permanent tender smile, seems to
be saying that she knows and is happy that Chen and Breakfaster are a couple.

That evening, before Chen and Breakfaster leave to return to Taipei, Chen's mother acknowledges Breakfaster as a part of the family by saying to her "Come home often with Yaling." In a sense, Chen's mother's words complete the homecoming trip. While I celebrate queer homecoming stories like this one in Chen's novel, I am also aware that I am treading on the dangerous terrain of theoretical debates among queer scholars on the politics of kinship. I am in no way dismissing or arguing against scholars like Lisa Duggan, who cautions that the struggle for same-sex marriage might run the risk of endorsing the legitimacy of the state-sanctioned institution of marriage, which is a form of equality that is still rather limiting.[1] Similarly, as I engage in a critical reading of Chen Xue's queer homecoming in and via *A Wife's Diary*, I am also conscious of the fact that recent queer cultural texts in literature, cinema, and media are products of a queer liberalism in Taiwan, a phenomenon similar to that in the United States examined by David Eng, which must be problematized.[2] I, however, want to open up the discussion on queer kinship in order to address the displaced connection and meaning of home to queer subjects. My agenda is not to cast queer subjects back into a heteronormative structure but to treat queer homecoming as an intervention into this seemingly stable heteronormative structure. Such intervention urges both queer subjects and their families to simultaneously navigate and negotiate a new type of kinship that is more inclusive than the traditional one. The above passage from Chen Xue's *A Wife's Diary* is one such example. It is no doubt tempting to read Chen's homecoming as giving in to heteronormativity. But I wonder if such a reading may be criticized for failing to consider the moment of homecoming itself as an intervention into old kinship structures in order to rethink new potential ones. Like Chen, her parents are forced to engage and negotiate with her homecoming trip to rethink their comfort zone, the home space, in order to feel at home again. The exchange is mutual.

Returning to literature, I want to propose that we begin thinking beyond the aesthetics of exile, a dominant trope in Taiwanese queer literature. Taiwan's *tongzhi wenxue* (同志文學; "gay and lesbian literature") or *ku'er wenxue* (酷兒文學; "queer literature") grew in popularity in the 1990s with award-winning works such as Chu T'ien-wen's 朱天文 *Notes of a Desolate Man* (荒人手記; 1994), Chi Ta-wei's 紀大偉 *Membrane* (膜; 1996), and Qiu Miaojin's 邱妙津 *The Crocodile's Journal* (鱷魚手記; 1994). Most of these works focus on the theme of transgressive sexuality, depicting the struggle of queer individuals to forge sexual identities against social pressures and cultural traditions. Even though the growth of *tongzhi wenxue* or *ku'er wenxue* over the last two decades has created its own community of queer readership, this particular literary movement is still nothing more than a subculture existing in the periphery of mainstream Taiwanese literary circles. With the recent debate on the legalization of same-sex marriage in Taiwan, there is a clear attempt to fight for LGBT rights in Taiwan by calling for the inclusion of the LGBT community in mainstream society. This emphasis on LGBT's rights to have families and raise children shifts the myopic focus of them as "deviant" (often sexual) subjects to that of individuals who have the basic needs and desires to form human relationships that could bring about diversity and harmony in a society.

Chen Xue's *A Wife's Diary* departs from her previous writings on the struggle of sexualities and social oppressions to adopt a different voice or representation for the LGBT community in Taiwan. *A Wife's Diary* is a diary novel jointly written with her partner, Breakfaster, and consists mainly of Chen's meditations on her relationship with Breakfaster as a married couple. The final section of the book is a collection of e-mails from Breakfaster to Chen. I see the shift in themes and content of Chen's recent work not as a compromise with the heteronormative structure of Taiwanese social makeup and traditional values, but as a negotiation for a reshaping of Taiwanese society into an inclusive space for queer desires and subjectivities.

This approach in Chen's works is what I call *queer homecoming*, an intervention into the traditional concept of family (patriarchal and heterosexual) in order to enable non-normative kinship relations to negotiate for a livable home space within a society. I propose to think of queer homecoming as both a practice and a metaphor. The former is an act that helps queer subjects reconnect and reintegrate into their families and society. The latter is a concept with a critical edge that ensures that the practice of queer homecoming is not a compromise with patriarchy and heteronormativity but an intervention that attempts at restructuring a state-endorsed hegemonic kinship system into an inclusive, nondiscriminatory one. Rather than feeling trapped in exile or locked in a perpetual pursuit of a queer utopia, Taiwanese queer literature can also promote in queer subjects a generative rethinking of kinship in a changing Taiwan society.

THE PROBLEMATIC HOME SPACE IN EARLY TAIWANESE QUEER LITERATURE

Sociologist Chou Wah-shan 周華山 in *Postcolonial Homosexual* (後殖民同志; 1997) and *Tongzhi: Politics of Same-Sex Eroticism in Chinese Societies* (2000) identifies "home" (*jia* 家) as an entrenched metaphor for Chinese kinship in the postcolonial Sinophone identity formation of queer subjects. He explains that social foundations of traditional Chinese culture are not isolated and unrelated structures; they are what constitute the clan network in Chinese kinship system. Chinese individuals are by birth a part of the close-knit kinship system defined by core ethical and moral values largely regulated by Confucianism. Under such a system, the space of "home" becomes the heart of this kinship network. Every individual's primary identity is defined by the social relations circumscribed by this particular kinship structure, such as the relations between father and son, husband and wife, and mother and daughter. Under this structure of sociality, to conform to such a network of relations is to affirm that the family under the metaphor of the "home" is a heterosexual space. It marginalizes or excludes those of alternative gender orientations and sexual practices. If queer subjects do not and cannot occupy a place in this heternormativized space, does it mean that their only option would be to resort to the struggle of perpetually living in a state of displacement and exile?

Writer and literary scholar Chi Ta-wei compares the queer subject's exilic experience to that of the diaspora.[3] He points out that queer classics from modern Taiwanese literature such as Pai Hsien-yung 白先勇 *Crystal Boys* (孽子; 1983) and *Notes of a Desolate Man* construct the imagery of a lost paradise for gay men in order to aestheticize their characters' state of being—one that is marked by exile and displacement. Other works such as Ku Dschau-sen's 顧肇森 "Zhang Wei" (張偉; 1984) and Hsu Yo-shen's 許佑生 "Stones on the Shore" (岸邊石; 1992) depict the inevitable departure from home to seek refuge in a new host country—leaving Taiwan for the United States. The characters in these stories are often social outcasts and misfits to their family and home. Their exile from home, voluntarily or involuntarily, adopts some form of physical distancing from their home, family, and country. Regardless of this physical distancing, Chi, in his essay "Sex and Exile of Gay Men in Taiwanese Novels" (台灣小說中男同性戀的性與流放; 1997), engages with the theory of the diaspora to argue that the experience of exile for queer subjects is not merely that of a physical displacement from one place to another but a state of being, one he calls "internal exile" (內在的驅除).[4]

The alternative identification to the kinship structure from which they are banished is either the new family structure constructed among the characters in *Crystal Boys*, who regard the 228 Memorial Park as their home space where alternative kinship is established, or the new host nation as the potential space and place of freedom and new identities in "Zhang Wei" and "Rock on the Riverbank." These new kinds of identification also come in the form of a physical space in the philosophical meditations of the characters in *Notes of a Desolate Man* as the main character wanders the streets of Taipei and on his overseas trips.

Although, as noted by Chi, these characters' exile from home is not merely a physical condition but rather a state of being, I want to highlight the implications of gay men's travel and movement in contrast to that of lesbian literary characters in Taiwan. In contrast to gay men's social mobility in Taiwanese gay literature, Gu Minlun 辜敏倫 contends that Taiwanese lesbian literature from the 1990s rarely includes characters who live in exile from their family home or escape abroad to start new lives. This discrepancy between the depiction of gay men and lesbians' relationship with their family or home leads Gu to conclude that there are at least two sets of relationships between queer subjects and their families in Taiwanese literature: one depicts those who live in exile in cities or foreign lands away from home, and the other portrays individuals who repress and distort their desires and identity by maintaining secrets and fabricating lies in order to fit in with the conventional kinship system into which they are interpellated.[5] The former is a common trope in queer literature from Taiwan. Often, the departure from home constitutes a new beginning of identity construction that depends intrinsically on the disavowal of the heteronormative and patrilineal structures of Chinese kinship. This disavowal is no doubt made possible by gay men's privilege to travel and move from place to place. Lesbian characters and their experience fall more into the latter paradigm. Colonized by the heteronormative structure of the traditional family, lesbian characters are bound to serve their fathers, husbands, and sons; in other words, they are doubly exploited as women and lesbians. Their "internal exile," unlike that of gay men, is further complicated by the fact that they are trapped at "home" without much alternative. It is precisely also because of this unique intimacy between gay women and their families, and the proximity between them and their home spaces, that Cambridge Hsu Chien-chiao 許劍橋 argues that gay women's identity clashes and negotiates more directly and frequently with the heteronormative Chinese kinship system mainly because their identity constructions or reconstructions are contingent on how they negotiate their movement within the home space.[6]

Despite the fact that lesbian and gay characters in Taiwanese queer literature are often presented as having very different relationships with their families, here I want to explore the possibility of locating some commonalities between the narratives of exile of gay men and the narratives of kinship entrapment of lesbian characters in Taiwanese literature to rethink their potential agency in order to intervene in the heteronormative kinship structure. In so doing, the "return" of queer subjects to the home space could potentially establish dialogues to negotiate a rethinking of the kinship system that is amicable to both queer subjects and their families. Before expounding on this concept, we need to first explore how kinship becomes normalized.

In *Antigone's Claim: Kinship Between Life and Death* (2000), Judith Butler challenges both Hegel's and Lacan's reading of Antigone's action in Sophocles' play. For Butler, Hegel affirms the interdependent relationship between state authority and kinship in Antigone's narrative, while Lacan places the kinship system in the realm of the symbolic, separating it from the social. Both readings naturalize kinship into a set of sacred rules above social practices and lived experience. For Lacan, kinship rules are what give the social its form, yet these rules cannot be reduced to the basic characteristics of the social. Butler asks, how do such rules function uniformly throughout the diverse cultures around the world?[7] If kinship, in the realm of the symbolic, represents a universal structure, then, can transgression and defiance exist within its reign? Butler takes issue with Lacan's attempt to equate Freud's Oedipus complex with the Law. She describes the Law as

> [a complex derived] from a primary or symbolic prohibition against incest, a prohibition that makes sense only in terms of kinship relations in which various "positions" are established within the family according to an exogamic mandate. In other words, a mother is someone with whom a son and daughter do not have sexual relations, and a father is someone with whom a son and daughter do not have sexual relations, a mother is someone who only had sexual relations with the father, etc. These relations of prohibition are thus encoded in the "position" that each of these family members occupies. To be in such a position is thus to be in such a crossed sexual relation, at least according to the symbolic or normative conception of what that "position" is. (18)

"Positions," according to Lacan, are linguistic products. If a position can be established and created as response to a set of symbolic kinship rules, then potentially some of these positions would not conform completely to such rules; they would perhaps transgress or even disavow the universal claims of the rules. Would that not imply the contingency of the symbolic? If we follow Lacan's train of thought in explicating kinship, would we not be acknowledging that human beings are inevitably trapped in a set of linguistic characteristics that shape the actions and meanings of their life? Instead of dwelling on Butler's critique of Lacan, I would like to examine how Butler theorizes the possibility of exploring other "normativities" of kinship structure that are not exclusively heteronormative.

Without rejecting the symbolic, Butler proposes that "the distinction between symbolic and social law cannot finally hold, that not only is the symbolic itself the sedimentation of social practices but that radical alterations in kinship demand a rearticulation of the structuralist presuppositions of psychoanalysis and, hence, of contemporary gender and sexual theory" (19). Hinting at the contingency of the symbolic under the influence of time and history, Butler aims at rethinking contemporary gender and sexual theory along with deconstructing the kinship system. For Butler, Antigone's piety for her dead brother does not in any way affirm the Law of kinship or reestablish the link between the state authority and the kinship system. Instead, Antigone ruptures the fixity of kinship by deforming and displacing its symbolic pattern, and eventually destabilizes the representational power of the reigning regime. Consequently, this enables "new schemes of intelligibility" for kinship structures that can exist within reigning regimes, such as state authority (25). In other words, new kinship structures can then evolve through a rethinking of kinship norms as diverse, contingent, and productive. I do not claim that Butler's proposal of "new schemes of intelligibility" is the solution to the family problems in Taiwanese queer literature, though I do think it can provide a catalyst for a rethinking of kinship normativities in contemporary Taiwan beyond the constraints of the dominant heteronormative family structure.

On (Not) Coming Out

Chen Xue's *A Wife's Diary* begins with an ambivalent sentiment that is split between the sweet remembrance of her wedding with Breakfaster and the lamentation of the fact that same-sex union in Taiwan is yet to be legalized.

> In the summer of 2009, at the beach
> We took a vow
>
> However, these few days
> I feel displaced in time and space
> As if we were only married after the news was reported in the papers
> Or
> During those sweetest moments, when we illogically claim
> That our wedding ceremony could be repeated in various styles

As our hair grows long
As wrinkles are inscribed around our lips
Layer on top of layer
Carving out traces of time on the LP record

二〇〇九年夏天的海邊
我們的盟誓

然而這幾日
我有一種時空錯置之感
彷彿消息見報後我們才真正結了婚
或者
像是最甜美時光時我們語無倫次地說著
那一場婚禮能以各種形式不斷重來
頭髮漸長
唇邊刻下皺紋
壘壘地
在唱片上雕劃時光 (8)

Two years after the wedding, which took place in 2009, Chen started posting *A Wife's Diary* on Facebook. Chen implies in her opening section of the print copy of her diary that the gap between the two moments of happiness and the lack of a sense of fulfillment widens as time passes. This, conversely, increases the urgency to push for the official legalization of same-sex unions in Taiwan. Without legal endorsement of the union between same-sex couples like herself and Breakfaster, the union will always lack some sort of concreteness and materiality. Without legal protections, the wedding vow between a same-sex couple, however comforting and assuring in terms of the couple's romantic connection, remains empty in its practicality: "Because there is no legal protection/Because it is even still a secret/Because it is still hard to tell others/As for the so-called vow we share/Would it return to its original form" (因為沒有法律保護/因為甚至是個秘密/因為難以對他人言說/所謂的盟誓/是否便還原到最初的樣子) (9).

The imagery of fleeting time exudes a sense of melancholia, which is soon counteracted by a persistence to make visible what is hidden from view—the rights and desires of the queer community in Taiwan.

What we can't see
What we incessantly attempt to capture
Prompts us to repeatedly face the challenges without letting go
Reiteration after reiteration
Fine-tune
Correct
Define
Examine
Comprehend
. . .

We believe
As time goes by
Something concrete will materialize

If we persist
If we persist

那看不見的
我們不斷努力去捕捉的
促使我們一次次面對困難而不鬆手的
那重複又重複
微調
校正
定義
審視
理解
. . .

我們以為
漫長時間過去
總有什麼會具體成形

如果一直一直地
如果一直一直地 (10–11)

The attempt to rescue the invisible from fading into the background and to recapture what is fleeting requires reiteration: "Reiteration after reiteration/ . . . /If we persist/ If we persist" (那重複又重複/ . . . /如果一直一直地/如果一直一直地). Reiteration, in various forms ("Fine-tune/Correct/Define/Examine/Comprehend"), can simultaneously destabilize heteronormativity and facilitate the taking form of what has been made invisible. Reiteration enables the acquisition of a new identity as the old one is transformed; it also establishes boundaries of fixity that contribute to the resistance against dominant, heteronormative expressions in this chapter.[8]

I want to return to the quote at the beginning of this section to discuss Chen's claim that "the past few days/I felt displaced in time and space/It was as if our wedding only became real after it appeared in the news." Even though Chen is a public figure whose sexuality is not a secret to her fans and those who know about her, she has never publicly come out. One could argue that she finally came out when she and Breakfaster did a photo shoot and interview with the lesbian magazine *Lesz*. But this interview was done a while after their wedding. The ambiguity surrounding Chen's coming out reveals that coming out as a practice is not necessarily a rite of passage for all queer individuals. In other words, the practice or process of coming out is not always monolithic.

In a Taiwanese or Sinophone context, *chugui* (出櫃), a literal translation of the Western expression "coming out of the closet," seems to remain more metaphorical than gestural. This is simply because there are various issues at stake for Taiwanese queer subjects, which could be different in context from those in other cultures, when it comes to deciding if they want to publicly pronounce their gender identities and prefer-ence. I think acknowledging this difference and specificity in Taiwanese cultural prac-tices is one of the first steps to rethinking the theoretical potential of queer studies in Asian contexts such as that of Taiwan.[9] The other potential area to theorize Taiwanese queer culture, especially in the twenty-first century, is to rethink a potential familial dialogue and dynamics through a sampling of recent Taiwanese literature.

As Chen Yaling and Breakfaster's wedding becomes public knowledge, Chen begins to wonder how her parents will react to the news, given that she has never come out to them in person. She is also not sure if they have even seen the announcement. She discusses the issue with her sister, and they conclude that if their parents found out about her relationship with Breakfaster, they probably would not have much reaction. In her heart, Chen reflects:

> I am not exactly sure about their views on gays and lesbians, but I know they have their own way of comprehending and accepting me. I am guessing that remaining silent is their way of accepting me.
> Every year, on Chinese New Year eve, I have reunion dinner with Breakfaster's family. On some other holidays she also visits my family with me. We hope that as time passes [literally, accumulates], a lot of things will become clear without us having to talk about them; those that are hard to articulate, time will clarify them for us. (50–51)

Unlike coming out—which is a performance and a speech act in the form of a confession—silence, on the part of her parents, can be read as either denial or accep-tance, or *neither* denial *nor* acceptance. But the bottom line is that their silence implies a consent coming from their unfaltering love for her. This consent over time extends to an acceptance on both sides of the family. What is worth noting is the notion of time passing. Though we often refer to the passing of time as procession, here, in Chinese, time "accumulates" (累積) year after year. This returns us to an earlier discussion on the politics of repetition. In this sense, repetition is not about active resistance but repeat negotiation through the accumulation of experience within a common temporal space—a milieu. This negotiation, even in its silent mode produces a shared expression that (re)marks the milieu into a territory, in which both queer subjects and their fami-lies coexist within a different set of kinship expressions.

In *A Thousand Plateaus: Capitalism and Schizophrenia*, Gilles Deleuze and Félix Guattari describe the *milieu* as

> a block of spacetime constituted by the periodic repetition of the component. Thus the living thing has an exterior milieu of materials, an interior milieu of composing elements and composed substances, an intermediary milieu of membranes and lim-its, and an annexed milieu of energy sources and actions-perceptions. Every milieu is coded, a code being defined by periodic repetition; but each code is in a perpetual state of transcoding or transduction. Transcoding or transduction is the manner in which one milieu serves as the basis for another, or conversely is established atop another milieu, dissipates in it or is constituted in it.[10]

I am particularly interested in Deleuze and Guattari's concept of the "intermediary milieu" and "annexed milieu" when thinking about Chen's symbolic homecoming as a process of refurnishing. If the intermediary milieu is the living thing's physical skin (membrane), it is also the semiotic parameters (limits) where individual identity can be located. The intermediary milieu does not exist independently but is repeatedly trans-coded or transduced when it passes or communicates with other milieus, such as the annexed milieu. The annexed milieu consists of materials that the living thing pos-sesses or occupies in its environment, such as language, food, clothing, and furniture. Hence, if the living thing is related to a combination of exterior, interior, intermediary, and annexed milieus, any attempt at substituting or moving a component in one of the milieus will inevitably constitute a transcoding or transduction. As a result, the milieu of the milieus (the larger environment of the living thing) undergoes negotia-tion to reconstitute a new expression. According to Deleuze and Guattari, expression is what marks a territory.[11] A territory can effect "*a reorganization of functions* [and/or] *a regrouping of forces*" such as "building a dwelling, or the transformation of old func-tions."[12] It is with the concepts of the transcoding and transduction of a milieu (envi-ronment) into an expressive and nonunitary identitarian territory that I read Chen's homecoming through the metaphor of refurnishing—moving furniture—in the fol-lowing section of this chapter.

QUEER HOMECOMING

In *Queer Phenomenology: Orientations, Objects, Others* (2006), Sara Ahmed explores how lived experience and object proximity shape bodies and social worlds through processes of orientation. Through her analysis of the relationship between queer sub-jects and their families, Ahmed argues that in order for a body to feel stable and secure, it must actively orient itself to, and around, objects in the space it inhabits. In this way, subjecthood is created, altered, and transformed. Familiarity is the affect of orienta-tion that motivates a body to navigate toward objects in a particular space. Familiarity is produced in the space of habitation to enable a body to orient itself toward and grow accustomed to objects in its vicinity. The act of becoming familiar makes bod-ies "feel at home" and, hence, establishes the familial. Orientation involves a negotia-tion between the familiar and the unfamiliar. This active negotiation gives the body agency to inhabit a space, and it also helps the body claim the space as home in order "to create new impressions, depending on which way we turn, which affects what is within reach."[13] Kinship systems evolve as contingent social relations as bodies orient themselves within the home space by negotiating, defining, and shaping bodies into a new collective. What is familiar becomes familial when the objects we inherit become our possessions as we orient ourselves toward them. This logic helps us rethink the structure of kinship without affirming a prescriptive heteronormative system.[14] The mobility of a body is what gives it agency to shape and be shaped by its surroundings in order to produce the affect of the familiar and the familial. The body as mobile agent facilitates the orientation of queer subjects toward a rethinking of the kinship system. In this context, I propose the concept of *queer homecoming* as a critical intervention to reconfigure normative patrilineal kinship structures. Queer homecoming as intervention enables articulations of alternative kinship structures; it helps queer subjects enter mainstream cultural expressions in order to destabilize the myth of consanguinity.

If Chen Xue's coming out (or not) had never been a rite of passage to a victorious identity formation that would liberate her or set her apart from her family, then her journey away from her family to establish a home with her same-sex partner offers her an insight into the potential reestablishing of a kinship that resists the reproduction and affirmation of a heteronormative system. She dedicates many pages to describing how she and Breakfaster move to their new apartment. There are details on how they assign the rooms (there is one for their cats, one serves as the master bedroom, another one as guestroom, which is also the room to which Breakfaster retreats when they fight, and so forth), how they decorate it with eclectic style, and how they arrange and rearrange furniture to make it fit:

> Last night, the workers came to install the shutters. We transformed the dinner room into a large study. It was unimaginable that shutters could so dramatically open up a room, making it look spacious and bright. We were both elated. At night, we excitedly checked out the catalogue and searched online to look for beautiful lights for our dining table and study. Since we moved in together, we have been economical in keeping our separate furniture and mix-matching them for our home. Besides the renovation we did on plumbing, electricity, and blinds, and the new dining sets we bought, we have not spent much on furniture. This shutter, which cost us NT 1,000, came from money we saved over time. It has "grown" to suit us, the owners of the home. (134)

Instead of adapting to the conventional layout of their new apartment and buying new furniture to match it, Chen and Breakfaster creatively repurpose the rooms in their new home. For example, they transform the kitchen into a large study and combine their furniture items to make it fit their new home. Here, I want to borrow Sara Ahmed's metaphorical extrapolation of furniture as a device of orientation that can be used to "create" meaning for a space as we employ it to "do" things for us. Though Ahmed acknowledges that furniture implicates "technologies of convention" that delineate and fix structures and patterns of how things function according to how they are arranged, she insists that furniture can offer a different kind of orientation to our understanding of kinship norms:

> Consider the expression, "You treat me like furniture"—which usually means, "You don't notice me; you make me part of the background." So, if furniture is conventional and indeed directs the bodies that use it, then furniture often disappears from view; indeed, what makes furniture "furniture" is this tendency to disappear from view. A queer furnishing might be about making what is in the background, what

is behind us, more available as "things" to "do" things with. . . . The chair moves as I fidget. As soon as we notice the background, then objects come to life, which already makes things rather queer.[15]

Furniture becomes queer when we make it do queer things. Queer orientation or queer furnishing is then a tactic to demystify the "technologies of convention" that furniture carries in order to bring what has disappeared under the influence of conventions to the foreground. There is one piece of furniture in Chen Xue's *A Wife's Diary* that harbors significant meanings for her in the home she grew up in and the present one she is building with her spouse:

> Today, I went to furnish our new home. A friend from Taichung helped deliver grandmother's wardrobe from the countryside to our new place. This wardrobe is almost eighty years old; it was grandmother's dowry. In my childhood, there was a time when I stayed with my grandparents in the side courtyard. In their tiny house, the wardrobe was the one piece of furniture that stood out the most. Grandmother liked to dress up. Every year, father would buy her beautiful clothes throughout the seasons. I used to think that it was made with black wood in my grandparents' badly lit house. Looking at it in the daylight, I realized that it was coated with dark red wood stain. There were minor defects among the drawers of various sizes and the flower-engraved mirror, but grandmother or grandfather fixed them by binding them with wire.
>
> . . .
>
> While I carefully wiped off the dust with a rag and scrutinized the nails used to repair the broken parts, I realized how much I loved this present. This was grandmother's dowry! It was as if my late grandmother was blessing me with happiness.
>
> Grandmother and grandfather lived to the age of ninety. They were deeply in love with one another (their relationship was also one in which the bride is older than the groom). (14–15)

This wardrobe Chen inherited from her grandmother is a piece of furniture her parents and siblings do not care to keep. Inheritance, in the form of this wardrobe, involves a sentimental affect produced through both proximity and likeness. By *proximity*, I am referring to the closeness that Chen feels towards her grandmother, a maternal figure, and by *likeness*, I mean the sense of fondness that one feels for someone, independent of blood ties. By inheriting the wardrobe, Chen deconstructs and reconstructs gender norms; what she inherits, indirectly, is not a patrilineal symbol but a maternal comfort, her grandmother's dowry. In addition, this act of inheritance is one that destabilizes heteronormativity through a form of queer intervention completed through (re)vision ("I used to think that it was made with black wood in my grandparents' badly lit house. Looking at it in the daylight, I realized that it was coated with dark red wood stain") and repair ("There were minor defects among the drawers of various sizes and the flower-engraved mirror, but grandmother or grandfather fixed them by binding them with wire"; "While I carefully wiped off the dust with a rag and scrutinized the nails used to repair the broken parts") of the wardrobe—or closet, the other name for a wardrobe—to engage more directly with a queer terminology and metaphor. The closet in this case is not exclusively a queer object but it becomes one when Chen inherits it. This (re)vision and repair also allows the wardrobe/closet to adopt new values and meanings as Chen places it within the new home space she shares with her same-sex spouse. This physical care and emotional engagement Chen invests in the closet renders the identification between her grandparents' romantic relationship and her own married life possible. On one hand, she seemingly reproduces the heteronormative structure by claiming that, like her grandparents, "the bride is older than the groom" (他們也是姐弟戀呢); on the other hand, it is also in this analogy that gender boundaries are crossed and hetero-normativity is threatened again via the act of queering. To push the allegorical reading further, the wardrobe, in a sense, is a movable "closet" that requires its owner to engage in the act of opening and closing the drawers in a more routine and ritualistic manner. Unlike the closet, which we use at times to store less frequently needed items (or secret identities that need to be kept hidden), the wardrobe contains daily necessities such as socks, undergarments, and causal outfits that we often wear with comfort. Hence, Chen indirectly inherits a sense of intimacy and freedom that comes with this particular piece of heritage furniture as she moves it to the new home she is building with Breakfaster.

By inheriting her grandmother's wardrobe, Chen also reconnects with her past, the past that is framed by the family from which she has grown apart. Chen notes in her diary that even as her perspective begins to change when she visits her parents with Breakfaster, so does that of her parents, judging from their response to Chen's new life:

> I missed my family but I never visited home. I buried the complex and conflicted emotions that I could not verbalize in my writing.
>
> Last night, my siblings and I decided that we would bring Breakfaster home to the countryside for Chinese New Year. My parents had met Breakfaster a couple of times. Even though they continued to refer to her as "your friend," I know they saw through our relationship. My sister told me that my father bought mutton so he could prepare mutton stew for our visit. It has been more than a decade since I last spent Chinese New Year united with my entire family. There is a mixed feeling of intimacy and fear with regard to home. (178)

This is another example of silence as consent as Chen's parents tacitly acknowledge Chen's new life, despite the fact that she has never openly come out to them. As Chen refers to this visit in the following paragraph as her "homecoming" (回娘家) on the second day of Chinese New Year, I read this as another example of the concept of a queer homecoming that I have developed here. First, there is the actual act of home-coming with Chen and Breakfaster's return to the countryside to visit Chen's parents and siblings. Second, this long-awaited family reunion is a homecoming to the self for Chen and her parents, since they each open up to themselves and others to reconnect via silent consent and acknowledgment. Lastly, this homecoming intervenes and rede-fines what "homecoming" means by queering the practice itself, supplementing a new form of (queer) home space that counters heteronormativity.

CONCLUSION

Queer homecoming, as both practice and metaphor, empowers queer subjects to resist their marginalization within the heteronormative kinship structure, in which their familial affinities are constantly put at risk. This in turn allows them to disturb the stability of heteronormativity and to challenge its claim of exclusivity in matters relating to the kinship system. Queer homecoming allows us to rearrange the furniture within the existing space of the home and thus create a more welcoming familial environment for all—queer, straight, and other.

In her 2011 Christmas Eve diary entry, Chen discusses the idea of "building a home" (成家) after returning from the book launch of My "Illegal" Family (我的違章家庭; 2011), a collection of twenty-eight stories of non-normative families in Taiwan, at the Fembooks Publishing House and Bookstore.[16] The heteronormative logic of homebuilding is the outcome of marriage; hence, for queer subjects to establish a home is inevitably a violation of that kinship structure. Because having a family for a queer individual is challenging due to issues of legality, Chen claims that many queer individuals are resigned to the fate of being alone for the rest of their lives: "It is not easy building a home. We all thought that we would grow old alone and have prepared ourselves to face that" (141). What is key here is the question of "choice." While queer scholars criticize moderate queer individuals for promoting a homonormativity that reifies the hegemony of heteronormative social structures, I think it is also important to consider the needs of others in the queer communities whose right to choose is not exclusive to the ones sanctioned by either straight conservatives or queer activists.[17]

By reading Chen Xue's recent work through the lens of the concept of queer homecoming, I have attempted to propose a different representation of queerness in contemporary Chinese literature. More importantly, I find Ahmed's shift from a focus on space and room to a focus on furniture in her theory of queer phenomenology helpful in making us rethink how queerness can help reshape the "appearance" of modern and contemporary Chinese literature by shifting our focus from defining boundaries to mapping a variety of literary expressions. The change in focus on space/room to a focus on furniture in Ahmed's work suggests that queerness can reshape the "appearance" of Chinese literature. This queer furnishing can only be accomplished by way of a queer homecoming that departs from the prevalent aesthetics of exile in queer modern Chinese literature and that reintroduces queerness at the heart of the familiar.

NOTES

Epigraph taken from Chen Xue and Breakfaster 陳雪與早餐人, Renqi riji 人妻日記 [A wife's diary] (Taipei: INK Publishing, 2012), 181. All translations of A Wife's Diary in this chapter are mine, and subsequent citations will be indicated parenthetically in the text.

1. See Duggan's The Twilight of Equality? Neoliberalism, Cultural Politics, and the Attack on Democracy (Boston: Beacon Press, 2004).

2. See David Eng's discussion on queer liberalism and the critique of homonormativity in "Queer Liberalism and the Racialization of Intimacy," in *The Feeling of Kinship: Queer Liberalism and the Racialization of Intimacy* (Durham: Duke University Press, 2010), 1–22.

3. See "Dai'esipola: 'Huangren shouji' de kuer yuedu" 帶餓思潑辣：《荒人手記》的酷兒閱讀 [Diaspora: A queer reading of *Notes of a Desolate Man*], *Zhongwai wenxue* 中外文學 [Chung-wai literary monthly] 24.3 (1995): 153–160.

4. See Chi Ta-wei 紀大偉, "Taiwan xiaoshuo zhong nan tongxinglian de xing yu liu-fang" 台灣小說中男同性戀的性與流放 [Sex and exile of gay men in Taiwanese novels], in *Leisi yu bianzi de jiaohuan: Dangdai Taiwan qingse wenxuelun* 蕾絲與鞭子的交歡：當代台灣情色文學論 [Intercourse between the lace and the whip: Theory of contemporary Taiwanese erotic literature], eds. Lin Shuifu 林水福 and Lin Yaode 林耀德 (Taipei: Shibao chubanshe, 1997), 136–137.

5. See Gu Minlun 辜敏倫, "Jia" 家 [Family], *Aifu haozizai bao* 愛福好自在報 [Love, happiness, freedom zine] 3.4–5 (1994); Gu Minlun 辜敏倫, "Nütongxinglian de shenti—muguang ningshi yu zhuti weizhi" 女同性戀的身體——目光凝視與主體位置 [Lesbian body—The gaze and subjectivity], *Lianhe wenxue* 聯合文學 [Unitas] 124 (1995): 134–139.

6. Cambridge Chien-chiao Hsu 許劍橋, "Jiajia youben nannian de jing—nütongzi xiaoshuozhong 'jia' de xiti" 家家有本難念的經-女同志小說中「家」的習題 [Every family has its issues—'Home' as problem in lesbian novels], in *"Tonghua" dashun? Jiuling niandai Taiwan nütongzhi xiaoshuolun* 「同花」大順? 九〇年代台灣女同志小說論 [Blossoming lesbian? A study of Taiwanese lesbian literature from the nineties] (Taipei: Shuiwen chubanshe, 2013), 205–255.

7. Judith Butler, *Antigone's Claim: Kinship Between Life and Death* (New York: Columbia University Press, 2000), 17. Further references will be provided in parentheses in the text.

8. Gilles Deleuze discusses repetition and newness: "*Repetition is a condition of action before it is a concept of* reflection. We produce something new only on condition that we repeat—once in the mode which constitutes the past, and once more in the present of metamorphosis. Moreover, what is produced, the absolute new itself, is in turn nothing but repetition"; in *Difference and Repetition* (New York: Columbia University Press, 1994), 90. See also James Williams, *Gilles Deleuze's Difference and Repetition: A Critical Introduction and Guide* (Edinburgh: Edinburgh University Press, 2013), 11–12.

9. For more discussion on theoretical approaches to queer Asia, see *Mobile Cultures: New Media in Queer Asia*, eds. Chris Berry, Fran Martin, and Audrey Yue (Durham: Duke University Press, 2003); *AsiaPacifiQueer: Rethinking Genders and Sexualities*, eds. Fran Martin, Peter Jackson, Mark McLelland, and Audrey Yue (Illinois: University of Illinois Press, 2008); Eng-Beng Lim, *Brown Boys and Rice Queens: Spellbinding Performance in the Asias* (New York: New York University Press, 2013).

10. For more on milieu, see Gilles Deleuze and Félix Guattari, "1837: Of the Refrain," in *A Thousand Plateaus: Capitalism and Schizophrenia*, trans. Brian Massumi (Minneapolis: University of Minnesota Press, 1987), 310–350, 313.

11. Deleuze and Guattari distinguishes milieu from territory by describing the function of the former as directional and the latter as dimensional. Nevertheless, they stress that the two are interdependent: "There is a territory precisely when milieu components cease to be directional, becoming dimensional instead, when they cease to be functional to become expressive . . . What defines the territory is the emergence of matters of expression (qualities)." See *A Thousand Plateaus: Capitalism and Schizophrenia*, trans. Brian Massumi (Minneapolis: University of Minnesota Press, 1987), 315.

12. Deleuze and Guattari, *A Thousand Plateaus*, 320–321.

13. See Sara Ahmed, *Queer Phenomenology: Orientations, Objects, Others* (Durham: Duke University Press, 2006), 8.

14. Sara Ahmed, *Queer Phenomenology*, 125–126.

15. Sara Ahmed, *Queer Phenomenology*, 168.

16. For details about the book, please see Awakening Foundation and Taiwan Alliance to Promote Civil Partnership Rights' story collection, *Wo de weizhang jiating—28 ge duoyuan chengjia gushi* 我的違章家庭—28 個多元成家故事 [My "illegal" family—stories of 28 multi-families] (Taipei: Fembooks Publishing, 2011).

17. See Lisa Duggan, "The New Homonormativity: The Sexual Politics of Neoliberalism," in *Materializing Democracy: Toward a Revitalized Cultural Politics* (Durham: Duke University Press, 2002), 175–194; Jack Halberstam, *In a Queer Time and Place: Transgender Bodies, Subcultural Lives* (New York: New York University Press, 2005); David L. Eng, *The Feeling of Kinship: Queer Liberalism and the Racialization of Intimacy* (Durham: Duke University Press, 2010); Judith Halberstam, "Queer Belongings: Kinship Theory and Queer Theory," in *A Companion to Lesbian, Gay, Bisexual, Transgender, and Queer Studies*, eds. George E. Haggerty and Molly McGarry (Malden, MA: Blackwell, 2007), 315–324; Martin F. Manalansan, "Queer Love in the Time of War and Shopping," in *A Companion to Lesbian, Gay, Bisexual, Transgender, and Queer Studies*, eds. George E. Haggerty and Molly McGarry (Malden, MA: Blackwell, 2007), 77–86.

WORKS CITED

Ahmed, Sara. *Queer Phenomenology: Orientations, Objects, Others*. Durham: Duke University Press, 2006.

Awakening Foundation and Taiwan Alliance to Promote Civil Partnership Rights 婦女新知基金會與台灣伴侶權益推動聯盟, ed. *Wo de weizhang jiating—28 ge duoyuan chengjia gushi* 我的違章家庭—28 個多元成家故事 [My "illegal" family—stories of 28 multi-families]. Taipei: Fembooks Publishing, 2011.

Berry, Chris, Fran Martin, and Audrey Yue, ed. *Mobile Cultures: New Media in Queer Asia*. Durham: Duke University Press, 2003.

Butler, Judith. *Antigone's Claim: Kinship Between Life and Death*. New York: Columbia University Press, 2000.

Chen Xue and Breakfaster 陳雪與早餐人. *Renqi riji* 人妻日記 [A wife's diary]. Taipei: INK Publishing, 2012.

Chi Ta-wei 紀大偉. "Dai'esipola: 'huangren shouji' de kuer yuedu" 帶餓思潑辣：《荒人手記》的酷兒閱讀 [Diaspora: A queer reading of *Notes of a Desolate Man*]. *Zhongwai wenxue* 中外文學 [Chung-wai literary monthly] 24.3 (1995): 153–160.

Chi Ta-wei 紀大偉. *Mo* 膜 [Membrane]. Taipei: Lianjing chubanshe, 1996.

Chi Ta-wei 紀大偉. "Taiwan xiaoshuo zhong nan tongxinglian de xing yu liufang" 台灣小說中男同性戀的性與流放 [Sex and exile of gay men in Taiwanese novels]. In *Leisi yu bianzi de jiaohuan: Dangdai Taiwan qingse wenxuelun* 蕾絲與鞭子的交歡：當代台灣情色文學論 [Intercourse between the lace and the whip: Theory of contemporary Taiwanese erotic literature]. Ed. Lin Shuifu 林水福 and Lin Yaode 林耀德. Taipei: Shibao chubanshe, 1997. 129–164.

Chou Wah-shan 周華山. *Houzhimin tongzhi* 後殖民同志 [Postcolonial homosexual]. Hong Kong: Xianggang tongzhi yangjiushe, 1997.

Chou, Wah-shan 周華山. *Tongzhi: Politics of Same-Sex Eroticism in Chinese Societies.* New York: Routledge, 2000.

Chu T'ien-wen 朱天文. *Huangren shouji* 荒人手記 [Notes of a desolate man]. Taipei: Shibao chubanshe, 1994.

Deleuze, Gilles. *Difference and Repetition.* Trans. Paul Patton. New York: Columbia University Press, 1994.

Deleuze, Gilles, and Félix Guattari. "1837: Of the Refrain." In *A Thousand Plateaus: Capitalism and Schizophrenia.* Trans. Brian Massumi. Minneapolis: University of Minnesota Press, 1987. 310–350.

Duggan, Lisa. "The New Homonormativity: The Sexual Politics of Neoliberalism." In *Materializing Democracy: Toward a Revitalized Cultural Politics.* Durham: Duke University Press, 2002. 175–194.

Duggan, Lisa. *The Twilight of Equality? Neoliberalism, Cultural Politics, and the Attack on Democracy.* Boston: Beacon Press, 2004.

Eng, David L. *The Feeling of Kinship: Queer Liberalism and the Racialization of Intimacy.* Durham: Duke University Press, 2010.

Gu Minlun 辜敏倫. "Jia" 家 [Family]. In *Aifu haozizai bao* 愛福好自在報 [Love, happiness, freedom Zine] 3 (1994): 4–5.

Gu Minlun 辜敏倫. "Nütongxinglian de shenti——muguang ningshi yu zhuti weizhi" 女同性戀的身體——目光凝視與主體位置 [The lesbian body—Gaze and subjectivity]. *Lianhe wenxue* 聯合文學 [Unitas] 124 (1995): 134–139.

Ku Dschau-sen 顧肇森. "Zhang wei" 張偉 [Zhang Wei]. In *Maolian de suiyue* 貓臉的歲月 [Traces of time on the cat's face]. Taipei: Jiuge chubanshe, 1986.

Halberstam, Jack. *In a Queer Time and Place: Transgender Bodies, Subcultural Lives.* New York: New York University Press, 2005.

Halberstam, Jack. "Queer Belongings: Kinship Theory and Queer Theory." In *A Companion to Lesbian, Gay, Bisexual, Transgender, and Queer Studies.* Eds. George E. Haggerty and Molly McGarry. Malden, MA: Blackwell, 2007. 315–324

Hsu, Cambridge Chien-chiao 許劍橋. "Jiajia youben nannian de jing—nütongzhi xiaoshuozhong 'jia' de xiti" 家家有本難念的經——女同志小說中「家」的習題 [Every family has its issues—'Home' as problem in lesbian novels]. In *"Tonghua" dashun? Jiuling niandai Taiwan nütongzhi xiaoshuolun* 「同花」大順? 九〇年代台灣女同志小說論 [Blossoming lesbian? A study of Taiwanese lesbian literature from the nineties]. Taipei: Shuiwen chubanshe, 2013. 205–255.

Hsu Yo-shen 許佑生. "Stones on the Shore." In *Angelwings: Contemporary Queer Fiction from Taiwan.* Trans. Fran Martin. Honolulu: University of Hawai'i Press, 2003. 95–126.

Hsu Yo-shen 許佑生. "Anbian shi" 岸邊石 [Stones on the shore]. In *Xuanshang langman* 懸賞浪漫 [Reward for romance]. Taipei: Yuanliu chubanshe, 1992.

Lim, Eng-Beng. *Brown Boys and Rice Queens: Spellbinding Performance in the Asias.* New York: New York University Press, 2013.

Manalansan, Martin F. "Queer Love in the Time of War and Shopping." In *A Companion to Lesbian, Gay, Bisexual, Transgender, and Queer Studies.* Eds. George E. Haggerty and Molly McGarry. Malden, MA: Blackwell, 2007. 77–86.

Martin, Fran, Peter Jackson, Mark McLelland, and Audrey Yue, eds. *AsiaPacifiQueer: Rethinking Genders and Sexualities*. Illinois: University of Illinois Press, 2008.

Pai Hsien-yung 白先勇. *Niezi* 孽子 [Crystal boys]. Taipei: Yunchen, 1996.

Qiu Miaojin 邱妙津. *Eyu shouji* 鱷魚手記 [The crocodile's journal]. Taipei: Shibao chubanshe, 1994.

Williams, James. *Gilles Deleuze's Difference and Repetition: A Critical Introduction and Guide*. Edinburgh: Edinburgh University Press, 2013.

CARE, VULNERABILITY, RESILIENCE

Ecologies of HIV/AIDS in Chinese Literature

KAREN THORNBER

EARLY in the 1994 novel *Notes of a Desolate Man* (荒人手記) by the Taiwanese writer Chu T'ien-wen 朱天文 (b. 1956), the narrator Xiao Shao, mourning the recent loss of his childhood friend Ah Yao to complications from AIDS, contemplates the very different ways in which Michael Jackson, Ingmar Bergman, Luis Buñuel, and Mel Gibson's Hamlet faced death.[1] Xiao Shao laments that, in contrast to these celebrities, who despite their differences all leave behind their names, he and Ah Yao are "doomed to be people without names, without miracles." And then he declares, "Living is difficult, and dying too is not easy, as with the nameless fish for whom I cared" (18). With this remark, the narrator launches into several pages on his experiences caring for a school of fish originally intended by his students as dinner for his cat; transferring the fish from a plastic bag to a fishbowl, moving them out of the feline's reach, and caring for them as best he could, he postponed but did not prevent and in fact arguably brought about their premature demise—many of the animals perished relatively quickly and none lived longer than a year. The fish are in many ways a distraction, one of any number in *Notes of a Desolate Man* that enable the narrator to think briefly about something other than the fate of Ah Yao and the HIV/AIDS crisis more generally. But probing more deeply into the dynamics of this episode, examining Chu T'ien-wen's novel from an environmentally conscious perspective, brings to light underrecognized aspects of the seemingly very "human" problem of HIV/AIDS.

Most important, although primarily a diversion for the narrator, the fish episode also provides an alternative model of giving care, one that is applicable to species of all types; whereas the narrator just assumes he knows how best to interact with his ailing friend, he agonizes over how best to care for his fish, continually questioning whether he should be doing something different and whether he is doing all that can be done. In the chapter preceding the fish episode, the narrator describes some of his interactions with the ailing Ah Yao, making abundantly clear his deep concern for his friend. Not only did he hurry from Taiwan to Ah Yao's bedside at a Tokyo clinic as soon as he learned the end was near, but in the preceding months Xiao Shao had served as Ah Yao's crutches while the two took short strolls, the latter's emaciated body so feeble that it threatened to crumble under the weight of falling cherry blossoms. But then, when Ah Yao became too weak to utter more than one word at a time, Xiao Shao describes himself as having known what he wanted to say and speaking for him: "Ah Yao was not strong enough to sustain a conversation, and before long, he could utter only single words, but I always knew what he wanted to say, and I helped him finish his sentences. He said, upstairs. I was able to help him continue to speak, the old are sent upstairs . . . Ah Yao and I, a couple of old palace maids, chatting endlessly until dawn" (9). Monologue becomes dialogue, at least in the imagination.

Xiao Shao means well, and he is caring for his friend as best he knows how, entertaining him with stories from the past while attempting to compensate for his lost voice, but his comments on communicating with Ah Yao bring to light a significant problem, one that applies to human relationships with the nonhuman as well—how to care best for those who cannot speak, who cannot articulate their needs and desires. Commenting at the beginning of *Notes of a Desolate Man* that "AIDS is horrible; but the price of loneliness is even greater" (3), the narrator makes clear his determination to be with his friend despite everything, for both of their sakes; loneliness can be devastating for patients and their loved ones alike. But what this means in practice is not as certain. The narrator describes himself and Ah Yao gossiping away, much as elderly women are wont to do, but in fact they are not talking to each other. Instead, Xiao Shao is speaking *for* Ah Yao, projecting—albeit with good intentions—what his friend wants to say. Whether his suppositions are correct, whether Ah Yao even wants him to try to speak on his behalf, is anyone's guess.

In contrast to his nearly reflexive treatment of his friend, the narrator questions repeatedly how to care for his fish and in so doing provides important insights into both intra- and interspecies interactions. Xiao Shao is deeply disturbed by how his students treat animals, and in particular fish and crabs, remarking on how, waiting for dinner to cook, the young adults dig for crabs and snap off their legs and scoop fish out of the water with newly purchased nets, only to abandon both the animals and the netting. Even more interesting is that Xiao Shao describes as "violent" the desire of his students to give fish to his cat; he greatly values all life, no matter how seemingly insignificant, no matter how "natural" its death.[2] Moreover, he describes being fully responsible for the lives of the fish his students meant for his cat as "cruel punishment" (18). Xiao Shao takes very seriously, almost surprisingly seriously, his obligation toward his new charges, seeking for them the proper home and nourishment, and he agonizes constantly over what he should be doing for them. When those fish that survive the initial transfer from plastic bag to fishbowl begin to die, the narrator is crushed, and he becomes even more apprehensive, thinking carefully about and eventually changing how he cares for these voiceless creatures. Believing that they might be at the mercy of something contagious, he changes their water more frequently; believing that overcrowding is killing his fish, he transfers some of them to a different bowl, declaring, "Moving mountains and emptying the sea, it was like a chemistry experiment, one that caused me great anxiety; I hated that I didn't have sufficient knowledge about fish to handle them; whether to change the water or not change the water, whether to feed them or not feed them, really frustrated me" (21). And when one of his two remaining fish dies from what Xiao Shao believes is overeating, he asserts, "This was entirely a result of human error, and it was now too late for regrets" (23).

Throughout, the narrator underlines his lack of understanding and ultimately helplessness vis-à-vis the fish, in sharp contrast to his attitude toward Ah Yao, whom he presumed to know so well that he could finish his friend's thoughts and in fact speak for him so convincingly that a monologue interspersed with occasional words was transformed in his mind into a true dialogue. To be sure, neither the fish nor Ah Yao survive; instead they all meet untimely deaths. And sometimes the fish perish despite Xiao Shao's devoting full attention to them, while at other times they perish when he believes that all has been resolved and he has "figured out" how best to care for them. *Notes of a Desolate Man* does not portray consciousness of relative ignorance as being a panacea and certainty of knowledge as necessarily harmful. But Chu T'ien-wen's novel does suggest that constantly questioning and consciously altering how care is given can improve the quality of life, both human and nonhuman. And ultimately it emphasizes the importance of remaining attentive. Xiao Shao became so comfortable with his last surviving fish that not only did it become "a part of [his] life," the two of them even "forgot about each other" (25). And so, when one day he found this fish lying belly-up, he was stunned and instantly blamed himself: "I had just read in the newspaper that in the south large numbers of milkfish had frozen to death, but I hadn't drawn the connection with the fish in my warm room. Separated by death, just like that. The moment I was most confident that all was well, suddenly a visit. The corporeal body, too fragile to endure" (25). Xiao Shao could do little more than bury the fish in a flowerpot to "commemorate" their year together.

Although briefly distracted by the power of life as embodied by the green leaves that continue to flourish in his fishbowl, the narrator of Chu T'ien-wen's novel turns quickly—after the fish episode—to a BBC documentary on the death of an elephant, commenting on the reaction of its companions, which have tried but ultimately failed to bring it to its feet: "The dying elephant lay on the ground, staring blankly ahead, while the densely bushed land was split apart by the animal's trampling, despairing companions" (25). This emotional, deafening scene is contrasted in the following paragraph with the death of a person succumbing to starvation: the death, also portrayed on film, of a woman in rural India whose food supply has been cut off by Japanese forces. Here people die silently and miserably, "like withered flowers disappearing from the earth" (26). *Notes* ironically depicts elephant herds as more traumatized by death than human societies, and engaging in more elaborate death rituals. This impresses the importance of respecting species of all kinds. It also underscores the necessity of at least trying to understand better the needs of those with whose care one is charged, and taking care not to take care for granted.

ECOCRITICISM AND *DREAM OF DING VILLAGE*

Chu T'ien-wen's *Notes* focuses far more on human than on nonhuman death, making this prose text at first glance an unusual choice for ecocritical analysis; to date, scholarly attention to the intersections between environment and disease has understandably centered on anthropocentric environmental diseases, especially health problems caused by exposure to toxic chemicals, not on conditions such as HIV/AIDS. Yet examining how the discourse on the nonhuman is integrated into depictions of primarily human tragedies deepens perspectives on the dynamics of caregiving and giving care, as well as the interplay of vulnerability and resilience vis-à-vis illness and death across species.

The Chinese have long been associated with belief systems that advocate reverence for nature, especially Buddhism, Confucianism, and Daoism, as well as numerous local philosophies and religions. Likewise, Chinese artists and philosophers have for millennia idealized people's interactions with their nonhuman surroundings. And popular perceptions both within and outside China often hold that environmental degradation there dates to the late nineteenth century, when, pressured by the West, China assimilated the latter's technologies and industries. But in fact, like most societies the Chinese have a long history of exploiting and transforming their environments; discourse on close, harmonious contacts between people and nature has more often defied than reflected empirical reality. Similarly, although marginalized by the scholarly field of ecocriticism (literature and environment studies; environmental criticism), and despite celebrating people's intimate connections with their environments, Chinese-language literature has from its beginnings also exposed the paradoxes of human encounters with the nonhuman and increasingly condemned human abuse of everything from single animals to entire landscapes.[3] Examining Chinese-language literature from an ecocritical perspective, and in particular analyzing how texts have grappled with interactions between people and ecosystems of all sizes, not only sheds new light on creative work from the Chinese mainland and other parts of the Sinosphere but also increases understanding of the important interplay between people's treatment of one another and their treatment of the nonhuman, as well as the vulnerability and resilience of human and nonhuman communities on multiple scales.

In this spirit, the remainder of this chapter discusses the ecological resonances of another work of Chinese-language literature set against the backdrop of the HIV/AIDS pandemic—the mainland Chinese writer Yan Lianke's 閻連科 (b. 1958) novel *Dream of Ding Village* (丁庄夢; 2006). In contrast with *Notes of a Desolate Man*, which contains only scattered references to large-scale environmental problems, Yan Lianke's *Dream of Ding Village* speaks repeatedly of razed landscapes, intermingling descriptions of human communities succumbing to AIDS with those of a devastated natural world.[4] Perhaps best known abroad for his provocative novel *Serve the People!* (為人民服務;

2005), a trenchant satire of the Cultural Revolution that, like others of his works, has been condemned by the Chinese government despite having been extensively self-censored, Yan Lianke is one of contemporary China's most celebrated writers. *Dream of Ding Village* is not his only work to engage with illness and health, both human and nonhuman. Another is *Lenin's Kisses* (受活; 2004), which centers on a remote Henan village whose residents, most of whom are physically handicapped, are persuaded to form a performance troupe in which they will travel the country exhibiting their disabilities. Also noteworthy is *Streams of Life and Time* (日光流年; 2004), which features impoverished rural villagers suffering from a condition that causes their throats to swell painfully and invariably kills them before they reach the age of forty. In an attempt to raise money to build an aqueduct to bring in uncontaminated water, the village women sell their bodies while the men sell their skin to a nearby hospital for burn victims.

For its part, *Dream of Ding Village*—based on the author's three years of undercover fieldwork in Henan province—caused a "severe earthquake" among readers, critics, and the Chinese government when it appeared in 2006, and was banned shortly after its release.[5] By censoring discourse on the blood-selling scandal and the HIV/AIDS crisis that followed, Chinese authorities launched what could be considered an autoimmune response against individuals and communities whose immune systems had already been compromised if not destroyed entirely. Official reaction to discourse on environmental degradation has been similar—silencing or heavily censoring reports of the destruction of ecosystems, Chinese authorities have in many ways mistaken an autoimmune for an immune response. That is to say, the system that is intended to protect the immune-suppressed body from harmful substances has in fact been attacking its own body.

Dream of Ding Village tells the story of a destitute Chinese rural community that has been destroyed by an unregulated blood plasma economy; rampant blood selling in Ding Village caused a lethal outbreak of HIV/AIDS that virtually destroyed the town. The novel thus gives insight into a frequently overlooked aspect of what continues to be, despite great medical advances, one of the world's most serious global health crises. It serves as a poignant reminder of the diverse ways in which this disease can be contracted and the vulnerability of the indigent and uneducated. Moreover, *Dream of Ding Village* devotes considerable space to the plight of the nonhuman, interweaving depictions of human death from AIDS with discourse on the human destruction of nature. In so doing, the novel emphasizes the interdependence of people and landscapes: not only how *readily* both can be obliterated but also the specific means by which they are being so readily obliterated.

Even as it underscores the vulnerability of both people and nature, Yan Lianke's novel also leaves space for different forms of survival, if not resilience.[6] On several occasions, the narrator speaks of landscapes being razed, most often in terms of trees having been felled, only to refer in a subsequent chapter to surviving and occasionally thriving foliage. Similarly, the narrator refers regularly to people dying one after another, of the town as disintegrating into oblivion, only to speak in a subsequent chapter about healthy survivors. And he comments repeatedly on the penetrating silences of both people and landscapes, only then occasionally to reveal the silence as shattered. This relative inconsistency can be attributed in part to the narrator's own positionality—he is the murdered son of the village's most powerful blood kingpin and is speaking from the grave. But the novel's ambiguity signals to an even greater degree the ability of both people and nature to challenge expectations, to survive, somehow, against incredible odds. *Dream of Ding Village* hardly depicts people and landscapes as impervious to corrupt officialdom, incurable diseases, and ruthless plundering. Yet it does point to their defiance and continued struggle, borne out in some ways by the failure of HIV/AIDS to become, in the years following the publication of *Dream of Ding Village*, the ravaging epidemic in China that many had predicted.

Following an initial *juan* ("volume"), which consists of only a single page and gives three brief dreams from Genesis, the second *juan* of Yan Lianke's novel opens in Ding Village with a brilliant red late-autumn sun setting over a village enveloped in silence. At first this silence appears "normal": the narrator states explicitly that the streets are deserted because it is cold. He also notes that the dogs are in their dens, chickens in their coops, and cows in their sheds. So when he declares on the next line that "the silence of Ding Village is an intense silence, severed from sound," it is almost possible still to believe that this silence is a simple consequence of people and animals barricading themselves indoors against the cold. But then everything appears to collapse, the narrator commenting that because of the absolute silence, the deep autumn, and the dusk, the village has fallen and withered (落萎), and the people too have withered (萎); the following lines speak of the crops likewise withering (萎), the grasses and trees both dry, the villagers "shrunken inside their homes, never to emerge again" (7). The novel is silent as to how long conditions have been like this and precisely why they are so dire, postponing until the next paragraph reference to the blood selling that spawned an AIDS epidemic.

The following pages reveal the horrors of the outbreak, primarily through the eyes of the narrator's grandfather Ding Shuiyang, who has learned from his talks with county officials that even though the village has already experienced considerable loss, the worst is yet to come. Shuiyang has been told that within a year AIDS will not only explode, it will burst upon and destroy his community like a flooding Yellow River, the waterway responsible for the four most devastating deluges in human history: [7]

> The fever would explode violently across the plain. It would explode violently upon Ding Village, Willow Village, Yellow Creek, Two-Li Village, and thousands of other hamlets like a flood. Like the Yellow River bursting through its dikes, it would surge through hundreds if not thousands of villages, and people would die like ants, people would die like falling leaves. Going out like lights, there would be no more people on the face of the earth, they would die like leaves floating down. At that time, **Ding Village would disappear forever. Ding Village would vanish from the face of the earth. Like leaves atop an old tree, the people of Ding Village, first withering, then yellow, and then with a gurgle, all would fall. After a gust of wind, the leaves, like the village, would go off somewhere unknown.** (10–11)

Repeating the phrase *explode violently* (大爆) in the first two sentences translated above, the narrator calls attention to the destructiveness of HIV/AIDS to any number of communities. People perishing like ants, like falling leaves, people going out like lights becomes one of the novel's most prominent refrains. Interestingly, however, attention soon turns to Ding Village itself; replacing regular type with boldface print, as he does throughout the text, the narrator emphasizes the traumatic plight of this one village.[8] Whereas in the opening paragraphs of the novel's second *juan* the narrator declared that Ding Village lives even as it dies, here he predicts this town's demise. The knowledge about AIDS is new to the narrator's grandfather, but there is little this awareness can do to alter the course of events; the time to do so is long past. First the villagers and now the village itself become little more than dead leaves, blown about and then disappearing. Interesting here is that the narrator moves from claiming that both people and village will disappear from the earth to stating instead that the leaves, like the village, will go off somewhere unknown and that the village, like the leaves, will also go off somewhere unknown. So the struggles do not end with death; even vanishing (after death) has become a challenge. Passages such as this recur throughout *Dream of Ding Village*; those that use the natural world as metaphor or simile call attention to just how many are dying if not already dead.

But the precise damage inflicted remains unclear. After completing his synopsis of what his grandfather has learned from speaking with county officials, the narrator gives statistics:

> In under two years this hamlet of fewer than 200 households and a population of under 800 had lost more than 40 people. Doing the numbers, in the time that had passed, every ten to fifteen days one person from the village had died, and every month about three people had died. Moreover, the season of the dead had only just begun, and when the following year arrived the dead were as numerous as the autumn grains. Graves were as numerous as the bundles of summer wheat . . . The fever spread widely, already clutching the throat of Ding Village, causing endless deaths in Ding Village, the screams never ceasing. (11–12)

As the rate of death increases, death comes to enjoy a chokehold on the town. But even as the bodies continue to pile up, the screams continue.

Initial changes to the natural world are notable, but they ultimately appear relatively benign. The narrator describes how Ding Village, when it was the site of twelve blood-collection stations sponsored by a plethora of government organizations, was littered with blood-filled plastic tubing, bottles of plasma, broken glass vials and syringes, discarded cotton balls, and used needles surrounded by red splashes of blood. Moreover, tree leaves in the village absorbed air "filled with the stench of fresh blood" and began to take on a faint reddish color (31). Even fresh verdure was affected: the narrator notes that in the past, the new leaves of the locust trees all had been thin and soft, and under the sunlight their color had been a pale yellow, with the threadlike ribs of the leaves appearing a brownish, darkish green. But during the blood boom years, the new leaves of these trees were tinged with pink and their veins a brownish purple. The locust tree by the veterinary hospital, beneath which had stood a particularly active blood bank, was especially affected; its yellow leaves became as red as those of persimmon trees in autumn and grew larger and thicker than in years past. Selling their blood also enables farmers to purchase chemical fertilizer, which allows them to grow plumper wheat than ever before.

Yet things change when people begin to die. Adding to the disaster is that far from leading to the regeneration of landscapes, which often happens when fields are left fallow, the ecosystems of Ding Village and its environs appear to be destroyed just as readily as, and in fact even before, the human population; Yan Lianke's novel is replete with descriptions of a damaged and then decimated natural world. Most notably, demand for coffins, and the demand for wood for other purposes that this triggers, depletes the village's wood supply.[9] Authorities so freely grant townspeople permission to fell trees for coffins both needed and anticipated that soon every tree is marked for destruction. The narrator devotes part of *juan* four to revealing, in bold characters, village ecosystems under siege. He describes how one evening, walking toward the village, his grandfather gradually began to hear saws buzzing and axes chopping. Shuiyang arrived at the nearest lights only to find them illuminating a large cottonwood under attack. When he questioned who gave the villagers permission to uproot this tree, they produced a letter on Ding Village party stationary. Shuiyang quickly discovered that authorities had authorized the felling of virtually every large tree in the village; the reader follows him through the hamlet as he surveys the extent of the (imminent) damage, remarking on the stark differences between the village now spreading before him and that of his dreams. He had envisioned Ding Village as a place of flowers (above) and gold (below). Instead, he finds a site of surreal destruction, trees being taken down no matter where in the village and its environs they are situated. The narrator observes, "Standing amid that torrential, unending sound of trees being felled, Grandpa once again caught sight [in his imagination] of the fresh flowers on the surface of the flatlands and of the gold beneath" (158). And the next morning all the trees are gone; it has taken just a single night to render the village treeless. The effects are immediate, the narrator noting that although the spring sun shone warm as usual, without foliage or shade to temper its rays it scorched the flesh of the villagers. So the townspeople stumble out of bed, stand in their doorways, grow white with surprise, and are rendered speechless.

And indeed, later in *Dream of Ding Village* the narrator elaborates:

> Because of the fever, on the plain people are dying **just like lights going out, just like leaves floating down from trees.** The dead needed coffins and the living needed houses. Used for coffins, the paulownia trees were as scarce as silver, and the cedar, used for crosspieces, as scarce as gold. But the coffins my father had delivered were not made of paulownia or cedar, but instead of ginkgo. The entire coffin was ginkgo . . . The entire coffin was made from planks, three inches thick, from a 1,000-year-old ginkgo. (218)

Noteworthy here are not only the refrain comparing human deaths with those of leaves and lights and the revelation that a venerable tree has been sacrificed for a coffin. Even more important is the comparison of the paucity of paulownia trees with that of silver and the scarcity of cedars with that of gold. The narrator earlier stated that all the trees had been felled, whereas here readers are informed that trees are as scarce as precious metals; it is not as though trees are now plentiful, and they are clearly exceptionally difficult to obtain, but they are no longer presented as being nonexistent.

After commenting on the lack of actual trees, the narrator describes in detail the specifics of his uncle's coffin—every surface of the coffin is engraved with scenes of people and nature, including "trees in parks, with people below trees" (218). To be sure, most of the engravings are products of material culture, everything from skyscrapers to overpasses to refrigerators, washing machines, and televisions. And the coffin features only pictures of trees rather than actual foliage. But nature has not vanished entirely, either from daily life or from memory.

Nor has nature disappeared from the imagination; the narrator describes his grandfather as seeing trees in his dreams. The human interactions are new, but the landscape is as of old. The narrator notes, in bold characters: "**Conditions in the courtyard were the same as before [the narrator's relatives] Uncle and Lingling had moved in. The crowns of the paulownia trees shaded one third of the courtyard, and the radiant sunlight streamed through the thick tree leaves . . . there wasn't anything that wasn't the same as before**" (212). The emphasis here is on continuity. Not all is perfect, to be sure; Grandpa also sees in his dream the two trees between which a washing line has been strung, and these trees have been "deeply scarred" by the wire that has been wrapped around them. But the narrator seems to forget that the trees are (presumably) alive only in the dream. He has Shuiyang wake up, tear himself away from his dream, and race toward Uncle's house, where "the cries of cicadas were dropping from the courtyard's paulownia trees, like falling, overripe fruit" (213). In fact, reality is here more fecund than the dream: it is in the experienced world that animal voices are as rich and full as succulent fruit.

These moments of resilience, however imagined, are few and far between, and circumstances deteriorate as the novel progresses. Nevertheless, people and plants prove irrepressible. Whereas the narrator earlier had stated that fields were left fallow, here he speaks of crops damaged by drought, revealing that people do continue to plant, on however limited a scale. The narrator repeats his claim that the trees that once shaded the village are gone. But he also depicts trees as being attacked by swarms of insects. And he declares that "The trees, those that still lived, could not support so many leaves, the leaves thinned out, so just the roots and the trunk still lived." And meanwhile, the cicadas hang from branches at night so that when the sun rises, "all the [cicada] shells emit a yellow light/A golden yellow light." Trees can hardly be said to be thriving, but they continue to support a robust insect population. Interestingly, the narrator almost immediately goes on to claim that at sunset the plain turns to fire and that by nightfall "throughout the land there are just lively cinders/lively cinders everywhere on earth" (234). But if this truly were the case, if the earth truly were reduced to nothing but burning cinders, then there would be nothing left to burn the following day. The fires cannot be as destructive as the narrator here indicates. And so the pattern continues, the narrator speaking in the following chapter of the extreme, deadly heat but also about how the wheat and grass are withering, the leaves curling up and dying, something they have been doing since the beginning of the novel. People too continue to die, "like chickens, like dogs, like trampled ants" (236).

Likewise, in the eighth and final *juan*, a short chapter of just four pages, the narrator reveals that trees have lived even as he reports their death: "The trees, trees that couldn't endure the drought, also died. Like the paulownias, locust trees, chinaberries, elms, toons . . . most of the trees, had all silently died./The big trees had been chopped down, and the small trees could not endure the drought, they all died . . . /The sun still lived./The wind also still lived./The sun and the moon, the stars and the planets, all still lived" (281). Moreover, the narrator notes that later into autumn sounds of life begin to be heard across the silent land. And, the narrator goes on to point out, despite everything some grass still lives, and it even puts out fresh green shoots whose scent mingles with the autumn's rotting grass; across the bright red skies an occasional bird takes flight. Shuiyang dreams that onto this barren wasteland falls a torrential downpour, one that turns the parched soil into mud. A woman—who closely resembles the legendary Chinese goddess Nüwa 女娲—dips down into the mud with a willow branch, then lifts up the branch and swings it back and forth. With each swing there appear many mud people (泥人) on the earth (285). Another dipping into the ground, another swing in the air, and on the ground there are hundreds, thousands of mud people. Touching and swinging again and again, never stopping, countless mud people are leaping and jumping, as numerous as the bubbles the rain makes on the ground, such that Grandpa finds himself gazing on a "new leaping jumping plain." The following sentence, in plain type, concludes the novel: "A new leaping and jumping world." Repeating three times in three lines the phrase "leaping [and] jumping" (蹦蹦[和]跳跳) the narrative highlights the vitality of this new space.[10] Yet nothing is said about the fate of the landscape beyond the rain-drenched soil. Perhaps its regeneration is so obvious as to render discussion redundant; people cannot survive long, much less "leap and jump" without the support of healthy ecosystems. But perhaps the region's regeneration is futile, and all the cavorting must remain in the realm of dreams.

Dream of Ding Village is not a story about overcoming disease. There is no real triumph. But voices—most audibly that of the narrator—continue to speak, even after death; people continue to live, even after communities are devastated; and trees and other foliage continue to grow, despite treacherous drought and rampant felling. Expectations are defied even as the future remains unclear. Perhaps a glimpse of hope is all it takes, that the mud people might not conform to current understandings of what constitutes a community, but that they mark a clear beginning of something new. On the other hand, the ending of Yan Lianke's novel comes back full circle to volume one, to Genesis, to the creation of humankind out of the soil. To be sure, here it is Nüwa, rather than God, who brings people to life. But there would seem to be little to prevent the "new" world just now being created from (d)evolving into the familiar world, little to prevent history from simply repeating itself, little to prevent people from continuing to attack and annihilate both one another and the nonhuman landscapes in which they are embedded.

Over the last century, improvements in human health worldwide have been monumental, and there is much to celebrate. Yet serious problems remain. Together, AIDS, malaria, and tuberculosis continue to kill six million people annually in the world's most impoverished countries; an additional seven million children perish each year from infectious diseases that have been virtually eradicated in wealthier parts of the globe.[11] Chronic diseases such as rheumatoid arthritis/rheumatoid disease, asthma, cancer, COPD (chronic obstructive pulmonary disease), diabetes, heart disease, and inflammatory bowel disease are on the rise worldwide and especially in industrialized nations.[12] The natural environment too is imperiled, despite numerous environmentalist movements and tremendous remediation worldwide during recent decades. In the words of the environmental lawyer Gustave Speth:

> Half the world's tropical and temperate forests are now gone. The rate of deforestation in the tropics continues at about an acre a second. About half the wetlands and a third of the mangroves are gone. An estimated 90 percent of the large predator fish are gone, and 75 percent of marine fisheries are now overfished or fished to capacity. . . . Species are disappearing at rates about a thousand times faster than normal. The planet has not seen such a spasm of extinction in sixty-five million years. . . .Persistent toxic chemicals can now be found by the dozens in essentially each and every one of us. (1–2)[13]

Chinese-language writers have grappled with the destruction of environments at home and abroad for millennia. Analyzing more closely precisely how they have done so, becoming more attentive to the ecological resonances in creative production of all types, exposes our vulnerabilities at the same time that it points to possibilities for the future, alternative ways of caregiving and giving care, and different types of resilience, if not immunity.

Notes

1. Chu T'ien-wen is one of contemporary Taiwan's most distinguished fiction writers, and her *Notes of a Desolate Man* is a celebrated work replete with both postmodernist markers and conventional modernist ideology. Chu T'ien-wen, *Huangren shouji* 荒人手記 [Notes of a desperate man] (Jinan: Shandong Huabao Chubanshe, 2009), 18. References will be provided as parentheses in the text. Where not indicated otherwise, translations are my own. Yvonne Chang remarks on how in *Notes of a Desolate Man* Chu interweaves extensive allusions to Foucault, Lévi-Strauss, and gay rights while at the same time featuring a narrator whose worldview is surprisingly conservative. See Sung-sheng Yvonne Chang, *Literary Culture in Taiwan: Martial Law to Market Law* (New York: Columbia University Press, 2004), 119.
2. What is ironic here is that if it is deprived of fish the cat is likely to catch birds and other creatures; the significant role outdoor cats have played in the decline in bird populations is well known. See Richard Conniff, "The Evil of the Outdoor Cat," *New York Times*, Sunday Review, March 23, 2014.

3. As Buell, Heise, and Thornber explain, ecocriticism comprises "an eclectic, pluriform, and cross-disciplinary initiative that aims to explore the environmental dimensions of literature and other creative media. . . .Ecocriticism begins from the conviction that the arts of imagination and the study thereof . . . can contribute significantly to the understanding of environmental problems. . . .At least as fundamental to their remediation as scientific breakthroughs and strengthened regimes of policy implementation is the impetus of creative imagination, vision, will, and belief" (418). The term "ecocriticism" was coined in the 1970s, but it was not until the 1990s that literature specialists—albeit primarily scholars of English literature—engaged in sustained environmental inquiry. Early ecocritical studies focused largely on nature preservation and human attachment to place, while the turn of the twenty-first century brought with it more attention to urbanization and industrialization, environmental justice, transnational concerns, and cross-pollination with postcolonial literary studies and with studies of indigenous and other ethnic minority literatures. See Lawrence Buell, Ursula K. Heise, and Karen Thornber, "Literature and Environment," *Annual Review of Environment and Resources* 36 (2011): 417–440. For a synopsis of ecologically themed literature in China and Taiwan from the *Shijing* 詩經 (Classic of Poetry, sixth century BCE) to the present, see Karen Laura Thornber, *Ecoambiguity: East Asian Literatures and Environmental Crises* (Ann Arbor: University of Michigan Press, 2012), 32–95.

4. For instance, the narrator despairs that the plastic bag in which he receives the fish will take many millennia to biodegrade. In addition, he portrays taking the train between Taipei in the north and Kaohsiung in the south as a journey past both endless flaming oil refineries and watery fields that appear like land covered with silver mines, leaving unclear the true extent of the damage to Taiwan's ecosystems (127).

5. Yan Lianke. *Ding Zhuang meng* 丁庄梦 [Dream of Ding Village] (Shanghai: Shanghai Wenyi Chubanshe, 2006), 7. References to this novel will be provided in parentheses in the text. Bookstores in China were permitted to sell their remaining stock even after the novel was banned. Moreover, *Dream of Ding Village* was also published in Taiwan, Hong Kong, and Singapore, and so remained readily available in Chinese even after it was technically banned in China. See Tian Yuan, "Kaisetsu: Shōchō to genjitsu no aida de—*Tei[Ding]shō* o yomu" [Commentary: Between symbol and reality—Reading Dream of Ding Village] in Yan Lianke, *Tei[Ding]shō no yume: Chūgoku no eizumura kidan* [Dream of Ding Village: Colorful tale of China's AIDS village], trans. Tanikawa Tsuyoshi (Tokyo: Kawade Shobō Shinsha, 2007), 352; and Chien-hsin Tsai, "In Sickness or in Health: Yan Lianke and the Writing of Autoimmunity," *Modern Chinese Literature and Culture* 23.1 (Spring 2011): 77.

6. Resilience—best understood as the ability of a system to absorb shocks and to adapt successfully to change, and arguably more a process than a characteristic—is an emergent and increasingly popular area of scholarly inquiry in a number of fields.

7. The Yellow River has a long history of devastating floods; for thousands of years, controlling this river has been the bane of many a Chinese ruler.

8. The narrator liberally employs boldface type, sometimes for emphasis and sometimes to provide a different perspective; boldface type is used for everything from single lines to entire chapter subdivisions.

9. Residents receive permission to fell trees for any number of reasons, including but not limited to constructing coffins.

10. The ending of Yan Lianke's novel provides an important contrast with that of Wang Lixiong's 王力雄 (b. 1953) novel *Yellow Peril* (黃禍; 1991). Wang Lixiong features a planet almost utterly destroyed, disparities among population, per capita demand, and available resources having become so great that ecosystems worldwide have reached their breaking points. *Yellow Peril* concludes, however, with a man walking by himself, carrying an "inflated baby/doll." Stopping to rest, he puts down both bags and baby/doll, the latter of which is soon confirmed to be, or becomes, an actual child; two paragraphs later the man, now sowing seeds, "hears the cries of the baby." People, or at least this one infant, appear to have somehow come back to life. And so too is the natural world beginning to revive, however slowly, the novel ending with the man "suddenly noticing the first pale green shoots" growing from seeds he had planted in the skeleton-infused, destitute, barren, and literally "dead soil" (死亡的土地). Wang Lixiong 王力雄, *Huanghuo* 黃禍, [Yellow peril] (Port Credit, ON: Jianda mingjing chubanshe, 1991), 3: 275–276.

11. Ruth Levine, *Case Studies in Global Health: Millions Saved* (Boston: Jones and Bartlett, 2007), xiii.

12. Autoimmune disease is arguably as much of a "medical frontier" today as syphilis and tuberculosis were in the nineteenth century, with the number of cases of such diseases rising at epidemic rates; it is estimated that as many as fifty million Americans suffer from autoimmunity, making it more prevalent than cancer. But unlike cancer, about which most people have heard, 85 percent of Americans cannot name an autoimmune disease, and finding donors to support research is difficult. Meghan O'Rourke, "What's Wrong with Me?" (*New Yorker*, August 26, 2013), 34.

13. James Gustave Speth, *The Bridge at the Edge of the World: Capitalism, The Environment, and Crossing from Crisis to Sustainability* (New Haven: Yale University Press, 2008), 1–2.

WORKS CITED

Buell, Lawrence, Ursula K. Heise, and Karen Thornber. "Literature and Environment." *Annual Review of Environment and Resources* 36 (2011): 417–440.

Chang, Sung-sheng Yvonne. *Literary Culture in Taiwan: Martial Law to Market Law.* New York: Columbia University Press, 2004.

Chu T'ien-wen. *Huangren shouji* 荒人手記 [Notes of a desolate man]. Jinan: Shandong Huabao Chubanshe, 2009.

Conniff, Richard. "The Evil of the Outdoor Cat." *New York Times*, Sunday Review, March 23, 2014.

Levine, Ruth. *Case Studies in Global Health: Millions Saved*. Boston: Jones and Bartlett, 2007.

O'Rourke, Meghan. "What's Wrong with Me?" *New Yorker*, August 26, 2013, 32–37.

Speth, James Gustave. *The Bridge at the Edge of the World: Capitalism, the Environment, and Crossing from Crisis to Sustainability*. New Haven: Yale University Press, 2008.

Thornber, Karen Laura. *Ecoambiguity: Environmental Crises and East Asian Literatures*. Ann Arbor: University of Michigan Press, 2012.

Tian Yuan. "Kaisetsu: Shōchō to genjitsu no aida de—*Tei[Ding]shō* o yomu" [Commentary: Between symbol and reality—Reading *Dream of Ding Village*]. In Yan Lianke, *Tei[Ding]shō no yume: Chūgoku no eizumura kidan* [*Dream of Ding Village*: Colorful tale of China's AIDS village]. Trans. Tanikawa Tsuyoshi. Tokyo: Kawade shobō shinsha, 2007. 349–358.

Tsai, Chien-hsin. "In Sickness or in Health: Yan Lianke and the Writing of Autoimmunity." *Modern Chinese Literature and Culture* 23.1 (Spring 2011): 77–104.

Wang Lixiong. *Huanghuo* 黄禍 [Yellow peril]. Port Credit, ON: Jianda Mingjing Chubanshe, 1991.

Yan Lianke 閻連科. *Ding Zhuang meng* 丁庄梦 [Dream of Ding Village]. Shanghai: Shanghai Wenyi Chubanshe, 2006.

Yan Lianke 閻連科. *Dream of Ding Village*. Trans. Cindy Carter. New York: Grove Press, 2009.

Yan Lianke 閻連科. *Riguang liunian* 日光流年 [Streams of life and time]. Shenyang: Chunfang Wenyi, 2004.

Yan Lianke 閻連科. *Shouhuo* 受活 [Lenin's kisses]. Beijing: Renmin Ribao Chubanshe, 2007.

Yan Lianke 閻連科. *Lenin's Kisses*. Trans. Carlos Rojas. New York: Grove Press, 2012.

MALAYSIA AS METHOD

Xiao Hei and Ethnolinguistic Literary Taxonomy

BRIAN BERNARDS

HANSHENG 漢生, the protagonist of the novella "A Literary Record of October 27 and Other Things" (十•廿七的文學記實與其他; 1989) by Xiao Hei 小黑 (which is the penname of the Malaysian author Tan Kee Keat 陳奇杰, b. 1951), is a character whose relationship to the surrounding Malaysian society is indelibly marked by his Chineseness. Hansheng's given name literally means "born Han Chinese," genealogically linking him to the Han people (China's ethnic majority) and to his Chinese ancestral homeland (as *Han* 漢 also alludes to China's Han dynasty). Hansheng's name not only symbolizes his seemingly unavoidable racialization as a perpetual Chinese "immigrant" in postcolonial Malaysia (even though he was actually born in a rural kampong in northern Malaysia, not China), it also predetermines his communal cultural orientation and life trajectory. A professor in the Chinese department at the University of Malaya in Kuala Lumpur, Hansheng is a staunch advocate for preserving the integrity of Mandarin-language education in Malaysia, composing fiery editorials in local Sinophone newspapers to publicly defend its important role in society against ongoing, corrosive interference from the Malay ruling government and majority *bumiputera* (the native "sons of the soil") population. In "A Literary Record," Xiao Hei unabashedly casts his protagonist as an allegorical and emblematic figure of a minority community which, alienated by the political apparatus of Malaysian nationhood, raises the banner of ethnolinguistic collectivity to wage resistance against the state authority and the discourse of official nationalism.

Whereas Hansheng's identity and cultural politics may appear simplistic and straightforward, those of Xiao Hei's novella are not. Setting aside the fact that the ultimate success or failure of Hansheng's struggle is left entirely uncertain (in fact the character mysteriously disappears), the larger formal structure in which Xiao Hei situates Hansheng's narrative features a collaborative, intertextual pastiche of citations and excerpts from other Sinophone literary works—poetry, fiction, and criticism—by several Malaysian Chinese authors, including other works by Xiao Hei himself. While such intertextual strategies bolster the collaborative literary record of the Chinese minority community that testifies to its collective sense of marginality and persecution at a given historical moment in the late 1980s, exemplifying what Malaysian scholar Khor Boon Eng 許文榮 describes as Xiao Hei's "poetics of resistance," these excerpts do not univocally embrace the same tactic of resistance—or even the same cultural politics and identity—as Hansheng.[1] Rather, their juxtaposition diversifies the literary record Xiao Hei constructs, producing a dialogue (indeed a cacophony) of voices that occasion critical self-reflection as much as they summon a common opponent and outward political strategy. Though the significance of (the fictional) Hansheng's ethnically inscribed name goes largely unchecked in the novella, several lines that Xiao Hei excerpts from a poem by fellow (real-life) author Fang Ang 方昂 outright reject the ascription of Chinese ethnolinguistic signifiers that are conflated with a foreign nationality and geography (*Zhongguo* 中國, "China"), that assign a permanent immigrant status of marginal, secondary citizenship (*Zhinaren* 支那人, "Chinaman"), or that altogether fail to specify a relationship to place of residence or homeland (*Huaren* 華人, "Overseas Chinese").[2]

In English translation, the geopolitical and ideological nuances of the three individual terms (*Zhongguo* 中國, *Zhina* 支那, *Hua* 華) invoked by Fang Ang—to which we may also add *Han* 漢—are lost or flattened by their general abstraction as variants of a seemingly singular *Chinese*. Read in this context, Fang Ang's need to reject each of them appears redundant. Yet, as I discuss later in this chapter, each term in Fang Ang's lyrical utterance invokes a separate interlocutor, a different ideological authority of ethnocultural identity ascription influencing the lives and fates of Malaysian Chinese (ethnic Chinese from Malaysia), including not only the nation-states of China and Malaysia but also the cultural engineers and proponents of diaspora. Through this collaborative invocation of multiple authorities, and its questioning from multiple perspectives (and literary forms) of the ideology behind various identitarian categories, Xiao Hei's novella not only serves as a collective record of a body of literature organized around an ethnolinguistic taxonomy (all the authors he excerpts are Malaysian Chinese, all the texts are written in Chinese), but also as a critical interrogation of the very taxonomy that constitutes that literary body. This taxonomy is *Ma Hua wenxue* 馬華文學, a term most often rendered in English as *Malaysian Chinese literature* or *Sinophone Malaysian literature*, but which I refer to here as *Ma Hua literature* to convey its dual ethnic and linguistic connotations. Although such a taxonomy appears more concerned with identity politics than with the aesthetic value or literariness of a given text, it is intended to serve as a reminder of the entangled relationship between politics and literature, or of the politics of literature itself.[3]

Starting from the assumption that Ma Hua literature provides fertile territory from which to rethink the taxonomical politics of modern Chinese literature more generally—as it encourages us to reconsider the ways in which the field and discipline are differentially constituted vis-à-vis language, ethnicity, and nationality—this chapter examines how Xiao Hei's "A Literary Record" is not only a work of collaborative protest fiction lamenting the marginalization of the ethnic and linguistic Chinese minority—the Ma Hua—in postcolonial Malaysia, but is also a dialogic reflection on how this community (and its literature) is constituted, mobilized, and represented in both the national sphere of Malaysia and in the transnational Sinophone sphere of the Chinese diaspora. I argue that it is not the multiple registers of Chineseness—the emphasis of what I call the practice of "China as method" in the study of Ma Hua literature—but rather Xiao Hei's multiangled (re) presentation of Malaysia as a historical experience, a contested political space, a claimed nation-space, and a rejected state apparatus that critically intervenes in and potentially undermines the ethnolinguistic taxonomy of a minor (diasporic) and minority (immigrant) literary tradition, showing how this organizational principle reinforces conditions of marginality. In calling this strategy *Malaysia as method*, I draw from Kuan-hsing Chen's proposal of *Asia as method*—which he offers as a historical corrective to the practice of *West as method* in contemporary knowledge production about Asian societies—to argue that Malaysia in Xiao Hei's novella functions as a mediating site for the decolonization of Malaysian national literature's ethnolinguistic basis (and bias) as well as the deimperialization of the overseas Chinese literary framework.[4]

A MINOR/ITY LITERARY RECORD: THE BURDEN OF COLLECTIVE REPRESENTATION AND RESISTANCE

As a work of fiction written in Chinese by a Malaysian Chinese author that not only extrapolates from other Ma Hua literary texts but also weaves the ongoing project and politics of Ma Hua writing into the story's plot, Xiao Hei's "A Literary Record of October 27 and Other Things" asserts its position within a Ma Hua minor/minority literary tradition as a collaborative document of Ma Hua literary history. To understand how "A Literary Record" engages this tradition, it is important to consider the overlapping but nevertheless distinct defining criteria of Ma Hua literature. Such criteria include the historical place and period in which a given work is written; the (primary) language in which it is composed; the assumed or assigned ethnic background and cultural affiliation of the author; the subjects of composition, both fictional and nonfictional; and finally, the national and transnational frames of intertextual reference, influence, and literary governance that both enable and delimit a given work's production, circulation, intelligibility, and appraisal.[5]

The taxonomical ambiguity of Ma Hua literature derives from the fact that *Ma* 馬 and *Hua* 華 are shorthand for related terms with variable connotative emphases. In the introduction to her study *Sinophone Malaysian Literature*, Alison Groppe provides a detailed overview of the various significations of *Ma* and *Hua* in relation to this literature, so I will not recapitulate this discussion here except to reflect on how *Ma* and *Hua* combine to simultaneously express a minor and minority literary tradition, as Xiao Hei's novella provides an excellent illustration of this fusion.[6]

Functioning as an abbreviation for both the British colony of Malaya (馬來亞) and subsequent nation-state of Malaysia (馬來西亞), *Ma* anchors this tradition in a specific place, a geopolitical territory whose modern borders—including its seats of administrative and cultural authority—have historically shifted. *Ma*-as-place implies flexible relations to readership (the origins of a Sinophone publication in Malaya/Malaysia, regardless of the origins of the author), authorship (works by Sinophone authors born and raised in Malaya/Malaysia, even if they subsequently settle elsewhere), and content (Malaya/Malaysia as fictional setting, poetic trope or motif, implicit or direct allusion, and object of political and historical critique, parody, dis/identification, celebration, alienation, or lament).

Xiao Hei's "A Literary Record" meets all three of these criteria concerning *Ma*-as-place: written in 1989, the novella is included in Xiao Hei's *The Eve* (前夕), a volume of short fiction first published in Kuala Lumpur. Xiao Hei is a secondary school administrator in Kuala Lumpur who hails from Padang Serai in the northern state of Kedah. In addition to editorials and prose essays, Xiao Hei has intermittently penned volumes of short fiction and novellas, including not only *The Eve* (1990), but also *Black* (黑; 1979) and *Clear Water, Dark Mountains* (白水黑山; 1993).[7] As in most of the author's published work, Malaysia is the primary setting and its national politics the main object of narrative concern in "A Literary Record."

While *Ma* connotes both the real historical and imagined creative space of Ma Hua literature, the standalone connotations of *Hua* produce greater taxonomical ambiguity. *Hua* (a Mandarin phonetic rendering) is an adjective indicating someone or something that is Chinese but that presumably evolves (or originates) outside or independent of China as a territory and geopolitical entity. In Ma Hua literature, the territorial displacement and decoupling of Chinese (a modifier) from China (a place) implied by *Hua* functions on two overlapping but distinct levels, one prioritizing ethnicity and the other language. As shorthand for an "overseas" (海外) or "diasporic" (離散) "person of Chinese descent" (*Huaren* 華人 or *Huayi* 華裔), *Hua*-as-ethnos operates on the assumption that the ethnic background or affiliation of the author as Chinese or being of Chinese descent profoundly determines the author's cultural orientation and life experiences and is therefore intimately tied to his or her literary endeavors. Ma Hua literature presumably speaks to what it is or means to be Chinese or of Chinese descent in a location estranged not only from the ancestral homeland but from the dominant political and cultural institutions in the space of historical settlement. *Hua* frequently conjures up experiences of marginalization, exclusion, and/or minoritization within its local context of articulation. In Ma Hua literature, *Hua* embodies one's racialized subjection to the British imperial regime in colonial Malaya, as well as one's minoritization under policies favoring Malays in postcolonial Malaysia.

Xiao Hei's "A Literary Record of October 27 and Other Things" addresses the political and historical circumstances of Chinese minoritization in Malaysia. Set in 1987, the novella concerns itself with the immediate postcolonial present, yet it appropriates the occasion of the thirty-year anniversary of *merdeka* (national independence) to reflect upon the country's inability to eliminate holdover colonial views of the Chinese as a temporary "foreign" population and the Malays as the indigenous host population, attitudes that seem to perpetuate and exacerbate interethnic conflicts. The historical backdrop to "A Literary Record" is Operation Lalang, or the "weeding operation," a police crackdown in late October 1987 on demonstrators and publications challenging the authority and policies of the government of Mahathir Mohamed (PM 1981–2003) and the Barisan Nasional (National Front or BN). As the ruling party since 1973, the BN maintains a triethnic structure, with the United Malays National Organization (UMNO) serving as the party's backbone and the Malaysian Chinese Association (MCA) and Malaysian Indian Congress (MIC) largely deferring to UMNO's supremacy.[8] In the spring and summer of 1987, as Malaysia celebrated thirty years of independence, there was a push for interethnic organizing at the grassroots level around various communal and noncommunal issues, such as press freedom, education, the environment, and consumer protection. At the University of Malaya, Sinophone educators rallied against the MCA's appointment of school administrators not fluent in Mandarin to oversee Chinese education in the country, expressing their concern that such appointments reflected state plans to eventually eliminate Chinese-medium schools altogether.[9] They were confronted with counterdemonstrations by UMNO supporters among the student body who accused them of fomenting ethnic antagonism. During Operation Lalang, the government and the police invoked the Internal Security Act and the Printing Presses Ordinance, draconian measures originally instituted under the British during the counterinsurgency period known as the Emergency (1948–1960), to arrest and detain over a hundred activists, as well as suspend or close down four national newspapers (two English, one Chinese, and one Malay).[10]

Xiao Hei's "A Literary Record" recounts the escalation of events leading up to Operation Lalang and the October 27 disappearance of Hansheng, a professor and essayist who published critiques of the BN's political, economic, and academic suppression in local newspapers. State media sources accuse him of being "hot-tempered" and "inflammatory," claiming his articles helped incite the student protests. Hansheng feels that he is simply appealing to the government to uphold rights protected by Malaysia's constitution. He wonders why Malays angrily accuse the Malaysian Chinese demonstrators of "chauvinism." Fearing he will be arrested and interrogated like some of his colleagues, Hansheng attempts to move into hiding with his family in his kampong hometown in the northern part of the country. As they make their final approach into the kampong, a sudden fog engulfs Hansheng's car, and even though he knows the area well he cannot find his way out. This is the last news of the family before its disappearance, and presumably Hansheng is "still circling in the fog" of his homeland.[11]

Hansheng is a rather flat allegorical character who shoulders the collective burden of the Ma Hua community. The open ending is an overt metaphor for the chaotic and uncertain present he faces as well as the foggy, unclear future of his community, implied by his children's presence in the car with him. As the common trope or idiom of a minoritized ethnos, or what in many cases scholars call *Chineseness*, the *Hua* in the

Ma Hua taxonomy symbolizes the vicissitudes of a minority community marked by its permanent immigrant or settler status.[12] It is not merely the name of an ethnic group but a consciously devised strategy of resistance and self-affirmation writers might cultivate to express the community's conflict with and distinction from the dominant culture or ideology of the local colonial or national regime. However, *Hua* may also be interpreted not as a purposeful tactic but as a possible symptom, outcome, or even unintended burden of this conflict. As Abdul JanMohamed and David Lloyd suggest, cultures "designated as minorities have certain shared experiences by virtue of their similar antagonistic relationship to the dominant culture, which seeks to marginalize them all." This relationship shapes what JanMohamed and Lloyd call the "collective nature of all minority discourse," which "derives from the fact that minority individuals are always treated and forced to experience themselves generically."[13] Within such a configuration, *Hua* denotes the sense of cultural crisis or endangerment that compels authors like Xiao Hei (and protagonists like Hansheng) to bear the "burden of representation," a collective responsibility seemingly inherent to the concept of minority cultural production that often trumps the privilege of narrative complexity.[14]

The various intertexts of Xiao Hei's "A Literary Record" further illuminate the process by which *Hua* comes to denote first a symptom of the ongoing ethnic conflict and second a repurposed strategy of minority resistance. However, rather than providing definitive conclusions or outcomes to these conflicts, the intertexts—like the case of Hansheng—merely ask open-ended questions, leaving unresolved the viability of *Hua* as an ethnic category and as a resistance strategy. First, an excerpt of "Thirty Years" (三十年; 1987), one of Xiao Hei's own essays, asks what improvements three decades of independence have brought the nation. Even though most Malaysians were poorer at the time of independence, their lives were "happier" and more "harmonious" because the "three major ethnic groups" (Malays, Chinese, and Indians) did not regard each other as enemies as a result of having cooperated to extricate the nation from British colonialism.[15] The comparison questions the logic of postcolonial "progress," suggesting instead an unexamined retrogression toward colonial attitudes and a hardening of racialized divisions. As an ethnic marker that sets a minority group apart from the nation, *Hua* here is a symptom of this process and lack of integration. Second, Xiao Hei's excerpt from the poem "Mid-Autumn—for My Classmates at the University of Malaya" (中秋——致國大一群同學) by fellow author He Naijian 何乃健, which the poet wrote in support of the Malaysian Chinese student demonstrations prior to the police crackdown, poignantly asks: "Why is a tropical arboretum enshrouded in the autumnal chill of the North Country?"[16] He Naijian deterritorializes the Mid-Autumn Festival as a trope of Chineseness to demonstrate against Malay cultural hegemony so that an occasion for celebration in China becomes a sign of distress in the tropics, where an autumnal distinction is a complete anomaly. Within the framework of a minority literature, such tropes exemplify strategies of Ma Hua literary resistance to Malay-centrism in the national arena.

This strategy of deterritorializing and recontextualizing a China-based trope (the idiom of Chineseness) for a local political purpose is not simply a matter of asserting one's ethnocultural difference (*Hua*-as-ethnos) within a national framework (*Ma*-as-place), but also relates to a linguistic difference (*Hua*-as-language) within a transnational sphere of Sinophone or Chinese-language writing, one that expresses the second connotation of *Hua* in Ma Hua literature. As an ethnic minority formation (Malaysian Chinese literature), Ma Hua literature theoretically does not exclude non-Sinophone works, such as Malay and Anglophone writing by Malaysian Chinese authors.[17] At the same time, *Hua* functions as not only an ethnic but also a linguistic marker, connoting a body of overseas literature written in Chinese.[18] More specifically, *Hua*-as-language has also come to indicate literature written in the modern vernacular script based on standard Mandarin, often called the "Hua language" (with "spoken" *huayu* 華語 and "written" *huawen* 華文 variants) outside China, especially in Southeast Asia. The term was adopted by Sinophone newspapers in colonial Malaya in the 1920s, following China's national revolution and vernacular language movement, as a language of modernity, diasporic Chinese nationalism, and literary realism. Scholars attribute the origins of Ma Hua literature to this moment in Malaya's colonial history, attesting to the integral role of script standardization and Mandarin education and dissemination in its early development.[19] In "A Literary Record," Xiao Hei portrays Hansheng's noble cause to preserve Mandarin education in postcolonial Malaysia, as well as the protests against the government's appointments of unqualified administrators to oversee Chinese education, as integral to the very survival of Ma Hua literature. The prose of Xiao Hei's novella, as a work of reportage or documentary realism that combines fiction and current events, highlights the intimate link between the vernacular of Sinophone literature and journalism in Malaysia.

Though absorbing the impact of script standardization, *Hua*-as-language should not be understood merely as Mandarin monolingual homogeneity. Inspired by Shu-mei Shih's theorization of Sinophone literature as literatures of the "Sinitic language family" (華語語系),[20] Tee Kim Tong 張錦忠 asserts the multilingualism of "Sinophone Malaysian literature" (馬來西亞華語語系文學) as one reading or translation of the *Ma Hua* abbreviation. The language family taxonomy suggests that Ma Hua literature may be written and read in other common Sinitic languages used in Malaya/Malaysia besides Mandarin.[21] Acknowledging the predominance of Mandarin-based writing since the vernacular movement of the 1920s, Tee's shift from "language" to "language family" is a gesture that recognizes what Ng Kim Chew 黃錦樹 identifies as the "multilingual environment" and translation/transliteration processes inherent in Ma Hua works: other Sinitic (or even non-Sinitic) languages spoken in Malaya/Malaysia inevitably inflect the standard written language deployed in the text.[22] *Hua*-as-language bears the traces of these multilingual inflections. Xiao Hei's fiction, despite its conscious composition in (and its narrative promulgation of) a standard vernacular Chinese based on Mandarin, must deploy local Malay terms in order to establish the political environment he is contesting. For example, in his short story "The Eve" (from which he excerpts at length in "A Literary Record"), Xiao Hei addresses the popular controversy surrounding the subjects tested in the SPM (Sijil Pelajaran Malaysia, literally the "Malaysian Certificate of Education"), a national university entrance examination taken by all fifth-year secondary school students in Malaysia. The author gives no Mandarin translation or explanation of SPM, either assuming readers are familiar with the term or encouraging them to do further research about the local context.

From his observations of Ma Hua literary language practice and its politics, Tee Kim Tong classifies Sinophone Malaysian literature as a "minor literature" (小文學), adopting the framework developed by Gilles Deleuze and Félix Guattari to analyze Franz Kafka's writing in Prague German.[23] Deleuze and Guattari use Kafka's example to identify three major characteristics of minor literature: its language is "deterritorialized," it exists in a "cramped space" and "fragile community" that renders it inherently "political," and its political immediacy gives it "collective value."[24] Following this line of thought, Tee asserts that the authorship and "textuality" of Ma Hua literature is "not constructed in the space of the little me or the private individual, but in the collective space of the social, the economic, and the political."[25] Tee's assertion provides some insight into the collaborative authorship of "A Literary Record." The pseudonym Xiao Hei, which literally means "little black," can be read as a kind of self-effacement: it evokes a small dark spot, a minor blotch, an insignificant but unpleasant detail, an untold story hidden in the shadows. The pseudonym positions Xiao Hei's authorship in a space of mediation between the individual (the "little me," 小我), the minor/minority Sinophone/Malaysian Chinese community, and the national body politic.

These characteristics, certainly analogous to the burden of collective representation and politics of opposition/recognition defining minority literature, align minor literature with that taxonomy, but minor literature begins from a focus on language use rather than ethnicity (though Kafka's Jewish background figures prominently in Deleuze and Guattari's argument). The "minor usage" of a dominant language deconstructs and deterritorializes the latter from a subject position outside its mainstream environment, inflecting it with the history, experience, and "polylingualism" of a different site.[26] *Hua*-as-language implies this minor usage inflecting the major language of Mandarin from a subject position "outside China" (中外) and the modern Chinese literary mainstream (China, Taiwan, and Hong Kong). For Tee, Ma Hua literature signals "the departure of Chinese from China" to Southeast Asia, where it becomes a kind of deterritorialized and "broken Mandarin," deficient yet exotic in its vocabulary and sentence structure.[27]

Not only is displacement from China insufficient to describe *Hua*-as-ethnos in Ma Hua literature as minority taxonomy, an additional estrangement related to locality—to *Ma*-as-place—also undergirds the function of *Hua*-as-language in its minor, deterritorialized usage. As Tee Kim Tong writes, "Sinophone Malaysian literature is deterritorialized in its own country because of the politics of recognition— as it is not written in Bahasa Malaysia, and therefore it is not recognized as national literature."[28] In postcolonial Malaysia, national literature (*sastera negara* or *sastera kebangsaan*)—as an official category with real ramifications for funding, institutional support, and awards—has been, since 1971, restricted to works composed in Malay. Literature written by Malaysian authors in other languages, including Chinese,

English, and Tamil (the other three major literary languages in Malaysia), are classified by the Institute of Language and Literature (Dewan Bahasa dan Pustaka) as sectional or ethnic literatures (*sastera sukuan* or *sastera etnik*) and deemed unfit for national representation.[29] By this definition, it is language, and not ethnicity, that offers the primary basis for categorizing literature in Malaysia. *Hua*-as-language embodies a paradoxical relationship to *Ma*-as-place: on one hand the historical experience of Malaya/Malaysia provides the minor, polylingual de-territorialization of standard Mandarin; on the other hand the experience of Malaysia as geopolitical entity estranges this language from the nation and confines it to its own ethnolinguistic space of literary dwelling.[30]

Such a dynamic shows that although I have thus far parsed *Ma* and *Hua* as distinct terms, the two should not be interpreted as stand-alone, mutually exclusive signifiers in the Ma Hua taxonomy. Rather, they are contrapuntal, defined in relation and sometimes in opposition to each other. Straddling Sinophone Malaysian literature (linguistic emphasis) and Malaysian Chinese literature (ethnic emphasis), the term *Ma Hua literature* functions as an ethnolinguistic literary taxonomy in which the ethnolinguistic signifier depends on Malaya/Malaysia as a colonial/national space for its very existence, regardless of whether this signifier functions to affirm or reject its position within that space. Ma Hua literature may lack the institutional support or positivism associated with the concept of national literature as an instrument of official, ideological hegemony, but it is not a "literature without nation." Although "the power to represent the nation is already the power to dominate it," as Neil Larsen suggests, the "power to contest this representation" or subvert its very logic either "preconditions the national-emancipatory act" or "stands in for it."[31] Ma Hua literature should thus not be read merely as the communal allegory for an ethnic minority or displaced language culture, but as a challenge to the hegemonic structure of national representation in Malaysia and as a defiant claim to that multicultural, multiethnic, and multilingual space. It is a literary formation that rejects the "state apparatus" but not necessarily the concept of national literature, maintaining an alternative vision of national literature as that produced in or about a nation, by its inhabitants or those invested in its greater welfare.[32]

From this perspective, Ma Hua literature may be read as a postcolonial mode of representing or envisioning the broader nation (with a prenational heritage, like all postcolonial literatures) that intervenes in and potentially undermines its own ethnolinguistic minor/ity taxonomy, because this category reinforces exclusionary state ideology. The ethnolinguistic taxonomy denies Ma Hua literature its own internal multiculturalism, thereby stripping it of any defiant claim to national representation. Reading Xiao Hei's "A Literary Record" through this lens, rather than merely that of collective ethnolinguistic resistance, reveals a more complex and self-reflexive metanarrative engagement with the postcolonial politics of identity and literature in Malaysia. This mode of engagement (and of critical interpretation) highlights what I mean by Malaysia as method, a subject to which I now turn.

INTER-REFERENCING OTHER
THINGS: MALAYSIA AS METHOD

To help articulate Malaysia as method as a potential alternative or complementary critical lens to that of China (or Chineseness) as method in reading and interpreting Xiao Hei's fiction (and Ma Hua literature in general), I draw from Kuan-hsing Chen's *Asia as Method: Toward Deimperialization* (2010).[33] Chen posits Asia as method as an "alternative horizon" for cultural studies, which have predominately taken the West as method, to approach Asia as an object or objective. Chen suggests that since certain resources, research methods, discourses, and other "elements of the West have become internal to base-entities in Asia," there is no longer a need "to stress our distinctiveness" by continuing to use the West as the primary referent point for different Asian societies and cultures. Chen proposes "a move toward Asia as a possible way of shifting points of reference and breaking away from the East-West binary structure."[34] For Chen, this shift has a critical objective:

> The implication of Asia as method is that using Asia as an imaginary anchoring point can allow societies in Asia to become one another's reference points, so that the understanding of the self can be transformed, and subjectivity rebuilt.[35]

Asia as method does not mean the homogenization or standardization of what it means to be Asian. Here, Asia functions not as a taxonomy or subjectivity but as an "inter-referencing process" necessary for the simultaneous movements of "decolonization, deimperialization," and "de-cold war" through which different local subjectivities are transformed.[36] To do Asia as method is to ask: how can we (re)imagine Asia from two (or more) points within Asia and the relationship between those points, whether they refer to specific nations, social classes, political formations, intersecting historical events, or minority cultures?

Whereas East/West is the schematic binary that for Chen requires Asia as method to critically intervene in cultural studies more broadly, China/Malaysia has been the dominant dichotomy in the study of Ma Hua literature. The latter dichotomy functions on two planes. On one hand, it consistently asserts the historical distinctiveness of Ma Hua literature from China—refusing tributary status to an imperial Chinese center—despite its appropriation of Chinese influence in terms of literary discourses, tools, trends, styles, and resources. On the other, the dichotomy stresses how this literature cultivates Chineseness as both victim and coping mechanism to reclaim cultural pride from the legacy of racialized exploitation at the hands of British and Japanese imperial regimes, and from postcolonial Malaysian political persecution and ethnic minoritization.[37]

Premised on the notion that its Chinese influences (vernacular script, modes of realism, modernism, etc.) are already—throughout a century of localization—internal to

Malaysia as base-entities, Malaysia as method recognizes that one no longer need assert the distinctiveness of Ma Hua literature from Chinese literature and instead shifts its imaginary anchoring points to Malaysia as a mediating site of subjectivity.[38] The critical imperative of Malaysia as method is to deimperialize a China-as-center/Malaysia-as-overseas model in which "Chinese literature" (namely the tradition of *Zhongguo wenxue* 中國文學) always serves as a primary methodology and epistemic interlocutor, as well as to decolonize the racialized colonial inheritance of Malaysian cultural production, a project that was stunted and intercepted by the creation of an ethnicized hierarchy in postcolonial Malaysia. The goal of Malaysia as method is not the homogenization or standardization of what it means to be Malaysian; such homogeneity is rather the unintended effect of a dichotomous China/Malaysia comparison, as Ma Hua literature is forced into a position of representing a distinct but singular Malaysian Chineseness to the Chinese literary center. Instead, the desired outcome of this project is the recognition of the ongoing transformation of local subjectivities through mediation between languages, ethnicities, sexes, gender identities, social classes, discursive structures, literary traditions, political parties and ideologies, and regions, states, cities, and villages in Malaysia as multiple touchstones for Ma Hua literature.

Although from the standpoint of China as method, Xiao Hei's "A Literary Record" is a univocal Ma Hua response to Malay political hegemony that underscores its Chineseness as resistance tactic (especially as only Ma Hua writers are featured in the intertext), Malaysia as method involves looking to the narrative spaces beyond the ethnolinguistic signifier to the "other things" which are not simply a matter of being Chinese or *Hua* in Malaysia, but that relate to other aspects, experiences, perspectives, and expressions of being (or feeling denied participation as) Malaysian. The "other things" (*qita* 其他) alluded to in the novella's title compose the key divisions within the narrative structure ("Other Thing 1", 2, 3, and so on): while framing Hansheng's story, they also serve as the point of departure for the first-person narrator to interreference the various perspectives expressed by his intertextual citations. At the beginning of the story, Hansheng's younger brother Hanxing 漢興 (literally "Han Chinese revival") visits Xiao Hei to inquire about his missing brother's whereabouts. The visit compels the narrator to not only reconstruct the story of what might have happened to Hansheng, but to also reflect on recent Ma Hua publications and the institutional constraints that actually prevent this literature from transcending its relegation to ethnolinguistic status.

Citing a review published in *Nanyang Siang Pau* (南洋商報; "South Seas Commercial Times") in July 1987 by Tang Lin 唐林 of Xiao Hei's own short story "The Eve,"[39] Xiao Hei proceeds to conceptualize an alternative, more inclusive ideal of Malaysian literature that begins from the individual courage to examine national issues from multiple angles, including those beyond one's own ethnolinguistic community. He acknowledges that the current institution of publication—which relies on media outlets only serving a certain cross-section of the public—hinders the realization of this ideal.[40] After mentioning Tang Lin's review, Xiao Hei includes three additional pages of excerpts from the story "The Eve" itself.[41] This choice to include such a lengthy excerpt from one of his short stories in another effectively documents a kind of composite reality from a diverse range of perspectives on Malaysia's political crisis at the time. The historical backdrop to "The Eve" is the 1986 federal elections. The story, which takes place on the eve of the voting, revolves around three unnamed brothers and their father, a retired Chinese schoolteacher, who live in an unnamed "mountain town." The unnamed youngest sister, who currently attends university, narrates the story. She paints a contrasting picture of the personalities and attitudes of her father and older brothers toward national politics: the father has experienced thirty years of betrayal by the MCA and refuses to give his blessing to his second son—a state assemblyman—to run as the local BN candidate for the federal legislature. The father even threatens to give his support to the opposition candidate, who is his former student. The oldest son, a successful merchant who favorably considers the economic advantages having a politician as a close relative will bring, offers financial support to his younger brother's candidacy. The third son, an individualistic, radical-minded "lone ranger" who has recently returned from studying in the West, has penned inflammatory editorials in the local newspaper that may undermine his older brother's candidacy. The narrator considers all of their stances: while she empathizes with the frustrations of her father and third brother, she appreciates her second brother's optimism, gentleness, and perseverance, and his willingness to enact steady change from within the BN administrative system rather than merely complain about it. If media censorship were as bad as his younger brother believes, the second brother asks, would he still be allowed to publish his harsh critiques?[42] The diverse positions taken by the father and three brothers demonstrate their different educations, their different friendships and associations not only with Malaysian Chinese but also non-Chinese and non-Malaysians as well, the different trajectories of their life travels, and their individual interests and personal goals, all leading to multiple ways of seeing themselves—and their responsibilities and commitments—as Malaysian citizens who are not limited to their self-understanding as part of a Chinese minority community.

Commenting on "The Eve," Tang Lin describes the narrative as an objective "videography" that abstracts a "realistic social portrait" of one family into the national body, so that the story could just as plausibly be set in any mountain town in Kedah, Penang, or Selangor.[43] In the commentary excerpted in "A Literary Record," Tang Lin cites Xiao Gu, a classmate of the story's narrator, as its most compelling character, suggesting that, despite a brief, marginal appearance, he best embodies the perspective of Xiao Hei himself. In "The Eve," Xiao Gu suggests to the narrator that her brothers' opposing views are limited by their "wavering back and forth within the confines of a single ethnic group." Responding to Tang in "A Literary Record," Xiao Hei claims that, "among the nine characters in the story," Xiao Gu possesses the "loftiest of ideals," but that this cultivates a sense of despair in him.[44] In the section directly reprinted from "The Eve," Xiao Hei cites several lines from Xiao Gu's dialogue with the narrator:

> Why is it that when we get to the highest level of schooling, we are segregated the most severely? In the countryside, we would all share one pack of Javanese cigarettes. . . . Sometimes I feel that we see each other more as enemies now than we did

thirty years ago. . . . Although it is difficult to seek unity across our differences, it is still an achievable ideal. The crux of the issue is: are our leaders willing to give up their emphasis on skin color and birth, language and religion, and truly try to create one race for the whole nation by not just being the heroes of one ethnic group?[45]

Reflecting on Xiao Gu's role, Xiao Hei asks why the hero of one ethnic group in Malaysia must always be someone who "stabs" another rather than one who strives to heal the wounds between them.[46] Combined with the excerpts from other authors in "A Literary Record," Xiao Hei uses the intertext to reveal the various ways Ma Hua literature—rather than reacting to political suppression merely with a retreat into ethnic defensiveness—also includes voices that resist discourses of racial "extremism."[47]

In addition to He Naijian's poem on the Mid-Autumn Festival, intertextual excerpts in "A Literary Record" from prominent Ma Hua poets of the 1980s include "Years of Torrential Rain" (濠雨歲月) by Fu Chengde 傅承得 and "For HCK" (給 HCK) by Fang Ang. Xiao Hei asserts that although each poem expresses "the painful sentiments of one person," they "basically capture the thoughts and feelings of most people at the time."[48] Despite their collective expression, the poems simultaneously reveal conflicted attitudes and a sense of self-reflexivity toward the adoption of tropes of Chineseness as a tactic of resistance.[49] Whereas He Naijian's poem deploys such a tactic, Fang Ang's reveals an awareness that China as method leaves Malaysian authors vulnerable to misappropriation and misinterpretation within the multiple national and transnational spheres of literary criticism and recognition, disavowing their claim to represent the nation by insinuating their eternal longing for the ancestral homeland and their essential dislocation from Malaysia as place.

Xiao Hei establishes the context for Fang Ang's poem by recounting a 1987 reception at Mimaland Park in Ulu Gombak for the visiting Taiwan poet Lin Huanzhang 林煥彰, who displays a sympathetic but overly patronizing view of Ma Hua literature as a lost tributary longing to return to the master tradition of Chinese literature. In response, Fang Ang gives an emotional reading of his poem "For HCK" (referring to Hwang Chong Kheow 方崇僑, the poet himself). Xiao Hei's "A Literary Record" reprints the entire poem:

之一
又有人說我們是移民了
說我們仍然
念念另一塊土地
說我們仍然
私藏另一條臍帶
這是一个風雨如晦的年代
該不該我們都問自己
究竟，我們愛不愛這塊土地
還是，我們去問問他們
如果土地不承認她的兒女，如何傾注心中的愛？

之二
說我們是中國人，我們不是
說我們是支那人，我們不願
說我們是馬來西亞人，誰說我們是
說我們是華人，哪一國的國民
我們擁有最滄桑的過去
與最荒涼的未來

One:
Yet another says that we are immigrants
That we still pine for another land
That we still cling to another umbilical cord
These are dark, stormy times
Should we ask ourselves
Whether we love this land
Or, should we go ask them
If this land doesn't recognize
Her sons and daughters,
Where can we pour the love in our hearts?

Two:
You say we are Chinese, but we are not
You say we are Chinamen,
But we won't play this role
You say we are Malaysians,
But who actually says this?
You say we are Overseas Chinese,
But then what country are we citizens of?
We possess the most turbulent of pasts
And the most desolate of futures.[50]

Rather than identity fragmentation, the two stanzas—with the clearly demarcated break between them—symbolize the poet's multiple interlocutors. Not only does the poet's reference to Chinamen target the ruling Malay elite, his invocation of Chinese (nationals) and Overseas Chinese targets mainland and diasporic Chinese readers, respectively. The identity of the poet's implied reader—the interlocutor with the power to ascribe certain identities to the poet and his community—is a crucial question, suggesting the poet's awareness that any rejection he makes of one interpellation may be interpreted as acceptance of another.

Knowing that his poem will be heard and interpreted by Chinese literary authorities outside Malaysia (including those invested in the concept of diaspora), Fang Ang rejects assignations of cultural identities from both national and transnational hegemonies of discursive signification. Whether to ascribe national, racial, or ethnic affinities and loyalties, most of these taxonomies invoke Chineseness, deploying what Ng Kim Chew calls the "symbolic violence" that compels "ancestral return," a process by which Malaysian Chinese "lose their position, their national identity, and their permission to establish roots on this land, as if their skin has been branded with the blood-red marking of 'immigrant.' "[51] Implicating and rejecting the ideological standpoint of these multiple interlocutors, Fang Ang questions the effectiveness of China as method as a resistance tactic for Malaysian Chinese authors. The poet does not flatly reject *Malaysian* as an alternative taxonomy, but he requires verification of its acceptance, since he doubts its flexible application. As long as integration is restricted to the conditions of Malaysian nationalism mandated by the ruling Malay elite, Fang Ang questions which interlocutors, or "implied others," will wholeheartedly accept—let alone initiate—the claim:[52] "We are Malaysians." The fact that the poem is, by virtue of its title, written for Fang Ang himself undermines his attempt to speak *on behalf* of a collective "we." Rather, it negotiates his own (re)constitution of and reconciliation with the larger community.

If China as method denotes Fang Ang's rejection of the various ethnolinguistic affiliations as the most privileged aspect of his identity, Malaysia as method represents not so much the poet's claim or disclaim to the Malaysian taxonomy but his questioning of the logic behind its construction and the ideology behind its deployment. Rather than deny *Malaysian* as an accurate label describing his relationship to the larger community, Fang Ang—whose voice Xiao Hei invokes here to perhaps reflect one aspect of his own consciousness—leaves his response open-ended. Through the diverse perspectives of Xiao Hei's intertext, "A Literary Record" allegorically and collaboratively constructs a minor/minority Ma Hua literary record/history, yet it defies and problematizes the collective function of its own ethnolinguistic literary taxonomy, especially when this collective is construed primarily through a China/Malaysia (or Chinese/Malaysian) dichotomy (China as method). Rather than representing the flipside of this dichotomy, Malaysia as method draws attention to the multiple angles from which "A Literary Record" approaches the historical events surrounding the 1987 Operation Lalang, making them the basis for a variety of relationships to the nation (and by extension a more inclusive national literature) which are not entirely bound by or limited to one's experience of being Chinese.

CONCLUSION

Straddling Malaysian Chinese and Sinophone Malaysian literature, Ma Hua literature is an ethnolinguistic taxonomy that alludes to both the minoritized political status of the ethnic Chinese settler community in Malaysia and the minor, deterritorializing function of literature in the Chinese script from Malaysia. This literature's creative renegotiation and deconstruction of the modern Chinese literary canon—as its presumed cultural heritage and primary discursive interlocutor—has deservedly drawn the attention of modern Chinese literary studies internationally; long a subject of inquiry in Sinophone scholarship, its significance has now garnered due recognition from scholars writing in English, with entire monographs declaring its history, politics, and cultural identity as "not made in China."[53] Such gestures are absolutely vital, especially considering the "spectacular rise of China as a superpower" in the twenty-first century.[54] They also raise the following question: must authors and texts assigned to the Ma Hua taxonomy always construct, constitute, and navigate the nationscape of Malaysia vis-à-vis their ethnolinguistic positioning and their relationship to the Ma Hua collective, a maneuver that subsequently necessitates asserting their distinction from China and Chinese literature?

Malaysia as method is not a facile, catch-all solution to this conundrum but a balancing gesture that opens up new readings, understandings, and interrogations of the multiple subjectivities produced in Ma Hua literature. To do Malaysia as method is to not take the ethnolinguistic taxonomy for granted as fixed and predetermined, but to consider seriously how this positioning reinforces a certain estrangement from Malaysia as place, since it replicates the ethnicized ideological hierarchy—a colonial holdover—undergirding the political apparatus of national literature in Malaysia. It is to examine, as Xiao Hei does through the intertext of "A Literary Record of October 27 and Other Things," the multiple relations to Malaysia as place that do not claim to speak from a common collective position determined by ethnicity and language, but are informed by region, class, and other political or social commitments and historical experiences. Finally, it is to consider Malaysia as the real mediating site—as well as the imaginary horizon—that emerges from the collaborative dialogues between these various positions.

Notes

The author wishes to thank Andrea Bachner and Carlos Rojas for their very constructive suggestions on a previous draft of this chapter that I presented at the "Remapping a Discipline: Modern Chinese Literary Studies" workshop at Duke University, April 4–6, 2014.

1. Khor Boon Eng 許文榮, *Nanfang xuanhua: Ma Hua wenxue de zhengzhi dikang shixue* 南方喧嘩：馬華文學的政治抵抗詩學 [Uproar in the south: The poetics of political resistance in Sinophone Malaysian literature] (Skudai, Johor: Nanfang xueyuan chubanshe/Singapore: Bafang wenhua chuangzuo shi), 96–111.

2. Xiao Hei 小黑, *Qianxi* 前夕 [The eve] (Kuala Lumpur: Shifang chubanshe, 1990), 146–147.

3. The politics of literature, according to Jacques Rancière, assumes that "literature does politics simply by being literature" and that "there is an essential connection between politics as a specific form of collective practice and literature as a well-defined practice of the art of writing." Jacques Rancière, *The Politics of Literature*, trans. Julie Rose (Cambridge, UK: Polity Press, 2011), 3.

4. Kuan-hsing Chen, *Asia as Method: Toward Deimperialization* (Durham: Duke University Press, 2010), 216–217.

5. By using "literary governance," I borrow from Jing Tsu's definition of the term to describe "the ways in which linguistic alliances and literary production organize themselves around incentives of recognition and power." Jing Tsu, *Sound and Script in Chinese Diaspora* (Cambridge: Harvard University Press, 2010), 12.

6. Alison Groppe, *Sinophone Malaysian Literature: Not Made in China* (Amherst, NY: Cambria Press, 2013), 4–7.

7. Xiao Hei began writing fiction around the time of the 1969 ethnic riots (the May 13 Incident) in Kuala Lumpur. His first volume, *Black*, features stories he wrote (many of them "slice-of-life" miniature narratives of less than a hundred words) between 1969 and 1978, a period during which he transitioned from being a student at the University of Malaya to teaching secondary school. After a hiatus, Xiao Hei published *The Eve* in 1990, which includes longer stories written between 1987 and 1989, focusing more on tumultuous national political events, such as political elections and demonstrations. Xiao Hei 小黑, *Hei: Xiaohei xiaoshuoji* 黑：小黑小說集 [Black: The collected fiction of Xiao Hei] (Petaling Jaya, Selangor: Jiaofeng chubanshe, 1979), i. See also *Qianxi*, 2–4.

8. Other ethnic and region-based political interests, such as the Sarawak People's Party and the United Sabah Party, are also constituents of the BN umbrella organization.

9. Clare Boulanger, "Government and Press in Malaysia," *Journal of Asian and African Studies* 28.1–2 (1993): 57–62.

10. Graham Brown, "The Rough and Rosy Road: Sites of Contestation in Malaysia's Shackled Media Industry," *Pacific Affairs* 78.1 (2005): 41–44.

11. Xiao Hei, *Qianxi*, 132, 149, 165, 174.

12. For an insightful treatment of Chineseness in Sinophone Malayan and Malaysian literature, see E. K. Tan, *Rethinking Chineseness: Translational Sinophone Identities in the Nanyang Literary World* (Amherst, NY: Cambria Press, 2013).

13. JanMohamed, Abdul R., and David Lloyd, "Toward a Theory of Minority Discourse: What Is To Be Done?" in *The Nature and Context of Minority Discourse*, ed. Abdul R. JanMohamed and David Lloyd (Oxford: Oxford University Press, 1990), 1 and 10.

14. For more on this issue in the British context, see Kobena Mercer, "Black Art and the Burden of Representation," *Third Text* 4.10 (1990): 61–78.

15. Xiao Hei, *Qianxi*, 147–148.

16. Qtd. in Xiao Hei, *Qianxi*, 137.

17. The scholar Tee Kim Tong reverses the abbreviations to categorize such works as "Chinese Malaysian" or Hua Ma 華馬 literature, short for "Malaysian literature [by those] with Chinese descent" 華裔馬來西亞文學. Tee Kim Tong 張錦忠, *Malaixiya Huayu yuxi wenxue* 馬來西亞華語語系文學 [On Sinophone Malaysian literature] (Petaling Jaya, Selangor: Youren chuban, 2011), 17–18.

18. Kim Tong Tee, "Sinophone Malaysian Literature: An Overview," in *Sinophone Studies: A Critical Reader*, ed. Shu-mei Shih, Chien-hsin Tsai, and Brian Bernards (New York: Columbia University Press, 2013), 305.

19. For more on this issue, see Kim Chew Ng, "Sinophone/Chinese: 'The South Where Language Is Lost' and Reinvented," trans. Brian Bernards, in *Sinophone Studies: A Critical Reader*, ed. Shu-mei Shih, Chien-hsin Tsai, and Brian Bernards (New York: Columbia University Press, 2013), 75–77.

20. "Sinophone literature should be translated in Mandarin as *Huayu yuxi wenxue*, literatures of the Sinitic language family, to denote the multiplicity of languages within the family, not *Huayu wenxue* or *Huawen wenxue*, literature written in standard Mandarin." Shu-mei Shih, "What Is Sinophone Studies?" in *Sinophone Studies: A Critical Reader*, ed. Shu-mei Shih, Chien-hsin Tsai, and Brian Bernards (New York: Columbia University Press, 2013), 9.

21. Tee, *On Sinophone Malaysian Literature*, 19–20.

22. Ng, "Sinophone/Chinese," 76–77.

23. Tee, *On Sinophone Malaysian Literature*, 25–29. Ng Kim Chew refutes the useful-ness of the minor literature taxonomy, suggesting that the framework does little to redress the marginality of Ma Hua literature. Kim Chew Ng, "Minor Sinophone Literature: Diasporic Modernity's Incomplete Journey," trans. Andy Rodekohr, in *Global Chinese Literature: Critical Essays*, ed. Jing Tsu and David Der-wei Wang (Leiden: Brill, 2010), 15–28. For a concise overview of the debate, see Groppe, *Sinophone Malaysian Literature*, 93–98.

24. Gilles Deleuze and Félix Guattari, *Kafka: Toward a Minor Literature*, trans. Dana Polan (Minneapolis: University of Minnesota Press, 1986), 16–18.

25. Tee, *On Sinophone Malaysian Literature*, 21.

26. Deleuze and Guattari, *Kafka*, 21–27.

27. Tee, *On Sinophone Malaysian Literature*, 25.

28. Kim Tong Tee, "(Re)mapping Sinophone Literature," in *Global Chinese Literature: Critical Essays*, ed. Jing Tsu and David Der-wei Wang (Leiden: Brill, 2010), 85.

29. Most critical discussions of Sinophone Malaysian literature reiterate this point. See Groppe, *Sinophone Malaysian Literature*, 2; Tee, *Malaixiya Huayu yuxi wenxue*, 22–23; Chong Fah Hing 莊華興, "Ma Hua wenxue yu Malai wenxue: Ruhe dingwei?" 馬華文學與馬來文學：如何定位? [Sinophone Malaysian literature and Malay lit-erature: How can their positions be determined?], *Renwen zazhi* 人文雜志 [Journal of humanities] 44.11 (2000): 14–18; and Brian Bernards, "Beyond Diaspora and Multiculturalism: Recuperating Creolization in Postcolonial Sinophone Malaysian Literature," *Postcolonial Studies* 15.3 (2012): 316.

30. Analogizing literary and architectural modernisms, David Spurr notes how *dwelling* con-notes both home and nomadism: it is "that idealized conception of space that prom-ises rootedness, permanence," yet *dwelling*'s own etymological origins are rooted in the sense of going "astray" and being "misled" and "hindered." David Spurr, *Architecture and Modern Literature* (Ann Arbor: University of Michigan Press, 2012), 52–53. The connota-tion of dwelling as nomadism in one's own homeland aptly illustrates the creative space of Ma Hua literature.

31. Neil Larsen, "Imperialism, Colonialism, Postcolonialism," in *A Companion to Postcolonial Studies*, ed. Henry Schwarz and Sangeeta Ray (Malden, MA: Blackwell, 2005), 48.

32. Tee, "(Re)mapping Sinophone Literature," 85: "Sinophone Malaysian literature does not resist the position of Malaysian national literature. On the contrary, it is the state apparatus of Malaysian national literature that refuses to acknowledge the legitimacy of Sinophone Malaysian literature as national literature."

33. For an incisive critique of Chen's proposal, see Akira Iriye, "*Asia as Method: Toward Deimperialization* (review)," *Journal of Cold War Studies* 13.3 (2011): 220–221.

34. Chen, *Asia as Method*, 216, 255.

35. Chen, *Asia as Method*, xv.

36. Chen, *Asia as Method*, x, 243. By "de-cold war," Chen refers first to the need to "de-Americanize" the contemporary knowledge structure of the "anticommunist" countries under US neocolonial influence, and second to the need to resume dialogues of decolo-nization and deimperialization begun after the Pacific War that were "intercepted, inter-rupted, and invaded" by the Cold War structure. Under this structure, "issues of Japanese colonialism in Taiwan and Korea could not be tackled because the Japanese, South Korean, and Taiwanese states were locked into the pro-American side" (*Asia as Method*, 7, 121).

37. Ng Kim Chew describes such expressions of Chineseness as "traumatic ritual." Ng Kim Chew 黃錦樹, "Dongnan Ya Huaren de shaoshu minzu de Huawen wenxue" 東南亞華人少數民族的華文文學——政治的馬來西亞個案：論大馬華人本地意識的限度 [The Sinophone literature of the Chinese Southeast Asian minority—the case of political Malaysia: On the limits of the local consciousness of Malaysian Chinese], in *Chongxie Ma Hua wenxue shilun wenji* 重寫馬華文學史論文集 [Essays on the rewriting of Sinophone Malaysian literary history], ed. Tee Kim Tong 張錦忠 (Puli: Jinan daxue dongnan ya yanjiu zhongxin, 2004), 119.

38. Lim Kien Ket offers a similar proposal, claiming that Sinophone Malaysian literature no longer needs to distinguish itself from Chinese literature but should instead articulate its relationship to other Malaysian literary traditions. Lim Kien Ket 林建國, "Weishenme Ma Hua wenxue?" 爲什麽馬華文學? [Why Sinophone Malaysian literature?], in *Chidao huisheng: Ma Hua wenxue duben* 赤道回聲：馬華文學讀本 [Equatorial echoes: A Sinophone Malaysian literary reader], ed. Chan Tah Wei 陳大爲, Choong Yee Voon 鍾怡雯, and Woo Kam Lun 胡金倫 (Taipei: Wanjuanlou chubanshe, 2004), 27.

39. Tang Lin 唐林, "Chentong de wan ge: du 'Qianxi' you gan" 沉痛的挽歌——讀〈前夕〉有感 [A painful elegy: Impressions on reading "The Eve"], in *Qianxi* 前夕 [The eve], by Xiao Hei 小黑 (Kuala Lumpur: Shifang chubanshe, 1990), 180.

40. Xiao Hei, *Qianxi*, 139–140.

41. Xiao Hei, *Qianxi*, 37–39, 133–136.

42. Xiao Hei, *Qianxi*, 25–36.

43. Tang, "Chentong de wan ge," 176–177.

44. Xiao Hei, *Qianxi*, 133–134.

45. Xiao Hei, *Qianxi*, 134–135.

46. Xiao Hei, *Qianxi*, 135.

47. Xiao Hei, *Qianxi*, 137. Khor Boon Eng 許文榮 argues that Xiao Hei was the first Sinophone author to consciously employ intertextuality as a resistance tactic against the official "discursive hegemony" of the "ruling Malay elite" (*Nanfang xuanhua*, 96).

48. Xiao Hei, *Qianxi*, 156.

49. Ng Kim Chew describes these poets as writing "nation-obsessed sentimental poetry" 感時憂國詩, expressing a sense of "floating on the margins of one's own nation" while adopting "candid resistance" to that positioning ("Dongnan Ya Huaren de shaoshu minzu de Huawen wenxue," 121). Khor Boon Eng notes how such authors engage in "a rich resistance discourse, from the exterior resistance to the social system to the interior critique of the subject itself." Khor Boon Eng 許文榮, *Jimu nanfang: Ma Hua wenhua yu Ma Hua wenxue huayu* 極目南方：馬華文化與馬華文學話語 [As far south as the eye can see: Sinophone Malaysian cultural and literary discourse] (Skudai, Johor: Nanfang xueyuan, Malaiya daxue Zhongwen biyesheng xiehui, 2001), 25.

50. Qtd. in Xiao Hei, *Qianxi*, 146–147. Translation mine.

51. Ng, "Dongnan Ya Huaren de shaoshu minzu de Huawen wenxue," 122.

52. Khor Boon Eng identifies the implied "other" as an integral aspect of Ma Hua literary discourse, functioning either as "a concrete object of representation, such as the colonial government, other social classes, other races," or as "an abstract object of representation, such as 'capitalism,' 'power,' 'cultural hegemony,' etc." (*Jimu nanfang*, 96).

53. This tagline is the subtitle of Alison Groppe's *Sinophone Malaysian Literature*.

54. Shu-mei Shih, "The Concept of the Sinophone," *PMLA* 126.3 (2011): 709.

WORKS CITED

Bernards, Brian. "Beyond Diaspora and Multiculturalism: Recuperating Creolization in Postcolonial Sinophone Malaysian Literature." *Postcolonial Studies* 15.3 (2012): 311–329.

Boulanger, Clare L. "Government and Press in Malaysia." *Journal of Asian and African Studies* 28.1–2 (1993): 54–66.

Brown, Graham. "The Rough and Rosy Road: Sites of Contestation in Malaysia's Shackled Media Industry." *Pacific Affairs* 78.1 (2005): 39–56.

Chen, Kuan-hsing. *Asia as Method: Toward Deimperialization.* Durham: Duke University Press, 2010.

Chong Fah Hing 莊華興. "Ma Hua wenxue yu Malai wenxue: Ruhe dingwei?" 馬華文學與馬來文學：如何定位? [Sinophone Malaysian literature and Malay literature: How can their positions be determined?]. *Renwen zazhi* 人文雜志 [Journal of humanities] 44.11 (2000): 14–18.

Deleuze, Gilles, and Félix Guattari. *Kafka: Toward a Minor Literature.* Trans. Dana Polan. Minneapolis: University of Minnesota Press, 1986.

Groppe, Alison M. *Sinophone Malaysian Literature: Not Made in China.* Amherst, NY: Cambria Press, 2013.

Iriye, Akira. "*Asia as Method: Toward Deimperialization* (review)." *Journal of Cold War Studies* 13.3 (2011): 220–221.

JanMohamed, Abdul R., and David Lloyd. "Toward a Theory of Minority Discourse: What Is To Be Done?" In *The Nature and Context of Minority Discourse.* Ed. Abdul R. JanMohamed and David Lloyd. Oxford: Oxford University Press, 1990. 1–16.

Khor Boon Eng 許文榮. *Jimu nanfang: Ma Hua wenhua yu Ma Hua wenxue huayu* 極目南方：馬華文化與馬華文學話語 [As far south as the eye can see: Sinophone Malaysian cultural and literary discourse]. Skudai, Johor: Nanfang xueyuan, Malaiya daxue Zhongwen biyesheng xiehui, 2001.

Khor Boon Eng 許文榮. *Nanfang xuanhua: Ma Hua wenxue de zhengzhi dikang shixue* 南方喧嘩：馬華文學的政治抵抗詩學 [Uproar in the south: The poetics of political resistance in Sinophone Malaysian literature]. Skudai, Johor: Nanfang xueyuan chubanshe/ Singapore: Bafang wenhua chuangzuo shi, 2004.

Larsen, Neil. "Imperialism, Colonialism, Postcolonialism." In *A Companion to Postcolonial Studies.* Ed. Henry Schwarz and Sangeeta Ray. Malden, MA: Blackwell, 2005. 23–52.

Lim Kien Ket 林建國. "Weishenme Ma Hua wenxue?" 爲什麼馬華文學? [Why Sinophone Malaysian literature?]. In *Chidao huisheng: Ma Hua wenxue duben* 赤道回聲：馬華文學讀本 [Equatorial echoes: A Sinophone Malaysian literary reader]. Ed. Chan Tah Wei 陳大爲, Choong Yee Voon 鍾怡雯, and Woo Kam Lun 胡金倫. Taipei: Wanjuanlou chubanshe, 2004.

Mercer, Kobena. "Black Art and the Burden of Representation." *Third Text* 4.10 (1990): 61–78.

Ng Kim Chew 黃錦樹. "Dongnan Ya Huaren shaoshu minzu de Huawen wenxue—zhengzhi de Malaixiya ge'an: lun da Ma Huaren bendi yishi de xiandu" 東南亞華人少數民族的華文文學——政治的馬來西亞個案：論大馬華人本地意識的限度 [The Sinophone literature of the Chinese Southeast Asian minority—the case of political Malaysia: On the limits of the local consciousness of Malaysian Chinese]. In *Chongxie Ma Hua wenxue shilun wenji* 重寫馬華文學史論文集 [Essays on the rewriting of Sinophone Malaysian literary history]. Ed. Tee Kim Tong 張錦忠. Puli: Jinan daxue Dongnan Ya yanjiu zhongxin, 2004. 115–132.

Ng Kim Chew 黃錦樹. "Minor Sinophone Literature: Diasporic Modernity's Incomplete Journey." Trans. Andy Rodekohr. In *Global Chinese Literature: Critical Essays*. Ed. Jing Tsu and David Der-wei Wang. Leiden: Brill, 2010. 15–28.

Ng Kim Chew 黃錦樹. "Sinophone/Chinese: 'The South Where Language Is Lost' and Reinvented." Trans. Brian Bernards. In *Sinophone Studies: A Critical Reader*. Ed. Shu-mei Shih, Chien-hsin Tsai, and Brian Bernards. New York: Columbia University Press, 2013. 74–92.

Rancière, Jacques. *The Politics of Literature*. Trans. Julie Rose. Cambridge, UK: Polity Press, 2011.

Shih, Shu-mei. "What Is Sinophone Studies?" In *Sinophone Studies: A Critical Reader*. Ed. Shu-mei Shih, Chien-hsin Tsai, and Brian Bernards. New York: Columbia University Press, 2013. 1–16.

Shih, Shu-mei. "The Concept of the Sinophone." *PMLA* 126.3 (2011): 709–718.

Spurr, David. *Architecture and Modern Literature*. Ann Arbor: University of Michigan Press, 2012.

Tan, E. K. *Rethinking Chineseness: Translational Sinophone Identities in the Nanyang Literary World*. Amherst, NY: Cambria Press, 2013.

Tang Lin 唐林. Appendix. "Chentong de wan ge: Du 'Qianxi' you gan" 沉痛的挽歌——讀〈前夕〉有感 [A painful elegy: Impressions on reading "The Eve"]. In *Qianxi* 前夕 [The eve]. By Xiao Hei 小黑. Kuala Lumpur: Shifang chubanshe, 1990. 175–189.

Tee Kim Tong 張錦忠. *Malaixiya Huayu yuxi wenxue* 馬來西亞華語語系文學 [On Sinophone Malaysian literature]. Petaling Jaya, Selangor: Youren chuban, 2011.

Tee Kim Tong 張錦忠. "(Re)mapping Sinophone Literature." In *Global Chinese Literature: Critical Essays*. Ed. Jing Tsu and David Der-wei Wang. Leiden: Brill, 2010. 77–91.

Tee Kim Tong 張錦忠. "Sinophone Malaysian Literature: An Overview." In *Sinophone Studies: A Critical Reader*. Ed. Shu-mei Shih, Chien-hsin Tsai, and Brian Bernards. New York: Columbia University Press, 2013. 304–314.

Tsu, Jing. *Sound and Script in Chinese Diaspora*. Cambridge: Harvard University Press, 2010.

Xiao Hei 小黑. *Bai shui, hei shan* 白水黑山 [Clear waters, dark mountains]. Sitiawan, Perak: Malaixiya Huawen zuojia xiehui, 1993.

Xiao Hei 小黑. *Hei: Xiaohei xiaoshuoji* 黑：小黑小說集 [Black: The collected fiction of Xiao Hei]. Petaling Jaya, Selangor: Jiaofeng chubanshe, 1979.

Xiao Hei 小黑. *Qianxi* 前夕 [The eve]. Kuala Lumpur: Shifang chubanshe, 1990.

A DISTANT SHORE

*Migration, Intextuation, and Postloyalism
in Chia Joo Ming's "Ambon Vacation"*

CHIEN-HSIN TSAI

A typhoon took place in the mid-seventeenth century, and centuries later its force was still strongly felt. "Had it not been for that typhoon, we would be Taiwanese today,"[1] remarks the narrator in the Singaporean writer Chia Joo Ming's 謝裕民 novella "Ambon Vacation" (安汶假期) after he learns about his family's migration history. Born and raised in Singapore, the narrator had never thought seriously about his ancestral homeland until he and his father embarked on a journey in search of their family roots. "Ambon Vacation" is the story of this journey.

The narrator's statement alludes to the transitional period between the Ming and the Qing dynasties. After storming Beijing and toppling the Ming in 1644, the Manchus established the Qing court, at which point one of the narrator's ancestors decided to retreat to Taiwan with his family. Martyrs and suicides who defied the Manchus, as well as others who refused to serve in the Qing court, were known as Ming "loyalists" (*yimin* 遺民). The narrator's ancestor fell into this category, and he originally planned to join Koxinga 國姓爺, also known as Zheng Chenggong 鄭成功, the Ming general who spearheaded the anti-Manchu campaign. However, a typhoon rerouted the ancestor's ship, and he and his family ended up on a remote Indonesian island. The rest got lost in time until father and son connect the dots and "reconstruct the image of the South Seas" (重構南洋圖像), which is the name of the collection from which "Ambon Vacation" comes.

Portending change and contingency, the typhoon is a powerful natural phenomenon that offers a potent trope. In reality, the typhoon throws order into disarray and plans into chaos. "Ambon Vacation" not only takes the reader back to the seventeenth century, it also brings about different interpretations of identity. It threads together the various notions of ancestry, history, identity, and loyalty, and presents them as the result of contingency. As the typhoon turned a historical loyalist and his family into migrants who accidentally settled in Indonesia, it prompts the contemporary narrator to reconsider how he may reconcile his ethnic identity and family history with his national identity. The narrator knows all too well that he cannot determine the origins of his family any more than he can select the family into which he was born. Neither nationality nor ancestry can adequately explain the narrator's connectedness with himself and others or, more broadly, the complexity of his interpersonal and institutional relations. Additionally, identity is relational; it manifests itself differently in space and time.

What distinguishes "Ambon Vacation" is not just its reflection on personal identity but also the dynamic way in which Chia Joo Ming questions his own allegiance to the various communities surrounding him—including family, society, and the nation. Chia recognizes loyalty as the irreplaceable lining of his Chinese Singaporean identity. Nevertheless, he holds a flexible set of beliefs when it comes to his loyalty, or loyalties, to whatever makes up and defines his existence. Loyalty like identity is contextual and relational. As Chia makes clear with the cyclonic trope, loyalty is as messy as history; and while ideologies and policies may shape the expression of loyalty and identity, they are themselves subject to contingency and change.

Although the mid-seventeenth-century wayfarer's displacement in "Ambon Vacation" is fictional, it parallels a nearly identical case that also occurred during the Ming-Qing transition. In 1649, a typhoon unexpectedly took the Ming loyalist Shen Guangwen 沈光文 away from his intended destination of Quanzhou and to Taiwan. Before Koxinga arrived in Taiwan in 1662 and recruited him, Shen led a precarious life, struggling miserably just to survive. In his seminal discussion of nationalism in contemporary Taiwan, "Postloyalist Writings," David Der-wei Wang problematizes the sort of loyalism Shen represents. For Wang, Shen embodies a delicate blending of loyalty to a homeland to which he could never return and a desire to set down roots in his adopted land. Wang captures this tension by juxtaposing the Chinese term *yimin* (遺民, "loyalist") with the homophonous term *yimin* (移民, meaning "migrant-settler"), and he adds the prefix *post* (*hou* 後) to mark the degree to which this new notion of loyalism differs from earlier understandings. Extrapolating from Shen Guangwen to consider the more general category of Chinese migrants, Wang concludes, "However much one remains loyal to his previous homeland, one nevertheless needs to put food on the table, and therefore he begins cultivating the foreign land into a new homeland."[2]

With a growing number of immigrants, mostly from Southeast Asia, Taiwan is becoming increasingly multiethnic and multilingual. Postcolonial Singapore is even more diversely so. Chia's story about a Chinese Singaporean who feels little attachment to the ancestral homeland fittingly attends to the complex postcolonial situations of Singapore. In this chapter, I reread Chia's novella through the lens of postloyalism and review the entanglements of travel routes and ancestral roots and the scattered fragments of memory and history, as well as cross-ethnic representations that further complicate the postcolonial conditions of Singapore, including the contingency of loyalism and the changing objectives of national identity.

MIGRATION

Chia's narrator initially shows scant interest in his father's project of ascertaining ancestral origins, remarking, "I do not have the time nor the heart to tend to his business, and I care even less about the fact that my forebears were in Indonesia" (56). The narrator's lack of interest reflects a sentiment shared by many descendants of Chinese immigrants, which is that ancestry does not beget familiarity. A busy stockbroker, the narrator reluctantly agrees to accompany his father when the stock market plummets during the 1997 Asian financial crisis, which he refers to as the "storm" (風暴) (57). This reference foreshadows the narrator's subsequent discovery of how his ancestors arrived in Ambon. The typhoon that disrupted the ancestors' travel plans and the storm that derailed the narrator's career were not, of course, the same event, but Chia highlights an unlikely connection between the two occurrences by way of the narrator's father, who considers the financial crisis the ancestors' act of "calling" (召喚) out to the narrator (58). As if responding to this calling, the narrator eventually agrees to the trip to Ambon.

Born in China, the father, who was known by the family name Choo, moved to Indonesia with his family as a young boy, and he consequently felt more connected to Indonesia than to China. In the 1960s, when Indonesia instituted a Chinese exclusion policy, Choo's family left Indonesia and returned to China, but before their departure they entrusted Choo to a relative, who later moved to Singapore, where Choo grew up and had his own family. Choo would not see his parents again during their lifetime. During one trip to China, Choo receives a note from his brother, which reads: "Before our father passed away, he mentioned that we are the Choos from the Fengyang region, descendants of the imperial family that founded the Ming dynasty. Our ancestor escaped from warfare and sojourned in Indonesia" (59). The "warfare" refers to none other than the conflict between Han Chinese and the Manchus in the seventeenth century. Besides this note, Choo also receives a few pages of an old travelogue written in literary Chinese, and after some research he determines that the pages come from an obscure text titled *Chance Encounter in the South Seas* (南洋述遇).

Chia thickens the plot by making many intertextual references to *Chance Encounter in the South Seas*, which is part of the voluminous collection *The Little Square Pot Studio Compilation of Cartographies and Travel Writings* (小方壺齋輿地叢鈔), compiled and published by Wang Xiqi 王錫祺 in the late nineteenth century. Since these references constitute the major plotline of the novella itself, "Ambon Vacation" is, to a considerable extent, an incarnation of *Chance Encounter in the South Seas*. Chia translates episodes from the old travelogue and intersperses them with his own narrative design. The odd-numbered sections in "Ambon Vacation" contain translated passages from *Chance Encounter in the South Seas*, while the even-numbered sections focus on what Chia's narrator hears and sees in present-day Ambon. In his own words, the narrator repeats events recorded in the old travelogue, making "Ambon Vacation" simultaneously an interpretation and reenactment of *Chance Encounter in the South Seas*. Chia's "Ambon Vacation," accordingly, is a metanarrative about a journey within a journey. The journey the narrator takes to ascertain the veracity of the journey recorded in *Chance Encounter in the South Seas* embodies a heuristic discovery, revealing and relating unexpected connections and meanings. In this way, the journey to search for roots exemplifies a journey of self-discovery. What the narrator finds rewarding in the end is not so much the connections per se, meaningful or not, but rather how these connections come into existence in the first place.

After the anonymous author of the late-Qing travelogue arrived on the island of Ambon, a middle-aged man dressed in local clothing greeted him "not in Cantonese or Fukianese, but in Mandarin," and proceeded to unravel his family history (60). An unexpected typhoon had caught the man's loyalist ancestor and his family by surprise and forced them to deviate from their destination. Unable to join Koxinga as planned, they could only settle on a small island far from both the Central Plains and Taiwan. "Fortunately," the man said, "the natives allowed us to stay.... We have been living here for a long time and have adopted local customs. But we have been passing down the old country's language and the genealogical records in the fear of forgetting about our roots" (61). This unexpected typhoon changed the course of the narrator's family history, motivated his journey, and prompted him to exclaim: "Had it not been for that typhoon, we would be Taiwanese today!"

Chia incorporates *Chance Encounter in the South Seas* to give his own narrative greater historical depth. As Chia's narrator explains, the man who greets the anonymous writer of *Chance Encounter in the South Seas* is his ancestor. This man, an heir of a Ming loyalist-migrant, makes a request as the anonymous writer boards his ship back to China: "I will probably never leave here for the rest of my life. To reinstate and pass down the family line in the old country, I bring my son here today and hope that you will take him with you" (122). The story does not tell us if he has other sons to continue the lineage in this homeland. Regardless, his wish is granted as the anonymous author takes the man's son back to China with him.[3] Chia's narrator then reveals that the son, who left the island for the mainland, was in fact his great-grandfather.

"Ambon Vacation," meanwhile, picks up where *Chance Encounter in the South Seas* leaves off, as the narrator speculates:

> My grandfather came to Indonesia not to make a living but to seek his roots. I believe my great-grandfather must have told my grandfather that we still have family on the island of Ambon. This is why he came southward to Indonesia. My grandfather had to leave for political reasons. He must have had an inkling that he would not come back again, and that was why he left my father behind just in case. (124)

The young child in *Chance Encounter in the South Seas* is the great-grandfather in "Ambon Vacation," who asks his own son, the narrator's grandfather, to return to Ambon. The involuntary migration to Indonesia in the seventeenth century leads to a reverse migration to China in the late nineteenth century, which then leads to another reverse migration to Indonesia at the beginning of the twenty-first century. As a result of these migrations, there is a proliferation of homelands as the very meaning of *homeland* multiplies. The series of (reverse) migrations move generations of the Choo family in full circle only to be interrupted by the narrator, who observes: "Indeed, my family had intended to have me stay on the island of Ambon so as to complete the grand cycle of family reunion of the century" (123). But Ambon is after all not his home, and he returns to Singapore.

Chia concludes "Ambon Vacation" with the narrator's contemplation of "the aftermath of a typhoon and the historical function of a travelogue" in his Singapore home (128). Interrelated migration experiences and diverse phases of lived time make up this grand cycle. Historical retrospection gives the narrator a better understanding of the phases his forefathers lived through but could not make much sense of as they were embedded in them. He understands his position in the genealogy, but views it as something outside of himself. Meanwhile, in another room, the narrator's father is planning to begin another round of migration: "I have decided to take the ancestor's ashes to Taiwan and bury them next to the Temple of Koxinga. He had planned to join Koxinga, and I should carry out his wish" (128). Fulfilling a Ming loyalist's wish, the father enacts his very own loyalism.

INTEXTUATION

From the preceding account of the novella's overlapping journeys, it is easy to observe Chia's blurring of boundaries between different levels of reality, whereby the author relies on intextuation to bring into focus notions of the contingency of history, the readability of the past, as well as the circuitous formation of loyalist identity. *Intextuation* describes the symbolic politics of writing as a process of knowledge production and, to a certain degree, indoctrination. On one hand, intextuation is incarnation, as it gives a concept, for instance *loyalism*, a materiality or "body" by transforming it into a text. On the other hand, writing is intextuation as it transfigures the body of a living being into signs and signifiers of loyalism. With *intextuation*, I call attention to the two complementary senses of the word *corpus*, as related to both body and text. Broadly speaking, history can be an example of intextuation, as it pertains to the construction of narratives about a variety of human subjects and their doings. Most obviously, "Ambon Vacation" grants history a body through its text. In addition to addressing the narrator's family history, the novella also acknowledges the *incorporation* of another historical text, *Chance Encounter in the South Seas*. On a symbolic level, to say that "Ambon Vacation" textualizes incidents of migration is to say that it is an intextuation of the bodies of the migrant-settlers, and that it is a telling form of the *incarnation* of histories of bodies in movements from one place to another. As Chia predicates the novella on an unlikely circulation of a family history in a century-old travelogue, his narrator also imagines himself as the Ming loyalist taken to a foreign shore. This is how "Ambon Vacation" begins:

> As the man slowly opened his eyes, needles of brilliant light pierced his pupils. Suddenly everything turned white. The man immediately closed his eyes, and instead used his ears. He heard a feeble sound of breathing; it was his own. Then, he heard the sound of waves.
>
> The man wiggled his fingers and raised them slowly to his eyebrows. He then carefully reopened his eyes to steal a glance at the unknown world.
>
> People were still on board, but their ship was now ashore. The man looked to his companions, hoping one or two were still alive. He was about to give them a nudge when a wave tossed him to the other end of the ship.
>
> There was a gust of wind, which chilled the man to the bone. His body gradually began to move again. He felt as though his entire body was on fire and the drought had gripped him by the throat.
>
> Water. The man raised his head only to see a pair of dark feet. A crowd of people who looked completely different from himself stood around him, waiting for his response. The man wondered, Why is Taiwan full of savages? Then he languidly closed his eyes. (55)

This is the first section of "Ambon Vacation," in its entirety. Chia begins and ends the section with descriptions of eyes opening and closing. The very next section begins with an image of the narrator with his eyes closed on a flight to Ambon. Together, the first two sections provide what the narrator sees in his mind's eye. The sight depicted in the first section is a result of the narrator's momentary engagement with fantasy.

Through this fantasy, Chia superimposes the narrator and his loyalist ancestor, as well as "Ambon Vacation" and *Chance Encounter in the South Seas*. Meanwhile, the smooth visual continuity conceals the actual time lapse between the ancestor and his descendant, rendering the superimposition a foreshadowing of their genealogical connection. Chia's superimposition is both a manipulation of time and a compression of space. The story makes clear the biological relations between the narrator and character in his imagination, as the narrator observes:

> If I may exaggerate, I am looking for my family roots. What you read in "the first section" is my imagination of what it looked like when my ancestor first arrived on the island of Ambon. We are going to find him. Rumor has it that this old ancestor and we are separated by three hundred years. Three hundred years. How unbelievable is that? (55–56)

If "Ambon Vacation" is a metanarrative that hinges on an old travelogue, then whenever Chia's narrator addresses the reader ("you"), which occurs sporadically throughout the story, he further instantiates the novella's metafictional quality. The narrator holds himself as an intermediary between history and reality: the diegetic time of "Ambon Vacation," the diegetic time of *Chance Encounter in the South Seas*, and versions of history in fiction. While Chia invites the reader to align with the narrator's perspective, as in the scenes of eyes opening and closing, his metareference often disrupts the self-identification of the reader with the narrator. As constant interruptions prevent any lengthy stays in the universe of the work, Chia skillfully urges the reader to avoid facile acceptance of whatever is presented. Consequently, the reader joins the narrator in a search for a rational explanation for the curious phenomena in life.

Imagination enables the narrator to fulfill his role as an intermediary and helps open the door to understanding the past and transforming it into narrative. By extension, the story functions as an intermediary between history and reality. Chia introduces and concludes the first section—a manifest of "my imagination"—with a description of eyes opening and closing. Similarly through the literary device of illustrative repetition, Chia starts and ends "Ambon Vacation" with repeated references to the imagination. The first section is nothing but the narrator's imagination, surely visualization, of his loyalist ancestor's first arrival on the island as *Chance Encounter in the South Seas* records it. He pretends to be his ancestor to initiate the hermeneutics of identity. In the last section, after returning from his exploration of ancestry, the narrator reflects on the fictionality of *Chance Encounter in the South Seas* as a result of historical imagination. He eventually unveils his skepticism, which he hides well throughout the journey: "I have been entertaining this hypothesis: the anonymous author has never been to the island of Ambon. *Chance Encounter in the South Seas* is but an imaginative writing that references other overseas travelogues, fictions, or hearsay. . . . I have actually been to Ambon, but I still don't know where it is" (128). This could have led to a serious reflection on the imaginary quality of the island, despite its physical presence, and on the ways Chia's novella may be a representation of representations from different historical moments. However, the narrator quickly dismisses this musing as inconsequential in his overall historical project. Chia does not scrutinize the volatile relationship between language and reality, at least not in "Ambon Vacation."[4] What counts for Chia is that the account of *Chance Encounter in the South Seas* would have remained obscure without the intextuation of "Ambon Vacation." The flipside of this, as he emphasizes, is that if the old travelogue had not spurred his imagination when he first read it in the 1990s, this novella would not have come into existence (134). Is this not another example of the contingency of history with which Chia seems preoccupied?

The issue of contingency aside, a further consideration of intextuation leads to an examination of the language—more specifically, the two written languages, literary Chinese and vernacular Chinese—used respectively by the anonymous late Qing author and by Chia himself. The issue here is not so much language's representational value, but rather its mechanical function. Whereas the anonymous author wrote *Chance Encounter in the South Seas* in literary Chinese, Chia unravels the twists and turns in "Ambon Vacation" in the contemporary vernacular. As mentioned above, the late-nineteenth-century travelogue enjoys a prominent position in the contemporary novella, though the incorporation of the earlier text is necessarily mediated through translation. Chia does not resort to a direct transplantation, and instead translates and transposes relevant passages from the travelogue into his novella. Translation brings together not only different languages but also their different users and their diverse geohistorical origins.

Chia's narrator initially must rely on his father to translate the travelogue's literary Chinese for him. In section four, for instance, he explains that part of the preceding section contains his father's translation of passages from *Chance Encounter in the South Seas*. However, by the end of the journey the narrator no longer has any trouble understanding literary Chinese. For the narrator, literary Chinese provides access to but does not authenticate Chinese history and heritage; it is also an inadequate identity marker and an unreliable gauge for nativity. Language connects individuals, defines communities, and forges allegiance, but it may also be used to keep people apart.[5] The narrator's acquisition of literary Chinese during his journey leads him to translate and incorporate the travelogue into his story, which in turn celebrates his Singaporean identity.

Later, the narrator reveals that he has even memorized certain parts of the travelogue. Memorization is a process through which not only culture and language but identity and history become inscribed upon the migrant-settlers and their descendants. Through translation and memorization the narrator recalls and incarnates his family history. Translation helps Chia mediate the negotiation between ancestry and posterity and facilitates his intextuation of history, which challenges a set of naturalized links between language, allegiance, identity, and nation, suggesting that these affiliations are not innate but rather constructed. As "Ambon Vacation" makes clear, blood does not guarantee any direct connection to the ancestral homeland. Rather, the meaning of homeland and heritage appears, disappears, and reappears during all sorts of practices in everyday life, from migration to translation, and from remembering to re-membering historical *passages*, in both senses of the word. Additionally, since the late-Qing travelogue is already about the settlement of migrant-settlers, its incarnation into "Ambon Vacation" precipitates a resettlement of established settlement. In the end, Chia presents the metanarrative as an impelling intextuation of histories of migration in which the narrator recursively displaces his ancestral origins.

TRANSLATOR, MOURNER; TRANSLATOR, LOYALIST; MOURNER, LOYALIST

A Chinese-Singaporean writer like Chia may assume more than one identity at any given time, thereby bringing about new meanings from the margins, where familiar situations and legitimacy have already vanished, for self-legitimation. The splitting of identity and the circuitous way in which Chia rescripts the past for self-reflection further reveals that a loyalist is also a translator. Chia's translation of an old travelogue from literary to vernacular Chinese starts the collateral migrations between languages. His mediation of the movement between languages, which makes possible the transposition between writings, is pertinent to the story's central plot—migration and loyalism as heritage. The conflicting identities a loyalist assumes—as a migrant who leaves the homeland for whatever reason, as a settler who begins a new legacy while maintaining a preexisting heritage, or as an heir who speaks no mother tongue—illustrate the tension between translator and traitor famously captured by the Italian proverb, *traduttore, traditore*. Chia is at once a translator of and a traitor to his own languages. His acknowledgment of Chinese heritage, ethnic or linguistic, is paradoxically implicated by its disavowal. The same applies to Lee Kuan Yew's 李光耀 "Speak Mandarin Campaign" (講華語運動), as well as contemporary Chinese Singaporeans' reverence for the English language, despite all the emphatic effort on heritage preservation.[6]

Chia's linguistic maneuver recalls the May Fourth intellectuals' insistence on using language and translation to modernize China. For them, the promotion of vernacular Chinese registered a break with tradition and an entry into modernity. Unlike his May Fourth predecessors, who sought to replace the old with the new, however, Chia aims to maintain his heritage language. Cultural contacts in China or other Sinophone communities often subject heritage language to change and translation.[7] As translation introduces novelties, it may produce unexpected consequences, such as mourning for the irrevocable loss and subsequent melancholia. Rey Chow utilizes the Freudian argument about mourning and melancholia as a new vantage point to think about cultural translation. For Chow, mourning and melancholia lurk behind the May Fourth intellectuals' project of modernizing China through translation:

> This proactive impulse to modernize—so as to catch up with the Western world—continues to describe much of the developing world to this day, and the figure of the translator thus stands, simultaneously, as a mourner, one whose betrayal of the native culture is an inevitable by-product of inequitable cultural contacts.[8]

The May Fourth generation betrayed the native culture in the name of modernization. Indeed, the more they tried to abolish everything traditional, the more rapidly tradition underwent a creative transformation and became an integral part of Chinese modernity. The mutual incorporation of modernity and tradition was a major source of their melancholy. Modernization is an unending project in the way that melancholia manifests itself as a continued process of grieving. In Chow's words, "As a compensation for the betrayal inherent to the cultural translation that is modernization, that produces the native original as barbarism, the melancholy turn has brought the task of the translator up-to-date."[9]

Paradoxically, insofar as the May Fourth intellectuals have succeeded in dismantling the Chinese tradition to some extent, their success may return their gaze to certain conditions that they deemed inassimilable and cast aside. One may even go so far as to ask if these intellectuals indulged in getting rid of tradition so as to initiate an interminable process of mourning and sustain an unfinished relationship with the lost. To put it differently, to the extent that these intellectuals insisted on eliminating certain traces of Chinese tradition as the inassimilable cultural other, they did so as the mournful or melancholic translator-traitors who stayed faithful to their Chinese heritage, just as the mutual implication of tradition and modernity, loyalty and betrayal, inscribe themselves on one another by way of translation.

In the meantime, the fervent supporters—indeed loyalists—of tradition were also mourners. As the negative feelings such as resentment and sense of loss they tried to work through lingered, mourning became melancholia, signaling an interminable relationship with the lost. The act of translation helps manifest melancholia's unexpected but meaningful relation to the plurality of languages, cultures, traditions, and as "Ambon Vacation" makes clear, loyalties. As the logic of translator, traitor; traitor, mourner dictates, loyalism, too, intextuates mourning. If the translator is concomitantly traitor and mourner, then the loyalist is fundamentally a mourner. As Wang explains:

> Bereavement, as a loyalist posture, is chosen. Even though bereavement is not conventionally understood as an optional condition, it is clear that, when faced with the loss of the desired object to the orbit of time, it is chosen. The dead remains of history are not easy to shirk. Likewise, the loyalist influence does not simply vanish. The dilemma of modernity appears subdued in memory or forgotten, abandoned yet passed on, in between the disenchantment with a modern state and the specters of summoned pasts.[10]

Not only does the intensity of Chinese loyalism show no signs of diminishment with the passage of time, even the most progressive reformers or radical denouncers of Chinese culture, as the logic of postloyalism dictates, may still be diehard loyalists.

POSTLOYALISM

Singapore is a multilingual and multiethnic country with four state languages: English, Malay, Mandarin, and Tamil. Officially, the Singapore government privileges no single ethnic or linguistic group, though in practice the situation is more complex. English is the language of bureaucracy, as the government emphasizes its instrumentality in making Singapore a cosmopolitan city-state. The prestige of the English language is a product of both the nation's colonial past and the cultural logics of the present-day transnationalism, though it is also at odds with postcolonial policies emphasizing heritage languages and heritage preservation.[11] When the posterity of migrant-settlers from China made up 74 percent of Singapore's population, its political history was closely related to the making and maintaining of Chinese heritage.[12] For many Chinese Singaporeans, learning their own heritage language is as important as keeping the customs of the old country, and many retain these heritage languages for generations. When Lee Kuan Yew, the former president of Singapore, launched the "Speak Mandarin Campaign" in 1979, he placed a particular emphasis on the importance of Mandarin. He understood many Chinese Singaporeans' emotional ties to various topolects, but believed Mandarin could become the new mother tongue for topolect speakers after a few generations. For Lee, who has shown great faith in China's "four modernizations" (四個現代化), Mandarin is at once a language of heritage and prosperity.[13] Lee's making of a Chinese Singaporean heritage through language is driven more by the market than by political allegiance. Heritage—cultural, ethnic, or linguistic—is at least an acknowledgment, if not always already an appropriation or a reconstruction, of the vast past that nourishes colonial resistance, inaugurates postcolonial development, and envisions a national future. As Daniel Herwitz aptly puts it, "The heritage turn was part of the logic of construction by which many late colonial societies were able to formulate their terms of identity and origin and found their national beginnings."[14] Singapore is one such late colonial society.

Singapore's multilingual and multiethnic conditions, as reflected in Chia's "Ambon Vacation," make it a revealing example of what Achille Mbembe calls a "postcolony":

> The postcolony is chaotically pluralistic; it has nonetheless an internal coherence. It is a specific system of signs, a particular way of fabricating simulacra or re-forming stereotypes. It is not, however, just an economy of signs in which power is mirrored and *imagined* self-reflectively. The postcolony is characterized by a distinctive style of political improvisation, by a tendency to excess and lack of proportion, as well as by distinctive ways identities are multiplied, transformed, and put into circulation.[15]

To be sure, Singapore's official language policy is not itself improvisational, but the politics of everyday language in Singapore are the politics of improvisation, or creative translation. Moreover, in "Ambon Vacation," Chia carries out his reflection on language, identity, legacy, and heritage. Mandarin and literary Chinese provide their own specific system of signs through which fabrication and self-reflection become possible. Chia superimposes multiple identities of migrants and puts *Chance Encounter in the South Seas* into circulation by translating and transposing it into "Ambon Vacation." By rescripting the past so as to construct a family heritage, the novella provides a window onto the relation of histories of migration to loyalist politics as it resurfaces in Singapore as a relatively young postcolony. The way Chia characterizes the son and the father as descendants of Ming loyalists who go on a journey to search for family roots substantiates a symbolic equation between loyalism and heritage.

In Chinese cultural and political writings, the figure of the "loyalist" (*yimin*) has traditionally referred to those who refused to serve a new regime, and hence has tended to connote resistance and political noncooperation. In the *Records of Zuo* (左傳), where the term first appeared, *yimin* referred simply to subjects who had survived state crisis, but over time the term became increasingly politicized and linked to Confucian notions of loyalty. In "Postloyalist Writings," however, David Wang argues that loyalism is always already postloyalism. Indeed, throughout history, Chinese loyalists' actions have assisted in the politicization of their identity, expanded the significance of their existence, and multiplied the definition of loyalism. For Wang, the prefix *post* underscores the polysemy of the term *yimin* itself, whether understood as meaning "loyalist," "migrant," or, to add a third homophonous term, "savage" (夷民).[16] During dynastic transitions, as soon as loyalist-migrants moved beyond the Central Plains, they put their civility and refinement in jeopardy. For centuries, the Han Chinese have considered the inhabitants of the Central Plains culturally and morally superior to aliens—the Eastern *Yi* (夷), Western *Rong* (戎), Northern *Di* (狄), and Southern *Man* (蠻)—outside its pale. The loyalist-*yimin* descendents risk becoming savage-*yimin* when they show attachment to their birthplace, which remains a foreign land in the eyes of their forefathers. Additionally, even when they display a strong nostalgia toward their ancestral homeland, their geographical locations still allow the Chinese to label them as alien. In present days, the principle of *jus sanguinis* often dictates that the descendents of migrants are Chinese. Meanwhile, the principle of *jus soli* can also conveniently label them as not Chinese enough whenever necessary, treating them as a dependency of the soil. Wang's notion of postloyalism, which purposefully blurs the line between loyalist-*yimin*, migrant-*yimin*, and savage-*yimin*, recalls what Ien Ang calls "post-Chinese"—relatively open-ended and plural identities that embody diasporic subjects' "investments in continuing cross-influences of diverse, lateral, unanticipated intercultural encounters in the world at large."[17]

The entanglement of migration, loyalism, and localism in "Ambon Vacation" is difficult to miss. By way of *Chance Encounter in the South Seas*, Chia explains that descendants of the Ming loyalists who arrived on the island have not only adopted local customs but also married the natives. This is no easy lineage to interpret. If the Ambon natives must necessarily be "savage" from a China-centric perspective, then the descendants who have engaged in interethnic marriage for generations are equally so.[18] Chia, however, gives this questionable typecasting another twist. Far removed from being pure-blood loyalists, the descendants are determined to pass on the Chinese language and family records. They hold onto a cultural attachment to the ancestral homeland they have never visited, and their fear of losing the linguistic and genealogical connection to an unfamiliar homeland is symptomatic of imaginary nostalgia. Such a strong desire to leave behind traces for future generations to remember also postpones any end date of diaspora.[19] As David Wang argues, "In post-loyalist writings, the diasporic condition does not conclude with death. Rather, it can never be put to rest. The most profoundly felt sense of diaspora emerges from the scattered entanglements of memory, forgetting, and vain fears."[20] In this regard, the descendants in "Ambon Vacation" are postloyalists who are out of touch with the times, and they are also postloyalists in the sense of representing a creolized hybrid of Chinese and Indonesian. By blood, they are Chinese, but by the accidental fact of birthplace, they are Indonesian. Additionally, as the narrator of "Ambon Vacation" reveals, because some of his predecessors have married the indigenous, he is not unadulteratedly Chinese.

One finds numerous references to contemporary Singapore's multicultural conditions in "Ambon Vacation." The novella also helps unpack the polysemy of *yimin* and provides concrete illustrations of the different meanings that the prefix *post* invokes. The Ming migrant who planned to move to Taiwan in the name of loyalism had to first leave the Mainland behind. The postloyalist project of heritage making extends over generations and beyond death as the father wishes to move the loyalist's ashes to Taiwan. As projects of writing history continue and diasporic sentiments linger, loyalism remains an incomplete project.

NOTES

1. Chia Joo Ming 謝裕民, *Chonggou nanyang tuxiang* 重構南洋圖像 [Reconstructing the image of the South Seas] (Singapore: Full House Communications, 2005), 65. All translations from this text are my own, and subsequent citations will be referenced parenthetically in the text itself.

2. David Der-wei Wang, "Post-loyalist Writings," in *Sinophone Studies: A Critical Reader*, ed. Shu-mei Shih, Chien-hsin Tsai, and Brian Bernards (New York: Columbia University Press, 2013), 96.

3. "Ambon Vacation" rewrites the ending of *Chance Encounter in the South Seas*. In the late-Qing travelogue, the anonymous author does not take the child with him to China.

4. Chia explores such a relationship in "Previous Incarnations of the Island" (島嶼前身), another story from the same collection of *Reconstructing the Image of the South Seas*. In the story, he frequently cites passages in literary Chinese from premodern historical records such as the *Rudimentary Records of Islands* (島夷志略) by Wang Dayuan 汪大淵 from the Yuan dynasty and the *Book of Han* (漢書), taking the reader as far back as to the Han dynasty. Chia himself considers "Previous Incarnations of the Island" an essay on the history of the naming of Singapore, from *Pulau*, *Tamasek*, and *Karimun* to *Singapore*. He insists that the study of place-names is important because it reveals the history and heritage of what is currently known as Singapore: "we must do so because this is the only small island we have. We must hold on to some evidence or we are as good as nonexistent." Chia Joo Ming, *Chonggou nanyang tuxiang*, 61.

5. See Jing Tsu's critical discussion of "linguistic nativity." Jing Tsu, *Sound and Script in Chinese Diaspora* (Cambridge: Harvard University Press, 2010), 1–17.

6. This deserves an in-depth discussion of the cultural logic of global capitalism at work beyond the scope of this essay. For a relevant discussion, see Wan-ling Wee, *The Asian Modern: Culture, Capitalist Development, Singapore* (Hong Kong: Hong Kong University Press, 2007), especially chaps. 2 and 3.

7. For a discussion of the changing definition of heritage language and of how Chinese heritage culture relates to Chinese heritage language, see Agnes Weiyun He, "Chinese as a Heritage Language: An Introduction," in *Chinese as a Heritage Language: Fostering Rooted Word Citizenry*, ed. Agnes W. He and Yun Xiao (Honolulu: University of Hawai'i Press, 2008), 1–12.

8. Rey Chow, "Translator, Traitor; Translator, Mourner (Or, Dreaming of Intercultural Equivalence)," *New Literary History* 39.3 Literary History in the Global Age (2008): 571.

9. Rey Chow, "Translator, Traitor; Translator, Mourner (Or, Dreaming of Intercultural Equivalence)," 573.

10. David Der-wei Wang, "Post-loyalist Writings," 98.

11. Singapore's literary field takes evidence of the country's multiethnicism and multilingualism. In terms of Chinese as ethnicity and Chinese as language, the discrepancy between being the largest population and not being the language of the bureaucracy not only provides much source material for political debates but also finds its way into the literary

work of Anglophone and Sinophone Singaporean writers alike. Many of the Post-65 Generation, which is to say writers born around the time of Singapore's independence, choose to depict Singapore's linguistic and cultural tensions in the English language. There are also bilingual Singaporean writers such as Xi Ni Er 希尼爾 and Eddie Tay 鄭竹文, both of whom write in fluent English and Mandarin. Chia Joo Ming is not one of them, as he writes and publishes essays and stories only in Mandarin.

12. 13 percent of the population are Malays, 9.1 percent are Indians, and others are listed at 3.3 percent. Department of Statistics Singapore, *Population Trends 2013* (Singapore: Department of Statistics, 2013), 3.

13. Intriguingly, Lee addressed the audience in Fukianese at the opening ceremony of the inaugural "Speak Mandarin Campaign" on September 6, 1979. The percentage of Chinese families speaking various Chinese dialects at home has decreased from 30.7 percent in 2000 to 19.2 percent in 2010, whereas the usage of Mandarin has made a minimal increase from 45.1 percent to 47.7 percent in the same decade. The "Speak Mandarin Campaign" has successfully decreased the number of dialect speakers in Singapore, but instead of Mandarin, more and more Chinese Singaporeans choose to speak English, as the percentage of English spoken at home has spiked from 23.9 percent to 32.6 percent in the first decade of the new millennium. Department of Statistics, *Consensus of Population 2010 Statistical Release 2: Households and Housing* (Singapore: Department of Statistics, 2011), x.

14. Daniel Herwitz, *Heritage, Culture, and Politics in the Postcolony* (New York: Columbia University Press, 2012), 4.

15. Achille Mbembe, *On the Postcolony* (Berkeley: University of California Press, 2001), 102.

16. David Der-wei Wang 王德威, "Huaihaizi Huang Jinshu: Huang Jinshu de mahua lunshu yu xushu" 壞孩子黃錦樹：黃錦樹的馬華論述與敘述 [Ng Kim Chew, enfant terrible: Ng Kim Chew's Sinophone Malaysian discourse and narrative], in Ng Kim Chew, *You dao zhi dao* 由島至島 [From island to island] (Taipei: Maitian, 2001), 11–35.

17. Ien Ang, "Can One Say No to Chineseness? Pushing the Limits of the Diasporic Paradigm," in *Sinophone Studies: A Critical Reader*, ed. Shu-mei Shih, Chien-hsin Tsai, and Brian Bernards (New York: Columbia University Press, 2013), 70.

18. In terms of interethnic relationships, Chia further complicates the plot by introducing a Dutch girl named Jolanda halfway through the story. Jolanda comes to Ambon to better understand the history of Dutch colonialism in Indonesia. As the critic Ko Chia-cian points out, Jolanda functions as a narrative device. The friendship between the son and Jolanda provides "a contrast between a romantic chance encounter and a desire for root searching." Ko Chia-cian 高嘉謙, "Chengshi huaren yu lishi shijian: Liang Wenfu yu Xie Yumin de Xinjiapo tuxiang" 城市華人與歷史時間：梁文福與謝裕民的新加坡圖像 [Urban Chinese and historical time: Liang Wern Fook and Chia Joo Ming's Singapore image], in *Wenxue dianfan de jianli yu zhuanhua* 文學典範的建立與轉化 [The creation and transformation of literary paradigms], ed. Cheng Yu-yu 鄭毓瑜 (Taipei: Xuesheng shuju, 2011), 514.

19. Shu-mei Shih writes of diaspora's end date: "When the (im)migrants settle and become localized, many choose to end their state of diaspora by the second or third generation." Shu-mei Shih, "Against Diaspora: The Sinophone as Places of Cultural Production," in *Sinophone Studies: A Critical Reader*, ed. Shu-mei Shih, Chien-hsin Tsai, and Brian Bernards (New York: Columbia University Press, 2013), 37.

20. David Der-wei Wang, "Post-loyalist Writings," 103.

WORKS CITED

Ang, Ien. "Can One Say No to Chineseness? Pushing the Limits of the Diasporic Paradigm." In *Sinophone Studies: A Critical Reader*. Ed. Shu-mei Shih, Chien-hsin Tsai, and Brian Bernards. New York: Columbia University Press, 2013. 57–73.

Chia Joo Ming 謝裕民. *Chonggou nanyang tuxiang* 重構南洋圖像 [Reconstructing the image of the south seas]. Singapore: Full House Communications, 2005.

Chow, Rey. "Translator, Traitor; Translator, Mourner (Or, Dreaming of Intercultural Equivalence)." *New Literary History*, 39.3 (2008): 565–580.

Department of Statistics. *Consensus of Population 2010 Statistical Release 2: Households and Housing*. Singapore: Department of Statistics, 2011.

Department of Statistics. *Population Trends 2013*. Singapore: Department of Statistics, 2013.

He, Agnes Weiyun. "Chinese as a Heritage Language: An Introduction." In *Chinese As a Heritage Language: Fostering Rooted Word Citizenry*. Ed. Agnes W. He and Yun Xiao. Honolulu: University of Hawai'i Press, 2008. 1–12.

Herwitz, Daniel. *Heritage, Culture, and Politics in the Postcolony*. New York: Columbia University Press, 2012.

Ko Chia-cian 高嘉謙. "Chengshi huaren yu lishi shijian: Liang Wenfu yu Xie Yumin de Xinjiapo tuxiang" 城市華人與歷史時間：梁文福與謝裕民的新加坡圖像 [Urban Chinese and historical time: Liang Wern Fook and Chia Joo Ming's Singapore image]. In *Wenxue dianfan de jianli yu zhuanhua* 文學典範的建立與轉化 [The creation and transformation of literary paradigms]. Ed. Cheng Yu-yu 鄭毓瑜. Taipei: Xuesheng shuju, 2011. 493–518.

Mbembe, Achille. *On the Postcolony*. Berkeley: University of California Press, 2001.

Shih, Shu-mei. "Against Diaspora: The Sinophone as Places of Cultural Production." In *Sinophone Studies: A Critical Reader*. Ed. Shu-mei Shih, Chien-hsin Tsai, and Brian Bernards. New York: Columbia University Press, 2013. 25–42.

Tsu, Jing. *Sound and Script in Chinese Diaspora*. Cambridge, MA: Harvard University Press, 2010.

Wang, David Der-wei. "Post-loyalist Writings." In *Sinophone Studies: A Critical Reader*. Ed. Shu-mei Shih, Chien-hsin Tsai, and Brian Bernards. New York: Columbia University Press, 2013. 93–116.

Wang, David Der-wei 王德威. "Huaihaizi Huang Jinshu: Huang Jinshu de mahua lunshu yu xushu" 壞孩子黃錦樹：黃錦樹的馬華論述與敘述 [Ng Kim Chew, enfant terrible: Ng Kim Chew's Sinophone Malaysian discourse and narrative]. In Ng Kim Chew, *You dao zhi dao* 由島至島 [From island to island]. Taipei: Maitian, 2001. 11–35.

Wee, C. J. W.-L. *The Asian Modern. Culture, Capitalist Development, Singapore*. Hong Kong: Hong Kong University Press, 2007.

CHAPTER 3.14

....

ON TIME

Anticipatory Nostalgia in Dung Kai-Cheung's Fiction

....

CARLOS ROJAS

> We came to a profound realization that this was a city that belonged com-
> pletely to tourists, and, for this reason, we were also in the end obliged
> to leave bearing with us the tourist's easily satisfied greed and quickly
> exhausted curiosity.
>
> (Dung Kai-Cheung, *Atlas: Archaeology of an Imaginary City*)

ORIGINALLY written and published in 1997, the year of the Hong Kong handover, Dung Kai-Cheung's 董啟章 novella *Atlas: Archaeology of an Imaginary City*
(地圖集：一個想像的城市的考古學) was subsequently reprinted in 2011 under the
shortened title *Atlas* (地圖集) as the first volume in Dung's "V-City series." The *V* in
V-City (V城) in the latter four-volume series is short for *Victoria*, and specifically the
municipality in central Hong Kong that was the colony's capital from 1842 until 1997.
Atlas itself describes Victoria as a "legendary city" originally located on a previously
barren island off China's southern coast, but notes that the city has long since disappeared, leaving behind only a handful of written texts and an array of material artifacts.
In fact, the novella speculates at one point that Victoria and even Hong Kong itself may
in fact be merely retrospective constructions, created from the vantage point of a future
present.

Atlas is structured as a series of (fictional) essays written by a group of archeologists
examining a set of historical maps of Hong Kong from an unspecified future point in
time. Part One of the novella is titled "Theory" and features discussions of a variety of
spatial and cartographic concepts, including half-invented concepts such as *counterplace, misplace, displace, antiplace, nonplace*, and so forth.[1] For instance, the novella's
first chapter opens with what is presented as an old saying that "every place that appears
on a map must have one or more counterplaces," and further observes that while this
folk notion has been disproved by "scientific mapmaking," it has nevertheless come to
receive renewed attention as a result of the investigation of old maps. The chapter then

describes an 1810 map of the territory that would later come to be known as Hong Kong, in which all of the sites are labeled with names (in Chinese) that phonetically resemble yet are semantically distinct from the names we know today. For instance, in the middle of the 1810 map there is an island called 紅江, which literally means "red river," and the text explains that in the local dialect this name would have been pronounced "hong kong," thereby making it a direct correlate—or "counterplace"—of Hong Kong itself (which is written with two different characters, 香港, that are similarly pronounced "hong kong" in the local dialect but literally mean "fragrant harbor") (21/4).[2]

Dung's novella may be viewed as an exploration of a set of "counterplaces," which is to say, imaginary correlates of contemporary Hong Kong. Composed against the backdrop of the Hong Kong handover—after which Victoria would no longer be the capital of Hong Kong, and Hong Kong itself would no longer be a British colony—*Atlas* uses the fictional conceit of a group of future archeologists investigating a set of historical maps to reflect on how the region and its community may be recalled in the future, after the city has already ceased to exist. The figure of Hong Kong in the novella, accordingly, may be seen as an imaginary counterpart, or "counterplace," of Hong Kong as it existed at the time the work was being written.

A chapter near the end of Dung's novella describes a 1997 tourist map that the future archeologists feel is capable of reflecting "the true circumstances of a place," and the archeologists proceed to use the map to create a life-sized replica of a portion of the original city:

> Using simulation software, they have reconstructed this twentieth-century urban space along the lines of the tourist map; what is more, they have also built a recreation on the same scale as the original. (152/145)

The chapter concludes, however, with a note written by a participant in the reconstruction project, who observes that the resulting simulacrum lacks one key element: the city's original residents. Given that the original tourist map was intended for tourists, the only people who appear in the subsequent reconstruction are the tourists themselves, together with the minority of Hong Kong residents involved in the tourist industry. The recreation of the city, in other words, is marked by the absence of the very residents whose presence defines an urban space in the first place.

On the other hand, to the extent that Hong Kong (as both a metropolis and a proto-nation) may be viewed as an example of what Benedict Anderson calls an imagined community, the sense of collective identity that it generates is grounded on residents' ability to projectively identify with a larger community of virtual strangers with whom they will probably never have meaningful direct interactions.[3] In this respect, accordingly, the putative failure of the reconstruction of a portion of the Hong Kong described in *Atlas* underscores what is already a defining quality of the city itself—namely, that the notion of a community of residents is itself an abstraction, and in practice the vast majority of Hong Kong residents are in fact strangers to one another, like the foreign tourists with whom they are figuratively contrasted.

Atlas approaches contemporary Hong Kong through a double temporal inversion that is simultaneously anticipatory and retrospective, and which reflects the imagined future legacy of the 1997 retrocession. As Dung notes in an afterword he composed for the novella when it was reprinted in 2011 as part of his "V-City series,"

> You cannot doubt [the retrocession], but neither can you rely on it. At the same time, however, it also should not become a black hole that we pretend doesn't exist so that we don't need to approach it or touch it. Therefore, in 1997 I resolved to write not about the retrocession itself but rather about its past, while at the same time writing about its future. From a future vantage point I seek to reconstruct the past, and from a past vantage point I seek to project the future. From this deliberate interweaving of past and future, I hope that a present that is more full of possibility will gradually be able to emerge.[4]

The approach Dung describes here may be viewed in grammatical terms as a hybrid of the future perfect and the past perfect tenses. Whereas the future perfect uses a future vantage point to refer back to an earlier future event and the past perfect uses a past vantage point to refer back to an even earlier past event, Dung instead uses an imaginary future vantage point to reassess both the present and the past, while at the same time using this newly reexamined historical perspective to reimagine both the present and the future. The result is that one's understanding of the present is conditioned by extrapolated visions of both the past and the future, each of which in turn mutually constitutes the other. The present, in other words, is no longer treated as a stable reference point from which one views the past and the future, but rather it is itself a product of a past and future that are themselves in a dialectical relationship with one another.

The resulting hybrid temporality is concisely captured in what cultural studies scholar Ackbar Abbas famously calls the sense of *déjà disparu*, literally "already disappeared," which Abbas argues characterizes contemporary Hong Kong.[5] Troping on the familiar use of the concept of *déjà vu* to refer to the uncanny experience of encountering something one feels one has already seen before, Abbas coins the phrase *déjà disparu* to describe the experience of observing something through the lens of its anticipated future disappearance, whereby something becomes an object of attention precisely when one realizes that it is in imminent danger of being lost. Published in 1997, the year of the Hong Kong retrocession, Abbas's *Hong Kong: Culture and the Politics of Disappearance* describes the surge in interest in Hong Kong culture during the years leading up to the retrocession, contending that the concern that Hong Kong might lose its autonomy and distinct character after 1997 helped encourage an energetic and wide-ranging reengagement with Hong Kong's history and culture. Abbas suggests, furthermore, that the resulting body of cultural production is not only driven by an anxiety that Hong Kong might soon lose its unique identity, it simultaneously comes to instantiate this same identity that appears to be in danger of being lost. He argues, in other words, that it is precisely a fear of loss that helps generate the very object that is perceived as being under threat.

If considered from a psychoanalytic perspective, Abbas's notion of *déjà disparu* may be viewed as a conjunction of two Freudian concepts dealing with states of anticipation and belatedness. In particular, Freud's concept of the fetish describes how a subject may create a set of symbolic substitutes of something valued in anticipation of its feared loss, while his concept of deferred action (*Nachträglichkeit*) describes instead how a subject may develop a substantially different understanding of a prior experience as a result of subsequent developments. Although Freud himself does not explicitly link these two concepts in his own writings, they may nevertheless be seen as precise inverses of one another, in that one concept approaches the present through the prism of an anticipated future loss, while the other approaches the present through a belated reassessment of a past event.

With respect to Abbas's analysis of contemporary Hong Kong, the array of cultural production produced on the eve of the Retrocession may be seen as a fetish, in that it functions as a preemptive substitute for the local cultural identity that many Hong Kongers had come to fear was in imminent danger. At the same time, this body of cultural production may also be seen as a form of deferred action, insofar as it is a product of a belated reassessment of Hong Kong's own history. Moreover, these logics of the fetish and of deferred action are, here, closely intertwined, in that the catalyst for the reassessment of the past is a set of eventualities that technically have not yet taken place, while the appreciation of this anticipated future loss is necessarily mediated through a new understanding of Hong Kong's past and present.

These overlapping qualities of anticipation and belatedness are evident in the text of *Atlas* itself. Although *Atlas* is now considered the first volume in Dung's V-City series, the abbreviation *V-City* actually doesn't appear at all in the 1997 novella itself, and in fact it is not introduced until the third volume of the series, the 1998 book *Visible Cities: A Chronicle of the Splendor of V-City* (V 城繁勝錄; reprinted in 2012 for the V-City series under the shortened title *Fansheng lu* 繁勝錄, or literally, "A chronicle of splendor"). Inspired by and modeled on Meng Yuanlao's 孟元老 Southern Song text *The Eastern Capital: A Dream of Splendor* (東京夢華錄), Dung's *Visible Cities* looks back at contemporary Hong Kong ("V-City") from a vantage point fifty years in the future. The twist, though, is that this future perfect narrative is simultaneously retrospective, insofar as it explicitly borrows from a mode of urban writing developed by Meng Yuanlao more than a millennium earlier. Standing as a fictional correlate of the city of Victoria—which itself functions as a synecdoche for Hong Kong—the figure of *V-City* introduced in this 1998 novella belatedly names the future perfect space previously explored in *Atlas* while at the same time anticipating the imaginary setting of many of Dung's later works, including the "Natural History trilogy" he has been working on for the past decade. The significance of *Atlas*, in other words, lies in the imaginary space of *V-City*, which will come to play an increasingly important role in Dung's later works but which technically had not yet been created when *Atlas* was first composed. To read *Atlas* through the figure of V-City, as the 2011 "V-City Series" explicitly invites us to do, accordingly, entails a version of the same Freudian notion of deferred action that Dung deploys in the work itself.

In the following discussion, I adopt a similar approach in my reading of Dung's Natural History trilogy, and particularly the first volume, *Works and Creations: Vivid and Lifelike* (天工開物: 栩栩如真). I draw on a dialectics of anticipatory loss and belated recognition to interpret the novel, while arguing that the work itself reflects on these same temporal logics and simultaneously suggests ways in which they may be extended from their original Freudian formulations.

WORKS AND CREATIONS

Currently standing at four volumes and more than 1.4 million Chinese characters, Dung Kai-Cheung's Natural History trilogy is a vast endeavor. In 2005, Dung published Part 1 of the trilogy, *Works and Creations*, and two years later he published the two volumes of Part 2, *Histories of Time: The Luster of Mute Porcelain* (時間繁史: 啞瓷之光). The first half of Part 3, *The Origin of Species: The Educational Age of Beibei's Rebirth* (物種源始：貝貝重生之學習年代), was published in 2010, but as of 2016 (as this handbook goes to press), the second and final volume of Part 3 has not yet been completed.[6] All five volumes were published in Taiwan, and collectively they offer a metatextual reflection on both Hong Kong history and on Dung's own career as an author. In particular, Hong Kong provides not only the setting and the conceptual focus of the novels, it also informs the linguistic structure of the works themselves, in the sense that they feature considerable amounts of Cantonese dialogue (this is particularly true beginning with Part 2, which even includes a multipage Cantonese-to-Mandarin glossary for the benefit of Mandarin-speakers readers who do not know Cantonese).

The Chinese title of the first volume in the trilogy, *Tiangong kaiwu: Xuxu ruzhen*, consists of several sets of overlapping conceptual pairs, with the first half of the title, *Tiangong kaiwu*, being borrowed from the title of a famous late-Ming encyclopedia by Song Yingxing 宋應星, which offers detailed and carefully illustrated discussions of a wide array of technologies ranging from agricultural irrigation to gemology. The title of Song's original text consists of the Chinese binomes *tiangong* (天工) and *kaiwu* (開物), which could be translated as "works of nature" and "human creations," respectively; in context, Song's title refers to the process of taking "works of nature" and transforming them into "manmade creations" (one common translation of the title of Song Yingxing's text is "The Exploitation of the Works of Nature"). In Dung's novel, however, the relationship between these two modes of creation is left somewhat more ambiguous, in that the novel offers a set of parallel narratives focusing on histories of a set of material technologies located in what the novel calls the "object world" (物件世界), on one hand, and an array of explicitly fictional characters inhabiting a "figural world" (人物世界) created in the narrator's "writing workshop," on the other. The "works" and "creations" in Dung's title, accordingly, may be parsed either as standing in a parallel relationship with one another or as interrelated components of a composite entity.

The second half of Dung's title, *Xuxu ruzhen* (栩栩如真), meanwhile, tropes on the phrase *xuxu rusheng* (栩栩如生), which means "vivid and lifelike." Dung, however, substitutes the final character in the original phrase, *sheng* (生, or "life"), with the near-homonym *zhen* (真, or "real"), yielding a new phrase that is almost like the original and could be translated as "vivid and real-like." At the same time, the new phrase also contains the names of two fictional characters in the novel who bear a distinct similarity to one another. In particular, Xuxu is a seventeen-year-old girl whom the narrator has created in his "writing studio," while Ruzhen was a close childhood friend of the narrator, whose subsequent disappearance is perceived as having provided one of the inspirations for his subsequent creation of Xuxu. The latter half of the novel's title, accordingly, may be read as referring to the "vivid and lifelike" phrase, to Xuxu and Ruzhen as distinct characters, or to a composite entity representing a synthesis of the two characters.

Reflecting the binary structure of the work's title, *Works and Creations* consists of two interlocking halves—alternating between one set of chapters describing Xuxu and the figural world she inhabits, and a second set consisting of a series of letters in which the narrator uses discussions of an array of different technologies to tell Xuxu about three generations of his family history, and in the process simultaneously offers her a miniature history of Hong Kong as well as of modern technologies of mechanical reproduction.

The novel begins, for instance, with a description of how Xuxu wakes up naked one morning with no memory of her past—or perhaps has no past to remember in the first place. Xuxu is described as though she were an actual girl, but her body is made up of material components. She has a metal bolt in her chest, and we learn later that her hair is made of pasta. The chapter concludes by observing that Xuxu did not exist before the story began, and had the author wished he could have had her be born a second or third time, but in the end he "was not willing to do so because, like in real life (*zhenru zhenshi shengming yiyang* 正如真實生命一樣), Xuxu could only live once. Otherwise, Xuxu would no longer be like-real (*ruzhen* 如真)."[7] This final sentence of the chapter features two instances of the two-character pair *ruzhen*, where in the first instance the characters are being used for their semantic value (in that they appear in separate binomes that happen to follow one after the other), while in the second there is a strategic ambiguity with respect to whether the characters *ru* and *zhen* are being used literally to mean "like-real," or whether they are instead being used as the proper name *Ruzhen* (as in, "Xuxu would no longer be Ruzhen").

The following chapter in the novel consists of a letter addressed to Xuxu, in which the narrator describes how hearing a radio broadcast triggers a childhood memory of having listened to a radio when he was a young boy. Starting with this moment of Proustian involuntary memory,[8] the narrator quickly shifts to a more distant memory of how his grandfather had given his grandmother a radio as a wedding gift. The following chapters use an array of other technologies, many of which are associated with mechanical reproduction, to trace the three generations of the narrator's family history, together with the space of Hong Kong that they come to call home.

As the novel progresses, however, Xuxu begins to bleed real blood and manifest other seemingly human traits, until eventually she leaves the "figural world" and crosses over into the "object world" inhabited by the narrator. It turns out that Xuxu has entered the narrator's world in search of her companion, Xiaodong—an androgynous figure whom she had met in the figural world shortly after she first awakened at the beginning of the novel.[9] Xuxu views the narrator as a correlate for Xiaodong, with the narrator's status as an author being mirrored by the fact that the figural Xiaodong literally has pens for hands (in the novel, he is explicitly compared to Edward Scissorhands). The narrator, meanwhile, is struck by how much Xuxu resembles his childhood friend Ruzhen, and the implication is that the narrator created Xuxu as a stand-in for his lost Ruzhen, even as Xuxu herself comes to perceive the narrator as stand-in for *her* lost Xiaodong.

Even as the novel presents Xuxu as the product of the narrator's very personal sense of loss, it simultaneously suggests that she also functions as a stand-in for a broader nostalgic and apprehensive relationship with Hong Kong itself. The first place the narrator takes Xuxu after she crosses over from the figural world into the object world, for instance, is to a Hong Kong history museum where he used to go with Ruzhen when they were young—suggesting that Xuxu functions as a surrogate not only for the narrator's memory of Ruzhen but also for his relationship with the imagined and imaginary space of Hong Kong as a whole.

Even before Xuxu crosses over to the object world and meets the narrator face-to-face, the narrator offers several other explanations for her origins and significance. In a chapter titled "The Sewing Machine," for instance, the narrator describes how his mother worked in garment factories while he was growing up, and would often accept piecemeal assignments to be completed at home. As the narrator is recalling this period of his life, at one point he remarks,

> Xuxu, I must honestly tell you that your form originated from a period even before I knew Ruzhen. When I was a child helping [my mother with] the piece work she had to do at home, I had already begun developing this idea. No, what I was developing wasn't merely an abstract idea, but rather it was in fact a prototype of you yourself. (129)

The narrator then describes how there had been a period during which the factory would send the narrator's mother "rag dolls" (布娃娃) to work on at home, and the narrator and his brother would help their mother make miniature clothing for them. One day, the factory accidently sent his mother an extra doll, which she offered to the narrator's younger sister. While the sister expressed little interest in the doll (she was more fascinated by mechanical toys like trains), the narrator became increasingly obsessed with this doll, secretly watching it every night before going to sleep.

One day when the narrator was home alone, he impulsively removed the doll's clothing. Noting the doll's expression never changed, and he felt as though the doll was either enjoying the procedure or else was secretly cursing him, as if saying "Look at you! You seem like a normal boy, yet you are hiding such dirty thoughts in your heart!

Did you think that I didn't know that you have been constantly trying to peek at me with those lascivious eyes of yours? Did you think that I didn't realize that you, even at such a young age, are already such a sex fiend?" In retaliation, the narrator got a needle and thread from his mother's sewing box, and proceeded to sew the doll's arms and legs behind its back—feeling an acute pulse of anguish each time the needle pierced the doll's tiny body. He then describes how the doll had an "empty lower body" (*xuwu xiati* 虛無下體), which he found to be

> as terrifying as a traditional ghost story account of an encounter with a faceless specter in a theater bathroom. That was a feeling of extreme terror, a terror of seeing *lack* (*wu* 無). I tightly half-closed my eyes and then, with a pair of scissors, cut up that site of *lack*, such that the doll looked as it were still unfinished. I wanted to see what was inside that *lack*, but all I found inside was cotton—snow-white cotton. (130)

The narrator describes how, once he realized what he had done, he tried to cover his tracks by putting the doll's clothes back on and even sewing its dress to its body so as to make it harder for someone else to remove. He recognizes, however, that in this way he is merely adding another layer of violence onto the previous one, as the act of sewing on clothes to cover over the doll's mutilated genital region ironically comes to acquire a traumatic significance in its own right.

After recounting this incident, the narrator again addresses Xuxu—telling her that it was precisely this sense of guilt that led him to decide to create her, so that he might then turn to her for redemption. The implication is that in creating Xuxu, the narrator is reenacting a version of the symbolic violence inherent in his act of sewing the maimed doll's clothes back onto its body, in that he is using Xuxu in order to figuratively cover over an earlier trauma while simultaneously reenacting that same trauma. In this respect, the narrator's creation of Xuxu may be seen as a form of repetition compulsion, whereby he continually repeats in symbolic form the conditions of an unresolved traumatic experience.

Moreover, the novel suggests that the rag doll incident was actually not the original trauma, but rather was *itself* a symbolic repetition of an even earlier incident. In particular, the narrator tells Xuxu about an incident that took place when he was so young that he now has only a hazy recollection of it, but which has subsequently come to assume the status of a "primal horror and trauma" (初始的驚慄和創傷; 131). The incident in question occurred when the narrator was about five, and one of his neighbors was a young woman named Xiaoling. The narrator was fascinated by Xiaoling, who would often chat with him as though he were a mere "cloth doll" (布公仔)—not really caring whether or not he was capable of understanding what she saying. After a while, the narrator began observing Xiaoling spending time with another boy, and one day he witnesses a peculiar scene in which Xiaoling puts on a garment she has just made. The garment immediately falls to the floor like a magician's cape, leaving Xiaoling standing there awkwardly in her underwear. The narrator notices that the left side of her chest protrudes more than the right, and it occurs to him that she—standing there naked and virtually motionless—resembles a department store mannequin.

Later that evening, the other boy is playing ball outside the narrator's house and the ball happens to roll inside. When the boy goes to retrieve it, he trips over an electrical cord and accidentally pulls a hot iron down onto his hand. The boy is taken to the hospital, where, in his dazed and feverish condition, he thinks he sees a naked figure being wheeled down the hallway. To him, the figure in the hallway resembles a "cloth doll" (布包娃娃) whose body appears to be covered in red stitches and is contorted in a bizarre manner—with one arm sewn onto her abdomen and the other wrist fastened to the back of her calf. After returning home, the other boy never sees Xiaoling again—but he knows intuitively that the "freakish figure" (怪胎) he glimpsed in the hospital corridor that night must have been her.

In this primal scene, which precedes not only the narrator's loss of Ruzhen but also the earlier episode in which he cuts up the doll his mother gave him, the narrator places *himself* in the position of the figurative rag doll with whom Xiaoling casually chats, while simultaneously projecting onto the other boy the anxieties about femininity and loss that the narrator will subsequently claim as his own. More specifically, the other boy's fantasy vision in the hospital of Xiaoling as a desecrated rag doll functions as a displaced projection of the narrator's subsequent traumatic encounter with his mother's rag doll. Accordingly, the other boy functions as a stand-in for the young narrator, who imagines that he occupies the status of a virtual rag doll in Xiaoling's eyes. The irony, however, is that in the final encounter in the hospital corridor it is actually Xiaoling herself who is perceived as a mutilated rag doll in the eyes of the other boy. The other boy views her as a "freakish figure" (怪胎), or literally a "strange fetus," and the narrator suggests that it is precisely this embryonic figure that subsequently develops into the fictional character Xuxu. The figure of Xiaoling in this scene anticipates the fictional Xuxu through a process of double displacement, in that Xiaoling here mirrors the figure of the narrator (whom she perceives as a mere rag doll) while also foreshadowing the rag dolls that will anticipate the narrator's eventual loss of Ruzhen, which will in turn constitute a key catalyst for the creation of the imaginary Xuxu. At the same time, however, it is important to note that it is not the narrator himself who equates Xiaoling with a rag doll, but rather it is a misperception that is projected onto the figure of the neighbor boy.

Works and Creations concludes with an epilogue that discusses several texts that have a particular significance for the narrator and his family, including not only the copy of the Ming dynasty encyclopedia *Works and Creations* that belonged to the narrator's grandfather but also a copy of the Qing dynasty text *Illustrated Handbook of the Principles of Myriad Objects* (萬物原理圖鑑) that had belonged to the narrator's father, as well as the narrator's own copies of several books, such as Darwin's *Origin of Species* and Stephen Hawking's *A Brief History of Time*. Perhaps the most intriguing of these texts, however, is an *Illustrated English-Chinese Dictionary* that the narrator had owned as a child. The dictionary contained an illustration of a female body with the various body parts labeled in both English and Chinese, and the narrator notes that it was from this illustration that he first learned the English word *breast*. He recalls that the only part of the illustration that was *not* labeled was the figure's crotch—which had been deliberately left blank so that young students would not learn inappropriate sexual terminology such as *genitals* and *labia*. Not only did this portion of the diagram lack any anatomical labels, it was explicitly labeled with the word *lack* (*wu*), and the narrator notes that "this was something that could not be named, and therefore it further stimulated my younger self's fascination with 'lack' (*wu*)."

The narrator then describes how he proceeded to rip the page with the diagram from the dictionary:

> Why? Perhaps it was because I felt that it was inappropriate for children, or perhaps it was because it gave me an ineffable feeling of terror. In any event, I carefully, compulsively, and spontaneously ripped the page out. This certainly did not mean that when I was young my thoughts were utterly pure. Not at all. At that time, when I was still maturing and before I had taken any sex ed classes, my mind was full of strange and fanciful notions. In my own personal material history, this had already been recorded in a manner that was detailed but difficult to read. However, I really did tear out that dictionary page with the female figure. Afterwards, I felt an alternating sense of pride and regret, but in any event this is something I will never forget. That torn-out page was preserved as a form of "lack" (*wu*). (476)

Just as the narrator's attempt to sew the doll's clothes back on, in the earlier rag doll scene, comes to function as a site of traumatic investment in its own right, in this latter description the narrator's act of tearing out the dictionary page with the disturbing diagram further reaffirms the symbolic "lack" that had been the focus of the diagram itself. The explicit focus on "lack" (*wu* 無) in this passage and the earlier discussion of the mutilated rag doll, meanwhile, invite an alternative reading of the novel's title. A near-homophone of *wu* 無 also appears in the novel's title, *Tiangong kaiwu* (天工開物), with the latter *wu* literally meaning "object" and being the same character that appears in the phrases "object world" (*wujian shijie* 物件世界) and "figural world" (*renwu shijie* 人物世界)—and while one reading of the novel is that material objects (*wujian* 物件) and fictional figures (*renwu* 人物) dialectically constitute one another, another, more intriguing, possibility is that both of the latter may in fact be the products of an anxiety about the possibility of loss and "lack" (*wu* 無).

In these parallel descriptions of the mother's rag doll, the neighbor Xiaoling, and the torn-out dictionary page, we find a precise articulation of the Freudian logic of the fetish. Freud argues that the fetish is rooted in a paradigmatic moment when a young boy accidentally glimpses his mother's naked body and discovers that she lacks a penis. Freud contends that the boy's anxiety about the possibility of losing his own penis leads him to create a series of symbolic substitutes that function both as preemptive replacements for this anxiety of future loss and also metonyms of that anxiety of loss itself. As Freud summarizes, "the fetish is a substitute for the woman's (the mother's) penis that the boy once believed in and—for reasons familiar to us—does not want to give up."[10] In *Works and Creations*, meanwhile, these descriptions of the narrator's childhood memories directly mirror Freud's iconic description of the boy accidentally glimpsing his mother's naked body—though here the mother's naked figure is already displaced onto a set of symbolic substitutes. In the dictionary scene, for instance, the figure of lack is displaced from the absent genitals in the dictionary diagram, onto the Chinese character *wu* that labels that absence, and again onto the ripped-out dictionary page itself. In Dung's work, in other words, the anxiety of loss that grounds the chain of symbolic substitutes is one that is itself always already characterized by a fetishistic logic in its own right.

Although the narrator was disturbed by these childhood incidents at the time, each episode comes to assume a more nuanced significance years later, after the narrator's memory of these sites of "lack" becomes conflated with his subsequent experience of losing Ruzhen. Moreover, to the extent that the fictional Xuxu also figures as a response to a set of collective anxieties about Hong Kong's fate in the years following the ret-rocession, the implication is that the significance of the earlier traumatic episodes is subsequently reshaped not only by the narrator's more recent experiences but also by a set of *anticipated future eventualities* that have been projected back onto the past and the present. Each of the earlier incidents helps generate the fictional character of Xuxu through a process that is simultaneously anticipatory and retrospective, and the result-ing temporal structure is one wherein the present functions not primarily as a reference point from which the past and the future are perceived, but rather as itself a product of a complex dialectical interaction of past and future.

Freud's paradigmatic example of deferred action involves a young child who is molested but does not perceive the event as sexually traumatic until years later. For instance, one of Freud's earliest allusions to the concept of deferred action can be found in his untitled 1895 manuscript that subsequently came to be known as "A Project for a Scientific Psychology," which contains a discussion of a patient, Emma, who was reluctant to go into stores alone, and who believed that this aversion was grounded on a memory of how, when she was twelve, she once went into a store and the two clerks laughed at her—in response, she explains that she felt that they were laughing at her clothes, even as she simultaneously found herself sexually attracted to one of them. Freud, however, concludes that the significance of this particular memory is actually grounded on an even earlier one from when Emma was about eight, in which a *different* store clerk twice fondled her genitals through her clothes. Freud contends that Emma didn't come to perceive this earlier experience as sexual until after entering puberty, whereupon she retrospectively linked the two sets of childhood memories. Freud notes that the earlier experience of having been fondled *through her clothing* appears to resurface in displaced fashion in the form of Emma's conviction that the latter two clerks, years later, were laughing *at her clothing*. He con-cludes that "we invariably find that a memory is repressed which has only become a trauma by deferred action (*nachträglich*)."[11]

Ironically, the genesis of Freud's notion of deferred action has followed a logic of deferred action of its own, in that although the concept can be traced back to the very beginning of Freud's psychoanalytic oeuvre (his analysis of Emma's case was written in 1895, a year before he first began using the term *psychoanalysis* to describe his approach), it was not until after his death that the concept began to be recognized as a theoretical intervention in its own right. Moreover, as Freud scholars Jean Laplanche and Jean-Bertrand Pontalis note, Freud "never offered a definition, much less a general theory" of the concept of deferred action, and they suggest that "the credit for drawing attention to the importance of this term must go to Jacques Lacan," who suggested that "the real implication of the *nachträglich* . . . has been ignored, though it was there all the time and had only to be picked up."[12]

Other aspects of Freud's psychoanalytic theory have undergone a similar trajectory. For instance, one of Freud's most significant contributions involves his attention to the ways in which issues of sexual desire and sexual difference are manifested in a displaced or mediated fashion in a wide range of other behaviors, but he has also been critiqued for his seemingly obsessive focus on sexual issues (and the normative attitudes that he frequently adopts). It was not until later, after other theorists helped translate key Freudian principles onto a more abstract plane, that the full implications of his psychoanalytical model finally began to emerge. Lacan, for instance, has famously proposed that Freudian notions of penis envy and the castration complex may be understood as referring primarily not to the anatomical penis but rather to the phallus as a symbolic abstraction that encompasses, but is not limited to, the anatomical sex organ. Similarly, the preceding reading of Dung Kai-Cheung's *Atlas* draws on Freudian notions of the fetish and deferred action, but uses them to theorize issues not of gender and desire but rather of cultural production and collective identity. The fetishistic logic of *Atlas*, in other words, revolves around the feared loss not of the anatomical penis, but rather of a distinctive Hong Kong identity, and the earlier experience that is belatedly reassessed is not a traumatic (pre-)sexual encounter but rather Hong Kong's colonial and imperial legacy.

Just as Freudian theory has often been critiqued for its seemingly excessive attention to sexual concerns, some scholarship on contemporary Hong Kong cultural production could similarly be criticized for relying on an allegorical approach wherein works are seen as commentaries on the condition of Hong Kong itself.[13] In Dung Kai-Cheung's case, a work like *Atlas* explicitly invites this sort of allegorical reading, and by extension it encourages readers to approach Dung's other works through a similar analytical lens. In *Works and Creations*, meanwhile, we find both an array of explicitly sexualized motifs (such as the focus on the rag doll and the dictionary illustration) that would appear to welcome a conventional Freudian analysis, as well as a set of sociohistorical elements (such as the visit to the Hong Kong history museum) that seem to invite an allegorical reading of the work as a commentary on the Hong Kong condition. At the same time, however, I would argue that *Works and Creations* is not simply recapitulating either a vulgar Freudian or a simplistic allegorical approach; instead, it emphasizes the status of textual production and cultural imagination within both these sexualized and allegorical approaches.

It is significant, for instance, that the narrator's traumatic childhood memory involves not an accidental glimpse of his mother's naked body, as in the classic Freudian model, but rather of a *schematic illustration* of a woman's body in a children's dictionary.

Similarly, it is equally noteworthy that the narrator's trip to the Hong Kong history museum is with Xuxu, who has just willed herself into existence—and to the extent that Xuxu represents a displaced manifestation of the work's interest in issues of Hong Kong identity, she also explicitly underscores processes of literary creation. Moreover, if we extend this reading of *Works and Creations* to its logical conclusion, we find that that novel encourages a retrospective reassessment of Dung's earlier works as offering a similar commentary on processes of literary imagination and cultural production.

CODA

Works and Creations opens with a preface attributed to a figure who calls himself the "Dictator" (獨裁者), who claims he belongs to the same generation as the novel's author, Dung Kai-Cheung. The preface notes that in *Works and Creations*, "the author sought to use a narrative of the protagonist's family's inheritances and the protagonist's own process of growing up, in order to establish *his own self-image* (自我的形象)" (4; emphasis in the original). This Dictator is one of the author's two alter-egos in the novel, the other being the main narrator, identified simply as Hei 黑 (meaning "black"). This figure of the Dictator plays a more central role in Part 2 of Dung's Natural History trilogy, *Histories of Time*, in which he is now paralyzed and living with his wife Yaci in the countryside. At the beginning of the latter work, the Dictator is visited by a Eurasian student named Virginia, who wishes to interview him.

Histories of Time makes numerous allusions to the Dictator's earlier writings, many of which correspond to works by Dung Kai-Cheung himself. At several points, for instance, the novel notes that the Dictator's first story collection is titled *The Rose of the Name* (名字的玫瑰), which is also the title of one of Dung's own early story collections.[14] The novel further specifies that *The Rose of the Name* collection contains a reprint of the Dictator's first published story, "The Piecing Together of Virginia in a Fast Food Restaurant" (快餐店拼湊維真尼亞的故事), and the narrative emphasizes not only how the Dictator uses this story to create a fictional "Virginia," but also his subsequent decision to permit this Virginia to commit suicide. The Eurasian Virginia who interviews him, meanwhile, criticizes him for this decision, saying:

> As the novel's author, you must bear responsibility for Virginia's death. From the perspective of the creation of the fictional character, you didn't provide a sufficient rationale for Virginia's suicide. And why is this? This is because you fundamentally didn't understand her. And yet, you have attempted to turn the tables and transform the guest into a host, transforming this loss into the grounds for the novel itself, in order to express that theme of a desire that will necessarily remain perpetually unfulfilled.[15]

Eventually, the Dictator and the Eurasian Virginia begin writing stories together, which are set in an unspecified future point in time after V-City has already become inundated. The protagonist of these stories is a fictional character also named Virginia, who has a mechanical clock in place of a heart and remains perpetually seventeen years old.

The fictional Virginia in the Dictator's early story is herself figuratively "pieced together" from a variety of other elements in *Histories of Time*. First, this fictional Virginia recalls the Eurasian Virginia who comes to interview the Dictator many years later, who in turn anticipates the fictional Virginia who appears in the stories that the Eurasian Virginia and the Dictator later compose together. Second, Virginia's Chinese name, *Weizhenniya* 維真尼亞, is the same length and shares two of the same characters as the Chinese transliteration of the *Victoria* in Victoria City, *Weiduoliya* 維多利亞— suggesting that the fictional Virginia may be viewed as a correlate of Victoria City, of V-Cheng, and even of Hong Kong itself.

Although Dung Kai-Cheung did indeed publish an early story titled "Piecing Together Shishi, Sisi, CC, and Virginia in a Fast Food Restaurant" (快餐店拼湊詩詩思思 CC 與維真尼亞的故事), a more suggestive parallel with the story mentioned in *Histories of Time* can be found in Dung's "Cecilia" (*Xixiliya* 西西利亞), which the author notes was his first published story.[16] This earlier story revolves around an uncanny figure named Cecilia, about whom the narrator remarks in the story's opening lines, "With respect to Cecilia, what else can I say? She is now finally before me, but has become so silent and her body has become so cold that I almost can't recognize her" (7). He adds matter-of-factly that Cecelia "doesn't have arms, doesn't have clothing, and doesn't have soft hair," and he compares her to the Venus de Milo.

The narrator describes how he has long been infatuated with Cecilia, to whom he writes countless impassioned love letters. Cecilia, however, never responds, and as the story progresses it is gradually revealed that she is not a person at all but rather a mannequin on display in the window of a clothing store across the street from the narrator's favorite coffee shop. The narrator emphasizes that his infatuation with Cecilia is not due to his failure to understand that she is merely an inanimate object, but rather is a result of his conviction that he may be able to animate her through sheer force of will. He hopes, in other words, that his desire for Cecilia will succeed in transforming her into a suitable object of that same desire.

It turns out that the narrator has a female coworker named Angela, who is romantically interested in him—but rather than reciprocate Angela's advances, the narrator instead displaces his attentions onto the inanimate mannequin. In this respect, Cecilia may be seen as Angela's spectral double, and the parallel between the two figures is reflected in the similarity of their Chinese names, which are the same length and share the same two final characters: *Anqiliya* 安琪利亞 and *Xixiliya* 西西利亞 (which also happen to be the same two characters that the names share with the Chinese transliteration of *Victoria, Weiduoliya* 維多利亞). This overdetermined significance of Cecilia's Chinese name is further underscored by the narrator's habit of referring to her not simply as Cecilia but rather as "the Cecilia who is named Cecilia" (名為西西利亞的 西西利亞)—thereby reflecting his conviction that the name supersedes the identity it ostensibly denotes. As the narrator remarks at one point,

And poor Cecilia, in addition to having lost her arms, she has also lost everything, including even her name. No, she has not lost her name—her name still exists, but what she has lost is herself as the referent of that name. An empty name and a disfigured body—what can they amount to?

Rather than presenting Cecilia's name as being anchored by its referent, the story instead imagines it as having an autonomous, free-floating status—as the name comes to constitute its own referent, even as that referent is itself a figure of loss and lack.

The story answers the narrator's rhetorical question of what an empty name and disfigured body might amount to by adopting Cecilia's point of view, suggesting that it was precisely the act of being named that helped grant Cecilia a "consciousness like that of a real person":

This is all because of a name, Cecilia, a name that a mannequin shouldn't have in the first place, and which made it possible for a consciousness comparable to that of a real person to enter my body. A physical object and a name—together, they constitute a person. (25)

Cecilia's very identity, therefore, is presented as a product of a synthesis of an empty name and dismembered body, and it is precisely out of this crisis of denotation and reference that Cecilia derives her consciousness and her voice.

Despite the story's putative focus on the narrator's infatuation with Cecilia, there is also an intriguing suggestion that the work may also be offering a broader commentary on the nature of social space itself. In particular, shortly after a discussion of how Cecilia's clothing begins to resemble Angela's, Angela gives the narrator a volume of photographs by the French photographer Eugène Atget (1857–1927). When the narrator opens the volume, the first image he sees is a photograph of a shop window:

In the display window there was a neat row of fabric and price tags, together with a male mannequin wearing a three-piece suit with white wing-tip collared shirt and bowtie. I could almost see him smiling, looking as though he were about to step out of the display window.

The reference here is to Atget's famous 1925 photograph "Avenue des Gobelins"—an image that is striking not only for its depiction of the lifelike mannequins, but also for how the view of the inside of the display window is juxtaposed with the street scene that is reflected on the surface of the window itself, making it appear as though the mannequins have entered into the streets of Paris. Just as the mannequins are uncanny simulacra of human beings, the reflection of the Parisian street scene visible on the glass surface of the display window is similarly a simulacrum of the urban space of Paris itself. Dung's allusion to the juxtaposition of the mannequins and the street reflection in Atget's photograph suggests that neither the fantasy world of Cecilia nor the urban space of the Hong Kong she inhabits exists independently of the other.

Dung's allusion to Atget's early-twentieth-century photograph points to a parallel between Cecilia (as a displaced figure of Angela), on one hand, and the image of the Parisian streets visible in the display window (as a displaced figure of the city itself), on the other. Just as the narrator's investment in the inanimate mannequin is presented as a displacement of his relationship with his coworker, the sorts of relationships that link each individual to a broader community of virtual strangers may similarly be viewed as extrapolations of the sort of immediate, embodied relationships that people have with their more immediate neighbors and acquaintances. "Cecilia" illustrates, in other words, another version of the cultural logic implicit in Benedict Anderson's theory of nations as imagined communities, in that the proto-nation of Hong Kong is implicitly presented as an extrapolation not of interactions between tourist-like strangers, as in the tourist-map chapter of *Atlas* discussed above, but rather of interactions with entities (human or otherwise) who have been projectively endowed with familiar qualities (like the department store mannequin in "Cecilia"). In other words, the story suggests that it is precisely as a result of a feeling of inadequacy with respect to direct interpersonal relations that one may project onto inanimate or anonymous objects (from the department store mannequin to the collective population of a city or a nation) a set of emotional investments, thereby making possible "imagined" relationships and communities.

"Cecilia" ends with four separate conclusions—including one narrated in Cecilia's own voice, in which she ironically laments the fact that she has no voice with which to inform the narrator that she is not real:

> About myself, Cecilia, what have I ever been able to say? When I stand here, in front of him, without arms, without clothing, without hair—but all of this is not important because, in the end, of what value are all of these things for me? However, what I don't have is a voice, and consequently I can't tell him that I fundamentally don't exist. But isn't it true that I have a very powerful voice, to tell him and her that they cannot doubt my existence? Is this not because I, myself, a lifeless mannequin, created this voice capable of causing someone to have a mental breakdown? (24)

This passage presents one of the story's central paradoxes: Cecilia, as a figure for lack, is in fact the central presence in the work, just as her voice is most powerful precisely when she is speaking about her own voicelessness. It is her status as an embodiment of absence, in other words, that makes it possible for her to help generate a set of projective displacements on which the very possibility of identity is predicated.

Dung's story then returns to the narrator's earlier rhetorical question of what an empty name and a disfigured body might amount to, suggesting that it was precisely the act of being named that helped grant Cecilia a "consciousness like that of a real person":

> But what he didn't realize as that for him, the name Cecilia and the mannequin named Cecilia would never again have any meaning; meanwhile, for me to be Cecilia and to be a mannequin was now equally pointless, since I was no longer able to model clothes. (25)

The story then concludes with the narrator, who is now addressed in the third person, walking out of a bookstore and boarding a tram. A short-haired young woman sits down next to him and introduces herself: "I am Cecilia."

Not only does Cecilia effectively will herself into existence, the story itself anticipates many of the central themes of Dung's subsequent literary oeuvre. At a practical level, "Cecilia"—which was completed at the end of the 1991 and was published in 1992—was later reprinted in Dung's *The Rose of the Name* collection in 1997, the same year as the initial publication of Dung's *Atlas*; and just as the implications of *Atlas* were further clarified by the work's subsequent inclusion in Dung's V-City series in 2011, the implicit significance of "Cecilia" was further realized by its republication in 1997, the year of the retrocession. In retrospect, we can see how the 1991 story anticipates some of the concerns with loss, displacement, and cultural creation that Dung will go on to explore not only in *Atlas* but also in later works like *Works and Creations*. Indeed, Cecilia's uncanny appearance in the 1991 story directly anticipates the narrator's recollection of the fantasy image of Xiaoling's resemblance to a "department store mannequin," which itself anticipates the narrator's subsequent obsession with Xuxu as a displaced substitute for the lost Ruzhen. To the extent that Xiaoling is presented as a foreshadowing of the fictional protagonist Xuxu, we may similarly see "Cecilia" as an anticipatory exploration of themes that will subsequently emerge as central concerns in Dung's *Works and Creations, Histories of Time*, and other recent works.

Read from the vantage point of the present, the fictional Cecilia, in other words, may be seen as an anticipatory version of Ruzhen, Xuxu, Virginia, and so forth, and it is only through this act of belated recognition that we can fully appreciate the degree to which the figure of Cecilia similarly offers a commentary on the fetish-like logic of contemporary Hong Kong culture and, more generally, on the process of literary creation itself.

NOTES

Dung Kai-Cheung 董啟章, *Dituji: Yige xiangxiang de chengshi de kaoguxue* 地圖集：一個想像的城市的考古學 [The atlas: The archaeology of an imaginary city] (Taipei: Lianhe wenxue, 1997); reprinted as *Dituji* 地圖集 [Atlas] (Taipei: Lianjing, 2011); translated as Dung Kai-Cheung, *Atlas: The Archaeology of an Imaginary City*, trans. Dung Kai-cheung, Anders Hansson, and Bonnie McDougall (New York: Columbia University Press, 2012). Subsequent quotes from this work will be referenced parenthetically in the main text, with page numbers corresponding first to the 2011 Chinese edition of the work, followed by the corresponding passage in the 2012 English edition.

1. These terms appear in both Chinese and English in Dung's text.
2. In Anders Hansson and Bonnie McDougall's translation of this work, this "Red River" (紅江) island is transliterated as "Hung Kong" (with a "u" in *Hung*), though Dung's original novella transliterates it as "Hong Kong," just as it does the (former) colony of Hong Kong itself.
3. Benedict Anderson, *Imagined Communities: Reflections on the Origin and Spread of Nationalism*, revised edition (New York: Verso, 2006).

4. Dung Kai-Cheung, "Houji: Zhencheng de youxi" 後記：真誠的遊戲 [Afterword: Reality games], in *Dituji* 地圖集 [Atlas] (Taipei: Lianjing, 2011), 161–162; quote taken from 162. Unless otherwise indicated, this and other translations from Dung's texts are my own.

5. Ackbar Abbas, *Hong Kong: Culture and the Politics of Disappearance* (Minneapolis: University of Minnesota Press, 1997).

6. Dung Kai-Cheung, *Tiangong kaiwu: Xuxu ruzhen* 天工開物：栩栩如真 [Works and creations: Vivid and lifelike] (Taipei: Maitian, 2005); *Shijian fanshi: Yaci zhiguang* 時間繁史：啞瓷之光 [Histories of time: The lustre of mute porcelain] (Taipei: Maitian, 2007); *Wuzhong yuanshi: Beibei chongsheng zhi xuexi niandai* 物種源始： 貝貝重生之學習年代 [The origin of species: The educational age of Beibei's rebirth] (Taipei: Maitian, 2010). For a useful discussion of this trilogy in the context of Dung's larger oeuvre, see David Der-wei Wang, "A Hong Kong Miracle of a Different Kind: Dung Kai-cheung's Writing/action and *Xuexi niandai* (The Apprenticeship)," *China Perspectives* 1 (2011): 80–85.

7. Dung Kai-Cheung, *Works and Creations*, 17. Subsequent quotations from this novel will be indicated parenthetically in the text.

8. Dung Kai-Cheung wrote his dissertation on Marcel Proust, and frequently alludes to Proust's *Remembrance of Things Past* in his own fictional work, including *Works and Creations*.

9. Xiaodong is a fictional character who appears in several of Dung Kai-Cheung's earlier works, including *Xiaodong xiaoyuan* 小冬校園 [Xiaodong's schoolyard], reprinted in *Lianxipu* 練習簿 [Exercise book] (Hong Kong: Tupo chubanshe, 2003).

10. Sigmund Freud, "Fetishism," trans. James Strachey in *The Standard Edition*, vol. 21, 147–157.

11. Although Freud mailed a portion of this manuscript to his friend Wilhelm Fliess shortly after completing it, he never published it in his lifetime. The full manuscript was finally published in 1950, after his death, in Marie Bonaparte, Anna Freud, and Ernst Kris, eds., *Aus den Anfängen der Psychoanalyse, Briefe an Wilhelm Fließ, Abhandlungen und Notizen aus den Jahren 1887–1902* (London: Imago, 1950), 387–477. An English translation was published four years later, under the title "Project for a Scientific Psychology." See Sigmund Freud, "Project for a Scientific Psychology," in *The Origins of Psychoanalysis* (New York: Basic Books, 1954), 349–455, esp. 410–412.

12. Jean Laplanche and Jean-Bertrand Pontalis, *The Language of Psycho-Analysis* (New York: W. W. Norton, 1974), 111; Jacques Lacan, *The Four Fundamental Concepts of Psycho-Analysis*, trans. Alan Sheridan (New York: Norton, 1998), 216. See also Jean Laplanche, *Problématiques VI: L'après-coup* (Paris: PUF, 2006). Jacques Derrida also offers an influential discussion of the concept of deferred action in "Freud and the Scene of Writing," in *Writing and Difference*, trans. Alan Bass (London and New York: Routledge, 1978), 247–248.

13. That is to say, many recent analyses of Hong Kong literature and culture have tended to follow a version of the logic that Fredric Jameson outlines in his well-known essay "Third-World Literature in the Era of Multinational Capitalism," *Social Text* 15 (Autumn 1986): 65–88.

14. The title of Dung's collection is a play on the title of Umberto Eco's novel *The Name of the Rose*.

15. Dung Kai-Cheung, *Histories of Time*, vol. 1.

16. Dung Kai-Cheung, "Xixiliya" 西西利亞 [Cecilia], in *Mingzi de meigui* 名字的玫瑰 [The rose of the name] (Hong Kong: Pupu congshu, 1997); reprinted the following year in

Taiwan under the same title (Taipei: Yuancun wenxue, 1998), 7–26. The quote cited here is taken from p. 9 of the latter edition. Further citations from this work will be noted parenthetically in the text, referencing the Taiwan edition of the work.

WORKS CITED

Abbas, Ackbar. *Hong Kong: Culture and the Politics of Disappearance*. Minneapolis: University of Minnesota Press, 1997.

Anderson, Benedict. *Imagined Communities: Reflections on the Origin and Spread of Nationalism*. Rev. ed. New York: Verso, 2006.

Bonaparte, Marie, Anna Freud, and Ernst Kris, eds. *Aus den Anfängen der Psychoanalyse, Briefe an Wilhelm Fließ, Abhandlungen und Notizen aus den Jahren 1887–1902*. London: Imago, 1950.

Derrida, Jacques. "Freud and the Scene of Writing." In *Writing and Difference*. Trans. Alan Bass. London and New York: Routledge, 1978. 247–248.

Dung Kai-Cheung 董啟章. "Xixiliya" 西西利亞 [Cecilia]. In *Mingzi de meigui* 名字的玫瑰 [The rose of the name]. Hong Kong: Pupu congshu, 1997.

Dung Kai-Cheung 董啟章. *Dituji: Yige xiangxiang de chengshi de kaoguxue* 地圖集: 一個想像的城市的考古學 [The atlas: The archaeology of an imaginary city]. Taipei: Lianhe wenxue, 1997. Reprinted as *Dituji* 地圖集 [Atlas]. Taipei: Lianjing, 2011.

Dung Kai-Cheung 董啟章. *Xiaodong xiaoyuan* 小冬校園 [Xiaodong's schoolyard]. Reprinted as *Lianxipu* 練習簿 [Exercise book]. Hong Kong: Tupo chubanshe, 2003.

Dung Kai-Cheung 董啟章. *Tiangong kaiwu: Xuxu ruzhen* 天工開物: 栩栩如真 [Works and creations: Vivid and lifelike]. Taipei: Maitian, 2005.

Dung Kai-Cheung 董啟章. *Shijian fanshi: Yaci zhiguang* 時間繁史: 啞瓷之光 [Histories of time: The lustre of mute porcelain]. 2 vols. Taipei: Maitian, 2007.

Dung Kai-Cheung 董啟章. *Wuzhong yuanshi: Beibei chongsheng zhi xuexi niandai* 物種源始: 貝貝重生之學習年代 [The origin of species: The educational age of Beibei's rebirth]. Taipei: Maitian, 2010.

Dung Kai-Cheung 董啟章. *Atlas: The Archaeology of an Imaginary City*. Trans. Dung Kai-cheung, Anders Hansson, and Bonnie McDougall. New York: Columbia University Press, 2012.

Freud, Sigmund. "Fetishism." Trans. James Strachey. In *The Standard Edition*, vol. 21. 147–157.

Freud, Sigmund. "Project for a Scientific Psychology." In *The Origins of Psychoanalysis*. New York: Basic Books, 1954. 349–455.

Jameson, Fredric. "Third-World Literature in the Era of Multinational Capitalism." *Social Text* 15 (Autumn 1986): 65–88.

Lacan, Jacques. *The Four Fundamental Concepts of Psycho-Analysis*. Trans. Alan Sheridan. New York: Norton, 1998.

Laplanche, Jean. *Problématiques VI: L'après-coup*. Paris: PUF, 2006.

Laplanche, Jean, and Jean-Bertrand Pontalis. *The Language of Psycho-Analysis*. New York: W. W. Norton, 1974.

Wang, David Der-wei. "A Hong Kong Miracle of a Different Kind: Dung Kai-cheung's Writing/action and *Xuexi niandai* (The Apprenticeship)." *China Perspectives* 1 (2011): 80–85.

CONCLUSION

Chinese Literatures in Conjunction

ANDREA BACHNER

As with all humanities disciplines, Chinese literary and cultural studies, as a field that requires particular time, application, and energy, is frequently called upon to justify its usefulness in pragmatic terms of investment and profit. The claim to study a fascinatingly rich tradition and bring it closer to students will no longer do, as even the flimsy façade of cultural capital is giving way to a more unabashed rhetoric of political and economic interests. For scholars in this field, it seems, depending on our disciplinary and institutional contexts, as well as our cultural, national, and linguistic positionalities, only a handful of options are open. And even these are continuations, extensions, but also, potentially, complications of recent and not so recent uses of the study of Chinese culture either as instrument in the forging of a Chinese national identity or as driven by political interest in the context of Western area studies in a Cold War climate:

(1) We can try to be the mouthpiece of Chinese culture and thus tread the fine line between producing an impression of culture that can be co-opted for national ideologies or constructions of otherness on one hand and investing in alternative versions of Chineseness on the other.[1]

(2) We can protest that globalized capital needs remedial interculturality, and thus become the handmaidens of globalization, accepting ever more precarious definitions of culture and interculturality while pleading for the continued importance, even the resistant potential, of cultural specificity.

(3) We can attempt to make a case for Chinese literary studies as an integral part of literary and cultural studies as such, in the name of intercultural comparison or world literature and thus risk framing Chinese literature either as a case of exception or as just another example of supposedly universal structures that are merely naturalized constructs of particular political and cultural interest.

Of course, disturbing the naturalized rhetoric of justification and justifiability itself—namely that our discipline and intellectual endeavor are in need of defending—has become crucial to our survival, since we need to fight the very discursive premises that put us at a disadvantage, rather than merely reacting to, and thus buying into, their logic. And yet we cannot but acknowledge that such pressures have played and continue to play an important role in the shape, scope, and methodologies of the field.

In past decades, the field of Chinese literary studies has been experiencing a double perspectival shift. On one hand, scholars have started to extend its scope and to expand the contours of the field. On the other, literary and cultural studies have increasingly started to pay attention to Chinese literature and culture and to integrate their articulations into broader intercultural, global, and comparative frameworks. Even though these disciplinary readjustments constitute distinct directions, they are also complementary. The first plots a centrifugal movement as it extends its scope to objects and phenomena situated at the outside or at the margins of its past purview. Rather than merely turning what was previously its outside into a new inside, however, such redefinitions often result from a closer attention to the "inside." New appreciations of the multiplicity and hybridity of the objects of Chinese literary studies also warrant other connections, affiliations, and alliances beyond the traditional scope of the field. The second movement consists in an inclusionary move by way of which Chinese literature becomes an area of interest for literary and cultural studies that aspire to an intercultural or global scope, such as comparative approaches or reflections on world literature. Of course, Chinese literature has been part of the literary production of our world all along, even before Goethe's much vaunted—but quite ambivalent—attention to a Chinese novel made it fit for inclusion into a Western definition of world literature (*Weltliteratur*),[2] and the origins of Chinese literature predate most of the literary traditions that are the subject of comparative and world literary approaches today. At the same time, however, although the discipline that continues to drive much of intercultural and interliterary research, comparative literature, has long preached global inclusion, its practice and methodology have nevertheless been slow to live up to this standard. Meanwhile, the increased inclusion of non-Western traditions within comparative frameworks has started to put pressure on its methodological premises, forcing East-West studies into new directions or creatively displacing the center of attention away from Europe or the "West," for instance, in the form of intraregional comparisons or those that circumvent models of center-periphery and trace connections beyond geographical contiguity and outside of the well-traveled paths of cultural influences.

Put in motion by these two complementary thrusts, the contours of the field of Chinese literary studies have become productively permeable. Or rather, as its methodologies become wary of essentialist definitions, such contours have come increasingly under scrutiny as strategically constructed and tightly policed boundaries masked as self-evident or natural—either as constructions of unified sameness in the interest of national politics or as visions of alterity as negative mirror for other cultures. On one hand, the modern study of Chinese literature as a new Western-style academic field implemented in China at the beginning of the twentieth century was inextricably linked to national interest, prized as a reflection of national spirit and sentiment—for instance in the form of "national learning" (*guoxue* 國學) or "rearranging the national heritage" (*zhengli guogu* 整理國故) rather than an attention to literariness or aesthetic qualities.[3] On the other, the emergence of Sinology as a non-Chinese discipline about things Chinese was coeval, if not always coextensive or in collusion with, Orientalism, and has remained marked by geopolitical interests throughout, for instance in the form of area studies with US political investment during the Cold War and beyond.[4]

To work within the field of Chinese literary studies means to reflect on the ties between politics and culture that determine the contours and limits of the discipline and to scrutinize the premises of our methodologies by, for instance, taking the label *Chinese literature* not as a given, but rather as itself an object of scrutiny in need of constant redefinition. To map the field of modern Chinese literatures by insisting on the plural—namely that there is not one coherent, unified corpus of literature, but rather a multiplicity of articulations—also entails that the link between these literatures and the adjective *Chinese* is complex and multiple. In fact, the recent trend of Sinophone studies, initiated by Shu-mei Shih, is seeking to open up the field of Chinese studies by highlighting differences within things Chinese, by a shift in categories from identity to language—irrespective of the divergent definitions of *Sinophone*. By shifting emphasis from a category of ethnic identity (where *Chinese* by metonymy has become a general sign for one of its parts, Han ethnicity and culture), to one based on linguistic practice and place, Shih also deterritorializes the assumed centrality of a standard Chinese language tied to the national and cultural hegemony of the PRC.[5] This is a welcome challenge to narrow and essentialist notions of Chinese identity and creates a category that both reformulates and points beyond things Chinese. As such, it strategically includes minor and diasporic articulations in Sinophone languages as well as in non-Sinitic languages (within Chinese cultural spheres), but excludes the cultural production in standard Chinese in the PRC. Consequently, in spite of the critical productivity of the Sinophone approach, reflected in a number of chapters in this volume, we need to continue to reshape what constitutes the scope, objects, and methodologies of Chinese literary studies by putting pressure on our definitions of Chineseness from different directions:[6] by critically rethinking how cultural traditions beyond national, ethnic, and even linguistic markers, such as art, music, food, medicine, or film for instance, are being coded as Chinese, by addressing wider networks of global connections with and of Chinese literature, and thus by carrying critical potential even to the political, cultural, national, and academic centers that hold authority over the construction of Chineseness. In fact, we have to scrutinize how literature's Chineseness (or Sinophonicity) is constructed in every instance, rather than taking it as an uncontested essence somehow inherent in certain literary texts and not others. If this pushes the notion of Chineseness to the margins of or even beyond the confines of conventional disciplinary comfort zones and thus makes the contours of the field of modern Chinese literature increasingly diffuse, it also allows for a richer, more complex understanding of our objects of study as well as enabling us to trace other constellations that inform our understanding of Chinese literature and are in turn transformed by taking Chinese literature into consideration.

CONNECTIONS

In recent years, the approach of world literature in vogue in much of contemporary comparative and intercultural work on literatures and cultures has started to provide a global framework for thinking about Chinese literature in a broader context by proposing to take the worlding or worldedness of literature into consideration. For critics such as David Damrosch, this means to scrutinize how literary texts that emerge in certain cultural, linguistic, and political contexts travel beyond their origins. In other words, what allows such texts to claim citizenship in the world republic of letters is the moment in which they exceed their original contexts. It is not the fact that they are of this world, which is to say that they form part of all the literature in the world, that makes them world literature, but their movement of being read elsewhere or of being translated into another language. Even though this approach reimagines the world from the vantage point of literature as a network of contact zones rather than confining literary texts to cultural, linguistic, or national monads, its intercultural openness and productivity risks cementing the very patterns that it seeks to transcend. On one hand, the worldedness or worldliness of literature depends on a movement of translation and transgression and thus threatens to reestablish a fixed ground or point of origin—of this world and yet not sufficient for the worlding of literature without which the movement of a text into the world would not be intelligible. On the other, world literature might also reproduce a problematically skewed map—a map that depends on unequally distributed literary markets and economic and geopolitical considerations rather than on aesthetic or cultural criteria per se. What kind of texts circulate beyond their languages and cultures, what kind of literature thus becomes world literature is often determined by factors of literary and economic prestige defined in the very cultural centers that produce the framework of world literature (such as western Europe and the United States), and world literary approaches from those places might focus on textual motions that include those cultural centers and be less knowledgeable about literary and cultural circulations elsewhere that might bypass them.

The problematic perspective of world literature emerges with particular salience in the case of Chinese literature, which, with its large readership with access to written Chinese (even though they might be communicating in a Sinophone language that is not Mandarin or standard Chinese), should certainly count as one of the major literatures of the world. And yet, according to Eurocentric critics like Pascale Casanova, Chinese literature can be described as a "small literature," a term that is intended to correct what the critic sees as Deleuze's and Guattari's mistranslation of Kafka's term *kleine Literatur*. Chinese literature falls under the fourth category of "small literature" that Casanova lists in *The World Republic of Letters* (*La république mondiale des lettres*): "Finally there are languages of broad diffusion, such as Arabic, Chinese, or Hindi that have great internal literary traditions but nonetheless are little known and largely unrecognized in the international marketplace, and are thus dominated at the center."[7]

Casanova's paradoxical characterization of Chinese literature as a "small literature" in spite of its "great literary tradition" might perpetuate in world-literary form the well-known Western stereotype of China as a self-enclosed, isolated, and stagnant culture, even as Casanova describes this situation critically.

That Chinese literature is "dominated at the center"—because it forms a negligible part of the "international marketplace"—shows the limit of approaches that trace and map patterns of circulation. From a world-literary perspective, domestic readership becomes almost negligible. And what about the global audience of Chinese speakers abroad who read Chinese texts in many international locales? What about the pre-modern circulation of Chinese texts as literary standard in dialogue with other traditions and languages within an Asian sphere? And what about the profound shaping and reshaping of modern Chinese culture by way of foreign influences? Would not the unprecedented creative translation, absorption, and reshaping of non-Chinese cultures make Chinese literature a world literature?[8] Or does worldedness only function as a colonial pattern in which texts triumph on the world literature market by becoming commodities abroad, rather than because of their receptivity to other influences? In other words, according to what kind of value system is the conquest of foreign markets more important than a role of playing host to world literature?

Rather than having to conform to the theorization of world literature, Chinese literature thus questions and contests the patterns highlighted by world literature. On one hand, it draws our attention to different regional and transregional circulations, ones that do not necessarily have to pass through Paris, London, or New York—as well as to movements between cultures and languages that do not have to conform necessarily to Western patterns of translation or cosmopolitan exchange.[9] On the other hand, looking at the Chinese context also allows us to critique the unequal distribution of original and copy or translation, or of literary exportation and importation. If world literature according to its prevalent understanding as based on spatial circulation can only produce a distorted picture from the outset, since, as Pheng Cheah explains in "World against Globe," it uses "global capitalist market exchange as model," the example of Chinese literature showcases the problematic premises of world literature in particularly glaring terms.[10] Chinese literature only finds a precarious position in the context of world literature because of a bias that values export over import; from such a perspective, Chinese literature is not an export commodity, but rather depends on absorbing original models from elsewhere. The insistence on the symbolic "smallness" of Chinese literature underlines rather than contests the model function of economic flows; after all, one of the nation-states that produces literature in Chinese, the PRC, has become one of the foremost global economic powers. But the symbolic equivalent of cultural capital is here wielded as a supplement of economic and political power, while necessarily following its structural logic and value.

Even more open formulations, such as Wai Chee Dimock's notion of "planetary literature," by way of which literary texts, as exemplars of an artificial species, circulate in idiosyncratic, highly personal ways—such as the adjacency between Osip Mandelstam and Dante by way of Mandelstam's fascination with Dante's *Commedia*—Chinese literature (among many other literary traditions) puts pressure on the claim that "the continuum of literature is anarchic: impossible to regulate or police."[11] After all, access to—or even knowledge of—literary works across cultures and languages is not open, even in the age of the Internet and its rhetoric of open access. Even such highly arbitrary individualistic connections rely on what Jing Tsu calls literary governance, on patterns of circulation and unequally distributed linguistic value.[12] In other words, if we want to indulge in biological metaphors of species and ecosystems, rather than symbiosis we might find ourselves in a Darwinian structure of the survival of the fittest that makes short work of literary and linguistic multiplicity or even results in a conglomerate of strictly policed, genetically engineered monocultures, closely protected from the incursion of weeds and hybrids.[13]

But Chinese literature also shows another problematic facet of a world literature approach. While Chinese literature might be at a disadvantage from a global perspective, in the face of the hegemony of Western literary paradigms and the prestige of English, it itself occupies the topmost position in a food chain comprised of other cultural and linguistic traditions, for instance vis-à-vis articulations in other Sinitic or non-Sinitic languages besides the standard Mandarin of the PRC, or even Sinophones such as Cantonese in Hong Kong or Taiwanese (Minnan) in Taiwan, which are already moderately minor while playing the role of official or at least educational and cultural languages in smaller regional contexts. In other words, while clamoring for paradigms of cultural circulation, aesthetic value, and linguistic distribution that include Chinese literature in less precarious ways, we cannot forget that a change of perspective and cultural scope will make Chinese literature morph from a moderately endangered or at least fringe species in some contexts to the predominant species that pushes others toward extinction in other contexts.

Since the strategic inclusionism of global frameworks, such as world literature, is suspect for the connections it naturalizes and the links it occludes, critics such as Emily Apter insist on mobilizing cultural differences against facile appropriations in the name of globalization.[14] In *Against World Literature*, Apter pits untranslatability—both as a feature of words and texts, as well as a more general theoretical concept—against the "translatability assumption" of world literature, especially in the form of anthologies, handbooks, and world literary histories that seem to implement a new universalist impetus. To counteract world literature's tendency to "zoom over the speed bumps of untranslatability in the rush to cover ground," Apter proposes a focus on "incommensurability and what has been called the Untranslatable" "as a deflationary gesture toward the expansionism and gargantuan scale of world-literary endeavors."[15] As a conceptual caveat, we certainly need to remind ourselves of the limits of translation and underscore cultural and textual specificities that ought not to be elided in the relational games of world literature or in the analogy machines of comparative literature. However, to wield incommensurability as a conceptual tool also conjures up the specter of essentialized and totalized cultural alterity. Where we place and how we script the limits of untranslatability—as a barrier of language, culture, nation, and so forth—is a matter of construction and a profoundly political act. For the sake of opening up Chinese literatures to other constellations and connecting them differently, we must beware of naturalizing the gap between what counts as Chinese and its cultural and linguistic others and introduce and wield the critical energy of untranslatability also within the field of Chinese literatures.

COMPARISONS

From the vantage point of a world literature approach, a somewhat reductive definition of the world imposes one type of global context for literary texts, which also often implies reducing the multiplicity of literary traditions to a univocal, coherent whole—not different literatures but rather *a* literature. Instead, other contexts and connections are needed to better account for the multiplicity and hybridity of Chinese literatures as well as to shape a more nuanced picture of its variegated affiliations, contiguities, and conjunctions—ones that do not privilege one type of link only. Focusing mainly on the circulation of literary texts creates, after all, only one type of constellation with naturalized units and thus might take us beyond the bounds of a nation-state or a culture only to tie us into a global straitjacket in the end.

Shu-mei Shih's "modest proposal" for a relational comparison in "Comparison as Relation" grounds literary comparison in historical, economic, and political connections and commonalities, such as the shared history of colonialism, forced migration, and indentured labor that characterizes the plantation arc and brings the Caribbean and South-East Asia into conjunction. This type of approach works by "setting into motion historical relationalities between entities brought together for comparison, and bringing into relation terms that have traditionally been pushed apart from each other due to certain interests, such as the European exceptionalism that undergirds Eurocentrism."[16] Shih sidesteps the problem of world literature by emphasizing historical and socioeconomic relations rather than dwelling on the intercourse of texts only, thus tracing new maps of connections. By insisting on relations, such as the global circulation of coolie laborers in the context of colonial economies, for instance, Shih's comparative methodology supplements models that use contextual similarities as analogical ground, such as David Porter's reflections on the commonalities of Chinese and English cultures during early modernity.[17] And yet, like analogical or ecological frameworks for literary and cultural comparison, Shih's approach also leaves literary texts and their literariness in an uncertain position. If the excavation—and thus, I would claim, construction—of historical connections and consequently of contextual commonalities suggests textual similarities, is literature then simply an indicator and symptom of such relations? Even though such an approach opens up different conjunctions between groups of texts belonging to minor constellations, not only to the monumental edifices of cultural traditions tied to nation-states or empires, this risks framing literary texts in the role of mere representations or expressions.

In spite of their methodological challenges, such approaches work as powerful anti-dotes to comparative approaches that have traditionally included Chinese cultures only in precarious ways, often through essentializing and totalizing units of compari-son (China as base unit) and polarizing comparative outcomes in meaningless (but strategically and ideologically important) binaries of difference and sameness. They have tended to create either a comfortable sense of similarity, of a cultural and civi-lizational commons—focused on problematically constructed and unequally distrib-uted universals—with no regard for specificities, or an equally comfortable sense of difference and alterity, where comparison simply underlines yet again that the other culture is other, in the discursive machines that churn out stereotypes and incessantly reinscribe and cement the structures of difference.

For centuries, China has been a positive or negative model of comparison, pre-cisely because it was thought of as belonging to an altogether different category. As modern colonial interests started to see China as a coveted object, the notion of a common civilization level between Europe and China started to give way to the rheto-ric of incommensurable difference. In the late seventeenth century, in the preface to *Novissima Sinica historiam nostri temporis illustrata* Gottfried Wilhelm Leibniz still described Europe and China as the cultured extremes of the Eurasian landmass, as if extending their civilizing reach toward each other across an uncultured expanse.[18] In the nineteenth century, however, overwhelmingly negative evaluations started to proliferate—such as Georg Wilhelm Friedrich Hegel's image of China as a stagnant culture eternally mired in the past, in the introduction to *Lectures on the Philosophy of History* (*Vorlesungen über die Philosophie der Geschichte*).[19] And at the turn of the twentieth century, from a Western perspective China's place in and access to the mod-ern world became a matter of contestation, as Western voices such as Henry Norman's denounced the barbarism of Chinese culture, even as Chinese intellectuals started to take up Western lenses and framed their critique of Chinese culture in similar terms.[20]

The paradigm of China as a foil and mirror of the West was (and sometimes still is) particularly compelling, since China could be construed as an extreme test case without the risk of any Chinese interference, since one could always script China stra-tegically in ways that would not interrupt a logic of exception or, alternatively, one of universal similarities. Although the discipline of comparative literature has embarked on courses beyond the discipline's Eurocentric roots and Orientalist legacies, it often still resonates with politically skewed world maps or treats Asian cultural traditions, as Gayatri Spivak remarks in "Rethinking Comparatism," with a "somewhat paternalistic approach."[21] Newer approaches to East-West comparisons in the context of compara-tive literature, for instance, have scrutinized European "sinographies," Western con-structions of Chinese culture, for their complex referentiality to and use of China.[22] Although this approach makes China thus "written" by Europeans an integral part of Western culture and its self-definition rather than treating it as merely a series of mis-readings, this still only captures one side of an intercultural dialogue. Even if China can become a method of cultural reflection, China and its sinographies are still only discursive objects that enrich and complicate the set-up of the West. Meanwhile, as Rey Chow points out in "How (the) Inscrutable Chinese Led to Globalized Theory," the power to either deconstruct or to leave cultural stereotypes intact depends on cultural and geopolitical power, as not "all cultures remain faithful to themselves while rethinking or deconstructing themselves in relation to others."[23] The distribution and circulation of (inter)cultural capital and the power of framing other cultures remains profoundly unequal, even as US and European academia remain safely ensconced as centers of critical, comparative engagement and analysis.[24]

Consequently, thrusts toward comparative studies of and among Asian or East Asian cultures have sought to allow for a less Western-centric ground for cultural comparison, in a shift of comparative focus after much of the work of comparative literature has been reframed not as a set of global analyses, but rather as a region-specific kind of comparison, one mainly concerned with Europe. In "Exquisite Cadavers Stitched from Fresh Nightmares," Haun Saussy singles out East Asia as an alternative and corrective to the Eurocentrism of comparative literature, while acknowledging that other cultural contexts might be similarly productive for comparative explorations:

> For the East Asianist, the other end of the Eurasian continent is a far more promising place to host the international, interlinguistic, intercultural investigation. A far longer temporal series; a single dominant literary idiom shared by multiple dynasties, nations, religions, and languages; a common canon, parsed and combated in many ways; the emergence of vernaculars from and against the literary language; exchanges with peoples from different cultural backgrounds, and the consequent adaptations and revaluations—these and other factors combine to make East Asia a more "normal" ground for comparative literary history.[25]

Of course, East Asia can and should be a productive ground for comparative approaches—as is any other place on this globe marked by human culture. Shifting the site of comparison away from its traditional focal points constitutes a powerful decentralization, which, however, cannot result in yet another privileged center of comparison. Nor can such a perspectival shift consolidate contiguity as necessary premise for comparison. Finding especially fertile grounds for comparison in some cultures, places, or regions can only ever be a temporary, markedly strategic move if it wants to eschew setting up new hierarchies defined by levels of comparative and intercultural productivity. Likewise, we have to beware of reifying and naturalizing new cultural and regional contours in the act. After all, as Arif Dirlik reminds us for the case of the Pacific Rim region, definitions of areas and regions instrumentalize physical space as ground for ideological constructs.[26] Consequently, physical contiguity or geographical continuity cannot eclipse other intercultural links and has to be scrutinized for its constructions of coherence or unity, for the multiple scales (from local spaces to megaregions) and different types of connections (continental, climatic, oceanic, and so forth) it relies on.

METHODS

What many of these approaches share—and what points beyond the risk of reifying cultural and regional delimitations or that of naturalizing some relations at the expense of others—is, either explicitly or implicitly, their attempt at rethinking the link between objects and methods of cultural inquiry. This responds to a situation in which non-Western cultures have been and are still being treated as particular objects or examples, while the theoretical frameworks for such a treatment are supposedly produced elsewhere. Whereas studies of Western cultures often claim universality, work on non-Western material is forced (by intellectual consensus based on prejudice, by academic and disciplinary structures, and by the mandates of academic publishing) to abide by its specific contexts and not overreach its place—for instance by claiming general validity or formulating theories and methodologies. This is equally true for area studies approaches and for certain tendencies in comparative literature. In fact, one way of detautologizing the system of comparison and of managing its conceptual circularity between pure difference and sameness has been to assign different functions to different cultures. Hence, for instance, China could become all object for a Western thought that desired itself all methodology or theory.

Especially in relation to the study of Asian cultures, the beginning of the twenty first century has produced work that sees different places and parts of Asia no longer merely as objects of study, but rather as a set of conditions, articulations, and constellations from which one can formulate different theories and methodologies. In the introduction to *Inhuman Conditions*, for instance, Pheng Cheah unapologetically describes his study of cosmopolitanism as a theoretical reflection partly based on Asian examples. In his book, postcolonial Asia is not merely a set of cases that theory can illuminate, but rather constitutes a ground for developing "fundamental theoretical issues concerning the nature of humanity."[27] Instead of provincializing Europe, Cheah proposes to universalize Asia. Instead of the distribution of labor according to which area studies is seen as the study of a particular cultural tradition—bounded and outside of she who studies it—while the universal framework that allows for theory building is formulated elsewhere and predates the data collection of the area studies scholar, Cheah proposes a different approach in "Universal Areas," one that means "neither to denigrate the universal nor to claim an alternative and usually antagonistic Asian modularity, but for Asian studies to claim that their subject is a *part* of the universal, not just as a check to a preformulated universal, but as something that actively *shares in* and *partakes of* the universal in a specific way."[28]

For Cheah's work or Kuan-hsing Chen's *Asia as Method: Toward Deimperialization*, the solution to the hegemonic position of the West as producer of theories and methodologies does not lie in looking for Asian theories—which is to say, supposedly indigenous traditions that would constitute a more appropriate frame for things Asian and as a corrective to Western theories. After all, as Chen points out, the "West as method" often played a crucial role in the formation of national and nationalist agendas in Asia, which makes the impulse of privileging indigenous theories somewhat paradoxical from the outset.[29] Instead, drawing on Naoki Sakai's critique of the binary between East and West that results also in shaping the West or Europe from a diffuse, hybrid cultural constellation without distinct essence or existence into a coherent, homogeneous whole, Chen further complicates essentialist constructions of cultural positionality, origin, and property by claiming that elements of the West have already become part of Asian culture.[30] Chen finds inspiration in Yuzo Mizoguchi's 溝口雄三 *China as Method* (方法としての中国), in which China, as a corrective to both Eurocentrism and Japancentrism, does not constitute a privileged field for conceptual thought—such as the formulation of world history—but merely a strategic entry point that calls up a multiplicity of other cultural references. Chen's shift from "China as method" to "Asia as method," in spite of the charged history of the term Asia, underlines a movement of deterritorialization:[31] in order to start to address parts of Asia, Asian studies needs to take into consideration multiple local, transborder, regional, and intercontinental practices.[32]

To convert non-Western phenomena into the basis for conceptual approaches, rather than treating them as objects to be scrutinized according to methods or theories developed elsewhere, is certainly conceptually and theoretically powerful, especially when such methods function according to a nonbinary understanding and do not essentialize cultural boundaries. Even though Chen envisions this method primarily as a new approach within Asian studies in Asia, it has clear implications for the studies of cultures across the globe—not only for the study of Asia outside of Asia, but also for the study of other non-Asian cultures, in and beyond Asia. In fact, this also means that no single culture has a monopoly of producing theories or methodologies, even as not all cultural objects and contexts will yield exactly the same kind of insights. As they cut through the false binary of objects and theories, Chen's and Cheah's approaches do not establish an equally problematic correlation between certain objects and certain theories. Positing China or Asia as methods implies decentering Western paradigms and assumptions not by establishing embargoes on anything supposedly Western or by reifying anything supposedly Asian. Instead, a reflection on one's own cultural, intellectual, and academic positionality needs to be accompanied by perspectives on other cultures, even as such cultures themselves are treated as internally hybrid and engaged in constant intercultural exchanges and transactions. Consequently, using Chinese or Asian cultures as ground and laboratory for methodologies and theories is never equivalent to the universalizing thrust of the "West as method," since it has to insist not on particulars that point toward a universal but on singularities whose different conjunctions and entanglements form larger constellations that are constantly being reshaped and redefined. This also means that we need to constantly reimagine the relationship between concrete, specific contexts and more general vectors of conceptual validity.

Inspired by these and other frameworks, our volume aims to provide models for and inspire new thought on Chinese literary texts not merely as objects in comparison or as parts of wider constellations, but also as phenomena that formulate new methodologies and trajectories in dialogue and contestation with existing concepts and frameworks. As such, this volume does not primarily constitute a survey of the state of the discipline; instead, it showcases a multiplicity of approaches that think Chinese literatures in conjunction and as conjunction, as object and method, as local, national, regional, diasporic, intercultural, and global—which also means throwing critical light on these very categories. Chinese literary studies as a field constantly undergoes shifts, incessantly delimits its contours as well as its understanding of Chineseness and, consequently, the potential relations and alliances with its "outsides," which also redefines its "inside." The phenomena that we investigate shape our perspectives, but are in turn shaped by our work. Our cultural, intellectual, and academic contexts as well as our choice of objects and methods—and both are intricately interconnected rather than constituting separate blocks—determine our work, but they also allow us to change and relativize perspectives, to strategically privilege and unprivilege specific sites, and to construct different junctures and conjunctions, keeping in mind the injunction to switch between and, in fact, engage the double or multiple vision of superimposed scopes, between the specific and the general, the minor and the molar, the local and the global, in their interconnectedness and inherent friction.

My conclusion thus invites us to continue to read Chinese literatures in conjunction. It does not understand itself as wedded to a temporality of the past, as a coda to an end, but rather as a new departure. The gesture of concluding—which, in the spirit of its Latin etymology, can be read as the strange addition of connection to closure, literally a "con-closure"—does not foreground closure or even foreclosure, but rather understands itself as a temporary, strategic, and intentionally precarious movement of pause; a rest, but not an arrest. With its nod toward conjunction, as well as because of its excessive, supplemental structure—after all, even as a conclusion indicates that something has come to an end, it effectively extends the duration of that which it is supposed to close—at the close of this volume, my conclusion undertakes also a motion of opening, of thinking modern Chinese literatures as beyond themselves, as a constellation that incessantly regroups and ungrounds itself. This is precisely the temporality and logic that I see at work in the project of this volume and in the discipline of modern Chinese literary studies in general. Not a preemptive, anticipatory mourning of its demise, the nostalgic overinvestment in the death of a discipline that is always in suspense and yet always impending, nor the attempt to fix the field in the Medusa gaze of disciplinary thinking, but rather an investment in a vitality that will endure precisely because it undergoes constant changes, even quite crucial and profound ones.

NOTES

1. Consequently, whenever I use the terms *Chinese* or *Chineseness* (or the *West*) here, I will dispense with quotation marks, since it is understood that these are not essential givens, but rather categories based on internally hybrid phenomena that are constantly shifting and subject to reconstruction.

2. The novel in question was the seventeenth-century novel *The Fortunate Union* or *The Well-Matched Lovers* (好逑傳), which Goethe discusses in contiguity with his famous formulation of the advent of world literature. Even though he dwells on the familiarity of much of the Chinese novel, he also disclaims its universal meaning or appeal; see David Damrosch, *What Is World Literature?* (Princeton: Princeton University Press, 2003), 10–12, and Jing Tsu, *Sound and Script in Chinese Diaspora* (Cambridge: Harvard University Press, 2014), 126–128.

3. See Chen Pingyuan's chapter, "The Story of Literary History," in this volume.

4. See the reshaping of Cold War paradigms in Xiaojue Wang's and Shuang Shen's chapters in this volume.

5. See Shu-mei Shih, *Visuality and Identity: Sinophone Articulations Across the Pacific* (Berkeley: University of California Press, 2007).

6. Several chapters in this volume push the envelope of what constitutes Chineseness, inspired by a Sinophone methodology; see the chapters by Brian Bernards, Belinda Kong, and Chien-hsin Tsai.

7. Pascale Casanova, *La république mondiale des lettres* (Paris: Seuil, 1999), 350; trans. M. B. DeBevoise as *The World Republic of Letters* (Cambridge: Harvard University Press, 2004), 256–257. I have slightly modified the English translation, which omits the phrase "and are thus dominated at the center" ("et sont par conséquent dominées au centre").

8. See Ji Jin's chapter in this volume.

9. Note, for example, the circulation and production of classical Chinese poetry in Japan of the nineteenth century, and the intersection of a common intellectual sphere (through patterns of poetry and a shared script culture of Chinese) and local inflections (such as the different Japanese readings of Chinese verse) that are posited between translation and reception in the original language. See Matthew Fraleigh's chapter in this volume.

10. Pheng Cheah, "World against Globe," *New Literary History* 45.3 (Summer 2014): 303–329, quotation at 303.

11. Wai Chee Dimock, "Literature for the Planet," *PMLA* 116.1 (January 2001): 173–188, quotation at 174.

12. See Jing Tsu, *Sound and Script in Chinese Diaspora*.

13. Recent comparative work, for instance Alexander Beecroft's *An Ecology of World Literature from Antiquity to the Present Day* (London and New York: Verso, 2015), has started to use ecological metaphors in productive ways.

14. See Rey Chow's critique of the inclusionist premise of globalization and global theories in "How (the) Inscrutable Chinese Led to Globalized Theory," *PMLA* 116.1 (2001): 69–74, quotation at 69.

15. Emily Apter, *Against World Literature: On the Politics of Untranslatability* (London and New York: Verso, 2013), 3.

16. Shu-mei Shih, "Comparison as Relation," in *Comparison: Theories, Approaches, Uses*, ed. Rita Felski and Susan Stanford Friedman (Baltimore: The Johns Hopkins University Press, 2013), 79–98, quotation at 79.

17. See David Porter's chapter in this volume.

18. See Gottfried Wilhelm Leibniz, *Novissima Sinica historiam nostri temporis illustrata*, 2nd ed. (Hanover: Förster, 1699), retrieved May 30, 2015, from http://digital.staatsbibliothek-berlin.de/werkansicht/?PPN=PPN666539251.

19. See Georg Wilhelm Friedrich Hegel, *Vorlesungen über die Philosophie der Geschichte* (Leipzig: Reclam, 1924 [1837]), retrieved May 30, 2015, from http://gutenberg.spiegel.de/buch/-1657/1.

20. See especially the chapter "Chinese Horrors," in Henry Norman, *The Peoples and Politics of the Far East: Travels and Studies in the British, French, Spanish and Portuguese Colonies, Siberia, China, Japan, Korea, Siam and Malaya* (New York: Charles Scribner's Sons, 1895), 219–230.

21. Gayatri Chakravorty Spivak, "Rethinking Comparatism," *New Literary History* 40 (2009): 609–626, quotation at 609.

22. For examples of such an approach, see Christopher Bush, *Ideographic Modernism: China, Writing, Media* (Oxford: Oxford University Press, 2010); Eric Hayot, *Chinese Dreams: Pound, Brecht, Tel quel* (Ann Arbor: University of Michigan Press, 2004); and *The Hypothetical Mandarin: Sympathy, Modernity, and Chinese Pain* (Oxford: Oxford University Press, 2009), as well as the volume *Sinographies: Writing China*, eds. Eric Hayot, Haun Saussy, and Steven G. Yao (Minneapolis: University of Minnesota Press, 2007).

23. Rey Chow, "How (the) Inscrutable Chinese Led to Globalized Theory," 73.

24. Precisely because Occidentalism is not a reverse Orientalism, Xiaomei Chen's *Occidentalism: A Theory of Counter-Discourse in Post-Mao China* (Oxford: Oxford University Press, 1995) shows the power differential between the West's framing of China and the West's overwhelmingly important—if not always equally welcome—influence on China.

25. Haun Saussy, "Exquisite Cadavers Stitched from Fresh Nightmares: Of Memes, Hives, and Selfish Genes," in *Comparative Literature in an Age of Globalization*, ed. Haun Saussy (Baltimore: The Johns Hopkins University Press, 2006), 3–42, quotation at 10.

26. See Arif Dirlik, "Introduction: Pacific Contradictions," in *What Is in a Rim? Critical Perspectives on the Pacific Region Idea*, ed. Arif Dirlik, 2nd ed. (Lanham, MD: Rowman & Littlefield, 1998), 3–13.

27. Pheng Cheah, *Inhuman Conditions: On Cosmopolitanism and Human Rights* (Cambridge: Harvard University Press, 2006), 13.

28. Pheng Cheah, "Universal Areas: Asian Studies in a World in Motion," in *The Postcolonial and the Global*, eds. Revathi Krishnaswamy and John C. Hawley (Minneapolis: University of Minnesota Press, 2007), 54–68, quotation at 62.

29. See Chen Kuan-Hsing, *Asia as Method: Toward Deimperialization* (Durham: Duke University Press, 2010), 216.

30. See Chen, *Asia as Method*, 217–218 and 255; Chen's reference is to Naoki Sakai's essay "Modernity and Its Critique: The Problem of Universalism and Particularism."

31. For a discussion and critique of the Western construction of Asia, see Gayatri Chakravorty Spivak, *Other Asias* (Malden, MA: Blackwell, 2008), 208–214.

32. See Chen, *Asia as Method*, 251–255.

Works Cited

Apter, Emily. *Against World Literature: On the Politics of Untranslatability*. London and New York: Verso, 2013.

Beecroft, Alexander. *An Ecology of World Literature from Antiquity to the Present Day*. London and New York: Verso, 2015.

Bush, Christopher. *Ideographic Modernism: China, Writing, Media*. Oxford: Oxford University Press, 2010.

Casanova, Pascale. *La république mondiale des lettres*. Paris: Seuil, 1999; trans. M. B. DeBevoise as *The World Republic of Letters*. Cambridge: Harvard University Press, 2004.

Cheah, Pheng. *Inhuman Conditions: On Cosmopolitanism and Human Rights*. Cambridge: Harvard University Press, 2006.

Cheah, Pheng. "Universal Areas: Asian Studies in a World in Motion." In *The Postcolonial and the Global*. Ed. Revathi Krishnaswamy and John C. Hawley. Minneapolis: University of Minnesota Press, 2007. 54–68.

Cheah, Pheng. "World against Globe." *New Literary History* 45.3 (Summer 2014): 303–329.

Chen, Kuan-Hsing. *Asia as Method: Toward Deimperialization*. Durham: Duke University Press, 2010.

Chen, Xiaomei. *Occidentalism: A Theory of Counter-Discourse in Post-Mao China*. Oxford: Oxford University Press, 1995.

Chow, Rey. "How (the) Inscrutable Chinese Led to Globalized Theory." *PMLA* 116.1 (2001): 69–74.

Damrosch, David. *What Is World Literature?* Princeton and Oxford: Princeton University Press, 2003.

Dimock, Wai Chee. "Literature for the Planet." *PMLA* 116.1 (January 2001): 173–188.

Dirlik, Arif. "Introduction: Pacific Contradictions." In *What Is in a Rim? Critical Perspectives on the Pacific Region Idea*. Ed. Arif Dirlik. 2nd ed. Lanham, MD: Rowman & Littlefield, 1998. 3–13.

Hayot, Eric. *Chinese Dreams: Pound, Brecht, Tel Quel*. Ann Arbor: University of Michigan Press, 2004.

Hayot, Eric. *The Hypothetical Mandarin: Sympathy, Modernity, and Chinese Pain*. Oxford: Oxford University Press, 2009.

Eric Hayot, Haun Saussy, and Steven G. Yao, eds. Sinographies: Writing China. Minneapolis: University of Minnesota Press, 2007.

Hegel, Georg Wilhelm Friedrich. *Vorlesungen über die Philosophie der Geschichte*. Leipzig: Reclam, 1924 [1837]. Retrieved May 30, 2015, from http://gutenberg.spiegel.de/buch/-1657/1.

Leibniz, Gottfried Wilhelm. *Novissima Sinica historiam nostri temporis illustrata*. 2nd ed. Hanover: Förster, 1699. Retrieved May 30, 2015, from http://digital.staatsbibliothek-berlin.de/werkansicht/?PPN=PPN666539251.

Norman, Henry. *The Peoples and Politics of the Far East: Travels and Studies in the British, French, Spanish and Portuguese Colonies, Siberia, China, Japan, Korea, Siam and Malaya*. New York: Charles Scribner's Sons, 1895.

Tsu, Jing. *Sound and Script in Chinese Diaspora*. Cambridge: Harvard University Press, 2014.

Saussy, Haun. "Exquisite Cadavers Stitched from Fresh Nightmares: Of Memes, Hives, and Selfish Genes." In *Comparative Literature in an Age of Globalization*. Ed. Haun Saussy. Baltimore: The Johns Hopkins University Press, 2006. 3–42.

Shih, Shu-mei. "Comparison as Relation." In *Comparison: Theories, Approaches, Uses*. Ed. Rita Felski and Susan Stanford Friedman. Baltimore: The Johns Hopkins University Press, 2013. 79–98.

Shih, Shu-mei. *Visuality and Identity: Sinophone Articulations Across the Pacific*. Berkeley: University of California Press, 2007.

Spivak, Gayatri Chakravorty. *Other Asias*. Malden, MA: Blackwell, 2008.

Spivak, Gayatri Chakravorty. "Rethinking Comparatism." *New Literary History* 40 (2009): 609–626.

APPENDIX: LIST OF LITERARY WORKS BY AUTHOR

Although this volume is neither a survey nor a literary history, it does cover considerable ground. To give readers a sense of the volume's breadth, we have compiled a necessarily incomplete list of the literary works discussed or mentioned in the preceding chapters. In addition to the conventional modern Chinese literary texts, this appendix also includes works that our contributors contend may be included in this category, broadly defined—including "early modern" novels from the Ming-Qing period, poetry in Literary Sinitic by Japanese authors, texts in the Yi language by an Yi author, essays in various Southeast Asian languages by migrant workers living in Taiwan, and foreign language works that have circulated in Chinese translation. We have included not only novels, stories, poems, and dramas, but also essays and literary histories, and even some films and songs that our contributors suggest may be approached as literary texts.

The appendix is organized by author (using the spellings and pen names by which the authors are most commonly known in English-language literature), and consequently for the most part the texts included here are limited to works with identifiable authors. To provide a sense of historical orientation we have dated each work, although for many works issues of dating are quite complicated. In most cases, the date is that of the first publication, though in some cases we have used the date of initial completion or a similar proxy. Chinese-language titles are provided for all works except for those either composed in a foreign language or which have circulated most widely in their foreign-language edition. For practical reasons, journals, newspapers, and other periodicals have been omitted, though in many cases they could be considered literary works in their own right.

For more information on any and all of these works, readers are invited to use the index to locate the corresponding discussions within the main body of the volume.

A

Ah Zhu 阿珠
    "Wandering for Eight Years" 流亡八年, 2013
Aku Wuwu 阿庫烏霧 (Luo Qingchun 羅慶春)
    Winter River 冬天的河流 (ꀕꅼꉬ), 1994
    Out of the Land of Sorcerers 走出巫界, 1995
    Tiger Tracks 虎跡 (ꄷꏸ), 1998
    Selected Poems of Aku Wuwu 阿庫烏霧詩歌選, 2004
    Appeal of the Mississippi River 密西西比河的傾訴, 2008
    The Wizard's Voice 神巫的祝咒, 2010
    Hybrid Age 混血時代, 2015
Angel Island Poems, 1910–1940

B

Ba Jin 巴金
>   *Family* 家, 1933

Bai Shouyi 白壽彝, ed.
>   *History of China* 中國通史, 1999

Bing Xin 冰心
>   *Jitanjiali* 吉檀迦利 [translation of Rabindranath Tagore's *Gitanjali*], 1955
>   *Stars* 星, 1921
>   *Spring Water* 春水, 1922

Bo Yang 柏楊
>   *Alien Lands* 異域, 1961

C

Cao Juren 曹聚仁
>   *The Hotel* 酒店, 1954

Cao Xueqin 曹雪芹 and Gao E 高鶚
>   *The Dream of the Red Chamber* 紅樓夢, 1790s

Chan Koonchung 陳冠中
>   *The Fat Years* 盛世: 中國二〇一三年, 2009

Chan, Rupert 陳鈞潤
>   *Cyrano de Bergerac* 美人如玉劍如虹 [translation of *Cyrano de Bergerac*], 1990
>   *Fooling Around with Heaven and the Emperor* 胡天胡帝 [translation of Alfred Jarry's Ubu Roi], 1990
>   *Hongkongers Speak* 港人自講, 1991
>   "Translating Drama for the Hong Kong Audience" 為香港觀眾翻譯戲劇, 1992
>   *Pygmalion* 窈窕淑女 [adaptation of George Bernard Shaw's *Pygmalion*], 1997
>   *A Small Family Business* 家庭作孽 [translation of Alan Ayckbourn's *A Small Family Business*], 2004

Chang, Eileen 張愛玲
>   "My Dream of Being a Genius" 天才夢, 1939
>   "Aloeswood Incense, the First Brazier" 沉香屑: 第一爐香, 1943
>   "The Golden Cangue" 金鎖記, 1943
>   "Love in a Fallen City" 傾城之戀, 1943
>   "Sealed Off" 封鎖, 1943
>   "Yin Baoyan Visits My Flat, Bringing a Bouquet" 殷寶灩送花樓會, 1944
>   *The Affinity of Half a Lifetime* 半生緣, 1948
>   *Love in the Redland* 赤地之戀, 1954
>   *Rice-Sprout Song*, 1954
>   *Naked Earth*, 1956
>   "A Return to the Frontier," 1963
>   *The Rouge of the North*, 1967
>   "Lust, Caution" 色·戒, 1977
>   *Small Reunions* 小團圓, 2009

Chen Jiying 陳紀瀅
 Fool in the Reeds 荻村傳, 1951
Chen Kaige 陳凱歌
 Yellow Earth 黃土地 (film), 1984
Chen Li 陳黎
 "War Symphony" 戰爭交響曲, 1995
 Worries and Freedom Well-Tempered 苦惱與自由的平均律, 2005
 Light/Slow 輕／慢, 2009
Chen Qiufan 陳楸帆
 The Waste Tide 荒潮, 2013
Chen Sihe 陳思和
 A Complete View of New Chinese Literature 中國新文學整體觀, 1987
Chen Xue 陳雪 and Breakfaster 早餐人
 A Wife's Diary 人妻日記, 2012
Chen Yinke 陳寅恪
 "On Love in Two Lives" 論再生緣, 1954
 Biography of Liu Rushi 柳如是別傳, 1963
Chen Zizhan 陳子展
 A History of the Chinese Literature of the Past Thirty Years 最近三十年中國文學史, 1930
Cheng Qianfan 程千帆
 "On the Problems of Teaching in Today's Chinese Literature Departments" 論今日大
  學中文系教學之蔽, 1943
Chi Ta-wei 紀大偉
 Membrane 膜, 1996
Chia Joo Ming's 謝裕民
 "Ambon Vacation" 安汶假期, 2005
Chu T'ien-wen 朱天文
 Notes of a Desolate Man 荒人手記, 1994
Chun Tao 春桃
 Chinese Peasant Investigation Report 中國農民調查報告, 2004
Clementi, Cecil
 "Hong Kong," 1925
Cui Jian 崔健
 "I Have Nothing" 一無所有 (song), 1997

D

Ding Cong 丁聰
 Images of Today 現象圖, 1944
Ding Ling 丁玲
 Miss Sophia's Diary 莎菲女士的日記, 1927
 Shanghai, Spring 1930 年春上海, 1930
 "In the Hospital" 在醫院中, 1941
Du Mingxin 杜鳴心 et al.
 The Red Detachment of Woman 紅色娘子軍 (ballet), 1964

Dung Kai-Cheung 董啟章

    The Rose of the Name 名字的玫瑰, 1997

    The Atlas: The Archaeology of an Imaginary City 地圖集: 一個想像的城市的考古學, 1997

    Visible Cities: A Chronicle of the Splendor of V-City V 城繁勝錄, 1998

    Works and Creations: Vivid and Lifelike 天工開物: 栩栩如真, 2005

    Histories of Time: The Luster of Mute Porcelain 時間繁史: 啞瓷之光, 2007

    The Origin of Species: The Educational Age of Beibei's Rebirth 物種源始: 貝貝重生之學習年代, 2010

F

Fan Wenlan 范文蘭, ed.

    Annotations to the History of China 中國通史簡編, 1964

Feng Zhi 馮至

    Northern Journey 北遊, 1929

    Sonnets 十四行詩, 1942

    A Biography of Du Fu 杜甫傳, 1952

    "My Thanks to Chairman Mao" 感謝毛主席, 1952

Fu Sinian 傅斯年

    "Differing Perspectives on Theater Reform" 戲劇改良各面觀, 1918

    "Another Consideration of Theater Reform" 再論戲劇改良, 1918

G

Gao Lan 高蘭

    "Developing Our Recited Poetry" 展開我們的朗誦詩歌, 1938

    "It's Time, My Comrades" 是時候了, 我的同胞, 1938

    "My Home is at the Heilong River" 我的家在黑龍江, 1939

Gao Xingjian 高興建

    Alarm Signal 絕對信號, 1982

    Bus Stop 車站, 1983

    Wild Man 野人, 1985

    The Other Shore 彼岸, 1986

    Flight 逃亡, 1990

    Soul Mountain 靈山, 1990

    Snow in August 八月雪, 1997

    One Man's Bible 一個人的聖經, 1999

    Roaming Spirit and Metaphysical Thinking: A Collection of Gao Xingjian's Poetry 遊神與玄思–高行健詩集, 2012

Ge Fei 格非

    "Greenish Yellow" 青黃, 1988

    "Ye Lang's Journey" 夜郎之行, 1989

Gu Jiegang, 顧頡剛, ed.

    Debates on Ancient History 古史辯 (book series), 1941

Gu Jiegang 顧頡剛 and Wang Zhonglin 王鐘麟
    Middle School Textbook in Modern Chinese History 現代初中本國史教科書, 1923
Guang Weiran 光未然
    "Yellow River Cantata" 黃河大合唱
Guo Moruo 郭沫若
    Preface to *Studies in Ancient Chinese Society* 中國古代社會研究, 1929
Guo Moruo 郭沫若 and Zhou Yang 周揚
    Red Flag Ballads 紅旗歌謠, 1958
Guo Shaoyu 郭紹虞
    The History of Chinese Literary Criticism 中國文學批評史上卷, 1934
Guo Xiaolu 郭小櫓
    20 Fragments of a Ravenous Youth 芬芳的三十七度二, 2000
    A Concise Chinese-English Dictionary for Lovers, 2007
    "Fragments of My Life," 2008
    UFO in Her Eyes, 2009
    Records of Three-Headed Bird Village 三頭鳥村記事錄 (film), 2011
Guo Zhenyi 郭箴一
    A History of the Chinese Novel 中國小說史, 1939

H

Han Shaogong 韓少功
    Dictionary of Maqiao 馬橋詞典, 1996
Han Song 韓松
    "The Fear of Seeing" 看的恐懼, 2002
    "My Fatherland Does Not Dream" 我的祖國不做夢, 2002
    Subway 地鐵, 2010
Hao Ran 浩然 (Liang Jinguang 梁金廣)
    Magpies on a Branch 喜鵲登枝, 1958
    "The New Bride" 新媳婦, 1958
    Bright Sunny Skies 艷陽天, 1966
    "Miscellaneous Memories of the Selection and Compilation of Songs of Spring"
        春歌集編選瑣憶, 1972
    The Golden Road 金光大道, 1974
Hirose Roshū 広瀬芦洲
    "Early Summer Pastorale," 1951
Hong Zicheng 洪子誠
    A History of Contemporary Chinese Literature 中國當代文學史, 1999
Hsu Yo-shen 許佑生
    "Stones on the Shore" 岸邊石, 1992
Hu Hanmin 胡漢民
    "Only Through Nationalism Can One Speak of Cosmopolitanism" 有民族主義
        才可以講世界主義, 1929
Hu Lancheng 胡蘭成
    China Through Time 山河歲月, 1954
Hu Shi 胡適

"Some Modest Proposals for the Reform of Literature" 文學改良芻議, 1917

"The Concept of Literary Evolution and Theater Reform" 文學進化觀念與戲劇改良, 1918

"The Importance of New Thought" 新思潮的意義, 1919

"On National Learning—in Response to Mao Zishui" 論國故學——答毛子水, 1919

"The Politics of Qing Scholars" 清代學者的治學方法, 1919

A Short History of Chinese Philosophy 中國哲學史大綱, 1919

A History of Ancient Chinese Philosophy 中國古代哲學史, 1919

The Greatest Event in Life 終身大事, 1919

Experiments 嘗試集, 1920

A Study of The Water Margin 水滸傳考証, 1920

"Uncontainable!" 關不住了 [translation of Sara Teasdale's "Over the Roofs"], 1920

Chinese Literature of the Past Fifty Years 五十年來中國之文學, 1922

Hu Shi 胡適 and Luo Jialun 羅家倫

Nora 娜拉 [translation of Henrik Ibsen's *A Doll's House*], 1918

Hua Gai 華蓋

"Lyricism in Nathan Road" 彌敦道抒情, 1964

Huang Kan 黃侃

Notes on the Literary Mind and the Carving of Dragons 文心雕龍札記, 1927

Huang Shiying 黃士英

"The Development of Chinese Manhua" 中國漫畫發展史, 1935

Huang Xiuyi 黃修已

A History of Chinese Literature in the Twentieth Century 20世紀中國文學史, 1998

Huang Yao 黃堯

Contradiction Collection 矛盾集, 1947

Huangjiang Diaosou 黃江釣叟

Tales of the Moon Colony 月球殖民地小說, 1904–1905

Hương Cỏ May 芒草香

"Dream of a Foreign Land" (Giấc mơ nơi xứ người), 2014

I

Ichikawa Wataru 市川渡 (Seiryū 清流)

A Leisurely Record of a Journey to Europe like a Fly on a Horse's Tail 尾蠅歐行漫録 (Biyō ōkō manroku), c. 1863

J

Jia Pingwa 賈平凹

Abandoned City *Abandoned City* 廢都, 1993

White Night 白夜, 1995

Earth Gate 土門, 1996

Gao laozhuang 高老庄, 1998

Nostalgia for the Wolf 懷念狼, 2000

Illness and Morbidity Report 病相報告, 2002

Ancient Furnace 古爐, 2011

 The Lantern Bearer 帶燈, 2013
Jian Bozan 翦伯贊, ed.
 Outline of the History of China 中國史綱要, 1962
Jiang Xiahun 姜俠魂, ed.
 A Record of the Words and Deeds of the Boxing Masters 拳師言行錄, 1923
Jin Yong 金庸 (Louis Cha 查良鏞)
 The Sword Stained with Royal Blood 碧血劍, 1956
Jin Zhimang 金枝芒
 Hunger 饑餓, 1960

K

Kang Youwei 康有為
 Great Unity 大同書, 1935
Ke Lan 柯藍
 Short Flute of Morning Mist 早霞短笛, 1957
Ke Zhongping 柯仲平
 "United Defense Army of the Border Region" 邊區自衛軍, 1938
 "Workers Will Ensure the Construction of an Industrialized Nation—Congratulations
  on Behalf of the Workers on the Occasion of the 28th Anniversary of the Chinese
  Communist Party" 創造工業國,工人敢保險--為中國工人慶祝中國共產黨二十八
  周歲作, 1949
Ku Dschau-sen 顧肇森
 "Zhang Wei" 張偉, 1984

L

Lao She 老舍
 The Cat Country 貓城記, 1932
Lee, C. Y.
 The Flower Drum Song, 1957
 Lover's Point, 1958
Leung Ping-kwan 梁秉鈞 (Yesi 也斯)
 "At the North Point Car Ferry" 北角汽車渡海碼頭, 1974
 Thunder and Cicada Songs 雷聲與蟬鳴, 1978
 The Book and the City 書與城市, 1985
 Islands and Continents 島和大陸, 1987
 "The Strange Banyan Tree" 古怪的大榕樹, 1987
 "Bittermelon" 給苦瓜的頌詩, 1989
 "In Response to Cecil Clementi" 悼逝去的——和金文泰香港詩, 1997
 "The Flame Tree" 鳳凰木, 1999
 Postcolonial Affairs of Food and of the Heart 後殖民食物與愛情, 2009
 "Land" 土地, 2011
 The Visible and the Invisible 顯與隱, 2012
 Fly Heads and Bird Claws 蠅頭與鳥爪, 2013
 "Transmigration of the Soul of Someone Who Drowned" 淹水者的超道, 2014

Li Ang 李昂
    Seeing Ghosts 看得見的鬼, 2004
Li Peifu 李佩甫
    The Gate for Sheep 羊的門, 1998
Li Rui 李銳,
    Trees Without Wind 無風之樹, 1996
Li Yiyun 李翊雲
    Kinder Than Solitude, 2014
Liang Qichao 梁啟超
    Commentaries on Chinese History 中國史敘論, 1901
    "On the Relationship between Fiction and Government of the People" 論小說與群治之關係, 1902
    New Historical Studies 新史學, 1902
    "Colloquy on Fiction" 小說叢話, 1903
Liang Qichao 梁啟超 et al.
    Two Years' Vacation 兩年假期 [translation of Jules Vernes's *Deux ans de vacances*], 1902
Liang Zongdai 梁宗岱
    Symbolism 象徵主義, 1934
Liao Bingxiong 廖冰兄
    Spring and Autumn in the Cat Kingdom 貓國春秋, 1946
Liao Yiwu 廖亦武
    Corpse Walker 中國底層訪談錄, 2001
Lin Chuanjia 林傳甲
    A History of Chinese Literature 中國文學史, 1904
Lin Shu 林紓
    Research on Classical Prose from Chunjuezhai 春覺齋論文, 1916
Lin Shu 林紓 and Wei Yi 魏易
    Stories of Paris's Lady of the Camellias 巴黎茶花女遺事 [translation of Alexandre Dumas fils's *The Lady of the Camellias*], 1899
    The Biography of Nell, a Filial Girl 孝女耐兒傳 [translation of Charles Dickens' *The Old Curiosity Shop*], 1908
Liu Cixin 劉慈欣
    China 2185 中國 2185, 1989
    "The Village Schoolteacher" 鄉村教師, 1999
    "Micro-cra" 微紀元, 1999
    The Era of the Supernova 超新星紀元, 2003
    The Three-Body Problem 三體, 2006
    The Dark Forest 黑暗森林, 2008
    Death's End 死神永生, 2010
    "Mountain" 山, 2010
Liu Huozi 劉火子
    "In the City, at Noon" 都市的午景, 1934
Liu Muxia 柳木下
    "Skyscraper" 大廈, 1938

Liu Shipei 劉師培
  "The Origins of Theater" 原戲, 1904
  A History of Ancient Chinese Literature 中國中古文學史, 1917
Lu Ling 路翎
  "Hungry Guo Su'e" 飢餓的郭素娥, 1942
  Children of the Rich 財主的兒女們, 1945
  "'Battle' of the Lowlands" 窪地上的"戰役," 1954
Lu Xun 魯迅 (Zhou Shuren 周樹人)
  "On the Refutation of Malevolent Voices" 破惡聲論, 1908
  "Concerning Imbalanced Cultural Development" 文化偏至論, 1908
  "On the Power of Mara Poetry" 摩羅詩力說, 1908
  "Diary of a Madman" 狂人日記, 1918
  "Hometown" 故鄉, 1921
  The True Story of Ah Q 阿Q正傳, 1922
  A Brief History of the Chinese Novel 中國小說史略, 1924
  "Upstairs in a Wineshop" 在酒樓上, 1924
  "What Happens after Nora Leaves?" 娜拉走後怎樣, 1924
  "New Year's Sacrifice" 祝福, 1924
  "Regret for the Past" 傷逝, 1925
  A Concise Outline of Chinese Literary History 漢文學史綱要, 1926
  Wild Grass 野草, 1927
  Dawn Blossoms Plucked at Dusk 朝花夕拾, 1928
  "On Relay Translation" 論重譯, 1934
  Compendium of New Chinese Literature 中國新文學大係: 小說二集序, 1935
  A History of Chinese Literature 中國文學史 (never completed)
Lu Zhiwei 陸志韋
  Crossing the River 渡河集
Lü Heruo 呂赫若
  Lü Heruo's Diary: (1942–1944) 呂赫若日記： (一九四二–一九四四年), 1944
  "Clear Autumn" 清秋, 1944

M

Ma Jian 馬建
  The Dark Road, 2013
Ma Lang 馬朗 (Ma Boliang 馬博良)
  "A Night in North Point" 北角之夜, 1957
Mao Dun 茅盾 (Shen Yanbing 沈雁冰)
  "Introduction" 引言 (to *Xiaoshuo yuebao* 小說月報), 1921
Mao Zedong 毛澤東
  "Talks at the Yan'an Forum on Literature and Art" 在延安文藝座談會上的講話,
   1942
Meng Bing 孟冰
  Searching for Li Dazhao 尋找李大釗, 2005

Meng Chao 孟超
  Li Huiniang 李慧娘, 1960
Mian Mian 棉棉
  Candy 糖, 2000
Mo Yan 莫言
  Garlic Ballads 天堂蒜臼之歌, 1988
  Republic of Wine 酒國, 1993
  Big Breasts and Wide Hips 豐乳肥臀, 1995
  Sandalwood Death 檀香刑, 2001
  Life and Death Are Wearing Me Out 生死疲勞, 2006
Mori Shuntō 森春濤
  Quatrains by Tokyo's Men of Talent 東京才人絶句, 1875
Morrison, Robert, ed.
  Dictionary of the Chinese Language, 1819
Mu Dan 穆旦
  "The Jungle's Apparition: To the Skulls on the Rivers of the Hukwang Valley"
    森林之魅: 祭胡康河上的白骨, 1945
Mu Mutian 穆木天
  "We Want to Seize Reality" 我們要捉住現實, 1933
Murong Xuecun 慕容雪村
  Leave Me Alone: A Novel of Chengdu 成都, 今夜請將我遺忘, 2002

N

Narushima Ryūhoku 成島柳北
  "Quatrain," 1874
Nie Gannu 聶紺弩 et al.
  The Complete Poems of Nie Gannu 聶紺弩诗全编, 1992
  Autobiographical Accounts by Nie Gannu 聶紺弩自序, 1998
  Nie Gannu's Case File 聶紺弩刑事檔案, 2009
Ng Kim Chew 黃錦樹
  "Inscribed Backs" 刻背, 2001

O

Okabe Keigoro 岡部啓五郎, ed.
  A Euphonious Meiji Collection 明治好音集 *Meiji kōinshū*, 1875
Ōtsuki Bankei 大槻磐溪
  Casual Drafts from the Hall of Fondness for Antiquity 愛古堂漫稿, 1874
Ou Jujia 歐榘甲
  "A Record of Observing Drama" 觀戲記, 1902
Ou Waiou 鷗外鷗
  Poems of Ou Waiou 鷗外鷗之詩, 1985
Ouyang Yuqian 歐陽予倩
  "Perspectives on Theater Reform" 戲劇改良各面觀, 1918
  The Shrew 破婦, 1922

P

Pai Hsien-yung 白先勇
  "Winter Night" 冬夜, 1970
  Crystal Boys 孽子, 1983
Phạm Thảo Vân 范草雲
  "When Mother is Away" (Mẹ vắng nhà), 2006

Q

Qian Liqun 錢理群
  Thirty Years of Modern Chinese Literary History 中國現代文學三十年, 1987
Qian Mu 錢穆
  Outline of Our National History 國史大綱, 1940
Qian Zhongshu 錢鍾書
  "Lin Shu's Translations" 林紓的翻譯, 1964
Qiu Miaojin 邱妙津
  The Crocodile's Journal 鱷魚手記, 1994
Qiu Tingliang 裘廷梁
  "The Vernacular is the Root of Reform" 論白話為維新之本, 1987
Qu Qiubai 瞿秋白
  "The Internationale" (*Yingtenaixiongnaier* 英特納雄耐爾) (Chinese lyrics), 1923
  "Superfluous Words" 多餘的話, 1935

R

Rou Shi 柔石
  February 二月, 1929
  "A Slave Mother" 為奴隸的母親, 1930

S

Sasakawa Taneo 笹川種郎
  Dynastic History of Chinese Literature 歷朝文學史, 1898/1903
Shen Congwen 沈從文
  "The Re-establishment of the Literary" 文運的重建, 1940
Shu Xiangcheng 舒巷城
  "Tsimshatsui" 尖沙咀 (year unknown)
Shui Hua 水華 (dir.)
  Living Forever in Burning Flames 烈火中永生, 1965
Song Chunfang 宋春舫
  "A Hundred Perspectives on Contemporary Drama" 近世名戲百種目, 1918
Su Manshu 蘇曼殊
  The Lone Swan 斷鴻零雁記, 1912
Sugawara no Michizane 菅原道真
  Literary Drafts of the Sugawara House; Later Collection of the Sugawara House 菅家文草·
  菅家後集 (*Kanke bunsō, Kanke kōshū*)

Sumarsini, Erin

    "The Story of Ye Feng and Carlos" (Kisah Ye Feng dan Carlos), 2014

Sun Lianggong 孫俍工, ed.

    Chinese Dictionary of Literature and Art 中國文藝辭典, 1931

Sun Yuxiu 孫毓修

    "An Essay on European and American Fiction" 歐美小說叢談, 1913

T

Tan Yiyuan 潭儀元 and Xu Hongsheng 許宏盛

    Guangzhou Thunder 廣州驚雷, 1997

Tian Han 田漢

    Guan Hanqing 關漢卿, 1958

    Shisanling Reservoir Fantasia 十三陵水庫暢想曲, 1958

    Princess Wencheng 文成公主, 1959

    Story of the Western Chamber 西廂記, 1959

    Xie Yaohuan 謝瑤環, 1961

Tonglingzhe 通靈者

    A Dream of Returning to 1997 夢回九七, 2005

W

Wang Anyi 王安憶

    Age of Enlightenment 啟蒙時代, 2007

Wang Guowei 王國維

    "An Investigation of the Origins of Xiqu" 戲曲考原, 1908

    Remarks on Song Lyrics and the Human Condition 人間詞話, 1910

    Study of Xiqu from the Song and the Yuan 宋元戲曲考, 1913

Wang Meng 王蒙

    A Young Newcomer in the Organization Department 組織部新來了個青年人, 1956

Wang Ping 王蘋 (dir.)

    The East is Red 東方紅 (performance), 1964

Wang Shiwei 王實味

    "Wild Lilies" 野百合花, 1942

Wang Tao 干韜

    Japan Travelogue 扶桑遊記, 1880

Wang Yaowen 王躍文

    Chinese Painting 國畫, 1999

Wang Zhefu 王哲甫

    A History of China's New Literature Movement 中國新文學運動史, 1933

Wang Zhongqi 王鍾麒

    "On the Relationship between Theater Reform and Government of the People" 論戲曲改良與群治之關係, 1906

Wang Zimei 汪子美

    "China's *manhua*: Evolution and Future Prospects" 中國漫畫之演進及展望, 1935

Wei Hui 衛慧 (Zhou Weihui 周衛慧)

    Shanghai Baby 上海寶貝, 1999

Wu Han 吳晗

    Hairui Dismissed from Office 海瑞罷官, 1959

Wu Jianren 吳趼人

    New Story of the Stone 新石頭記, 1904

Wu Jingzi 吳敬梓

    The Scholars 儒林外史, 1750

Wu Mei 吳梅

    "Lectures on Drama" 詞餘講義, 1919

Wu Yu 吳虞

    "Theory of the Family System as the Basis of Totalitarianism" 家族制度為專制主義
之根據論, 1917

Wu Zhaodi (dir.)

    Heroic Sons and Daughters 英雄兒女, 1964

Wu Zhuoliu 吳濁流,

    Mixed Feelings about Nanjing 南京雜感, 1977

X

Xiao Hei 小黑 (Tan Kee Keat 陳奇杰)

    Black: The Collected Fiction of Xiao Hei 黑：小黑小說集, 1979

    The Eve 前夕, 1990

    Clear Waters, Dark Mountains 白水黑山, 1993

Xiaoxiao Sheng 蘭陵笑笑生

    The Plum in the Golden Vase 金瓶梅, 1610

Xiang Kairan 向愷然 (Pingjiang Buxiaosheng 平江不肖生)

    Marvelous Gallants of the Rivers and Lakes 江湖奇俠傳, 1923

    Righteous Heroes of Modern Times 近代俠義英雄傳, 1923

Xu Nianci 許念慈

    "New Tales of Mr. Bragadoccio" 新法螺先生譚, 1904

Xu Su 徐速

    The Star, the Moon, the Sun 星星月亮太陽, 1953

    The Girl Called Sakurako 櫻子姑娘, 1959

Xu Zhenya 徐枕亞

    Jade Pear Spirit 玉梨魂, 1912

    The Snow Crane's Tears 雪鴻淚史, 1914

Y

Yan Geling 嚴歌苓

    The Banquet Bug, 2006

Yan Lianke 閻連科

    Streams of Life and Time 日光流年, 1998

    Hard Like Water 堅硬如水, 2001

Serve the People! 為人民服務, 2005
Dream of Ding Village 丁庄夢, 2006
The Four Books 四書, 2011
The Explosion Chronicles 炸裂志, 2013
Yang Jisheng 楊繼繩
Tombstone 墓碑, 2008
Yao Yongpu 姚永樸
A Method for Literary Research 文學研究法, 1914
Ye Songshi 葉松石
Collected Farewell Songs from Japan 扶桑驪唱集, 1891
Yip Fai 葉輝
"Nathan Road" 彌敦道, 2001
Yu Dafu 郁達夫
"Sinking" 沈淪, 1921
Yu Hua 余華
Brothers 兄弟, 2006
Yu Shangyuan 余上沅
"Drama," 1931
Yu Shangyuan 余上沅 et al.
Yang Guifei, 1924

Z

Zhang Guangyu 張光宇
Journey to the West in Cartoons 西遊漫記, 1945
Zhang Houzai 張厚載
"My Views on Old-Style Chinese Theater" 我的中國舊戲觀, 1918
Zhang Wenhuan 張文環
"Night Monkeys" 夜猿, 1942
Zhang Yihe 章詒和
The Past is Not Like Smoke 往事并不如烟, 2004
Zheng Zhenduo 鄭振鐸
"Three Problems in the Translation of Literature" 譯文學書的三個問題, 1921
Zhou Enlai 周恩來
The East is Red 東方紅 (performance), 1964
Zhou Guisheng 周桂笙
In the Serpent's Coil 毒蛇圈 [translation of Fortuné du Boisgobey's *Margot la balafrée*], 1903
Zhou Zuoren 周作人
"History of European Literature" 歐洲文學史, 1918
Zhu Ziqing 朱自清
An Outline of Research on New Chinese Literature 中國新文學研究綱要, 1933
"A Review of a History of Chinese Literary Criticism by Guo Shaoyu, Volume 1" 評郭紹虞《中國文學批評史》上卷, 1934
"The Development of Criticism on Poetry and Prose" 詩文評的發展, 1946

INDEX